The Law of
Tax-Exempt Organizations

The Law of
Tax-Exempt Organizations

EIGHTH EDITION

BRUCE R. HOPKINS

WILEY

JOHN WILEY & SONS, INC.

This book is printed on acid-free paper. (∞)

Published by John Wiley & Sons, Inc., Hoboken, New Jersey.
Published simultaneously in Canada.

For general information on our other products and services, or technical support, please contact our Customer Care Department within the United States at 800-762-2974, outside the United States at 317-572-3993 or fax 317-572-4002.

Wiley also publishes its books in a variety of electronic formats. Some content that appears in print may not be available in electronic books.

For more information about Wiley products, visit our web site at www.wiley.com.

Library of Congress Cataloging-in-Publication Data:

Hopkins, Bruce R.
    The law of tax-exempt organizations / Bruce R. Hopkins.—8th ed.
      p. cm.
    Includes bibliographical references and index.
    ISBN 0-471-26820-8 (cloth)
    1. Nonprofit organizations—Taxation—Law and legislation—United States. 2. Charitable uses, trusts, and foundations—Taxation—United States. I. Title.
    KF6449 .H6 2003
    343.7306'68—dc21   2002192261

Printed in the United States of America.

10 9 8 7 6 5 4 3 2

This book is dedicated to my son,
Christopher B. Hopkins, Esq.,
with love.

Update Service

BECOME A SUBSCRIBER!

Did you purchase this product from a bookstore?

If you did, it's important for you to become a subscriber. John Wiley & Sons, Inc. may publish, on a periodic basis, supplements and new editions to reflect the latest changes in the subject matter that you *need to know* in order to stay competitive in this ever-changing industry. By contacting the Wiley office nearest you, you'll receive any current update at no additional charge. In addition, you'll receive future updates and revised or related volumes on a 30-day examination review.

If you purchased this product directly from John Wiley & Sons, Inc., we have already recorded your subscription for this update service.

To become a subscriber, please call **1-877-762-2974** or send your name, company name (if applicable), address, and the title of the product to:

mailing address: **Supplement Department**
John Wiley & Sons, Inc.
One Wiley Drive
Somerset, NJ 08875

e-mail: **subscriber@wiley.com**
fax: **1-732-302-2300**
online: **www.wiley.com**

For customers outside the United States, please contact the Wiley office nearest you:

Professional & Reference Division
John Wiley & Sons Canada, Ltd.
22 Worcester Road
Etobicoke, Ontario M9W 1L1
CANADA
Phone: 416-236-4433
Phone: 1-800-567-4797
Fax: 416-236-4447
Email: canada@wiley.com

John Wiley & Sons Australia, Ltd.
33 Park Road
P.O. Box 1226
Milton, Queensland 4064
AUSTRALIA
Phone: 61-7-3859-9755
Fax: 61-7-3859-9715
Email: brisbane@johnwiley.com.au

John Wiley & Sons, Ltd.
The Atrium
Southern Gate, Chichester
West Sussex PO19 8SQ
ENGLAND
Phone: 44-1243-779777
Fax: 44-1243-775878
Email: customer@wiley.co.uk

John Wiley & Sons (Asia) Pte., Ltd.
2 Clementi Loop #02-01
SINGAPORE 129809
Phone: 65-64632400
Fax: 65-64634604/5/6
Customer Service: 65-64604280
Email: enquiry@wiley.com.sg

About the Author

Bruce R. Hopkins is a lawyer in Kansas City, Missouri, with the firm of Polsinelli Shalton Welte, P.C., having practiced law in Washington, D.C., for 26 years. He specializes in the representation of tax-exempt organizations. His practice ranges over the entirety of tax matters involving exempt organizations, with emphasis on the formation of nonprofit organizations, acquisition of recognition of tax-exempt status for them, the private inurement and private benefit doctrines, the intermediate sanctions rules, legislative and political campaign activities issues, public charity and private foundation rules, unrelated business planning, use of exempt and for-profit subsidiaries, joint venture planning, review of annual information returns, Internet communications developments, the law of charitable giving (including planned giving), and fundraising law issues.

Mr. Hopkins served as Chair of the Committee on Exempt Organizations, Tax Section, American Bar Association; Chair, Section of Taxation, National Association of College and University Attorneys; and President, Planned Giving Study Group of Greater Washington, D.C. He was accorded the Assistant Commissioner's (IRS) Award in 1984.

Mr. Hopkins is the series editor of Wiley's Nonprofit Law, Finance, and Management Series. In addition to *The Law of Tax-Exempt Organizations, Eighth Edition*, he is the author of *The Tax Law of Charitable Giving, Second Edition*; *The Law of Fundraising, Third Edition*; *The Nonprofits' Guide to Internet Communications Law*; *The Law of Intermediate Sanctions: A Guide for Nonprofits*; *The First Legal Answer Book for Fund-Raisers*; *The Second Legal Answer Book for Fund-Raisers*; *The Legal Answer Book for Nonprofit Organizations*; *The Second Legal Answer Book for Nonprofit Organizations*; *The Nonprofit Law Dictionary*; *Starting and Managing a Nonprofit Organization: A Legal Guide, Third Edition*; and is the co-author, with Jody Blazek, of *Private Foundations: Tax Law and Compliance, Second Edition*; also with Ms. Blazek, *The Legal Answer Book for Private Foundations*; with D. Benson Tesdahl, of *Intermediate Sanctions: Curbing Nonprofit Abuse*; and with Thomas K. Hyatt, of *The Law of Tax-Exempt Healthcare Organizations, Second Edition*. He also writes *The Nonprofit Counsel*, a monthly newsletter, published by John Wiley & Sons.

Mr. Hopkins earned his J.D. and L.L.M. degrees at the George Washington University and his B.A. at the University of Michigan. He is a member of the bars of the District of Columbia and the state of Missouri.

Preface

A highlight of my life is writing books about the law applicable to nonprofit organizations. This started in 1975 and I haven't been able to stop. Sixteen books have been authored or co-authored by me over the years, and more await their turn. *The Law of Tax-Exempt Organizations*, however, was the first book I wrote. I find it extraordinary that it is now in its eighth edition.

By the time this edition is available, it will be over 28 years of age (1975–2003). As is the case with my law partners, I prefer not to think of the thousands of hours that underlie this project. Certainly the field of tax-exempt organizations has been dynamic, volatile at times, and the fact that this book is now in this edition is testament to the complexity of the subject matter and its astounding growth. In fact, the number of books in the Wiley Nonprofit Law, Finance, and Management Series, and the wonderful range of that material, evidences the explosiveness of the nonprofit sector in recent years.

Most of the law reflected in this book did not exist 33 years ago. Tax exemption was provided for in the Revenue Act of 1913 and the unrelated business income rules came in 1950, but that was about it. A considerable portion of the statutory law of tax-exempt organizations is the product of enactment of the Tax Reform Act of 1969. (I am often asked how I found myself practicing in the realm of tax-exempt organizations. My law practice started in 1969, I got caught up in the writing and interpreting of the law Congress passed that year, and I just kept on going.) This body of statutory law has been significantly expanded by over a dozen major tax acts. In recent years alone, the field has been enlarged by reason of enactment of the Taxpayer Bill of Rights 2 (1996), the Small Business Job Protection Act of 1996, the Health Insurance Portability and Accountability Act of 1996, the Taxpayer Relief Act of 1997, the IRS Restructuring and Reform Act of 1998, the Ticket to Work and Work Incentives Improvement Act (1999), the political organizations disclosure legislation (2000), the Economic Growth and Tax Relief Reconciliation Act of 2001, and the Victims of Terrorism Relief Act of 2001.

But the tax law affecting exempt organizations is by no means confined to statutes. Like other areas of tax law, the field is heavily informed by Treasury Department regulations, Internal Revenue Service revenue rulings and revenue procedures, and opinions from various federal courts. More so than in other aspects of the tax law, the world of tax-exempt organizations is dramatically affected almost daily by IRS "private" determinations, usually in the form of private letter rulings or technical advice memoranda. All of this has resulted in a mammoth body of law.

The last decade or so alone bears witness to an immense augmentation of the law of tax-exempt organizations. Developments in the health care, higher education, private foundations, and associations fields, just to name a few, have been awesome to watch and challenging to chronicle. Other notable expansions of this law have occurred and are occurring in the realms of private inurement and private benefit, legislative and political activities, the applications for recognition of exemption and the annual information returns, the use of partnerships and subsidiaries, the commerciality doctrine, and the unrelated business rules.

New bodies of law have also emerged. While perhaps the most notable are the intermediate sanctions rules, others include disclosure and document distribution requirements, exempt organizations and insurance, mergers and other reorganizations, and fundraising regulation. On the immediate horizon is applicability in the exempt organizations area of the concepts emanating from the for-profit corporate responsibility legislation.

This book evolved out of materials developed for the course on tax-exempt organizations that I taught for 19 years at the George Washington University National Law Center, in Washington, D.C., beginning in 1973. It reflects hundreds of questions asked by law students and seminar and conference attendees over the years. It also has been shaped by the inquiries of clients and colleagues. At the same time, the task has been to capture all of the law and developments across the entire field.

I have tried to provide a summary of the law of tax-exempt organizations, one that is sufficiently general to present the subject in all of its marvelous expanse, yet with enough particularity to give the reader the specifics when needed. Thus, the book has been written in as nontechnical a way as I can muster, yet with footnotes and other sources that lead to more detailed information. The latter include references to Internal Revenue Code provisions, tax regulations, court opinions, and public and private rulings from the IRS.

It is hoped that lawyers, managers, accountants, directors and officers, fundraising executives, and students of the field can use this book to learn particular aspects of the subject matter or to refresh their minds about one rule or another. The book is designed for the newcomer as well as for the expert practitioner.

One aspect of this book that has been a problem over the years has been its size. Each edition, up to the seventh, had been larger than the previous one. The cumulative supplements end up being books in their own right. While I admit to, in exuberance, occasional overwriting, the core difficulty has been the sheer number of ways in which this area of the law has broadened.

This edition, while somewhat longer than the Seventh, is shorter than the Sixth. This was accomplished in part by tightening the writing and jettisoning various sections. The single most important reason for this shrinkage, however, is that nearly 200 pages of the law concerning private foundations was removed and incorporated into a separate book (i.e., *Private Foundations: Tax Law and Compliance, Second Edition* John Wiley & Sons, Inc., 2003, co-authored with Jody Blazek). Private foundation law is still covered in this book (see Chapter 11), but the details in this area are now in this companion volume.

There have been other instances of this nature. I have authored or co-authored books on charitable giving, fundraising regulation, intermediate sanctions, Internet communications, and health law. These efforts, too, have helped to trim the size of the book. There isn't enough space in the book for a detailed analysis of cases, rulings, and the like. I try to do this, however, in my monthly newsletter, *The Nonprofit Counsel*, which is now in its twentieth year. The format of the newsletter includes references to this book for additional reading and background information. Thus, the newsletter will continue as a stand-alone publication; at the same time, for those with the book, it will also serve as a monthly update.

The flow of this edition has been substantially revised. Subjects like private inurement, legislative and political activities, and insurance activities have been newly placed and discussed from the standpoint of several types of exempt organizations. Some chapters have been consolidated. There are 33 chapters in this edition compared to 46 in the book's most expansive form. It is hoped that this format will make the book more useful.

It was observed earlier that the law of tax-exempt organizations is mammoth. All indications are that more, perhaps much more, is in the offing. For example, the IRS will be testing its authority to levy penalties in instances of excess benefit transactions, there will be litigation over charities in politics, law will emanate concerning application of the doctrine of private inurement and the concepts of corporate responsibility, the annual return will be revised and expanded, and more creativity and ensuing regulation will evolve as the result of reorganizations, mergers, affiliations, use of subsidiaries, conversions, and liquidations.

Clichés about a book like this can abound. "Labor of love" and "work in progress" come to mind. The most important one of all, however, has to be said: There have been a lot of people along the way who have helped enormously, doing so much to nurture the book over the years, particularly my friends and colleagues at John Wiley & Sons, Inc. Most notable in the past have been Jeffrey Brown, Marla Bobowick, Martha Cooley, and Robin Goldstein. I thank my editor, Susan McDermott, for her support in the development of this edition of the book and Kerstin Nasdeo, associate managing editor, for her skills in the production of it.

Revising and updating a book of this nature is a time-consuming project, requiring much intense focus. In reflection of these facts, I also extend my gratitude to my dear wife, Bonnie J. Buchele, for her patience, understanding, and support.

BRUCE R. HOPKINS
April, 2003

Contents

CONTENTS

PART TWO: TAX-EXEMPT CHARITABLE ORGANIZATIONS

5   Scope of Term *Charitable*   103

6   Charitable Organizations   135

7   Educational Organizations   193

8   Religious Organizations   219

CONTENTS

CONTENTS

CONTENTS

PART FOUR: GENERAL EXEMPT ORGANIZATION LAWS

19 Private Inurement, Private Benefit, and Excess Benefit Transactions 483

20 Legislative Activities by Tax-Exempt Organizations 543

21 Political Campaign Activities by Tax-Exempt Organizations 583

CONTENTS

CONTENTS

PART SIX: INTER-ORGANIZATIONAL STRUCTURES AND OPERATIONAL FORMS

PART ONE

Introduction to the Law
of Tax-Exempt Organizations

CHAPTER ONE

Philosophy Underlying and Rationales for Tax-Exempt Organizations

Nearly all of federal and state law pertains, directly or indirectly, to tax-exempt organizations; there are few areas of law that have no bearing whatsoever on these entities. The fields of federal law that directly apply to exempt organizations include tax exemption and charitable giving requirements, and the laws concerning antitrust, contracts, employee benefits, the environment, estate planning, health care, labor, the postal system, securities, and fundraising for charitable and political purposes. The aspects of state law concerning exempt organizations are much the same as the federal ones, along with laws pertaining to the formation and operation of corporations and trusts, and charitable solicitation acts. Both levels of government have much constitutional and administrative law directly applicable to exempt organizations. A vast array of other civil and criminal laws likewise apply. The principal focus of this book is the federal tax law as it applies to nonprofit organizations, although other laws applicable to exempt organizations are referenced throughout.

§ 1.1 *NONPROFIT* ORGANIZATIONS

A tax-exempt organization is a unique entity; among its features is the fact that it is (with few exceptions) a nonprofit organization. Most of the laws that pertain to the concept and creation of a nonprofit organization originate at the state level, while most laws concerning tax exemption are generated at the federal level. Although almost every nonprofit entity is incorporated or otherwise formed under state law, a few nonprofit organizations are chartered by federal statute. The nonprofit organizations that are the chief focus from a federal tax law standpoint are corporations, trusts, and unincorporated associations. There may, however, be increasing use of limited liability companies in this regard.

A nonprofit organization is not necessarily a tax-exempt organization. To be exempt, a nonprofit organization must meet certain criteria. As noted, most of these criteria are established under federal law. State law, however, may embody additional criteria; those rules can differ in relation to the tax from which exemption is sought (such as taxes on income, sales of goods or services, use of property, tangible personal property, intangible personal property, or real property).[1] Thus, there are nonprofit organizations that are taxable entities, under both federal and state law.

(a) Definition of *Nonprofit Organization*

The term *nonprofit organization* does not refer to an organization that is prohibited by law from earning a *profit* (that is, an excess of earnings over expenses). In fact, it is quite common for nonprofit organizations to generate profits. Rather, the definition of nonprofit organization essentially relates to requirements as to what must be done with the profits earned or otherwise received. This fundamental element is found in the doctrine of *private inurement*.[2]

The legal concept of a nonprofit organization is best understood through a comparison with a *for-profit* organization. The essential difference between nonprofit and for-profit organizations is reflected in the private inurement doctrine.[3] Nonetheless, the characteristics of the two categories of organizations are often identical, in that both mandate a legal form,[4] one or more directors or trustees, and usually officers, and both of these types of entities can have employees (and thus pay compensation), face essentially the same expenses, make investments, enter into contracts, sue and be sued, produce goods and/or services, and, as noted, generate profits.

A fundamental distinction between the two entities is that the for-profit organization has owners that hold the equity in the enterprise, such as stockholders of a corporation. The for-profit organization is operated for the benefit of its owners; the profits of the business undertaking are passed through to them, such as by the payment of dividends on shares of stock. That is what is meant by the term

---

[1] In establishing its criteria for tax exemption, however, a state may not develop rules that are discriminatory to the extent that they unconstitutionally burden interstate commerce (Camps Newfound/Owatonna, Inc. v. Town of Harrison, et al., 520 U.S. 564 (1997)). In general, Brody, "Hocking the Halo: Implications of the Charities' Winning Briefs in *Camps Newfound/Owatonna, Inc.*," 20 *Exempt Org. Tax Rev.* (No. 1) 31 (1998).

[2] The doctrine states that the entity be organized and operated so that "no part of . . . [its] net earnings . . . inures to the benefit of any private shareholder or individual" (e.g., Internal Revenue Code of 1986, as amended, section (IRC §) 501(c)(3)). The technical aspects of the private inurement doctrine are the subject of Chapter 19.

[3] The word *nonprofit* should not be confused with the term *not-for-profit* (although it often is). The former describes a type of organization; the latter describes a type of activity. For example, in the federal income tax setting, expenses associated with a not-for-profit activity (namely, one conducted without the requisite profit motive) are not deductible as business expenses (IRC § 183).

[4] See § 4.1.

for-profit organization: It is one that is designed to generate a profit for its owners. The transfer of the profits from the organization to its owners is the inurement of net earnings to them in their private capacity.

By contrast, the nonprofit organization generally is not permitted to distribute its profits (net earnings) to those who control it (such as directors and officers).[5] (A nonprofit organization rarely has owners.[6]) Simply stated, a nonprofit organization is one that cannot engage in private inurement. Consequently, the private inurement doctrine is the substantive defining characteristic that distinguishes nonprofit organizations from for-profit organizations for purposes of the federal tax law.

To reiterate: Both nonprofit and for-profit organizations are legally able to generate a profit. Yet, as the comparison between the two types of organizations indicates, there are two categories of profit: one at the *entity level* and one at the *ownership level*. Both can yield the former type of profit; the distinction between the two types of entities pivots on the latter category of profit.[7] The for-profit organization endeavors to produce a profit for its owners—what one commentator called its "residual claimants."[8] For-profit organizations are supposed to engage in private inurement; nonprofit entities may not do so. Indeed, the nonprofit organization often seeks to devote its profit to ends that are beneficial to society.

(b) The Nonprofit Sector

Critical to an understanding of the nonprofit organization is appreciation of the concept of the *nonprofit sector* of society. This sector of society has been termed, among other titles, the *independent sector*, the *third sector*, the *voluntary sector*, and the *philanthropic sector*. The English language has yet to capture the precise nature of this sector; in a sense, none of these appellations is appropriate.[9] (The author prefers the term *nonprofit sector*.)

A tenet of political philosophy is that a democratic state—or, as it is sometimes termed, civil society—has three sectors. These sectors contain institutions and organizations that are governmental, for-profit, and nonprofit in nature. Thus, in the United States, the governmental sector includes the branches, de-

---

[5] The U.S. Supreme Court wrote that a "nonprofit entity is ordinarily understood to differ from a for-profit corporation principally because it 'is barred from distributing its net earnings, if any, to individuals who exercise control over it, such as members, officers, directors, or trustees' " (Camps Newfound/Owatonna, Inc. v. Town of Harrison, et al., *supra* note 1 at 585, quoting from Hansmann, "The Role of Nonprofit Enterprise," 89 *Yale L. J.* 835, 838 (1980)).

[6] A few states allow nonprofit organizations to issue stock. This is done as an ownership (and control) mechanism only; this type of stock does not carry with it any rights to earnings (such as dividends).

[7] One commentator stated that charitable and other nonprofit organizations "are not restricted in the amount of profit they may make; restrictions apply only to what they may do with the profits" (Weisbrod, "The Complexities of Income Generation for Nonprofits," Chapter 7, Hodgkinson, Lyman, and Assocs., *The Future of the Nonprofit Sector* (Jossey-Bass, Inc., 1989)).

[8] Norwitz, " 'The Metaphysics of Time': A Radical Corporate Vision," 46 *Bus. Law* (No. 2) 377 (Feb. 1991).

[9] A discussion of these sectors appears in Ferris & Graddy, "Fading Distinctions among the Nonprofit, Government, and For-Profit Sectors," Chapter, 8, Hodgkinson, Lyman, and Assocs., *supra* note 7. An argument that the sector should be called the "first sector" is advanced in Young, "Beyond Tax Exemption: A Focus on Organizational Performance versus Legal Status," *id.* at Chapter 11.

partments, agencies, and bureaus of the federal, state, and local governments; the class of for-profit entities comprises the business, trade, professional, and commercial segment of society; and nonprofit entities constitute the balance of this society. The nonprofit sector is seen as being essential to the maintenance of freedom for individuals and a bulwark against the excesses of the other two sectors, particularly the governmental sector.

There are subsets within the nonprofit sector. Tax-exempt organizations represent a subset of nonprofit organizations. Organizations that are eligible to attract deductible charitable gifts, charitable organizations (using the broad definition[10]), and other types of exempt organizations are subsets of exempt organizations. Charitable

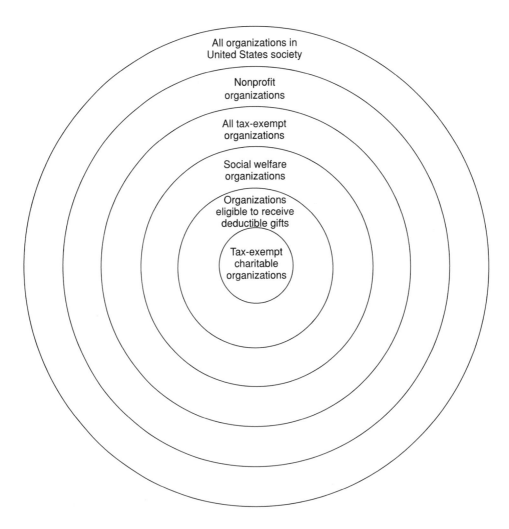

[10] This broad definition carries with it connotation of *philanthropy* (e.g., Van Til, "Defining Philanthropy," Chapter 2, Van Til & Assocs., *Critical Issues in American Philanthropy* (Jossey-Bass, Inc., 1990)). Also Payton, *Philanthropy: Voluntary Action for the Public Good* (Macmillan Pub. Co., 1998); O'Connell, *Philanthropy in Action* (The Foundation Center, 1987).

organizations (in the narrow, technical sense of that term) are subsets of charitable organizations (as defined in the broader sense).[11] These elements of the nonprofit sector may be portrayed (see previous page) as a series of concentric circles.

§ 1.2   *TAX-EXEMPT* ORGANIZATIONS

For the most part in this book, the term *tax-exempt organization* refers to a non-profit organization that is exempt from (excused from paying) the federal income tax. There are, of course, other federal taxes (such as excise and employment taxes), and there are categories of exemptions from them. At the state level, there are exemptions associated with income, sales, use, excise, and property taxes.

Nonetheless, there is no category of nonprofit organization that is not subject to some form of federal tax. The income tax that is potentially applicable to nearly all tax-exempt organizations is the tax on unrelated business income.[12] Exempt entities can be taxed for engaging in political activities;[13] public charities are subject to tax in the case of substantial efforts to influence legislation[14] or participation in political campaign activities;[15] and some exempt organizations, such as social clubs, are taxable on their investment income.[16] Associations and like organizations can be subject to a proxy tax when engaged in attempts to influence legislation or engage in political activities.[17] Private foundations can be caught up in a variety of excise taxes.[18]

There is no entitlement in a nonprofit organization to tax exemption; there is no entity that has some inherent right to exempt status. The existence of tax exemption and the determination of entities that have it are essentially the whim of the legislature involved. There is no constitutional law principle mandating tax exemption.[19]

An illustration of this point is the grant by Congress of tax-exempt status to certain mutual organizations—albeit with the stricture that to qualify for the exemption, an organization must be organized before September 1, 1957.[20] Prior to that date, exemption was available for all savings and loan associations. This exemption was repealed because Congress determined that the purpose of the

---

[11] The complexity of the federal tax law is such that the charitable sector (using the term in its broadest sense) is also divided into two segments: charitable organizations that are considered *private* (private foundations) and charitable organizations that are considered *public* (all charitable organizations other than those that are considered private); these nonprivate charities are frequently referred to as *public charities*. See Chapter 11.

[12] See Part Five.

[13] See § 17.5.

[14] See § 20.5.

[15] See § 21.4.

[16] See § 14.3.

[17] See §§ 20.7, 21.7.

[18] See § 11.3.

[19] Nonetheless, see *supra* note 1.

[20] IRC § 501(c)(14)(B).

exemption, which was to afford savings institutions that did not have capital stock the benefit of exemption so that a surplus could be accumulated to provide the depositors with greater security, was no longer appropriate, because the savings and loan industry had developed to the point where the ratio of capital account to total deposits was comparable to nonexempt commercial banks. A challenge to this law by an otherwise qualified organization formed in 1962 failed, with the U.S. Supreme Court holding that Congress did not act in an arbitrary and unconstitutional manner in declining to extend the exemption beyond the particular year.[21]

There are other illustrations of this point. For years, organizations like Blue Cross and Blue Shield entities were tax-exempt;[22] Congress, however, determined that these organizations had evolved to be essentially no different from commercial health insurance providers and thus generally legislated this exemption out of existence.[23] (Later, Congress realized that it had gone too far in this regard and restored exemption for some providers of insurance that function as charitable risk pools.[24]) Congress allowed the exempt status for group legal services organizations[25] to expire without ceremony in 1992; it also created a category of exemption for state-sponsored workers' compensation reinsurance organizations, with the stipulation that they be established before June 1, 1996.[26] Indeed, in 1982, Congress established exemption for a certain type of veterans' organization, with one of the criteria being that the entity be established before 1880.[27]

There is a main list of tax-exempt organizations,[28] to or from which Congress periodically adds or deletes categories of organizations. Occasionally, Congress extends the list of organizations that are exempt as charitable entities.[29] Otherwise, it may create a new provision describing the particular exemption criteria.[30]

A compendium of tax law containing an analysis of the law of tax-exempt organizations proclaims that exempt status is the "most prized of all tax concessions sanctioned by Congress."[31] That bit of hyperbole, intending to confer momentum and stature to the exempt organizations field, is in fact a considerable overstatement. For example, in the case of some charitable organizations, the eligibility to receive tax-deductible contributions is a far more prized attribute than tax exemption. From an economic viewpoint, there are several tax expenditures that are worth more (in terms of revenue losses to the federal

---

[21] Maryland Sav.-Share Ins. Corp. v. United States, 400 U.S. 4 (1970).
[22] By reason of IRC § 501(c)(4).
[23] See § 22.1.
[24] See § 10.6.
[25] See § 16.6.
[26] See § 18.5.
[27] See § 18.10(b).
[28] IRC § 501(c).
[29] IRC §§ 501(e), 501(f), 501(k), 501(m), 501(n).
[30] IRC §§ 521, 526–529.
[31] 8 Stand. Fed. Tax Rep. (CCH) ¶ 22, 604.01 (1996).

fisc) than the charitable contribution deduction or the federal tax exemption for nonprofit organizations.[32]

§ 1.3   PRINCIPLES OF EXEMPT ORGANIZATIONS LAW PHILOSOPHY

The definition in the law of the term *nonprofit organization* and the concept of the nonprofit sector as critical to the creation and functioning of a civil society do not distinguish nonprofit organizations that are tax-exempt from those that are not. This is because the tax aspect of nonprofit organizations is not relevant to either subject. Indeed, rather than defining either the term *nonprofit organization* or its societal role, the federal tax law principles respecting tax exemption of these entities reflect and flow out of the essence of these subjects.

This is somewhat unusual; many provisions of the federal tax laws are based on some form of rationale that is inherent in tax policy. The law of tax-exempt organizations has very little to do with any underlying tax policy. Rather, this aspect of the tax law is grounded in a body of thought far distant from tax policy: political philosophy as to the proper construct of a democratic society.

This raises, then, the matter of the rationale for the eligibility of nonprofit organizations for tax-exempt status. That is, what is the fundamental characteristic that enables a nonprofit organization to qualify as an exempt organization? In fact, there is no single qualifying feature; the most common one is, as noted, the doctrine of private inurement. This circumstance mirrors the fact that the present-day statutory exemption rules are not the product of a carefully formulated plan. Rather, they are a hodgepodge of statutory law that has evolved over 90 years, as various Congresses have deleted from (infrequently) and added to (frequently) the roster of exempt entities, causing it to grow substantially over the decades. One observer wrote that the various categories of exempt organizations "are not

---

[32] The staff of the Joint Committee on Taxation and the Department of the Treasury measure the economic value (revenue "losses") of various tax preferences, such as tax deductions, credits, and exclusions (termed *tax expenditures*). Although the income tax charitable contribution deduction tends to be the fifth or sixth largest tax expenditure, the ones that are greater than it include the net exclusions for pension plan contributions and earnings, the exclusion from gross income of employer contributions for health insurance premiums and health care, the deductibility of mortgage interest on personal residences, the reduced rates of tax on long-term capital gains, and the deduction for state and local governments' income and personal property taxes. The Joint Committee on Taxation staff estimated that, for the federal government's fiscal years 2003–2007, the tax expenditure for the income tax charitable deduction is $248 billion, of which $38 billion is for gifts to educational institutions and $27 billion is for gifts to health organizations (*Estimates of Federal Tax Expenditures for Fiscal Years 2003–2007* (JCS-5-02)).

Tax exemption for qualified nonprofit organizations is not considered a tax expenditure. There are two rationales for this approach. One is that exempt status is not a tax expenditure because the nonbusiness activities of these organizations, such as charities, generally must predominate and their unrelated business activities are subject to tax. The exemption of certain nonprofit cooperative business organizations, including trade and business associations, is not treated as a tax expenditure because the tax benefits are available to any entity that chooses to organize itself and operate in the required manner to avoid the entity-level tax.

the result of any planned legislative scheme" but were enacted over the decades "by a variety of legislators for a variety of reasons."[33]

There are six basic rationales underlying qualification for tax-exempt status for nonprofit organizations. On a simplistic plane, a nonprofit entity is exempt because Congress wrote a provision in the Internal Revenue Code according exemption to it. Thus, some organizations are exempt for no more engaging reason than that Congress said so. Certainly, there is no grand philosophical construct buttressing this type of exemption.

Some of the federal income tax exemptions were enacted in the spirit of being merely declaratory of, or furthering, then-existing law. The House Committee on Ways and Means, in legislating a forerunner to the provision that exempts certain voluntary employees' beneficiary associations,[34] commented that "these associations are common today [1928] and it appears desirable to provide specifically for their exemption from ordinary corporation tax."[35] The exemption for nonprofit cemetery companies[36] was enacted to parallel then-existing state and local property tax exemptions.[37] The exemption for farmers' cooperatives[38] has been characterized as an element of the federal government's policy of supporting agriculture.[39] The provision exempting certain U.S. corporate instrumentalities from tax[40] was deemed declaratory of the exemption simultaneously provided by the particular enabling statute.[41] The provision according exemption to multiparent title-holding corporations was derived from the IRS's refusal to recognize exempt status for title-holding corporations serving more than one unrelated parent entity.[42]

Tax exemption for categories of nonprofit organizations can arise as a by-product of enactment of other legislation. In these instances, exemption is granted to facilitate accomplishment of the purpose of another legislative end. Thus, exempt status was approved for funds underlying employee benefit programs.[43] Other examples include exemption for professional football leagues that emanated out of the merger of the National Football League and the American Football League,[44] and for state-sponsored providers of health care to the needy, which was required to accommodate the goals of Congress in creating health care delivery legislation.[45]

---

[33] McGovern, "The Exemption Provisions of Subchapter F," 29 *Tax Law* 523 (1976). Other overviews of the various tax exemption provisions are in Hansmann, "The Rationale for Exempting Nonprofit Organizations from Corporate Income Taxation," 91 *Yale L. J.* 69 (1981); Bittker & Rahdert, "The Exemption of Nonprofit Organizations from Federal Income Taxation," 85 *Yale L. J.* 299 (1976).
[34] See § 16.3.
[35] H. Rep. No. 72, 78th Cong., 1st Sess. 17 (1928).
[36] See § 18.6.
[37] Lapin, "The Golden Hills and Meadows of the Tax-Exempt Cemetery," 44 *Taxes* 744 (1966).
[38] See § 18.11.
[39] Comment, 27 *Iowa L. Rev.* 128, 151–155 (1941).
[40] See § 18.1.
[41] H. Rep. No. 704, 73d Cong., 2d Sess. 21–25 (1934). This policy has changed, however (see § 18.1, text accompanying note 1).
[42] See § 18.2(b).
[43] See Chapter 16.
[44] See § 13.5.
[45] See § 18.14.

There is a pure tax rationale for a few tax-exempt organizations. The exemption for social clubs, homeowners' associations, and political organizations is reflective of this rationale.[46]

The fourth rationale for tax-exempt status is a policy one—not tax policy, but policy with regard to less essential elements of the structure of a civil society. This is why, for example, exempt status has been granted to fraternal organizations,[47] title-holding companies,[48] and qualified tuition programs.[49]

The fifth rationale for tax-exempt status is one that rests solidly on a philosophical principle. Yet there are degrees of scale here; some principles are less grandiose than others. Thus, there are nonprofit organizations that are exempt because their objectives are of direct importance to a significant segment of society and indirectly of consequence to all society. Within this frame lies the rationale for exemption for entities such as labor organizations,[50] trade and business associations,[51] and veterans' organizations.[52]

The sixth rationale for tax-exempt status for nonprofit organizations is predicated on the view that exemption is required to facilitate achievement of an end of significance to the entirety of society. Most organizations that are generally thought of as *charitable* in nature[53] are entities that are meaningful to the structure and functioning of society in the United States.[54] At least to some degree, this rationale embraces social welfare organizations.[55] This rationale may be termed the *political philosophy* rationale.

§ 1.4   POLITICAL PHILOSOPHY RATIONALE

The policy rationale for tax exemption, particularly for charitable organizations, is, as noted, one involving political philosophy rather than tax policy. The key concept underlying this philosophy is *pluralism*; more accurately, the pluralism of institutions, which is a function of competition between various institutions within the three sectors of society. In this context, the competition is between the nonprofit and governmental sectors. This element is particularly critical in the

---

[46] See *infra* § 5.

[47] See § 18.4.

[48] See § 18.2.

[49] See § 18.6.

[50] See § 15.1.

[51] See Chapter 13.

[52] See § 18.10.

[53] These are the charitable, educational, religious, scientific, and like organizations referenced in IRC § 501 (c)(3).

[54] In general, Brody, "Charities in Tax Reform: Threats to Subsidies Overt and Covert," 66 *Tenn. L. Rev.* (No. 3) 687 (Spring 1999); Brody, "Of Sovereignty and Subsidy: Conceptualizing the Charity Tax Exemption," 23 *J. Corp. Law* (No. 4) 585 (Summer 1998); 22 *Exempt Org. Tax Rev.* (No. 3) 421 (Dec. 1998). This book is written from the perspective of U.S. law. The philosophical principles are, however, applicable with respect to any society. In general, Hopkins & Moore, "Using the lessons learned from US and English law to create a regulatory framework for charities in evolving democracies," 3 *Voluntas* 194 (1992).

[55] See Chapter 12. Tax exemption for social welfare organizations also originated in 1913; the promotion of social welfare is one of the definitions of the term *charitable* for federal tax purposes (see § 6.7).

United States, the history of which originates in distrust of government. (Where the issue is unrelated business income taxation, the matter is one of competition between the nonprofit and for-profit sectors.) Here, the nonprofit sector serves as an alternative to the governmental sector as a means for addressing society's problems.

One of the greatest exponents of pluralism was John Stuart Mill. He wrote in *On Liberty*, published in 1859:

> In many cases, though individuals may not do the particular thing so well, on the average, as officers of government, it is nevertheless desirable that it should be done by them, rather than by the government, as a means to their own mental education—a mode of strengthening their active faculties, exercising their judgment, and giving them a familiar knowledge of the subjects with which they are thus left to deal. This is a principal, though not the sole, recommendation of . . . the conduct of industrial and philanthropic enterprises by voluntary associations.

Following a discussion of the importance of "individuality of development, and diversity of modes of action," Mill continued:

> Government operations tend to be everywhere alike. With individuals and voluntary associations, on the contrary, there are varied experiments, and endless diversity of experience. What the State can usefully do is to make itself a central depository, and active circulator and diffuser, of the experience resulting from many trials. Its business is to enable each experimentalist to benefit by the experiments of others, instead of tolerating no experiments but its own.

This conflict among the sectors—a sorting out of the appropriate role of governments and nonprofit organizations—is, in a healthy society, a never-ending process, ebbing and flowing with the politics of the day. A Congress may work to reduce the scope of the federal government and a U.S. president may proclaim that the "era of big government is over," while a preceding and/or succeeding generation may celebrate strong central government.

Probably the greatest commentator on the impulse and tendency in the United States to utilize nonprofit organizations was Alexis de Tocqueville. Writing in 1835, he observed in *Democracy in America*:

> Feelings and opinions are recruited, the heart is enlarged, and the human mind is developed only by the reciprocal influence of men upon one another. I have shown that these influences are almost null in democratic countries; they must therefore be artificially created, and this can only be accomplished by associations.

De Tocqueville's classic formulation on this subject came in his portrayal of the use by Americans of "public associations" as a critical element of societal structure:

> Americans of all ages, all conditions, and all dispositions constantly form associations. They have not only commercial and manufacturing companies, in

which all take part, but associations of a thousand other kinds, religious, moral, serious, futile, general or restricted, enormous or diminutive. The Americans make associations to give entertainments, to found seminaries, to build inns, to construct churches, to diffuse books, to send missionaries to the antipodes; in this manner they found hospitals, prisons, and schools. If it is proposed to inculcate some truth or to foster some feeling by the encouragement of a great example, they form a society. Wherever at the head of some new undertaking you see the government in France, or a man of rank in England, in the United States you will be sure to find an association.

This was the political philosophical climate concerning nonprofit organizations in place when Congress, toward the close of the nineteenth century, began considering enactment of an income tax. Although courts would subsequently articulate policy rationales for tax exemption, one of the failures of American jurisprudence is that the Supreme Court and the lower courts have never fully articulated this political philosophical doctrine.

Contemporary Congresses legislate by writing far more intricate statutes than their forebears, and in doing so usually leave in their wake rich deposits in the form of extensive legislative histories. Thus, it is far easier to ascertain what a recent Congress meant when creating law than is the case with respect to an enactment nearly a century ago.

At the time a constitutional income tax was coming into existence (the first enacted in 1913[56]), Congress legislated in spare language and rarely embellished on its statutory handiwork with legislative histories. Therefore, there is no contemporary record in the form of legislative history of what members of Congress had in mind when they first started creating categories of tax-exempt organizations. Congress, it is generally assumed, saw itself doing what other legislative bodies have done over the centuries. One observer stated that the "history of mankind reflects that our early legislators were not setting precedent by exempting religious or charitable organizations" from income tax.[57] That is, the political philosophical policy considerations pertaining to nonprofit organizations were such that taxation of these entities—considering their contributions to the well-being and functioning of society—was unthinkable.

Thus, in the process of writing the Revenue Act of 1913, Congress viewed tax exemption for charitable organizations as the only way to consistently correlate tax policy to political theory on the point, and saw the exemption of charities in the federal tax statutes as an extension of comparable practice throughout the whole of history. There is no legislative history that enlarges on the point. Presumably, Congress believed that these organizations ought not be taxed and

---

[56] In 1894, Congress imposed a tax on corporate income. This was the first time Congress was required to define the appropriate subjects of tax exemption (inasmuch as prior tax schemes specified the entities subject to taxation). The Tariff Act of 1894 provided exemption for nonprofit charitable, religious, and educational organizations, fraternal beneficiary societies, certain mutual savings banks, and certain mutual insurance companies. The 1894 legislation succumbed to a constitutional law challenge (Pollock v. Farmers' Loan & Trust Co., 157 U.S. 429 (1895), overruled on other grounds, State of S.C. v. Baker, 485 U.S. 505 (1988)), the Sixteenth Amendment was subsequently ratified, and the Revenue Act of 1913 was enacted.

[57] McGovern, *supra* note 33, at 524.

found the proposition sufficiently obvious so that extensive explanation of its actions was not necessary.

Some clues in this regard are found in the definition of *charitable activities* in the income tax regulations,[58] which are considered to be reflective of congressional intent. The regulations refer to purposes such as relief of the poor, advancement of education and science, erection and maintenance of public buildings, and lessening of the burdens of government. These definitions of charitable undertakings have an obvious derivation in the Preamble to the Statute of Charitable Uses,[59] written in England in 1601. Reference is there made to certain charitable purposes:

> . . . some for relief of aged, impotent and poor people, some for maintenance of sick and maimed soldiers and mariners, schools of learning, free schools, and scholars in universities, some for repair of bridges, ports, havens, causeways, churches, seabanks and highways, some for education and preferment of orphans, some for or towards relief, stock or maintenance for houses of correction, some for marriages of poor maids, some for supportation, aid and help of young tradesmen, handicraftsmen and persons decayed, and others for relief of redemption of prisoners or captives . . .

As this indicates, a subset of this political philosophical doctrine implies that tax exemption for charitable organizations derives from the concept that they perform functions that, in the absence of these organizations, government would have to perform. This view leads to the conclusion that government is willing to forgo the tax revenues it would otherwise receive in return for the public interest services rendered by charitable organizations. This rationale is, of course, inapplicable in the case of many religious organizations.[60]

Since the founding of the United States and beforehand in the colonial period, tax exemption—particularly with respect to religious organizations—was common.[61] Churches were uniformly spared taxation.[62] This practice has been sustained throughout the history of the nation—not only at the federal level but also at the state and local levels of government, which grant property tax exemptions, as an example.

The U.S. Supreme Court concluded, soon after enactment of the income tax, that the foregoing rationalization was the basis for the federal tax exemption for charitable entities (although in doing so it reflected a degree of uncertainty in the strength of its reasoning, undoubtedly based on the paucity of legislative history). In 1924, the Court stated that "[e]vidently the exemption is made in recognition of the benefit which the public derives from corporate activities of the class named, and is intended to aid them when [they are] not conducted for private gain."[63] Nearly 50 years later, in upholding the

---

[58] Income Tax Regulations ("Reg.") § 1.501(c)(3)-1(d)(2).
[59] Stat. 43 Eliz. i, ch. 4.
[60] See § 8.1.
[61] Cobb, *The Rise of Religious Liberty in America* 482–528 (1902).
[62] Torpey, *Judicial Doctrines of Religious Rights in America* 171 (1948).
[63] Trinidad v. Sagrada Orden de Predicadores de la Provincia del Santisimo Rosario de Filipinas, 263 U.S. 578, 581 (1924).

constitutionality of income tax exemption for religious organizations, the Court observed that the "State has an affirmative policy that considers these groups as beneficial and stabilizing influences in community life and finds this classification [tax exemption] useful, desirable, and in the public interest."[64] Subsequently, the Court wrote that, for most categories of nonprofit organizations, "exemption from federal income tax is intended to encourage the provision of services that are deemed socially beneficial."[65]

Other courts have taken up this theme. A federal court of appeals wrote that the "reason underlying the [tax] exemption granted" to charitable organizations "is that the exempted taxpayer performs a public service."[66] This court continued:

> The common element of charitable purposes within the meaning of the . . . [federal tax law] is the relief of the public of a burden which otherwise belongs to it. Charitable purposes are those which benefit the community by relieving it pro tanto from an obligation which it owes to the objects of the charity as members of the community.[67]

This federal appellate court subsequently observed, as respects tax exemption for charitable organizations, that one "stated reason for a deduction or exemption of this kind is that the favored entity performs a public service and benefits the public or relieves it of a burden which otherwise belongs to it."[68] Another federal court opined that the justification of the charitable contribution deduction was "historically . . . that by doing so, the Government relieves itself of the burden of meeting public needs which in the absence of charitable activity would fall on the shoulders of the Government."[69]

Only one federal court has fully articulated this political philosophical doctrine, noting that the "very purpose" of the charitable contribution deduction is "rooted in helping institutions because they serve the public good."[70] The doctrine was explained as follows:

> [A]s to private philanthropy, the promotion of a healthy pluralism is often viewed as a prime social benefit of general significance. In other words, society can be seen as benefiting not only from the application of private wealth to specific purposes in the public interest but also from the variety of choices made by individual philanthropists as to which activities to subsidize. This decentralized choice-making is arguably more efficient and responsive to public needs than the cumbersome and less flexible allocation process of government administration.[71]

---

[64] Walz v. Tax Comm'n, 397 U.S. 664, 673 (1970).

[65] Portland Golf Club v. Comm'r, 497 U.S. 154, 161 (1990).

[66] Duffy v. Birmingham, 190 F.2d 738, 740 (8th Cir. 1951).

[67] Id.

[68] St. Louis Union Trust Co. v. United States, 374 F.2d 427, 432 (8th Cir. 1967).

[69] McGlotten v. Connally, 338 F. Supp. 448, 456 (D.D.C. 1972).

[70] Green v. Connally, 330 F. Supp. 1150, 1162 (D.D.C. 1971), *aff'd sub nom.* Coit v. Green, 404 U.S. 997 (1971).

[71] Id., 330 F. Supp. at 1162.

Occasionally, Congress issues a pronouncement on this subject. One of these rare instances occurred in 1939, when the report of the House Committee on Ways and Means, part of the legislative history of the Revenue Act of 1938, stated:

> The exemption from taxation of money or property devoted to charitable and other purposes is based upon the theory that the government is compensated for the loss of revenue by its relief from financial burden which would otherwise have to be met by appropriations from public funds, and by the benefits resulting from the promotion of the general welfare.[72]

The doctrine is also referenced from time to time in testimony before a congressional committee. For example, the Secretary of the Treasury testified before the House Committee on Ways and Means in 1973, observing:

> These organizations [which he termed "voluntary charities, which depend heavily on gifts and bequests"] are an important influence for diversity and a bulwark against over-reliance on big government. The tax privileges extended to these institutions were purged of abuse in 1969 and we believe the existing deductions of charitable gifts and bequests are an appropriate way to encourage those institutions. We believe the public accepts them as fair.[73]

The literature on this subject is extensive. The contemporary versions of it are traceable to 1975, when the public policy rationale was reexamined and reaffirmed by the Commission on Private Philanthropy and Public Needs. The Commission observed:

> Few aspects of American society are more characteristically, more famously American than the nation's array of voluntary organizations, and the support in both time and money that is given to them by its citizens. Our country has been decisively different in this regard, historian Daniel Boorstin observes, "from the beginning." As the country was settled, "communities existed before governments were there to care for public needs." The result, Boorstin says, was that "voluntary collaborative activities" were set up to provide basic social services. Government followed later.
>
> The practice of attending to community needs outside of government has profoundly shaped American society and its institutional framework. While in most other countries, major social institutions such as universities, hospitals, schools, libraries, museums and social welfare agencies are state-run and state-funded, in the United States many of the same organizations are privately controlled and voluntarily supported. The institutional landscape of America is, in fact, teeming with nongovernmental, noncommercial organizations, all the way from some of the world's leading educational and cultural institutions to local garden clubs, from politically powerful national associations to block associations—literally millions of groups in all. This vast and varied array is, and has long been widely recognized as part of the very fabric of American life. It reflects a national belief in the philosophy of pluralism and in the profound importance to society of individual initiative.

---

[72] H. Rep. No. 1860, 75th Cong., 3d Sess. 19 (1939).
[73] Department of the Treasury, "Proposals for Tax Change," Apr. 30, 1973.

Underpinning the virtual omnipresence of voluntary organizations, and a form of individual initiative in its own right, is the practice—in the case of many Americans, the deeply ingrained habit—of philanthropy, of private giving, which provides the resource base for voluntary organizations.

These two interrelated elements, then, are sizable forces in American society, far larger than in any other country. And they have contributed immeasurably to this country's social and scientific progress. On the ledger of recent contributions are such diverse advances as the creation of noncommercial "public" television, the development of environmental, consumerist and demographic consciousness, community-oriented museum programs, the protecting of land and landmarks from the often heedless rush of "progress." The list is endless and still growing; both the number and deeds of voluntary organizations are increasing. "Americans are forever forming associations," wrote de Tocqueville. They still are: tens of thousands of environmental organizations have sprung up in the last few years alone. Private giving is growing, too, at least in current dollar amounts.[74]

Here the concept of *philanthropy* enters, with the view that charitable organizations, maintained by tax exemption and nurtured by the ability to attract deductible contributions, reflect the American philosophy that not all policy-making and problem-solving should be reposed in the governmental sector. Thus, a jurist wrote that philanthropy is the "very possibility of doing something different than government can do, of creating an institution free to make choices government cannot—even seemingly arbitrary ones—without having to provide a justification that will be examined in a court of law, which stimulates much private giving and interest."[75]

A component part of the public policy doctrine is its emphasis on *voluntarism*. This principle was expressed as follows:

> Voluntarism has been responsible for the creation and maintenance of churches, schools, colleges, universities, laboratories, hospitals, libraries, museums, and the performing arts; voluntarism has given rise to the public and private health and welfare systems and many other functions and services that are now an integral part of the American civilization. In no other country has private philanthropy become so vital a part of the national culture or so effective an instrument in prodding government to closer attention to social needs.[76]

One of the modern-day exponents of the role and value of the independent sector in the United States was John W. Gardner, former Secretary of Health, Education, and Welfare, founder of Common Cause, and one of the founders of Independent Sector, an exempt organization that advocates on behalf of the charitable sector. Mr. Gardner wrote extensively on the subject of the necessity for and significance of the nation's nonprofit sector. He wrote that the "area of

---

[74] *Giving in America: Toward a Stronger Voluntary Sector*, Report of the Commission on Private Philanthropy and Public Needs 9-10 (1975).

[75] Friendly, "The Dartmouth College Case and the Public-Private Penumbra," 12 *Tex. Q.* (2d Supp.) 141, 171 (1969). Two other sources of prominence are Rabin, "Charitable Trusts and Charitable Deductions," 41 *N.Y.U.L. Rev.* 912 (1966); Saks, "The Role of Philanthropy: An Institutional View," 46 *Va. L. Rev.* 516 (1960).

[76] Fink, "Taxation and Philanthropy—A 1976 Perspective," 3 *J. Coll. & Univ. L.* 1, 6–7 (1975).

our national life encompassed by the deduction for religious, scientific, educational, and charitable organizations lies at the very heart of our intellectual and spiritual strivings as a people, at the very heart of our feeling about one another and about our joint life."[77] He added that the "private pursuit of public purpose is an honored tradition in American life"[78] and believed that "[a]ll elements in the private sector should unite to maintain a tax policy that preserves our pluralism."[79] Likewise, Robert J. Henle, formerly president of Georgetown University, wrote of how the "not-for-profit, private sector promotes the free initiative of citizens and gives them an opportunity on a nonpolitical basis to join together to promote the welfare of their fellow citizens or the public purposes to which they are attracted."[80]

A book of this nature cannot fully capture the philosophical underpinnings of the nonprofit sector. Yet this task was accomplished by Brian O'Connell while president of Independent Sector.[81] In a foreword to one of Mr. O'Connell's works, John W. Gardner stated that "[a]ll Americans interact with voluntary or nonprofit agencies and activities regularly, although they are often unaware of this fact."[82] Still, the educational process must continue, for as Mr. Gardner wrote, the nonprofit sector "enhances our creativity, enlivens our communities, nurtures individual responsibility, stirs life at the grassroots, and reminds us that we were born free."[83] Mr. O'Connell's collection included thoughts from sources as diverse as Max Lerner (the "associative impulse is strong in American life; no other civilization can show as many secret fraternal orders, businessmen's 'service clubs,' trade and occupational associations, social clubs, garden clubs, women's clubs, church clubs, theater groups, political and reform associations, veterans' groups, ethnic societies, and other clusterings of trivial or substantial importance"[84]); Daniel J. Boorstin (in "America, even in modern times, communities existed before governments were here to care for public needs"[85]); Merle Curti ("voluntary association with others in common causes has been thought to be strikingly characteristic of American life"[86]); John W. Gardner (for "many countries . . . monolithic central support of all educational, scientific, and charitable activities would be regarded as normal . . . [b]ut for the United States it would mean the end of a great tradition"[87]); Richard C. Cornuelle ("[w]e have been unique because another sector, clearly distinct from the other two, has, in the past, borne a heavy load of public responsibility"[88]); John D. Rockefeller III (the "third sector is . . . the seedbed for organized efforts to deal with social problems"[89]); Waldemar A.

---

[77] Gardner, "Bureaucracy vs. the Private Sector," 212 Current 17–18 (May 1979).
[78] Id. at 17.
[79] Id. at 18.
[80] Henle, "The Survival of Not-for-Profit, Private Institutions," America 252 (Oct. 23, 1976).
[81] O'Connell, America's Voluntary Spirit (The Foundation Center, 1983).
[82] Id. at xi.
[83] Id. at xv.
[84] Id. at 81.
[85] Id. at 131.
[86] Id. at 162.
[87] Id. at 256.
[88] Id. at 278.
[89] Id. at 356.

Neilsen (the "ultimate contribution of the Third Sector to our national life—namely what it does to ensure the continuing responsiveness, creativity and self-renewal of our democratic society"[90]); Richard W. Lyman (an "array of its [the independent sector's] virtues that is by now fairly familiar: its contributions to pluralism and diversity, its tendency to enable individuals to participate in civic life in ways that make sense to them and help to combat that corrosive feeling of powerlessness that is among the dread social diseases of our era, its encouragement of innovation and its capacity to act as a check on the inadequacies of government"[91]); and himself (the "problems of contemporary society are more complex, the solutions more involved and the satisfactions more obscure, but the basic ingredients are still the caring and the resolve to make things better").[92]

Consequently, it is error to regard tax exemption (and, where appropriate, the charitable contribution deduction) as anything other than a reflection of this larger political philosophical construct. Congress is not merely "giving" eligible nonprofit organizations "benefits"; the exemption from income taxation (or charitable deduction) is not a "loophole," a "preference," or a "subsidy"—it is not really an "indirect appropriation."[93] Rather, the various provisions of the federal and state tax exemption system exist as a reflection of the affirmative policy of American government to refrain from inhibiting by taxation the beneficial activities of qualified tax-exempt organizations acting in community and other public interests.[94]

Regrettably, however, the tax law is not evolving in conformity with this political philosophical framework; long-term political philosophical principles are being sacrificed to short-term views as to practical economical realities. This is reflected in the U.S. Supreme Court's confusion in thinking; the court has been correct on some occasions as to the rationale for tax exemption for nonprofit organizations,[95] yet in its fear of misuse of exemptions, such as to promote racial discrimination,[96] or in furtherance of unconstitutional ends, such as government promotion of religion,[97] has on other occasions inexplicably ignored the political philosophical construction. Thus, for example, in striking down a state sales tax exemption solely for the sale of religious publications, the Court wrote that it is "difficult to view" this "narrow exemption as anything but state sponsorship of religious belief."[98]

From a constitutional law perspective, it may have been appropriate for the Court to use the word "sponsorship" in that setting. Certainly it would

---

[90] *Id.* at 368.

[91] *Id.* at 371.

[92] *Id.* at 408. A companion book by the author addresses this point in additional detail, and traces the origins and development of a hypothetical charitable organization to illustrate the applicability of various federal and state laws concerning nonprofit organizations (*Starting and Managing a Nonprofit Organization: A Legal Guide, Third Edition* (John Wiley & Sons, Inc., 2001)).

[93] Cf. *supra* note 32.

[94] In general, Brody, "Of Sovereignty and Subsidy: Conceptualizing the Charity Tax Exemption," 23 *J. of Corp. L.* (No. 4) 585 (Summer 1998); Pappas, "The Independent Sector and the Tax Law: Defining Charity in an Ideal Democracy," 64 *S. Cal. L. Rev.* 461 (Jan. 1991).

[95] See text accompanied by *supra* notes 63-65.

[96] E.g., Bob Jones Univ. v. United States, 461 U.S. 574 (1983).

[97] Texas Monthly, Inc. v. Bullock, 489 U.S. 1 (1989).

[98] *Id.* at 15.

have been preferable, not to mention more accurate, for the Court to have confined this characterization to that word. Unfortunately, the Court found it necessary to amplify this point by observing that "[e]very tax exemption constitutes a subsidy that affects nonqualifying taxpayers."[99] While this "subsidy" is accurate terminology from the standpoint of the pure economics of the matter,[100] it misconstrues and distorts the larger (and far more important) political philosophical rationalization for tax exemption for nonprofit organizations. The policy underlying this tax exemption simply reflects the nature of the way U.S. society is structured. Inasmuch as it is not the government's money to begin with, the governmental sector should not be seen as "subsidizing" the nonprofit sector.

§ 1.5 INHERENT TAX RATIONALE

Aside from considerations of public policy, there exists an inherent tax theory for tax exemption. The essence of this rationale is that the receipt of what otherwise might be deemed income by an exempt organization is not a *taxable event*, in that the organization is merely a convenience or means to an end, a vehicle by which each of those participating in the enterprise may receive and expend money in much the same way as they would if the money was expended by them individually.

This rationale chiefly underlies the tax exemption for certain social clubs, which enable individuals to pool their resources for the purpose of provision of recreation and pleasure more effectively than can be done on an individual basis.[101] This tax rationale was summarized by a federal court as follows:

> Congress has determined that in a situation where individuals have banded together to provide recreational facilities on a mutual basis, it would be conceptually erroneous to impose a tax on the organization as a separate entity. The funds exempted are received only from the members and any "profit" which results from overcharging for the use of the facilities still belongs to the

---

[99] *Id.* at 14. The lower courts, not surprisingly, follow the Supreme Court's view that tax exemption is a government-provided subsidy (e.g., American Civil Liberties Union Foundation of Louisiana v. Crawford, 2002 WL 461649 (E.D. La. 2002)) (where the court enjoined application of three state statutes providing tax exemptions only for religious organizations).

Actually, the matter is somewhat worse. The Supreme Court, in addition to asserting that these tax exemptions are subsidies, also regarded nonexempted taxpayers as "indirect and vicarious donors" (Bob Jones University v. United States, *supra* note 96, at 591, quoted in Texas Monthly, Inc. v. Bullock, *supra* note 97, at 14). Persons who are required to pay a tax because they do not qualify for an exemption, however, are hardly "donors," indirect or otherwise; characterization of such persons as "donors" is wholly inconsistent with the Court's jurisprudence on that subject (e.g., Comm'r v. Duberstein, 363 U.S. 278, 285 (1960), where the Court stated that a *gift* is a transfer of money or property motivated by "detached or disinterested generosity"). In general, Hopkins, *The Tax Law of Charitable Giving, Second Edition* (John Wiley & Sons, Inc., 2000) § 3.1.

[100] Usually, every tax exemption, deduction, credit, or other preference accorded to certain persons causes other persons to pay more tax; that almost always is an inevitable outcome when a tax base is narrowed (see *supra* note 32).

[101] See Chapter 14.

same members. No income of the sort usually taxed has been generated; the money has simply been shifted from one pocket to another, both within the same pair of pants.[102]

This rationale is likewise reflected in congressional committee reports.[103] It was invoked by Congress when enacting the tax exemption for homeowners' associations.[104] Thus, the Senate Finance Committee observed that, "[s]ince homeowners' associations generally allow individual homeowners to act together in order to maintain and improve the area in which they live, the committee believes it is not appropriate to tax the revenues of an association of homeowners who act together if an individual homeowner acting alone would not be taxed on the same activity."[105]

This rationale, however, operates only where "public" money is not unduly utilized for private gain.[106]

The inherent tax theory also serves as the rationale for the tax exemption for political organizations.[107] Thus, the legislative history underlying this exemption stated that these organizations should be treated as exempt organizations, inasmuch as "political activity (including the financing of political activity) as such is not a trade a business which is appropriately subject to tax."[108]

§ 1.6 OTHER RATIONALES AND REASONS FOR TAX-EXEMPT ORGANIZATIONS

(a) Rationales in Law

There are, as noted,[109] rationales for exempting organizations from tax other than the public policy rationale and the inherent tax rationale. One of these, less lofty than that accorded charitable and social welfare organizations, is extended as justification for the exemption of trade associations and other forms of business leagues.[110] These entities function to promote the welfare of a segment of society: the business, industrial, and professional community. An element of the philosophy supporting this type of exemption is that a healthy business climate advances the public welfare. The exemption for labor unions and other labor organizations rests on a comparable rationale.

The tax exemption for fraternal beneficiary organizations also depends, at least in part, on this concept. A study of the insurance practices of large fraternal

---

[102] McGlotten v. Connally, *supra* note 69 at 458.
[103] H. Rep. No. 91-413, 91st Cong., 1st Sess. 48 (1969); S. Rep. No. 91-552, 91st Cong., 1st Sess. 71 (1969). A similar rationale for the income tax exemption of churches (see Chapter 8) has been advanced (Bittker, "Churches, Taxes and the Constitution," *78 Yale L. J.* 1285 (1969)).
[104] See § 18.13.
[105] S. Rep. No. 938, 94th Cong. 2d Sess. 394 (1976).
[106] West Side Tennis Club v. Comm'r, 111 F.2d 6 (2d Cir. 1940), *cert. den.*, 311 U.S. 674 (1940).
[107] See Chapter 17.
[108] S. Rep. No. 1357, 93d Cong., 2d Sess. 26 (1974).
[109] See *supra* § 3.
[110] See Chapter 13.

societies by the U.S. Department of the Treasury[111] concluded that this rationale is inapplicable with respect to the insurance programs of these entities because the "provision of life insurance and other benefits is generally not considered a good or service with significant external benefits" to society generally. This report added, however, that "tax exemption for these goods and services [insurance and like benefits] may be justified in order to encourage" the charitable activities conducted by these organizations. The inherent tax rationale[112] "may" provide a basis for exemption for "certain" of these societies' services, according to the report. Further, the report observed that "[i]nsurance is not a type of product for which consumers may lack access to information on the appropriate quantity or quality that they need." Therefore, the market failure rationale[113] "may not be applicable" in this instance.

Other federal tax exemption provisions may be traced to an effort to achieve a particular objective. These provisions tend to be of more recent vintage, testimony to the fact of a more complex Internal Revenue Code. For example, exemption for veterans' organizations[114] was enacted to create a category of organizations entitled to use a particular exemption from the unrelated business income tax,[115] and exemption for homeowners' associations[116] came about because of a shift in the policy of the Internal Revenue Service[117] regarding the scope of exemption provided for social welfare organizations. The exemption for college and university investment vehicles was the result of Congress's effort to salvage the exempt status of a common investment fund in the face of a determination by the IRS to the contrary.[118] As is so often the case with respect to the tax law generally, a particular exemption provision can arise as the result of case law, or to clarify it; this was the origin of statutes granting exemption to cooperative hospital service organizations,[119] charitable risk pools,[120] child care organizations,[121] public safety testing entities,[122] and prepaid tuition programs.[123]

All of the foregoing rationales for tax-exempt organizations have been described in philosophical, historical, political, policy, or technical tax terms. Yet another approach to an understanding of exempt organizations can be found in economic theory.

---

[111] "Report to the Congress on Fraternal Benefit Societies," U.S. Department of the Treasury, January 15, 1993. See § 18.4(a), note 96.
[112] See *supra* § 3.
[113] See text accompanied by infra notes 127–129.
[114] See § 18.10(a).
[115] See § 28.3, text accompanied by note 26.
[116] See § 18.13.
[117] Hereinafter IRS.
[118] See § 10.5.
[119] See § 10.4
[120] See § 10.6.
[121] See § 7.7.
[122] See § 10.3.
[123] See § 18.16.

(b) Rationales in Economic Theory

Principles of economics are founded on the laws of supply (production) and demand (consumption). Using the foregoing analyses, tax-exempt organizations appear to have arisen in response to the pressures of the supply side, namely, to provide goods and services, and the force of pluralistic institutions and organizations in society. Others, however, view exempt organizations as responses to sets of social needs that can be described in demand-side economic terms, a "positive theory of consumer demand."[124]

According to the demand-side analysis, consumers in many contexts prefer to deal with nonprofit, tax-exempt organizations in purchasing goods and services, because the consumer knows that a nonprofit organization has a "legal commitment to devote its entire earnings to the production of services,"[125] while for-profit organizations have an incentive to raise prices and decrease quality. Generally, it is too difficult for consumers to monitor these forces. This means that consumers have a greater basis for trusting exempt organizations to provide the services. Thus, the consumer, pursuant to this analysis, "needs an organization that he [or she] can trust, and the non-profit, because of the legal constraints under which it must operate, is likely to serve that function better than its for-profit counterpart."[126]

This phenomenon has been described as *market failure* as far as for-profit organizations are concerned, in that, in certain circumstances, the market is unable to police the producers by means of ordinary contractual devices.[127] This, in turn, has been described as *contract failure*, which occurs where "consumers may be incapable of accurately evaluating the goods promised or delivered" and "market competition may well provide insufficient discipline for a profit-seeking producer."[128] Hence, according to this theory, the consuming public selects the nonprofit organizations, which operate without the profit motive[129] and offer the consumer the "trust element" that the for-profit organizations cannot always provide.

Although the economic demand-side theory is fascinating and undoubtedly contains much truth, it probably overstates the aspect of consumer demand and downplays historical realities, tax considerations, and human frailties. The nonprofit organization antedates the for-profit corporation, and many of today's tax-exempt organizations may be nonprofit because their forebears started out as such. In addition, the forces of pluralism of institutions and organizations continue to shape much of the contemporary independent sector.

Another application of economic theory to the rationale for tax exemption (and the charitable contribution deduction) occurred when Congress was considering fundamental tax system reform in 2000. In an analysis, the staff of

---

[124] Hansmann, "The Role of Nonprofit Enterprise," *supra* note 5, at 896.
[125] *Id.* at 844.
[126] *Id.* at 847.
[127] *Id.* at 845.
[128] *Id.* at 843.
[129] See § 4.9.

the Joint Committee on Taxation wrote: "One rationale for the charitable contribution deduction is that income given to a charity should not be taxed because it does not enrich the giver. Or, stated differently, the charitable contribution reduces the taxpayer's ability to pay income tax. A contrasting view would be that charitable giving is a purely personal expenditure, a deduction for which should be denied under a theoretically pure income tax system."[130]

The second rationale for the deduction, according to this analysis, "relates to the view that charitable organizations are providing many services at little or no direct cost to taxpayers. It is argued that such services would otherwise have to be provided by the government at full cost to taxpayers. In this view, the tax deduction for voluntary charitable contributions is seen as equivalent to deductions permitted for many State and local taxes. The charitable contribution deduction can be said to provide neutrality in the choice to provide certain services to the public through direct government operation or through the private operation and mixed private and public financing of a charitable organization."[131]

A third rationale for the deduction, as reflected in this analysis, is that "many charitable organizations are public in nature or provide significant spillover benefits to the public at large. For example, some charitable organizations maintain open spaces such as bird refuges. Open space is an example of a public good, that is, a good or service that may be simultaneously enjoyed by all. Other charitable organizations provide benefits that improve the health of specific individuals, such as through the provision of vaccinations, which provide spillover benefits to the population in general. Economists generally argue that, in the absence of a subsidy, the private market may provide insufficient levels of public goods or goods that create spillover benefits. Thus, it is argued that the tax deduction for charitable contributions under present law encourages donations to charities that provide public goods or significant spillover benefits and, therefore, promotes the provision of such benefits."[132]

As to this third rationale, the analysis noted that economists refer to these "spillover benefits" as "positive externalities," which are "benefits that accrue to the individual who consumes the good and also to other individuals who are 'external' to the initial consumption of the good."

As interesting as these rationales for the charitable deduction are, it is disheartening to read this cold recitation of them in such stark economic terms. As discussed, the basis for tax exemption and the charitable deduction lies in the domain of political philosophy, rather than the realm of the "dismal science." The ultimate purpose of the exemption and deduction is to sustain and grow the charitable sector, which is an integral and necessary component of U.S. society. The purpose of tax exemption and the charitable deduction is not to cause the ac-

---

[130] "Overview of Present Law and Analysis Relating to Selected Provisions of the President's Individual Income Tax Proposals" (JCX-15-01), 106th Cong., 2d Sess. (2000).
[131] *Id.*
[132] *Id.*

crual of positive externalities to consumers of goods who are external to the initial consumption of those goods.

§ 1.7 FREEDOM OF ASSOCIATION

Tax exemption for nonprofit membership organizations may be viewed as a manifestation of the constitutionally protected right of association accorded the members of these organizations. There are two types of *freedoms of association*. One type—termed the *freedom of intimate association*—is the traditional type of protected association derived from the right of personal liberty. The other type—the *freedom of expressive association*—is a function of the right of free speech protected by the First Amendment to the U.S. Constitution.

By application of the doctrine of freedom of intimate association, the formation and preservation of certain types of highly personal relationships are afforded a substantial measure of sanctuary from interference by government.[133] These personal bonds are considered to foster diversity and advance personal liberty.[134] In assessing the extent of constraints on the authority of government to interfere with this freedom, a court must make a determination of where the objective characteristics of the relationship, which is created where an individual enters into a particular association, are located on a spectrum from the most intimate to the most attenuated of personal relationships.[135] Relevant factors include size, purpose, policies, selectivity, and congeniality.[136]

The freedom to engage in group effort is guaranteed under the doctrine of freedom of expressive association[137] and is viewed as a way of advancing political, social, economic, educational, religious, and cultural ends.[138] Government, however, has the ability to infringe on this right where compelling state interests, unrelated to the suppression of ideas and not achievable through means significantly less restrictive of associational freedoms, are served.[139]

These two associational freedoms were the subject of a U.S. Supreme

---

[133] Pierce v. Society of Sisters, 268 U.S. 510 (1925); Meyer v. Nebraska, 262 U.S. 390 (1923).

[134] Zablocki v. Redhail, 434 U.S. 374 (1978); Quilloin v. Walcott, 434 U.S. 246 (1978); Smith v. Organization of Foster Families, 431 U.S. 494 (1977); Carey v. Population Servs. Int'l, 431 U.S. 678 (1977); Moore v. East Cleveland, 431 U.S. 494 (1977); Cleveland Bd. Of Educ. v. LaFleur, 414 U.S. 632 (1974); Wisconsin v. Yoder, 406 U.S. 205 (1973); Stanley v. Illinois, 405 U.S. 645 (1972); Stanley v. Georgia, 394 U.S. 557 (1969); Griswold v. Connecticut, 381 U.S. 479 (1965); Olmstead v. United States, 277 U.S. 438 (1928).

[135] Runyon v. McCrary, 427 U.S. 160 (1976).

[136] Roberts v. United States Jaycees, 468 U.S. 609 (1984).

[137] Rent Control Coalition for Fair Housing v. Berkeley, 454 U.S. 290 (1981).

[138] NAACP v. Claiborne Hardware Co., 458 U.S. 886 (1982); Larson v. Valente, 456 U.S. 228 (1982); In re Primus, 436 U.S. 412 (1978); Abood v. Detroit Bd. of Educ. 431 U.S. 209 (1977).

[139] Brown v. Socialist Workers '74 Campaign Comm., 459 U.S. 87 (1982); Democratic Party v. Wisconsin, 450 U.S. 107 (1981); Buckley v. Valeo, 424 U.S. 1 (1976), Cousins v. Wigoda, 419 U.S. 477 (1975); American Party v. White. 415 U.S. 767 (1974); NAACP v. Button, 371 U.S. 415 (1963); Shelton v. Tucker, 364 U.S. 486 (1960), NAACP v. Alabama, 347 U.S. 449 (1958).

Court analysis concerning an organization's right to exclude women from its voting membership.[140] The Court found that the organization and its chapters were too large and unselective to find shelter under the doctrine of freedom of intimate association. While the Court conceded that the "[f]reedom of association therefore plainly presupposes a freedom not to associate," it concluded that the governmental interest in eradicating gender-based discrimination is superior to the associational rights of the organization's male members.[141] In general, the Court held that to tolerate this form of discrimination would be to deny "society the benefits of wide participation in political, economic, and cultural life."[142]

A state supreme court held that the state's antidiscrimination law was violated when a youth organization expelled a member, who was in a leadership position, because he was gay.[143] The court found that the organization was a "public accommodation" rather than a private organization, so the doctrine of freedom of association did not operate to protect the expulsion decision. The organization was held not to be private, in part, because it was "inclusive, not selective, in its membership practice."[144] The free speech doctrine argument failed before this court, in part, because the organization's members "do not associate for the purpose of disseminating the belief that homosexuality is immoral."[145]

Nonetheless, the U.S. Supreme Court, holding that the organization has a constitutional right, under the First Amendment, to exclude gays from leadership positions because of their sexual orientation, overruled this opinion.[146] Application of the state's antidiscrimination law was found to be a "severe intrusion" on the organization's rights to freedom of expressive association.[147] The Court's review of the record resulted in a finding that there was a sufficient basis to conclude that the organization does "not want to promote homosexual conduct as a legitimate form of behavior."[148] The Court wrote: "The forced inclusion of an unwanted person in a group infringes the group's freedom of expressive association if the presence of that person affects in a significant way the group's ability to advocate public or private viewpoints."[149]

The Court observed that organizations do not have to associate for the "purpose" of disseminating a certain message to be entitled to First Amendment protections.[150] Rather, an organization need merely engage in expressive

---

[140] Roberts v. United States Jaycees, *supra* note 136.

[141] *Id.* at 622–629.

[142] *Id.* at 625. In general, Linder, "Freedom of Association after *Roberts v. United States Jaycees*," 82 *Mich. L. Rev.* (No. 8) 1878 (1984).

[143] Dale v. Boy Scouts of America, 734 A.2d 1196 (N.J. Super. Ct. 1998).

[144] *Id.* at 1216.

[145] *Id.* at 1223.

[146] Boy Scouts of America et al v. Dale, 530 U.S. 640 (2000).

[147] *Id.* at 659.

[148] *Id.* at 651.

[149] *Id.* at 648.

[150] *Id.* at 2448. In general, Brody, "Entrance, Voice, and Exit: The Constitutional Bounds of the Right of Association," 35 *U.C. Davis L. Rev.* (No. 4) 821 (April 2002).

activity that could be impaired to be entitled to protection. The Court also noted that the First Amendment does not require that every member of a group agree on every issue in order for the group's policy to be expressive association. The dissenters wrote that the organization did not engage in the requisite level of expression on the subject to trigger the constitutional law protections.

CHAPTER TWO

Overview of Nonprofit Sector and Tax-Exempt Organizations

The nonprofit sector in the United States and the federal tax law with respect to it have a common feature: enormous and incessant growth. As to the sector, this expansion is reflected in all of the principal indicators, such as the number of organizations, the sector's asset base, the amount of charitable giving and granting, its annual expenditures, its share of the gross national product, and the size of its workforce. There is, however, this direct correlation: As the nonprofit sector expands, so too does the body of federal and state law regulating it. No end to either of these expansions is in sight.[1]

Over the years, there have been many efforts to analyze and portray the nonprofit sector. One of the first of these significant undertakings, utilizing statistics, conducted jointly by the Survey Research Center at the University of Michigan and the U.S. Census Bureau, was published in 1975 as part of the findings of the Commission on Private Philanthropy and Public Needs, informally known as the Filer Commission.[2] The data compiled for the Commission's use were for 1973. Contemporary charitable giving statistics are explored below, but one striking basis of comparison cannot be resisted at this point: Charitable giving in the year the first edition of this book was published—1975—was $28.56 billion,[3] while for 2001 the amount was about $212 billion.

Research of the nature developed for the Filer Commission spawned recurring statistical portraits of the sector. One of the most comprehensive of these analyses is that provided in the periodic almanac now prepared by Independent

---

[1] "The rapid growth of the nonprofit sector in the last half century has led to greatly increased attention from the media, scholars, the government, and the public" (O'Neill, *Nonprofit Nation: A New Look at the Third America* 34 (Jossey-Bass, Inc., 2002) (*Nonprofit Nation*)).

[2] *Giving in America: Toward a Stronger Voluntary Sector*, Report of the Commission on Private Philanthropy and Public Needs (1975).

[3] See text accompanied by *infra* note 31.

Sector and the Urban Institute.[4] Others include a fascinating portrait of the "third America"[5] and the annual survey of charitable giving published by the American Association of Fund Raising Counsel Trust for Philanthropy.[6] The IRS's Statistics of Income Division collects data on tax-exempt organizations.[7] Further, various subsets of the nonprofit sector are the subject of specific portrayals.[8]

The nonprofit sector in the United States is not uniformly labeled; it goes by many names. In addition to *nonprofit,*[9] adjectives used include *tax-exempt, voluntary, nongovernmental, independent,* and *voluntary.* (In the author's view, *nonprofit sector* endures as the sturdiest of the terms.) In its most expansive definition, the nonprofit sector comprises all tax-exempt organizations and some entities that cannot qualify for exemption. Independent Sector defines the *independent sector* as all charitable[10] and social welfare organizations.[11]

As Independent Sector defines the sector, it is comprised of "many, varied" organizations, such as "religious organizations, private colleges and schools, foundations, hospitals, day-care centers, environmental organizations, museums, symphony orchestras, youth organizations, advocacy groups, and neighborhood organizations, to name a few." This analysis continued: "What is common among them all is their mission to serve a public purpose, their voluntary and self-governing nature, and their exclusion from being able to distribute profits to stockholders."[12]

§ 2.1 PROFILE OF NONPROFIT SECTOR

Any assessment of any consequence of the nonprofit sector includes a discussion of the number of organizations in the sector. Yet, it is "surprisingly difficult to answer the seemingly simple question, How many nonprofit organizations are

---

[4] Weitzman, Jalandoni, Lampkin, & Pollak, *The New Nonprofit Almanac and Desk Reference: The Essential Facts and Figures for Managers, Researchers, and Volunteers* (Jossey-Bass, Inc., various editions). The edition referenced in this chapter (the sixth) was published in 2002 (*Nonprofit Almanac*).

[5] *Nonprofit Nation.*

[6] These annual publications of this organization (Trust for Philanthropy) are titled *Giving USA.*

[7] The IRS publishes various editions of the *Statistics of Income Bulletins.*

[8] E.g., *Yearbook of American and Canadian Churches* (National Council of the Churches of Christ in the United States of America, various editions); *Foundation Giving: Yearbook of Facts and Figures on Private, Corporate and Community Foundations* (The Foundation Center, various editions); *Foundation Management Report* (Council on Foundations, various editions). The American Hospital Association publishes statistics concerning hospitals; the National Center for Education Statistics publishes data on independent colleges and universities; and the American Society of Association Executives publishes information concerning the nation's trade, business, and professional associations. There are several other of these analyses.

[9] Indeed, there is no uniformity as to this term (see § 1.1(b)).

[10] That is, organizations that are tax-exempt pursuant to IRC § 501(a) because they are described in IRC § 501(c)(3) (see Part Two).

[11] That is, organizations that are tax-exempt pursuant to IRC § 501(a) because they are described in IRC § 501(c)(4) (see Chapter 12). This definition of the independent sector is in *Nonprofit Almanac* 7–8.

[12] *Nonprofit Almanac* at 3.

there in the United States?"[13] The simple answer is: millions. There are "several million" nonprofit organizations, although "no one really knows how many."[14]

In an understatement, the observation was made that "[m]easuring the number of organizations in the independent sector is a complex activity, largely because of the diversity of its components."[15] There are several reasons for this. One reason is that church organizations (of which there are an estimated 354,000[16]) are not required to file annual information returns with the IRS,[17] so that data concerning them is difficult to amass. Also, hundreds of organizations are under a group exemption[18] and thus not separately identified. Further, smaller nonprofit organizations need not seek recognition of tax exemption from the IRS[19] and/or need not annually report to the agency.[20]

Certainly, it appears that the number of nonprofit organizations that are formally recognized by a government is approaching 2 million. The most recent analysis posits the number at 1.8 million nonprofit organizations.[21] The number of them in 1998 was estimated to be approximately 1.6 million.[22] This number, however, was principally based on entities reporting to the IRS.

In 1998, nonprofit organizations represented 6 percent of total U.S. operating organizations (27.7 million entities). (For-profit organizations constituted 94 percent of total entities.) The number of reporting charitable and social welfare organizations (874,000) increased by 31 percent between 1987 and 1997, surpassing the growth rate of the business and governmental sectors.[23] The IRS data on this subject are discussed below.[24]

In 1998, total national income was $7.27 trillion. The nonprofit organizations sector's share of this was 6.7 percent. The value of volunteer time for that year was $225.9 billion. The value of volunteer time as a share of national income increased from 121.8 billion in 1977 to 221.8 billion in 1998.[25] In 1998, an estimated 144.1 million individuals received compensation for work. Charitable and social welfare organizations increased their share of total employment from 5.3 percent in 1977 to 7.1 percent in 1998. With volunteer time taken into account, the 1998 percentage of the sector's total national employment was 10.8 percent.[26] In 1998,

---

[13] *Nonprofit Nation* at 8.

[14] *Id.* at 1.

[15] *Id.* at 8. The point was articulated more forcefully (albeit less elegantly) in the fifth edition of this almanac, where it was stated that "[c]ounting the number of institutions in the independent sector is a challenge" (Hodgkinson & Weitzman, *Nonprofit Almanac: Dimensions of the Independent Sector* 25 (Jossey-Bass, Inc., 1996)).

[16] *Nonprofit Almanac* at 5. The term *church* includes analogous religious congregations, such as temples and mosques.

[17] See § 24.3.

[18] See § 23.6.

[19] These are organizations that normally do not generate more than $5,000 in revenue. See § 23.3(b).

[20] These are organizations that normally do not generate more than $25,000 annually in revenue. See § 24.3.

[21] *Nonprofit Nation* at 1.

[22] *Nonprofit Almanac* at 8.

[23] *Id.* at 7.

[24] See the text accompanied by *infra* notes 32–34.

[25] *Nonprofit Almanac* at 15.

[26] *Id.* at 19.

the annual earnings from work (including volunteer employment) totaled $5 trillion. In that year, nonprofit sector organizations accounted for $383.5 billion of total earnings.[27]

In 1999, current operating expenditures for all nonprofit organizations were said to be $784.6 billion. In constant (1996) dollars, these expenditures increased from $172.2 billion in 1959 to $723.4 billion in 1999. In constant dollars, nonprofit organizations expended in 1999 for each individual in the country $2,649.[28]

Also in 1999, the current operating expenditures of nonprofit organizations were 21.5 percent of total services. In that year, these expenditures were 12.5 percent of personal consumption expenditures and 8.5 percent of the gross domestic product. Current operating expenditures of nonprofit organizations as a percentage of gross domestic product peaked at 8.6 percent in 1993–1996, decreasing slightly to 8.5 percent in recent years.[29]

In 1998, there were 10.3 million paid employees in the nonprofit sector, representing 9.3 percent of all paid employees in the economy. Employment in the nonprofit sector grew at an annual rate of 3.2 percent from 1977 to 1997. In 1998, the nonprofit sector's share of total wages and salaries was 6.3 percent ($259 billion). Within the framework of charitable and social welfare organizations, the health services subsector's share of total wages and salaries in 1998 was 43 percent. The education and research subsector's share of total wages and salaries was 21.6 percent in that year. Comparable percentages are 17.5 percent for social and legal services; 11.6 percent for religious organizations; 4.2 percent for civic, social, and fraternal organizations; 1.9 percent in the field of arts and culture; and 0.3 percent for private foundations and charitable trusts.[30]

In 1997, total revenues for charitable and social welfare organizations were estimated to be $665 billion. The major sources of funds for these organizations were forms of exempt function revenue (dues, fees, and other charges) (38 percent), government grants and contracts (31 percent), contributions (20 percent), and other forms of revenue (11 percent). In that year, total revenues in the health services subsector were $326 billion, in the education and research subsector were $119 billion, in the social and legal services subsector were $76.9 billion, in the religion subsector were $76.3 billion, and in the arts and cultural subsector were $15.4 billion.[31]

On the basis of data in the IRS Business Master File of Exempt Organizations and in annual information returns, it was estimated that there were over 632,000 charitable organizations, other than religious ones, in 1998. In that year, these charitable entities consisted of 567,237 public charities and 64,903 private foundations. Thus, in 1998, when the 354,000 congregations were taken into account, there were about 986,000 charitable organizations.[32]

[27] *Id.* at 23.
[28] *Id.* at 25.
[29] *Id.* at 28–29.
[30] *Id.* at 39–44.
[31] *Id.* at 90–92.
[32] *Id.* at 124–125.

Of these public charities, 224,272 reported to the IRS. This was an increase of 39 percent, compared with the number of charitable organizations that reported in 1992. About two-thirds of these organizations are relatively small. About 73 percent of these organizations had total expenses under $500,000; about 4 percent of these entities had total expenses exceeding $10 million.[33]

Total annual revenue received by these organization was nearly $693 billion in 1998, an increase of about 47 percent in relation to 1992. About 12.4 percent of this sum was in the form of contributions and 8 percent as government grants. The largest amount of revenue—68 percent—was exempt function (related business) revenue. The remaining revenue came in the form of investment income (7.7 percent) and other sources, such as dues, rental income, and income from special events.[34]

Of these reporting charitable organizations, 35 percent were in the human services field; 16 percent were in education; and 15 percent were in the health field or were in the arts, culture, humanities, and other charitable subsectors. Health organizations received $392.5 billion in 1998, while revenue to educational organizations was nearly $129 billion, revenue to human services charities was $91.7 billion; revenue to arts, culture, and humanities was $19.4 billion; and revenue to environment and animal organizations was $6.3 billion. Expenses for reporting public charities were over $621.2 billion in 1998, an increase of almost 41 percent compared to 1992.[35]

Assets for all reporting charitable organizations grew to $1.2 trillion in 1998, a mammoth 83 percent increase compared to 1992. Two major categories, health (44 percent) and education (29 percent), accounted for nearly 75 percent of the assets of filing institutions. The subsector with the largest number of organizations—human services—held only 11 percent of total assets.[36]

The net assets of reporting public charities increased by 100 percent, from nearly $396 billion in 1992 to $791 billion in 1998. The health subsector accounted for 38 percent of the net assets of the nonprofit sector, with educational organizations holding 33 percent and human services organizations accounting for 9 percent of net assets.[37]

The Trust for Philanthropy calculated that charitable giving in the United States in 2001 totaled about $212 billion.[38] The sources of these contributions were as follows: living individuals, $160.72 billion; private foundations (other than corporate foundations), $25.9 billion; bequests, $16.33 billion; and corporations, $9.05 billion. Giving by individuals constituted 75.8 percent of all charitable giving in 2001; that sum amounted to 1.8 percent of personal income for that year. Private foundation granting increased by 5.4 percent. Giving by corporations dropped by 12.1 percent.

[33] *Id.* at 124.
[34] *Id.*
[35] *Id.* at 124–126.
[36] *Id.* at 127.
[37] *Id.*
[38] *Giving USA* (2002). This was a change of 0.5 percent (–2.3 percent in inflation-adjusted terms) from an estimate of $210.89 billion in giving in 2000.

These gifts were allocated as follows: religion, $80.96 billion; education, $31.84 billion; health, $18.43 billion; human services, $20.71 billion; arts, culture, and humanities, $12.14 billion; public-society benefit organizations, $11.82 billion; environment/animals, $6.41 billion; and international affairs, $4.14 billion. Giving to religious entities comprised 38.2 percent of charitable giving in 2001.

There were 516,554 charitable organizations registered with the IRS in 1991; there were 865,096 in 2001. There were 46,088 of these entities added in 2001. Growth in the number of charities from 2000 to 2001 was 5.6 percent.

Here are some other perspectives on the nonprofit sector; it:

- Accounts for 5 to 10 percent of the nation's economy.

- Accounts for 8 percent of the nation's noninstitutional civilian employees.

- Has more civilian employees than the federal government and the 50 state governments combined.

- Employs more people than any of the following industries: agriculture; mining; construction; transportation, communications, and other public utilities; and finance, insurance, and real estate.

- Generates revenue that exceeds the gross domestic product of all but six foreign countries: China, France, Germany, Italy, Japan, and the United Kingdom.[39]

Statistics, of course, cannot provide the entire nonprofit sector picture. As the Commission on Private Philanthropy and Public Needs observed (albeit nearly 30 years ago), the "arithmetic of the nonprofit sector finds much of its significance in less quantifiable and even less precise dimensions—in the human measurements of who is served, who is affected by nonprofit groups and activities." The Commission added:

> In some sense, everybody is [served or affected by the sector]: the contributions of voluntary organizations to broadscale social and scientific advances have been widely and frequently extolled. Charitable groups were in the forefront of ridding society of child labor, abolitionist groups in tearing down the institution of slavery, civic-minded groups in purging the spoils system from public office. The benefits of non-profit scientific and technological research include the great reduction of scourges such as tuberculosis and polio, malaria, typhus, influenza, rabies, yaws, bilharziasis, syphilis and amoebic dysentery. These are among the myriad products of the nonprofit sector that have at least indirectly affected all Americans and much of the rest of the world besides.
>
> Perhaps the nonprofit activity that most directly touches the lives of most Americans today is noncommercial "public" television. A bare concept twenty-five years ago, its development was underwritten mainly by foundations. Today it comprises a network of some 240 stations valued at billions of

---

[39] *Nonprofit Nation* at 12.

dollars, is increasingly supported by small, "subscriber" contributions and has broadened and enriched a medium that occupies hours of the average American's day.

More particularly benefited by voluntary organizations are the one quarter of all college and university students who attend private institutions of higher education. For hundreds of millions of Americans, private community hospitals, accounting for half of all hospitals in the United States, have been, as one Commission study puts it, "the primary site for handling the most dramatic of human experiences—birth, death, and the alleviation of personal suffering." In this secular age, too, it is worth noting that the largest category in the non-profit sector is still very large indeed, that nearly two out of three Americans belong to and evidently find comfort and inspiration in the nation's hundreds of thousands of religious organizations. All told, it would be hard to imagine American life without voluntary nonprofit organizations and associations, so entwined are they in the very fabric of our society, from massive national organizations to the local Girl Scouts, the parent-teachers association or the bottle recycling group.[40]

§ 2.2   CATEGORIES OF TAX-EXEMPT ORGANIZATIONS

Data compiled by the IRS, through 1998, indicate that there were 1,273,336 organizations in its Master File of Tax-Exempt Organizations.[41] This compilation, as noted, does not include nonprofit organizations that are not required to file applications for recognition of tax exemption with the IRS, including churches, integrated auxiliaries of churches, conventions and associations of churches, and certain subordinate units of churches.[42] As also noted, however, it is estimated that there were, in 1998, 354,000 churches.[43] Further, taking into account small organizations and those covered by a group exemption (such as scout troops and fraternal lodges), there are, as noted, millions of nonprofit organizations in the United States, with the current number of "registered" tax-exempt organizations in the nation set at 1.8 million.

The breakdown as to these tax-exempt organizations is as follows:[44] 20 instrumentalities of the United States,[45] 7,009 single-parent title-holding companies,[46] 819,008 charitable organizations,[47] 137,037 social welfare organizations,[48] 63,456 labor and agricultural organizations,[49] 82,246 business leagues,[50] 67,246

---

[40] *Giving in America—Toward a Stronger Voluntary Sector, supra* note 1, at 34–38.
[41] *Nonprofit Almanac* at 6.
[42] See § 24.3.
[43] See the text accompanied by *supra* note 12.
[44] *Nonprofit Nation* at 4–5.
[45] Organizations described in IRC § 501(c)(1) (see § 18.1).
[46] Organizations described in IRC § 501(c)(2) (see § 18.2(a)).
[47] Organizations described in IRC § 501(c)(3) (see Part Two). The entities referenced *infra* notes 72–73 are also charitable organizations.
[48] Organizations described in IRC § 501(c)(4) (see Chapter 12).
[49] Organizations described in IRC § 501(c)(5) (see Chapter 15).
[50] Organizations described in IRC § 501(c)(6) (see Chapter 13).

social and recreational clubs,[51] 81,890 fraternal beneficiary societies,[52] 13,595 voluntary employees' beneficiary societies,[53] 23,487 domestic fraternal beneficiary societies,[54] 15 teachers' retirement funds,[55] 6,489 benevolent life insurance associations,[56] 10,132 cemetery companies,[57] 4,320 credit unions,[58] 1,342 mutual insurance companies,[59] 22 crop operations finance corporations,[60] 501 supplemental unemployment benefit trusts,[61] 2 employee-funded pension trusts,[62] 35,249 war veterans' organizations,[63] 56 group legal services organizations,[64] 28 black lung benefit trusts,[65] 2 veterans' organizations founded prior to 1880,[66] 1 trust described in section 4049 of the Employee Retirement Income Security Act,[67] 1,192 title-holding companies for multiple beneficiaries,[68] 9 organizations providing medical insurance for those difficult to insure,[69] 7 state-formed workers' compensation organizations,[70] 127 religious and apostolic organizations,[71] 41 cooperative hospital service organizations,[72] 1 cooperative service organization of educational institutions,[73] 1,330 farmers' cooperatives,[74] 12,877 political organizations,[75] and 126,548 homeowners' associations.[76]

This enumeration of tax-exempt organizations does not include references to multiemployer pension trusts,[77] day care centers,[78] or shipowners' protection and indemnity organizations.[79] Because there are no data yet com-

[51] Organizations described in IRC § 501(c)(7) (see Chapter 14).
[52] Organizations described in IRC § 501(c)(8) (see § 18.4(a)).
[53] Organizations described in IRC § 501(c)(9) (see § 16.3).
[54] Organizations described in IRC § 501(c)(10) (see § 18.4(b)).
[55] Organizations described in IRC § 501(c)(11) (see § 16.6).
[56] Organizations described in IRC § 501(c)(12) (see § 18.5).
[57] Organizations described in IRC § 501(c)(13) (see § 18.6).
[58] Organizations described in IRC § 501(c)(14) (see § 18.7).
[59] Organizations described in IRC § 501(c)(15) (see § 18.8).
[60] Organizations described in IRC § 501(c)(16) (see § 18.9).
[61] Organizations described in IRC § 501(c)(17) (see § 16.4).
[62] Organizations described in IRC § 501(c)(18) (see § 16.6).
[63] Organizations described in IRC § 501(c)(19) (see § 18.10(a)).
[64] Organizations that were described in IRC § 501(c)(20), prior to its expiration in 1992.
[65] Organizations described in IRC § 501(c)(21) (see § 16.5).
[66] Organizations described in IRC § 501(c)(23) (see § 18.10(b)).
[67] Organizations described in IRC § 501(c)(24) (see § 16.6).
[68] Organizations described in IRC § 501(c)(25) (see § 18.2(b)).
[69] Organizations described in IRC § 501(c)(26) (see § 18.14).
[70] Organizations described in IRC § 501(c)(27) (see § 18.15).
[71] Organizations described in IRC § 501(d) (see § 8.7).
[72] Organizations described in IRC § 501(e) (see § 10.4).
[73] Organizations described in IRC § 501(f) (see § 10.5.)
[74] Organizations described in IRC § 521 (see § 18.11)
[75] Organizations described in IRC § 527 (see Chapter 17).
[76] Organizations described in IRC § 528 (see § 18.13).
[77] Organizations described in IRC § 501(c)(22) (see § 16.6).
[78] Organizations described in IRC § 501(k) (see § 7.7).
[79] Organizations described in IRC § 526(d) (see § 18.12).

piled as to them, there is no listing of charitable risk pools[80] or prepaid tuition plan trusts.[81]

The federal tax law recognizes 68 categories of tax-exempt organizations.[82]

§ 2.3   ORGANIZATION OF THE IRS

The Internal Revenue Service is an agency of the U.S. Department of the Treasury. It is best known for being the nation's tax collection agency. The mission of the IRS, as it sees the matter, is to "provide America's taxpayers with top quality service by helping them understand and meet their tax responsibilities and by applying the tax law with integrity and fairness to all."[83] One of the functions of the Treasury Department is to formulate national tax policy, including that pertaining to tax-exempt organizations. This policy formulation is the responsibility of the Assistant Treasury Secretary for Tax Policy.

Recent years have brought substantive restructuring of the IRS. This is due in part to legislation enacted in 1998[84] and in part to initiatives undertaken by the agency as the result of a reorganization plan announced in early 1998.[85] An Oversight Board is responsible for overseeing the IRS in its administration, conduct, direction, and supervision of the execution and application of the internal revenue laws.[86] One function of this board is to recommend to the President candidates for Commissioner of Internal Revenue; the board may recommend removal of the Commissioner.[87] The Commissioner, who need not be a tax lawyer or accountant but must have a "demonstrated ability in management," is appointed to serve a five-year term.[88]

The IRS is administered at the national level from its office in Washington, D.C. (the National Office),[89] and is headed by the Commissioner, who generally

---

[80] Organizations described in IRC § 501(n) (see § 10.6).

[81] Organizations described in IRC § 529 (see § 18.16). This illustrates in part why it is difficult to tabulate the number of tax-exempt organizations at any point in time. *Nonprofit Nation* stated that there are 0 tuition plans (at 5). Yet, this cannot be; the IRS has issued rulings concerning these entities (see § 18.16, note 391). Moreover, the *New York Times* of August 12, 2002, reported in a front-page article that Americans created over 2 million of these plans in the past two and a half years, including $500,000 worth of accounts in the first three months of 2002; by the close of March 2002, assets in these accounts totaled $19 billion. This article concluded: "With the development of the 529 plans in the past few years, Congress and the IRS have created a whole industry."

As the preceding footnotes indicate, the many categories of tax-exempt organizations are discussed in various chapters throughout the book. Nonetheless, as the following observation by the U.S. Tax Court affirms, "[t]rying to understand the various exempt organization provisions of the Internal Revenue Code is as difficult as capturing a drop of mercury under your thumb" (Weingarden v. Comm'r, 86 T.C. 669, 675 (1986), *rev'd* (on other grounds), 825 F.2d 1027 (6th Cir. 1987)).

[82] See Appendix C.

[83] IRS Web site.

[84] Internal Revenue Service Restructuring and Reform Act of 1998, 112 Stat. 685 (Pub. L. No. 105-26, 105th Cong., 2d Sess. (1998) (for purposes of this section, Act)).

[85] See *infra* note 91.

[86] IRC § 7801(c)(1)(A).

[87] IRC § 7801(d)(3)(A).

[88] IRC § 7803(a)(1)(A).

[89] Reg. § 601.101(a).

superintends the assessment and collection of all taxes imposed by any law providing for federal revenue.[90] There are at present two deputy commissioners.

Congress in 1998 directed the Commissioner to reorganize the IRS in a way that substantially altered the then-existing structure (which was based on regional divisions), by restructuring the agency into units serving groups of taxpayers and other organizations with similar needs.[91] As a result, the IRS organization now includes four operating divisions, one of which serves tax-exempt organizations (and employee plans and state and local governments). This structure is reflected in the IRS's regional offices. As stated in one summary, in each of these three categories are four structures: "education and communication to identify taxpayer concerns early on; rulings and agreements to facilitate development of a voluntary compliance initiative; customer account services to process forms filed by exempt organizations; and examinations to identify compliance issues."[92] The first of these four divisions—the Tax Exempt and Government Entities Division—was established on December 5, 1999.[93] Within this arrangement is the Exempt Organizations Division, which functions to develop policy and administer the law in the realm of tax-exempt organizations. The Director of this division, who reports to the Tax Exempt Entities/Government Entities Division Commissioner, supervises the activities of the offices of Customer Education and Outreach, Rulings and Agreements, and Examinations.

Another aspect of the reorganization of the IRS is centralization of certain functions. Thus, all applications for recognition of exemption are sent to Cincinnati, Ohio; all annual information returns are sent to Ogden, Utah; and the exempt organization audit function is concentrated in Dallas, Texas.

The IRS began issuing Exempt Organizations Implementing Guidelines in 2002, which outline how the tax-exempt organizations component of the IRS will be applying its resources in support of the agency's major strategies and operational priorities in the exempt organizations area. One of the principal aspects of these guidelines is the IRS's view of the exempt organizations community as a cluster of *market segments*, 42 of which have been identified and will be or are in the process of being studied. The initial focus is on social clubs, labor organizations, business leagues, community foundations, social service organizations, and religious organizations other than churches. Other priority projects include enhancing the staffing of those who engage in determination work, implementing the IRS's customer education and outreach programs,[94] and redirecting the type and emphasis of audit programs.

Another component of the IRS at the national level is the Office of the IRS Chief Counsel, which is part of the Legal Division of the Treasury Department.

---

[90] IRC § 7802(a).

[91] Act § 1001(a)(3). This approach was a reinforcement of a plan announced by the Commissioner on January 28, 1998.

[92] Hirani, "Exempt Sector Will See Regional Offices, Ultimately More Funding for Operations," *Daily Tax Rep.* (No. 225) G-1 (Nov. 23, 1998).

[93] IRS News Release IR-1999-101. In general, McGovern, "The Tax Exempt and Government Entities Division—The Pathfinder," 27 *Exempt Org. Tax Rev.* (No. 2) 239 (Feb. 2000); Boisture, Davis, and Mayer, "How the IRS Plans to Restructure Its Exempt Organizations Operations," 10 *J. Tax Exempt Orgs.* (No. 5) 195 (Mar./Apr. 1998).

[94] An aspect of this program is the issuance of "plain language" publications; the IRS seeks suggestions for topics for these publications (Ann. 2001-14, 2001-7 L.R.B. 648).

The Chief Counsel is the principal legal adviser on federal tax matters to the Commissioner. Among the Associate Chief Counsels is the Associate Chief Counsel (Employee Benefits and Exempt Organizations). One of the functions of this Associate Chief Counsel's office, which includes an Assistant Chief Counsel with direct responsibility in the exempt organizations area and seven branches, is to develop legal policy and strategy in the field of tax-exempt organizations.

§ 2.4   EVOLUTION OF THE STATUTORY SCHEME

The statutory law of tax-exempt organizations was initiated in 1913, and given major boosts in 1950 and 1969. Indeed, today's statutory structure (along with the charitable giving rules[95]) was shaped substantially by the 1969 legislation. Nearly every tax act of any consequence since then (particularly in 1974, 1976, 1982, 1984, 1986, 1987, 1993, 1996, 1997, 2000, and 2002) has added to this body of law. (Additional legislation that would have augmented this collection of law, passed in 1992, 1995, and 1998, was vetoed.)

The original statutory tax exemption for nonprofit organizations in U.S. law for charitable organizations was contained in the Tariff Act of 1894.[96] The provision stated that "nothing herein contained shall apply to . . . corporations, companies, or associations organized and conducted solely for charitable, religious, or educational purposes."[97]

After ratification of the Sixteenth Amendment by the states in 1913, which provided Congress with the authority to enact an income tax, Congress enacted the Tariff Act of that year, exempting from federal income tax "any corporation or association organized and operated exclusively for religious, charitable, scientific, or educational purposes, no part of the net income of which inures to the benefit of any private shareholder or individual."[98]

In the Revenue Act of 1918, the enumeration of tax-exempt organizations was expanded to include those organized "for the prevention of cruelty to children or animals."[99] The Revenue Act of 1921 expanded the statute to exempt "any community chest, fund, or foundation" and added "literary" groups to the list of exempt entities.[100] The Revenue Acts of 1924,[101] 1926,[102] 1928,[103] and 1932[104] did not provide for any changes in the law of exempt organizations.

The Revenue Act of 1934 carried forward the tax exemption requirements as stated in the prior revenue measures and added the rule that "no substantial

---

[95] See *infra* § 5.
[96] 28 Stat. 556 (Act ch. 349).
[97] The income tax law enacted in 1894 was declared unconstitutional by the U.S. Supreme Court in Pollock v. Farmer's Loan & Trust Co., 158 U.S. 601 (1895), overruled on other grounds in State of S.C. v. Baker, 485 U.S. 505 (1988). Congress first created the office of the Commissioner of Internal Revenue and enacted an income tax in 1862, to finance Civil War expenses; that tax was repealed in 1872.
[98] 38 Stat. 114, 166.
[99] 40 Stat. 1076.
[100] 42 Stat. 253.
[101] 43 Stat. 282.
[102] 44 Stat. 40.
[103] 45 Stat. 813.
[104] 47 Stat. 193.

part" of the activities of an exempt charitable organization can involve the carry-ing on of "propaganda" or "attempting to influence legislation."[105] The Revenue Acts of 1936[106] and 1938[107] brought forward these rules, as did the Internal Rev-enue Code of 1939.[108]

The unrelated business rules were enacted in 1950.[109] This was a radical ad-dition to the law, in part because it introduced the concept that some or all other-wise tax-exempt organizations could be taxed. This would lead to many more federal taxes on or in connection with "tax-exempt" organizations. Today, the un-related business body of law is the dreadnought of the law of tax-exempt organi-zations.

The rules for charitable and like organizations, as stated in the tax exemp-tion law provision that remains in use today,[110] came into being as a consequence of enactment of the Internal Revenue Code in 1954.[111] The previous rules were re-tained and two additions to the statute were made: The listing of exempt organi-zations was amplified to include entities that are organized and operated for the purpose of "testing for public safety,"[112] and organizations otherwise described in the provision became forbidden to "participate in, or intervene in (including the publishing or distributing of statements), any political campaign on behalf of any candidate for public office."[113]

Enactment of the Revenue and Expenditure Control Act of 1968 brought rules concerning cooperative hospital service organizations.[114] These rules would be amended by provisions of the Revenue Act of 1988, the Tax Reform Act of 1976, and the Taxpayer Relief Act of 1997. The rules pertaining to cooperative ser-vice organizations of operating educational organizations were enacted in 1974,[115] as was statutory law concerning political organizations.[116]

The Tax Reform Act of 1969[117]—the most significant of the tax acts from the standpoint of the law of tax-exempt organizations—brought a stupendous array of exempt organizations laws, including rules differentiating public charities from private foundations, imposing taxes on various aspects of the operations of private foundations, and revising the unrelated debt-financed property rules and the tax treatment of social clubs.[118]

The Tax Reform Act of 1976 brought law concerning declaratory judgment

---

[105] 48 Stat. 700.
[106] 49 Stat. 1674.
[107] 52 Stat. 481.
[108] 53 Stat. 1.
[109] See Part Five.
[110] IRC § 501(c)(3).
[111] 68A Stat. 163.
[112] See § 10.3.
[113] See § 21.1.
[114] 82 Stat. 269.
[115] 88 Stat. 235.
[116] 88 Stat. 2108.
[117] 83 Stat. 487.
[118] While, as discussed, there was law pertaining to, and law practices concerning, tax-exempt organi-zations before 1969, enactment of the Tax Reform Act of 1969 ushered in the contemporary bases of this area of the law (other than the unrelated business law structure) and the modern exempt organi-zations law practice.

rules for charitable organizations, lobbying by public charities (the expenditure test), amateur sports organizations, social clubs, homeowners' associations, definition of the term agricultural, and tax exemption for group legal services plans (the latter of which expired in 1992).[119] The next year saw enactment of the Black Lung Benefits Revenue Act of 1977.[120]

The Tax Equity and Fiscal Responsibility Act of 1982 revised the rules pertaining to veterans' organizations and amended the law concerning amateur sports organizations.[121] The Tax Reform Act of 1984 caused the church audit rules, changes in the U.S. instrumentalities rules, and the child care organizations rules to become law.[122] The Deficit Reduction Act of 1984 brought the tax-exempt entity leasing rules.[123]

The Tax Reform Act of 1986 changed the Internal Revenue Code formal reference to the Code of 1986 (which, as amended, is its status today).[124] This act also introduced the law concerning provision of commercial-type insurance, liquidations of for-profit entities into tax-exempt organizations, and multiparent title-holding corporations; also, it revised the exempt entity leasing rules.

The Revenue Act of 1987 brought taxes on public charities for engaging in excessive lobbying and political campaign activities, as well as fundraising disclosure requirements for noncharitable organizations.[125] Enactment of the Omnibus Budget Reconciliation Act of 1993 introduced rules concerning the nondeductibility of expenses for lobbying and political campaign activities, and disclosure rules as to these activities for associations.[126] The 1993 legislation also introduced law in the charitable giving arena, concerning substantiation requirements and quid pro quo contributions.[127]

Legislation known as the Taxpayer Bill of Rights 2, enacted in 1996, added the intermediate sanctions rules,[128] expanded the penalties for failure to timely file complete annual information returns, expanded the contents of these returns, revised disclosure rules, and added the private inurement language to the law pertaining to tax-exempt social welfare organizations.[129] The Small Business Job Protection Act of 1996 added revisions to the unrelated business rules, exemption opportunities for charitable risk pools and state tuition programs, and the ability of exempt charitable organizations to own stock in small business corporations.[130]

The Health Insurance Portability and Accountability Act of 1996 brought two new categories of tax-exempt organizations.[131] The enactment of the Tax-

---

[119] 90 Stat. 1520.
[120] 92 Stat. 11.
[121] 96 Stat 324.
[122] 98 Stat. 494.
[123] *Id.*
[124] 100 Stat. 1951.
[125] 101 Stat. 1330.
[126] 107 Stat. 312.
[127] See Hopkins, *The Law of Fundraising, Third Edition* (John Wiley & Sons, Inc., 2002 (annually supplemented)).
[128] See Hopkins, *The Law of Intermediate Sanctions: A Guide for Nonprofits* (John Wiley & Sons, Inc., 2003).
[129] 110 Stat. 1452.
[130] 110 Stat. 1755.
[131] 110 Stat. 1936.

payer Relief Act of 1997 caused several changes and additions to the law of exempt organizations, including various modifications of the unrelated business income rules and treatment of associations of holders of timeshare interests as homeowners' associations.[132]

In 2000, Congress enacted rules requiring political organizations to disclose their funding and activities.[133] The Victims of Terrorism Tax Relief Act, which was signed into law in 2002,[134] brought rules concerning the provision of assistance by charitable organizations to individuals who are victims of terrorism and clarified the law concerning exempt organization-funded disaster relief programs.

§ 2.5 CHARITABLE CONTRIBUTION DEDUCTION RULES

The tax laws pertaining to tax-exempt charitable organizations and deductible charitable giving are closely intertwined.[135] Not only are the two subject matters intimately related conceptually, but the Internal Revenue Code also frequently cross-references one to the other. For example, many of the organizations that are considered public charities are described in the income tax charitable contribution deduction rules.[136]

The basic concept of the federal income tax charitable contribution deduction is that individuals who itemize deductions, as well as taxable corporations, can deduct, subject to a variety of limitations, an amount equivalent to the value of a contribution made to a qualified donee. A *charitable contribution* for income tax purposes is a gift to or for the use of one or more qualified donees.[137]

Aside from the nature of the donee, another basic element in determining whether a charitable contribution is deductible is, in the case of gifts of property, the nature of the property contributed. There are important distinctions between current giving and planned giving, between gifts of cash and of property, and between outright gifts and those of partial interests or in trust. The value of a qualified charitable contribution of an item of property generally is its fair market value.[138]

The tax treatment of gifts of property is dependent on whether the property is *capital gain property*, that is, a capital asset that has appreciated in value, which if sold would result in long-term capital gain.[139] (To be capital gain property, the property must be held for the long-term capital gain holding period, which is 12 months.[140]) Other property is *ordinary-income property* (including short-term capital gain property).

---

[132] 111 Stat. 788.

[133] 114 Stat. 477.

[134] 115 Stat. 2427.

[135] The federal tax laws pertaining to charitable giving are the subject of Hopkins, *The Tax Law of Charitable Giving, Second Edition* (John Wiley & Sons, Inc., 2000 (annually supplemented)).

[136] See § 11.3.

[137] IRC § 170(c).

[138] Reg. § 1.170A-1(c).

[139] IRC § 170(b)(1)(C)(iv).

[140] IRC § 1222(1), (2).

The deductibility of charitable contributions for a tax year is confined by certain percentage limitations, which in the case of individuals are a function of the donor's *contribution base*, which is essentially the same as adjusted gross income.[141] These percentage limitations are (1) 50 percent of the donor's contribution base for contributions of cash and ordinary-income property to public charities and private operating foundations;[142] (2) 20 percent of contribution base for contributions of capital gain property to organizations other than public charities and operating foundations, including private foundations;[143] (3) 30 percent of contribution base for contributions of capital-gain property to public charities;[144] (4) 30 percent of contribution base for contributions of cash and ordinary-income property to private foundations and certain other recipients;[145] and (5) 50 percent of contribution base for contributions of capital-gain property to public charities where the amount of the contribution is reduced by all of the unrealized appreciation in the value of the property.[146]

Where an individual makes a contribution to a public charity or certain other recipients to the extent that a percentage limitation is exceeded, the excess generally may be carried forward and deducted in subsequent years, up to five.[147] In the case of gifts of cash and ordinary-income property to private foundations in excess of the 30 percent limitation, the five-year carryforward rule also is applicable.[148]

Deductible charitable contributions by corporations in any tax year may not exceed 10 percent of taxable income, as adjusted.[149] A corporation on the accrual method of accounting can elect to treat a contribution as having been paid in a tax year if it is actually paid during the first two and one-half months of the following year.[150] While corporate gifts of property are generally subject to the rules discussed below, special rules apply to the deductibility of gifts of inventory.[151] The making of a charitable gift by a business corporation is not an *ultra vires* act and may be deductible where the general interests of the corporation and its shareholders are advanced.[152]

A donor (individual or corporation) who makes a gift of ordinary income property to any charity (public or private) must reduce the deduction by the full amount of any gain.[153] A donor who makes a gift of capital gain property to a public charity generally can compute the deduction using the property's fair

---

[141] IRC § 170(b)(1)(E).
[142] IRC § 170(b)(1)(A).
[143] IRC § 170(b)(1)(B). See Hopkins & Blazek, *Private Foundations: Tax Law and Compliance, Second Edition* (John Wiley & Sons, Inc., 2003 (annually supplemented)).
[144] IRC § 170(b)(1)(C)(i).
[145] IRC § 170(b)(1)(B)(i).
[146] IRC § 170(b)(1)(C)(iii).
[147] IRC §§ 170(b)(1)(C)(ii), 170(d)(1)(A).
[148] IRC § 170(b)(1)(B), last sentence.
[149] IRC § 170(b)(2).
[150] IRC § 170(a)(2).
[151] IRC § 170(e)(3).
[152] E.g., A. P. Smith Mfg. Co. v. Barlow, 98 A.2d 581 (N.J. 1953), *app. dis.*, 356 U.S. 861 (1953).
[153] IRC § 170(e)(1)(A). E.g., IRC § 1221(3).

market value at the time of the gift, regardless of basis and with no taxation of the appreciation.[154] An individual donor who makes a gift of capital gain tangible personal property to a public charity must reduce the deduction by all of the long-term capital gain that would have been recognized had the donor sold the property at its fair market value as of the date of contribution, where the use by the donee is unrelated to its tax-exempt purposes.[155] Generally, an individual donor who makes a gift of capital gain property to a private foundation must reduce the amount of the otherwise allowable deduction by all of the appreciation element.[156]

A deduction for a contribution of less than the donor's entire interest in property (that is, a partial interest), including the right to use property, is generally denied.[157] The exceptions are gifts of interests in trust;[158] gifts of an outright remainder interest in a personal residence or farm;[159] gifts of an undivided portion of one's entire interest in property;[160] gifts of a lease on, option to purchase, or easement with respect to real property granted in perpetuity to a public charity exclusively for conservation purposes;[161] and a remainder interest in real property that is granted to a public charity exclusively for conservation purposes.[162]

Contributions of income interests in property in trust are basically confined to the use of charitable lead trusts.[163] Aside from the charitable gift annuity and gifts of remainder interests in personal residences or farms, there is no deduction for a contribution of a remainder interest in property unless it is in trust and the trust is one of three types:[164] a charitable remainder annuity trust or unitrust[165] or a pooled income fund.[166] Defective charitable split-interest trusts may be reformed to preserve the charitable deduction where certain requirements are satisfied.[167]

Other notable features of the income tax charitable contribution deduction are the lack of a charitable deduction for contributions of services[168] and the re-

---

[154] IRC § 170(e).

[155] IRC § 170(e)(1)(B)(i).

[156] IRC § 170(e)(1)(B)(ii). There is a special rule in this regard: A donor is allowed to base the charitable deduction, for a gift of certain publicly traded stock to a private foundation, on the full fair market value of the property (IRC § 170(e)(5)).

[157] IRC § 170(f)(3).

[158] IRC § 170(f)(3)(A).

[159] IRC § 170(f)(3)(B)(i).

[160] IRC § 170(f)(3)(B)(ii).

[161] IRC § 170(f)(3)(B)(iii).

[162] IRC § 170(f)(3)(B)(iv).

[163] IRC § 170(f)(2)(B).

[164] IRC § 170(f)(2)(A).

[165] IRC § 664(d).

[166] IRC § 642(c)(5).

[167] IRC §§ 170(f)(7), 664(f), 2055(e)(3), 2522(c)(4).

[168] Reg. § 1.170A-1(g).

quirement of the filing of an information return with respect to certain transfers of income-producing property to charity.[169]

Charitable gifts are not subject to the gift tax[170] or to the estate tax.[171] There is no percentage ceiling on the amount of an estate that may be subject to the estate tax charitable deduction, and appreciated property may pass to charity from estates without any taxation on the appreciation element.

---

[169] IRC § 6050.
[170] IRC § 2522.
[171] IRC § 2055.

CHAPTER THREE

Sources, Advantages, and Disadvantages of Tax Exemption

As subsequent chapters indicate, there are many categories of tax-exempt organizations and, accordingly, the advantages and disadvantages of tax exemption will differ, depending upon the particular category.

§ 3.1 SOURCE OF TAX EXEMPTION

Section 61(a) of the Internal Revenue Code provides that "[e]xcept as otherwise provided in this subtitle [Subtitle A—income taxes], gross income means all income from whatever source derived . . ." including items such as interest, dividends, compensation for services, and receipts derived from business. The Code provides for a variety of deductions, exclusions, and exemptions in computing taxable income. Many of these are contained in Internal Revenue Code Subtitle A, Subchapter B, entitled "Computation of taxable income." Of pertinence in the tax-exempt organizations context, however, is the body of exemption provisions contained in Subtitle A, Subchapter F, captioned "Exempt organizations."

Exemption from federal income taxation is derived from a specific provision to that end in the Internal Revenue Code. *Derivation* of exemption is here used in the sense of *recognition* of exemption by the appropriate administrative agency (the IRS) or as a matter of law, as opposed to exemption that is a by-product (albeit a resolutely sought one) of some other tax status (such as a cooperative or a state instrumentality).

A federal tax exemption is a privilege (a matter of legislative grace), not an entitlement,[1] and—being an exception to the norm of taxation—is often strictly

---

[1] As discussed, however, the federal tax exemption for many nonprofit organizations (such as charitable ones) is a reflection of the heritage and societal structure of the United States (see § 1.3).

construed.[2] (The same principle applies with respect to tax deductions[3] and tax exclusions.[4]) This type of exemption must be by enactment of Congress and will not be granted by implication.[5] Two related tax precepts are that a person requesting exemption must demonstrate compliance with the requirements set forth in the statute that grants the exemption[6] and the party claiming the exemption bears the burden of proof of eligibility for the exemption.[7] Thus, a court wrote that the federal tax statutory law "generally consists of narrowly defined categories of exemption" and is "replete with rigid requirements which a putatively exempt organization must demonstrate it meets."[8] The IRS and the courts are alert for efforts to gain a tax exemption where the underlying motive is the purpose of "confounding tax collection."[9]

At the same time, provisions giving exemption for charitable organizations are usually liberally construed. Thus, a court wrote that the "judiciary will liberally construe, and rightfully so, provisions giving exemptions for charitable, religious, and educational purposes."[10] Another court said that "in view of the fact that bequests for public purposes operate in aid of good government and perform by private means what ultimately would fall upon the public, exemption from taxation is not so much a matter of grace or favor as

---

[2] E.g., Knights of Columbus Bldg. Ass'n of Stamford, Conn., Inc. v. United States, 88-1 U.S.T.C. ¶ 9336 (D. Conn. 1988) ("A tax exemption is a benefit conferred by the legislature in its discretion. Because there is no entitlement to an exemption absent allowance by the legislature, the exemption provisions are strictly construed"); Mercantile Bank & Trust Co. v. United States, 441 F.2d 364 (8th Cir. 1971) ("Special benefits to taxpayers, such as tax exemption status, do not turn upon general equitable considerations but are matters of legislative grace" (at 366)). Also Conference of Major Religious Superiors of Women, Inc. v. District of Columbia, 348 F.2d 783 (D.C. Cir. 1965); American Automobile Ass'n v. Comm'r, 19 T.C. 1146 (1953); Associated Indus. of Cleveland v. Comm'r, 7 T.C. 1449 (1946); Bingler v. Johnson, 394 U.S. 741 (1969) and authorities cited therein. In general, Murtagh, "The Role of the Courts in the Interpretation of the Internal Revenue Code," 24 *Tax Law.* 523 (1971).

[3] Deputy v. Du Pont, 308 U.S. 488 (1940); White v. United States, 305 U.S. 281 (1938). In a case involving tax deductions claimed by a trust, the court wrote that the deductions "must fit into a statutory category of deductibility, else the trustees must carry out their fiduciary duty at the expense of the trust, rather than the public fisc" (Alfred I. duPont Testamentary Trust v. Comm'r, 514 F.2d 917, 922 (5th Cir. 1975)).

[4] E.g., Estate of Levine v. Comm'r, 526 F.2d 717 (2d Cir. 1975) (where the court was prompted to observe that "[o]ne suspects that because the Internal Revenue Code . . . piles exceptions upon exclusions, it invites efforts to outwit the tax collector" (at 717)).

[5] E.g., Mescalero Apache Tribe v. Jones, 411 U.S. 145 (1973).

[6] E.g., Christian Echoes Nat'l Ministry v. United States, 470 F.2d 849 (10th Cir. 1972), *cert. den.*, 414 U.S. 864 (1973); Parker v. Comm'r, 365 F.2d 792 (8th Cir. 1966), *cert. den.*, 385 U.S. 1026 (1967).

[7] E.g., United States v. Olympic Radio & Television, Inc., 349 U.S. 232 (155); Bubbling Well Church of Universal Love v. Comm'r, 670 F.2d 104 (9th Cir. 1981); Senior Citizens Stores, Inc. v. United States, 602 F.2d 711 (5th Cir. 1979); Kenner v. Comm'r, 318 F.2d 632 (7th Cir. 1963).

[8] Knights of Columbus Ass'n of Stamford, Conn., Inc. v. United States, *supra* note 2.

[9] Granzow v. Comm'r, 739 F.2d 265, 268–269 (7th Cir. 1984).

[10] American Inst. for Economic Research v. United States, 302 F.2d 934, 937 (Ct. Cl. 1962), *cert. den.*, 372 U.S. 976 (1963), *reh'g den.*, 373 U.S. 954 (1963).

rather an act of justice."[11] Similarly, the exemption of income devoted to charity by means of the charitable contribution deductions has been held to not be narrowly construed.[12] These provisions respecting income destined for charity are accorded favorable construction, since they are "begotten from motives of public policy"[13] and any ambiguity therein has been traditionally resolved against taxation.[14]

The provision in the Internal Revenue Code that is the general source of the federal income tax exemption is IRC § 501(a),[15] which states an "organization described in subsection (c) or (d) or section 401(a) shall be exempt from taxation under this subtitle [Subtitle A—income taxes] unless such exemption is denied under section 501 or 503."

The U.S. Supreme Court characterized IRC § 501(a) as the "linchpin of the statutory benefit [exemption] system."[16] The Court summarized the exemption provided by IRC § 501(a) as according "advantageous treatment to several types of nonprofit corporations [and trusts and unincorporated associations], including exemption of their income from taxation and [for those that are also eligible charitable donees] deductibility by benefactors of the amounts of their donations."[17]

Thus, to be recognized as tax-exempt under IRC § 501(a), an organization must conform to the appropriate descriptive provisions of IRC § 501(c), IRC § 501(d), or IRC § 401(a). This exemption, however, does not extend to an organization's unrelated business taxable income.[18] Thus, the term *tax-exempt organization* is often not literally accurate, inasmuch as this type of nonprofit organization may be subject to the tax on unrelated income, as well as other taxes, such as those imposed on private foundations,[19] on organizations that engage in excessive lobbying,[20] on organizations that engage in certain political activities,[21] or on the investment income of certain nonprofit organizations.[22]

As will be discussed,[23] an organization that seeks to obtain tax-exempt

---

[11] Harrison v. Barker Annuity Fund, 90 F.2d 286, 288 (7th Cir. 1937). The court also said that the "courts quite generally have extended liberal construction to statutes furthering the encouragement of bequests for purposes which tend toward the public good, without reference to personal or selfish motives" (*id.*).

[12] SICO Found. v. United States, 295 F.2d 924, 930, note 19 (Ct. Cl. 1962), and cases cited therein.

[13] Helvering v. Bliss, 293 U.S. 144, 151 (1934).

[14] C. F. Mueller Co. v. Comm'r, 190 F.2d 210 (3d Cir. 1951).

[15] Also IRC §§ 521, 526–529.

[16] Simon v. Eastern Ky. Welfare Rights Org., 426 U.S. 26, 29, note 1 (1976).

[17] *Id.*, at 28.

[18] IRC § 501(b); Reg. § 1.501(a)-1(a)(1). See Part Five.

[19] See § 11.4.

[20] See §§ 20.2, 20.3.

[21] See § 21.2.

[22] See Chapters 14, 17, § 18.13.

[23] See Chapter 21.

status, therefore, bears the burden of proving that it satisfies all the requirements of the exemption statute involved.[24]

§ 3.2 ADVANTAGES OF TAX-EXEMPT STATUS

(a) Tax Exemption

Of course, the one advantage looming over all the rest, shared by all categories of tax-exempt organizations, is that—barring loss of exemption and/or imposition of the tax on income other than exempt function income, the unrelated business income tax, the tax on excessive legislative activities, the tax on certain political activities, or (if private foundations) a variety of excise taxes and the tax on net investment income[25]—these entities are spared federal income taxation. In some instances, exempt status under federal law will mean comparable or similar status under state and local law; in other cases, additional requirements must be satisfied.[26]

Federal income tax exemption may also involve exemption from certain federal excise and employment taxes. If, however, an exempt organization is a private foundation, it is subject to an excise tax on investment income[27] and perhaps a tax on termination of its private foundation status.[28] Generally, the private foundation rules carry sanctions in the form of taxes.[29]

Many organizations that are tax-exempt under federal law also qualify for exemption from state and local taxes. These exemptions may pertain to purchases of items of property, sales of items of property, use of property, the ownership of tangible personal property, ownership of intangible personal property, ownership of real property, and other activities.[30] In some jurisdictions, only some of these exemptions are available; the real property tax exemption is usually the most difficult to obtain. Some jurisdictions assert that exemption is harmful, in that it erodes the tax base;[31] nonprofit organizations will, on occasion, voluntarily pay taxes in lieu of taxation.

[24] E.g., Harding Hosp. v. United States, 505 F.2d 1068, 1071 (6th Cir. 19); Haswell v. United States, 500 F.2d 1133, 1140 (Ct. Cl. 1974).
[25] See *supra* notes 13–16.
[26] E.g., in the District of Columbia, franchise (income) tax exemption is available to charitable (IRC § 501(c)(3)) organizations only if they are "organized and operated to a substantial extent" within the District of Columbia (9 D.C. Code, Title 47 § 47-1802.1(4)).
[27] See § 11.4(f).
[28] *Id.*
[29] See § 11.4. The intermediate sanctions excise taxes are imposed on disqualified persons, not tax-exempt organizations (see § 19.11).
[30] E.g., University v. People, 99 U.S. 309 (1878).
[31] In general, see Balk (ed.), *The Free List* (1971).

(b) Deductibility of Contributions

Certain tax-exempt organizations[32] are eligible to attract deductible charitable contributions from individuals and corporations. With one exception, this advantage is extended only to organizations that are regarded as *charitable* in nature.[33] This exception pertains to organizations that test for public safety;[34] while these entities are tax-exempt, contributions to them are not deductible.

Nonetheless, an organization the exemption of which is based on a status other than charitable can achieve the essentially same result with respect to deductibility of contributions. This is accomplished by means of *bifurcation*: a division of the organization so that one of the entities qualifies as a charitable one, usually named a "foundation."[35] A common example of this type of entity-splitting is the ability of tax-exempt trade associations and other business leagues[36] to establish and maintain related foundations.[37] Often, these associated organizations are *supporting organizations*.[38] Indeed, often charitable organizations utilize related charitable organizations in this manner.[39]

Some organizations can attract financial support that is deductible, not as charitable contributions but as business expenses.[40] For example, dues paid to tax-exempt business leagues are usually deductible business expenses.[41]

(c) Grants

Many tax-exempt organizations are the likely subject of grants from private foundations. This is especially the case with charitable organizations that have achieved public charity status, since a foundation generally may distribute funds to a public charity in satisfaction of the mandatory payout requirements[42] without having to assume expenditure responsibility for the grant.[43] Public charities and other exempt organizations also may engage in grant-making.

---

[32] That is, those that qualify under IRC § 170(c).

[33] That is, are described in IRC § 501(c)(3). See IRC § 170(c)(2). Cf. IRC §§ 170(c)(1), 170(c)(3)–170(c)(5), 170(h).

[34] See § 11.3(d).

[35] See Chapter 30.

[36] See Chapter 13.

[37] See § 30.2(a).

[38] See § 11.3(c). In general, Hopkins & Blazek, *Private Foundations: Tax Law and Compliance, Second Edition* (John Wiley & Sons, Inc., 2003), § 15.7; Hopkins & Blazek, *The Legal Answer Book for Private Foundations* (John Wiley & Sons, Inc., 2002), Chapter 12, Q 12:15-Q 12:31.

[39] See § 30.3. Also Hyatt & Hopkins, *The Law of Tax-Exempt Healthcare Organizations, Second Edition* (John Wiley & Sons, Inc., 2001), Chapter 14 (concerning development foundations related to tax-exempt health-care entities).

[40] IRC § 162.

[41] Reg. § 1.162-6.

[42] See § 11.4(b).

[43] See § 11.4(e).

In some instances, federal and state governmental agencies only make grants to or enter into contracts with nonprofit, tax-exempt organizations, oftentimes only those organizations determined to be charitable entities.

(d) Preferential Postal Rates

Several types of tax-exempt organizations are eligible for the preferential postal rates.[44] This body of law, however, excludes from the qualification for reduced mailing rates mailings that are not in furtherance of the organizations' exempt purposes.[45]

(e) Employee Benefits

The employees of a tax-exempt charitable organization may take advantage of rules providing favorable tax treatment for contributions for certain annuity benefit programs.[46] There are unique rules concerning a variety of deferred compensation arrangements that exist for the benefit of employees of exempt organizations.[47] Services performed for a tax-exempt organization may be exempt from federal unemployment taxation.[48]

(f) Antitrust Laws

In general, tax-exempt organizations—including charitable ones—can be subject to the antitrust laws, including (at the federal level) the Clayton Act[49] and the Sherman Act.[50] As the U.S. Supreme Court observed, "[t]here is no doubt that the sweeping language of section 1 [of the Sherman Act] applies to nonprofit entities."[51] This conclusion is based on the proposition that the absence of a profit motive by those who operate a nonprofit entity is no guarantee that the organization will act in the best interest of consumers. Thus, although "pure charity" is beyond the ambit of antitrust law, "commercial transactions with a 'public service aspect' " are not.[52]

This distinction is not always easy to make, as illustrated by the finding that increasing the percentage of minority-group students at a group of schools

---

[44] 39 U.S.C. §§ 4355(a), 4452(d). The organizations entitled to the preferential postal rates (essentially charitable entities) are defined in the Domestic Mail Manual.
[45] This body of law is summarized in Hopkins, *The Second Legal Answer Book for Fund-Raisers* (John Wiley & Sons, Inc., 2000), Chapter 8.
[46] IRC § 403(b). See § 16.1(g).
[47] IRC § 457. See § 16.1(f).
[48] IRC § 3306(c).
[49] 15 U.S.C. § 12.
[50] 15 U.S.C. § 9.
[51] NCAA v. University of Okla., 468 U.S. 85, 100, note 22 (1984).
[52] United States v. Brown Univ., 5 F.3d 658, 666 (3d Cir. 1993).

through a "need-blind" admissions program was too commercial because even reduced tuition is a commercial payment for educational services.[53] The solicitation of contributions by charitable organizations, however, while considerably regulated,[54] is not an activity that amounts to engaging in trade or commerce and thus is not covered by the Sherman Act.[55]

There is, nonetheless, an advantage for tax-exempt charitable organizations in this context in that they may use, or agree to use, the same annuity rate for the purpose of issuing one or more charitable gift annuities[56] without violation of the federal or state antitrust laws.[57] This protection is not confined to charities: It extends to lawyers, accountants, actuaries, consultants, and others retained or employed by a charitable organization when assisting in the issuance of a charitable gift annuity or the setting of charitable annuity rates.[58] Moreover, this antitrust exemption also sweeps within its ambit the act of publishing suggested annuity rates. Thus, organizations cannot be in violation of the antitrust laws as a result of publication of actuarial tables or annuity rates for use in issuing gift annuities.[59]

(g) Securities Laws

The federal securities laws consist principally of the Securities Act of 1933,[60] the Securities Exchange Act of 1934,[61] the Investment Company Act of 1940,[62] and the Investment Advisers Act of 1940.[63] There are also securities laws at the state level.

Exempt from the provisions of the Securities Act (other than the antifraud provisions) are securities issued by an entity organized and operated exclusively for religious, educational, benevolent, fraternal, charitable, or reformatory purposes, and not for pecuniary profit, as long as there is no private inurement.[64] A comparable exemption is available with respect to the Securities Exchange Act.[65] Likewise, an organization of this type is excluded

---

[53] *Id.*

[54] See Hopkins, *The Law of Fundraising, Third Edition* (John Wiley & Sons, Inc., 2002).

[55] DELTA v. Humane Soc'y, 50 F.3d 710 (9th Cir. 1995).

[56] This term has the same meaning as in IRC § 501(m)(5). See § 22.1, text accompanied by notes 25–26.

[57] 15 U.S.C. § 37, 109 Stat. 687. This law was created upon enactment of the Charitable Gift Annuity Antitrust Relief Act of 1995 (Pub. L. No. 104-63).

[58] H. Rep. 336, 104th Cong., 1st Sess. 6 (1995).

[59] *Id.* This legislation was enacted to shield charitable organizations from litigation based on the use of agreed-upon annuity rates, as well as to provide a complete defense to then-pending litigation (Richie v. American Council on Gift Annuities (Civ. No. 9:94-CV-128-X)). The scope of this legislation was clarified and tightened by the enactment of Pub. L. No. 105-26. This body of law is summarized in Hopkins, *supra* note 39, Chapter 9.

[60] 15 U.S.C. § 77b.

[61] 15 U.S.C. § 78c.

[62] 15 U.S.C. § 80a.

[63] 15 U.S.C. § 80b.

[64] 15 U.S.C. § 77c-3(a)(4).

[65] 15 U.S.C. § 781-12(g)(2)(D).

from the definition of an investment company under the Investment Company Act.[66]

Another advantage of classification as a charitable or similar organization is the limitation on the applicability of federal and state securities laws to the activities of charitable organizations in connection with the maintenance of charitable income funds.[67] This limitation provides certain exemptions under the federal securities laws for charitable organizations that maintain these funds.

A *charitable income fund* is a fund maintained by a charitable organization exclusively for the collective investment and reinvestment of one or more assets of a charitable remainder or similar trust; of a pooled income fund; contributed in exchange for the issuance of charitable gift annuities; of a charitable lead trust; of the general endowment fund or other funds of one or more charitable organizations; or of certain other trusts the remainder interests of which are revocably dedicated to or for the benefit of one or more charitable organizations.[68] The Securities and Exchange Commission (SEC) has the authority to expand the scope of the exemptive provisions of the legislation to include funds that may include assets not expressly defined.[69]

A fund that is excluded from the definition of *investment company* under the Investment Company Act must provide to each donor to a charity by means of the fund written information describing the material terms of operation of the fund.[70] This disclosure requirement is not, however, a condition of exemption from the Investment Company Act.[71] Thus, a charitable income fund that fails to provide the requisite information is not subject to the securities laws, although the fund may be subject to an enforcement or other action by the SEC. Charitable organizations have flexibility in determining the contents of the required disclosure.

This exemption in the Investment Company Act is also engrafted onto the Securities Act, although charitable income funds are not exempted from that law's anti-fraud provisions.[72] A similar rule operates with respect to the Securities Exchange Act.[73]

A charitable organization is not subject to the Securities Exchange Act's broker-dealer regulation solely because the organization trades in securities on its behalf, or on behalf of a charitable income fund, or the settlors, potential settlors, or beneficiaries of either.[74] This protection is extended to trustees, direc-

---

[66] 15 U.S.C. § 80b-3(c)(10).

[67] 15 U.S.C. § 80a, 109 Stat. 682. This body of law was created on enactment of the Philanthropy Protection Act of 1995 (Pub. L. No. 104-62).

[68] 15 U.S.C. §§ 80a-3(c)(10)(B)(i)-80a-3(c)(10)(B)(vii). These trusts and funds are the subject of Hopkins, *The Tax Law of Charitable Giving, Second Edition* (John Wiley & Sons, Inc., 2000), Part Four.

[69] 15 U.S.C. § 80a-3(c)(10)(B)(viii).

[70] 15 U.S.C. § 80a-7(e).

[71] H.R. Rep. 333, 104th Cong., 1st Sess. 13 (1995).

[72] 15 U.S.C. § 77c(a)(4).

[73] 15 U.S.C. § 78c(a)(12)(A)(v).

[74] 15 U.S.C. § 78c(e).

tors, officers, employees, or volunteers of a charitable organization, acting within the scope of their employment or duties with the organization. Similar exemptions are provided for charitable organizations, and certain persons associated with them, in connection with the provision of advice, analyses, or reports, from the reach of the Investment Advisors Act of 1940 (other than its anti-fraud elements).[75]

Interests in charitable income funds excluded from the definition of *investment company*, and any offer or sale of these interests, are exempt from any state law that requires registration or qualification of securities.[76] A charitable organization or trustee, director, officer, employee, or volunteer of a charity (acting within the scope of his or her employment or duties) is not subject to regulation as a dealer, broker, agent, or investment adviser under any state securities law because the organization or person trades in securities on behalf of a charity, charitable income fund, or the settlors, potential settlors, or beneficiaries of either.[77] These rules do not alter the reach or scope of state anti-fraud laws.[78]

(h) Other Advantages

Numerous other advantages can be derived from tax-exempt status. These other advantages may be more important to an organization than tax exemption. In one instance, an organization (unsuccessfully) sought categorization as an exempt charitable entity so that its child day-care centers would qualify for a food reimbursement program administered by the U.S. Department of Agriculture.[79]

---

[75] 15 U.S.C. § 80b-3(b)(4).

[76] 15 U.S.C. § 80a-3a(a).

[77] 15 U.S.C. § 80a-3a(b).

[78] Prior to the enactment of this legislation, the applicability of the Securities Act, the Securities Exchange Act, and the Investment Company Act to charitable income funds was addressed by the staff of the SEC. This administration approach can be traced back to 1972, when the American Council on Education received a no-action letter as to pooled income funds, which was predicated on the fact that these entities are the subject of federal tax law and are subject to the oversight of the IRS. One of the principal conditions of this no-action assurance was that each prospective donor receive written disclosures fully and fairly describing the fund's operations. (Also, the SEC staff has consistently maintained that the anti-fraud provisions of the securities laws apply to the activities of these funds and their associated persons.) This no-action position has always been rationalized by the view that (1) the primary purpose of those who transfer money and property to these funds is to make a charitable gift, rather than to make an investment, and (2) this field has historically been regulated by the IRS.

Until this legislation ensued, the oversight by the IRS and the no-action position of the SEC worked in tandem rather nicely. As a lawsuit (see *supra* note 59) illustrated, however, a favorable letter from the SEC staff does not necessarily insulate the recipient of it from liability asserted by a private litigant who alleges that the same transaction violates the securities laws. For the most part, the Philanthropy Protection Act of 1995 codified the approach taken over the past 23 years by the staff of the SEC.

The scope of this legislation was clarified and tightened by the enactment of Pub. L. No. 105-26. This body of law is the subject of Hopkins, *supra* note 39, Chapter 9.

[79] Baltimore Regional Joint Bd. Health & Welfare Fund, Amalgamated Clothing & Textile Workers Union v. Comm'r, 69 T.C. 554 (1978).

One advantage of tax exemption for charitable organizations once was exemption of services performed for them from taxation under the Federal Insurance Contributions Act (Social Security).[80] This general exemption was, however, repealed as of January 1, 1984.[81] Nonetheless, a one-time irrevocable election by a church[82] or a qualified church-controlled organization to exclude from the FICA tax base remuneration for all services performed for it (other than in an unrelated trade or business) is available, with the employees of electing organizations liable for self-employment taxes with respect to the excluded services.[83] This election may be made only where the employer organization states that it is opposed for religious reasons to the payment of the FICA tax.[84] A *qualified church-controlled organization* is any charitable organization controlled by a church, other than an organization that (1) offers goods, services, or facilities for sale, except on an incidental basis, to the general public, other than goods, services, or facilities that are sold at a nominal charge that is substantially less than the cost of providing the goods, services, or facilities; and (2) normally receives more than 25 percent of its support from either governmental sources or receipts from admissions, sales of merchandise, performance of services, or furnishing of facilities, in activities that are not unrelated trades or businesses, or both.[85]

Although obviously relatively minor in scope, another advantage to tax exemption for charitable organizations is that it provides exemption from the Organized Crime Control Act,[86] which prohibits certain gambling businesses. This law exempts from its application any "bingo game, lottery, or similar game of chance conducted by an organization exempt from tax under paragraph (3) of subsection (c) of section 501 of the Internal Revenue Code of 1954, as amended, if no part of the gross receipts derived from such activity inures to the benefit of any private shareholder, member, or employee of such organization except as compensation for actual expenses incurred by him in the conduct of such activity."[87]

Still another advantage of income tax exemption is the exemption that a nonprofit organization may have from the federal price discrimination law, known as the Robinson-Patman Act. This law makes it "unlawful for any person engaged in commerce, in the course of such commerce, either directly or indirectly, to discriminate in price between different purchasers of commodi-

---

[80] IRC § 3121(b).

[81] Social Security Amendments of 1983 (Pub. L. No. 98-21), 97 Stat. 65 § 102.

[82] For this purpose, the term *church* means a church, a convention or association of churches, or an elementary or secondary school that is controlled, operated, or principally supported by a church or by a convention or association of churches (IRC § 3121(w)(3)(A)). See §§ 8.4, 8.5.

[83] IRC §§ 3121(b)(8)(B), 3121(w)(1), (2).

[84] IRC § 3121(w)(1). This election is made by means of Form 8274.

[85] IRC § 3121(w)(3)(B). A federal district court upheld these rules against a challenge to the constitutionality of them in Bethel Baptist Church v. United States, 629 F. Supp. 1073 (M.D. Pa. 1986), aff'd, 822 F.2d 1334 (3d Cir. 1987), cert. den., 485 U.S. 959 (1988).

[86] 18 U.S.C. § 1955.

[87] See, e.g., United States v. Hawes, 529 F.2d 472, 481 (5th Cir. 1976).

ties of like grade and quality, where either or any of the purchasers involved in such discrimination are in commerce, or such commodities are sold for use, consumption, or resale within the United States . . ., and where the effect of such discrimination may be substantially to lessen competition or tend to create a monopoly in any line of commerce. . . ."[88] Exempted from coverage of this law are certain nonprofit institutions that purchase supplies for their own use at lower prices than can be obtained by other purchasers. This exemption is accorded to "schools, colleges, universities, public libraries, churches, hospitals, and charitable institutions not operated for profit."[89] The purpose of the exemption is to enable nonprofit institutions to operate as inexpensively as possible.[90]

Another advantage that flows from income tax exemption relates to the federal excise tax on wagers.[91] A lottery, raffle, drawing, or other form of *wagering* conducted by an exempt organization[92] is excluded from the tax as long as no part of the net proceeds from the wagering inures to the benefit of any individual in his or her private capacity.[93]

Another federal tax advantage for certain tax-exempt organizations is an exemption from user fees on permits for industrial use of specially denatured distilled spirits. This exemption is available for any "scientific university, college of learning, or institution of scientific research," where the entity is issued a permit and, as to any year in which the permit is in effect, procures less than 25 gallons of the spirits for "experimental or research use but not for consumption (other than organoleptic tests) or sale."[94]

Still another federal tax advantage for tax-exempt organizations is the exemption from the harbor maintenance tax. This exemption is applicable to any nonprofit organization or cooperative for cargo that is owned or financed by the entity and that is certified by the U.S. Customs Service as intended for use in "humanitarian or developmental assistance overseas."[95]

There are programs or other tax advantages that are available to tax-exempt organizations, although their involvement in the program or utilization of the tax advantage has been subject to (unsuccessful) constitutional law challenge. For example, tax-exempt religious private schools may participate in a city school voucher plan,[96] a public school may be required to permit a religious organization

---

[88] 15 U.S.C. § 13(a).
[89] 15 U.S.C. § 13(c).
[90] Logan Lanes, Inc. v. Brunswick Corp., 378 F.2d 212 (9th Cir. 1967).
[91] IRC §§ 4401(a), 4411, 4421.
[92] That is, an organization described in IRC § 501 or IRC § 521.
[93] IRC § 4421; Reg. § 44.4421-1(b)(2)(ii).
[94] IRC § 5276(c).
[95] IRC § 4462(h).
[96] Zelman v. Simmons-Harris et al., 122 S.Ct. 2460 (2002).

to use its after-school facilities pursuant to a community use policy,[97] and a sectarian university may be the beneficiary of tax-exempt revenue bonds issued by a state industrial development board.[98] A federal appellate court considered the possibility that the parsonage housing allowance exclusion[99] is unconstitutional[100] but dismissed the appeal in the aftermath of the enactment of legislation designed to moot the case.[101]

It is clear, nonetheless, that an organization is not exempt from a statutory requirement merely because it is a nonprofit entity. That is, in the absence of an express or implied exception in a statute, a nonprofit organization (irrespective of tax exemption) is required to comply with the statute in the same manner as a for-profit organization.[102]

§ 3.3 DISADVANTAGES OF TAX-EXEMPT STATUS

In general, it may seem that an ability to avoid income taxation affords little opportunity for a disadvantage. While often this is the case, the law usually imposes one or more organizational and/or operational limitations on a nonprofit organization in exchange for tax-exempt status. The most common of these limitations is the rule that the exempt organization may not engage in forms of private inurement.[103]

Therefore, qualification as a tax-exempt organization may entail disadvantages. Tax-exempt charitable organizations are prohibited from engaging in substantial legislative activities[104] and in campaign or similar political activities.[105] In other instances, most notably in the field of private foundations, qualification as an exempt organization brings with it a host of limitations that must be adhered to if exempt status is to be maintained.[106] Exempt status also will likely involve extensive annual reporting requirements, including the filing of an annual information return with the IRS and a tax return for each year in which there is unrelated business income.[107] Unlike tax returns, these information returns are open to public inspection.[108] Exempt noncharitable organizations must disclose the nondeductibility of contributions to them[109] and

---

[97] Good News Club et al. v. Milford Central School, 533 U.S. 98 (2001).

[98] Steele v. Nashville Industrial Development Bd., 301 F. 3d 401 (6th Cir. 2002).

[99] IRC § 107(2).

[100] Warren v. Comm'r, 114 T.C. 343 (2000), appealed to the U.S. Court of Appeals for the Ninth Circuit.

[101] Clergy Housing Allowance Clarification Act of 2002 (P. L. No. 107-181). Two law professors serving as amicis curiae to the appellate court concluded that the exclusion is unconstitutional. In general, see § 8.1.

[102] Tony and Susan Alamo Found. v. Secretary of Labor, 471 U.S. 290 (1985).

[103] See Chapter 19.

[104] See Chapter 20.

[105] See Chapter 21.

[106] See, e.g., Chapter 11.

[107] See § 24.3.

[108] See § 24.4.

[109] IRC § 6113. See § 22.2.

exempt organizations are subject to a penalty if they fail to disclose that information or services being offered are available without charge from the federal government.[110]

In some instances, these limitations and forms of regulation may be more extensive than those imposed on for-profit organizations. In occasional instances, the requirement of adherence to these limitations will not be worth qualification as a conventional tax-exempt organization, particularly where a more preferable alternative is available. Payment of income tax is not always to be abhorred; it can be viewed as an indicator of success.

§ 3.4 ALTERNATIVES TO TAX-EXEMPT STATUS

An organization may elect or be required to operate without formal recognition as a tax-exempt entity and yet achieve the same basic objective: the nonpayment of income tax. The legitimate alternatives to this type of exempt status are, however, few.

Alternatives to conventional tax-exempt organizations include a variety of trusts, partnerships,[111] and limited liability companies.[112] For the most part, these entities do not pay tax.[113]

Perhaps the simplest illustration of this principle is the organization (nonprofit or not) that is operated so that its deductible expenses equal or exceed income in any tax year. In essence, this is the basis upon which cooperatives function without having to pay tax.

The rules as to nonexempt cooperatives[114] apply to any "corporation operating on a cooperative basis" (with exceptions) and to certain farmers' cooperatives.[115] Basically, a qualified cooperative escapes taxation because, in computing taxable income, a deduction is available for "patronage dividends" and qualified and nonqualified "per-unit retain allocations."[116] Moreover, a farmers' cooperative is entitled to certain deductions for nonpatronage dividends.[117] Generally, amounts received as patronage dividends and qualified per-unit retain certificates are includable in the patrons' gross income.

An organization that loses its tax-exempt status may continue to operate without taxation by conversion to operation as a cooperative.[118] Similarly, an or-

---

[110] IRC § 6711. See § 24.6.
[111] See § 32.1.
[112] See §§ 4.1(b), 4.3(d), 32.6(b).
[113] See § 32.1.
[114] IRC §§ 1381-1383.
[115] See § 18.11.
[116] IRC §§ 1382(b), 1388.
[117] IRC § 1382(c).
[118] E.g., A. Duda & Sons Coop. Ass'n v. United States, 495 F.2d 193 (5th Cir. 1974). This decision was subsequently withdrawn and superseded by the decision reported at 504 F.2d 970 (5th Cir. 1975).

ganization that cannot qualify as an exempt entity may choose to function as a co-operative.[119]

If a nonexempt organization that does not operate on a cooperative basis seeks to avoid taxation by matching deductions and income, federal tax law may foil the scheme if the organization is a social club or other membership organization operated to furnish goods or services to its members.[120] In this situation, the expenses of furnishing services, goods, or other items of value (such as insurance) to members are deductible only to the extent of income from members (including income from institutes or trade shows primarily for members' education). This means that any expenses attributable to membership activities in excess of membership income may not be deducted against membership income (although the increment may be carried forward). Prior to enactment of these rules, the courts had upheld contrary treatment.[121]

There is a line of law that permits nontaxability of an organization where it is merely a conduit for the expenditure of a fund established for a specific purpose. Thus, a soft drink manufacturer that received funds from bottlers for a national advertising fund was held to not be taxable on these funds, inasmuch as they were earmarked for advertising purposes; the manufacturer was considered merely an administrator of a trust fund.[122] Initially, the IRS took the position that this precept would be followed only where the recipient of the funds received them with the obligation to expend them solely for a particular purpose.[123] This position was subsequently superseded, however, by a ruling that taxes to the recipient organization the amounts received and the permits related deductions, subject to the previously discussed expense allocation rules.[124] Also, the IRS distinguished the above-described factual setting involving a soft drink manufacturer from one in which the participants (dealers, bottlers, and the like) form an unincorporated organization to conduct a national advertising program; the IRS ruled that the organization is separately taxable as a corporation.[125]

If tax-exempt status is unavailable, lost, or not desired, and if deductions do not or cannot equal income, and cooperative status is either unavailable or unwanted, and if the organization is not formally incorporated, perhaps the

[119] E.g., Rev. Rul. 69-633, 1969-2 C.B. 121.
[120] IRC § 277.
[121] E.g., Anaheim Union Water Co. v. Comm'r, 321 F.2d 253 (9th Cir. 1963). An application of IRC § 277 appears in Boating Trade Ass'n of Metro. Houston v. United States, 75-1 U.S.T.C. ¶ 9398 (S.D. Tex. 1975).
[122] The Seven-Up Co. v. Comm'r, 14 T.C. 965 (1950). Also Rev. Rul. 69-96, 1969-1 C.B. 32; Ford Dealers Advertising Fund, Inc. v. Comm'r, 55 T.C. 761 (1971), aff'd, 456 F.2d 255 (5th Cir. 1972); Park Place, Inc. v. Comm'r, 57 T.C. 767 (1972); Greater Pittsburgh Chrysler Dealers Ass'n of W. Pa. v. United States, 77-1 U.S.T.C. ¶ 9293 (W.D. Pa. 1977); Insty-Prints, Inc. Nat'l Advertising Fund Trust v. Comm'r, 44 T.C.M. 556 (1982); Broadcast Measurement Bureau v. Comm'r, 16 T.C. 988 (1951).
[123] Rev. Rul. 58-209, 1958-1 C.B. 19.
[124] Rev. Rul. 74-318, 1974-2 C.B. 14.
[125] Rev. Rul. 74-319, 1974-2 C.B. 15. Also Michigan Retailers Ass'n v. United States, 676 F. Supp. 151 (W.D. Mich. 1988)); Dri-Power Distribrs. Ass'n Trust v. Comm'r, 54 T.C. 460 (1970); N.Y. State Ass'n Real Est. Bd. Group Ins. Fund v. Comm'r, 54 T.C. 1325 (1970); Angelus Funeral Home v. Comm'r, 47 T.C. 391 (1967), aff'd, 407 F.2d 210 (9th Cir. 1969), cert. den., 396 U.S. 824 (1969).

entity can escape taxation by contending it is nonexistent for tax purposes. This is generally unlikely, in view of the authority of the IRS to treat an unincorporated entity as a taxable corporation.[126] Yet this is what political campaign committees did for many years, as the IRS failed or refused to assert tax liability. In 1974, however, the IRS ruled that campaign committees are to be treated as taxable corporations (although contributions remained nontaxable).[127] This ruling was in turn superseded by the enactment of legislation on the point[128] and related law[129] late in 1974.[130] Nonetheless, even after this ruling, the IRS continued to uphold the per-donee gift tax exclusion for separate fundraising campaign committees,[131] despite opposition in the courts.[132] In 1974, however, contributions to political parties or committees were exempted from the gift tax.[133]

Thus, to be exempt from federal income taxation, an organization generally must formally qualify as a tax-exempt organization (by means of recognition or otherwise), operate as a cooperative, legally marshall deductions against income, or seek a change in the law. Otherwise, it is nearly certain that the entity will be liable for tax as a taxable corporation, even if it is organized as a nonprofit organization. That is, it is possible that an entity will be a taxable, nonprofit organization.[134]

---

[126] E.g., Rev. Rul. 75-258, 1972-2 C.B. 503 (where the IRS ruled that the "Family Estate" trust is an association taxable as a corporation under IRC § 7701) and Rev. Rul. 77-214, 1977-1 C.B. 408 (where the IRS determined that a type of German unincorporated business organization—"Gesellschaft mit beschränkter Haftung" or "GmbH"—was taxable as a corporation). Also, the court concluded that real estate syndicates organized under the California limited partnership act are associations taxable as corporations with the meaning of IRC § 7701(a)(3) (Larson v. Comm'r, 65 T.C. No. 10 (1975) (withdrawn), 66 T.C. 159 (1976)). In general, Morrissey v. Comm'r, 296 U.S. 344 (1935); Reg. § 301.7701-29a)(1).

[127] Rev. Rul. 74-21, 1974-1 C.B. 14.

[128] IRC § 527.

[129] IRC §§ 41 (as amended), 84, 2501(a)(5).

[130] See Chapter 17.

[131] Rev. Rul. 72-355, 1972-2 C.B. 532; Rev. Rul. 74-199, 1974-1 C.B. 285.

[132] Tax Analysts & Advocates v. Schultz, 376 F. Supp. 889 (D.D.C. 1974), aff'd, 75-1 U.S.T.C. ¶ 13,052 (D.C. Cir. 1975).

[133] IRC § 2501(a)(5).

[134] See §§ 1.1, 1.2.

CHAPTER FOUR

Organizational, Operational, and Similar Tests

In addition to other rules underlying tax-exempt status, the federal tax law mandates adherence to certain general organizational and operational requirements as a condition of tax exemption. These requirements are the most pronounced with respect to charitable organizations.[1]

§ 4.1 CONSIDERATIONS OF FORM

(a) General Rules

Generally, the Internal Revenue Code does not prescribe a specific organizational form for entities to qualify for tax exemption. Basically, the choices are nonprofit corporation, trust (*inter vivos* or testamentary), or unincorporated association.[2] Some provisions of the Code, however, mandate, in whole or in part, the corporate form,[3] and other Code provisions (particularly in the employee plan context[4]) mandate the trust form for exempt organizations.[5] Throughout the categories of exempt organizations are additional terms such as *clubs, associations, so-*

[1] That is, organizations described in IRC § 501(c)(3) and tax-exempt by reason of IRC § 501(a).
[2] Rev. Proc. 82-2, 1982-1 C.B 367.
[3] IRC §§ 501(c)(1), 501(c)(2), 501(c)(3), 501(c)(14), 501(c)(16).
[4] See Chapter 16.
[5] IRC §§ 501(c)(17), 501(c)(18), 501(c)(19), 501(c)(20), 401(a).

cieties, leagues, companies, boards, orders, posts, and *units,* which are not terms referencing legal forms. For tax purposes, an organization may be deemed a corporation even though it is not formally incorporated.[6]

The federal tax provision which describes charitable organizations provides that an organization described in that provision must be a corporation, community chest, fund, or foundation. An unincorporated association or trust can qualify under this provision, presumably as a fund or foundation or perhaps, as noted, as a corporation.[7] A partnership cannot, however, be tax-exempt as a charitable organization.[8]

An organization already exempt from federal taxation may establish a separate fund or like entity that is itself an exempt organization.[9] The attributes of this type of a fund include a separate category of exemption (for example, an educational research and scholarship fund established by a bar association[10]), a separate governing body, and separate books and accounts.[11] A mere bank deposit cannot, however, amount to a requisite fund; thus, a contribution to it would be considered a nondeductible gift to an individual rather than a possibly deductible gift to a qualified organization.[12]

For purposes of the rules concerning charitable organizations, an organization tax-exempt by reason of those rules may be a unit of government[13] or a foreign organization,[14] or may conduct all or part of its activities in foreign countries.[15]

The formalities of organization of an entity may have a bearing on the tax exemption. This is the case not only in connection with the sufficiency of the governing instruments,[16] but also, and more fundamentally, with regard to whether there is a separate organization in the first instance. An individual may perform worthwhile activities, such as providing financial assistance to needy students, but will receive no tax benefits from his or her beneficence, unless he or she establishes and funds a qualified organization that in turn renders the charitable works, such as scholarship grants. One court observed, in the process of denying a charitable contribution deduction, that the federal tax law makes no provision for a charitable deduction in the context of personal ventures, however praiseworthy in character. The court noted that "[t]here is no evidence of

---

[6] IRC § 7701(a)(3).

[7] Fifth-Third Union Trust Co. v. Comm'r, 56 F.2d 767 (6th Cir. 1932).

[8] IRS Exempt Organizations Handbook (IRM 7751) § 315.1. Also Emerson Inst. v. United States, 356 F.2d 824 (D.C. Cir. 1966), *cert. den.*, 385 U.S. 822 (1966). In one opinion, a court, in deciding that an organization could not qualify for tax-exempt status because of its role as a general partner in a limited partnership (see § 32.2), placed emphasis on the fact that the partnerships involved "are admittedly for-profit entities" and that none of these partnerships is "intended to be nonprofit" (Housing Pioneers, Inc. v. Comm'r, 65 T.C.M. 2191, 2195 (1993)); however, the law does not make provision for an entity such as a nonprofit partnership.

[9] E.g., IRC § 509(a), last sentence.

[10] American Bar Ass'n v. United States, 84-1 U.S.T.C. ¶ 9179 (N.D. Ill. 1984); Rev. Rul. 58-293, 1958-1 C.B. 146.

[11] Rev. Rul. 54-243, 1954-1 C.B. 92.

[12] E.g., Pusch v. Comm'r, 39 T.C.M. 838 (1980).

[13] Rev. Rul. 60-384, 1960-2 C.B. 172.

[14] Rev. Rul. 66-177, 1966-1 C.B. 132.

[15] Rev. Rul. 71-460, 1971-2 C.B. 231.

[16] Cone v. McGinnes, 63-2 U.S.T.C. ¶ 9551 (E.D. Pa. 1963). Also *infra* § 2.

such enterprise being a corporation, community chest, fund, or foundation and little information, if any, as to its organization or activities."[17] Assuming the organization is not operated to benefit private interests, its tax exemption will not be endangered because its creator serves as the sole trustee and exercises complete control,[18] although state law may limit or preclude close control.

It is the position of the IRS that a "formless aggregation of individuals" cannot be tax-exempt as a charitable entity.[19] At a minimum, the entity—to be exempt—must have an organizing instrument, some governing rules, and regularly chosen officers.[20] These rules have been amply illustrated in the cases concerning so-called personal churches.[21]

Among the nontax factors to be considered in selecting an organizational form are legal liabilities in relation to the individuals involved (the corporate form can limit certain personal liabilities), local law requirements, necessities of governing instruments, local annual reporting requirements, organizational expenses, and any membership requirements.[22] Federal law, other than the tax laws, may also have a bearing on the choice, such as the organization's comparable status under the postal laws.[23]

A change in form may require a tax-exempt organization to reapply for recognition of exempt status. For example, an unincorporated organization that has been recognized by the IRS as an exempt charitable entity must commence the application process anew if it incorporates.[24]

(b) Check-the-Box Regulations

(i) Basic Rules. In general, the classification of an entity as a particular type of organization can have significant federal tax consequences. Although this

---

[17] Hewitt v. Comm'r, 16 T.C.M. 468, 471 (1957). Also Doty, Jr. v. Comm'r, 6 T.C. 587 (1974); Walker v. Comm'r, 37 T.C.M. 1851 (1978).

[18] Rev. Rul. 66-219, 1966-2 C.B. 208.

[19] IRS Exempt Organizations Handbook (IRM 7751) §§ 315.1, 315.2(3), 315.4(2).

[20] Kessler v. Comm'r, 87 T.C. 1285 (1986); Trippe v. Comm'r, 9 T.C.M. 622 (1950). Cf. Morey v. Riddell, 205 F. Supp. 918 (S.D. Cal. 1962). A claim that it is unconstitutional not to permit individuals to be tax-exempt was dismissed (Fields v. United States, Civ. No. 96-317 (D.D.C. 1998)).

[21] E.g., United States v. Jeffries, 88-2 U.S.T.C. ¶ 9,459 (7th Cir. 1988). In general, see § 8.2(c).

[22] A separate form (even the corporate form), however, is not always respected. For example, courts find charitable organizations to be the "alter ego" of their founders or others in close control and operating proximity, so that IRS levies against the organizations for their income and assets to satisfy the individuals' tax obligations are upheld (e.g., Towe Antique Ford Found. v. Internal Revenue Serv., 999 F.2d 1387 (9th Cir. 1993); United States v. Kitsos, 770 F. Supp. 1230 (N.D. Ill. 1991), *aff'd*, 968 F.2d 1219 (7th Cir. 1992); Zahra Spiritual Trust v. United States, 910 F.2d 240 (5th Cir. 1990); Loving Savior Church v. United States, 556 F. Supp. 688 (D.S.D. 1983), *aff'd*, 728 F.2d 1085 (8th Cir. 1984); Faith Missionary Baptist Church v. Internal Revenue Serv., 174 B.R. 454 (U.S. Bankr. Ct. E.D. Tex. 1994); Church of Hakeem v. United States, 79-2 U.S.T.C. ¶ 9651 (N.D. Cal. 1979)). In general, Henn & Pfeifer, "Nonprofit Groups: Factors Influencing Choice of Form," 11 *Wake Forest L. Rev.* 181 (1975).

[23] 39 C.F.R. Part 132 (second class), Part 134 (third class).

[24] See § 24.1(6).

is an issue principally for for-profit entities, there are some ramifications in this area for tax-exempt organizations.

In the for-profit context, classification of this nature can be problematic for unincorporated business organizations. (That is, this issue does not pertain to entities that are formed as corporations.) Under old law, an unincorporated entity was classified as a trust or an association, depending on certain characteristics. If an entity was determined to be an association, it was then classified as a corporation or partnership for tax purposes, according to criteria as to limited liability, centralized management, continuity of life, and free transferability of member interests.[25]

The IRS decided to simplify the entity classification process and did so by means of new regulations which generally took effect in 1997. These rules are known as the *check-the-box* regulations.[26] Basically, under these rules, an organization is either a trust[27] or a *business entity*.[28] A business entity with two or more members is classified for federal tax purposes as a corporation or a partnership. A business entity with only one owner either is classified as a corporation or is disregarded. When an entity is disregarded, its activities are treated as those of the owner, in the manner of a sole proprietorship.[29] A *corporation* includes a business entity organized under a federal or state statute, an *association*, or a business entity owned by a state or political subdivision of a state.[30]

A business entity that is not classified as a corporation is an *eligible entity*. An eligible entity with at least two members can elect to be classified as either an association (and thus a corporation[31]) or a partnership. An eligible entity with a single owner can elect to be classified as an association or to be disregarded as an entity separate from its owner.[32] If there is no election, an eligible entity with two or more members is a partnership and an eligible entity with a single member is disregarded as an entity separate from its owner.[33] Thus, an eligible entity is required to act affirmatively only when it desires classification as a corporation.[34]

---

[25] Prior Reg. § 301.7701-2.

[26] This name is derived from the simple way in which entity classification is made: by checking the appropriate box on Form 8832 (Reg. § 301.7701-3(c)(1)).

[27] A *trust* essentially is a nonbusiness entity; it is an arrangement created by a will or life-time instrument by which trustees take title to property for the purpose of protecting or conserving it for designated beneficiaries (Reg. § 301.7701-4(a)).

[28] Reg. § 301.7701-2(a).

[29] *Id*. Also Reg. § 301.7701-2(c).

[30] Reg. § 301.7701-2(b). An organization wholly owned by a state is not recognized as a separate entity for these purposes if it is an integral part of a state (Reg. § 301.7701-1(a)(3)).

[31] Reg. § 301.7701-2(b)(2).

[32] Reg. § 301.7701-3(a).

[33] Reg. § 301.7701-3(b)(1).

[34] In general, Pillow, Schmalz & Starr, "Simplified Entity Classification Under the Final Check-the-Box Regulations," 86 *J. Tax.* (No. 4) 197 (April 1997). Rules as to the tax consequences associated with entity conversions by election were proposed, as amendments to the check-the-box regulations, on Oct. 27, 1997 (REG-105162-97). In general, Pillow, Schmalz & Starr, "Changing an Entity's Classification by Election: The First Modifications to Check-the-Box," 88 *J. Tax.* (No. 3) 143 (March 1998).

(ii) Exempt Organization Rules.   There is a *deemed election* in the tax-exempt organization's context. That is, an eligible entity that has been determined to be, or claims to be, exempt from federal income taxation[35] is treated as having made the election to be classified as an association.[36] As noted, this in turn causes the exempt entity to be regarded as a corporation.[37]

Some organizations are tax-exempt because of a relationship to a state or a political subdivision of a state.[38] When a state or political subdivision conducts an enterprise through a separate entity, the entity may be exempt from federal income tax[39] or its income may be excluded from federal income tax.[40] Generally, if income is earned by an enterprise that is an integral part of a state or political subdivision of a state, that income is not taxable. In determining whether an enterprise is an integral part of a state, it is necessary to consider all the facts and circumstances, including the state's degree of control over the enterprise and the state's financial commitment to the enterprise.

These distinctions are reflected in the check-the-box regulations. A business entity can be recognized as a distinct entity when it is wholly owned by a state or a political subdivision of a state; it then is classified as a corporation.[41] Yet, an entity formed under local law is not always recognized as a separate entity for federal tax purposes. The regulations state that an "organization" wholly owned by a State is not recognized as a separate entity for federal tax purposes if it is an integral part of the State."[42]

Another instance of an interrelationship between the law of tax-exempt organizations and the check-the-box regulations is the matter of formation by exempt charitable organizations of single-member limited liability companies (LLCs) for various purposes. Under a default rule,[43] these LLCs are disregarded for federal income tax purposes; these entities are known as *disregarded LLCs*.[44]

The IRS contemplated whether a single-member LLC can qualify for tax-exempt status.[45] In the case of an LLC owned wholly by a charitable organization, the issue was whether the LLC, like its owner,[46] is obligated to file an application

---

[35] That is, exempt from tax by reason of IRC § 501(a).

[36] Reg. § 301.7701-3(c)(1)(v)(A).

[37] See the text accompanied by *supra* note 30.

[38] See, e.g., §§ 6.9, 18.17.

[39] That is, exempt from tax by reason of IRC § 501(a).

[40] IRC § 115.

[41] Reg. § 301.7701-2(b)(6). See § 18.17, text accompanied by note 416.

[42] Reg. § 301.7701-1(a)(3). See § 18.17, text accompanied by notes 414 and 417.

[43] See the text accompanied by *supra* note 33.

[44] Many interesting IRS rulings concerning the use of disregarded LLCs by charitable organizations are emerging. As an illustration, the IRS ruled that a charitable organization may transfer parcels of contributed real property to separate LLCs—for the purpose of sheltering other properties from legal liability that may be caused by the gifted property—yet report the gift properties on its annual information return as if it owned them directly (Priv. Ltr. Rul. 200134025).

[45] An LLC is not taxable; that is, it is treated, for federal income tax purposes, as a partnership (IRC § 701). The issue, however, is whether an LLC can qualify for tax-exempt status under IRC § 501.

[46] See § 23.3.

for recognition of tax-exempt status. The IRS decided that a disregarded LLC is regarded as a branch or division of its member owner.[47] Thus, separate recognition of tax exemption for these LLCs is not required (or available).[48] The IRS subsequently addressed the matter of the tax-exempt status of LLCs that have more than one tax-exempt member.[49]

§ 4.2 GOVERNING INSTRUMENTS

An organization must have governing instruments to qualify for tax exemption, if only to satisfy the appropriate organizational test. This is particularly the case for charitable organizations, as to which the federal tax law imposes specific organizational requirements.[50] These rules are more stringent if the charitable organization is a private foundation.[51]

If the corporate form is used, the governing instruments will be articles of incorporation and bylaws. An unincorporated organization will have articles of organization, perhaps in the form of a constitution, and, undoubtedly, also bylaws. If a trust, the basic document will be a declaration of trust or trust agreement.

The articles of organization should contain provisions stating the organization's purposes; whether there will be members and, if so, their qualifications and classes; the initial board of directors or trustee(s); the registered agent and incorporators (if a corporation); the dissolution or liquidation procedure; and the required language referencing the appropriate tax law (federal and state) requirements and prohibitions. If the organization is a corporation, particular attention should be given to the appropriate state nonprofit corporation statute, which will contain requirements that may supersede the provisions of the articles of incorporation and bylaws or may apply where the governing instruments are silent.

The bylaws may also contain the provisions of the articles of organization and, in addition, should contain provisions amplifying or stating the purposes of the organization; the terms and conditions of membership (if any); the manner of selection and duties of the directors or trustees, and officers; the voting requirements; the procedure for forming committees; the accounting period; any indemnification provisions; the appropriate tax provisions; and the procedure for amendment of the bylaws.[52]

---

[47] Ann. 99-102, 1999-43 I.R.B. 545.

[48] E.g., Priv. Ltr. Rul. 200134025. The IRS has before it the issue of whether a contribution of money or property directly to a single-member LLC, where the member is a charitable (IRC § 501(c)(3)) organization, is deductible as a charitable contribution.

[49] See *infra* § 3(e).

[50] See *infra* § 4.

[51] See § 11.1(g).

[52] In general, see Oleck, *Non-Profit Corporations, Organizations, and Associations* (6th ed. 1996); Webster, *The Law of Associations* (Matthew Bender); Chaffe, "The Internal Affairs of Associations Not For Profit," 43 *Harv. L. Rev.* 993 (1930).

§ 4.3 ORGANIZATIONAL TEST

An organization, to be tax-exempt as a charitable entity, must be both organized and operated exclusively for one or more of the permissible exempt purposes. This requirement has given rise to an *organizational test* and an *operational test* for charitable organizations. If an organization fails to meet either the organizational test or the operational test, it cannot qualify for exemption from federal income taxation as a charitable entity.[53] (The organizational and operational tests of other categories of exempt organizations—such as they are—are discussed in the respective chapters.)

The income tax regulations contemplate two types of governing instruments for a charitable organization: the instrument by which the organization is created (*articles of organization*) and the instrument stating the rules pursuant to which the organization is operated (*bylaws*).[54] For the incorporated organization, the articles of organization are *articles of incorporation*. For the unincorporated entity, the articles of organization may be so termed or may be termed otherwise, such as a *constitution*, *agreement of trust*, or *declaration of trust*. Occasionally, an unincorporated organization will combine these two types of instruments in one document; while this is technically inappropriate, the IRS is unlikely to find the practice a violation of the organizational test.

An organization is organized exclusively for one or more tax-exempt, charitable purposes only if its articles of organization limit its purposes to one or more exempt purposes[55] and do not expressly empower it to engage, otherwise than as an insubstantial part of its activities, in activities that in themselves are not in furtherance of one or more exempt purposes.[56] Additional requirements are imposed for the governing instruments of private foundations.[57]

(a) Statement of Purposes

In meeting the organizational test, the charitable organization's purposes, as stated in its articles of organization, may be as broad as, or more specific than, the particular exempt purposes, such as religious, charitable, or educational ends. Therefore, an organization that, by the terms of its articles of organization, is formed for "literary and scientific purposes within the meaning of section 501(c)(3) of the Internal Revenue Code" shall, if it otherwise meets the requirements of the organizational test, be considered to have met the test. Similarly, articles of organization stating that the organization is created solely to "receive contributions and pay them over to organizations which are described in section 501(c)(3) and exempt from taxation under section 501(a) of the Internal Revenue Code" are sufficient for purposes of the organizational test. If the

---

[53] Reg. § 1.501(c)(3)-1(a); Levy Family Tribe Found. v. Comm'r, 69 T.C. 615, 618 (1978).
[54] Reg. § 1.501(c)(3)-1(b)(2).
[55] See Reg. § 1.501(c)(3)-1(d).
[56] Reg. § 1.501(c)(3)-1(b)(1)(i).
[57] IRC § 508(e). See § 11.1(g).

articles of organization state that the organization is formed for "charitable purposes," the articles ordinarily will be adequate for purposes of the organizational test.[58]

Articles of organization of charitable entities may not authorize the carrying on of nonexempt activities (unless they are insubstantial), even though the organization is, by the terms of its articles, created for a purpose that is no broader than the specified charitable purposes.[59] Thus, an organization that is empowered by its articles to "engage in a manufacturing business" or to "engage in the operation of a social club" does not meet the organizational test, regardless of the fact that its articles of organization may state that the organization is created for "charitable purposes within the meaning of section 501(c)(3) of the Internal Revenue Code."[60]

In no case will an organization be considered to be organized exclusively for one or more tax-exempt charitable purposes if, by the terms of its articles of organization, the purposes for which the organization is created are broader than the specified charitable purposes. The fact that the actual operations of the organization have been exclusively in furtherance of one or more exempt purposes is not sufficient to permit the organization to meet the organizational test. An organization wishing to qualify as a charitable entity should not provide in its articles of organization that it has all of the powers accorded under the particular state's nonprofit corporation act, since those powers are likely to be broader than those allowable under federal tax law.[61] Similarly, an organization will not meet the organizational test as a result of statements or other evidence that its members intend to operate only in furtherance of one or more exempt purposes.[62]

An organization is not considered organized exclusively for one or more exempt charitable purposes if its articles of organization expressly authorize it to (1) devote more than an insubstantial part of its activities to attempting to influence legislation by propaganda or otherwise;[63] (2) directly or indirectly participate in, or intervene in (including the publishing or distributing of statements), any political campaign on behalf of or in opposition to any candidate for public office;[64] or (3) have objectives and engage in activities that characterize it as an *action* organization.[65] The organizational test is not violated, however, where an organization's articles empower it to make the expenditure test election (relating to expenditures for legislative activities)[66] and, only if it so elects, to make direct lobbying or grassroots lobbying expenditures that are not in excess of the ceiling amounts

---

[58] Reg. § 1.501(c)(3)-1(b)(1)(ii).
[59] Rev. Rul. 69-279, 1969-1 C.B. 152; Rev. Rul. 69-256, 1969-1 C.B. 151.
[60] Reg. § 1.501(c)(3)-1(b)(iii). Also Interneighborhood Housing Corp. v. Comm'r., 45 T.C.M. 115 (1982); Santa Cruz Bldg. Ass'n v. United States, 411 F. Supp. 871 (E. D. Mo. 1976).
[61] E.g., Gen. Couns. Mem. 39633.
[62] Reg. § 1.501(c)(3)-1(b)(1)(iv).
[63] See Chapter 20.
[64] See Chapter 21.
[65] Reg. § 1.501(c)(3)-1(b)(3). See *infra* § 5(b).
[66] See § 20.5(a).

prescribed by that test.[67] The organizational test, however, does not require that references be made in the organizational document to the prohibitions on private inurement, substantial private benefit, substantial lobbying, and political campaign activities.

It is the position of the IRS that only a *creating document* may be looked to in meeting the organizational test:

> Accordingly, the organizational test cannot be met by reference to any document that is not the creating document. In the case of a corporation, the bylaws cannot remedy a defect in the corporate charter. A charter can be amended only in accordance with state law, which generally requires filing of the amendments with the chartering authority. In the case of a trust, operating rules cannot substitute for the trust indenture. In the case of an unincorporated association, the test must be met by the basic creating document and the amendments thereto, whatever that instrument may be called. Subsidiary documents that are not amendments to the creating document may not be called on.[68]

It is the view of one court, however, that the organizational test entails a "purely . . . factual inquiry" and that it is not required to "myopically consider *only*" articles of incorporation or another creating document; in the case, an organization was found to qualify as a charitable organization meeting the organizational test because of suitable language in its bylaws.[69]

The law of the state in which an organization is created is controlling in construing the terms of its articles of organization.[70] An organization that contends that the terms have, under state law, a different meaning from their generally accepted meaning must establish the special meaning by clear and convincing reference to relevant court decisions, opinions of the state attorney general, or other evidence of applicable state law.[71]

An organization that would be classified as a private foundation[72] if it were recognized as a charitable entity does not satisfy the organizational test by virtue of having complied with the special governing instrument provisions applicable only to private foundations.[73] In so ruling, the IRS considered a case where an organization's articles of incorporation lacked the requisite provision requiring the distribution of its assets for charitable purposes upon dissolution. The state law under which the organization operates had not been construed to assure dedication of assets to charitable purposes,[74] although the state had a statute that mandates reference to the various private foundation

---

[67] Reg. § 1.501(c)(3)-1(b)(3).
[68] IRS Exempt Organizations Handbook (IRM 7751) § 332(2).
[69] Colorado State Chiropractic Soc'y v. Comm'r, 93 T.C. 487, 495 (1989) (emphasis in the original).
[70] Estate of Sharf v. Comm'r, 38 T.C. 15 (1962), aff'd 316 F.2d 625 (7th Cir. 1963); Holden Hosp. Corp. v. Southern Ill. Hosp. Corp., 174 N.E. 2d 793 (Ill. 1961).
[71] Reg. § 1.501(c)(3)-1(b)(5).
[72] See Chapter 11.
[73] IRC § 508(e). See § 11.1(g).
[74] See text accompanying *supra* note 71.

rules in the foundation's articles of incorporation on all private foundations formed in the state.[75] The IRS reasoned that a private foundation is a charitable organization, yet an organization cannot be so classified where its governing instrument fails to include a dissolution clause, and the special governing instrument provisions only apply to private foundations. Also, the IRS reviewed the legislative history of the private foundation rules, which makes it clear that these rules comprise requirements that are in addition to the general tax exemption requirements.[76]

(b) Dissolution Requirements

An organization is not organized exclusively for one or more exempt charitable purposes unless its assets are dedicated to an exempt purpose. An organization's assets will be considered dedicated to an exempt purpose, for example, if, upon dissolution, the assets would, by reason of a provision in the organization's articles of organization or by operation of law, be distributed for one or more exempt purposes, or to the federal government, or to a state or local government, for a public purpose or would be distributed by a court to another organization to be used in a manner as in the judgment of the court will best accomplish the general purposes for which the dissolved organization was organized. A charitable organization does not, however, meet the organizational test if its articles of organization or the law of the state in which it was created provide that its assets would, upon dissolution, be distributed to its members or shareholders.[77] Consequently, federal income tax exemption as a charitable organization will be denied where, upon dissolution of the organization, its assets would revert to the individual founders rather than to one or more qualifying charities.[78] A charitable organization's assets may, upon dissolution, be transferred for charitable purposes without necessarily being transferred to a charitable organization.[79]

The dedication-of-assets requirement contemplates that, notwithstanding the dissolution of a charitable entity, the assets will continue to be devoted to a charitable purpose (albeit a substituted one). Under the *cy pres* rule, a state court, in the exercise of its equity power, may modify the purpose of a charitable trust or place the funds of a charitable corporation in a new entity.[80] Organizations that

---

[75] Rev. Rul. 75-38, 1975-1 C.B. 161.

[76] Rev. Rul. 85-160, 1985-2 C.B. 162.

[77] Reg. § 1.501(c)(3)-1(b)(4). E.g., Chief Steward of the Ecumenical Temples and the Worldwide Peace Movement and His Successors v. Comm'r, 49 T.C.M. 640 (1985). Cf. Bethel Conservative Mennonite Church v. Comm'r, 746 F.2d 388 (7th Cir. 1984).

[78] Church of Nature in Man v. Comm'r, 49 T.C.M. 1393 (1985); Stephenson v. Comm'r, 79 T.C. 995 (1982); Truth Tabernacle v. Comm'r, 41 T.C.M. 1405 (1981); Calvin K. of Oakknoll v. Comm'r, 69 T.C. 770 (1978), aff'd, 603 F.2d 211 (2d Cir. 1979); General Conference of the Free Church of Am. v. Comm'r, 71 T.C. 920 (1979).

[79] Gen. Couns. Mem. 37126, clarifying Gen. Couns. Mem. 33207. Moreover, the absence of a dissolution clause has been held to not be fatal to IRC § 501(c)(3) status, in Universal Church of Scientific Truth, Inc. v. United States, 74-1 U.S.T.C. ¶ 9360 (N.D. Ala. 1973).

[80] Scott, *The Law of Trusts* (2d ed. 1956) §§ 397, 339.3; IRS Exempt Organizations Handbook (IRM 7751) § 335(4), (6). Also Davis v. United States, 201 F. Supp. 92 (S.D. Ohio 1961).

are organized for both exempt and nonexempt purposes fail to satisfy the organizational test.[81]

The IRS published guidelines for identification of states and circumstances where an express dissolution clause for charitable organizations is not required. Basically, these guidelines are a function of the type of organization that is involved. For example, the IRS has determined that the *cy pres* doctrine in any jurisdiction is insufficient to prevent an *inter vivos* charitable trust or an unincorporated association from failing, and thus that an adequate dissolution clause is essential for satisfaction of the organizational test. By contrast, the law of several states applies the *cy pres* doctrine to testamentary charitable trusts and the law of a few states applies the doctrine to nonprofit charitable corporations.[82] Consequently, from the standpoint of the IRS, an organization in a jurisdiction where the *cy pres* doctrine is inapplicable must have an express, qualifying distribution or liquidation clause to satisfy the organizational test.[83]

(c) Judicial Gloss on Test

In most respects, the courts have adhered to the IRS-mandated requirements of the organizational test. Prior to the effective date of the organizational test requirements in the income tax regulations (July 27, 1959),[84] however, there was a tendency to read into the term *organized* in the federal tax law rules for charitable organizations a greater flexibility than is contemplated by the regulations.[85] That is, the courts tended to blur the technical distinction between the organizational test and the operational test by viewing the former in the light of the predominant purpose for forming the organization and its manner of operations.[86] In one case,[87] for example, a court concluded that the word *organized* does not state a "narrowly limited formal requirement" and that the term largely requires only the requisite inurement:

> Our conclusion is that a corporation satisfies the requirement of being "organized" for a charitable purpose if, at the time in question, its setup or organization of ownership, directors, and officers is such that its earnings must inure to a charity.[88]

---

[81] Rev. Rul. 69-256, *supra* note 59; Rev. Rul. 69-279, *supra* note 59.

[82] Rev. Proc. 82-2, 1982-1 C.B. 367.

[83] The IRS will accept the following phraseology of a dissolution clause: "Upon the dissolution of [this organization], assets shall be distributed for one or more exempt purposes within the meaning of section 501(c)(3) of the Internal Revenue Code, or corresponding section of any future Federal tax code, or shall be distributed to the Federal government, or to a state or local government, for a public purpose" (Rev. Proc. 82-2, *supra* note 82 § 3.05).

[84] Reg. § 1.501(c)(3)-1(b)(6).

[85] Rev. Rul. 60-193, 1969-1 C.B. 195.

[86] Passaic United Hebrew Burial Ass'n v. United States, 216 F. Supp. 500 (D. N.J. 1963).

[87] Dillingham Transp. Bldg. v. United States, 146 F. Supp. 953 (Ct. Cl. 1957).

[88] *Id.* at 955.

The organization in this case remained organized as a for-profit corporation with stockholders. Once all of its stock became held by a tax-exempt hospital and the hospital's trustees assumed control over it, however, the organization was deemed qualified as a charitable entity even though the corporate charter was never amended—with the court finding that it was properly organized "for all practical purposes."[89]

By contrast, another court had elected to follow the "reasonable interpretation" of the word *organized*.[90] The organization involved was organized as a for-profit corporation and the fact that it was a holding company for a tax-exempt art museum was considered insufficient for passage of the organizational test. The court held that the term " 'organized' means 'incorporated' and not 'operated' " and that, in line with the IRS requirements, the "right of the corporation to an exemption is to be determined by the powers given it in its charter."[91]

Some courts sought a middle ground. In one case, the court wrote:

> The better view, based in part upon the doctrine of liberality of construction respecting charitable exemptions which resolves ambiguities in favor of the taxpayer and in part upon a refusal to allow form to control over substance, is that "organized" means "created to perform" or "established to promote" charitable purposes rather than meaning merely "incorporated" with powers limited solely to charitable activities.[92]

Thus, this court dismissed the approach that focuses only on "recitations in a charter or certificate" and held that the analysis must extend to the "actual objects motivating the organization and the subsequent conduct of the organization" and the "manner in which the corporation has been operated."[93]

Since promulgation of the regulations containing the organizational test, the courts have been somewhat silent on the subject. One court, however, hinted that a provision in an organization's articles of organization that is contrary to the requirements of the organizational test (such as permitting substantial lobbying activities) may not be a bar to tax exemption where that aspect of the organization's activities is "dormant."[94] Another court observed that the "mere existence of power to engage in activities other than those set out in section 501(c)(3) does not in itself prevent . . . [an organization] from meeting the organizational test."[95]

In the final analysis, however, prudence dictates compliance with the or-

---

[89] Also Roche's Beach, Inc. v. Comm'r, 96 F.2d 776 (2d Cir. 1938).

[90] Sun-Herald Corp. v. Duggan, 73 F.2d 298 (2d Cir. 1934), *cert. den.*, 294 U.S. 719 (1934). Also Sun-Herald Corp. v. Duggan, 160 F.2d 475 (2d Cir. 1947). Cf. Universal Oil Prods. Co. v. Campbell, 181 F.2d 451 (7th Cir. 1950).

[91] Sun-Herald Corp. v. Duggan, *supra* note 90, 73 F.2d at 300.

[92] Samuel Friedland Found. v. United States, 144 F. Supp. 74, 84 (D. N.J. 1956).

[93] *Id.* at 85. Also Comm'r v. Battle Creek, Inc., 126 F.2d 405 (5th Cir. 1942); Forest Press, Inc. v. Comm'r, 22 T.C. 265 (1954); Lewis v. United States, 189 F. Supp. 950 (D. Wyo. 1961).

[94] Center on Corporate Responsibility v. Shultz, 368 F. Supp. 863, 878, note 31 (D. D.C. 1973).

[95] Peoples Translation Service/Newsfront Int'l v. Comm'r, 72 T.C. 42, 48 (1979).

ganizational test whenever possible. There can be many barriers to tax-exempt status and problems with the organizational test are among the easiest to avoid. This point is underscored by the approach of the IRS that, since articles of organization that fail to meet the organizational test are ordinarily amendable and since after amendment the exemption may be retroactive to the period before amendment, the "resolution of an organizational test question is only the first step in determining whether an organization is exempt."[96] Even if doing battle with the IRS over the tax-exempt status of an organization appears inevitable, presumably the struggle can be joined over matters of greater substance.

(d) Rules for Limited Liability Companies

The IRS concluded that an LLC,[97] with two or more members that are charitable or governmental entities,[98] can qualify for tax exemption as a charitable organization itself, if it satisfies 12 conditions.[99] They are:

1. The LLC's organizational documents must include a specific statement limiting its activities to one or more exempt (charitable) purposes.

2. The organizational language must specify that the LLC is operated exclusively to further the charitable purposes of its members.

3. The organizational language must require that the LLC's members be charitable organizations, governmental units, or wholly owned instrumentalities of a state or political subdivision of a state.

4. The organizational language must prohibit any direct or indirect transfer of any membership interest in the LLC to a transferee other than a charitable organization, governmental unit, or instrumentality.

5. The organizational language must state that the LLC, interests in the LLC (other than a membership interest), or its assets may only be availed of or transferred to, directly or indirectly, any nonmember (other than a charitable organization, governmental unit, or instrumentality) in exchange for fair market value.

6. The organizational language must guarantee that, upon dissolution of the LLC, the assets devoted to the LLC's charitable purposes will continue to be devoted to charitable purposes.

---

[96] IRS Exempt Organizations Handbook (IRM 7751) § 338(2).
[97] See *supra* § 1(b), § 32.6(b).
[98] A single-member LLC is a disregarded entity for tax purposes (see *supra* § 1(b)(ii)).
[99] These elements are stated in the IRS's exempt organizations continuing professional education technical instruction text for fiscal year 2001.

7. The organizational language must require that any amendments to the LLC's articles of organization and operating agreement be consistent with the general organizational test applicable to charitable organizations.[100]

8. The organizational language must prohibit the LLC from merging with, or converting into, a for-profit entity.

9. The organizational language must require that the LLC not distribute any assets to members who cease to be charitable organizations, governmental units, or instrumentalities.

10. The organizational language must contain an acceptable contingency plan in the event one or more members ceases at any time to be a charitable organization, a governmental unit, or instrumentality.

11. The organizational language must state that the LLC's exempt members will "expeditiously and vigorously" enforce all of their rights in the LLC and will pursue all legal and equitable remedies to protect their interests in the LLC.

12. The LLC must represent that all its organizing document provisions are consistent with state LLC laws, and are enforceable at law and in equity.

Because of conflict and confusion among the states as to the role of LLC articles of organization and operating agreement, the IRS is requiring that both documents separately comply with the first 11 of these conditions. The last one is met in a separate written statement from the organization.

An LLC that meets each of these 12 conditions can also qualify as a tax-exempt social welfare organization,[101] if it otherwise meets the requirements for that category of tax exemption. The IRS has yet to establish its position as to whether an LLC can qualify as any other type of exempt organization.

§ 4.4 PRIMARY PURPOSE TEST

Section 501(c)(3) of the Internal Revenue Code provides that an organization must, to qualify as a tax-exempt organization by reason of that provision, be organized and operated *exclusively* for an exempt purpose. It is clear that the term *exclusively* as employed in this context does not mean *solely* but rather *primarily*.[102]

Although the term *exclusively* is not used with respect to categories of tax-exempt organizations other than charitable ones, its presence may be presumed. That is, as a general precept, any type of tax-exempt organization must

---

[100] See *supra* § 3(a), (b).
[101] See Chapter 12.
[102] Reg. § 1.501(c)(3)-1(c)(1). Also Reg. § 1.501(c)(3)-1(a)(1).

operate primarily for its exempt purpose to remain exempt.[103] This is the *primary purpose* test.

The law could not reasonably be interpreted in any other way. That is, if *exclusively* truly meant *exclusively*, there would not be an opportunity for the conduct of unrelated business activity. Since that interpretation would render the entire law of unrelated business income taxation[104] meaningless, the interpretation would not be reasonable. Consequently, by treating the word *exclusively* as if it meant *primarily*, the law accommodates the co-existence of some unrelated activities with related ones.

The general rule, as stated by the U.S. Supreme Court, is that the "presence of a single . . . [nonexempt] purpose, if substantial in nature, will destroy the exemption regardless of the number or importance of truly . . . [exempt] purposes."[105] A federal court of appeals held that nonexempt activity will not result in loss or denial of exemption where it is "only incidental and less than substantial" and that a "slight and comparatively unimportant deviation from the narrow furrow of tax approved activity is not fatal."[106] In the words of the IRS, the rules applicable to charitable organizations in general have been "construed as requiring all the resources of the organization [other than an insubstantial part] to be applied to the pursuit of one or more of the exempt purposes therein specified."[107] So, the existence of one or more truly exempt purposes of an organization will not be productive of tax exemption as a charitable entity if there is present in its operations a substantial nonexempt purpose.[108]

There is no definition of the term *insubstantial* in this context. Thus, application of these rules is an issue of fact to be determined under the facts and circumstances of each case.[109] A court opinion in one case suggested that, where a function represents less than 10 percent of total efforts, the primary purpose test will not be contravened.[110] By contrast, another court opinion stated that an organization that received approximately one-third of its revenue from an unrelated business could not qualify for tax-exempt status.[111]

---

[103] E.g., Orange County Agric. Soc'y, Inc. v. Comm'r, 55 T.C.M. 1602 (1988), *aff'd*, 893 F.2d 647 (2d Cir. 1990).

[104] See Part Five.

[105] Better Business Bureau of Washington, D.C. v. United States, 326 U.S. 279, 283 (1945). Also Universal Church of Jesus Christ, Inc. v. Comm'r, 55 T.C.M. 143 (1988).

[106] St. Louis Union Trust Co. v. United States, 374 F.2d 427, 431–432 (8th Cir. 1967). Also Seasongood v. Comm'r, 227 F.2d 907, 910 (6th Cir. 1955).

[107] Rev. Rul. 77-366, 1977-2 C.B. 192.

[108] Stevens Bros. Found. v. Comm'r, 324 F.2d 633 (8th Cir. 1963), *cert. den.*, 376 U.S. 969 (1964); Scripture Press Found. v. United States, 285 F.2d 800, 806 (Ct. Cl. 1961), *cert. den.*, 368 U.S. 985 (1962); Fides Publishers Ass'n v. United States, 263 F. Supp. 924, 935 (N.D. Ind. 1967); Edgar v. Comm'r, 56 T.C. 717, 755 (1971); The Media Sports League, Inc. v. Comm'r, 52 T.C.M. 1093 (1986).

[109] E.g., Kentucky Bar Found. v. Comm'r, 78 T.C. 921 (1982).

[110] World Family Corp. v. Comm'r, 81 T.C. 958 (1983).

[111] Orange County Agric. Soc'y, Inc. v. Comm'r, *supra* note 103 (where the unrelated business was held to have "exceeded the benchmark of insubstantiality" (55 T.C.M., at 1604)). This view of the law may be changing, in the aftermath of increasing emphasis on the *commensurate test* (see *infra* § 7).

The primary purpose test looks—in a rule frequently honored in its breach—to an organization's purposes rather than its activities.[112] The focus should not be on an organization's primary activities as the test of tax exemption but on whether the activities accomplish one or more tax-exempt purposes.[113] This is why, for example, an organization may engage in nonexempt or profit-making activities and nonetheless qualify for exemption.[114]

The proper approach to be taken, therefore, when determining whether an organization qualifies as a tax-exempt entity, is to assume *arguendo* one or more tax-exempt purposes and endeavor to ascertain whether the organization has a commercial or other nonexempt purpose. Upon finding a nonexempt purpose, an inquiry should then be made as to whether it is primary or incidental to the exempt purposes.[115] Then, if there is a nonexempt purpose that is substantial in nature, the exemption would be precluded. This approach was adhered to by a court, in concluding that a policemen's benevolent association could not qualify for tax exemption as a charitable organization because the payment of retirement benefits to its members was a substantial nonexempt activity.[116] This approach was again followed by the court in a case holding that a religious organization was ineligible for tax exemption because a substantial portion of its receipts was expended for the nonexempt function of medical care of its members.[117] The second of these two holdings was reversed on appeal, however, with the appellate court holding that the medical aid plan was carried out in furtherance of the church's religious doctrines and therefore was an exempt purpose.[118]

This approach is not always followed, as illustrated by a case involving a would-be religious organization that was denied tax exemption on the basis of the primary purpose test.[119] The disqualifying aspect of its activities was that the organization made grants that "carried with them no legal obligation to repay any interest or principal" and as to which the organization was "unable to

---

[112] Reg. § 1.501(c)(3)-1(c)(1).

[113] Aid to Artisans, Inc. v. Comm'r, 71 T.C. 202 (1978).

[114] Nonetheless, the courts occasionally stretch this criterion, as illustrated by the decision denying tax-exempt status to a scholarship fund, for violation of the primary purpose test, because its fundraising activities were conducted in a cocktail lounge and attracted customers to the lounge (P.L.L. Scholarship Fund v. Comm'r, 82 T.C. 196 (1984); also KJ's Fund Raisers, Inc. v. Comm'r, 74 T.C.M. 669 (1997) *aff'd*, 166 F.3d 1200 (2nd Cir. 1998)). Cf. Hope Charitable Found. v. Ridell, 61-1 U.S.T.C. ¶ 9437 (S.D. Cal. 1961).

[115] American Inst. for Economic Research Inc. v. United States, 302 F.2d 934 (Ct. Cl. 1962); Edward Orton, Jr., Ceramic Found. v. Comm'r, 56 T.C. 147 (1971); Pulpit Resource v. Comm'r, 70 T.C. 594 (1978); Aid to Artisans, Inc. v. Comm'r, *supra* note 113.

[116] Policemen's Benevolent Ass'n of Westchester County, Inc. v. Comm'r, 42 T.C.M. 1750 (1981). Also Police Benevolent Ass'n of Richmond, Va. v. United States, 87-1 U.S.T.C. ¶ 9238 (E.D. Va. 1987).

[117] Bethel Conservative Mennonite Church v. Comm'r, 80 T.C. 352 (1983).

[118] Bethel Conservative Mennonite Church v. Comm'r, *supra* note 77. The court wrote that "[r]eligions by their very nature provide many services that benefit only the members of the individual congregation, and to say that any church which so provides these benefits must be denied tax exemption would disrupt many organized churches as we know them," citing, *inter alia*, O'Leary v. Social Security Bd., 153 F.2d 704 (3d Cir. 1946); Passaic United Hebrew Burial Ass'n v. United States, *supra* note 86.

[119] Church in Boston v. Comm'r, 71 T.C. 102 (1978).

furnish any documented criteria which would demonstrate the selection process of a deserving recipient, the reason for specific amounts given, or the purpose of the grant."[120] The statutory and regulatory law, however, does not contain any criteria by which public charities are to consider and award grants.[121]

The difficulties inherent in applying the primary purpose test were illustrated by a court opinion, where the opinion initially prepared as the majority holding was converted by the full court into a dissenting opinion. At issue was the tax status of an organization that operated a pharmacy that sold prescription drugs at cost to the elderly and handicapped. The court held that the organization did not constitute a tax-exempt charitable entity, inasmuch as it did not use its surplus receipts to provide drugs to these persons below cost and it was in competition with profit-making drug stores. Contrary arguments that the organization operated to promote health and relieve the financial distress of a charitable class were unavailing. The dissenting opinion took the position that an organization's activities are not to be evaluated in a vacuum but in the context of accomplishment of exempt purposes, that generation of a profit is not a *per se* bar to exemption, and that the organization was not being operated for commercial ends but rather to promote health.[122]

The primary purpose test was subsequently applied in an opinion denying tax-exempt status as a religious entity to an organization that operated a mountain lodge as a retreat facility.[123] While the organization contended that its "primary purpose is to provide a religious retreat facility for Christian families where they may come to reflect upon and worship the Lord in a setting free from the outside interferences of everyday life," the government asserted that its "substantial, if not sole, purpose is to provide a facility where guests can relax, socialize and engage in recreational activities, or, in other words, to operate a vacation resort."[124] The court held that the organization was not operated exclusively for religious (or other exempt) purposes largely because of the organization's inability to demonstrate that the recreational facilities "were not used extensively and were not used in more than an insubstantial manner."[125] The court also appeared concerned with the fact that a guest at the lodge was not required to participate in any type of religious activity and that the organization was governed and was initially funded by members of the same family.[126]

---

[120] *Id.* at 106–107.

[121] Cf. IRC § 4945(d), applicable only to private foundations (see § 11.4 (e)).

[122] Federation Pharmacy Servs., Inc. v. Comm'r, 72 T.C. 687 (1979), *aff'd*, 625 F.2d 804 (8th Cir. 1980).

[123] The Schoger Found. v. Comm'r, 76 T.C. 380 (1981).

[124] *Id.* at 386.

[125] *Id.* at 388.

[126] At the same time, in a showing as to how the exclusivity doctrine can dictate the outcome of a case, the court observed that, in a "proper factual case, the operation of a lodge as a religious retreat facility would no doubt constitute an exempt religious purpose under [IRC] section 501(c)(3), and the presence of some incidental recreational or social activities might even be found to be activities to further or accomplish that exempt purpose" (*id.* at 389).

By contrast, an organization formed to construct, and sell or lease, housing at a religious retreat facility owned and operated by a church was held to be tax-exempt as a charitable entity because the predominant use of the housing units was inextricably tied to the religious activities of the church.[127] While housing construction is not inherently an exempt function, in this instance the organization was found to be organized and operated exclusively for exempt purposes because of the manner of the development of the project, in that the organization had not advertised, it confined sale of the units to those who would take an active part in the religious activities, restrictions were placed on the properties as to resale, and otherwise was not operating for commercial purposes or private benefit. In general, the organization's function of providing additional housing was held essential to its continuing ability to carry out the purposes of the church.

The primary purpose test was also invoked to deny tax exemption to an organization formed to provide a service through which public and private libraries, commercial organizations, and others centrally pay license fees for the photocopying of certain copyrighted publications. In this capacity, the organization functioned as a clearinghouse for licensing photocopying and as a conduit for the transfer of license fees to copyright holders. The organization sought exempt status as a charitable organization because it operated channels of communication necessary to implement the copyright clause of the U.S. Constitution and the federal copyright law as revised in 1976. To this end, it showed that it promoted social welfare, lessened the burdens of government, and promoted education and science.[128] The court involved conceded that the organization served exempt purposes and did so to a substantial degree. Nonetheless, the court found a substantial nonqualifying purpose, precluding the organization from exemption. The organization was founded by a division of the American Association of Publishers and was funded almost entirely by commercial publishers. The court wrote that there was "little persuasive evidence that . . . [the organization's] founders had interests of any substance beyond the creation of a device to protect their copyright ownership and collect license fees."[129] Finding that the "potential for a substantial private profit was the driving force behind the organization and operation" of the entity, the court concluded that the nonexempt purpose was not incidental but represented the "dominant and overriding concern of those who organized, sponsored, and promoted" the organization.[130] Consequently, the court determined that the organization could not qualify for exemption as a charitable entity.

Thereafter, in application of the primary purpose test, the same court analyzed the tax status of a scholarship fund. While normally a scholarship fund is a charitable entity because it advances education,[131] in this case the court was

[127] Junaluska Assembly Housing, Inc. v. Comm'r, 86 T.C. 1114 (1986).
[128] See §§ 6.3, 6.5, 6.6.
[129] Copyright Clearance Center, Inc. v. Comm'r, 79 T.C. 793, 805 (1982).
[130] *Id.* at 807, 808.
[131] See § 6.5.

moved to decide to the contrary by reason of the fact that the fund was established pursuant to a collective bargaining agreement between a labor union and an employers' association. The only recipients of the scholarships were children of the employees. The court concluded that the class of persons served was "too restricted" to confer the requisite "public benefit."[132] The court also held that the benefits were compensation in the form of a "negotiated fringe benefit,"[133] so that the fund was not operated exclusively for an exempt purpose and therefore did not qualify as a charitable organization.

The primary purpose test was applied by a federal district court to deny tax-exempt status as charitable entities to two cemetery associations.[134] The court found that the cemetery associations generally conducted charitable activities, on two grounds. First, the "fundamental responsibility" of the associations for the "proper disposal of human remains is critical to society and would otherwise have to be assumed by the government." This was in recognition of the fact that an organization can be charitable where it lessens the burdens of government.[135] Second, the associations had a long-standing policy in providing free burial to indigents. This practice, said the court, served to "historically infuse" the cemetery associations with "a charitable concept." The court, however, applied the primary purpose test to preclude the associations from being eligible recipients of deductible charitable bequests. In so doing, the court concluded that two of the cemetery associations' activities were the sale of burial plots and maintenance of the cemeteries. Since the court found these two activities to be substantial in nature, the associations were found to not be charitable entities.

This test is applied with respect to amateur sports organizations. Thus, when an organization promotes, advances, and sponsors recreational and amateur sports, with an emphasis on training and education, the organization can qualify as a charitable and educational entity.[136] If, however, the principal purpose of the organization is the advancement of the social and recreational interests of the players, the organization cannot be that type of exempt organization.[137]

As another example, the retail sale of goods and services normally is a nonexempt business activity. This is the case, for example, when a tax-exempt museum is selling souvenir items relating to the city in which the museum is located.[138] Yet, an organization with the primary purpose of providing assistance

[132] Local Union 712, I.B.E.W. Scholarship Trust Fund v. Comm'r, 45 T.C.M. 675, 678 (1983).
[133] Id.
[134] Smith v. United States, 84-2 U.S.T.C. ¶ 13,595 (W.D. Mo. 1984).
[135] See § 6.3.
[136] Reg. § 1.501(c)(3)-1(a)(1).
[137] Rev. Rul. 72-369, 1972-2 C.B. 245.
[136] E.g., Hutchinson Baseball Enters., Inc. v. Comm'r, 73 T.C. 144 (1979), aff'd, 696 F.2d 757 (10th Cir. 1982). See §§ 6.10(c), 7.4.
[137] E.g., Wayne Baseball, Inc. v. Comm'r, 78 T.C.M. 437 (1999). This type of organization may, however, qualify as a social club (see Chapter 14).
[138] Rev. Rul. 73-105, 1973-1 C.B. 264.

to needy women to enable them to earn income was held to be exempt as a charitable entity because it operated a market for the cooking and needlework of this category of women, who are not otherwise able to support themselves and their families.[139] Likewise, an organization that operated a consignment shop as a place where "industrious and meritorious" women can sell articles and foodstuffs prepared by them was held to be exempt.[140]

The primary purpose of an organization is not taken into account only when determining whether it qualifies for tax-exempt status. This purpose can also be a critical factor in application of the unrelated business rules.[141]

§ 4.5 OPERATIONAL TEST

(a) In General

An organization, to qualify as a charitable entity, is regarded as operated exclusively for one or more tax-exempt purposes only if it engages primarily in activities that accomplish one or more of its exempt purposes.[142] The IRS observed that, to satisfy this *operational test*, the organization's "resources must be devoted to purposes that qualify as exclusively charitable within the meaning of section 501(c)(3) of the Code and the applicable regulations."[143] An organization will not be so regarded if more than an insubstantial part of its activities is not in furtherance of an exempt purpose.[144] An organization is not considered as operated exclusively for one or more exempt purposes if its net earnings inure in whole or in part to the benefit of private shareholders or individuals.[145] An organization can be substantially dominated by its founder without, for that reason alone, failing to satisfy the operational test.[146] A court concluded, however, that an organization cannot qualify for tax exemption where one individual controls all aspects of the organization's operations and "is not checked" by any governing body.[147]

A deficiency in an organization's operations that causes failure of the operational test cannot be cured by language in its governing instruments. Thus, the

[139] Rev. Rul. 68-167, 1968-1 C.B. 255.
[140] Tech. Adv. Mem. 200021056.
[141] See § 26.4.
[142] Reg. § 1.501(c)(3)-1(c)(1).
[143] Rev. Rul. 72-369, 1972-2 C.B. 245.
[144] Reg. § 1.501(c)(3)-1(c)(1). In one instance, the operational test was found to be unmet because the organization involved, which was organized for the study and promotion of the philately of the Central American republics, operated a mail bid stamps sales service for its members as a substantial activity (Society of Costa Rica Collectors v. Comm'r, 49 T.C.M. 304 (1984)).
[145] Reg. §§ 1.501(c)(3)-1(c)(2), 1.501(a)-1(c). Also Wildt's Motorsport Advancement Crusade, Bill v. Comm'r, 56 T.C.M. 1401 (1989); Athenagoras I Christian Union of the World, Inc. v. Comm'r, 55 T.C.M. 781 (1988); Levy Family Tribe Found. v. Comm'r, *supra* note 53. See Chapter 19.
[146] E.g., The Church of the Visible Intelligence That Governs the Universe v. United States, 83-2 U.S.T.C. ¶ 9726 (Cl. Ct. 1983).
[147] Chief Steward of the Ecumenical Temples and the Worldwide Peace Movement and His Successors v. Comm'r, *supra* note 77, at 643. Likewise, it was held that an organization was not entitled to exemption because the affairs of the entity and the individual who was its founder, sole director, and officer were "irretrievably intertwined" (Salvation Navy, Inc. v. Comm'r, T.C. Mem. 2002-275).

IRS stated that an organization "whose activities are not within the statute cannot be exempt by virtue of a well-written charter."[148]

An organization may meet the federal tax law requirements for charitable entities even though it operates a trade or business as a substantial part of its activities.[149] If the organization has as its primary purpose the carrying on of a trade or business, however, it may not be tax-exempt.[150] The core issue is whether the substantial business activity accomplishes or is in furtherance of an exempt purpose.[151] (The existence of an operating profit is not conclusive as to a business purpose.[152]) Even though the operation of a business does not deprive an organization of classification as a charitable entity, there may be unrelated trade or business tax consequences.[153]

The operational test focuses on the actual purposes the organization advances by means of its activities, rather than on the organization's statement of purposes or the nature of its activities, in recognition of the fact that an organization may conduct a business in furtherance of a tax-exempt purpose and qualify as a charitable entity:

> Under the operational test, the purpose towards which an organization's activities are directed, and not the nature of the activities themselves, is ultimately dispositive of the organization's right to be classified as a section 501(c)(3) organization exempt from tax under section 501(a). . . . [I]t is possible for . . . an activity to be carried on for more than one purpose. . . . The fact that . . . [an] activity may constitute a trade or business does not, of course, disqualify it from classification under section 501(c)(3), provided the activity furthers or accomplishes an exempt purpose. . . . Rather, the critical inquiry is whether . . . [an organization's] primary purpose for engaging in its . . . activity is an exempt purpose, or whether its primary purpose is the nonexempt one of operating a commercial business producing net profits for . . . [the organization]. . . . Factors such as the particular manner in which an organization's activities are conducted, the commercial hue of those activities and the existence and amount of annual or accumulated profits are relevant evidence of a forbidden predominant purpose.[154]

---

[148] IRS Exempt Organizations Handbook (IRM 7751) § 320(2).

[149] E.g., Rev. Rul. 64-182, 1964-1 (Part 1) C.B. 186.

[150] Reg. § 1.501(c)(3)-1(e)(1).

[151] Federation Pharmacy Services, Inc. v. Comm'r, 72 T.C. 687 (1979), aff'd, 625 F.2d 804 (8th Cir. 1980); est of Hawaii v. Comm'r, 71 T.C. 1067 (1979), aff'd, 647 F.2d 170 (9th Cir. 1981).

[152] Rev. Rul. 68-26, 1968-1 C.B. 272; Elisian Guild, Inc. v. United States, 412 F.2d 121 (1st Cir. 1969). Cf. Fides Publishers Assn. v. United States, 263 F. Supp. 924 (N.D. Ind. 1967).

[153] See Part Five.

[154] B.S.W. Group, Inc. v. Comm'r, 70 T.C. 352, 356–357 (1978). Also American Campaign Academy v. Comm'r, 92 T.C. 1053 (1989); Goldsboro Art League, Inc. v. Comm'r, 75 T.C. 337 (1980); Aid to Artisans, Inc. v. Comm'r, supra note 113; Ohio Teamsters Educ. & Safety Training Fund v. Comm'r, 77 T.C. 189 (1981), aff'd, 692 F.2d 432 (6th Cir. 1982). To determine whether the operational test has been satisfied, the Tax Court wrote that it looks beyond the "four corners of the organization's charter to discover the actual objects motivating the organization' " (American Campaign Academy v. Comm'r., 92 T.C. at 1064).

This important distinction between activities and purpose is sometimes over-looked by the IRS and the courts. For example, in one case a court concluded that the operational test was not satisfied because the organization failed to describe its activities in sufficient detail in its application for recognition of tax exemption.[155]

Although an organization might be engaged in only a single activity, that activity may be directed toward multiple purposes, both exempt and nonexempt. If the nonexempt purpose is substantial in nature, the organization will not sat-isfy the operational test.[156]

Whether an organization has a substantial nonexempt purpose is a ques-tion of fact, to be resolved on the basis of all the appropriate evidence.[157] The Tax Court observed: "Factors such as the particular manner in which an orga-nization's activities are conducted, the commercial hue of those activities, and the existence and amount of annual or accumulated profits are relevant evi-dence of a forbidden predominant purpose."[158]

An illustration of the application of the operational test rules was pro-vided by a case concerning the tax-exempt status of an organization estab-lished to provide a fund for the purpose of giving scholarships to contestants in a state pageant.[159] As a condition for qualifying for the scholarships, the or-ganization required the participants to enter into a contract obligating them, in the event they are selected to participate in the pageant, to abide by its rules and regulations. A court ruled that the ostensible scholarships were compen-satory in nature, being payment for the contestants' agreement to perform the requirements of the contract, thus not constituting tax-excludable[160] scholar-ships. Because the grant of the scholarships was the organization's sole activ-ity, and because the primary purpose of the payments was to provide compensation, the court concluded that the organization did not qualify for exemption as a charitable organization.

Another illustration of the application of these rules is inherent in a court decision concluding that an organization that principally administered donor-advised funds qualified as a tax-exempt charitable entity.[161] The government unsuccessfully contended in court that the organization lacked exempt pur-poses, being instead an association of individuals for which it performs com-mercial services for fees. Rejecting the thought that the organization was a mere conduit for its donors, the court—conceding that the entity's "methods of operating may be somewhat unique and innovative"—found that its "goal is to create an effective national network to respond to many worthy charitable needs at the local level which in many cases might go unmet" and that its ac-tivities "promote public policy and represent the very essence of charitable

---

[155] General Conference of the Free Church of America v. Comm'r, 71 T.C. 920 (1979).

[156] KJ's Fund Raisers, Inc. v. Comm'r, *supra* note 114; Manning Association v. Comm'r, 93 T.C. 596 (1989); Copyright Clearance Center, Inc. v. Comm'r., *supra* note 129.

[157] Church by Mail, Inc. v. Comm'r, 765 F.2d 1387 (9th Cir. 1985), *aff'g* 48 T.C.M. 471 (1984).

[158] B.S.W. Group, Inc. v. Comm'r, 70 T.C. 352, 358 (1978).

[159] Miss Georgia Scholarship Fund, Inc. v. Comm'r, 72 T.C. 267 (1979).

[160] IRC § 117.

[161] National Found., Inc. v. United States, 87-2 U.S.T.C. ¶ 9602 (Cl. Ct. 1987). See § 11.6.

benevolence as envisioned by Congress in enacting" exempt status for charitable organizations.

Still another example illustrating application of the operational test rules involved a court opinion that invoked the concept of private benefit, holding that when an organization operates to confer a private benefit, where the benefit is more than incidental, it cannot satisfy the test. The case concerned an otherwise qualifying school that trained individuals for careers as political campaign professionals, because of the benefit accruing to entities of a political party and its candidates, since nearly all of the school's graduates became employed by or consultants to these entities or candidates.[162] The court was not concerned with the "primary" private benefit accruing to the students but with the "secondary" private benefit accruing to the party's organizations and candidates.[163]

The operational test is used to apply the tests of *commerciality* and *competition* to charitable and other categories of tax-exempt organizations. Previously, the test has been used in conjunction with the *exclusivity* requirement[164] and the rules defining *business* for unrelated income taxation purposes.[165] This application of the commerciality doctrine has largely been by the U.S. Tax Court, where, for example, it denied exempt status, as a charitable and religious entity, to an organization associated with the Seventh-day Adventist Church that, in advancement of Church doctrine, operated vegetarian restaurants and health food stores; the court wrote that the organization's activity was "conducted as a business and was in direct competition with other restaurants and health food stores" and that "[c]ompetition with commercial firms is strong evidence of a substantial nonexempt commercial purpose."[166] Likewise, the Tax Court held that an organization that supported religious missionary work properly had its exemption revoked because it conducted a mail order business in tape and electronic equipment, as a substantial part of its activities and purposes,[167] and that an organization cannot be exempt because it functioned the same as a purchasing, brokering, or consulting organization in the private sector.[168] The only prior opinion from the Tax Court that invoked the commerciality standard is one that looked at the issue from a somewhat different slant, in that the court wrote that the operational test is violated where the

---

[162] American Campaign Academy v. Comm'r, *supra* note 154.

[163] See § 19.10. Other cases in which the operational test has been found to have been transgressed include Larry D. Bowen Family Found. v. Comm'r, 77 T.C.M. 1954 (1999); Tate Family Found. v. Comm'r, 77 T.C.M. 2016 (1999); Tamaki Found. v. Comm'r, 77 T.C.M. 2020 (1999); Share Network Found. v. Comm'r, 78 T.C.M. 6 (1999); Resource Management Found. v. Comm'r, 78 T.C.M. 44 (1999); Hart Found. v. Comm'r, 78 T.C.M. 57 (1999); Oliver Family Found. v. Comm'r, 78 T.C.M. 104 (1999).

[164] See *infra* § 6.

[165] See § 26.2.

[166] Living Faith, Inc. v. Comm'r, 60 T.C.M. 710, 713 (1990), *aff'd*, 950 F.2d 365 (7th Cir. 1991).

[167] United Missionary Aviation, Inc. v. Comm'r, 60 T.C.M. 1152 (1990), *rev'd and rem'd*, 89-2 U.S.T.C. ¶ 9595 (8th Cir. 1989), *cert. den.*, 506 U.S. 816.

[168] Public Indus., Inc. v. Comm'r, 61 T.C.M. 1626 (1991).

organization's "primary purpose is the nonexempt one of operating a commercial business producing net profits for" the organization.[169]

(b) Action Organizations

An organization is not operated exclusively for one or more exempt purposes if it is an action organization.[170]

An organization is an *action organization* if a substantial part of its activities is attempting to influence legislation by propaganda or otherwise. For this purpose, an organization is regarded as attempting to influence legislation if the organization contacts, or urges the public to contact, members of a legislative body for the purpose of proposing, supporting, or opposing legislation or if it advocates the adoption or rejection of legislation. The term *legislation* includes action by the U.S. Congress, a state legislature, a local council or similar governing body, or the public in a referendum, initiative, constitutional amendment, or similar procedure. An organization will not fail to meet the operational test merely because it advocates, as an insubstantial part of its activities, the adoption or rejection of legislation.[171] Also, an organization for which the expenditure test election (relating to expenditures for legislative activities)[172] is in effect for a tax year is not considered an action organization for the year if it avoids loss of tax exemption by reason of that test.[173]

An organization is an action organization if it participates or intervenes, directly or indirectly, in any political campaign on behalf of or in opposition to any candidate for public office. The phrase *candidate for public office* means an individual who offers himself or herself, or is proposed by others, as a contestant for an elective public office, whether the office is national, state, or local. Activities that constitute participation or intervention in a political campaign on behalf of or in opposition to a candidate include, but are not limited to, the publication or distribution of written or printed statements or the making of oral statements on behalf of or in opposition to the candidate.[174]

An organization is an action organization if it has the following two characteristics: (1) Its main or primary objective or objectives (as distinguished from its incidental or secondary objectives) may be attained only by legislation or a defeat of proposed legislation, and (2) it advocates or campaigns for the attainment of this main or primary objective or objectives as distinguished from engaging in nonpartisan analysis, study, or research, and making the results thereof available to the public. In determining whether an organization has these characteristics, all the surrounding facts and circumstances, including one or more provisions in the articles of organization and all activities of the organization, are considered.[175]

---

[169] B.S.W. Group, Inc. v. Comm'r, *supra* note 154 at 356.
[170] Reg. § 1.501(c)(3)-1(c)(i).
[171] Reg. § 1.501(c)(3)-1(c)(3)(ii).
[172] See § 20.5(a).
[173] Reg. § 1.501(c)(3)-1(c)(3)(ii).
[174] Reg. § 1.501(c)(3)-1(c)(3)(iii).
[175] Reg. § 1.501(c)(3)-1(c)(3)(iv).

The IRS is aware that the regulations' terms *exclusively, primarily,* and *insubstantial* present "difficult conceptual problems."[176] The IRS concluded that "[q]uestions involving the application of these terms can more readily be resolved on the basis of the facts of a particular case."[177]

Application of the operational test is, therefore, intertwined with the proscriptions on private inurement, and legislative and political campaign activities.[178] In essence, however, to meet the operational test, an organization must be engaged in activities that further public rather than private purposes.[179]

The entwining of the operational test with the other requirements of the federal tax rules governing charitable organizations was recognized by a court in a decision refusing to reclassify a health and welfare fund, which was tax-exempt as an employee beneficiary association,[180] as a charitable organization.[181] The court ruled against the organization on the ground that it was not operated exclusively for charitable purposes[182] and that its activities were furthering private interests[183] but cloaked its opinion in the mantle of the operational test. (The organization's activities consisted of operating child day-care centers—which the court implied was not a charitable activity[184]—and providing services to members, and the organization charged the employees less tuition for the day-care services than it charged other parents.)

An organization deemed to be an action organization, other than because of more than merely incidental political campaign activities, though it cannot for that reason qualify as a charitable organization, may nonetheless qualify as a social welfare organization.[185]

The activities of a partnership or other form of joint venture are often considered to be the activities of the partners; this is termed the *aggregate principle.*[186] This principle applies for purposes of the operational test, in that the operations of a joint venture that includes a tax-exempt organization are attributed to the exempt organization when it is being evaluated pursuant to the test.[187]

§ 4.6   THE EXCLUSIVELY STANDARD

To be tax-exempt as a charitable organization, an entity must be organized and operated *exclusively* for exempt purposes. As noted,[188] this rule is reflected in the

---

[176] IRS Exempt Organizations Handbook (IRM 7751) § 341.1(2).
[177] *Id.*
[178] See Chapters 19–21.
[179] Reg. § 1.501(c)(3)-1(d)(1)(ii). E.g., American Campaign Academy v. Comm'r., *supra* note 154.
[180] See § 16.3.
[181] Baltimore Regional Joint Bd. Health & Welfare Fund, Amalgamated Clothing & Textile Workers Union v. Comm'r, 69 T.C. 554 (1978).
[182] See *infra* § 6.
[183] See Chapter 19.
[184] Cf. Rev. Rul. 70-533, 1970-2 C.B. 112; San Francisco Infant School, Inc. v. Comm'r, 69 T.C. 957 (1978); Michigan Early Childhood Cent., Inc. v. Comm'r, 37 T.C.M. 808 (1978). See § 7.7.
[185] Reg. § 1.501(c)(3)-1(c)(3)(v). See Chapter 12.
[186] Butler v. Comm'r, 36 T.C. 1097 (1961).
[187] Rev. Rul. 98-15, 1998-1 C.B. 718. See § 32.4(b).
[188] See § 4.4.

primary purpose test. There is, however, additional law pertaining to the *exclusivity* rule.

A more controversial opinion in this regard was authored by a federal court of appeals, which accorded tax exemption to a public parking facility as a charitable organization.[189] The organization was formed by several private businesses and professional persons to construct and operate the facility, utilizing a validation stamp system in an effort to attract shoppers to a center city. The government contended that the operation of a commercial parking facility is not an exempt activity[190] and that a substantial objective of the organization was to encourage the general public to patronize the businesses that participate in the validation stamp system, which constituted private inurement and only incidental public benefit.[191] Concluding that the city involved was the primary beneficiary of the organization's activities, the district court had held that the "business activity itself is similar to that which others engage in for profit, but it is not carried on in the same manner; it is carried on only because it is necessary for the attainment of an undeniably public end."[192] On appeal, the appellate court observed that the lower court "made a quantitative comparison of the private versus the public benefits derived from the organization and operation of the plaintiff corporation" and determined that the requirements for exemption were "adequately fulfilled."[193] The opinion is not illustrative of blind adherence to the *exclusively* doctrine.

The IRS does not subscribe to the principles of the public parking corporation case and announced that it does not follow the decision.[194] The IRS asserts that this type of a public parking corporation does not operate exclusively for charitable purposes and carries on a business with the general public in a manner similar to organizations that are operated for profit. This position was made clear earlier when the IRS ruled that an organization formed to revive retail sales in an area suffering from continued economic decline by constructing a shopping center that would complement the area's existing retail facilities could not qualify for tax exemption as a charitable entity. The IRS, then taking no notice of the appellate court decision, said that the activities of the organization "result in major benefits accruing to the stores that will locate within the shopping center," thereby precluding the exemption.[195] (An organization that provided free parking to persons visiting a downtown area can, however, qualify as an exempt social welfare organization.[196])

Application of the concept of *exclusively* may require even more flexibility than has been previously displayed. This may be particularly unavoidable as re-

---

[189] Monterey Pub. Parking Corp. v. United States, 481 F.2d 175 (9th Cir. 1973), *aff'd.* 321 F. Supp. 972 (N.D. Cal. 1970).

[190] See Chapter 25.

[191] See Chapter 19.

[192] Monterey Pub. Parking Corp. v. United States, *supra* note 189, 321 F. Supp., at 977.

[193] Monterey Public Parking Corp. v. United States, *supra* note 189, 481 F. 2d at 177. Cf. Rev. Rul. 73-411, 1973-2 C.B. 180.

[194] Rev. Rul. 78-86, 1978-1 C.B. 151.

[195] Rev. Rul. 77-111, 1977-1 C.B. 144. Also Rev. Rul. 64-108, 1964-1 (Part I) C.B. 189.

[196] Rev. Rul. 81-116, 1981-1 C.B. 333. Social welfare organizations are the subject of Chapter 12.

spects organizations performing services that are considered necessary in today's society, even where the services are parallel with those rendered in commercial settings. For example, the provision of medical services can obviously be an enterprise for profit, yet the IRS was able to rule that an organization formed to attract a physician to a medically underserved rural area, by providing the doctor with a building and facilities at a reasonable rent, qualified as a charitable organization.[197] "In these circumstances," said the IRS, any "personal benefit derived by the physician (the use of the building in which to practice medicine) does not detract from the public purpose of the organization nor lessen the public benefit flowing from its activities."[198] Similarly, an organization formed to provide legal services for residents of economically depressed communities was ruled to be engaged in charitable activities.[199] Even though those providing the services were subsidized by the organization, the IRS minimized this personal gain by the rationale that they were merely the instruments by which the charitable purposes were accomplished.[200]

A court considered the tax status of an organization, the primary purpose of which was to promote, improve, and expand the handicraft output of disadvantaged artisans in developing societies of the world.[201] The organization's primary activities were the purchase, import, and sale of handicrafts—taken alone, clearly commercial activities—undertaken to alleviate economic deficiencies in communities of disadvantaged artisans, educate the American public in the artistry, history, and cultural significance of handicrafts from these communities, preserve the production of authentic handicrafts, and achieve economic stabilization in disadvantaged communities where handicrafts are central to the economy. The court found that these activities advanced charitable and educational objectives[202] and that the furtherance of nonexempt purposes (benefit to nondisadvantaged artisans) was an insubstantial part of the organization's activities. The essence of the case is captured in the following excerpt: "Thus, the sale of handicrafts to exempt organizations [museums] is neither an exempt purpose as argued by . . . [the organization] nor a non-exempt purpose as argued by . . . [the IRS]. Rather, such sale is merely an activity carried on by . . . [the organization] in furtherance of its exempt purposes."[203]

By contrast, the same court refused to find a scholarship fund established pursuant to a collective bargaining agreement to be a charitable entity, holding it to be a voluntary employees' beneficiary association[204] instead.[205] The court con-

---

[197] Rev. Rul. 73-313, 1973-2 C.B. 174.
[198] *Id.* at 176 citing In re Estate of Carlson, 358 P.2d 669 (Kan. 1961). Cf. Rev. Rul. 69-266, 1969-1 C.B. 151.
[199] Rev. Rul. 72-559, 1972-2 C.B. 247. Also Rev. Rul. 70-640, 1970-2 C.B. 117; Golf Life World Entertainment Golf Championship, Inc. v. United States, 65-1 U.S.T.C. ¶ 9174 (S. D. Cal. 1964). Cf. Rev. Rul. 72-369, *supra* note 143.
[200] See § 5.5(d).
[201] Aid to Artisans, Inc. v. Comm'r, *supra* note 113.
[202] The court held that the first of these activities relieved the poor and distressed or the underprivileged (see § 6.1) and that the fourth of these activities promoted social welfare (see § 6.7).
[203] Aid to Artisans, Inc. v. Comm'r, *supra* note 113 at 214.
[204] See § 16.3.
[205] The Newspaper Guild of N.Y., Times Unit–The New York Times College Scholarship Fund v. Comm'r, 57 T.C.M. 812 (1989).

cluded that the fund failed the exclusively test because one of the substantial purposes of the entity was the provision of compensation for services rendered by employees pursuant to the agreement. The court also found that an organization failed the exclusively test because its primary purpose was to operate bingo games for other tax-exempt organizations.[206]

The IRS revoked the tax-exempt status of a charitable organization which had as its purpose the promotion of understanding among the people of the world through learning of nations' sports activities, because of its extensive golf and tennis tours. Those on the tours were regarded as "sports ambassadors"; they (and their families and friends) were the beneficiaries of "good parties" and enjoyable accommodations, meals, and transportation. These facts were aggravated by the fact that two for-profit travel agencies had exclusive accounts for planning and operation of the tours. The operation of the golf and tennis programs in this fashion was found to be a substantial nonexempt purpose of the organization.[207]

In another instance, a nonprofit organization was created by three restaurant owners in a city on the East Coast for the purpose of making "travel grants" to indigent and antisocial persons. The court found that the true purposes of the organization were to rid the downtown area (where the restaurants are located) of disruptive homeless persons and to protect the commercial interests of the restaurateurs (who were the organization's officers). The organization was found to not be "genuinely concerned with the fate of the homeless persons it was relocating, but rather with relocating such persons out of" the city and toward the West Coast, and thus not be operating exclusively for the advancement of charitable purposes.[208]

In another case, tax-exempt status was denied pursuant to the exclusively doctrine to an organization that is part of the Scientology hierarchy of churches and other organizations.[209] The court found that the organization was established for the primary purpose of obtaining exempt status to serve the financing interests of other, nonexempt entities. In reaching its decision, the court took into account the overall structure and financing of the Scientology organization. The court observed that the organization was linked by "a cat's cradle of connections" to a range of Scientology organizations; the court wrote of the "commercial character" of the organization, its "scripturally-based hostility to taxation," and its role as a "shelter from taxation."[210] Its ostensible exempt purpose was to create an archive of Scientology scriptures but the court concluded that that purpose was secondary to its principal (nonexempt) purposes.

[206] Make a Joyful Noise, Inc. v. Comm'r, 56 T.C.M. 1003 (1989).
[207] Tech. Adv. Mem. 9540002.
[208] Westward Ho v. Comm'r, 63 T.C.M. 2617 (1992).
[209] Church of Spiritual Technology v. United States, 92-1 U.S.T.C. ¶ 50,305 (Cl. Ct. 1992), aff'd, 991 F.2d 812 (Fed. Cir. 1993), cert. den., 510 U.S. 870 (1993).
[210] Id., 92-1 U.S.T.C. ¶ 50,305, at 84,217.

§ 4.7   THE COMMENSURATE TEST

Somewhat related to the operational test is another test that the IRS has developed but, until recently, had rarely used. This test is termed the *commensurate test*, which was first articulated in 1964.[211] Under this test, the IRS is empowered to assess whether a charitable organization is maintaining program activities that are commensurate in scope with its financial resources.

In the particular facts underlying the 1964 ruling, the organization derived most of its income from rents, yet was successful in preserving its tax-exempt status because it satisfied the test, in that it was engaging in an adequate amount of charitable functions notwithstanding the extent of its rental activities.

The commensurate test lay dormant for years, then surfaced again in 1990, when the IRS began a close review of the fundraising practices of charitable organizations. In that connection, the IRS developed an 82-question "checksheet" for use by its auditing agents; its full title was "Exempt Organizations Charitable Solicitations Compliance Improvement Program Study Checksheet." One question asked the reviewing agent to determine whether the charitable organization being examined is meeting the *commensurate* test.[212] In this context, the agent was to ascertain whether the charitable organization was engaging in sufficient charitable activity in relation to its available resources, including gifts received through fundraising campaigns, as measured against the time and expense of fundraising.

Later in 1990, the IRS revoked the tax-exempt status of a charitable organization on a variety of rationales, including the ground that its fundraising costs were too high and thus violated the *commensurate* test. In a technical advice memorandum,[213] the IRS concluded that the test was transgressed because of its finding that the charity involved expended, during the two years examined, only about 1 percent of its revenue for charitable purposes; the rest was allegedly spent for fundraising and administration. (The matter of the organization's tax-exempt status was ultimately resolved in court, albeit without application of the commensurate test; the case turned out to be one involving private inurement.[214])

Wrote the IRS:

> The "commensurate test" does not lend itself to a rigid numerical distribution formula—there is no fixed percentage of income that an organization must pay out for charitable purposes. The financial resources of any organization may be affected by such factors as startup costs, overhead, scale of operations, whether labor is voluntary or salaried, phone or postal costs, etc. In each case, therefore, the particular facts and circumstances of the organization must be

---

[211] Rev. Rul. 64-182, *supra* note 149.

[212] This checksheet is discussed in detail in Hopkins, *The Law of Fundraising, Third Edition* (NY: John Wiley & Sons, Inc., 1996), § 5.1(c).

[213] This technical advice memorandum is reproduced at 4 *Exempt Org. Tax Rev.* (No. 5) 726 (July 1991), and is discussed in detail in Hopkins, *supra* note 212, at § 5.15.

[214] United Cancer Council, Inc. v. Comm'r, 109 T.C. 326 (1997), *rev'd and rem'd*, 165 F.3d 1173 (7th cir. 1999).

considered. Accordingly, a specific payout percentage does not automatically mandate the conclusion that the organization under consideration has a primary purpose that is not charitable. In each case, it should be ascertained whether the failure to make real and substantial contributions for charitable purposes is due to reasonable cause.

The IRS added:

> While there is no specified payout percentage, and while special facts and circumstances may control the conclusion, distribution levels that are low invite close scrutiny. The "commensurate" test requires that organizations have a charitable program that is both real and, taking the organization's circumstances and financial resources into account, substantial. Therefore, an organization that raises funds for charitable purposes but consistently uses virtually all its income for administrative and promotional expenses with little or no direct charitable accomplishments cannot reasonably argue that its charitable program is commensurate with its financial resources and capabilities.

The commensurate test and the primary purpose test have an awkward coexistence. For example, a charitable organization was allowed to retain its tax-exempt status while receiving 98 percent of its support from unrelated business income, since 41 percent of the organization's activities were charitable programs.[215]

§ 4.8 BOARDS OF DIRECTORS

There is nothing in the federal statutory law, the federal tax regulations, or the rulings from the IRS that, as a general rule, dictates the composition of the board of directors (or other governing body) of a tax-exempt organization.[216]

Nonetheless, the courts are building up some presumptions in this area. For example, it is the view of the U.S. Tax Court that "where the creators [of an organization] control the affairs of the organization, there is an obvious opportunity for abuse, which necessitates an open and candid disclosure of all facts bearing upon the organization, operation, and finances so that the Court can be assured that by granting the claimed exemption it is not sanctioning an abuse of the revenue laws."[217] The court added that, where this disclosure is not made, the "logical inference is that the facts, if disclosed, would show that

---

[215] Tech. Adv. Mem. 9711003. The IRS concluded, by application of the commensurate test, that the tax-exempt status of four charities should not be revoked because of the small amount of money they grant for charitable purposes (Field Service Advice Mem. 199910007).

[216] A charitable organization that wishes to avoid private foundation status as a donative publicly supported organization by means of the *facts-and-circumstances test* (see § 11.3(6)(ii)) may have to meet certain criteria as to the composition of its governing board. Also, the rules with respect to supporting organizations (see § 11.3(c)) can operate to affect the composition of the board of directors of a charitable organization.

[217] United Libertarian Fellowship, Inc. v. Comm'r, 65 T.C.M. 2175, 2181 (1993).

the taxpayer [organization] fails to meet the requirements" for tax-exempt status.[218]

In another case, the Tax Court found that all of the directors and officers of an organization were related and it could not find the "necessary delineation" between the organization and these persons acting in their personal and private capacity.[219] Earlier, a court found the fact that a husband and wife were two of three members of an organization's board of directors required a special justification of certain payments by the organization to them.[220] Before that, an appellate court concluded that one individual who had "complete and unfettered control" over an organization had a special burden to explain certain withdrawals from the organization's bank account.[221]

In still another setting, a court considered an organization with three directors, namely, the founder, his wife, and their daughter; these three individuals were among the membership base of five. The small size of the organization was held to be "relevant," with the court finding private inurement and private benefit because of the "amount of control" the founder exercised over the organization's operations and the "blurring of the lines of demarcation between the activities and interests" of the organization.[222] The court observed that "[t]his is not to say that an organization of such small dimensions cannot qualify for tax-exempt status."[223]

Thus, while there is nothing specific in the operational test concerning the size or composition of the governing board of a charitable organization, the courts are engrafting onto the test greater burdens of proof when the organization has a small board of directors, dominated by an individual.

§ 4.9   OPERATIONS FOR PROFIT

The IRS, when alleging that an organization is not operated exclusively for an exempt purpose, may base its contention on a finding that the organization's operation is similar to a commercial enterprise operated for profit. As one court observed, however, the "presence of profitmaking activities is not *per se* a bar to qualification of an organization as exempt if the activities further or accomplish an exempt purpose."[224] Similarly, the IRS acknowledged that a charitable organization can have a qualified[225] profit-sharing plan for its employees without endangering its tax exemption.[226]

---

[218] *Id.* Identical language was used by the court in a prior opinion (Bubbling Well Church of Universal Love, Inc. v. Comm'r, 74 T.C. 531, 535 (1980), *aff'd*, 670 F.2d 104 (9th Cir. 1981)).

[219] Levy Family Tribe Found., Inc. v. Comm'r, *supra* note 53, at 619.

[220] Founding Church of Scientology v. United States, 412 F.2d 1197, 1201 (Ct. Cl. 1969), *cert. den.*, 397 U.S. 1009 (1970).

[221] Parker v. Comm'r, 365 F.2d 792, 799 (8th Cir. 1966), *cert. den.*, 385 U.S. 1026 (1967).

[222] Western Catholic Church v. Comm'r, 73 T.C. 196, 213 (1979).

[223] *Id.* In Blake v. Comm'r, 29 T.C.M. 513 (1970), an organization of similar dimensions was ruled to be tax-exempt, although private inurement or private benefit was not at issue in the case.

[224] Aid to Artisans, Inc. v. Comm'r, *supra* note 113, at 211.

[225] IRC § 401(a).

[226] See § 19.4(i)

In one instance, a plan was designed by a hospital as an employee incentive plan, with "profits" defined in the general accounting sense of excess of receipts over expenses.[227] Plan distributions must be reasonable; the distributions were held to not be "dividends" and to not constitute private inurement.[228]

The question as to whether, and if so to what extent, a tax-exempt organization (particularly one that is classified as a charitable entity) can earn a profit is at once difficult and easy to answer. The question is easy to answer in the sense that it is clear that the mere showing of a profit (excess of revenue over expenses) for one or more tax years will not bar tax exemption. If the profit is from what is perceived as a business activity and the fact of a profit is used to show the commercial hue of the activity, the answer to the question will depend upon the facts and circumstances of the particular case. That is, the decisive factor is likely to be the nature of the activities that give rise to the profits.[229]

An illustrative body of law is that concerning organizations that prepare and sell publications at a profit.[230] In one case, an organization sold religious publications to students attending classes it sponsored and to members of its religious following, for a relatively small profit.[231] In rejecting the government's argument that the receipt of the income indicated that the organization was not operated exclusively for religious purposes, a court held that the sale of religious literature was an activity "closely associated with, and incidental to" the organization's tax-exempt purposes and bore "an intimate relationship to the proper functioning" of it, and thus that the receipt of the income did not prevent the organization from being an organization organized and operated exclusively for religious purposes.[232]

By contrast, a court denied status as a tax-exempt charitable entity to an organization that prepared and sold religious literature on a nondenominational basis. Because the organization's materials were competitively priced and the sales over a seven-year period yielded substantial accumulated profits that greatly exceeded the amount expended for its activities, the court concluded that the sales activities were the organization's primary concern and that it was engaging in the conduct of a trade or business for profit.[233] Another organization was denied exemption for publishing on a for-profit basis, with the court observing that, were the law otherwise, "every publishing house would be entitled to an exemption on the ground that it furthers the education of the public."[234] Likewise, an organization could not achieve exemption because its primary activity—the publication and sale of books that are religiously

---

[227] Gen. Couns. Mem. 38283.
[228] Priv. Ltr. Rul. 8442064. In general, Note, "The Semantic Anomaly: Maintenance of Qualified Profit-Sharing Plans by Non-Profit Organizations—A Concept Whose Time Has Come," 59 *Notre Dame L. Rev.* (No. 3) 754 (1984).
[229] See the discussion of the *commerciality doctrine* in Chapter 25.
[230] See § 8.4.
[231] Saint Germain Found. v. Comm'r, 26 T.C. 648 (1956).
[232] *Id.* at 658. Also Elisian Guild, Inc. v. United States, 412 F.2d 121 (1st Cir. 1969), *rev'g* 292 F. Supp. 219 (D. Mass. 1968).
[233] Scripture Press Found. v. United States, *supra* note 108.
[234] Fides Publishers Ass'n v. United States, *supra* note 108, at 936.

inspired and oriented and written by its founder—was conducted in a commercial manner, at a profit.[235]

Each case on this point, therefore, must reflect one of these two analyses. In one case, a court accepted the contention by an organization that its publishing activities furthered its religious purpose of improving the preaching skills and sermons of the clergy of the Protestant, Roman Catholic, and Jewish faiths. Subscriptions for the publications were obtained by advertising and direct mail solicitation, and the publications were sold at a modest profit. The court found that the organization was not in competition with any commercial enterprise and that the sale of religious literature was an integral part of the organization's religious purposes. Said the court: "The fact that . . . [the organization] intended to make a profit, alone, does not negate [the fact] that . . . [it] was operated exclusively for charitable purposes."[236]

By contrast, an organization was denied tax exemption as a charitable entity because it was directly engaged in the conduct of a commercial leasing enterprise for the principal purpose of realizing profits. The enterprise was regarded as its principal activity (measured by total gross income), in which it was an active participant, and not related to an exempt purpose. Further, its charitable activities were deemed to be of relatively minimal consequence.[237] Similarly, a court reflected upon a nonprofit organization's accumulated profits and decided that this was evidence that the primary function of the organization was commercial in nature.[238]

One court determined that "[c]ases where a tax-exempt organization conducts only one activity present particular difficulty" in this area and singled out for uniquely stringent review "religious publishing companies."[239] In one of the leading cases on the subject, an organization had as its sole function the publication of literature in furtherance of a religious doctrine, although it was not affiliated with any particular church. This the organization had done since 1931, and over the years it achieved what the court characterized as "substantial profits" and "consistent and comfortable net profit margins."[240] The issue thus became whether the publishing activities were exempt functions because they were primarily carried on in advancement of charitable, educational, and religious purposes or whether the organization was engaged in a business activity that was carried out in a manner similar to a commercial enterprise. In the case, the court concluded that, due to a "gradual growth and eventual engulfing," a "commercial purpose assumed such significance that we cannot conclude that it was merely incidental to its religious mission."[241]

In arriving at its conclusions, the court first set forth its preliminary premise: "If . . . an organization's management decisions replicate those of com-

---

[235] Christian Manner Int'l, Inc. v. Comm'r, 71 T.C. 661 (1979).
[236] Pulpit Resource v. Comm'r, *supra* note 115, at 611. Also Junaluska Assembly Housing, Inc. v. Comm'r, *supra* note 127; Industrial Aid for the Blind v. Comm'r, 73 T.C. 96 (1979).
[237] Greater United Navajo Dev. Enters., Inc. v. Comm'r, 74 T.C. 69 (1980).
[238] Elisian Guild, Inc. v. United States, *supra* note 232, at 412 F. 2d 124.
[239] Presbyterian & Reformed Publishing Co. v. Comm'r, 70 T.C. 1070, 1083, 1087 (1982).
[240] *Id.* at 1085.
[241] *Id.* at 1087.

mercial enterprises, it is a fair inference that at least one purpose is commercial, and hence nonexempt," and "if this nonexempt goal is substantial, tax exempt status must be denied."[242] Having found that the organization's "conduct of a growing and very profitable publishing business must imbue it with some commercial hue," the court articulated the factors to determine "[h]ow deep a tint these activities impart."[243] Four of the factors were deemed to be the principal ones: the presence of substantial profits, the method of pricing the books sold, consistent and comfortable net profit margins, and competition with commercial publishers.[244] Other factors were considered that showed, to the court, that the organization "consciously attempted to transform itself into a more mainline commercial enterprise"[245]: it searched out additional readers, employed paid workers, dropped money-losing plans, paid substantial royalties, made formal contracts with some authors, expanded into a new facility "from which it could continue to reap profits," and was not affiliated or controlled by any particular church.[246]

The criteria recognized by the court as indicating a "nonprofit-oriented approach" were: reliance on volunteers, payment of "modest amounts" to those that are paid, publication of books even if they would not sell well, and the making of interest-free loans and contributions to tax-exempt organizations.[247] The court hastened to state that it "reject[ed] the notion . . . that efficiency and success automatically negate tax-exempt status."[248] Nevertheless, this opinion went a long way toward establishing the principle that efforts to be efficient, productive, and successful will be equated with substantial commercialism, and that tax exemption is fostered by volunteers struggling to keep an organization afloat in a sea of red ink. Some of these criteria simply reflected a misunderstanding of the reality of operation of a nonprofit organization today. Others—such as employing workers and entering into contracts—would produce nonsensical results if applied to "mainline" tax-exempt institutions that conduct many activities, such as colleges, universities, hospitals, and large, national charities.

A federal court of appeals, however, rejected these views, as it was "troubled by the inflexibility" of the approach of the lower court.[249] The appellate court wrote that the federal tax law does not "define the purpose of an organization claiming tax-exempt status as a direct derivative of the volume of business of that organization"; instead, said the court, "the inquiry must remain that of determining the purpose to which the increased business activity is directed."[250] Thus, the court of appeals concluded that financial expansion and success experienced by a nonprofit organization does not, in and of itself, lead to revocation of tax-exempt status.

---

[242] *Id.* at 1083.
[243] *Id.*
[244] *Id.* at 1083–1086.
[245] *Id.* at 1086.
[246] *Id.*
[247] *Id.* at 1086–1087.
[248] *Id.* at 1087.
[249] Presbyterian & Reformed Publishing Co. v. Comm'r, 743 F.2d 148 (3d Cir. 1984).
[250] *Id.* at 156.

An aspect of the facts that generated much attention from the appellate court was the accumulation by the organization of capital for the purchase of land and the construction of buildings. While the court of appeals observed that "[t]here is no doubt that unexplained accumulations of cash may properly be considered as evidence of commercial purpose,"[251] it refused to endorse the thought that aggregations of funds automatically constitute a form of undue commerciality. Instead, it initiated a precept in the law of tax-exempt organizations by analogizing to the accumulated earnings tax, which is imposed on businesses that accumulate earnings beyond their reasonable needs.[252] In the case, the higher court found no evidence of improper motives for the accumulation.

This court of appeals stated that "success in terms of audience reached and influence exerted, in and of itself, should not jeopardize the tax-exempt status of organizations that remain true to their stated goals."[253] The appellate court expressed concern that, under the lower court's approach, organizations seeking charitable status may be "forced to choose between expanding their audience and influence on the one hand, and maintaining their tax-exempt status on the other"—a concern that would "evaporate," wrote the court, were this a "stagnant society in which various ideas and creeds preserve a hold on a fixed proportion of the population."[254] But, said the appellate court, the view of the lower court "does not reflect either the dynamic quality of our society or the goals that generated the grant of tax-exempt status to religious publishers."[255] The approach of the lower court would, said the appellate court, allow a large institution to engage in an activity such as publishing without loss of exemption, yet deny exemption to an entity where that activity is its only function; the court of appeals refused to uphold this "inequitable disparity in treatment,"[256] thereby voiding the determination of the lower court that single-purpose organizations are to be subject to more stringent review than multipurpose organizations.

Moreover, a federal court of appeals held that the unrelated income rules are not triggered solely by virtue of the "commercial character" of the activity in question.[257] The appellate court reversed the lower court, which had found unrelated activity, and commented that the lower court was "apparently distracted by the commercial character" of the activity and thus "place[d] too great an emphasis on the similarity of the activity to commercial" undertakings.[258] The court reiterated the fact that the essential test is the relationship between the activity under examination and the tax-exempt purposes of the organization.[259]

---

[251] *Id.* at 157.

[252] IRC § 531 *et seq.*

[253] Presbyterian & Reformed Publishing Co. v. Comm'r, *supra* note 249, at 158.

[254] *Id.* at 159.

[255] *Id.*

[256] *Id.*

[257] American College of Physicians v. United States, 743 F.2d 1570, 1576 (Fed. Cir. 1984), *rev'd*, 475 U.S. 834 (1986).

[258] *Id.*, 743 F.2d at 1576.

[259] See *supra* § 1. Cf. Petersen v. Comm'r, 53 T.C.M. 235 (1987).

Nonetheless, one court revoked the tax-exempt status of an organization, using the commerciality rationale, before it became aware of either of these appellate court decisions.[260] The court adhered to its earlier tests, utilizing the same language, relying on the "commercial hue" of the activities, the existence and amount of accumulated profits, the charging of fees for services, the organization's pricing policies, its promotional efforts, the presence of cash reserves, and the fact of contractual arrangements.[261] Likewise, another court refused to grant exempt status to an adoption agency, on the ground that it operated in a manner indistinguishable from, and in competition with, commercial entities.[262]

Yet, given an appropriate set of circumstances, the greater the extent of profits, the greater the likelihood that the revenue-producing activity may be considered to be in furtherance of tax-exempt purposes. In one case, an activity—which the organization regarded as fundraising and the IRS considered a business—was held to not be a business because the activity generated a "staggering amount of money" and "astounding profitability" in a manner that could not be replicated in a commercial context.[263] Also, the organization was much more candid with its supporters than would be the case in a commercial setting, leading the court to note that, "[b]y any standard, an enterprise that depends on the consent of its customers for its profits is not operating in a commercial manner and is not a trade or business."[264]

---

[260] Church of Scientology of Cal. v. Comm'r, 83 T.C. 381 (1984), aff'd, 823 F.2d 1310 (9th Cir. 1987), cert. den., 486 U.S. 1015 (1988).

[261] Id. at 473–490. The Tax Court subsequently held that payments to the Church of Scientology for "auditing and training" services are not deductible as charitable contributions, in part because the Church was found to be "commercial" in nature (Graham v. Comm'r, 83 T.C. 575 (1984), aff'd, 822 F.2d 844 (9th Cir. 1987)). Likewise, Hernandez v. Comm'r, 819 F.2d 1212 (1st Cir. 1987); Miller v. Internal Revenue Serv., 829 F.2d 500 (4th Cir. 1987); Christiansen v. Comm'r, 843 F.2d 418 (10th Cir. 1988). Cf. Staples v. Comm'r, 821 F.2d 1324 (8th Cir. 1987); Foley v. Comm'r, 844 F.2d 94 (2d Cir. 1988); Neher v. Comm'r, 852 F.2d 848 (6th Cir. 1988). This matter seemingly was resolved by the U.S. Supreme Court, when it held that payments to the Church of Scientology are not deductible as charitable contributions (Hernandez v. Comm'r, 490 U.S. 680 (1989)). In general, Shaller, "Tax Exemption of Charitable Organizations and Deductibility of Charitable Contributions: Dangerous New Tests," 8 *Bridgeport L. Rev.* 77 (1987); Colliton, "The Meaning of 'Contribution or Gift' for Charitable Contribution Deduction Purposes," 41 *Ohio St. L. J.* 973 (1980).

Also, the Tax Court found that the performance of the sacrament of "spinology" is not a religious function, in that a substantial purpose of the activity is the "training and practicing of an art akin to chiropractic" (Triune of Life Church, Inc. v. Comm'r, 85 T.C. 45 (1985), aff'd, 791 F.2d 922 (3d Cir. 1986)). Likewise, the Tax Court found that an organization, formed to facilitate the transfer of technology from the laboratories of tax-exempt research institutions to public use and generate royalty income for the institutions, was not qualified for tax exemption as a charitable entity because its activities of developing patentable products and licensing them to private industry were commercial in nature (Washington Research Found. v. Comm'r, 50 T.C.M. 1457 (1985)). This latter case was, however, "overruled" by Congress when it enacted § 1605 of the Tax Reform Act of 1986 (see H. Rep. 841, 99th Cong., 2d Sess. II-827 (1986)).

[262] Easter House v. United States, 87-1 U.S.T.C. ¶ 9359 (Cl. Ct. 1987), aff'd, 846 F.2d 78 (Fed. Cir. 1988), cert. den., 488 U.S. 907 (1988).

[263] American Bar Endowment v. United States, 84-1 U.S.T.C. ¶ 9204 (Cl. Ct. 1984).

[264] Id. at 83, 353.

A federal court of appeals, in considering this latter case, took that occasion to strongly state that "[u]nlike what some other courts may do, this court does not find 'profits,' or the maximization of revenue, to be the controlling basis for a determination" as to whether the activity involved is a "business."[265]

Thus, the mere fact of profit-making activities should not, as a matter of law, adversely affect an organization's tax-exempt status. As another federal court of appeals has noted, the "pertinent inquiry" is "whether the [organization's] exempt purpose transcends the profit motive rather than the other way around."[266] The IRS may use the existence of a profit, however, to characterize the activity as being commercial in nature, thus placing at issue the question as to whether the organization's activities are devoted exclusively to tax-exempt purposes. This approach is sometimes also taken by the courts, such as in a case where the publications of an organization were held to produce an unwarranted profit, thereby depriving it of qualification as an educational organization.[267]

[265] American Bar Endowment v. United States, 761 F.2d 1573 (Fed. Cir. 1985). (This case was resolved by the U.S. Supreme Court, in favor of the government (see § 26.2(a), text accompanied by notes 43–44)). The reference to the "other courts" is to the U.S. Courts of Appeal for the Fourth Circuit (e.g., Carolinas Farm & Power Equip. Dealers v. United States, 699 F.2d 167 (1983)); Fifth Circuit (e.g., Louisiana Credit Union League v. United States, 693 F.2d 525 (1982)); and Sixth Circuit (e.g., Professional Ins. Agents of Mich. v. Comm'r, 726 F.2d 1097 (1984)).
[266] The Incorporated Trustees of the Gospel Worker Soc'y v. United States, 510 F. Supp. 374 (D.D.C. 1981), aff'd, 672 F.2d 894 (D.C. Cir. 1981), cert. den., 456 U.S. 944 (1982).
[267] American Institute for Economic Research, Inc. v. United States, supra note 115. See § 7.6.

PART TWO

Tax-Exempt Charitable Organizations

CHAPTER FIVE

Scope of Term *Charitable*

Organizations that are exempt from federal income tax by reason of IRC § 501(c)(3) are often simply referred to as *charitable* organizations. The pertinent portion of this provision is the basis of tax exemption for

> Corporations, and any community chest, fund or foundation, organized and operated exclusively for religious, charitable, scientific, testing for public safety, literary, or educational purposes, or to foster national or international amateur sports competition (but only if no part of its activities involve the provision of athletic facilities or equipment), or for the prevention of cruelty to children or animals . . .

The term *charitable* is often used in this broader context notwithstanding the fact that *charitable* is only one of the eight descriptive words and phrases used in the federal tax law to describe the various organizations embraced by this provision. That is, the term *charitable* is considered a generic term and, in its expansive sense, includes *religious, scientific, educational*, and the other entities.[1]

The use of the term *charitable* to describe all IRC § 501(c)(3) organizations has arisen in part because, with one exception, all of these organizations are also qualified charitable donees[2] and thus are eligible to attract charitable contributions that are deductible for federal tax purposes. (The exception is public safety

---

[1] E.g., United States v. Proprietors of Social Law Library, 102 F.2d 481 (1st Cir. 1939). Indeed, the U.S. Supreme Court, in Bob Jones University v. United States, 461 U.S. 574 (1983), *aff'g* 639 F.2d 147 (4th Cir. 1980), *rev'g* 468 F. Supp. 890 (D.S.C. 1978), held that all organizations described in IRC § 501(c)(3) and tax-exempt under IRC § 501(a) are charitable entities for purposes of exempt organizations and charitable gift deductibility law analysis. Frequently, therefore, throughout this book, the term *charitable* is used to reference any category of organization described in IRC § 501(c)(3).

[2] IRC §§ 170(c)(2) (income tax deduction), 2055(a)(2) (estate tax deduction), 2522(b)(2) (gift tax deduction).

testing organizations.[3]) Thus, the focus of this chapter is on the parameters of the term *charitable* as it is used to portray all of the organizations described in IRC § 501(c)(3).

§ 5.1 DEFINITION OF *CHARITABLE* IN LAW

The term *charitable* is usually thought to mean assistance to the poor, the indigent, the destitute. For many, this seems to be the only definition of charity. Thus, often churches, synagogues, mosques, universities, colleges, schools, hospitals, and similar institutions are not understood to be charitable entities—even though contributors to them receive a charitable deduction for their support.

This concept of charity is known in the law as the "popular and ordinary" (or "vulgar"[4]) usage of the term. In this setting, the word *charity* means *relief of the poor*.

The term *charitable* has been given formal recognition in the law for centuries, inasmuch as the term emanates from the English common law of charitable trusts.[5] This definition is broad, meaning essentially that a function promoting the general welfare is charitable. The general rule is that the word *charitable* at common law encompassed "trusts for the relief of poverty; trusts for the advancement of education, trusts for the advancement of religion; and trusts for other purposes beneficial to the community, not falling under any of the preceding heads."[6]

The term *charitable*, under the English common law, had a broadly inclusive scope, yet it remained a definable legal concept. The definition of the term *charitable* dates back to the definition of *charitable purposes* in the Preamble to the Statute of Charitable Uses of 1601.[7] The Statute itself is based upon holdings of the English Court of Chancery before 1601 and upon earlier experiences (such as the Codes of Justinian) of previous civilizations including those of Rome and Greece and in early Judaism, as well as in many other early cultures and religions. The Statute enumerates certain charitable purposes:

> . . . some for relief of aged, impotent and poor people, some for maintenance of sick and maimed soldiers and mariners, schools of learning, free schools, and scholars in universities, some for repair of bridges, ports, havens, causeways, churches, seabanks and highways, some for education and preferment of orphans, some for or towards relief, stock or maintenance for houses of correction, some for marriages of poor maids, some for supportation, aid and help of young tradesmen, handicraftsmen and persons decayed, and others for relief or redemption of prisoners or captives, and for aid or ease of any

---

[3] See § 10.3.

[4] See *infra* note 7.

[5] Of course, the definition of the term *charitable* is independent of and predates modern tax systems. Thus, for example, in the Bible, it is stated that "also we certify you, that, touching any of the priests and Levites, singers, porters, Nethinim, or Ministers of this House of God, it shall not be lawful to impose toll, tribute, or customs upon them" (Ezra 7:24).

[6] Comm'rs for Special Purposes of Income Tax v. Pemsel, A.C. 531, 583 (1891).

[7] Stat. 43 Eliz., c.4.

poor inhabitants concerning payments of fifteens, setting out of soldiers and other taxes.

These and other classifications of the concept of charity were discussed by Lord Macnaghten in 1891, who said:

> Of all words in the English language bearing a popular as well as a legal significance I am not sure that there is one which more unmistakably has a technical meaning in the strictest sense of the term, that is a meaning clear and distinct, peculiar to the law as understood and administered in this country, and not depending upon or coterminous with the popular or vulgar use of the word.[8]

Lord Macnaghten's discussion was cited with approval by the U.S. Supreme Court.[9]

The English common law concept of *philanthropy* is considerably broader than that of *charity*. The basic opinion on this point was authored in 1896, wherein Lindley, L.J., wrote: "Philanthropy and benevolence both include charity; but they go further, and include more than mere charitable purposes. 'Philanthropic' is a very wide word, and includes many things which are only for the pleasure of the world, and cannot be called 'charitable.' "[10] In the case, Sterling, J., wrote that the word *philanthropic*, in meaning "goodwill to mankind at large," is "wide enough to comprise purposes which are not charitable in the technical sense."[11] This approach is traceable into the common law of the United States.[12]

Consequently, the categories of organizations described in IRC § 501(c)(3) may be referred to on occasion as *philanthropic* or also as *benevolent* or *eleemosynary*.[13] These terms, however, are generally regarded, from a federal tax law standpoint, as overbroad in relation to IRC § 501(c)(3) organizations, as being less descriptive, or invoking peculiarities of local law.[14] The term *charitable*, then, has a legal meaning and is regarded as a term of art, while terms such as *philanthropy* remain popularized words lacking in legal significance.[15]

---

[8] Comm'rs for Special Purposes of Income Tax v. Pemsel, *supra* note 6.

[9] Evans v. Newton, 382 U.S. 296, 303 (1966). In general, Bogert, *Trusts and Trustees* (2d ed. 1959) § 369.

[10] 2 Ch. 451, 459 (1896).

[11] *Id.* at 457.

[12] E.g., Drury v. Inhabitants of Natick, 10 Allen 169 (Mass. 1865). A minority view evident in English common law and reflected in U.S. cases was that the terms *philanthropic* and *charitable* are synonymous (e.g., Comm'rs for Special Purposes of Income Tax v. Pemsel, *supra* note 6; Jackson v. Phillips, 14 Allen 539 (Mass. 1867); Rotch v. Emerson, 105 Mass. 431 (1870)).

[13] In general, Clark, "Charitable Trusts, the Fourteenth Amendment and the Will of Stephen Girard," 66 *Yale L. J.* 979 (1957).

[14] Westchester County Soc'y for Prevention of Cruelty to Animals v. Mengel, 54 N.E. 329, 330 (N.Y. 1944); Schall v. Comm'r, 174 F.2d 893, 894 (5th Cir. 1949); Allebach v. City of Friend, 226 N.W. 440, 441 (Neb. 1929); In re Downer's Estate, 142 A. 78 (Sup. Ct. Ver. 1938); Thorp v. Lund, 116 N.E. 946 (Mass. 1917). Several state charitable solicitation (charitable fundraising regulation) statutes, however, use terms such as *philanthropic* and *eleemosynary* to define charitable organizations (see Hopkins, *The Law of Fundraising, Third Edition* (John Wiley & Sons, Inc., 2002), § 3.2(b)).

[15] Bogert, *Trusts and Trustees* (2d ed. 1959) § 370.

§ 5.2 FEDERAL TAX LAW DEFINITION OF *CHARITABLE*

Congress, in enacting and perpetuating federal income tax exemption for organizations described in IRC § 501(c)(3), did not and has not clearly indicated whether it was influenced by the common law definition of the term *charitable* or by the use of that term in its "popular and ordinary" sense. This fact has two ramifications: the meaning to be ascribed to the term *charitable* as used in IRC § 501(c)(3) and whether the entirety of that section is intended to describe organizations that are in some sense *charitable*.

The latter point can be regarded as an exercise in construing the statute itself. That is, pursuant to the canons of statutory construction, the search for congressional intent is to begin with the express words of the statute.[16]

The provision—IRC § 501(c)(3)—describes as organizations that are eligible for federal income tax exemption those that are "organized and operated exclusively for" eight specifically enumerated purposes or functions. These purposes or functions include those that are considered *charitable, educational, religious*, and *scientific*. However—and this is absolutely fundamental to those who in these regards place heavy emphasis on the statutory construction argument—the enumeration of the exempt functions or purposes is framed in the disjunctive: The law describes "religious, charitable, scientific . . . or educational purposes . . ." This use of the disjunctive can be regarded as evidence of congressional intent to accord tax exemption to any organization organized and operated for any *one* of the designated purposes or functions. As the U.S. Supreme Court has noted: "Canons of construction ordinarily suggest that terms connected by a disjunctive be given separate meanings, unless the context dictates otherwise."[17] Thus, the distinct references in IRC § 501(c)(3) to charitable *or* educational *or* scientific *or* like organizations can be read as confirming "Congress' intent that [for example] not all educational institutions must also be charitable institutions (as that term was used in the common law) in order to receive tax-exempt status."[18]

There is another applicable canon of statutory construction, which is that related statutory provisions should be interpreted together.[19] This has considerable relevance in this context, inasmuch as sister provisions of IRC § 501(c)(3) (both those in existence and those since repealed) reiterate the separate and disjunctive purposes or functions described in IRC § 501(c)(3).[20] The principal one of these sister provisions is IRC § 170(c)(2)(B), which defines the term *charitable contribu-*

---

[16] E.g., Northwest Airlines, Inc. v. Transport Workers Union, 451 U.S. 77 (1981); United States v. Oregon, 366 U.S. 643 (1961).

[17] Reiter v. Sonotone Corp., 442 U.S. 330, 339 (1979).

[18] Prince Edward School Found. v. United States, 450 U.S. 944, 947 (1981) (dissent from denial of certiorari).

[19] E.g., Kokoska v. Belford, 417 U.S. 642 (1974); United States v. Cooper Corp., 312 U.S. 600 (1941).

[20] For example, phraseology in the disjunctive similar to that in IRC § 501(c)(3) can be found in IRC §§ 170(c)(2) (income tax charitable contribution deduction), 503(b)(3) (references to IRC § 501(c)(3) organizations repealed in 1969), 504(a)(1) and 504(a)(3) (repealed in 1969), 513(a) (defining the phrase *unrelated trade or business*), 2055(a)(2) (estate tax charitable contribution deduction), and 2522(a)(2) (gift tax charitable contribution deduction).

tion for purposes of the federal income tax charitable contribution deduction.[21] This provision also recites the eight separate and independent categories of exempt functions, thereby providing further support for the proposition that Congress intended to recognize each category of purpose or function enumerated in IRC § 501(c)(3) as a distinct basis for tax exemption.[22]

Thus, it can be argued that, in IRC § 501(c)(3) and its sister provisions, Congress has "spoken in the plainest of words"[23] in intending to accord federal income tax exemption to any organization organized and operated exclusively for any one of the purposes or functions enumerated in IRC § 501(c)(3).

For example, it can be readily asserted that if Congress had intended that all organizations embraced by IRC § 501(c)(3) must qualify as charitable entities in the common law sense of the term, it would not have made reference in 1894 to "charitable, religious, or educational purposes," since the references to *religious* and *educational* purposes would have been subsumed within the references to the term *charitable*. Likewise, the subsequent additions of the references to *scientific* purposes (in 1913), the *prevention of cruelty to children or animals* (in 1918), *literary* purposes (in 1921), testing for public safety (in 1934), and for certain amateur sports organizations (in 1976) arguably would have been unnecessary if the term *charitable* were used in its common law sense. Similarly, it can be contended that if Congress had intended to condition tax exemption on satisfaction of the requirements of a common law charity, there would have been no need to add to the statutory law (as was done in 1913) the prohibition concerning the inurement of net earnings to private persons,[24] inasmuch as, under the common law, the income of a charitable organization cannot inure to the benefit of private persons.[25]

Therefore, one can regard the overall structure of the federal tax law regarding tax exemption and charitable giving as evidence that each of the eight purposes enumerated in IRC § 501(c)(3) are not overlain with a requirement that all organizations, to be exempt under that section, must qualify as entities that are *charitable* in the common law sense.[26]

Aside from the matter of whether the entirety of IRC §§ 170(c)(2)(B) and 501(c)(3) is subject to overarching requirements imposed by the common law of charitable trusts, there is the ambiguity of Congress's intent when it employed the term *charitable* in those two, and related, provisions. That is, did Congress have in mind the common law definition of the term *charitable* or did it intend to

---

[21] See § 2.5.

[22] A contrasting argument (ultimately adopted by the U.S. Supreme Court) is stated in Bob Jones University v. United States, 639 F.2d 147 (4th Cir. 1980), where, in part because contributions to all organizations described in IRC § 170(c)(2)(B) are referred to as *charitable contributions*, the court concluded that each of the separately enumerated purposes are to be considered as within a broad classification of *charitable*.

[23] TVA v. Hill, 437 U.S. 153, 194 (1978).

[24] See Chapter 19.

[25] 4 Scott, *The Law of Trusts* (2d ed. 1956) § 376.

[26] This reading of the law is in conformance with still another axiom of statutory construction, which is that statutes are to be construed to give effect to each word and that no one part of a statute should be interpreted so as to render another part of the statute redundant (Jarecki v. G. D. Searle & Co., 367 U.S. 303 (1961); United States v. Menasche, 348 U.S. 528 (1955)).

apply the word in its "popular and ordinary" sense? There is little concrete evidence to support a proposition that Congress intended the application of either definition.

The strongest argument that Congress did not intend the use of the common law definition of the term *charitable* is the statutory construction argument, discussed above, which is that application of the broad, common law definition of the word would render other words and phrases in the provisions redundant.[27] There is no legislative history, however, that gives much (if any) support for the proposition that Congress intended use of the narrower, "popular" meaning of the term.

In fact, the scarce legislative history that exists is usually cited in support of the view that the common law public policy definition is the one to be applied. The chief component of this legislative history is a portion of a report of the House of Representatives issued in 1939, explaining the theory that inspired Congress to exempt from taxation organizations devoted to charitable and other purposes:

> The exemption from taxation of money or property devoted to charitable and other purposes is based upon the theory that the Government is compensated for the loss of revenue by its relief from financial burdens which would otherwise have to be met by appropriations from other public funds, and by the benefits resulting from the promotion of the general welfare.[28]

This phraseology, which includes words such as "public" and "general welfare," can thus be read as evidencing the need to follow the dictates of the common law meaning of *charitable*, including the public policy doctrine. (At the same time, this legislative history speaks of "charitable and other purposes," which can be read as evidence of an intent to invoke a narrower meaning of the term *charitable*.) Another element of legislative history that suggests a broader use of the term *charitable* is a statement by the sponsor of the 1909 tax exemption statute that the provision was designed to relieve from the income tax (then imposed only on corporations) those organizations "devoted exclusively to the relief of suffering, to the alleviation of our people, and to all things which commend themselves to every charitable and just impulse."[29]

As noted below, the courts will occasionally look to contemporaneous administrative agency interpretation of a statute in an attempt to divine the statute's true meaning.[30] It is, therefore, instructive to note that, as early as 1923, in reviewing the law that is now IRC § 501(c)(3), the IRS interpreted the word *charitable* in its "popular and ordinary sense" and not in its common law sense.[31]

---

[27] *Id.*

[28] H.R. Rep. No. 1860, 75th Cong., 3d Sess. 19 (1938).

[29] 44 *Cong. Rec.* 4150 (1909).

[30] See *infra* text accompanying notes 39–41.

[31] I.T. 1800, II-2 C.B. 152, 153 (1923), which discussed the intended meaning of the word *charitable* in section 231(6) of the Revenue Acts of 1918 and 1921. As the U.S. Supreme Court observed, "a consistent and contemporaneous construction of a statute by the agency charged with its enforcement is entitled to great deference" (NLRB v. Boeing Co., 412 U.S. 67, 75 (1973); Power Reactor Dev. Co. v. Electricians, 367 U.S. 396 (1961)).

As revenue acts were subsequently enacted, the accompanying regulations stated: "Corporations organized and operated exclusively for charitable purposes comprise, in general, organizations for the relief of the poor"[32]—clearly the "popular and ordinary" meaning of the term *charitable*. During the 15 years that the Internal Revenue Code of 1939[33] was in effect, three sets of regulations were issued, each of which defined the term *charitable* in its popular and ordinary sense.[34] When the Internal Revenue Code of 1954 was enacted, IRC § 501 was derived from the 1939 Code.[35] As to IRC § 501, a report of the House Committee on Ways and Means stated that "[n]o change in substance has been made. . . ."[36] Consequently, it appears rather apparent that, as of the adoption of the Internal Revenue Code of 1954, the "popular and ordinary" meaning of the term *charitable* governed the definition of that word for federal tax purposes.

Nonetheless, in 1959 new regulations were promulgated that vastly expanded the federal tax definition of the term *charitable*. This regulation (which is currently in effect) reads as follows:

> The term "charitable" is used in section 501(c)(3) in its generally accepted legal sense and is, therefore, not to be construed as limited by the separate enumeration in section 501(c)(3) of other tax-exempt purposes which may fall within the broad outlines of "charity" as developed by judicial decisions. Such term includes: Relief of the poor and distressed or of the underprivileged; advancement of religion; advancement of education or science; erection or maintenance of public buildings, monuments, or works; lessening of the burdens of Government; and promotion of social welfare by organizations designed to accomplish any of the above purposes, or (i) to lessen neighborhood tensions; (ii) to eliminate prejudice and discrimination; (iii) to defend human and civil rights secured by law; or (iv) to combat community deterioration and juvenile delinquency.[37]

This regulation has several striking features. One of these is its claim that the definition of the term *charitable* in IRC § 501(c)(3) is used in its "generally accepted legal sense," which is at least somewhat akin to its common law meaning. Another is that "[r]elief of the poor"[38] is now only one of several ways in which an organization can qualify as a charitable entity.

Thus, the above-quoted tax law definition of the term *charitable*, as supplemented and amplified by subsequent court cases and IRS rulings, is the existing

---

[32] Reg. 65, Art. 517 (Revenue Act of 1924, 43 Stat. 282); Reg. 69, Art. 517 (Revenue Act of 1926, 44 Stat. 40); Reg. 74, Art. 527 (Revenue Act of 1928, 45 Stat. 813); Reg. 77, Art. 527 (Revenue Act of 1932, 47 Stat. 193); Reg. 86, Art. 101(6)-1 (Revenue Act of 1934, 48 Stat. 700); Reg. 94, Art. 101(6)-1 (Revenue Act of 1936, 49 Stat. 1674); Reg. 101, Art. 101(6)-1 (Revenue Act of 1938, 52 Stat. 481).

[33] See *infra* note 183.

[34] Reg. 103, § 19.101(6)-1; Treas. Reg. 111, § 29.101(6)-1; Reg. 118, § 39.101(6)-1(b).

[35] Specifically, 1939 Code §§ 101, 421.

[36] H.R. Rep. No. 1337, 83d Cong., 2d Sess. A165 (1954).

[37] Reg. § 1.501(c)(3)-1(d)(2).

[38] See § 6.1.

law on the subject. To that extent, any concern as to the original intended meaning of the term charitable for federal tax purposes may (or seems to) be academic. Thus, there is almost no likelihood that an argument that the 1959 regulations are of suspect validity because they are so inconsistent with the intent of Congress at the time would be successful.[39] The sheer passage of time since promulgation of the 1959 regulations gives these regulations ongoing validity simply because Congress has—despite many opportunities to do so—refrained from enacting a statutory definition of the term *charitable* and thus has tacitly accepted the broader meaning of the word as articulated by the Department of the Treasury and the IRS.

These regulations clearly reflect an interpretation of IRC § 501(c)(3) that affords tax-exempt status to any organization qualifying under *one* of the eight categories enumerated in the statute, without regard to whether it also accords with the characteristics of a common law charity. Under the regulations, an organization may be exempt if it is "organized and operated exclusively for *one or more of the following purposes*: (a) Religious, (b) Charitable, (c) Scientific, (d) Testing for public safety, (e) Literary, (f) Educational, or (g) Prevention of cruelty to children or animals."[40] As if this regulation was not adequately clear as to the independence of the separate exempt purposes, the regulations continue with the observations that "*each* of the[se] purposes . . . is an exempt purpose in itself" and that an organization may be "exempt if it is organized and operated exclusively for any one or more of such purposes."[41]

Therefore, the pertinent regulations take the position that each purpose or function stated in IRC §§ 170(c)(2)(B) and 501(c)(3) is an independent basis for qualification as a tax-exempt charitable donee. As noted, however, these regulations were adopted in 1959 and thus cannot be reflective of congressional intent in, for example, 1894 or 1913.[42]

This background notwithstanding, the position taken by various courts since the inception of the income tax exemption for charitable entities emphasized the breadth of the meaning of the term *charitable*.

For example, the Supreme Court seemingly emphasized the overarching application of the term *charitable* when it observed that "Congress, in order to encourage gifts to religious, educational *and other charitable objects*, granted the privilege of deducting such gifts from gross income."[43] Earlier, the Court wrote that "[e]vidently the exemption [was] made in recognition of the benefit which the public derives from corporate activities of the class named, and [was] intended to aid them when not conducted for private gain."[44]

[39] As the U.S. Supreme Court observed, an administrative agency has the authority only to "adopt regulations to carry into effect the will of Congress as expressed by the statute" and that a regulation "which does not do this, but operates to create a rule out of harmony with the statute, is a mere nullity" (Manhattan Gen. Equip. Co. v. Comm'r, 297 U.S. 129, 134 (1936)).
[40] Reg. § 1.501(c)(3)-1(d)(1)(i) (emphasis supplied).
[41] Reg. § 1.501(c)(3)-1(d)(1)(iii) (emphasis supplied).
[42] Cf. National Muffler Dealers Ass'n v. United States, 440 U.S. 472, 477 (1979), where the Supreme Court wrote of a "substantially contemporaneous construction of the statute by those presumed to have been aware of congressional intent."
[43] Helvering v. Bliss, 293 U.S. 144, 147 (1934) (emphasis supplied).
[44] Trinidad v. Sagrada Orden de Predicadores de la Provincia del Santisimo Rosario de Filipinas, 263 U.S. 578, 581 (1924). Likewise, St. Louis Union Trust Co. v. United States, 374 F.2d 427, 432 (8th Cir. 1967).

This approach is also reflected in a variety of appellate court opinions. Thus, a federal court of appeals determined that the "term 'charitable' is a generic term and includes literary, religious, scientific and educational institutions."[45] Likewise, another federal court of appeals stated: "That Congress had in mind these broader definitions is confirmed by the words used in the [District of Columbia Code] for by its terms it embraces religious, charitable, scientific, literary or educational corporations, thus including within the exemption clause every nonprofit organization designed and operating for the benefit and enlightenment of the community, the State, or the Nation."[46] Similarly, still another federal court of appeals (and later the U.S. Supreme Court) held that the structure of the statutory framework (IRC §§ 170 and 501(c)) demonstrates that an organization seeking tax exemption under IRC § 501(c)(3) must show that it is charitable, irrespective of the particular nature of its activities (e.g., religious, educational, or scientific).[47]

A federal court of appeals observed that "we must look to established [trust] law to determine the meaning of the word 'charitable.' "[48] Subsequently, the same appellate court stated that Congress intended to apply these tax rules to "those organizations commonly designated charitable in the law of trusts."[49]

This approach thus makes certain fundamental criteria applicable to all IRC §§ 501(c)(3) and 170(c)(2) organizations. As the Supreme Court observed well over 100 years ago, a "charitable use, where neither law nor public policy forbids, may be applied to almost any thing that tends to promote the well-doing and well-being of social man."[50] A federal district court later held, in application of the broader definitional approach to educational entities, that this "doctrine operates as a necessary exception to or qualifier of the precept that in general trusts for education are considered to be for the benefit of the community."[51]

Thus, it is clear today that all of the organizations described in IRC § 501(c)(3) share certain common characteristics of *charitable* organizations. This clarity has come about by reason of application of the *public policy doctrine*.

§ 5.3   THE PUBLIC POLICY DOCTRINE

The U.S. Supreme Court ruled that tax exemption for charitable organizations may be granted only where the organizations are operating in conformance with a public policy doctrine.[52]

---

[45] United States v. Proprietors of Social Law Library, *supra* note 1, at 483.

[46] International Reform Fed'n. v. District Unemployment Bd., 131 F.2d 337, 339 (D.C. Cir. 1942).

[47] Bob Jones Univ. v. United States, *supra* note 22.

[48] Pennsylvania Co. for Ins. on Lives v. Helvering, 66 F.2d 284, 285 (D.C. Cir. 1933).

[49] International Reform Fed'n. v. District Unemployment Bd., *supra* note 46, at 339.

[50] Ould v. Washington Hosp. for Foundlings, 95 U.S. 303, 311 (1877).

[51] Green v. Connally, 330 F. Supp. 1150, 1160 (D.D.C. 1971), *aff'd sub nom.* Coit v. Green, 404 U.S. 997 (1971).

[52] Bob James Univ. v. United States, *supra* note 1.

Authority for this proposition is traceable to a 1958 U.S. Supreme Court opinion, holding that tax benefits such as deductions and exclusions generally are subject to limitation on public policy grounds.[53] At issue in that case was the deductibility of fines paid for violation of state maximum weight laws applicable to motor vehicles (enacted to protect state highways from damage and to ensure the safety of highway users) as "ordinary and necessary" business expenses.[54] The Supreme Court held that an expense is not "necessary" to the operation of a business if "allowance of the deduction would frustrate sharply defined national or state policies proscribing particular types of conduct, evidenced by some governmental declaration thereof."[55] Observing that "[d]eduction of fines and penalties uniformly has been held to frustrate state policy in severe and direct fashion by reducing the 'sting' of the penalty prescribed by the state legislature," the Court concluded that Congress did not intend to allow income tax deductions for fines incurred to punish violations of state penal laws.[56]

The U.S. Supreme Court in 1983 generally resolved the issues as to the scope of the term *charitable* in favor of those who asserted that all organizations described in IRC §§ 501(c)(3) and 170(c)(2) must satisfy the common law test as to what is charitable—finding specifically that private schools must (to be tax-exempt) meet "certain common law standards of charity."[57] In so doing, the Court relied heavily on the classification of deductible gifts to nearly all IRC § 501(c)(3) entities as charitable contributions, concluding that IRC § 170 "reveals that Congress' intention was to provide tax benefits to organizations serving charitable purposes."[58] This reliance led the Court to decide that the "form and history of the charitable exemption and deduction sections of the various income tax acts reveal that Congress was guided by the common law of charitable trusts."[59]

---

[53] Tank Truck Rentals, Inc. v. Comm'r, 356 U.S. 30 (1958).

[54] The deduction there at issue was that available pursuant to the predecessor of IRC § 162(a).

[55] Tank Truck Rentals, Inc. v. Comm'r, *supra* note 53, at 33.

[56] *Id.* at 35–36. After this opinion, Congress (in 1969 and 1971) enacted rules explicitly limiting the public policy doctrine of nondeductibility of expenses of this nature to fines paid for violations of law and to illegal bribes, kickbacks, and similar payments (IRC §§ 162(c), 162(f)). The statutory law addition in 1969 involved an item of legislative history, stating: "Public policy, in other circumstances, generally is not sufficiently clearly defined to justify the disallowance of deductions" (S. Rep. No. 552, 91st Cong., 1st Sess. (1969), at 2 *U.S. Code Cong. & Admin. News* 2311 (1969)). This was presaged by a Supreme Court admonishment that the public policy exception to the general rule of deductibility is "sharply limited and carefully defined" (Comm'r v. Tellier, 383 U.S. 687, 691, 693–694 (1966)). In *Tellier*, the Court added: "[T]he federal income tax is a tax on net income, not a sanction against wrongdoing. That principle has been firmly imbedded in the tax statute from the beginning. One familiar facet of the principle is the truism that the statute does not concern itself with the lawfulness of the income it taxes" (*id.* at 691). These words of restraint did not, however, prevent the Supreme Court from applying the public policy doctrine in the context of tax exemption for charitable entities.

[57] Bob Jones Univ. v. United States, *supra* note 1, at 586.

[58] *Id.* at 587.

[59] *Id.* at 587–588. The Court added that "[w]e need not consider whether Congress intended to incorporate into the Internal Revenue Code any aspects of charitable trust law other than the requirements of public benefit and a valid public purpose" (*id.*). An unexpected application of the *Bob Jones University* opinion materialized when a court ruled that these concepts cause at least some nonprofit cemetery organizations to be charitable (Mellon Bank v. United States, 590 F. Supp. 160 (W.D. Pa. 1984)). This decision was, however, reversed on appeal (Mellon Bank v. United States, 762 F.2d 283 (3d Cir. 1985)). See §§ 6.10(f), 18.6.

Having formulated this breadth of the federal tax doctrine of *charity*, the Court consequently adopted the view that, based upon the common law of charitable trusts, the purpose of a charitable entity "may not be illegal or violate established public policy."[60] The Court thus concluded as follows:

> History buttresses logic to make clear that, to warrant [tax] exemption under [IRC] § 501(c)(3), an institution must fall within a category specified in that section and must demonstrably serve and be in harmony with the public interest. [footnote omitted] The institution's purpose must not be so at odds with the common community conscience as to undermine any public benefit that might otherwise be conferred.[61]

(In the setting of the case, the Supreme Court found that racial discrimination in education is contrary to public policy and that the IRS is vested with the authority to determine what is public policy. The Court concluded that "[c]learly an educational institution engaging in practices affirmatively at odds with [the] declared position of the whole government cannot be seen as exercising a 'beneficial and stabilizing influenc[e]' in community life,' . . . and is not 'charitable,' within the meaning of [IRC] § 170 and [IRC] § 501(c)(3)."[62])

The Court majority took notice of the fact that "determinations of public benefit and public policy are sensitive matters with serious implications for the institutions affected" and wrote that a "declaration that a given institution is not 'charitable' should be made only where there can be no doubt that the activity involved is contrary to a fundamental public policy."[63] Yet, in a concurring opinion, one justice stated that he was "troubled by the broader implications of the Court's opinion,"[64] "find[ing] it impossible to believe that all or even most of . . . [the IRC § 501(c)(3)] organizations could prove that they 'demonstrably serve and [are] in harmony with the public interest' or that they are 'beneficial and stabilizing influences in community life.'"[65] Quoting other passages of the majority's opinion that impart the "element of conformity that appears to inform the Court's analysis," this justice wrote that "these passages suggest that the primary function of a tax-exempt organization is to act on behalf of the Government in carrying out governmentally approved policies."[66] Moreover, he disassociated himself from the majority by being "unwilling to join any suggestion that the Internal Revenue Service is invested with authority to decide which public policies are sufficiently 'fundamental' to require denial of tax exemptions."[67]

In dissent, another justice viewed the matter as largely one of statutory construction; he summarized the statutory scheme and traced its history, and

[60] *Id.* at 591.
[61] *Id.* at 591–592.
[62] *Id.* at 598–599.
[63] *Id.* at 592.
[64] *Id.* at 606.
[65] *Id.* at 609.
[66] *Id.* at 609.
[67] *Id.* at 611.

concluded that the Court majority's public policy standard reflects an unconstitutional attempt by the Court to act where Congress has failed to legislate. He also expressed his view that Congress has legislated the requirements for achieving tax-exempt status and that, therefore, the IRS is powerless to enforce the application of other criteria, such as satisfaction of a public policy test.[68]

Although the reach of this Supreme Court decision has not been extensive, certainly the public policy doctrine will be applied far beyond the scope of racial discrimination in private schools. In one case, the government contended that an organization was ineligible for tax exemption because it engaged in violent and illegal activities. The case was dismissed but the court nonetheless concluded that the requirements articulated by the Supreme Court could have been applied in the case had the court decided the matter on its merits.[69]

Subsequently, a court revoked the tax exemption of an organization on the ground that it violated fundamental notions of public policy. The court found a violation of the public policy requirement in the organization's "conspir[acy] to impede the IRS in performing its duty to determine and collect taxes" from the organization, in contravention of federal criminal laws.[70]

It is clear that the IRS will continue to apply the rule that an organization must satisfy the public policy test to qualify under IRC § 501(c)(3).[71] For example, in determining whether activities such as demonstrations, economic boycotts, strikes, and picketing are permissible means for furthering charitable ends,[72] the IRS adheres to the public policy doctrine.[73]

§ 5.4 PUBLIC POLICY DOCTRINE AND DISCRIMINATION

(a) Racial Discrimination

A private educational institution that has racially discriminatory policies cannot qualify for tax-exempt status under federal law as a charitable organization.

---

[68] *Id.* at 612–623.

[69] Synanon Church v. United States, 579 F. Supp. 967, 978–979 (D.D.C. 1984), *aff'd*, 820 F.2d 421 (D.C. Cir. 1987).

[70] Church of Scientology of Cal. v. Comm'r, 83 T. C. 381 (1984), *aff'd*, 823 F.2d 1310 (9th Cir. 1987).

[71] Congress is not evidencing any interest in legislating on this subject.

[72] See Bachmann, *Nonprofit Litigation* (John Wiley & Sons, Inc., 1991), Chapter 4.

[73] Gen. Coun. Mem. 37858. In general, Thompson, "Public Policy Limitations on the Tax Exemption for Charitable Organizations," 2 *Tax L. J.* (No. 1) 1 (1984); Galston, "Public Policy Constraints on Charitable Organizations," 3 *Va. Tax Rev.* (No. 2) 291 (Winter 1984); McNulty, "Public Policy and Private Charity: A Tax Policy Perspective," 3 *Va. Tax Rev.* 229 (Winter 1984); Bender, "Has the Supreme Court Laid Fertile Ground for Invalidating the Regulatory Interpretation of Code Section 501(c)(3)?," 58 *Notre Dame L. R.* (No. 3) 564 (1983); Dye & Webster, "Sup. Ct. in Bob Jones holds that exempt organizations are bound by law of charity," 59 *J. Tax.* (No. 2) 70 (1983).

The rationale in the federal tax law for this principle was articulated by the Supreme Court in 1983, when it held that private schools may not racially discriminate and at the same time be tax-exempt and eligible for deductible charitable contributions.[74] This conclusion was expressly made applicable to all nonprofit private schools, including those that engage in racial discrimination on the basis of sincerely held religious beliefs. As to the religious schools, the Court found that the "governmental interest at stake here is compelling" and that this interest substantially outweighs the burden the denial of the tax benefits places on the schools' exercise of their religious beliefs.[75] The application of its holding to religious schools was played down by the Court as follows: "Denial of tax benefits will inevitably have a substantial impact on the operation of private religious schools, but will not prevent those schools from observing their religious tenets."[76]

The Court majority unabashedly adopted a public policy argument. The Court found in the "Congressional purposes" underlying this tax exemption "unmistakable evidence" of an "intent that entitlement to tax exemption depends on meeting certain common law standards of charity—namely, that an institution seeking tax-exempt status must serve a public purpose and not be contrary to established public policy."[77]

Persuaded that the use by Congress of the term *charitable* in the charitable contribution deduction context meant that the common law of charitable trusts fully applies, the Court concluded that a "corollary principle" also is applicable, which is that the "purpose of a charitable trust may not be illegal or violate established public policy."[78] Therefore, wrote the Court, an institution that is to be tax-exempt because it is a charitable entity "must demonstrably serve and be in harmony with the public interest" and its "purpose must not be so at odds with the common community conscience as to undermine any public benefit that might otherwise be conferred."[79]

As to the requisite public policy involved in this context, the Court concluded that "there can no longer be any doubt that racial discrimination in education violates deeply and widely accepted views of elementary justice."[80] "It would be wholly incompatible with the concepts underlying tax exemption," held the Court, "to grant the benefit of tax-exempt status to racially discriminatory educational entities. . . ."[81] The Court added: "Whatever may be the rationale for such private schools' policies, and however sincere the rationale may be, racial discrimination in education is contrary to public policy."[82]

[74] Bob Jones Univ. v. United States, *supra* note 1. See *supra* § 3.
[75] *Id.* at 604.
[76] *Id.* at 603–604.
[77] *Id.* at 586.
[78] *Id.* at 591–592.
[79] *Id.* at 592.
[80] *Id.*
[81] *Id.* at 595.
[82] *Id.* Also Clarksdale Baptist Church v. Green (Green v. Regan), 731 F.2d 995 (D.C. Cir. 1984), *cert. den.*, 469 U.S. 834 (1984).

The Court confronted the fact that Congress, while it clearly has the authority to revise the statutory law on this subject, has not done so. Congress, held the Court, had known about the posture of the IRS in these regards for a dozen years and thus had acquiesced in and had impliedly ratified IRS rulings in 1970 and 1971.[83] In fact, the Court cited the failure by Congress to enact bills that would statutorily override the IRS position as providing "added support for concluding that Congress acquiesced in" the IRS determinations.[84] Moreover, the Court concluded that the enactment by Congress of antidiscrimination rules in 1976, applicable to tax-exempt social clubs,[85] represented that "Congress affirmatively manifested its acquiescence in the IRS policy" pertaining to private schools.[86]

Prior to the Supreme Court's forceful pronouncement, the law was not so clear. The IRS had taken the position since 1967 that private educational institutions may not, to be tax-exempt, have racially discriminatory policies. In a 1971

[83] *Id.* at 598–602.
[84] *Id.* at 601.
[85] See § 14.5.
[86] Bob Jones Univ. v. United States, *supra* note 1, at 601–602. In general, Shaviro, "From *Big Mama Rag* to *National Geographic:* The Controversy Regarding Exemptions for Educational Publications," 41 *Tax L. Rev.* (No. 4) 693 (1986); Schweizer, "Federal Taxation—Exempt Organizations—Constitutional Law—First Amendment—Right to Free Exercise of Religion," 30 *N. Y. Law Sch. L. Rev.* (No. 4) 825 (1986); "*Bob Jones University v. United States*: For Whom Will the Bell Toll?," 29 *St. Louis U. L. J.* (No. 2) 561 (1985); Simon, "Applying the *Bob Jones* public-policy test in light of *TWR* and *U.S. Jaycees*," 62 *J. Tax.* (No. 3) 166 (1985); Thompson, "The Availability of the Federal Educational Tax Exemption for Propaganda Organizations," 18 *U. C. Davis L. Rev.* (No. 2) 487 (1985); Thornton, "Taxation in Black and White: The Disallowance of Tax-Exempt Status to Discriminatory Private Schools," 27 *Howard L. J.* (No. 4) 1769 (1984); Miller, "Applying a Public Benefit Requirement to Tax-Exempt Organizations," 49 *Mo. L. Rev.* (No. 2) 353 (1984); Johnston, Jr., "Federal Taxation—*Bob Jones University v. United States*: Segregated Sectarian Education and IRC Section 501(c)(3)," 62 *N. C. L. Rev.* (No. 5) 1038 (1984); Note, "IRS Acted Within Its Authority in Determining that Racially Discriminatory Non-Profit Schools Are Not 'Charitable' Institutions Entitled to Tax-Exempt Status," 15 *St. Mary's L. J.* (No. 2) 461 (1984); Kee, "The I.R.S. Fights Racial Discrimination in Higher Education: No Tax Exemption for Religious Institutions That Discriminate Because of Race," 10 *S. U. L. Rev.* (No. 2) 291 (1984); Galvin & Devine, "A Tax Policy Analysis of *Bob Jones University v. United States*," 36 *Vand. L. Rev.* (No. 6) 1353 (1983); Asaki, Jacobs, & Scott, "Racial Segregation and the Tax-Exempt Status of Private Educational and Religious Institutions," 25 *Howard L. J.* (No. 3) 545 (1982); Note, "Federal Income Taxation—Tax-Exempt Status for Educational Organizations in Treasury Regulation § 1.501(c)(3)-1(d)(3) is Unconstitutionally Vague in Violation of the First Amendment," 49 *Geo. Wash. L. Rev.* (No. 3) 623 (1981); Winslow & Ash, "Effects of *Big Mama Rag* on Exempt Educational Organizations," 55 *J. Tax.* 20 (1981); Note, "*Big Mama Rag*: An Inquiry into Vagueness," 67 *Va. L. Rev.* (No. 8) 1543 (1981); Laycock, "Observation: Tax Exemptions for Racially Discriminatory Religious Schools," 60 *Tex. L. Rev.* (No. 2) 259 (1982); Milich, "Racially Discriminatory Schools and the IRS," 33 *Tax Law.* 571 (1980); Comment, "Tax Exemptions for Educational Institutions: Discretion and Discrimination," 128 *U. Pa. L. Rev.* 849 (1980); Anderson, "Tax-Exempt Private Schools Which Discriminate on the Basis of Race: A Proposed Revenue Procedure," 55 *Notre Dame Law.* 356 (1980); Christians, "The IRS, Discrimination, and Religious Schools: Does the Revised Proposed Revenue Procedure Exact Too High a Price?," 56 *Notre Dame Law.* 141 (1980); Neuberger & Crumplar, "Tax Exempt Religious Schools under Attack: Conflicting Goals of Religious Freedom and Racial Integration," 48 *Fordham L. Rev.* 229 (1979); Note, "The Judicial Role in Attacking Racial Discrimination in Tax-Exempt Private Schools," 93 *Harv. L. Rev.* 378 (1979); Connell, "The Tax-Exempt Status of Sectarian Educational Institutions That Discriminate on the Basis of Race," 65 *Iowa L. Rev.* 258 (1979); Drake, "Tax Status of Private Segregated Schools: The New Revenue

case,[87] the Secretary of the Treasury and the Commissioner of Internal Revenue were enjoined from approving any application for recognition of tax exemption, continuing any current exemption, or approving charitable contribution deductions for any private school in Mississippi that failed to show that it has a publicized policy of nondiscrimination. The court found a "Federal public policy against support for racial segregation of schools, public or private" and held that the law "does not contemplate the granting of special Federal tax benefits to trusts or organizations . . . whose organization or operation contravene Federal public policy."[88] Thus, this decision was essentially founded on the principle that the statutes providing tax deductions and exemptions are not construed to be applicable to actions that are either illegal or contrary to public policy.[89] The court in this case concluded: "Under the conditions of today they [the federal tax law rules allowing tax exemption for and deductibility of gifts to charitable organizations] can no longer be construed so as to provide to private schools operating on a racially discriminatory premise the support of the exemptions and deductions which Federal tax law affords to charitable organizations and their sponsors."[90]

The IRS in 1971 stated that it would deny recognition of tax-exempt status to any private school that otherwise meets the requirements for tax exemption and charitable donee status but that "does not have a racially nondiscriminatory policy as to students."[91] The IRS initially announced its position on the exempt status of private nonprofit schools in 1967, stating that exemption and deductibility of contributions would be denied if a school was operated on a segregated basis.[92] This position was basically reaffirmed early in 1970 and the IRS

Procedure," 20 *Wm. & Mary L. Rev.* 463 (1979); Bagni, "Discrimination in the Name of the Lord: A Critical Evaluation of Discrimination by Religious Organizations," 79 *Columbia L. Rev.* 1514 (1979); Myers, "The Internal Revenue Service's Treatment of Religiously Motivated Racial Discrimination by Tax Exempt Organizations," 54 *Notre Dame Law.* 925 (1979); Kurtz, "Difficult Definitional Problems in Tax Administration: Religion and Race," 23 *Cath. Law.* 301 (1978); Colvin, "Contesting Loss of Exemption Under I.R.C. Section 501(c)(3) after *Bob Jones University* and '*Americans United*' *Inc.*," 34 *Fed. Bar J.* 182 (1975).

The reach of the decision by the U.S. Supreme Court in the *Bob Jones University* case may have been significantly augmented by its opinions in Shaare Tefila Congregation v. Cobb, 481 U.S. 615 (1987), and Saint Francis College v. Al-Khazraji, 481 U.S. 604 (1987), holding that the term "race," as used in the Civil Rights Act of 1866 and the voting rights act of 1870 (now reflected in 42 U.S.C. §§ 1981–1983) is to be interpreted in accordance with its usage in the nineteenth century, rather than in the context of modern scientific theory, so that the term embraces intentional discrimination on the basis of ancestry or ethnicity.

[87] Green v. Connally, 330 F. Supp. 1150 (D.D.C. 1971), *aff'd sub nom.* Coit v. Green, 404 U.S. 997 (1971).

[88] *Id.*, 330 F. Supp. at 1162, 1163.

[89] In general, Note, "Charities, Exempt Status and Public Policy," 50 *Tex. L. Rev.* 544 (1972); also Notes at 100 *Harv. L. Rev.* 1606 (1987); 19 *Wayne L. Rev.* 1629 (1973); 72 *Col. L. Rev.* 1215 (1972); 23 *Syr. L. Rev.* 1189 (1972); 68 *Mich. L. Rev.* 1410 (1970); 23 *Tax L. Rev.* 399 (1968); 68 *Col. L. Rev.* 992 (1968); 21 *Vand. L. Rev.* 406 (1968).

[90] Green v. Connally, *supra* note 87, 330 F. Supp. at 1164. Also Note, "Constitutionality of Federal Tax Benefits to Private Segregated Schools," 11 *Wake Forest L. Rev.* 289 (1975).

[91] Rev. Rul. 71-447, 1971-2 C.B. 230.

[92] Rev. Rul. 67-325, 1967- 2 C.B. 113. In general, Spratt, "Federal Tax Exemption for Private Segregated Schools: The Crumbling Foundation," 12 *Wm. & Mary L. Rev.* 1 (1970).

began announcing denials of exemption later that year. A clamor began for stricter guidelines, however, when the recognition of exemptions resumed to allegedly segregated schools.[93]

In 1972, the IRS issued guidelines and record-keeping requirements for determining whether private schools that have tax exemption rulings or are applying for recognition of tax exemption have racially nondiscriminatory policies as to students.[94] In 1975, the IRS promulgated new guidelines on the subject, which superseded the 1972 rules.[95] Under the 1975 guidelines, the racially nondiscriminatory policy of every private school must be stated in its governing instruments or governing body resolution, and in its brochures, catalogs, and similar publications. This policy must be publicized to all segments of the general community served by the school, either by notice in a newspaper or by use of broadcast media. All programs and facilities must be operated in a racially nondiscriminatory manner and all scholarships or comparable benefits must be offered on this basis. Each school must annually certify its racial nondiscrimination policy.[96]

The 1975 guidelines describe the information that must be provided by every school filing an application for recognition of tax-exempt status. Also included are an assortment of record-keeping requirements, mandating the retention for at least three years of records indicating the racial composition of the school's student body, faculty, and administrative staff; records documenting the award of financial assistance, copies of all brochures, catalogs, and advertising dealing with student admissions, programs, and scholarships; and copies of all materials used by or on behalf of the school to solicit contributions. Failure to maintain or to produce the required reports and information ostensibly creates a presumption that the school has failed to comply with the guidelines and thus has a racially discriminatory policy as to students.

In general, a private school must be able to affirmatively demonstrate (for example, as upon audit) that it has adopted a racially nondiscriminatory policy as to students that is made known to the general public, and that since the adoption of that policy it has operated in a bona fide manner in accordance with that policy.

It is the position of the IRS that church-related schools that teach secular subjects and generally comply with state law requirements for public education for the grades for which instruction is provided may not rely on the First Amendment to avoid the bar on tax exemption to those educational institutions that practice racial discrimination.[97] It is therefore the view of the IRS that a

---

[93] E.g., "Equal Educational Opportunity," Hearings Before the Senate Select Committee on Equal Educational Opportunity, at 1991–2038, 91st Cong., 2d Sess. (1970).

[94] Rev. Proc. 72-54, 1972-2 C.B. 834.

[95] Rev. Proc. 75-50, 1975-2 C.B. 587. These guidelines are applicable only to organizations that are classified as schools under IRC § 170(b)(1)(A)(ii) (see §§ 7.3, 11.3(a)), although the doctrine of the *Bob Jones University* opinion (see text accompanying *supra* notes 74-86) may nonetheless be applicable (Gen. Coun. Mem. 39757).

[96] TIR-1449 (Mar. 19, 1976); also Ann. 76-57, 1976-16 I.R.B. 24.

[97] Rev. Rul. 75-231, 1975-1 C.B. 158. In general, Brown v. Dade Christian Schools, Inc., 556 F.2d 310 (5th Cir. 1977); Goldsboro Christian Schools, Inc. v. United States, 436 F. Supp. 1314 (E.D.N.C. 1977), *aff'd in unpub. op.* (4th Cir. 1981).

church-sponsored school (that is not an entity separate from the church) that has racially discriminatory policies (in violation of IRS guidelines[98]) causes the sponsoring church to fail to qualify for tax exemption.[99]

The Supreme Court held that private schools are barred by federal law from denying admission to children solely for the reason of race.[100] The Court held that a statute that grants equal rights to make and enforce contracts is contravened where a minority applicant is denied a contractual right that would have been granted to him or her if he or she were a member of the racial majority. This statute has been characterized as a limitation on private discrimination and, by virtue of the Court's decision, applies to private schools irrespective of state action or tax exemption.[101]

The IRS ruled that an organization that was formed to conduct an apprentice training program offering instruction in a skilled trade is a charitable entity, even though it confined its instruction to native Americans. Admissions were so limited in accordance with the Adult Vocational Training Act (which authorizes programs of vocational and on-the-job training to help adult Native American living on or near reservations obtain gainful employment) and with a Bureau of Indian Affairs funding contract. The IRS concluded that the organization's "admission policy is designed to implement certain statutorily defined Federal policy goals that are not in conflict with Federal public policy against racial discrimination in education" and that it is not a "type of racial restriction that is contrary to Federal public policy."[102]

In an effort to further regulate in this field, the IRS proposed guidelines, on August 21, 1978,[103] and again in revised form on February 13, 1979,[104] for ascertaining whether private schools have racially discriminatory policies toward students. These rules would have established certain presumptions as to discriminatory practices by a private school, such as the nature of its minority enrollment and the relationship between formation or expansion of the school and local public school desegregation.

While these guidelines were pending, Congress, in enacting the fiscal year 1980 appropriations act for the Department of the Treasury,[105] prohibited the IRS from using funds appropriated under that law to implement the guidelines. In addition to specifically precluding the use of these appropriations to carry out the proposed guidelines, the legislation stated that none of the appropria-

---

[98] Rev. Proc. 75-50, *supra* note 95.

[99] Gen. Couns. Mem. 39574.

[100] This position is based upon 42 U.S.C. § 1981.

[101] Runyon v. McCrary, 424 U.S. 941 (1976), as limited by Patterson v. McLean Credit Union, 491 U.S. 164 (1989).

[102] Rev. Rul. 77-272, 1977-2 C.B. 191.

[103] 43 Fed. Reg. 37296.

[104] 44 Fed. Reg. 9451. In general, Sanders, "Exemptions for private schools threatened by service's latest controversial guidelines," 50 *J. Tax.* 234 (1979); Wilson, "An Overview of the IRS's Revised Proposed Revenue Procedure on Private Schools as Tax-Exempt Organizations," 57 *Taxes* 515 (1979).

[105] Pub. L. No. 96-74, 93 Stat. 559 (1979).

tions "shall be used to formulate or carry out any rule, policy, procedure, guideline, regulation, standard, or measure which would cause the loss of tax-exempt status to private, religious, or church-operated schools under section 501(c)(3) of the Internal Revenue Code of 1954 unless in effect prior to August 22, 1978."[106]

The position of the IRS in this regard became particularly aggravated when, notwithstanding the prohibition on the use of appropriated funds, a court ordered the IRS to refrain from according or continuing tax-exempt status for racially discriminatory private schools in the state of Mississippi.[107] This court order likewise used certain criteria concerning the timing of establishment of the school to raise an inference of discrimination, to be overcome only by clear and convincing evidence to the contrary. This prohibition was dropped from the House of Representatives' version of the measure to provide the fiscal year 1981 appropriations for the Department of the Treasury.[108]

A federal court subsequently gave considerable impetus to the philosophy underlying the proposed IRS guidelines, when it upheld the IRS's revocation of tax-exempt status of a private school on the ground that the institution maintained a racially discriminatory admissions policy. In so holding, the court noted that the school did not directly prove a nondiscriminatory admissions policy and that the government did not directly prove that the policy was discriminatory. Nonetheless, the court inferred from the circumstances surrounding the establishment of the school that it administered a racially discriminatory policy. The court also upheld the revocation of exemption retroactive to 1970.[109]

Although this area of law had seemed relatively settled as of 1981, in early 1982, the Reagan Administration announced that it had decided to abandon the 12-year-old effort to deny tax exemption and the eligibility to receive deductible contributions to private schools that have racially discriminatory practices, essentially on the ground that the IRS lacked the authority to develop this type of law and that only Congress, by statute, could cause racially discriminatory practices to be a prohibition on exemption. As part of this announcement, the Reagan Administration stated that it was going to accord tax-exempt and charitable donee status to Bob Jones University and Goldsboro Christian Schools, and claimed that cases then before the Supreme Court concerning these institutions were thereby rendered moot. Ten days later, the Administration submitted legislation on the subject, intended to place regulation

---

[106] Congress, in this legislation, also barred the IRS from carrying out any ruling to the effect "that a taxpayer is not entitled to a charitable deduction for general purpose contributions which are not used for educational purposes by [an exempt] religious organization," thereby prohibiting enforcement of Rev. Rul. 79-99, 1979-1 C.B. 108, during fiscal year 1980. Rev. Rul. 79-99 was subsequently revoked by Rev. Rul. 83-104, 1983-2 C.B. 46, which stated guidelines as to when payments to private schools are deductible charitable contributions or nondeductible tuition payments.

[107] Green v. Miller, 80-1 U.S.T.C. ¶ 9401 (D.D.C. 1980).

[108] H.R. 7583, 96th Cong., 2d Sess. (1980).

[109] Prince Edward School Found. v. United States, 80-1 U.S.T.C. ¶ 9295 (D.D.C. 1980), *aff'd in unpub. op.* (D.C. Cir. 1981), *cert. den.*, 450 U.S. 944 (1981).

in this field on a statutory basis, rather than on the foundation of "federal public policy."

Five weeks later, a federal court of appeals ordered the Reagan Administration not to grant recognition of tax exemption to any private schools with racially discriminatory practices.[110] The order, which applied to Bob Jones University and Goldsboro Christian Schools, appeared to erase any basis the Administration may have had for contending that the cases before the Supreme Court were mooted by its earlier announcement. Much speculation arose thereafter as to what the Reagan Administration would do next. Many believed that the President would not reverse his mootness claim, and wait for Congress or the courts to act. One week later, however, the Reagan Administration asked the Supreme Court to consider the private school issue. The court did so, responding with its historic decision in mid-1983.[111]

With the issue as to the appropriate tax policy for private schools with racially discriminatory policies now generally resolved, the ramifications of this policy are beginning to have an impact on the tax status of other types of racially discriminatory organizations. This development is amply illustrated by litigation involving an organization known as the National Alliance, which disseminates several publications including the monthly newsletter *Attack!* A lawsuit concerning the tax-exempt status of the National Alliance was instituted in federal district court, which remanded the case to the IRS for further review.[112]

The National Alliance was formed as a nonprofit organization in 1974 to, according to its articles of incorporation, develop in "those with whom communication is established" an "understanding of and a pride in their racial and cultural heritage and an awareness of the present dangers to that heritage," with a view to establishing an "effective force for building a new order in American life." Its membership is confined to "persons of the European race"; its primary activities are the publication and distribution of a newspaper, a bulletin, and books and pamphlets. In the words of an amici curiae brief filed by the American Jewish Congress, the Anti-Defamation League, and the National Association for the Advancement of Colored People, the organization is engaged in the "propagation of racial hatred and advocacy of the extermination of Jews and Blacks (as well as other 'non-European' peoples)."

The IRS determined that the National Alliance could not qualify for tax exemption because it is neither charitable nor educational. In return, the organization took the matter to court, contending that denial of exemption was an infringement of its constitutional rights. This argument was largely based on the fact that a federal court of appeals had concluded that the tax regulations defining the term *educational* were unconstitutionally vague.[113]

[110] Wright v. Regan, 49 A.F.T.R. 2d 82-757 (D.C. Cir. 1982).
[111] See text accompanying *supra* notes 74–76.
[112] National Alliance v. United States, 81-1 U.S.T.C. ¶ 9464 (D.D.C. 1981).
[113] *Big Mama Rag*, Inc. v. United States, 631 F.2d 1030 (D.C. Cir. 1980).

The correlation with this case and the private school issue is the reach of the doctrine that an organization cannot be charitable where it engages in an activity that is contrary to public policy.[114] In the school context, the position reflected in court decisions is that racially discriminatory policies are contrary to public policy. The counterargument was that schools are *educational*, not *charitable*, so that the public policy doctrine is inapplicable. The National Alliance case presented this issue in a somewhat larger context. Neither the district court[115] nor the appellate court[116] directly faced the issue of whether the propagation of racial hatred and violence can be considered charitable or educational. Moreover, the two courts did not resort to applicability of the public policy doctrine (or something approximating it) in reaching their decisions, although the appellate court twice found the occasion to favorably cite the private school case.[117]

The appellate court in the National Alliance case declined to address the issue directly from the standpoint of whether or not the organization is educational.[118] Indeed, the court concluded that "[e]ven under the most minimal requirement of a rational development of a point of view, National Alliance's materials fall short."[119] As the court's opinion made starkly clear, there was no direct precedent for resolving this issue. There is caselaw holding that organizations that engage in political agitation or in propagandizing cannot be educational.[120] The political agitation cases may not be on point; however, the court elected to avoid becoming ensnarled in the "propaganda" issue by concluding that the material fell short of being educational to begin with. Thus, the National Alliance case did not resolve the controversy of whether an organization can advocate racial discrimination and simultaneously be educational where the advocacy is preceded by reasoned development of the viewpoint—something akin to compliance with the *full and fair exposition* standard.[121]

There are also First Amendment considerations. The appellate court had "no doubt that publication of the National Alliance material is protected by the First Amendment from abridgment by law."[122] The court, however, rejected the idea that a denial of tax exemption is a contravention of free speech rights,[123] stating that "it does not follow [from free speech protection of material] that the First Amendment requires a construction of the term 'educational' which embraces every continuing dissemination of views."[124] Thus, racially discriminatory activity that is protected by the free speech doctrine is not

---

[114] See *supra* § 3.
[115] *Supra* note 112.
[116] National Alliance v. United States, 710 F.2d 868 (D.C. Cir. 1983).
[117] *Id.* at notes 4, 15.
[118] See § 7.1.
[119] National Alliance v. United States, *supra* note 116, at 873.
[120] See Chapters 20 and 21.
[121] See § 7.2.
[122] National Alliance v. United States, *supra* note 116, at 875.
[123] Citing Regan v. Taxation With Representation of Washington, 461 U.S. 54 (1983). See § 20.9.
[124] National Alliance v. United States, *supra* note 116, at 875.

automatically educational simply because it is not merely propagandizing.[125]

The U.S. Supreme Court subsequently ruled that parents of black schoolchildren lack standing to challenge the process being utilized by the IRS in denying recognition of exemption to racially discriminatory private schools.[126] Another court ruled that an organization that made grants to private schools is not entitled to exemption, because a substantial portion of its funds was granted to schools that have failed to adopt racially nondiscriminatory policies with respect to students.[127]

In application of its guidelines, the IRS adheres to a judicially recognized position that, under certain circumstances, rebuttable inferences of discriminatory policies as to students can arise.[128] Thus, for example, where a school has a history of racial discrimination, efforts by the school to attract minority group applicants will be regarded as ineffective in relation to the guidelines unless they are "reasonably calculated to succeed," such as active and vigorous recruitment of minority students and teachers, financial assistance to minority students, and effective communication of the nondiscriminatory policy to the minority population.[129] "[A]ctual enrollment of minority students," the IRS's lawyers observed, "while not determinative of the issue, is generally the most convincing evidence of the existence of a non-discriminatory policy as to students."[130] These principles have been applied by a court, that, holding that a private school seeking tax exemption must prove racial nondiscrimination by a preponderance of the evidence, concluded that a school failed to meet this burden of proof because it was founded at a time when courts were forcing desegregation in public schools, had never enrolled a black student, and did not adequately publicize a policy of racial nondiscrimination.[131]

The IRS applies the rule denying recognition of tax-exempt status as a char-

---

[125] *Id.* In general, Morris and White, "Beware a Forgotten Trap for Tax-Exempt Schools," 3 *J. Tax. Exempt Orgs.* 13 (Spring 1991); Note, "Granting Charitable Tax Exemptions to Racially Discriminatory Schools," 70 *Ky. L. J.* 807–829 (1981–1982); Nevin & Bills, *The Schools That Fear Built* (1977); Comment, "The Tax Exempt Status of Sectarian Educational Institutions That Discriminate on the Basis of Race," 65 *Iowa L. Rev.* 258 (1979); Note, "Racial Exclusion by Religious Schools, Brown v. Dade Christian Schools, Inc.," 91 *Harv. L. Rev.* 879 (1978); Adams, "Racial and Religious Discrimination in Charitable Trusts: A Current Analysis of Constitutional and Trust Law Solutions," 25 *Clev. St. L. Rev.* 1 (1976); Note, "Constitutionality of Federal Tax Benefits to Private Segregated Schools," 11 *Wake Forest L. Rev.* 289 (1975); Horvitz, "Tax Subsidies to Promote Affirmative Action in Admission Procedures for Institutions of Higher Learning—Their Inherent Danger," 52 *Taxes* 452 (1974); Comment, "Denial of Tax Exempt Status to Southern Segregation Academies," 6 *Harvard Civil Rights—Civil Liberties L. Rev.* 179 (1970); Note, "Federal Tax Exempt Status of Private Segregated Schools," 7 *Wake Forest L. Rev.* 121 (1970).
[126] Allen v. Wright, 468 U.S. 737 (1984); Regan v. Wright, 468 U.S. 737 (1984).
[127] Virginia Educ. Fund v. Comm'r, 85 T.C. 743 (1985), *aff'd*, 799 F.2d 903 (4th Cir. 1986). Also Estate of Clopton v. Comm'r, 93 T.C. 275 (1989).
[128] Norwood v. Harrison, 382 F. Supp. 921, 924–926 (N.D. Miss. 1984).
[129] Gen. Couns. Mem. 39525.
[130] Gen. Couns. Mem. 39524.
[131] Calhoun Academy v. Comm'r, 94 T.C. 284 (1990).

itable organization because of racially discriminatory policies to all entities seeking that classification, not just private educational institutions.[132]

(b) Gender-Based Discrimination

While there is a recognized federal public policy against support for racial segregation in private schools (and, presumably, other varieties of racial discrimination[133]), a somewhat comparable federal public policy against support for institutions that engage in gender-based discrimination may be developing.[134] The question is whether this is a sufficiently established federal policy so that its contravention would have an impact on the tax status of these institutions and other charitable organizations.[135] The issue has been raised, with the courts concluding that sex discrimination does not bar federal tax exemption.[136] One court, however, having concluded that the charitable contribution deduction is equivalent to a federal matching grant, found that by allowing the deduction of charitable contributions, the federal government has conferred a "benefit" on the recipient organization and that the Fifth Amendment is applicable.[137]

Nonetheless, the U.S. Supreme Court determined that a national nonprofit membership organization is compelled to accept women as regular members, by direction of a state human rights act, notwithstanding the organization's free speech and associational rights.[138] The organization's chapters were found to be "place[s] of public accommodations," the skills it develops were held to be "goods," and business contacts and employment promotions were ruled to be "privileges" and "advantages"—all so that the state's law banning gender-based discriminatory practices in access to places of public accommodation could be made applicable.

This opinion broadly exposes the Court's interest in eradicating gender-based discrimination in all feasible quarters, including the nonprofit organization context. In some respects, it is strongly analogous to the Court's efforts to elimi-

---

[132] Priv. Ltr. Rul. 8910001.

[133] Bob Jones Univ. v. Simon, 416 U.S. 725 (1974); Crenshaw County Private School Found. v. Connally, 474 F.2d 1185 (3d Cir. 1973), *cert. den.*, 417 U.S. 908 (1973).

[134] E.g., McGlotten v. Connally, 388 F. Supp. 448 (D.D.C. 1972). Also Bittker & Kaufman, "Taxes and Civil Rights: 'Constitutionalizing' the Internal Revenue Code," 82 *Yale L. J.* 51 (1972).

[135] E.g., Executive Order 11246, as amended, 30 Fed. Reg. 12319 (1965); Title VII of the Civil Rights Act of 1964, as amended, 42 U.S.C. § 2000e *et seq.*; Equal Employment Opportunity Commission regulations, 29 C.F.R. § 1604 *et seq.*; Title IX of the Education Amendments of 1972, 20 U.S.C. § 1681 *et seq.*; the Equal Pay Act of 1963, 29 U.S.C. § 206 *et seq.*; Califano v. Webster, 430 U.S. 313 (1977); Alexander v. Louisiana, 405 U.S. 625 (1972); Reed v. Reed, 404 U.S. 71 (1971).

[136] McCoy v. Shultz, 73-1 U.S.T.C. ¶ 9233 (D.D.C. 1973); Junior Chamber of Commerce of Rochester, Inc., Rochester, New York v. U.S. Jaycees, 495 F.2d 883 (10th Cir. 1974), *cert den.*, 419 U.S. 1026 (1974); New York City Jaycees, Inc. v. United States Jaycees, Inc., 512 F.2d 856 (2d Cir. 1975).

[137] McGlotten v. Connally, *supra* note 134, at 456–457, note 37. Also Stearns v. Veterans of Foreign Wars, 500 F.2d 788 (D.C. Cir. 1974) (remand).

[138] Roberts, Acting Comm'r, Minn. Dep't of Human Rights v. United States Jaycees, 468 U.S. 609 (1984).

nate race discrimination in private education.[139] Indeed, the Court, recalling its upholding of Title II of the Civil Rights Act of 1964, which forbids race discrimination in public accommodations, wrote that injuries caused by discrimination are "surely felt as strongly by persons suffering discrimination on the basis of their sex as by those treated differently because of their race."[140] The Court wrote that "discrimination based on archaic and overbroad assumptions about the relative needs and capacities of the sexes forces individuals to labor under stereotypical notions that often bear no relationship to their actual abilities."[141] This discrimination, added the Court, "both deprives persons of their individual dignity and denies society the benefits of wide participation in political, economic, and cultural life."[142]

(c) Other Forms of Discrimination

It may also be quite validly asserted that there is a federal public policy, either presently in existence or in the process of development, against other forms of discrimination, such as discrimination on the basis of marital status, national origin, religion, handicap, sexual preference, and age.[143] Thus, the law may develop to the point where a charitable organization will jeopardize its tax status where it engages in one or more of these forms of discrimination. The IRS itself has displayed some sensitivity to these matters, such as by including discrimination on the ground of national origin as being within the scope of racial discrimination for purposes of the nondiscrimination rules applicable to private educational in-

---

[139] See this chapter, *supra* text accompanying notes 73–131.

[140] Roberts, Acting Comm'r, Minn. Dep't of Human Rights v. United States Jaycees, *supra* note 138, at 625.

[141] *Id.*

[142] *Id.* Also New York State Club Ass'n. v. New York City, 487 U.S. 1 (1987); Board of Directors of Rotary Int'l v. Rotary Club of Duarte, 481 U.S. 537 (1987). Cf. Trustees of Smith College v. Board of Assessors of Whately, 434 N.E.2d 182 (Mass. 1982) (successful defense of single-sex admissions policy at private college). In general, Comment, "Taxing Sex Discrimination: Revoking Tax Benefits of Organizations Which Discriminate on the Basis of Sex," 1976 *Ariz. State L. J.* 641 (1976); Note, "Sex Restricted Scholarships and the Charitable Trust," 59 *Iowa L. Rev.* 1000 (1974).

Where the educational institution is operated by a government, the maintenance of it exclusively for the members of one gender is likely to be a violation of the equal protection doctrine (e.g., the operation by the Commonwealth of Virginia of the military college, Virginia Military Institute, exclusively for males) (United States v. Virginia, 518 U.S. 515 (1996)).

[143] E.g., Title VII of the Civil Rights Act of 1964, as amended, 42 U.S.C. § 2000e *et seq.*; Executive Order 11246, as amended, 30 Fed. Reg. 12319 (1965); Title IX of the Education Amendments of 1972, 20 U.S.C. § 1681 *et seq.*; the Rehabilitation Act Amendments of 1974, 29 U.S.C. §§ 793, 794; the Age Discrimination in Employment Act, 29 U.S.C. § 621 *et seq.*; and the Age Discrimination Act of 1975, 89 Stat. 713.

For example, where a university was held by a court to be in violation of the District of Columbia human rights act, which prohibits an educational institution from discriminating against any individual on the basis of his or her sexual orientation (D.C. Code, Title 1 § 1-2520), the court wrote that the "eradication of sexual orientation discrimination is a compelling governmental interest" (Gay Rights Coalition of Georgetown Univ. Law Cent. & D.C. v. Georgetown Univ., 536 A.2d 1 (D.C. Ct. App. 1987)). In general, Duttle, "God and Gays at Georgetown: Observations on Gay Rights Coalition of Georgetown University Law Center v. Georgetown University," 15 *J.C.U.L.* (No. 1) 1 (1988).

stitutions[144] and by evincing concern that a 1965 ruling carries overtones of a condonation of age discrimination.[145]

§ 5.5 COLLATERAL CONCEPTS

Conceptually, the term *charitable* has a broad, wide-ranging, multifaceted meaning. While specific applications of the concept are continually generating new illustrations of charitable organizations, the basic categories of charity are encompassed by the common law definition of the term[146] as opposed to terms such as *philanthropy, eleemosynary,* or *benevolent.*[147] The IRS observed that the provisions in the federal tax statutory law relating to charitable organizations "do not reflect any novel or specialized tax concept of charitable purposes, and that . . . [those provisions] should be interpreted as favoring only those purposes which are recognized as charitable in the generally accepted legal sense."[148] The concept of *charitable* thus includes relief of poverty by assisting the poor, distressed, and underprivileged, advancement of religion, advancement of education and science, performance of government functions and lessening of the burdens of government, promotion of health, and promotion of social welfare for the benefit of the community. Viewing the foregoing categories as substantially the totality of the concept of *charitable,* there is a striking similarity between the Preamble to the Statute of Charitable Uses enacted in 1601 and the Department of the Treasury regulation under IRC § 501(c)(3).[149]

There are, however, some collateral principles derived from the law of charitable trusts with respect to the concept of charity as applied for federal income tax purposes that should be distilled at this point.[150]

(a) Requirement of *Charitable Class*

The persons who are to benefit from the purported charitable activity must constitute a sufficiently large or indefinite class. Thus, it is inadequate if the beneficiaries of the alleged charitable works are specifically named, are solely relatives of the donor or donors, or are organizations such as social clubs and fraternal organizations.[151] Conversely, an adequate class may be present even where the beneficiaries are confined to the inhabitants of a particular town or are employees of a particular company. For example, a foundation established to award scholar-

---

[144] Rev. Proc. 75-50, *supra* note 95.

[145] Rev. Rul. 77-365, 1977-2 C.B. 192. The U.S. Supreme Court held, however, that a tax-exempt organization had the constitutional right, pursuant to the freedom of association principle (see § 1.7), to exclude gays from leadership positions because of their sexual orientation (Boy Scouts of America v. Dale, 530 U.S. 64. (2000)). In general, Brennan, "The Power of the Treasury: Racial Discrimination, Public Policy, and 'Charity' in Contemporary Society," 33 *U. C. Davis L. Rev.* (No. 2) 389 (Winter 2000).

[146] Reg. § 1.501(c)(3)-1(d)(2). See *supra* note 37.

[147] E.g., People v. Thomas Walters Chapter of Daughters of Am. Revolution, 142 N.E. 566 (Ill. 1924); In re Dol's Estate, 187 P. 428 (Cal. 1920); Hamburger v. Cornell Univ., 166 N.Y.S. 46 (Sara. Cty. 1917).

[148] Rev. Rul. 67-325, 1967-2 C.B. 113.

[149] See Chapter 6. Also *Restatement of Trusts* 2d §§ 368–374.

[150] It is commonplace for the law of charitable trusts to be analogized to in exploring the meaning of terms used in IRC § 501(c)(3). E.g., Green v. Connally, *supra* note 51, 330 F. Supp. at 1157–1159.

[151] Rev. Rul. 56-403, 1956-2 C.B. 307.

ships solely to members of a designated fraternity was ruled exempt as an educational organization.[152] Another foundation, however, lost its tax-exempt status because it expended a considerable portion of its funds on a scholarship grant to the son of a trustee of the foundation.[153] Basically, where a class of persons is involved as beneficiaries, the sufficiency of the class for purposes of ascertaining whether charitable activities are being engaged in becomes a question of degree.[154]

A case in point is the regard of the IRS for the elderly. Until the 1970s, the IRS's position was that the aged were not a charitable class per se, even the unemployed aged.[155] There was some support for this stance from the courts.[156] When an organization operated to assist the elderly, any exemption as a charitable entity was tied to the concept that they were also impoverished, as illustrated by the charitable and educational status accorded an organization to aid elderly unemployed persons of limited means in obtaining employment by providing these persons with free counseling and placement services and by educating the general public in the employment capabilities of the elderly.[157]

This position of the IRS began to soften in the early 1970s, as evidenced by its change of heart with respect to homes for the aged, when the IRS first articulated the thought that the elderly face forms of distress other than financial distress and have special needs for housing, health care, and economic security in general.[158] Thereafter, the IRS held that charitable status could be extended to an organization that established a service center providing information, referrals, counseling services relating to health, housing, finances, education, employment, and recreational facilities for a particular community's senior citizens,[159] that operated a rural rest home to provide, at a nominal charge, two-week vacations for elderly poor people,[160] and that provided home delivery of meals to elderly and handicapped people by volunteers.[161]

In 1977, the IRS first recognized that the elderly can constitute a charitable class *per se*. In so doing, the IRS continued to impose as a touchstone the corollary requirement that the elderly also be distressed, but the facts reveal that the presence of this element was minimal. The circumstances involved an organization that provided low-cost bus transportation to senior citizens and the handicapped in a community where public transportation was unavailable or inadequate. The IRS observed: "Providing the elderly and the handicapped with necessary transportation within the community is an activity directed toward meeting the spe-

---

[152] *Id.*

[153] Charleston Chair Co. v. United States, 203 F. Supp. 126 (E.D.S.C. 1962). Also Rev. Rul. 67-367, 1967-2 C.B. 188.

[154] E.g., *Restatement of Trusts* (2d ed. 1959) § 375; Bogert, *Trusts and Trustees* (2d ed. 1959) § 365; Rev. Rul. 57-449, 1957-2 C.B. 622. Also Rev. Rul. 67-325, *supra* note 148, where the IRS discussed this concept in the context of ruling, following the decision in Peters v. Comm'r, 21 T.C. 55 (1953), that community recreational facilities may be classified as charitable if they are provided for the use of the general public in the community. Cf. Rev. Rul. 59-310, 1959-2 C.B. 146.

[155] Rev. Rul. 68-422, 1968-2 C.B. 207; Rev. Rul. 56-138, 1956-1 C.B. 202.

[156] Watson v. United States, 355 F.2d 269 (3d Cir. 1965).

[157] Rev. Rul. 66-257, 1966-2 C.B. 212.

[158] Rev. Rul. 72-124, 1972-1 C.B. 145.

[159] Rev. Rul. 75-198, 1975-1 C.B. 157.

[160] Rev. Rul. 75-385, 1975-2 C.B. 205.

[161] Rev. Rul. 76-244, 1976-1 C.B. 155.

cial needs of these charitable classes of individuals."[162] Subsequently, the IRS ruled that an organization that provided specially designed housing that is "within the financial reach of a significant segment of the community's elderly persons" qualified as a charitable entity.[163]

The IRS ruled that a law library qualified as a tax-exempt educational organization, even though the organization's rules limit "access to and use of the library facilities . . . to a designated class of persons . . ."[164] The IRS, on this point, said that "[w]hat is of importance is that the class benefited be broad enough to warrant a conclusion that the educational facility or activity is serving a broad public interest rather than a private interest." The rationale for the favorable ruling was that the library facilities are available to a "significant number" of people and that the restrictions were placed on use of the library because of the limited size and scope of the facilities.[165]

Therefore, the requirements as to what is charitable generally contemplate the presence of a sufficient class or community. On occasion, however, the IRS will attempt to use this requirement as a basis for denial of exemption, by characterizing the beneficiaries as being too small in number or too limited in interests, such as where benefits are confined to an organization's membership. There are, nonetheless, reasonable limitations on the reach by the IRS in applying this doctrine. As one court has observed: "To our knowledge, no charity has ever succeeded in benefiting *every* member of the community. If to fail to so benefit *everyone* renders an organization noncharitable, then dire times must lie ahead for this nation's charities."[166]

A charitable purpose may be served regardless of whether corpus is immediately distributed or is continued indefinitely, or whether the number of persons actually relieved is small as long as they are selected from a valid charitable class. Nor is the economic status of the individuals benefited necessarily a factor, except where relief of poverty is the basis for designation of the purpose as charitable. That is, it is not necessary that the beneficiaries of a charitable organization's program be members of a charitable class in the colloquial sense of that term (such as the poor or the distressed). Rather, the essential requirement for achieving charitable status is that benefits be accorded the general public or the community, or some sufficiently general subgroup thereof, such as students, patients, or the aged.[167] For example, the IRS determined that community recreational facilities are classifiable as charitable if they are provided for the use of the general public of a community.[168] As one court stated, "[r]elief of poverty is not a condition of

---

[162] Rev. Rul. 77-246, 1977-2 C.B. 190.

[163] Rev. Rul. 79-18, 1979-1 C.B. 194.

[164] Rev. Rul. 75-196, 1975-2 C.B. 155.

[165] Rev. Rul. 68-504, 1968-2 C.B. 211, and Rev. Rul. 65-298, 1965-2 C.B. 163, held that an organization formed to conduct educational programs for a specific group is entitled to IRC § 501(c)(3) classification.

[166] Sound Health Ass'n v. Comm'r, 71 T.C. 158, 185 (1978) (emphasis in the original). A contemporary application of the charitable class requirement was provided by the IRS when it held that a bequest for scholarships at two universities failed to qualify for the estate tax charitable deduction inasmuch as the only other criterion for the grants was that the recipients have the same surname as the decedent; the IRS determined that only 603 families have that name (Priv. Ltr. Rul. 9631004).

[167] E.g., Rev. Rul. 68-422, *supra* note 155.

[168] Rev. Rul. 67-325, *supra* note 148.

charitable assistance. If the benefit conferred is of sufficiently widespread social value, a charitable purpose exists."[169] Likewise, another court accorded tax exemption to an organization that functioned primarily as a crop seed certification entity, despite the government's contention that its activities only incidentally benefit the public, with the court observing that the "fact that the majority of persons interested in seed technology may well come from the agricultural community does not mean that farmers and gardeners are not an important part of the general public."[170]

(b) Community Benefit

A limited number of persons may be benefited as the result of an organization's activities and the assistance considered charitable in nature as long as the effect is to benefit the community rather than merely individual recipients. Thus, the funding of a chair at a university will benefit individual professors although the actual effect is to promote education, and is therefore an exempt activity. In these instances, the individuals benefited are frequently regarded as "means" or "instruments" to a charitable end. As an illustration, an organization was ruled exempt as a charitable entity for providing substantially free legal services to low-income residents of economically depressed communities by providing financial and other assistance to legal interns; the IRS recognized that the interns themselves are not members of a charitable class but that they are "merely the instruments by which the charitable purposes are accomplished."[171] Likewise, proxy contests when conducted in the public interest are charitable activities, in that there is a "community benefit" (i.e., the "beneficiary of this activity and educational process to promote socially responsible corporations will be the public"), even though the exempt organization's resources are being devoted to direct participation in the processes of corporate management.[172] Similarly, a member of an organization may properly obtain financial benefit from the organization where the members are the means by which public purposes are served.[173] The same principle obtains as respects the operation of public interest law firms.[174] The IRS has accepted the view that a charitable organization may provide services or make distributions to nonexempt organizations where done in furtherance of its exempt purpose.[175]

Thus, the IRS ruled that an organization did not fail to qualify as a charitable and educational entity because its tax-exempt function (the training of unem-

---

[169] In re Estate of Henderson, 112 P.2d 605, 607 (Sup. Ct. Cal. 1941).
[170] Indiana Crop Improvement Ass'n, Inc. v. Comm'r, 76 T.C. 394, 400 (1981). The provision of charitable assistance does not always require a charitable class, as illustrated by the evolving law concerning the provision of aid to those who are victims of a disaster (see § 6.2).
[171] Rev. Rul. 72-559, 1972-2 C.B. 247.
[172] Center on Corporate Responsibility, Inc. v. Shultz, 368 F. Supp. 863, 874, note 21 (D.D.C. 1973).
[173] Gen. Couns. Mem. 38459.
[174] Rev. Proc. 71-39, 1971-2 C.B. 575. See § 6.10(d).
[175] Rev. Rul. 81-29, 1981-1 C.B. 329; Rev. Rul. 68-489, 1968-2 C.B. 210. Where, however, a grant is for the improvement of a study room, the room must be used primarily for educational purposes, according to the IRS Chief Counsel, analogizing to IRC § 280A(c)(1)(A) (concerning the business deduction for a home office), in Gen. Couns. Mem. 39288, as mod. by Gen. Couns. Mem. 39612.

ployed and underemployed individuals) was carried out through the manufacturing and selling of toy products.[176] The IRS observed:

> The question in this case is whether the organization is conducting its manufacturing and merchandising operation as an end in itself or as the means by which it accomplished a charitable purpose other than through the production of income. Here, the facts clearly support the conclusion that the manufacturing and merchandising operation is the means of accomplishing the organization's declared charitable objectives. Thus, there is a clear and distinct causal relationship between the manufacturing activity and the training of individuals for the purpose of improving their individual capabilities. There is likewise no evidence that the scale of the endeavor is such as to suggest that it is being conducted on a larger scale than is reasonably necessary to accomplish the organization's charitable purpose.

Similarly, the IRS stated that:

> The performance of a particular activity that is not inherently charitable may nonetheless further a charitable purpose. The overall result in any given case is dependent on why and how that activity is actually being conducted.[177]

(c) *Charity* as Evolutionary Concept

The concept of what is charitable is continually changing and evolving. This principle may be illustrated by the abandonment by the IRS of its prior rule that homes for the aged may be exempt only where services are provided free or below cost, to be replaced by the requirement that housing, health care, and financial security needs be met.[178] Thus, the old law that focused solely upon relief of financial distress of the aged has been supplanted by a recognition of other forms of "distress": need for housing, health care services, and financial security. Changes in the concept are expounded in constitutions, statutes, and, for the most part, court decisions. In the latter instance, the changes are "wrought by changes in moral and ethical precepts generally held, or by changes in relative values assigned to different and sometimes competing and even conflicting interests of society."[179]

A particular charitable activity may partake of more than one of the basic six categories, such as a scholarship program for impoverished youths, which constitutes both the relief of poverty and the advancement of education.

---

[176] Rev. Rul. 73-128, 1973-1 C.B. 222.

[177] Rev. Rul. 69-572, 1969-2 C.B. 119. Also Rev. Rul. 80-279, 1980-2 C.B. 176; Rev. Rul. 80-278, 1980-2 C.B. 175; Rev. Rul. 67-4, 1967-1 C.B. 121. Cf. Senior Citizens Stores, Inc. v. United States, 602 F.2d 711 (5th Cir. 1979).

[178] Rev. Rul. 72-124, *supra* note 158, superseding Rev. Rul. 57-467, 1957-2 C.B. 313.

[179] Green v. Connally, *supra* note 51, 330 F. Supp. at 1159; Bogert, *Trusts and Trustees* (2d ed. 1959) § 369 and Scott, *The Law of Trusts* (2d ed. 1956) §§ 368, 374.2.

(d) Motive

The motive of the founder in initiating the alleged charitable activity is immaterial in terms of ascertaining whether the activity is in fact charitable in nature.[180] This principle was illustrated by the case of a decedent's bequest to a cemetery association formed to maintain a cemetery and sell burial plots. In the absence of proof that the cemetery was operated exclusively for charitable purposes or that the bequest was to be used exclusively for such purposes, a court held that the bequest was not a charitable bequest for federal estate tax purposes.[181] The court stated that it is the "use to which a bequest is to be applied that determines its deductibility and not the motive prompting the bequest."[182]

(e) Private Use

A charitable purpose cannot be served where the property involved or the income therefrom is directed to a private use.[183] Thus, a tax-exempt charitable organization cannot be one organized and operated for a profit or for other private ends. For example, a book publishing venture was denied exemption as a charitable and/or educational organization because a substantial purpose of the organization was found to be the derivation of substantial profits by the organization and the authors to which it made grants.[184] Other illustrations include an organization that was denied exemption because its principal activity was the making of research grants for the development of new machinery to be used in a commercial operation[185] and an association that was denied exemption as a business league because its "research program" benefited its members rather than the public.[186]

It was for this reason that the IRS refused to recognize an organization as being charitable where its primary purpose was to encourage individuals to contribute funds to charity and its primary activity was the offering of free legal services for personal tax and estate planning to individuals who wish to make current and planned gifts to charity as part of their overall tax and estate planning. Stating that "[a]iding individuals in their tax and estate planning is not a charitable activity in the generally accepted legal sense," the IRS ruled that the "benefits to the public are tenuous in view of the predominantly private purpose served by arranging individuals' tax and estate plans."[187]

The fact that private individuals or organizations incidentally derive a benefit from a charitable undertaking, however, does not destroy the charitable nature of the endeavor. For example, an organization of educational institutions

[180] Bogert, *Trusts and Trustees* (2d ed. 1959) §§ 366.
[181] Estate of Amick v. Comm'r, 67 T.C. 924 (1977).
[182] *Id.* at 928. Also Wilbur Nat'l Bank v. Comm'r, 17 B.T.A. 654 (1929); Estate of Wood v. Comm'r, 39 T.C. 1 (1962); Rev. Rul. 67-170, 1967-1 C.B. 272. Cf. Estate of Audenried v. Comm'r, 26 T.C. 120 (1956).
[183] *Restatement of Trusts* (2d ed. 1959) § 376.
[184] Rev. Rul. 66-104, 1966-1 C.B. 135; Christian Manner Int'l, Inc. v. Comm'r, 71 T.C. 661 (1979).
[185] Rev. Rul. 65-1, 1965-1 C.B. 226.
[186] Rev. Rul. 69-632, 1969-2 C.B. 120.
[187] Rev. Rul. 76-442, 1976-2 C.B. 148. In general, Note, "The Twilight Zone of Charity: The IRS Denies Exemption for a Free Tax Planning Service under Section 501(c)(3)," 55 *N.C .L. Rev.* 721 (1977).

that accredited schools and colleges was found to foster excellence in education and to qualify as a charitable and educational entity even though its membership contained a small number of proprietary schools, since any private benefit that "may accrue to the few proprietary members because of accreditation is incidental to the purpose of improving the quality of education."[188] Thus, the IRS, which accorded status as a tax-exempt charitable entity to an organization formed and supported by residents of an isolated rural community to provide a medical building and facilities at reasonable rent to attract a physician who would provide medical services to the community, stated:

> In these circumstances, any personal benefit derived by the doctor (the use of the building in which to practice his profession) does not detract from the public purpose of the organization nor lessen the public benefit flowing from its activities and is not considered to be the type of private interest prohibited by the regulations.[189]

Likewise, the IRS ruled that the fact that lawyers use an exempt library to derive personal benefit in the practice of their profession is incidental to the exempt purpose of the library and is, in most instances, a "logical by-product" of an educational process.[190] Similarly, a court held that a day care center qualified as an exempt educational organization and that the provision of custodial care was "merely a vehicle for or incidental to achieving petitioner's only substantial purpose, education of the children, and is not ground for disqualification from exemption."[191] The same court subsequently reiterated this position, holding that an early childhood center is a tax-exempt educational organization, "with custodial care being incidental only because of the needs of the children for such care if they are to receive the education offered."[192] Likewise, this court held that an organization may sell artworks without jeopardizing its exemption because the sales activities "are but a means to the end of increasing public appreciation of the arts."[193] Still another illustration is the ability of an exempt organization to provide services (such as research) in furtherance of an exempt function where nonexempt entities are among the recipients of the services.[194] In still another illustration of this point, the IRS determined that a professional standards review organization can qualify as a charitable entity, as promoting health and lessening the burdens of government, because the benefits accorded by it to members of the medical profession were incidental to the charitable benefits it provided.[195]

---

[188] Rev. Rul. 74-146, 1974-1 C.B. 129. An IRS private letter ruling suggested that an association of this nature may receive up to 15 percent of its resources from for-profit members without endangering its tax-exempt status (Priv. Ltr. Rul. 9237034).

[189] Rev. Rul. 73-313, 1973-2 C.B. 174.

[190] Rev. Rul. 75-196, *supra* note 164. Also Rev. Rul. 75-471, 1975-2 C.B. 207; Rev. Rul. 78-85, 1978-1 C.B. 150.

[191] San Francisco Infant School, Inc. v. Comm'r, 69 T.C. 957, 966 (1978). See § 7.7.

[192] Michigan Early Childhood Cent., Inc. v. Comm'r, 37 T.C.M. 808, 810 (1978).

[193] Cleveland Creative Arts Guild v. Comm'r, 50 T.C.M. 272 (1985).

[194] Rev. Rul. 81-29, *supra* note 175.

[195] Rev. Rul. 81-276, 1981-2 C.B. 128. Also Fraternal Medical Specialist Servs., Inc. v. Comm'r, 49 T.C.M. 289 (1984).

(f) Illegal Activities

A charitable purpose cannot be one that is illegal or contrary to public policy.[196] The IRS determined that an organization formed to promote world peace and disarmament could not qualify as either a tax-exempt charitable or social welfare organization, because its primary activity was the sponsorship of antiwar protest demonstrations, where it urged its participants to commit violations of local ordinances and breaches of public order.[197] The IRS held:

> In this case the organization induces or encourages the commission of criminal acts by planning and sponsoring such events. The intentional nature of this encouragement precludes the possibility that the organization might unfairly fail to qualify for exemption due to an isolated or inadvertent violation of a regulatory statute. Its activities demonstrate an illegal purpose which is inconsistent with charitable ends. Moreover, the generation of criminal acts increases the burdens of government, thus frustrating a well recognized charitable goal, i.e., relief of the burdens of government. Accordingly, the organization is not operated exclusively for charitable purposes and does not qualify for exemption from Federal income tax under section 501(c)(3) of the Code.

> Illegal activities, which violate the minimum standards of acceptable conduct necessary to the preservation of an orderly society, are contrary to the common good and the general welfare of the people in a community and thus are not permissible means of promoting the social welfare for purposes of section 501(c)(4) of the Code. Accordingly, the organization in this case is not operated exclusively for the promotion of social welfare and does not qualify for exemption from Federal income tax under section 501(c)(4).

The fact that a particular purpose requires efforts to bring about a change in the statutory law does not, however, preclude the purpose from being charitable. Thus, the proscription on substantive legislative activities by charitable organizations is a statutory constraint on otherwise permissible charitable activities rather than a declaration of a feature of the term *charitable* in the common law.[198]

In conclusion, the "common element of all charitable purposes is that they are designed to accomplish objects which are beneficial to the community."[199] A frequently cited case on this point is a venerable U.S. Supreme Court pronouncement, where the Court stated: "A charitable use, where neither law nor public policy forbids, may be applied to almost any thing that tends to promote the well-doing and well-being of social man."[200]

---

[196] *Restatement of Trusts* (2d ed. 1959) § 377; Tank Truck Rentals, Inc. v. Comm'r, *supra* note 53.

[197] Rev. Rul. 75-384, 1975-2 C.B. 204.

[198] See § 20.2.

[199] *Restatement of Trusts* (2d ed. 1959) § 368, comment a.

[200] Ould v. Washington Hosp. for Foundlings, *supra* note 50, at 311. In general, Reiling, "What is a Charitable Organization?" 44 *A.B.A.J.* 528 (1958); Annot. 12 A.L.R. 2d 849, 855 (1950). Also Peters v. Comm'r, *supra* note 154, at 59.

CHAPTER SIX

Charitable Organizations

Section 501(a) of the Internal Revenue Code provides federal income tax exemption for organizations described in IRC § 501(c)(3), including entities that are organized and operated exclusively for charitable purposes.

The term *charitable* has the most extensive history and the broadest meaning of any of the terms referencing categories of tax-exempt organizations in IRC § 501(c)(3). It is used in this context in its "generally accepted legal sense" and is, therefore, not construed as being limited by the other purposes stated in the section that may fall within the broad outlines of *charity* as developed by judicial decisions.[1] These uses of the word *charitable* involve the definitions of the term as used in its technical sense (rather than in its broader, more encompassing sense[2]). The various categories of purposes comprehended by the term *charitable* in the federal tax law are discussed in this chapter.

---

[1] Reg. § 1.501(c)(3)-1(d)(2). Also Reg. § 1.501(c)(3)-1(d)(1)(i)(b).
[2] See § 5.2.

§ 6.1   RELIEF OF THE POOR

The regulations underlying the federal tax statutory law concerning charitable organizations define the term *charitable* as including "[r]elief of the poor and distressed or of the underprivileged."[3]

The relief of poverty is the most basic and historically founded form of charitable activity. The *poor* constitute a charitable class. The provision of nearly any type of aid to the poor constitutes a charitable undertaking. A traditional definition of this type of assistance is that it encompasses aid in the form of the "distribution of money or goods among the poor, by letting land to them at low rent, by making loans to them, by assisting them to secure employment, by establishment of a home or other institution, by providing soup kitchens and the like."[4] Thus, relieving poverty can entail direct financial assistance or, just as likely in contemporary society, the provision of services.

Organizations deemed tax-exempt because they relieve the poor, distressed, or underprivileged may be categorized on the basis of the types of services they provide. Some organizations provide assistance to enable the impoverished to secure employment, such as vocational training,[5] establishment of a market for products of the needy,[6] or employment assistance for the elderly.[7] Others provide assistance to maintain employment, such as operation of a day care center,[8] promotion of the rights and welfare of public housing tenants,[9] provision of technical and material assistance under foreign self-help programs,[10] provision of financial assistance in securing a private hospital room,[11] or operation of a service center providing information, referral, and counseling services relating to health, housing, finances, education, and employment, as well as a facility for specialized recreation for a community's senior citizens.[12]

Others of these organizations provide services more personal in nature, such as provision of low-income housing,[13] legal services,[14] money management advice,[15] vacations for the elderly poor at a rural rest home,[16] home delivery of meals to the elderly,[17] and transportation services for the elderly and

[3] Reg. § 1.501(c)(3)-1(d)(2).
[4] *Restatement of Trusts* (2d ed. 1959) § 369, comment a.
[5] Rev. Rul. 73-128, 1973-1 C.B. 222.
[6] Industrial Aid for the Blind v. Comm'r, 75 T.C. 96 (1979); Rev. Rul. 68-167, 1968-1 C.B. 255; Tech. Adv. Mem. 200021056.
[7] Rev. Rul. 66-257, 1966-2 C.B. 212.
[8] Rev. Rul. 70-533, 1970-2 C.B. 112; Rev. Rul. 68-166, 1968-1 C.B. 255.
[9] Rev. Rul. 75-283, 1975-2 C.B. 201.
[10] Rev. Rul. 68-165, 1968-1 C.B. 253; Rev. Rul. 68-117, 1968-1 C.B. 251.
[11] Rev. Rul. 79-358, 1979-2 C.B. 225.
[12] Rev. Rul. 75-198, 1975-1 C.B. 157. Also Rev. Rul. 77-42, 1977-1 C.B. 142.
[13] Rev. Rul. 70-585, 1970-2 C.B. 115; Rev. Rul. 68-17, 1968-1 C.B. 247; Rev. Rul. 67-250, 1967-2 C.B. 182; Rev. Rul. 67-138, 1967-1 C.B. 129.
[14] Rev. Rul. 78-428, 1978-2 C.B. 177; Rev. Rul. 72-559, 1972-2 C.B. 247; Rev. Rul. 69-161, 1969-1 C.B. 149.
[15] Rev. Rul. 69-441, 1969-2 C.B. 115.
[16] Rev. Rul. 75-385, 1975-2 C.B. 205.
[17] Rev. Rul. 76-244, 1976-1 C.B. 155.

handicapped.[18] Still others of these organizations seek to render assistance to the poor and distressed by helping them at a time when they are particularly needy, such as prisoners requiring rehabilitation,[19] the elderly requiring specially designed housing,[20] the physically handicapped requiring specially designed housing,[21] hospital patients needing the visitation and comfort provided by their relatives and friends,[22] and widow(er)s and orphans of police officers and firefighters killed in the line of duty.[23] Similarly, tax exemption on this basis was accorded to an organization that posted bail for individuals who were otherwise incapable of paying for bail, as part of its integrated program for their release and rehabilitation,[24] to a legal aid society that provided free legal services and funds to pay fees of commercial bondsmen for indigent persons who were otherwise financially unable to obtain these services,[25] and to an organization that provided rescue and emergency services to persons suffering because of a disaster.[26] Under appropriate circumstances,[27] an organization can qualify as a charitable one where the impoverished being assisted are in countries other than the United States.[28]

As noted, the provision of low-income housing can be a charitable purpose.[29] The IRS held that an organization formed to develop a program to provide housing not otherwise affordable to low-income families is a form of relief to the poor and thus is a charitable activity.[30] Providing affordable housing to persons who are not poor or otherwise members of a charitable class is not a charitable undertaking; thus, the IRS ruled that a nonprofit housing organization created to aid moderate-income families did not qualify for tax exemption because its program is not designed to carry out a charitable purpose.[31]

Nevertheless, inclusion of some individuals who are not poor and distressed or underprivileged in a housing project for the poor may indirectly advance charitable purposes by providing some degree of stability, resource, and role model function. The IRS developed safe-harbor guidelines for determining whether organizations that provide low-income housing will be considered tax-exempt charitable entities on the ground that they relieve the poor and distressed, as well as a facts-and-circumstances test for these organizations that are

---

[18] Rev. Rul. 77-246, 1977-2 C.B. 190.
[19] Rev. Rul. 70-583, 1970-2 C.B. 114; Rev. Rul. 67-150, 1967-1 C.B. 133.
[20] Rev. Rul. 79-18, 1979-1 C.B. 194.
[21] Rev. Rul. 79-19, 1979-1 C.B. 195.
[22] Rev. Rul. 81-28, 1981-1 C.B. 328.
[23] Rev. Rul. 55-406, 1955-1 C.B. 73.
[24] Rev. Rul. 76-21, 1976-1 C.B. 147.
[25] Rev. Rul. 76-22, 1976-1 C.B. 148; Rev. Rul. 69-161, *supra* note 14.
[26] Rev. Rul. 69-174, 1969-1 C.B. 149. Cf. Rev. Rul. 77-3, 1977-1 C.B. 140.
[27] See § 30.2(d).
[28] E.g., Rev. Rul. 68-165, *supra* note 10, Rev. Rul. 68-117, *supra* note 10.
[29] See *supra* note 13.
[30] Rev. Rul. 70-585, *supra* note 13, Situation 1.
[31] *Id.*, Situation 4.

outside the safe harbor.[32] In general, this type of organization must demonstrate, for each project, that at least 75 percent of the units are occupied by low-income residents; either at least 20 percent of the units are occupied by residents that also meet a very-low-income limit for the area or 40 percent of the units are occupied by residents that also do not exceed 120 percent of the area's very-low-income limit; up to 25 percent of the units may be provided at market rates to individuals who have incomes in excess of the low-income limit; the project is actually occupied by poor and distressed residents; the housing is affordable to the charitable beneficiaries; and, if the project consists of multiple buildings, they share the same grounds.[33]

The breadth of the meaning of the term *charity* was dramatically illustrated in the litigation that followed the pronouncement by the IRS in 1969 of new criteria for defining a charitable hospital.[34] In that year, the IRS issued a ruling that the promotion of health was itself a charitable purpose as long as the requisite charitable class was present; specifically, the ruling enables a hospital to qualify for tax exemption where it provides emergency room services to all individuals requiring health care irrespective of their ability to pay.[35] A lawsuit ensued, with a federal district court holding that a hospital, to be exempt, must significantly serve the poor for a reduced or forgone charge. The court concluded that "Congress and the judiciary have consistently insisted that the application of sections 501 and 170 [the federal income tax exemption and charitable deduction provisions] to hospitals be conditioned upon a demonstration that ameliorative consideration be given poor people in need of hospitalization."[36] To find otherwise, said the court, would be "to disregard what has been held to be the underlying rationale for allowing charitable deductions."[37] On appeal, however, this construction of the term *charitable* was reversed. On finding that the law of charitable trusts has promotion of health as a charitable purpose and noting the IRS citation of the appropriate authority, the appeals court held that the term *charitable* is "capable of a definition far broader than merely relief of the poor."[38] After reviewing the changes in the financing of health care in the United States over past decades (including the advent of Medicare and Medicaid), the court found that the rationale

[32] Rev. Proc. 96-32, 1996-1 C.B. 717.
[33] An organization that is engaged in housing activities but cannot qualify for tax exemption on the basis of relieving the poor and distressed may nonetheless be exempt because it combats community deterioration (see *infra* § 7) or lessens a burden of government (see *infra* § 4) (e.g., Priv. Ltr. Rul. 9731038). In general, Wexler, "IRS Proposes Useful New Safe Harbor for Nonprofits That Provide Low-Income Housing," 83 *J. Tax.* (No. 2) 100 (Aug. 1995); Roady, "New Guideline Sets Standards for Low-Income Housing Organizations," 6 *J. Tax Exempt Orgs.* (No. 3) 99 (Nov./Dec. 1994); Harlan, "Housing for the Elderly: Federal Income Tax Concerns," 5 *Exempt Org. Tax Rev.* (No. 1) 39 (1992).
[34] See *infra* § 3(a).
[35] Rev. Rul. 69-545, 1969-2 C.B. 117.
[36] Eastern Ky. Welfare Rights Org. v. Shultz, 370 F. Supp. 325, 332 (D.D.C. 1973).
[37] *Id.* at 333.
[38] Eastern Ky. Welfare Rights Org. v. Simon, 506 F.2d 1278, 1287 (D.C. Cir. 1974).

by which hospitals' charitable status is confined to the extent they provide for the poor "has largely disappeared."[39] Indeed, the court noted, "[t]oday, hospitals are the primary community health facility for both rich and poor."[40] (These developments, of course, preceded the managed care revolution.)

On occasion, a view is expressed that assistance to the poor is the only basis on which an organization can achieve tax-exempt status as a charity under the federal tax law. There is no requirement, however, in the federal statutory law or in the tax regulations that an organization must provide services only to the poor and distressed or to the underprivileged to qualify as an exempt charitable organization. As one writer stated, it is a "general rule in the construction of exemptions from taxation that the word 'charity' is not to be restricted to the relief of the sick or the poor, but extends to any form of philanthropic endeavor or public benefit."[41] Thus, as discussed throughout, an organization may achieve status as a charitable entity if it functions, for example, to promote health, to advance education, or to lessen the burden of a government. These are independent grounds for acquiring classification as a charitable organization and do not require proof that the organization is also operated to relieve the poor and distressed. This principle was noted by the IRS in 1975 when it observed, when considering exemption for public interest law firms, that these organizations are regarded as "charities because they provide a service which is of benefit to the community as a whole."[42]

Another case in point involved consumer credit counseling agencies that offer their services to the general public. That is, the definition of eligibility for assistance is not limited to a low-income classification that indicates a need for credit counseling assistance. It was the initial view of the IRS that these agencies cannot qualify as tax-exempt charitable organizations, because they do not confine the provision of their services to low-income individuals. The issue of exempt status of these agencies was resolved in court, where it was held that the IRS cannot condition a nonprofit organization's tax status solely on the extent to which it provides assistance to the indigent.[43] The court said that the status of consumer credit counseling agencies as charitable entities cannot be regarded by the IRS as dependent on whether they confine their assistance to low-income individuals (or provide their services without charge). These agencies were found to be entitled to classification as charitable organizations as long as they can

---

[39] *Id.* at 1288.

[40] *Id.* The *Eastern Kentucky* case was heard by the U.S. Supreme Court, which did not address the merits of the case because it held that the plaintiffs lacked standing to bring the action (426 U.S. 26 (1976)).

[41] Black, *A Treatise in the Law of Income Taxation* 40 (2d ed. 1950).

[42] Rev. Rul. 75-74, 1975-1 C.B. 152.

[43] Consumer Credit Counseling Serv. of Ala., Inc. v. United States, 78-2 U.S.T.C. ¶ 9660 (D.D.C. 1978). Also Credit Counseling Centers of Okla., Inc. v. United States, 79-2 U.S.T.C. ¶ 9468 (D.D.C. 1979).

demonstrate that they satisfy at least one of the definitions of the term *charitable* (or qualify as *educational* organizations).[44]

Thus, it is clear that a charitable purpose is not necessarily dependent on a showing that the poor are being relieved. Functions such as promotion of health,[45] lessening of the burdens of government,[46] promotion of social welfare,[47] and promotion of the arts[48] are, therefore, charitable enterprises that need not involve any nexus with relief of the poor. At the same time, the belief persists in some quarters that a charitable purpose cannot be present where "the rich, the poor and the in-between are treated alike."[49] As discussed next, this clearly is not the law.[50]

§ 6.2 RELIEF OF THE DISTRESSED

As noted, a charitable undertaking may be present where the beneficiaries of the program are the "poor and distressed."[51] Yet the IRS based a finding of tax-exempt charitable status for an organization solely on the ground that it relieved individuals who were *distressed*, irrespective of whether they are also *poor*. The occasion was the IRS's consideration of the tax treatment of a non-profit hospice that operated on both inpatient and outpatient bases, to assist persons of all ages, who have been advised by a physician that they are terminally ill, in coping with the distress arising from their medical condition.[52] Thus, the classification of the organization as a charitable entity was predicated on the fact that the hospice "alleviat[ed] the mental and physical distress of persons terminally ill." What the IRS did, beginning with three rulings issued in 1979,[53] was change the phraseology from poor *and* distressed to poor *or* distressed.

---

[44] Subsequently, the Department of Justice elected to not appeal these cases and the IRS decided that any "further litigation of this issue would be futile" (Gen. Couns. Mem. 38881). This conclusion was also reached by the U.S. Court of Appeals for the Sixth Circuit in Lugo v. Miller, 640 F.2d 823 (6th Cir. 1981), *rev'g* Lugo v. Simon, 453 F. Supp. 677 (N.D. Ohio). It is because of this expansion of the patient base of contemporary tax-exempt health care providers that the principle that promotion of health is a separate basis for exemption (see *infra* § 3) is of such significance.

[45] See *infra* § 3.

[46] See *infra* § 4.

[47] See *infra* § 7.

[48] See *infra* § 8.

[49] Child v. United States, 540 F.2d 579, 582 (2d Cir. 1976). Likewise, Bank of Carthage v. United States, 304 F. Supp. 77, 80 (W.D. Mo. 1969).

[50] Also: "Although the relief of the poor, or benefit to them, is in its popular sense a necessary ingredient in charity, this is not so in the view of the law" (Zollman, *American Law of Charity* 135–136 (1924)).

[51] See the text accompanied by *supra* note 3.

[52] Rev. Rul. 79-17, 1979-1 C.B. 193. A similar discussion, concerning similar forms of distress facing the elderly, appears in the IRS ruling concerning homes for the aged (see *infra* § 3(d)). Also Rev. Rul. 79-19, *supra* note 21, which discussed the distress confronting the physically disabled.

[53] See *supra* note 51.

The confusion inherent in the interplay between *relief of the poor* and *relief of the distressed*, as meanings of the term *charitable*, is being vividly reflected in the matter of the application of contributions raised by charitable organizations in the aftermath of the terrorist attacks on September 11, 2001, for disaster relief purposes, and the huge controversy as to who is eligible for monetary relief and/or services. This brouhaha is about whether an individual who has sufficient economic resources is nonetheless entitled to this form of assistance. The IRS, some tax law practitioners, and some in the media in the weeks following the attacks stated that to be eligible for this aid an individual must demonstrate a financial need. This, however, is not required as a matter of law. Aside from assistance in the form of scholarships and health care (which clearly does not have to be need-based), monetary relief can be provided to those who are distressed, irrespective of financial condition. Funds can be distributed, such as to families of those killed in or otherwise harmed as a result of the attacks, when objective criteria are in place.

Considerable misunderstanding followed testimony by the IRS at a congressional hearing on November 8, 2001. On that occasion, the IRS correctly stated that charitable purposes can be accomplished by "providing relief to persons who are poor and/or distressed." It was pointed out that some charitable organizations provide assistance in the form of emergency food, shelter, clothing, crisis counseling, or medical services. The IRS added that charitable organizations can offer "longer-term relief for victims and dependents of victims, such as annuities, permanent housing, long-term counseling, or scholarships for children."

Then, this testimony added the proposition that a charitable organization, whether providing immediate or long-term relief, must "serve persons who belong to a charitable class." That, however, is not always the case.[54] The testimony stated that victims of disaster, such as the one that occurred on September 11, 2001, "generally represent a charitable class." That is not always the case, either; police and firefighters and members of their families, for example, are not automatically members of a charitable class. The statement that generated most of the uncertainty was this: "An affected individual generally is not entitled to charitable funds without a showing of need." This was widely interpreted as meaning *financial* need; the concept of *distressed* was not mentioned in this context. Further confusion ensued when the agency said that a charity's funds "cannot be distributed among the victims simply on a pro-rata basis because that method is not based on meeting individual victims' needs." That, too, is not the state of the law.[55]

Then suddenly the IRS shifted its position, issuing an announcement on November 16, 2001, stating that charities can provide assistance to those victimized by the terrorist attacks without regard to financial need, as long as the payments are made "in good faith using objective standards."[56] This, however, has been the essence of this area of the law all along.

---

[54] See § 5.5(a).

[55] The IRS did not cite any authority for any of these statements.

[56] Notice 2001-78, 2001-50 I.R.B. 576.

Thereafter, Congress decided to weigh in on the debate. One of the major items of legislation that was passed in 2001 was a measure that contains provisions codifying rules for provision of assistance by charitable organizations to individuals who are victims of terrorism.[57] By reason of this legislation, charitable organizations that make payments to individuals by reason of the death, injury, wounding, or illness of an individual incurred as a result of the September 11, 2001, attacks, or as a result of an attack involving anthrax occurring on or after September 11, 2001, and before January 1, 2002, are not required to make a specific assessment of need for the payments to be considered made for charitable purposes. The grantor organization must make the payments in good faith using a reasonable and objective formula that is consistently applied.

A summary of this legislation, prepared by the staff of the Joint Committee on Taxation,[58] provides some examples. A charitable organization that assists families of firefighters killed in the line of duty can make a pro rata distribution to the families of firefighters killed in the attacks, even though the specific financial needs of each family are not directly considered. Similarly, if the amount of a distribution is based on the number of dependents of a charitable class of individuals killed in the attacks and this standard is applied consistently, the specific needs of each recipient do not have to be taken into account. It would not be appropriate, however, for a charity to make pro rata payments based on the recipients' living expenses before September 11 if the result generally is to provide significantly greater assistance to individuals in a better position to provide for themselves than to individuals with fewer financial resources.

Charities providing assistance pursuant to this standard are asked to indicate this on the relevant page of their annual information return. If a private foundation makes payments in reliance on this standard, the payments are not treated as made to disqualified persons for the purposes of the self-dealing rules.[59]

The legislative history of this measure addresses the matter of the provision of disaster relief assistance by a private foundation controlled by an employer where those who are assisted are employees of the employer. The position of the IRS in this regard, prior to enactment of this legislation, was that the practice is not consistent with the rules for tax exemption, largely on a private benefit rationale.[60] The legislative history, however, articulates this presumption: "If payments in connection with a qualified disaster are made by a private foundation to employees (and their family members) of an employer that controls the foundation, the presumption that the charity acts consistently with the requirements of section 501(c)(3) applies if the class of beneficiaries is large or indefinite and if recipients are selected based on an objective determina-

[57] Victims of Terrorism Tax Relief Act, Pub. Law No. 107-124, 107th Cong., 1st Sess. (2001).
[58] JCX-91-01.
[59] See § 11.4(a).
[60] See § 19.10.

tion of need by an independent committee of the private foundation, a majority of the members of which are persons other than persons who are in a position to exercise substantial influence over the affairs of the controlling employer (determined under principles similar to those in effect under section 4958)."[61] This analysis states that the IRS is expected to reconsider its ruling position of this new standard.[62]

This Joint Committee summary perpetuated the confusion in this area of the law. For example, it stated that this legislation does not change the "other substantive standards" for tax exemption as a charitable (and educational) organization, then identifies one of these standards as the "need for a charitable class." As noted, a charitable class is not always required. The summary also states that for charities making payments in connection with the September 11 attacks or attacks involving anthrax, but not in reliance on this standard, "present law rules apply." But the summary does not indicate what the "present law" is. In fact, this new statutory standard basically is codification of previous law.

Then, the summary offers examples of charitable assistance that may be provided, on a basis other than the statutory standard. Inexplicably, the examples go beyond the new standard. Payments to permit a surviving spouse with young children to remain at home with them rather than entering the workforce are permitted (to maintain the "psychological well-being of the entire family"). Assistance with elementary and secondary school tuition to permit a child to remain in the "same educational environment" is appropriate. Assistance "needed for higher education" is allowable. Also permissible is assistance with rent or mortgage payments for the family's principal residence or car loans, to "forestall losses of a home or transportation that could cause additional trauma to family already suffering." This summary concludes that, in situations where the statutory standard is not followed, still "[o]ther types of assistance that the scope of the tragedy makes it difficult to anticipate may also serve a charitable purpose."

Later in the summary, there is this characterization of the law, which is essentially correct but is wholly inconsistent with what was written before: "Providing assistance to relieve distress for individuals suffering the effects of a disaster generally serves a public rather than a private interest if the assistance benefits the community as a whole, or if the recipients otherwise lack the resources to meet their physical, mental and [should be "or"] emotional needs."

Again, the law in this area does not always require the presence of a charitable class. (The "community as a whole" is not a charitable class.) Outside of fields such as scholarships and medical assistance, the fundamental determinant is whether the recipients of this type of assistance are *distressed*—physically, mentally, financially, or emotionally.

---

[61] The reference to "section 4958" is to the intermediate sanctions rules. See § 19.11.
[62] For these purposes, IRC § 139 defines the term *qualified disaster*.

Prior to the terrorist attacks, the IRS was in the process of revising its view as to the state of the law concerning disaster relief programs in general. A common pattern for these programs is the plan maintained by a corporation employing hundreds, perhaps thousands of employees, providing emergency assistance (small grants, short-term loans, and the like) to employees in the event they are adversely affected by a disaster. Often, these programs are funded by a foundation related to the corporation. At the outset, the IRS ruled that these programs were charitable, with any benefit to the employer being incidental.[63] Then, the agency reversed course, concluding that charitable activity was not occurring, that the private benefit to the corporation was more than incidental, and that the foundations were engaging in acts of self-dealing[64] and making taxable expenditures[65] when funding these programs.[66] The legislation enacted in 2001 is causing the IRS to return to its original position.

As of mid-2002, the position of the IRS concerning disaster relief as a charitable activity is stated in an unnumbered document available only on its Web site.[67] This document perpetuated the uncertainty as to this aspect of the law. There the IRS said that "[p]roviding aid to relieve human suffering that may be caused by a natural or civil disaster or an emergency hardship is charity in its most basic form." The agency wrote that disaster relief or emergency hardship organizations "may provide assistance in the form of funds, services, or goods to ensure that victims have the basic necessities, such as food, clothing, housing (including repairs), transportation, and medical assistance (including psychological counseling)." Examples of distressed individuals provided by the IRS included those who are (1) temporarily in need of food or shelter when stranded, injured, or lost because of a disaster; (2) temporarily unable to be self-sufficient as a result of a sudden and severe personal or family crisis, such as victims of crimes of violence or physical abuse; (3) in need of long-term assistance for housing, child care, or educational expense because of a disaster; and (4) in need of counseling because of trauma experienced as a result of a disaster or crime.

Nonetheless, this publication also stated that the "group of individuals that may properly receive assistance from a charitable organization is called a charitable class." Also: "When a disaster or emergency hardship occurs, a charitable organization may help individuals who are needy or otherwise distressed because they are part of a general class of charitable beneficiaries." Further: "Generally, a disaster relief or emergency hardship organization must make a specific assessment that a recipient of aid is financially or otherwise in need." These either were misstatements of the law or a redefinition of the concept of a charitable class. Thus, the IRS continued to assert that "[u]nder estab-

[63] E.g., Priv. Ltr. Rul. 9314058.
[64] See § 11.4(a).
[65] See § 11.4(e).
[66] E.g., Priv. Ltr. Rul. 199917079.
[67] *Disaster Relief: Providing Assistance Through Charitable Organizations.* Also, Gitterman & Friedlander, "Disaster Relief—Current Developments," IRS Exempt Organizations Technical Instruction Program for Fiscal Year 2003, item M.

lished rules, charitable funds cannot be distributed to individuals merely because they are victims of a disaster" without identifying what such rules might be.[68]

§ 6.3   PROMOTION OF HEALTH

The promotion of health as a charitable purpose includes the establishment or maintenance of hospitals, clinics, homes for the aged, and other providers of health care; advancement of medical and similar knowledge through research; and the maintenance of conditions conducive to health. The term *health*, for this purpose, includes mental health and would include, were it not for a separate enumeration in the federal tax law description of charitable organizations, the prevention of cruelty to children.[69] The tax regulations defining the types of charitable entities do not contain any specific reference to the promotion of health as a charitable purpose, but this aspect of charitable activity has been reaffirmed by the courts and the IRS on several occasions.[70]

(a) Hospitals

The most common example of an organization established and operated for the promotion of health is a hospital.[71] To qualify for tax exemption as a charitable organization, however, a hospital must demonstrate that it serves a public rather than a private interest.[72] The Supreme Court observed that "[n]onprofit hospitals have never received these benefits [tax exemption and eligibility to receive deductible contributions] as a favored general category, but an individual nonprofit hospital has been able to claim them if it could qualify" as a charitable entity.[73] The Court added: "As the Code does not define the term charitable,

---

[68] The evolution of these developments is nicely illustrated by three front-page headlines in the *New York Times*. The IRS's initial announcement of its position in November 2001 made it appear that some charities were transgressing the law in providing assistance to individuals without regard to financial need: "Victims' Funds May Violate U.S. Tax Law," *New York Times*, Nov. 12, 2001. When the IRS quickly revised its position, the following appeared: "IRS Makes An Exception on Terror Aid," *New York Times*, Nov. 17, 2001. The fact is that the agency did not make any "exception"; rather, it made a *correction*. Nearly a year later, the newspaper announced "what may be the most ambitious effort ever undertaken by charitable organizations to address the emotional needs of disaster victims": "Program to Cover Psychiatric Help For 9/11 Families" (*New York Times*, Aug. 21, 2002), describing a program involving major charities to "underwrite the expense of extended mental health treatment for anyone directly affected by the terrorist attacks last year." In general, Shortill, "Company-Sponsored Disaster Relief Programs," 36 *Exempt Org. Tax Rev.* (No. 1) 39 (Apr. 2002).

[69] *Restatement of Trusts* (2d ed. 1959) § 372, comment b.

[70] E.g., Rev. Rul. 69-545, *supra* note 35; also *Restatement of Trusts* (2d ed. 1959) §§ 368, 372 (1959); IV *Scott on Trusts* (3d ed. 1967) §§ 368, 372.

[71] IRC § 170(b)(1)(A)(iii); Bogert, *Trusts and Trustees* (rev. 2d ed. 1977) § 374.

[72] Reg. § 1.501(c)(3)-1(d)(1)(ii); *Restatement of Trusts* (2d ed. 1959) § 372, comment b.

[73] Simon v. Eastern Ky. Welfare Rights Org., *supra* note 40 at 29.

the status of each nonprofit hospital is determined on a case-by-case basis by the IRS."[74]

The initial position of the IRS in this regard was published in 1956, in which the IRS set forth requirements for tax exemption, including a rule requiring patient care without charge or at below cost.[75] At that time, the IRS stated that a hospital, to be charitable, "must be operated to the extent of its financial ability for those not able to pay for the services rendered and not exclusively for those who are able and expected to pay."[76] This approach (the *charity care* standard) was a reflection of the charitable hospital as it once was—a health care provider emphasizing care more for the poor than for the sick.

Today's tax-exempt hospital provides health services for its community, funded by patient care revenue and charitable contributions. Prepayment plans cover hospital expenses for much of the citizenry, and reimbursement programs under Medicare and Medicaid have substantially reduced the number of patients who lack an ability to pay, directly or indirectly, for health care services. Because of these changes in the health care delivery system, in 1969 the IRS modified its 1956 position by recognizing that the promotion of health is inherently a charitable purpose and is not obviated by the fact that the cost of services is borne by patients or third-party payors.[77] Under the 1969 ruling, to be tax-exempt, a hospital must adhere to a *community benefit standard*; that is, it must promote the health of a class broad enough to benefit the community and must be operated to serve a public rather than a private interest. In practical terms, this means that the emergency room must be open to all and that hospital care is provided to all who can pay, directly or indirectly. The hospital may generate a surplus of receipts over

---

[74] *Id.* at 29 (emphasis in original). In general, Schaffer & Fox, "Tax Administration as Health Policy: The Tax Exemption of Hospitals, 1969–1990," 4 *Exempt Org. Tax Rev.* (No. 9) 1185 (1991); Simpson & Strum, "How Good a Samaritan? Federal Income Tax Exemption for Charitable Hospitals Reconsidered," 4 *Exempt Org. Tax Rev.* (No. 8) 1084 (1991); Peregrine & McNulty, "Emerging Standards: The Impact of Medicare Law on Hospital Tax-Exempt Status," 4 *Exempt Org. Tax Rev.* (No. 7) 941 (1991). Also Comment, "Income Taxation—A Pauper a Day Keeps the Taxman Away: Qualification of Hospitals as Charitable Institutions under Section 501(c)(3)," 54 *N.C.L. Rev.* 1195 (1976); Note, "Federal Income Tax Exemptions for Private Hospitals," 36 *Fordham L. Rev.* 747 (1968). Cf. Barker, "Re-Examining the 501(c)(3) Exemption of Hospitals as Charitable Organizations," 3 *Exempt Org. Tax. Rev.* (No. 5) 539 (1990); Congdon, "With Charity for All: Did the I.R.S. Comply with the Administrative Procedure Act in Changing the Requirements for Charitable Exemptions of Hospitals?," 1 *ISL L. Rev.* (No. 1) 41 (1976).

The various types of nonprofit health care entities that qualify for tax-exempt status are discussed more fully in Hyatt & Hopkins, *The Law of Tax-Exempt Healthcare Organizations, Second Edition* (John Wiley & Sons, Inc., 2001), particularly Chapters 8–13.

[75] Rev. Rul. 56-185, 1956-1 C.B. 202.

[76] *Id.* at 203.

[77] Rev. Rul. 69-545, *supra* note 35. Also *Restatement of Trusts* (2d ed. 1959) § 372, comment b. This ruling was upheld in Eastern Ky. Welfare Rights Org. v. Simon, *supra* note 38.

disbursements and nonetheless be exempt. The requirement that health care must be provided free or at reduced costs was abandoned.

Other factors that may indicate that a hospital is operating for the benefit of the public include control of the institution by a board of trustees composed of individuals who do not have any direct economic interest in the hospital; maintenance by the hospital of an open medical staff, with privileges available to all qualified physicians, consistent with the size and nature of the facilities; a hospital policy enabling any member of the medical staff to rent available office space; hospital programs of medical training, research, and education; and involvement by the hospital in various projects and programs to improve the health of the community.[78] These and similar factors are of particular help in the qualification for tax exemption of hospitals that do not operate an emergency room, either because other institutions provide emergency care sufficient to adequately serve the community or because the hospital is a specialized institution (e.g., an eye hospital or cancer center) that offers medical care under conditions unlikely to necessitate emergency care.[79]

For tax purposes, the term *hospital* includes federal government hospitals; state, county, and municipal hospitals that are instrumentalities of governmental units; rehabilitation institutions; outpatient clinics; extended care facilities; community mental health or drug treatment centers; and cooperative hospital service organizations,[80] if they otherwise qualify. The term does not, however, include convalescent homes, homes for children or the aged, or institutions the principal purpose or function of which is to train handicapped individuals to pursue a vocation,[81] nor does it include free clinics for animals.[82]

The term *medical care* includes the treatment of any physical or mental disability or condition, whether on an inpatient or an outpatient basis, as long as the cost of the treatment is eligible for deductibility[83] by the person treated.[84]

The state of the law of tax-exempt organizations today regarding exempt charitable hospitals is heavily influenced by the emergence of the for-profit hospital. The principal reason for this is the acquisition of charitable health care institutions by for-profit (investor-owned) chains of proprietary health care providers. Another reason is the advent of the large hospital systems or networks, involving many institutions and organizations (often a mix of for-profit and nonprofit entities). These facts, accompanied by the greater reliance by hospitals on patient fees rather than charitable gifts and the change in the demographics of patients, have convinced some that there is now no material difference between nonprofit and

---

[78] IRS Exempt Organizations Handbook (IRM 7751) § 343.5(2).
[79] Rev. Rul. 83-157, 1983-2 C.B. 94.
[80] As to the latter, see § 10.4. Cf. Rev. Rul. 76-452, 1976-2 C.B. 60.
[81] Reg. § 1.170A-9(c)(1).
[82] Rev. Rul. 74-572, 1974-2 C.B. 82.
[83] IRC § 213.
[84] Reg. § 1.170A-9(c)(1).

for-profit hospitals.[85] Although as a matter of law there remains a fundamental difference between the two types of health care entities,[86] this superficial similarity between the two types of hospitals continues to sow confusion.[87]

(b) Hospital Clinical Departments

Application of the concept that the term *charitable* embraces the function of promoting health continues to trouble the IRS as the courts persist in allowing various forms of the practice of medicine (generally, a for-profit endeavor) to lodge

---

[85] A court opinion reflecting this viewpoint lamented the "gradual disappearance of the traditional charitable hospital for the poor" and concluded that it has been replaced by a "medical-industrial complex" (County Board of Utilization of Utah County v. Intermountain Healthcare, Inc., 709 P.2d 265, 270, 271 (Utah 1985)). This court wrote that it is "precisely because such a vast system of third-party payers has developed to meet the expense of modern hospital care that the historical distinction between for-profit and nonprofit hospitals has eroded" (*id.* at 274). The court noted that, in its view, the primary care services of both types of hospitals are largely the same, the rates are similar, both types accumulate capital, and both types have comparable operations; the nonprofit hospital was criticized for using its "profits" to acquire "capital improvements and new, updated equipment" (*id.* at 275). Also Hospital Utilization Project v. Commonwealth, 487 A.2d 1306 (Sup. Ct. Pa. 1985).

[86] See Hyatt & Hopkins, *supra* note 74, Chapters 3, 6, and 26.

[87] The overlap of charitable health care activities and the private practice of medicine was illustrated by the IRS's approval of the transfer of components of a physicians' group's medical practice to an exempt charitable organization (Priv. Ltr. Rul. 9710030).

An organization will not fail to be treated as organized and operated exclusively for a charitable purpose solely because a hospital that is owned and operated by it participates in a provider-sponsored organization (as defined in § 1853(e) of the Social Security Act), irrespective of whether the provider-sponsored organization is tax-exempt (IRC § 501(o)). For purposes of private inurement (see Chapter 19), a person with a material financial interest in one of these provider-sponsored organizations is regarded as an insider with respect to the hospital (*id.*).

In general, Kramer, "Nonprofit Hospitals: A Charitable Cause or Unjustified Tax Subsidy?," 19 *Exempt Org. Tax Rev.* (No. 3) 341 (1998); Copeland, "Nonprofit Versus For-Profit Hospitals," 18 *Exempt Org. Tax Rev.* (No. 1) 35 (1997); Columbo, "Health Care Reform and Federal Tax Exemption: Rethinking the Issues," 10 *Exempt Org. Tax Rev.* (No. 2) 335 (1994); Gourevitch, "CRS Report: Tax Aspects of Health Care Reform: The Tax Treatment of Health Care Providers," 9 *Exempt Org. Tax Rev.* (No. 6) 1317 (1994); Flynn, "Hospital Charity Care Standards: Reexamining the Grounds for Exempt Status," 3 *J. Tax. Exempt Orgs.* 13 (Winter 1992); Bove, "When Should a Hospital Be Treated as a Charity?," 3 *J. Tax Exempt Orgs.* 10 (Spring 1991); Sullivan & Moore, "A Critical Look at Recent Developments in Tax-Exempt Hospitals," 23 *J. Health & Hosp. Law* (No. 3) 65 (1990); Copeland & Rudney, "Federal Tax Subsidies for Not-for-Profit Hospitals," 46 *Tax Notes* (No. 13) 1559 (1990); Barker, "Reexamining the 501(c)(3) Exemption of Hospitals as Charitable Organizations," 48 *Tax Notes* (No. 3) 339 (1990); Hall, "The Charitable Status of Nonprofit Hospitals: Toward a Donative Theory of Tax Exemption," 66 *Wash. L. Rev.* 307 (Apr. 1991); Simpson & Strum, "How Good a Samaritan? Federal Income Tax Exemption for Charitable Hospitals Reconsidered," 14 *U. Puget Sound L. Rev.* 633 (Spring 1991); Note, "Nonprofit Hospitals and the State Tax Exemption: An Analysis of the Issues Since *Utah County v. Intermountain Healthcare, Inc.*," 9 *Va. Tax Rev.* (No. 3) 599 (Winter 1990); Roska, "Nonprofit Hospitals: The Relationship Between Charitable Tax Exemptions and Medical Care for Indigents," 43 *Sw. L. J.* (No. 2) 759 (1989); Milligan, Jr., "Provision of Uncompensated Care in American Hospitals: The Role of the Tax Code, the Federal Courts, Catholic Health Care Facilities, and Local Governments in Defining the Problem of Access for the Poor," 31 *Cath. Law.* (No. 1) 7 (1987); McGovern, "Restructured Nonprofit Hospitals," 33 *Tax Notes* (No. 4) 405 (1987); McCoy, "Health Care and the Tax Law: Reorganizations, Structural Changes, and Other Contemporary Problems of Tax-Exempt Hospitals," 44 *N.Y.U. Inst. on Fed. Tax.* 58-1 (1986); Hopkins & Beckwith, "The Federal Tax Law of Hospitals: Basic Principles and within its ambit. Of course, the practice of medicine occurs in hospitals but, as noted, the law has rationalized the classification of most nonprofit hospitals as charitable. Thereafter, also as noted, charitable entities have been determined to include a variety of clinics, centers, research agencies, plans, and health maintenance organizations. The IRS has been confronted with another type of noncommercial health provider: the incorporation of clinical departments of teaching hospitals associated with medical schools.

In one instance, at issue was the tax-exempt status of a professional corporation, all of the stockholders (who were also its employees) of which were physicians on the clinical staff of a teaching hospital operated by a state university and full-time members of the faculty of the university's school of medicine. The corporation consisted of four departments of the medical school and, in addition to the provision of medical care, was empowered to provide academic and clinical instruction of medical students, medical research, and ancillary administrative services solely for the benefit of the medical school and the teaching hospital. The financial support of the organization was derived from the receipt of fees for medical care performed by its employees at the teaching hospital; approximately 25 percent of the billable value of the services performed by the employees was rendered to patients who were unable to pay and were not required to pay for the services.

Rejecting the position of the IRS, a court found that the corporation was organized and operated for charitable, educational, and scientific purposes, in that it, in part, "delivers health care to the general public."[88] The fact that the organization was authorized to engage in the general practice of medicine did not deter the court since the organization's activities were limited to serving the interest of the medical school and hospital involved; thus, it was not authorized to practice medicine for profit. The court also excused the form of the professional corporation, rationalizing it as necessary because that is the only corporate entity permitted to practice medicine in the state. Further, the court tolerated the existence of stockholders and dismissed the fact that each shareholder was entitled to receive the par value of his or her single share ($1.00) in the event of dissolution as being insubstantial and thus not a violation of the rule requiring dedication of assets for a charitable purpose.[89]

Consequently, on the basis of this and prior court decisions,[90] this type of

---

Current Developments," 24 *Duq. L. Rev.* (No. 2) 691 (Winter 1985); Richeda, "Comment—Hospitals, Tax Exemption, and the Poor," 10 *Harv. Civil Rights-Civil Liberties L. Rev.* 653 (1975); Dwyer, "Income Tax—Section 501(c)(3)—Qualification of Hospitals for Tax Exempt Status as Charitable Organizations," 7 *U. Tol. L. Rev.* 278 (1975); Rose, "The IRS Contribution to the Health Problems of the Poor," 21 *Cath. U. L. Rev.* 35 (1971); Bromberg, "The Charitable Hospital," 20 *Cath. U. L. Rev.* 237 (1970).

[88] University of Md. Physicians, P.A. v. Comm'r, 41 T.C.M. 732, 735 (1981). Other tax-exempt activities were held to be the rendering of services without charge to the indigent (§ 1 hereof), provision of clinical training to the students, interns, and residents of the medical school (§ 6 hereof; Chapter 8 § 2), and medical research for the advancement of the healing arts (§ 6 hereof; Chapter 10).

[89] See § 4.3(b).

[90] University of Mass. Medical School Group Practice v. Comm'r, 74 T.C. 1299 (1980); B.H.W. Anesthesia Found. v. Comm'r, 72 T.C. 681 (1979). In general, Columbo, "Are Associations of Doctors Tax-Exempt? Analyzing Inconsistencies in the Tax-Exemption of Health Care Providers," 9 *Va. Tax. Rev.* (No. 3) 469 (1990).

corporate collective of physicians is tax-exempt, even though it generates fees for the performance of medical care services and pays the resulting earnings to individuals who are its stockholders. In these instances, of course, it is the close nexus with a medical school and teaching hospital that provides the underlying basis for the tax exemption.[91]

Occasionally, the IRS will rule that an organization is a tax-exempt charitable entity because it is carrying out an integral part of the activities of another charitable organization.[92] The IRS used this rationale to find that a trust created by an exempt hospital to accumulate and hold funds for the settlement of malpractice claims against the hospital, and from which the hospital directed the trustee to make payments to claimants, is a charitable organization for federal tax purposes.[93]

(c) Medical Research Organizations

Charitable organizations that promote health include certain medical research organizations that are "directly engaged in the continuous active conduct of medical research in conjunction with a hospital."[94] The term *medical research* means the conduct of investigations, experiments, and studies to discover, develop, or verify knowledge relating to the causes, diagnosis, treatment, prevention, or control of physical or mental diseases and impairments of humans. To qualify, the organization must have the appropriate equipment and professional personnel necessary to carry out its principal function.[95] Medical research encompasses the associated disciplines spanning the biological, social, and behavioral sciences.

This type of organization must have the conduct of medical research as its principal purpose or function[96] and be primarily engaged in the continuous active conduct of medical research in conjunction with a hospital, which itself is a public charity. The organization need not be formally affiliated with a hospital to be considered primarily engaged in the active conduct of medical research in conjunction with a hospital. There must be, however, a joint effort on the part of the research organization and the hospital pursuant to an understanding that the two organizations will maintain continuing close cooperation in the active conduct of medical research.[97] An organization will not be considered to be "primarily engaged directly in the continuous active conduct of medical research" unless it, during the applicable computation period,[98] devoted more than one-half of its assets to the continuous active conduct of med-

---

[91] E.g., Priv. Ltr. Rul. 9434041, superseded by Priv. Ltr. Rul. 9442025.
[92] Rev. Rul. 75-282, 1975-2 C.B. 201.
[93] Rev. Rul. 78-41, 1978-1 C.B. 148.
[94] IRC § 170(b)(1)(A)(iii).
[95] Reg. § 1.170A-9(c)(2)(iii).
[96] Reg. § 1.170A-9(c)(2)(iv).
[97] Reg. § 1.170A-9(c)(2)(vii).
[98] Reg. § 1.170A-9(c)(2)(vi)(a).

ical research or it expended funds equaling at least 3.5 percent of the fair market value of its endowment for the continuous active conduct of medical research.[99] If the organization's primary purpose is to disburse funds to other organizations for the conduct of research by them or to extend research grants or scholarships to others, it is not considered directly engaged in the active conduct of medical research.[100]

(d) Homes for the Aged

Another well-recognized health care provider is the home for the aged. Until 1972, the chief basis for tax exemption for a home for the aged as a charitable entity was that free or below-cost services must be provided, in conformance with the early IRS view of hospitals.[101] This approach was abandoned in that year and replaced with a requirement that the exempt charitable home for the aged be operated as to satisfy the primary needs of the aged: housing, health care, and financial security.[102]

The need for housing is generally satisfied if the home "provides residential facilities that are specifically designed to meet some combination of the physical, emotional, recreational, social, religious, and similar needs" of the aged. As for health care, that need is generally satisfied where the home "either directly provides some form of health care, or in the alternative, maintains some continuing arrangement with other organizations, facilities, or health personnel, designed to maintain the physical, and if necessary, mental well-being of its residents." Satisfaction of the financial security need has two aspects: The home must (1) maintain in the residence "any persons who become unable to pay their regular charges" and (2) provide its services "at the lowest feasible cost."

A home for the aged will qualify for tax-exempt status as a charitable organization, assuming it otherwise qualifies, if it operates in a manner designed to meet these primary needs of the aged. A home for the aged may, however, in the alternative, qualify under prior IRS rulings for exempt status, if the home is primarily concerned with providing care and housing for financially distressed aged persons.[103]

---

[99] Reg. § 1.170A-9(c)(2)(v)(b).

[100] Reg. § 1.170A-9(c)(2)(v)(c). For purposes of the charitable contribution deduction, the organization must be committed, during the calendar year in which the contribution is made, to expend the contribution for medical research before January 1 of the fifth calendar year that begins after the date the contribution is made (Reg. § 1.170A-9(c)(2)(ii), (viii)).

[101] Rev. Rul. 56-185, *supra* note 75. Also Rev. Rul. 57-467, 1957-2 C.B. 313.

[102] Rev. Rul. 72-124, 1972-1 C.B. 145. Also Rev. Rul. 75-198, 1975-1 C.B. 157.

[103] Rev. Rul. 64-231, 1964-2 C.B. 139; Rev. Rul. 61-72, 1961-1 C.B. 188. In general, Note, "The Property Tax Exemption and Non-Profit Homes for the Aged," 53 *Marq. L. Rev.* 140 (Spring 1970); Bromberg, "Non-Profit Homes for the Aged: An Analysis of Their Current Tax Exempt Status," 38 *J. Tax.* 54, 120 (1973); Bromberg, "Tax Exemption of Homes for the Aged," 46 *Taxes* 68 (1968).

(e) Health Maintenance Organizations

One of the most controversial of the health provider institutions—from the standpoint of federal tax categorization—is the health maintenance organization (HMO).[104] Many tax-exempt HMOs provide health care services by means of facilities and programs, in adherence to standards of what is *charitable* comparable to those followed by exempt hospitals. It is a membership organization; its services are provided to members on a prepaid basis and to nonmembers on a fee-for-service basis. In most instances, the HMO handles emergency cases without regard to whether the patient is a member and annually provides care either free or at reduced rates to a limited number of indigent patients. Frequently, HMOs sponsor education programs and research efforts to study ways to deliver better health care services. The HMO governing board is usually elected by and from its membership.

The position of the IRS originally was that an HMO may qualify for tax exemption as a social welfare organization[105] but cannot qualify for exemption as a charitable organization, on the ground that the preferential treatment accorded its member-subscribers constitutes the serving of private interests and because the prepayment feature constitutes a form of insurance that is not a charitable activity. This position was rejected in court, however, in connection with one model of an HMO, where it was held that (1) the persons benefited by an HMO represent a class large enough to constitute a requisite community,[106] (2) the HMO meets all of the IRS criteria applied to determine charitable status for nonprofit hospitals,[107] and (3) while the risk of illness is spread throughout its entire membership, the HMO operates not for commercial purposes but for charitable purposes, and thus the risk-spreading feature[108] is not a bar to designation of an HMO as a charitable organization.[109]

Following the issuance of this court opinion, the IRS relented somewhat, agreeing that where an HMO possesses certain characteristics, it qualifies as a tax-exempt charitable entity.[110] Essentially, an HMO will qualify for charitable status in the eyes of the IRS when it operates primarily to benefit the community, rather than private interests.

The IRS has determined, however, that certain HMOs cannot qualify as charitable organizations, because they are not operating for the benefit of a community. An IRS pronouncement distilled the key factors that, in the view of the agency, differentiate a tax-exempt HMO from a nonexempt HMO.[111]

---

[104] HMOs are authorized under federal law pursuant to Title XIII of the Public Health Service Act, 42 U.S.C. § 300e.
[105] See Chapter 12.
[106] See § 5.5(b).
[107] Rev. Rul. 69-545, *supra* note 35.
[108] The IRS ruled that prepaid group practice plans are not insurance companies for federal tax law purposes (IRC Subchapter L) (Rev. Rul. 68-27, 1968-1 C.B. 315).
[109] Sound Health Ass'n v. Comm'r, 71 T.C. 158 (1978). This type of HMO is known as the *staff model HMO*; this test for qualification as a charitable entity is known as the *direct provider community benefit test* (or *rigid community benefit test*).
[110] Gen. Couns. Mem. 38735.
[111] Gen. Couns. Mem. 39828.

These factors include: actual provision of services to nonmembers on a fee-for-service basis; care and reduced rates for the indigent; care for those covered by Medicare, Medicaid, or similar assistance programs; emergency room facilities available to the community without regard to ability to pay (and communication of this fact to the community); a meaningful subsidized membership program; a board of directors broadly representative of the community; health education programs open to the community; health research programs; health care providers who are paid on a fixed fee basis; and the application of any surplus to improving facilities, equipment, patient care, or to any of the above programs.

This pronouncement stated additional factors that must be considered in connection with the HMO membership element. The relevant factors in this determination include a membership composed of both groups and individuals, where the individuals comprise a substantial portion of the membership; a program to attract individuals to become members; a community rating system that provides uniform rates for prepaid care; similar rates charged to individuals and groups (with a possible modest initiation fee for individuals); and no substantive age or health barriers to eligibility for either individuals or groups.

The two plans that were the subject of this IRS pronouncement were found to not qualify as tax-exempt charitable organizations, because there were "substantial discrepancies" between their operations and the operations of the exempt HMO described in the prior IRS pronouncement and the court opinion. The disqualifying features of the HMOs included denial of health care services to nonmembers; failure to make emergency care available to the community; a noncomprehensive, cost-based scope of care; absence of need-based cost reduction or a subsidized dues program; absence of health education or research programs; and failure to show an "overt attempt" to increase membership.[112]

A federal court of appeals held that a nonprovider HMO does not qualify as a tax-exempt charitable organization.[113] The government won this case by distinguishing the facts from those in the prior litigation.[114] In the previous case, the HMO provided health care services itself, rather than arranging for others to provide that care. It employed physicians and other health care providers who were not affiliated with the HMO to provide health care services. It provided services to both subscribers and members of the general public through an outpatient clinic that it operated and through which it treated emergency patients, subscribers or not, regardless of ability to pay. It adjusted rates for and provided some free care to patients who were not subscribers. It offered public educational programs regarding health.

---

[112] In general, Neal & Papiewski, "Taxation of HMOs Now and Under Health Care Reform—Separating Fact From Fiction," 9 *Exempt Org. Tax Rev.* (No. 3) 577 (1994).
[113] Geisinger Health Plan v. Comm'r, 985 F.2d 1210 (3d Cir. 1993), *rev'g* 62 T.C.M. 1656 (1991).
[114] Sound Health Ass'n v. Comm'r, *supra* note 109.

The court in that litigation concluded that, as noted, the criteria to be applied in this context are those that are used to determine the tax-exempt status of nonprofit hospitals. It thus applied the community benefit standard to find that the HMO in that case was exempt. The appellate court in the subsequent case agreed that the community benefit standard could be used. It went on to find, however, that the HMO did not provide any health services itself, it did not ensure that people who are not its subscribers had access to health care or information about health care, it did not conduct research, and it did not offer educational programs open to the public. In short, wrote the court, "it benefits no one but its subscribers."[115]

In a 1998 technical advice memorandum, the IRS considered the case of an HMO that had been recognized by the IRS as a tax-exempt charitable organization since 1985. Although licensed as a third-party administrator, it was not federally qualified. This HMO was a member of a nonprofit health care system; the parent of this system (the HMO's sole member) also was an exempt charitable organization. The parent entity was as well the parent of another charitable organization, which owned or operated 25 acute care hospitals that provided inpatient and outpatient care to patients in three states. The HMO did not provide medical services by employed physicians at its own facilities; medical care services were provided through contracts with various physicians. It did not operate an emergency room open to the public and did not offer health care services to all persons in the community who cannot afford to pay. It provided coverage only through accepted employer groups; its services were provided almost exclusively to its enrollees. The IRS ruled that this HMO did not satisfy the direct provider community benefit test[116] or the flexible community benefit test,[117] and thus could not qualify as a charitable organization; the exemption was revoked retroactively.[118]

The IRS has acknowledged that it is possible for an HMO that is not a direct provider of care to qualify for tax exemption as a charitable organization. This

---

[115] Geisinger Health Plan v. Comm'r, *supra* note 113, at 1219. This test for qualification as a tax-exempt entity is known as the *flexible community benefit test*. This opinion contains some odd statements. The court seemed to endorse this view: "The IRS argues that the relevant precedents require at least some 'indicia of charity' in the form of serving the public and providing some services free of charge" (*id.*); that is not the law (see § 26.2(c)). Another is that this organization could not be charitable because it does not provide health care services itself—it "simply arrang[es] for others to provide them" (*id.*, 1217); this is not the law—if it were, peer review organizations (PROs) and health system agencies (HSAs) (see *infra* §§ (g), (h)) could not qualify for tax exemption.

The appellate court remanded the case for a decision as to whether the HMO could be tax-exempt because it is an integral part of a health care system. That approach, however, also failed (see § 23.7(a), text accompanied by notes 188–192).

In general, Rasman, "Third Circuit's 'Boost' Test Denies Section 501(c)(3) Status to HMO," 6 *J. Tax Exempt Orgs.* (No. 4) 147 (Jan./Feb. 1995); Gerhart & Rasman, "HMO Denied Section 501(c)(3) Status by Third Circuit," 4 *J. Tax. Exempt Orgs.* (No. 6) 17 (May/June 1993).

[116] See *supra* note 109.

[117] See *supra* note 115.

[118] Tech. Adv. Mem. (not released); see BNA, Inc. TaxCore, Dec. 17, 1998; 98 TNT 243-2 (Doc. 98-37129).

type of exempt HMO is the *Medicaid HMO*, which is a managed care organization expressly organized and designed to serve Medicaid beneficiaries under the auspices of state statutes encouraging the development of this form of health care delivery for the indigent population.[119] This type of HMO qualifies as a charitable organization because, in addition to promoting health, it is providing relief to the poor and distressed.[120]

Subsequent to these developments, a court upheld the revocation by the IRS of the tax-exempt status of a nonprofit HMO, on the ground that it no longer provided the requisite community benefit.[121] One of the factors the court emphasized was the difference in treatment of the enrollees in the setting of premiums; the court inferred that this HMO was benefiting larger employers. Likewise, the composition of the HMO's board of trustees, "lacking in representation of the community at large, furthers the inference that [the HMO] predominantly served the private interests of the larger employers participating in its plans."[122] The court concluded that the HMO "failed to show that it provides any community benefit that accomplishes a charitable purpose."[123]

(f) Integrated Delivery Systems

Another of the organizations eligible for tax exemption as charitable organizations because they promote health is the *integrated delivery system* (IDS). Private determination letters (from the National Office of the IRS) recognizing the exempt status of these entities first appeared in early 1993.

An IDS is a health provider (or a component entity of an affiliated network of providers) created to integrate the provision of hospital services with medical services provided by physicians. Previously, these services were provided (and paid for by patients, their insurers, or government programs) separately; the hospital provided its services and facilities (such as diagnostic services, surgery, nursing, emergency care, room, and board), while physicians provided medical services to patients by means of private medical practices, admitting and treating patients in hospital facilities. In an IDS, an entity provides and bills for both hospital and physician services, either itself or by contract with another organization.

There are several models of a tax-exempt IDS. In one, a charitable organization obtains (by purchase, lease, license, stock transfer, or contribution) all of the assets needed to operate one or more hospitals, clinics, and physician offices.

---

[119] Brauer & Friedlander, "Exemption of Medicaid HMOs and Medicaid Service Organizations under IRC 501(c)(3)," Chapter D, *IRS FY 1999 Exempt Organization Continuing Professional Education Technical Instruction Program Textbook.*

[120] See *supra* § 1; § 22.1(c).

[121] IHC Health Plans, Inc. v. Comm'r, 82 T.C.M. 593 (2001).

[122] *Id.* at 605.

[123] *Id.* Also IHC Group, Inc. v. Comm'r, 82 T.C.M. 606 (2001); IHC Care, Inc. v. Comm'r, 82 T.C.M. 617 (2001).

(There is concern on this point about the potential for forms of private inurement or private benefit,[124] particularly in connection with leasing and licensing arrangements; the IRS prefers arrangements where the system's assets are purchased for fair market value and the IDS controls them.) It acquires the services of physicians, through direct employment or independent contract (the latter known as a professional services agreement). The organization is the provider of health care services—hospital and medical, inpatient and outpatient. It enters into all payor contracts, provides all nonprofessional personnel for the system, maintains all assets, and collects all revenues for services provided. Other models have the exempt IDS as a subsidiary of a hospital, hospital system, or clinic. (Another type of IDS, which is jointly controlled by a health care provider and physicians, cannot qualify for exemption as a charitable entity because of the ownership and control by physicians.[125])

Tax exemption for an IDS is tested against the community benefit standard. In this connection, the exempt IDS can minimize or eliminate duplication of tests, procedures, and treatments, resulting in greater efficiency and reduced costs to the public; provide increased accessibility to Medicare, Medicaid, and charity care patients; undertake research in primary care or areas of specialization that benefit the public; and conduct health education programs open to the public. The IRS expects (as it does in the exempt hospital setting) the governing board, and most committees and subcommittees, of an IDS to be independent (that is, not controlled by the physicians) and reflective of the community.[126]

---

[124] See Chapter 19.

[125] Somewhat similar to an IDS is a *medical service organization* (MSO). Typically, with the MSO structure, a hospital or affiliate, in return for a share of revenues, provides to an independent physician or group of physicians all real and personal property, support staff, and management and billing services required to manage an otherwise private medical practice. An MSO is not an IDS because there is no one entity with responsibility for providing both types of services.

The IRS ruled that hospitals may form a health care delivery system, using a supporting organization (see § 11.3(c)) as the coordinating mechanism, pursuant to a *joint operating agreement* (JOA) (e.g., Priv. Ltr. Rul. 9651047). These hospitals ceded authority under the JOA to the governing body of the supporting organization to establish their budgets, including major expenditures, debts, contracts, managed care agreements, and capital expenditures; to direct their provision of health care services; and to monitor and audit their compliance with its directives. In addition, the governing body and its committees meet regularly to exercise overall responsibility for operational decisions involving the day-to-day and long-range strategic management decisions that have been delegated by the participating entities. The IRS concluded that this arrangement is analogous to circumstances where the hospitals are subsidiaries of the coordinating entity. (See § 11.3(c).)

[126] In general, Jedrey, "Standards Evolve for Hospital-Affiliated Group Practice Exemption," 6 *J. Tax Exempt Orgs.* (No. 1) 3 (July/Aug. 1994); Peregrine & Broccolo, "IRS Releases Detailed Position on Exempt Status of Integrated Delivery Systems," 8 *Exempt Org. Tax Rev.* (No. 5) 903 (Nov. 1993); Bromberg, "Tax Considerations in Forming MSOs and Clinics without Walls," 8 *Exempt Org. Tax Rev.* (No. 5) 887 (Nov. 1993).

(g) Peer Review Organizations

Another category of organization posing problems with regard to eligibility for tax exemption as a charitable entity is the *utilization and quality control peer review organization* (PRO), which was authorized by statute in 1972.[127] PROs are qualified groups of physicians that establish mandatory cost and quality controls for medical treatment rendered in hospitals and financed under Medicare and Medicaid and that monitor this care. PROs were conceived as part of a larger effort to curb the rising costs of health care, in this instance by minimizing or eliminating unnecessary services (those services termed *overutilization*) by assuring that payments under these governmental health care programs are made only when and to the extent that the health care services provided are medically necessary.

Congress views PROs as entities that act in the public interest, their chief purpose being to generally improve the quality of medical care in the United States and to obtain maximum value for every federal health dollar expended.[128] Assuming that the tax law requirements for tax-exempt charitable organizations are otherwise satisfied, this purpose would seem to clearly constitute a charitable activity, the rationales being the promotion of health, lessening of the burdens of government,[129] and/or promotion of social welfare.[130] There may, however, be a private purpose served by PROs, namely, enhancement of and establishment of confidence in the medical profession (even though, ironically, much of the medical community initially was bitterly opposed to the PRO concept).

PROs must be nonprofit organizations; they are reimbursed by the federal government for administrative costs. Members of a PRO must be licensed practitioners of medicine or osteopathy. The basic question with respect to tax-exempt charitable status is whether a PRO functions primarily to benefit the general public or to serve the interests of the medical profession. The inclination of the IRS is to treat certain health care organizations as business leagues rather than as charitable organizations.[131] The IRS recognized that incidental benefit to physicians will not defeat exemption as a charitable organization,[132] but also made it clear that, when it concludes a profession is itself receiving substantial benefit from an organization's activities, status as a business league

---

[127] Social Security Amendments of 1972 (Pub. L. No. 603) § 249F, 86 Stat. 1429 (adding new Title XI to the Social Security Act); 42 U.S.C. § 1320c *et seq.* These organizations were formerly known as professional standards review organizations (PSROs).

[128] The law states that the purpose of these organizations is to perform medicine and osteopathy peer reviews of the "pattern of quality of care in an area of medical practice where actual performance is measured against objective criteria which define acceptable and adequate practice" (42 U.S.C. § 1320c-1(2)).

[129] See *infra* § 4.

[130] See *infra* § 7.

[131] See Chapter 13.

[132] Rev. Rul. 73-313, 1973-2 C.B. 174.

is the likely result.[133] Prior to litigation, it was the position of the IRS that the public benefits flowing from physician peer review activities were overshadowed by the benefits ostensibly accorded physicians in their professional capacities, and thus that these organizations could not qualify as exempt charitable entities.[134]

By contrast, the IRS recognized a health systems agency (HSA), an organization established by federal law[135] to establish and maintain a system of health planning and resources development aimed at providing adequate health care for a specified geographic area, to be a tax-exempt charitable organization.[136] Among the functions of the agency is the establishment of a health systems plan after appropriate consideration of the recommended national guidelines for health planning policy issued by the Department of Health and Human Services. The agency receives planning and matching grants from the federal government. Finding the basis of the designation of the agency as a charitable entity to be the promotion of health, the IRS observed that, by "establishing and maintaining a system of health planning and resources development aimed at providing adequate health care, the HSA is promoting the health of the residents of the area in which it functions."[137]

The adverse position of the IRS regarding PROs was rejected by a court, in a case involving PRO support centers.[138] The court held that Congress's principal purpose in establishing PROs was to ensure the economical and effective delivery of health care services under Medicare and Medicaid, and that any benefits that physicians and others may derive (including reimbursement for services, limitation on tort liability, or promotion of esteem for the medical profession) have only a "tenuous, incidental, and non-substantial connection with the [PRO] scheme."[139] On this latter point, the court added that the PRO support centers did not engage in financial transactions "designed to benefit the members of the organizations or the organizations themselves, activities in the nature of a patient referral service, or other potential money-making activities designed to benefit members or participants."[140]

As a sidelight of this PRO decision, the court found it "difficult to reconcile" the position of the IRS against PROs and the ruling granting classification as tax-exempt charitable entities to HSAs. Said the court: "The similarity between HSAs

[133] Rev. Rul. 74-553, 1974-2 C.B. 168; Rev. Rul. 73-567, 1973-2 C.B. 178; Rev. Rul. 70-641, 1970-2 C.B. 119. Cf. Kentucky Bar Found., Inc. v. Comm'r, 78 T.C. 921 (1982). This posture of the IRS may be contrasted with the fact that the medical profession instituted an (unsuccessful) action to enjoin implementation of the PSRO law and to declare the 1972 act unconstitutional (Ass'n of Amer. Physicians & Surgeons v. Weinberger, 395 F. Supp. 125 (N.D. Ill. 1975)). Cf. Amer. Ass'n of Councils of Medical Staffs v. Mathews, 421 F. Supp. 848 (E.D. La. 1976).
[134] Bromberg, "The Effect of Tax Policy on the Delivery and Cost of Health Care," 53 Taxes 452, 475–478 (1975).
[135] National Health Planning and Resources Development Act of 1974, 42 U.S.C. § 300k et seq.
[136] Rev. Rul. 77-69, 1977-1 C.B. 143.
[137] Id. at 144.
[138] Virginia Professional Standards Review Found. v. Blumenthal, 466 F. Supp. 1164 (D.D.C. 1979).
[139] Id. at 1170.
[140] Id. at 1173.

and PROs and [PRO] support centers is obvious. [PROs] collect and analyze data, establish regional norms and criteria of care, and coordinate activities with HSAs and other federal state health planning entities."[141]

In the aftermath of these two court decisions,[142] the IRS revised its position concerning physician peer review organizations and concluded that, in certain circumstances, this type of entity is a tax-exempt charitable organization because it is "promoting the health of the beneficiaries of governmental health care programs by preventing unnecessary hospitalization and surgery."[143] The IRS regards these factors as essential for exemption of a PRO as an exempt charitable entity: Membership in it is open by law to all physicians without charge; it is an organization mandated by federal statute as the exclusive method of assuring appropriate quality and utilization of care provided to Medicare and Medicaid patients; the composition of the board of directors of the PRO is not tied to any membership or association with any medical society; and the PRO has the authority to make final decisions regarding quality and utilization of medical care for purposes of payment under the Medicare and Medicaid programs. The fact that the activities of the PRO "may indirectly further the interests of the medical profession by promoting public esteem for the medical profession, and by allowing physicians to set their own standards for the review of Medicare and Medicaid claims and thus prevent outside regulation" was dismissed as being "incidental" to the charitable benefits provided by the organization.[144]

(h) Fitness Centers

Fitness centers and similar facilities, whether freestanding or operated by institutions such as hospitals, can be tax-exempt organizations (or programs), considered charitable in nature because they promote health. In this setting, the IRS once again applies the community benefit doctrine. Thus, when the health facility provides a benefit for the entire community the organization serves, operation of the facility is an exempt function.[145] By contrast, if the fees for use of a health club are sufficiently high to restrict use of the club's facilities to a limited segment of a community, the club operation will be a nonexempt one.[146]

In one instance, the IRS expressed the view that the standard as to tax exemption for a health club is whether its "operations promote health in a manner which is collateral to the providing of recreational facilities which advances the

---

[141] *Id.* at 1172. Also Professional Standards Review Org. of Queens County, Inc. v. Comm'r, 74 T.C. 240 (1980).

[142] See *supra* notes 108, 110.

[143] Rev. Rul. 81-276, 1981-2 C.B. 128.

[144] *Id.* at 129. Analogous entities are the Medicaid Service Organizations, which can qualify as tax-exempt charitable organizations because they lessen the burdens of government (see *infra* § 4; Brauer & Friedlander, "Exemption of Medicaid HMOs and Medicaid Service Organizations Under IRC 501(c)(3)," *supra* note 119).

[145] E.g., Tech. Adv. Mem. 8505002.

[146] Rev. Rul. 79-360, 1979-2 C.B. 236.

well-being and happiness of the community in general."[147] Similarly, a fitness center was held to be exempt inasmuch as it furthered the accomplishment of certain of the other programs of the health care organization that operated it (including an occupational and physical therapy program), its facilities and programs were specially designed for the needs of the disabled and the treatment plans of patients in other programs, its fee structure was designed to make it available to the general public (its rates were comparable to those charged by similar fitness centers), and it offered a range of programs that focused on wellness.[148] Likewise, a freestanding state-of-the-art cardiovascular rehabilitation and heart disease prevention center, which included a fitness facility, was found to be a related activity of an exempt hospital, with the IRS emphasizing the existence of a nutrition program and a scholarship plan for those who could not afford the programs and services of the center.[149]

The IRS's treatment of fitness and health centers as tax-exempt charitable functions that promote health extends to the most elaborate of facilities. In one instance, exemption was accorded a hospital-run sports and fitness center, the components of which included exercise rooms, racquetball and tennis courts, a two-pool aquatic area, an indoor track, tanning beds, a roller skating rink, and a juice bar. The agency held that the rehabilitation of hospital inpatients and outpatients in connection with treatment plans prescribed by physicians or other appropriate hospital personnel furthered the hospital's exempt purpose of serving the health care needs of the community involved.[150]

(i) Other Health Care Organizations

There are various other types of health provider institutions that qualify as exempt charitable organizations for federal tax purposes. These include entities such as preferred provider organizations, drug rescue centers,[151] blood banks,[152] halfway houses,[153] organizations that minister to the nonmedical needs of patients in a proprietary hospital,[154] nursing bureaus,[155] senior citizens centers,[156] organizations that provide private hospital rooms when medically necessary,[157] Christian Science medical care facilities,[158] and medical research organizations.[159]

[147] Tech. Adv. Mem. 8505002.
[148] Priv. Ltr. Rul. 9329041.
[149] Priv. Ltr. Rul. 9736047. The IRS issued a similar ruling in the case of a university-based fitness center (Priv. Ltr. Rul. 9732032).
[150] Priv. Ltr. Rul. 200051049.
[151] Rev. Rul. 70-590, 1970-2 C.B. 116.
[152] Rev. Rul. 66-323, 1966-2 C.B. 216, as modified by Rev. Rul. 78-145, 1978-1 C.B. 169.
[153] Rev. Rul. 72-16, 1972-1 C.B. 143. Also Rev. Rul. 75-472, 1975-2 C.B. 208.
[154] Rev. Rul. 68-73, 1968-1 C.B. 251.
[155] Rev. Rul. 55-656, 1955-2 C.B. 262.
[156] Rev. Rul. 75-198, *supra* note 102.
[157] Rev. Rul. 79-358, *supra* note 11.
[158] Rev. Rul. 80-114, 1980-1 C.B. 115, superseding Rev. Rul. 78-427, 1978-2 C.B. 176. This determination is consistent with the IRS's position that payments to Christian Science practitioners for services rendered are deductible medical expenses (Rev. Rul. 55-261, 1955-1 C.B. 307).
[159] IRC § 170(b)(1)(A)(iii).

Moreover, recognition of tax-exempt status has been accorded to several types of organizations providing specialized health care services. Thus, for example, a home health agency, an organization that provides low-cost health care to patients in their homes, can be an exempt charitable entity.[160] Similarly, an organization created to attract a physician to a medically underserved community by providing a medical building and facilities was ruled to be exempt, notwithstanding the fact that the physician charged for services provided and received some personal benefit (use of a building) under the arrangement.[161] Also, an organization was determined to be furthering the charitable purpose of promoting the health of its community where it built and leased a public hospital and related facilities to an exempt charitable association that operated the facilities for an amount sufficient only to retire indebtedness and meet necessary operating expenses.[162] Likewise, organizations that conduct medical research are frequently ruled to be exempt as charitable organizations, although these organizations may instead be considered as engaged in scientific research.[163] As another illustration, an organization that operated a free computerized donor authorization retrieval system to facilitate transplantation of body organs on the death of donors qualified as an exempt charitable organization as engaged in the promotion of health.[164] Still another example is an organization that provided services (such as housing, transportation, and counseling) for relatives and friends who traveled to the organization's community to visit and comfort patients at local health care facilities.[165] Further, an organization that provided medical care to indigent individuals through five medical clinics, including the funding of emergency room care and related inpatient care to the indigent, was ruled by the IRS to be promoting health.[166]

The IRS stated that the term *charitable* includes the promotion of *public health,* in ruling that an organization formed to provide individual psychological and educational evaluations, as well as tutoring and therapy, for children and adolescents with learning disabilities qualified as a charitable organization for federal income tax purposes.[167] The organization's psychologists and other professionals administered tests designed to determine intellectual capacity, academic achievement, psychological adjustment, speech and language difficulties, and perceptual-motor abilities. Therapy was available through staff professionals specially trained in the various areas of learning disabilities.

Despite the efforts of the IRS to deny tax-exempt status to nearly all forms of referral services,[168] a court held that an organization that operated a medical and

---

[160] Rev. Rul. 72-209, 1972-1 C.B. 148.
[161] Rev. Rul. 73-313, *supra* note 132. Also In re Carlson's Estate, 358 P.2d 669 (Kan. 1961). Cf. Rev. Rul. 69-266, 1969-2 C.B. 151.
[162] Rev. Rul. 80-309, 1980-2 C.B. 183.
[163] E.g., Rev. Rul. 69-526, 1969-2 C.B. 115. See Chapter 9.
[164] Rev. Rul. 75-197, 1975-1 C.B. 156.
[165] Rev. Rul. 81-28, *supra* note 22.
[166] Priv. Ltr. Rul. 200233024.
[167] Rev. Rul. 77-68, 1977-1 C.B. 142.
[168] Kentucky Bar Found., Inc. v. Comm'r, *supra* note 133.

dental referral service was a charitable entity because it promoted health.[169] Users of the service (subscribers) paid the organization an annual fee and were provided an array of information concerning the availability of health-related supplies, equipment, and services at a discount. The service providers did not pay any fees to be listed with the referral service, although many made contributions to the organization. Other program activities of the organization were the publication of a health care newsletter, sponsorship of a community health fair, the provision of speakers, and the presentation of an annual conference for physicians and dentists. The court said that the referral service "serves its charitable purpose by providing a resource whereby subscribers can be made aware of and referred to medical specialists who can serve their health care needs" and that any financial benefit inuring to the referral service is merely incidental to the overall charitable purposes being served.[170]

Thus, there is a variety of types of nonprofit organizations that promote health. Many of these entities, including hospitals, operate as members of a health care provider system. Generally, an aggregation of organizations, even where they have a common purpose (sometimes termed *system*), cannot itself qualify for tax exemption as a charitable entity.[171] Usually, each organization must separately establish (if it can) a basis in law for its claim to exemption.[172] In this context, at least, the IRS resists the concept of "exemption by attachment" or "derivative exemption."[173]

§ 6.4 LESSENING THE BURDENS OF GOVERNMENT

The regulations accompanying the federal tax law concerning exempt charitable organizations define the term *charitable* as including "lessening of the burdens of Government" and the "erection or maintenance of public buildings, monuments, or works."[174] This first concept relates more to the provision of governmental or municipal services rather than facilities, because of inclusion in the regulations of the exempt activity of erection or maintenance of public facilities.

According to the IRS, a determination as to whether an organization is lessening the burdens of a government requires consideration of whether the organization's activities are activities that a governmental unit considers to be its burdens and whether the activities actually lessen a governmental burden.[175] For an activity to be a burden of a government, there must be an "objective manifes-

---

[169] Fraternal Med. Specialist Servs., Inc. v. Comm'r, 49 T.C.M. 289 (1984).
[170] *Id.* at 292.
[171] Cf. § 6.2(d).
[172] Gen. Couns. Mem. 39508. See Chapter 23.
[173] Gen. Couns. Mem. 31433. In general, Holdenreid, "Common Threads Link Revocation and Denial of Exemption for Health Care Organizations," 10 J. *Tax. Exempt Orgs.* (No. 1) 18 (July/Aug. 1998).
[174] Reg. § 1.501(c)(3)-1(d)(2).
[175] Rev. Rul. 85-2, 1985-1 C.B. 178.

tation" by a governmental unit that it considers the activity to be part of its burden. It is insufficient that an organization engages in an activity that is sometimes undertaken by a government or that a government or a governmental official expresses approval of an organization and its activities. The interrelationship between a governmental unit and an organization may provide evidence that the governmental unit considers the activity to be its burden. All relevant facts and circumstances are considered in determining whether an organization is actually lessening the burdens of a government.

A favorable working relationship between a government and an organization is "strong evidence" that the organization is actually lessening the burdens of the government. For example, an organization that provided funds to a county's law enforcement agencies to police illegal narcotic traffic was held to lessen the burdens of government and thus be charitable, in that governmental funds were not available to purchase the drugs used to apprehend drug traffickers.[176] Likewise, an organization that provided legal advice and training to guardians *ad litem* representing neglected or abused children before a juvenile court was found to lessen governmental burdens, because otherwise the government would have to train the law volunteers or appointed lawyers as guardians.[177]

Some organizations that are tax-exempt under this category of *charitable* provide services directly in the context of governmental activity, such as assisting in the preservation of a public lake,[178] beautifying a city,[179] operating a prisoner correctional center,[180] assisting in the operation of a mass transportation system,[181] maintaining a volunteer fire company,[182] conserving natural resources,[183] or encouraging plantings of public lands.[184]

Other organizations that are charitable, because they reduce a governmental burden, provide services in tandem with existing governmental agencies. As examples, tax exemption on this basis was ruled to be obtainable for an organization that made funds available to a police department for use as reward money;[185] an organization that assisted firefighters, police, and other personnel to perform their duties more efficiently during emergency conditions;[186] an organization that provided bus transportation to isolated areas of a community not served by the city bus system as a Model Cities demonstration project

[176] Rev. Rul. 85-1, 1985-1 C.B. 177.
[177] Rev. Rul. 85-2, *supra* note 175. In one instance, claims for tax exemption on this basis failed because the organization did not show that the entities ostensibly assisted were government agencies, that activities they undertook were those that a government considers its burden, and that the activities lessened any burdens (University Med. Resident Servs., P.C. v. Comm'r, 71 T.C.M. 3130 (1996)).
[178] Rev. Rul. 70-186, 1970-1 C.B. 128.
[179] Rev. Rul. 68-14, 1968-1 C.B. 243. Cf. Rev. Rul. 75-286, 1975-2 C.B. 210.
[180] Rev. Rul. 70-583, *supra* note 19.
[181] Rev. Rul. 71-29, 1971-1 C.B. 150.
[182] Rev. Rul. 74-361, 1974-2 C.B. 159.
[183] Rev. Rul. 67-292, 1967-2 C.B. 184.
[184] Rev. Rul. 66-179, 1966-1 C.B. 139.
[185] Rev. Rul. 74-246, 1974-1 C.B. 130.
[186] Rev. Rul. 71-99, 1971-1 C.B. 151.

performed under the authority of the federal and local governments;[187] a community foundation that participated in an investment plan to retain a for-profit baseball team in a city (when the governmental units involved demonstrated an "intense and unique interest" in professional sports franchises);[188] and an organization that provided expert opinions to local government officials concerning traffic safety.[189] A government internship program may likewise come within this category of charitable activities,[190] as does a program of awards to citizens for outstanding civic achievements.[191] Likewise, physician peer review organizations[192] can qualify as exempt charitable entities because they enable the medical profession to assume the government's responsibility for reviewing the appropriateness and quality of services provided under the Medicare and Medicaid programs.[193]

In an application of these rules, an organization that certified crop seed within a state was found to be performing a service required by federal and state law—a service performed in other states by a governmental agency—and thus to be charitable because it was lessening the burdens of government. The organization, functioning in conjunction with one of the state's universities, was held to be protecting the "purchasing public—generally farmers and gardeners—from perceived abuses in the sale of agricultural and vegetable seed which is impure, mislabeled or adulterated," and therefore to be undertaking a "public service" and a "recognized governmental function."[194]

Organizations that qualify for *charitable* status because they perform functions for the benefit of a government also include those that supply a community with facilities ordinarily provided at the taxpayers' expense or maintain the facilities, such as town halls, bridges, streets, parks, trees, and monuments.[195] Examples of organizations in this category include those that engage in activities such as solid waste recycling,[196] community improvement,[197] and community land-use analysis,[198] as well as those that provide public parks,[199] other recreational facilities,[200] and public parking lots.[201]

A corollary of the foregoing law is that an organization that frustrates attempts to relieve the burdens of government and thereby increases these burdens

---

[187] Rev. Rul. 78-68, 1978-1 C.B. 149. Cf. Rev. Rul. 78-69, 1978-1 C.B. 156.
[188] Priv. Ltr. Rul. 9530024.
[189] Rev. Rul. 76-418, 1976-2 C.B. 145. Cf. Rev. Rul. 70-79, 1970-1 C.B. 127.
[190] Rev. Rul. 70-584, 1970-2 C.B. 114.
[191] Rev. Rul. 66-146, 1966-1 C.B. 136.
[192] See *supra* § 3(g).
[193] Rev. Rul. 81-276, *supra* note 143.
[194] Indiana Crop Improvement Ass'n, Inc. v. Comm'r, 76 T.C. 394, 398, 399 (1981).
[195] *Restatement of Trusts* (2d ed. 1959) § 373, comment a.
[196] Rev. Rul. 72-560, 1972-2 C.B. 248.
[197] Rev. Rul. 68-15, 1968-1 C.B. 244.
[198] Rev. Rul. 67-391, 1967-2 C.B. 190.
[199] Rev. Rul. 66-358, 1966-2 C.B. 218.
[200] Rev. Rul. 70-186, *supra* note 178; Rev. Rul. 59-310, 1959-2 C.B. 332.
[201] Monterey Pub. Parking Corp. v. United States, 481 F.2d 175 (9th Cir. 1973).

cannot qualify as a charitable organization.[202] Likewise, where an organization engages in activities that are specifically proscribed under federal and applicable state law, it cannot be regarded as a charitable organization that is lessening the burdens of government.[203]

§ 6.5   ADVANCEMENT OF RELIGION

The regulations accompanying the federal tax law concerning charitable organizations provide that the term *charitable* includes the "advancement of religion."[204]

The advancement of religion has long been considered a charitable purpose, although the scope of this category of charitable endeavors is imprecise because of the separate enumeration in the federal tax law of religious activities as being in furtherance of exempt purposes.[205] The concept of *advancement of religion* includes the construction or maintenance of a church building, monument, memorial window, or burial ground, and collateral services such as the provision of music, payment of salaries to employees of religious organizations, dissemination of religious doctrines, maintenance of missions, and distribution of religious literature.[206] This category of tax exemption includes organizations the works of which extend to the advancement of particular religions, religious sects, or religious doctrines, as well as religion in general.[207]

Organizations that are tax-exempt as charitable entities because they advance religion also include those maintaining a church newspaper,[208] providing material for a parochial school system,[209] providing young adults with counseling,[210] and undertaking genealogical research.[211] The IRS ruled that an organization that supervised the preparation and inspection of food products prepared commercially in a particular locality to ensure that they satisfy the dietary rules of a particular religion was exempt as advancing religion.[212] An organization that provided funds for the defense of members of a religious sect in legal actions involving a state's abridgement of religious freedom was ruled exempt as a charitable organization by virtue of "promoting social welfare by defending hu-

---

[202] Rev. Rul. 75-384, 1975-2 C.B. 204.
[203] Public Indus., Inc. v. Comm'r, 61 T.C.M. 1626 (1991). In general, Criddle & Malvey, "Ensuring Exemption for Lessening the Burdens of Government," 8 *J. Tax. Exempt Orgs.* (No. 6) 243 (May/June 1997).
[204] Reg. § 1.501(c)(3)-1(d)(2).
[205] See Chapter 8.
[206] *Restatement of Trusts* (2d ed. 1959) § 371, comment a.
[207] *Id.*, comments b, d.
[208] Rev. Rul. 68-306, 1968-1 C.B. 257. Cf. Foundation for Divine Meditation, Inc. v. Comm'r, 24 T.C.M. 411 (1965), *aff'd sub nom.* Parker v. Comm'r, 365 F.2d 792 (8th Cir. 1966), *cert. den.*, 385 U.S. 1026 (1967).
[209] Rev. Rul. 68-26, 1968-1 C.B. 272.
[210] Rev. Rul. 68-72, 1968-1 C.B. 250.
[211] Rev. Rul. 71-580, 1971-2 C.B. 235.
[212] Rev. Rul. 74-575, 1974-2 C.B. 161.

man and civil rights secured by law,"[213] although it would seem that it was also advancing religion.[214]

An organization formed and controlled by an exempt conference of churches, that borrowed funds from individuals and made mortgage loans at less than the commercial rate of interest to affiliated churches to finance the construction of church buildings, qualified as a charitable organization because it advanced religion.[215] An organization that provided a continuing education program in an atmosphere conducive to spiritual renewal for ministers, members of churches, and their families may qualify as an exempt organization because it advanced religion.[216] An organization that provided traditional religious burial services, which directly support and maintain basic tenets and beliefs of religion regarding burial of its members, was ruled to advance religion.[217] Likewise, an organization that conducted weekend religious retreats, open to individuals of diverse religious denominations, at a rural lakeshore site at which the participants may enjoy recreational facilities in their limited amount of free time, qualified as an organization that advances religion.[218]

Religion may be advanced by a tax-exempt organization that operates a noncommercial broadcasting station presenting programming on religious subjects.[219] Similarly, a nonprofit religious broadcasting entity may acquire classification as an exempt charitable organization even though it operates on a commercial license, as long as it does not sell commercial or advertising time[220] or, if it does so, sells the time as an incidental part of its activities.[221]

The IRS determined that an organization established to provide temporary low-cost housing and related services for missionary families on furlough for recuperation or training in the United States from their assignments abroad qualified as a charitable organization acting to advance religion because the assistance to the missionaries was provided them in their official capacities for use in furtherance of and as part of the organized religious program with which they were associated.[222] The IRS cautioned, however, that the provision of "assistance to individuals in their individual capacities solely by reason of their identification with some form of religious endeavor, such as missionary work, is not a charitable use."[223]

---

[213] See *infra* § 7.
[214] Rev. Rul. 73-285, 1973-2 C.B. 174.
[215] Rev. Rul. 75-282, *supra* note 92.
[216] Rev. Rul. 77-366, 1977-2 C.B. 192.
[217] Rev. Rul. 79-359, 1979-2 C.B. 226.
[218] Rev. Rul. 77-430, 1977-2 C.B. 194.
[219] Rev. Rul. 66-220, 1966-2 C.B. 209.
[220] Rev. Rul. 68-563, 1968-2 C.B. 212.
[221] Rev. Rul. 78-385, 1978-2 C.B. 174.
[222] Rev. Rul. 75-434, 1975-2 C.B. 205. Also World Family Corp. v. Comm'r, 81 T.C. 958 (1983).
[223] The IRS ruled that an organization formed to aid immigrants in the United States qualified as a tax-exempt charitable organization (Rev. Rul. 76-205, 1976-1 C.B. 154).

§ 6.6   ADVANCEMENT OF EDUCATION OR SCIENCE

The regulations accompanying the federal tax law concerning charitable organizations include among the definitions of the term *charitable* the "advancement of education or science."[224]

The *advancement of education* includes the establishment or maintenance of nonprofit educational institutions, financing of scholarships and other forms of student assistance, establishment or maintenance of institutions such as public libraries and museums, advancement of knowledge through research, and dissemination of knowledge by publications, seminars, lectures, and similar activities. The *advancement of science* includes comparable activities devoted to the furtherance or promotion of science and the dissemination of scientific knowledge. Inasmuch as the federal tax law exemption for charitable organizations also contains the terms *educational* and *scientific*,[225] organizations coming within one or both of these two terms will qualify as tax-exempt organizations on that basis.

Thus, for federal income tax purposes, the more traditional forms of advancement of education, such as the establishment or maintenance of educational institutions, libraries, museums, and the like, will fall within the scope of the term *educational*, leaving to the broader term *charitable* related concepts of advancement of education in the collateral sense. Nonetheless, the IRS, in ruling that an organization is educational, frequently also finds it to be charitable.[226]

For example, while the operation of a college or university is an educational undertaking, many satellite endeavors are regarded as charitable in nature. Thus, the provision of scholarships is a charitable activity,[227] as are the making of low-interest loans to attend college[228] and the provision of free housing, books, or supplies.[229] Other charitable activities that constitute the advancement of education include publication of student journals such as law review journals,[230] maintenance of a training table for athletes,[231] provision of assistance to law students to obtain experience with public interest law firms and legal aid societies,[232] operation of a foreign student center,[233] selection of students for enrollment at foreign universities,[234] operations of an alumni association,[235] provision of work experience in selected trades and professions

---

[224] Reg. § 1.501(c)(3)-1(d)(2).
[225] See Chapters 7 and 9, respectively.
[226] E.g., Rev. Rul. 77-272, 1977-2 C.B. 191.
[227] Rev. Rul. 69-257, 1969-1 C.B. 151; Rev. Rul. 66-103, 1966-1 C.B. 134.
[228] Rev. Rul. 63-220, 1963-2 C.B. 208; Rev. Rul. 61-87, 1961-1 C.B. 191.
[229] Rev. Rul. 64-274, 1964-2 C.B. 141.
[230] Rev. Rul. 63-235, 1963-2 C.B. 610.
[231] Rev. Rul. 67-291, 1967-2 C.B. 184.
[232] Rev. Rul. 78-310, 1978-2 C.B. 173.
[233] Rev. Rul. 65-191, 1965-2 C.B. 157.
[234] Rev. Rul. 69-400, 1969-2 C.B. 114.
[235] Rev. Rul. 60-143, 1960-1 C.B. 192; Rev. Rul. 56-486, 1956-2 C.B. 309; Estate of Thayer v. Comm'r, 24 T.C. 384 (1955).

to high school graduates and college students,[236] the operation of interscholastic athletic programs,[237] and the provision of housing for students of a college.[238] Still other activities that are charitable because they advance education are more institutionally oriented, such as bookstores,[239] organizations that accredit schools, colleges, and universities,[240] and provide financial and investment assistance[241] or computer services[242] to educational organizations. One type of organization operated closely with colleges and universities, however—fraternities and sororities—generally is not regarded as being charitable or educational in nature.[243]

With regard to college, university, or school bookstores, it is clear that the sale to students and faculty of books, supplies, materials, athletic wear necessary for participation in the institution's athletic and physical education programs, and other items that are required by or are otherwise necessary for courses at the institution (including computer hardware and software) is an activity that is charitable in nature.[244] Some bookstores associated with educational institutions, however, sell items that are not related to education of the students; the sale of these items is likely to be an unrelated business activity,[245] unless the sales are within the scope of the *convenience doctrine*.[246]

Colleges and universities frequently utilize affiliated nonprofit organizations in connection with the carrying out of their charitable and educational programs. These related organizations can be charitable in character. As illustrations, the IRS recognized as tax-exempt an organization that operated a book and supply store that sold items only to students and faculty of a college,[247] that operated a cafeteria and restaurant on the campus of a university primarily for the convenience of its students and faculty,[248] and that provided housing and food service exclusively for students and faculty of a university.[249]

For this category of tax exemption to be available, the organization must in fact engage in advancement activities. In one instance, a court rejected two orga-

---

[236] Rev. Rul. 75-284, 1975-2 C.B. 202; Rev. Rul. 70-584, *supra* note 190.

[237] Rev. Rul. 55-587, 1955-2 C.B. 261.

[238] Rev. Rul. 76-336, 1976-2 C.B. 143.

[239] Squire v. Students Book Corp., 191 F.2d 1018 (9th Cir. 1951).

[240] Rev. Rul. 74-146, 1974-1 C.B. 129.

[241] Rev. Rul. 71-529, 1971-2 C.B. 234; Rev. Rul. 67-149, 1967-1 C.B. 133.

[242] Rev. Rul. 74-614, 1974-2 C.B. 164, *amp. by* Rev. Rul. 81-29, 1981-1 C.B. 329.

[243] Rev. Rul. 69-573, 1969-2 C.B. 125; Phinney v. Dougherty, 307 F.2d 357 (5th Cir. 1962); Davison v. Comm'r, 60 F.2d 50 (2d Cir. 1932); Alumnae Chapter Beta of Clovia v. Comm'r, 46 T.C.M. 297 (1983); Johnson v. Southern Greek Hous. Corp., 307 S.E.2d 491 (Ga. 1983); Alford v. Emory Univ., 116 S.E.2d 596 (Ga. 1960). Also Rev. Rul. 64-118, 1964-1(Part 1) C.B. 182 (fraternity housing corporations); Rev. Rul. 64-117, 1964-1 (Part 1) C.B. 180 (student clubs). These entities are tax-exempt social clubs (see Chapter 14).

[244] College and university examination guidelines (see § 24.8(d)) § 342.(13).

[245] See § 26.5(a)(i).

[246] See § 27.2(b).

[247] Rev. Rul. 69-538, 1969-2 C.B. 116.

[248] Rev. Rul. 58-194, 1958-1 C.B. 240.

[249] Rev. Rul. 67-217, 1967-2 C.B. 181.

nizations' claims for tax exemption based on this ground, because they provided "minimal, if any" assistance to educational and other entities.[250]

The nature of the law regarding organizations the functions of which represent assistance to other organizations that are tax-exempt can shift radically where the assistance is directed to two or more exempt entities. Exempt organizations, such as colleges and universities, often turn to cooperative ventures to reduce costs and improve the quality of performance. Colleges and universities often find it productive and more efficient to share, for example, data processing or library resources.[251]

Organizations not affiliated with an institution of learning but that provide instruction may also be deemed to advance education, such as those that teach industrial skills,[252] conduct work experience programs,[253] provide apprentice training,[254] act as a clearinghouse and course coordinator for instructors and students,[255] instruct in the field of business,[256] evaluate the public service obligations of broadcasters,[257] and provide services to relieve psychological tensions and improve the mental health of children and adolescents.[258]

The advancement of education can consist of making a grant to a tax-exempt fraternity or sorority[259] for the purpose of constructing or maintaining educational facilities, such as financing of allocable construction costs of the fraternity or sorority house, maintaining a library, and funding study facilities.[260] Where the grantor is a private foundation,[261] it should be certain that the grant is a qualifying distribution[262] and not a taxable expenditure.[263]

Education may be advanced through activities such as the publication and dissemination of research,[264] maintenance of collections,[265] the provision of anthropological specimens,[266] the operation of a foreign exchange program,[267] and the operation of an honor society.[268] Likewise, the IRS determined that the provision of bibliographic information by means of a computer network to researchers at both tax-exempt and nonexempt libraries constituted the advancement of edu-

[250] University Med. Resident Servs. P.C. v. Comm'r, *supra* note 177.
[251] See *infra* § 8.
[252] Rev. Rul. 72-101, 1972-1 C.B. 144. Cf. Rev. Rul. 78-42, 1978-1 C.B. 158.
[253] Rev. Rul. 78-310, *supra* note 232; Rev. Rul. 76-37, 1976-1 C.B. 146; Rev. Rul. 75-284, *supra* note 236; Rev. Rul. 70-584, *supra* note 190.
[254] Rev. Rul. 67-72, 1967-1 C.B. 125.
[255] Rev. Rul. 71-413, 1971-2 C.B. 228.
[256] Rev. Rul. 68-16, 1968-1 C.B. 246.
[257] Rev. Rul. 79-26, 1979-1 C.B. 196.
[258] Rev. Rul. 77-68, *supra* note 167.
[259] These entities are tax-exempt by reason of IRC § 501(c)(7). See Chapter 14.
[260] E.g., Priv. Ltr. Rul. 9014061.
[261] See Chapter 11.
[262] See § 11.4(b).
[263] See § 11.4(e).
[264] Rev. Rul. 67-4, 1967-1 C.B. 121.
[265] Rev. Rul. 70-321, 1970-1 C.B. 129.
[266] Rev. Rul. 70-129, 1970-1 C.B. 128.
[267] Rev. Rul. 80-286, 1980-2 C.B. 179.
[268] Rev. Rul. 71-97, 1971-1 C.B. 150.

cation.[269] Similarly, the IRS held that an organization formed to preserve the natural environment by acquiring ecologically significant underdeveloped land and to maintain the land or to transfer it to a government conservation agency qualified for exemption at least in part for the reason that it was advancing education and science.[270]

Although an organization that is deemed to be a scientific entity is usually engaged in scientific research,[271] an organization may be classified as one that advances education and/or science where it publishes or otherwise distributes scientific information without having performed the supporting research.[272]

§ 6.7 PROMOTION OF SOCIAL WELFARE

The promotion of social welfare is one of the more indefinite categories of charitable purposes. In the general law of charitable trusts, the concept includes a broad spectrum of activities, such as the promotion of temperance, prevention of alleviation of suffering of animals, promotion of national security, inculcation of patriotism, promotion of the happiness or well-being of the members of the community, promotion of the happiness or well-being of persons who have few opportunities for recreation and enjoyment, and (perhaps) the erection of maintenance of a tomb or monument.[273] As was observed, "[n]o attempt . . . can successfully be made to enumerate all of the purposes which fall within the scope" of this category of charitable purpose, and the question in each case is whether the "purpose is one the accomplishment of which might reasonably be held to be for the social interest of the community."[274]

The federal tax regulations defining *charitable purpose* state five types of endeavors that constitute the promotion of social welfare: activities "designed to accomplish any of the above [charitable] purposes," "lessen neighborhood tensions," "eliminate prejudice and discrimination," "defend human and civil rights secured by law," and "combat community deterioration and juvenile delinquency."[275]

The types of organizations that are tax-exempt as charitable organizations because they are operated to eliminate prejudice and discrimination are illustrated by three rulings issued by the IRS. One of these organizations worked to educate the public about integrated housing and conducted pro-

---

[269] Rev. Rul. 81-29, *supra* note 242.
[270] Rev. Rul. 76-204, 1976-1 C.B. 152. Cf. Rev. Rul. 78-384, 1978-2 C.B. 174.
[271] See Chapter 9.
[272] E.g., Gen. Couns. Mem. 38459.
[273] *Restatement of Trusts* (2d ed. 1959) § 374, comments b–h.
[274] *Id.*, comment a. One of the sources of confusion in this area is use of the term *social welfare* to reference organizations that are tax-exempt by reason of IRC § 501(c)(4) (see Chapter 12).
[275] Reg. § 1.501(c)(3)-1(d)(2).

grams to prevent panic selling when neighborhoods were integrated.[276] Another entity conducted investigations and research to obtain information regarding discrimination against minority groups and housing and public accommodations.[277] The third operated to advance equal job opportunities in a particular community for qualified workers discriminated against because of race or creed.[278]

An organization qualified as a tax-exempt charitable organization because it functioned to eliminate discrimination against members of minorities seeking employment in the construction trades by recruiting, educating, and counseling workers, providing technical assistance to lawyers involved in litigation to enforce workers' rights, and acting as a court-appointed monitor after successful lawsuits.[279] Combating community deterioration in the charitable sense involves remedial action leading to the elimination of the physical, economic, and social causes of the deterioration,[280] such as by purchasing and renovating deteriorating residences and selling or leasing them to low-income families on a nonprofit basis,[281] and by operating a self-help home building program.[282] The charitable activity of combating community deterioration can be present "whether or not the community is in a state of decline."[283]

Discrimination in this context is not confined to racial discrimination. Thus, an organization formed to promote equal rights for women in employment and other economic contexts was ruled to be tax-exempt as promoting social welfare by eliminating prejudice and discrimination.[284] Also, an organization created to aid immigrants to the United States in overcoming social, cultural, and economic problems by personal counseling or referral to appropriate agencies was granted federal income tax exemption on this basis.[285]

The position of the IRS once was that the phrase "human and civil rights secured by law" refers only to the individual liberties, freedoms, and privileges involving human dignity that are either specially guaranteed by the U.S. Constitution or by a special statutory provision coming directly within the scope of the Thirteenth or Fourteenth Amendment or some other comparable constitutional provision, or that otherwise fall within the protection of the Constitution by reason of their long-established recognition in the common law as rights that are essential to the orderly pursuit of happiness by free people. Consequently, tax exemption as a charitable organization was denied by the agency to an organization the primary activity of which was the provision of legal assistance to em-

---

[276] Rev. Rul. 68-655, 1968-2 C.B. 613.
[277] Rev. Rul. 68-438, 1968-2 C.B. 609.
[278] Rev. Rul. 68-70, 1968-1 C.B. 248.
[279] Rev. Rul. 75-285, 1975-2 C.B. 203.
[280] Rev. Rul. 67-6, 1967-1 C.B. 135.
[281] Rev. Rul. 68-17, *supra* note 13; also Rev. Rul. 76-408, 1976-2 C.B. 145; Rev. Rul. 70-585, *supra* note 13.
[282] Rev. Rul. 67-138, *supra* note 13.
[283] Rev. Rul. 76-147, 1976-1 C.B. 151.
[284] Rev. Rul. 72-228, 1972-1 C.B. 148.
[285] Rev. Rul. 76-205, *supra* note 223.

ployees whose rights were violated under compulsory unionization arrangements, on the theory that its criterion for intervention in a case is whether there is a grievance arising out of a compulsory union membership requirement, and that the right to work is not a protected constitutional right. A court disagreed, however, holding that the right to work is an individual liberty involving a human dignity that is guaranteed by the Constitution, and is therefore a human and civil right secured by law. The organization was thus ruled to be tax-exempt as a charitable entity.[286]

One of the ways in which an organization can qualify for tax exemption as a charitable entity is by preserving the historic or architectural character of a community, which promotes social welfare by combating community deterioration. This can be accomplished, for example, with a program of acquiring historic structures, restoring them, and selling them subject to restrictive covenants.[287]

With regard to the promotion of social welfare by combating juvenile delinquency, the IRS found the activity of an organization that promoted sports for children to be tax-exempt. This organization developed, promoted, and regulated a sport for individuals under 18 years of age, and generally provided a recreational outlet for young people.[288] Similarly, an organization that provided teaching of a particular sport to children, by holding clinics conducted by qualified instructors and by providing free instruction, equipment, and facilities, was found to be combating juvenile delinquency and thus to be charitable in nature.[289]

Obviously, these five categories of social welfare activities tend to overlap. Thus, one organization that was ruled to be engaged in the elimination of prejudice and discrimination was also found to operate to "lessen neighborhood tensions" and "prevent deterioration of neighborhoods,"[290] while another was ruled to also act to lessen neighborhood tensions and to defend "human and civil rights secured by law."[291] An organization that counseled residents of a community and city officials in the best use of vacant lots in order to eliminate potential gathering places for "unruly elements" was held to be engaged in combating juvenile delinquency, as well as, because of other activities, the elimination of prejudice and discrimination, the lessening of neighborhood tensions, and the combating of community deterioration.[292]

[286] National Right to Work Legal Defense & Educ. Found., Inc. v. United States, 487 F. Supp. 801 (E.D.N.C. 1979).
[287] Rev. Rul. 86-49, 1986-1 C.B. 243; Rev. Rul. 75-470, 1975-2 C.B. 207.
[288] Rev. Rul. 80-215, 1980-2 C.B. 174.
[289] Rev. Rul. 65-2, 1965-1 C.B. 227. Cf. Rev. Rul. 70-4, 1970-1 C.B. 126 (holding that an organization promoting and regulating a sport for amateurs qualified under IRC § 501(c)(4) (see Chapter 12) but not under IRC § 501(c)(3) because it directed its activities to all members of the general public irrespective of age).
[290] Rev. Rul. 68-655, *supra* note 276.
[291] Rev. Rul. 68-438, *supra* note 277. Also Rev. Rul. 73-285, *supra* note 214.
[292] Rev. Rul. 68-15, *supra* note 197. Also Rev. Rul. 81-284, 1981-2 C.B. 130; Rev. Rul. 76-419, 1976-2 C.B. 146; Rev. Rul. 74-587, 1974-2 C.B. 162. Cf. Rev. Rul. 77-111, 1977-1 C.B. 144.

There can also be an overlap of categories of charitable organizations where they operate to eliminate prejudice and discrimination and to educate the public. Thus, an organization educating the public as to how to invest in housing made available to the public on a nondiscriminatory basis was ruled to be tax-exempt.[293] Similar illustrations include an organization that informed the public, through lectures and discussions, of the advantages of nondiscriminatory hiring[294] and an organization that operated programs to prevent panic selling from resulting integration of a neighborhood.[295]

As noted, the regulation defining *charitable* endeavors states that the promotion of social welfare includes activities that seek to accomplish otherwise charitable ends. By nature, these activities tend to be characterized as lessening the burdens of government.[296] Thus, an organization created to assist local governments of a metropolitan region by studying and recommending regional policies directed at the solution of mutual problems was held to be involved in both the combating of community deterioration and lessening of the burdens of government.[297] Yet, social welfare activities of this nature may traverse the gamut of charitable works, as illustrated by the case of an organization that made awards to individuals who have made outstanding contributions and achievements in the field of commerce, communications, creative arts and crafts, education, finance, government, law, medicine and health, performing arts, religion, science, social services, sports and athletics, technology, and transportation.[298]

§ 6.8   PROMOTION OF THE ARTS

Organizations devoted to promotion of the arts may qualify for tax exemption as charitable entities. For example, an organization that functioned to arouse and give direction to local interest in a community for the establishment of a repertory theater qualified as a charitable entity.[299] The repertory theater company itself can be charitable in nature.[300] This type of charitable activity was initially recognized by the IRS as being "cultural," with emphasis on the musical arts.[301]

One feature of this aspect of charitable endeavor is the effort akin to the advancement of education,[302] that is, to promote public appreciation of one or more of the arts. Thus, an organization formed to perpetuate group harmony

---

[293] Rev. Rul. 67-250, *supra* note 13.
[294] Rev. Rul. 68-70, *supra* note 278.
[295] Rev. Rul. 68-655, *supra* note 276.
[296] See *supra* § 4.
[297] Rev. Rul. 70-79, *supra* note 189.
[298] Rev. Rul. 66-146, *supra* note 191; Bok v. McCaughn, 42 F.2d 616 (3d Cir. 1930).
[299] Rev. Rul. 64-174, 1964-1 (Part I) C.B. 183.
[300] Rev. Rul. 64-175, 1964-1 (Part I) C.B. 185.
[301] S.M. 176, 1 C.B. 147 (1919); I.T. 1475, 1-2 C.B. 184 (1922).
[302] See *supra* § 6.

singing and to educate the general public as to this type of music was ruled to be tax-exempt.[303] Similarly, an organization formed to promote an appreciation of jazz music as an American art form was held to be an exempt organization,[304] as was a nonprofit school of contemporary dancing.[305] This exemption for charitable entities may likewise extend to an organization that seeks to encourage the creative arts and scholarship by making grants to needy artists,[306] by promoting interest in and appreciation of contemporary symphonic and chamber music,[307] or by sponsoring public exhibits of art works by unknown but promising artists.[308]

Other organizations are tax-exempt because they function to promote and encourage the talent and ability of young artists. The scope of types of these activities include the training of young musicians in concert technique,[309] the promotion of filmmaking by conducting festivals to provide unknown independent filmmakers with opportunities to display their films,[310] and the encouragement of musicians and composers through commissions and scholarships and the opportunity for students to play with accomplished professional musicians.[311] Organizations in this category frequently promote (and finance) their charitable function through the sponsorship of public festivals, concerts, exhibits, and other productions.[312] In nearly all of these instances, the artists are amateurs, performing solely for the onstage experience or to enable the charitable organization to meet expenses.

Organizations operated to promote the arts, which otherwise qualify as charitable entities, may find themselves engaging in an activity the IRS regards as serving a private interest. Thus, while the preservation of classical music programming can be a charitable purpose,[313] an organization that undertook a variety of activities to enable a for-profit radio station to continue broadcasting classical music was denied tax exemption.[314] Likewise, although the displaying of art works often is a charitable activity,[315] an organization will not achieve exemption as a charitable entity where it sells the artworks it exhibits and remits the proceeds to the artists.[316] (The fact that exhibited artworks are available for sale,

---

[303] Rev. Rul. 66-46, 1966-1 C.B. 133.
[304] Rev. Rul. 65-271, 1965-2 C.B. 161.
[305] Rev. Rul. 65-270, 1965-2 C.B. 160.
[306] Rev. Rul. 66-103, *supra* note 227.
[307] Rev. Rul. 79-369, 1979-2 C.B. 226.
[308] Rev. Rul. 66-178, 1966-1 C.B. 138.
[309] Rev. Rul. 67-392, 1967-2 C.B. 191.
[310] Rev. Rul. 75-471, 1975-2 C.B. 207.
[311] Rev. Rul. 65-271, *supra* note 304.
[312] E.g., Priv. Ltr. Rul. 9217001.
[313] Rev. Rul. 64-175, *supra* note 300.
[314] Rev. Rul. 76-206, 1976-1 C.B. 154.
[315] Goldsboro Art League, Inc. v. Comm'r, 75 T.C. 337 (1980) (where the artworks displayed were selected by jury procedures and the organization maintained the only art gallery in the geographic area); Rev. Rul. 66-178, *supra* note 308.
[316] St. Louis Science Fiction Ltd. v. Comm'r, 49 T.C.M. 1126 (1985) (where the organization did not apply any controls to ensure the quality of artworks sold and the "tone" of its annual convention was predominantly social and recreational); Rev. Rul. 76-152, 1976-1 C.B. 151. Also Rev. Rul. 71-395, 1971-2 C.B. 228.

however, will not necessarily deprive the organization sponsoring the show of exemption as a charitable entity.[317])

Status as tax-exempt charitable organizations has been accorded organizations that sponsor professional presentations, such as plays, musicals, and concerts. The chief rationale for extending exemption to these organizations is that they operate to foster the development in a community of an appreciation for the dramatic and musical arts, such as by staging theatrical productions that are not otherwise available.[318] At the same time, these exempt theaters may be perceived as placing the commercial theaters in the same locale at a competitive disadvantage. Defenders of the exempt cultural centers claim that they champion theatrical presentations that otherwise would never be produced, while their critics insist that they are frequently presenting popular entertainment in unfair competition with privately owned theaters.

A court discussed the distinctions between tax-exempt performing arts organizations and commercial theaters as follows:

> Admittedly, the line between commercial enterprises which produce and present theatrical performances and nonprofit, tax-exempt organizations that do the same is not always easy to draw. Indeed, the theater is the most prominent area of the performing arts in which commercial enterprises co-exist, often in the same city, with nonprofit, tax-exempt charitable organizations that also sponsor professional presentations. . . .
>
> However, there are differences. Commercial theaters are operated to make a profit. Thus, they choose plays having the greatest mass audience appeal. Generally, they run the plays so long as they can attract a crowd. They set ticket prices to pay the total costs of production and to return a profit. Since their focus is perennially on the box office, they do not generally organize other activities to educate the public and they do not encourage and instruct relatively unknown playwrights and actors.
>
> Tax-exempt organizations are not operated to make a profit. They fulfill their artistic and community obligations by focusing on the highest possible standards of performance; by serving the community broadly; by developing new and original works; and by providing educational programs and opportunities for new talent. Thus, they keep the great classics of the theater alive and are willing to experiment with new forms of dramatic writing, acting, and staging. Usually nonprofit theatrical organizations present a number of plays over a season for a relatively short specified time period. Because of a desired quality in acoustics and intimacy with the audience, many present their performances in halls of limited capacity. The combination of the shortness of the season, the limited seating capacity, the enormous costs of producing quality performances of new or experimental works coupled with the desire to keep ticket prices at a level which is affordable to most of the community means that except in rare cases, box of-

[317] Cleveland Creative Arts Guild v. Comm'r, 50 T.C.M. 272 (1985) (where the organization's art sales activity was found to be a means to the end of increasing public appreciation of the arts); Rev. Rul. 78-131, 1978-2 C.B. 156.
[318] Rev. Rul. 73-45, 1973-1 C.B. 220.

fice receipts will never cover the cost of producing plays for nonprofit performing arts organizations.... We feel that ... [the arts organization involved in the case] has shown that it is organized and operated similar to other nonprofit theater organizations, rather than as commercial theatre.[319]

§ 6.9   CONSORTIA

Tax-exempt organizations frequently utilize cooperative ventures to further their purposes. The early position of the IRS toward cooperative venturing by or for charitable (including educational) organizations was relatively favorable. This is reflected in an IRS ruling concerning an organization that was created to construct and maintain a building to house member agencies of a community chest.[320] The purpose of this organization was to facilitate coordination among the agencies and to make more efficient use of the available voluntary labor force. The rental rate charged the agencies was substantially lower than commercial rates for comparable facilities (the organization leased the land from a city and itself paid only a nominal rental) and the organization's annual rental income was approximately equal to its total annual operating costs. Citing the concept that the "performance of a particular activity that is not inherently charitable may nonetheless further a charitable purpose,"[321] the IRS ruled that the organization was exempt as a charitable entity, emphasizing the low rental rates and the close relationship between its purposes and functions and those of the tenant organizations.[322]

The contemporary state of the law in this regard, however, is that these cooperative ventures are likely to be nonexempt entities, even where the venture is controlled by and performs a function for its members that each tax-exempt institution would otherwise have to undertake for itself, without adverse tax consequences. The IRS has two exceptions to this policy, in that exemption as a charitable organization will be granted where the consortium conducts substantive programs that are inherently exempt in nature[323] or where at least 85 percent of the organization's revenue is derived from outside sources (the *donative element* test).[324] The agency bases its position on a passage in the regulations accompanying the federal tax rules pertaining to feeder organizations.[325] The IRS policy to-

---

[319] Plumstead Theatre Soc'y, Inc. v. Comm'r, 74 T.C. 1324, 1332-1333 (1980), *aff'd*, 675 F.2d 244 (9th Cir. 1982).

[320] Rev. Rul. 69-572, 1969-2 C.B. 119.

[321] Rev. Rul. 67-4, *supra* note 264.

[322] Also Rev. Rul. 64-182, 1964-1 C.B. (Part I) 186; Rev. Rul. 58-147, 1958-2 C.B. 275.

[323] Rev. Rul. 74-614, *supra* note 242, *amp. by* Rev. Rul. 81-29, *supra* note 242.

[324] Rev. Rul. 72-369, 1972-2 C.B. 245; Rev. Rul. 71-529, *supra* note 241. A corollary policy of the IRS is that, where neither of the exceptions is present, the provision of services by one tax-exempt organization to one or more other exempt (or nonexempt) organization may be the conduct of an unrelated trade or business (see Part Five) (Rev. Rul. 69-528, 1969-2 C.B. 127). But, however, see § 26.5(i).

[325] Rev. Rul. 69-528, *supra* note 324. The feeder organization rules are discussed in § 28.6.

ward cooperative ventures had, for many years, been rejected in the courts on nearly every occasion when it was considered,[326] and Congress had legislated in this area, contravening the IRS's policy three times.[327]

The direction of the law regarding tax exemption for consortia began to shift as a result of consideration of the issue by the U.S. Tax Court. The case involved a cooperative hospital laundry service owned and operated by exempt hospitals. Finding the regulations under the feeder organization rules to have the force of law because of long-standing congressional awareness of them, and concluding that the legislative history of related statutes evidenced congressional intent to not allow exemption for hospital-controlled laundries, the court found that the hospital laundry service organization was a feeder organization and thus not exempt from taxation.[328] Because of the emphasis placed on this legislative history, however, it was not clear whether consortia other than hospital laundry enterprises would receive like treatment by the Tax Court. Shortly after the Tax Court reached this decision, the Third,[329] Ninth,[330] and Sixth Circuit courts of appeal arrived at the same conclusion.[331]

Despite this policy, the IRS recognized the necessity and utility of cooperative endeavors in the field of higher education. Thus, the IRS stated:

> Many activities normally carried on by colleges and universities can be more effectively accomplished through the combined efforts of a group of such institutions. . . . Associations composed entirely of privately supported nonprofit colleges and universities have been created and are operated exclusively to carry out these activities.
>
> [These associations] aid and promote the educational endeavors of their members and interpret to the public the aims, functions, and needs of the institutions, with a view to better understanding and cooperation.[332]

---

[326] Hospital Bur. of Standards & Supplies v. United States, 158 F. Supp. 560 (Ct. Cl. 1958); United Hosp. Serv., Inc. v. United States, 384 F. Supp. 766 (S.D. Ind. 1974); Hospital Central Serv. Ass'n v. United States, 77-2 U.S.T.C. ¶ 9601 (W.D. Wash. 1977); Metropolitan Detroit Area Hosp. Serv., Inc. v. United States, 445 F. Supp. 857 (E.D. Mich. 1978); Northern Calif. Central Serv. Inc. v. United States, 591 F.2d 620 (Ct. Cl. 1979); Community Hosp. Services, Inc. v. United States, 79-1 U.S.T.C. ¶ 9301 (E.D. Mich. 1979); HCSC-Laundry v. United States, 473 F. Supp. 250 (E.D. Pa. 1979). In general, Gailey, "Tax-Exempt Auxiliary Corporations and Major Public Institutions," 14 *Bus. Off.* (No. 5) 24 (1980); Hopkins, "Cooperative Ventures of Colleges and Universities: The Current Tax Law Developments," 4 *Coll. & Univ. Bus. Off.* (No. 5) (1975); Whaley, "Interinstitutional Cooperation Among Educational Organizations," 1 *J. Coll. & Univ. Law* (No. 2) 93 (1973).

[327] IRC §§ 501(e), 501(f), 513(e).

[328] Associated Hosp. Serv., Inc. v. Comm'r, 74 T.C. 213 (1980), *aff'd, unrep. dec.* (5th Cir. 1981).

[329] HCSC-Laundry v. United States, 624 F.2d 428 (3d Cir. 1980), *rev'g supra* note 326, *aff'd,* 450 U.S. 1 (1981).

[330] Hospital Central Servs. Ass'n v. United States, 623 F.2d 611 (9th Cir. 1980), *cert. den.,* 450 U.S. 911 (1980), *rev'g supra* note 326. Also Community Hosp. Serv., Inc. v. United States, 81-1 U.S.T.C. ¶ 9198 (6th Cir. 1981), *rev'g supra* note 326.

[331] Metropolitan Detroit Area Hosp. Serv. v. United States, 634 F.2d 330 (6th Cir. 1980), *cert. den.,* 450 U.S. 1031 (1980), *rev'g supra* note 326.

[332] Rev. Rul. 63-15, 1963-1 C.B. 189.

The IRS subscribed to this view in the intervening years.[333]

Some IRS rulings are contradictory to its announced position on college, university, and similar consortia. For example, the IRS ruled that an organization, the members of which are educational (including some proprietary) institutions, qualified as a tax-exempt charitable organization because it accredits these institutions.[334] The rationale for exemption was that the organization advanced education and thus was charitable in nature;[335] it engaged in activities that "support and advance education by providing significant incentive for maintaining a high quality educational program."

Similarly, the IRS accorded charitable entity status to an organization controlled by a tax-exempt conference of churches, where its purpose was to issue mortgages to the churches to enable them to finance the construction of church buildings.[336] The rationale for exemption was that the organization was advancing religion.[337] The making of loans is not, of course, an inherently religious activity; rather, exemption was derived from the fact that the loans were made at lower than commercial interest rates to churches of the conference to enable them to construct buildings at reduced cost for religious purposes.

Also, the IRS granted tax-exempt charitable status to a consortium of counties located in the same state.[338] This exemption was accorded on the ground that the organization's activities contribute to the "more efficient operation of county government." Efficiency of operation is, as noted, one of the principal reasons for the establishment and operation of consortia.

Further, it has long been the position of the IRS that an organization formed and operated for the purpose of providing financial assistance to organizations that are regarded as charitable is itself qualified for tax exemption as a charitable entity.[339]

A federal court had occasion to reaffirm its original position concerning consortia,[340] stating that "[t]his court has held in the past that where one organization provides a service which is necessary and indispensable to the operations of another, the first will take on the tax status of the second."[341] Invoking an *adjunct theory*, the court added:

---

[333] E.g., Rev. Rul. 63-208, 1963-2 C.B. 468; Rev. Rul. 63-209, 1963-2 C.B. 469 (where offices formed by a tax-exempt religious entity to administer its statewide parochial school system and a convent to house teachers in parochial schools organized by the religious institution was held to function as integral parts of the educational activities of the schools); Rev. Rul. 64-286, 1964-2 C.B. 401 (holding that the general board of a church that made purchases for the exclusive use of parochial schools and missions shared the exempt status of the primary educational organization); Rev. Rul. 71-553, 1971-2 C.B. 404 (where a student government association was ruled to be an integral part of a university).

[334] Rev. Rul. 74-146, *supra* note 240.

[335] See *supra* § 6.

[336] Rev. Rul. 75-282, *supra* note 92.

[337] See *supra* § 5.

[338] Rev. Rul. 75-359, 1975-2 C.B. 79.

[339] Rev. Rul. 67-149, *supra* note 241; Rev. Rul. 78-310, *supra* note 232.

[340] See *supra* note 326.

[341] Trustees of Graceland Cemetery Improvement Fund v. United States, 515 F.2d 763, 770 (Ct. Cl. 1975).

These cases clearly indicate that where one organization serves as a mere adjunct for a primary organization by providing services which are essential to the functioning of the primary organization and which would be normally performed by it, the adjunct will acquire the tax status of the primary company.[342]

The adjunct theory was initially invoked by a federal court of appeals in 1934.[343] The first application of this theory to adjunct entities of charitable organizations occurred in 1951. In that year, another federal appellate court reviewed the tax status of a corporation organized to operate a bookstore and restaurant on the campus of a tax-exempt college. Despite the fact that these operations were not inherently charitable or educational activities, the court of appeals invoked the rationale of the adjunct theory, writing that the "business enterprise in which [the] taxpayer is engaged obviously bears a close and intimate relationship to the functioning of the [c]ollege itself."[344] The appellate court concluded that this corporation was entitled to exemption as an educational organization.

The adjunct theory was subsequently espoused by a court, which concluded that a museum was a tax-exempt educational organization because it was an integral part of and a valuable adjunct to a public school system.[345] At issue in this case was the availability of the pre-1969 additional charitable contribution deduction of 10 percent of a taxpayer's adjusted gross income for contributions to operating educational institutions that engage in the presentation of formal instruction.[346] The court concluded that gifts to the museum qualified for the bonus charitable contribution deduction, even though the museum itself did not satisfy the statutory requirements, because it was an integral part of the school system and thus was clothed with the educational status of the system.[347]

The adjunct theory, however, does not have broad application. That is, it cannot be used to sidestep the prerequisites for tax exemption that an organization must meet under the statutory rules. As a court stated, the "adjunct doctrine has developed in unique factual settings which when reconciled do not stand for a general principle capable of eroding the statutory limitations on exemptions."[348]

---

[342] *Id.* at 771.

[343] Produce Exchange Stock Clearing Ass'n v. Helvering, 71 F.2d 142 (2d Cir. 1934).

[344] Squire v. Students Book Corp., *supra* note 239, at 1020. Also Rev. Rul. 78-41, *supra* note 93.

[345] Brundage v. Comm'r, 54 T.C. 1468 (1970). Cf. Miller v. United States, 527 F.2d 231 (8th Cir. 1975).

[346] See IRC § 170(b)(1)(A)(ii).

[347] Also Rosehill Cemetery Co. v. United States, 285 F. Supp. 21 (N.D. Ill. 1968); Industrial Aid for the Blind v. Comm'r, *supra* note 6.

[348] Knights of Columbus Bldg. Ass'n of Stamford, CT, Inc. v. United States, 88-1 U.S.T.C. ¶ 9336 (D. Conn. 1988) (holding that an organization, while closely affiliated with and principally holding title to property for a tax-exempt organization, could not qualify for exempt status under the adjunct theory because it failed to meet the requirements for exempt title-holding corporations under IRC § 501(c)(2) (see § 18.2)).

One of the principal reasons that the government has opposed tax-exempt status for a consortium entity is the fear that an organization that is not formed and controlled by charitable entities will by its own choice confine its services to charitable entities and thereby itself acquire exempt charitable status, even where the provision of its services is in competition with commercial enterprises. Of course, this factual situation is easily distinguishable from the normal consortium arrangement, but this concern nonetheless persists.

The government's concerns in this regard were presumably largely alleviated by a court decision holding that an organization that planned to offer consulting services for a fee to a class of nonprofit (but not all tax-exempt) organizations did not qualify as an exempt charitable entity but was taxable as a business.[349] The court's opinion might have been different, however, had the organization confined its clientele to charitable organizations (even though not controlled by them), not set its fees to return a considerable net profit, and been able to demonstrate that its services would not be in competition with commercial businesses.

An IRS private letter ruling is at odds with its public pronouncements and positions on this point. The matter concerned an organization the members of which were nonprofit universities and municipal libraries, and that operated a computer network to enable its members to exchange information concerning the availability of books and other research materials in the libraries throughout a particular state. The IRS previously determined that the organization was tax-exempt as a charitable entity, apparently for the reason that its programs were inherently exempt in nature.[350] The issue was whether the organization could, without jeopardy to its exempt status or receipt of unrelated business income, extend its services to various private businesses (such as banks, utilities, and automotive, chemical, and pharmaceutical industries). The IRS held that "in making your information dissemination services available to private institutions on the same basis, and for the same fee, as services are provided to your members you are serving your exempt purpose of disseminating useful bibliographic information to researchers."[351]

A well-known consortium is The Common Fund, a cooperative arrangement formed by a group of colleges and universities for the collective investment of their funds, which the IRS ruled was a tax-exempt charitable organization. During its formative years, the administrative expenses of the Fund were largely met by start-up grants from a private foundation. As the Fund became more reliant on payments from its member institutions, however, it became unqualified for status as an exempt charitable entity, according to the IRS, because of the donative element test, in that the Fund's services were no longer being provided to members at a charge of no more than 15 percent of costs. In the face of prospective loss of the Fund's exemption, Congress legis-

---

[349] B.S.W. Group, Inc. v. Comm'r, 70 T.C. 352 (1978).
[350] Rev. Rul. 74-614, *supra* note 242.
[351] Priv. Ltr. Rul. 7951134.

lated the rule that cooperative arrangements such as The Common Fund are exempt charitable organizations.[352]

The legislative history of The Common Fund provision stated that it applies only to cooperative organizations formed and controlled by the participating institutions themselves, rather than to private organizations furnishing the same services, even where those services might be made available only to educational organizations. Congress stated that, in enacting this statute, "it is not intended that any inference be drawn as to the exempt status of other organizations formed by educational institutions or by other charities on their behalf to carry out their normal functions in a cooperative manner."[353]

Congress changed the law in this area in one respect in 1976.[354] It had been the position of the IRS that income derived by a tax-exempt hospital from providing services to other exempt hospitals constitutes unrelated business income to the hospital providing the services, on the rationale that the provision of services to other hospitals is not an activity that is substantially related to the exempt purposes of the provider hospital.[355] Congress acted to override this position in the case of small hospitals where an exempt hospital[356] provides services only to other exempt hospitals, as long as each of the recipient hospitals has facilities to serve no more than 100 inpatients and the services are consistent with the recipient hospitals' exempt purposes if performed by them on their own behalf.[357]

This law change was implemented to enable a number of small hospitals to receive services from a single institution instead of providing them directly or creating a tax-exempt organization to provide the services. Language in the legislative history, however, is somewhat broader than the specifics of this rule, inasmuch as the Senate Finance Committee explanation stated that a hospital is not engaged in an unrelated trade or business "simply because it provides services to other hospitals if those services could have been provided, on a tax-free basis, by a cooperative organization consisting of several tax-exempt hospitals."[358]

The U.S. Supreme Court held that a cooperative hospital laundry organization did not qualify for tax exemption as a charitable entity.[359] Such an organization is, of course, a type of consortium. The Court ruled in opposition to

---

[352] IRC § 501(f). See § 10.5.

[353] S. Rep. No. 93-888, 93d Cong., 2d Sess. 3 (1974).

[354] IRC § 513(e). See § 27.2(g).

[355] Rev. Rul. 69-633, 1969-2 C.B. 121. The IRS, however, held that the provision by a tax-exempt organization of administrative services for unrelated exempt organizations constitutes the performance of an unrelated business (Tech. Adv. Mem. 8032039), which held open the possibility that services to related organizations may be considered related activities. This aspect of the law has been clarified (see § 26.5(i)).

[356] IRC § 170(b)(1)(A)(iii). See §§ 6.2(a), 11.3(a).

[357] The services provided must be confined to those described in IRC § 501(e)(1)(A). See § 10.4.

[358] S. Rep. No. 94-938 (Part 2), 94th Cong., 2d Sess. 76 (1976).

[359] HCSC-Laundry v. United States, 450 U.S. 1 (1981).

exemption in this context, however, because the facts necessitated application of the rules concerning cooperative hospital organizations—a unique set of circumstances[360]—and not because the tax law is generally in opposition to exemption for consortia. Thus, for example, a court held that an organization, operated on a cooperative basis, was entitled to exempt status as a charitable organization because it was controlled by its member exempt organizations (libraries) and provided indispensable program and administrative services to them.[361] The court stated that "where a group of tax exempt organizations forms a cooperative to provide services exclusively to those tax exempt organizations, and the services provided are necessary and indispensable to the operations of the tax exempt organizations, the cooperative is a tax exempt organization."[362]

§ 6.10   INSTRUMENTALITIES OF GOVERNMENT

A wholly owned state or municipal instrumentality that is a separate entity may qualify for tax exemption as a charitable entity if it is a *clear counterpart* of a charitable, educational, religious, or like organization.[363] The test set by the IRS is based on the scope of the organization's purposes and powers, that is, whether the purposes and powers are beyond those of a charitable organization. For example, a state or municipality itself cannot qualify as a charitable organization, inasmuch as its purposes are not exclusively those inherent in charities, nor can an integral component of the state or municipality.[364]

An otherwise qualified instrumentality meeting the *counterpart* requirement, such as a school, college, university, or hospital, can be deemed a charitable organization.[365] If, however, an instrumentality is clothed with powers other than those described in the federal tax rules for charitable organizations, such as enforcement or regulatory powers in the public interest (for example, health, welfare, safety), it would not be a clear counterpart organization.

Two IRS rulings draw the contrast. In one ruling,[366] a public housing author-

---

[360] See § 10.4.

[361] The Council for Bibliographic & Information Technologies v. Comm'r, 63 T.C.M. 3186 (1992).

[362] *Id.* at 3188. This court concluded that the Supreme Court decision, *supra* note 359, is confined to cooperative hospital organizations, *citing* Chart, Inc. v. United States, 491 F. Supp. 10 (D.D.C. 1979), *rev'd*, 652 F.2d 195 (D.C. Cir. 1981).

This "necessary and indispensable" analysis was applied in a case involving an organization providing insurance services to its member charitable organizations; in denying tax exemption on this ground, the court wrote that "providing insurance to 487 unrelated exempt organizations is not an activity that is vital to each member's exempt purpose" and that such a service "neither goes to the essence of running each of . . . [the] member organizations nor constitutes an activity which would normally be performed by the member organizations" (Nonprofits' Ins. Alliance of Calif. v. United States, 94-2 U.S.T.C. ¶ 50,593 (Cl. Ct. 1994)). See, however, § 10.6.

[363] Rev. Rul. 60-384, 1960-2 C.B. 172; Rev. Rul. 55-319, 1955-1 C.B. 119; Estate of Slayton v. Comm'r, 3 B.T.A. 1343 (1926).

[364] Cf. IRC § 115(a).

[365] E.g., Estate of Ethel P. Green v. Comm'r, 82 T.C. 843 (1984); Rev. Rul. 67-290, 1967-2 C.B. 183.

[366] Rev. Rul. 74-14, 1974-1 C.B. 125.

ity was denied tax exemption as a charitable organization, even though its purpose was to provide safe and sanitary dwelling accommodations for low-income families in a particular municipality. The state statute under which it was incorporated conferred upon it the power to conduct examinations and investigations, administer oaths, issue subpoenas, and make its findings and recommendations available to appropriate agencies; these powers were ruled to be regulatory or enforcement powers. By contrast, in the other ruling,[367] a public library organized under a state statute was ruled to be a counterpart to a charitable organization and hence exempt. The organization had the power to determine the tax rate necessary to support its operations within specified maximum and minimum rates; since the organization lacked the power to impose or levy taxes, the power was deemed not regulatory or enforcement in nature.

Until 1975, the IRS had not specifically distinguished between state instrumentalities and state political subdivisions.[368] In that year, the IRS made the distinction, ruling that an association of counties in a state constituted an instrumentality of the state or the counties (themselves political subdivisions) but not a political subdivision of the state.[369]

In 1957,[370] the IRS promulgated criteria for classification of an entity as an instrumentality of a state:

> In cases involving the status of an organization as an instrumentality of one or more states or political subdivisions, the following factors are taken into consideration: (1) whether it is used for a governmental purpose and performs a governmental function; (2) whether performance of its function is on behalf of one or more states or political subdivisions; (3) whether there are any private interests involved, or whether the states or political subdivision involved have the powers and interests of an owner; (4) whether control and supervision is vested in public authority or authorities; (5) if express or implied statutory or other authority is necessary for the creation and/or use of such an instrumentality and whether such authority exists; and (6) the degree of financial autonomy and the source of its operating expenses.

According to the government, however, an additional characteristic differentiates a political subdivision from a state instrumentality: the former has been delegated the right to exercise part of the sovereign government power of the governmental unit of which it is a division (or is a municipal corporation).[371] Thus, the association of counties referenced above was denied status as a political subdivision of the state because it was not delegated any of the counties' or state's sovereign powers. The IRS ruled that the association was nonetheless a qualified donee for charitable contribution purposes, however, with contribu-

[367] Rev. Rul. 74-15, 1974-1 C.B. 126.
[368] See § 18.17.
[369] Rev. Rul. 75-359, *supra* note 338.
[370] Rev. Rul. 57-128, 1957-1 C.B. 311.
[371] Reg. § 1.103(b).

tions deductible as being "for the use of" political subdivisions (that is, the counties), subject to the annual limitation of 20 percent of the donor's contribution base.[372]

A state law characterization of an entity's status as a governmental unit is overridden for federal tax purposes by the criteria established in 1957. For example, the University of Illinois has been determined by the supreme court of that state to be a "public corporation."[373] Because the University met the criteria promulgated in 1957 and has been delegated the right to exercise part of the sovereign power of the State of Illinois, it constitutes a political subdivision of the state. (The IRS and the courts have recognized that the education of its citizens is an essential governmental function of a state.[374]) Thus, a state college or university (and comparable entities such as state hospitals) may qualify as both a clear counterpart state instrumentality (and thus have tax exemption as a charitable entity) and a political subdivision because its activities, in addition to those described in the 1957 criteria, are neither regulatory nor enforcement powers.[375] It is the position of the IRS, however, that most state universities cannot qualify as political subdivisions.[376]

The foregoing analysis by the IRS did not take into account the consequence of operation of the adjunct theory.[377] By this theory, the association of counties could have been regarded as a political subdivision of the state rather than an instrumentality of the state, inasmuch as the characteristics of the counties are attributable to the association.[378]

The IRS ruled on several occasions as to whether an entity is a political subdivision or a state instrumentality. The IRS characterized a county board of education as an instrumentality of a state in the fact statement of a ruling, but then concluded that the board qualified as a political subdivision.[379] Similarly, the IRS ruled that a governor's conference was a political subdivision of a state.[380] Also, an organization created by the governors of 11 states to foster interstate cooperation and to otherwise coordinate action among these states was ruled to be an instrumentality of the states.[381] Likewise, the IRS held that an industrial commission established by a state legislature to study the problems of industrial life in a geographic area are qualified as a charitable donee.[382]

Reversing an earlier position, the IRS ruled that an incorporated integrated

---

[372] IRC § 170(b)(1)(B).

[373] The People ex rel. The Board of Trustees of the Univ. of Ill. v. Barrett, 46 N.E.2d 951 (Ill. 1943).

[374] Rev. Rul. 75-436, 1975-2 C.B. 217; Gilliam v. Adams, 171 S.W.2d 813 (Tenn. 1943).

[375] Cf. Rev. Rul. 74-14, *supra* note 366.

[376] Rev. Rul. 77-165, 1977-1 C.B. 21. See the discussion in § 18.17.

[377] See text accompanied by *supra* notes 340–348.

[378] E.g., Brundage v. Comm'r, *supra* note 345. Cf. Miller v. United States, *supra* note 345; Puerto Rico Marine Mgt., Inc. v. International Longshoremen's Ass'n, 398 F. Supp. 118 (D.P.R. 1975).

[379] Rev. Rul. 70-562, 1970-2 C.B. 63.

[380] Rev. Rul. 69-459, 1969-2 C.B. 35.

[381] Priv. Ltr. Rul. 7935043.

[382] Rev. Rul. 79-323, 1979-2 C.B. 106.

state bar did not qualify as an instrumentality or political subdivision of a state.[383] The IRS reasoned that the state bar was a "dual purpose" organization, in that it had public purposes (such as admission, suspension, disbarment, and reprimand of licensed lawyers) and private purposes (such as the protection of professional interests of its members), and thus that it was "not an arm of the state because it is a separate entity and has private as well as public purposes." The IRS also held that the state bar was "not a political subdivision because it has no meaningful sovereign powers."

A committee, created by joint resolution of a state legislature, established to receive and expend contributions to provide state units for a parade incident to a presidential inauguration, was ruled to be a political subdivision.[384] A committee that was created by a governor's executive order to educate the public about the activities of the United Nations was considered a political subdivision of the state.[385] Under appropriate circumstances, a nonprofit corporation may qualify as a political subdivision of a state.[386]

The IRS considered the question of whether a nonprofit membership corporation qualified as a political subdivision.[387] The members of the corporation consisted of representatives of the local chambers of commerce and other private business groups in a particular county, the county commissioners, and officials of participating municipalities. There was no private inurement, and the corporation's articles provided that upon any dissolution of the corporation the beneficial interest in any property owned by the corporation would pass the county.

The IRS held that obligations of this type of a corporation would be considered issued *on behalf* of the state or political subdivision of the state, provided each of the following requirements was met: the corporation engaged in activities that are essentially public in nature; the corporation must be one that is not organized for profit (except to the extent of retiring indebtedness); the corporate income must not inure to any private person; the state or a political subdivision thereof must have a beneficial interest in the corporation while the indebtedness remains outstanding and it must obtain full legal title to the property of the corporation with respect to which the indebtedness was incurred upon the retirement of such indebtedness; and the corporation must have been approved by the state or a political subdivision of the state.[388]

State liquor stores are generally considered political subdivisions, as being part of the states' effort to regulate the use of alcohol.[389] Lawyers' trust accounts,

---

[383] Rev. Rul. 77-232, 1977-2 C.B. 71, revoking Rev. Rul. 59-152, 1959-1 C.B. 54. This change in classification also means that contributions to these state bars are not deductible under IRC §§ 170(c)(1), 2055(a)(1), and 2522(a)(1).

[384] Rev. Rul. 58-265, 1958-1 C.B. 172.

[385] Rev. Rul. 62-66, 1962-1 C.B. 83.

[386] Rev. Rul. 59-41, 1959-1 C.B. 13; Rev. Rul. 54-296, 1954-2 C.B. 59.

[387] Rev. Rul. 63-20, 1963-1 C.B. 24.

[388] Also Rev. Rul. 60-243, 1960-2 C.B. 35; Rev. Rul. 57-187, 1957-1 C.B. 65.

[389] Rev. Rul. 71-132, 1971-1 C.B. 29; Rev. Rul. 71-131, 1971-1 C.B. 28.

created and supervised by a state's supreme court, are exempt from federal income tax as an integral part of the state.[390]

A federal court of appeals held that a *political subdivision* is any division of any state that has been delegated the right to exercise part of the sovereign power of the state.[391] The appellate court observed that the term *political subdivision* is "broad and comprehensive and denotes any division of the State made by the proper authorities thereof, acting within their constitutional powers, for the purpose of those functions of the State which by long usage and the inherent necessities of government have always been regarded as public."[392]

A state supreme court observed that the "[i]mportant factors, among others, which must be considered in determining that . . . [a]n agency is an instrument of government are [whether]: (1) [i]t was created by the government; (2) it is wholly owned by the government; (3) it is not operated for profit; (4) it is primarily engaged in the performance of some essential governmental function; [and] (5) the proposed tax will impose an economic burden upon the government, or it serves to materially impair the usefulness or efficiency of the agency, or to materially restrict it in the performance of its duties."[393]

An organization may seek instrumentality status rather than tax exemption as a charitable entity to avoid the annual reporting requirements, the private foundation rules, other federal tax limitations on charitable groups, or because it cannot qualify as charitable in nature. Contributions to instrumentalities are deductible as long as they qualify as a *governmental unit* and the gift is made for exclusively public purposes;[394] the interest they pay on their borrowings generally is exempt from the lender's gross income.[395]

§ 6.11 OTHER CATEGORIES OF CHARITABLE ORGANIZATIONS

There are several other categories of tax-exempt charitable organizations. Many of these do not fit within any of the traditional definitions of *charitable* function.

---

[390] Rev. Rul. 87-2, 1987-1 C.B. 18. Also Rev. Rul. 81-209, 1981-2 C.B. 16.
[391] Comm'r v. Estate of Alexander J. Shamberg, 3 T.C. 131 (1944), *aff'd*, 144 F.2d 998 (2d Cir. 1944), *cert. den.*, 323 U.S. 792 (1944).
[392] *Id.*, 144 F.2d 16 1004.
[393] Unemployment Compensation Comm'n of N.C. v. Wachovia Bank & Trust Co., 2 S.E.2d 592, 596 (N.C. 1939). Also City of Bay Minette v. Quinly, 82 So.2d 192 (Ala. 1955); War Memorial Hosp. of District No. 1 v. Bd. of County Comm'rs of County of Park, 279 P.2d 472 (Wyo. 1955); City of Cincinnati v. Gamble, 34 N.E.2d 226 (Ohio 1941); Gebhardt v. Village of La Grange Park, 188 N.E. 372, 374 (Ill. 1933).
[394] IRC §§ 170(c)(1), 170(b)(1)(A)(v).
[395] IRC § 103(a)(1). Cf. State of S.C. v. Baker, 485 U.S. 505 (1988). In general, Aprill, "The Integral, the Essential, and the Instrumental: Federal Income Tax Treatment of Governmental Affiliates," 23 *Exempt Org. Tax Rev.* (No. 2) 263 (Feb. 1999).

(a) Environmental Protection

An organization established to promote environmental conservancy is a tax-exempt charitable entity.[396] The IRS ruled that it is "generally recognized that efforts to preserve and protect the natural environment for the benefit of the public serve a charitable purpose."[397] The IRS concluded that the organization involved was "enhancing the accomplishment of the express national policy of conserving the nation's unique natural resources."[398] The IRS, however, refused to classify an organization as an exempt charitable entity where it merely restricted land uses that did not change the environment, where the land lacked any "distinctive ecological significance," and where any public benefit was "too indirect and insignificant."[399]

Nonetheless, the position of the IRS that only land of "distinctive ecological significance" can qualify as a tax-exempt function holding of an environmental conservation organization was implicitly rejected by a court when it accorded classification as an exempt charitable organization to a model farm operated as a conservation project.[400] The organization's land was "generally representative of the surrounding farmland in the county" and the organization "readily admit[ed] its land does not have special environmental attributes, nor is the land part of an ecologically significant undeveloped area such as a swamp, marsh, forest, or other wilderness tract."[401] Instead, the organization's "goal is to test and demonstrate the restoration of over-cultivated, exhausted land to a working ecological balance."[402] The organization simply "encourages more local practice of the farming and conservation techniques it is developing."[403] Rather than focus on the nature of the land as such, the court emphasized the use of the land: The organization's "agricultural program seeks to demonstrate the commercial viability of ecologically sound farming techniques not yet practiced in the surrounding community."[404]

(b) Promotion of Patriotism

The IRS concluded that the promotion of patriotism is a charitable objective. The ruling came in the case of a membership organization, formed by citizens of a community to promote "civic pride in the community, state, and the country," by providing a color guard and conducting flag-raising and other ceremonies at patriotic and community functions.[405] As authority for this position, the IRS stated

---

[396] Rev. Rul. 76-204, *supra* note 270. Also Rev. Rul. 80-279, 1980-2 C.B. 176, Rev. Rul. 80-278, 1980-2 C.B. 175; Rev. Rul. 75-207, 1975-1 C.B. 361; Rev. Rul. 70-186, *supra* note 178; Rev. Rul. 67-292, *supra* note 183.
[397] Rev. Rul. 76-204, *supra* note 270, at 153.
[398] *Id.*
[399] Rev. Rul. 78-384, *supra* note 270.
[400] Dumaine Farms v. Comm'r, 73 T.C. 650 (1980).
[401] *Id.* at 653.
[402] *Id.*
[403] *Id.*
[404] *Id.* at 656.
[405] Rev. Rul. 78-84, 1978-1 C.B. 150.

that trusts created for the purpose of "inculcating patriotic emotions have been upheld as charitable, as have trusts for the purchase and display of a flag, and for the celebration of a patriotic holiday."[406]

(c) Promotion of Sports

A court held that the promotion, advancement, and sponsoring of recreational and amateur sports is a charitable activity.[407] The organization involved owned and operated an amateur baseball team that played in a semiprofessional league, leased and maintained a baseball field used by its team and other teams, furnished instructors and coaches for a baseball camp, and provided coaches for Little League teams. The players were not paid for their participation on the team, although they received free lodging and were guaranteed employment in local industries during the season. The government's contention that the team was semiprofessional, and thus that the operation of it was a nonexempt activity, was rejected.[408]

(d) Public Interest Law

Organizations structured as *public interest law firms*—entities that provide legal representation for important citizen interests that are unrepresented because the cases are not economically feasible for private law firms—can qualify as tax-exempt charitable organizations where they provide a "service which is of benefit to the community as a whole," with "[c]haritability ... also dependent upon the fact that the service provided by public interest law firms is distinguishable from that which is commercially available."[409] The recognition by the IRS that public interest law firms can be charitable in nature was significant, in that beforehand the agency would not recognize as exempt an organization operating in support of interests of a majority of the public since that segment of society does not constitute a charitable class.[410]

In guidelines containing criteria for these firms, the IRS acknowledged that legal representation for disadvantaged minorities, victims of racial discrimination, and those denied human and civil rights has long been recognized as a charitable activity.[411]

---

[406] Citing IV *Scott on Trusts* (3d ed. 1967) § 374.3; Bogert, *Trusts and Trustees* (2d ed. 1964) § 378. Also Buder v. United States, 7 F.3d 1382 (8th Cir. 1993) (where a trust, established to foster and promote the cause of patriotism, loyalty, and fundamental constitutional government (and to combat subversive activities, socialism, and communism), was held to qualify as a tax-exempt charitable entity).

[407] Hutchinson Baseball Enters., Inc. v. Comm'r, 73 T.C. 144 (1979), aff'd, 696 F.2d 757 (10th Cir. 1982). Where, however, the sports organization is primarily established to further social or recreational interests, tax exemption as a charitable organization will not be available (Wayne Baseball, Inc. v. Comm'r, 78 T.C.M. 437 (1999); North Am. Sequential Sweepstakes v. Comm'r, 77 T.C. 1087 (1981)).

[408] This case did not involve the IRC § 501(c)(3) provision for certain amateur sports organizations. See § 10.2.

[409] Rev. Rul. 75-74, *supra* note 42.

[410] See § 5.5(a).

[411] Rev. Proc. 71-39, 1971-2 C.B. 575. In general, see *supra* § 7.

These guidelines state that the "engagement of the organization in litigation can reasonably be said to be in representation of a broad public interest rather than a private interest." In addition to generally complying with the requirements of the federal tax law rules concerning charitable organizations, the IRS guidelines for the public interest law firm require the following: (1) it may accept fees for services rendered but only in accordance with specific IRS procedures; (2) it may not have a program of "disruption of the judicial system, illegal activity, or violation of applicable canons of ethics"; (3) it files with its annual information return a description of cases litigated and the "rationale for the determination that they would benefit the public generally";[412] (4) its policies and programs are the responsibility of a "board or committee representative of the public interest," not controlled by its employees or those who litigate on its behalf nor by noncharitable organizations; (5) it is not operated so as to create "identification or confusion with a particular private law firm"; and (6) there is no "arrangement to provide, directly or indirectly, a deduction for the cost of litigation which is for the private benefit of the donor."

Subsequently, the IRS promulgated procedures for the acceptance of fees by these firms.[413] In essence, these procedures forbid a firm from seeking fees from clients; allow the acceptance of fees where paid by opposing parties under court or agency award; require the firm to use awarded fees solely to defray normal operating expenses, with no more than one-half of such costs (calculated over five years) so defrayed; and require the firm to file with its annual information return a report of all fees sought and recovered.

The IRS recognized that the awarding of lawyers' fees serves to effectuate a legislative or judicial policy in deterring or encouraging certain actions.[414] Thus, the agency concluded, the "award or acceptance of attorneys' fees by public interest law firms in these situations is consistent with and tends to support the statutory and public policy objectives in awarding such fees," and this type of a firm constitutes a tax-exempt charitable organization as long as it is "clear that neither the expectation nor the possibility, however remote, of an award of fees is a substantial motivating factor in the selection of cases."[415] By contrast, where the firm has an "established policy of charging or accepting attorneys' fees from its clients, the representation provided cannot be distinguished from that available through traditional private law firms" and the exemption as a charitable entity will be denied or revoked.[416] Similarly, a public interest law firm will lose its exemption if it enters into a fee-sharing arrangement with a private lawyer who will keep a portion of a

---

[412] Failure, absent reasonable cause, by a public interest law firm to comply with this filing requirement constitutes a failure to file a return under IRC § 6652(d)(1) (see § 24.3(vii)) and revocation of tax exemption is a valid sanction, according to the IRS (Gen. Couns. Mem. 37159).

[413] Rev. Proc. 75-13, 1975-1 C.B. 662.

[414] Citing Mills v. Electric Auto-Lite Co., 396 U.S. 375 (1970); Newman v. Piggie Park Enters., Inc., 309 U.S. 400 (1968).

[415] Rev. Rul. 75-76, 1975-1 C.B. 154.

[416] Rev. Rul. 75-75, 1975-1 C.B. 154.

court-awarded fee that exceeds the amount paid by the firm to the lawyer for services rendered.[417]

(e) Local Economic Development Corporations

A form of tax-exempt charitable organization is the *local economic development corporation* (LEDC). LEDCs engage in a variety of activities, including investment in local businesses; direct operation of job-training, housing, and other programs; business counseling; and encouragement to established national businesses to open plants or offices in economically depressed areas. A prime purpose of an LEDC is to alleviate poverty—clearly a charitable purpose.[418] By necessity, however, LEDCs render assistance to commercial business enterprises and make investments in businesses as part of their principal function. While these activities are not normally regarded as charitable in nature, there is authority for a determination that these LEDCs engage in charitable endeavors.

The IRS ruled that an organization is tax-exempt as a charitable entity (as promoting social welfare[419]) where it maintained a program of providing low-cost financial assistance and other aid designed to improve economic conditions and economic opportunities in economically depressed areas.[420] The organization undertook to combat these conditions by providing funds and working capital to business corporations or individual proprietors who were unable to obtain funds from conventional commercial sources because of the poor financial risks involved. The IRS noted that "these loans and purchases of equity interest are not undertaken for purpose of profit or gain but for the purpose of advancing the charitable goals of the organization and are not investments for profit in any conventional business sense."[421]

It is possible for an LEDC to qualify for tax exemption as a charitable entity even though it is licensed as a nonprofit small business investment company (SBIC) under the Small Business Investment Act.[422] A SBIC licensee is required to comply with certain regulations promulgated by the Small Business Administration (SBA) that set requirements as to the level of interest rates charged by a licensee and impose various restrictions on the degree of financial support that may be offered to a prospective recipient. The difficulty is that an SBA-regulated SBIC may be prevented from engaging in certain loan transac-

---

[417] Rev. Rul. 76-5, 1976-1 C.B. 146. In general, Houck, "With Charity for All," 93 *Yale L. J.* 1415 (1984); Note, "Public Interest Law Firms and Client-Paid Fees," 33 *Tax Law.* 915 (1980); Hobbet, "Public Interest Law Firms—To Fee or Not to Fee," 27 *Nat'l Tax J.* 45 (1974); Chomsky, "Tax-Exempt Status of Public Interest Law Firms," 45 *S. Cal. L. Rev.* 228 (1972); Note, "IRS Man Cometh: Public Interest Law Firms Meet the Tax Collector," 13 *Ariz. L. Rev.* 857 (1971); Goldberg & Cohen, "Does higher authority than IRS guidelines exist for public interest law firms?," 34 *J. Tax.* 77 (1971).

[418] See *supra* § 1.

[419] See *supra* § 7.

[420] Rev. Rul. 74-587, supra note 292.

[421] *Id.* at 163.

[422] 15 U.S.C. § 681(d).

tions in which it would otherwise be able to engage in furtherance of charitable purposes. Although a "narrower range of permissible transactions" is available to an SBIC than to non-SBA regulated LEDCs, the IRS concluded that the SBIC "may still provide loans to businesses that cannot secure financing through conventional commercial sources, the operation of which businesses will achieve charitable purposes. . . ."[423] Thus, although this ruling does not mean that all SBA-regulated SBICs are automatically exempt LEDCs, it does not mean that the mere fact that the organization is subject to the SBA regulations does not preclude it from exemption.

Subsequently, the IRS distinguished the situation involved in its prior ruling from that where the primary purpose of the organization is to promote business in general rather than to provide assistance only to businesses owned by minority groups or to businesses experiencing difficulty because of their location in a deteriorated section of the community. Thus, the IRS denied classification as a tax-exempt charitable entity to an organization formed to increase business patronage in a deteriorated area mainly inhabited by minority groups by providing information on the area's shopping opportunities, local transportation, and accommodations, and to an organization the purpose of which was to revive retail sales in an area suffering from continued economic decline by constructing a shopping center in the area to arrest the flow of business to competing centers in outlying areas.[424]

(f) Other Charitable Organizations

The IRS ruled that the term *charitable* includes the "care of orphans."[425] The occasion was consideration of the tax status of an organization that arranged for the placement of orphan children living in foreign countries with adoptive parents in the United States. The agency also determined that "facilitating student and cultural exchanges" is a charitable activity.[426]

Although a federal court allowed an estate tax charitable contribution deduction for a bequest to a "public" cemetery because of the "important social function" it performed and the "concurrent lessening of the burden of the public fisc,"[427] the decision was overturned on appeal on the grounds that Congress has not enacted an estate tax counterpart to the income tax exemption provision for cemetery companies[428] and that the common-law definition of the term *charity* in the income tax context cannot be imported into the estate tax field.[429] The appel-

---

[423] Rev. Rul. 81-284, *supra* note 292. The IRS likewise recognized that an IRC § 501(c)(3) organization can provide funding for a minority enterprise small business investment company (Gen. Couns. Mem. 38497).

[424] Rev. Rul. 77-111, *supra* note 292. In general, Buehler, "Community Development and Tax-Exempt Business Incubators," 2 *J. Tax. Exempt Orgs.* 16 (Spring 1990).

[425] Rev. Rul. 80-200, 1980-2 C.B. 173.

[426] Rev. Rul. 80-286, *supra* note 267.

[427] Mellon Bank v. United States, 509 F. Supp. 160 (W.D. Pa. 1984).

[428] IRC § 501(c)(13). See § 18.6.

[429] Mellon Bank v. United States, 762 F.2d 283 (3d Cir. 1985), *cert. den.,* 475 U.S. 1031 (1986).

late court was unable to discern why Congress elected to treat contributions to cemetery organizations differently for income and estate tax deduction purposes, regarding the matter as an "anomaly" that must be left to "congressional wisdom."[430] The attempt by the lower court to categorize public cemeteries as charities because the "maintenance of cemetery facilities by cemetery associations benefits the community both through its aesthetic effects and by the performance of a necessary social task"[431] thus failed.[432]

A court concluded that the purpose of "maintain[ing] public confidence in the legal system" through "various means of improving the administration of justice" is charitable.[433] By contrast, a court refused to regard as charitable the object to "encourage, foster, promote and perpetuate outdoor activities."[434]

---

[430] *Id.* at 286. Also Child v. United States, 540 F.2d 579 (2d Cir. 1976), *cert. den.*, 429 U.S. 1092 (1977).

[431] Mellon Bank v. United States, *supra* note 427, at 164.

[432] In general, Note, "Estate Tax—Charitable Deduction: Cemetery Not a Charitable Organization," 18 *B.C. Ind. & Comm. L. Rev.* 955 (1977).

[433] Kentucky Bar Found., Inc. v. Comm'r, *supra* note 133, at 930.

[434] Greiss v. United States, 57-1 U.S.T.C. ¶ 11,659 (N. D. Ill. 1956) (where the court observed that such a "wide-sweeping, dragnet purpose would embrace many varied activities not contemplated by" the concept of charity).

CHAPTER SEVEN

Educational Organizations

Section 501(a) of the Internal Revenue Code provides federal income tax exemption for organizations described in IRC § 501(c)(3), including entities that are organized and operated exclusively for *educational* purposes.[1] There is some overlap in this area with the classification of organizations as being charitable entities, inasmuch as the term *charitable* includes the *advancement of education*.[2]

§ 7.1 FEDERAL TAX LAW DEFINITION OF *EDUCATIONAL*

Federal tax law defines the term *educational* as encompassing far more than formal schooling. Basically, the concept of *educational* as used for federal tax purposes is defined as relating to the "instruction or training of the individual for the purpose of improving or developing his capabilities" or the "instruction of the public on subjects useful to the individual and beneficial to the community."[3]

For many years, the definition accorded the term *educational* by the Department of the Treasury and the IRS was routinely followed. In 1980, however, a federal court of appeals found portions of the regulation defining the term unconstitutionally vague.[4] That segment of the regulation—pertaining to a *full and fair exposition test*[5]—permits materials that advocate a viewpoint to qualify as being educational in nature but only if the advocacy is preceded by an objective discussion of the issue or subject involved. Subsequently, this appellate court—albeit recognizing the "inherently general nature of the term 'educational' and the

---

[1] Also Reg. § 1.501(c)(3)-1(d)(1)(i)(f).
[2] See § 6.6.
[3] Reg. § 1.501(c)(3)-1(d)(3)(i).
[4] Big Mama Rag, Inc. v. United States, 631 F.2d 1030 (D.C. Cir. 1980).
[5] See *infra* § 2.

wide range of meanings Congress may have intended to convey," and stating that "[w]e do not attempt a definition" of the term—set forth some general criteria as to what material may qualify as educational.[6]

In the subsequent case, this federal appellate court decided that the materials there at issue "fall short" of being educational, "[e]ven under the most minimal requirement of a rational development of a point of view."[7] Said the court: "It is the fact that there is no reasoned development of the conclusions which removes it [the material at issue] from any definition of 'educational' conceivably intended by Congress."[8] Moreover, the court ruled, "in order to be deemed 'educational' and enjoy tax exemption some degree of intellectually appealing development of or foundation for the views advocated would be required."[9] The court wrote: "The exposition of propositions the correctness of which is readily demonstrable is doubtless educational. As the truth of the view asserted becomes less and less demonstrable, however, 'instruction' or 'education' must, we think, require more than mere assertion and repetition."[10] Thereafter, the court observed that, in "attempting a definition suitable for all comers, IRS, or any legislature, court, or other administrator is beset with difficulties which are obvious."[11]

Thus, the federal tax law does not contain a threshold, generic definition of the term *educational*, but rests on the concept that subjects spoken or written about must be objectively developed or founded.

§ 7.2 *EDUCATION* VERSUS *PROPAGANDA*

Inherent in the concept of *educational* is the principle that an organization is not educational in nature where it zealously propagates particular ideas or doctrines without presentation of them in any reasonably objective or balanced manner. The point is reflected in the income tax regulations that define the term *educational*, where it is stated: "An organization may be educational even though it advocates a particular position or viewpoint so long as it presents a sufficiently full and fair exposition of the pertinent facts as to permit an individual or the public to form an independent opinion or conclusion. On the other hand, an organization is not educational if its principal function is the mere presentation of unsupported opinion."[12]

This requirement is designed to exclude from the concept of *educational* the technique of the dissemination of *propaganda*, a term that also is considered in the

[6] National Alliance v. United States, 710 F.2d 868, 873 (D.C. Cir. 1983).
[7] *Id.*
[8] *Id.*
[9] *Id.*
[10] *Id.*
[11] *Id.*
[12] Reg. § 1.501(c)(3)-1(d)(3)(i).

context of the rules governing legislative activities by charitable organizations.[13] In this context, it can be said that the term *educational* does not extend to "public address with selfish or ulterior purpose and characterized by the coloring or distortion of facts."[14]

An organization may avoid the charge that its principal function is the mere presentation of unsupported opinion either by presenting a sufficiently full and fair exposition of the pertinent facts in the materials it prepares and disseminates or by circulating copies of materials that contain this type of an exposition.[15] As discussed below, this precept is now embodied in the IRS's *methodology* test. The test bears that name in reflection of the point that the method used by an organization in advocating its position, rather than the position itself, is the standard for determining whether the organization has educational purposes.

These regulations were applied by the IRS in a case involving an organization that endeavored to educate the public concerning the obligations of the broadcast media to serve the public interest. Periodically, the organization prepared evaluations of the performance of local broadcasters and made the evaluations available to the general public and governmental agencies. The IRS ruled that these evaluations were "objective" (members of the organization with a personal, professional, or business interest in a particular evaluation did not participate in the consideration) and that the organization qualified as a tax-exempt educational entity.[16]

Also, an educational organization, for federal tax purposes, may not so carry on its work as to become an *action organization*.[17] Thus the income tax regulations provide as follows:

> The fact that an organization, in carrying out its primary purpose, advocates social or civic changes or presents opinion on controversial issues with the intention of molding public opinion or creating public sentiment to an acceptance of its views does not preclude such organization from qualifying under section 501(c)(3) so long as it is not an "action" organization of any one of the types described in paragraph (c)(3) of this section.[18]

The foregoing points were illustrated by a ruling from the IRS holding that an organization operated to educate the public about homosexuality in order to foster an understanding and tolerance of homosexuals and their problems qualified as an educational entity.[19] The IRS noted that the information disseminated

---

[13] See Chapter 20.
[14] Seasongood v. Comm'r, 227 F.2d 907, 911 (6th Cir. 1955).
[15] National Ass'n for the Legal Support of Alternative Schools v. Comm'r, 71 T.C. 118 (1978).
[16] Rev. Rul. 79-26, 1979-1 C.B. 196, 197.
[17] See Chapters 20 and 21.
[18] Reg. § 1.501(c)(3)-1(d)(2).
[19] Rev. Rul. 78-305, 1978-2 C.B. 172.

by the organization was "factual" and "independently compiled," and that the materials distributed "contain a full documentation of the facts relied upon to support conclusions contained therein."[20] Further, the IRS observed that the organization "does not advocate or seek to convince individuals that they should or should not be homosexuals."[21]

By contrast, an organization, the principal activity of which was publication of a feminist monthly newspaper, was found by a federal district court to not qualify as a tax-exempt educational entity because it failed to meet the *full and fair exposition* standard.[22] The newspaper contained material designed to advance the cause of the women's movement; the organization refused to publish items it considered damaging to that cause. The court, characterizing the organization as an "advocate" that had eschewed a policy of offering any balancing facts, said that its holding "is not to say that a publication may not advocate a particular point of view and still be educational, or that it must necessarily present views inimical to its philosophy, only that in doing so it must be sufficiently dispassionate as to provide its readers with the factual basis from which they may draw independent conclusions."[23] The court rejected the assertion that the standard is a *per se* violation of the First Amendment,[24] although it observed that the regulation does not allow the IRS to censor views with which it does not agree.

On appeal, in an upset of the tax regulations concerning educational organizations, a federal court of appeals concluded that the *full and fair exposition* requirement is so vague as to violate the First Amendment.[25] The appellate court conceded that the terms in the tax-exempt organizations field, such as "religious," "charitable," and "educational," easily "lend themselves to subjective definitions at odds with the constitutional limitations."[26] The court said, however, that the full and fair exposition test lacks the "requisite clarity, both in explaining which applicant organizations are subject to the standard and in articulating its substantive requirements."[27]

The regulations state that only an organization that "advocates a particular position or viewpoint" must pass the test. The rules looked to by the IRS classify this type of an organization as one that is "controversial."[28] That, held the court, was too vague to pass First Amendment muster, because the IRS lacked any "objective standard by which to judge which applicant organizations are advocacy groups," in that the determination is made solely on the basis of a subjective evaluation of what is "controversial."[29]

---

[20] *Id.* at 173.

[21] *Id.*

[22] Big Mama Rag, Inc. v. United States, 494 F. Supp. 473 (D.D.C. 1979).

[23] *Id.* at 479.

[24] In so doing, the court relied largely upon Cammarano v. United States, 358 U.S. 498 (1959), and Hannegan v. Esquire, 327 U.S. 146 (1946).

[25] Big Mama Rag, Inc. v. United States, *supra* note 4.

[26] *Id.* at 1035.

[27] *Id.* at 1036.

[28] E.g., IRS Exempt Organizations Handbook § 345 (12); Rev. Rul. 78-305, *supra* note 19.

[29] Big Mama Rag, Inc. v. United States, *supra* note 4, at 1036.

Also, the court found wanting the requirements of the full and fair exposition standard. The court posed these questions: What is a "full and fair" exposition? Can an exposition be "fair" but not "full"? What is a "pertinent" fact? When is the exposition "sufficient" to permit persons to form an independent opinion? and who makes these determinations?[30] Noting the "futility of attempting to draw lines between fact and unsupported opinion," the appeals court observed that the district court did not actually apply the test but instead found the organization too "doctrinaire."[31] This approach was severely criticized, with the higher court writing that it "can conceive of no value-free measurement of the extent to which material is doctrinaire, and the district court's reliance on that evaluative concept corroborates for us the impossibility of principled and objective application of the fact/opinion distinction."[32]

Summarizing its findings (in words with implications reaching far beyond the specific case), the court said: "Applications for tax exemption must be evaluated, however, on the basis of criteria capable of neutral application. The standards may not be so imprecise that they afford latitude to individual IRS officials to pass judgment on the content and quality of an applicant's views and goals and therefore to discriminate against those engaged in protected First Amendment activities."[33]

In the aftermath of the voiding of the full and fair exposition test, the IRS advanced the *methodology test*, pursuant to which a presentation is evaluated by that agency to determine whether it may be *educational*, as opposed to *propaganda*. Pursuant to the methodology test, initially unveiled in litigation, the federal government endeavors (because of the free speech considerations) to avoid being the "arbiter of 'truth' " and accordingly "test[s] the method by which the advocate proceeds from the premises he furnishes to the conclusion he advocates . . ."[34]

Although a federal district court found the methodology test itself unconstitutionally vague,[35] on appeal, the appellate court did not reach the question of the constitutionality of the test, having concluded that the material at issue was not, in the first instance, educational in nature.[36] Nonetheless, the appellate court implicitly endorsed the methodology test by observing that "starting from the breadth of terms in the regulation, application by IRS of the methodology test would move in the direction of more specifically requiring, in advocacy material, an intellectually appealing development of the views advocated," that the "four criteria tend toward ensuring that the educational exemption be restricted to material which substantially helps a reader or listener in a learning process," and

---

[30] *Id.* at 1037.

[31] *Id.* at 1038.

[32] *Id.*

[33] *Id.* at 1040. In general, Comment, "Tax Exemptions for Educational Institutions: Discretion and Discrimination," 128 *U. Pa. L. Rev.* 849 (1980).

[34] National Alliance v. United States, *supra* note 6, at 874.

[35] National Alliance v. United States, 81-1 U.S.T.C. ¶ 9464 (D.D.C. 1981).

[36] National Alliance v. United States, *supra* note 6.

that the "test reduces the vagueness found" to be present in the full and fair exposition standard.[37] Indeed, the appellate court noted—without contradiction—that the "government does argue that the methodology test goes as far as humanly possible in verbalizing a line separating education from noneducational expression."[38]

The criteria of the methodology test as developed by the IRS were enunciated in a court opinion[39] and subsequently by the IRS administratively.[40] This test rests on the predicate that the IRS "renders no judgment as to the viewpoint or position of the organization." Under this test, the "method used by the organization will not be considered educational if it fails to provide a factual foundation for the viewpoint or position being advocated, or if it fails to provide a development from the relevant facts that would materially aid a listener or reader in a learning process."[41]

The "presence of any of the following factors in the presentations made by an organization is indicative that the method used by the organization to advocate its viewpoints or positions is not educational": the "presentation of viewpoints or positions unsupported by facts in a significant portion of the organization's communications," the "facts that purport to support the viewpoints or positions are distorted," the "organization's presentations make substantial use of inflammatory and disparaging terms and express conclusions more on the basis of strong emotional feelings than of objective evaluations," and the "approach used in the organization's presentations is not aimed at developing an understanding on the part of the intended audience or readership because it does not consider their background or training in the subject matter."[42] The criteria stated that "[t]here may be exceptional circumstances, however, where an organization's advocacy may be educational even if one or more of the factors listed" above are present.[43] The IRS stated that it "will look to all the facts and circumstances to determine whether an organization may be considered educational despite the presence of one or more of such factors."[44] The IRS observed that, in applying these rules, it "has attempted to eliminate or minimize the potential for any public official to impose his or her preconceptions or beliefs in determining whether the particular viewpoint or position is educational."[45] "It has been, and it remains," read the guidelines, "the policy of the Service to maintain a position of disinterested neutrality with respect to the beliefs advocated by an organization."[46]

Thus, the IRS "recognizes that the advocacy of particular viewpoints or po-

[37] National Alliance v. United States, *supra* note 6, at 875.
[38] *Id.*
[39] *Id.*
[40] Rev. Proc. 86-43, 1986-2 C.B. 729.
[41] *Id.* § 3.02.
[42] *Id.* § 3.03.
[43] *Id.* at § 3.04.
[44] *Id.*
[45] *Id.* § 2.02.
[46] *Id.*

sitions may serve an educational purpose even if the viewpoints or positions being advocated are unpopular or are not generally accepted."[47]

A court applied the methodology test and concluded that an organization's publication and other activities violated three of the four standards of the test and thus were not educational, including a finding that a significant portion of the activities "consists of the presentation of viewpoints unsupported by facts."[48] As to *substantiality*, it was written that whether an activity is substantial is a "facts-and-circumstances inquiry not always dependent upon time or expenditure percentages";[49] on the basis of the record showing the activities in question to be one of two sets of programs, the court found the noneducational activity to be substantial. The court held that the test is "not unconstitutionally vague or overbroad on its face, nor is it unconstitutional as applied."[50] It added: "Its provisions are sufficiently understandable, specific, and objective both to preclude chilling of expression protected under the First Amendment and to minimize arbitrary or discriminatory application by the IRS," because it "focuses on the method rather than the content of the presentation."[51]

§ 7.3   FORMAL EDUCATIONAL INSTITUTIONS

(a) Schools, Colleges, and Universities

Nonprofit educational institutions, such as primary, secondary, and postsecondary schools, colleges and universities, early childhood centers,[52] and trade schools, are educational organizations for federal tax law purposes.[53] These organizations all have, as required, a "regularly scheduled curriculum, a regular faculty, and a regularly enrolled body of students in attendance at the place where the educational activities are regularly carried on."[54] To be tax-exempt, however, the schools must, like all charitable organizations (as the term is used in its broadest sense), meet all of the tax law requirements pertaining to these entities, including a showing that they are operated for public, rather than private, interests.

---

[47] *Id.* § 3.01. In general, Shaviro, "From *Big Mama Rag* to *National Geographic*: The Controversy Regarding Exemptions for Educational Publications," 41 *Tax L. Rev.* (No. 4) 693 (1986); Thompson, "The Availability of the Federal Educational Tax Exemption for Propaganda Organizations," 18 *U.C. Davis L. Rev.* (No. 2) 487 (1985); Note, "Federal Income Taxation—Tax-Exempt Status for Educational Organizations in Treasury Regulation § 1.501(c)(3)-1(d)(3) is Unconstitutionally Vague in Violation of the First Amendment," 49 *Geo. Wash. L. Rev.* (No. 3) 623 (1981); Winslow & Ash, "Effects of *Big Mama Rag* on exempt educational organizations," 55 *J. Tax.* 20 (1981); Note, "*Big Mama Rag*: An Inquiry Into Vagueness," 67 *Va. L. Rev.* (No. 8) 1543 (1981).

[48] The Nationalist Movement v. Comm'r, 102 T.C. 558, 592 (1994), *aff'd*, 37 F.3d 216 (5th Cir. 1994).

[49] *Id.* 102 T.C. at 589.

[50] *Id.* at 588–589.

[51] *Id.* at 589.

[52] Michigan Early Childhood Center, Inc. v. Comm'r, 37 T.C.M. 808 (1978); San Francisco Infant School, Inc. v. Comm'r, 69 T.C. 957 (1978); Rev. Rul. 70-533, 1970-2 C.B. 112. See *infra* § 7.

[53] Reg. § 1.501(c)(3)-1(d)(3)(ii)(1).

[54] *Id.* Also IRC § 170(b)(1)(A)(ii).

This type of institution must have as its primary function the presentation of formal instruction.[55] Thus, an organization that has as its primary function the presentation of formal instruction, has courses that are interrelated and given in a regular and continuous manner (thereby constituting a regular curriculum), normally maintains a regular faculty, and has a regularly enrolled student body in attendance at the place where its educational activities are regularly carried on, qualifies as a tax-exempt educational institution.[56]

An organization may not achieve status as a tax-exempt operating educational institution where it is engaged in both educational and noneducational activities, unless the latter activities are merely incidental to the former.[57] Thus, the IRS denied tax-exempt status in the case of an organization the primary function of which was not the presentation of formal instruction but the maintenance and operation of a museum.[58]

An organization may be regarded as presenting formal instruction even though it lacks a formal course program or formal classroom instruction. Thus, an organization that provided elementary education on a full-time basis to children at a facility maintained exclusively for that purpose, with a faculty and enrolled student body, was held to be an operating educational institution despite the absence of a formal course program.[59] Similarly, an organization that conducted a survival course was granted classification as an operating educational institution, although its course periods were only 26 days and it used outdoor facilities more than classrooms, since it had a regular curriculum, faculty, and student body.[60] Similarly, an organization that operated a wilderness camping program to rehabilitate adolescents with emotional and behavioral problems was ruled to be an operating educational institution, notwithstanding the fact that its program comprised 26-day hiking and camping trips; other aspects of its program included daily demonstrations, group counseling sessions, and instruction in hiking and camping skills.[61]

By contrast, a tax-exempt organization, the primary activity of which was providing specialized instruction by correspondence and a five-to-ten-day seminar program of personal instruction for students who have completed the correspondence course, was ruled to not be an operating educational organization "[s]ince the organization's primary activity consists of providing instruction by correspondence."[62] In another instance, tutoring on a one-to-one basis in the stu-

---

[55] Reg. § 1.170A-9(b). In one instance, an organization was held to not lose its classification as an operating educational institution where it made a grant of over one half of its annual income to another organization, because the grant did not affect its instructional activities and involved almost none of its employees' time and effort (Gen. Couns. Mem. 38437).

[56] Rev. Rul. 78-309, 1978-2 C.B. 123.

[57] Reg. § 1.170A-9(b).

[58] Rev. Rul. 76-167, 1976-1 C.B. 329.

[59] Rev. Rul. 72-430, 1972-2 C.B. 105.

[60] Rev. Rul. 73-434, 1973-2 C.B. 71. Also Rev. Rul. 79-130, 1979-1 C.B. 332; Rev. Rul. 73-543, 1973-2 C.B. 343, *clar. by* Ann. 74-115, 1974-52 I.R.B. 29; Rev. Rul. 75-215, 1975-1 C.B. 335; Rev. Rul. 72-101, 1972-1 C.B. 144; Rev. Rul. 69-492, 1969-2 C.B. 36; Rev. Rul. 68-175, 1968-1 C.B. 83.

[61] Rev. Rul. 83-140, 1983-2 C.B. 185, *revoking* Rev. Rul. 80-21, 1980-1 C.B. 233.

[62] Rev. Rul. 75-492, 1975-2 C.B. 80.

dents' homes was ruled insufficient to make the tutoring organization an operating educational entity.[63]

The fact that an otherwise qualifying organization offers a variety of lectures, workshops, and short courses concerning a general subject area, open to the general public and to its members, is not sufficient for it to acquire nonprivate foundation status as an educational institution.[64] This is because this type of an "optional, heterogeneous collection of courses is not formal instruction" and does not constitute a "curriculum."[65] Where the attendees are members of the general public and can attend the functions on an optional basis, there is no "regularly enrolled body of pupils or students."[66] Further, where the functions are led by various invited authorities and personalities in the field, there is no "regular faculty."[67]

Even if an organization qualifies as a school or other type of formal educational institution, it will not be able to achieve tax-exempt status if it maintains racially discriminatory admissions policies[68] or if it benefits private interests to more than an insubstantial extent.[69] As an illustration of the latter point, an otherwise qualifying school, which trained individuals for careers as political campaign professionals, was denied exempt status because of the secondary benefit accruing to entities of a political party and its candidates, since nearly all of the school's graduates became employed by or consultants to these entities or candidates.[70]

One federal court rejected the contention of the IRS that a board of education cannot qualify as an operating educational organization. While this type of entity does not actually present formal instruction, it employs all of the teachers in a school system and maintains control over a community's school districts. The court viewed the board as an entity that merely delegated the conduct of the formal educational process to the schools administered by the school districts.[71]

(b) Museums and Similar Organizations

Museums and similar organizations may qualify as institutions that provide formal instruction and training, and therefore as tax-exempt educational entities.[72] Thus, a sports museum was held by the IRS to be an exempt educational institution, although the ruling lacked any discussion of the criteria for qualification.[73] Likewise, the agency concluded that an organization established to operate a mu-

---

[63] Rev. Rul. 76-384, 1976-2 C.B. 57. Also Rev. Rul. 76-417, 1976-2 C.B. 58.
[64] Rev. Rul. 78-82, 1978-1 C.B. 70.
[65] Rev. Rul. 62-23, 1962-1 C.B. 200.
[66] Rev. Rul. 64-128, 1964-1 (Part I) C.B. 191.
[67] Rev. Rul. 78-82, *supra* note 64.
[68] Bob Jones Univ. v. United States, 461 U.S. 574 (1983). See § 5.4(a).
[69] See § 19.10.
[70] American Campaign Academy v. Comm'r, 92 T.C. 1053 (1989).
[71] Estate of Ethel P. Green v. Comm'r, 82 T.C. 843 (1984).
[72] Reg. § 1.501(c)(3)-1(d)(3)(ii), Example (4).
[73] Rev. Rul. 68-372, 1968-2 C.B. 205.

seum, which offered, in sponsorship with an exempt university, a degree program in museology, was an exempt educational organization.[74]

The law as to what constitutes a tax-exempt *museum* is sparse. The IRS, relying on a dictionary, ruled that a museum is an institution "devoted to the procurement, care, and display of objects of lasting interest or value."[75] The agency ruled that, by obtaining items of lasting interest or value relating to a particular sport, caring for and displaying these items in an institution open to the general public, and sponsoring and carrying on activities that foster a better understanding of the history and development of the sport and people associated with it, the organization qualified as an exempt museum. Activities can include courses, seminars, and a lecture series.[76]

The IRS observed, in the context of issuance of a ruling preserving an organization's tax-exempt status, that the purpose of the organization was to "hold and manage" a "collection of works of art, artifacts, books, writings, materials and miscellaneous memorabilia pertaining to the historical and architectural heritage" of the organization's area, noting that, as part of its management of these assets, the entity will operate a museum.[77]

In another ruling, the IRS noted, in finding a museum to be tax-exempt, that it conducted the "usual activities of an art museum," namely, it maintained displays of the art for public viewing and operated a shop which offered related items for sale, such as books, posters, reproductions, and art periodicals.[78] In another ruling finding exempt status for an organization, the IRS stated that the entity "owns approximately 80 pieces of artwork in its permanent collection, and obtains for exhibition touring art collections."[79]

A court held that an organization was tax-exempt where it furnished "various educational and charitable services to the community."[80] These services were said to include the sponsorship of classes and demonstrations, and the conduct of a lecture and film series. The organization owned pieces of art which it held as a "permanent collection" and displayed in public buildings.

Still another IRS ruling involving a tax-exempt museum concerned the issue as to whether the museum could operate a gift shop and restaurant as related businesses.[81] In passing, the IRS observed that the purpose of the organization was to promote interest in and educate the public as to decoy carvings and baymen's artifacts. To that end, the organization operated a museum and acquired artifacts for display in it; it "will house, free to the public, a number of maritime exhibits and related literature." A floor of its building was used as classroom space. In addition to the exhibit, the organization engaged in "demonstrations, instructional classes, and workshops," all as educational activities.[82]

---

[74] Rev. Rul. 76-167, *supra* note 58.
[75] Rev. Rul. 68-372, *supra* note 73.
[76] Rev. Rul. 76-167, *supra* note 58.
[77] Priv. Ltr. Rul. 8444097.
[78] Priv. Ltr. Rul. 8040014.
[79] Priv. Ltr. Rul. 8634001.
[80] Goldsboro Art League, Inc. v. Comm'r, 75 T.C. 337, 339 (1980).
[81] See § 26.5(c).
[82] Priv. Ltr. Rul. 200222030.

The IRS seems most concerned about the aspect of displays of objects and public access to them. In one instance, a private foundation placed paintings in the residence of a disqualified person, as part of a large private collection; although there were occasional tours of the premises, the IRS concluded that placement of the foundation's paintings in the residence amounted to self-dealing.[83] In another case, where there was a lack of publicity and public access to a museum, an examination by the agency led to the following changes: (1) the museum facility has regular open hours, plus access at other times by appointment; (2) visitors are provided detailed material describing the history, architecture, and furnishings of the facility; (3) visitors are provided tours; (4) a permanent sign is placed at the main entrance to the facility, with information concerning the times of public access to it; (5) publication of a brochure with information about the facility, including its telephone number and times of operation; (6) distribution of the brochure to area tourism groups, such as chambers of commerce, for distribution and display at their visitor centers; (7) advertisement at least annually in a historical or antiquities interest periodical of wide circulation, with more frequent publication elsewhere; and (8) maintenance of a visitor register.[84]

An illustration of what the IRS regards as an institution *similar* to a museum was provided when the IRS categorized as a museum an organization formed to create and operate a replica of an early American village.[85] The organization, which made the village open to the public, was determined by the IRS to be "engaging in activities similar to those of a museum" and thus to be educational in nature. In so finding, the IRS relied upon one of its prior determinations in which an organization was found to be educational because it promoted an appreciation of history through the acquisition, restoration, and preservation of homes, churches, and public buildings having special historical or architectural significance and opened the structures for viewing by the general public.[86]

(c) Other Educational Organizations

Other tax-exempt educational institutions include zoos, planetariums, libraries, and symphony orchestras.[87] In this regard, a bird and animal sanctuary,[88] an international exposition,[89] and a bar association library[90] were ruled by the IRS to be educational organizations.

---

[83] Rev. Rul. 74-600, 1974-2 C.B. 385. The self-dealing rules are the subject of § 11.4(a).
[84] Tech. Adv. Mem. 9646002.
[85] Rev. Rul. 77-367, 1977-2 C.B. 193.
[86] Rev. Rul. 75-470, 1975-2 C.B. 207.
[87] Reg. § 1.501(c)(3)-1(d)(3)(ii), Example (4).
[88] Rev. Rul. 67-292, 1967-2 C.B. 184.
[89] Rev. Rul. 71-545, 1971-2 C.B. 235.
[90] Rev. Rul. 75-196, 1975-1 C.B. 155.

§ 7.4 INSTRUCTION OF INDIVIDUALS

As noted, the term *educational* for federal tax law purposes relates to the instruction or training of the individual for the purpose of improving or developing his or her capabilities.[91]

Within this category of tax-exempt educational organizations are entities the primary function of which is to provide instruction or training for a general purpose or on a particular subject, although they may not have a regular curriculum, faculty, or student body. Thus, an organization that provided educational and vocational training and guidance to nonskilled persons to improve employment opportunity was ruled to be an exempt educational organization,[92] as was an organization that conducted an industrywide apprentice training program,[93] operated community correctional centers for the rehabilitation of prisoners,[94] provided a facility and program for the rehabilitation of individuals recently released from a mental institution,[95] provided apprentice training in a skilled trade to native Americans,[96] offered instruction in basic academic subjects, speech, perceptual motor coordination, and psychological adjustment for children and adolescents with learning disabilities,[97] and provided room, board, therapy, and counseling for persons discharged from alcoholic treatment centers.[98]

Similarly, the IRS ruled tax-exempt as educational in nature an organization that maintained a government internship program for college students,[99] that provided high school graduates and college students with work experience in selected trades and professions,[100] that provided assistance to law students to obtain experience with public interest law firms and legal aid societies,[101] and that promoted student and cultural exchanges.[102] As for instruction on a particular subject, organizations that provided instruction in se-

---

[91] See the text accompanied by *supra* note 3.

[92] Rev. Rul. 73-128, 1973-1 C.B. 222.

[93] Rev. Rul. 67-72, 1967-1 C.B. 125. This conclusion was reached because the primary purpose (see § 4.4) of the organization was educational. If, however, the provision of education is secondary and the primary purpose of the organization is the betterment of the working conditions of the apprentices, the organization would be classified as a tax-exempt labor entity (see § 15.1)(Rev. Rul. 59-6, 1959-1 C.B. 121).

[94] Rev. Rul. 70-583, 1970-2 C.B. 114; Rev. Rul. 67-150, 1967-1 C.B. 133.

[95] Rev. Rul. 72-16, 1972-1 C.B. 143.

[96] Rev. Rul. 77-272, 1977-2 C.B. 191.

[97] Rev. Rul. 77-68, 1977-1 C.B. 142.

[98] Rev. Rul. 75-472, 1975-2 C.B. 208.

[99] Rev. Rul. 70-584, 1970-2 C.B. 114.

[100] Rev. Rul. 75-284, 1975-2 C.B. 202.

[101] Rev. Rul. 78-310, 1978-2 C.B. 173.

[102] Rev. Rul. 80-286, 1980-2 C.B. 179; Rev. Rul. 69-400, 1969-2 C.B. 114; Rev. Rul. 68-165, 1968-1 C.B. 253; Rev. Rul. 65-191, 1965-2 C.B. 157. By contrast, an organization that merely arranged group tours for students and faculty members of a university was ruled to not be tax-exempt as an educational organization (Rev. Rul. 67-327, 1967-2 C.B. 187).

curities management,[103] dancing,[104] sailboat racing,[105] drag car racing,[106] and the promotion of sportsmanship[107] were ruled to be tax-exempt as educational entities. The training of animals is not an educational activity, however, even where the animals' owners also receive some instruction.[108]

Another category of tax-exempt educational organizations that relates to the instruction or training of individuals includes those that conduct discussion groups, panels, forums, lectures, and the like.[109] For example, the operation of a coffee house by a number of churches, where church leaders, educators, businesspersons, and young people discussed a variety of topics, was held to be an educational endeavor.[110] Comparable organizations include those that instruct individuals as to how to improve their business or professional capabilities, such as the conduct of seminars and training programs on the subject of managing credit unions (for individuals in developing nations),[111] the practice of medicine (for physicians),[112] and banking (for bank employees).[113] Other exempt organizations in this category include an organization that conducted discussion groups and panels in order to acquaint the public with the problems of ex-convicts and parolees,[114] an organization that sponsored public workshops for training artists in concert technique,[115] and an organization that conducted clinics for the purpose of teaching a particular sport.[116] Organizations that present courses of instruction by means of correspondence or through the utilization of television or radio (and presumably the Internet) may qualify as educational in nature.[117]

If the functions of a discussion group are to a significant extent fraternal or social in nature, and where the speeches and discussions are deemed subjective and more akin to the exchanges of personal opinions and experiences in the informal atmosphere of a social group or club, the organization will not qualify as organized and operated exclusively for educational purposes.[118] Likewise, an organization that does not employ any faculty and does not provide any classes, lectures, or instructional material may be regarded, for federal tax purposes, as a social or recreational group rather than an educational organization, as was the

---

[103] Rev. Rul. 68-16, 1968-1 C.B. 246.

[104] Rev. Rul. 65-270, 1965-2 C.B. 160.

[105] Rev. Rul. 64-275, 1964-2 C.B. 142.

[106] Lions Assoc. Drag Strip v. United States, 64-1 U.S.T.C. ¶ 9283 (S.D. Cal. 1963).

[107] Rev. Rul. 55-587, 1955-2 C.B. 261.

[108] Ann Arbor Dog Training Club, Inc. v. Comm'r, 74 T.C. 207 (1980); Rev. Rul. 71-421, 1971-2 C.B. 229.

[109] Reg. § 1.501(c)(3)-1(d)(3)(ii), Example (2).

[110] Rev. Rul. 68-72, 1968-1 C.B. 250.

[111] Rev. Rul. 74-16, 1974-1 C.B. 126.

[112] Rev. Rul. 65-298, 1965-2 C.B. 163.

[113] Rev. Rul. 68-504, 1968-2 C.B. 211.

[114] Rev. Rul. 67-150, *supra* note 94.

[115] Rev. Rul. 67-392, 1967-2 C.B. 191.

[116] Rev. Rul. 65-2, 1965-1 C.B. 227, as amplified by Rev. Rul. 77-365, 1977-2 C.B. 192. Also Hutchinson Baseball Enters., Inc. v. Comm'r, 73 T.C. 144 (1979), *aff'd*, 696 F.2d 757 (10th Cir. 1982); Wayne Baseball, Inc. v. Comm'r, 78 T.C.M. 437 (1999) (see § 4.4).

[117] Reg. § 1.501(c)(3)-1(d)(3)(ii), Example (3).

[118] North Am. Sequential Sweepstakes v. Comm'r, 77 T.C. 1087 (1981).

case with a flying club that merely provided its members with an opportunity for unsupervised flight time.[119] This conclusion was also reached in a case involving an organization that arranged chess tournaments for its members, provided chess magazines and books to libraries, and offered instruction in and sponsored exhibitions of the game of chess, yet was denied classification as an educational organization because a substantial activity of the organization was the promotion and conduct of the tournaments, which were found to serve "recreational interests."[120] In another instance, an organization that was originally classified as a tax-exempt social club was denied reclassification as a charitable or educational organization because of the "substantial social and personal aspects" of the organization.[121] Another application of this principle occurred when an organization, the principal function of which was an annual science fiction convention, was denied classification as an educational organization because of its substantial "social and recreational purposes."[122] Another instance of application of this rule occurred when it was held that an association of descendants of a settler from England in the United States in the 1600s did not qualify for exemption as an educational organization, in part because its annual meeings and other activities were held to be "family-focused" and "social and recreational."[123]

A third category of educational organizations that instruct individuals are those that primarily engage in study and research. As an illustration, educational status was accorded an organization that undertook a program of study, research, and assembly of materials relating to court reform in a particular state.[124] Other organizations ruled to be tax-exempt under this category of *educational* include an organization that researched and studied Civil War battles[125] and one that conducted and published research in the area of career planning and vocational counseling.[126]

A subject of considerable controversy in this context is the tax-exempt status of organizations that conduct "study tours," with the IRS concerned that exemption not be attached to activities amounting to sightseeing or other forms of vacation travel. An organization that conducted study tours for the purpose of educating individuals about the culture of the United States and other countries was ruled to be exempt,[127] although the commercial travel industry challenged the policy of the IRS in granting exempt status to organizations that substantially provided commercial travel services, claiming a competitive disadvantage.[128]

---

[119] Syrang Aero Club, Inc. v. Comm'r, 73 T.C. 717 (1980).

[120] Minnesota Kingsmen Chess Ass'n, Inc. v. Comm'r, 46 T.C.M. 1133, 1135 (1983). Also Spanish Am. Cultural Ass'n of Bergenfield v. Comm'r, 68 T.C.M. 931 (1994).

[121] Alumnae Chapter Beta of Clovia v. Comm'r, 46 T.C.M. 297, 298 (1983).

[122] St. Louis Science Fiction Ltd. v. Comm'r, 49 T.C.M. 1126, 1129 (1985).

[123] Manning Ass'n v. Comm'r, 93 T.C. 596, 606 (1989).

[124] Rev. Rul. 64-195, 1964-2 C.B. 138.

[125] Rev. Rul. 67-148, 1967-1 C.B. 132.

[126] Rev. Rul. 68-71, 1968-1 C.B. 249.

[127] Rev. Rul. 70-534, 1970-2 C.B. 113; Rev. Rul. 69-400, *supra* note 102.

[128] American Soc'y of Travel Agents, Inc. v. Simon, 36 A.F.T.R. 2d 75-5142 (D.D.C. 1975) (complaint dismissed), *aff'd*, 566 F.2d 145 (D.C. Cir. 1977) (finding of no standing to sue), *cert. den.*, 435 U.S. 947 (1978).

Where a tax-exempt educational program involving travel (such as wintertime ocean cruises) is intermixed with substantial social and recreational activities, exempt status will not be forthcoming.[129] Thus, as noted, an organization, the sole purpose and activity of which was to arrange group tours for students and faculty members of a university, was ruled to not be educational for federal tax purposes,[130] while an organization that arranged for and participated in the temporary exchange of children between families of a foreign country and the United States was found to be exempt because it was fostering the cultural and educational development of children.[131]

According to the IRS, the tax status of travel tours is dependent on how they are structured, what they consist of, and what they accomplish. This amounts to a facts and circumstances test, which examines the "nature, scope and motivation for a tour in making a determination as to whether there is a connection between a particular tour and the accomplishment of an exempt purpose."[132] A "critical factor" is the methods used, such as organized study, reports, lectures, library access, and reading lists. To be an exempt function, each tour must have the achievement of exempt ends as its primary purpose. Another factor the IRS evaluates is other relevant facts that demonstrate the advancement of exempt objectives, such as mandated classroom and other structured activities and "choice of destination." An exempt function tour is likely to consist of an "intensive learning experience," rather than tours and visits that are essentially social and recreational experiences.

The IRS was constrained to rule that the definition of the term *educational* relating to the instruction of individuals (and, presumably, also as respects instruction of the public) "contains no limitation with regard to age in defining that term."[133] The issue arose when the IRS, in ruling that an organization organized and operated for the purpose of teaching a particular sport qualified as a tax-exempt educational entity,[134] observed in the facts that the program of instruction was offered only to children. This earlier ruling was amplified to make it clear that the concept of *educational* extends to the instruction of individuals "of all ages."[135]

The instruction of individuals is thus inherently a tax-exempt function, and tax exemption is not dependent on the subjects under instruction or the number or motives of those being instructed (unless the facts demonstrate the presence of a practice contrary to public policy or an unwarranted private benefit[136]). There is,

---

[129] Rev. Rul. 77-366, 1977-2 C.B. 192. Also International Postgraduate Med. Found. v. Comm'r, 56 T.C.M. 1140 (1989).

[130] Rev. Rul. 67-327, *supra* note 102.

[131] Rev. Rul. 80-286, *supra* note 102.

[132] Tech. Adv. Mem. 9702004. These criteria are refinements of the IRS position articulated in 1990 (Tech. Adv. Mem. 9027003). The criteria the IRS follows in this regard were further clarified by the development of regulations in the unrelated business area (see § 26.5(k)).

[133] Rev. Rul. 77-365, *supra* note 116, at 192.

[134] Rev. Rul. 65-2, *supra* note 116.

[135] Rev. Rul. 77-365, *supra* note 116, at 192.

[136] See §§ 5.3, 19.10.

then, no requirement that the *general public* be directly instructed; in this context, there is nothing akin to any requirement that a charitable class be served.[137] For example, an organization may conduct a seminar for lawyers on some aspect of the law and the lawyers may attend solely for the purpose of augmenting their law practices, yet the seminar is clearly an educational undertaking. The fact is that, generally, exempt educational activities provide direct benefits to parties in their private capacity. The dissemination of information and the training of individuals is seen as serving public purposes (and thus as being educational) in that the increased capabilities of those receiving the instruction serves to improve the public welfare. In one instance, the IRS advised that an "educational activity may be performed in the public interest even if members of the public have no access to the activity whatsoever."[138]

§ 7.5 INSTRUCTION OF THE PUBLIC

As noted, the income tax regulations state that the term *educational* as used for federal tax purposes relates, in part, to the "instruction of the public on subjects useful to the individual and beneficial to the community."[139] In many instances, an organization is considered educational because it is regarded as instructing the public as well as the individual. Nonetheless, even though it is difficult (and usually unnecessary) to formulate rigid distinctions between the two types of educational purposes, various categories of the former purpose have evolved.

One category of this type of tax-exempt educational organization is the one that provides certain personal services deemed beneficial to the general public. The IRS, under this rationale, ruled to be exempt organizations that disseminated information concerning hallucinatory drugs,[140] conducted personal money management instruction,[141] and educated expectant mothers and the public in a method of painless childbirth.[142] Similarly, an organization that functioned primarily as a crop seed certification entity was held to be educational because of its adult education classes, seminars, newsletter, and lending library.[143]

Another way an organization can be educational in this regard is by providing instruction in the form of counseling. The IRS wrote that "[p]ersonal counseling has been recognized as a valid method of instruction for educational organizations."[144] For example, an organization that provided free counseling to men concerning methods of voluntary sterilization was held to be a tax-exempt

---

[137] Cf. § 5.5(a).
[138] Gen. Couns. Mem. 38459. In general, Rev. Rul. 75-196, *supra* note 90. Cf. American Campaign Academy v. Comm'r, *supra* note 70.
[139] See the text accompanied by *supra* note 3.
[140] Rev. Rul. 70-590, 1970-2 C.B. 116.
[141] Rev. Rul. 69-441, 1969-2 C.B. 115.
[142] Rev. Rul. 66-255, 1966-2 C.B. 210.
[143] Indiana Crop Improvement Ass'n, Inc. v. Comm'r, 76 T.C. 394 (1981).
[144] Rev. Rul. 73-569, 1973-2 C.B. 178.

educational entity.[145] Other exempt personal counseling organizations include those that offered group counseling to widows and widowers to assist them in legal, financial, and emotional problems caused by the death of their spouses;[146] counseling to women on methods of resolving unwanted pregnancies;[147] marriage counseling;[148] vocational counseling;[149] counseling of immigrants to the U.S. enabling them to overcome social, cultural, and economic problems;[150] and counseling as to personal health and fitness.[151]

Another category of tax-exempt educational organization consists of those that endeavor to instruct the public in the field of civic betterment. This type of organization frequently also qualifies under one or more varieties of the concept of *charitable* or *social welfare*. Thus, an organization that disseminated information, in the nature of results of its investigations, in an effort to lessen racial and religious prejudice in the fields of housing and public accommodations, was ruled to be exempt.[152] Other organizations in this category include ones that distributed information about the results of a model demonstration housing program for low-income families conducted by it,[153] disseminated information on the need for international cooperation,[154] educated the public as to the means of correcting conditions such as community tension and juvenile delinquency,[155] enlightened the public in a particular city as to the advantages of street planning,[156] developed and distributed a community land-use plan,[157] and educated the public regarding environmental deterioration due to solid waste pollution,[158] radio and television programming,[159] and accuracy of news coverage by newspapers.[160]

The fourth category of tax-exempt educational organization that exists to instruct the public is those that conduct study and research. The variety of efforts encompassed by these organizations is nearly limitless. As illustrations, these organizations include those that conducted analyses, studies, and research into the problems of a particular region (pollution, transportation, water resources, waste disposal) and published the results,[161] instructed the public on agricultural matters by conducting fairs and exhibitions,[162] and published a

[145] Rev. Rul. 74-595, 1974-2 C.B. 164.
[146] Rev. Rul. 78-99, 1978-1 C.B. 152.
[147] Rev. Rul. 73-569, *supra* note 144.
[148] Rev. Rul. 70-640, 1970-2 C.B. 117.
[149] Rev. Rul. 68-71, *supra* note 126.
[150] Rev. Rul. 76-205, 1976-1 C.B. 154.
[151] Priv. Ltr. Rul. 9732032.
[152] Rev. Rul. 75-285, 1975-2 C.B. 203; Rev. Rul. 68-438, 1968-2 C.B. 209; Rev. Rul. 68-70, 1968-1 C.B. 248; Rev. Rul. 67-250, 1967-2 C.B. 182.
[153] Rev. Rul. 68-17, 1968-1, C.B. 247; Rev. Rul. 67-138, 1967-1 C.B. 129.
[154] Rev. Rul. 67-342, 1967-2 C.B. 187.
[155] Rev. Rul. 68-15, 1968-1 C.B. 244.
[156] Rev. Rul. 68-14, 1968-1 C.B. 243.
[157] Rev. Rul. 67-391, 1967-2 C.B. 190.
[158] Rev. Rul. 72-560, 1972-2 C.B. 248.
[159] Rev. Rul. 64-192, 1964-2 C.B. 136.
[160] Rev. Rul. 74-615, 1974-2 C.B. 165.
[161] Rev. Rul. 70-79, 1970-1 C.B. 127.
[162] Rev. Rul. 67-216, 1967-2 C.B. 180.

journal to disseminate information about specific types of physical and mental disorders.[163]

The publication of printed material can be an educational activity in a variety of other contexts. For example, an organization that surveyed scientific and medical literature and prepared, published, and distributed abstracts of it was recognized as tax-exempt.[164] Similarly, an organization was ruled tax-exempt for assisting the National Park Service by preparing, publishing, and distributing literature concerning a park.[165] Likewise, a nonprofit corporation that compiled and published a manual on the standard library cataloguing system was ruled to be engaged in educational activities.[166] By contrast, where a publication effort is operated by an entity akin to normal commercial practices, tax exemption as an educational organization will be denied.[167] Thus, the IRS held that an organization, the only activities of which were the preparation and publication of a newspaper of local, national, and international news articles with an ethnic emphasis, soliciting advertising and selling subscriptions to the newspaper in a manner indistinguishable from ordinary commercial publishing practices, was not operated exclusively for educational purposes.[168]

In general, an organization engaged in publishing can qualify as a tax-exempt educational entity where the content of the publication is inherently educational; the preparation of the material follows methods generally accepted as educational in character; the distribution of the materials is necessary or valuable in achieving the organization's exempt purposes; and the manner in which the distribution is accomplished is distinguishable from ordinary commercial publishing practices.[169] The IRS relied on these criteria in concluding that the recording and sale of musical compositions that were not generally produced by the commercial recording industry was educational because it was a means for presenting new works of unrecognized composers and the neglected works of more recognized composers.[170] By contrast, a publication of an exempt organization was held to not be educational because its contents were found to be primarily news concerning the organization's members and current events affecting the organization, with the information provided of limited interest to the general public.[171]

The educational activities of organizations may be carried on through a tax-exempt club, such as a gem and mineral club[172] or a garden club,[173] or by means of public lectures and debates.[174] These organizations may function as broad-based

---

[163] Rev. Rul. 67-4, 1967-1 C.B. 121.

[164] Rev. Rul. 66-147, 1966-1 C.B. 137.

[165] Rev. Rul. 68-307, 1968-1 C.B. 258.

[166] Forest Press, Inc. v. Comm'r, 22 T.C. 265 (1954).

[167] Rev. Rul. 60-351, 1960-2 C.B. 169.

[168] Rev. Rul. 77-4, 1977-1 C.B. 141. Also Christian Manner Int'l, Inc. v. Comm'r, 71 T.C. 661 (1979).

[169] Rev. Rul. 67-4, *supra* note 163.

[170] Rev. Rul. 79-369, 1979-2 C.B. 226.

[171] Phi Delta Theta Fraternity v. Comm'r, 90 T.C. 1033 (1988), *aff'd*, 887 F.2d 1302 (6th Cir. 1989).

[172] Rev. Rul. 67-139, 1967-1 C.B. 129.

[173] Rev. Rul. 66-179, 1966-1 C.B. 139.

[174] Rev. Rul. 66-256, 1966-2 C.B. 210.

membership organizations,[175] as organizations formed to promote a specific cause,[176] or as a transitory organization, such as one to collect and collate campaign materials of a particular candidate for ultimate donation to a university or public library.[177]

A somewhat controversial ruling from the IRS concerning this category of educational organization is one involving a society of heating and air conditioning engineers and others having a professional interest in this field that was held to be educational in nature.[178] Its educational purposes were the operation of a library, dissemination of the results of its scientific research, and the making available of model codes of minimum standards for heating, ventilating, and air conditioning. The IRS went to considerable lengths to distinguish this type of professional society from a business league.[179]

Organizations that are charitable, educational, or scientific societies have been recognized by the IRS as being exempt organizations. Frequently, their membership base is composed of individuals (rather than organizations); these persons share common professional and/or disciplinary interests. In most instances, these organizations satisfy the criteria for classification as charitable, educational, or like entities, but, because they provide services to individual members, the tendency of the IRS may be to categorize or reclassify them as business leagues, on the ground that they serve to enhance the professional development of the members rather than advance a charitable purpose.[180]

An otherwise tax-exempt organization that produced and distributed free, or for small, cost-defraying fees, educational, cultural, and public interest programs for public viewing via public educational channels of commercial cable television companies was held to be operated for educational purposes and thus qualified for exemption because an organization may achieve its educational purposes through the production of television programs where it does so in a noncommercial manner.[181] Similarly, a nonprofit organization established to operate a noncommercial educational broadcasting station presenting educational, cultural, and public interest programs qualified as an exempt educational entity,[182] as did an organization that produced educational films concerning a particular subject and that disseminated its educational material to the public by means of commercial television, where the films were presented in a noncommercial manner.[183]

With these three rulings as precedent, the IRS considered the case of an organization that made facilities and equipment available to the general public for the production of noncommercial educational or cultural television programs intended for communication to the public via the public and educational access channels of a commercial cable television company. The programs did

---

[175] Rev. Rul. 68-164, 1968-1 C.B. 252.
[176] Rev. Rul. 72-228, 1972-1 C.B. 148.
[177] Rev. Rul. 70-321, 1970-1 C.B. 129.
[178] Rev. Rul. 71-506, 1971-2 C.B. 233.
[179] Cf. Rev. Rul. 70-641, 1970-2 C.B. 119.
[180] See § 13.3.
[181] Rev. Rul. 76-4, 1976-1 C.B. 145.
[182] Rev. Rul. 66-220, 1966-2 C.B. 209.
[183] Rev. Rul. 67-342, *supra* note 154.

not support or oppose specific legislation and, where a particular viewpoint was advocated, the organization ensured that the program presented a full and fair exposition of the pertinent facts. The organization was informally affiliated with, but did not control and was not controlled by, the commercial cable television company. The IRS ruled that, by "providing members of the general public with the opportunity to produce television programs of an educational or a cultural nature for viewing on the public access channels of a commercial cable television company," the organization was operating exclusively for educational purposes.[184]

In this ruling, the IRS characterized the prior three rulings as "clearly indicat[ing] that an organization may achieve its educational purposes through the production of television programs, regardless of whether the programs are to be broadcast over the airwaves or over a cable system, so long as the programs are presented in a noncommercial manner."[185] The IRS added: "The absence of commercial advertising is a key factor in determining the noncommercial nature of the programming activity."[186] Where an organization engages in educational programming by means of television to a substantial extent, however, it can be accorded designation as an educational entity, even though the organization owns and operates the station under a commercial broadcasting license.[187]

§ 7.6 EDUCATIONAL ACTIVITY AS COMMERCIAL BUSINESS

One of the most troublesome aspects of the law of tax-exempt organizations is differentiation between exempt and commercial functions.[188] While this aspect of the law is by no means confined to educational organizations,[189] much of the clashing of principles occurs in this context because what may be an exempt educational activity in one context may be a commercial business in another. Certainly, for example, in the general world of commerce, operation of a restaurant, bookstore, broadcasting station, portfolio management service, publishing company, and the like is a trade or business. This type of an operation may qualify as an exempt educational organization, however, as, for example, has a university restaurant,[190] a museum restaurant,[191] a university

[184] Rev. Rul. 76-443, 1976-2 C.B. 149, 150.
[185] *Id.* at 149.
[186] *Id.* With regard to programs prepared for cable television, Federal Communications Commission regulations prohibit cable operators from advertising commercially on their educational or "public access" channels.
[187] Rev. Rul. 78-385, 1978-2 C.B. 174.
[188] The *commerciality doctrine* is the subject of Chapter 25.
[189] Indeed, many of the difficulties in this area occur in the health care field (see § 6.3).
[190] Rev. Rul. 67-217, 1967-2 C.B. 181.
[191] Priv. Ltr. Rul. 200222030. Inexplicably, however, the IRS does not follow this policy in settings other than colleges, universities, hospitals, and museums (e.g., Tech. Adv. Mem. 200021056).

store,[192] a broadcasting station,[193] an endowment fund management service,[194] a retail sales enterprise,[195] a money lending operation,[196] and an organization publishing a law school journal.[197]

It is difficult to formulate guidelines to determine when a given purpose or activity is *educational* or a commercial business. Of course, an exempt purpose or activity must be one that benefits the public, or an appropriate segment of the public, rather than any private individual or individuals and the organization must not be operated for the benefit of private shareholders or individuals.[198] Nevertheless, even these rules, aside from the essential questions as to what constitutes an educational activity, require some subjective judgments.

The task of making these judgments befell a federal court, in a case involving an organization created to disseminate knowledge of economics with a view to advancing the welfare of the American people. The court concluded that the primary purpose of the organization was not an educational but a commercial one.[199] The organization published periodicals containing analyses of securities and industries and of general economic conditions; no forecasting of stock market trends was made, although the publications did contain recommendations as to the purchase and sale of securities. These publications were sold at subscription at a cost above production expenses, as was a separate service providing advice for sales and purchases of securities in a particular portfolio; the organization also published special studies prepared by its research staff and maintained fellowship and scholarship programs.

In this case, the court developed an instructive process of reasoning. First, it noted that *education* is an "extremely broad concept."[200] Second, recognizing that the tax exemption provision is to be liberally construed, the court "first assume[d] *arguendo* an educational purpose without giving definitive meaning to that concept."[201] Third, the court then "ascertain[ed] whether or not the tax-

---

[192] Rev. Rul. 68-538, 1968-2 C.B. 116; Rev. Rul. 58-194, 1958-1 C.B. 240; Squire v. Students Book Corp., 191 F.2d 1018 (9th Cir. 1951).

[193] Rev. Rul. 66-220, *supra* note 182.

[194] Rev. Rul. 71-529, 1971-2 C.B. 234.

[195] Rev. Rul. 68-167, 1968-1 C.B. 255. For this rationale to be successful, however, the business function must be related to exempt purposes. Thus, an organization wholly owned by an exempt college that manufactured and sold wood and metal products was ruled to not be exempt, notwithstanding the fact that the entity furnished employment to the students of the college (Rev. Rul. 69-177, 1969-1 C.B. 150).

[196] Rev. Rul. 63-220, 1963-2 C.B. 208; Rev. Rul. 61-87, 1961-1 C.B. 191. Cf. Rev. Rul. 69-177, 1969-1 C.B. 150.

[197] Rev. Rul. 63-234, 1963-2 C.B. 210. As noted, publishing can obviously be a commercial undertaking. Thus, even though an organization published "better teaching materials," it was found by the IRS to be an "enterprise conducted in an essentially commercial manner, in which all the participants expect to receive a monetary return" (Rev. Rul. 66-104, 1966-1 C.B. 135). Likewise, while a magazine had some educational aspects, it was published and sold to the "general public in accordance with ordinary commercial publishing practices" (Rev. Rul. 60-351, *supra* note 168, at 171).

[198] Reg. §§ 1.501(c)(3)-1(c)(ii), 1.501(c)(3)-1(c)(2).

[199] American Inst. for Economic Research v. United States, 302 F.2d 934 (Ct. Cl. 1962).

[200] *Id.* at 937.

[201] *Id.* at 938.

payer has an additional commercial purpose."[202] Fourth, on finding a commercial purpose, the court had to decide "whether the commercial purpose is primary or incidental to the exempt purpose."[203] The court found the commercial purpose to be primary and not incidental to any exempt purpose, and thus held the organization to not be exempt as an educational organization.

This court held that the required element of *exclusivity* was absent and that the tax exemption was thus unavailable, citing the Supreme Court that "the presence of a single [nonexempt] . . . purpose, if substantial in nature, will destroy the exemption regardless of the number or importance of truly [exempt] . . . purposes."[204] The court, in concluding that the publications of the organization merely provided investment advice to subscribers for a fee, noted that the existence of profits, while not conclusive, is some evidence that the business purpose is primary[205] and that the services of the organization are those "commonly associated with a commercial enterprise."[206] The argument of the organization that any profits gained from the sale of its publications were used for exempt purposes was unavailing.[207]

Subsequently, the IRS determined that an association of investment clubs, formed for the mutual exchange of investment information among its members and prospective investors to enable them to make sound investments, was not a tax-exempt educational organization, inasmuch as the association was serving private economic interests.[208] Likewise, an organization operated to protect the financial stability of a teachers' retirement system, and the contributions and pensions of retiree members of the system, was held to not be educational and to serve its members' private interests, notwithstanding its publication of a newsletter.[209]

The same result occurred with respect to a nonprofit organization that clearly engaged in educational activities, namely, the sponsorship of programs involving training, seminars, lectures, and the like in areas of intrapersonal awareness and communication.[210] The educational activities were conducted pursuant to licensing arrangements with for-profit corporations that amounted to substantial control over the functioning of the nonprofit organization. In rejecting tax-exempt status for the nonprofit organization, the court held that it is part of a "franchise system which is operated for private benefit and that its affiliation with this system taints it with a substantial commercial purpose."[211] Thus, the organization's entanglements with for-profit corporations were such that

---

[202] *Id.* 302 F.2d at 938.

[203] *Id.* This line of reasoning was followed in, for example, Pulpit Resource v. Comm'r, 70 T.C. 594 (1978).

[204] *Id.* at 937. The quote is from Better Business Bureau v. United States, 326 U.S. 279, 283 (1945). See § 4.6.

[205] Scripture Press Found. v. United States, 285 F.2d 800 (Ct. Cl. 1961), *cert. den.*, 368 U.S. 985 (1962).

[206] American Inst. for Economic Research v. United States, *supra* note 199, at 938.

[207] See IRC § 502; § 28.6.

[208] Rev. Rul. 76-366, 1976-2 C.B. 144.

[209] Retired Teachers Legal Defense Fund, Inc. v. Comm'r, 78 T.C. 280 (1982).

[210] est of Hawaii v. Comm'r, 71 T.C. 1067 (1979), *aff'd*, 647 F.2d 170 (9th Cir. 1981).

[211] *Id.* at 1080.

commercial ends were imputed to it, notwithstanding the inherently exempt nature of its activities.

Likewise, an organization, originally exempted from federal income tax as an educational and religious entity, had its tax exemption revoked as a result of evolving into a commercial publishing entity.[212] Both the IRS and a court concluded that the publishing activities had taken on a "commercial hue" and the organization had "become a highly efficient business venture."[213] In reaching this conclusion, the court noted that the organization followed publishing and sales practices used by comparable nonexempt commercial publishers, had generated increasing profits in recent years,[214] was experiencing a growth in accumulated surplus, and had been paying substantially increased salaries to its top employees.[215]

This line of law is troublesome for tax-exempt organizations. Nonprofit organizations (particularly charitable ones) are often criticized for not operating more efficiently and prudently (for not functioning "like a business"). For example, the IRS considered the status of an organization that operated a retail grocery store to sell food to residents in a poverty area at substantially lower-than-usual prices, that maintained a free delivery service for the needy, and that allocated about 4 percent of its earnings for use in a training program for the hard-core unemployed. The IRS held that the operation of the grocery store was a substantial nonexempt activity, since it was conducted on a scale larger than reasonably necessary for the training program (an exempt activity[216]) and since the operation could not be characterized as an investment or business undertaking for the production of income for use in carrying on qualified charitable purposes, and denied the exemption.[217] Similarly, the IRS ruled nonexempt an organization, wholly owned by an exempt college, that manufactured and sold wood products primarily to employ students of the college to enable them to continue their education, on the ground that the enterprise itself was not an instructional or training activity.[218] Conversely, the IRS recognized that an exempt organization may engage in a commercial activity without endangering its tax status where the business is not an end in itself but is a means by which charitable purposes are accomplished and where the endeavor is not conducted on a scale larger than is reasonably necessary to accomplish the organization's tax-exempt purpose.[219] Likewise, an organization that provided training of procurement officials for countries receiving United States aid was found to be educational in nature, despite an IRS contention that procurement activity is not inherently exempt, since the procurement activity furthered the organization's educational and training program.[220]

---

[212] The Incorporated Trustees of the Gospel Worker Soc'y. v. United States, 510 F. Supp. 374 (D.D.C. 1981), aff'd , 672 F.2d 894 (D.C. Cir. 1981), cert. den., 456 U.S. 944 (1982).
[213] Id. at 381.
[214] See § 4.9.
[215] See 19.4(a).
[216] See supra § 4.
[217] Rev. Rul. 73-127, 1973-1 C.B. 221.
[218] Rev. Rul. 69-177, supra note 180.
[219] Rev. Rul. 73-128, supra note 80.
[220] Afro-American Purchasing Center, Inc. v. Comm'r, 37 T.C.M. 184 (1978).

A case involving an organization's tax-exempt status, where the IRS is claiming that the organization is operated for a substantial commercial purpose, may be dependent upon the organization's charges for services or products in relation to its costs.[221] Where the fees are set at a level less than costs, the courts and sometimes the IRS will be spurred on to the conclusion that the organization is not operated in an ordinary commercial manner.[222] Other considerations govern where a nonprofit organization is experiencing net receipts.[223]

This aspect of the law is being greatly influenced by developments in the field of unrelated income taxation.[224] The courts have developed law concerning the scope of the phrase *trade or business* that ranges considerably beyond the criteria set forth in the statutory definition of the phrase.[225] As this aspect of the law is evolving, great consideration is being given to the concepts of *unfair competition* and *profit motive*.[226] More contemporaneously, the courts are focusing on the question as to whether or not a particular activity is being operated in a *commercial manner*.[227]

Thus, some courts will, in characterizing an activity as a trade or business, place emphasis on the conclusion that the undertaking was conducted with a profit motive.[228] This conclusion is usually buttressed by a finding that the particular activity was in fact profitable. This approach is a reflection of the test for business expense deduction purposes,[229] which looks to determine whether the activity was entered into with the dominant hope and intent of realizing a profit.[230] One appellate court commented that where an activity is not substantially related to exempt purposes (the principal statutory test), is "conducted in a competitive profit seeking manner, and regularly earns significant profits, a heavy burden must be placed on the organization to prove profit is not its motive" for engaging in the activity.[231]

Other courts place more emphasis on the question as to whether the activity constitutes unfair competition with taxable business.[232] This is understandable, given the legislative history of the unrelated income rules, which clearly reflects the intent of Congress to eliminate unfair competitive advan-

---

[221] See § 26.2(c).
[222] Peoples Translation Service/Newsfront Int'l v. Comm'r, 72 T.C. 42 (1979).
[223] See § 4.9.
[224] See Part Five.
[225] See § 26.2.
[226] See § 26.2(a), (b).
[227] See Chapter 25.
[228] E.g., Professional Ins. Agents of Mich. v. Comm'r, 726 F.2d 1097 (6th Cir. 1984); Carolinas Farm & Power Equip. Dealers Ass'n, Inc. v. United States, 699 F.2d 167 (4th Cir. 1983); Louisiana Credit Union League v. United States, 693 F.2d 525 (5th Cir. 1982); Professional Ins. Agents of Wash. v. Comm'r, 53 T.C.M. 9 (1987).
[229] IRC § 162.
[230] E.g., United States v. American Bar Endowment, 477 U.S. 105, 110, note 1 (1986).
[231] Carolinas Farm & Power Equip. Dealers Ass'n, Inc. v. United States, *supra* note 228, at 171.
[232] E.g., Disabled Am. Veterans v. United States, 650 F.2d 1178 (Ct. Cl. 1981); Hope School v. United States, 612 F.2d 298 (7th Cir. 1980); Carle Found. v. United States, 611 F.2d 1192 (7th Cir. 1979).

tages that tax-exempt organizations may otherwise have over for-profit business entities.[233]

The U.S. Supreme Court indicated a tendency to favor both of these lines of cases, noting the rationale for the profit motive approach[234] and that a focus should be on whether the activity under examination is the kind of activity that is "provided by private commercial entities in order to make a profit."[235] Lower courts are now reflecting a willingness to utilize both of these lines of cases.[236]

§ 7.7   CHILD CARE ORGANIZATIONS

The term *educational* purposes includes the "providing care of children away from their homes if—(1) substantially all of the care provided by the organization is for purposes of enabling individuals [their parents] to be gainfully employed, and (2) the services provided by the organization are available to the general public."[237] It is the view of the IRS that a child care facility will not qualify under these rules if it provides preference in enrollment for the children of employees of a specific employer.[238]

The Office of the Chief Counsel of the IRS issued an opinion that the provision of day care referrals and assistance information to the general public is not a charitable or educational activity but, rather, a commercial one.[239] In so doing, the IRS modified an earlier opinion from that office which indicated that these activities were considered to not be unrelated business when undertaken by an organization the primary purpose of which was the operation of day care centers.[240] In the earlier opinion, the IRS also took the position that the provision of specialized child care assistance to employers in the organization's locale is not a tax-exempt activity because of the substantial benefit provided the employers in connection with the operation of their qualified dependent care assistance programs.[241]

This statutory definition was enacted because of the reach of the ruling policy by the IRS in this area. This policy has been described as follows: "The IRS has recognized that nonprofit day care centers may be eligible for tax exemption and tax-deductible contributions where enrollment is based on the financial need of

---

[233] See § 26.1.

[234] United States v. American Bar Endowment, *supra* note 230, at 112–114.

[235] *Id.* at 111.

[236] E.g., Illinois Ass'n of Professional Ins. Agents, Inc. v. Comm'r, 86-2 U.S.T.C. ¶ 9702 (7th Cir. 1986), *aff'g* 49 T.C.M. 925 (1985).

[237] IRC § 501(k). The reference to the words *general public* means that the IRC § 501(k) organization cannot be racially discriminatory (see § 5.4(a)), although it does not have to satisfy the IRS guidelines on the subject (*id.*, text accompanied by notes 94–98), unless it is also classified under IRC § 170(b)(1)(A)(ii) (see § 11.3(a)) (Gen. Couns. Mem. 39757).

[238] Gen. Couns. Mem. 39613.

[239] Gen. Couns. Mem. 39872.

[240] Gen. Couns. Mem. 39622.

[241] *Id.* These specialized child care assistance plans are operated pursuant to IRC § 129, which provides that the gross income of an employee does not include amounts paid or incurred by the employer for eligible dependent care assistance.

the family and the need of the child for the program, or where the center provides preschool-age children of working parents with an educational program through a professional staff of qualified teachers."[242]

This definition of *educational* purposes is "not intended to affect the meaning of terms 'educational' or 'charitable' for any purpose other than considering the child care organizations described in the provision as having educational purposes."[243]

---

[242] H. Rep. No. 98-861, 98th Cong., 2d Sess. 1100 (1984). See *supra* note 52.
[243] *Id.*

CHAPTER EIGHT

Religious Organizations

Section 501(c)(3) of the Internal Revenue Code provides that an organization may be exempt from federal income tax if it is organized and operated exclusively for a *religious* purpose.[1] Because of policy and constitutional law constraints, the IRS and the courts are usually reluctant to enter, let alone dwell in, the realm of religion. The difficulties of enforcement of the law concerning tax-exempt religious organizations by the IRS are compounded by exceptions for churches and certain other religious organizations from the requirements of filing an application for recognition of exemption[2] and annual information returns,[3] and by rules making examinations of churches by the IRS more difficult to undertake and administer.[4]

§ 8.1 CONSTITUTIONAL LAW FRAMEWORK

With few exceptions, the IRS, other governmental agencies, and the courts have either refused to or been quite cautious in attempting to define *religious* activities or organizations, or the word *religion*. This reticence by policymakers at the federal and state levels stems largely from First Amendment considerations, as articulated in opinions from the judiciary in tax and other cases. Constitutional law

---

[1] Also Reg. § 1.501(c)(3)-1(d)(1)(i)(a).
[2] See § 23.3(b).
[3] See § 24.3(b)(i).
[4] See § 24.8(b).

principles in this context are imposed on the states by operation of the Fourteenth Amendment.[5]

(a) Constitutional Law Principles in General

The First Amendment provides that "Congress shall make no law respecting an establishment of religion, or prohibiting the free exercise thereof." These two religion clauses are known as the *establishment clause* and the *free exercise clause*. Both of these clauses are directed toward the same goal: government neutrality with respect to matters pertaining to religion. The U.S. Supreme Court observed that the First Amendment "rests upon the premise that both religion and government can best work to achieve their lofty aims if each is left free from the other within its respective sphere."[6]

The jurisprudence in this area is extensive, replete with controversy, and sometimes inconsistent.

(i) Free Exercise Clause. Free exercise clause cases arise out of conflict between secular laws and individuals' religious beliefs. This clause was aptly characterized by the Supreme Court when it wrote that the "door of the Free Exercise Clause stands tightly closed against any governmental regulation of religious beliefs as such," and that "[g]overnment may neither compel affirmation of a repugnant belief, nor penalize or discriminate against individuals or groups because they hold religious views abhorrent to the authorities."[7] The Court also wrote that the First Amendment "requires the state to be neutral in its relations with groups of religious believers and nonbelievers."[8] Also, the "State must confine itself to secular objectives, and neither advance nor impede religious activity."[9]

Conversely, the Court rejected challenges under the free exercise clause to governmental regulation of "certain overt acts prompted by religious beliefs or principles, for 'even when the action is in accord with one's religious convictions, [it] is not totally free from legislative restrictions.' "[10] The Court added that "in this highly sensitive constitutional area, '[o]nly the gravest abuses, endangering paramount interest, give occasion for permissible limitation.' "[11]

The more significant free exercise clause cases, relating to tax-exempt organizations, include the clash between the secular law prohibiting polygamy and the precepts at the time of the Mormon religion,[12] military service requirements and conscientious objectors' principles,[13] state unemployment compensation law

---

[5] E.g., Lee v. Weisman, 505 U.S. 577 (1992).
[6] Illinois ex rel. McCollum v. Bd. of Educ., 333 U.S. 203, 212 (1948).
[7] Sherbert v. Verner, 374 U.S. 398, 402 (1963).
[8] Everson v. Bd. of Educ., 330 U.S. 1, 18 (1947).
[9] Roemer v. Bd. of Pub. Works of Md., 426 U.S. 736, 747 (1976).
[10] Sherbert v. Verner, *supra* note 7, at 403.
[11] *Id.* at 406, quoting from Thomas v. Collins, 323 U.S. 516, 530 (1937).
[12] Reynolds v. United States, 98 U.S. 145 (1878).
[13] Gillette v. United States, 401 U.S. 437 (1971).

requiring Saturday work and the dictates of the Seventh-Day Adventists' religion,[14] compulsory school attendance laws and the doctrines of the Amish religion,[15] and a license tax on canvassing and the missionary evangelism objectives of Jehovah's Witnesses.[16] Where there is to be permissible government regulation notwithstanding free exercise of religion claims, there must be a showing by the government of "some substantial threat to public safety, place or order."[17] Thus, courts have upheld a compulsory vaccination requirement,[18] prosecution of faith healers practicing medicine without a license,[19] and a prohibition on snake handling as part of religious ceremonies.[20]

Short of such a *substantial threat*, however, the government may not investigate or review matters of ecclesiastical cognizance. This principle frequently manifests itself in the area of alleged employment discrimination in violation of civil rights laws.[21] Thus, there must be a compelling governmental interest in regulation before free exercise of religion rights may be infringed. For example, a city ordinance prohibiting animal sacrifice for religious purposes was found to be violative of the constitutional right to the free exercise of religion.[22]

(ii) Establishment Clause.   Establishment clause cases are usually more relevant to the law of tax-exempt organizations, inasmuch as they involve governmental regulation of religious organizations and institutions. These cases frequently arise in the form of attacks on the propriety of state aid to schools (including religious schools) or special treatment to religious entities (such as tax exemption).[23] For example, the Supreme Court held that a city's voucher plan, which funded private school tuition, was constitutional, notwithstanding the fact that some of the schools involved were religious entities.[24] Likewise, the proposed issuance by an industrial development board of tax-exempt revenue bonds for campus improvements to a tax-exempt sectarian university was found to not be a violation of the establishment clause.[25]

This clause is designed to prohibit the government from establishing a religion, aiding a religion, or preferring one religion over another. The Supreme Court observed that the establishment clause is intended to avoid "sponsor-

---

[14] Sherbert v. Verner, *supra* note 7.

[15] Wisconsin v. Yoder, 406 U.S. 205 (1972).

[16] Watchtower Bible & Tract Soc'y v. Village of Stratton, 122 S. Ct. 2080 (2002); Murdock v. Pennsylvania, 319 U.S. 105 (1943).

[17] Sherbert v. Verner, *supra* note 7, at 403.

[18] Jacobson v. Massachusetts, 197 U.S. 11 (1905).

[19] People v. Handzik, 102 N.E.2d 340 (Ill. 1964).

[20] Kirk v. Commonwealth, 44 S.E. 3d 409 (Va. 1947).

[21] E.g., McClure v. Salvation Army, 460 F.2d 553 (5th Cir. 1972).

[22] Church of the Lukumi Babalu Aye, Inc. v. City of Hialeah, 508 U.S. 520 (1993).

[23] E.g., Committee for Public Educ. v. Nyquist, 413 U.S. 756 (1973); Engle v. Vitale, 370 U.S. 421 (1962); Abington School Dist. v. Schempp, 374 U.S. 203 (1953); Zorach v. Clausen, 343 U.S. 306 (1952); Illinois ex rel. McCollum v. Bd. of Educ., *supra* note 6; Everson v. Bd. of Educ., *supra* note 8. See infra § (b).

[24] Zelman v. Simmons-Harris et al., 122 S. Ct. 2460 (2002).

[25] Steele v. Nashville Industrial Development Bd., 301 F.3d 401 (6th Cir. 2002)). Also Johnson v. Economic Development Corp., 241 F.3d 501 (6th Cir. 2001); Hunt v. McNair, 413 U.S. 734 (1973).

ship, financial support, and active involvement of the sovereign in religious activity."[26] As will be discussed, the governing principal in this context is government *neutrality*.

The Supreme Court has repeatedly held that a function of the First Amendment is the avoidance of substantial entanglement of church–state relationships. In one case, where state aid to religious schools, conditioned on pervasive restrictions, was held to be excessive entanglement, the Court stated:

> ... [A] comprehensive, discriminating, and continuing state surveillance will inevitably be required to ensure that these restrictions are obeyed and the First Amendment otherwise respected. ... This kind of state inspection and evaluation of religious content of a religious organization is fraught with the sort of entanglement that the Constitution forbids. It is a relationship pregnant with dangers of excessive government direction of church schools and hence of churches ... and we cannot ignore here the danger that pervasive modern governmental power will ultimately intrude on religion and thus conflict with the Religion Clauses.[27]

The Court's establishment clause caselaw basically entails three tests: for a statute to be constitutional, it must have a "secular legislative purpose," its "principal or primary effect must be one that neither advances nor inhibits religion," and it must not foster an "excessive government entanglement with religion."[28] Other tests applied by the Court are an *endorsement test*[29] and a *coercion test*.[30] Thus, where there is significant government investigation and/or surveillance, particularly analysis of the sincerity or application of religious beliefs, of a religious institution, there is likely to be a violation of the establishment clause.[31]

Again, the essence of the standard applied in these cases is neutrality—the basis for the constitutionality of tax exemptions in general, albeit where religious organizations are benefited.[32] Thus, in the school voucher case, the Court wrote that "where a government aid program is neutral with respect to religion, and provides assistance directly to a broad class of citizens who, in turn, direct government aid to religious schools wholly as a result of their own genuine and independent private choice, the program is not readily subject to challenge under the Establishment Clause."[33] Similarly, in the case involving proposed issuance of exempt revenue bonds for the benefit of a sectarian university, the court wrote that,

---

[26] Lemon v. Kurtzman, 403 U.S. 602, 612 (1971).

[27] *Id.* at 619-620.

[28] *Id.* at 612-613. Other courts add refining tests, such as a measurement of whether a government "has directed a formal religious exercise in such a way as to oblige the participation of objectors" or a prohibition on a government "from conveying or attempting to convey a message that religion is preferred over nonreligion" (citations omitted) (Doe v. Beaumont Independent School Dist., 240 F.3d 462, 468 (5th Cir. 2001)).

[29] E.g., County of Allegheny v. ACLU, 492 U.S. 573 (1989).

[30] E.g., Lee v. Weisman, *supra* note 5.

[31] E.g., Presbyterian Church v. Hull Church, 393 U.S. 440 (1969).

[32] See *infra* § (b).

[33] Zelman v. Simmons-Harris et al., *supra* note 24, at 2467.

because the proposed bond issuance is "part of a neutral program to benefit education, including that provided by sectarian institutions, and confers at best only an indirect benefit to the school, we hold that the issuance of the bonds does not violate the First Amendment."[34]

There are many cases decided by the Supreme Court finding government assistance programs involving tax-exempt religious programs constitutional, including programs that provided educational materials and equipment to religious schools;[35] allowed remedial public school teachers and counselors to assist at religious schools;[36] provided printing facilities for all qualified student publications including religious publications;[37] provided a sign language interpreter for a deaf child in a religious secondary school;[38] funded abstinence-based family planning programs offered by a religious social welfare agency;[39] offered vocational education scholarship to a visually disabled seminarian;[40] reimbursed religious schools for performance of state-mandated standardized tests and record-keeping;[41] provided textbook loans, vocational training, diagnostic services, therapeutic and remedial services, and standardized testing and scoring for religious schools;[42] provided subsidies on a per-student basis to a religious college;[43] provided construction grants to a religiously affiliated college;[44] provided loans of textbooks for a religious school;[45] reimbursed parents for bus transportation costs to a religious school;[46] provided loans of textbooks to a religious school;[47] and allowed use of federal funds to build a religious hospital.[48]

Establishment clause cases also include Supreme Court decisions holding unconstitutional the practice of including invocations and benedictions in the form of ostensibly nonsectarian prayers in public school graduation ceremonies,[49] striking down a school district's policy of permitting student-led invocations before high school football games,[50] upholding the inclusion of a nativity scene in a city's Christmas display,[51] sanctioning a state legislature's practice of opening each day's session with a prayer by a state-paid chaplain,[52] and finding unconstitutional a school district's wartime policy of punishing students who refused to

---

[34] Steele v. Nashville Industrial Development Bd., *supra* note 25, at 416.
[35] Mitchell v. Helms, 530 U.S. 793 (2000).
[36] Agostini v. Felton, 521 U.S. 203 (1997).
[37] Rosenberger v. Rector & Visitors of Univ. of Virginia, 515 U.S. 819 (1995).
[38] Zobrest v. Catalina Foothills Sch. Dist., 509 U.S. 1 (1993).
[39] Bowen v. Kendrick, 487 U.S. 598 (1988).
[40] Witters v. Washington Dept. of Services for the Blind, 474 U.S. 481 (1986).
[41] Committee for Pub. Educ. & Religious Liberty v. Regan, 444 U.S. 646 (1980).
[42] Wolman v. Walter, 433 U.S. 229 (1977).
[43] Roemer v. Bd. of Pub. Works of Maryland, *supra* note 9.
[44] Tilton v. Richardson, 403 U.S. 672 (1971).
[45] Bd. of Educ. v. Allen, 392 U.S. 236 (1968).
[46] Everson v. Bd. of Educ., *supra* note 8.
[47] Cochran v. Louisiana State Bd. of Educ., 281 U.S. 370 (1930).
[48] Bradfield v. Roberts, 175 U.S. 291 (1899).
[49] Lee v. Weisman, *supra* note 5.
[50] Santa Fe Independent School Dist. v. Doe, 530 U.S. 290 (2000).
[51] Lynch v. Donnelly, 465 U.S. 668 (1984).
[52] Marsh v. Chambers, 463 U.S. 783 (1983).

recite the pledge of allegiance and salute the flag.[53] A federal court of appeals upheld the inscription of the phrase "In God We Trust" on the nation's coins and currency,[54] and found unconstitutional the practice of recitation in schools of the pledge of allegiance because of inclusion of the words "one nation under God."[55]

(iii) Free Speech Considerations. Another aspect of this body of law, again from the perspective of tax-exempt religious and other organizations, are First Amendment free speech principles, such as *viewpoint discrimination.* For example, the Supreme Court considered a case concerning the policy of a public school as to community use of its building, afer school hours, for instruction in fields such as education, civics, and the arts. Use of the facilities by a nonprofit club—a Christian organization where children sing, hear Bible lessons, memorize scripture, and pray—was denied on the ground that the club's program content was religious. The Court, however, concluded that the school violated the club's free speech rights by excluding it from conducting its meetings at the school.[56]

This school, assumed by the Court to be a limited public forum, was found by the Court to have acted in a discriminatory manner because the teaching of morals and character was permissible under the school's community use policy. The Court wrote that "speech discussing otherwise permissible subjects cannot be excluded from a limited public forum on the ground that the subject is discussed from a religious viewpoint."[57] That is, the Court disagreed that "something that is 'quintessentially religious' or 'decidely religious in nature' cannot also be characterized properly as the teaching of morals and character development from a particular viewpoint."[58] For purposes of free speech rights, the Court saw "no logical difference in kind between the invocation of Christianity by the [c]lub and the invocation of teamwork, loyalty, or patriotism by other associations to provide a foundation for their lessons."[59]

(b) Constitutional Law Principles and Tax Exemption

Exemption from income and/or other taxes is an economic benefit that is accorded to a wide variety of organizations, including religious entities. This type of exemption is not unconstitutional, however, even though it is extended by government to religious organizations, because the tax preference, like the deduction for charitable contributions and the other programs discussed above, is neutral with respect to religion.

Thus, the Supreme Court, in the seminal case on the point, involving an attack on tax exemption for properties held by religious organization as being violative of the establishment clause, said that the government may become

[53] West Virginia State Bd. of Educ. v. Barnette, 319 U.S. 624 (1943).
[54] Aronow v. United States, 432 F.2d 242 (9th Cir. 1970).
[55] Newdow v. U.S. Congress et al., 292 F.3d 597 (9th Cir. 2002).
[56] Good News Club v. Milford Central School, 533 U.S. 98 (2001).
[57] *Id.* at 111-112.
[58] *Id.* at 111.
[59] *Id.*

involved in matters relating to religious organizations in this regard so as to "mark boundaries to avoid excessive entanglement" and to adhere to the "policy of neutrality that derives from an accommodation of the Establishment and Free Exercise Clauses that has prevented that kind of involvement that would tip the balance toward government control of [c]hurch or governmental restraint on religious practice."[60] Recognizing that either tax exemption or taxation of churches "occasions some degree of involvement with religion," the Court held that "[g]ranting tax exemptions to churches necessarily operates to afford an indirect economic benefit and also gives rise to some, but yet a lesser, involvement than taxing them."[61]

The Court added that the "grant of a tax exemption is not sponsorship since the government does not transfer part of its revenues to churches but simply abstains from demanding that the church support the state."[62] Consequently, the Court concluded that "[t]here is no genuine nexus between tax exemption and establishment of religion."[63]

Consequently, tax exemption for religious organizations is not violative of the religion clauses, as long as it is provided in the context of neutrality, inasmuch as the alternative of nonexemption would necessarily lead to prohibited excessive entanglements, such as valuation of property held by religious organizations, imposition of tax liens, and foreclosures.[64] This approach to the constitutionality of tax exemptions generally was presaged in the literature[65] and in state court opinions.[66]

Nonetheless, although tax exemption for a variety of nonprofit organizations, including religious ones, is constitutional, a tax exemption solely for religious organizations violates the establishment clause. Thus, the Supreme Court held a state sales tax exemption "confined to religious organizations" to be a form of "state sponsorship of religion," and wrote that it should be struck down as

---

[60] Walz v. Tax Comm'r, 397 U.S. 664, 669–670 (1970).

[61] *Id.* at 674

[62] *Id.* at 675.

[63] *Id.* Also Mueller v. Allen, 463 U.S. 388 (1983) (where the Court upheld a tax deduction for amounts paid as school tuition, textbooks, and transportation, even though "religious institutions benefit very substantially from the allowance" of the deduction (at 396, note 5)).

[64] The point may be viewed from the other perspective: "If the Establishment Clause barred the extension of general benefits to religious groups 'a church could not be protected by the police and fire departments or have its public sidewalk kept in repair' " (Widmer v. Vincent, 454 U.S. 263, 274-275 (1981), citing Roemer v. Bd. of Pub. Works, *supra* note 9, at 747).

[65] E.g., Harpster, "Religion, Education, and the Law," 36 *Marq. L. Rev.* 24 (1952); Note, "Exemption of Property Owned and Used by Religious Organizations," 11 *Minn. L. Rev.* 541 (1927).

[66] E.g., Murray v. Comptroller of Treas., 216 A.2d 897 (Md. 1966), *cert. den.*, 385 U.S. 816 (1966); General Fin. Corp. v. Archetto, 176 A.2d 73 (R.I. 1961), *app. dis.*, 369 U.S. 424 (1962); Fellowship of Humanity v. County of Alameda, 315 P.2d 394 (N.Y. 1957); Lundberg v. County of Alameda, 298 P.2d 1 (Cal. 1956), *app. dis. sub nom.*, Heisey v. County of Alameda, 352 U.S. 921 (1956); Franklin St. Soc'y v. Manchester, 60 N.H. 342 (1880). Cf. Sostre v. McGinnes, 334 F.2d 906 (2d Cir. 1964); Washington Ethical Soc'y v. District of Columbia, 249 F.2d 127 (D.C. Cir. 1957); Cooke v. Tramburg, 205 A.2d 889 (Sup. Ct. N.J. 1964).

"lacking a secular purpose and effect."[67] The Court added that "[w]hat is crucial [to sustaining the validity of a tax exemption] is that any subsidy afforded religious organizations be warranted by some overarching secular purpose that justifies like benefits for nonreligious groups."[68] In the aftermath of this decision, a federal district court held that another state's sales and use tax exemptions, available only to religious and faith-based organizations, violated the establishment clause and thus were unconstitutional.[69]

As regards nonprofit organizations seeking tax exemption as religious entities, it is difficult to mark the boundary between proper government regulation and unconstitutional entanglement. Not infrequently, for example, a religious organization will claim a violation of its constitutional rights when the IRS probes too extensively in seeking information about it in the context of evaluation of an application for recognition of exemption. The courts appear to agree that the IRS is obligated, when processing an exemption application, to make inquiries and gather information to determine whether the organization's purposes and activities are in conformance with the statutory requirements, and that this type of an investigation is not precluded by the First Amendment's guarantee of freedom of religion.[70]

[67] Texas Monthly, Inc. v. Bullock, 489 U.S. 1, 11 (1989). Also Arkansas Writers' Project, Inc. v. Ragland, 481 U.S. 221 (1987); Finlator v. Secretary of Revenue of N.C., 902 F.2d 1158 (4th Cir. 1990).
[68] Id. at 15, note 4. As to the matter of a *subsidy*, see § 1.4.
[69] American Civil Liberties Union Foundation of Louisiana v. Crawford, 2002 WL 461649 (E.D. La. 2002). A federal court of appeals requested briefs from parties in a case concerning an interpretation of the parsonage allowance (IRC § 107) (Warren v. Comm'r, 282 F.3d 1119 (9th Cir. 2002); the court considered questioning the constitutionality of the parsonage allowance, notwithstanding the fact that that issue was not considered by the trial court (114 T.C. 343 (2000)). In the aftermath of enactment of the Clergy Housing Allowance Clarification Act of 2002 (116 Stat. 583), however, the appellate court dismissed the appeal and denied the motion of amici curiae to intervene (302 F.3d 1012 (9th Cir. 2002)).
In another manifestation of the intertwining of constitutional law and the law of tax-exempt organizations, some consideration is being given by Congress to amendment of the law to permit churches and certain other religious organizations to engage in a limited amount of political campaign activity; this type of activity is prohibited under present law (see Chapter 21). For example, the House Subcommittee on Oversight held a hearing on the subject on May 14, 2002 ("Review of Internal Revenue Code Section 501(c)(3) Requirements for Religious Organizations," Serial No. 107-69, 107th Cong., 2d Sess. (2002)). At this hearing, the issue of the constitutionality of such a law change was discussed, as was exemption for churches from the tax on political campaign expenditures (see § 21.2). Legislation to this end failed to pass the House of Representatives on October 2, 2002.
[70] Church of Scientology of Calif. v. Comm'r, 83 T.C. 381 (1984), aff'd, 823 F.2d 1310 (9th Cir. 1987); United States v. Toy Nat'l Bank, 79-1 U.S.T.C. ¶ 9344 (N.D. Iowa 1979); General Conference of the Free Church of Am. v. Comm'r, 71 T.C. 920, 930–932 (1979); Coomes v. Comm'r, 572 F.2d 554 (6th Cir. 1978); United States v. Holmes, 614 F.2d 985 (5th Cir. 1980); United States v. Freedom Church, 613 F.2d 316 (1st Cir. 1980); Bronner v. Comm'r, 72 T.C. 368 (1979). Cf. United States v. Dykema, 80-2 U.S.T.C. ¶ 9735 (E.D. Wis. 1980). It is the position of the IRS that the tax-exempt status of a church is to be revoked where the church fails to produce its books and records following a proper request for them (Gen. Couns. Mem. 38248).

§ 8.2   FEDERAL TAX LAW CONSIDERATIONS

(a) Definition of Religion

Although the federal income tax law provides tax exemption for religious organizations, there is no statutory or regulatory definition of the terms *religious* or *religion* for this purpose. Indeed, by reason of the religion clauses of the First Amendment, it would be unconstitutional for the federal government to adopt and apply a strict definition of these terms. As one court stated, the "lack of a precise definition [of the terms *religious* or *religion*] is not surprising in light of the fact that a constitutional provision is involved."[71]

Nonetheless, government officials, judges, and justices have, from time to time, grappled with the meaning of the term *religious*. The Supreme Court ventured the observation, authored over a century ago, that the term *religion* has "reference to one's views of his relations to his Creator, and to the obligations they impose of reverence for his being and character, and of obedience to his will."[72] Subsequently, the Court wrote that the "essence of religion is belief in a relation to God involving duties superior to those arising from any human relation."[73] In other than the constitutional law and federal tax law contexts, these instances have arisen in cases concerning, for example, conscientious objector status,[74] employment discrimination,[75] state and local real property tax exemptions,[76] and zoning restrictions.[77]

State courts have ventured into this area. One court stated that the term *religion* has "reference to man's relation to Divinity; to reverence, worship, obedience, and submission to the mandates and precepts of supernatural or superior beings" and in its broadest sense "includes all forms of belief in the existence of superior beings, exercising power over human beings by volition, imposing rules of conduct with future rewards and punishments."[78] Many courts have advanced definitions, including the following: "Religion as generally accepted may be defined as a bond uniting man to God and a virtue whose purpose is to render God the worship due to him as the source of all being and the principle of all govern-

---

[71] Malnak v. Yogi, 440 F. Supp. 1284, 1315 (D.N.J. 1977), *aff'd*, 592 F.2d 197 (3d Cir. 1979).

[72] Davis v. Beason, 133 U.S. 333, 342 (1890).

[73] United States v. Macintosh, 283 U.S. 605, 633 (1931).

[74] Welsh v. United States, 398 U.S. 333 (1970); United States v. Seeger, 380 U.S. 163 (1965); Berman v. United States, 156 F.2d 377 (9th Cir. 1946), *cert. den.*, 329 U.S. 795 (1946); United States ex rel. Phillips v. Downer, 135 F.2d 521 (2d Cir. 1943); United States v. Kauten, 133 F.2d 703 (2d Cir. 1943).

[75] Braunfield v. Brown, 366 U.S. 599 (1961); Johnson v. U.S. Postal Serv., 364 F. Supp. 37 (N.D. Fla. 1973); Powers v. State Dept. of Social Welfare, 493 P.2d 590 (Kan. 1972); Martin v. Industrial Accident Comm'n, 304 P.2d 828 (D.C. Cal. 1956).

[76] Walz v. Tax Comm'n, *supra* note 60; Washington Ethical Soc'y v. District of Columbia, *supra* note 66; American Bible Soc'y v. Lewisohn, 351 N.E.2d 697 (Ct. App. N.Y. 1976); Watchtower Bible & Tract Soc'y, Inc. v. Lewisohn, 315 N.E.2d 801 (N.Y. 1974); People ex rel. Watchtower Bible & Tract Soc'y, Inc. v. Haring, 170 N.E.2d 677 (Ct. App. N.Y. 1960); Fellowship of Humanity v. County of Alameda, *supra* note 66.

[77] In re Community Synagogue v. Bates, 136 N.E.2d 488 (N.Y. 1956).

[78] McMasters v. State of Okla., 29 A.L.R. 292, 294 (Okla. Crim. App. 1922).

ment of things;"[79] and the "Christian religion, in its most important ultimate aspect, recognizes, has faith in and worships a Divine Being or Spirit—one Father of all mankind—who has the power to and will forgive the transgressions of repentants and care for the immortal souls of the believers, and which belief brings earthly solace and comfort to and tends to induce right living in such believers."[80] One summary definition of the term is: "Religion is squaring human life with superhuman life. . . . What is common to all religions is belief in a superhuman power and an adjustment of human activities to the requirements of that power, such adjustment as may enable the individual believer to exist more happily."[81]

The literature contains many definitions of the term *religious*.[82] For example, one author posits six "dimensions of religion." These are the:

- Doctrinal dimension. "A religion typically has a system of doctrines."
- Mythic dimension. "Typically a religion has a story or stories to tell. . . . In the field of religion such stories are called myths."
- Ethical dimension. "A religion has an ethical dimension. Believers are enjoined to observe certain rules and precepts."
- Ritual dimension. "[T]ypically a religion has a ritual dimension" such as "acts of worship, praying, singing . . . and . . . sacraments."
- Experiential dimension. "Ritual helps to express feelings—awe and wonder, for instance—and can itself provide a context of dramatic experience."
- Social dimension. "Any tradition needs some kind of organization in order to perpetuate itself. It thus embeds itself in society."[83]

One student of the subject believes that religion comprises a set of beliefs that assists human beings in giving meaning to otherwise unanswerable questions. Religion is a way that human beings orient themselves to the reality of the world. Religion often involves a ritual (tradition), prayer, ethics, a figurehead, a center of worship, a text (for example, the Bible or the Koran), one or more practices (for example, in Christianity, baptism), symbols (for example, in Christianity, the cross), and a goal (an ideal state of existence). Religion usually entails a belief in a realm of existence that lies beyond humans' planetary existence, efforts to progress toward a goal, and the achievement of personal benefits through techniques such as prayer, offerings, rituals, and pilgrimages.[84]

The federal government and the courts have generally been reluctant to take the position that a particular activity, function, or purpose is not religious in nature. One court succinctly stated the reason why:

---

[79] Nikulnikoff v. Archbishop & Consistory of Russian Orthodox Greek Catholic Church, 255 N.Y.S. 653, 663 (Sup. Ct. N.Y. Cty. 1932).
[80] Taylor v. State, 11 So.2d 663, 673 (Miss. 1943).
[81] Hopkins, *The History of Religions*, 2 (Macmillan, 1918), quoted in Minersville School Dist. v. Gobitis, 108 F.2d 683, 685 (3d Cir. 1939).
[82] The author thanks Christopher B. Hopkins, Esq., for his contribution to this portion of the text.
[83] Smart, *Worldviews: Crosscultural Explorations of Human Beliefs* 7–8 (Charles Scribner's Sons, 1983). Also Elide, *The Sacred & the Profane: The Nature of Religion* (Harcourt Brace Jovanovich, 1959).
[84] *Supra* note 82.

> Neither this Court, nor any branch of this Government, will consider the merits or fallacies of a religion. Nor will the Court compare the beliefs, dogmas, and practices of a newly organized religion with those of an older, more established religion. Nor will the Court praise or condemn a religion, however excellent or fanatical or preposterous it may seem. Were the Courts to do so, it would impinge upon the guarantees of the First Amendment.[85]

Similarly, a federal court of appeals observed that it is not the "province of government officials or courts to determine religious orthodoxy."[86] Another court evidenced a like attitude, when it wrote that, "[a]s a judicial body, we are loathe to evaluate and judge ecclesiastical authority and duties in the various religious disciplines."[87]

This approach has been sanctioned by the Supreme Court, which has repeatedly held[88] that freedom of thought and religious belief "embraces the right to maintain theories of life and of death and of the hereafter which are rank heresy to followers of the orthodox faiths," and that, if triers of fact undertake to examine the truth or falsity of the religious beliefs of a sect, "they enter a forbidden domain."[89] Subsequently, the Court observed that it is "not within the judicial ken to question the centrality of particular beliefs or practices to a faith, or the validity of particular litigants' interpretations of those creeds."[90] Yet some courts are not reluctant to attempt to separate secular beliefs from religious ones, as illustrated by a court opinion involving an organization that, in addition to lacking "external manifestations analogous to other religions," had as its major doctrine a "single-faceted doctrine of sexual preference and secular lifestyle."[91]

A court observed that, in "implementing the establishment clause, the Supreme Court has made clear that an activity may be religious even though it is neither part of nor derives from a societally recognized religious sect."[92] In another instance, a court held that an organization was a religious entity because it held regular prayer meetings and weekly services, and published a newsletter.[93]

An illustration of the courts' policy to abstain from a determination of what is and is not religious is an opinion of a federal court concerning an organization,

---

[85] Universal Life Church, Inc. v. United States, 372 F. Supp. 770, 776 (E.D. Cal. 1974). This decision has not estopped subsequent federal court actions adverse to the Universal Life Church and to those who establish "congregations" with respect to it (see *infra* § (c)) (Universal Life Church, Inc. v. United States, 86-1 U.S.T.C. ¶ 9271 (Ct. Cl. 1986); Universal Life Church v. United States, 76-2 U.S.T.C. ¶ 9548 (E.D. Cal. 1976)).

[86] Teterud v. Burns, 522 F.2d 357 (8th Cir. 1975).

[87] Colbert v. Comm'r, 61 T.C. 449, 455 (1974).

[88] See *supra* § 1.

[89] United States v. Ballard, 322 U.S. 78, 86, 87 (1943). Also United States v. Seeger, *supra* note 74, at 174–176.

[90] Hernandez v. Comm'r, 490 U.S. 680 (1989).

[91] Church of the Chosen People (North Am. Panarchate) v. United States, 548 F. Supp. 1247, 1252, 1253 (D. Minn. 1982).

[92] Malnak v. Yogi, *supra* note 71, 440 F. Supp. at 1313.

[93] The Church of the Visible Intelligence That Governs the Universe v. United States, 83-2 U.S.T.C. ¶ 9726 (Ct. Cl. 1983).

the founder of which received "revelations" from "Ascended Masters," princi-pally Saint Germain.[94] The founder's spouse continued to receive the revelations after his death. The entity was organized and operated to propagate the teachings of the "I AM Religious Activity." In this case, the IRS did not allege that the orga-nization was not religious but principally sought to convince the court that net in-come of the organization inured to the benefit of private individuals. The court devoted little effort to finding the organization religious in nature but largely re-lied on its statement in a prior case:

> Religion is not confined to a sect or a ritual. The symbols of religion to one are anathema to another. What one may regard as charity another may scorn as foolish waste. And even education is today not free from divergence of view as to its validity. Congress left open the door of tax exemption to all corpora-tions meeting the test, the restriction being not as to the species of religion, charity, science or education under which they might operate, but as to the use of its profits and the exclusive purpose of its existence.[95]

The court, noting that it was not "compelled to decide whether the objectives of the . . . [organization] are worthy or desirable," concluded that the organization was established exclusively for religious purposes.[96]

Another federal court reflected the same degree of caution when deciding a case involving an organization formed as the parent church of Scientology.[97] The court concluded that the organization was not exempt from tax—not because it was not religious (that issue was not even considered)—but because the net in-come of the entity inured to the founders in their private capacity.[98]

Occasional attempts made in the literature to define the term *religion*[99] usu-ally become criticized for being or becoming incomplete or outdated.[100]

---

[94] Saint Germain Found. v. Comm'r, 26 T.C. 648 (1956).

[95] Unity School of Christianity v. Comm'r, 4 B.T.A. 61, 70 (1926).

[96] Saint Germain Found. v. Comm'r, *supra* note 94, at 657. Also Rev. Rul. 68-563, 1968-2 C.B. 212, *amp. by* Rev. Rul. 78-385, 1978-2 C.B. 174; Rev. Rul. 68-26, 1968-1 C.B. 272.

[97] Founding Church of Scientology v. United States, 412 F.2d 1197 (Ct. Cl. 1969), *cert. den.*, 397 U.S. 1009 (1970). Cf. Church of Scientology of Hawaii v. United States, 485 F.2d 313 (9th Cir. 1973); Church of Sci-entology of Calif. v. United States, 75-2 U.S.T.C. ¶ 9584 (9th Cir. 1975); Founding Church of Scientology of Washington, D.C. v. United States, 409 F.2d 1146 (D.C. Cir. 1968), *cert. den.*, 396 U.S. 963 (1969).

[98] The U.S. Tax Court held that the expenses of Scientology processing and auditing are not deductible medical expenses in Brown v. Comm'r, 62 T.C. 551 (1974), *aff'd*, 523 F.2d 365 (8th Cir. 1975). Cf. Hande-land v. United States, 75-2 U.S.T.C. ¶ 9586 (9th Cir. 1975); Rev. Rul. 78-188, 1978-1 C.B. 40; Rev. Rul. 78-190, 1978-1 C.B. 74. The Supreme Court held that payments to the Church of Scientology for auditing sessions are not deductible as charitable contributions, in Hernandez v. Comm'r, *supra* note 90. The IRS adopted the same position in 1978 (Rev. Rul. 78-189, 1978-1 C.B. 68), although it rendered that ruling ob-solete in 1993 (Rev. Rul. 93-73, 1993-2 C.B. 75). Also in 1993, the IRS recognized the tax-exempt status of 25 Church of Scientology organizations in rulings issued by the IRS National Office (61 *Tax Notes* 279 Oct. 18, 1993). A federal appellate court, in ruling that tuition payments made to a religious private school which the payors' children attend are not deductible as charitable gifts, questioned the constitu-tionality of the closing agreement between the IRS and the Church (Sklar v. Comm'r, 279 F.3d 697 (9th Cir. 2002)). In general, United States v. Moon, 718 F.2d 1210 (2d Cir. 1983), *cert. den.*, 466 U.S. 971 (1984).

[99] E.g., Note, "Toward a Constitutional Definition of Religion," 91 *Harv. L. Rev.* 1056 (1978).

[100] E.g., Worthing, " 'Religion' and 'Religious Institutions' Under the First Amendment," 7 *Pepp. L. Rev.* 313, 320–321 (1980).

There are, nonetheless, some explicit discussions of what may constitute *religion* or *religious belief*. In one case, it was said that "[r]eligious belief . . . is a belief finding expression in a conscience which categorically requires the believer to disregard elementary self-interest and to accept martyrdom in preference to transgressing its tenets."[101] Another court found an activity religious because it was centered around belief in a higher being "which in its various forms is given the name 'god' in common usage" and because a form of prayer was involved.[102] Still another court formulated a three-part test for determining the religious nature of an organization's goals: whether the beliefs address fundamental and ultimate questions concerning the human condition, are comprehensive in nature, and constitute an entire system of belief instead of merely an isolated teaching, and are manifested in external forms.[103] The Supreme Court placed emphasis on belief in a "supreme being," and looked to see whether a "given belief that is sincere and meaningful occupies a place in the life of its possessor parallel to that filled by the orthodox belief in God"[104] and whether the belief occupies in the life of the individual involved " 'a place parallel to that filled by . . . God' in traditional religious persons."[105] Some courts have been reluctant, however, to confine the concept of *religious belief* to theistic beliefs.

For example, one court held that the permissible inquiry on this subject is "whether or not the belief occupies the same place in the lives of its holders that the orthodox beliefs occupy in the lives of believing majorities, and whether a given group that claims the exemption conducts itself the way groups conceded to be religious conduct themselves."[106] This court added that the appropriate test is whether the activities of the organization in question "serve the same place in the lives of its members, and occupy the same place in society, as the activities of the theistic churches."[107] Indeed, this court developed what is apparently the most expansive, yet definitional statement as to the general characteristics of the concept of *religion*:

> Religion simply includes: (1) a belief, not necessarily referring to supernatural powers; (2) a cult, involving a gregarious association openly expressing the beliefs; (3) a system of moral practice directly resulting from an adherence to the belief; and (4) an organization within the cult designed to observe the tenets of belief.[108]

---

[101] United States v. Kauten, *supra* note 74 at 708.

[102] Malnak v. Yogi, *supra* note 71, 440 F. Supp. at 1320, 1323.

[103] Africa v. Commonwealth of Pa., 662 F.2d 1025, 1032 (3d Cir. 1981), *cert. den.*, 456 U.S. 908 (1982).

[104] United States v. Seeger, *supra* note 74, 380 U.S. at 165–166.

[105] Welsh v. United States, *supra* note 74, 398 U.S. at 340.

[106] Fellowship of Humanity v. County of Alameda, *supra* note 66, 315 P.2d at 406.

[107] *Id.*, 315 P.2d at 409–410.

[108] *Id.*, 315 P.2d at 406. This finding that secular humanism is a religion applied only to a particular group of humanists. The debate as to whether humanism is a *religion* or merely a *philosophy* has not been stilled. For example, an appellate court observed that "traditional notions of religion surely would not include humanism" (Kalka v. Hawk, 215 F.3d 90, 98 (D.C. Cir. 2000)) (holding that, even assuming humanism is a religion, that principle has not been clearly established, so that officials of the Federal Bureau of Prisons were qualifiedly immune from liability for refusing to allow a prisoner to promote humanism within prison chapels).

Indeed, the difficulties contemporary courts are having in grappling with a definition of the term *religion* can be seen in court holdings that the use of basic reader textbooks, offensive to the religious beliefs of some, in public schools does not advance "secular humanism" or inhibit theistic religion.[109]

Consequently, federal tax law lacks a crisp and workable definition of the term *religious*. There is, nonetheless, an approach to application of the term that adheres to the admonition offered concerning the meaning of the term *obscenity*, that one "knows it when one sees it."[110] As the foregoing citations reflect, there are unabashed references in the court opinions to "traditional," "orthodox," and "majority" religious beliefs, and at least one opinion differentiates between groups "conceded to be religious" and others. Also, as noted, it is relatively clear that religious belief is not confined to theistic belief. Indeed, the most pertinent one-sentence summary on this point is that the term *religion* as employed in federal and state statutes "has been held to encompass nontheistic beliefs which occupy a place in the lives of their possessors parallel to that occupied by belief in God in persons with traditional religious faith."[111]

An organization that is deemed to be a religious entity may well engage in activities that by themselves may not be regarded as religious, such as charitable, educational, social welfare, and community activities. It appears generally recognized that the conduct of these activities will not deprive an otherwise religious organization of its classification as a religious group. For example, one court held that "[s]trictly religious uses and activities are more than prayer and sacrifice" and include social activities, study, and community service.[112] A commentator observed that "[r]eligious activities or uses have been held to include incidental social, charitable, and maintenance activities (for both persons and property) as well as religious worship."[113]

(b) Other Bases for Denial of Exemption

Typically, when a court finds an alleged religious organization to not be tax-exempt, it does so not on the ground that the organization's purpose is not religious but rather on a finding that the activity smacks too much of a commercial enterprise operated for private gain or that the organization engages in an inappropriate

---

[109] Smith v. Board of School Comm'rs of Mobile County, 827 F.2d 684, 688–689 (11th Cir. 1987), *rev'g* 655 F. Supp. 939 (S.D. Ala. 1987); also Mozert v. Hawkins County Board of Educ., 827 F.2d 1058 (6th Cir. 1987), *rev'g* 647 F. Supp. 1194 (E.D. Tenn. 1986), where it was observed that "[a]lthough the Supreme Court has shied away from attempting to define religion, the past forty years has witnessed an expansion of the court's understanding of religious belief," so that the "concept of religion has shifted from a fairly narrow religious theism . . . to a broader concept providing protection for the views of unorthodox and nontheistic faiths" (concurring opinion, 827 F.2d at 1078).

[110] In Jacobellis v. Ohio, 378 U.S. 184 (1964), Justice Potter Stewart, conceptualizing as to the meaning of the word "obscene," observed that one may not succeed in intelligibly defining the term but would "know it when I see it" (at 197).

[111] Worthing, " 'Religion' and 'Religious Institutions' Under the First Amendment," *supra* note 100 at 332.

[112] In re Community Synagogue v. Bates, *supra* note 77, 136 N.E.2d at 493.

[113] Worthing, " 'Religion' and 'Religious Institutions' Under the First Amendment," *supra* note 100 at 332.

amount of lobbying or political activities.[114] In one case, a restaurant was operated as a private business for profit with the net profits going to a church, which itself was engaged in commercial activities; contributions to the church were held to not be deductible because the organization's business activities defeated the requisite tax status.[115] Another purported religious organization's exempt status was precluded because its primary activity was the operation of a (religious) publishing house.[116]

An illustration of the application of the legislative activities rules in this context was the government's successful revocation of the tax-exempt status of a national ministry organization. The organization maintained religious radio and television broadcasts, authored publications, engaged in evangelistic campaigns and meetings, operated the Summer Anti-Communist University, and conducted other activities. All parties (the IRS and courts) recognized this organization as being a religious entity; its tax exemption was lost on the grounds that a substantial part of its activities consisted of carrying on propaganda, attempting to influence legislation, and intervening in political campaigns.[117] Similarly, the IRS successfully revoked the tax-exempt status of an organization the purpose of which is to defend and maintain religious liberty in the United States by the dissemination of knowledge concerning the constitutional principle of the separation of church and state, on the ground that the organization engaged in a substantial amount of lobbying.[118]

A court found that an organization's social aspects were so predominant as to relegate any religious activities to secondary status.[119] The organization, formed to further the doctrine of "ethical egoism," was found to have as its principal purpose the social functions of sponsoring dinner meetings and publishing a newsletter. While "church meetings" were also held, the court believed they were in reality merely an extension of the social gatherings. In general, the court concluded that the "religious aspects of such conclaves seems . . . indistinct."[120] Likewise, an organization was determined to not qualify as a religious organization because its primary activity was the investment and accumulation of funds, albeit for the purpose of eventually building a church.[121]

---

[114] See Chapters 25, 20, and 21, respectively.

[115] Riker v. Comm'r, 244 F.2d 220 (9th Cir. 1957), *cert. den.*, 355 U.S. 839 (1957). Also Parker v. Comm'r, 365 F.2d 792 (8th Cir. 1966), *cert. den.*, 385 U.S. 1026 (1967).

[116] Scripture Press Found. v. United States, 285 F.2d 800 (Ct. Cl. 1961), *cert. den.*, 368 U.S. 985 (1962). Also Christian Manner Int'l, Inc. v. Comm'r, 71 T.C. 661 (1979); Fides Publishers Ass'n v. United States, 263 F. Supp. 924 (N.D. Ind. 1967); Unitary Mission Church of Long Island v. Comm'r, 74 T.C. 507 (1980), *aff'd*, 647 F.2d 163 (2d Cir. 1981); Bubbling Well Church of Universal Love, Inc. v. Comm'r, 74 T.C. 531 (1980), *aff'd*, 670 F.2d 104 (9th Cir. 1981); Loiler v. Comm'r, 53 T.C.M. 785 (1987). Cf. Elisian Guild, Inc. v. United States, 412 F.2d 121 (1st Cir. 1969); Rev. Rul. 68-26, *supra* note 96.

[117] Christian Echoes Nat'l Ministry, Inc. v. United States, 470 F.2d 849 (10th Cir. 1972), *cert. den.*, 414 U.S. 864 (1973).

[118] Alexander v. "Americans United," Inc., 416 U.S. 752 (1974).

[119] First Libertarian Church v. Comm'r, 74 T.C. 396 (1980).

[120] *Id.* at 405.

[121] Western Catholic Church v. Comm'r, 73 T.C. 196 (1979), *aff'd*, 631 F.2d 736 (7th Cir. 1980), *cert. den.*, 450 U.S. 981 (1981).

RELIGIOUS ORGANIZATIONS

(c) Abuse of Exemption for Religious Organizations

There is no question but that the current state of the law on this subject poses perplexing and probably unresolvable burdens on regulatory officials and judges. These difficulties are exacerbated as new religions emerge and as new forms of approach to the practice of religion evolve (for example, the "electronic churches" and the "mail-order ministries"[122]). In some instances, such as with re-

---

[122] The IRS has been particularly concerned with the tax status of mail-order ministries, such as those chartered by the Universal Life Church (ULC). In 1977, the IRS commenced a study of illegal tax protestor activities, which culminated in a report published in 1979. One finding of this report was that illegal protest schemes are increasingly employing the technique of establishing "bogus churches," where "a secularly employed individual places all of his or her wages in an organization created through the use of a mail-order charter whereby the organization pays for his or her living expense." To date, the courts have uniformly rejected claims for tax exemption for, or the deductibility of gifts to, these "organizations." E.g., Davis v. Comm'r, 81 T.C. 806 (1983), aff'd, 767 F.2d 931 (9th Cir. 1985), holding that the payment of personal expenses from a ULC congregation bank account constitutes private inurement (see Chapter 19) and that the transfer of funds to the account was not a bona fide gift; also Richardson v. Comm'r, 70 T.C.M. 14 (1995); Page v. Comm'r, 66 T.C.M. 571 (1993); Bruce Goldberg, Inc. v. Comm'r, 58 T.C.M. 519 (1989); Gookin v. United States, 707 (N.D. Cal. 1988); Bullock v. Comm'r, 56 T.C.M. 636 (1988); Johnston v. Comm'r, 56 T.C.M. 520 (1988); Bray v. Comm'r, 56 T.C.M. 430 (1988); Mulvaney v. Comm'r, 55 T.C.M. 998 (1988); Boharski v. Comm'r, 55 T.C.M. 604 (1988); Jackson v. Comm'r, 55 T.C.M. 537 (1988); Webb v. Comm'r, 55 T.C.M. 245 (1988), aff'd, 872 F.2d 380 (11th Cir. 1989); Dunn v. Comm'r, 55 T.C.M. 66 (1988); Burwell v. Comm'r, 89 T.C.M. 590 (1987), app. dis. (9th Cir., May 4, 1988); Ruberto v. Comm'r, 54 T.C.M. 1388 (1987); Goodnight v. Comm'r, 54 T.C.M. 1272 (1987); Roughen v. Comm'r, 54 T.C.M. 510 (1987); Randolph v. Comm'r, 54 T.C.M. 339 (1987); Bobbit v. Comm'r, 53 T.C.M. 1285 (1987); Graboske v. Comm'r, 53 T.C.M. 896 (1987); Krause v. Comm'r, 53 T.C.M. 589 (1987); Fowler v. Comm'r, 53 T.C.M. 377 (1987); Fowler v. Comm'r, 53 T.C.M. 373 (1987); Petersen v. Comm'r, 53 T.C.M. 235 (1987); Adamson v. Comm'r, 52 T.C.M. 699 (1987); McMains v. Comm'r, 51 T.C.M. 1297 (1986); Mathis v. Comm'r, 51 T.C.M. 1067 (1986); Starks v. Comm'r, 51 T.C.M. 500 (1986); Zollo v. Comm'r, 51 T.C.M. 443 (1986); Roben v. Comm'r, 51 T.C.M. 407 (1986); Grew v. Comm'r, 51 T.C.M. 405 (1986); Martin v. Comm'r, 51 T.C.M. 403 (1986); Van Cleve v. Comm'r, 50 T.C.M. 1353 (1985), Rager v. Comm'r, 775 F.2d 1081 (9th Cir. 1985); Bell v. Comm'r, 85 T.C. 436 (1985); Gambardella v. Comm'r, 50 T.C.M. 1331 (1985); Neil v. Comm'r, 50 T.C.M. 1254 (1985); Gookin v. Comm'r, 50 T.C.M. 1163 (1985); Botwinick v. Comm'r, 50 T.C.M. 1161 (1985); Woo v. Comm'r, 50 T.C.M. 1115 (1985); Elliott v. Comm'r, 50 T.C.M. 1111 (1985); Pryor v. Comm'r, 50 T.C.M. 1093 (1985); Weaver v. Comm'r, 50 T.C.M. 1020 (1985); Sensing v. Comm'r, 50 T.C.M. 973 (1985); Cox v. Comm'r, 50 T.C.M. 971 (1985); Eutsler v. Comm'r, 50 T.C.M. 872 (1985); Marinovich v. Comm'r, 50 T.C.M. 839 (1985); Conlow v. Comm'r, 50 T.C.M. 832 (1985); Layden v. Comm'r, 50 T.C.M. 527 (1985); Rutter v. Comm'r, 50 T.C.M. 506 (1985); Taylor v. Comm'r, 50 T.C.M. 313 (1985); Morgan v. Comm'r, 50 T.C.M. 114 (1985); Ebner v. Comm'r, 49 T.C.M. 1541 (1985); Brown v. Comm'r, 49 T.C.M. 1531 (1985); Wilcox v. Comm'r, 49 T.C.M. 1525 (1985); Lufkin v. Comm'r, 49 T.C.M. 1462 (1985); Dummler v. Comm'r, 49 T.C.M. 1460 (1985); Witherow v. Comm'r, 49 T.C.M. 1458 (1985); Uhrig v. Comm'r, 49 T.C.M. 1355 (1985); Beauvais v. Comm'r, 49 T.C.M. 1346 (1985); Howard v. Comm'r, 49 T.C.M. 1344 (1985); Green v. Comm'r, 49 T.C.M. 1320 (1985); Estate of Sweeney v. Comm'r, 49 T.C.M. 1249 (1985); Porter v. Comm'r, 49 T.C.M. 1015 (1985); Williamson v. Comm'r, 49 T.C.M. 928 (1985); Booker v. Comm'r, 49 T.C.M. 854 (1985); Lane v. Comm'r, 49 T.C.M. 837 (1985); Nelson v. Comm'r, 49 T.C.M. 799 (1985); Schmidel v. Comm'r, 49 T.C.M. 351 (1984); Abercrombie v. Comm'r, 49 T.C.M. 347 (1984); Shade v. Comm'r, 49 T.C.M. 212 (1984); Moriarty v. Comm'r, 48 T.C.M. 1345 (1984) Hoskinson v. Comm'r, 48 T.C.M. 678 (1984); Hodges v. Comm'r, 48 T.C.M. 617 (1984); Hawbaker v. Comm'r, 47 T.C.M. 231 (1983); Universal Life Church, Inc. (Full Circle) v. Comm'r, 83 T.C. 292 (1984); Lee v. Comm'r, 48 T.C.M. 1454 (1984); Ruberto v. Comm'r, 48 T.C.M. 1438 (1984), rev'd, 774 F.2d 61 (2d Cir. 1985), on remand, 54 T.C.M. 1388 (1988); Beck v. Comm'r, 48 T.C.M. 1425 (1984); Pollard v. Comm'r, 48 T.C.M. 1303 (1984), aff'd, 786 F.2d 1063 (11th Cir. 1986); Martinez v. Comm'r, 48 T.C.M. 1271 (1984); Swanson v. Comm'r, 48 T.C.M. 1267 (1984); Ford v. Comm'r, 48 T.C.M. 1173 (1984); Brennan v. Comm'r, 48 T.C.M. 1165 (1984); Wert v. Comm'r, 48 T.C.M. 1158 (1984); Di Pierri v. Comm'r, 48 T.C.M. 1156 (1984); Addeo v. Comm'r, 48 T.C.M. 1126 (1984); Bradfield v. Comm'r, 48 T.C.M. 1071 (1984);

spect to personal churches,[123] the matter has evolved away from the law of tax-exempt organizations and into the realm of criminal tax fraud.[124] Indeed, personal churches have been added to the concept of tax shelters, so that special penalties for substantial understatements of federal income tax[125] are

Kent v. Comm'r, 48 T.C.M. 952 (1984); Snodgrass v. Comm'r, 48 T.C.M. 883 (1984); Makkay v. Comm'r, 47 T.C.M. 869 (1984); Poldrugovaz v. Comm'r, 47 T.C.M. 860 (1984); Hoskinson v. Comm'r, 48 T.C.M. 678 (1984); Clark v. Comm'r, 48 T.C.M. 371 (1984); Fowler v. Comm'r, 48 T.C.M. 309 (1984); Johnson v. Comm'r, 48 T.C.M. 289 (1984); Beasley v. Comm'r, 48 T.C.M. 287 (1984); Kalgaard v. Comm'r, 48 T.C.M. 106 (1984); aff'd, 764 F.2d 1322 (9th Cir. 1985); Winston v. Comm'r, 48 T.C.M. 55 (1984); Odd v. Comm'r, 47 T.C.M. 1483 (1984); Chicone v. Comm'r, 47 T.C.M. 980 (1984); Schreiber v. Comm'r, 47 T.C.M. 680 (1984); Stephenson v. Comm'r, 79 T.C. 995 (1982); Mendenhall v. Comm'r, 46 T.C.M. 1120 (1983); Bronner v. Comm'r, 45 T.C.M. 738 (1983); Solanne v. Comm'r, 45 T.C.M. 657 (1983); Owens v. Comm'r, 45 T.C.M. 157 (1982); Mustain v. Comm'r, 45 T.C.M. 153 (1982); Harcourt v. Comm'r, 44 T.C.M. 1506 (1982); Neil v. Comm'r, 44 T.C.M. 1237 (1982); Magin v. Comm'r, 44 T.C.M. 397 (1982); Murphy v. Comm'r, 45 T.C.M. 621 (1983); Hall v. Comm'r, 44 T.C.M. 151 (1982), aff'd, 729 F.2d 632 (9th Cir. 1984); Schilberg v. Comm'r, 44 T.C.M. 148 (1982); Kellman v. Comm'r, 42 T.C.M. 1508 (1981); Riemers v. Comm'r, 42 T.C.M. 838 (1981); Brown v. Comm'r, 41 T.C.M. 542 (1980). A ULC congregation seems doomed to noncharitable status in the U.S. Tax Court, due to the "cynical abuse of the church concept for tax purposes in recent years" (Church of Ethereal Joy v. Comm'r, 83 T.C. 20, 27 (1984)). Likewise, a federal court of appeals has referenced the "patently frivolous appeals filed by abusers of the tax system [who create unqualified religious groups] merely to delay and harass the collection of public revenues" (Granzow v. Comm'r, 739 F.2d 265, 267 (7th Cir. 1984), aff'g 46 T.C.M. 223 (1983)). In general, those who establish a Life Science Church congregation fare no better (e.g., Troyer v. Comm'r, 57 T.C.M. 334 (1989)). See also Woods v. Comm'r, 58 T.C.M. 673 (1989), aff'd without op. (6th Cir. 1991).

In one instance, an appeal of a ULC congregation case was deemed by the court to be so frivolous that double costs and lawyers' fees were awarded the government (Larsen v. Comm'r, 765 F.2d 939 (9th Cir. 1985)). In another instance, the deduction for alleged gifts to a ULC congregation was denied on the ground that the receipts offered as evidence were hearsay (McMains v. Comm'r, 53 T.C.M. 118 (1987)). Further, charitable contribution deductions were denied by the U.S. Tax Court for payments made by ULC charter holders to other ULC congregations, where the payments were repaid by means of a check-swapping arrangement, with the court noting that the claimants "present[ed] more tiresome claims to deductions for alleged contributions" to the ULC (Wedvik v. Comm'r, 87 T.C. 1458, 1465 (1986)). Also Dew v. Comm'r, 91 T.C. 615 (1988) (where the court found a "daisy chain" sequence of payments to be a "perifidious twist to the usual Universal Life Church" case, a "brazen scheme," and "as blatant an example of [private] inurement as this Court has encountered in the innumerable ULC scams and check-swapping schemes it has been called upon to rule on" (id., at 625, 624); Svedahl v. Comm'r, 89 T.C. 245 (1987), app. dis. (9th Cir., June 24, 1988). Yet these cases are not automatically won by the government on appeal; in one case, the appellate court refused to find private inurement for purposes of a summary judgment request, and the case was remanded for trial on the point (Carter v. United States, 973 F.2d 1479 (9th Cir. 1992)).

The courts are upholding summonses served on banks in connection with investigations into the legitimacy of deductions for contributions made to ULC congregations (e.g., LaMura v. Comm'r, 765 F.2d 974 (11th Cir. 1985)). On September 4, 1984, the IRS announced that it will no longer recognize the tax-exempt status of the "parent" Universal Life Church (Ann. 84-90, 1984-36 I.R.B. 32). This revocation was subsequently upheld by the U.S. Claims Court in Universal Life Church, Inc. v. United States, 87-2 U.S.T.C. ¶ 9617 (Cl. Ct. 1987), aff'd, 862 F.2d 321 (Fed. Cir. 1988). The practices represented by these cases can amount to tax fraud (e.g., Braswell v. Comm'r, 66 T.C.M. 627 (1993); Mobley v. Comm'r, 65 T.C.M. 1939 (1993), aff'd in unpub. op. (11th Cir. 1994)).

In general, Petkanics & Petkanics, "Mail Order Ministries, the Religious Purpose Exemption, and the Constitution," 33 Tax Law. 959 (1980).

[123] E.g., Rev. Rul. 81-94, 1981-1 C.B. 330; Rev. Rul. 78-232, 1978-1 C.B. 69.
[124] E.g., United States v. Daly, 756 F.2d 1076 (5th Cir. 1985).
[125] IRC § 6661.

applicable.[126] Other instances involving blatant abuses are generating numerous court opinions, which contribute to the shaping of the evolving law, often in ways not complimentary to the religious sector.[127] Yet policymakers are to tread carefully even when confronting the nontraditional, minority, and/or unorthodox religious groups; the First Amendment applies to them as well. As one court noted, "[n]ew religions appear in this country frequently and they cannot stand outside the first amendment merely because they did not exist when the Bill of Rights was drafted."[128] Nonetheless, the IRS's concerns about abuse in this area are leading to stringent decisions by the courts, so that the law is often shaping up as being appropriately tough with respect to the sham situations, but it is formulating some legal principles that are questionable when applied outside the areas of abuse.[129]

Still, church abuse cases abound, with tax avoidance clearly taking precedence over religion.[130] The U.S. Tax Court has been inundated with these cases; in 1983, the court wrote that "our tolerance for taxpayers who establish churches solely for tax avoidance purposes is reaching a breaking point."[131] The court added: "Not only do these taxpayers use the pretext of a church to avoid paying their fair share of taxes, even when their brazen schemes are uncovered many of them resort to the courts in a shameless attempt to vindicate themselves."[132] Consequently, the court gave notice that it will impose damages in these cases for using the court for purposes of delay.[133]

The Tax Court imposes the penalty for fraudulently intending to evade and defeat the payment of taxes legally due[134] in a situation where an individual established a bogus church. In one of these cases, a correctional officer, while attending a "tax strike convention," obtained information on how to form an "independent church." The church was formed with the assistance of materials acquired from the "Church of the Golden Rule." Banking accounts were opened in the name of the "church." The minister, his wife, and his daughter were signatories on the accounts, and personal expenses were paid from these accounts. The minister executed an ostensible vow of poverty but did not change his lifestyle in any way. A delinquent tax return included a sizable gift deduction for a transfer made to the "church." Reviewing all of the facts, the

[126] Rev. Rul. 89-74, 1989-1 C.B. 311; Tweeddale v. Comm'r, 92 T.C. 501 (1989).
[127] E.g., The Southern Church of Universal Brotherhood Assembled, Inc. v. Comm'r, 74 T.C. 1223 (1980) (concerning a "religious" organization that held its "services" on a boat in a large bay; the acronym for the entity is SCUBA).
[128] Malnak v. Yogi, *supra* note 71, 440 F. Supp. at 1315.
[129] E.g., Basic Bible Church v. Comm'r, 74 T.C. 846 (1980); Truth Tabernacle v. Comm'r, 41 T.C.M. 1405 (1981). Cf. McGahen v. Comm'r, 76 T.C. 468 (1981), aff'd, 720 F.2d 664 (3d Cir. 1983).
[130] E.g., Self-Realization Brotherhood, Inc. v. Comm'r, 48 T.C.M. 344 (1984); The Ecclesiastical Order of the Ism of Am v. Comm'r, 80 T.C. 833 (1983), aff'd, 740 F.2d 967 (6th Cir. 1984), cert. den., 471 U.S. 1015 (1985). Also King Shipping Consum, Inc. v. Comm'r, 58 T.C.M. 574 (1989) (alleged church operated for the purpose of selling illegal drugs held not tax-exempt); Baustert v. Comm'r, 54 T.C.M. 673 (1987).
[131] Miedaner v. Comm'r, 81 T.C. 272, 282 (1983).
[132] *Id.*
[133] IRC § 6673. Also Sommer v. Comm'r, 45 T.C.M. 1271 (1983); Van Dyke v. Comm'r, 45 T.C.M. 1233 (1983); Noberini v. Comm'r, 45 T.C.M. 587 (1983).
[134] IRC § 6653(b).

court concluded that the "minister" "fraudulently intended to evade and defeat the payment of taxes legally due from him." Thus, the court upheld the imposition of the addition to tax. The "deliberate willful nature" of his intent was divined from the establishment of "his purported church," the claiming of unsubstantiated contributions to it, the submission of a false letter to his employer concerning tax withholdings, and his failure to timely file a tax return.[135]

There are several categories of institutions that are regarded, for federal tax purposes, as *religious* organizations. These include churches, conventions and associations of churches, integrated auxiliaries of churches, religious orders, and apostolic organizations. There are a variety of church-administered organizations (usually tax-exempt but not necessarily religious in nature), such as schools, hospitals, orphanages, nursing homes, broadcasting and publishing entities, and cemeteries.

§ 8.3   CHURCHES AND SIMILAR INSTITUTIONS

A bona fide *church* (including institutions such as synagogues and mosques) is, of course, a religious entity. Yet, just as is the case with respect to the term *religious*, there is no definition in the Internal Revenue Code or in a currently applicable tax regulation of the term *church*. Again, a rigid regulatory definition of the term church would undoubtedly be unconstitutional. As one court observed: "We can only approach this question with care for all of us are burdened with the baggage of our own unique beliefs and perspectives."[136]

The concept of a tax-exempt church is recognized in the Internal Revenue Code.[137] Federal tax law applies the term *church* in a variety of contexts. One of

---

[135] Butler v. Comm'r, 50 T.C.M. 218 (1985). Another approach used by the courts to deny tax-exempt status to a mail-order church is that it failed to keep adequate financial records to demonstrate entitlement to tax exemption as required by IRC § 6001 (Church of Gospel Ministry, Inc. v. United States (D.D.C. 1986)). In general, Flynn, "Witchcraft and Tax Exempt Status Under Section 501(c)(3) of the Internal Revenue Code," 21 *U. San Fran. L. Rev.* (No. 4) 763 (1987); Slye, "Rendering Unto Caesar: Defining 'Religion' for Purposes of Administering Religion-Based Tax Exemptions," 6 *Harv. J. Law Public Policy* 219 (1983); Peacock, "Emerging Criteria for Tax-Exempt Classification for Religious Organizations," 60 *Taxes* (No. 1) 61 (1982).

[136] Foundation of Human Understanding v. Comm'r, 88 T.C. 1341, 1356–1357 (1987).

[137] IRC § 170(b)(1)(A)(i). The term *church* has been defined for state law purposes in a variety of ways. One of the most straightforward definitions is that a church is "an organization for religious purposes, for the public worship of God" (Bennett v. City of La Grange, 112 S.E. 482, 485 (Ga. 1922)). Other definitions of the term *church* include the following: "A body or community of Christians, united under one form of government by the same profession of the same faith, and the observance of the same ritual and ceremonies" (McNeilly v. First Presbyterian Church in Brookline, 137 N.E. 691 (Mass. 1923)); "The term may denote either a society of persons who, professing Christianity, hold certain doctrines or observances which differentiate them from other like groups, and who use a common discipline, or the building in which such persons habitually assemble for public worship" (Baker v. Fales, 16 Mass. 488, 498, quoted in First Indep. Missionary Baptist Church of Chosen v. McMillan, 153 So.2d 337, 342 (Fla. 1963)); and "A church society is a voluntary organization whose members are associated together, not only for religious exercises, but also for the purpose of maintaining and supporting its ministry and providing the conveniences of a church home and promoting the growth and efficiency of the work of the general church of which it forms a co-ordinate

the oldest of these instances is reflected in tax regulations issued in 1958 and applicable for tax years before 1970, which defined the term *church* (in the unrelated business and charitable contribution deduction settings).[138] Those regulations focused on the "duties" of a church, which were said to include the "ministration of sacerdotal [priestly] functions and the conduct of religious worship." The existence of these elements was said to depend on the "tenets and practices of a particular religious body."

The IRS has since formulated the criteria that it uses to ascertain whether or not an organization qualifies as a church. The IRS position is that, to be a church for tax purposes, an organization must satisfy at least some of the following criteria: a distinct legal existence, a recognized creed and form of worship, a definite and distinct ecclesiastical government, a formal code of doctrine and discipline, a distinct religious history, a membership not associated with any other church or denomination, a complete organization of ordained ministers ministering to their congregations and selected after completing prescribed courses of study, a literature of its own, established places of worship, regular congregations, regular religious services, Sunday schools for the religious instruction of the young, and schools for the preparation of its ministers.[139]

The Commissioner of Internal Revenue first made these criteria public in 1977.[140] He observed that "few, if any, religious organizations—conventional or unconventional—could satisfy all of these criteria" and that the IRS does "not give controlling weight to any single factor." Further, he asserted that "[t]his is obviously the place in the decisional process requiring the most sensitive and discriminating judgment." He concluded by noting that the IRS has "been criticized for the scope and breadth of the criteria we use and it has been implied that the Service has been trying in recent years to discourage new religions and new churches"; he offered the assurance "that this is not the case with the IRS."

part" (First Presbyterian Church of Mt. Vernon v. Dennis, 161 N.W. 183, 187 (Iowa 1917)). Thus, the term *church* carries many meanings, including the congregation and the physical facilities themselves. As one court observed, the term "may refer only to the church building or house of worship; it may mean in a more consecrated way the great body of persons holding the Christian belief, or in a restricted sense confined to those adhering to one of the several denominations of the Christian faith, at large or in a definite territory; and it may mean the collective membership of persons constituting the congregation of a single permanent place of worship" (Forsberg v. Zehm, 143 S.E. 284, 286 (Va. 1928)).

[138] Reg. §§ 1.170-2 (b)(2), 1.511-2 (a)(3)(ii) (inapplicable with respect to tax years after 1969).

[139] Internal Revenue Manual § 321.3. Also Rev. Rul. 59-129, 1959-1 C.B. 58. The Chief Counsel of the IRS advised against formal publication of the church criteria on the theory that the publication would prejudice criminal cases under review by the Department of Justice (e.g., Gen. Couns. Mem. 38699). One federal court of appeals reversed the U.S. Tax Court in one of these cases, holding that the lower court abused its discretion in refusing to give the individuals involved a reasonable opportunity to produce evidence to substantiate their alleged contributions to the Universal Life Church (Roberto v. Comm'r, *supra* note 122).

[140] "Difficult Definitional Problems in Tax Administration: Religion and Race," remarks by then Commissioner Jerome Kurtz before the Practicing Law Institute Seventh Biennial Conference on Tax Planning for Foundations, Tax-Exempt Status and Charitable Contributions, on Jan. 9, 1977, reproduced at Bureau of National Affairs, *Daily Executive Report*, Jan. 11, 1977, at page J8.

Although the IRS continues to utilize these criteria,[141] it—on advice of its chief counsel[142]—made it clear that the criteria are not exclusive and are not to be mechanically applied, and added another criterion that embraces "any other facts and circumstances which may bear upon the organization's claim to church status."[143] The IRS has resisted suggestions to publish these criteria in a revenue ruling because of concern for potential prejudice to various church cases under review by the government and concern that the criteria could be interpreted as providing a "safe harbor" for certain alleged churches.[144]

As has been discussed, the courts have been reluctant to pass on the question as to what is a religious organization, let alone what is a church. Still, an extreme factual setting may embolden a court to make a distinction between religious activities and personal codes of conduct that lack spiritual import. This was the case with the Neo-American Church, the chief precept of which was that psychedelic substances, such as LSD and marijuana, are the "true Host of the Church," thereby specifying that it is "the Religious *duty* of all members to partake of the sacraments on regular occasions." The Church had the equivalent of bishops (known as "Boo Hoos"), a symbol (a three-eyed toad), official songs (e.g., "Puff, the Magic Dragon"), a church key (a bottle opener), a catechism and handbook (excerpt: "we have the *right* to practice our religion, even if we are a bunch of filthy, drunken bums"), and a motto ("Victory over Horseshit"). Recognizing that judges "must be ever careful not to permit their own moral and ethical standards to determine the religious implications of beliefs and practices of others," a court nonetheless concluded that the Neo-American Church was not a religious entity, in the absence of any "solid evidence of a belief in a supreme being, a religious discipline, a ritual, or tenets to guide one's daily existence."[145]

Nonetheless, some courts are becoming more willing to enunciate criteria for a church. Thus, in the view of the U.S. Tax Court, a church is an organization that, in addition to having a "religious-type function," holds services or meetings on a regular basis, has ministers or other "representatives," has a record of performance of "marriages, other ceremonies or sacraments," has a place of worship,

---

[141] The Chief Counsel of the IRS invoked another criterion, which is whether the organization involved characterized itself as a church from its inception (Gen. Couns. Mem. 38982).

[142] Gen. Couns. Mem. 38699.

[143] Internal Revenue Manual—Administration § 321.3.

[144] Gen. Couns. Mem. 38699. The IRS criteria are not without their critics. One commentator stated that they "tend to require an organization to be a developed denomination according to the pattern reflected in the most accepted mainline churches"; they "tend to . . . limit the religious scene to the denominations already in existence, in violation of the establishment clause"; and "Christ and His band of disciples certainly did not meet these criteria" (Worthing, " 'Religion' and 'Religious Institutions' Under the First Amendment," *supra* note 100, at 344–345). A challenge to these criteria, on the ground that they are unconstitutional, was dismissed (Fields v. United States, Civ. No. 96-317 (D.D.C. 1998)).

[145] United States v. Kuch, 288 F. Supp. 439, 443–444 (D.D.C. 1968). Also Puritan Church of Am. v. Comm'r, 10 T.C.M. 485 (1951), *aff'd*, 209 F.2d 306 (D.C. Cir. 1953), *cert. den.*, 347 U.S. 975 (1954), 350 U.S. 810 (1955). Cf. Malnak v. Yogi, *supra* note 71; People v. Woody, 394 P.2d 813 (Cal. 1964); Heller v. Comm'r, 37 T.C.M. 643 (1978); Baker v. Comm'r, 40 T.C.M. 983 (1980); Clippinger v. Comm'r, 37 T.C.M. 484 (1978).

ordains ministers, requires some financial support by its members, has a form of "formal operation," and satisfies all other requirements of the federal tax law rules for religious organizations.[146]

In the first instance of a court's utilization of the IRS criteria as to the definition of the term *church*, the Tax Court concluded that an organization, albeit religious, could not qualify as a church because there was no "congregation," nor requisite "religious instruction" nor "conduct of religious worship."[147] Laying down a "minimum" definition of a church as including a "body of believers or communicants that assembles regularly in order to worship," the court said that of "central importance" is the "existence of an established congregation served by an organized ministry, the provision of regular religious services and religious education for the young, and the dissemination of a doctrinal code."[148] In the case, no "congregation" was found present, in that the only communicants were the founder of the church and his wife who "pray together in the physical solitude of their home"; the organization's "religious instruction" consisted of "a father preaching to his son"; and its "organized ministry" was a "single self-appointed clergyman."[149] Because the organization "does not employ recognized, accessible channels of instruction and worship" and was merely a "quintessentially private religious enterprise," the court concluded that it was not a church.[150] The U.S. Claims Court also endorsed these criteria, concluding that, while a "new religious organization should not be held to a standard only an established church can satisfy," "one man's publication of a newsletter and extemporaneous discussion of his beliefs, even when advertised, is not sufficient to constitute a church within the common understanding of that word."[151]

Courts are evidencing acceptance of the IRS criteria. Thus, a federal court of appeals concluded that a social service agency, substantially connected with a particular faith, was not a church because it did not hold regular worship services, and because it provided services to individuals irrespective of their reli-

---

[146] Pusch v. Comm'r, 39 T.C.M. 838 (1980), *aff'd*, 628 F.2d 1353 (5th Cir. 1980). Also Pusch v. Comm'r, 44 T.C.M. 961 (1982); Abney v. Comm'r, 39 T.C.M. 965 (1980); Manson v. Comm'r, 40 T.C.M. 972 (1980); Lynch v. Comm'r, 41 T.C.M. 204 (1980). Cf. Morey v. Riddell, 205 F. Supp. 918 (S.D. Cal. 1962); Peek v. Comm'r, 73 T.C. 912 (1980); Chapman v. Comm'r, 48 T.C. 358 (1967).

[147] American Guidance Found. Inc. v. United States, 490 F. Supp. 304, 306 (D.D.C. 1980), *aff'd (without opinion)* (D.C. Cir. 1981).

[148] *Id.* at 306.

[149] *Id.* at 307.

[150] *Id.* Likewise The Church of Eternal Life & Liberty, Inc. v. Comm'r, 86 T.C. 916 (1986); Universal Bible Church, Inc. v. Comm'r, 51 T.C.M. 936 (1986).

In a subsequent case, the Tax Court wrote that the court does not adopt the IRS criteria as to the definition of the term church "as a test," then went on to explicitly find the organization at issue to be a church because it "possess[es] most of the criteria to some degree" and because "most of the factors considered to be of critical importance are satisfied" (Foundation of Human Understanding v. Comm'r, *supra* note 136, at 1360).

[151] The Church of the Visible Intelligence That Governs the Universe v. United States, *supra* note 93, at 88, 597.

gious beliefs and counseling without any particular religious orientation.[152] Another appellate court held that an organization that did not meet enough of the IRS criteria could not qualify as a church.[153]

The U.S. Supreme Court offered a partial definition of the term *church* in the tax context, in an opinion construing an exemption from unemployment compensation taxes imposed by the Federal Unemployment Tax Act and complementary state law. The issue was the eligibility for the exemption for services performed for church-related schools that do not have a separate legal existence, pursuant to provision of exemption for employees "of a church or convention or association of churches."[154] The Court rejected the view that the term *church* means no more than the "actual house of worship used by a congregation" and held that the word "must be construed, instead, to refer to the congregation or the hierarchy itself, that is, the church authorities who conduct the business of hiring, discharging, and directing church employees."[155] Thus, in one instance, a church-operated day school, financed by the church's congregation and controlled by a board of directors elected from that congregation, was considered part of the church, and a secondary school owned, supported, and controlled by a synod was considered part of a convention or association of churches; neither school was separately incorporated. Although the Court recognized that the issue carries with it potential constitutional law questions,[156] it also expressly "disavow[ed] any intimations in this case defining or limiting what constitutes a church under FUTA or under any other provision of the Internal Revenue Code."[157]

Traditionally, courts have enunciated only two guides as to what constitutes a church in the federal tax context: it must be a religious organization and it must be the equivalent of a "denomination" or a "sect." For example, in 1967, a court held that "though every church may be a religious organization, every religious organization is not per se a church" and that the "concept of 'church' appears to be synonymous with the concept of 'denomination.'"[158] Then the court hastened to add that its holding "is not to imply that in order to

[152] Lutheran Social Servs. of Minn. v. United States, 758 F.2d 1283 (8th Cir. 1985). A court concluded that a "church is a coherent group of individuals and families that join together to accomplish the religious purposes of mutually held beliefs" and that a "church's principal means of accomplishing its religious purposes must be to assemble regularly a group of individuals related by common worship and faith" (The Church of Eternal Life & Liberty, Inc. v. Comm'r, *supra* note 150, at 924.) An organization unsuccessfully contested an IRS finding that it was not a church; a motion for summary judgment on the point, relying on dicta in a bankruptcy court opinion, failed (Gates Community Chapel of Rochester, Inc. d/b/a Freedom Village USA v. United States, 96-1 U.S.T.C. ¶ 50,093 (Cl. Ct. 1996)).

[153] Spiritual Outreach Soc'y v. Comm'r, 91-1 U.S.T.C. ¶ 50,111 (8th Cir. 1991)).

[154] IRC § 3309(b)(1)(A).

[155] St. Martin Evangelical Lutheran Church v. South Dakota, 451 U.S. 772, 784 (1981).

[156] *Id.* at 780.

[157] *Id.* at 784, note 15.

[158] Chapman v. Comm'r, *supra* note 146, at 363. As to the latter element, the court observed that the organization involved is "merely a religious organization comprised of individual members who are already affiliated with various churches" (*id.* at 364).

be constituted a church, a group must have an organizational hierarchy or maintain church buildings."[159]

From this standpoint, a church is, in the absence of a statutory definition, an organization that is a church under the "common meaning and usage of the word."[161] Pursuant to this approach, an organization "established to carry out 'church' functions, under the general understanding of the term, is a 'church.' "[162] These functions, according to this view, principally are forms of conduct of religious worship (such as a mass or communion) but are not activities such as the operation of schools, religious orders, wineries, and missions, even where these "religious organizations . . . [or functions are] formed [or conducted] under church auspices."[163] If the latter categories of activities predominate, the organization cannot be a church, inasmuch as the "tail cannot be permitted to wag the dog" and the conduct of such "incidental activities" cannot make an organization a church.[164] Some subsequent cases follow this approach, such as the court finding that an organization is not a church because "there is no showing in the record of any marriages, other ceremonies or sacraments performed by any 'minister' or representative of the Church."[165] Other cases reject this narrow reading of the term and embrace within the ambit of church functions activities such as "mission or evangelistic program[s]" and efforts for the "care of the needy, the sick, or the imprisoned, traditionally the beneficiaries of the ministration of churches."[166]

Thus, just as the law cannot formulate a tax definition of the term *religion*, it seems unable to formulate a formal definition of the term *church*. This is not surprising, in that the religion clauses preclude the strict application of definitions of this nature.[167]

---

[159] *Id.* at 363.

[160] See § 6.4.

[161] De La Salle Inst. v. United States, 195 F. Supp. 891, 903 (N.D. Cal. 1961).

[162] *Id.* at 903.

[163] *Id.* at 902.

[164] *Id.* at 901.

[165] Pusch v. Comm'r, *supra* note 146, 39 T.C.M., at 841. An organization formed to promote "wellness" among its members, through education in exercise, nutrition, and stress management, was held to not qualify as a church (VIA v. Comm'r, 68 T.C.M. 212 (1994)).

[166] Bubbling Well Church of Universal Love, Inc. v. Comm'r, *supra* note 116, 74 T.C. at 536.

[167] In general, Shaller, "Churches and Their Enviable Tax Status," 51 *U. of Pittsburgh L. Rev.* (No. 2) 345 (1990); Lashbrooke, Jr., "An Economic and Constitutional Case for Repeal of the I.R.C. Section 170 Deduction for Charitable Contributions to Religious Organizations," 27 *Duq. L. Rev.* (No. 4) 695 (1989); Scialabba, Kurzman, & Steinhart, "Mail-Order Ministries Under the Section 170 Charitable Contribution Deduction: The First Amendment Restrictions, the Minister's Burden of Proof, and the Effect of TRA '86," 11 *Campbell L. Rev.* (No. 1) 1 (1988); Whelan, " 'Church' in the Internal Revenue Code: The Definitional Problems," 45 *Fordham L. Rev.* 885 (1977); Worthing, "The Internal Revenue Service as a Monitor of Church Institutions: The Excessive Entanglement Problem," 45 *Fordham L. Rev.* 929 (1977); Schwarz, "Limiting Religious Tax Exemptions: When Should the Church Render Unto Caesar," 29 *U. Fl. L. Rev.* 50 (1976); Burns, "Constitutional Aspects of Church Taxation," 9 *Col. J. Law & Social Problems* 646 (1973).

§ 8.4. CONVENTIONS OR ASSOCIATIONS OF CHURCHES

Another type of religious organization is the *convention or association of churches*.[168] The IRS recognizes that the phrase has a historical meaning generally referring to a cooperative undertaking by a church of the same denomination.[169] The agency ruled that the term also applies to a cooperative undertaking by churches of differing denominations, assuming that the convention or association otherwise qualifies as a religious organization.[170]

The phrase "convention or association of churches" was used by Congress to refer to the organizational structures of congregational churches. The term was employed to accord them the comparable tax treatment granted to hierarchical churches.[171]

§ 8.5 INTEGRATED AUXILIARIES OF CHURCHES

An integrated auxiliary of a church is a religious organization.[172] The phrase *integrated auxiliary of a church* means an organization that is a tax-exempt charitable entity,[173] a public charity,[174] affiliated with a church or a convention or association of churches, and internally supported.[175]

An organization is *affiliated* with a church or a convention or association of churches, for this purpose, if the organization is covered by a group exemption letter issued to a church or a convention or association of churches;[176] the organization is operated, supervised, or controlled by or in connection with[177] a church or a convention or association of churches; or relevant facts and circumstances show that it has the requisite affiliation.[178]

The following factors are among those used to determine whether an organization is affiliated with a church or a convention or association of churches (although the absence of one or more of them does not necessarily preclude a finding of affiliation): the organization's enabling instrument[179] or bylaws affirm that the organization shares common religious doctrines, principles, disciplines, or practices with a church or a convention or association of churches; a church or a convention or association of churches has the authority to appoint

[168] IRC § 170(b)(1)(A)(i). A discussion of the legislative history of this phrase appears in De La Salle Inst. v. United States, *supra* note 161, at 897-910. See Reg. § 1.170A-9(a).
[169] Rev. Rul. 74-224, 1974-1 C.B. 61. Cf. Chapman v. Comm'r, *supra* note 146.
[170] *Id.*
[171] Lutheran Social Servs. of Minn. v. United States, *supra* note 152, at 1288.
[172] IRC § 170(b)(1)(A)(i).
[173] That is, an organization described in IRC § 501(c)(3).
[174] That is, an organization described in IRC § 509(a)(1), 509(a)(2), or 509(a)(3). See § 11.3.
[175] Reg. § 1.6033-2(h)(1).
[176] See § 23.6.
[177] This phraseology is the same as that used in connection with the supporting organization rules (see § 11.3(c), text accompanied by note 189).
[178] Reg. § 1.6033-2(h)(2).
[179] That is, its corporate charter, trust instrument, articles of association, constitution, or similar document. This is what the IRS refers to in other contexts as the *articles of organization* (see, e.g., § 4.2).

or remove, or to control the appointment or removal of, at least one of the organization's officers or directors; the corporate name of the organization indicates an institutional relationship with a church or a convention or association of churches; the organization reports at least annually on its financial and general operations to a church or a convention or association of churches; an institutional relationship between the organization and a church or a convention or association of churches is affirmed by the church, or convention or association of churches, or a designee of one or more of them; and, in the event of dissolution, the organization's assets are required to be distributed to a church or a convention or association of churches, or to an affiliate (as defined by these rules) of one or more of them.[180]

An organization is *internally supported*, for these purposes, unless it both offers admissions, goods, services, or facilities for sale, other than on an incidental basis, to the general public (except goods, services, or facilities sold at a nominal charge or for an insubstantial portion of the cost) and normally receives more than 50 percent of its support from a combination of government sources, public solicitation of contributions, and receipts from the sale of admissions, goods, performance of services, or furnishing of facilities in activities that are not unrelated trades or businesses.[181]

Men's and women's organizations, seminaries, mission societies, and youth groups that meet all of the criteria for qualification of an integrated auxiliary of a church or a convention or association of churches are such integrated auxiliaries irrespective of whether these entities satisfy the internal support requirement.[182]

Under previous rules, the term *integrated auxiliary of a church* meant an organization that is a tax-exempt charitable organization, affiliated with a church, and engaged in a principal activity that is "exclusively religious."[183] An organization's principal activity was not considered to be exclusively religious, however, if that activity was of a nature other than religious that would serve as a basis for tax exemption (such as charitable, educational, or scientific activity).[184]

Litigation ensued as the consequence of issuance of these previous rules. A federal court of appeals invalidated the requirement that an organization must be exclusively religious to qualify as an integrated auxiliary of a church.[185] This court held that that portion of the regulation was inconsistent with clear congressional policy,[186] thus ruling that the organization involved—a social service agency that was affiliated with various synods of a church—was an integrated auxiliary of the church because it "performs functions of the church bodies to which it is related by satisfying the tenet of the . . . faith [of the church] which requires the

---

[180] Reg. § 1.6033-2(h)(3).
[181] Reg. § 1.6033-2(h)(4).
[182] Reg. § 1.6033-2(h)(5).
[183] Former Reg. § 1.6033-2(g)(5)(i).
[184] Former Reg. § 1.6033-2(g)(5)(ii).
[185] Lutheran Social Servs. of Minn. v. United States, *supra* note 152, *rev'g* 583 F. Supp. 1298 (D. Minn. 1984). Also Lutheran Children & Family Serv. of Eastern Pa. v. United States, 86-2 U.S.T.C. ¶ 9593 (E.D. Pa. 1986).
[186] The appellate court was particularly influenced by the fact that Congress specifically imposed the "exclusively religious" standard upon religious orders (IRC § 6033(a)(2)(A)(iii)) but did not do so with respect to integrated auxiliaries of churches (IRC § 6033(a)(2)(A)(i)).

stimulation of works of mercy through social action ministries developed to promote human welfare."[187] By contrast, a federal district court found these regulations to be valid, but only after finding an organization to be an integrated auxiliary of a church because the entity was exclusively religious.[188]

§ 8.6   RELIGIOUS ORDERS

Another type of religious organization is the *religious order*, a term that is not defined in the Internal Revenue Code or the tax regulations. The IRS promulgated guidelines for determining whether an organization qualifies as a religious order, utilizing a variety of characteristics drawn from the caselaw.[189] These characteristics are as follows: the organization is a charitable one;[190] the members of the organization vow to live under a strict set of rules requiring moral and spiritual self-sacrifice and dedication to the goals of the organization at the expense of their material well-being; the members of the organization, after successful completion of the organization's training program and probationary period, make a long-term commitment to the organization (normally more than two years); the organization is, directly or indirectly, under the control and supervision of a church or convention or association of churches, or is significantly funded by a church or convention or association of churches; the members of the organization normally live together as part of a community and are held to a significantly stricter level of moral and religious discipline than that required by lay church members; the members of the organization work or serve full-time on behalf of the religious, educational, or charitable goals of the organization; and the members of the organization participate regularly in activities such as public or private prayer, religious study, teaching, care of the aging, missionary work, or church reform or renewal.[191]

In determining whether an organization is a religious order, all of the facts and

---

[187] Lutheran Social Serv. of Minn. v. United States, *supra* note 152, 758 F.2d at 1291.

[188] Tennessee Baptist Children's Homes, Inc. v. United States, 604 F. Supp. 210 (M.D. Tenn. 1984), *aff'd*, 790 F.2d 534 (6th Cir. 1986). Under prior law, for example, schools that were operated, supported, and controlled by a church or a convention or association of churches were integrated auxiliaries (St. Martin Evangelical Lutheran Church v. South Dakota, *supra* note 155), an organization was held to not qualify as an integrated auxiliary because the church involved lacked any control over the assets or income of the organization (Parshall Christian Order v. Comm'r, 45 T.C.M. 488 (1983)), and a church-affiliated college that trained ministers and lay workers to serve religious functions in the church qualified as an integrated auxiliary (Rev. Rul. 77-381, 1977-2 C.B. 462). Private letter rulings issued by the IRS provided illustrations of organizations that were integrated auxiliaries of a church under prior law (e.g., Priv. Ltr. Rul. 8416065) and of those that did not qualify as an integrated auxiliary of a church (e.g., Priv. Ltr. Rul. 8402014).

In general, Blaine, "The Unfortunate Church-State Dispute Over the I.R.C. Section 6033 'Exclusively Religious' Test," 23 *New Eng. L. Rev.* (No. 1) 1 (1988); Reed, "Integrated Auxiliaries, Regulations and Implications," 23 *Cath. Law.* 211 (Summer 1978).

[189] Rev. Proc. 91-20, 1991-1 C.B. 524. The cases cited by the IRS in this regard are St. Joseph Farms of Indiana Bros. of the Congregation of Holy Cross, SW, Inc. v. Comm'r, 85 T.C. 9 (1985), *app. dis.* (7th Cir. 1986); De La Salle Inst. v. United States, *supra* note 161; Eighth Street Baptist Church, Inc. v. United States, 295 F. Supp. 1400 (D. Kan. 1969), *aff'd*, 431 F.2d 1193 (10th Cir. 1970); Kelley v. Comm'r, 62 T.C. 131 (1974); Estate of Callaghan v. Comm'r, 33 T.C. 870 (1960).

[190] That is, it is described in IRC § 501(c)(3).

[191] Rev. Proc. 91-20, *supra* note 189, § 3.

circumstances must be considered. Generally, the presence of all of these characteristics is determinative that the organization is a religious order; however, the absence of the first of these characteristics is determinative that the organization is not a religious order. The absence of one or more of the other enumerated characteristics is not necessarily determinative in a particular case. If application of these characteristics to the facts of a particular case does not clearly indicate whether the organization is a religious order, the IRS's procedures call for it to contact the particular authorities affiliated with the organization for their views concerning the characterization of the organization, which views are to be "carefully considered."[192]

§ 8.7 APOSTOLIC ORGANIZATIONS

Certain *religious or apostolic* organizations are exempt from federal income taxation, even though they are not embraced by the general reference to religious organizations. These are "religious or apostolic associations or corporations, if such associations or corporations have a common treasury or community treasury, even if such associations or corporations engage in business for the common benefit of the members, but only if the members thereof include (at the time of filing their returns) in their gross income their entire pro rata shares, whether distributed or not, of the taxable income of the association or corporation for such year."[193] Any amount so included in the gross income of a member is treated as a dividend received.[194] It is the position of the IRS that a member of a religious or apostolic organization may not claim his or her minor children as dependents for tax purposes because the organization provides their food, clothing, medical care, and the like, the members cannot claim the investment tax credit on their proportionate shares of property purchased by the organization,[195] the members cannot claim the fuel tax credit on fuels purchased by the organization, the costs of personal goods and services provided by such an organization for its members are not deductible business expenses, and the amounts distributed to the members of the organization do not constitute self-employment income.[196]

The requirement that there be a "common treasury or community treasury" does not mean that the members of the apostolic organization must take a vow of poverty and irrevocably contribute all of their property to the organization upon becoming members and not be entitled to any part of that property upon leaving the organization.[197] The concept of this type of treasury "connotes that the property of such organizations not be held by members individually but rather held in a 'community capacity' with all members having equal interests in the commu-

---

[192] *Id.*
[193] IRC § 501(d).
[194] Reg. § 1.501(d)-1(a); Rev. Rul. 58-328, 1958-1 C.B. 327; Rev. Rul. 57-574, 1957-2 C.B. 161; Riker v. Comm'r, *supra* note 115.
[195] Kleinsasser v. United States, 707 F.2d 1024 (9th Cir. 1983), *aff'g* 522 F. Supp. (D. Mont. 1981).
[196] Priv. Ltr. Rul. 7740009.
[197] Twin Oaks Community, Inc. v. Comm'r, 87 T.C. 1233 (1986).

nity property" and does not mean "that members are necessarily prohibited from owning property outside and apart from the organization."[198] This requirement is satisfied "when all of the income generated internally by community-operated business and any income generated from property owned by the organization is placed into a common fund that is maintained by such organization and is used for the maintenance and support of its members, with all members having equal, undivided interests in this common fund, but no right to claim title to any part thereof."[199]

For purposes of determining the pro rata shares of the taxable income of an apostolic organization (to be included in the members' gross income), the membership in the organization is to be determined in accordance with the rules of the organization itself and applicable state law. Individuals qualified to be members of this type of an organization must consent to this membership status; parents may consent to the membership on behalf of their minor children to the extent allowed under applicable state law.[200]

The origins of these rules (in 1936) are reflected in the following excerpt from its legislative history:

> It has been brought to the attention of the committee that certain religious and apostolic associations and corporations, such as the House of David and the Shakers, have been taxed as corporations, and that since their rules prevent their members from being holders of property in an individual capacity the corporations would be subject to the undistributed-profits tax. These organizations have a small agricultural or other business. The effect of the proposed amendment is to exempt these corporations from the normal corporations tax and the undistributed-profits tax, if their members take up their shares of the corporations' income on their own individual returns. It is believed that this provision will give them relief, and their members will be subject to a fair tax.[201]

Subsequently, a federal court of appeals, in commenting on the type of organization contemplated by these rules, said: "One might assume, then, that Congress intended an association somewhat akin to the ordinary association or partnership in which each member has a definite, though undivided, interest in the business conducted for the common benefit of the members, as well as a common interest in the community treasury and property."[202]

Also, the statute's beginnings are traceable to the fact that apostolic organizations were early found to not qualify for tax exemption under the general rules for religious organizations because of the presence of commercial activities and private inurement, as discussed in the cases concerning the tax status of the Hut-

---

[198] *Id.* at 1248.
[199] *Id.* at 1254.
[200] Rev. Rul. 77-295, 1977-2 C.B. 196.
[201] 80 *Cong. Rec.* 9074 (1936).
[202] Riker v. Comm'r, *supra* note 115 at 230.

terische Church.[203] Few exemptions under this provision have been granted; the most notable example may be the 1939 determination of exemption thereunder accorded the Israelite House of David.[204] The courts appear to prefer to cope with organizations of this nature in the context of the law applicable to religious groups generally.[205]

Organizations contemplated by these rules are those that are supported by internally operated businesses in which all the members have an individual interest. In one instance, a communal religious organization did not conduct any business activities and instead was supported by the wages of some of its members who were engaged in outside employment and thus was ruled to not qualify as an apostolic organization.[206]

It is the position of the IRS (general counsel) that failure to qualify as an apostolic organization under these rules does not preclude the possibility that an organization may qualify as a communal religious organization.[207] In other

---

[203] Hofer v. United States, 64 Ct. Cl. 672 (1928); Hutterische Bruder Gemeinde v. Comm'r, 1 B. T. A. 1208 (1925).

[204] Blume v. Gardner, 262 F. Supp. 405, 408 (W.D. Mich. 1966), aff'd, 397 F.2d 809 (6th Cir. 1968). Also Israelite House of David v. United States, 58 F. Supp. 862 (W.D. Mich. 1945); People v. Israelite House of David, 225 N.W. 638 (Mich. 1929).

[205] Golden Rule Church Ass'n v. Comm'r, 41 T.C. 719 (1964), State v. King Colony Ranch, 350 P.2d 841 (Mont. 1960).

[206] Rev. Rul. 78-100, 1978-1 C.B. 162.

[207] Gen. Couns. Mem. 38827. See *infra* § 8. In general, Wylie & Pfeifer, "Distinguishing Among Churches, Religious Orders, and Other Religious Organizations," 7 *J. Tax. Exempt Orgs.* (No. 2) 6557 (Sept./Oct. 1995); Spirtos, "Draft IRS Publication Details Tax Constraints for Churches and Religious Organizations," 6 *J. Tax. Exempt Orgs.* (No. 5) 213 (Mar./Apr. 1995). Marshall & Blomgren, "Regulating Organizations Under the Establishment Clause," 47 *Ohio St. L. J.* 316 (1986); Mangrum, "Naming Religion (and Eligible Cognates) in Tax Exemption Cases," 19 *Creighton L. Rev.* (No. 4) 821 (1985); Sciarrino, "United States v. Sun Myung Moon: Precedent For Tax Fraud Prosecution of Local Pastors?," 1984 *S. Ill. L. J.* (No. 2) 237 (1985); Nomady, "Mail Order Ministries: Application of the Religious Purpose Exemption Under the First Amendment," 17 *J. Mar. L. Rev.* 895 (1984); Hageman, "An Examination of Religious Tax Exemption Policy Under Section 501(c)(3) of the Internal Revenue Code," 17 *Val. Law Rev.* 405 (1983); Comment, "Real Property Tax Exemptions for Religious Organizations: The Dilemma of *Holy Spirit Association v. Tax Commissioner*," 47 *Albany L. Rev.* 1117 (1983); Note, "The Forbidden Fruit of Church-State Contacts: The Role of the Entanglement Theory in Its Ripening," 16 *Suffock U. L. Rev.* 725 (1982); Peacock, "Emerging Criteria for Tax-Exempt Classification for Religious Organizations," 61 *Taxes* 61 (Sept. 1982); Choper, "Defining 'Religion' in the First Amendment," 1982 *U. Ill. L. Rev.* 579 (Summer 1982); Moore, "Piercing the Religious Veil of the So Called Cults," 7 *Pepp. L. Rev.* 655 (1980); Note, "Mail Order Ministries, the Religious Purpose Exemption, and the Constitution," 33 *Tax Law.* 959 (1980); Kelley, "Why Churches Do Not Pay Taxes," XIII *The Philanthropy Monthly* 20 (Nov. 1980); Jackson, "Are Churches Charitable or Public Trusts?," XIII *The Philanthropy Monthly* 21 (Nov. 1980); Brancato, "Characterization in Religious Property Tax-Exemption: What is Religious? A Survey and a Proposed Definition and Approach," 44 *Notre Dame Law.* 60 (1968); Considine & Whelan, "Church Tax Exemptions," 15 *Cath. Law.* 93 (1969); Hurvich, Religion and the Taxing Power," 35 *U. Cinn. L. Rev.* 531 (1966); Katz, "Radiations from Church Tax Exemption," 1970 *Sup. Ct. Rev.* 93 (1970); Korbel, "Do the Federal Income Tax Laws Involve an 'Establishment of Religion'?," 53 *A.B.A.J.* 1018 (1967); Note, "Aid to Religion Through Taxation," 43 *Notre Dame Law.* 756 (1968); Boyan, "Defining Religion in Operational and Institutional Terms," 116 *U. Pa. L. Rev.* 479 (1967–1968); Note, "Constitutionality of Tax Exemptions Accorded American Church Property," 30 *Albany L. Rev.* 58 (1966); Van Alstyne, "Tax Exemption of Church Property," *Ohio State L. J.* 461 (1959); Stimson, "The Exemption of Churches from Taxation," 18 *Taxes* 361 (1940); Paulsen, "Preferment of Religious Institutions in Tax and Labor Legislation," 14 *Law & Contemp. Prob.* 144 (1949); Zollman, "Tax Exemption of American Church Property," 14 *Mich. L. Rev.* 646 (1916); Zollman, *American Church Law* 328–329 (1933).

words, the IRS does not believe that Congress occupied the field with respect to tax exemption of all communal religious organizations in enacting the rules for apostolic organizations.

§ 8.8   COMMUNAL GROUPS

The IRS invokes the private inurement doctrine in still another context involving religious organizations: the tax treatment of communal groups. The IRS position is that, generally, where individuals reside in a communal setting in the context of professing religious beliefs, with room, board, and other costs provided by the organization, the result is unwarranted private benefit to the individuals which precludes tax exemption. This position has been upheld by the courts.[208]

These and similar cases have enormous implications. Certainly, the "traditional" church, for example, may provide lodging, food, and the like to its ministers and family,[209] or operate a school, and not attract any difficulties with the IRS. Parsonages and parochial schools are not likely to be the basis for IRS revocation of a church's tax-exempt status. Perhaps the publicity given to "cults" and the uncovering of immense property holdings of and substantial government infiltration by controversial "churches" have influenced the IRS to shy away from any aid and comfort to burgeoning "nontraditional" churches by merely denying them tax exemption.

Regardless of individual attitudes toward new religions or new religious structures, the full consequences of the government's position are yet to unfold. As respects the tax status of monasteries, nunneries, and religious orders, the IRS has recognized that support of monks, nuns, and other clerics (in the form of shelter, food, clothing, medical care, and other necessities) is an exempt religious function.[210]

Repercussions of this attitude toward communal groups were felt soon after these court decisions, as the IRS quickly recognized the extremity of its position (notwithstanding the court approval) and moved to confine the scope of the above-noted three court decisions. Now, the IRS position—as manifested in a 1981 general counsel memorandum (overruling the IRS rulings division[211])—is that communal groups can qualify as religious organizations where the facilities and benefits provided by the organization to its membership "do not exceed those strictly necessary to exist in a communal religious organization . . ."; references such as "primitive," "stark," and "deprivation in material terms of life" are used in the memorandum. Also, the IRS found a distinguishing feature in the fact that, in the case of the organization that achieved tax exemption, "few" of its

---

[208] E.g., Canada v. Comm'r, 82 T.C. 973 (1984); Beth-El Ministries, Inc. v. United States, 79-2 U.S.T.C. ¶ 9412 (D.D.C. 1979); Martinsville Ministries, Inc. v. United States, 80-2 U.S.T.C. ¶ 9710 (D.D.C. 1979).

[209] E.g., IRC § 107. See *supra* note 69.

[210] The IRS held that a monastery of the Order of Cistercians of the Strict Observance, a Roman Catholic order, engages in an exempt function when it provides the monks "with food, shelter, clothing, and the other necessities of life" (e.g., Priv. Ltr. Rul. 7838028).

[211] Gen. Couns. Mem. 38827.

members worked outside the community. (These allegedly "distinguishing" factors were not discussed in the court opinions, however, where the very fact of a communal existence was found to be the barrier to classification as a religious organization.)

In describing the activities of this (religious) organization, the IRS observed that the members believe that their religious beliefs (noted as being "Christian in origin") require them to "live together and in relative isolation . . . under primitive living conditions." Said the IRS: "They eat, work, and worship together in a tightly ordered Christian environment in which work and prayer are viewed as worship." The IRS added that the "community's minimum food and shelter needs are met by the mutual efforts of all. . . ." Finding, as noted, the organization to be religious, the IRS concluded that the members of the organization "have a sincere and meaningful belief in a set of doctrines," that the "provision of minimum food and lodging to the members primarily furthers its religious purposes," that the members "may be viewed as proper participants in an exempt activity acting in the public interest rather than in their private capacities as members" of the organization, and that the provision of food and lodging in this context "constitutes an indirect benefit which is qualitatively incidental because it is a necessary concomitant to . . . operation [of the organization] as a communal religious organization with its particular religious tenets."

One of the difficulties with the original IRS position is that it would have precluded federal tax exemption for monasteries, nunneries, and religious orders. For these entities, the IRS previously recognized the support of monks, nuns, and other clerics (in the form of shelter, food, clothing, medical care, and other necessities) as an exempt function. This general counsel memorandum states, however, that "many religious orders that practice communal living in furtherance of their religious goals, or churches that have such religious orders" are recognized as tax-exempt entities. Added the IRS: "It is implicit to the recognition of these organizations' exempt status, that communal living with the inherent provision of support in the nature of food and lodging to its members can, depending on all the facts and circumstances, be primarily in furtherance of a religious purpose.[212]

§ 8.9   RETREAT FACILITIES

In one instance, an organization attempted to become recognized as a religious organization by virtue of its operation of a retreat facility.[213] The facility was a mountain lodge; the activities available at the lodge—being religious, recreational, and social—were not regularly scheduled nor required. The religious activities revolved around individual prayer and contemplation, with optional

---

[212] Also New Life Tabernacle v. Comm'r, 44 T.C.M 309 (1982); Rev. Rul. 76-323, 1976-2 C.B. 18; Rev. Rul. 68-123, 1968-1 C.B. 35. In general, Emory & Zelenak, "The Tax Exempt Status of Communitarian Religious Organizations: An Unnecessary Controversy?," 50 *Fordham L. Rev.* 1085 (1982).
[213] The Schoger Found. v. Comm'r, 76 T.C. 380 (1981).

daily devotions and occasional Sunday services available. The IRS asserted that the organization's "substantial, if not sole, purpose is to provide a facility where guests can relax, socialize and engage in recreational activities, or, in other words, to operate a vacation resort."[214] Conversely, the organization contended that "its primary purpose is to provide a religious retreat facility for Christian families where they may come to reflect upon and worship the Lord in a setting free from the outside interferences of everyday life."[215] The court involved, holding that the organization failed to sustain its burden of proof that the facilities were not used in more than an insubstantial manner for recreational purposes, concluded that tax exemption as a religious organization could not be found, in that "[w]holesome family recreation or just sitting on a rock contemplating nature may well provide a family or an individual with a religious, or at least a spiritually uplifting experience, but it is difficult to see how that experience differs, if it does, from the same experience one can have at any quiet inn or lodge located in the beautiful mountains of Colorado."[216]

Nonetheless, retreat facilities can be regarded as religious organizations, particularly where the IRS or a court is not burdened with the thought that something other than authentic religious pursuits dominate the establishment and operation of the entity. For example, an organization, controlled by an auxiliary of a major church denomination, formed to contract for the construction of housing at a conference and retreat center owned and operated by the church, was held to be a religious organization, in that the housing it was to provide was predominantly to aid and enhance the religious purposes of the auxiliary and ultimately the church.[217] The court observed that the auxiliary had served the church since 1910 and the facilities had been used as a "gathering place of missionaries on leave, retired clergy, active laymen and pastors for religious services, religious seminars, and religious training."[218] The court cautioned, however, that if the "housing units are in fact utilized substantially for vacation or recreational purposes, or otherwise by individuals who do not have active roles in the planning, organization, operation of or participation in the [auxiliary's] ... programs and religious activities, then a substantial nonexempt purpose would be served" and the organization would not qualify for tax exemption.[219] Nonetheless, despite the government's assertion that the housing to be constructed at the "beautiful surroundings" of the retreat grounds is "primarily to provide an enviable vacation spot not unlike others situated in the neighboring Smokey Mountains," the court wrote that the "tax law, however, does not require churches to hold their retreats or other gatherings for religious purposes in the wilderness or to eschew recreation incident to gatherings held primarily for religious activity."[220]

---

[214] *Id.* at 386.

[215] *Id.* at 387.

[216] *Id.* at 388. Also Petersen v. Comm'r, 53 T.C.M. 235 (1987).

[217] Junaluska Assembly Hous., Inc. v. Comm'r, 86 T.C. 1114 (1986).

[218] *Id.* at 1122.

[219] *Id.* at 1123.

[220] *Id.* at 1122–1123. Previously, the Tax Court upheld the tax-exempt status of an organization that operated religious facilities in an idyllic setting, finding the social and recreational aspects of its program insubstantial (Alive Fellowship of Harmonious Living v. Comm'r, 47 T.C.M. 1134 (1984)).

CHAPTER NINE

Scientific Organizations

Section 501(c)(3) of the Internal Revenue Code provides that an organization may be exempt from federal income tax under IRC § 501(a) if it is organized and operated exclusively for *scientific* purposes.[1]

§ 9.1 FEDERAL TAX LAW DEFINITION OF *SCIENCE*

Neither the Internal Revenue Code, nor any income tax regulation, nor IRS ruling defines the term *scientific* as used in the tax-exempt organizations context. A dictionary definition states that *science* is a "branch of study that is concerned with observation and classification of facts and especially with the establishment ... of verifiable general laws chiefly by induction and hypotheses."[2] Another dictionary defines *science* as "[k]nowledge, as of facts and principles, gained by systemic study."[3] A more technical definition of the term is that science is a "branch of study in which facts are observed, classified, and, usually, quantitative laws are formulated and verified; [or] involves the application of mathematical reasoning and data analysis to natural phenomena."[4]

A federal district court, however, offered the view that, "while projects may vary in terms of degree of sophistication, if professional skill is involved in the design and supervision of a project intended to solve a problem through a search for a demonstrable truth, the project would appear to be scientific research."[5] Another federal court was of the view that the term *science* means the

---

[1] Reg. § 1.501(c)(3)-1(d)(1)(i)(c).

[2] *Webster's Third New International Dictionary.*

[3] *Random House Dictionary of the English Language* (Stein, ed., 1967).

[4] *McGraw-Hill Dictionary of Scientific and Technical Terms* (Lapedes, ed., 2d ed. 1978).

[5] Midwest Research Inst. v. United States, 554 F. Supp. 1379, 1386 (W.D. Mo. 1983), *aff'd* 744 F.2d 635 (8th Cir. 1984). Also Oglesby v. Chandler, 288 P. 1034 (1930); In re Massachusetts General Hosp., 95 F. 973 (C.C. Mass. 1899).

"process by which knowledge is systematized or classified through the use of observation, experimentation, or reasoning."[6]

In one instance, concerning an organization the exempt purpose of which was to provide multidisciplinary scientific research for government and industry, the court found all of the contractual arrangements challenged by the government to consist of scientific research. The contracts, said the court, involved "work performed by, and capable of being performed only by, qualified engineers and scientists with expertise in particular technological fields."[7] The court observed that the organization was not involved in the commercialization of the products or processes developed as a result of its research, nor did it conduct consumer or market research, social science research, or ordinary testing of the type carried on incident to commercial operations (see below). Said the court: "The fact that research is directed towards solving a particular industrial problem does not necessarily indicate that the research is not scientific."[8]

Basically, then, a *scientific* organization is one engaged in scientific research or otherwise operated for the dissemination of scientific knowledge. A fundamental requirement underlying this form of tax exemption is that the organization must serve a public rather than a private interest.[9] Thus, the tax-exempt scientific organization must, among the other criteria for exemption, be organized and operated in the public interest.[10]

An organization composed of members of an industry to develop new and improved uses for products of the industry was ruled to not be a tax-exempt scientific organization on the ground that it was serving the private interests of its creators.[11] By contrast, an organization formed by a group of physicians specializing in heart disease to research the cause and publish treatments of heart defects was found to be an exempt scientific organization.[12] In the latter instance, any personal benefit (in the form of increased prestige and enhanced reputation) derived by the physician-creators was deemed not to lessen the public benefits flowing from the organization's operations.

§ 9.2 CONCEPT OF *RESEARCH*

In this area, the focus is largely on the concept of *research*. *Research*, when taken alone, is a word with various meanings—it is not synonymous with *science*. Inasmuch as the nature of particular research depends upon the purpose that it serves, for research to be scientific, it must be carried on in furtherance of a scien-

---

[6] IIT Research Inst. v. United States, 85-2 U.S.T.C. ¶9734 (Cl. Ct. 1985).

[7] *Id.*

[8] *Id.* In general, Simpson & Powell, "Does Income of Exempt Scientific Research Organizations Come from Unrelated Business?," 64 *J. Tax* (No. 4) 210 (1986).

[9] Reg. §§ 1.501(a)-1(c), 1.501(c)(3)-1(c)(2).

[10] Reg. § 1.501(c)(3)-1(d)(5)(i).

[11] Rev. Rul. 69-632, 1969-2 C.B. 120. Also Medical Diagnostic Ass'n v. Comm'r, 42 B.T.A. 610 (1940).

[12] Rev. Rul. 69-526, 1969-2 C.B. 115.

tific purpose. Thus, the term *scientific* includes the carrying on of scientific research in the public interest.

The determination of whether research is scientific can depend on whether the research is classified as *fundamental* or *basic* as contrasted with *applied* or *practical*. Federal tax law, however, excludes from unrelated business taxable income, in the case of an organization operated primarily for purposes of carrying on fundamental research the results of which are freely available to the general public, all income derived from research performed for any person and all deductions directly connected with the activity.[13] For purposes of the unrelated income rules, therefore, it is necessary to determine whether the organization is operated primarily for purposes of carrying on fundamental, as contrasted with applied, research.[14]

Consequently, scientific research does not include activities ordinarily carried on incident to commercial operations, as, for example, the testing or inspection of materials or products or the designing or construction of equipment or buildings.[15] For example, an organization that fostered the development of machinery in connection with a commercial operation, and was empowered to sell, assign, and grant licenses with respect to its copyrights, trademarks, trade names, or patent rights, was held by the IRS to not be engaged in scientific research.[16] Similarly, an organization that tested drugs for commercial pharmaceutical companies was held by the IRS to not qualify for tax exemption as a scientific organization because the testing was regarded as principally serving the private interests of the manufacturers.[17] Likewise, an organization that inspected, tested, and certified for safety shipping containers used in the transport of cargo, and engaged in related research activities, was determined by the IRS to not be undertaking scientific research because these activities were incidental to commercial or industrial operations.[18]

Scientific research is regarded as carried on in the public interest if the results of the research (including any patents, copyrights, processes, or formulas) are made available to the public on a nondiscriminatory basis, if the research is performed for the United States, or any of its agencies or instrumentalities, or for a state or political subdivision thereof, or if the research is directed toward benefiting the public.[19] Examples of scientific research that is considered as meeting this last criterion include scientific research carried on for the purpose of aiding in the scientific education of college or university students, obtaining scientific information that is published in a form that is available to the interested public, dis-

---

[13] IRC § 512(b)(9).
[14] Reg. § 1.501(c)(3)-1(d)(5)(i).
[15] Reg. § 1.501(c)(3)-1(d)(5)(ii). Also Rev. Rul. 68-373, 1968-2 C.B. 206. In one case, this type of activity was described as "generally repetitive work done by scientifically unsophisticated employees for the purpose of determining whether the item tested met certain specifications, as distinguished from testing done to validate a scientific hypothesis" (Midwest Research Inst. v. United States, *supra* note 5, at 1386).
[16] Rev. Rul. 65-1, 1965-1 C.B. 226.
[17] Rev. Rul. 68-373, *supra* note 15.
[18] Rev. Rul. 78-426, 1978-2 C.B. 175.
[19] Reg. § 1.501(c)(3)-1(d)(5)(iii).

covering a cure for a disease, or aiding a community or geographical area by at-tracting new industry thereto or by encouraging the development of, or reten-tion of, an industry in the community or area.[20] Publication of research results, consequently, is not the only means by which scientific research can be in the public interest.[21] Scientific research is regarded as carried on in the public inter-est even though research is performed pursuant to a contract or agreement un-der which the sponsor of the research has the right to obtain ownership or control of any patents, copyrights, processes, or formulas resulting from re-search.[22] Thus, an organization formed by physicians to research heart disease was ruled to be tax-exempt as a scientific organization.[23] An organization en-gaged in conducting research programs in the social sciences may qualify as an exempt scientific organization.[24]

The IRS unsuccessfully asserted that an organization that conducted a crop seed certification program and scientific research in seed technology was engaged in activities of a type ordinarily conducted incident to commercial op-erations and served the private interests of commercial seed producers and commercial farmers. A court concluded that the scientific research involved qualified the organization for tax exemption because the research was being conducted either pursuant to its delegated authority as the official seed certifi-cation agency for a state or in conjunction with the state's designated agency for agricultural research and experimentation. Also, the research was consid-ered carried on for public rather than private interests because the research was performed for a state or political subdivision thereof, because the results of the research were made available to the public on a nondiscriminatory basis, and because the research was directed toward benefiting the public. While conceding that the "majority of persons interested in seed technology may well come from the agricultural community," the court stated that that "does not mean that farmers and gardeners are not an important part of the general public."[25]

It is often difficult to ascertain whether a particular activity constitutes *scien-tific research* or *commercial testing*. This is particularly the case where the activity is conducted in the public interest.[26]

The IRS accorded categorization as a tax-exempt scientific organization to a membership organization formed to encourage and assist in the establishment of nonprofit regional health data systems, conduct scientific studies and propose improvements with regard to quality, utilization, and effectiveness of health care

---

[20] In one case, an organization that engaged in research projects for nongovernmental sponsors on a contract basis, in the fields of physics, chemistry, economic development, engineering, and biological sciences, was held to be a scientific entity (as defined; see *supra* notes 2–8), rather than engaged in commercial testing; it satisfied the public benefit test because the research was intended to attract and develop industry in a particular geographic area (the Midwest) (Midwest Research Inst. v. United States, *supra* note 5).

[21] IIT Research Inst. v. United States, *supra* note 6.

[22] *Id.*

[23] Rev. Rul. 69-526, *supra* note 12. Also Comm'r v. Orton, 173 F.2d 483 (6th Cir. 1949).

[24] Rev. Rul. 65-60, 1965-1 C.B. 231.

[25] Indiana Crop Improvement Ass'n, Inc. v. Comm'r, 76 T.C. 394, 400 (1981).

[26] See *infra* § 3.

and health care agencies, and to educate those involved in furnishing, administering, and financing health care.[27] The IRS observed that by "improving and enlarging the body of knowledge concerning current usage of health facilities and methods of treatment, the organization seeks to create a more efficient use of the nation's health facilities, and to aid in the planning of better care for future health needs."[28] The IRS also ruled that an organization formed to develop scientific methods for the diagnosis, prevention, and treatment of diseases, and to disseminate the results of its developmental work to members of the medical profession and the general public, qualified for exemption as a scientific entity.[29]

§ 9.3   REQUIREMENT OF *PUBLIC INTEREST*

An organization is regarded as not organized or operated for the purpose of carrying on scientific research in the *public interest* and, consequently, will not qualify as a scientific organization for federal tax exemption purposes if (1) it performs research only for persons that are (directly or indirectly) its creators and that are not charitable organizations, or (2) it retains (directly or indirectly) the ownership or control of more than an insubstantial portion of the patents, copyrights, processes, or formulas resulting from its research and does not make the items available to the public on a nondiscriminatory basis.[30] In addition, although one person may be granted the exclusive right to the use of a patent, copyright, process, or formula, it is considered as made available to the public if the granting of the exclusive right is the only practicable manner in which the patent, copyright, process, or formula can be utilized to benefit the public.[31] In this case, however, the research from which the patent, copyright, process, or formula resulted will be regarded as carried on in the public interest only if it is carried on for the United States (or instrumentality thereof) or a state (or political subdivision thereof) or if it is scientific research that is directed toward benefiting the public.[32]

These distinctions were the subject of an IRS ruling discussing the federal tax treatment, in the exempt organizations context, of commercially sponsored scientific research, which is scientific research undertaken pursuant to contracts with private industries.[33] Under these contracts, the sponsor pays for the research

---

[27] Rev. Rul. 76-455, 1976-2 C.B. 150.

[28] *Id.* at 150–151.

[29] Rev. Rul. 65-298, 1965-2 C.B. 163. Cf. Rev. Rul. 74-553, 1974-2 C.B. 168. A 25 percent tax credit for certain research and experimental expenditures paid in carrying on a trade or business (IRC § 41) is available for, *inter alia*, "basic research" expenses. That term is defined to mean any "original investigation for the advancement of scientific knowledge not having a specific commercial objective, except that such term shall not include (i) basic research conducted outside of the United States, and (ii) basic research in the social sciences, arts, or humanities" (IRC § 41(e)(7)(A)).

[30] Reg. § 1.501(c)(3)-1(d)(5)(iv).

[31] *Id.*

[32] *Id.*

[33] Rev. Rul. 76-296, 1976-2 C.B. 141.

and receives the right to the results of the research and all ownership rights in any patents resulting from work on the project.

Where the results and other relevant information of the commercially sponsored projects are "generally published in such form as to be available to the interested public either currently, as developments in the project warrant, or within a reasonably short time after completion of the project," the organization is considered to be engaging in scientific research in the public interest.[34] Publication of the research is not required "in advance of the time at which it can be made public without jeopardy to the sponsor's right by reasonably diligent action to secure any patents or copyrights resulting from the research."[35] By contrast, the carrying on of sponsored research is considered the conduct of an unrelated trade or business[36] where the organization agrees, at the sponsor's request, to "forego publication of the results of a particular project in order to protect against disclosure of processes or technical data which the sponsor desires to keep secret for various business reasons" or where the research results are withheld beyond the time reasonably necessary to obtain patents or copyrights.[37]

§ 9.4 *SCIENTIFIC* AS *CHARITABLE* OR *EDUCATIONAL*

Organizations qualifying as tax-exempt scientific entities may also be tax-exempt as charitable and/or educational entities.[38]

For example, an organization formed to survey scientific and medical literature published throughout the world and to prepare and distribute free abstracts of the literature was ruled to be both charitable and scientific in nature for federal tax purposes.[39] This is because the federal tax definition of the term *charitable* embraces the concept of *advancement of science*.[40]

An organization engaged in research on human diseases, developing scientific methods for treatment, and disseminating its results through physicians' seminars was determined to be a tax-exempt educational organization.[41] Also, an engineering society created to engage in scientific research in the areas of heating, ventilating, and air conditioning for the benefit of the general public was deemed to qualify as an educational and scientific organization.[42]

---

[34] *Id.* at 142.
[35] *Id.* at 143.
[36] See Part VI.
[37] Rev. Rul. 76-296, *supra* note 33, at 142. In general, see *infra* § 5.
[38] See Chapters 6, 7.
[39] Rev. Rul. 66-147, 1966-1 C.B. 137. Also Science & Research Found. Inc. v. United States, 181 F. Supp. 526 (S.D. Ill. 1960); Forest Press, Inc. v. Comm'r, 22 T.C. 265 (1954).
[40] See § 6.5.
[41] Rev. Rul. 65-298, *supra* note 29.
[42] Rev. Rul. 71-506, 1971-2 C.B. 233. Also American Kennel Club, Inc. v. Hoey, 148 F.2d 920 (2d Cir. 1945).

§ 9.5   TECHNOLOGY TRANSFERS

The IRS is struggling to determine the criteria by which an organization that has the primary purpose of transferring technology can qualify for tax exemption as a scientific or other charitable organization. The difficulty lies in the essence of *technology transfer*: the conduct of scientific or other research by and within the organization and the subsequent transfer of the results of that research to others for development commercially and for the marketing and sale of the resulting products or services to the general public. The technology transfer function can place a nonprofit organization in a position where it is, or appears to be, engaging in commercial activities that are not related to its tax-exempt functions (and/or is receiving income that may be taxed as unrelated business income).[43]

Part of the problem is that the other areas of federal law, which are being developed to facilitate technology transfer, involve concepts that the authors of the federal tax law are finding awkward to assimilate. Contemporary "public/private partnerships" and other ventures that blend the efforts of charitable organizations and commercial businesses are not easily accommodated by the existing tax law. Colleges and universities are leading the way in this regard, because of the immense volume of research being funded by private firms and governments. Indeed, one recent federal law encourages universities and businesses to collaborate and "commercialize," and to license federally funded technology to U.S. businesses.[44] The relationships among these institutions of higher education (or other types of tax-exempt organizations), their faculty, and the licensees or other for-profit users of the technology raise issues of private inurement,[45] private benefit,[46] and unrelated income taxation.

The initial reaction of the IRS to technology transfer organizations was to resist granting them tax exemption as charitable entities.[47] In the one court case on the point, the IRS prevailed on the issue.[48] As technology transfer became more commonplace in the large colleges, universities, and scientific research institutions (and with much of the research activity protected from taxation[49]), however, the views of the IRS began to change. The first indication of this alteration in policy came in the fall of 1982. The IRS ruled that, when a foundation, as its primary activity, assisted colleges and universities in bringing their scientific inventions into public use under the patent system, the foundation qualified for tax exemption as a charitable organization. Twelve years earlier,

---

[43] See Part Five.
[44] Patent and Trademark Amendments of 1980, 35 U.S.C. § 200 *et seq.*
[45] See Chapter 19.
[46] See § 19.10.
[47] An IRS technical advice memorandum issued in 1970, discussed in Tech. Adv. Mem. 8306006, concluded that a technology transfer program constituted a business activity ordinarily carried on in a commercial manner for profit (and thus an unrelated trade or business).
[48] Washington Research Found. v. Comm'r, 50 T.C.M. 1457 (1985). See § 4.9, note 261, second paragraph.
[49] See § 27.1(l).

the activity, then much smaller in scope, was ruled to be an unrelated business.[50]

Subsequent rulings have involved organizations that were created in implementation of a state program; the basis for their exemption is the lessening of the burdens of a government.[51] Other organizations have transferred the technology they created through research to for-profit subsidiaries, which thereafter develop and manufacture the resulting products.[52] Still other organizations simply contract with unrelated commercial entities for the transfer of technology, often by means of a license agreement for a patent and technical information that results in tax-free royalties—the type of practice that the IRS found to be private inurement at the outset.[53]

The IRS seems particularly concerned about the financing associated with technology transfers. Thus, the IRS grudgingly ruled that a scientific technology transfer organization would not lose its tax exemption by taking title and copyright to software developed at universities, introducing the software into public use by means of licenses, and paying the universities royalties from consumer use of the software. The IRS went out of its way to note that the software transfer program was incidental in relation to the other operations of the organization.[54]

Another IRS ruling on technology transfer organizations is one of its most extensive rulings on the point.[55] The organization involved was a scientific research organization that concentrated its efforts in biotechnology (the use of biological materials to create and facilitate useful processes and products) with the objective of economic development and job creation in a particular region of states. The IRS wrote that the organization "conducts research and development to the stage where the technical risk is reduced and the technology is acceptable to the private sector for commercialization." The organization sought a ruling because of its shift away from basic research and toward applied research, its focus on the maximization of the potential for creating marketable technologies (such as by entering into research agreements with industry businesses), and its establishment of a for-profit subsidiary to seek commercial application of resultant products. Although the IRS ruled that these new facts would not alter the organization's tax exemption, it did not do so by directly addressing the technology transfer issue. Instead, the organization's continuing exemption was predicated on the fact that it is "operated for the purpose of aiding a geographical area by attracting new industry to the area or by encouraging the development of, or retention of, an industry in the area"; the use of a subsidiary or of licensees was cast as the "only practicable manner" in which the organization's technology can be used to benefit the public.

In its examination guidelines developed for use in the audits of colleges and universities,[56] the IRS observed that these and other institutions are being

---

[50] Tech. Adv. Mem. 8306006 (see *supra* note 47).
[51] E.g., Priv. Ltr. Rul. 9243008 (see § 6.4, particularly the text accompanied by note 187).
[52] E.g., Priv. Ltr. Rul. 8606056.
[53] E.g., Priv. Ltr. Rul. 9527031.
[54] Priv. Ltr. Rul. 8512084.
[55] Priv. Ltr. Rul. 9316052.
[56] See § 24.8(d).

encouraged to "collaborate with business and to 'commercialize' and license federally-funded technology to U.S. businesses," and that, as a result, the "relationship between institutions and these licensees is growing more complex."[57] These guidelines add, "To gain access to research and/or faculty and students, industry may fund university research through many forms, such as research contracts, joint ventures, venture capital funds, industry liaison programs, spin-off companies, consortia, jointly-owned research facilities, material transfers, commercial licenses, consultations and clinical trial agreements."[58] The auditing agent is to examine research activities for private inurement or impermissible private benefit and for unrelated business activities.[59]

[57]*Id.*, § 342(10)(1).
[58]*Id.*
[59]*Id.* In general, Monroe, "Collaboration Between Tax-Exempt Research Organizations and Commercial Enterprises—Federal Income Tax Limitations," 62 *Taxes* 297 (1984); Sugarman & Mancino, "Tax Aspects of University & Patent Policy," 3 *J. Coll. U.L.* (No. 1) 41 (1976); Wolfman, "Federal Tax Policy and the Support of Science," 114 *U. Pa. L. Rev.* 171 (1965); Gray, "What Is 'Research' for the Purpose of Exemption?," 5th *Biennial N.Y.U. Conf. on Char. Fdns.* 233 (1961).

CHAPTER TEN

Other Charitable Organizations

Aside from the organizations discussed in the previous four chapters, Section 501(c)(3) of the Internal Revenue Code provides the basis for tax exemption for certain other organizations. These are entities that are organized and operated to prevent cruelty to children and animals, amateur sports organizations, public safety testing organizations, certain cooperative service organizations, charitable risk pools, and literary organizations.

§ 10.1 PREVENTION-OF-CRUELTY ORGANIZATIONS

Charitable organizations include those that are organized and operated exclusively for the *prevention of cruelty to children or animals*.[1]

An organization that prevented the birth of unwanted animals and their eventual suffering by providing funds for pet owners who cannot afford the spaying or neutering operation was ruled tax-exempt under this provision,[2] as was an organization that sought to secure humane treatment of laboratory animals.[3]

An organization to protect children from working at hazardous occupations in violation of state laws and in unfavorable work conditions was held by the IRS to be an organization established to prevent cruelty to children.[4]

§ 10.2 AMATEUR SPORTS ORGANIZATIONS

Another category of charitable organization is the *amateur athletic organization*. This exemption was established in 1976 by adding to the tax-exempt organiza-

---

[1] Reg. § 1.501(c)(3)-1(d)(1)(i)(g).
[2] Rev. Rul. 74-194, 1974-1 C.B. 129.
[3] Rev. Rul. 66-359, 1966-2 C.B. 219.
[4] Rev. Rul. 67-151, 1967-1 C.B. 134.

tions rules[5] and the charitable contribution deduction rules[6] the following phraseology: ". . . or to foster national or international amateur sports competition (but only if no part of its activities involve the provision of athletic facilities or equipment)."[7]

The legislative history of this provision contained the observation that, under prior law, organizations that "teach youth or which are affiliated with charitable organizations" may qualify as charitable entities and may receive charitable contributions but that organizations that foster national or international sports competition may be granted tax exemption as social welfare organizations[8] or business leagues[9] and be ineligible to receive deductible contributions. This history also stated, as respects the parenthetical limitation, that this "restriction . . . is intended to prevent the allowance of these benefits for organizations which, like social clubs, provide facilities and equipment for their members."[10]

At issue in the first court case to interpret this parenthetical restriction was the federal tax status of an organization that promoted the building and use of a particular class of racing sailboats by, in part, maintaining the design character of the class of boat (the "International E22 Class"). Its activities included the supervision of the conduct of builders of the E22 class of sailboats through the measurement of hulls, spars, and sails, and the formulation and enforcement of measurement rules relating to the shape of, and equipment and materials used in, E22 Class sailboats to ensure that all of these boats conform to a standard design. The organization maintained a precisely measured, full-size shape of the hull of an E22 Class sailboat (the "master plug") and precisely measured pieces of aluminum or mylar that represent the required shapes of different parts of an E22 Class sailboat, such as the rudder, keel, mast, and boom (the "measurement templates"). The IRS contended that the organization's use of the master plug and measurement templates for enforcing measurement rules and for providing measurement control services at the time of construction and in connection with races constituted the proscribed provision of athletic facilities or equipment. The U.S. Tax Court, however, declined to support that interpretation, ruling instead that the items are "tools" that are necessary to standardize competitive categories in the amateur competition that the organization fosters.[11] The court wrote that the term "athletic facilities" refers to physical structures such as clubhouses, swimming pools, and gymnasiums, and that the term "athletic equipment" means "property used directly in athletic endeavors."[12] The court concluded that "[w]e know of no athletic exercise, game, competition, or other endeavor in which

---

[5] IRC § 501(c)(3).

[6] IRC §§ 170(c)(2)(B), 2055(a)(2), 2522(a)(2).

[7] In general, Hutchinson Baseball Enters. v. Comm'r, 73 T.C. 144 (1979), aff'd 696 F.2d 757 (10th Cir. 1982). Cf. The Media Sports League, Inc. v. Comm'r, 52 T.C.M. 1093 (1986).

[8] IRC § 501(c)(4). See Chapter 12.

[9] IRC § 501(c)(6). See Chapter 13.

[10] Joint Committee on Taxation, "General Explanation of the Tax Reform Act of 1976," 94th Cong., 2d Sess. 423–424 (1976).

[11] International E22 Class Ass'n v. Comm'r, 78 T.C. 93 (1982).

[12] Id. at 99.

those items [the master plug and the measurement templates] may be used," and thus held that the items were not "athletic facilities or equipment."[13]

The parenthetical prohibition is a limitation only upon the purpose added in 1976; that is, it is not a limitation on the tax exemption and charitable contribution provisions generally. Thus, a private foundation was advised by the IRS that it could make a grant to a state university-related foundation for the purpose of constructing an aquatic complex as an integral part of the university's educational program, with the grant constituting a qualifying distribution,[14] because it would be made to accomplish educational and charitable purposes.[15]

This aspect of the law of tax-exempt organizations was modified again in 1982.[16] Thus, in the case of a *qualified amateur sports organization*, the requirement in the law that no part of the organization's activities may involve the provision of athletic facilities or equipment does not apply.[17] Also, a qualified amateur sports organization will not fail to qualify as a charitable entity merely because its membership is local or regional in nature.[18] A qualified amateur sports organization is any organization organized and operated exclusively to foster national or international amateur sports competition if the organization is also organized and operated primarily to conduct national or international competition in sports or to support and develop amateur athletes for national or international competition in sports.[19]

§ 10.3   PUBLIC SAFETY TESTING ORGANIZATIONS

A federal appellate court held that an organization that conducted tests, experiments, and investigations into the causes of losses against which insurance companies provided coverage was neither charitable, scientific, nor educational.[20] Congress responded by providing tax-exempt status for organizations that engage in *testing for public safety*.[21] This term includes the "testing of consumer products, such as electrical products, to determine whether they are safe for use by the general public."[22]

This provision was the basis for tax exemption for an organization that tested boating equipment and established safety standards for products used

---

[13] *Id.* at 98.
[14] See § 11.4(b).
[15] Priv. Ltr. Rul. 8037103.
[16] IRC § 501(j).
[17] IRC § 501(j)(1)(A).
[18] IRC § 501(j)(1)(B).
[19] IRC § 501(j)(2). The legislative history of this provision is discussed in Gen. Couns. Mem. 39775, which held that an organization that assists in securing and conducting state, regional, national, and international sports competitions in a particular geographic area and an organization that sponsors a postseason college football game are qualified amateur sports organizations. In general, Moot, Jr., "Tax-Exempt Status of Amateur Sports Organizations," 40 *Wash. & Lee L. Rev.* (No. 4) 1705 (1983).
[20] Underwriters' Laboratory, Inc. v. Comm'r, 135 F.2d 371 (7th Cir. 1943), *cert. den.*, 320 U.S. 756 (1943).
[21] IRC § 501(c)(3).
[22] Reg. § 1.501(c)(3)-1(d)(4). Also Reg. § 1.501(c)(3)-1(d)(1)(i)(d).

aboard pleasure craft by the boating public.[23] An organization that clinically tested drugs for commercial pharmaceutical companies was denied tax exemption under this provision, however, on the ground that the testing principally served the private interests of the manufacturer and that a drug is not a "consumer product" until it is approved for marketing by the Food and Drug Administration.[24] Similarly, an organization whose activities included the inspection, testing, and safety certification of cargo shipping containers and research, development, and reporting of information in the field of containerization was denied tax exemption under this provision because these activities served the private interests of manufacturers and shippers by facilitating their operations in international commerce.[25]

An organization that performed flammability tests and evaluations for manufacturers of building materials qualified under this category of tax exemption.[26] By contrast, an organization that had as its principal activity pre-service and in-service examinations and evaluations of nuclear reactor power plants, to ensure their safe operation, did not qualify for this exemption because the examinations did not involve the testing of consumer products.[27] Likewise, an organization that tested various hydraulic and mechanical devices designed for the protection of a public water supply from contamination and pollution did not qualify because the devices were not consumer products.[28] This approach was also reflected in a ruling holding that testing performed for commercial entities, of either products for pre-market clearance or air samples or like substances for compliance with environmental laws, is unrelated business activity.[29]

These organizations are expressly exempted from classification as private foundations.[30] Contributions, bequests, or gifts to public safety testing organizations (as such) are not deductible as charitable gifts, however, inasmuch as provision has not been made for them in the charitable contribution deduction rules.[31]

§ 10.4 COOPERATIVE HOSPITAL SERVICE ORGANIZATIONS

Qualifying *cooperative hospital service organizations* are tax-exempt entities by virtue of being charitable organizations.[32] These organizations must be organized and operated solely for two or more exempt member hospitals and must be orga-

---

[23] Rev. Rul. 65-61, 1965-1 C.B. 234.
[24] Rev. Rul. 68-373, 1968-2 C.B. 206.
[25] Rev. Rul. 78-426, 1978-2 C.B. 175.
[26] Priv. Ltr. Rul. 7930005.
[27] *Id.*
[28] Priv. Ltr. Rul. 7820007.
[29] Priv. Ltr. Rul. 8409055. An organization that developed and administered a program setting safety and other standards in a field of engineering qualified as a charitable organization because its quality control program lessened the burdens of a local government (see § 6.3) (Gen. Couns. Mem. 38577).
[30] IRC § 509(a)(4). See § 11.3(d).
[31] IRC §§ 170, 2055, 2106, 2522.
[32] IRC § 501(e).

nized and operated on a cooperative basis. They must perform certain specified services[33] on a centralized basis for their members, namely, data processing, purchasing (including the purchasing of insurance on a group basis),[34] warehousing, billing and collection (including the purchase of patron accounts receivable on a recourse basis), food, clinical, industrial engineering,[35] laboratory, printing, communications, records center, and personnel (including selection, testing, training, and education of personnel) services. To qualify, these services must constitute exempt activities if performed on its own behalf by a participating hospital.[36] Although this type of cooperative must have hospitals as members (patrons), its membership may include comparable entities, such as the outpatient component of a county health department.[37]

The IRS takes the position that, to qualify as a cooperative hospital service organization, the organization may provide only the services specified in the specific authorizing legislation.[38] This position is based upon the legislative history of the provision.[39] Thus, the IRS ruled that a cooperative hospital laundry service cannot be tax-exempt as a charitable organization by reason of these rules, and observed that this type of an entity may qualify as a tax-exempt cooperative.[40] (As discussed below, the IRS prevailed on this point. Thus, although it had been expressly held by a court that an organization that qualifies under the cooperative hospital service organization rules may nonetheless also qualify as a charitable organization generally,[41] this opinion was reversed on appeal, with the appellate court holding that these cooperatives can qualify (if at all) only under the cooperative hospital service organization rules.[42])

A court, in a case involving a centralized laundry service operated for tax-exempt hospitals, held that the organization qualified for status as a charitable entity, notwithstanding these specific rules.[43] The court maintained that the "question of whether it [the plaintiff organization] is organized and operated for an exempt purpose is a question of fact for this Court to decide."[44] Commenting on the rules for certain hospital cooperatives, the court said: "The clearly expressed Congressional purpose behind the enactment of Section

---

[33] IRC § 501(e)(1)(A).

[34] An organization performs the service of *purchasing* when it buys equipment for one of its patron hospitals, even though it holds legal title to the equipment, where that arrangement is used merely as a convenience to the hospital, which remains the beneficial owner of and solely responsible for paying for the equipment (Rev. Rul. 80-316, 1980-2 C.B. 172).

[35] Rev. Rul. 74-443, 1974-2 C.B. 159.

[36] Rev. Rul. 69-633, 1969-2 C.B. 121.

[37] Gen. Couns. Mem. 39692.

[38] Rev. Rul. 69-160, 1969-1 C.B. 147.

[39] H. Rep. No. 1533, 90th Cong., 2d Sess. 1, 20 (1968). Also S. Rep. No. 744, 90th Cong., 1st Sess. 200–201 (1967); H. Rep. No. 1030, 90th Cong., 1st Sess. 73 (1967).

[40] Rev. Rul. 69-633, *supra* note 36. (The rules concerning cooperative organizations are at IRC §§ 1381–1383.) Services performed in the employ of a cooperative hospital service organization described in IRC § 501(e) are exempted from "employment" for purposes of the F.U.T.A. (Rev. Rul. 74-493, 1974-2 C.B. 327).

[41] Chart, Inc. v. United States, 491 F. Supp. 10 (D.D.C. 1979).

[42] Chart, Inc. v. United States, 652 F.2d 195 (D.C. Cir. 1981).

[43] United Hosp. Servs., Inc. v. United States, 384 F. Supp. 776 (S.D. Ind. 1974).

[44] *Id.* at 780.

501(e) was to enlarge the category of charitable organizations under Section 501(c)(3) to include certain cooperative hospital service organizations, and not to narrow or restrict the reach of Section 501(c)(3)."[45] Inasmuch as the organization was operational prior to the enactment of these rules, the court, having concluded that it was charitable in nature, found the specific rules irrelevant to the case.[46]

The Senate Finance Committee's version of the Tax Reform Act of 1976 contained a provision[47] that would have inserted "laundry" services in the statutory enumeration of permissible services. The Finance Committee observed that "it is appropriate to encourage the creation and operation of cooperative service organizations by exempt hospitals because of the cost savings to the hospitals and their patients that result from providing certain services, such as laundry and clinical services, on a cooperative basis."[48] This provision was, however, defeated on the floor of the Senate.[49]

Following the enactment of these rules in 1968,[50] there was controversy as to the meaning and scope of the provision in relation to the general rules defining charitable entities.[51] There were two competing views: the hospital cooperative rules were enacted to (1) provide the exclusive and controlling means by which a cooperative hospital service organization can achieve tax exemption, so that this type of an organization that fails to satisfy the requirements of the rules thereby fails to qualify as a charitable organization,[52] or (2) enlarge the category of charitable organizations to include certain types of cooperative hospital service organizations, so that it does not narrow or restrict the reach of the rules defining charitable organizations generally.[53]

In a 1981 decision, the U.S. Supreme Court ruled that the first of these two views is the correct one.[54] In reaching this conclusion, the Court utilized a statutory construction rationale (namely, the rule that a specific statute controls over a general provision, particularly where the two are interrelated and closely positioned[55]), but principally relied on the legislative history underlying the rules for hospital cooperatives. The case involved a cooperative laundry organization serving tax-exempt entities and, as noted, laundry service is not specifically refer-

---

[45] *Id.* at 781.
[46] *Id.* Also Northern Calif. Central Servs., Inc. v. United States, 591 F.2d 620 (Ct. Cl. 1979).
[47] H.R. 10612 (1976) (as reported by the Senate Committee on Finance) § 2509.
[48] S. Rep. No. 94-938 (Part 2), 94th Cong., 2d Sess. 76 (1976).
[49] Amendment No. 315, 122 *Cong. Rec.* 25915 (1976).
[50] Pub. L. No. 374, 90th Cong. 2d Sess. (1968), § 109(a), 82 Stat. 269.
[51] IRC § 501(c)(3).
[52] E.g., HCSC-Laundry v. United States, 624 F.2d 428 (3d Cir. 1980), *rev'g* 473 F. Supp. 250 (E.D. Pa. 1979); Metropolitan Detroit Area Hosp. Servs., Inc. v. United States, 634 F.2d 330 (6th Cir. 1980), *rev'g* 445 F. Supp. 857 (E.D. Mich. 1978); Community Hosp. Servs., Inc. v. United States. 47 AFTR 2d 81-999 (6th Cir. 1981), *rev'g* 43 AFTR 2d 79-934 (E.D. Mich. 1979): Hospital Central Servs. Ass'n v. United States, 623 F.2d 611 (9th Cir. 1980), *rev'g* 40 AFTR 2d 77-5646 (W.D. Wash. 1977).
[53] E.g., Northern Calif. Central Servs., Inc. v. United States, 591 F.2d 620 (Ct. Cl. 1979); United Hosp. Servs., Inc. v. United States, *supra* note 43; Chart, Inc. v. United States, *supra* note 41.
[54] HCSC-Laundry v. United States, 450 U.S. 1 (1981), *aff'g* 624 F.2d 428 (3d Cir. 1980).
[55] Citing Bulova Watch Co. v. United States, 365 U.S. 753, 761 (1961).

enced in the rules despite efforts in 1978 and 1976 to include such a reference.[56] The Court thus determined that:

> In view of all this, it seems to us beyond dispute that subsection (e)(1)(A) of § 501, despite the seemingly broad general language of subsection (c)(3), specifies the types of hospital service organizations that are encompassed within the scope of § 501 as charitable organizations. Inasmuch as laundry service was deliberately omitted from the statutory list and, indeed, specifically was refused inclusion in that list, it inevitably follows that petitioner is not entitled to tax-exempt status. The Congress easily can change the statute whenever it is so inclined.[57]

A public charity, formed to provide and maintain a variety of cooperatively planned hospital and health-related programs and facilities, performed services on a centralized basis for tax-exempt hospitals. The IRS reviewed these services to test them against the statutory requirements for cooperative hospital service organizations. Some of the services clearly qualified because they were expressly referenced in the statute, such as printing, warehousing of records, and purchasing. Some qualified because of interpretation of the law; thus, courier services and alarm installation and maintenance services were held to fall within the meaning of "communications," while maintenance of biomedical equipment, environmental monitoring, and infectious waste disposal were found to be within the ambit of "clinical" or "laboratory" services. The IRS, however, rejected as nonqualifying services those conducted for security, parking, and housekeeping and grounds maintenance; it also held that the organization could not subcontract for impermissible services. Consequently, the organization was found not to be operating solely as a cooperative hospital entity and its tax-exempt status was revoked.[58]

This provision pertains to hospital cooperative service organizations that perform qualified administrative and other services directly for hospitals. It is not controlling in situations where an organization provides patient care services to the general public.[59]

§ 10.5   COOPERATIVE EDUCATIONAL SERVICE ORGANIZATIONS

Cooperative service organizations of operating educational organizations are regarded as charitable organizations.[60]

---

[56] *Supra* notes 39, 47–49.

[57] HCSC-Laundry v. United States, *supra* note 54, at 8. The decision in HCSC-Laundry v. United States, may be contrasted with another 1981 Supreme Court decision, where the Court went out of its way to ignore directly pertinent legislative history and to interpret a statute in a manner wholly inconsistent with congressional intent, so as to avoid constitutional law difficulties, finding that approach "simpler and more reasonable" (St. Martin Evangelical Lutheran Church v. South Dakota, 451 U.S. 772, 782 (1981)). The IRS has, in reliance upon the *HCSC-Laundry* decision, ruled that, if an organization fails to qualify under a specific category of tax exemption, it is therefore precluded from qualifying under a more general category of tax exemption (Rev. Rul. 83-166, 1983-2 C.B. 96).

[58] Tech. Adv. Mem. 9542002. In general, Tuthill, "Qualifying as a Tax Exempt Cooperative Hospital Service Organization," 50 *Notre Dame Law.* 448 (1975).

[59] Tech. Adv. Mem. 200151045.

[60] IRC § 501(f).

These organizations must be organized and controlled by and composed solely of members that are private or public educational institutions.[61] They must be organized and operated solely to hold, commingle, and collectively invest and reinvest (including arranging for and supervising the performance by independent contractors of investment services), in stocks and securities, the monies contributed to it by each of the members of the organization, and to collect income from the investments and turn over the entire amount, less expenses, to its members. While this type of organization may not invest in assets other than stocks and other securities, it may use a taxable subsidiary to make these investments.[62]

These rules were enacted to forestall the contemplated revocation by the IRS of the tax-exempt status of The Common Fund, a cooperative arrangement formed by a large group of colleges and universities for the collective investment of their funds. During its formative years, the management and administrative expenses of the Fund were largely met by start-up grants from a private foundation. As the Fund became more reliant upon payments from its member institutions, however, the IRS decided that this factor alone disqualified the Fund for exempt status.[63] In the face of loss of the Fund's exemption, Congress made it clear that cooperative arrangements for investments of the type typified by The Common Fund are eligible for exemption as charitable entities.

§ 10.6 CHARITABLE RISK POOLS

Still another category of charitable organization is the *qualified charitable risk pool*, added to the federal tax statutory law in 1996.[64] This body of statutory law overrides otherwise applicable caselaw denying tax-exempt status to eligible charitable risk pools.[65]

A qualified charitable risk pool is an entity that is organized and operated solely to pool insurable risks of its members (other than medical malpractice risks) and to provide information to its members with respect to loss control and risk management.[66] No profit or other benefit may be accorded to any member of the organization other than through the provision of members with insurance coverage below the cost of comparable commercial coverage (and loss control and risk management information).[67] Only charitable organizations can be members of these pools.[68]

This type of pool is required to be organized as a nonprofit organization under state law authorizing risk pooling for charitable organizations, to be exempt

[61] That is, organizations defined in IRC § 170(b)(1)(A)(ii) or § 170(b)(1)(A)(iv). See § 11.3(a).
[62] Gen. Couns. Mem. 39776.
[63] See S. Rep. No. 888, 93d Cong. 2d Sess. 2–3 (1974). See § 6.8.
[64] IRC § 501(n)(1)(A).
[65] See § 22.1.
[66] IRC § 501(n)(2)(A).
[67] H.R. Rep. No. 737, 104th Cong., 2d Sess. 189 (1996).
[68] IRC § 501(n)(2)(B).

from state income tax, to obtain at least $1 million in start-up capital[69] from non-member charitable organizations,[70] to be controlled by a board of directors elected by its members, and to provide three elements in its organizational documents, namely, that members must be tax-exempt charitable organizations at all times, that if a member loses that status it must immediately notify the organization, and that no insurance coverage applies to a member after the date of any final determination that the member no longer qualifies as a tax-exempt charitable organization.[71]

The rule that a charitable organization cannot be exempt from tax if a substantial part of its activities consists of providing commercial-type insurance[72] is not applicable to charitable risk pools.[73] Because this category of tax exemption is based on qualification as a charitable organization, a risk pool must satisfy all of the other requirements for achievement of this exempt status.[74]

§ 10.7   LITERARY ORGANIZATIONS

Although there is a statutory basis for tax exemption as a *literary* organization,[75] there is no law on the subject. The concept is encompassed by the terms *charitable* and *educational*.[76]

There is, in a sense, a variety of charitable organizations other than those surveyed in this chapter. Most of these entities are (or will be) derived from interpretations of the term *charitable* in its more technical sense.[77] As discussed, the term *charitable* has an ongoing, dynamic meaning.[78] There is, of course, always the possibility that Congress will legislate into existence one or more types of charitable organizations (using that term in the largest sense) that are not presently recognized as such.

---

[69] This term means any capital contributed to, and any program-related investments (see § 11.4(d)) made in, the risk pool before the pool commences operations (IRC § 501(n)(4)(A)).

[70] A *nonmember charitable organization* is a tax-exempt organization described in IRC § 501(c)(3), which is not a member of the risk pool and does not benefit, directly or indirectly, from the insurance coverage provided by the pool to its members (IRC § 501(n)(4)(B)).

[71] IRC §§ 501(n)(2)(C), (3).

[72] See § 22.1.

[73] IRC § 501(n)(1)(B).

[74] See Part Two. In general, Larue, Jr., "Small Business Act Grants Exempt Status to Charitable Risk Pools," 8 *J. Tax. Exempt Orgs.* 103 (Nov./Dec. 1996).

[75] IRC § 501(c)(3); Reg. § 1.501(c)(3)-1(d)(1)(i)(e). In general, Trenberry, "A Literary Pilgrim's Progress Along Section 501(c)(3)," 51 *A.B.A.J.* 252 (1965).

[76] See Chapters 6, 7.

[77] See Chapter 6.

[78] See § 5.1.

CHAPTER ELEVEN

Public Charities and Private Foundations

The federal tax law relating to charitable organizations[1] differentiates between *public charities* and *private foundations*. This is done for a variety of reasons, including the fact that the charitable giving rules make this distinction[2] and because

---

[1] That is, organizations described in IRC § 501(c)(3) and tax-exempt by reason of IRC § 501(a). See Part Two.

[2] See § 2.5.

special regulatory requirements specifically target private foundations.[3] Despite the relative scarcity of private foundations,[4] the extent and growth of the law governing them is extraordinary.[5]

§ 11.1 FEDERAL TAX LAW DEFINITION OF *PRIVATE FOUNDATION*

(a) Definition of *Private Foundation*

The federal tax law does not define the term *private foundation*. Rather, it enumerates the types of charitable organizations that are not private foundations.[6] From a statutory law perspective, a private foundation is a charitable organization, domestic or foreign, that does not qualify as a public charity; a public charity is an institution (such as a university or a hospital), an organization that has broad public support, or an organization that functions in a supporting relationship to one or more institutions or publicly supported entities.[7] A charitable entity is presumed to be a private foundation; this presumption may be rebutted by a showing that the entity is a public charity.[8]

A standard private foundation is a type of tax-exempt organization that has four characteristics: It is a charitable organization; it is funded from one source (usually an individual, married couple, family, or corporation); its ongoing funding is in the form of investment income (rather than from a flow of investment income); and it makes grants for charitable purposes to other persons (rather than conducting its own programs). (In many respects, then, a private foundation is much like an endowment fund.) The *private* aspect of a private foundation thus relates principally to the nature of its financial support.

---

[3] See *infra* § 4.

[4] There are about 65,000 private foundations, compared to more than 1 million charitable organizations (see § 2.1).

[5] The law in this area originated with the Tax Reform Act of 1969; it was written in an anti–private foundation environment. One of the principal stimuli for this legislation was a report prepared by the Department of the Treasury in 1965 ("Treasury Report on Private Foundations," Committee on Finance, United States Senate, 89th Cong., 1st Sess. (1969)). In the intervening years, however, the general perception is that private foundations are being properly operated and are in conformity with the tax law requirements. One court stated that Congress enacted these rules "to put an end, so far as it reasonably could, to the abuses and potential abuses associated with private foundations" (Hans S. Mannheimer Charitable Trust v. Comm'r, 93 T.C. 35, 39 (1989)). This objective of Congress seems to have been successfully reached. In general, Hopkins & Blazek, *Private Foundations: Tax Law and Compliance, Second Edition* (John Wiley & Sons, Inc., 2003); Hopkins & Blazek, *The Legal Answer Book for Private Foundations* (John Wiley & Sons, Inc., 2002).

[6] IRC § 509(a), the deceptive heading of which is "Private Foundation Defined."

[7] Reg. § 1.509(a)-1. The term *public charity* is the subject of *infra* § 3.

[8] IRC § 508(b); Reg. § 1.508-1(b).

(b) Private Operating Foundations

The *private operating foundation* is a private foundation that operates its own programs, in contrast to the standard private foundation which is a grantmaking entity. This type of foundation devotes most of its earnings and much of its assets directly to the conduct of its charitable programs.[9]

A private operating foundation must meet an *income test*.[10] To satisfy this test, a private foundation must expend an amount equal to substantially all[11] of the lesser of its adjusted net income or its minimum investment return,[12] in the form of qualifying distributions,[13] directly for the active conduct of its exempt charitable activities.[14]

The term *adjusted net income* means any excess of a private foundation's gross income for a year over the sum of deductions allowed to a taxable corporation.[15] This amount of gross income is determined using certain *income modifications*[16] and the allowable deductions are determined using certain *deduction modifications*.[17]

The funds expended must be applied by the private foundation itself; these outlays are termed *direct expenditures*, while grants to other organizations are *indirect expenditures*.[18] Amounts paid to acquire or maintain assets that are used directly in the conduct of exempt activities are direct expenditures, as are administrative expenses and other operating costs necessary to conduct exempt activities. An amount set aside[19] by a foundation for a specific project involving the active conduct of exempt activities may qualify as a direct expenditure.[20] The making or awarding of grants or similar payments to individuals to support active tax-exempt programs constitutes direct expenditures only if the foundation maintains some significant involvement in the programs.[21]

To qualify as a private operating foundation, an organization must also satisfy an *assets test*,[22] an *endowment test*,[23] or a *support test*.[24]

A private foundation will satisfy the assets test where substantially more than one half[25] of its assets is (1) devoted directly to the active conduct of its tax-

---

[9] IRC § 4942(j)(3).
[10] IRC § 4942(j)(3)(A); Reg. § 53.4942(b)-1(a).
[11] Namely, at least 85 percent (Reg. § 53.4942(b)-1(c)).
[12] See *infra* § 4(b), text accompanied by note 243.
[13] *Id.*, text accompanied by note 241.
[14] Reg. § 53.4942(b)-1(a)(1).
[15] IRC § 4942(f)(1); Reg. § 53.4942(a)-2(d)(1).
[16] IRC § 4942(f)(2); Reg. § 53.4942(a)-2(d)(2).
[17] IRC § 4942(f)(3); Reg. § 53.4942(a)-2(d)(4).
[18] Reg. § 53.4942(b)-1(b)(1).
[19] See *infra* § 4(b).
[20] Reg. § 53.4942(b)-1(b)(1). E.g, Rev. Rul. 74-450, 1974-2 C.B. 388.
[21] Reg. § 53.4942(b)-1(b)(2). E.g., The "Miss Elizabeth" D. Leckie Scholarship Fund v. Comm'r, 87 T.C. 251 (1986); Rev. Rul. 78-315, 1978-2 C.B. 271.
[22] IRC § 4942(j)(3)(B)(i).
[23] IRC § 4942(j)(3)(B)(ii).
[24] IRC § 4942(j)(3)(B)(iii).
[25] Namely, at least 65 percent (Reg. § 53.4942(b)-2(a)(5)).

exempt activities, to functionally related businesses,[26] or to a combination of these functions; (2) stock of a corporation that is controlled by the foundation and substantially all of the assets of which are devoted to charitable activities; or (3) in part assets described in the first category and in part stock described in the second category.[27]

An asset, to qualify under this test, must actually be used by the foundation directly for the active conduct of its tax-exempt purpose. It can consist of real estate, physical facilities or objects, and intangible assets, but it cannot include assets held for the production of income, investment, or other similar use. Property used for both exempt and other purposes will meet the assets test (assuming it otherwise qualifies) as long as the exempt use represents at least 95 percent of total use.[28]

A private foundation will satisfy the endowment test where it normally expends its funds, in the form of qualifying distributions, directly for the active conduct of exempt activities, in an amount equal to at least two thirds of its minimum investment return.[29] The concept of expenditures directly for the active conduct of exempt activities under the endowment test is the same as that under the income test.[30]

A private foundation will satisfy the support test if (1) substantially all of its support (other than gross investment income[31]) is normally received from the general public and from at least five tax-exempt organizations that are not disqualified persons[32] with respect to each other or the foundation involved; (2) not more than 25 percent of its support (other than gross investment income) is normally received from any one of these exempt organizations; and (3) not more than one half of its support is normally received from gross investment income.[33]

An organization may satisfy the income test and either the assets, endowment, or support test by one of two methods: meeting the requirements for any three years during a four-year period consisting of the year involved and the three immediately preceding tax years, or on the basis of an aggregation of all pertinent amounts of income or assets held, received, or distributed during the four-year period. The same method must be used for satisfying the tests.[34] A foundation, to be regarded as a private operating foundation, generally must satisfy the income test and one of the other tests for its first year.[35]

Contributions to a private operating foundation are treated as if made to a public charity.[36]

---

[26] See *infra* § 4(c).
[27] Reg. § 53.4942(b)-2(a)(1).
[28] Reg. § 53.4942(b)-2(a)(2).
[29] Reg. § 53.4942(b)-2(b)(1).
[30] Reg. § 53.4942(b)-2(b)(2).
[31] IRC § 509(e).
[32] See *infra* § 2.
[33] Reg. § 53.4942(b)-2(c)(1).
[34] Reg. § 53.4942(b)-3(a).
[35] Reg. § 53.4942(b)-3(b)(1).
[36] IRC §§ 170(b)(1)(A)(vii), 170(b)(1)(E)(i); Reg. § 1.170A-9(f).

(c) Exempt Operating Foundations

Another variant of private foundation is the *exempt operating foundation*.[37] This type of private foundation is termed an *exempt* entity because it does not have to pay the private foundation excise tax on investment income[38] nor are grants to it subject to the expenditure responsibility requirement.[39] The reason this category of foundation was established is to provide organizations that are not, in a generic sense, private foundations (such as many museums and libraries) some of the attributes of public charities.[40]

To be an exempt operating foundation for a year, a private foundation is required to have these characteristics: It qualifies as a private operating foundation; it has been publicly supported[41] for at least 10 years; its governing body consists of individuals at least 75 percent of whom are not *disqualified individuals*[42] and is broadly representative of the general public; and at no time during the year did it have an officer who is a disqualified individual.[43]

(d) Conduit Foundations

A *conduit private foundation* is not a separate category of private foundation but is a standard private foundation that, under certain circumstances, is regarded as a public charity for charitable contribution deduction purposes.[44]

This type of foundation makes qualifying distributions that are treated as distributions from its corpus[45] in an amount equal in value to 100 percent of all contributions received in the year involved, whether as money or property.[46] The distributions must be made not later than the fifteenth day of the third month after the close of the private foundation's year in which the contributions were received, and the foundation must not have any remaining undistributed income for the year.

The qualifying distribution may be of the contributed property or of the proceeds from its sale. In making the calculation in satisfaction of the 100 percent requirement, the amount distributed generally must be equal to the fair market value of the contributed property on the date of its distribution. The amount of this fair market value may, however, be reduced by any reasonable selling expenses incurred by the foundation in disposing of the contributed property. At the option of the private foundation, if the contributed property is sold or distributed within 30 days of its receipt by the foundation, the amount of the fair market

---

[37] IRC § 4940(d).
[38] IRC § 4940(d)(1). See *infra* § 4(f).
[39] IRC § 4945(d)(4)(A). See *infra* § 4(e).
[40] H. Rep. No. 98-861, 98th Cong., 2d Sess. 1084 (1984).
[41] IRC § 4940(d)(3)(A).
[42] Namely, substantial contributors (see *infra* § 2(a)) and certain related persons (IRC §§ 4940(d)(3)(B)–4940(d)(3)(E)).
[43] IRC § 4940(d)(2).
[44] IRC §§ 170(b)(1)(A)(vii), 170(b)(1)(E)(ii). See § 2.5.
[45] IRC § 4942(h).
[46] IRC § 170(b)(1)(E)(ii); Reg. § 1.170A-9(g)(1).

value is either the gross amount received from the sale of the property (less reasonable selling expenses) or an amount equal to the fair market value of the property on the date of its distribution to a public charity.[47]

These distributions are treated as made first out of contributions of property and then out of contributions of money received by the private foundation in the year involved. The distributions cannot be made to an organization controlled directly or indirectly by the private foundation or by one or more disqualified persons[48] with respect to the private foundation or to a private foundation that is not a private operating foundation.[49]

(e) Common Fund Foundations

A special type of standard private foundation (that is, it is not a private operating foundation) is one that pools contributions received in a common fund but allows the donor or his or her spouse (including substantial contributors[50]) to retain the right to designate annually the organizations to which the income attributable to the contributions is given (as long as the organizations qualify as certain types of entities that are not private foundations[51]) and to direct (by deed or will) the organizations to which the corpus of the contributions is eventually to be given. Moreover, this type of private foundation must pay out its adjusted net income to public charities by the fifteenth day of the third month after the close of the tax year in which the income is realized by the fund and the corpus must be distributed to these charities within one year after the death of the donor or his or her spouse.[52]

Contributions to this type of private foundation are treated as if made to a public charity.[53]

(f) Other Types of Foundations

There are various types of tax-exempt charitable organizations that are termed *foundations* although they are not private foundations. For example, a form of publicly supported charity is the *community foundation*, which is a fund established to support charitable organizations in an identified geographical area.[54] Various *supporting organizations* are termed foundations, although they are public charities.[55] Public colleges and universities often have related "foundations," that are in fact public charities.[56]

---

[47] Reg. § 1.170A-9(g)(2)(iv).
[48] See *infra* § 2.
[49] Reg. § 1.170A-9(g).
[50] See *infra* § 2.
[51] IRC § 509(a)(1). See *infra* § 3(a), (b).
[52] Reg. § 170A-9(h).
[53] IRC §§ 170(b)(i)(A)(vii), 170(b)(i)(E)(iii). See *infra* §§ 2-5.
[54] This entity is a publicly supported charity by reason of IRC §§ 170(b)(1)(A)(vi) and 509(a)(1). See *infra* § 3.
[55] See *infra* § 3(c).
[56] See *infra* § 3(b)(v).

One of the types of organizations eligible to receive funding, that qualifies for the scientific research tax credit,[57] is a fund organized and operated exclusively to make basic research grants to qualified institutions of higher education.[58] This type of fund must be a charitable organization that is not a private foundation and must make its grants pursuant to written research contracts. A fund must elect this status; by doing so, it becomes treated as a private foundation, although the tax on net investment income[59] is not applicable.[60]

(g) Organizational Rules

An organization must satisfy the applicable organizational test in order to achieve tax-exempt status.[61] There are organizational rules for private foundations, which must be met in addition to the organizational test applicable for charitable organizations generally.[62]

A private foundation cannot be exempt from tax (nor will contributions to it be deductible as charitable gifts) unless its governing instrument includes provisions the effects of which are to require distributions at such time and in such manner as to comply with the payout rules and prohibit the foundation from engaging in any act of self-dealing, retaining any excess business holdings, making any jeopardizing investments, and making any taxable expenditures.[63] Generally, these elements must be in the foundation's articles of organization and not solely in its bylaws.[64]

The provisions of a foundation's governing instrument must require or prohibit, as the case may be, the foundation to act or refrain from acting so that the foundation, and any foundation managers or other disqualified persons with respect to it, will not be liable for any of the private foundation excise taxes.[65] The governing instrument of a nonexempt split-interest trust[66] must make comparable provision as respects any of the applicable private foundation excise taxes.[67] Specific reference in the governing instrument to the appropriate sections of the Internal Revenue Code is generally required, unless equivalent language is used that is deemed by the IRS to have the same full

---

[57] IRC § 41.
[58] IRC § 41(e)(6)(D).
[59] See *infra* § 4(f).
[60] IRC § 41(e)(6)(D)(iv).
[61] The law contains an express organizational test for charitable organizations; there is an implied test of this nature for other categories of exempt organizations. For the latter, the requirement essentially is that the organizational document be reflective of the organization's primary exempt purposes (see § 4.4).
[62] See § 4.3.
[63] IRC § 508(e)(1).
[64] Reg. § 1.508-3(c).
[65] Rev. Rul. 70-270, 1970-1 C.B. 135, contains sample governing instrument provisions.
[66] That is, entities described in IRC § 4947(a)(1).
[67] Reg. § 1.508-3(e). Rev. Rul. 74-368, 1974-2 C.B. 390, contains sample governing instrument provisions.

force and effect. A governing instrument that contains only language sufficient to satisfy the requirements of the organizational test for charitable entities generally does not meet the specific requirements applicable with respect to private foundations, regardless of the interpretation placed on the language as a matter of law by a state court, and a governing instrument does not meet the organizational requirements if it expressly prohibits the distribution of capital or corpus.[68]

A foundation's governing instrument is deemed to conform with the organizational requirements if valid provisions of state law have been enacted that require the foundation to act or refrain from acting so as to not subject it to any of the private foundation excise taxes or that treat the required provisions as contained in the foundation's governing instrument.[69] The IRS ruled as to which state statutes contain sufficient provisions in this regard.[70]

Any provision of state law is presumed valid as enacted, and in the absence of state law provisions to the contrary, applies with respect to any foundation that does not specifically disclaim coverage under state law (either by notification to the appropriate state official or by commencement of judicial proceedings).[71] If a state law provision is declared invalid or inapplicable with respect to a class of foundations by the highest appellate court of the state or by the U.S. Supreme Court, the foundations covered by the determination must meet certain requirements[72] within one year from the date on which the time for perfecting an application for review by the Supreme Court expires. If such an application is filed, these requirements must be met within a year from the date on which the Supreme Court disposes of the case, whether by denial of the application for review or decision on the merits. In addition, if a provision of state law is declared invalid or inapplicable with respect to a class of foundations by any court of competent jurisdiction, and the decision is not reviewed by the highest state appellate court of the Supreme Court, and the IRS notifies the general public that the provision has been so declared invalid or inapplicable, then all foundations in the state must meet these requirements, without reliance upon the statute to the extent declared invalid or inapplicable by the decision, within one year from the date such notice is made public. These rules do not apply to any foundation that is subject to a final judgment entered by a court of competent jurisdiction, holding the law invalid or inapplicable with respect to the foundation.[73]

---

[68] Reg. § 1.508-3(b).
[69] Reg. § 1.508-3(d)(1).
[70] Rev. Rul. 75-38, 1975-1 C.B. 161.
[71] Reg. § 1.508-3(b)(6).
[72] IRC § 508(e).
[73] Reg. § 1.508-3(d)(2).

§ 11.2 DISQUALIFIED PERSONS

A basic concept of the tax laws relating to private foundations is that of the *disqualified person*. Essentially, a disqualified person is a person (including an individual, corporation, partnership, trust, or estate) that has a particular, usually intimate, relationship with respect to a private foundation.[74]

(a) Substantial Contributor

One category of disqualified person[75] is a *substantial contributor* to a private foundation.[76] A substantial contributor generally is any person who contributed or bequeathed an aggregate amount of more than $5,000 to the private foundation involved, where the amount is more than 2 percent of the total contributions and bequests received by the foundation before the close of its year in which the contribution or bequest is received by the foundation from that person.[77] In making this computation, all contributions and bequests to the private foundation, made since its establishment, are taken into account.[78]

In the case of a trust, the term *substantial contributor* also means the creator of the trust.[79] The term *person* includes tax-exempt organizations[80] (except as discussed below) but does not include governmental units.[81] The term *person* also includes a decedent, even at the point in time preceding the transfer of any property from the estate to the private foundation.[82] With one exception, once a person becomes a substantial contributor to a private foundation, it can never escape that status,[83] even though it might not be so classified if the determination were first made at a later date.[84]

Only one exception enables a person's status as a substantial contributor to terminate in certain circumstances after 10 years with no connection with the private foundation.[85] This requires that, during the 10-year period, (1) the person (and any related persons) did not make any contributions to the private foundation, (2) neither the person (nor any related person) was a foundation manager of

---

[74] The term *disqualified person* is defined, for these purposes, in IRC § 4946(a). The term is defined somewhat differently in the setting of excess benefit transactions involving public charities and social welfare organizations (see § 19.11(c)).

[75] IRC § 4946(a)(1)(A); Reg. § 53.4946-1(a)(1)(i).

[76] IRC §§ 4946(a)(2), 507(d)(2).

[77] IRC § 507(d)(2)(A).

[78] Reg. § 1.507-6(a)(1). In the first case on the point, a court concluded that an individual was not a substantial contributor to a private foundation (Graham v. Comm'r, 83 T.C.M. 1137 (2002)).

[79] *Id.*

[80] That is, organizations encompassed by IRC § 501(a).

[81] That is, entities described in IRC § 170(c)(1).

[82] Rockefeller v. United States, 572 F. Supp. 9 (E.D. Ark. 1982), *aff'd*, 718 F.2d 290 (8th Cir. 1983), *cert. den.*, 466 U.S. 962 (1984).

[83] IRC § 507(d)(2)(B)(iv).

[84] Reg. § 1.507-6(b)(1).

[85] IRC § 507(d)(2)(C).

the private foundation, and (3) the aggregate contributions made by the person (and any related person) are determined by the IRS "to be insignificant when compared to the aggregate amount of contributions to such foundation by one other person,"[86] taking into account appreciation on contributions while held by the private foundation. For these purposes, the term *related person* means related disqualified persons, and in the case of a corporate donor includes the officers and directors of the corporation.[87]

For certain purposes,[88] the term *substantial contributor* does not include most organizations that are not private foundations[89] or an organization wholly owned by a public charity. Moreover, for purposes of the self-dealing rules,[90] the term does not include any charitable organization,[91] since to require inclusion of charitable organizations for this purpose would preclude private foundations from making large grants to or otherwise interacting with other private foundations.[92] In computing the support fraction for purposes of one category of publicly supported organization,[93] however, the term *substantial contributor* includes public charities where the $5,000/2 percent test is exceeded, although the support may qualify as a material change in support or an unusual grant.

In determining whether a contributor is a substantial contributor, the total of the amounts received from the contributor and the total contributions and bequests received by the private foundation must be ascertained as of the last day of each tax year commencing with the first year ending after October 9, 1969.[94] Generally, all contributions and bequests made before October 9, 1969, are deemed to have been made on that date, and each contribution or bequest made after that is valued at its fair market value on the date received, with an individual treated as making all contributions and bequests made by his or her spouse.[95]

(b) Foundation Manager

Another category of disqualified person[96] is the *foundation manager*. A foundation manager is an officer, director, or trustee of a private foundation, or an individual

---

[86] IRC § 507(d)(2)(C)(i)(III).
[87] IRC § 507(d)(2)(C)(ii).
[88] IRC §§ 170(b)(1)(D)(iii), 507(d)(1), 508(d), 509(a)(1), 509(a)(3), and IRC Chapter 42.
[89] That is, organizations described in IRC §§ 509(a)(1), 509(a)(2), or 509(a)(3).
[90] See *infra* § 4(a).
[91] For these purposes, an organization described in IRC § 501(c)(3), other than an organization that tests for public safety (IRC § 509(a)(4)). See *infra* § 3(a)-(c).
[92] Reg. § 1.507-6(a)(2). This exception also applies to IRC § 4947(a)(1) trusts (Rev. Rul. 73-455, 1973-2 C.B. 187).
[93] IRC § 509(a)(2)(A). See *infra* § 3(b)(iv).
[94] Reg. § 1.507-6(b)(i).
[95] IRC § 507(d)(2)(B)(i)–(iii).
[96] IRC § 4946(a)(1)(B); Reg. § 53.4946-1(f)(1).

having powers or responsibilities similar to one or more of these three positions.[97] An individual is considered an *officer* of a private foundation if he or she is specifically designated as such under the documents by which the foundation was formed or if he or she regularly exercises general authority to make administrative or policy decisions on behalf of the foundation.[98] Independent contractors acting in that capacity—such as lawyers, accountants, and investment managers and advisers—are not officers.[99]

An organization can be a foundation manager, such as a bank, a similar financial institution, or an investment adviser.[100]

(c) Twenty Percent Owner

An owner of more than 20 percent of the total combined *voting power* of a corporation, the *profits interest* of a partnership, or the *beneficial interest* of a trust or unincorporated enterprise, any of which is (during the ownership) a substantial contributor to a private foundation, is a disqualified person.[101]

The term combined voting power[102] includes voting power represented by holdings of voting stock, actual or constructive,[103] but does not include voting rights held only as a director or trustee.[104]

The term *voting power* includes outstanding voting power and does not include voting power obtainable but not obtained, such as voting power obtainable by converting securities or nonvoting stock into voting stock, by exercising warrants or options to obtain voting stock, and voting power that will vest in preferred stockholders only if and when the corporation has failed to pay preferred dividends for a specified period or has otherwise failed to meet specified requirements.[105]

The profits interest[106] of a partner is that equal to his or her distributive share of income of the partnership as determined under special federal tax rules.[107] The term *profits interest* includes any interest that is outstanding but not any interest that is obtainable but has not been obtained.[108]

The beneficial interest in an unincorporated enterprise (other than a trust or estate) includes any right to receive a portion of distributions from profits of the enterprise or, in the absence of a profit-sharing agreement, any right to receive a portion of the assets (if any) upon liquidation of the enterprise, except as

---

[97] IRC § 4946(b)(1).
[98] Reg. § 53.4946-1(f)(1). An example of the latter is in Rev. Rul. 74-287, 1974-1 C.B. 327.
[99] Reg. § 53.4946-1(f)(2).
[100] E.g., Priv. Ltr. Rul. 9535043.
[101] IRC § 4946(a)(1)(C).
[102] IRC § 4946(a)(1)(C)(i).
[103] See IRC § 4946(a)(3).
[104] Reg. § 53.4946-1(a)(5).
[105] Reg. § 53.4946-1(a)(6).
[106] IRC § 4946(a)(1)(C)(ii).
[107] IRC §§ 707(b)(3), 4946(a)(4); Reg. § 53.4946-1(a)(2).
[108] Reg. § 53.4946-1(a)(6).

a creditor or employee.[109] A right to receive distribution of profits includes a right to receive any amount from the profits other than as a creditor or employee, whether as a sum certain or as a portion of profits realized by the enterprise. Where there is no agreement fixing the rights of the participants in an enterprise, the fraction of the respective interests of each participant therein is determined by dividing the amount of all investments or contributions to the capital of the enterprise made or obligated to be made by the participant by the amount of all investments or contributions to capital made or obligated to be made by all of them.[110]

A person's beneficial interest in a trust is determined in proportion to the actuarial interest of the person in the trust.[111]

The term *beneficial interest* includes any interest that is outstanding but not any interest that is obtainable but has not been obtained.[112]

(d) Family Member

Another category of disqualified person is a member of the family of an individual who is a substantial contributor, a foundation manager, or one of the previously discussed 20 percent owners.[113] The term *member of the family* is defined to include only an individual's spouse, ancestors, children, grandchildren, great-grandchildren, and the spouses of children, grandchildren, and great-grandchildren.[114] Thus, these family members are themselves disqualified persons.

A legally adopted child of an individual is treated for these purposes as a child of the individual by blood.[115] A brother or sister of an individual is not, for these purposes, a member of the family.[116] For example, the spouse of a grandchild of an individual is a member of his or her family for these purposes.[117]

(e) Corporation

A corporation is a disqualified person if more than 35 percent of the total combined voting power in the corporation (including constructive holdings[118]) is owned by substantial contributors, foundation managers, 20 percent owners, or members of the family of any of these individuals.[119]

---

[109] IRC § 4946(a)(1)(C)(iii).
[110] Reg. § 53.4946-1(a)(3).
[111] Reg. § 53.4946-1(a)(4).
[112] Reg. § 53.4946-1(a)(6).
[113] IRC § 4946(a)(1)(D).
[114] IRC § 4946(d).
[115] Reg. § 53.4946-1(h).
[116] *Id.*
[117] *Id.*
[118] IRC § 4946(a)(3).
[119] IRC § 4946(a)(1)(E).

(f) Partnership

A partnership is a disqualified person if more than 35 percent of the profits interest in the partnership (including constructive holdings[120]) is owned by substantial contributors, foundation managers, 20 percent owners, or members of the family of any of these individuals.[121]

(g) Trust or Estate

A trust or estate is a disqualified person if more than 35 percent of the beneficial interest in the trust or estate (including constructive holdings[122]) is owned by substantial contributors, foundation managers, 20 percent owners, or members of the family of any of these individuals.[123]

(h) Private Foundation

A private foundation may be a disqualified person with respect to another private foundation but only for purposes of the excess business holdings rules.[124] The disqualified person private foundation must be effectively controlled,[125] directly or indirectly, by the same person or persons (other than a bank, trust company, or similar organization acting only as a foundation manager) who control the private foundation in question, or must be the recipient of contributions substantially all of which were made, directly or indirectly, by substantial contributors, foundation managers, 20 percent owners, and members of their families who made, directly or indirectly, substantially all of the contributions to the private foundation in question.[126] One or more persons are considered to have made *substantially all* of the contributions to a private foundation for these purposes if the persons have contributed or bequeathed at least 85 percent of the total contributions and bequests that have been received by the private foundation during its entire existence, where each person has contributed or bequeathed at least two percent of the total.[127]

(i) Governmental Official

A governmental official may be a disqualified person with respect to a private foundation but only for purposes of the self-dealing rules.[128] The term *governmental official* means (1) an elected public official in the U.S. Congress or executive branch, (2) presidential appointees to the U.S. executive or judicial branches, (3)

---

[120] IRC § 4946(a)(4).
[121] IRC § 4946(a)(1)(F).
[122] IRC § 4946(a)(4).
[123] IRC § 4946(a)(1)(G).
[124] IRC § 4946(a)(1)(H). See *infra* § 4(c).
[125] Reg. § 1.482-1(a)(3).
[126] Reg. § 53.4946-1(b)(1).
[127] Reg. § 53.4946-1(b)(2).
[128] IRC § 4946(a)(1)(I).

certain higher compensated or ranking employees in one of these three branches, (4) House of Representatives or Senate employees earning at least $15,000 annually, (5) elected or appointed public officials in the U.S. or D.C. governments (including governments of U.S. possessions or political subdivisions or areas of the United States) earning at least $15,000 annually, or, as regards compensation received after December 31, 1985, $20,000 annually, or (6) the personal or executive assistant or secretary to any of the foregoing.[129]

In defining the term *public office* for purposes of the fifth category of governmental officials, this term must be distinguished from mere public employment. Although holding a public office is one form of public employment, not every position in the employ of a state or other governmental subdivision[130] constitutes a public office. Although a determination as to whether a public employee holds a public office depends on the facts and circumstances of the case, the essential element is whether a significant part of the activities of a public employee is the independent performance of policy-making functions. Several factors may be considered as indications that a position in the executive, legislative, or judicial branch of the government of a state, possession of the United States, or political subdivision or other area of any of the foregoing, or of the District of Columbia, constitutes a public office. Among the factors to be considered, in addition to that set forth above, are that the office is created by Congress, a state constitution, or a state legislature, or by a municipality or other governmental body pursuant to authority conferred by Congress, state constitution, or state legislature, and the powers conferred on the office and the duties to be discharged by the official are defined either directly or indirectly by Congress, a state constitution, or a state legislature, or through legislative authority.[131]

§ 11.3 CATEGORIES OF PUBLIC CHARITIES

A *public charity* is a charitable organization[132] that does not constitute a private foundation. There are, in essence, four categories of charitable organizations that are not private foundations: *public institutions, publicly supported charities, supporting organizations,* and *organizations that test for public safety.*

(a) Public Institutions

There are types of charitable organizations that generally are recognized as entities that are not private foundations, under any reasonable definition of that term, by virtue of the nature of their programs, how they are structured, and their relationship with the general public. These are the *public institutions.*

---

[129] IRC § 4946(c).
[130] IRC § 4946(c)(5).
[131] Reg. § 53.4946-1(g)(2).
[132] That is, an entity described *supra* note 1.

The category of public institutions comprises churches, and conventions and associations of churches;[133] educational organizations that normally maintain a regular faculty and curriculum, and normally have a regularly enrolled body of pupils or students in attendance at the place where the educational activities are regularly carried on, that is, schools, colleges, and universities;[134] hospitals and medical research organizations;[135] and governmental units,[136] including a state, a possession of the United States, a political subdivision of either of the foregoing, the United States, or the District of Columbia.[137]

(b) Publicly Supported Charities

(i) Donative Publicly Supported Charities—In General. An organization qualifies as a *donative* type of publicly supported charity if it normally receives a substantial part of its support (other than exempt function revenue) from a governmental unit[138] or from direct or indirect contributions from the general public.[139]

The principal requirement for a charitable organization to qualify as a donative publicly supported organization is that it normally derives at least one-third of its financial support from qualifying contributions and grants.[140] This type of entity must maintain a *support fraction* (using the cash basis method of accounting), the denominator of which is total eligible support received during the computation period and the numerator of which is the amount of eligible public support for the period.

The term *support* means amounts received as contributions, grants, net income from unrelated business activities,[141] gross investment income,[142] tax revenues levied for the benefit of the organization and either paid to or expended on behalf of it, and the value of services or facilities (exclusive of services or facilities generally furnished to the public without charge) furnished by a governmental unit to the organization without charge.[143] All of these items are amounts that, if received by the organization, represent the denominator of the support fraction.

Support does not include any gain from the disposition of property that would be considered gain from the sale or exchange of a capital asset, or the value of exemption from any federal, state, or local tax or any similar benefit.[144]

---

[133] IRC §§ 170(b)(1)(A)(i), 509(a)(1). See §§ 8.3, 8.4.
[134] IRC §§ 170(b)(1)(A)(ii), 509(a)(1). See § 7.3.
[135] IRC §§ 170(b)(1)(A)(iii), 509(a)(1). See § 6.2.
[136] IRC §§ 170(b)(1)(A)(v), 509(a)(1). See § 6.9.
[137] IRC § 170(c)(1).
[138] *Id.*
[139] IRC §§ 170(b)(1)(A)(vi), 509(a)(1).
[140] Reg. § 1.170A-9(e)(2).
[141] See Part Five.
[142] IRC § 509(e).
[143] IRC § 509(d).
[144] *Id.*

A loan is not a form of support; however, should the lender forgive the debt, the amount becomes support in the year of the forgiveness.[145]

In general, contributions and grants constitute public support to the extent that the total amount of gifts or grants from a source during the computation period does not exceed an amount equal to 2 percent of the organization's total includible support for the period.[146] (Where a contributor or grantor provides an amount that is in excess of the 2 percent threshold, the portion that does not exceed the threshold qualifies as public support.) Therefore, the total amount of support from a donor or grantor is included in full in the denominator of the support fraction, while the amount determined by application of the 2 percent threshold is included in the numerator of the support fraction. Persons who have a defined relationship with one another (such as spouses) are considered as one source for purposes of computing the two percent threshold amount.

Qualifying gifts and grants constitute support in the form of *direct* contributions from the general public. Support received from governmental units and other donative publicly supported organizations, in the form of grants, are forms of *indirect* contributions from the general public (in that these grantors are considered conduits of direct public support).

This 2 percent threshold does not generally apply to support received by a donative publicly supported charity from other donative publicly supported charities nor to support from governmental units. That is, this type of support is, in its entirety, public support.[147] This is also the case concerning grants from a public institution, the support of which satisfies the rules for donative publicly supported charities.[148]

In constructing the support fraction, an organization must exclude from the numerator and denominator of it amounts that constitute *exempt function revenue*, which are amounts received from the exercise or performance of its exempt purpose or function and contributions of services for which a deduction is not allowable.[149] The organization is not treated as meeting the support test, however, if it receives almost all of its support in the form of exempt function revenue and an insignificant amount of its support from governmental units and the general public.[150] The organization also may exclude from the support fraction an amount equal to one or more qualifying *unusual grants*.[151]

The determination of whether a payment is a contribution rather than exempt function revenue, or whether a payment is a grant rather than an amount paid pursuant to a contract (the latter being a form of exempt function revenue)

---

[145] Priv. Ltr. Rul. 9608039.
[146] Reg. § 1.170A-9(e)(6)(i).
[147] *Id.*
[148] E.g., Rev. Rul. 78-95, 1978-1 C.B. 71 (grants by a church).
[149] Reg. § 1.170A-9(e)(7)(i).
[150] Reg. § 1.170A-9(e)(7)(ii).
[151] Reg. §§ 1.170A-9(e)(6)(ii), 1.170A-9(e)(6)(iii). E.g., Rev. Rul. 76-440, 1976-2 C.B. 58.

can be controversial. As to the former, a membership fee is not a contribution.[152] As to the latter, an amount paid by a governmental unit to an organization is not regarded as received from the exercise or performance of its exempt functions, and thus is a grant, if the purpose of the payment is primarily to enable the organization to provide a service to the direct benefit of the public rather than to serve the direct and immediate needs of the payor.[153]

Calculation of the support fraction entails an assessment of the organization's support that is *normally* received. This means that the organization must meet the one-third support test for a period encompassing the four years immediately preceding the year involved, on an aggregate basis. Where this is done, the organization is considered as meeting the one-third support test for its current year and the year immediately succeeding it.[154] (A five-year computational period for meeting the support test is used for organizations in the initial years of their existence.[155])

(ii) Facts-and-Circumstances Test.   There are some charitable organizations that are not private foundations in the generic sense, yet are not publicly supported under the general rules. Organizations in this position include entities such as museums and libraries that rely principally on endowments for their financial support. The *facts-and-circumstances test* offers a way for an organization of this type to qualify as a donative publicly supported charity, even though it does not receive at least one third of its support from the public.

An organization may qualify as a publicly supported donative organization—where it cannot satisfy the one-third public support requirement—as long as the amount normally received from governmental and/or public sources is *substantial*.[156] To meet this test, the organization must demonstrate the existence of three elements: (1) The total amount of governmental and public support normally received by the organization is at least 10 percent of its total support normally received; (2) the organization has a continuous and bona fide program for solicitation of funds from the general public, governmental units, or public charities; and (3) all other pertinent facts and circumstances, including

---

[152] Reg. § 1.170A-9(e)(7)(iii). E.g., Williams Home, Inc. v. United States, 540 F. Supp. 310 (W.D. Va. 1982) (monies paid to a home for the aged by incoming residents as a condition of admission are not contributions but are a form of exempt function revenue).

[153] Reg. § 1.170A-9(e)(8)(ii). E.g., payments by the federal government to a professional standards review organization were held to not be excludable gross receipts but instead includable public support because the payments compensated the organization for a function that promoted the health of the beneficiaries of government health care programs in the areas in which the organization operated (Rev. Rul. 81-276, 1981-2 C.B. 128). By contrast, Medicare and Medicaid payments to tax-exempt health care organizations constitute gross receipts derived from the performance of exempt functions and thus are not forms of public support, inasmuch as the patients control the ultimate recipients of the payments by their choice of a health care provider, so that they, not the governmental units, are the payors (Rev. Rul. 83-153, 1983-2 C.B. 48).

[154] Reg. § 1.170A-9(e)(4)(i).

[155] See § 23.4.

[156] Reg. § 1.170A-9(e)(3). An illustration of an organization that failed both the general rules and the facts and circumstances test appears in Collins v. Comm'r, 61 T.C. 693 (1974).

the percentage of its support from governmental and public sources, the public nature of the organization's governing board, the extent to which its facilities or programs are publicly available, its membership dues rates, and whether its activities are likely to appeal to persons having some broad common interest or purpose.[157]

Concerning the governing board factor, the organization's nonprivate foundation status will be enhanced where it has a governing body that represents the interests of the public, rather than the personal or private interests of a limited number of donors. This can be accomplished by the election of board members by a broadly based membership or otherwise by having the board composed of public officials, persons having particular expertise in the field or discipline involved, community leaders, and the like.

(iii) Community Foundations. A community trust (or community foundation) may qualify as a donative publicly supported charity if it attracts, receives, and depends on financial support from members of the general public on a regular, recurring basis. Community foundations are designed primarily to attract large contributions of a capital or endowment nature from a small number of donors, with the gifts often received and maintained in the form of separate trusts or funds. They are generally identified with a particular community or area and are controlled by a representative group of persons from that community or area. Individual donors relinquish control over the investment and distribution of their contributions and the income generated from them, although donors may designate the purposes for which the assets are to be used, subject to change by the governing body of the community trust.[158]

A community foundation, to qualify as a publicly supported organization, must meet the support requirements for a donative publicly supported charity[159] or meet the facts-and-circumstances test for donative charities.[160] As to the latter, the requirement of attraction of public support will generally be satisfied if a community foundation seeks gifts and bequests from a wide range of potential donors in the community or area served, through banks or trust companies, through lawyers or other professional individuals, or in other appropriate ways that call attention to the community foundation as a potential recipient of gifts and bequests made for the benefit of the community or area served. A community foundation is not required to engage in periodic, community-wide, fundraising campaigns directed toward attracting a large number of small contributions in a manner similar to campaigns conducted by a community chest or united fund.

---

[157] Reg. § 1.170A-9(e)(3). In a case concerning the public charity status of a home for the elderly, a court held that the practice of the home to encourage lawyers to mention to their clients the possibility of bequests to the home was inadequate compliance with the requirement of an ongoing development program (Trustees for the Home for Aged Women v. United States, 86-1 U.S.T.C. ¶ 9290 (D. Mass. 1986)).

[158] Reg. § 1.170A-9(e)(10).

[159] See *supra* § 3(b)(i).

[160] See *supra* § 3(b)(ii).

A community foundation wants to be treated as a single entity, rather than as an aggregation of funds. To be regarded as a component part of a community foundation, a trust or fund must be created by gift or like transfer to a community foundation that is treated as a separate entity and may not be subjected by the transferor to any material restriction[161] with respect to the transferred assets.[162] To be treated as a separate entity, a community foundation must be appropriately named, be so structured as to subject its funds to a common governing instrument, have a common governing body, and prepare periodic financial reports that treat all funds held by the community foundation as its funds.[163] The governing body of a community foundation must have the power to modify any restriction on the distribution of funds where it is inconsistent with the charitable needs of the community, must commit itself to the exercise of its powers in the best interests of the community foundation, and must commit itself to seeing that the funds are invested pursuant to accepted standards of fiduciary conduct.[164]

Grantors, contributors, and distributors to community trusts may rely on the publicly supported charity status of these trusts under circumstances that are the same as those applicable to reliance in the case of other categories of public charities[165] or of private operating foundations.[166]

(iv) Service Provider Publicly Supported Organizations. An organization qualifies as a *service provider* type of publicly supported charity[167] if it satisfies two tests.[168] One test requires that the charity normally receive more than one third of its support from any combination of (1) contributions, grants, or membership fees, and (2) gross receipts from admissions, sales of merchandise, performance of services, or furnishing of facilities in activities related to exempt purposes, as long as the support is from *permitted sources*.[169] (As discussed below, there is an additional limitation on the qualification of exempt function revenue as public support.) Thus, an organization seeking to qualify under this set of rules must construct a *support fraction* (using the cash basis method of accounting), with the amount of qualified support received from these two sources constituting the numerator of the fraction and the total amount of support received being the denominator.[170]

Permitted sources are public institutions, donative publicly supported organizations, and persons other than disqualified persons with respect to the

---

[161] See Reg. §§ 1.507-2(a)(7), (8).

[162] Reg. § 1.170A-9(e)(11)(ii).

[163] Reg. §§ 1.170A-9(e)(11)(iii)–(vi).

[164] Reg. § 1.170A-9(e)(11)(v).

[165] Reg. § 1.509(a)-7.

[166] See *supra* § 1(b). The reliance rule for community trusts appears at Reg. § 1.508 1(b)(4)(i).

[167] This term was adopted by the U.S. Supreme Court in Camps Newfound/Owatonna, Inc. v. Town of Harrison, et al., 520 U.S. 564, 572 (1997).

[168] IRC § 509(a)(2).

[169] IRC § 509(a)(2)(A). Revenue derived from the sale of pickle cards (a form of gambling) is not public support (Education Athletic Ass'n. v. Comm'r, 77 T.C.M. 1525 (1999)).

[170] Reg. § 1.509(a)-3(a)(2).

organization.[171] The term *support* means the two types of public support, along with net income from unrelated business activities,[172] gross investment income,[173] tax revenues levied for the benefit of the organization and either paid to or expended on behalf of it, and the value of services or facilities (exclusive of services or facilities generally furnished to the public without charge) furnished by a governmental unit to the organization without charge.[174] All of these items are amounts that, if received by the organization, comprise the denominator of the support fraction.

Support does not include any gain from the disposition of property that would be considered gain from the sale or exchange of a capital asset, or the value of exemption from any federal, state, or local tax or any similar benefit.[175] A loan is not a form of support; however, should the lender forgive the debt, the amount becomes support in the year of the forgiveness.[176]

The second test requires that an organization, to qualify as a service provider publicly supported charity, normally receive not more than one-third of its support from the sum of gross investment income[177] and any excess of the amount of unrelated business taxable income over the amount of the tax imposed on that income.[178] This entails the construction of a *gross investment income fraction*, with the amount of gross investment income and any unrelated income (less the tax paid on it) received constituting the numerator of the fraction and the total amount of support received being the denominator.[179]

These support and investment income tests are computed on the basis of the organization's *normal* sources of support. Generally, an organization is considered as *normally* receiving one-third of its support from permitted sources and not more than one-third of its support from gross investment income for its current year and immediately succeeding year if, for the four years immediately preceding its current year, the aggregate amount of support received over the four-year period from permitted sources is more than one-third of its total support and the aggregate amount of support over the four-year period from gross investment income is not more than one-third of its total support.[180] Substantial contributions and bequests that are unusual or unexpected in terms of the amount—termed *unusual grants*—may be excluded from these calculations.[181]

In computing the amount of support received from gross receipts that is allowable toward the one-third support requirement, gross receipts from related

---

[171] IRC § 509(a)(2)(A).
[172] See Part Five.
[173] IRC § 509(e).
[174] IRC § 509(d).
[175] *Id.*
[176] Priv. Ltr. Rul. 9608039.
[177] IRC § 509(e).
[178] IRC § 509(a)(2)(B).
[179] Reg. § 1.509(a)-3(a)(3).
[180] Reg. § 1.509(a)-3(c)(1)(i).
[181] Reg. § 1.509(a)-3(c)(3). E.g., Rev. Rul. 76-440, *supra* note 151. The IRS has promulgated "safe haven" criteria that automatically cause a contribution or a grant to be considered *unusual* (Rev. Proc. 81-7, 1981-1 C.B. 621).

activities (other than from membership fees) received from any person or from any bureau or similar agency of a governmental unit are includable in a year to the extent that the receipts do not exceed the greater of $5,000 or one percent of the organization's support for the year.[182]

(v) *Foundations Supporting Public Colleges and Universities.* Public charity status is provided for certain organizations providing support for public colleges and universities.[183] The organization must normally receive a substantial part of its support (exclusive of income received in the exercise or performance of its tax-exempt activities) from the United States or from direct or indirect contributions from the general public. It must be organized and operated exclusively to receive, hold, invest, and administer property and to make expenditures to or for the benefit of a college or university (including a land grant college or university) that is a public charity and that is an agency or instrumentality of a state or political subdivision thereof, or that is owned or operated by a state or political subdivision thereof or by an agency or instrumentality of one or more states or political subdivisions.

These expenditures include those made for any one or more of the regular functions of colleges and universities, such as the acquisition and maintenance of real property representing part of the campus area; the construction of college or university buildings; the acquisition and maintenance of equipment and furnishings used for, or in conjunction with, regular functions of colleges and universities; or expenditures for scholarships, libraries, and student loans.[184]

Another frequently important feature of the state college or university related foundation is its ability to borrow money for or on behalf of the supported institution, with the indebtedness bearing tax-excludable interest.[185]

(c) Supporting Organizations

A category of organization that is a public charity is the *supporting organization.*[186] This type of entity must be sufficiently related to one or more qualified organizations, which include public institutions and publicly supported organizations.[187]

A supporting organization must be organized and operated exclusively for the benefit of, to perform the functions of, or to carry out the purposes of one or more specified qualified supported organizations.[188] A supporting organization must be operated, supervised, or controlled by or in connection with one or more

---

[182] IRC § 509(a)(2)(A)(ii); Reg. § 1.509(a)-3(b)(1). E.g., Rev. Rul. 83-153, 1983-2 C.B. 48; Rev. Rul. 75-387, 1975-2 C.B. 216.
[183] IRC § 170(b)(1)(A)(iv).
[184] Reg. § 1.170A-9(b)(2).
[185] IRC § 103.
[186] IRC § 509(a)(3).
[187] Reg. § 1.509(a)-4(a)(5).
[188] IRC § 509(a)(3)(A); Reg. § 1.509(a)-4(a)(2).

supported organizations.[189] A supporting organization may not be controlled directly or indirectly by one or more disqualified persons (other than foundation managers).[190]

A supporting organization must engage solely in activities that support or benefit one or more supported organizations.[191] These activities may include making payments to or for the use of, or providing services or facilities for, individual members of the charitable class benefited by one or more supported public charities. A supporting organization may, but need not, pay over its income to a supported organization. It may carry on an independent program that supports or benefits one or more supported organizations.[192]

The relationship between a supporting organization and a supported organization must be one of three types: *operated, supervised or controlled by, supervised or controlled in connection with,* or *operated in connection with*.[193] The first of these types of relationships requires a relationship comparable to that of a parent and a subsidiary.[194] The third of these relationships entails a programmatic interlock, where the supporting organization is responsive to and significantly involved in the operations of the supported organization.[195]

As noted, a supporting organization must be organized and operated to support or benefit one or more *specified* supported organizations. This specification must be in the articles of organization of the supporting organization, with the manner of the specification dependent on which of the three types of relationships is involved.[196]

A supporting organization may operate to support and benefit a social welfare organization,[197] a labor or agricultural organization,[198] or a business league.[199] The principal requirement in this regard is that the beneficiary organization meet the one-third public support test of the rules concerning the service provider publicly supported charitable organization.[200]

(d) Public Safety Testing Organizations

Another category of organization that is deemed to not be a private foundation is an organization that is organized and operated exclusively for testing for public safety.[201] These entities are described in the analysis of charitable organizations.

[189] IRC § 509(a)(3)(B).
[190] IRC § 509(a)(3)(C); Reg. § 1.509(a)-4(a)(4).
[191] Reg. §§ 1.509(a)-4(e)(1), (2).
[192] Reg. § 1.509(a)-4(e)(2).
[193] Reg. §§ 1.509(a)-4(a)(3), 1.509(a)-4(f)(2).
[194] Reg. §§ 1.509(a)-4(f)(4), 1.509(a)-4(g)(1)(i).
[195] Reg. § 1.509(a)-4(f)(4).
[196] Reg. § 1.509(a)-4(c)(1).
[197] See Chapter 12.
[198] See Chapter 15.
[199] See Chapter 13.
[200] IRC § 509(a), last sentence of Reg. § 1.509(a)-4(k).
[201] IRC § 509(a)(4). See § 10.3.

§ 11.4   PRIVATE FOUNDATION RULES

The federal tax law governing the operations of private foundations is a composite of rules pertaining to self-dealing, mandatory payout requirements, business holdings, investment practices, various types of expenditures, and more. The sanctions for violation of these rules are five sets of excise taxes, with each set entailing three tiers of taxation. The three tiers are known as the *initial tax*,[202] the *additional tax*,[203] and the *involuntary termination tax*.[204] In general, when there is a violation, the initial tax must be paid; the additional tax is levied only when the initial tax is not timely paid and the matter not timely corrected; the termination tax is levied when the other two taxes have been imposed and there continues to be willful, flagrant, or repeated acts or failures to act, giving rise to one or more of the initial or additional taxes.

The IRS generally has the authority to abate these initial taxes, where the taxable event was due to reasonable cause and not to willful neglect, and the event was timely corrected.[205] This abatement authority, however, does not extend to initial taxes imposed in the context of self-dealing.[206] Where a taxable event is timely corrected, any additional taxes that may have been assessed or paid are abated.[207]

Because of the stringency of these rules, the sanctions are far more than merely taxes, being rather a system of absolute prohibitions.

(a) Self-Dealing

In general, the federal tax law prohibits acts of self-dealing between a private foundation and a disqualified person.[208] An act of self-dealing may be direct or indirect. The latter generally is a self-dealing transaction between a disqualified person and an organization controlled by a private foundation.[209]

The sale or exchange of property between a private foundation and a disqualified person generally constitutes an act of self-dealing.[210] The transfer of real or personal property by a disqualified person to a private foundation is treated as a sale or exchange if the property is subject to a mortgage or similar lien that the foundation assumes or if it is subject to a mortgage or similar lien that a disqualified person placed on the property within the 10-year period ending on the date of transfer.[211]

The leasing of property between a private foundation and a disqualified

---

[202] IRC §§ 4941(a), 4942(a), 4943(a), 4944(a), 4945(a).
[203] IRC §§ 4941(b), 4942(b), 4943(b), 4944(b), 4945(b).
[204] IRC § 507(a)(2).
[205] IRC § 4962(a).
[206] IRC § 4962(b).
[207] IRC § 4961.
[208] IRC § 4941.
[209] Reg. § 53.4941(d)-1(b).
[210] IRC § 4941(d)(1)(A); Reg. § 53.4941(d)-2(a)(1). E.g., Rev. Rul. 76-18, 1976-1 C.B. 355.
[211] IRC § 4941(d)(2)(A); Reg. § 53.4941(d)-2(a)(2).

person generally constitutes self-dealing.[212] The leasing of property by a disqualified person to a private foundation without charge is not, however, an act of self-dealing.[213]

The lending of money or other extension of credit between a private foundation and a disqualified person generally constitutes an act of self-dealing.[214] This rule does not apply to an extension of credit by a disqualified person to a private foundation if the transaction is without interest or other charge and the proceeds of the loan are used exclusively for charitable purposes.[215]

The furnishing of goods, services, or facilities between a private foundation and a disqualified person generally constitutes an act of self-dealing.[216] The furnishing of goods, services, or facilities by a disqualified person to a private foundation is not an act of self-dealing, however, if they are furnished without charge and used exclusively for charitable purposes.[217] The furnishing of goods, services, or facilities by a private foundation to a disqualified person is not self-dealing if the furnishing is made on a basis no more favorable than that on which the goods, services, or facilities are made available to the general public.[218]

The payment of compensation (or payment or reimbursement of expenses) by a private foundation to a disqualified person generally constitutes an act of self-dealing.[219] Except in the case of a governmental official, however, the payment of compensation (or payment or reimbursement of expenses) by a private foundation to a disqualified person for the performance of personal services that are reasonable and necessary to carrying out the charitable purpose of the foundation is not self-dealing if the compensation (or payment or reimbursement) is not excessive.[220]

The transfer to, or use by or for the benefit of, a disqualified person of the income or assets of a private foundation generally constitutes self-dealing.[221] Unlike the other sets of rules describing specific categories of acts of self-dealing, this one is a catch-all provision designed to sweep into the ambit of self-dealing a variety of transactions that might otherwise technically escape the discrete transactions defined to be self-dealing ones. The fact that a disqualified person receives an incidental or tenuous benefit from the use by a private foundation of its income or assets will not, by itself, make the use an act of self-dealing.[222]

---

[212] IRC § 4941(d)(1)(A); Reg. § 53.4941(d)-2(b)(1).
[213] Reg. § 53.4941(d)-2(b)(2).
[214] IRC § 4941(d)(1)(B): Reg. § 53.4941(d)-2(c)(1).
[215] IRC § 4941(d)(2)(B); Reg. § 53.4941(d)-2(c)(2).
[216] IRC § 4941(d)(1)(C); Reg. § 53.4941(d)-2(d)(1).
[217] IRC § 4941(d)(2)(C); Reg. § 53.4941(d)-2(d)(3).
[218] IRC § 4941(d)(2)(D); Reg. § 53.4941(d)-3(b).
[219] IRC § 4941(d)(1)(D); Reg. § 53.4941(d)-2(e).
[220] IRC § 4941(d)(2)(E); Reg. § 53.4941(d)-3(c).
[221] IRC § 4941(d)(1)(E); Reg. § 53.4941(d)-2(f)(1). There are special rules concerning indemnification and the purchase of insurance by private foundations for the benefit of foundation managers (Reg. § 53.4941(d)-2(f)(3)–(8)).
[222] Reg. § 53.4941(d)-2(f)(2).

An agreement by a private foundation to make a payment of money or other property to a government official generally constitutes self-dealing, unless the agreement is to employ the individual for a period after termination of his or her government service if he or she is terminating service within a 90-day period.[223] In the case of a government official, the self-dealing rules do not apply to the receipt of certain prizes and awards, scholarship and fellowship grants, annuities, gifts, and traveling expenses.[224]

There are several other exceptions to the self-dealing rules, one of which holds that a transaction between a private foundation and a corporation that is a disqualified person with respect to the foundation is not an act of self-dealing if the transaction is engaged in pursuant to a liquidation, merger, redemption, recapitalization, or other corporate adjustment, organization, or reorganization.[225] For this exception to apply, all the securities of the same class as that held by the foundation prior to the transfer must be subject to the same terms and these terms must provide for receipt by the foundation of no less than fair market value.[226]

An act of self-dealing *occurs* on the date on which all of the terms and conditions of the transaction and the liabilities of the parties have been fixed.[227] The *amount involved* generally is the greater of the amount of money and the fair market value of the other property given or the amount of money and the fair market value of the other property received.[228] *Correction* of an act of self-dealing means undoing the transaction that constituted the act to the extent possible, but in no case may the resulting financial position of the private foundation be worse than would be the case if the disqualified person was dealing under the highest fiduciary standards.[229]

An initial tax is imposed on each act of self-dealing between a disqualified person and a private foundation; the tax is imposed on the self-dealer at a rate of 5 percent of the amount involved with respect to the act for each year in the taxable period or part of a period.[230] Where this initial tax is imposed, a tax of $2\frac{1}{2}$ percent of the amount involved is imposed on the participation of any foundation manager in the act of self-dealing, where the manager knowingly participated in the act.[231] This tax is not imposed, however, where the participation is

---

[223] IRC § 4941(d)(1)(F); Reg. § 53.4941(d)-2(g).
[224] IRC § 4941(d)(2)(G); Reg. § 53.4941(d)-3(e).
[225] IRC § 4941(d)(2)(F); Reg. § 53.4941(d)-3(d).
[226] Reg. § 53.4941(d)-3(d)(1).
[227] Reg. § 53.4941(e)-1(a)(2).
[228] IRC § 4941(e)(2); Reg. § 53.4941(e)-1(b)(1).
[229] IRC § 4941(e)(3); Reg. § 53.4941(e)-1(c).
[230] IRC § 4941(a)(1); Reg. § 53.4941(a)-1(a)(1). The *taxable period* is the period beginning with the date on which the transaction occurred and ending on the earliest of the date of mailing of a notice of deficiency with respect to the initial tax, the date on which the initial tax is assessed, or the date on which correction of the transaction is completed (IRC § 4941(e)(1); Reg. § 53.4941(e)-1(a)). The calculation of the initial self-dealing tax in the case of a multi-year loan to a disqualified person is illustrated in Rev. Rul. 2002-43, 2002-28 I.R.B. 85.
[231] IRC § 4941(a)(2); Reg. § 53.4941(a)-1(b).

not willful and is due to reasonable cause.[232] This tax, which must be paid by the foundation manager, may not exceed $10,000.[233]

Where an initial tax is imposed and the self-dealing act is not timely corrected, an additional tax is imposed in an amount equal to 200 percent of the amount involved; this tax must be paid by the disqualified person (other than a foundation manager) who participated in the act of self-dealing.[234] An additional tax equal to 50 percent of the amount involved, up to $10,000,[235] is imposed on a foundation manager (where the additional tax is imposed on the self-dealer) who refuses to agree to all or part of the correction.[236]

In a case where more than one person is liable for any initial or additional tax with respect to any one act of self-dealing, all of the persons are jointly and severally liable for the tax or taxes.[237]

Willful repeated violations of these rules will result in involuntary termination of the private foundation's status and the imposition of additional taxes.[238] The termination tax thus serves as a third-tier tax.

(b) Mandatory Distributions

A private foundation is required to distribute, for each year, at least a minimum amount of money and/or property for charitable purposes.[239] The amount that must annually be distributed by a private foundation is the *distributable amount*.[240] That amount must be in the form of *qualifying distributions*, which essentially are grants, outlays for administration, and payments made to acquire charitable assets.[241] Generally, the distributable amount for a private foundation is an amount equal to 5 percent of the value of the noncharitable assets of the foundation;[242] this is the *minimum investment return*.[243] The distributable amount also includes amounts equal to repayments to a foundation of items previously treated as qualifying distributions (such as scholarship loans), amounts received on disposition of assets previously treated as qualifying distributions, and amounts previously set aside for a charitable project but not so used.[244]

---

[232] *Id.*
[233] IRC § 4941(c)(2); Reg. § 53.4941(c)-1(b).
[234] IRC § 4941(b)(1); Reg. § 53.4941(b)-1(a).
[235] IRC § 4941(c)(2); Reg. § 53.4941(c)-1(b).
[236] IRC § 4941(b)(2); Reg. § 53.4941(b)-1(b).
[237] IRC § 4941(c)(1); Reg. § 53.4941(c)-1(a).
[238] IRC § 507(a)(2).
[239] IRC § 4942.
[240] IRC § 4942(d).
[241] IRC § 4942(g)(1); Reg. § 53.4942(a)-3(a), (c).
[242] Reg. §§ 53.4942(a)-2(c)(1), 53.4942(a)-2(c)(5). A private foundation is required to ascertain the aggregate fair market value of its assets, although those used or held for use for charitable purposes are not considered when determining its minimum investment return (IRC § 4942(e)(1)(A)).
[243] IRC §§ 4942(d)(1), 4942(e)(1)(A); Reg. § 53.4942(a)-2(b)(1). The minimum investment return is reduced by any acquisition indebtedness (see § 29.3) with respect to the assets (IRC § 4942(e)(1)(B)).
[244] IRC §§ 4942(d)(1), 4942(f)(2)(C).

The charitable assets of a private foundation are those actually used by the foundation in carrying out its charitable objectives or assets owned by the foundation where it has convinced the IRS that its immediate use for exempt purposes is not practical and that definite plans exist to commence a related use within a reasonable period.[245] Thus, the assets that are in the minimum investment return base are those held for the production of income or for investment (such as stocks, bonds, interest-bearing notes, endowment funds, and leased real estate).[246] Where property is used for both exempt and other purposes, it is considered to be used exclusively for tax-exempt purposes where the exempt use represents at least 95 percent of the total use; otherwise, a reasonable allocation between the two uses is required.[247]

An exception to the timing of distributions by a private foundation for mandatory payout purposes is the *set-aside*, where funds are credited for a charitable purpose, rather than immediately granted; where the requirements are met, the set aside is regarded as a qualifying distribution.[248] One type of set aside is that referenced in the *suitability test*; this requires a specific project, a payment period not to exceed 60 months, and a ruling from the IRS.[249] The other type of set aside is that of the *cash distribution test*; this test entails set percentages of distributions over a multi-year period and does not require an IRS ruling.[250]

An initial tax of 15 percent is imposed on the undistributed income of a private foundation for any year that has not been distributed on a timely basis in the form of qualifying distributions.[251] In a case in which an initial tax is imposed on the undistributed income of a private foundation for a year, an additional tax is imposed on any portion of the income remaining undistributed at the close of the taxable period.[252] This tax is equal to 100 percent of the amount remaining undistributed at the close of the period.[253]

Payment of these taxes is required in addition to, rather than in lieu of, making the required distributions.[254]

The termination taxes[255] serve as third-tier taxes.

---

[245] Reg. § 53.4942(a)-2(c)(3). These assets include interests in a functionally related business (see the text accompanied by *infra* notes 262–263) and in a program-related investment (see the text accompanied by *infra* notes 277–278).

[246] IRC § 4942(e)(1)(A).

[247] Reg. § 53.4942(a)-2(c)(3).

[248] Reg. § 53.4942(a)-3(b)(1).

[249] Reg. § 53.4942(a)-3(b)(2), (7)(i).

[250] IRC § 4942(g)(2); Reg. § 53.4942(a)-3(b)(3)–(7)(ii).

[251] IRC § 4942(a); Reg. § 53.4942(a)-1(a)(1).

[252] IRC § 4942(b); Reg. § 53.4942(a)-1(a)(2). The *taxable period* is the period beginning with the first day of the year involved and ending on the date of mailing of a notice of deficiency with respect to the initial tax or the date on which the initial tax is assessed (IRC § 4942(j)(1); Reg. § 53.4942(a)-1(c)(1)).

[253] IRC § 4942(b); Reg. § 53.4942(a)-1(a)(2).

[254] Reg. § 53.4942(a)-1(a)(3).

[255] IRC § 507(a)(2).

(c) Excess Business Holdings

Private foundations are limited as to the extent to which they can own interests in commercial business enterprises.[256] A private foundation and all disqualified persons with respect to it generally are permitted to hold no more than 20 percent of a corporation's voting stock or other interest in a business enterprise; these are *permitted holdings*.[257] If effective control of the business can be shown to be elsewhere, a 35-percent limit may be substituted for the 20 percent limit.[258] A private foundation must hold, directly or indirectly, more than 2 percent of the value of a business enterprise before these limitations become applicable.[259]

There are three principal exceptions to these rules. One is for a business at least 95 percent of the gross income of which is derived from passive sources.[260] These sources generally include dividends, interest, annuities, royalties, and capital gain.[261] The second exception is for holdings in a *functionally related business*.[262] This is a business that is substantially related to the achievement of the foundation's exempt purposes (other than merely providing funds for the foundation's programs); in which substantially all the work is performed for the private foundation without compensation; that is carried on by a private foundation primarily for the convenience of its employees; that consists of the selling of merchandise, substantially all of which was received by the foundation as contributions; or that is carried on within a larger aggregate of similar activities or within a larger complex of other endeavors that is related to the exempt purposes of the foundation.[263] The third exception is for program-related investments.[264]

If a private foundation obtains holdings in a business enterprise, in a transaction that is not a purchase by the foundation or by disqualified persons with respect to it, and the additional holdings would result in the foundation having an excess business holding, the foundation has five years to reduce the holdings to a permissible level without penalty.[265] The IRS has the authority to allow an additional five-year period for the disposition of excess business holdings in the case of an unusually large gift or bequest of diverse business holdings or holdings with complex corporate structures.[266] This latter rule entails several requirements, including a showing that diligent efforts were made to dispose of the holdings within the initial five-year period and that disposition

---

[256] IRC § 4943.
[257] IRC §§ 4943(c)(2)(A), 4943(c)(3); Reg. §§ 53.4943-1, 53.4943-3(b)(1), 53.4943-3(b)(2), 53.4943-3(b)(3)(c).
[258] IRC § 4943(c)(2)(B); Reg. § 53.4943-3(b)(3).
[259] IRC § 4943(c)(2)(C); Reg. § 53.4943-3(b)(4).
[260] IRC § 4943(d)(3)(B).
[261] Reg. § 53.4943-10(c).
[262] IRC § 4943(d)(3)(A).
[263] IRC § 4942(j)(4), Reg. § 53.4943-10 (b).
[264] Reg. § 53.4943-10(b) (see the text accompanied by *infra* notes 277–278).
[265] IRC § 4943(c)(6); Reg. § 53.4943-6(a).
[266] IRC § 4943(c)(7).

within that five-year period was not possible (except at a price substantially below fair market value) by reason of the size and complexity or diversity of the
holdings.

An initial excise tax is imposed on the excess business holdings of a private foundation in a business enterprise for each tax year that ends during
the taxable period.[267] The amount of this tax is 5 percent of the total value of all
of the private foundation's excess business holdings in each of its business
enterprises.[268]

If the excess business holdings are not disposed of during the period, an additional tax is imposed on the private foundation; the amount of this tax is 200
percent of the value of the excess business holdings.[269]

The termination taxes[270] serve as third-tier taxes.

(d) Jeopardizing Investments

There are rules governing the type of investments that a private foundation is
allowed to make.[271] In general, a private foundation cannot invest any
amount—income or principal—in a manner that would jeopardize the carrying
out of any of its tax-exempt purposes.[272] An investment is considered to jeopardize the carrying out of the exempt purposes of a private foundation if it is determined that the foundation managers, in making the investment, failed to
exercise ordinary business care and prudence, under the facts and circumstances prevailing at the time of the investment, in providing for the long-term
and short-term financial needs of the foundation in carrying out its charitable
activities.[273]

A determination as to whether the making of a particular investment jeopardizes the exempt purposes of a private foundation is made on an investment-
by-investment basis, in each case taking into account the private foundation's
portfolio as a whole.[274] Although the IRS will not rule as to an investment procedure governing investments to be made in the future, it will rule as to a currently
proposed investment.[275]

No category of investments is treated as a per se violation of these rules. The
types or methods of investment that are closely scrutinized to determine whether
the foundation managers have met the requisite standard of care and prudence

---

[267] IRC § 4943(a)(1); Reg. § 53.4943-2(a)(1). The *taxable period* is the period beginning on the first day
on which there are excess business holdings and ending on the earlier of the date of mailing of a notice of deficiency with respect to the initial tax or the date on which the initial tax is assessed (IRC §
4943(d)(2); Reg. § 53.4943-9(a)(1)).
[268] IRC § 4943(a)(1); Reg. § 53.4943-2(a)(1).
[269] IRC § 4943 (b); Reg. § 53.4943-2(b).
[270] IRC § 507(a)(2).
[271] IRC § 4944.
[272] IRC § 4944(a)(1).
[273] Reg. § 53.4944-1(a)(2)(i).
[274] *Id.*
[275] E.g., Priv. Ltr. Rul. 9451067.

include trading in securities on margin, trading in commodity futures, investments in oil and gas syndications, the purchase of puts and calls (and straddles), the purchase of warrants, and selling short.[276]

A *program-related investment* is not a jeopardizing investment. This is an investment the primary purpose of which is to accomplish one or more charitable purposes and no significant purpose of which is the production of income or the appreciation of property.[277] No purpose of the investment may be the furthering of substantial legislative or political campaign activities.[278]

If a private foundation invests an amount in a manner as to jeopardize the carrying out of any of its charitable purposes, an initial tax is imposed on the foundation on the making of the investment, at the rate of 5 percent of the amount so invested for each year or part of a year in the taxable period.[279]

In any case in which this initial tax is imposed, a tax is imposed on the participation of any foundation manager making an investment in the knowledge that it jeopardizes the carrying out of any of the foundation's exempt purposes; the tax is equal to 5 percent of the amount so invested for each year of the foundation (or part of the year) in the period.[280] With respect to any one investment, the maximum amount of this tax is $5,000.[281] This tax, which must be paid by any participating foundation manager, is not imposed where the participation was not willful and was due to reasonable cause.[282]

An additional tax is imposed in any case in which this initial tax is imposed and the investment is not removed from jeopardy within the period; this tax, which is to be paid by the private foundation, is at the rate of 25 percent of the amount of the investment.[283] In any case in which this additional tax is imposed and a foundation manager has refused to agree to all or part of the removal of the investment from jeopardy, a tax is imposed at the rate of 5 percent of the amount of the investment.[284] With respect to any one investment, the maximum amount of this tax is $10,000.[285]

Where more than one foundation manager is liable for an initial tax or an additional tax with respect to a jeopardizing investment, all of the managers are jointly and severally liable for the taxes.[286]

The termination taxes[287] serve as third-tier taxes.

---

[276] Reg. § 53.4944-1(a)(2)(i).

[277] IRC § 4944(c); Reg. § 53.4944-3(a).

[278] Reg. § 53.4944-3(a)(1)(iii).

[279] IRC § 4944(a)(1); Reg. § 53.4944-1(a)(1). The *taxable period* is the period beginning with the date of the jeopardizing investment and ending on the earliest of the date of mailing of a notice of deficiency with respect to the initial tax, the date on which the initial tax is assessed, or the date on which the amount invested is removed from jeopardy (as defined in IRC § 4944(e)(2); Reg. § 53.4944-5(b)) (IRC § 4944(e)(1); Reg. § 53.4944-5(a)).

[280] IRC § 4944(a)(2); Reg. § 53.4944-1(b)(1).

[281] IRC § 4944(d)(2); Reg. § 53.4944-4(b).

[282] IRC § 4944(a)(2); Reg. § 53.4944-1(b)(1).

[283] IRC § 4944(b)(1); Reg. § 53.4944-2(a).

[284] IRC § 4944(b)(2); Reg. § 53.4944-2(b).

[285] IRC § 4944(d)(2); Reg. § 53.4944-4(b).

[286] IRC § 4944(d)(1); Reg. § 53.4944-4(a).

[287] IRC § 507(a)(2).

(e) Taxable Expenditures

The federal tax law provides restrictions, in addition to those discussed above, on the activities and purposes for which private foundations may expend their funds.[288] These rules pertain to matters such as legislative activities, electioneering, grants to individuals, and grants to noncharitable organizations. Improper and, in effect, prohibited expenditures are termed *taxable expenditures*.

One form of taxable expenditure is an amount paid or incurred by a private foundation to carry on propaganda or otherwise attempt to influence legislation.[289] Thus, the general rule, by which charitable organizations can engage in a certain amount of legislative activity,[290] is inapplicable to private foundations.

Attempts to influence legislation generally include certain communications with a member or employee of a legislative body or with an official or employee of an executive department of a government who may participate in formulating legislation or efforts to affect the opinion of the general public or a segment of it.[291] An expenditure is an attempt to influence legislation if it is for a *direct lobbying communication* or a *grassroots lobbying communication*.[292]

Engaging in nonpartisan analysis, study, or research and making the results of this type of an undertaking available to the general public (or a segment of it) or to governmental bodies or officials is not a prohibited form of legislative activity.[293] Likewise, amounts paid or incurred in connection with the provision of technical advice or assistance to a governmental body or committee (or other subdivision of it) in response to a written request from the entity do not constitute taxable expenditures.[294] Another exception is that the taxable expenditures rules do not apply to any amount paid or incurred in connection with an appearance before or communication to a legislative body with respect to a possible decision of that body which might affect the existence of the private foundation, its powers and duties, its tax-exempt status, or the deductibility of contributions to the foundation.[295] Expenditures for examinations and discussions of broad social, economic, and similar issues are not taxable even if the problems are of the types with which government would be expected to deal ultimately.[296]

The term *taxable expenditure* includes an amount paid or incurred by a private foundation to influence the outcome of a specific public election or to conduct, directly or indirectly, a voter registration drive.[297] The first of these prohibitions generally parallels the prohibition on political campaign activities

---

[288] IRC § 4945.
[289] IRC § 4945(d)(1).
[290] See Chapter 20.
[291] IRC § 4945(e).
[292] Reg. § 53.4945-2(a)(1).
[293] IRC § 4945(e); Reg. § 53.4945-2(d)(1).
[294] IRC § 4945(e)(2); Reg. § 53.4945-2(d)(2).
[295] IRC § 4945(e) (last sentence); Reg. § 53.4945-2(d)(3).
[296] Reg. § 53.4945-2(d)(4).
[297] IRC § 4945(d)(2); Reg. § 53.4945-3(a)(1).

by all charitable organizations.[298] A private foundation may engage in election-eering activities (including voter registration drives), however, without making a taxable expenditure, where a variety of criteria are satisfied, such as not confining the activity to one election period and carrying it on in at least five states.[299]

The term *taxable expenditure* includes an amount paid or incurred by a private foundation as a grant to an individual for travel, study, or other similar purposes.[300] This type of grant is not prohibited, however, if it is awarded on an objective and nondiscriminatory basis pursuant to a procedure approved in advance by the IRS and the IRS is satisfied that the grant is one of three specified types: (1) a scholarship or fellowship grant that is excludable from the recipient's gross income and used for study at an educational institution; (2) a prize or award that is excludable from the recipient's gross income, where the recipient is selected from the general public; or (3) a grant the purpose of which is to achieve a specific objective, produce a report or similar product, or improve or enhance a literary, artistic, musical, scientific, teaching, or other similar capacity, skill, or talent of the grantee.[301]

The requirement as to objectivity and nondiscrimination generally requires that the group from which grantees are selected be chosen on the basis of criteria reasonably related to the purposes of the grant. The group must be sufficiently broad so that the making of grants to members of the group would be considered to fulfill a charitable purpose.[302] The individual or group of individuals who select grant recipients should not be in a position to derive a private benefit as the result of the selection process.[303]

These rules as to individual grants generally require (1) the receipt by a private foundation of an annual report from the beneficiary of a scholarship or fellowship;[304] (2) that a foundation investigate situations indicating that all or a part of a grant is not being used in furtherance of its purposes;[305] and (3) recovery or restoration of any diverted funds, and withholding of further payments to a grantee in an instance of improper diversion of grant funds.[306] A private foundation must maintain certain records pertaining to grants to individuals.[307]

A private foundation may make grants to an organization that is not a public charity;[308] however, when it does so it must exercise *expenditure responsibility*

---

[298] Reg. § 53.4945-3(a)(2). See Chapter 21.
[299] IRC § 4945(f); Reg. § 53.4945-3(b).
[300] IRC § 4945(d)(3); Reg. § 53.4945-4(a)(1), (2).
[301] IRC § 4945 (g); Reg. § 53.4945-4(a)(3)(ii).
[302] Reg. § 53.4945-4(b)(2).
[303] Reg. § 53.4945-4(b)(4).
[304] Reg. § 53.4945-4(c)(2), (3).
[305] Reg. § 53.4945-4(c)(4).
[306] Reg. § 53.4945-4(c)(5).
[307] Reg. § 53.4945-4(c)(6).
[308] See *supra* § 3.

with respect to the grant.[309] A private foundation is considered to be exercising expenditure responsibility in connection with a grant as long as it exerts all reasonable efforts and establishes adequate procedures to see that the grant is spent solely for the purpose for which it was made, obtain full and complete reports from the grantee on how the funds are spent, and make full and detailed reports with respect to the expenditures to the IRS.[310]

The term *taxable expenditure* includes an amount paid or incurred by a private foundation for a *noncharitable* purpose.[311] Ordinarily, only an expenditure for an activity that, if it were a substantial part of the organization's total activities, would cause loss of tax exemption is a taxable expenditure.[312]

Expenditures ordinarily not treated as taxable expenditures under these rules are (1) expenditures to acquire investments entered into for the purpose of obtaining income or funds to be used in furtherance of charitable purposes, (2) reasonable expenses with respect to investments, (3) payment of taxes, (4) any expenses that qualify as deductions in the computation of unrelated business income tax,[313] (5) any payment that constitutes a qualifying distribution[314] or an allowable deduction pursuant to the investment income tax rules,[315] (6) reasonable expenditures to evaluate, acquire, modify, and dispose of program-related investments,[316] or (7) business expenditures by the recipient of a program-related investment. Conversely, expenditures for unreasonable administrative expenses, including compensation, consultants' fees, and other fees for services rendered, are ordinarily taxable expenditures, unless the private foundation can demonstrate that the expenses were paid or incurred in the good faith belief that they were reasonable and that the payment or incurrence of the expenses in amounts was consistent with ordinary business care and prudence.[317]

An excise tax is imposed on each taxable expenditure of a private foundation, which is to be paid by the private foundation at the rate of 10 percent of the amount on each taxable expenditure.[318] An excise tax is imposed on the agreement of any foundation manager to the making of a taxable expenditure by a private foundation.[319] This latter initial tax is imposed only where the private foundation initial tax is imposed, the manager knows that the expenditure to which he or she agreed was a taxable one, and the agreement is not willful and not due to reasonable cause. This initial tax, which is at the rate of

---

[309] IRC § 4945(d)(4); Reg. § 53.4945-5(a). For this purpose, exempt operating foundations (see *supra* § 1(c)) are regarded the same as public charities.
[310] IRC § 4945(h); Reg. § 53.4945-5(b)–(d).
[311] IRC § 4945(d)(5).
[312] Reg. § 53.4945-6(a).
[313] See § 28.2.
[314] IRC § 4942(g). See *supra* § 4(b).
[315] IRC § 4940.
[316] See *supra* § 4(d).
[317] Reg. § 53.4945-6(b).
[318] IRC § 4945(a)(1); Reg. § 53.4945-1(a)(1).
[319] IRC § 4945(a)(2).

$2\frac{1}{2}$ percent of each taxable expenditure, must be paid by the foundation manager.[320]

An excise tax is imposed in any case in which an initial tax is imposed on a private foundation because of a taxable expenditure and the expenditure is not corrected within the taxable period; this additional tax is to be paid by the private foundation and is at the rate of 100 percent of the amount of each taxable expenditure.[321] An excise tax in any case in which an initial tax has been levied is imposed on a foundation manager because of a taxable expenditure and the foundation manager has refused to agree to part or all of the correction of the expenditure; this additional tax, which is at the rate of 50 percent of the amount of the taxable expenditure, is to be paid by the foundation manager.[322]

Where more than one foundation manager is liable for an excise tax with respect to the making of a taxable expenditure, all the foundation managers are jointly and severally liable for the tax.[323] The maximum aggregate amount collectible as an initial tax from all foundation managers with respect to any one taxable expenditure is $5,000 and the maximum aggregate amount so collectible as an additional tax is $10,000.[324]

The second-tier excise taxes will be imposed at the end of the *taxable period*, which begins with the event giving rise to the expenditure tax and ends on the earlier of (1) the date a notice of deficiency with respect to the first-tier tax is mailed or (2) the date the first-tier tax is assessed if no deficiency notice is mailed.[325]

The termination taxes[326] serve as third-tier taxes.

(f) Other Provisions

An excise tax of 2 percent is generally imposed on the net investment income of private foundations for each tax year.[327] This tax must be estimated and paid quarterly, generally following the estimated tax rules for corporations.[328] Under certain circumstances, this tax rate is reduced to one percent in a year where the foundation's payout for charitable purposes is increased by an equivalent amount.[329] Exempt operating foundations[330] are exempt from this tax on investment income.[331]

---

[320] Reg. § 53.4945-1(a)(2).
[321] IRC §§ 4945(b)(1), 4945(i); Reg. § 53.4945-1(b)(1). The *taxable period* begins with the event giving rise to the expenditure tax and ends on the earlier of the date a notice of deficiency with respect to the first-tier tax is mailed or the date the first-tier tax is assessed if there has not been a mailing of a deficiency notice (IRC § 4945(i)(2); Reg. § 53.4945-1(e)(1)).
[322] IRC § 4945(b)(2); Reg. § 53.4945-1(b)(2).
[323] IRC § 4545(c)(1); Reg. § 53.4945-1(c)(1).
[324] IRC § 4545(c)(2); Reg. § 53.4945-1(c)(2).
[325] IRC § 4945(i)(2); Reg. § 53.4945-1(e)(1).
[326] IRC § 507(a)(2).
[327] IRC § 4940(a), Reg. § 53.4940-1(a).
[328] IRC § 6655.
[329] IRC § 4940(e)(1).
[330] See *supra* § 1(c).
[331] IRC § 4940(d)(1).

As to certain of the private foundation rules, non-exempt charitable trusts[332] and split-interest trusts[333] are treated as private foundations.[334] A 4 percent tax is imposed on the gross investment income derived from sources within the United States by foreign organizations that constitute private foundations.[335]

§ 11.5   CONSEQUENCES OF PRIVATE FOUNDATION STATUS

Because there are no advantages, from the standpoint of the law, to a charitable organization in classification of it as a private foundation, these organizations almost always attempt (when they can) to become characterized as a public charity.[336] The disadvantages are several, and the importance of any of them largely depends upon the circumstances of the particular charitable organization.

The disadvantages to private foundation status include (1) the obligation of payment of a tax on net investment income;[337] (2) probable inability of the organization to be funded by private foundations, because of the requirement that such grants be the subject of expenditure responsibility;[338] (3) a lesser degree of deductibility of charitable contributions to the organization;[339] (4) the fact that the charitable deduction for a gift of appreciated property to a private foundation generally is confined to its basis rather than the full fair market value of the property;[340] (5) requirement of compliance with a broad range of onerous rules and limitations as to programs and investment policy;[341] and (6) more extensive record-keeping and annual reporting requirements.[342]

It may be asserted that the ability of a small number of individuals to preside over an aggregation of investment assets and "privately" determine how to apply the income from the assets for charitable purposes is an "advantage." The same opportunities can be available, however, for a charitable entity that is regarded by the federal tax law as a public charity.

§ 11.6   DONOR-ADVISED FUNDS

An alternative to the private foundation is an account within a charitable organization that is classified as a public charity, such as a community foundation,

---

[332] That is, entities described in IRC § 4947(a)(1).
[333] That is, entities described in IRC § 4947(a)(2), including charitable remainder trusts (IRC § 664) and pooled income funds (IRC § 642(c)(5)).
[334] IRC § 4947.
[335] IRC § 4948.
[336] The various ways in which public charity status can be achieved are described in *supra* § 3.
[337] IRC § 4940.
[338] *Supra* § 4(e).
[339] See § 2.5.
[340] *Id.*
[341] See *supra* § 4.
[342] See § 24.3.

a college, a university, a church, or a charitable gift fund.[343] These accounts are usually referred to as *funds*; the most common of them is known as the *donor-advised fund*.

(a) Basics of Donor-Advised Funds

This vehicle has been part of the federal tax law of charity for nearly a century, yet only recently has it become the subject of considerable scrutiny and criticism. Indeed, several federal tax issues are involved, all rested on the fundamental fact that the donor-advised fund is an alternative to a private foundation. Some choose to state the matter somewhat differently, regarding donor-advised funds as a means of sidestepping or avoiding the private foundation rules.

These accounts can be in the name of an individual, family, corporation, or cause, or used to facilitate anonymous gifts. They often bear the name of the contributor or the contributor's family or business. Because of its name, a donor-advised fund can appear to be a separate legal entity—seemingly a charitable organization with many of the attributes of a private foundation.

The donor-advised fund is to be contrasted with the *donor-directed fund*. In the case of a donor-directed fund, the donor or a designee of the donor retains the right to direct investment of the fund's assets and/or to direct grants from the fund for charitable purposes. By contrast, with the donor-advised fund, the donor has the ability (but not a legal right) to make recommendations (proffer advice) as to investment policy and/or the making of grants.

The donor-advised fund has, as noted, long been a staple of community foundations. In recent years, other types of charitable organizations and commercial investment companies have created donor-advised funds, recognized as public charities by the IRS. As long as the use of these funds was confined to community foundations, there was no controversy; the attention accorded these funds, including criticism, started when other public charities began utilizing them.

These funds can be viable alternatives to the formation of private foundations. The individual or individuals involved may wish to avoid the administrative responsibilities (including the annual reporting and other regulatory requirements) of operating a private foundation. Another factor may be that the amount of money or property involved is too small to warrant the establishment of a private foundation.

(b) Types of Donor-Advised Funds

The Internal Revenue Code and the income tax regulations offer only two significant methods for donors to charitable organizations to exercise any posttransfer control or direction over the use of money or property irrevocably transferred to charity for which the donor is entitled to a charitable deduction in the year of the transfer. One method is use of a special type of private foundation that is, in

---

[343] See *supra* § 3.

essence, a donor-directed fund. This entity is referred to as the *common fund foundation*.[344] The other method is utilization of the community foundation or community trust.[345] The community foundation regulations and another regulation[346] only allow donor designation at the time of the gift and donor advice (not donor direction) after the date of the gift.

There is little specific law on donor-advised funds and donor-directed funds, however. The closest reference in the Internal Revenue Code to the concept is the provision authorizing the common fund foundation; deductible charitable contributions are allowed in these circumstances.[347] This is the case even though the donor and his or her spouse can annually designate public charities to which the foundation must grant the income and principal of the original contribution. Thus, the common fund foundation is a type of private foundation that is closely comparable to a donor-directed fund. Nothing in the Internal Revenue Code defines an entity comparable to a donor-advised fund.

In the case of community foundations, which hold themselves out as a bundle of donor-advised funds, a donor at the time of the gift (that is, at the time of creation of the component fund) is permitted to designate the charitable purpose of the gift or the specific charity that will receive the income or principal, consistent with the community foundation's exempt purposes.[348] These regulations do not permit the donor to direct, aside from the original designation, which charity may receive distributions or the timing of the distributions to the charitable recipient.[349] The donor may also offer nonbinding advice to the community fund manager regarding payouts from the component fund. (When a donor offers advice of this nature, the IRS is likely to carefully examine the facts involved to determine whether the giving of such "advice" by the donor is in actuality an exercise of a right to direct the distributions.)

The law concerning prohibited material restrictions[350] is very similar to the concepts distinguishing donor-directed funds and donor-advised funds. This body of law is in the federal income tax regulations.[351] The test under these restrictions is whether the transferee of assets is prevented from freely and effectively employing the transferred assets or the income from them for charitable purposes. For example, if the transferor reserved the right to direct one or more public charities to which the transferee must distribute the transferred assets and/or income, that would constitute a prohibited material restriction. The same is true with respect to restrictions on the transferee's ability to maintain or manage the assets or to any other condition imposed on the transferee that prevents it from exercising ultimate control over the assets received from the transferor.

[344] See *supra* § 1(e).
[345] See *supra* § 3(b)(iii).
[346] Reg. § 1.170A-9(h)(i).
[347] IRC § 170(b)(1)(A)(vii).
[348] Reg. §§ 1.170A-9(e)(11)(B), 1.507-2(a)(8)(iii)(B).
[349] Cf. Reg. § 1.507-2(a)(8)(iv)(A)(1).
[350] See *infra* § (d).
[351] Reg. § 1.507-2(a)(8)(iii).

(c) IRS Challenges to Donor-Advised Funds

The IRS challenged the donor-advised fund/donor-directed fund technique in court; the government lost the case for reasons articulated in an opinion issued in 1987.[352] The IRS attempted to deny tax-exempt status to a public charity maintaining donor-advised funds, contending that the entity was merely an association of donors for which commercial services were being performed for fees, and that it was violating the prohibitions on private inurement and private benefit.[353] The IRS asserted that the organization's "activities are all originated, funded and controlled by small related groups, by single individuals, or by families" and that "these individual donors retain full control of the funds."[354] The court, however, found that donors to the organization "relinquish all ownership and custody of the donated funds or property" and that the organization is "free to accept or reject any suggestion or request made by a donor."[355] Indeed, the court enthused that the "goal" of the organization "is to create an effective national network to respond to many worthy charitable needs at the local level which in many cases might go unmet" and that its activities "promote public policy and represent the very essence of charitable benevolence as envisioned by Congress in enacting" tax-exempt status for charitable organizations.[356]

Ten years later, the IRS prevailed on the point.[357] The entity involved was structured much the same as the collective of donor-advised funds in the previous case. The trustee of the fund was bound by the donor's enforceable conditions as to disposition of its funds to ultimate charities. The fund was ruled not to be tax-exempt as a charitable organization. The court wrote: "The manner in which the Fund's investment activity would be conducted makes clear that one of the purposes of the Fund is to allow persons to take a charitable deduction for a donation to the Fund while retaining investment control over the donation."[358] This opinion did not differentiate between material and other restrictions. Nevertheless, the IRS's victory was short-lived. This decision was appealed, which led to settlement negotiations.[359] The trustee of the fund agreed, as requested by the IRS, to eliminate the language in the fund's document that gave donors the control that had been found by the lower court to be unwarranted private benefit. Nonetheless, for more than one year, the IRS refused to grant the fund recognition of tax-exempt status (although settlement negotiations took place), eventually causing the court of appeals, in frustration, to vacate the district court's decision and to direct that court to issue an order that the fund is an exempt charitable entity.[360]

---

[352] National Found., Inc. v. United States, 87-2 U.S.T.C. ¶ 9602 (Cl. Ct. 1987).
[353] See Chapter 19.
[354] National Found., Inc. v. United States, *supra* note 352, at 89,830.
[355] *Id.* at 89,831.
[356] *Id.* at 89,832.
[357] The Fund for Anonymous Gifts v. Internal Revenue Serv., 97-2 U.S.T.C. ¶ 50,710 (D.D.C. 1997).
[358] *Id.* at 89,854.
[359] See text accompanied by *infra* note 360.
[360] Fund for Anonymous Gifts v. Internal Revenue Serv., 99-1 U.S.T.C. ¶ 50,440 (D.C. Cir. 1999).

The government is of the view that this amendment did not "sufficiently address the inadequacies" of the fund's operations. It contended that the administrative record showed that the fund would not "take complete control over the contributions." Rather, the government is of the view that the fund will "adhere to the directions of its donors regarding the investment and the ultimate distribution of the contributed funds." This amendment does not, the government asserts, prevent the fund from "providing investment services and acting as an administrative conduit for its donors' funds."[361]

It may be anticipated that this issue as to tax exemption of donor-advised funds will be the subject of, and will be shaped by, further litigation.[362] In addition, the IRS was expected to assert that funds of this nature do not qualify as publicly supported donative entities, although the agency, in its initial rulings, has not taken that position.[363]

(d) Prohibited Material Restrictions

One of the reasons for focus on these types of donor funds is the need for a judgment as to whether a transaction that is otherwise a charitable gift is not, in law, a completed gift at all because the donor retains too much control over the subsequent use and disposition of the gift money or property. At least in the context of donor-advised gift funds (and thus presumably in most other donor fund contexts, including donor-directed funds), the IRS uses the criteria in the private foundation termination rules to determine whether a completed gift has been made.

A charitable organization can terminate its private foundation status by transferring all of its income and assets to one or more public charities.[364] An issue that can arise is whether the "transfer" is in fact a completed one. The income tax regulations provide criteria for making this determination.

The regulations concerning termination of private foundation status focus on whether a grantor private foundation has transferred "all of its right, title, and interest in and to" the funds (including any property) transferred.[365] To effectuate such a transfer, a grantor private foundation "may not impose any material restriction or condition" that prevents the grantee from "freely and effectively employing the transferred assets, or the income derived therefrom, in furtherance of its exempt purposes."[366] Whether a particular condition or restriction imposed upon a transfer of assets is *material* must be determined from all the facts and circumstances of the transfer.[367]

The presence of some or all of the following *nonadverse factors* (or positive

[361] *IRS Exempt Organizations Continuing Professional Education Text for Fiscal Year 2000* (IRS CPE Text FY 2000), Technical Topic P 2 B (2).
[362] E.g., New Dynamics Found. v. United States (No. 99-197T Fed. Cl. 1999).
[363] E.g., Priv. Ltr. Rul. 200037053.
[364] IRC § 507(b)(i)(A).
[365] Reg. § 1.507-2(a)(7).
[366] Reg. § 1.507-2(a)(8)(i).
[367] *Id.*

characteristics) is not considered as preventing the grantee from "freely and effectively employing the transferred assets, or the income derived therefrom, in furtherance of its exempt purposes":

1. The transfer is to a fund that is given a name or other designation which is the same as or similar to that of the grantor private foundation or otherwise memorializes the creator of the foundation or his or her family.

2. The income and assets of the fund are to be used for a designated purpose or for one or more particular public charities, and that use is consistent with the public charity's charitable purpose.

3. The transferred money or property is administered in an identifiable or separate fund, some or all of the principal of which is not to be distributed for a specified period, if the grantee public charity is the legal and equitable owner of the fund and the governing body of the public charity exercises ultimate and direct authority and control over the fund.[368]

4. The grantor private foundation transfers property the continued retention of which by the grantee is required by the transferor if the retention is important to the achievement of charitable purposes.[369]

The presence of any of seven factors is considered as preventing the grantee from "freely and effectively employing the transferred assets, or the income derived therefrom, in furtherance of its exempt purposes" (the *adverse factors*).[370]

The first of these factors concerns control over distributions. The issue is whether the transferor private foundation, a disqualified person with respect to it (such as a board member, officer, or substantial contributor), or any person or committee designated by, or pursuant to the terms of an agreement with, such a person (collectively, the *grantor*) reserved the right, directly or indirectly, to name the persons to which the transferee public charity must distribute, or to direct the timing of such distributions.[371]

With respect to this factor, the IRS will carefully examine whether the seeking of advice by the transferee from, or the giving of advice by, any grantor after the assets have been transferred to the transferee constitutes an indirect reservation of a right to direct the distributions.[372] In such a case, the reservation of this type of a right will be considered to exist when the only criterion considered by the public charity in making a distribution of income or principal from a grantor's fund is advice offered by the grantor.[373] Whether there is a reservation of this type of right is to be determined on the basis of all of the facts and

[368]A donor-advised fund established within a community trust must be administered in or as a component part of the trust (Reg. § 1.170A-9(e)(1)). See § 13.5(d).
[369]Reg. § 1.507-2(a)(8)(iii).
[370]Reg. § 1.507-2(a)(8)(iv).
[371]Reg. § 1.507-2(a)(8)(iv)(A)(1).
[372]*Id.*
[373]*Id.*

circumstances.[374] In making this determination, the elements contained in the six factors, in addition to the five factors (both of which are discussed next), are to be taken into consideration.[375]

The presence of some or all of the following six factors indicates that a reservation of this type of right does not exist:

1. There has been an independent investigation by the staff of the public charity evaluating whether the grantor's advice is consistent with specific charitable needs most deserving of support by the recipient charity (as determined by it).

2. The public charity has promulgated guidelines enumerating specific charitable needs consistent with the charitable purposes of the public charity.

3. The grantor's advice is consistent with these guidelines.

4. The public charity has instituted an educational program publicizing these guidelines to donors and other persons.

5. The public charity distributes funds in excess of amounts distributed from the grantor's fund to the same or similar types of organizations or charitable needs as those recommended by the grantor.

6. The solicitations for funds of the public charity specifically state that the public entity will not be bound by advice offered by the grantor (the *six factors*).[376]

The presence of some or all of the following five factors indicates that the reservation of a right exists:

1. The solicitation of funds by the public charity states or implies that the grantor's advice will be followed.

2. A pattern of conduct on the part of that charity creates an expectation that the grantor's advice will be followed.

3. The advice of a grantor (whether or not restricted to a distribution of income or principal from the grantor's trust or fund) is limited to distributions of amounts from the grantor's fund (and certain factors are not present (namely, the first two of the six factors)).

4. Only the advice of the grantor as to distributions from the grantor's fund is solicited by the public charity and no procedure is provided for considering advice from persons other than the grantor with respect to the fund.

---

[374]*Id.*
[375]*Id.*
[376]Reg. § 1.507-2(a)(8)(iv)(A)(2).

5. For the year involved and all prior years, the public charity follows the advice of all grantors with respect to their funds substantially all of the time (the *five factors*).[377]

The other factor of the seven factors that may be relevant pertains to any agreement entered into between the transferor private foundation and the transferee public charity "which establishes irrevocable relationships with respect to the maintenance or management of assets transferred to the public charity."[378] This factor is additionally described by a reference to relationships "such as continuing relationships with banks, brokerage firms, investment counselors, or other advisors with regard to the investments or other property transferred to the public charity."[379]

Of the seven factors, the remaining five are irrelevant to this matter. They pertain to certain mandatory actions or withholding of actions, assumptions of leases, retentions of investment assets, rights of first refusal, and any other condition that prevents the transferee public charity "from exercising ultimate control over the assets received from the transferor private foundation for purposes consistent with its exempt purposes."[380]

The presence of any of the seven factors is, as noted, considered as preventing the transferee from "freely and effectively" utilizing the transferred assets or income from them in furtherance of charitable purposes. To have application of these rules be deemed to cause something less than a full transfer for purposes of termination of private foundation status, and thus for purposes of determining whether a transfer is a qualifying distribution,[381] however, a restriction, right, or condition must also be material.[382]

Whether a particular condition or restriction imposed upon a transfer of assets is *material* must be determined from all the facts and circumstances of the transfer.[383] The tax regulations state that some of the "more significant" facts and circumstances to be considered in making this determination are whether:

1. The public charity is the owner in fee of the assets it received from the private foundation.

2. The assets are to be held and administered by the public charity in a manner consistent with one or more of its exempt purposes.

3. The governing body of the public charity has the ultimate authority and control over the assets and the income derived from them.

[377]Reg. § 1.507-2(a)(8)(iv)(A)(3).
[378]Reg. § 1.507-2(a)(8)(iv)(F).
[379]*Id.*
[380]Reg. § 1.507-2(a)(8)(iv)(B)–(E), (G).
[381]See *supra* § 4(b).
[382]Reg. § 1.507-2(a)(8)(i).
[383]*Id.*

4. The extent to which the governing body of the public charity is organized and operated so as to be independent from the transferor (the *materiality factors*).[384]

As to the fourth of these factors, it also must be determined from all the facts and circumstances.[385] Some of the "more significant" of these facts and circumstances to be considered are:

1. Whether, and to what extent, members of the governing body are individuals selected by the transferor private foundation or its disqualified persons, or are themselves disqualified persons with respect to the foundation.

2. Whether, and to what extent, members of the governing body are selected by public officials acting in their capacities as such.

3. How long a period of time each member of the governing body may serve in that capacity (the *independence factors*).[386]

In one instance, a private foundation proposed to provide an endowment to fund the operating expenses of a public charity, including those for construction of a facility. The funds were to be paid to an escrow agent, who would hold the funds until certain conditions were satisfied. The purpose for establishment of the endowment, before construction took place, was to assure bond holders and contributors that funds would be available to support the entity. In finding the restrictions not to be material, the IRS observed that the private foundation had given up any right to control use of the funds in the grantee's possession, other than through the restrictions set forth in the escrow agreement; the private foundation retained no right of reversion or other interest in the transferred assets; ultimate distribution of the funds would occur within a reasonable period of time; and the ultimate grantee was a public charity.[387]

(e) Public Charity Status of Funds

Another issue being raised by the functions of charitable organizations that maintain donor-advised funds—particularly those that maintain these funds as their sole function, such as charitable gift funds and national foundations[388]—is whether these entities qualify as publicly supported charities.

Community foundations, charitable gift funds, and other entities maintaining donor-advised funds to a significant extent are classified as donative-type publicly supported charities.[389] This is because the contributions to these

---

[384]*Id.*
[385]Reg. § 1.507-2(a)(8)(ii).
[386]*Id.*
[387]Priv. Ltr. Rul. 9014004.
[388]A term of disparagement occasionally promoted by certain members of congressional staff to describe these entities is *accommodation charities.*
[389]See *supra* § 3(b)(iii).

organizations, albeit earmarked for donor-advised funds, are treated, in whole or in part, as public support for the charity. The IRS, however, frets over the propriety of treating donor-advised funds as publicly supported charities, on the theory that these charities may not be *supported* in a technical, legal sense.

When a grant is made from a donor-advised fund to a charity—which may be termed the *ultimate beneficiary*—the grant amount can be regarded (in whole or in part) as public support for the ultimate beneficiary. For some time, it was the view of the IRS that these gifts to charities maintaining donor-advised funds amounted to public support for both the "intermediate" and "ultimate" beneficiary charities.[390] As the controversy widened, however, the IRS withdrew its views on the subject.[391] The agency's present views on the subject have not been published.

Still, it is clear that this issue festers. This fact is reflected in an IRS publication issued in 1995.[392] The IRS is not troubled by the concept that "earmarked" gifts are forms of public support for the "ultimate" charitable recipient. It is the treatment of these gifts as public support for the "intermediate" entity—the collective of donor-advised funds—that is giving the IRS pause.

The IRS's publication feigns objectivity in places, then loses even that in others. Thus, it was written: "There is no authority in the regulations or elsewhere that the earmarked funds are treated as support for the intermediary organizations as well as the ultimate recipient." It is true that the law is silent on the point, but that does not necessarily mean that this dual characterization of the funds for tax purposes is inappropriate. This is particularly the case with donor-advised funds, where the gifts are not really earmarked. The statement is thus loaded, rendered predisposed to the conclusion.

This analysis posited a second approach, in that it applied the distinction between contributions *to* a charitable organization and those *for the use of* a charitable organization.[393] The idea is that only contributions to a charitable organization can be treated as public support, because the charity is free to use the gifts in its charitable program. The IRS essay asserts that an "earmarked" gift and a gift "for the use of" a charity are similar in that "both have qualities of property held in trust." That is, this view asserts that the "intermediary" entity is the functional equivalent of a trustee for the "ultimate" charity, so that these "earmarked" contributions ought not to be regarded as public support for the intermediate entity (the organization housing charitable gift funds).

There are fundamental problems with this approach. This analysis often fails to differentiate between donor-advised funds and donor-directed funds. Given the limited recommendatory authority associated with the former, it is not credible to assert that the arrangement involves a trust relationship. Also, it is common for donors to make restricted gifts, where the restriction is a program-

---

[390] Gen. Couns. Mem. 39748.
[391] Gen. Couns. Mem. 39875.
[392] *1995 Exempt Organizations Continuing Professional Education Technical Instruction Program Textbook*, which contains an essay on donor-advised and donor-directed funds.
[393] See Hopkins, *The Tax Law of Charitable Giving, Second Edition* (John Wiley & Sons, Inc., 2000) § 10.2.

matic one (such as for research or scholarships); there is no authority for a proposition that these restrictions give rise to a trust. Moreover, the statutory definition of *support*[394] does not embody this dubious dichotomy in this context between gifts to and for the use of charity.

The foregoing notwithstanding, in its first ruling on the point, the IRS held that contributions to a charitable organization, destined for its donor-advised fund, qualify as public support from the general public.[395] The IRS wrote that the core issue is whether an organization exercises "dominion and control" over a gifted asset so as to be considered its owner. While the IRS did not say so, the issue was whether the ability of donors to make recommendations and the policy of the organization to generally follow these recommendations amounted to a form of material restriction or condition; the answer, in this case at least, was no.[396]

(f) Interrelationship of Private Foundation Rules

If tax exemption is to be recognized, the IRS expects donor-advised funds to adhere to certain of the private foundation rules. The following expected representations are being required, at least in certain circumstances:[397]

1. The organization expects that its grants for the year will equal or exceed 5 percent of its average net assets on a fiscal-year rolling basis. (This is adherence to the private foundations payout requirements.[398]) If this level of grant activity is not attained, the organization will identify the named accounts (donor-advised funds) from which grants over the same period totaled less than 5 percent of each account's average assets. The organization will contact the "donor-advisors" of these accounts to request that they recommend grants of at least this amount. If a donor-advisor does not provide the qualified grant recommendations, the organization is authorized to transfer an amount up to 5 percent of assets from the donor-advisor's named account to the charity or charities selected by the organization.

2. The organization will add language to its promotional materials stating that the organization will investigate allegations of improper use of grant funds for the private benefit of donor-advisors.

3. The organization will add language to its grantee letters to the effect that grants are to be used by grantees exclusively in furtherance of charitable purposes and that grants cannot be used for the private benefit of donor-advisors. (This is intended to parallel the prohibitions on private foundations as to the making of taxable expenditures.[399])

---

[394] IRC § 509(d).

[395] That is, public support for purposes of IRC § 170(b)(1)(A)(vi). See *supra* § 3(b)(i).

[396] Priv. Ltr. Rul. 200037053.

[397] These are referenced in IRS CPE Text FY 2000, Technical Topic P, 2C.

[398] See *supra* § 4(b).

[399] See *supra* § 4(e).

PART THREE

Noncharitable Tax-Exempt Organizations

CHAPTER TWELVE

Social Welfare Organizations

§ 12.1 Concept of *Social Welfare*
    (a) General Rules
    (b) Benefits to Members
§ 12.2 The Requisite *Community*

§ 12.3 Advocacy Organizations
§ 12.4 Comparison with Charitable Organizations

The federal tax law provides tax exemption for "[c]ivic leagues or organizations not organized for profit but operated exclusively for the promotion of social welfare . . ."[1]

The reference to organizations operated for the promotion of *social welfare* is somewhat confusing and outdated. It is confusing because of the considerable similarity between these entities and those that are *charitable* in nature; *promotion of social welfare* is one of the definitions of a tax-exempt charitable organization.[2] It is outmoded in the sense that the principal type of organization that is tax-exempt by reason of this category of exemption is one that is advocacy-oriented—in the sense of focus on community, state, and/or national policymaking, including lobbying—rather than one that is generally functioning to promote some vague form of social betterment.

§ 12.1 CONCEPT OF *SOCIAL WELFARE*

(a) General Rules

There is no precise definition of the term *social welfare* for federal law tax exemption purposes. The regulations amplifying the law concerning this category of tax-exempt organization offer two basic precepts: (1) "Social welfare" is commensurate with the "common good and general welfare" and "civic betterments and social improvements,"[3] and (2) the promotion of social welfare does not include activities that primarily constitute "carrying on a business with the general public in a manner similar to organizations which are operated for profit."[4] The regula-

---

[1] IRC § 501(c)(4); Reg. § 1.501(c)(4)-1(a)(1).
[2] See §§ 6.6, 12.4.
[3] Reg. § 1.501(c)(4)-1(a)(2)(i).
[4] Reg. § 1.501(c)(4)-1(a)(2)(ii). E.g., Industrial Addition Ass'n v. Comm'r, 149 F.2d 294 (6th Cir. 1945); Club Gaona, Inc. v. United States, 167 F. Supp. 741 (S.D. Cal. 1958); Harvey v. Campbell, 107 F. Supp. 757 (N.D. Tex. 1952); Interneighborhood Housing Corp. v. Comm'r, 45 T.C.M. 115 (1982).

tions also contain a prohibition on political campaign activity[5] and state that an organization is not operated primarily for the promotion of social welfare "if its primary activity is operating a social club for the benefit, pleasure, or recreation of its members."[6] The conduct of social functions for the benefit of its members will not defeat social welfare status for an organization, however, where these activities are something less than primary,[7] or are otherwise incidental to a primary function.[8]

Like all tax-exempt organizations, the social welfare organization, to be operated *exclusively* for the promotion of social welfare, must be operated *primarily* for that purpose.[9] The key principle is that, to qualify as a tax-exempt social welfare organization, the activities of the organization must be those that will benefit the community as a whole, rather than merely benefit the organization's membership or other select group of individuals or organizations.[10] Thus, an organization that restricted its membership to individuals of good moral character and health belonging to a particular ethnic group residing in a geographical area and that provided sick benefits to members and death benefits to their beneficiaries was ruled to not be tax-exempt as a social welfare organization, as it was essentially a mutual, self-interest type of organization.[11] Likewise, an individual practice association was denied categorization as a tax-exempt social welfare organization because its primary beneficiaries were its member-physicians, in that it provided an available pool of physicians who abided by its fee schedule when rendering medical services to the subscribers of a health maintenance organization and provided its members with access to a large group of patients (the subscribers) who generally may not be referred to nonmember-physicians.[12]

As an additional example, a nonprofit organization, incorporated for the purpose of furnishing television reception to its members on a cooperative basis in an area not adaptable to ordinary reception, where the members contracted for services and the payment of installment fees, was deemed to not be a tax-exempt social welfare organization because it was "operate[d] for the benefit of its members rather than for the promotion of the welfare of mankind."[13] Yet, a similar organization, which obtained memberships and contributions on a voluntary basis, was found to be a tax-social welfare organization, since it "operate[d] its system for the benefit of all television owners in the community."[14]

[5] See § 21.4.

[6] Reg. § 1.501(c)(4)-1(a)(2)(ii). There is a separate category of tax exemption for social clubs (see Chapter 14), which can encompass entities that do not qualify as social welfare organizations (e.g., Ye Mystic Krewe of Gasparilla v. Comm'r, 80 T.C. 755 (1983); Polish Am. Club v. Comm'r, 33 T.C.M. 925 (1974)).

[7] Rev. Rul. 66-179, 1966-1 C.B. 139; Rev. Rul. 63-190, 1963-2 C.B. 212.

[8] Rev. Rul. 74-361, 1974-2 C.B. 159. Also Rev. Rul. 68-224, 1968-1 C.B. 262 (annual festival); Priv. Ltr. Rul. 9220010 (recreational activities).

[9] See § 4.4.

[10] Reg. § 1.501(c)(4)-1(a)(2)(i).

[11] Rev. Rul. 75-199, 1975-1 C.B. 160, *mod'g* Rev. Rul. 55-495, 1955-2 C.B. 259.

[12] Rev. Rul. 86-98, 1986-2 C.B. 74.

[13] Rev. Rul. 54-394, 1954-2 C.B. 131. Also Rev. Rul. 55-716, 1955-2 C.B. 263, *mod. by* Rev. Rul. 83-170, 1983-2 C.B. 97.

[14] Rev. Rul. 62-167, 1962-2 C.B. 142.

Similarly, because of the lack of sufficient benefit to the entire community, a trust to provide group life insurance only for members of an association was not considered a tax-exempt social welfare organization.[15] Likewise, a resort operated for a school's faculty and students was held to not be an exempt social welfare organization.[16] In the latter instance, a federal court of appeals wrote that the "exemption granted to social welfare . . . organizations is made in recognition of the benefit which the public derives from their social welfare activities."[17] Conversely, a consumer credit counseling service that assisted families and individuals with financial problems was ruled to qualify as a tax-exempt social welfare organization because its objectives and activities "contribute to the betterment of the community as a whole" by checking the rising incidence of personal bankruptcy in the community.[18] Also, exempt social welfare status was accorded an organization that processed consumer complaints concerning products and services provided by businesses, met with the parties involved to encourage resolution of the problem, and recommended an appropriate solution, and (where the solution was not accepted) informed the parties about the administrative or judicial remedies available to resolve the dispute.[19] Likewise, an organization created to maintain a system for the storage and distribution of water to raise the underground water level in a community was ruled a tax-exempt social welfare organization because of the benefits to those whose wells were thereby supplied.[20]

Organizations that operate in a manner inimical to principles of what constitutes the common good and the general welfare of the people in a community will not, of course, qualify as a tax-exempt social welfare organization. In part for that reason, the IRS denied tax exemption to an antiwar protest organization that urged demonstrators to commit violations of local ordinances and breaches of public order.[21] Said the IRS: "Illegal activities, which violate the minimum standards of acceptable conduct necessary to the preservation of an orderly society, . . . are not a permissible means of promoting social welfare . . ."[22]

Other examples of tax-exempt social welfare organizations include an organization that provided a community with supervised facilities for the teaching of the safe handling and proper care of firearms,[23] encouraged industrial development to relieve unemployment in an economically depressed area,[24] helped to secure accident insurance for the students and employees in a school district,[25] provided bus transportation between a community and the major employment centers in a metropolitan area during rush hours when the regular bus service

---

[15] N.Y. State Ass'n of Real Estate Boards Group Ins. Fund v. Comm'r, 54 T.C. 1325 (1970).
[16] People's Educ. Camp Soc'y, Inc. v. Comm'r, 331 F.2d 923 (2d Cir. 1964), *aff'g* 39 T.C. 756 (1963), *cert. den.*, 379 U.S. 839 (1964).
[17] *Id.* at 932.
[18] Rev. Rul. 65-299, 1965-2 C.B. 165.
[19] Rev. Rul. 78-50, 1978-1 C.B. 155.
[20] Rev. Rul. 66-148, 1966-1 C.B. 143.
[21] Rev. Rul. 75-384, 1975-2 C.B. 204.
[22] *Id.* at 205.
[23] Rev. Rul. 66-273, 1966-2 C.B. 222.
[24] Rev. Rul. 67-294, 1967-2 C.B. 193.
[25] Rev. Rul. 61-153, 1961-2 C.B. 114. Cf. Rev. Rul. 66-354, 1966-2 C.B. 207.

was inadequate,[26] conducted a community art show for the purpose of encouraging interest in painting, sculpture, and other art forms,[27] provided assistance to low-income farm families in a particular state,[28] conducted a free public radio forum for the dissemination of progressive social views,[29] maintained parking for visitors to a downtown business district,[30] provided low-cost rural electrification,[31] and established and maintained a roller-skating rink for residents of a particular county.[32] Junior chambers of commerce usually qualify as tax-exempt social welfare organizations.[33]

Organizations formed to promote sports frequently are a type of nonprofit organization likely to gain status as tax-exempt social welfare organizations. A corporation formed to initiate programs designed to stimulate the interest of youth in organized sports, by furnishing youths virtually free admission and encouraging their attendance at sporting events, was considered a tax-exempt social welfare organization because it provided "wholesome entertainment for the social improvement and welfare of the youths of the community."[34] Sports organizations can fall short of the requisite criteria in this regard, however, as illustrated by the fate of a nonprofit corporation that was organized to provide facilities for training men and horses for use in emergencies, and obtained qualification as a tax-exempt social welfare organization, only to subsequently lose its tax exemption because it evolved into a commercial riding stable.[35] Said the court: "[T]he few persons eligible to use . . . [the organization's] facilities as members or on any basis other than by paying a regular commercial fee for such use causes . . . [the] operation (no matter how laudable) to be such as not to come within the meaning of 'social welfare.' "[36]

In one instance, a corporation maintained a vacation home for "working girls and women of proper character."[37] All of the trustees were required to be employees of a particular business corporation; the use of the farm's facilities was by invitation only to a select and limited number of women who were predominantly (80 percent) employees of the same business corporation. The government unsuccessfully asserted that the vacation home did not benefit the community as a whole, by virtue of the predominance of the employees of a single business or the invitational process. Indeed, the court concluded that the organization "is an institution which has served a broad community need in the sense that Congress intended, that is, that when one segment or slice of the community, in this case

---

[26] Rev. Rul. 78-69, 1978-1 C.B. 156. Cf. Rev. Rul. 78-68, 1978-1 C.B. 149; Rev. Rul. 55-311, 1955-1 C.B. 72.
[27] Rev. Rul. 78-131, 1978-1 C.B. 156. Cf. § 6.7.
[28] Scofield v. Rio Farms, Inc., 205 F.2d 68 (5th Cir. 1953).
[29] Debs Memorial Radio Fund, Inc. v. Comm'r, 148 F.2d 948 (2d Cir. 1945).
[30] Rev. Rul. 81-116, 1981-1 C.B. 333. Cf. Rev. Rul. 78-86, 1978-1 C.B. 151.
[31] United States v. Pickwick Elec. Membership Corp., 158 F.2d 272 (6th Cir. 1946).
[32] Rev. Rul. 67-109, 1967-1 C.B. 136.
[33] Rev. Rul. 65-195, 1965-2 C.B. 164.
[34] Rev. Rul. 68-118, 1968-1 C.B. 261. Also Rev. Rul. 70-4, 1970-1 C.B. 126; Rev. Rul. 69-384, 1969-2 C.B. 122. As discussed in § 10.2, Congress amended IRC § 501(c)(3) in 1976 to provide tax exemption for organizations the primary purpose of which is to foster national or international sports competition.
[35] Los Angeles County Remount Ass'n v. Comm'r, 27 T.C.M. 1035 (1968).
[36] Id. at 1044. Also Rev. Rul. 55-516, 1955-2 C.B. 260.
[37] Eden Hall Farm v. United States, 389 F. Supp. 858 (W.D. Penn. 1975).

thousands of working women ... , are [sic] served, then the community as a whole benefits."[38]

(b) Benefits to Members

A related criterion of the tax-exempt social welfare organization is that it must not be operated primarily for the economic benefit or convenience of its members.

Thus, a corporation that purchased and sold unimproved land, invested proceeds received from the sales, and distributed profits to members, was deemed to not be a tax-exempt social welfare organization.[39] Similarly, as noted, an organization formed to manage low- and moderate-income housing property for a fee was ruled to not qualify for tax-exempt social welfare status.[40] Likewise, a federal court of appeals held that a consumer and producer membership cooperative that rebated a percentage of net income to members as patronage dividends made the disbursements "primarily to benefit the taxpayer's membership economically" and not exclusively for promotion of social welfare,[41] and that a membership corporation composed of buyers of ready-to-wear apparel and accessories was not a tax-exempt social welfare organization, since its functions were largely social and many of its activities were designed to enable presently employed members to earn more money.[42] Subsequently, another federal court of appeals denied tax-exempt social welfare status to a mutual assistance association established by a church in furtherance of its "mutual aid" practices, because its practices and policies were found to benefit only its members, rather than the requisite community.[43] Similarly, an association of police officers primarily engaged in providing retirement benefits to members and death benefits to beneficiaries of members was held to not qualify for tax exemption as a social welfare organization because the primary benefits from the organization were limited to its members,[44] although the exemption may be available where this type of an association is established and is maintained by, and where the benefits provided are funded primarily by, a government.[45] Likewise, an individual practice association providing health services through written agreements with health maintenance organizations was ruled to not qualify as a social welfare or-

---

[38] *Id.* at 866. The IRS does not follow the *Eden Hall Farm* decision, *supra* note 37, on the ground that an organization providing recreational facilities to the employees of selected corporations cannot qualify as a tax-exempt social welfare organization (Rev. Rul. 80-205, 1980-2 C.B. 184).

[39] Rev. Rul. 69-385, 1969-2 C.B. 123.

[40] Rev. Rul. 70-535, 1970-2 C.B. 117.

[41] Consumer-Farmer Milk Coop. v. Comm'r, 186 F.2d 68, 71 (2d Cir. 1950), *aff'g* 13 T.C. 150 (1949), *cert. den.*, 341 U.S. 931 (1951).

[42] American Women Buyers Club, Inc. v. United States, 338 F.2d 526 (2d Cir. 1964).

[43] Mutual Aid Ass'n of the Church of the Brethren v. United States, 759 F.2d 792 (10th Cir. 1985), *aff'g* 578 F. Supp. 1451 (D. Kan. 1983). Also American Ass'n of Christian Schools Voluntary Employees Beneficiary Ass'n Welfare Plan Trust v. United States, 850 F.2d 1510 (11th Cir. 1988), *aff'g* 663 F. Supp. 275 (M.D. Ala. 1987); El Paso Del Aguila Elderly v. Comm'r, 64 T.C.M. 376 (1992).

[44] Rev. Rul. 81-58, 1981-1 C.B. 331. Also Police Benevolent Ass'n of Richmond, Va. v. United States, 661 F. Supp. 765 (E.D. Va. 1987).

[45] Rev. Rul. 87-126, 1987-2 C.B. 150.

ganization because the primary beneficiaries were its member physicians,[46] and an organization carrying on a business with the general public was found to not qualify as an exempt social welfare entity because it was operated primarily for the benefit of its members.[47]

Many other types of membership service groups have been denied categorization as tax-exempt social welfare organizations, such as an automobile club,[48] an organization that operated a dining room and bar for the exclusive use of its members,[49] and a national sorority controlled by a business corporation that furnished the member chapters with supplies and services.[50] In another instance, an organization formed to purchase groceries for its membership at the lowest possible prices on a cooperative basis was denied tax-exempt social welfare status.[51] The rationale: "The organization . . . is a private cooperative enterprise [operated primarily] for the economic benefit or convenience of the members."[52] Similarly, the IRS denied classification as a tax-exempt social welfare entity to a cooperative organization providing home maintenance services to its members, even though payments for the services were made in kind.[53] In another instance, an organization, the membership of which was limited to persons who owned shares of public utility companies, was ruled to not qualify as an exempt social welfare entity because it was operated to serve private interests, in that it promoted the interests of the public utility industry and its stockholders by preparing and filing statements concerning public utility matters pending before state and federal agencies and legislative bodies, and by publishing a newsletter about matters affecting the stockholders.[54]

The rendering of services to members does not, however, necessarily work a denial or loss of tax-exempt social welfare status. For example, a memorial association formed to develop methods of achieving simplicity and dignity in funeral services and to maintain a registry for the wishes of its members in regard to funeral arrangements qualified for tax exemption as a social welfare organization,[55] as did an organization engaged in rehabilitation and job placement of its members.[56] Likewise, an organization that promoted the legal rights of all tenants in a particular community and occasionally initiated litigation to contest the validity of legislation adversely affecting tenants was held to qualify as a tax-exempt social welfare organization because its activities were directed toward benefiting all tenants in the community.[57] By contrast, a tenants' rights group was denied tax-

---

[46] Rev. Rul. 86-98, 1986-2 C.B. 74.
[47] Santa Cruz Bldg. Ass'n v. United States, 411 F. Supp. 871 (D. Mo. 1976).
[48] Smyth v. California State Automobile Ass'n, 175 F.2d 752 (9th Cir. 1949), *cert. den.*, 338 U.S. 905 (1949). Also Automobile Club of St. Paul v. Comm'r, 12 T.C. 1152 (1949).
[49] Rev. Rul. 61-158, 1961-2 C.B. 115.
[50] Rev. Rul. 66-360, 1966-2 C.B. 228.
[51] Rev. Rul. 73-349, 1973-2 C.B. 179.
[52] *Id.* at 180.
[53] Rev. Rul. 78-132, 1978-1 C.B. 157.
[54] Rev. Rul. 80-107, 1980-1 C.B. 117.
[55] Rev. Rul. 64-313, 1964-2 C.B. 146.
[56] Rev. Rul. 57-297, 1957-2 C.B. 307.
[57] Rev. Rul. 80-206, 1980-2 C.B. 185.

exempt social welfare organization status because its activities were directed primarily toward benefiting only tenants who were its members.[58]

Also, qualification as a tax-exempt social welfare entity will not be precluded where an organization's services are equally available to members and non-members. As an illustration of this point, the IRS accorded tax-exempt social welfare classification to an organization formed to prevent oil and other liquid spills in a city port area, and to contain and clean up any spills that occur.[59] The organization's membership included business firms, primarily oil and chemical companies, that stored or shipped liquids in the port area. Because the organization cleaned up spills of both members and nonmembers, the IRS found that it was acting to prevent deterioration of the port community and not merely to prevent damage to the facilities of its members, so that any benefits to its members were incidental. Had the organization confined its repairs to property damaged by its members, the tax exemption would not have been available.[60]

Veterans' organizations frequently qualify as tax-exempt social welfare organizations;[61] however, the IRS has ruled to the contrary.[62] Organizations that have a membership of veterans may qualify as exempt social welfare groups,[63] although tax exemption may also be available under a separate category of exemption enacted for the benefit of veterans' groups.[64] The IRS, from time to time, reviews the status of a veterans' organization and concludes that the entity cannot qualify for tax exemption.[65] A subsidiary organization must establish exempt status on its own rather than on the basis of the functions of the parent veterans' organization.[66]

§ 12.2   THE REQUISITE *COMMUNITY*

As discussed, a social welfare organization may not—if it is to qualify for tax exemption—operate for the benefit of a select group of individuals but must be engaged in the promotion of the common good and general welfare of those in a community.[67] It has proved difficult to quantify the meaning of the term *community*, as can be seen, for example, as respects the question of the appropriate tax

---

[58] Rev. Rul. 73-306, 1973-2 C.B. 179.

[59] Rev. Rul. 79-316, 1979-2 C.B. 228.

[60] Contracting Plumbers Coop. Restoration Corp. v. United States, 488 F.2d 684 (2d Cir. 1973), *cert. den.*, 419 U.S. 827 (1974).

[61] Rev. Rul. 66-150, 1966-1 C.B. 147. Cf. Rev. Rul. 58-117, 1958-2 C.B. 196.

[62] Rev. Rul. 68-46, 1968-1 C.B. 260. Also see Veterans Found. v. United States, 281 F.2d 912 (10th Cir. 1960).

[63] Rev. Rul. 68-455, 1968-2 C.B. 215; Rev. Rul. 68-45, 1968-1 C.B. 259; Rev. Rul. 55-156, 1955-1 C.B. 292; Polish Army Veterans Post 147 v. Comm'r, 236 F.2d 509 (3d Cir. 1956), *vac'g and rem'g* 24 T.C. 891 (1956).

[64] IRC § 501(c)(19). See § 18.10.

[65] E.g., Tech. Adv. Mem. 199912033.

[66] Rev. Rul. 66-150, *supra* note 61.

[67] Reg. § 1.501(c)(4)-1(a)(2)(i). Also Rev. Rul. 76-147, 1976-1 C.B. 151; Erie Endowment v. United States, 316 F.2d 151 (3d Cir. 1963).

status of community associations, principally, homeowners' associations. The typical homeowners' association is a nonprofit membership corporation composed of landowners and tenants in a housing development. The association may have been created by the real estate developer or subsequently by the homeowners themselves. These associations are normally supported by annual assessments or membership dues; membership in these organizations may be voluntary or involuntary. A homeowners' association typically engages in one or more of the following functions: It owns and/or maintains common green areas, streets, and sidewalks for the use of all residents; it administers and enforces covenants for preserving the architecture and general appearance of the development; and/or it participates in the formulation of public policies having an impact on the development, such as the expansion of nearby principal roads, development of nearby lands, or encroachment of commercial enterprises. In this latter capacity, the association is functioning much as a conventional civic league.[68]

The IRS ruled, in relation to an association performing the first two of the above functions, that the association is exempt from federal income tax as a social welfare organization.[69] The association was found to be "serving the common good and the general welfare of the people of the entire development," with the IRS noting that a "neighborhood, precinct, subdivision, or housing development" may constitute the requisite community.[70] Thus, even though the association was established by the developer and its existence may have aided the developer in selling housing units, any benefits to the developer were dismissed as incidental. Also deemed incidental were the benefits that accrued to the individual members, such as the preservation and protection of property values.[71]

Following issuance of this ruling in 1972, the IRS quickly concluded that its "increasing experience" with homeowners' associations demonstrated that the ruling was being misconstrued as to its scope. Consequently, in 1974, the IRS issued a "clarifying" ruling.[72] The IRS said that homeowners' associations, as described in the 1972 ruling, are *prima facie* presumed to be essentially and primarily formed and operated for the benefit of the individual members and, accordingly, not tax-exempt—a position wholly absent from the 1972 ruling. Subsequently, however, the IRS ruled that an organization with membership limited to the residents and business operators within a city block and formed to preserve and beautify the public areas in the block, thereby benefiting the community as a whole as well as enhancing the members' property rights, may qualify as a tax-exempt social welfare entity.[73] Moreover, a membership organization formed to help preserve, beautify, and maintain a public park was ruled to qualify as a tax-exempt charitable organization.[74]

---

[68] Rev. Rul. 67-6, 1967-1 C.B. 135, *mod. by* Rev. Rul. 76-147. *supra* note 67.
[69] Rev. Rul. 72-102, 1972-1 C.B. 149, *mod. by* Rev. Rul. 74-99, 1974-1 C.B. 131.
[70] Rev. Rul. 72-102, *supra* note 69 at 149.
[71] Cf. Rev. Rul. 69-280, 1969-1 C.B. 152.
[72] Rev. Rul. 74-99, *supra* note 69.
[73] Rev. Rul. 75-286, 1975-2 C.B. 210. Cf. Rev. Rul. 68-14, 1968-1 C.B. 243.
[74] Rev. Rul. 78-85, 1978-1 C.B. 150.

The position of the IRS as to the definition of the word *community*, as stated in this 1974 ruling, is that the term has "traditionally been construed as having reference to a geographical unit bearing a reasonably recognizable relationship to an area ordinarily identified as a governmental subdivision or a unit or district thereof."[75] Thus, the IRS held that a community is "not simply an aggregation of homeowners bound together in a structured unit formed as an integral part of a plan for the development of a real estate subdivision and the sale and purchase of homes therein."[76]

The IRS, in this 1974 ruling, also held that, where the association's activities include those directed to exterior maintenance of private residences, the above *prima facie* presumption is reinforced. Moreover, the 1974 ruling stated that, as far as ownership and maintenance of common areas is concerned, the IRS's approval is only extended to those areas "traditionally recognized and accepted as being of direct governmental concern in the exercise of the powers and duties entrusted to governments to regulate community health, safety, and welfare."[77] That is, the IRS's "approval" was extended only to ownership and maintenance by a homeowners' association of areas such as "roadways and parklands, sidewalks and street lights, access to, or the use and enjoyment of which is extended to members of the general public, as distinguished from controlled use or access restricted to the members of the homeowners' association."[78]

Subsequent pronouncements by the IRS in this area illustrate that the IRS has continued to issue a variety of determinations as to the meaning of the term *community*. In 1975, the IRS issued a ruling that, assuming the presence of a community, accorded tax-exempt social welfare status to an organization formed to provide the community with security protection, improved public services, recreational and holiday activities, and a community newspaper.[79] Because these services clearly redounded to the benefit of the individual residents in the community, it is difficult to reconcile this ruling with the foregoing 1974 ruling. This is particularly the case in view of still another ruling, this one denying classification as an exempt social welfare entity to an organization formed to promote the common interest of tenants in an apartment complex, by negotiating with the apartment management and engaging in litigation activities.[80]

The IRS granted tax-exempt social welfare classification to an organization that operated an airport that was used by the public.[81] In the face of the prohibition in the income tax regulations on according tax-exempt social welfare classification to an organization carrying on a business with the general public,[82] the IRS decided that the rule was not contravened because the organization used volunteer services and received government grants. The requirement of a benefited

---

[75] Rev. Rul. 74-99, *supra* note 69, at 132.
[76] Comm'r v. Lake Forest, Inc., 305 F.2d 814, 820 (4th Cir. 1962), *rev'g and rem'g* 36 T.C. 510 (1962); Rev. Rul. 56-225, 1956-1 C.B. 58.
[77] Rev. Rul. 74-99, *supra* note 69, at 133.
[78] *Id.*
[79] Rev. Rul. 75-386, 1975-2 C.B. 211.
[80] Rev. Rul. 73-307, 1973-2 C.B. 186.
[81] Rev. Rul. 78-429, 1978-2 C.B. 178.
[82] See text accompanied by *supra* note 4.

community was held met because the airport served a rural area that had no other airport facilities; at the same time, most of the airplanes berthed at the airport were owned by key local businesses that were essential to the area's economy and the airport was used predominantly by executives, employees, and clients of the companies. The organization was deemed responsive to the community because it was supervised by a city council, inasmuch as the airport was located on land owned by a municipality.[83]

Thereafter, the IRS moderated its position in these regards somewhat, by stating that whether a particular homeowners' association meets the requirements of conferring benefit on a community must be determined according to the facts and circumstances of each case. The IRS also indicated that, although an area represented by an association may not be a community, the association may nonetheless still qualify for tax exemption if its activities benefit a community (such as owning and maintaining common areas and facilities for the use and enjoyment of the general public). The agency continues to insist, however, that tax exemption as a social welfare organization is not available to a homeowners' association (that does not represent a community) if it restricts the use of its facilities (such as parking and recreational facilities) to its members.[84] This position of the IRS is generally being accepted by the courts.[85]

Nonetheless, a federal district court rejected some of the positions of the IRS concerning the eligibility of homeowners' associations for tax-exempt status as social welfare organizations, holding that the association in the case represented a development that is an "independent community" (with 3,000 members and 6,100 acres of land), so that its benefits were provided to persons within the requisite community.[86] "There is no requirement," wrote the court, "that if the work of the association benefits the entire community, that it must also benefit the general public in terms of the world-at-large."[87] The court also stated: "Thus, only where an association represents less than the entire community is it a concern whether the benefits of the association are made available to the general public, because in that situation the benefits which are restricted to association members are not benefiting the community as a whole."[88] Therefore, held the court, the association was not required to give unlimited access to its golf course and tennis courts "beyond the community it serves to the world-at-large" to be tax-exempt.[89]

As noted, another court was in agreement with the IRS position in these regards, holding that an association of homeowners, which owned, controlled, leased, and sold real estate and built, maintained, and operated recreational facilities for the pleasure and convenience of its members, did not qualify as a tax-exempt social welfare organization.[90] The court noted that membership in the

---

[83] Cf. § 6.3.
[84] Rev. Rul. 80-63, 1980-1 C.B. 116, *clar.* Rev. Rul. 74-99, *supra* note 69.
[85] E.g., Flat Top Lake Ass'n, Inc. v. United States, 86-2 U.S.T.C. ¶ 9756 (S.D. W. Va. 1986), *rev'd*, 89-1 U.S.T.C. ¶ 9180 (4th Cir. 1989); Lake Petersburg Ass'n v. Comm'r, 33 T.C.M. 259 (1974).
[86] Rancho Santa Fe Ass'n v. United States, 84-2 U.S.T.C. ¶ 9536 (S.D. Cal. 1984).
[87] *Id.* at 84, 530.
[88] *Id.*
[89] *Id.*
[90] Flat Top Lake Ass'n, Inc. v. United States, *supra* note 85.

association was mandatory and was restricted to lot owners in the development, the association prohibited certain structures and uses of property, it provided road maintenance for the common roadways, and the facilities of the association were strictly limited to members and their guests. Holding that "a private association of homeowners which restricts its facilities to the exclusive use of its members" cannot be tax-exempt, the court observed that in other court holdings to the contrary there was "availability of taxpayer's facilities to the general public."[91]

The tax status of homeowners' associations has become even more important with the popularity of condominiums and the condominium management corporation. Basically, a condominium involves an ownership arrangement whereby individuals own a unit in a building and—with the other owners—the underlying land and commonly used improvements. The condominium management corporation, formed and supported by the unit owners, performs the maintenance and repair activities of the commonly owned properties.[92]

The position of the IRS is that condominium management corporations do not qualify as tax-exempt social welfare organizations inasmuch as the organizations' activities are for the private benefit of the members.[93] The IRS's rationale underlying this position is of two parts. First, the IRS ruled that, because of the essential nature and structure of the condominium system of ownership, the rights, duties, privileges, and immunities of the members are "inextricably and compulsorily tied to the owner's acquisition and enjoyment of his property in the condominium."[94] Second, the IRS noted that "condominium ownership necessarily involves ownership in common by all condominium unit owners of a great many so-called common areas, the maintenance and care of which necessarily constitutes the provision of private benefits for the unit owners."[95]

The IRS traces its position as to condominium management organizations to a 1962 federal court of appeals opinion.[96] There, the court held that a cooperative housing corporation was not a tax-exempt social welfare organization, since its activities were in the nature of an economic and private cooperative undertaking. In 1965, the IRS ruled that a cooperative organization operating and maintaining a housing development and providing housing facilities did not qualify as an exempt social welfare organization.[97] Again, in 1969, the IRS ruled that a nonprofit organization formed to provide maintenance of exterior walls and roofs of members' homes in a development was not tax-exempt as a social welfare entity.[98]

---

[91] *Id.* at 85, 865. Cf. Columbia Park & Recreation Assn, Inc. v. Comm'r, 88 T.C. 1 (1987).

[92] E.g., Garrett, "The Taxability of Condominium Owners' Associations," 12 *San Diego L. Rev.* 778 (1975); Curry, "Tax Considerations of Condominiums," 19 *Tul. Tax Inst.* 347 (1970); Anderson, "Tax Aspects of Cooperative and Condominium Housing," 25 *N.Y.U. Inst. on Fed. Tax.* 79 (1967).

[93] Rev. Rul. 74-17, 1974-1 C.B. 130. Cf. Rev. Rul. 70-604, 1970-2 C.B. 9.

[94] Rev. Rul. 74-17, *supra* note 93, at 131.

[95] *Id.*

[96] See *supra* note 77.

[97] Rev. Rul. 65-201, 1965-2 C.B. 170.

[98] Rev. Rul. 69-280, *supra* note 71. Cf. Rev. Rul. 74-563, 1974-2 C.B. 38. Also Eckstein v. United States, 452 F.2d 1036 (Ct. Cl. 1971).

A homeowners' association or condominium management organization may, if attempts to qualify as a tax-exempt social welfare organization fail, qualify as an exempt social club.[99] That is, an organization may have as its primary purpose the establishment and operation of social facilities, such as a swimming pool, for the benefit of the homeowners in a community.[100]

Also, a tax-exempt homeowners' association may establish a separate but affiliated organization, to own and maintain recreational facilities and restrict their use to members of the association, as long as the organization is operated totally separate from the association.[101]

Congress, in 1976, brought some clarification of the tax law concerning homeowners' associations.[102] This provision provides an elective tax exemption for condominium management and residential real estate management associations.[103]

§ 12.3 ADVOCACY ORGANIZATIONS

As noted at the outset, the contemporary tax-exempt social organization often is an advocacy organization. The term *advocacy* is used to embrace attempts to influence legislation and involvement in political campaign activities. Thus, a social welfare organization can be what a charitable organization may not be—an *action organization*.[104] (The requirement that an exempt social welfare organization serve a community[105] is ignored when the purpose of the entity is to function as an advocacy entity.)

Thus, a tax-exempt social welfare organization may draft legislation, present petitions for the purpose of having legislation introduced, and circulate speeches, reprints, and other material concerning legislation.[106] This type of organization may appear before a federal or state legislative body, or a local council, administrative board, or commission, and may encourage members of the community to contact legislative representatives in support of its programs.[107]

The IRS ruled that a tax-exempt social welfare organization can operate to inform the public on controversial subjects, "even though the organization advocates a particular viewpoint."[108] The IRS noted that "seeking of legislation germane to the organization's program is recognized by the regulations . . . as

---

[99] See Chapter 14.
[100] Rev. Rul. 69-281, 1969-1 C.B. 155. Cf. Rev. Rul. 75-494, 1975-2 C.B. 214. In general, Frank, "IRS Takes Harsh Position on Exempting Condominium and Homeowners' Association," 44 *J. Tax.* 306 (1976); Snowling. "Federal Taxation of Homeowners' Associations," 28 *Tax Law.* 117 (1974).
[101] Rev. Rul. 80-63, *supra* note 84.
[102] IRC § 528.
[103] See § 18.13.
[104] See § 20.2.
[105] See *supra* § 2.
[106] Rev. Rul. 68-656, 1968-2 C.B. 216.
[107] Rev. Rul. 67-6, 1967-1 C.B. 135.
[108] Rev. Rul. 68-656, *supra* note 105, at 216.

permissible means of attaining social welfare purposes."[109] Offering a rationale for allowing a tax-exempt social welfare organization to engage in legislative activities, the IRS stated: "The education of the public on [controversial subjects] is deemed beneficial to the community because society benefits from an informed citizenry."[110] Likewise, the IRS extended exempt status as a social welfare organization to an organization formed to educate the public on the subject of abortions, promote the rights of the unborn, and support legislative and constitutional changes to restrict women's access to abortions, recognizing that the organization "advocates objectives that are controversial."[111]

Similarly, an organization that engaged in attempts to influence legislation intended to benefit animals, animal owners, persons interested in the welfare of animals, and the community at large was considered a tax-exempt social welfare organization, although it was denied exempt status as a charitable entity (as an organization operated for the prevention of cruelty to animals) because it was deemed to be an action organization.[112]

Like tax-exempt charitable organizations, exempt social welfare organizations generally are forbidden from participating or intervening in any political campaign on behalf of or in opposition to any candidate for public office.[113] The IRS has traditionally been strict in applying this restriction, as illustrated by the denial of classification as an exempt social welfare organization to a group that rated candidates for public office on a nonpartisan basis and disseminated its ratings to the general public, on the theory that its rating process was intervention or participation on behalf of those candidates favorably rated and in opposition to those less favorably rated.[114]

Nor will objectivity necessarily ward off an unfavorable determination, as evidenced by the nonprofit group that selected slates of candidates for school board elections and engaged in campaigns on their behalf, and that was accordingly denied tax exemption as a charitable organization (and thus presumably as a social welfare organization) because of these political campaign activities, "even though its process of selection may have been completely objective and unbiased and was intended primarily to educate and inform the public about the candidates."[115]

The foregoing does not mean, however, that a tax-exempt social welfare organization is completely foreclosed from participation in governmental and political affairs. An organization the activities of which were primarily directed, on a nonprofit and nonpartisan basis, toward encouraging individuals in business to become more active in politics and government and toward promoting business, social, or civic action was held to qualify for exemption as a social welfare organization.[116] Likewise, a group that engaged in nonpartisan analysis, study, and re-

---

[109] *Id.* at 216–217.
[110] *Id.* at 216.
[111] Rev. Rul. 76-81, 1976-1 C.B. 156.
[112] Rev. Rul. 67-293, 1967-2 C.B. 185.
[113] Reg. § 1.501(c)(4)-1(a)(2)(ii). See Chapter 21.
[114] Rev. Rul. 67-368, 1967-2 C.B. 194.
[115] Rev. Rul. 67-71, 1967-1 C.B. 125.
[116] Rev. Rul. 60-193, 1960-1 C.B. 145.

search, made the results available to the public, and publicized the need for a code of fair campaign practices, was ruled to be an exempt educational organization.[117] Also, an organization that recruited college students for an internship program providing employment with local municipal agencies qualified as a tax-exempt educational and charitable organization.[118] Thus, an exempt social welfare organization could similarly undertake these activities.

The IRS, therefore, in determining an organization's tax-exempt status in light of the requirements for a social welfare entity, carefully adheres to the distinction between those groups that actively participate or intervene in a political campaign for or against candidates for public office and those that more passively seek to stimulate public interest in improved government, better campaign practices, and the like.

This prohibition on political campaign activities by tax-exempt social welfare organizations is not absolute, in that the requirement is that these organizations must be *primarily* engaged in activities that promote social welfare. Thus, an exempt organization primarily engaged in social welfare functions may also carry on activities (such as financial assistance and in-kind services) involving participation and intervention in political campaigns on behalf of or in opposition to candidates for nomination or election to public office.[119]

An organization that was tax-exempt as a charitable entity and lost that status as the result of excessive legislative activities may be precluded from thereafter converting to an exempt social welfare organization.[120]

§ 12.4   COMPARISON WITH CHARITABLE ORGANIZATIONS

In several ways, the tax-exempt charitable organization and the exempt social welfare organization are identical. Neither may be organized nor operated for private gain.[121] Neither may, to any appreciable degree, participate or intervene in any political campaign on behalf of or in opposition to any candidate for public office.[122] Both are liable for taxation on unrelated business income.[123] Moreover, of greatest importance, the concepts of what is charitable and what constitutes social welfare can be very much alike. Thus, the same organization may simultaneously qualify under both categories of tax exemption.[124]

As noted,[125] the promotion of social welfare is one of the definitions of *chari-*

---

[117] Rev. Rul. 66-258, 1966-2 C.B. 213.

[118] Rev. Rul. 70-584, 1970-2 C.B. 114.

[119] Rev. Rul. 81-95, 1981-1 C.B. 332. These political campaign activities may, however, cause the organization to be subject to the tax imposed by IRC § 527(f) on the expenditures for political activities that are within the meaning of IRC § 527(e)(2) (see § 17.3(b)).

[120] IRC § 504. See § 20.7.

[121] Rev. Rul. 69-385, 1969-2 C.B. 123; Amalgamated Hous. Corp. v. Comm'r, 37 B.T.A. 817 (1938), *aff'd*, 108 F.2d 1010 (2d Cir. 1940).

[122] See § 21.4.

[123] See Part Five.

[124] E.g., Rev. Rul. 74-361, 1974-2 C.B. 159. In general, Reg. § 1.501(c)(4)-1(a)(2)(i).

[125] See § 6.6.

table activity for purposes of tax exemption.[126] Thus, a variety of activities and programs may be characterized as tax-exempt functions for purposes of either charitable entities or social welfare entities. For example, the following charitable efforts have been treated as promoting social welfare: furnishing of housing to low-income groups,[127] relieving unemployment by area development,[128] and rehabilitating the elderly unemployed.[129]

The principal distinction, as regards its federal tax status, between a charitable and social welfare organization is that the former is prohibited from "carrying on propaganda, or otherwise attempting to influence legislation" as a "substantial part" of its activities.[130] Conversely, a social welfare organization, while not so circumscribed as to permissible legislative activities,[131] cannot attract charitable contributions that are deductible for income, gift, and estate tax purposes. Federal tax law provides, however, that a *charitable contribution* includes a gift to a "state, a possession of the United States, or any political subdivision of the foregoing, or the United States or the District of Columbia, but only if the contribution or gift is made for exclusively public purposes."[132] Thus, contributions to a social welfare organization that was organized to build a stadium and lease it to a school district, which would eventually get title, were ruled deductible as charitable contributions;[133] but deductible charitable contributions in this context are infrequent.

Thus, the basic trade-off between these two types of tax-exempt organizations is a greater scope of permissible legislative activities as opposed to deductible contributions as a source of revenue.

The basic operational difference between tax-exempt charitable and social welfare organizations, then, is embodied in the regulations accompanying both sections by the concept of the *action organization*. An exempt charitable organization must not have any of the characteristics of an action organization,[134] while an exempt social welfare organization may be a certain type of action organization.[135] A social welfare organization that is not exempt from taxation as a charitable organization may qualify as an exempt social welfare entity even though it is an action organization because of its legislative activities.[136] Stated another way, a social welfare organization may qualify for tax exemption as a charitable organization, as long as it is not deemed an action organization.[137]

---

[126] Reg. § 1.501(c)(3)-1(d)(2).

[127] Rev. Rul. 55-439, 1955-2 C.B. 257; Garden Homes Co. v. Comm'r, 64 F.2d 593 (7th Cir. 1932).

[128] Rev. Rul. 64-187, 1964-1 (Part 1) C.B. 187.

[129] Rev. Rul. 57-297, 1957-2 C.B. 307.

[130] See § 20.7.

[131] Tax-exempt social welfare organizations that engage in lobbying activities are, however, ineligible for the receipt of federal funds by means of a grant, contract, loan, award, or the like (Lobbying Disclosure Act of 1995 (2 U.S.C. 1601) § 1611).

[132] IRC § 170(c)(1).

[133] Rev. Rul. 57-493, 1957-2 C.B. 314.

[134] Reg. § 1.501(c)(3)-1(c)(3).

[135] Reg. § 1.501(c)(4)-1(a)(2)(ii).

[136] *Id.*

[137] Reg. § 1.501(c)(4)-1(a)(2)(i).

Action organization is defined as being any one of three types of organizations.[138] In contrast to the tax-exempt charitable organization, the tax-exempt social welfare organization may be an action organization, as long as it is not the type of action organization that is substantively involved in political campaigns.[139] An exempt social welfare organization can undertake legislative activities within the general framework established by the regulations describing the two types of action organizations that may engage in activities involving legislation.[140]

---

[138] See § 4.3.
[139] Reg. §§ 1.501(c)(3)-1(c)(3)(v), 1.501(c)(4)-1(a)(2)(ii).
[140] In general, Admur, "Tax Exemption of Social Welfare Organizations," 45 *Taxes* 292 (1967).

CHAPTER THIRTEEN

Associations and Other Business Leagues

The federal tax law provides tax exemption for "[b]usiness leagues . . . not organized for profit and no part of the net earnings of which inures to the benefit of any private shareholder or individual."[1] This exemption also extends to chambers of commerce, real estate boards, boards of trade, and professional football leagues (whether or not administering a pension fund for football players).

§ 13.1 BUSINESS LEAGUES IN GENERAL

A tax-exempt business league is an association of persons having some common business interest, the purpose of which is to promote that common interest and not to engage in a regular business of a kind ordinarily carried on for profit. Its activities must be directed to the improvement of business conditions of one or more lines of business, as distinguished from the performance of particular services for individual persons. An organization whose purpose is to engage in a regular business of a kind ordinarily carried on for profit, even though the business is conducted on a cooperative basis or produces only sufficient income to be

---

[1] IRC § 501(c)(6).

self-sustaining, cannot be an exempt business league.[2] An exempt business league is not required to promote the general commercial welfare.[3]

(a) Meaning of *Business*

The term *business* is broadly construed and includes nearly any activity carried on for the production of income,[4] including the professions[5] and efforts to promote the cooperative method of service, production, and distribution.[6]

Tax exemption has been denied for lack of a sufficient common business interest in situations involving an organization of individuals engaged in different trades or professions not in competition who exchanged business information,[7] an association of motorists,[8] and an association of dog owners, most of whom were not in the business of raising dogs.[9] At a minimum, to qualify as an exempt business league, an organization must have some program directed to the improvement of business conditions; for example, the mere provision of bar and luncheon facilities is insufficient.[10] Organizations that promote the common interests of hobbyists do not qualify as business leagues, although exemption may be found within some other category of exempt organization.[11]

(b) Line-of-Business Requirement

In this context, a *line of business* is a "trade or occupation, entry into which is not restricted by a patent, trademark, or similar device which would allow private parties to restrict the right to engage in the business."[12]

The line-of-business requirement was upheld by the U.S. Supreme Court as being consistent with the intent of Congress in granting tax exemption to business leagues. The occasion for the Court's review of the pertinent regulations was a

---

[2] Reg. § 1.501(c)(6)-1; Engineers Club of San Francisco v. United States, 791 F.2d 686 (9th Cir. 1986) (where this definition was said to have been given the "imprimatur of Congress and is thus entitled to the effect of law" (at 689)); United States v. Oklahoma City Retailers Ass'n, 331 F.2d 328 (10th Cir. 1964); Retailers Credit Ass'n of Alameda County v. Comm'r, 90 F.2d 47 (9th Cir. 1937); Credit Union Ins. Corp. v. United States, 95-1 U.S.T.C. ¶ 50,286 (D. Md. 1995), aff'd, 96-2 U.S.T.C. ¶ 50,323 (4th Cir. 1996). A discussion of the legislative history of this exemption appears in National Muffler Dealers Ass'n, Inc. v. United States, 440 U.S. 472, 477–479 (1979).

[3] Rev. Rul. 59-391, 1959-2 C.B. 151; Comm'r v. Chicago Graphic Arts Fed'n, Inc., 128 F.2d 424 (7th Cir. 1942).

[4] See § 26.2.

[5] Rev. Rul. 70-641, 1970-2 C.B. 119; I.T. 3182, 1938-1 C.B. 168.

[6] Rev. Rul. 67-264, 1967-2 C.B. 196. In reliance on this ruling, the IRS concluded that an association that promotes a certain philosophy as to the conduct of business is an exempt business league (Priv. Ltr. Rul. 200223067). Indeed, on that occasion, the agency wrote that "[u]pholding the integrity of a particular industry/profession is an activity properly engaged in by" exempt business leagues.

[7] Rev. Rul. 59-391, *supra* note 3.

[8] American Automobile Ass'n v. Comm'r, 19 T.C. 1146 (1953).

[9] American Kennel Club v. Hoey, 148 F.2d 920 (2d Cir. 1945).

[10] Rev. Rul. 70-244, 1970-1 C.B. 132.

[11] Rev. Rul. 66-179, 1966-1 C.B. 144.

[12] IRS Exempt Organizations Handbook (IRM 7751) § 652(1).

case involving the tax-exempt status of a trade organization of muffler dealers that confined its membership to dealers franchised by Midas International Corporation and that had as its principal activity the bargaining with the corporation on behalf of its members. The Court held that Midas Muffler franchisees do not constitute a line of business, in that their efforts do not benefit a sufficiently broad segment of the business community, as would the efforts of the entire muffler industry.[13] Thus, concluded the Court, exemption as a business league is "not available to aid one group in competition with another within an industry."[14]

Consequently, the line-of-business rule generally requires that a tax-exempt trade group represent an entire industry.[15] Thus, in one instance, an organization was held to not be entitled to exemption as a business league because "[n]othing is done to advance the interests of the community or to improve the standards or conditions of a particular trade."[16] The courts (including the U.S. Supreme Court), however, have recognized as exempt a business league that represents all components of an industry within a geographic area.[17]

Where business groups have a narrower range of purposes and/or membership base, classification as a tax-exempt business league will not be forthcoming. For example, the IRS denied tax exemption to groups composed of businesses that market a single brand of automobile[18] or bottle one type of soft drink.[19] In these and similar cases, the IRS reasoned that groups of this nature are not designed to better conditions in an entire industrial *line* but rather are devoted to the promotion of a particular product at the expense of others in the industry.[20] That is, tax exemption as a business league is not available for organizations that endeavor to improve business conditions in only "segments" of lines of business.[21]

Thus, tax exemption was denied an association composed of the licensees of a patent on a particular product, since its activities did not benefit those who manufactured competing products of the same type as that covered by the

---

[13] National Muffler Dealers Ass'n, Inc. v. United States, *supra* note 2, *aff'g* 565 F.2d 845 (2d Cir. 1977). The Supreme Court thus rejected the contrary view of the U.S. Court of Appeals for the Seventh Circuit, which had held that an association composed solely of bottlers of a single brand of soft drink was an exempt business league (Pepsi-Cola Bottlers' Ass'n, Inc. v. United States, 369 F.2d 250 (7th Cir. 1966)).

[14] National Muffler Dealers Ass'n, Inc. v. United States, *supra* note 2 at 488. Three justices dissented from the majority view, in part because the pertinent regulation originally promulgated (in force from 1919 to 1929) embodied a position opposite to the one contained in the present regulation and they believed that was "strong evidence of the understanding of the meaning of the law at the time it was enacted" in 1913. *Id.* at 489. The Court majority deferred to the revised regulation, however, which has been the administrative law on the point since 1929 and which reflects the view of those who originally advocated tax exemption for business leagues. *Id.* at 472–484.

[15] E.g., American Plywood Ass'n v. United States, 267 F. Supp. 830 (W.D. Wash. 1967); National Leather & Shoe Finders Ass'n v. Comm'r, 9 T.C. 121 (1947).

[16] Produce Exch. Stock Clearing Ass'n v. Helvering, 71 F.2d 142, 144 (2d Cir. 1934).

[17] E.g., Comm'r v. Chicago Graphic Arts Fed'n, Inc., *supra* note 3; Crooks v. Kansas City Hay Dealers Ass'n, 37 F.2d 83 (8th Cir. 1929); Washington State Apples, Inc. v. Comm'r, 46 B.T.A. 64 (1942).

[18] Rev. Rul. 67-77, 1967-1 C.B. 138.

[19] Rev. Rul. 68-182, 1968-1 C.B. 263 (wherein the IRS announced its nonacquiescence in Pepsi-Cola Bottlers' Association, Inc. v. United States, *supra* note 13).

[20] Rev. Rul. 76-400, 1976-2 C.B. 153.

[21] Rev. Rul. 83-164, 1983-2 C.B. 95.

patent.[22] Likewise, an organization of users of a manufacturer's computers, formed to discuss computer use operational and technical problems, was ruled by the IRS to not qualify as an exempt business league, in part because the organization helped to provide a competitive advantage to the manufacturer and its customers.[23] This position of the IRS was endorsed by a federal district court, holding that a computer users' group did not qualify as an exempt business league, because it promoted a single manufacturer's computers, in that the group's "activities advance the interests of . . . [the vendor] and fail to bestow a benefit upon either an entire industry or all components of an industry within a geographic area" as the federal tax law requires.[24] By contrast, an organization formed by members of an industry that contracted with research organizations to develop new and improved uses for existing products was recognized as an exempt business league, in part because none of the organization's patents and trademarks was licensed to any member on an exclusive basis.[25] As one federal court of appeals observed, the line-of-business requirement is "well suited to assuring that an organization's efforts do indeed benefit a sufficiently broad segment of the business community."[26]

Examples of activities that promote a common business interest include the development and distribution of publications of pertinence to the interests of an organization's members (such as journals and newsletters), the conduct of annual conventions and educational seminars, other means by which information pertaining to the field is disseminated, presentation of information and opinions to government agencies,[27] promotion of improved business standards and methods and uniform business practices,[28] advocacy of the open shop principle,[29] attempts to influence legislation germane to the members' common business interests,[30] other annual events (such as sports tournaments, forums, and holiday parties),[31] and the holding of luncheon meetings for the purpose of discussing the problems of a particular industry.[32] In other instances, the IRS ruled that an organization formed to promote the acceptance of women in business and the professions was a tax-exempt business league because it attempted to seek to improve conditions in one or more lines of business,[33] as was an organization formed to attract conventions to a city for the benefit of the economic interest of business throughout the community.[34]

---

[22] Rev. Rul. 58-294, 1958-1 C.B. 244.

[23] Rev. Rul. 83-164, *supra* note 21.

[24] National Prime Users Group, Inc. v. United States, 667 F. Supp. 250 (D. Md. 1987)). Also Guide Int'l Corp. v. United States, 948 F.2d 360 (7th Cir. 1991).

[25] Rev. Rul. 69-632, 1969-2 C.B. 120.

[26] National Muffler Dealers Ass'n v. United States, *supra* note 13, at 565 F.2d 847.

[27] American Refractories Inst. v. Comm'r, 6 T.C.M. 1302 (1947); Atlanta Master Printers Club v. Comm'r, 1 T.C.M. 107 (1942).

[28] Rev. Rul. 68-657, 1968-2 C.B. 218.

[29] Associated Indus. of Cleveland v. Comm'r, 7 T.C. 1449 (1946).

[30] Rev. Rul. 61-177, 1961-2 C.B. 117, *mod'g* Rev. Rul. 54-442, 1954-2 C.B. 131.

[31] Priv. Ltr. Rul. 9550001.

[32] Rev. Rul. 67-295, 1967-2 C.B. 197.

[33] Rev. Rul. 76-400, *supra* note 20.

[34] Rev. Rul. 76-207, 1976-1 C.B. 158.

Even though it is essential to qualification as a tax-exempt business league that the organization be an association of persons having a common business interest, the persons do not necessarily have to be engaged in a business at the time they are acting in association. As an illustration, an organization of persons studying for a degree in a particular profession can qualify as an exempt business league if the purpose of the organization is to promote their common interests as future members of that profession and if it otherwise qualifies.[35] Also, an exempt association will not jeopardize its business league status if it characterizes as nonvoting "associate members" persons who are merely sponsors of the organization and lack a common business interest with the regular members.[36]

The typical business league has as its membership—in conformity with the requirement that it be an "association of persons"—business corporations or individuals. A tax-exempt business league may, however, have exempt organizations as its membership, even where there are only two entities as members. For example, the IRS held that a trust created by a labor union and a business league qualified as an exempt business league.[37] Likewise, a trust created pursuant to collective bargaining agreements between a labor union and several business leagues was ruled to be exempt as a business league.[38]

The IRS considered the tax-exempt status of a membership organization, the primary activity of which was the provision of the required certification of origin ("clearing document" for shipment) to American suppliers of goods and services to another country. The organization was the only entity in the United States authorized to certify commercial and legal documents related to transactions between the two countries. The certification fees provided more than 95 percent of the organization's total revenue. The IRS observed that an exempt business league must be "financed, at least in part, through membership dues." An organization "which is not in fact membership supported lacks the most significant characteristics common to" exempt business leagues. An organization that has "demonstrated a pattern of nonmembership support must necessarily fail a critical test of exemption" for business leagues, the IRS said. In this case, however, because the certification fees were received for an activity that contributed importantly to the accomplishment of the organization's exempt functions, this income had a "substantial causal relationship to the achievement of exempt purposes," and the IRS ruled that the income is "therefore considered to be membership support."[39]

---

[35] Rev. Rul. 77-112, 1977-1 C.B. 149.

[36] In one case, the requirement that there be an "association of persons" was deemed met solely because the organization was created by three incorporators and had a board of directors (North Carolina Ass'n of Ins. Agents, Inc. v. United States, 83-2 U.S.T.C. ¶ 9445 (E.D.N.C. 1983)). However, the government secured a reversal of this opinion (739 F.2d 949 (4th Cir. 1984)).

[37] Rev. Rul. 70-31, 1970-1 C.B. 130.

[38] Rev. Rul. 82-138, 1982-2 C.B. 106.

[39] Priv. Ltr. Rul. 200020056.

(c) Business Leagues in General

Varieties of tax-exempt business leagues abound, in part because the term lacks a well-defined meaning or common usage outside the parameters of the federal tax law rules concerning business leagues.[40]

For example, an organization created under state statute to pay claims against (that is, act as guarantor for) insolvent insurance companies, where the companies were mandatory members of the organization, was ruled to be a tax-exempt business league, with the IRS holding that the organization is serving a "quasi-public function imposed by law which is directed at relieving a common cause of hardship and distress of broad public concern in the field of insurance protection."[41] Likewise, an association of insurance companies created pursuant to a state's no-fault insurance statute to provide personal injury protection for residents of the state who sustain injury and are not covered by any insurance was ruled to qualify as an exempt business league because its activities "promote the common business interests of its members by fulfilling an obligation that the state has imposed upon the insurance industry as a prerequisite for doing business within the state and by enhancing the image of the industry."[42] Exempt business league status was accorded an organization of representatives of diversified businesses that own or lease one or more digital computers produced by various manufacturers; the IRS found that the "primary objective of the organization is to provide a forum for the exchange of information which will lead to the more efficient utilization of computers by its members and other interested users, and thus improve the overall efficiency of the business operations of each."[43] Similarly, an organization that operated a "plan room" and published a news bulletin that contained information about plans available at the plan room, bid results and activities of concern to persons in the industry, was ruled to be an exempt business league.[44]

Other tax-exempt business leagues include an organization composed of members of a particular industry formed to develop new and improved uses for existing products of the industry,[45] an organization composed of advertising agencies that verified the advertising claims of publications selling advertising space and made reports available to members of the advertising industry generally,[46] an organization that collected contributions to further an industry's programs,[47] an organization that promoted convention and tourism business in a particular town,[48] an organization that effected improvement in public awareness of thoroughbred racing,[49] an organization that made recommendations con-

---

[40] Helvering v. Reynolds Co., 306 U.S. 110, 114 (1939).
[41] Rev. Rul. 73-452, 1973-2 C.B. 183.
[42] Rev. Rul. 76-410, 1976-2 C.B. 155.
[43] Rev. Rul. 74-147, 1974-1 C.B. 136. Cf. Rev. Rul. 83-164, *supra* note 21; Rev. Rul. 74-116, 1974-1 C.B. 127.
[44] Rev. Rul. 72-211, 1972-1 C.B. 150, clarifying Rev. Rul. 56-65, 1956-1 C.B. 199. Also Builder's Exch. of Tex., Inc. v. Comm'r, 31 T.C.M. 844 (1972).
[45] Rev. Rul. 69-632, *supra* note 25.
[46] Rev. Rul. 69-387, 1969-2 C.B. 124.
[47] Priv. Ltr. Rul. 8422170.
[48] Priv. Ltr. Rul. 9032005.
[49] Priv. Ltr. Rul. 9050002.

cerning the establishment and revision of regulations and rates for its members who were regulated by the Interstate Commerce Commission,[50] an organization of packaging manufacturers with an industry advertising program,[51] an organization that provided its member small loan companies with information concerning borrowers,[52] an organization of individuals who advanced their spouses' profession,[53] and an organization formed to improve the business conditions of financial institutions by offering rewards for information leading to the arrest and conviction of individuals committing crimes against its members.[54] Also, an organization, the members of which were involved in the commercial fishing industry in a state, that published a monthly newspaper of commercial fishing technical information and news, and that derived its income primarily from membership dues and sales of advertising, may qualify as an exempt business league.[55] A merger, consolidation, or other reorganization of business leagues can result in one or more exempt business leagues.[56]

The IRS recognized that programs of testing and certification of an industry's products is a tax-exempt function for a business league.[57] In a speech in 1973, the Commissioner of Internal Revenue, analogizing to organizations that accredit television repairers and automobile mechanics, commented that organizations that accredit physicians in their fields of specialization will be treated as exempt business leagues and not as tax-exempt charitable organizations.[58] Thus, in the view of the IRS, enhancement of the medical profession, not delivery of adequate health care, is the primary objective of these organizations. The Commissioner's observations are memorialized in a ruling published in 1973.[59]

Similarly, the IRS ruled that an organization formed by physicians of a state medical society to operate peer review boards for the purpose of establishing and maintaining standards for quality, quantity, and reasonableness of the costs of medical services qualified as a tax-exempt business league.[60] The IRS recognized that these organizations are being established in response to concern over the rising costs of medical care, in an effort to curb these expenses by reviewing medical procedures and utilization of medical facilities. Nonetheless, ruled the IRS, "[al]though this activity may result in a measurable public benefit, its primary objective is to maintain the professional standards, prestige, and independence of the organized medical profession and thereby further the common business interest of the organization's members."[61] The promotion of health

---

[50] Rev. Rul. 67-393, 1967-2 C.B. 200.
[51] Rev. Rul. 67-344, 1967-2 C.B. 199.
[52] Rev. Rul. 67-394, 1967-2 C.B. 201.
[53] Rev. Rul. 67-343, 1967-2 C.B. 198.
[54] Rev. Rul. 69-634, 1969-2 C.B. 124.
[55] Rev. Rul. 75-287, 1975-2 C.B. 211.
[56] E.g., Priv. Ltr. Rul. 9003045.
[57] Rev. Rul. 70-187, 1970-1 C.B. 131; Rev. Rul. 81-127, 1981-1 C.B. 357.
[58] Remarks of then-Commissioner of Internal Revenue Donald C. Alexander, August 29, 1973, before the American Society of Association Executives (IR-1326).
[59] Rev. Rul. 73-567, 1973-2 C.B. 178. Cf. Kentucky Bar Found., Inc. v. Comm'r, 78 T.C. 921 (1982).
[60] Rev. Rul. 74-553, 1974-2 C.B. 168.
[61] Id. at 169.

is a charitable purpose,[62] however, and some courts are of the view that improvements in the delivery of health care is a charitable function, even if the profession is somewhat benefited.[63]

As discussed below,[64] the performance of particular services for individuals can preclude an otherwise qualified business league from tax-exempt status. An activity may be found to benefit a common business interest even though services are being rendered to members, however, as long as a member's benefit is incidental. Examples of this include organizations that conduct negotiations for members and nonmembers in an industry,[65] mediate and settle disputes affecting an industry,[66] operate a bid registry,[67] investigate criminal aspects of claims against members,[68] subsidize litigation,[69] operate an insurance rating bureau,[70] negotiate the sale of broadcast rights,[71] conduct fire patrols and salvage operations for insurance companies,[72] provide for equitable distribution of high-risk insurance policies among member insurance companies,[73] and publish a magazine containing information of interest to an entire industry.[74]

(d) Ban on For-Profit Activities

The requirement that a tax-exempt business league not engage in business for profit had more significance before enactment of the unrelated business income rules in 1950.[75] Before that date, business activities could preclude tax exemption, as occurred with respect to an organization selling credit information and collection services,[76] operating an employment agency,[77] and testing the safety of electrical products.[78] Today, tax exemption will not be threatened where a business is not an organization's principal activity, such as a chamber of commerce operating a credit bureau as one of 15 departments,[79] a chamber of commerce developing an industrial park to attract new industry to the community,[80] and an association of

---

[62] See § 6.2.

[63] San Antonio District Dental Soc'y v. United States, 340 F. Supp. 11 (W.D. Tex. 1972); Huron Clinic Found. v. United States, 212 F. Supp. 847 (S.D. 1962).

[64] See *infra* § 4.

[65] American Fishermen's Tuna Boat Ass'n v. Rogan, 51 F. Supp. 933 (S.D. Cal. 1943).

[66] Rev. Rul. 65-164, 1965-1 C.B. 238.

[67] Rev. Rul. 66-223, 1966-2 C.B. 224.

[68] Rev. Rul. 66-260, 1966-2 C.B. 225.

[69] Rev. Rul. 67-175, 1967-1 C.B. 139.

[70] Oregon Casualty Ass'n v. Comm'r, 37 B.T.A. 340 (1938).

[71] Priv. Ltr. Rul. 7922001.

[72] Minneapolis Bd. of Fire Underwriters v. Comm'r, 38 B.T.A. 1532 (1938).

[73] Rev. Rul. 71-155, 1971-1 C.B. 152.

[74] National Leather & Shoe Finders Ass'n v. Comm'r, *supra* note 15.

[75] See Part Five.

[76] Credit Bur. of Greater N.Y. Inc. v. Comm'r, 162 F.2d 7 (2d Cir. 1947), *aff'g* 5 T.C.M. 826 (1947).

[77] American Ass'n of Eng'rs Employment, Inc. v. Comm'r, 11 T.C.M. 207 (1952), *aff'd*, 204 F.2d 19 (7th Cir. 1953).

[78] Underwriters Laboratories, Inc. v. Comm'r, 135 F.2d 371 (7th Cir. 1943), *cert. den.*, 320 U.S. 756 (1943). Cf. § 10.3.

[79] Milwaukee Ass'n of Commerce v. United States, 72 F. Supp. 310 (E.D. Wis. 1947).

[80] Rev. Rul. 70-81, 1970-1 C.B. 131, *amp.*, Rev. Rul. 81-138, 1981-1 C.B. 358.

insurance agents collecting (as an insubstantial activity) commissions on municipal insurance placed through its members.[81] Even where its principal purpose is not the operation of a business, however, an association may nonetheless be subject to liability for the unrelated business income tax, notwithstanding the fact that the business is conducted with its members.[82] It is the view of the Chief Counsel of the IRS that a business league must have meaningful support in the form of members' dues and revenue from related activities, and cannot—to be tax-exempt—receive its principal support from unrelated business activities.[83]

§ 13.2 BUSINESS AND TRADE ASSOCIATIONS

The most common form of tax-exempt business league is the business or trade association. This type of association has as its membership companies or other persons engaged in the same line of business or operating within the same industry. Its purpose is to promote and improve the conditions of the business or industry. One non–tax law definition of *business or trade association* characterized it as "a nonprofit, cooperative, voluntarily-joined, organization of business competitors designed to assist its members and its industry in dealing with mutual business problems."[84]

The criteria in the tax regulations for the tax-exempt business or trade association are generally followed by the courts, but there has been disagreement, such as over the scope of the proscription in the regulations that an exempt association's activities should not be the "performance of particular services for individual persons."[85] In one case, however, a court did not deny an association exemption even though it maintained laboratories for quality control testing and promoted the association's trademark through television advertising, because these activities were incidental.[86] Nonetheless, the IRS ruled that an association of manufacturers, the principal activity of which was the promotion of its members' products under its required trademark, did not qualify for exemption.[87] Further, the regulations maintain that an exempt association's activities must be directed to the "improvement of business conditions of one or more lines of business" and not just for a limited group (such as a single brand or product)[88] within a line of business. Nonetheless, an association of bottlers of a particular brand of soft drink was held to be an exempt trade association (although this holding is now inconsistent with the law).[89]

An organization may fail to qualify as a tax-exempt business league because

[81] King County Ins. Ass'n v. Comm'r, 37 B.T.A. 288 (1938).
[82] Rev. Rul. 66-151, 1966-1 C.B. 152.
[83] E.g., Gen. Couns. Mem. 39108. The IRS has ruled, however, that an organization can qualify as a tax-exempt business league, notwithstanding the fact that the organization does not have a membership.
[84] Judkins, *National Associations of the United States*, vii (1949).
[85] See *infra* § 4.
[86] American Plywood Ass'n v. United States, *supra* note 15. Cf. Rev. Rul. 56-65, *supra* note 44.
[87] Rev. Rul. 70-80, 1970-1 C.B. 130.
[88] Rev. Rul. 68-182, 1968-1 C.B. 263; Rev. Rul. 58-294, *supra* note 22.
[89] Pepsi-Cola Bottlers' Ass'n, Inc. v. United States, *supra* note 13.

it disseminates advertising carrying the name of its members. Illustrations of this include an association created to attract tourism to a particular area, the principal activity of which was publication of a yearbook consisting primarily of paid advertisements by its members[90] and an association that published catalogs that listed only products manufactured by the members.[91] Conversely, if the organization advertises the products and services of an entire industry, exemption will not be denied,[92] even if the advertising incidentally results in the performance of services by occasionally mentioning the names of its members.[93] Often, however, the advertising function is treated as an unrelated business,[94] so that the exempt status of the association is not affected.

Other areas of controversy as respects the tax status of trade associations include the requisite availability of association research,[95] operation of trade shows,[96] provision of credit information,[97] and provision of group insurance for the employees of employer-members.[98]

§ 13.3 PROFESSIONAL ORGANIZATIONS

Some nonprofit membership organizations operate for the benefit of a profession, rather than a trade or business. These entities are often known as *professional societies*. This can cause tax exemption classification controversies, in that the likelihood is greater than these entities engage in at least some charitable, educational, scientific, or like activities.

In many instances, the rules concerning business leagues serve as the basis of tax exemption for professional societies. For example, the IRS presumes that

---

[90] Rev. Rul. 65-14, 1965-1 C.B. 236.

[91] Automotive Elec. Ass'n v. Comm'r, 168 F.2d 366 (6th Cir. 1948), *aff'g* 8 T.C. 894 (1947). Also Rev. Rul. 56-84, 1956-1 C.B. 201.

[92] Washington State Apples, Inc. v. Comm'r, *supra* note 17.

[93] Rev. Rul. 55-444, 1955-2 C.B. 258.

[94] E.g., Priv. Ltr. Rul. 9440001.

[95] Rev. Rul. 69-106, 1969-1 C.B. 153; Glass Container Indus. Research Corp. v. United States, 70-1 U.S.T.C. ¶ 9214 (W.D. Pa. 1970).

[96] E.g., Rev. Rul. 58-224, 1958-1 C.B. 242; Rev. Rul. 67-219, 1967-2 C.B. 212; Orange County Builders Ass'n, Inc. v. United States, 65-2 U.S.T.C. ¶ 9679 (S.D. Cal. 1956); Texas Mobile Home Ass'n v. Comm'r, 324 F.2d 691 (5th Cir. 1963); American Inst. of Interior Designers v. United States, 204 F. Supp. 201 (N.D. Cal. 1962); American Woodworking Mach. & Equip. Show, v. United States, 249 F. Supp. 392 (M.D.N.C. 1966); Men's & Boys' Apparel Club of Fla. v. United States, 64-2 U.S.T.C. ¶ 9840 (Ct. Cl. 1964); National Ass'n of Display Indus. v. United States, 64-1 U.S.T.C. ¶ 9285 (S.D.N.Y. 1964).

[97] E.g., Rev. Rul. 70-591, 1970-2 C.B. 118; Rev. Rul. 68-265, 1968-1 C.B. 265; Oklahoma City Retailers Ass'n v. United States, 331 F.2d 328 (10th Cir. 1964).

[98] Rev. Rul. 70-95, 1970-1 C.B. 137; Rev. Rul. 67-176, 1967-1 C.B. 140; Rev. Rul. 66-151, *supra* note 82; Oklahoma Cattlemen's Ass'n v. United States, 310 F. Supp. 320 (W.D. Okla. 1969). Also United States v. Omaha Live Stock Traders Exch., 366 F.2d 749 (8th Cir. 1966); Retail Credit Ass'n of Minneapolis v. United States, 30 F. Supp. 855 (D. Minn. 1938); Little Rock Grain Exch. v. Thompson, 30 F. Supp. 571 (E.D. Ark. 1950); Leaf Tobacco Exporters Ass'n, Inc. v. Comm'r, 10 T.C.M. 706 (1951), *appeal dis.* (4th Cir. 1952); National Retail Credit Ass'n v. Comm'r, 45 B.T.A. 1160 (1941); Waynesboro Mfg. Ass'n v. Comm'r, 1 B.T.A. 911 (1925); Priv. Ltr. Rul. 8623006.

bar associations, medical societies, and similar organizations are business leagues, even though some of these organizations' activities are clearly charitable and educational.[99] That is, the IRS applies the primary purpose test[100] and usually concludes that these organizations' activities are directed primarily at the promotion of the particular profession and that they are operated to further the common business purpose of their members.

A tax-exempt medical society may engage in the following charitable and educational activities: meetings where technical papers are presented, maintenance of a library, publication of a journal, provision of lecturers and counseling services at medical schools, and the support of public health programs. This type of a society may also undertake the following activities: provision of a patient referral service, maintenance of a grievance committee, meetings concerned with the promotion and protection of the practice of medicine, operation of a legislative committee, and conduct of a public relations program. Where the latter category of activities is primary, charitable status is denied, and exempt status as a business league is accorded.[101] A bar association may likewise engage in charitable and educational activities, such as law institutes, law review journal, moot court program, speakers' panels, and legal assistance to indigents. The bar association, however, will be an exempt business league where the following activities predominate: preparation of studies on the economics of law office administration, programs directed toward making the practice of law more profitable, enforcement of standards of conduct, and sponsorship of social events (for example, holiday parties, golf tournaments, and travel plans).[102] Some court opinions have implied that bar associations may qualify as exempt charitable organizations.[103] In fact, one court decision held that the maintenance of "public confidence in the legal system" is a "goal of unquestionable importance in a civil and complex society" and that activities such as the operation of a client security fund, an inquiry tribunal, a fee arbitration plan, and a lawyer referral service are "devoted to that goal through various means of improving the administration of justice."[104]

If a professional society's dominant activities are noncommercial research, maintenance of a library, publication of a journal, and the like, it will qualify for tax exemption as being charitable, educational, or perhaps scientific, as long as no substantial activities are directed at or are concerned with the protection or promotion of the professional practice or business interests of any of the professions represented by its membership.[105] A professional society, then, may fail to qualify as a tax-exempt charitable organization and will be deemed a tax-exempt busi-

---

[99] See Chapters 6, 7.

[100] See § 4.4.

[101] Rev. Rul. 71-504, 1971-2 C.B. 231. Also Rev. Rul. 77-232, 1977-2 C.B. 71.

[102] Rev. Rul. 71-505, 1971-2 C.B. 232. Also Hammerstein v. Kelly, 349 F.2d 928 (8th Cir. 1965); Colonial Trust Co. v. Comm'r, 19 B.T.A. 174 (1930).

[103] St. Louis Union Trust Co. v. United States, 374 F.2d 427 (8th Cir. 1967); Dulles v. Johnson, 273 F.2d 362 (2d Cir. 1959); Rhode Island Hosp. Trust Co. v. United States, 159 F. Supp. 204 (D.R.I. 1958).

[104] Kentucky Bar Found., Inc. v. Comm'r, *supra* note 59, at 930. Also Fraternal Med. Specialist Serv., Inc. v. Comm'r, 59 T.C.M. 289 (1984).

[105] Rev. Rul. 71-506, 1971-2 C.B. 233.

ness league where it, other than incidentally, engages in public relations activities, polices a profession, seeks to improve the condition of its members, seeks to develop good will or fellowship among its members, engages in social and recreational activities, maintains facilities (for example, restaurant, lounge, or club house) for its members, or engages in legislative or political campaign activities.[106] In one instance, an organization of individuals from various public health and welfare professions (seemingly charitable undertakings) was ruled to be an exempt business league, for the reasons that its "activities promote the business and professional interests of the members by increasing the effectiveness of the interaction among the various professions, by developing greater efficiency in the professions, and by solving problems common to the professions."[107] It is the position of the IRS that activities such as the operation of certification programs and the maintenance of codes of ethics are suitable programs for professional organizations that are business leagues but not for professional organizations that are charitable, educational, and/or scientific organizations, because these programs are designed and operated to achieve professional standing for the line of business represented and to enhance the respectability of those who are certified.[108]

§ 13.4 NONQUALIFYING BUSINESS LEAGUES

There are several bases on which tax-exempt status may be denied to an otherwise qualifying business league.

(a) For-Profit Business Activities

One is the prohibition on business activities for profit. Thus, an organization that issued shares of stock carrying the right to dividends was denied exemption as a business league.[109] Also, an association of insurance companies that provided

---

[106] As to the latter, see Chapters 20, 21.

[107] Rev. Rul. 70-641, *supra* note 5, at 119. Also I.T. 3182, *supra* note 5.

[108] Gen. Couns. Mem. 39721. There can be interplay between the rules describing a qualifying business league and those defining a tax-exempt social club (see Chapter 14). In one instance, the IRS attempted to classify an engineering society as a social club, claiming that it was regularly engaged in substantial restaurant, beverage, and other social operations. This approach was rejected in litigation, however, inasmuchas the court concluded that the primary purpose of the organization was the promotion of the profession of engineering (through the conduct of professional education, training, and information dissemination activities) with the food, beverage, and social activities deemed either incidental or related to the professional activities (The Engineers Club of San Francisco v. United States, 609 F. Supp. 519 (N.D. Cal. 1985)). Also United States v. Engineers Club of San Francisco, 325 F.2d 204 (9th Cir. 1963).) Nonetheless, on appeal, the government prevailed, albeit on another argument, namely, that the society could not qualify as a tax-exempt business league because the food and beverage service constituted a service performed for individual persons rather than the engineering profession as a whole (Engineers Club of San Francisco v. United States, *supra* note 2). For a discussion of this principle, see *infra* § 4.

[109] Northwestern Jobbers Credit Bur. v. Comm'r, 37 F.2d 880 (8th Cir. 1930). Cf. Crooks v. Kansas City Hay Dealers Ass'n, 37 F.2d 83 (8th Cir. 1929).

medical malpractice insurance to doctors, nurses, hospitals, and other health care providers in a particular state, where that type of insurance was not available from for-profit insurers in the state, was denied classification as an exempt business league on the ground that the provision of medical malpractice insurance is a business of a kind ordinarily carried on for profit.[110] Similarly, an association of insurance companies that accepted for reinsurance high-risk customers who would ordinarily be turned down by the member companies was ruled to not qualify as an exempt business league, because reinsurance is a business ordinarily carried on by commercial insurance companies for a profit.[111]

(b) Performance of Particular Services

The chief basis on which tax exemption as a business league may be denied is a finding that the organization is performing particular services for its members, as distinguished from the improvement of business conditions in the particular business or industry.[112] Thus, the IRS denied tax-exempt business league status to a telephone answering service for tow truck operators, on the ground that it provided its members with economy and convenience in the conduct of their individual businesses.[113] A nurses' registry was denied categorization as a exempt business league on a finding that it was no more than an employment service for the benefit of its members.[114] Similarly, an independent practice association was ruled to not qualify as an exempt business league, with the IRS portraying it as akin to a billing and collection service that provided an economy or convenience to its members relating to the operation of their private medical practices.[115] By contrast, a lawyer referral service was ruled to be an exempt business league, since (because of the manner in which it was operated) it was more than a mere business referral service and served to improve the image and functioning of the legal profession in general.[116]

Under limited circumstances, a tax-exempt business league can operate a "warranty or guarantee" program, which is a program designed to assure purchasers of a product that it meets acceptable standards and to provide insurance and arbitration services, without deprivation of its exempt status on the ground that it is providing services to its membership. These circumstances are as follows: The program must primarily benefit the industry in its entirety rather than the private interests of its members, the advertisements do not have the purpose of giving members a competitive edge over nonmembers (where the membership does not encompass an industry), and the activity is not ordinarily carried on for

---

[110] Rev. Rul. 81-174, 1981-1 C.B. 335.

[111] Rev. Rul. 81-175, 1981-1 C.B. 337.

[112] Southern Hardware Traffic Ass'n v. United States, 283 F. Supp. 1013 (W.D. Tenn. 1968), aff'd, 411 F.2d 563 (6th Cir. 1969).

[113] Rev. Rul. 74-308, 1974-2 C.B. 168.

[114] Rev. Rul. 61-170, 1961-2 C.B. 112. Also Rev. Rul. 71-175, 1971-1 C.B. 153 (concerning a telephone-answering service for physicians). Cf. Rev. Rul. 55-656, 1955-2 C.B. 262.

[115] Rev. Rul. 86-98, 1986-2 C.B. 74.

[116] Rev. Rul. 80-287, 1980-2 C.B. 185. Also Kentucky Bar Found., Inc. v. Comm'r, *supra* note 59.

profit; also, the IRS favors an enforced policy of a business league of obtaining reimbursement from the members responsible for defects.[117] The IRS, however, is likely to conclude that unwarranted private interests are being conferred on an organization's members in this setting where only a small portion of the eligible sellers participate in the program.[118]

Other organizations providing services to individual persons and denied tax exemption as business leagues include entities promoting and selling national advertising in members' publications,[119] providing insurance,[120] operating a traffic bureau,[121] appointing travel agents to sell passages on members' ships,[122] making interest-free loans to member credit unions,[123] operating commodity and stock exchanges,[124] promoting its members' writings,[125] supplying management services and supplies and equipment,[126] operating a multiple listing service,[127] conducting a trading stamp plan,[128] operating a laundry and dry cleaning plant,[129] operation of a warehouse,[130] promoting the exchange of orders by wire,[131] acting as a receiver and trustee for a fee,[132] appraising properties,[133] performing services in connection with bond investments,[134] estimating quantities of building materials for its members' projects,[135] ensuring the discharge of its members' obligations to pay taxes,[136] publishing and distributing a directory of its members to businesses likely to require the members' services,[137] administration of a welfare benefit plan pursuant to a collective bargaining agreement,[138] and maintaining a library for its members' use.[139]

In one case, a court held that an organization did not qualify as a tax-exempt business league, because it both engaged in a regular business of a kind

[117] Gen. Couns. Mem. 34608.

[118] Gen. Couns. Mem. 39105.

[119] Rev. Rul. 56-84, *supra* note 91.

[120] Rev. Rul. 74-81, 1974-1 C.B. 135.

[121] Rev. Rul. 68-264, 1968-1 C.B. 264.

[122] Rev. Rul. 74-228, 1974-1 C.B. 136.

[123] Rev. Rul. 76-38, 1976-1 C.B. 157.

[124] Reg. § 1.501(c)(6)-1. Cf. Rev. Rul. 55-715, 1955-2 C.B. 263.

[125] Rev. Rul. 57-453, 1957-2 C.B. 310.

[126] Rev. Rul. 66-338, 1966-2 C.B. 226; Indiana Retail Hardware Ass'n v. United States, 366 F.2d 998 (Ct. Cl. 1966); Apartment Operators Ass'n v. Comm'r, 136 F.2d 435 (9th Cir. 1943); Uniform Printing & Supply Co. v. Comm'r, 33 F.2d 445 (7th Cir. 1929), *cert. den.*, 280 U.S. 69 (1929).

[127] Rev. Rul. 59-234, 1959-2 C.B. 149. Also Evanston-North Shore Bd. of Realtors v. United States, 320 F.2d 375 (Ct. Cl. 1963).

[128] Rev. Rul. 65-244, 1965-2 C.B. 167.

[129] A-1 Cleaners & Dyers Co. v. Comm'r, 14 B.T.A. 1314 (1929).

[130] Growers Cold Storage Warehouse Co. v. Comm'r, 17 B.T.A. 1279 (1929).

[131] Florists' Telegraph Delivery Ass'n, Inc. v. Comm'r, 47 B.T.A. 1044 (1942).

[132] O.D. 786, 4 C.B. 269 (1921).

[133] Central Appraisal Bur. v. Comm'r, 46 B.T.A. 1281 (1942).

[134] Northwestern Mun. Ass'n, Inc. v. United States, 99 F.2d 460 (8th Cir. 1938).

[135] General Contractors Ass'n v. United States, 202 F.2d 633 (7th Cir. 1953).

[136] Rev. Rul. 66-354, 1966-2 C.B. 207.

[137] Rev. Rul. 76-409, 1976-2 C.B. 154.

[138] Gen. Couns. Mem. 39411, revoking Gen. Couns. Mem. 38458.

[139] Rev. Rul. 67-182, 1967-1 C.B. 141.

ordinarily carried on for profit and its activities were directed to the performance of particular services for individual members.[140] As respects the business activity, the court found that the organization was engaging in an insurance business to a substantial extent (measured in terms of time and finances), as its officers and employees were involved on a daily basis with record keeping, processing claims for benefits, paying claims, and performing other administrative duties in connection with the insurance activities. The court distinguished this insurance activity from that conducted by associations only on a passive basis (that is, mere sponsorship of the insurance program) and where a self-insurance program was not involved.[141] With respect to the provision of services, the court observed that the organization offered its members, in addition to the many insurance programs, an eyeglass and prescription lens replacement service, and sold its local chapters and members various supplies, charts, books, shop emblems, and association jewelry. The court concluded that the organization was undertaking activities that "serve as a convenience or economy to . . . [its] members in the operation of their businesses" and was not promoting a common business interest or otherwise conducting itself like a qualified business league.[142]

In reliance upon this case, the IRS denied tax exemption as a business league to two types of associations of insurance companies because they engaged in a business of a kind ordinarily carried on for profit and were performing particular services for their members. In one instance, an association of insurance companies in a state that provided medical malpractice insurance to health care providers where the insurance was not available from for-profit insurers in the state was held to be "performing particular services for its member companies and policyholders" because its "method of operation involves it in its member companies' insurance business, and since the organization's insurance activities serve as an economy or convenience in providing necessary protection to its policyholders engaged in providing health care."[143] The same rationale was applied to the activities of an association of insurance companies that accepted for reinsurance high-risk customers who would ordinarily be turned down by its member companies.[144] The rule remains, however, that an association of insurance companies that assigns applications for insurance to member companies that perform the actual insurance functions can qualify as an exempt business league because it does not assume the risk on the policies.[145]

Likewise, an engineering society that provided food and beverage service to its individual members was found to be providing a service for individual persons, and thus was deprived of qualification for tax-exempt status as a business league.[146]

---

[140] Associated Master Barbers & Beauticians of America, Inc. v. Comm'r, 69 T.C. 53 (1977).

[141] Oklahoma Cattlemen's Ass'n, Inc. v. United States, *supra* note 98, San Antonio District Dental Soc'y v. United States, *supra* note 63. See § 26.5(d).

[142] Associated Master Barbers & Beauticians of America, Inc. v. Comm'r, *supra* note 140, at 70.

[143] Rev. Rul. 81-174, *supra* note 110, at 336.

[144] Rev. Rul. 81-175, *supra* note 111.

[145] Rev. Rul. 71-155, *supra* note 73.

[146] Engineers Club of San Francisco v. United States, *supra* note 2.

Also, an association of life insurance companies that operated an insurance underwriting information exchange among its members was ruled to not qualify as a tax-exempt business league, despite the contention that its primary purpose was to benefit the entire life insurance industry by deterring fraud in the application process and that any benefits to its members were incidental. In the latter instance, the court agreed that the organization's activities advanced the members' interests generally but concluded that the member companies were also provided "particular services."[147] The court held that a major factor in determining whether services are *particular* is whether they are supported by fees and assessments in approximate proportion to the benefits received.

One court concluded that a nonprofit organization that itself functioned as an insurance agent was a tax-exempt business league. The organization's sole client was a state, which it served in the purchase of all insurance and bonding coverage required by the state and its agencies. The court held that the organization functioned on behalf of agents in the state in that its competent handling of the state's insurance needs enhanced the image of the insurance industry in the eyes of the public.[148] On appeal, however, it was held that the organization was not an exempt business league because it conducted a business of a kind ordinarily carried on for profit and did so more than incidentally.[149]

Despite the express prohibition as stated in the regulations, it is the position of the IRS that a tax-exempt business league will lose its exemption because it performs particular services for individual members only where the services are a principal or sole undertaking of the organization.[150] Where these services are less than a primary function of a business league, the IRS will characterize them as a business of a kind ordinarily carried on for profit and treat the business as an unrelated activity.[151] For example, the IRS concluded that an executive referral service conducted by an exempt association constituted the performance of particular services for individual persons but, because other activities were the association's primary ones, the IRS ruled that the service was an unrelated, taxable business.[152] Similarly, a compensation consulting service, while a particular service, did not jeopardize an association's exemption because it was not a primary activity of the organization.[153]

It is frequently difficult in a specific instance to distinguish between the performance of particular services and activities directed to the improvement of business conditions. Perhaps the best illustration of this difficulty is the case of organizations that maintain a "plan room." In one case, an organization of contractors operated a plan room, containing information about plans available, bid results, and activities of concern to persons in the industry. The IRS ruled that the

---

[147] MIB, Inc. v. Comm'r, 734 F.2d 71, 78–81 (1st Cir. 1984).
[148] North Carolina Ass'n of Ins. Agents, Inc. v. United States, *supra* note 36.
[149] North Carolina Ass'n of Ins. Agents, Inc. v. United States, *supra* note 36.
[150] E.g., Rev. Rul. 68-265, *supra* note 97; Rev. Rul. 68-264, *supra* note 121. In general, Retailers Credit Ass'n of Alameda County v. Comm'r, *supra* note 2.
[151] See Part Five.
[152] Priv. Ltr. Rul. 8524006.
[153] Priv. Ltr. Rul. 9128003.

organization was a tax-exempt business league because its activities improved the business conditions of the line of business served inasmuch as it made the information on construction projects freely available to the construction industry as a whole. Clearly, the existence of this type of a plan room is a significant convenience or economy for the member contractors. The IRS dismissed this aspect of the facts, however, on the ground that the information on file at the plan room generally duplicated the information already available to its members.[154]

One court, in addressing this issue, concluded that an activity of a business league was a tax-exempt function where the activity benefited its membership as a group, rather than in their individual capacities.[155] The benefit to the group occurred where the business league provided a product or service to its members for a fee, with the benefit not directly proportional to the fees (for example, seminars, legislative activities). This court wrote that "[s]ervices which render benefits according to the fee that is paid for them are taxable business activities, not tax exempt services."[156] The court added: "Therefore, the activities that serve the interests of individual . . . [members] according to what they pay produce individual benefits insufficient to fulfill the substantial relationship test, since those activities generally do not generate inherent group benefits that inure to the advantage of its members as members."[157]

Subsequently, the IRS grappled with these distinctions, differing between "an industry-wide benefit or a particular service to members." The IRS held that activities that provide an industry-wide benefit "usually possess certain characteristics," such as being an "activity for which individual members could not be expected to bear the expense and thus lends itself to cooperative effort" and the fact that the "benefits are intangible and only indirectly related to the individual business." Activities constituting particular services "can usually be characterized as either a 'means of bringing buyers and sellers together' or a 'convenience or economy' to members in conducting their business," wrote the IRS, which also cautioned that "[f]ull participation by industry components does not guarantee that the activity provides an industry-wide benefit."[158] Thus, for example, the IRS held that the operation, by an exempt association of members in the trucking industry, of an alcohol and drug testing program for members and nonmembers was a particular service (as opposed to an incident of membership), notwithstanding the fact that the prevention of alcohol and drug abuse is a "legitimate goal" of trucking companies.[159]

---

[154] Rev. Rul. 72-211, *supra* note 44. Also Rev. Rul. 56-65, *supra* note 44.

[155] Professional Ins. Agents of Mich. v. Comm'r, 726 F.2d 1097 (6th Cir. 1984).

[156] *Id.* at 1104.

[157] *Id.*

[158] Priv. Ltr. Rul. 8524006.

[159] Tech. Adv. Mem. 9550001. Business leagues should be contrasted with organizations operating to better the conditions of persons engaged in agriculture or to improve the grade of their products. These organizations may qualify for tax exemption as labor, agricultural, or horticultural organizations (see Chapter 15) rather than as business leagues. If the organization is promoting the common business interests of persons in an industry related to agricultural pursuits, however, tax-exempt business league designation would be appropriate assuming the organization otherwise qualifies (Rev. Rul. 70-31, *supra* note 37; Rev. Rul. 67-252, 1967-2 C.B. 195).

(c) Other Bases for Nonqualification

Another basis for nonqualification as a tax-exempt business league is a finding that the organization is not structured along particular business or industry lines.[160] Still another basis for failure to qualify as a business league is violation of the private inurement doctrine.[161]

§ 13.5 CHAMBERS OF COMMERCE, BOARDS OF TRADE, AND THE LIKE

A chamber of commerce or a board of trade that is tax-exempt is an organization the "common business interest" of which is the general economic welfare of a community.[162] That is, it is an organization whose efforts are directed at promoting the common economic interests of all the commercial enterprises in a given trade community. For example, the attraction of business to a particular community is an appropriate exempt activity in this context, even where it necessitates the development of an industrial park.[163] Similarly, an organization formed for the purpose of encouraging national organizations to hold their conventions in a city was recognized by the IRS as being an exempt chamber of commerce.[164]

One court observed that the terms *chamber of commerce* and *board of trade* are "nearly synonymous," although there is a "slight distinction" between their meanings. The court explained: "The former relates to all businesses in a particular geographic location, while the latter may relate to only one or more lines of business in a particular geographic location, but need not relate to all."[165]

By contrast, a business league serves only the common business interests of the members of a single line of business or of closely related lines of business

---

Other illustrations of organizations denied classification as business leagues are in Contracting Plumbers Coop. Restoration Corp. v. United States, 488 F.2d 684 (2d Cir. 1974); Credit Managers Ass'n of N. & Cent. Calif. v. United States, 148 F.2d 41 (9th Cir. 1945); Clay Sewer Pipe Ass'n v. United States, 139 F.2d 130 (3d Cir. 1943); Park West-Riverside Assocs., Inc. v. United States, 110 F.2d 1023 (2d Cir. 1940); Motor & Equip. Mfrs. Ass'n v. United States, 57-1 U.S.T.C. ¶ 9253 (D. Ill. 1957); Jockey Club v. United States, 137 F. Supp. 419 (Ct. Cl. 1956), *cert. den.*, 352 U.S. 834 (1956); Cook County Loss Adjustment Bur. v. United States, 42-2 U.S.T.C. ¶ 9638 (D. Ill. 1942); Durham Merchants Ass'n v. United States, 34 F. Supp. 71 (M.D.N.C. 1940); Louisville Credit Men's Ass'n v. United States, 39-2 U.S.T.C. ¶ 9649 (D. Ky. 1939); Louisville Credit Men's Adjustment Bur. v. United States, 6 F. Supp. 196 (W.D. Ky. 1934); Lake Petersburg Ass'n v. Comm'r, 33 T.C.M. 259 (1974); National Automobile Dealers Ass'n v. Comm'r, 2 T.C.M. 291 (1943); Adjustment Bur. of St. Louis Ass'n of Credit Men v. Comm'r, 21 B.T.A. 232 (1930); Rev. Rul. 64-108, 1964-1 C.B. (Part 1) 189; Priv. Ltr. Rul. 7902006.

[160] See *supra* § 1(b).
[161] See Chapter 19.
[162] IRC § 501(c)(6).
[163] Rev. Rul. 70-81, *supra* note 80; Rev. Rul. 81-138, *supra* note 80.
[164] Rev. Rul. 76-207, *supra* note 34.
[165] Retailers Credit Ass'n of Alameda County v. Comm'r, *supra* note 2, at 51.

within a single industry. Also, as respects a chamber of commerce or a board of trade, membership is voluntary and generally open to all business and professional persons in the community.[166]

The IRS ruled that a tenants' association (specifically, an association of shopping center merchants) did not qualify as a tax-exempt chamber of commerce or a board of trade.[167] The IRS noted that membership in the association was compulsory, imposed by the landlord owner of the shopping center, and that the requisite *community* was not being served, as the "community represented by the membership of the present organization is a closed, non-public aggregation of commercial enterprises having none of the common characteristics of a community in the usual geographical or political sense."[168] Also, the IRS invoked a private inurement rationale, holding that the organization was designed to serve the tenants' business interests in the center. (Exempt status as a business league was denied because the association was not structured along particular industry or business lines.[169]) Similarly, a board of trade was denied exemption because its principal activity was the provision of services to individuals (grain analysis laboratory services to both members and nonmembers) and because the board was supported almost entirely from the substantial profits of the laboratory.[170] Likewise, a board of trade does not encompass "organizations which provide conveniences or facilities to certain persons in connection with buying, selling, and exchanging goods."[171] By contrast, an organization regulating the sale of an agricultural commodity to assure equal treatment of producers, warehousers, and purchasers was ruled to be an exempt board of trade.[172]

A neighborhood community association may qualify for tax exemption in this context where the following criteria are satisfied: The organization has a voluntary membership, it is not concerned with tenants' matters, and the organization is operated to improve the business conditions of a community (rather than a single one-owner shopping mall).[173] This may be the case even though a majority of the association's member businesses is located in one shopping center.

Tax exemption for real estate boards, added in 1928, came into being as an overturning of a court decision. A court, in 1927, denied exemption as a

---

[166] A self-insurer guaranty trust fund was ruled tax-exempt by reason of IRC § 501(c)(6) because it was "of the same general class" as a chamber of commerce or board of trade (Georgia Self-Insurers Guar. Trust Fund v. United States, 78 A.F.T.R. 2d 6552 (N.D. Ga. 1996)).

[167] Rev. Rul. 73-411, 1973-2 C.B. 180.

[168] *Id.* at 182. Also Rev. Rul. 59-391, *supra* note 3.

[169] Rev. Rul. 64-315, 1964-2 C.B. 147, *clar. by* Rev. Rul. 73-411, *supra* note 167.

[170] Rev. Rul. 78-70, 1978-1 C.B. 159. Also Fort Worth Grain & Cotton Exch. v. Comm'r, 27 B.T.A. 983 (1933).

[171] L.O. 1123, III-1 C.B. 275 (1924).

[172] Rev. Rul. 55-715, *supra* note 124.

[173] Rev. Rul. 78-225, 1978-1 C.B. 159.

business league to a corporation organized by associations of insurance companies to provide printing services for member companies.[174] Thereafter, the statute was revised so as to specifically exempt real estate boards from taxation.

Tax exemption for professional football leagues was added in 1966.[175] This was done to forestall any claim that a football league's pension plan would be considered inurement of benefits to a private individual. The amendment was part of a larger legislative package that paved the way for a merger that created an "industry-wide" professional football league.

§ 13.6 CONSEQUENCES OF ABANDONMENT OF TAX-EXEMPT STATUS

The advantages and benefits of the classification of tax exemption are many: (1) exemption from federal income taxation (thereby sheltering from tax the receipt of dues and other items of income, except with respect to any tax on unrelated income); (2) exemption from taxation (such as income, sales, excise, franchise, and property taxes) at state and local levels; (3) access to contract and grant funds under programs where contractees and grantees must be nonprofit organizations; (4) enhancement of the public's perception and acceptance of the organization and its programs as the result of being designated tax-exempt; (5) much greater flexibility as respects accumulation of funds without adverse tax consequences; and (6) a deduction of $1,000[176] in computing taxable income.[177]

Nonetheless, a business league with a membership base may contemplate abandonment of its tax exemption, in the hope that it can achieve the equivalent of exemption by using the expenses of some related activities and those associated with investments to offset the net income from other related activities. The thought is that, by converting to a taxable organization, the entity can escape the various forms of regulation with which it is burdened as an exempt organization.

Prior to 1969, this strategem would have worked, because the income of the organization from business activities (including services to nonmembers) and in-

---

[174] Uniform Printing & Supply Co. v. Comm'r, *supra* note 126.

[175] Pub. L. No. 89-800, 80 Stat. 1515, Sess. (1966) § 6(a).

[176] See § 28.2.

[177] Classification of an organization under IRC § 501(c)(3) brings the same advantages and benefits as classification under IRC § 501(c)(6), except for the limitation on legislative activities, along with the preferences of charitable donee status and various postal privileges. See § 3.2.

vestments could have been offset by deductions in the form of expenses of providing services to members (as related activities), thereby generating little if any overall net income. This approach was tolerated by a federal court of appeals, which held that the investment income of a nonexempt water company could be offset by its losses in supplying water to its members.[178] Other courts, however, were not permitting this result.[179]

In 1969, Congress created special rules in an attempt to resolve the matter.[180] These rules are applicable with respect to any membership organization that is not exempt from taxation and is operated primarily to furnish services or goods to its members. This provision allows deductions for a tax year attributable to the furnishing of services, insurance, goods, or other items of value to the organization's membership only to the extent of income derived during the year from members or transactions with members (including income derived during the year from institutes and trade shows that are primarily for the education of members).

The intent of these rules is to preclude the result previously sanctioned by the above-referenced appellate court, that is, to prevent a taxable membership organization from offsetting its business and investment income with deductions created by the provision of related services to members. Stated another way, these rules are designed to make taxable membership organizations allocate and confine their deductions to the corresponding sources of income.[181] As a result, an organization that operated in a particular year at an overall loss may still have to pay tax if its unrelated business and investment activities produced net income. In this fashion, these rules are intended to serve as a deterrent to the abandonment of tax-exempt status by membership organizations, particularly those that are serving their members at less than cost.[182]

---

[178] Anaheim Union Water Co. v. Comm'r, 321 F.2d 253 (9th Cir. 1963), rev'g 35 T.C. 1972 (1961). Also Bear Valley Mut. Water Co. v. Riddell, 283 F. Supp. 949 (C.D. Cal. 1968), aff'd, 427 F.2d 713 (9th Cir. 1970); San Antonio Water Co. v. Riddell, 285 F. Supp. 297 (C.D. Cal. 1968), aff'd, 427 F.2d 713 (9th Cir. 1970).

[179] Adirondack League Club v. Comm'r, 55 T.C. 796 (1971), aff'd, 458 F.2d 506 (2d Cir. 1972); Five Lakes Outing Club v. United States, 468 F.2d 443 (8th Cir. 1972); Iowa State Univ. of Science & Technology v. United States, 500 F.2d 508 (Ct. Cl. 1974).

[180] IRC § 277.

[181] E.g., Concord Consumers Hous. Coop. v. Comm'r, 89 T.C. 105 (1987); Armour-Dial Men's Club, Inc. v. Comm'r, 77 T.C. 1 (1981). Also Rev. Rul. 90-36, 1990-1 C.B. 59.

[182] H. Rep. No. 91-413 (Part 1), 91st Cong., 1st Sess. 49 (1969); S. Rep. No. 91-552, 91st Cong., 1st Sess. 74 (1969).

Where, for a tax year, a taxable membership organization's deductions attributable to the furnishing of items of value to members exceed income from its members, the excess may be carried forward and used as a deduction against income from its members in the succeeding tax year.[183]

---

[183] Certain nonprofit membership organizations that receive prepaid dues income (such as the American Automobile Association) are not subject to the IRC § 277 restrictions on deductions. See IRC §§ 277(b)(2), 456(c). IRC § 277 is applicable to any nonexempt membership organization that otherwise meets the requirements of the section and was previously tax-exempt under any provision of IRC § 501(c), including IRC §§ 501(c)(3), 501(c)(4), 501(c)(5), 501(c)(6), or 501(c)(7). It has been held that IRC § 277 does not apply to cooperatives subject to IRC subchapter T (§§ 1381–1388) (Buckeye Countrymark, Inc. v. Comm'r, 103 T.C. 547 (1994); Landmark, Inc. v. United States, 25 Cl. Ct. 100 (1992)).

In general, Brittain & Crotty, "Creation of Tax-Exempt Business Leagues: For the Section 501(c)(6) 'First Timer'," 16 *Washburn L.J.* 628 (1977); Crawford, "The Money Side: Associations," XXX *Golf J.* (No. 2) 24 (1977); Denny, "Professional and Social Organizations," 25 *Tul. Tax Inst.* 2200 (1975); Combs, "Tax Implications of Association Efforts for Members," 69 *The Brief* 155 (1974); Fox & Jackson, "Trade Associations: Present and Future Problems," 26 *Tax L. Rev.* 781 (1971); Bodner, "Antitrust Restrictions on Trade Association Membership and Participation," 54 *A.B.A.J.* 37 (1968); Cooper, "The Tax Treatment of Business Grassroots Lobbying: Defining and Attaining the Public Policy Objectives," 68 *Columbia L. Rev.* 801 (1968); Orrick, "Risks Inherent in Trade Associations," *Nat'l Oil Jobber* 11 (May 1967); Note, "Tax-Exempt Business League and Its Functions," 8 *B.C. Ind. & Com. L. Rev.* 953 (1967); Note, "Taxation—Business Leagues—Noncompetitive Membership Does Not Preclude Exempt Status," 13 *Wayne L. Rev.* 611 (1967); Van De Linder, "Trade Associations: Retaining Exemption, Unrelated Business Income Problems," 24 *J. Tax.* 250 (1966); Webster, "Current Federal Tax Aspects of Association Activities," 27 *A.B.A. Sec. Antitust Law* 150 (1965); Webster, "Should a Trade Association Give Up Its Tax Exemption? The Pros and Cons," 23 *J. Tax.* 358 (1962); Teschner, "Business Leagues, Tax Exemption v. Service to Members," 37 *Taxes* 669 (1959).

As to the IRC § 277 rules, see Crimm, "Should Internal Revenue Code Section 277 Be Applied to Cooperative Housing Organizations?" 7 *Akron Tax J.* (No. 2) 87 (1990); Miller, "Condominiums and Cooperatives: IRS Tiers Section 277 Allowances So As to Minimize Reduction of Tenant-Stockholder Deductions," 18 *J. Real Estate Tax.* (No. 2) 167 (1991); Fleck, "Cooperatives—Accounting and Tax Developments: Section 277 Issues in Private Letter Rulings," 11 *J. Agric. Tax. & Law* (No. 1) 86 (1989).

CHAPTER FOURTEEN

Social Clubs

Tax-exempt social clubs have as the essential prerequisite of their exemption the provision of pleasure and recreation to their members. By contrast, many other exempt organizations find their classification as such rationalized by a concept of public service (charitable works, promotion of social welfare, economic betterment, or the like).

§ 14.1 SOCIAL CLUBS IN GENERAL

The federal tax law provides tax exemption for qualified social clubs, which are "organized for pleasure, recreation, and other nonprofitable purposes, substantially all of the activities of which are for such purposes and no part of the net earnings of which inures to the benefit of any private shareholder."[1] Generally, this tax exemption extends to social and recreation clubs that are supported primarily by membership fees, dues, and assessments.[2] An organization that otherwise qualifies as an exempt social club will not, however, be denied exemption solely because it adopts a method of raising revenue from members by means other than fees, dues, and assessments.[3]

(a) Rationale for Tax Exemption

Social clubs are tax-exempt because Congress recognized that these organizations are generally not appropriate subjects of taxation, that is, that the operation of a social club does not involve the requisite shifting of income.[4] One court summarized the rationale as follows:

[1] IRC § 501(c)(7).
[2] Reg. § 1.501(c)(7)-1(a); Maryland Country Club, Inc. v. United States, 539 F.2d 345 (4th Cir. 1976).
[3] Rev. Rul. 53-44, 1953-1 C.B. 109.
[4] See § 1.5.

> Congress has determined that in a situation where individuals have banded together to provide recreational facilities on a mutual basis, it would be conceptually erroneous to impose a tax on the organization as a separate entity. The funds exempted are received only from the members and any "profit" which results from overcharging for the use of the facilities still belongs to the same members. No income of the sort usually taxed has been generated; the money has simply been shifted from one pocket to another, both within the same pair of pants.[5]

The Department of the Treasury acknowledged the legitimacy of the tax exemption for social clubs for essentially the same reason:

> [T]he tax exemption for social clubs is designed to allow individuals to join together to provide recreational or social facilities on a mutual basis, without further tax consequences . . . [where] the sources of income of the organization are limited to receipts from the membership . . . the individual is in substantially the same position as if he had spent his income on pleasure or recreation without the intervening separate organization.[6]

This theme was echoed in the legislative history accompanying the extension, in 1969, of the tax on unrelated business income to social clubs.[7] Thus, one committee report explained:

> Since the tax exemption for social clubs and other groups is designed to allow individuals to join together to provide recreational or social facilities or other benefits on a mutual basis, without tax consequences, the tax exemption operates properly only when the sources of income of the organization are limited to receipts from the membership. Under such circumstances, the individual is in substantially the same position as if he had spent his income on pleasure or recreation (or other benefits) without the intervening separate organization. However, where the organization receives income from sources outside the membership, such as income from investments . . . upon which no tax is paid, the membership receives a benefit not contemplated by the exemption in that untaxed dollars can be used by the organization to provide pleasure or recreation (or other benefits) to its membership . . . In such a case, the exemption is no longer simply allowing individuals to join together for recreation or pleasure without tax consequences. Rather, it is bestowing a substantial additional advantage to the members of the club by allowing tax-free dollars to be used for their personal recreational or pleasure purposes. The extension of the exemption to such investment income is, therefore, a distortion of its purpose.[8]

Reflecting on this rationale, the U.S. Supreme Court concluded that the federal tax exemption for social clubs has a "justification fundamentally different

---

[5] McGlotten v. Connally, 338 F. Supp. 448, 458 (D.D.C. 1972).
[6] Treasury Department, *Tax Reform Studies and Proposals* (Comm. Prt.), 91st Cong., 1st Sess. 317 (1969).
[7] The applicability of the unrelated business income tax was broadened for the following reason: "In recent years, many of the exempt organizations not subject to the unrelated business income tax—such as churches, social clubs, fraternal beneficiary societies, etc.—began to engage in substantial commercial activity. . . . [I]t is difficult to justify taxing a university or hospital which runs a public restaurant or hotel or other business and not tax a country club or lodge engaged in similar activity" (Joint Committee on Internal Revenue Taxation, *General Explanation of Tax Reform Act of 1969* 66-67 (91st Cong., 2d Sess. (1970)).
[8] S. Rep. No. 91-552, 91st Cong., 1st Sess. 71 (1969).

from that which underlies the grant of tax exemption to other nonprofit entities."[9] That is, while for most nonprofit organizations "exemption from federal
income tax is intended to encourage the provision of services that are deemed
socially beneficial," social clubs are "exempted from tax not as a means of conferring tax *advantages*, but as a means of ensuring that the members are not subject to tax *disadvantages* as a consequence of their decision to pool their resources
for the purpose of social or recreational services."[10] The Court restated this rationale by observing that the "statutory scheme for the taxation of social clubs was
intended to achieve tax *neutrality*, not to provide these clubs a tax advantage:
even the exemption for income derived from members' payments was designed
to ensure that members are not disadvantaged as compared with persons who
pursue recreation through private purchases rather than through the medium of
an organization."[11]

(b) Club Functions

To qualify as a tax-exempt social club, an organization not only must be a nonprofit entity[12] but must meet both an organizational test and an operational test.[13]
To satisfy the requirement of a pleasure, recreation, or other permissible
purpose,[14] the club must have an established membership of individuals, personal contacts, and fellowship.[15] A commingling of the members must play a material part in the life of the organization.[16]

Where the requisite degree of fellowship is absent, tax exemption may be denied, as occurred with respect to an organization formed to furnish television an-
tenna service to its members[17] and associations composed primarily of "artificial"
persons or other clubs.[18] Thus, a club operated to assist its members in their business endeavors through study and discussion of problems and similar activities at
weekly luncheon meetings was denied exemption as a social club on the ground
that any social activities at the meetings were merely incidental to the business

---

[9] Portland Golf Club v. Comm'r., 497 U.S. 154, 161 (1990).

[10] *Id.* at 161–162 (emphasis in original).

[11] *Id.* at 163 (emphasis in original).

[12] West Side Tennis Club v. Comm'r, 111 F.2d 6 (2d Cir. 1940), *cert. den.*, 311 U.S. 674 (1940).

[13] E.g., Rev. Rul. 70-32, 1970-1 C.B. 140.

[14] Discussions of the scope of the phrase *other nonprofitable purposes* appear in Allgemeiner Arbeiter
Verein v. Comm'r, 237 F.2d 605 (3d Cir. 1956); Allied Trades Club v. Comm'r, 228 F.2d 906 (3d Cir.
1956); The Associates v. Comm'r, 28 B.T.A. 521 (1933). Clubs providing sickness and death benefits to
their members do not qualify as exempt social clubs (e.g., Polish Army Veterans Post 147 v. Comm'r,
24 T.C. 891 (1955), *rev'd on another issue*, 236 F.2d 509 (3d Cir. 1956); St. Albert's American-Polish Citizens & Social Club v. Comm'r, 14 T.C.M. 196 (1955); Spokane Commercial Travelers v. United States,
126 F. Supp. 424 (W. D. Wash. 1954); Rev. Rul. 63-190, 1963-2 C.B. 212).

[15] Kanawha-Roane Lands, Inc. v. United States, 136 F. Supp. 631 (D. W. Va. 1956); Barstow Rodeo &
Riding Club v. Comm'r, 12 T.C.M. 1351 (1953).

[16] Rev. Rul. 58-589, 1958-2 C.B. 266.

[17] Rev. Rul. 55-716, 1955-2 C.B. 263, *mod. by* Rev. Rul. 83-170, 1983-2 C.B. 97; also Gen. Couns. Mem.
39063. Cf. Rev. Rul. 62-167, 1962-2 C.B. 142.

[18] Rev. Rul. 67-428, 1967-2 C.B. 204.

purpose of the organization.[19] A related concept is that a club, to be exempt, must have members actively sharing interests or goals, as evidenced, for example, by appropriate prerequisite conditions or limitations upon members.[20] It is insufficient, for purposes of exemption, for an organization to be able to demonstrate a common objective or interest of the members. Consequently, for example, most nonprofit automobile clubs are denied exemption as social clubs.[21]

To the IRS, the criterion of providing pleasure or recreation by a tax-exempt social club to its members is paramount to the qualification of the club for tax exemption. Thus, gambling can be an exempt purpose for a social club, even where substantial income is derived from the practice, as long as the source of the revenue is the club's members and their guests. The IRS will refrain from denying or revoking an organization's exemption on this basis, notwithstanding the fact that the gambling activities are illegal under state or local law.[22]

While country clubs, dinner clubs, variety clubs, swim, golf, and tennis clubs, and the like set the norm for the tax-exempt social club,[23] the concept of an exempt social club is considerably broader. Thus, a flying club was ruled to qualify for exemption, where the members were interested in flying as a hobby, commingled in informal meetings, maintained and repaired aircraft owned by the club, and flew together in small groups,[24] as opposed to a club that was operated primarily to provide flying facilities suitable for members' individual business or personal use.[25] Social club status was accorded an organization composed solely of persons who were members of a political party and those interested in party affairs,[26] and of members of a specific family to bring them into closer communication through social, family history, and newsletter activities.[27] Gem and mineral clubs or a federation of these clubs may qualify as exempt social clubs.[28] Other illustrations of exempt social clubs include pet clubs,[29] garden clubs,[30] fraternities and sororities,[31] a sponsor of bowling

[19] Rev. Rul. 69-527, 1969-2 C.B. 125.

[20] Arner v. Rogan, 40-2 U.S.T.C. ¶ 9567 (S.D. Cal. 1940).

[21] Warren Automobile Club v. Comm'r, 182 F.2d 551 (6th Cir. 1950); Keystone Automobile Club v. Comm'r, 181 F.2d 402 (3d Cir. 1950); Chattanooga Automobile Club v. Comm'r, 182 F.2d 551 (6th Cir. 1950); Smyth v. California State Automobile Ass'n, 175 F.2d 752 (9th Cir. 1949), cert. den., 338 U.S. 905 (1949); Automobile Club of St. Paul v. Comm'r, 12 T.C. 1152 (1949); Rev. Rul. 69-635, 1969-2 C.B. 126; Rev. Rul. 67-249, 1967-2 C.B. 179.

[22] Rev. Rul. 69-68, 1969-1 C.B. 153.

[23] Hillcrest Country Club, Inc. v. United States, 152 F. Supp. 896 (D. Mo. 1957); Slovene Workers Home v. Dallman, 56-1 U.S.T.C. ¶ 9205 (S.D. Ill. 1956); Coeur D'Alene Athletic Round Table, Inc. v. Comm'r, 21 T.C.M. 1430 (1962); Rev. Rul. 69-281, 1969-1 C.B. 155.

[24] Rev. Rul. 74-30, 1974-1 C.B. 137. Also Syrang Aero Club, Inc. v. Comm'r, 73 T.C. 717 (1980).

[25] Rev. Rul. 70-32, supra note 13. Also Rev. Rul. 56-475, 1956-2 C.B. 308.

[26] Rev. Rul. 68-266, 1968-1 C.B. 270. Cf. Thomas J. McGee Regular Democratic Club, Inc. v. Comm'r, 1 T.C.M. 18 (1942) (where public use was too extensive).

[27] Rev. Rul. 67-8, 1967-1 C.B. 142.

[28] Rev. Rul. 67-139, 1967-1 C.B. 129.

[29] Rev. Rul. 73-520, 1973-2 C.B. 180; Rev. Rul. 71-421, 1971-2 C.B. 229.

[30] Rev. Rul. 66-179, 1966-1 C.B. 139.

[31] Rev. Rul. 69-573, 1969-2 C.B. 125; Rev. Rul. 64-118, 1964-1 C.B. (Part 1) 182; Phinney v. Dougherty, 307 F.2d 357 (5th Cir. 1962); Alumnae Chapter Beta of Clovia v. Comm'r, 46 T.C. 297 (1983).

tournaments,[32] a promoter of golf,[33] a horse-riding club,[34] and clubs affiliated with exempt lodges.[35]

A tax-exempt social club may provide social and recreational facilities to its members who are limited to homeowners of a housing development and nonetheless qualify for tax exemption. This exemption will be precluded, however, where any of the following services are provided by the club: owning and maintaining residential streets, administering and enforcing covenants for the preservation of the architecture and appearance of the housing development, or providing police and fire protection and a trash collection service to residential areas.[36]

(c) Other Tax Matters

A social club constitutes a *welfare benefit fund*[37] and therefore a *disqualified benefit*[38] provided by the organization will give rise to tax liability.[39]

There is no business expense or other tax deduction for amounts paid or incurred for membership in a social club, whether or not tax-exempt.[40]

§ 14.2   PUBLIC USE OF FACILITIES

Under the income tax regulations (which antedate the 1976 statutory revision, discussed below), a "club which engages in business, such as making its social and recreational facilities available to the general public . . ., is not organized and operated exclusively for pleasure, recreation, and other nonprofitable purposes, and is not exempt" from federal income tax.[41] Solicitation of the general public to utilize club facilities will disqualify the social club for tax exemption.[42]

---

[32] Rev. Rul. 74-148, 1974-1 C.B. 138.

[33] Augusta Golf Ass'n v. United States, 338 F. Supp. 272 (S.D. Ga. 1971).

[34] Clements Buckaroos v. Comm'r, 21 T.C.M. 83 (1962).

[35] Rev. Rul. 66-150, 1966-1 C.B. 164; Rev. Rul. 56-305, 1956-2 C.B. 307.

[36] Rev. Rul. 75-494, 1975-2 C.B. 214.

[37] IRC § 419(e)(3)(A).

[38] IRC § 4976(b).

[39] IRC § 4976(a).

[40] IRC § 274(a)(3). For this purpose, a *club* organized for business, pleasure, recreation, or other social purpose includes any membership organization "if a principal purpose of the organization is to conduct entertainment activities for members of the organization or their guests or to provide members or their guests with access to entertainment facilities" (Reg. § 1.274-2(a)(2)(iii)(a)). These clubs include country clubs, golf and athletic clubs, airline clubs, and clubs operated to provide meals under circumstances generally considered to be conducive to business discussion (*id.*). Unless a principal purpose of the organization is to conduct or provide entertainment, this rule is inapplicable to (1) trade associations, professional organizations (such as bar and medical associations), other business leagues, chambers of commerce, boards of trade, or real estate boards (see Chapter 13); or (2) civic or public service organizations (including those described in Chapter 12) (Reg. § 1.274-2(a)(2)(iii)(b)).

[41] Reg. § 1.501(c)(7)-1(b).

[42] Keystone Automobile Club v. Comm'r, *supra* note 21; United States v. Fort Worth Club of Fort Worth, Texas, 345 F.2d 52 (5th Cir. 1965), *mod. and reaff'd*, 348 F.2d 891 (5th Cir. 1965); Polish American Club, Inc. v. Comm'r, 33 T.C.M. 925 (1974).

(a) Nonmember Use in General

The IRS promulgated guidelines for determining the effect on a social club's tax exemption of gross receipts derived from nonmember use of the club's facilities.[43] The concern in this regard is not with the situation where a club member entertains a few guests at his or her club, but where a club's facilities are made available to the general public on a regular and recurring basis, thereby removing that segment of the public from the marketplace of competing commercial operations.[44] Infrequent use of an exempt social club by the general public is permissible, since it is an incidental use.[45] Thus, for example, a club cannot be exempt when a significant portion of its revenue is derived from greens fees charged to the general public,[46] yet can be exempt where fees of this nature are incidental.[47]

This matter concerning the permissible extent of public use of the facilities of social clubs has long been the subject of debate. In perhaps the most well-known case on the point, a tennis club was held not to be entitled to tax exemption because it received more than one-half of its income from the conduct of national championship tennis matches. The court mused that, were it not for limitations on nonmember income, a club would be able to maintain "as large and luxurious a plant as the members might like without the payment of burdensome dues."[48]

In another instance, a court nicely stated the consequence arising from a situation when a club derives substantial income from nonmember sources: The club "has eschewed that mutuality which is the basis for its exemption."[49] "In such a situation," the court continued, "revenue derived from nonmembers is used to benefit members since the outside revenue permits the club to assess lower dues than would otherwise be required to support the club's facilities and operations."[50]

---

[43] Rev. Proc. 71-17, 1971-1 C.B. 683. Also The Minnequa Univ. Club v. Comm'r, 30 T.C.M. 1305 (1971). Litigation concerning these guidelines is reflected in Pittsburgh Press Club v. United States, 388 F. Supp. 1269 (W.D. Pa. 1975), *rev. and rem.*, 536 F.2d 572 (3d Cir. 1976), *on remand*, 426 F. Supp. 553 (W.D. Pa. 1977), *rem.*, 579 F.2d 751 (3d Cir. 1978), *on remand*, 462 F. Supp. 322 (W.D. Pa. 1978), *rev'd*, 615 F.2d 600 (3d Cir. 1980).

[44] Rev. Rul. 60-324, 1960-2 C.B. 173. Also Rev. Rul. 69-220, 1969-1 C.B. 154; Rev. Rul. 69-217, 1969-1 C.B. 115; Rev. Rul. 68-638, 1968-2 C.B. 220; Rev. Rul. 65-63, 1965-1 C.B. 240; United States v. Fort Worth Club of Fort Worth, Texas, *supra* note 42; Spokane Motorcycle Club v. United States, 222 F. Supp. 151 (E.D. Wash. 1963); Sabers of Denver, Inc. v. United States, 65-2 U.S.T.C. ¶ 9670 (D. Col. 1965); Matter of The Breakfast Club, Ltd., 35-1 U.S.T.C. ¶ 9265 (D. Cal. 1935).

[45] Rev. Rul. 60-323, 1960-2 C.B. 173; Rev. Rul. 66-149, 1966-1 C.B. 146; Town & Country Club v. Comm'r, 1 T.C.M. 334 (1942).

[46] Rev. Rul. 69-219, 1969-1 C.B. 153.

[47] Coeur d'Alene Country Club v. Viley, 64 F. Supp. 540 (D. Idaho 1946).

[48] West Side Tennis Club v. Comm'r, *supra* note 12, 111 F.2d at 8.

[49] Pittsburgh Press Club v. United States, *supra* note 43, 579 F.2d at 761. See *supra* § 1.

[50] *Id.*

A corporation may pay for individual club memberships without jeopardizing the club's tax exemption,[51] although an organization the membership of which is entirely in corporations' names does not qualify for exemption.[52] To the extent an exempt social club has corporate members, however, the individuals who use the club's facilities under the memberships are treated as part of the general public for these purposes.[53] Amounts paid to an exempt social club by visiting members of another exempt social club, pursuant to a reciprocity arrangement, are forms of nonmember income.[54]

Where the group includes eight or fewer individuals, the tax-exempt social club must maintain records that substantiate that the group included no more than eight individuals, at least one of whom was a member, and that payment was received from the member or his or her employer. Where 75 percent or more of the group are members of the club, records must be maintained that substantiate that at least 75 percent of the group were club members and that payment was received directly from members or members' employers.

On all other occasions involving nonmembers, the tax-exempt social club must maintain records showing each use and the income derived from the use, even though a member pays initially for the use. The club's records must also include the following: the date, the total number in the party, the number of nonmembers in the party, the total charges, the charges attributable to nonmembers, and the charges paid by nonmembers. If a member pays all or part of the charges, there must be a statement signed by the member as to whether he or she has been or will be reimbursed and to what extent by the nonmembers.

Further, where a member's employer reimburses the member, or pays the social club directly for nonmember charges, there must be a statement indicating the name of the employer, the amount attributable to nonmember use, the nonmember's name and business or other relationship to the member, and the business, personal, or social purpose of the member served by the nonmember use. If a nonmember (other than a member's employer) makes payment to the club or reimburses a member and claims the amount was paid gratuitously, the member must sign a statement indicating the donor's name, relationship to the member, and information demonstrating the gratuitous nature of the payment.

The requirements for record keeping under these IRS guidelines are extensive, and the penalty for failing to maintain adequate records is severe. If these records are not maintained, the IRS will not apply the minimum gross receipts standard or the audit assumptions and all income will be treated as unrelated business income. Therefore, tax-exempt social clubs must maintain adequate records for the purpose of labeling income from members as *exempt function income*.

Excessive use of tax-exempt social club facilities by the general public is not the only way in which a club may be considered as engaging in business. In one instance, a swim club was held to be operated as a commercial venture for the fi-

---

[51] Rev. Rul. 74-168, 1974-1 C.B. 139.
[52] Rev. Rul. 67-428, *supra* note 18.
[53] Rev. Rul. 74-489, 1974-2 C.B. 169.
[54] Gen. Couns. Mem. 39343.

nancial benefit of its manager and thus was denied exemption.[55] (A club may, however, without jeopardizing its exemption, enter into a management and lease agreement for the operation of its facilities.[56]) In another case, a club had such a large number of "associate members" that the IRS treated it as selling services for profit to these individuals.[57]

(b) Limitations on Outside Income

As referenced, one of the statutory requirements for tax exemption of social clubs was that they must be organized and operated *exclusively* for pleasure, recreation, and other nonprofitable purposes.[58] Congress in 1976 changed this rule so that now *substantially all* of a club's activities must be for these purposes.[59] This allows an exempt social club to receive some outside income (including investment income) and a higher level of income from nonmembers using its facilities or services than the IRS previously allowed without losing its tax-exempt status. The underlying rationale was that the extension of the unrelated business income tax to social clubs[60] meant that the "extent to which a club can obtain income from nonmember sources can be somewhat liberalized."[61] This rule is not contained in a statute (nor is it reflected in the tax regulations); it is stated in the legislative history to the 1976 tax legislation.[62]

This legislative history provided for "safe-harbor" guidelines: A tax-exempt club can receive as much as 35 percent of its *gross receipts*, including investment income, from sources outside of its membership without losing tax-exempt status.[63] Within that 35 percent amount, no more than 15 percent of the gross receipts can be derived from the use of a social club's facilities or services by the general public. It is not intended that social clubs be permitted to receive, within either percentage allowance, income from the active conduct of businesses not traditionally carried on by these organizations.[64]

The term *gross receipts*, for this purpose, means those receipts from normal and usual activities of these clubs (that is, those activities they have traditionally conducted), including charges, admissions, membership fees, assessments, investment income, and normal recurring gain. Initiation fees and capital contributions

---

[55] Rev. Rul. 65-219, 1965-2 C.B. 168.
[56] Rev. Rul. 67-302, 1967-2 C.B. 203.
[57] Rev. Rul. 58-588, 1958-2 C.B. 265.
[58] See text accompanying *supra* note 41.
[59] Pub. L. No. 94-568, 94th Cong., 2d Sess. (1976).
[60] See *infra* § 3.
[61] S. Rep. No. 94-1318, 94th Cong., 2d Sess. 2 (1976).
[62] H. Rep. No. 94-1353, 94th Cong., 2d Sess. 4 (1976); S. Rep. No. 94-1318, *supra* note 61, at 4. Also I.R. 1731 (Jan. 11, 1977). The guidelines created by Congress in 1976 supersede the criteria created by the IRS in 1971 (*supra* note 43), although the latter remain valid as a basis for recordkeeping requirements.
[63] Case law embodying prior law as to the nonmember income issue loosely used words like *income*, *revenue*, and *subsidy*. As to the concept of *subsidy*, for example, see Pittsburgh Press Club v. Comm'r, *supra* note 49. These words have been replaced by the term *gross receipts*.
[64] Tech. Adv. Mem. 199912033.

are excluded.[65] The concept of gross receipts entails some form of tangible economic benefit, such as revenue derived from a club's sale of cookbooks;[66] revenue derived by a club from the sale of fox hounds;[67] revenue derived from a club's conduct of a sports tournament;[68] revenue derived from commercial advertising appearing in a club's periodicals;[69] fees paid by "apprentice members";[70] revenue derived by a club from the conduct of luncheons, banquets, and receptions;[71] and revenue derived from the sale of timber by a club.[72] Court opinions likewise reflect this view, such as characterization of a club's receipts of income from concessions and the sale of souvenirs,[73] revenue from the conduct of nonmember golf tournaments,[74] and revenue from the sale of food and beverages to nonmembers.[75]

In computing this percentage, a tax-exempt social club need not take into consideration "unusual amounts of income." This rule was generally intended to cover receipts from the sale of a clubhouse or similar facility. Presumably, the rule is also applicable to receipts from a major sporting event (such as a golf or tennis tournament) that is open to the public but is held by the club on an irregular basis. This interpretation would be in conformance with prior caselaw.[76]

Some clubs hold tournaments on a regularly recurring basis (for example, annually). In this situation, the exclusion for unusual amounts is presumably unavailable. Thus, the tax exemption of a social club in this circumstance would be adversely affected if the 15 percent limitation was exceeded[77] but, even if the level of receipts did not trigger revocation of tax exemption, the return from the tournament would nonetheless be subject to taxation as non-exempt function income.[78]

A tax-exempt social club that makes its facilities available to the general public in hosting an athletic tournament generates receipts from nonmember use

---

[65] The rule as to capital contributions does not reference any categories of providers of capital; presumably, then, excludable capital contributions can come from members and nonmembers. As a practical matter, it is uncommon for a social club to receive contributions to its capital from any source other than its members, although it does happen. An analogy may be made to the law concerning contributions of capital to for-profit corporations by shareholders and nonshareholders (IRC § 118(a); Reg. § 1.118-1). The principal cases on the law pertaining to nonshareholder contributions to capital are Brown Shoe Co. v. Comm'r, 339 U.S. 583 (1950), and United States v. Chicago, Burlington & Quincy Railroad Co., 412 U.S. 401 (1973). A IRS ruling on nonshareholder capital contributions is Priv. Ltr. Rul. 200133036.

[66] Priv. Ltr. Rul. 8141019.

[67] Priv. Ltr. Rul. 8242003.

[68] Priv. Ltr. Rul. 8426001.

[69] Priv. Ltr. Rul. 8446008.

[70] Priv. Ltr. Rul. 8541008.

[71] Priv. Ltr. Rul. 8542003.

[72] Priv. Ltr. Rul. 9533015.

[73] Ye Mystic Krewe of Gasparilla v. Comm'r, 80 T.C. 755 (1983).

[74] North Ridge Country Club v. Comm'r, 877 F.2d 750 (9th Cir. 1989), rev'g 89 T.C. 563 (1987).

[75] The Cleveland Athletic Club, Inc. v. United States, 779 F.2d 1160 (6th Cir. 1985); Inter-Com Club, Inc. v. United States, 721 F. Supp. 1112 (D. Neb. 1989); The Brook, Inc. v. Comm'r, 50 T.C.M. 959 (1985); Polish American Club v. Comm'r, supra note 42.

[76] E.g., Santee Club v. White, 87 F.2d 5 (1st Cir. 1936).

[77] West Side Tennis Club v. United States, supra note 12; Rev. Rul. 68-638, supra note 44.

[78] E.g., Priv. Ltr. Rul. 8426001.

of the facilities, with these receipts subject to the 15 percent test. For example, the IRS ruled that an association of professional tournament golfers that maintained a championship course may make the course available to the general public when the tournament is not being held, without disturbing its exempt status but with the income from the use subject to taxation as unrelated business income.[79]

The tax-exempt status of a social club is not automatically lost, however, if these percentages are exceeded, because the guidelines are, as noted, a safe harbor. If the guidelines are exceeded, then all of the facts and circumstances are taken into account in determining whether the organization qualifies for exempt status. Indeed, the IRS sometimes analyzes cases of this nature by reviewing the facts and circumstances first and then, if necessary, applying the safe-harbor guidelines.[80] The overarching standard used in application of this facts and circumstances test is whether the activity or support is "necessary to preserve the assets of the club used for exempt purposes."[81] On another occasion, when a club exceeded the percentage guidelines, the IRS used the facts and circumstances test to enable the club to retain its tax exemption because of a "lack of profits."[82] Indeed, in one instance, the IRS applied the test (the safe-harbor guidelines having been exceeded), concluding that revocation was inappropriate because the "officers and [other] representatives [of the club] held a good faith belief that the income from the functions at issue constituted member income."[83]

Nonetheless, this safe harbor rule notwithstanding, there is *some* limit as to the amount of investment income a social club can receive and still remain tax-exempt. Thus, a court held that a club could not be tax-exempt when it received 100 percent of its gross receipts in the form of investment income.[84] This court referenced an appellate court opinion (albeit one issued before 1976) which contained the observation that the "source of a club's revenues, as well as their destination, is crucial in determining the purpose for which the club is 'organized and operated.' "[85]

It is the view of the Chief Counsel of the IRS, however, that the revision of the law in 1976 did not modify the preexisting rule that revenue derived by an activity that does not advance exempt purposes, whether engaged in for the benefit of members or nonmembers, will lead to revocation of a social club's tax-exempt status. These activities, known as *nontraditional* activities, may not cause loss of tax-exempt status if the income from them represents only *de minimis* amounts of income. In one instance, the IRS's lawyers considered the tax status of a social club that rented rooms as temporary principal residences, rented offices, operated a barber shop, provided a take-out service, operated a service station and parking garage, and maintained in its lobby a commercial ticket agency, a flower and gift shop, and a liquor store. The sale of petroleum products and services, and of take-out food, were found to be nontraditional activities; the rental of rooms, opera-

---

[79] Priv. Ltr. Rul. 7838108.
[80] E.g., Tech. Adv. Mem. 199912033.
[81] Priv. Ltr. Rul. 9533015.
[82] Priv. Ltr. Rul. 8426001.
[83] Priv. Ltr. Rul. 8542003.
[84] The Skillman Family Reunion Fund, Inc. v. Comm'r, 196 F. Supp. 2d 543 (N.D. Ohio 2002).
[85] United States v. Fort Worth Club of Fort Worth, Texas, *supra* note 42, at 56.

tion of the barber shop and parking garage, and maintenance of the ticket agency were termed "questionable."[86]

§ 14.3   TAXATION OF SOCIAL CLUBS

The income tax regulations deprive tax exemption for a social club that "engages in business, such as by selling real estate, timber or other products," unless a sale of property is incidental.[87] Nonetheless, abuses were prevalent, perhaps fostered by the courts' willingness to salvage a social club's exemption. For example, a federal court of appeals held that two golf clubs did not lose exemption because of the execution of oil leases on their properties that generated substantial income, on the theory that the leases were "incidental" to club operations.[88] Of course, the profits from the oil leases went untaxed.[89]

In 1969, Congress adhered to the Department of the Treasury's recommendation for reform in this area. The Treasury Department had, in effect, relied on the basic rationale for the tax exemption of social clubs[90] and ran the rationale in reverse, contending that the investment income of social clubs was equivalent to income earned by the club members in their individual capacity. Thus, the Senate Finance Committee stated:

> Since the tax exemption for social clubs and other groups is designed to allow individuals to join together to provide recreational and social facilities or other benefits on a mutual basis, without tax consequences, the exemption operates properly only when the sources of income of the organization are limited to the receipts from the membership. . . . However, where the organization receives income from sources outside the membership, such as income from investments . . . upon which no tax is paid, the membership receives a benefit not contemplated by the exemption in that untaxed dollars can be used by the organization to provide pleasure or recreation (or other benefits) to its membership.[91]

---

[86] Gen. Couns. Mem. 39115.

[87] Reg. § 1.501(c)(7)-1(b); Rev. Rul. 69-232, 1969-1 C.B. 154.

[88] Scofield v. Corpus Christi Golf & Country Club, 127 F.2d 452 (5th Cir. 1942); Koon Kreek Klub v. United States, 108 F.2d 616 (5th Cir. 1940). Cf. The Coastal Club, Inc. v. Comm'r, 43 T.C. 783 (1965), aff'd, 368 F.2d 231 (5th Cir. 1966), cert. den., 386 U.S. 1032 (1967).

[89] Another case involving a social club that was a nonexempt businesses is Aviation Club of Utah v. Comm'r, 162 F.2d 984 (10th Cir. 1947), cert. den., 332 U.S. 837 (1947). Where the business activity was incidental, however, tax exemption was permitted (e.g., Town & Country Club v. Comm'r, supra note 45; Aviation Country Club, Inc. v. Comm'r, 21 T.C. 807 (1954)).

[90] See text accompanying supra notes 5–11.

[91] S. Rep. No. 91-552, supra note 8; also H. Rep. No. 91-413, 91st Cong., 1st Sess. 47 (1969) (Part 1); Rev. Rul. 69-220, supra note 44. Applying this doctrine, a federal court of appeals held that the regular drawings with the public by a Knights of Columbus council (an IRC § 501(c)(8) fraternal society (see § 18.4(a))) were subject to the wagering excise and occupational taxes (IRC § 4421), in that the exception from the taxes for activities where there is no inurement of net earnings was ruled to not apply, on the theory that the revenues derived from the gaming are used to preclude dues increases, so that the "subsidization" constitutes a form of private inurement to the council's members (Knights of Columbus Council No. 3660 v. United States, 83-2 U.S.T.C. ¶ 16,410 (S.D. Ind. 1983), aff'd, 783 F.2d 69 (7th Cir. 1986)).

In that year, Congress subjected income unrelated to the normal operation of a social club to the tax on unrelated business income.

For most types of tax-exempt organizations, revenue is nontaxable other than net income from unrelated business activities.[92] Thus, for nearly all exempt organizations, nontaxable revenue embraces gifts, grants, income from the performance of exempt functions, and passive (investment) income. The income of a tax-exempt social club, however, is taxed in a significantly different manner: rather than isolate and tax unrelated business taxable income (the general rule), the law isolates the exempt function income of social clubs and subjects the balance of its revenue (including investment income) to taxation. (Thus, one of the principal disadvantages of classification as a "tax-exempt" social club is that all of its investment income—including passive income—generally is taxable.[93])

Specifically, a tax-exempt social club's *unrelated business taxable income* is defined as "gross income (excluding any exempt function income), less the deductions allowed . . . [for business expenses] which are directly connected with the production of the gross income (excluding exempt function income) . . ."[94] This income is computed for tax purposes by deducting all expenses directly connected with production of the income and by applying certain of the modifications generally used in determining unrelated business taxable income.[95]

There has been a substantial dispute (eventually resolved by the U.S. Supreme Court, as discussed below) as to the extent to which deductions may be taken in determining a tax-exempt social club's taxable income, leading to differing positions by federal appellate courts. This dispute was stimulated by the practice of social clubs of deducting from investment income losses incurred in connection with the sale of meals and beverages to nonmembers. Thus, an effort commenced to develop a theory to preclude an exempt social club from generating losses from the performance of nonexempt functions that could be offset against gross investment income.

The IRS announced in 1981 that, when a tax-exempt social club operates a food and beverage concession catering to nonmembers and has consistently sold the food and beverages at prices insufficient to recover the cost of sales, the club "may not, in determining its unrelated business taxable income . . . , deduct from its net investment income its losses from such sales to nonmembers."[96] The concept underlying this position was that, where an exempt social

---

[92] See Part Five.

[93] E.g., Carlson, "The Little Known Repeal of the Income Tax Exemption of Social Clubs," 26 *Tax L. Rev.* 45 (1970).

[94] IRC § 512(a)(3)(A); Prop. Reg. § 1.512(a)-3(a), (b). Thus, in one case, the interest earned by a tax-exempt social club on deposits required for its charter flights was held taxable as unrelated income (Council of British Societies in S. Calif. v. United States, 78-2 U.S.T.C. ¶ 9744 (C.D. Cal. 1978), *aff'd*, 587 F.2d 931 (9th Cir. 1978)). Also Deer Park Country Club v. Comm'r, 70 T.C.M. 1445 (1995); Confrerie De La Chaine Des Rotisseuers v. Comm'r, 66 T.C.M. 1845 (1993); Inter-Com Club, Inc. v. United States, *supra* note 75.

[95] IRC §§ 162, 512(b). The foregoing rules are also applicable to organizations described in IRC §§ 501(c)(9), 501(c)(17), and 501(c)(20). See Chapter 16.

[96] Rev. Rul. 81-69, 1981-1 C.B. 351, 352.

club does not endeavor to realize a profit from the sales to nonmembers, the expenses cannot be deductible as business expenses under the general rules for that deduction.[97]

This position was tested in the U.S. Tax Court and was upheld, albeit on a different theory. The Tax Court, relying on the statutory language that states that a social club's taxable income is gross nonexempt income less the deductions that are "directly connected" with the production of gross income, held that a tax-exempt social club's expense may only be offset against income it directly helped to generate, thereby precluding a club from deducting the expenses of service to nonmembers against investment income.[98] On appeal, however, it was held that the Tax Court's interpretation of the statute was incorrect and that federal tax law "authorizes deductions to be taken from the sum total of a club's non-exempt gross income, not merely from the portion of the income connected to the particular deduction."[99] This appellate court returned to the IRS position and concluded that exempt social clubs can only deduct the expenses of activities engaged in with the intention of making a profit, thereby precluding the club in the case from reducing its taxable investment income with nonmember service expenses.

The stance of the IRS in this regard was initially upheld in another case,[100] but was rejected on appeal by the U.S. Court of Appeals for the Sixth Circuit. This appellate court's position, which is founded on the difference in tax treatment, in the unrelated income context, of social clubs,[101] was that a social club has a business expense deduction for outlays associated with activities engaged in with "a basic purpose of economic gain."[102] Under this principle, with which the Second Circuit expressly disagreed, a club could deduct, as business expenses, all expenses of providing food and beverages to nonmembers against investment income.

The U.S. Court of Appeals for the Ninth Circuit sided with the Second Circuit on this point, holding that a tax-exempt social club must pursue a nonmember activity with a profit motive before it can properly deduct its losses.[103] The appellate court agreed with the IRS that the omission of the term *trade or business* from the definition of *unrelated business taxable income* as applied to tax-exempt social clubs[104] does not allow social clubs to deduct losses in nonmember activities that are not businesses, writing that it is "well-established" that, to qualify as a trade or business, an activity must be "regular and profit-seeking."[105] In the case,

---

[97] IRC § 162. Thus, a tax-exempt social club was permitted to deduct the donations of the net proceeds of beano games it conducted, where the payments were a condition of its license for the games (South End Italian Independent Club, Inc. v. Comm'r, 87 T.C. 168 (1986)).

[98] The Brook, Inc. v. Comm'r, *supra* note 75, 51 T.C.M. 133 (1985).

[99] The Brook, Inc. v. Comm'r, 799 F.2d 833 (2d Cir. 1986).

[100] The Cleveland Athletic Club, Inc. v. United States, 588 F. Supp. 1305 (N.D. Ohio 1984).

[101] See text accompanied by *supra* notes 92–95.

[102] The Cleveland Athletic Club, Inc. v. United States, *supra* note 75, at 1165.

[103] North Ridge Country Club v. Comm'r, *supra* note 74.

[104] IRC § 512(a)(3)(A). See text accompanied by *infra* note 112.

[105] North Ridge Country Club v. Comm'r, *supra* note 74, at 753, citing Comm'r v. Groetzinger, 480 U.S. 23 (1987) (see § 26.2(a)).

the club's nonmember food and bar activity was held to not be profit-seeking, because of consistent losses for six years.[106]

As noted, this matter was resolved by the U.S. Supreme Court in 1990, when it held that a tax-exempt social club may use losses incurred in connection with sales to nonmembers to offset investment income only if the sales were motivated by an intent to generate a profit.[107] The Court held that the requisite "profit motive" means "an intent to generate receipts in excess of costs" and concluded that there is "no basis for dispensing with the profit-motive requirement" in these circumstances.[108] The Court explained that elimination of the profit motive standard would create "considerable tension" with the overall statutory scheme of tax treatment of social clubs, in that "Congress intended that the investment income of social clubs (unlike the investment income of most other exempt organizations) should be subject to the same tax consequences as the investment income of any other taxpayer," so that the allowance of the offset for social clubs "would run counter to the principle of tax neutrality which underlies the statutory scheme."[109]

Under the general rules of unrelated income taxation,[110] unrelated business taxable income is defined as the "gross income derived by any organization from any unrelated trade or business . . . regularly carried on by it, less the deductions . . . which are directly connected with the carrying on of such trade or business."[111] The *trade or business* requirement is not in the definition of unrelated business taxable income applicable to social clubs, thereby, as noted, subjecting these organizations to, in the words of the Second Circuit Court of Appeals, a "much more far-reaching tax than" most other categories of tax-exempt organizations.[112]

Exempt function income is gross income from dues, fees, charges, or similar amounts paid by members of the tax-exempt organization in connection with the

---

[106] Cf. Portland Golf Club v. Comm'r, 55 T.C.M. 212 (1988); West Va. State Med. Ass'n v. Comm'r, 91 T.C. 651 (1988), *aff'd*, 882 F.2d 123 (4th Cir. 1989), *cert. den.*, 493 U.S. 1044 (1990). In general, Chiechi & Munk, "When Can Social Clubs Offset Investment Income with Losses from Nonmember Activities?," 73 *J. Tax.* (No. 3) 184 (1990).

[107] Portland Golf Club v. Comm'r, *supra* note 9.

[108] *Id.* at 165, 166.

[109] *Id.* at 165. There is confusion resulting from this Supreme Court opinion concerning the manner in which social clubs demonstrate the necessary profit motive; the Court majority held that the same method of determining "costs" (both direct and indirect) used to ascertain intent to profit must be used in computing actual profit or loss. This holding was criticized in a partial concurring opinion, on the ground that economic reality and statements of income and expenses for tax purposes may be different. Miller, "U.S. Supreme Court in *Portland Golf Club* Reserves on a Key Profit-Intent Question and Adopts a Pervasive Estoppel-by-Reporting Rule," 15 *Rev. of Tax. of Indivs.* 108 (1991); Falk, "Portland Golf Club—Uncertain Direction from the Supreme Court," 2 *J. Tax Exempt Orgs.* 11 (Fall 1990).

Thereafter, the U.S. Tax Court ruled that a tax-exempt social club was not entitled to offset losses from its nonmember activities against investment income because it did not undertake the activities with the requisite profit motive (Atlanta Athletic Club v. Comm'r, 61 T.C.M. 2011 (1991), overruled on another issue, 980 F.2d 1409 (11th Cir. 1993)).

[110] See Part Five.

[111] IRC § 512(a)(1).

[112] The Brook, Inc. v. Comm'r, *supra* note 99, at 841.

purposes constituting the basis for the exemption of the club.[113] Also, the passive income of an exempt social club is generally not taxed if it is set aside to be used for charitable and similar purposes.[114] In one instance, an attempted set-aside failed to immunize net investment income from taxation because the activity funded by the investment income, which was publication of a magazine, was found to not be educational.[115]

In an illustration of these rules, the Tax Court ruled that a tax-exempt social club, the principal activity of which was to annually stage a mock pirate invasion and a parade, incurred taxable income from the sale of refreshments along the parade route, souvenirs, and advertising, inasmuch as the concession and other income was derived from dealings with nonmembers. The court also held that the expenses of staging the invasion and parade could not be used to offset concession revenue, because the expenses did not have the requisite "direct" relationship with the income.[116]

It is the view of the Department of the Treasury that the dividends received deduction[117] is not allowed in computing the taxable income of these organizations.[118] Believing that the reason for this deduction is inapplicable in the context

---

[113] IRC § 512(a)(3)(B); Prop. Reg. §§ 1.512(a)-3(c)(1), (2).

[114] IRC § 170(c)(4); Prop. Reg. §§ 1.512(a)-3(c)(3), (4). In 1926, the U.S. District Court for the Southern District of New York had occasion to review a set-aside provision contained in the Revenue Act of 1918, in Slocum v. Bowers, 15 F.2d 400 (S.D. N.Y. 1926), the classic opinion on the subject of set-asides. Noting that the "policy of exempting" charitable and similar organizations "is firmly established," the court wrote that the set-aside rule should be read "in such a way as to carry out this policy and not to make the result turn on accidental circumstances or legal technicalities" (at 403). The tax consequences depend, said the court, "upon who is ultimately entitled to the property constituting [the] income" (at 404). Consequently, the court interpreted the set-aside rule to exempt from taxation the income of an estate that was destined for charitable purposes even though the representative of the estate still held legal title to the underlying property during the period of administration and even though there was no entry made on the books of the representative crediting the charitable organizations with the income. This decision was affirmed on appeal, with the U.S. Court of Appeals for the Second Circuit holding that it was the intent of Congress to not tax income going to charitable entities and that the designation made by the decedent in the will was the "most effective method" of setting the income aside (Bowers v. Slocum, 20 F.2d 350, 352, 353 (2d Cir. 1927)). Comparable caselaw invokes the law of trusts, where the courts have concluded that the segregated funds are housed in a constructive trust, an implied trust, or a resulting trust. For example, the U.S. Tax Court, having found in the facts a "reasonable certainty as to the property, the objects and the beneficiaries," held that funds transferred to an organization for the purpose of carrying out the objects "were impressed with a trust upon their receipt" (Broadcast Measurement Bur., Inc. v. Comm'r, 16 T.C. 988, 997 (1951)). "No express words of trust were used, but none are necessary," wrote the court in concluding that the recipient organization "was merely a designated fiduciary" (at 997, 1000). In finding that the funds did not constitute gross income to the organization, this court singled out the essential criteria for what is also known as the set-aside: The organization's "books showed the total amount of such fees it received and the unexpended balance thereof at all times" (at 1001). A commingling of the funds with other receipts was expressly held to "not destroy their identity as a trust fund" (id.; also The Seven-Up Co. v. Comm'r, 14 T.C. 965 (1950)). Further, Reg. § 1.512(a)-4(b)(5); Phi Delta Theta Fraternity v. Comm'r, 887 F.2d 1302 (6th Cir. 1989), aff'g, 90 T.C. 1033 (1988) (set aside not found); Alpha Tau Omega Fraternity, Inc. v. Comm'r (U.S. Tax Court Dkt. No. 2810-84 (settled)).

[115] Phi Delta Theta Fraternity v. Comm'r, supra note 114.

[116] Ye Mystic Krewe of Gasparilla v. Comm'r, supra note 73.

[117] IRC § 243.

[118] Prop. Reg. § 1.512(a)-3(b)(2) (withdrawn).

of these organizations, Congress clarified this point by agreeing to the Treasury Department's position.[119] (A similar law change was made for nonexempt membership organizations.[120]) Although the statutory revision took effect in 1976, it has been held that tax-exempt social clubs are not entitled to the dividends-paid deduction for prior years (back to 1970) because the deduction is not for an expense incurred in the production of income but comes into being as a consequence of the existence of the income.[121]

§ 14.4 SALE OF CLUB ASSETS

Congress, in 1969, relegated to statute the law governing nonrecurring sales of club assets. A common example of this is a country club that sells land that has become encroached upon by developers to buy land further out in the countryside for new facilities.[122] Where the purpose of this type of a sale is not profit but to facilitate relocation or a comparable purpose, the law provides a carryover of basis, that is, nonrecognition of gain.[123] Specifically, where property used directly in the performance of the club's tax-exempt function is sold and the proceeds reinvested in exempt function property, within a period beginning one year before the sale date and ending three years thereafter, any gain from the sale is recognized only to the extent that the sale price of the old property exceeds the purchase price of the new property.[124]

There can be controversy over the meaning of the term *used directly*. In one case, the government argued that there must be "actual, direct, continuous, and regular usage," and that the property involved must form an "integral part of the exempt functions of a social club"; it lamented the club's "desultory activities" on the property, which it regarded as essentially investment property. But the court involved held that these requirements are not in the statute and, if they should be, Congress should expand the statute.[125]

By contrast, where the sale of tax-exempt social club assets occurs more than once, the IRS is likely to resist application of this special rule, particularly in any case where the sale transactions substantially deplete the club of its assets and the club has not evidenced an intention to replace the property that is being sold.[126] Also, where a club derives revenue as the result of a grant of an option on

---

[119] IRC § 512(a)(3)(A), last sentence. Pub. L. No. 94-568, *supra* note 59; H. Rep. No. 1353, 94th Cong. 2d Sess. 6 (1976).

[120] IRC § 277. See § 13.6.

[121] Rolling Rock Club v. United States, 85-1 U.S.T.C. ¶ 9374 (W.D. Pa. 1985) *aff'd* 785 F.2d 93 (3d Cir. 1986).

[122] Rev. Rul. 69-232, *supra* note 87; Rev. Rul. 65-64, 1965-1 C.B. 241; Rev. Rul. 58-501, 1958-2 C.B. 262; Santee Club v. White, *supra* note 76; Mill Lane Club v. Comm'r, 23 T.C. 433 (1954); Anderson Country Club, Inc. v. Comm'r, 2 T.C. 1238 (1943); Juniper Hunting Club, Inc. v. Comm'r, 28 B.T.A. 525 (1933).

[123] IRC § 512(a)(3)(D).

[124] Cf. IRC § 1034. E.g., Tamarisk Country Club v. Comm'r, 84 T.C. 756 (1985).

[125] Atlanta Athletic Club v. Comm'r, *supra* note 109; 980 F.2d at 1414. By contrast, in another instance, the government prevailed in a case involving the "used directly" requirement (Deer Park Country Club v. Comm'r, *supra*, note 94).

[126] E.g., Priv. Ltr. Rul. 8337092.

the sale of the property, rather than from the sale of the property itself, this non-recognition rule is inapplicable, so that the option income is taxable as unrelated income.[127]

In another of these instances, a tax-exempt social club sold a painting that had been prominently displayed in its dining room for decades. The club was of the view that the painting was an important part of its exempt function because it enhanced a room where exempt activities took place; the room was named for the painting. Due to concerns over adequate security for the painting, the club sold the painting to an unrelated party and used the proceeds in furtherance of its exempt purposes. The IRS ruled that the gain on the sale of the painting qualified for exclusion from unrelated income taxation.[128]

---

[127] Framingham Country Club v. United States, 659 F. Supp. 650 (D. Mass. 1987).
[128] Priv. Ltr. Rul. 200051046.

CHAPTER FIFTEEN

Labor, Agricultural, and Horticultural Organizations

§ 15.1 Labor Organizations   § 15.3 Horticultural Organizations
§ 15.2 Agricultural Organizations

The federal tax law provides tax exemption for qualified labor, agricultural, or horticultural organizations. No part of the net earnings of this type of an organization may inure to the benefit of any member.[1] Moreover, this category of organization must have as its principal object the betterment of the conditions of those engaged in the exempt pursuits, the improvement of the grade of their products, and the development of a higher degree of efficiency in the particular occupation.[2]

§ 15.1 LABOR ORGANIZATIONS

The principal purpose of a tax-exempt labor organization is to engage in collective action to better the working conditions of individuals engaged in a common pursuit. The most common example of the exempt labor entity is labor unions that negotiate with employers on behalf of workers for improved wages, fringe benefits, and hours and similar working conditions. Nonetheless, the exempt labor organization category encompasses a broader range of entities, including union-controlled organizations that provide benefits to workers that enhance the union's ability to bargain effectively. This classification includes, for example, an organization of exempt labor unions representing public employees,[3] an organization to provide strike and lockout benefits (strike funds),[4] the "labor temple"

---

[1] Reg. § 1.501(c)(5)-1(a)(1). The pro rata refund of excess dues to members by an exempt agricultural organization does not constitute private inurement and thus does not disqualify the organization from continuing tax exemption (Rev. Rul. 81-60, 1981-1 C.B. 335).
[2] Reg. § 1.501(c)(5)-1(a)(2).
[3] Rev. Rul. 74-596, 1974-2 C.B. 167.
[4] Rev. Rul. 67-7, 1967-1 C.B. 137.

(offices, meeting rooms, auditoriums, and the like for labor union members),[5] and an organization publishing a labor newspaper.[6]

According to the IRS, "[g]eneral usage defines a labor organization as an association of workmen who have combined to protect or promote the interests of the members by bargaining collectively with their employers to secure better working conditions, wages, and similar benefits."[7] One court characterized the term *labor organization* as "bespeak[ing] a liberal construction to embrace the common acceptation of the term, including labor unions and councils and groups which are ordinarily unions and councils and the groups which are ordinarily organized to protect and promote the interests of labor."[8] Subsequently, another court observed that a tax-exempt labor organization is a "voluntary association of workers which is organized to pursue common economic and social interests."[9]

Thus, a tax-exempt labor organization must have authority to represent or speak for its members in matters relating to their employment, such as wages, hours of labor, conditions, or economic benefits. An organization that does not function, or directly support the efforts of any labor organization, to better employment conditions cannot qualify as an exempt labor organization. For example, an organization (controlled by individuals in their private capacity) that provided weekly income to its members in the event of a lawful strike by the member's labor union by reason of its contractual agreements with and payments from the workers was ruled to not qualify as an exempt labor organization.[10]

A tax-exempt labor organization is generally composed of employees or representatives of the employees (such as collective bargaining agents) and similar groups. An organization whose membership is composed principally of laborers will not, for that reason alone, however, qualify as an exempt labor organization.[11] An exempt labor organization's membership must be composed of those who are employees. For example, an organization the members of which were independent contractors and entrepreneurs (persons engaged in harness racing in a specific geographical area as drivers, trainers, and horse owners) was held to not qualify as an exempt labor organization because the members were not employees.[12]

One case concerned the appropriateness of the membership of a tax-exempt labor organization, a union, with the government asserting that certain associate members were not bona fide members. The court disagreed, holding that the "membership of a union is a matter of self-definition, found in the organization's constitution or other governing documents."[13] This court observed that "neither

---

[5] Portland Co-Operative Labor Temple Ass'n v. Comm'r, 39 B.T.A. 450 (1939).

[6] Rev. Rul. 68-534, 1968-2 C.B. 217.

[7] IRS Exempt Organizations Handbook (IRM 7751) § 521.

[8] Portland Co-Operative Labor Temple Ass'n v. Comm'r, *supra* note 5, at 455.

[9] American Postal Workers Union, AFL-CIO v. United States, 90-1 U.S.T.C. ¶ 50,013 (D.D.C. 1989).

[10] Rev. Rul. 76-420, 1976-2 C.B. 153.

[11] Workingmen's Co-Op. Ass'n of the United States Ins. League of N.Y. v. Comm'r, 3 B.T.A. 1352 (1978). Cf. Rev. Rul. 78-287, 1978-2 C.B. 146.

[12] Rev. Rul. 78-288, 1978-2 C.B. 179. On this point, the IRS will look to see whether the members are self-employed for purposes of IRC § 1402.

[13] American Postal Workers Union, AFL-CIO v. United States, *supra* note 9, at 83,055.

the Congress, the Treasury, the Internal Revenue Service nor the courts have made exemption for labor organizations dependent on the identity of the particular group or groups of employees represented or the types of economic benefits provided" and that "[t]here is no authority for limiting a labor union's exempt purposes to representing a particular classification of employees or providing particular kinds of benefits to its members."[14] The court added that "[t]here is no requirement in the Internal Revenue Code that a union member receive any particular quantum of benefit in order to be considered a bona fide member," so that a union or other type of labor organization can have different classes of membership.[15] The consequence of these findings was that the dues revenue from the associate members was held nontaxable.

By contrast, another case, on essentially the same facts, produced the opposite conclusion of law. The court involved found taxable the income paid to the organization by its "limited benefit members" for the opportunity to obtain insurance under its health plan.[16] The organization operated for the economic well-being of its regular and associate members, the court found, but these operations were held to benefit the limited benefit members only incidentally and indirectly. The court held that the provision of the insurance to limited benefit members, who could not vote or hold office in the organization, was not related to the organization's tax-exempt purposes (which were to serve the regular and associate members) and thus was taxable as income from the performance of unrelated services.

Labor organizations may also meet the requirements of exemption by providing benefits that directly improve working conditions or compensate for unpredictable hazards that interrupt work. Thus, the IRS recognized as a tax-exempt labor organization a committee formed pursuant to a collective bargaining agreement to improve working conditions for apprentices in various skilled crafts and to aid in the settlement of disputes between employers and apprentices.[17] The agency so held, even though the committee's membership consisted of an equal number of employer and employee representatives, and the committee was financed primarily by employer and union contributions. Another example was an organization that operated a dispatch hall to match union members with work assignments.[18] Exempt labor organization classification was also recognized in the case of a trust organized pursuant to a collective bargaining agreement, funded and administered solely by the employers in an industry, because the purpose of the trust was to compensate a multiemployer steward who was under a union's direct control with responsibility to settle disputes, investigate complaints, and otherwise encourage compliance with the agreement throughout the entire industry.[19] Similarly, the IRS determined that a nurses' as-

[14] *Id.*

[15] *Id.* This opinion was reversed on appeal, on the issue of unrelated income taxation (925 F.2d 480 (D.C. Cir. 1991)) (see § 26.5(e)).

[16] National Ass'n of Postal Supervisors v. United States, 90-2 U.S.T.C. ¶ 50,445 (Cl. Ct. 1990). See *supra* note 15.

[17] Rev. Rul. 59-6, 1959-1 C.B. 121. Also Rev. Rul. 78-42, 1978-1 C.B. 158.

[18] Rev. Rul. 75-473, 1975-2 C.B. 213.

[19] Rev. Rul. 77-5, 1977-1 C.B. 148.

sociation, which had as its primary purposes the acting as a collective bargaining agent for its members in contract negotiations between various institutions and the nurses employed by them and the operation of a health and welfare fund for its membership, constituted an exempt labor organization.[20]

In another illustration, the IRS ruled that a city school teachers' association was a tax-exempt labor organization.[21] The organization was formed to improve the professional abilities of its members and to secure for them better salaries and working conditions. It sponsored seminars and courses for its members, participated in teacher conventions, bargained collectively and processed grievances, and kept its members informed of its activities through regular meetings and a newsletter.

Generally, a tax-exempt labor organization is one that operates to better the conditions of those (frequently its members) engaged in a particular trade, such as by striking for better wages and working conditions. Where the labor organization has members, they will mostly be employees, although the inclusion of some self-employed persons in the membership will not deprive the organization of its classification as an exempt labor group if it otherwise qualifies.[22] Similarly, the payment by a labor organization of death, sick, accident, and similar benefits to its members generally will not preclude exemption, even in circumstances in which a majority of the organization's members are retired.[23] Likewise, the payment by an organization of law enforcement officers for its members' legal defense in actions brought against them in connection with the performance of their official duties did not adversely affect the organization's exempt status as a labor organization.[24]

The IRS had occasion to consider the tax status of a nonprofit organization that was established pursuant to a collective bargaining agreement between a union and an employers' association to enable members of the union to save money under a plan by which a fixed amount was withheld from their pay and deposited in a bank account. The funds were paid to the union's members annually, along with any interest remaining after payment of administrative expenses. In determining that this organization did not qualify as a tax-exempt labor organization, the IRS noted that, to so qualify, the activities of this type of an organization must be those "commonly or historically recognized as characteristic of labor organizations, or be closely related and necessary to accomplishing the principal purposes of exempt labor organizations."[25] Thus, the IRS concluded that "savings plans that disburse money on an annual basis are not closely related to the labor organization's principal activities of negotiating wages, hours, and working conditions nor are such savings plans closely related

[20] Rev. Rul. 77-154, 1977-1 C.B. 148.
[21] Rev. Rul. 76-31, 1976-1 C.B. 157.
[22] Rev. Rul. 77-154, *supra* note 20; Rev. Rul. 74-167, 1974-1 C.B. 134.
[23] Rev. Rul. 62-17, 1962-1 C.B. 87. This position represents a reversal of the IRS's prior stance, as stated in Rev. Rul. 58-143, 1958-1 C.B. 239. Also American Postal Workers Union v. United States, *supra* note 9.
[24] Rev. Rul. 75-288, 1975-2 C.B. 212.
[25] Rev. Rul. 77-46, 1977-1 C.B. 147.

and necessary to providing the mutual benefits characteristically associated with labor organizations."[26]

As noted, one of the purposes of a tax-exempt labor organization may be the development among its members of a higher degree of efficiency in their occupations. To this end, an exempt labor organization may administer bona fide skill-improvement or self-improvement programs as part of its tax-exempt activity, as long as the programs are administered by the organization specifically for, and involve substantial participation by, its members. Thus, this doctrine does not embrace programs substantially developed and administered by other organizations (even though they improve the skills of the labor organization's membership) or that require only insubstantial participation by a labor organization's members in educational activities. For example, a labor organization was advised that its conduct of travel tours for nonmembers and members who do not substantially participate in educational programs administered by it was not a tax-exempt activity.[27]

An organization cannot qualify as a tax-exempt labor organization if its principal activity is to receive, hold, invest, disburse, or otherwise manage funds associated with savings or investment plans or programs, including pension or other retirement savings plans or programs.[28] For example, a trust organized pursuant to a collective bargaining agreement between a labor union and multiple employers, that as most of its activities (1) receives funds from the employers who are subject to the agreement, (2) invests the funds and uses them and accumulated earnings to pay retirement benefits to union members as specified in the agreement, (3) provides information to union members about their retirement benefits and assists them with administrative tasks associated with the benefits, and (4) participates in the renegotiation of the agreement, cannot qualify as an exempt labor organization.[29] This regulation is a reflection of the view of the IRS that, a decision of an appellate court[30] notwithstanding, managing saving and investment plans for workers, including retirement plans, does not bear directly on working conditions.[31] Nonetheless, the IRS continues to recognize that negotiation of the terms of a retirement plan and other postretirement benefits, and designation of one or more representatives to the board of a multiemployer pension trust, are appropriate activities for an exempt labor organization.[32]

A labor union owned-and-controlled company organized to provide em-

---

[26] *Id.*

[27] Priv. Ltr. Rul. 7944018.

[28] Reg. § 1.501(c)(5)-1(b)(1). There is an exception for certain dues-financed pension plans that do not have any employer involvement (Reg. § 1.501(c)(5)-1(b)(2)).

[29] Reg. § 1.501(c)(5)-1(b)(2).

[30] Morganbesser v. United States, 984 F.2d 560 (2d Cir. 1993). The court relied heavily on IRS general counsel memoranda (37942, 37726, and 35862) in its decision. The IRS Office of Chief Counsel recommended nonacquiescence in this case (AOD 1995-016).

[31] Rev. Rul. 77-46, *supra* note 25. A federal district court subsequently refused to follow the *Morganbesser* rationale, holding that the term *labor organization* does not encompass a pension fund that exists only to provide retirement benefits for its members (Stichting Pensioenfonds Voor de Gezondheid v. United States, 950 F. Supp. 373 (D.D.C. 1996), *aff'd*, 129 F.3d 195. (D.C. Cir. 1997)). Also Tupper v. United States, 134 F.3d 444 (1st Cir. 1998).

[32] In general, Note, "Can a Pension Plan be a Labor Organization?, 47 *Tax Law.* (No. 2) 501 (Winter 1994).

ployment to the union's members did not qualify for tax exemption, even though its net profits were turned in to the union's treasury.[33] Exemption was also denied an organization established by an employer and a union under a collective bargaining agreement to ensure the efficient discharge of the employer's obligation to pay withheld employment taxes to federal and state authorities.[34] An organization of farmers formed to furnish farm laborers for individual farmers also did not qualify for exemption as a labor organization.[35] With the advent of the unrelated business income taxation scheme,[36] tax-exempt labor organizations may engage in some nonexempt activities, in the nature of "business" functions or services, and nonetheless continue to remain exempt from federal income taxation.[37]

The effectiveness of labor organizations, particularly unions, on the legislative and political fronts continually generates controversy. The matter came before the courts in a case brought by aerospace workers covered by compulsory union-shop contracts and thus required to pay union dues, to enjoin the government from continuing to recognize tax exemption in the case of any labor organization that expended membership dues for partisan political campaigns.[38] The court rejected the idea that tax exemption of unions should be terminated where union dues are used in political campaigns, stating that Congress has considered and not adopted that result.[39] The court also rejected the argument that the exemption amounts to a federal subsidy and consequently that general political activity of labor organizations should be proscribed, finding that the exemption is "benevolent neutrality" and that there is not the requisite "nexus" between the exemption and any government "involvement" in union activities.[40]

§ 15.2 AGRICULTURAL ORGANIZATIONS

As respects agricultural organizations, the principal tax issue is likely to be the scope of the term *agricultural*. For many years, the IRS relied on the narrow dictionary definition of the term *agriculture* as meaning "the science or art of cultivating the soil, harvesting crops and raising livestock."[41]

Prior to 1976, neither the federal statutory tax law nor the income tax regulations defined the term *agricultural*. There was a body of law holding that this

---

[33] Rev. Rul. 69-386, 1969-2 C.B. 123.

[34] Rev. Rul. 66-354, 1966-2 C.B. 207.

[35] Rev. Rul. 72-391, 1972-2 C.B. 249.

[36] See Part Five.

[37] E.g., Rev. Rul. 62-191, 1962-2 C.B. 146; Rev. Rul. 59-330, 1959-2 C.B. 153.

[38] Marker v. Schultz, 485 F.2d 1003 (D.C. Cir. 1973), *aff'g* 337 F. Supp. 1301 (D.D.C. 1972).

[39] E.g., 18 U.S.C. § 610.

[40] Marker v. Schultz, *supra* note 38, at 1006, citing Waltz v Tax Comm'n, 397 U.S. 664 (1970). This characterization of tax exemption was, however, expressly rejected in Regan v. Taxation with Representation of Washington, 461 U.S. 540 (1983). In general, Graves, "When Will Political Activities of Unions and Associations Cost Them Their Exemption?," 35 *J. Tax* 254 (1971); Albert & Hansell, "The Tax Status of the Modern Labor Union," 111 *U. Pa. L. Rev.* 137 (1962).

[41] Citing *Webster's Third New International Dictionary.* Also Dorrell v. Norida Land & Timber Co., 27 P.2d 960 (Id. 1933).

term must, for tax purposes, be given its normal and customary meaning.[42] This approach did not entail mere reference to dictionary definitions, inasmuch as statutes are to be interpreted in effectuation of intended congressional policy, which may not be identical to the meaning of certain words in lay terms. Certainly, the principal dictionary meaning of *agriculture* is the cultivation of land, as in the raising of crops. *Agriculture*, however, also means *husbandry*, which connotes *farming* as well as *agriculture*. *Agriculture* means "farming (in a broad sense, including . . . stock raising, etc.)."[43] Certainly, *stock* raising can be interpreted as broader than the raising of *livestock*.[44] Thus, it was contended that the meaning reflected in the statutory scheme should be relied upon, rather than dictionary definitions.[46]

An illustration of the foregoing was the IRS's refusal to accord tax-exempt status to organizations engaged in the harvesting of aquatic resources (often termed *aquaculture*). Yet it appeared that, in the face of contemporary food, health, and related needs, any distinction in this context between land farming and sea resource gathering was artificial. In other statutory and regulatory contexts, this distinction has disappeared. For example, the Farm Credit Act, as amended, provided that those engaging in commercial fishing may qualify for the benefits of the Act as "producers or harvesters of aquatic products." The Rural Development Act of 1972 authorized individuals involved in producing fish and fishery products to obtain loans in the same manner as farmers. Additionally, the Federal Energy Office's Petroleum Allocation and Price Regulations included fishing under the definition of *agricultural production*. In other contexts, the IRS has readily turned, in the process of assessing organizations' claims to exemption, to nontax statutes to divine congressional intent or the basis for federal public policy bearing on the organizations' activities.[46]

Unlike the term *farmer*,[47] it is clear that the term *agriculture*, for federal tax purposes, is to be liberally construed. Thus, for example, an organization that annually hosted a rodeo was recognized as being a tax-exempt agricultural organization.[48] An organization that was concerned with methods of raising fur-bearing animals and marketing pelts was ruled to be a tax-exempt agricultural organization,[49] as was an organization that tested soil for farmers and nonfarmers and furnished test results for educational purposes.[50] It is not mandatory that the membership of the organization desiring tax categorization as an agricultural entity be engaged in agricultural pursuits.[51] For example, an organization

---

[42] United States v. Byrum, 408 U.S. 125, 136 (1972). Also Comm'r v. Caulkins, 144 F.2d 482, 484 (6th Cir. 1944), *aff'g* 1 T.C. 656 (1944).
[43] *The American College Dictionary*.
[44] Fromm Bros. Inc. v. United States, 35 F. Supp. 145 (W.D. Wis. 1940); Rev. Rul. 57-588, 1957-2 C.B. 305.
[45] Mitchell v. Cohn, 333 U.S. 411 (1948).
[46] E.g., Rev. Rul. 76-204, 1976-1 C.B. 152.
[47] IRC § 521; § 18.11.
[48] Campbell v. Big Spring Cowboy Reunion, 210 F.2d 143 (5th Cir. 1954).
[49] Rev. Rul. 56-245, 1956-1 C.B. 204.
[50] Rev. Rul. 54-282, 1954-2 C.B. 126.
[51] Rev. Rul. 60-86, 1960-1 C.B. 198.

of women who had no relationship to agriculture other than the fact that their husbands were farmers in a particular state, was ruled to be an exempt agricultural organization.[52]

Efforts were made to invest the law in this area with a broader interpretation of the term agriculture. A federal court of appeals provided precedent for this undertaking:

> According to the lexicographers, agriculture is defined as the art or science of cultivating the ground including the harvesting of crops and *in a broader sense the science or art of the production of plants and animals useful to man*, including in a variable degree the preparation of these products for man's use.[53]

The IRS did not, however, accept this broader view, conceding only that an organization formed for the purpose of encouraging better and more economical methods of fish farming was an agricultural organization.[54] Also, the IRS determined that an organization, the members of which were involved in the commercial fishing industry in a state, that published a monthly newspaper of commercial fishing technical information and news, and that derived its income primarily from membership dues and sale of advertising, did not qualify as a tax-exempt agricultural organization but instead as a business league.[55]

In an attempt to settle this controversy, Congress, in 1976, authored a rule[56] providing that, for purposes of tax exemption as an agricultural organization, the term *agriculture* includes (but is not limited to) the art or science of cultivating land, harvesting crops or aquatic resources, or raising livestock. The insertion of the phrase "harvesting . . . aquatic resources" was designed to encompass fishing and related pursuits (such as the taking of lobsters and shrimp), the cultivation of underwater vegetation, and the cultivation or growth of any edible organism. This change resulted from Congress's realization that there is no tax policy to be served under the provision for exempt agricultural groups for differentiating between occupations devoted to the production of foodstuffs and other items from the earth and from the waters. The statutory definition became effective for tax years beginning after 1975, although inasmuch as the statute may be declaratory of what Congress perceived the law should have been beforehand,[57] it can be contended that the definition is of utility with respect to pre-1976 tax years.

Another dimension of this dilemma for organizations engaged in or associated with aquatic harvesting is that the Postal Service followed the position of the IRS and categorized them as business leagues rather than agriculture organizations, thereby depriving them of the preferential postal rates under the second and third classes. Congress also remedied this aspect of the problem in 1976,

---

[52] Rev. Rul. 74-118, 1974-1 C.B. 134.
[53] Sancho v. Bowie, 93 F.2d 323, 324 (1st Cir. 1937) (emphasis added).
[54] Rev. Rul. 74-488, 1974-2 C.B. 166. Cf. Rev. Rul. 76-241, 1976-1 C.B. 131.
[55] Rev. Rul. 75-287, 1975-2 C.B. 211. See Chapter 13.
[56] IRC § 501(g).
[57] 121 *Cong. Rec.* 34442 (1975).

when it enacted the Postal Reorganization Act Amendments of 1976.[58] This law added a definition of the term agriculture to the postal laws, as including the "art or science of cultivating land, harvesting crops or marine resources, or raising of livestock," thereby removing these organizations from business league status under the postal laws as well.[59] For postal law purposes, this definition also extends to "any organization or association which collects and disseminates information or materials relating to agricultural pursuits."

Other tax-exempt agricultural organizations include an organization engaged in ways to improve the breed of cattle,[60] an association engaged in the promotion of the artificial insemination of cattle,[61] an association formed to guard the purity of Welsh ponies,[62] an organization established to advance agriculture, that purchased supplies and equipment for resale to its members,[63] a local association of dairy farmers that participated in the U.S. Department of Agriculture's National Cooperative Dairy Herd Improvement Program,[64] a local association of farmers formed to promote more effective agricultural pest control,[65] an organization that produced and distributed certified seed to a state's corn producers,[66] an organization of agricultural growers and producers formed principally to negotiate with processors for crop prices,[67] and an organization that participated in furthering research, sales, and distribution of seed stock.[68]

A tax-exempt agricultural organization usually has a membership; those served by the entity must represent a significant portion of the interested agricultural community.[69] The performance of services directly on behalf of an individual member, however, is not improving the grade of the person's product or developing a higher degree of efficiency in the person's agricultural-related pursuits.[70] Yet, where an activity benefits agriculture as a whole and only incidentally benefits individual members, tax exemption is available.[71]

The IRS will not recognize, as a tax-exempt agricultural entity, an organi-

[58] P.L. 94-421, 94th Cong., 2d Sess. (1976).
[59] 39 U.S.C. § 3626(d). While the tax law definition of the term *agricultural* encompasses the "harvesting . . . [of] aquatic resources," the postal law definition of the term includes the "harvesting . . . [of] marine resources." The dictionary definition of *aquatic* is "of or pertaining to water," whereas the dictionary definition of *marine* is "of or pertaining to the sea," thereby holding open the possibility that an organization engaged in or associated with the harvesting of fresh waters will acquire classification as an agricultural organization for federal tax purposes but as a business league for postal law purposes.
[60] Minnesota Holstein-Friesian Breeders Ass'n v. Comm'r, 64 T.C.M. 1319 (1992). Also California Thoroughbred Breeders Ass'n v. Comm'r, 57 T.C.M. 962 (1989).
[61] East Tenn. Artificial Breeders Ass'n v. United States, 63-2 U.S.T.C. ¶ 9748 (E.D. Tenn. 1963).
[62] Rev. Rul. 55-230, 1955-1 C.B. 71.
[63] Rev. Rul. 57-466, 1957-2 C.B. 311. Cf. Rev. Rul. 67-252, 1967-2 C.B. 195.
[64] Rev. Rul. 74-518, 1974-2 C.B. 166, clarifying Rev. Rul. 70-372, 1970-2 C.B. 118.
[65] Rev. Rul. 81-59, 1981-1 C.B. 334.
[66] Priv. Ltr. Rul. 8429010.
[67] Rev. Rul. 76-399, 1976-2 C.B. 152.
[68] Priv. Ltr. Rul. 9732022.
[69] Id.
[70] Rev. Rul. 70-372, *supra* note 64; Rev. Rul. 66-105, 1966-1 C.B. 145; Rev. Rul. 57-466, *supra* note 63.
[71] Rev. Rul. 81-59, *supra* note 65; Rev. Rul. 74-518, *supra* note 64.

zation the principal purpose of which is to provide a direct business service for its members' economic benefit. Thus, an organization engaged in the management, grazing, and sale of its members' cattle was denied exempt status as an agricultural entity.[72] The same fate befell an organization composed of agricultural producers the principal activity of which was marketing livestock for its members.[73] Similarly, the IRS denied an organization classification as an exempt agricultural entity where it furnished farm laborers for individual farmers, ruling that the organization was "merely providing services to individual farmers that they would have to provide for themselves or get someone else to provide for them."[74] In another illustration of this rule, the IRS denied exempt agricultural status to an organization that owned and operated a livestock facility and leased it to local members of a nonexempt national association of farmers for use in implementing the association's collective bargaining program with processors. The facility was used to collect, weigh, sort, grade, and ship livestock marketed through the program. The IRS determined that the operation and leasing of the facility is the "providing of a business service to those members who make use of the national association's collective bargaining program" and that this service "merely relieves the members of the organization of work they would either have to perform themselves or have performed for them."[75]

As noted, to be tax-exempt as an agricultural organization, the organization must have as its objective the betterment of the conditions of those *engaged in* agricultural pursuits. The IRS on one occasion used this rule as the rationale for denying exempt agricultural status to an institute of butter and cheese manufacturers, concluding that those who benefit directly from its activities were not engaged in agricultural pursuits (allowing, however, that it may qualify as a business league).[76] Similarly, the IRS was successful, using the rationale that activities only remotely promoting the interests of those engaged in agricultural pursuits cannot qualify an organization for this exemption, in refusing an organization tax exemption where it was organized to hold agricultural fairs, stock shows, and horse race meets but actually devoted itself solely to horse racing.[77]

As was pointed out, the IRS may conclude that an organization is being operated in the furtherance of interests other than agriculture and that, consequently, it is more properly classifiable as a tax-exempt business league rather than as an agricultural organization.[78] The exemptions for agricultural and charitable organizations may also overlap, such as where an organization conducts a state or county fair or otherwise presents expositions and exhibitions in an educational manner.[79]

---

[72] Rev. Rul. 74-195, 1974-1 C.B. 135.
[73] Rev. Rul. 66-105, *supra* note 70. Also Rev. Rul. 70-372, *supra* note 64.
[74] Rev. Rul. 72-391, *supra* note 35, at 249.
[75] Rev. Rul. 77-153, 1977-1 C.B. 147, 148.
[76] Rev. Rul. 67-252, *supra* note 63.
[77] Forest City Live Stock & Fair Co. v. Comm'r, 26 B.T.A. 1494 (1932).
[78] E.g., Rev. Rul. 67-252, *supra* note 63; Rev. Rul. 56-245, *supra* note 49.
[79] Rev. Rul. 67-216, 1967-2 C.B. 180. Also Indiana Crop Improvement Ass'n, Inc. v. Comm'r, 76 T.C. 394 (1981).

§ 15.3 HORTICULTURAL ORGANIZATIONS

Horticulture is the art or science of cultivating fruits, flowers, and vegetables.[80]

Tax exemption as a horticultural organization was determined by the IRS to be appropriate for a garden club formed for the purpose of bettering the conditions of persons engaged in horticultural pursuits and improving their products, by publishing a monthly journal, reporting new developments in horticultural products to its members, and encouraging the development of such products through a system of awards.[81]

---

[80] Guerrero v. United States Fidelity & Guar. Co., 98 S.W.2d 796 (Tex. 1936).
[81] Rev. Rul. 66-179, 1966-1 C.B. 139.

CHAPTER SIXTEEN

Employee Benefit Funds[1]

The law of tax-exempt organizations and the law of employee benefits are inextricably intertwined. This is because the funding underlying the various forms of employee benefits plans is derived from assets contributed to and held for investment in a trust or fund, and the law provides for federal income tax exemption for these funds, so as to maximize the resources available to provide the benefits.

This interrelationship is also reflected in the organization of the IRS. A component of the agency is the Tax Exempt and Government Entities Division. This division serves three IRS "customer segments": tax-exempt organizations, government entities, and employee (public and private retirement) plans.

The tax-exempt organizations aspect of the law of employee benefits is reflected in the opening passage of the statutory law of tax-exempt organizations, where it is provided that organizations referenced in the rules concerning retirement, profit-sharing, and similar plans[2] are exempt from federal income taxation.[3] That section makes reference to trusts that are part of qualified stock bonus, pension, or profit-sharing plans.

---

[1] The author extends his thanks to Gregory L. Ash, Esq., of Spencer Fane Britt & Browne, LLP, Kansas City, Missouri, for his considerable assistance in the preparation of this chapter.
[2] IRC § 401(a).
[3] IRC § 501(a).

The law of employee benefits as such is outside the scope of this book.[4] Nonetheless, as a prelude to a summary of the law concerning various employee benefit funds that are tax-exempt, a brief overview of this aspect of the law is appropriate to provide a context.

§ 16.1 OVERVIEW OF EMPLOYEE BENEFITS LAW

Basically, employees—whether of nonprofit, for-profit, or governmental employers—are individuals who provide services to an employer. That is, these individuals are provided compensation, in a context where they are not functioning as independent contractors, in exchange for their services. There are employees of nonprofit, tax-exempt organizations who choose to earn less than what they would receive were they working in the for-profit sector, but for the most part those who work for nonprofit organizations (other than volunteers) expect and must have remuneration for their services. Indeed, the law is clear that an individual need not necessarily accept reduced compensation merely because he or she renders services to a tax-exempt, as opposed to a taxable, organization.[5] Thus, an analysis concluded that those who work for nonprofit organizations "display few characteristics that set them off from other service workers."[6]

Compensation in general is provided in three forms: current, deferred, and retirement. Each of these forms of compensation is available to employees of tax-exempt organizations. Whatever the mode of compensation—be it wages, salaries, bonuses, commissions, fringe benefits, deferred compensation, and/or retirement benefits—most exempt organizations are constrained by the doctrines of private inurement, private benefit, and/or the intermediate sanctions rules.[7] This essentially means that all compensation, no matter how determined or whatever the form, must, for the employer to be or remain exempt, be *reasonable*.

(a) Current Compensation in General

A nonprofit organization may pay a salary or wage. This is a form of *current*, as opposed to *deferred* (see below), compensation. Generally, the payments must be reasonable, largely using the community's standard, taking into account factors such as the value of the services being rendered and pertinent experience.[8] (The same rule essentially applies with respect to for-profit employers,

---

[4] See, however, Pianko & Samuels, *Nonprofit Employment Law: Compensation, Benefits, and Regulation* (John Wiley & Sons, Inc., 1998).

[5] H. Rep. 104-506, 104th Cong., 2d Sess. 56, note 5 (1996).

[6] Johnston & Rudney, "Characteristics of Workers in Nonprofit Organizations," 110 *Monthly Labor Rev.* (No. 7) 28, 29 (July 1987).

[7] See Chapter 19. In this regard, public charities and social welfare organizations must take into account the rules concerning excess benefit transactions (see § 19.11) and private foundations must take into account the self-dealing rules (see § 11.4(a)).

[8] See Hopkins, *The Law of Intermediate Sanctions: A Guide for Nonprofits* (John Wiley & Sons, Inc., 2003), §§ 2.4, 4.6.

in that, to be deductible as a business expense, a payment of compensation must be ordinary and necessary.[9]) For this purpose, reasonable current compensation includes appropriate salary increases based on merit and appropriate cost-of-living adjustments.

Nonprofit organizations may pay bonuses. A bonus amount also is subject to the standard of reasonableness. A bonus, however, may be more closely scrutinized than regular current compensation, because it is additional compensation and thus more susceptible than regular compensation to the allegation that it is excessive or otherwise a form of inurement of net earnings. The sensitivity is increased where a bonus is paid to one who is a director, officer, key employee, or similar insider with respect to the nonprofit organization.[10]

In many respects, commissions are subject to the same rules as bonuses, in that both are forms of incentive compensation. Commissions and other forms of percentage-based compensation can, however, result in heightened inquiry, because they are, by definition, computed using percentages and thus tend to approximate, if not constitute, private inurement. Consequently, the IRS and/or a court may scrutinize compensation programs of tax-exempt organizations that are predicated on an incentive feature where compensation is a function of revenues received or guaranteed, or is otherwise outside the boundaries of conventional compensation arrangements.

(b) Fringe Benefits

Federal tax and other law do not prohibit the payment of fringe benefits by tax-exempt organizations. A *fringe benefit* usually is a form of noncash compensation to an employee, although it may well entail a cash outlay by the employer. Once again, a fringe benefit (or a package of them), paid by an exempt employer to an employee, usually must be reasonable to preserve the tax exemption of the employer.

Typically, an employer that is a tax-exempt organization will pay for fringe benefits such as health insurance, medical insurance, dental insurance, disability insurance, and perhaps travel insurance. For the most part, exempt organizations can pay for one or more of these benefits without tax law difficulties.

Other common forms of fringe benefits paid (either directly or by reimbursement) by employers in general are entertainment costs, costs of an automobile, moving expenses, costs of attending conventions and/or educational seminars, costs of parking, club memberships, and costs of certain professional fees (such as physicians' charges for physical examinations, financial planning fees, and stress management expenses).

These latter types of fringe benefits may cause tax law problems for the tax-exempt organizations that pay them. Some exempt entities may be able to pay

---

[9] IRC § 162(a)(1).

[10] In the case of public charities, social welfare organizations, and private foundations, these persons are known as *disqualified persons* (see §§ 11.2, 19.11 (c)).

moving expenses, continuing education expenses, and perhaps automobile and parking expenses, without attracting too much investigation by the IRS. Generally, however, an exempt organization will be suspect, in the eyes of legislators and regulators (and perhaps the general public), if its employees are granted fringe benefits such as country club memberships, financial planning services, or substantial entertainment allowances.

(c) Deferred Compensation

It is becoming more common for tax-exempt organizations to provide *deferred compensation* to their employees, in part because this practice is widespread in the for-profit sector. Many unique tax and other issues arise when deferred compensation arrangements are offered by exempt employers. As with current compensation, deferred compensation is subject to the rule of reasonableness.

Deferred compensation programs may take many forms, including retirement plans and profit-sharing plans. (A nonprofit organization can maintain a profit-sharing plan; the words *excess of revenue over expenses* are used instead of *profit*.) These plans are usually subject to the law laid down by the Employee Retirement Income Security Act of 1974 (ERISA),[11] as well as subsequent enactments, such as those extending rules of nondiscrimination.

Deferred compensation plans are basically divided into qualified and nonqualified plans.

(d) Qualified Plans

A *qualified plan* is a plan that satisfies a variety of tax law requirements,[12] as to coverage, contributions, other funding, vesting, nondiscrimination, and distributions.

For for-profit organizations, it is desirable for a plan to be a qualified one, to enable employer contributions to the plan to be deductible as business expenses. This, of course, is not of relevance to tax-exempt organizations. Other considerations of a qualified plan are that the income and capital gains from the assets underlying the plan are not subject to federal income tax, in that they are held in an exempt trust, and that employees are usually not taxed until the benefits of the plans are actually received.

Qualified plans may be either defined benefit plans or defined contribution plans, the latter also referred to as individual account plans.

(i) Defined Benefit Plans. A *defined benefit plan* is a plan established and maintained by an employer primarily to systematically provide for the payment of definitely determinable benefits to the employees over a period of years, usually life, following retirement. Retirement benefits under a defined benefit plan are measured by and based on various factors, such as years of service rendered, and compensation earned, by the employee. The determination of the amount of

---

[11] Pub. L. No. 406, 93d Cong., 2d Sess. (1974).
[12] IRC § 401(a).

benefits and the contributions made to the plan are not dependent upon the profits of the employer. Under a defined benefit plan, the benefits are established in advance by a formula and the employer contributions are treated as the variable factor.

Any plan that is not a defined contribution plan is a defined benefit plan.

(ii) Defined Contribution Plans.   A *defined contribution plan* is a plan that provides an individual account for each participant and bases benefits solely on the amount contributed to the participant's account and any expense, investment return, and forfeitures allocated to the account.

This type of plan defines the amount of contribution to be added to each participant's account. This may be done in one of two ways: by directly defining the amount the employer will contribute on behalf of each employee or by leaving to the employer's discretion the amount of the contribution but defining the method of allocation. The individual accounts must receive, at least annually, their share of the total investment return, including investment income received and realized, and unrealized gain.

Ordinarily, all of a defined contribution plan's assets are allocated to the individual accounts of plan participants. If a participant terminates his or her employment before becoming vested, the nonvested portion of the account balance is forfeited and is applied either to reduce future employer contributions or to increase the accounts of other participants. When a participant becomes eligible to receive a benefit, his or her benefit equals the amount that can be provided by the account balance. The benefit may be paid in the form of a lump-sum distribution, a series of installments, or an annuity.

Defined contribution plans may be structured in many ways. Where the undertaking is to set aside periodic contributions according to a predetermined formula, the plan is referred to as a *money purchase pension plan*. Employer contributions to a money purchase pension plan are mandatory, and generally are expressed as a percentage of each participant's compensation. A *target benefit plan* is a money purchase pension plan that sets a targeted benefit to be met by actuarily determined contributions. Special antidiscrimination rules apply to target benefit plans.

Another type of defined contribution plan is a *profit-sharing plan*. A profit-sharing plan is one established and maintained by an employer to provide for participation in profits by employees or their beneficiaries. The sponsor of this type of a plan must make substantial and recurring contributions, but unlike money purchase pension plan contributions, employer contributions to a profit-sharing plan may be discretionary. The plan must have a definite, predetermined formula for allocating any contributions made under the plan among the participants, and for distributing the funds accumulated under the plan after a fixed number of years, the attainment of a stated age, or on the prior occurrence of an event, such as layoff, illness, disability, retirement, death, or severance of employment. A profit-sharing plan may, but is not required to, have a definite, predetermined formula for computing the amount of annual employer contributions.

Tax-exempt employers (other than governmental employers) also may sponsor *cash or deferred arrangements*, also known as *401(k) plans*.[13] Legislation enacted in 1996 removed a decade-old prohibition that had prevented exempt employers from sponsoring these plans.[14] A 401(k) plan is a qualified profit-sharing or stock bonus plan pursuant to which participants may choose to reduce their current compensation and have that amount contributed to the plan. These contributions, and any earnings or losses on them, are excluded from the participant's taxable income until they are distributed to the participant. Distributions generally may not be made without penalty until the participant retires, becomes disabled, dies, or attains age $59\frac{1}{2}$.

Other defined contribution plans (some of which are profit-sharing plans) include stock bonus plans, employee stock ownership plans, and, simplified employee pension plans (which can be a form of individual retirement accounts).

(iii) The Funding Mechanism. The usual method of funding a pension or profit-sharing plan is through a tax-exempt trust. A trusteed plan uses a trust to receive and invest the funds contributed under the plan, and to distribute the benefits to participants and/or their beneficiaries. In order for a trust forming part of a pension, profit-sharing, or like plan to constitute a qualified trust, (1) the trust must be created or organized in the U.S. and must be maintained at all times as a U.S. domestic trust; (2) the trust must be established by an employer for the exclusive benefit of the employees and/or their beneficiaries; (3) the trust must be formed or availed of for the purpose of distributing to employees and/or their beneficiaries the corpus and income of the fund accumulated by the trust in accordance with the plan; (4) it must be impossible under the trust instrument at any time before all liabilities, with respect to employees and their beneficiaries, are satisfied for any part of the trust's corpus or income to be used for, or diverted to, purposes other than for the exclusive benefit of employees and/or their beneficiaries; (5) the trust must be part of a plan that benefits a nondiscriminatory classification of employees under IRS guidelines and provides nondiscriminatory benefits; and (6) the plan of which such trust is a part must satisfy various other federal tax law requirements.[15]

The tax advantages of a qualified plan can be obtained without the use of a trust through an *annuity plan*, under which contributions are used to purchase retirement annuities directly from an insurance company. An annuity contract is treated as a qualified trust if it would, except for the fact that it is not a trust, satisfy all the requirements for qualification. In that case, the annuitant is treated as if he or she were the trustee.

A segregated asset account of a life insurance company can be used as an investment medium for assets of a qualified pension, profit-sharing, or annuity plan. Assets of a qualified plan may be held in this type of account without the use of a trust.

A custodial account can be another nontrusteed funding device. Under this

---

[13] These plans are authorized by IRC § 401(k).
[14] Small Business Job Protection Act of 1996, Pub. L. No. 104-188, 110 Stat. 1755 (1996).
[15] IRC § 401(a).

approach, the employer arranges with a bank or other qualified institution to act as custodian of the plan funds placed in the account. Although a custodial account is not a trust, a qualifying custodial account is treated for tax purposes as a qualified trust.

(e) 403(b) Plans

Another form of deferred compensation arrangement in the tax-exempt organizations context is the tax-sheltered (or tax-deferred) annuity. This is an annuity paid out of a *403(b) plan*.[16] A tax-sheltered annuity is treated as a defined contribution plan but it is not a qualified plan because it is not subject to the general qualified employer benefit plan requirements.[17]

Tax-sheltered annuity programs are available only to employees of charitable organizations[18] and employees of public educational institutions. Essentially, if amounts are contributed by a qualified employer toward the purchase of an annuity contract for an employee, then, to the extent that the amounts do not exceed federal tax law limits for the tax year of the employee, the employee is not required to include the amounts in gross income for the tax year. These plans are usually represented by an individual annuity contract purchased by the employee or a group annuity contract with the employer where a separate account is maintained for each participant. As an alternative, funding may be through a custodial account.

Contributions to a tax-sheltered annuity plan—usually made on a salary reduction basis—are excluded from the employees' taxable income, with certain limitations. Generally, elective (employee) contributions may not exceed an annual dollar limit set forth in the statutory law. That limit, which was modified by legislation enacted in 2001,[19] will increase in steps, from $12,000 in 2003 to $15,000 in 2006. The funds contributed to a tax-sheltered annuity accumulate without taxation.

As a consequence of this legislation, tax-sheltered annuity plans (as well as 401(k) plans) may permit any employee who will reach age 50 by the end of the year, and who has already made the maximum contribution permitted under the terms of the plan and the law, to make an additional (or catch-up) contribution for that year. The maximum additional contribution will increase to $5,000 by 2006.

Amounts contributed by an employee to a tax-sheltered annuity plan are not required to be included in the employee's gross income to the extent that such contributions do not exceed a limit set forth in federal tax law. For decades, this cumulative limit has been referred to as the employee's *maximum exclusion allowance*. The legislation enacted in 2001, however, repealed the complicated ex-

---

[16] These plans are authorized by IRC § 403(b).

[17] IRC § 401(a).

[18] That is, organizations that are tax-exempt pursuant to IRC § 501(a) as organizations described in IRC § 501(c)(3).

[19] Economic Growth and Tax Relief Reconciliation Act of 2001, Pub. Law. No. 107-16, 115 Stat. 38 (2001).

clusion allowance limit, replacing it with the general limit that applies to annual additions that may be made to an employee's account in a qualified defined contribution plan.[20] At the same time, the legislation eliminated the special "A," "B," and "C" elections previously available to participants in tax-sheltered annuity plans. These elections had allowed participants to exceed the maximum exclusion allowance limit in some circumstances.

Tax-sheltered annuity plans generally are subject to less federal regulation than other employee benefit plans. Many of these plans are exempt from the requirements of the Employee Retirement Income Security Act. In general, this exemption applies if an employer makes no contributions of its own to the plan, limits its involvement with the plan, and affords employees a reasonable choice of funding media.[21] If the employer's role is more extensive, however, various provisions of this law apply, as do many of the nondiscrimination, distribution, and other limitations (including restrictions on loans) on qualified plans.

Distributions from a tax-sheltered annuity plan are taxed in the same way as are periodic distributions from qualified plans.

(f) Nonqualified Plans

Nonqualified plans are used as a means to provide supplemental benefits and/or to avoid the technical requirements imposed upon qualified plans. The advantages of nonqualified plans for many employers (particularly for-profit ones), however, have been substantially eroded in recent years. Yet, nonqualified plans are of great importance to tax-exempt employers.

The federal tax consequences of nonqualified plans vary, depending on whether the plan is funded or unfunded. Where the plan is funded, contributions by an employer to a nonexempt employees' trust are includible in an employee's gross income in the first tax year in which the rights of the individual having the beneficial interest in the trust are transferable and are not subject to a substantial risk of forfeiture. Unfunded plans are those plans that do not constitute qualified employees' trusts nor certain nonqualified annuity contracts. The tax consequences to an employee under an unfunded arrangement are determined by application of the doctrines of constructive receipt or economic benefit.

Funds in these plans can be deemed constructively received by employees and accessible by creditors of the employer.

Nonqualified deferred compensation programs afford tax-exempt employers an additional means of compensating certain of their top executives. In order to avoid the strictures of the Employee Retirement Income Security Act, which generally restricts an employer's ability to tailor a benefit plan in a manner that favors highly paid employees, nonqualified plan benefits under an unfunded plan must be provided solely to a "select group of management or other highly

---

[20] That limit is the subject of IRC § 415(c). It is defined generally to be the lessor of $40,000 or 100 percent of the employee's compensation.
[21] 29 C.F.R. § 2510.3-2(f).

compensated employees."[22] This group often is referred to as a "top-hat" group and these programs as "top-hat" programs. Although the Department of Labor has not formally defined the contours of the top-hat group, its most authoritative statement on the subject limits the group to individuals who "by virtue of their position or compensation level have the ability to affect or substantially influence, through negotiation or otherwise, the design and operation of their deferred-compensation plan, taking into consideration any risks attendant thereto, and [who], therefore, would not need the substantive rights and protections" of the Act.[23]

There are two types of top-hat plans available to tax-exempt employers. Both of these methods of providing nonqualified, unfunded deferred compensation receives some favorable tax treatment under the federal tax law[24] and they are referred to as *457 plans*. These plans also are available to employees of state and local governments.

A 457 plan enables an employee to defer the current taxation of income. In exchange for this favorable tax treatment, however, the employee's deferrals must be unfunded and thus remain subject to the claims of the employer's general creditors in the event that the employer becomes insolvent. The employee's only assurance of receiving the benefits from such a plan is the employer's contractual promise to pay.

(i) 457(b) Plans.   Top-hat plans that are *457(b) plans*[25] generally provide more favorable tax treatment than the other type of top-hat plan available to tax-exempt employers. A 457(b) plan may allow each executive to defer up to $12,000 per year (increasing to $15,000 per year by 2006) on a tax-deferred basis. Under some circumstances, catch-up deferrals are permitted, up to twice the annual limit that would otherwise apply. Deferral of the tax on 457(b) plan contributions continues even after the contributions become vested. An executive is not taxed on these deferrals, or earnings on the deferrals, until he or she receives a distribution from the plan.

Distributions from a 457(b) plan cannot be made before the earlier of the date the employee has a severance from employment, attains age 70½, or is faced with an unforeseeable emergency.

Legislation enacted in 2001 made 457(b) plans even more advantageous for employees of tax-exempt employers. Previously, 457(b) plan deferrals counted against the dollar limit on elective contributions to 403(b) plans, with the reverse also true. Thus, there had been little incentive for an employer to maintain both types of plans. This coordination requirement was repealed, however, beginning in 2002, making it possible for an employee who participates in both a 403(b) plan and a 457(b) plan to defer much more compensation.

---

[22] Employee Retirement Income Security Act § 201(2), 29 U.S.C. § 1015(2).
[23] Dep't of Labor Advisory Opinion 90-014A.
[24] IRC § 457.
[25] That is, are described in IRC § 457(b).

(ii) 457(f) Plans.   A *457(f) plan* is a top-hat plan that does not satisfy the requirements applicable to 457(b) plans. The tax advantages attendant to 457(f) plans are far more limited than those accorded 457(b) plans. Although participants in 457(f) plans may defer an unlimited amount of their compensation, these deferrals are taxed as soon as they become vested, as are any earnings that have accumulated prior to the vesting date. Earnings that accrue after the deferrals are fully vested are not taxed until the participant has an immediate right to receive them, such as at a specified retirement age.

(iii) Rabbi Trusts.   Although both 457(b) plans and 457(f) plans generally must be unfunded in order to avoid regulation by the Employee Retirement Income Security Act and preserve their principal tax advantages, the assets of these plans may nevertheless be held in a particular form of trust fund. This type of trust—commonly referred to as a *rabbi trust* because the first such trust for which the IRS issued a private letter ruling involved the payment of deferred compensation to a rabbi—essentially is treated as a mere extension of the sponsoring employer. The trust document must provide that deferred amounts will remain subject to the claims of the employer's general creditors in the event of the insolvency of the employer. Any income, deductions, or credits attributable to such a trust are treated as being attributable to the employer for tax purposes. The primary advantage of a rabbi trust is that plan participants are protected against losing their benefits on account of most corporate events short of insolvency.

(g) Options for Tax-Exempt Employers

When Congress in 1996 relaxed the rules that had prohibited tax-exempt organizations from sponsoring 401(k) plans, it caused these organizations to consider more carefully which type of deferred compensation arrangement best suits the needs of their employees. Each plan—401(k), 403(b), 457(b), or 457(f) type—comes with its own set of advantages and drawbacks.[26] Often, the suitability of a particular deferred compensation arrangement depends on the nature of the employer.

A non-charitable tax-exempt employer[27] generally is limited to a 401(k) plan or a 457 plan. For these employers, a 401(k) plan may be preferable, inasmuch as 457 plans receive less protection from the operation of the constructive receipt doctrine than do 401(k) plans, and because 457 plans must be unfunded and restricted to a small group of management employees.

In addition to a 401(k) plan and a 457 plan, a charitable tax-exempt employer also may sponsor a 403(b) plan. Although the attributes of 401(k) plans and 403(b) plans are similar, 401(k) plans afford broader investment flexibility

---

[26] In general, Mason, "Should a Tax-Exempt Employer Adopt a Section 401(k) Plan?," *Pension & Benefits Week* 7 (Oct. 28, 1996).

[27] That is, an exempt employer the tax exemption of which is not based on IRC § 501(c)(3).

than do 403(b) plans. The assets of 403(b) plans must be held in either annuity contracts or mutual funds, while 401(k) plans can permit participants to invest their accounts in common stocks, limited partnerships, and other investment options. That flexibility as to investment, however, comes at a cost. A 401(k) plan must comply with nondiscrimination requirements that may limit the contributions that can be made to highly compensated employees and also is subject to regulation by the Employee Retirement Income Security Act. A 403(b) plan need not comply with these rules.

(h) Perspective

The law in this field is complex, with Congress repeatedly visiting the subject. The enactment of the Employee Retirement Income Security Act in 1974 brought a vast amount of statutory law on the subject, for tax-exempt and for-profit employers alike. In 1986, Congress, as noted above, extended deferred compensation plan rules for the benefit of employees of tax-exempt organizations and made it clear that exempt organizations can maintain qualified profit-sharing plans.[28] In 1996, Congress decided that exempt organizations may maintain the qualified cash or deferred arrangements known as 401(k) plans.[29] The year 2001 brought even more changes to the rules governing retirement arrangements sponsored by tax-exempt employers. Congress, Treasury, and the IRS will assuredly add more law in this field in the coming years—much of it of direct applicability in the exempt organizations context.[30]

§ 16.2   SPECIAL RULES FOR WELFARE BENEFIT FUNDS

There are several categories of tax-exempt organizations, other than those entities that are exempt as retirement or profit-sharing plans, that are funds underlying employee benefit plans or are otherwise principally concerned with employee compensation.[31] Two of these are termed *welfare benefit funds:*[32] the voluntary employees' beneficiary association (VEBA) and the supplemental unemployment benefit trust (SUB).

---

[28] IRC § 401(a)(27).

[29] IRC § 401(k)(4)(B)(i).

[30] In general, Mason, "EGTRRA Requires Immediate Decisions by § 403(b) and § 457(b) Plan Sponsors," 29 *Tax Mgmt. Compensation Planning J.* (No. 12) 309 (Dec. 2001); Rasman & Olivieri, "How Pre-Tax Retirement Plans Stack Up for Tax-Exempt Employers," 8 *J. Tax. Exempt Orgs.* (No. 5) 206 (Mar./Apr. 1997); Walsh Skelly, "Getting More for Less: Tax-Advantaged Compensation Packages for Employees of Tax-Exempt Organizations," 3 *Exempt Org. Tax. Rev.* (No. 10) 1135 (1990); Altieri, "Nonqualified Deferred Compensation and the Tax-Exempt Employer," 16 *J. Pension Planning & Compliance* (No. 3) 229 (1990).

[31] See *infra* § 2.4.

[32] IRC § 505.

(a) Nondiscrimination Requirements

A VEBA cannot be tax-exempt unless it meets certain nondiscrimination requirements.[33] In general, a plan meets these requirements only if (1) each class of benefits under the plan is provided to a classification of employees that is set forth in the plan and that is found by the IRS not to be discriminatory in favor of employees who are highly compensated individuals, and (2) in the case of each class of benefits, the benefits do not discriminate in favor of employees who are highly compensated individuals.[34]

The following categories of employees may be excluded from consideration in this regard: employees who have not completed three years of service, employees who have not attained age 21, seasonal employees or less than half-time employees, employees covered by a collective bargaining agreement that was the subject of good faith bargaining, and employees who are nonresident aliens and who do not receive earned income from U.S. sources.[35]

(b) Tax-Exempt Status

A VEBA or SUB is not an organization that is tax-exempt for federal income purposes unless it has made timely application to the IRS for recognition of exempt status.[36]

§ 16.3 VOLUNTARY EMPLOYEES' BENEFICIARY ASSOCIATIONS

The federal tax law accords tax-exempt status to voluntary employees' beneficiary associations "providing for the payment of life, sick, accident or other benefits to the members of such association or their dependents or designated beneficiaries," as long as there is no private inurement.[37]

One of the basic requirements for achievement of tax exemption as a VEBA is that the organization must be an association of employees.[38] Thus, a trust that provides benefits to only one employee cannot qualify as an exempt

---

[33] IRC § 505(a)(1). This rule does not apply to any organization that is part of a plan maintained pursuant to an agreement between employee representatives and one or more employers if the IRS finds that the agreement is a collective bargaining agreement and that the plan was the subject of good faith bargaining between the employee representatives and the employer or employers (IRC § 505(b)).

[34] IRC § 505(b)(1). A life insurance, disability, severance pay, or supplemental unemployment compensation benefit will not fail the second of these requirements merely because the benefits available bear a uniform relationship to the total compensation, or the basic or regular rate of compensation, of employees covered by the plan (*id.*, last sentence).
The term *compensation* is defined in IRC § 414(s) and the term *highly compensated individual* is defined in IRC § 414(q).

[35] IRC § 505(b)(2).

[36] IRC § 505(c). The concept of recognition of tax-exempt status by the IRS is the subject of § 23.1.

[37] IRC § 501(c)(9); Reg. § 1.501(c)(9)-1. See Chapter 19.

[38] Reg. § 1.501(c)(9)-2(b).

VEBA.[39] Typically, those eligible for membership in a VEBA are defined by reference to a common employer (or affiliated employers), to coverage under one or more collective bargaining agreements (with respect to benefits provided by reason of the agreement(s)), to membership in a labor union, or to membership in one or more locals of a national or international labor union. Employees of one or more employers engaged in the same line of business in the same geographic locale are considered to share an employment-related bond for purposes of an organization through which their employers provide benefits. Employees of a labor union are considered to share an employment-related common bond with members of the union, and employees of a VEBA are considered to share an employment-related common bond with members of the VEBA. Whether a group of individuals is defined by reference to a permissible standard or standards is a question to be determined with regard to all the pertinent facts and circumstances.[40]

Despite the foregoing criteria, a federal court of appeals declared the tax regulations invalid to the extent of the *same geographic locale* requirement. The court reviewed the legislative history of the statute and the phraseology of other tax exemption provisions, and concluded that Congress intentionally elected to not place a geographic restriction on exempt VEBAs. Noting that the "quintessential element" of an exempt VEBA is the "commonality of interests among its employee members," the court wrote that the "relatedness among a group of employees is neither established nor dissipated upon the geographic locale of the group's members."[41]

Eligibility for membership in a VEBA may be restricted by geographic proximity, or by objective conditions or limitations reasonably related to employment, such as a limitation as to a reasonable classification of workers, a limitation based on a reasonable minimum period of service, a limitation based on maximum compensation, or a requirement that members be employed on a full-time basis. Also, eligibility for benefits may be restricted by objective conditions relating to the type or amount of benefits offered. Any objective criteria used to restrict eligibility for membership or benefits may not, however, be selected or administered in a manner that limits membership or benefits to officers, shareholders, or highly compensated employees of an employer contributing to or otherwise funding a VEBA. Similarly, eligibility for benefits may not be subject to conditions or limitations that have the effect of entitling officers, shareholders, or highly compensated employees of an employer contributing to or otherwise funding the VEBA to benefits that are disproportionate in relation to benefits to which other members of the VEBA are entitled.[42] Whether the selection or administration of objective conditions has the effect of providing disproportionate benefits to officers, shareholders, or highly compensated employees generally is determined on the

---

[39] Rev. Rul. 85-199, 1985-2 C.B. 163.
[40] Reg. § 1.501(c)(9)-2(a)(1).
[41] Water Quality Ass'n Employees' Benefit Corp. v. United States, 795 F.2d 1303, 1310-1311 (7th Cir. 1986), *rev'g* 609 F. Supp. 91 (N.D. III. 1985).
[42] E.g., Lima Surgical Assocs., Inc. Voluntary Employees' Beneficiary Ass'n Plan Trust v. United States, 90-1 U.S.T.C. ¶ 50,329 (Cl. Ct. 1990), *aff'd*, 944 F.2d 885 (Fed. Cir. 1991).

basis of all the facts and circumstances.[43] This tax exemption does not apply to pension funds distributing benefits to partners.[44]

Membership in a VEBA must be voluntary. Membership is *voluntary* if an affirmative act is required on the part of an employee to become a member rather than the designation as a member due to employee status. A VEBA is considered voluntary even though membership is required of all employees, however, as long as the employees do not incur a detriment (such as deductions from compensation) as the result of membership in the VEBA. An employer is not deemed to have imposed involuntary membership on the employees if membership is required as the result of a collective bargaining agreement or as an incident of membership in a labor organization.[45]

A tax-exempt VEBA must be controlled either by its membership, an independent trustee (such as a bank), or trustees, at least some of whom are designated by or on behalf of the membership.[46] Loose forms of affiliation are inadequate.[47]

The life, sick, accident, or other benefits provided by a VEBA must be payable to its members, their dependents, or their designated beneficiaries.[48] Life, sick, accident, or other benefits may take the form of cash or noncash benefits. To be tax-exempt, the VEBA must function so that substantially all of its operations are in furtherance of the provision of the requisite benefits.[49] The income tax regulations define the terms *life benefit*[50] and *sick and accident benefit*,[51] and provide that the term *other benefits* includes only benefits that are similar to life, sick, or accident benefits, namely, a benefit that is intended to safeguard or improve the health of a member or a member's dependents, or that protects against a contingency that interrupts or impairs a member's earning power.[52] Other benefits include paying vacation benefits, providing vacation facilities, reimbursing vacation expenses, subsidizing recreational activities, the provision of child-care facilities for preschool and school-age dependents, and personal legal service benefits.[53] Other benefits do not include the payment of commuting expenses, the provision of accident or homeowner's insurance benefits for damage to property,

[43] Reg. § 1.501(c)(9)-2(a)(2)(i). The income tax regulations enumerate certain generally permissible restrictions or conditions (Reg. § 1.501(c)(9)-2(a)(2)(ii); also Reg. § 1.501(c)(9)-4(b)).

[44] Nelson v. Joyce, 404 F. Supp. 489 (N.D. Ill. 1975); Rev. Rul. 70-411, 1970-2 C.B. 91; Rev. Rul. 69-144, 1969-1 C.B. 115.

[45] Reg. § 1.501(c)(9)-2(c)(2).

[46] Reg. § 1.501(c)(9)-2(c)(3)(iii). E.g., Lima Surgical Assocs., Inc. Voluntary Employees' Beneficiary Ass'n Plan Trust v. United States, *supra* note 42.

[47] E.g., American Ass'n of Christian Schools Voluntary Employees Beneficiary Ass'n Welfare Plan Trust v. United States, 663 F. Supp. (N.D. Ala. 1987), *aff'd*, 850 F.2d 1510 (11th Cir. 1988).

[48] E.g., Milwaukee Sign Painters Welfare Fund v. United States, 66-1 U.S.T.C. § 9170 (E.D. Wis. 1965).

[49] Reg. § 1.501(c)(9)-3(a). The IRS appears to apply a de minimis standard to determine whether less than substantially all of a VEBA's assets are used to provide permissible benefits to members (Gen. Couns. Mem. 39873, 39817).

[50] Reg. § 1.501(c)(9)-3(b).

[51] Reg. § 1.501(c)(9)-3(c).

[52] Reg. § 1.501(c)(9)-3(d).

[53] Reg. § 1.501(c)(9)-3(e).

the provision of malpractice insurance,[54] the provision of loans to members (except in times of distress), the provision of pension and annuity benefits payable at the time of mandatory or voluntary retirement, or the provision of savings facilities for members.[55]

An illustration of VEBAs, under the law prior to the promulgation of the pertinent income tax regulations, was an organization that reimbursed its members for premiums paid under the Medicare program.[56] An association that merely ensured the discharge of an obligation imposed by law upon an employer corporation (for example, workers' compensation benefits) was held to not qualify for tax exemption as a VEBA because the employees did not receive any additional benefits.[57]

The private inurement doctrine as applied to VEBAs means not only a prohibition on matters such as unreasonable compensation or self-dealing, but also the payment to any member of disproportionate benefits.[58] Thus, a plan was held to be merely a separate fund controlled by a company's sole shareholder for his own benefit, with coverage of other employees incidental, in part because deducted contributions were found to be excessive in relation to amounts paid out for insurance premiums and costs, and because funds of the plan were invested in a speculative manner.[59] The rebate of excess insurance premiums, based on the mortality or morbidity experience of the insurer to which the premiums were paid, to the person or persons whose contributions were applied to the premiums, is not prohibited inurement.[60] Also, the termination of a VEBA, with the remaining assets used to provide permissible benefits (such as a transfer of assets from one VEBA to another[61]), or certain distributions to members upon dissolution of a VEBA, are not forms of prohibited inurement.[62]

VEBAs may merge, with the successor entity retaining its status as a tax-exempt VEBA.[63] Surplus assets may be transferred from a trust to a VEBA without

[54] E.g., Anesthesia Serv. Med. Group, Inc., Employee Protective Trust, San Diego Trust & Sav. Bank, Trustee v. Comm'r, 85 T.C. 1031 (1985).
[55] Reg. § 1.501(c)(9)-3(f). This regulation was upheld in Canton Police Benevolent Ass'n of Canton, Ohio v. United States, 658 F. Supp. 411 (N.D. Ohio 1987), aff'd, 88-1 U.S.T.C. ¶ 9285 (6th Cir. 1988); Bricklayers Benefit Plans of Delaware Valley, Inc. v. Comm'r, 81 T.C. 735 (1983).
[56] Rev. Rul. 66-212, 1966-2 C.B. 230.
[57] Rev. Rul. 74-18, 1974-1 C.B. 139. Also Rev. Rul. 66-354, 1966-2 C.B. 207.
[58] Reg. § 1.501(c)(9)-4(a), (b). E.g., Lima Surgical Assocs, Inc. Voluntary Employees' Beneficiary Ass'n Plan Trust v. United States, *supra* note 42.
[59] Sunrise Constr. Co., Inc. v. Comm'r, 52 T.C.M. 1358 (1987).
[60] Reg. § 1.501(c)(9)-4(c).
[61] E.g., Priv. Ltr. Rul. 9414044.
[62] Reg. § 1.501(c)(9)-4(d). An insurance-based scheme to utilize tax-exempt VEBAs to generate business expense deductions and tax-free income is being thwarted by the courts, with the excess contributions treated as taxable disguised dividends and the individuals involved held liable for the accuracy-related negligence penalties (e.g., Neonatology Associates P.A. v. Comm'r, 299 F.3d 221 (3rd Cir. 2002)); these cases do not concern the exempt status of the VEBAs, although private inurement presumably occurred.
[63] E.g., Priv. Ltr. Rul. 200009051.

altering the exempt status of the VEBA.[64] A transfer of assets from a subsidiary's VEBA to a parent's VEBA will not disqualify either entity for exempt status,[65] nor will the transfer of assets to, and use by, the VEBA of an acquiring corporation from the VEBA of a corporation acquired in a merger.[66]

A VEBA cannot be tax-exempt unless it meets certain nondiscrimination requirements.[67] This rule is inapplicable, however, to a VEBA that is part of a plan maintained pursuant to one or more collective bargaining agreements between one or more employee organizations and one or more employers.[68]

A VEBA constitutes a *welfare benefit fund*.[69] Therefore, a *disqualified benefit*[70] provided by a VEBA will give rise to tax liability.[71]

VEBAs are subject to the unrelated income rules,[72] including the special rules by which only exempt function revenue is excluded from taxation.[73] Employer contributions to VEBAs are contributions to capital, rather than forms of gross income.[74] Net passive income of VEBAs constitutes unrelated business income, unless it is properly set aside for charitable purposes or to provide for the payment of life, sick, accident, or other benefits.[75]

Congress, in 1969, removed a limitation that no more than 15 percent of a VEBAs annual receipts could be in the form of investment income, thereby enabling VEBAs to accumulate reserves at reasonable levels. (VEBAs must conform to the requirements of the Employee Retirement Income Security Act, however, including those governing investment practices.) With this restriction eliminated, business corporations are utilizing VEBAs to provide employee benefits on a self-insurance basis, because the benefits program can be fashioned to meet the employers' desires and because it is less expensive than insurance premium costs.[76]

---

[64] Priv. Ltr. Rul. 9840050.
[65] Priv. Ltr. Rul. 200211053.
[66] Priv. Ltr. Rul. 200225041.
[67] IRC § 505(a)(1), (b).
[68] IRC § 505(a)(2).
[69] IRC § 419(e)(3)(A).
[70] IRC § 4976(b).
[71] IRC § 4976(a).
[72] See Part Five.
[73] See § 28.3.
[74] Priv. Ltr. Rul. 8512058.
[75] IRC § 512(a)(3)(B). See § 28.3. IRC § 512(a)(3)(E)(i) limits the amount that can be treated as exempt function income, because it is set aside, to an amount that does not exceed the account limits imposed by IRC § 419A(c). These limits are, however, inapplicable to collectively bargained plans (IRC § 419A(f)(5)(A)). Thus, there are no set-aside limits where the VEBA is a plan that is collectively bargained (e.g., Priv. Ltr. Ruls. 200003053, 9216033).
[76] In general, Hoffman & Lerner, "Pension Funds and Exempt Organizations: Prefunding Welfare Benefits with VEBAs," 8 *J. Tax. Inv.* (No. 1) 66 (1990); Paxton, "26 U.S.C. Sec 501(c)(9): Tax-Exempt Status of Voluntary Employees' Benefit Associations," 5 *Akron Tax J.* 253 (1988); Ryan, "DEFRA Requires a Current Look at VEBAs," 15 *Col. Law.* (No. 7) 1184 (1986); Sollee, "Analyzing the New Temporary Regulations for Welfare Benefit Plans: Part II," 64 *J. Tax.* (No. 6) 322 (1986); Sollee, "Analyzing the New Temporary Regulations for Welfare Benefit Plans," 64 *J. Tax.* (No. 5) 258 (1986); Hira & Perry, "IRS Provides Much Guidance on Welfare Benefit Funds," 17 *Tax Adviser* (No. 9) 585 (1986); Miller, "Legal Issues: New Rules for Funded Welfare Plans," 2 *Comp. & Benefits Man.* (No. 1) 185 (1985); Lurie, "Why

§ 16.4   SUPPLEMENTAL UNEMPLOYMENT BENEFIT TRUSTS

The federal tax law provides tax exemption for certain trusts forming part of a plan providing for the payment of supplemental unemployment compensation benefits, which satisfy five requirements.[77] Among other criteria, the SUB must be part of a plan the eligibility conditions and benefits of which do not discriminate in favor of supervisory or highly compensated employees and that requires that benefits be determined according to objective standards. Also, the SUB must be a part of a plan that provides that the corpus and income of the SUB cannot (before the satisfaction of all liabilities to employees covered by the plan) be used for, or diverted to, any purpose other than the provision of supplemental unemployment compensation benefits. Termination of a SUB, with distribution of its remaining assets to employees covered by the plan (after the satisfaction of all liabilities) will not result in loss of its exempt status (even though technically the assets will not be used solely for the purpose of providing benefits).[78] Moreover, the excess assets of a SUB, after paying all benefits and outstanding administrative costs, may be transferred to, and the SUB effectively merged with, a VEBA without threatening the exempt status of either.[79]

SUBS are intended to provide benefits to laid-off (or perhaps ill) employees, frequently in conjunction with other payments such as state unemployment benefits.

The term *supplemental unemployment compensation benefits* means separation-from-employment benefits and sick and accident benefits that are subordinate to the separation benefits.[80] These benefits encompass short-week benefits paid

Not a Salary-Reduction VEBA? Its Time Has Come," 1 *Comp. & Benefits Man.* (No. 2) 149 (1985); Sacks, "How Excess Assets of Terminating VEBAs May Best Be Utilized by the Employer," 62 *J. Tax.* (No. 4) 194 (1985); Eggertsen & Hainer, "1984 Tax Act: Changes Affecting Many Group Insurance Contracts and VEBAs," 64 *Mich. Bar J.* (No. 9) 932 (1985); Porcano, "Reconsidering Voluntary Employees' Beneficiary Associations Under the DRA," 16 *Tax Adv.* (No. 3) 130 (1985); Greenblatt, "VEBA Changes and Planning Under DEFRA," 37 *U.S.C. Inst. on Fed. Tax.* 2 (1985); Fuchs, "New VEBA Rules—Changes Under the 1984 Tax Act," 12 *Comp. Planning J.* (No. 9) 259 (1984); Tauber, "Voluntary Employees' Beneficiary Associations—Their Uses and Abuses," 10 *N.Y.U. Conf. on Employee Benefit Tax.* 11 (1984); Cole, Jr., "Voluntary Employee Beneficiary Associations and IRC Section 501(c)(9) Trusts," 42 *N.Y.U. Inst. on Fed. Tax.* 45 (1984); Boyers, "Using VEBAs to Complement Qualified Plan Benefits After TEFRA," 42 *N.Y.U. Inst. on Fed. Tax.* 43 (1984); Greenblatt, "Tax Planning for Fringe Benefits Provided by VEBAs Requires Changes Due to New Tax Law," 33 *Tax. Accts.* (No. 2) 82 (1984); Greenblatt, "Planning for VEBAs Under The Tax Reform Act of 1984," 62 *Taxes* (No. 9) 605 (1984); Smith, "An Examination of VEBAs and Deductions: Current or Deferred Compensation?," 17 *U.C. Davis L. Rev.* (No. 3) 925 (1984); Cirino, "Benefits: The Quiet Debut of 501(c)(9) Trusts," 11 *Institutional Investor* (No. 5) 57 (1977); Haneberg, " The 501(c)(9) Trust Revisited," 114 *Tr. & Est.* 622 (1975); Note, "Self-Insured Employee Welfare Plans and the 501(c)(9) Trust: The Specter of State Regulation," 43 *U. Cincinnati L. Rev.* 325 (1974); Stuchiver, "Using a 501(c)(9) Trust to Fund Employee Benefits," 112 *Tr. & Est.* 242 (1973).

[77] IRC § 501(c)(17); Reg. § 1.501(c)(17)-1(a).
[78] Rev. Rul. 81-68, 1981-1 C.B. 349.
[79] Priv. Ltr. Rul. 200206056.
[80] IRC § 501(c)(17)(D); Reg. § 1.501(c)(17)-1(b)(1).

to employees not wholly separated from employment[81] and relocation payments to employees who would otherwise be separated from employment.[82] Payments from a SUB to union members to compensate them for anticipated lost wages because of the adoption of a new industrial process were, however, ruled to not qualify as this type of benefit since there was no showing that all union members receiving the benefits were involuntarily separated from employment or actually incurred a reduction in the number of hours worked because of the new process.[83]

An otherwise qualified SUB can invest in low-risk, income-producing investments that serve social purposes, do not accrue for the benefit of related parties, and are not contrary to the employees' interests without jeopardizing its tax exemption.[84] Distribution to employees of funds representing contributions in excess of maximum funding will, however, adversely affect a SUB's exempt status.[85] The trustee of an exempt plan may, upon authorization from an employee, deduct and pay the employee's union dues from his or her benefit payments.[86]

A SUB constitutes a *welfare benefit fund*.[87] Accordingly, a *disqualified benefit*[88] provided by a SUB will give rise to tax liability.[89]

§ 16.5 BLACK LUNG BENEFITS TRUSTS

Another type of tax-exempt organization is the black lung benefits trust (BLBT).[90] The purpose of this body of law is to provide income tax exemption for a qualifying trust used by a coal mine operator to self-insure for liabilities under federal and state black lung benefits laws. Under the federal black lung benefits statute, a coal mine operator in a state not deemed to provide adequate worker's compensation coverage for pneumoconiosis must secure the payment of benefits for which the operator may be found liable under the statute, either by means of commercial insurance or through self-insuring. Since state laws presently are deemed inadequate for this purpose, all operators subject to this liability must obtain insurance or self-insure. Because this insurance is unavailable or is of high cost, Congress established this form of

[81] Rev. Rul. 70-189, 1970-1 C.B. 134. Also Rev. Rul. 80-124, 1980-1 C.B. 212; Rev. Rul. 56-249, 1956-2 C.B. 488.
[82] Rev. Rul. 70-188, 1970-1 C.B. 133.
[83] Rev. Rul. 77-43, 1977-1 C.B. 151.
[84] Rev. Rul. 70-536, 1970-2 C.B. 120.
[85] Rev. Rul. 71-156, 1971-2 C.B. 153.
[86] Rev. Rul. 73-307, 1973-2 C.B. 185.
[87] IRC § 419(e)(3)(A).
[88] IRC § 4976(b).
[89] IRC § 4976(a). Also, an organization described in IRC § 501(c)(17) cannot be tax-exempt if it engaged in a prohibited transaction as defined in IRC § 503(b) (IRC § 503(a)(1)(A), (B)).
[90] IRC § 501(c)(21).

self-insurance program, with similar tax consequences (from the point of view of the operator) as would result if the operator had purchased noncancellable accident and health insurance.[91]

A qualified BLBT must be irrevocable, must be established by a written instrument, must be created or organized in the United States, and may be contributed to by any person (other than an insurance company). The trust instrument may be amended or restated for appropriate purposes, such as to enable subsidiaries of the corporation that initially created the BLBT to self-insure their obligations under the black lung benefits law.[92]

The tax-exempt BLBT has as its exclusive purpose the (1) satisfaction, in whole or in part, of the liability of a contributor to the trust for, or with respect to, claims for compensation for disability or death due to pneumoconiosis under Black Lung Acts;[93] (2) payment of premiums for insurance exclusively covering this type of liability; and (3) payment of administrative and other incidental expenses of the trust (including legal, accounting, actuarial and trustee expenses) in connection with the operation of the trust and the processing of claims under Black Lung Acts against a contributor to the trust.[94]

No part of the assets of a tax-exempt BLBT may be used for, or diverted to, any purpose other than the foregoing three purposes, or investment.[95] Investment can, however, occur only to the extent that the trustee determines that the invested assets are not currently needed for the trust's exempt purposes. Moreover, the investment may only be in (1) public debt securities of the U.S., (2) obligations of a state or local government that are not in default as to principal or interest, or (3) time or demand deposits in a bank[96] or an insured credit union located in the United States.[97] A division of a BLBT and the transfer of its assets to one or more new BLBTs is not a prohibited diversion of assets.[98]

The assets of a qualified BLBT also may be paid into the Black Lung Disability Trust Fund[99] or into the general fund of the U.S. Treasury (other than in satisfaction of any tax or other civil or criminal liability of the person who established or contributed to the trust).

The income of a qualified BLBT is not taxable to the operator making contributions to it. Similarly, the trust's income is not taxable to the trust, except that

[91] S. Rep. No. 95-336, 95th Cong., 2d Sess. 11–12 (1978).
[92] E.g., Priv. Ltr. Rul. 9428030.
[93] These laws are Part C, Title IV, of the Federal Coal Mine Health and Safety Act of 1969 and any state law providing compensation for disability or death due to pneumoconiosis.
[94] IRC § 501(c)(21)(A).
[95] IRC § 501(c)(21)(B).
[96] As defined in IRC § 581.
[97] As defined in the Federal Credit Union Act, 12 U.S.C. § 1752(b).
[98] E.g., Priv. Ltr. Ruls. 200102056, 9428029.
[99] See § 3 of the Black Lung Benefits Revenue Act of 1977, Pub. L. No. 227, 95th Cong., 2 Sess. (1978).

the trust is subject to tax on any unrelated business taxable income.[100] The trust must, however, file annual information returns with the IRS.[101]

The contributions by a coal mine operator to a tax-exempt BLBT are deductible by the operator for federal income tax purposes.[102] This provision imposes alternative limitations on the deductibility of these contributions for a tax year, based on actual benefit claims approved or filed during the taxable year, as well as on the amount of anticipated liabilities for claims filed or expected to be filed in the future by past or present employees of the operator determined by using reasonable actuarial methods and assumptions, and any excess contributions may be taxable.[103] A contribution of property will be treated as a sale or exchange of the property for tax purposes, unless it is transferred without consideration and is not subject to a mortgage or similar lien.

A trust that is tax-exempt under these rules is subject to prohibitions on self-dealing[104] and the making of certain expenditures[105] (and is the only type of exempt organization, other than a private foundation,[106] to be governed by such statutory restrictions). These prohibitions are similar to those imposed on private foundations and are sanctioned by excise taxes upon the trust, its trustees, and/or the disqualified person(s) involved. The Senate Finance Committee observed that the investment limitations imposed on these trusts "are intended to preclude speculative or other investments of corpus or income which might jeopardize the carrying out of the trust's exempt purposes and permit the [C]ommittee [which authored these provisions] to simplify the self-dealing restrictions and avoid the necessity of certain other restrictions to prevent potential abuses."[107]

§ 16.6   RETIREMENT PLAN TRUST FUNDS

The federal tax law provides that an organization "described in . . . [IRC] section 401 (a) shall be exempt from taxation under this subtitle . . ." This provision of the Internal Revenue Code defines the qualified trust fund that is part of a stock bonus, pension, or profit-sharing plan[108] maintained by an employer for the exclusive benefit of its employees or their beneficiaries. While the fund is the tax-

---

[100] See Part Five.
[101] See § 24.3. Although the exemption application and annual information returns of an IRC § 501(c)(21) trust are subject to the public disclosure requirements (IRC § 6104(a)(1), 6104(b); see § 24.4(b)), disclosure is not required of confidential business information of a coal mine operator who establishes and contributes to such a trust (Pub. L. No. 488, 95th Cong., 2d Sess. (1978) § (e); H. Rep. No. 1656, 95th Cong., 2d Sess. 6 (1978)).
[102] IRC § 192.
[103] IRC § 4953.
[104] IRC § 4951. Cf. IRC § 4941.
[105] IRC § 4952. Cf. IRC § 4945.
[106] See Chapter 11.
[107] S. Rep. No. 95-336, *supra* note 91, at 14.
[108] IRC § 501(a).

exempt organization, the principal focus of the law in this area is on the terms and conditions of the retirement plan.[109]

The law of retirement plans was substantially modified by the Employee Retirement Income Security Act of 1974.[110] Government supervision of retirement plans is largely the responsibility of the IRS and the Department of Labor. This body of law imposes requirements relating to employee participation, coverage, vesting of interests, funding, portability of benefits, fiduciary responsibility, prohibited transactions, preparation of plan summaries, and annual reporting and disclosure to the Department of Labor. The Pension Benefit Guaranty Corporation administers a program of plan termination insurance applicable to defined benefit plans.[111]

§ 16.7   OTHER BENEFIT FUNDS

Another type of tax-exempt organization is a trust established by the sponsors of a multiemployer pension plan as a vehicle to accumulate funds in order to provide withdrawal liability payments to the plan.[112]

Also, a type of tax-exempt organization is a trust described in section 4049 of the Employee Retirement Income Security Act of 1974 (as in effect on the date of the enactment of the Single-Employer Pension Plan Amendments Act of 1986).[113]

The federal tax law references a trust or trusts, created before June 25, 1959, forming part of a plan providing for the payment of benefits under a pension plan funded only by employees' contributions, where three requirements are satisfied.[114]

Tax exemption is provided for teachers' retirement fund associations of a purely local character, if there is no private inurement (other than through payment of retirement benefits) and the income consists wholly of amounts received from public taxation, amounts received from assessments on the teaching salaries of members, and income from investments.[115] Tax regulations have not been issued under this provision, nor have there been any IRS rulings or court opinions concerning it, prompting the IRS to conclude that the section "has very limited application." The phrase *of a purely local character* has the same meaning in this context as it does with respect to benevolent or mutual organizations.[116]

---

[109] See *supra* § 1.
[110] 29 U.S.C. § 1001 *et seq.*
[111] See *supra* § 1(d)(i).
[112] IRC § 501(c)(22).
[113] IRC § 501(c)(24). Section 4049 was repealed on Dec. 22, 1987 (Pub. L. No. 100-203, § 9312(a)).
[114] IRC § 501(c)(18); Reg. § 1.501(c)(18)-1. An organization described in IRC § 501(c)(18) cannot be tax-exempt if it engaged in a prohibited transaction as defined in IRC § 503(b) (IRC § 503(a)(1)(C)).
[115] IRC § 501(c)(11).
[116] IRS Exempt Organizations Handbook (IRM 7751) § (12) 21.

CHAPTER SEVENTEEN

Political Organizations

Since the inception of the federal tax laws and until 1974, there were no rules as to whether political campaign committees and similar organizations were appropriate subjects of taxation. This absence of tax exposure resulted from the belief that virtually all of the receipts of political organizations were in the form of gifts and that, consequently, these organizations would not have taxable income.[1]

For many years, the IRS either failed or refused to assert tax liability against political campaign committees.[2] Early in 1974, however, the IRS ruled that an unincorporated campaign committee was not exempt from federal income taxation and must file tax returns, showing, as elements of gross income, items such as interest, dividends, and net gains from the sale of securities and related deductions (although contributions to the organization remained nontaxable).[3] This ruling was superseded by the enactment in 1974 of a tax law

---

[1] S. Rep. No. 93-1357, 93d Cong., 2d Sess. 25 (1974). The philosophy underlying the enactment of the tax rules concerning political organizations is much the same as that for social clubs (see Chapter 14) and homeowners' associations (see § 18.13). That is, in the case of social clubs and homeowners' associations, the law is designed to preclude income from sources other than members (i.e., nonmember and investment income) from subsidizing the members in their personal capacity.

[2] See Ann. 73-84, 1973-2 C.B. 461, which noted that it had been the historical practice of the IRS not to require the filing of tax returns by political parties and organizations, and that this policy had been previously communicated to the field offices of the IRS more than 25 years beforehand, but was never made public.

[3] Rev. Rul. 74-21, 1974-1 C.B. 14. Also Rev. Rul. 74-23, 1974-1 C.B. 17, *mod. and clar. by* Rev. Rul. 74-475, 1974-2 C.B. 22.

provision on the point[4] and related rules (including a per donee gift tax exclusion).[5]

Nonetheless, even after its 1974 ruling, the IRS continued to uphold the per donee gift tax exclusion for separate fundraising campaign committees,[6] despite opposition in the courts.[7] Later in 1974, as noted, Congress exempted contributions to political parties or committees from the gift tax.[8]

The granting of tax exemption to political organizations by Congress in 1974 resulted from a congressional belief that "political activity (including the financing of political activity) as such is not a trade or business that is appropriately subject to tax."[9]

§ 17.1 *POLITICAL ORGANIZATIONS* DEFINED

(a) Political Organizations in General

This category of tax exemption is available for the *political organization*.[10] A political organization is a party, committee, association, fund, or other organization (whether or not incorporated) organized and operated primarily for the purpose

---

[4] IRC § 527.

[5] IRC §§ 84, 2501(a)(5). IRC § 84 and Reg. § 1.84-1 provide that if any person transfers appreciated property to a political organization, the transferor is treated as having sold the property to the political organization on the date of the transfer and as having realized an amount equal to the property's fair market value on that date.

[6] Rev. Rul. 72-355, 1972-2 C.B. 532; Rev. Rul. 74-199, 1974-1 C.B. 285.

[7] E.g., Tax Analysts & Advocates v. Schultz, 376 F. Supp. 889 (D.D.C. 1974), *vacated*, 75-1 U.S.T.C. ¶ 13,052 (D.C. Cir. 1975).

[8] IRC § 2501(a)(5); Reg. § 25.2501-1(a)(5). The IRS contended that gifts to political organizations made before May 8, 1974 (the effective date of the statutory revision), were subject to the gift tax. Litigation ensued, with the U.S. Tax Court holding that the gift tax did not apply to amounts contributed for political purposes during the period there at issue (1967–1971) (Carson v. Comm'r, 71 T.C. 252 (1978), *aff'd*, 641 F.2d 864 (10th Cir. 1981)). A similar decision had been reached by the U.S. Court of Appeals for the Fifth Circuit, for years 1959–1961 (Stern v. United States, 426 F.2d 1327 (5th Cir. 1971)). The *Carson* decision rejected the government's contention that the enactment of this gift tax exclusion represented a change in the law. The IRS subsequently acquiesced in the *Carson* decision (Rev. Rul. 82-216, 1982-2 C.B. 220). This acquiescence was as to the result of, and not necessarily in the rationale of, the decision. That is, in the acquiescence ruling, the IRS stated that it "continues to maintain that gratuitous transfers to persons . . . [other than political organizations] are subject to the gift tax absent any specific statute to the contrary, even though the transfers may be motivated by a desire to advance the donor's own social, political or charitable goals" (*id.* at 220). For example, the IRS stated that the gift tax exclusion in the charitable gift context (IRC § 2522(a)) is not available for transfers to organizations that have been disqualified from classification under IRC § 501(c)(3) for engaging in legislative or political campaign activities (*id.* at 220).

[9] S. Rep. No. 93-1357, *supra* note 1, at 26.

[10] Political organizations generally cannot qualify under any of the other categories of tax-exempt organizations, such as IRC § 501(c)(3) (e.g., Lonsdale v. Comm'r, 41 T.C.M. 1106 (1981); Cavell v. Comm'r, 40 T.C.M. 395 (1980), *aff'd*, 661 F.2d 71 (5th Cir. 1981)).

of directly or indirectly accepting contributions[11] or making expenditures[12] for an exempt function.[13]

Although the *political action committee* (PAC) is perhaps the most recognized form of the political organization, the term includes a much broader range of entities. For example, it has been held that a bank account used by a candidate for depositing political contributions and disbursing bona fide political campaign expenses qualifies as a tax-exempt political organization.[14] Additionally, a candidate's newsletter fund can constitute a political organization.[15]

As noted, a political organization is exempt from taxation when it accepts contributions or makes expenditures for an exempt function. An *exempt function* is the activity of influencing or attempting to influence the selection, nomination, election, or appointment of any individual to any federal, state, or local public office[16] or office in a political organization, or the election of presidential or vice-presidential electors, whether or not these individuals or electors are selected,

---

[11] The term *contribution* includes a gift, subscription, loan, advance, or deposit of money, or anything of value, and includes a contract, promise, or agreement to make a contribution, whether or not legally enforceable (IRC § 527(e)(3), which incorporated the definition in IRC § 271(b)(2)).

[12] The term *expenditures* includes a payment, distribution, loan, advance, deposit, or gift of money, or anything of value, and includes a contract, promise, or agreement to make an expenditure, whether or not legally enforceable (IRC § 527(e)(4), which incorporated the definition in IRC § 271)(b)(3)).

[13] IRC § 527(e)(1). Accordingly, a political organization may include a committee or other group that accepts contributions or makes expenditures for the purpose of promoting the nomination of an individual for an elective public office in a primary election, or in a meeting or caucus of a political party (Reg. § 1.527-2(a)).

[14] Rev. Rul. 79-11, 1979-1 C.B. 207. Also Rev. Rul. 79-12, 1979-1 C.B. 208; Rev. Rul. 79-13, 1979-1 C.B. 208. A nonprofit and nonpartisan committee organized to provide a corporation's employees, shareholders, and their families an opportunity to join together to financially support candidates for public office was ruled to be a political organization (Tech. Adv. Mem. 7742008).

[15] See *infra* § 1(b).

[16] The facts and circumstances of each case determine whether a particular federal, state, or local office is a *public office*. In making the determination, the IRS uses principles consistent with those found in Reg. § 52.4946-1(g)(2) (Reg. § 1.527-2(d)). This regulation, which is part of the private foundation rules, contains a definition of *public office* for purposes of determining who is a government official under IRC § 4946(c). The regulation states:

> In defining the term "public office" . . . such term must be distinguished from mere public employment. Although holding a public office is one form of public employment, not every position in the employ of a State or other governmental subdivision . . . constitutes a "public office." Although a determination whether a public employee holds a public office depends on the facts and circumstances of the case, the essential element is whether a significant part of the activities of a public employee is the independent performance of policymaking functions. In applying this subparagraph, several factors may be considered as indications that a position in the executive, legislative, or judicial branch of the government of a State, possession of the United States, or political subdivision or other area of any of the foregoing, or of the District of Columbia, constitutes a "public office." Among such factors to be considered in addition to that set forth above, are that the office is created by the Congress, a State constitution, or the State legislature, or by a municipality or other governmental body pursuant to authority conferred by the Congress, State constitution, or State legislature, and the powers conferred on the office and the duties to be discharged by such office are defined either directly or indirectly by the Congress, State constitution, or State legislature, or through legislative authority.

nominated, elected, or appointed.[17] The term includes the making of expenditures relating to an eligible office that, if incurred by the individual, would be a deductible business expense.[18]

The term *exempt function* has been construed by the IRS to encompass a wide range of activities. For example, the IRS ruled that exempt function expenditures include:

1. Expenses for parties or other celebrations given on election night by a candidate's campaign committee for the candidate's campaign workers;[19]
2. Cash awards to campaign workers after the election, if the amount is reasonable;[20]
3. Amounts expended to enable an elected legislator to attend a political party's national convention as a delegate;[21]
4. Amounts expended for voter research, public opinion polls, and voter canvasses on behalf of an elected legislator who becomes a candidate for another political office;[22]
5. Payments made for a direct mail campaign (for grass-roots lobbying purposes) in support of a nonbinding referendum promoting fiscal responsibility where a potential candidate's name, picture, and political philosophy were included in the mailing;[23]
6. Payments of salary to a candidate who took a leave of absence from his employment to campaign on a full-time basis, when the amounts are reasonable;[24]
7. Disbursements for the distribution of voter guides and incumbents' voting records;[25]
8. Expenditures for grassroots lobbying,[26] where the lobbying is of a "dual character," in that the targeting of materials and the timing of their distribution is in relation to one or more elections, so that there is a "link" between issues and candidates.[27]

---

[17] IRC § 527(e)(2).

[18] *Id.*, last sentence.

[19] Rev. Rul. 87-119, 1987-2 C.B. 151. An exempt function does not, however, include the payment of an elected official's trade or business expenses (e.g., the cost of food for individuals working through lunch on legislative matters) and the payment of these expenses is gross income to the elected official (*id.*).

[20] *Id.* The amount of the cash award, however, is includible in the campaign worker's gross income.

[21] Rev. Rul. 79-12, *supra* note 14. The delegate's expenses were paid from surplus funds from an earlier campaign maintained in a separate bank account; these expenses are not includible in the delegate's gross income.

[22] Rev. Rul. 79-13, *supra* note 14. The voter research expenses were paid from surplus funds from an earlier campaign maintained in a separate bank account.

[23] Tech. Adv. Mem. 9130008.

[24] Priv. Ltr. Rul. 9516006.

[25] Priv. Ltr. Rul. 9652026.

[26] See § 20.2.

[27] E.g., Priv. Ltr. Rul. 9652026.

9. Disbursements for distribution of incumbents' voting records, voter guides, and information about incumbents and other candidates or potential candidates.[28]

10. Contributions and advertising in support of particular candidates, mass media campaigns, initiative campaigns, and litigation.[29]

The income tax regulations also contain several examples of exempt function expenditures[30] and state that the individual for whom these expenditures are made does not have to be an announced candidate, "nor is it critical that he [or she] ever become a candidate for an office."[31] Even activities engaged in "between elections" can be exempt function activities, as long as they are directly related to the process of selection, nomination or election of an individual in the next applicable political campaign.[32] Also, *indirect expenses*[33] and *terminating activities*[34] fall within the definition of *exempt function*.

The IRS will look at all the facts and circumstances in determining whether an expenditure constitutes an exempt function.[35] For example, a proper exempt function expenditure includes expenses for "voice and speech lessons to improve [a candidate's] skills," but does not include expenses of a political incumbent for "periodicals of general circulation in order to keep himself informed on national and local issues."[36]

(b) Principal Campaign Committees and Newsletter Funds

There are two aspects of the tax law for political organizations that are of particular benefit to those seeking election or reelection to public office, especially office

---

[28] Priv. Ltr. Rul. 9808037.

[29] Priv. Ltr. Rul. 199925051.

[30] Reg. § 1.527-2(c)(5).

[31] Reg. § 1.527-2(c)(1).

[32] *Id.* For example, funds held by a political organization and expended at the direction of a public officeholder after the individual had assumed office were found to be exempt function expenditures because the funds were expended for activities that were directly related to the process of influencing or attempting to influence the reelection of the individual (Tech. Adv. Mem. 8650001). The expenditures in question included a trip to a conference, where the political committee paid for the travel expenses of an entourage of political leaders, press staff, civic leaders, administrative staff, extra body guards, and certain spouses; the travel expenses of the family members of a politically influential official; donations to various charities and politically active groups; donations to certain families calculated to ingratiate the officeholder politically with certain ethnic constituencies; and the expenditure of funds to entertain certain political figures in an effort to facilitate fundraising on behalf of the officeholder's upcoming reelection campaign (*id.*).

[33] Indirect expenses include items such as overhead, record keeping, and expenses incurred in soliciting contributions to the political organization (Reg. § 1.527-2(c)(2)).

[34] Terminating expenses are expenses incurred in furtherance of the process of terminating a political organization's existence. They can include payment of campaign debts after the conclusion of a campaign (Reg. § 527-2(c)(3)).

[35] Reg. § 1.527-2(c)(1); Tech. Adv. Mem. 8147009 (the determining factor in categorizing an activity as an exempt function is the character and nature of the activity itself and not the identity of the organization that is conducting the activity).

[36] Reg. §§ 1.527-2(c)(5)(iii),(v).

in the U.S. Congress. The first provision provides a more favorable rate of tax on the political organization taxable income of congressional candidate campaign committees, while the second provision includes within the definition of a *political organization* any newsletter funds established by candidates or incumbents at any level of elective public office. This latter provision alters tax rules that were perceived as unfairly distorting elected officials' taxable income.[37]

As stated above, political organizations generally are subject to the highest rate, rather than the graduated rates, of corporate tax on their political organization taxable income. In 1981, however, Congress changed the law so that the political organization taxable income of a congressional candidate's *principal campaign committee*[38] is taxed at the graduated corporate income tax rates. A principal campaign committee is that designated by a congressional candidate pursuant to the federal election law.[39] A designation is not required where there is only one political committee with respect to a candidate.[40]

In addition, a newsletter fund is treated as if the fund constituted a political organization.[41] A newsletter fund is a fund established and maintained by an individual who holds, has been elected to, or is a candidate[42] for nomination or election to any federal, state, or local elective public office for use by the individual exclusively for the preparation and circulation of the individual's newsletter.[43] The exempt function of a newsletter fund is limited to the preparation and circulation of the newsletter, which includes secretarial services, printing, ad-

---

[37] Under tax laws prior to 1974, if an elected official received contributions to a fund established to pay for his or her newsletter, the IRS treated the contributions as income in the year received. Amounts spent in printing, addressing, and mailing the newsletter were deductible as ordinary and necessary business expenses, if the elected official itemized his or her deductions. The Senate Committee on Finance noted that this tax treatment could unfairly distort an elected official's tax items. For example, since the official's gross income would be higher than normal due to the inclusion of the contributions to his or her newsletter fund, this would increase the amount of charitable deductions he or she could take, while raising the nondeductible floor for medical expense deductions. To avoid these and other distortions, the Committee decided not to make taxable the newsletter contributions received and not to allow any deductions for newsletter expenses paid by the official (S. Rep. No. 93-1357, *supra* note 1, at 33).

[38] IRC § 527(h); Reg. § 1.527-9. If a campaign committee is not a principal committee, it is taxed at the highest corporate rate.

[39] 2 U.S.C. § 432(e); IRC § 527(h)(2)(B). Designation is made by appending a copy of the Statement of Candidacy (Federal Election Form 2 or equivalent statement filed with the Federal Election Commission under 11 C.F.R. § 101.1(a)) to the Form 1120-POL filed by the principal campaign committee (Reg. § 1.527-9(b)). This designation can only be revoked with the consent of the IRS (Reg. § 1.527-9(c)).

[40] IRC § 527(h)(2)(B), last sentence.

[41] IRC § 527(g). The exempt function of a newsletter fund, however, is narrower (see text accompanying *infra* notes 42 and 43) and the $100.00 specific deduction allowed to other political organizations is not applicable to a newsletter fund (Reg. § 1.527-7(b)).

[42] For purposes of newsletter funds, the term *candidate* means an individual who "publicly announces" that he or she is a candidate for nomination or election to an office and who meets the qualifications prescribed by law to hold such office (IRC § 527(g)(3)). This differs from the definition of *candidate for public office*, contained in Reg. § 1.501(c)(3)-1(c)(3)(iii), which does not require public announcement of a candidacy. (For a discussion of this term, see § 21.1(f).)

[43] IRC § 527(g)(1).

dressing, and mailing.[44] Thus, unlike other types of political organizations, newsletter fund assets may not be used for campaign activities.[45] Furthermore, newsletter fund assets used for purposes other than the preparation and circulation of the newsletter must be included in the gross income of the individual who established and maintained the fund.[46]

§ 17.2   ORGANIZATIONAL AND OPERATIONAL TESTS

A political organization satisfies the requisite organizational test if its articles of organization provide that the primary purpose of the organization is to carry on one or more exempt functions. If the organization has no formal articles of organization, consideration will be given to statements of the organization's members at the time it was formed that they intend to carry on an exempt function.[47]

To satisfy an operational test, a political organization does not have to engage exclusively in exempt function activities.[48] For example, a political organization may sponsor nonpartisan educational workshops, carry on social activities unrelated to an exempt function, support the enactment or defeat of a ballot proposition, or pay an incumbent's office expenses, as long as these are not the organization's primary activities.[49] In contrast, an organization that engages wholly in legislative activities cannot qualify as a political organization.[50]

§ 17.3   TAXATION OF ORGANIZATIONS

(a) Taxation of Political Organizations

Although political organizations are generally tax-exempt, they are subject to the highest rate[51] of corporate tax on their *political organization taxable income*.[52] A po-

---

[44] Reg. § 1.527-7(c). Congressional incumbents also can mail their newsletters without charge under the congressional franking privilege, although these mailings are not supposed to be used to solicit political support (39 U.S.C. § 3210). Both the House and the Senate prohibit their members from making franked mass mailings that were printed or prepared with private or political funds, since the franking privilege is reserved for "official documents." See The Committee on Standards of Office Conduct, Ethics Manual for Members, Officers, and Employees of the U.S. House of Representatives, 100th Cong., 1st Sess., Chap. 6 (1987); Rule XL, Standing Rules of the Senate, S. Doc. No. 101-25, 101st Cong., 2d Sess. 59 (1990).

[45] Reg. § 1.527-7(d). Thus, a newsletter fund cannot transfer assets to another political organization, unless that organization also is a newsletter fund.

[46] Reg. § 1.527-7(a). Additionally, any future contributions to the fund also are treated as income to that individual (*id.*).

[47] Reg. § 1.527-2(a)(2).

[48] Reg. § 1.527-2(a)(3).

[49] *Id.* As noted, the payment of an incumbent's office expenses is not an exempt function and will be treated as gross income to the incumbent (*supra* note 19).

[50] E.g., Priv. Ltr. Rul. 9244003.

[51] Cf. *supra* §1(b).

[52] IRC § 527(b).

litical organization's taxable income is its gross income,[53] less *exempt function income* and allowable deductions directly connected with the production of gross income (other than exempt function income).[54]

A political organization's exempt function income is any amount received as:

1. Contributions[55] of money or other property;[56]
2. Membership dues, fees, or assessments[57] from a member of the organization;
3. Proceeds from a political fundraising or entertainment event;[58]

[53] *Gross income* can include amounts expended for other than an exempt function, if the expenditure results in direct or indirect financial benefit to the political organization. For example, a political organization must include in its gross income amounts expended for improvements to its facilities or for equipment that is not necessary for or used in carrying out an exempt function (Reg. § 1.527-5(a)(1)). Amounts expended for illegal activities also must be included in the political organization's taxable income (Reg. § 1.527-5(a)(2)).

[54] IRC § 527(c). A specific deduction of $100.00 is also allowed, but no net operating loss deduction and none of the special deductions for corporations may be taken (IRC § 527(c)(2)). The IRS ruled that state income taxes paid by a political organization on its nonexempt function income are deductible in computing its taxable income (Rev. Rul. 85-115, 1985-2 C.B. 172). A political organization's tax return is filed on Form 1120-POL (IRC § 6012(a)(6); Reg. 1.6012-6).

[55] Generally, money or other property solicited personally, by mail, or through advertising will qualify as a *contribution*. Additionally, to the extent a political organization receives federal, state, or local funds under the "checkoff" provisions of IRC § 9001 *et* seq. or other provisions for campaign financing, those amounts are also treated as a contribution (Reg. § 1.527-3(b)).

[56] Some businesses establish "charity-PAC" matching programs, which allow employees of the business to designate a charitable organization to be the recipient of a contribution from the corporate employer; the contribution made by the corporation is an amount equal to the sum of the contributions that the employee made to the corporation's political action committee during the previous year. The Federal Election Commission is of the view that this type of matching is not a means of exchanging corporate funds for voluntary contributions (which is illegal (11 C.F.R. 114.5(b))) but instead is a permissible solicitation expense (2 U.S.C. 441b(b)(2) (Federal Election Commission Advisory Opinion 1989-7)). It is the position of the IRS, as expressed by its Chief Counsel's Office, however, that a business corporation's contribution to a charitable organization, designated by an employee of the corporation, is not deductible as a charitable gift by the corporation where the contribution is made under a charity-PAC matching program (Gen. Couns. Mem. 39877). The reason for this lack of deduction is the fact that the corporation received a quid pro quo, for the payment to the charity, in the form of the contribution to the political action committee. In general, see Hopkins, *The Tax Law of Charitable Giving* § 3.1(b).

[57] For example, filing fees paid by an individual directly or indirectly to a political party in order that the individual may run as a candidate in a primary or general election as a candidate of that party are treated as exempt function income (Reg. § 1.527-3(c)).

[58] Events intended to rally and encourage support for an individual for public office would be proper political fundraising events. Examples of these events are dinners, breakfasts, receptions, picnics, dances, and athletic exhibitions (Reg. § 1.527-3(d)(1)). By contrast, the IRS ruled that the mere use of funds generated by an event for political purposes does not transform the event into a political event; thus, for example, the sale of raffle tickets by a political organization did not result in exempt function revenue (Tech. Adv. Mem. 9847006). In response to outcries from the political fundraising community, the IRS (in a memorandum from the Exempt Organizations Division to the regional chief compliance officers, dated December 1, 1999) clarified this matter by stating that raffle proceeds can escape taxation as long as the sponsors of the raffle make the political purpose clear to those who purchase tickets (such as by placing a sign to that effect in the place where the tickets are sold).

4. Proceeds from the sale of political campaign materials,[59] which are not received in the ordinary course of any trade or business;[60] or

5. Proceeds from the conduct of any bingo game,[61] to the extent the amount is segregated for use only for the exempt function of the political organization.[62]

For political organizations that limit their activities solely to exempt functions, the effect of the foregoing tax rules is to subject only their investment income to taxation. For example, assume that a political organization receives $100,000 in political contributions, which it keeps segregated for appropriate exempt function use. In addition, assume the organization earns $10,000 in interest income (for example, from depositing the political contributions in an interest-bearing account). Under these circumstances, the political organization taxable income would include only the $10,000 in interest income.

By contrast, where a political organization expends money that results in a direct or indirect benefit to the organization itself[63] or expends money for an illegal activity,[64] the entire amount of the expenditure will be included in the political organization's gross income. Further, where a political organization makes a dual use of facilities or personnel (that is, use for both an exempt function and for the production of political organization taxable income), the expenses, depreciation, and similar items attributable to the facility or personnel must be allocated between the two uses on a "reasonable and consistent basis."[65]

---

[59] Proceeds from the sale of political memorabilia, bumper stickers, campaign buttons, hats, shirts, political posters, stationery, jewelry, or cookbooks are related to political activity as long as these items can be identified as relating to distributing political literature or organizing voters to vote for a candidate for public office (Reg. § 1.527-3(e)).

[60] The IRS looks at all the facts and circumstances in determining whether an activity is in the ordinary course of a trade or business. Usually, proceeds from "casual, sporadic fund raising or entertainment events" are not considered in the ordinary course of a trade or business (Reg. § 1.527-3(d)(2)). However, the IRS ruled that the proceeds received by a political organization from the sales of art reproductions did not qualify as exempt function income, because the sales activity was considered to be a trade or business (Rev. Rul. 80-103, 1980-1 C.B. 120).

[61] This term uses the definition in IRC § 513(f)(2). See § 27.2(h).

[62] IRC § 527(c)(3). As noted above, exempt function income must be segregated. Reg. § 1.527-2(b) defines a *segregated fund* as any fund that is established and maintained by a political organization or an individual separate from the assets of the organization or the personal assets of the individual. The purpose of the fund must be to receive and segregate exempt function income (and earnings on this income) for use only for an exempt function or for an activity necessary to fulfill an exempt function. If an organization that has a segregated fund for purposes of segregating amounts referred to in IRC § 527(c) expends more than an insubstantial amount from the segregated fund for activities that are not for an exempt function during the taxable year, the fund will not be treated as a segregated fund for that tax year (*id.*).

[63] An illustration would be the expenditure of exempt function income to purchase building improvements or equipment not necessary to carry on an exempt function.

[64] Although expenses for illegal activity are includable in the organization's gross income, expenses incurred in the defense of civil or criminal suits against the organization are not taxable to the organization (Reg. § 1.527-5(a)(2)). In addition, voluntary reimbursement to the participants in the illegal activity for similar expenses incurred by them are not taxable to the organization if it can demonstrate that such payments were not a part of the inducement to engage in the illegal activity or part of the agreed upon compensation for such activity (*id.*).

[65] Reg. § 1.527-4(c)(3).

In addition to the above activities, which result in gross income to the political organization, certain activities by political organizations can result in gross income to a candidate or other individual affiliated with the political organization.[66] For example, where a political organization expends any amount for the personal use of any individual, such as for paying a candidate's income tax liability, the amount expended is included in the individual's gross income.[67] Also, excess funds controlled by a political organization or other person after a campaign or election are treated as expended for the personal use of the person having control over the ultimate use of the funds, unless the funds are held in reasonable anticipation of use by the political organization for future exempt functions or the funds are transferred within a reasonable period of time to certain political, tax-exempt, or governmental organizations described in the regulations.[68]

(b) Taxation of Exempt Organizations other than Political Organizations

Although a political organization is exempt from taxation on amounts expended for an exempt function, if another type of tax-exempt organization[69] expends any amount during a tax year, either directly[70] or through another organization,[71] for what would be a political organization exempt function, it must include in its gross income for the year an amount equal to the lesser of (1) its net

---

[66] Activities that will not be treated as income to a candidate or other person affiliated with a political organization include contributions to another political organization or newsletter fund; contributions to organizations described in IRC § 509(a)(1) or § 509(a)(2) (see § 11.3(a), (b)); and deposits in the general fund of the U.S. Treasury or the general fund of any state or local governments (IRC § 527(d); Reg. § 1.527-5(b)).

[67] Reg. § 1.527-5(a)(1).

[68] Reg. § 1.527-5(c)(1). The organizations to which funds can be transferred are described in Reg. § 1.527-5(b). For example, a political organization can contribute amounts "to or for the use of" a public or publicly supported charitable organization (i.e., those entities described in IRC § 509(a)(1) or § 509(a)(2) (see § 11.3(a), (b)) (Reg. § 1.527-5(b)(2)). The IRS ruled that campaign committees could transfer funds to a private foundation and remain within this exception, where the foundation was obligated by its corporate documents to make grants only to these types of charitable entities; the foundation was characterized as a "trust" under state law, with the funds transferred "for the use of" the charitable organizations (Priv. Ltr. Rul. 9425032). Contributions to these organizations are not deductible (Reg. § 1.527-5(b)(2), last sentence). Where excess funds are held by an individual who dies before the funds have been properly transferred, the funds are generally considered income of the decedent and will be included in the decedent's gross estate, unless the estate transfers the funds within a reasonable period to an eligible organization in accordance with Reg. § 1.527-5(b) (Reg. § 1.527-5(c)(2)). In general, Friedman, "How Political Organizations Are Taxed," 8 J. Tax Exempt Orgs. (No. 5) 221 (Mar./Apr. 1997).

[69] That is, an organization described in IRC § 501(c) that is exempt from tax under IRC § 501(a).

[70] See Tech. Adv. Mem. 8502003 (contributions made by an exempt labor organization from its general checking fund directly to state and local candidates were taxable expenditures).

[71] Although an expenditure can be made for an exempt function "through another organization" (e.g., by making a contribution to another organization, which then uses the contribution for an exempt function), an IRC § 501(c) organization will not be absolutely liable for tax under IRC § 527(f)(1) for amounts transferred to an organization, as long as "reasonable steps" are taken to ensure that the transferee does not use these amounts for an exempt function (Reg. § 1.527-6(b)(1)(ii)).

investment income[72] for the year or (2) the aggregate amount expended during the year for the exempt function.[73] Generally, this amount is taxed at the highest corporate tax rate.[74]

The foregoing rules are not intended to change the prohibition on political activities applicable to charitable and social welfare organizations.[75] Indeed, public charities engaging in any amount of political campaign intervention stand to lose their tax-exempt status, in addition to facing the political organization tax. The concept of political organization exempt function, however, is broader than the political campaign intervention limitation.[76] For example, an exempt function includes an attempt to influence the appointment of an individual to a federal public office, such as a presidential nomination of a Supreme Court justice.[77] Since the effort to secure Senate confirmation of a Supreme Court nominee does not involve a political campaign, a charitable organization is not precluded from participating in that process.[78]

The purpose of taxing exempt organizations on their exempt function activity is to treat them on an equal basis for tax purposes with political organizations, and, at the same time, to ensure that they are taxed only to the extent they actually operate in a fashion similar to political organizations.[79] Tracing of funds is not required, and the tax will apply even though the tax-exempt organization uses its investment income exclusively for nonpolitical purposes and makes its political expenditures entirely out of other funds.[80]

Not all politically related expenditures by exempt organizations, however, are considered exempt function expenditures subject to taxation. For example, ex-

---

[72] *Net investment income* is defined as the excess of gross income from interest, dividends, rents, and royalties, plus the excess of gains from the sale or exchange of assets over losses from the sale or exchange of assets, over allowable deductions directly connected with the production of investment income (IRC § 527(f)(2)). To avoid double taxation, however, items taken into account for purposes of the unrelated business income tax imposed by IRC § 511 are not taken into account when calculating net investment income (*id.*, last sentence).

[73] IRC § 527(f)(1). The IRS adopted protest and conference procedures for contesting the tax imposed by IRC § 527(f) (Rev. Proc. 90-27, 1990-1 C.B. 514).

[74] IRC § 527(b). Special rules apply, however, in cases where the organization has a net capital gain (IRC § 527(b)(2)). The IRS may revoke a ruling letter that recognized an organization's tax exemption, without retroactive effect, pursuant to IRC § 7805(b), but in this type of case the organization would be subject to taxation on any political activity during the IRC § 7805(b) relief period (Gen. Couns. Mem. 39811).

[75] S. Rep. No. 93-1357, *supra* note 1, at 29; Reg. § 1.527-6(g). For example, the IRS ruled that a tax-exempt social welfare (IRC § 501(c)(4)) organization may, without adversely affecting its exempt status, participate in political campaign activities as long as it is primarily engaged in the promotion of social welfare but that the amounts expended for the activities may be treated as political organization taxable income (Rev. Rul. 81-95, 1981-1 C.B. 332) (see § 21.4).

The U.S. Tax Court held that a tax-exempt labor organization (see § 15.1) was liable for the IRC § 527(f) tax as the result of the transfer of monies to its political action committee (Alaska Pub. Serv. Employees Local 71 v. Comm'r, 67 T.C.M. 1664 (1991)).

[76] In general, § 21.1.

[77] *Id.*

[78] *Id.*

[79] S. Rep. No. 93-1357, *supra* note 1, at 29.

[80] *Id.*

penditures for nonpartisan activity are not considered exempt function expenditures. *Nonpartisan activities* include voter registration and "get-out-the-vote" campaigns, as long as they are not specifically identified with any candidate or political party.[81] Additionally, where an exempt organization appears before a legislative body in response to a "written request . . . for the purpose of influencing the appointment or confirmation of an individual to a public office," expenditures related to the appearance are not treated as exempt function expenditures.[82] Also, the IRS ruled that an exempt social welfare organization is not subject to the political activities tax when it provides administrative services to a related political action committee in exchange for a fee based on fair market value.[83]

§ 17.4 AVOIDING THE POLITICAL ORGANIZATIONS TAX

Although tax-exempt organizations are subject to tax on their exempt function expenditures, these entities can avoid this political activities tax in a number of ways.

First, it may be possible for a tax-exempt organization to establish a related political organization (usually a political action committee, or PAC). From a tax law perspective, the law on this point is sparse. It is clear that tax-exempt organizations, such as social welfare organizations, trade and business associations, labor unions, and chambers of commerce can establish related PACs.[84] Presumably this is also true with respect to other types of exempt organizations, such as social clubs and veterans' organizations.

Also, a tax-exempt organization will not be taxed where it merely receives contributions from its members for political action and promptly and directly[85] transfers the funds to the political organization that solicited them.[86] Furthermore, the IRS ruled that, where an exempt organization deposits political contributions into an interest-bearing checking account for administrative efficiency

[81] Reg. § 1.527-6(b)(5).
[82] Reg. § 1.527-6(b)(4).
[83] Priv. Ltr. Rul. 9850025.
[84] E.g., Priv. Ltr. Rul. 9652026. The Senate Finance Committee stated that "generally, a section 501(c) organization that is permitted to engage in political activities would establish a separate organization that would operate primarily as a political organization, and directly receive and disburse all funds related to nomination, etc. activities. In this way, the campaign-type activities would be taken entirely out of the section 501(c) organization, to the benefit both of the organization and the administration of the tax laws" (S. Rep. No. 93-1357, *supra* note 1, at 30).
[85] A transfer is considered promptly and directly made if the organization's procedures satisfy requirements of applicable federal or state campaign laws, the organization maintains adequate records to demonstrate that amounts transferred are in fact political contributions or dues (rather than investment income), and the political contributions or dues transferred were not used to earn investment income for the organization (Reg. § 1.527-6(e)(3)).
[86] Reg. § 1.527-6(e).

before their transfer to a PAC, it has still satisfied the regulation's requirements to promptly and directly transfer the funds to the PAC.[87]

A separate segregated fund that is maintained by an eligible tax-exempt organization is treated as a separate entity from that organization for purposes of the rules pertaining to political organizations.[88] Thus, an exempt organization that engaged in a political organization exempt function as a relatively small part of its operations may have much or all of its net investment income taxed, while the exempt organization that maintains a separate segregated fund can segregate contributions for use in an exempt function, with the result that only the net investment income of the fund is subject to tax.[89]

A tax-exempt organization can make *soft-dollar* expenditures (i.e., expenditures for indirect expenses allowed by the federal election law) in support of a separate segregated fund. These expenditures generally are not considered an exempt function outlay and, thus, will not subject a tax-exempt organization to the political activities tax. It is important to note, however, that this type of expenditure is an exempt function outlay when made by a political organization.[90] There is some confusion on this point because of the dual use of the term *exempt function expenditure*, and the IRS has indicated that, if it should conclude in the future that some or all of the indirect expenses allowed by the federal election law constitute exempt function expenditures for purposes of the political activities tax, that interpretation of the law will apply only on a prospective basis.[91]

---

[87] Tech. Adv. Mems. 9105001, 9105002. Also Gen. Couns. Mem. 39837, which is the background document for these two technical advice memoranda. The IRS stated that the primary objective of the test stated in Reg. § 1.527-6(e)(3) is to prevent tax-exempt organizations from needlessly retaining the PAC funds in order to invest those funds. In this case, even though a small amount of interest was earned and retained by the organization when it briefly held the PAC funds in its interest-bearing checking account, the PAC funds were placed in the checking account primarily for administrative efficiency, rather than for investment purposes (*id.; also* Tech. Adv. Mem. 9042004, reaching the same result with respect to a business league; Tech. Adv. Mem. 8628001, reaching the same result with respect to a labor union).

[88] IRC § 527(f)(3); Reg. § 1.527-6(f). A *separate segregated fund* is defined as a fund within the meaning of 18 U.S.C. § 610 or any similar state statute, or within the meaning of any state statute that permits the segregation of dues moneys for political organization exempt functions (IRC § 527(f)(3)). However, 18 U.S.C. § 610 was repealed by the Federal Election Campaign Act Amendments of 1976, Pub. L. No. 94-382. § 112, 90 Stat. 490, and was recodified at 2 U.S.C. § 441b. The term *separate segregated fund* is not further defined in the recodified section. Although the focus of IRC § 527(f)(3) is on separate segregated funds that are maintained by an IRC § 501(c) organization, the IRS stated that there is nothing in the legislative history to indicate that was to be the only type of segregated fund to which amounts could be transferred (Tech. Adv. Mem. 8147008).

[89] Ann. 88-114, 1988-37 I.R.B. 26; S. Rep. No. 93-1357, *supra* note 1, at 30.

[90] Reg. § 1.527-6(b)(1).

[91] Tech. Adv. Mem. 8516001. A soft-dollar expenditure by a tax-exempt membership organization, which is not an exempt function expenditure, may cause a portion of the members' dues to be nondeductible as a business expense, as a political campaign expense (IRC § 162(e)(2)) (Tech. Adv. Mem. 8202019). The same may be the case in connection with certain types of lobbying expenditures (Tech. Adv. Mem. 7946009). The business expenses deduction is disallowed where either of these disqualifying activities is substantial in relation to total activities (Reg. § 1.162-20(c)(3)).

As discussed,[92] charitable organizations are not permitted to engage in political campaign activities; that is, they cannot intervene in a campaign on behalf of or in opposition to a candidate for public office.[93] A charitable organization, however, may establish and use a political organization (such as a PAC) if the purpose of the PAC is to engage in political activities[94] that are not political campaign activities.[95] In other words, a noncampaign PAC affiliated with a charitable organization may be used to promote the organization's viewpoint on particular issues. In the view of the IRS, however, a corporate sponsor of a PAC may not deduct the organizational and administrative costs of the PAC.[96] In the instance under review, the expenses sought to be deducted were legal fees and interest expenses. The IRS concluded that the expenditures for the PAC were for intervention in political campaigns on behalf of candidates for public office and/or in connection with attempts to influence the general public, and thus were nondeductible.[97]

It is possible for the managers of a charitable organization and/or others, acting as individuals, to establish and use an *independent* political action committee, even if the PAC has the function of supporting a candidate's political campaign. While the IRS has yet to address this topic, the Federal Election Commission published an advisory opinion[98] sanctioning the concept of what the federal campaign law recognizes as a "non-connected political committee."[99] According to the FEC, a nonconnected political committee has the following characteristics:

1. It is established by the members of the governing board of the charitable organization acting in their individual capacities;

2. The committee operates and is governed independently of the charitable organization;

3. The committee is not financially supported by the charitable organization;

4. The committee appropriately reimburses the charitable organization for expenses incurred on behalf of the committee;

5. The committee pays a fair rent to the charitable organization for the use of any office space and/or facilities;

[92] See Chapter 21.
[93] IRC § 501(c)(3).
[94] That is, IRC § 527 exempt functions.
[95] Ann. 88-114, 1988-37 I.R.B. 26.
[96] Priv. Ltr. Rul. 8202019. The IRS also held that the portion of the salaries of the corporation's officers and employees allocable to work on the PAC (including time spent after regular working hours) is nondeductible expenses. Further, the IRS also ruled as nondeductible the corporation's overhead expenses relating to the withholding of contributions to the PAC from employee's salaries and agents' commissions.
[97] IRC § 162(e)(2).
[98] FEC Advisory Opinion 1984-12.
[99] Cf. 2 U.S.C. §§ 431(7), 411b.

6. The committee pays a "commercially reasonable" consideration for the services of individuals who are employees or agents of the charitable organization;

7. The charitable organization does not engage in conduct that favors or appears to favor the solicitation activity of the committee; and

8. Neither the charitable organization nor the committee asserts a proprietary interest in or control over use of the name of the political committee.[100]

[100] *Id.* In general, Tesdahl, "Taxation and Representation—How to Use Political Organizations," 4 *J. Tax Exempt Orgs.* 29 (Spring 1992); Forman, "PAC Contributions and Effective Corporate Tax Rates," 45 *Tax Notes* (No. 11) 1363 (1990); Schoenblum, "From De Facto to Statutory Exemption: An Analysis of the Evolution of Legislative Policy Regarding the Federal Taxation of Campaign Finance," 65 *Va. L. Rev.* 513 (1979); Golden, "Federal Taxation and the Political Process," 24 *Kan. L. Rev.* 221 (1976); Streng, "The Federal Tax Treatment of Political Contributions and Political Organizations," 29 *Tax Law.* 139 (1975); Kaplan, "Taxation and Political Campaigns: Interface Resolved," 53 *Taxes* 340 (1975); Boehm, "Taxes and Politics," 22 *Tax L. Rev.* 369 (1967).

CHAPTER EIGHTEEN

Other Tax-Exempt Organizations

Several categories of organizations are exempt from federal income tax, in addition to those that are the subject of previous chapters. The law as to these categories of entities is summarized in this chapter, in order of the accompanying Internal Revenue Code section provisions, followed by law summaries as to other types of exempt organizations.

§ 18.1 UNITED STATES INSTRUMENTALITIES

The federal income tax law references "[c]orporations organized under Act of Congress, if such corporations are instrumentalities of the United States and if it is specifically provided in this title [Internal Revenue Title] (or under such Act as amended and supplemented before . . . [July 18, 1984]) that such corporations are exempt from Federal income taxes."[1] This third criterion was added to the Internal Revenue Code in 1984 to stipulate that tax exemptions for *United States instrumentalities* must be specified in the Code or in a revenue act. Under prior law (and for pre-1984 instrumentalities), it was sufficient to have tax exemption provided in any act of Congress.

Organizations exempt from federal income tax as U.S. instrumentalities include the Federal Deposit Insurance Corporation, the Reconstruction Finance Corporation, Federal Land Banks, Federal National Mortgage Association, Federal Reserve Banks, the Federal Savings and Loan Insurance Corporation, and the Pennsylvania Avenue Development Corporation.[2]

Federal credit unions organized and operated under the Federal Credit Union Act are instrumentalities of the United States[3] and therefore are entitled to tax exemption under this body of law. These credit unions are included in a group exemption ruling[4] issued to the National Credit Union Administration.[5] Certain other credit unions that fail to qualify under this provision may secure tax exemption as non-stock mutual credit unions.[6]

When Congress enacted the Employee Retirement Income Security Act of 1974 (ERISA), it established the Pension Benefit Guaranty Corporation (PBGC) primarily to administer a pension plan termination program. ERISA exempted the PBGC from state and local taxation but was silent on the matter of federal taxation. By enactment of the Tax Reform Act of 1976, Congress also exempted the PBGC from federal income taxation.

Congress amended ERISA[7] to exempt the PBGC from taxation by the United States. (The PBGC, however, remains subject to the taxes imposed under the Federal Insurance Contributions Act and the Federal Unemployment Tax Act.) This action by Congress qualified the PBGC for tax-exempt status as an instrumentality of the United States. The applicability of the PBGC provision was retroactive to September 2, 1974 (the date of enactment of ERISA).

In other illustrations, the Supreme Court held that the concept of a *federal instrumentality* includes army post exchanges[8] and the American National Red Cross.[9] While neither is directly controlled by the United States, they have an "unusual relationship" with the federal government, such as operation pursuant to a federal charter, federal government audit, involvement of a presidential appointee or government employees, and government funding or provision of ser-

---

[1] IRC § 501(c)(1).

[2] Tax exemption as a U.S. instrumentality extends to the Central Liquidity Facility established under the Federal Credit Union Act, and the Resolution Trust Corporation and the Resolution Funding Corporation established under the Federal Home Loan Bank Act (IRC § 501(1)).

[3] Rev. Rul. 55-133, 1955-1 C.B. 138.

[4] See § 23.6.

[5] Rev. Rul. 89-94, 1989-2 C.B. 233.

[6] Rev. Rul. 69-283, 1969-1 C.B. 156. See *infra* § 7.

[7] ERISA § 4002(g)(1).

[8] Standard Oil Co. v. Johnson, 316 U.S. 481 (1942).

[9] Department of Employment v. United States, 85 U.S. 355 (1966). Also United States v. Livingston, 179 F. Supp. 9 (E.D.S.C. 1959), *aff'd*, 364 U.S. 281 (1960).

vices. Applying these criteria, a federal court found the U.S. Capital Historical Society to be a federal instrumentality, also finding that it performs an essential function for the federal government (with the result that the District of Columbia was held to lack the power to tax sales by the historical society).[10]

§ 18.2   TITLE-HOLDING CORPORATIONS

The *title-holding corporation* is an entity that serves only one or more tax-exempt organizations. Its purpose, as the name indicates, is to function as a subsidiary organization, holding title to property that would otherwise be held by the parent exempt organization or organizations and remitting any net income from the property to the parent or parents. Originally designed to circumvent state law restrictions on the holding of property by nonprofit organizations, the title-holding company today is used to house the title to property in the subsidiary for the purpose of reducing the exposure of liability from use of the property by the parent entity, otherwise facilitate administration, and increase borrowing power.[11]

Title-holding corporations are most useful where—for management and/or law reasons—it is deemed appropriate that the title to an item of property be held in the name of another (albeit related) organization. There is no limitation on the type of property the title to which may be held by a title-holding corporation; it may be real property, such as an office building, or an item of personal property, such as capital equipment. As the IRS observed, the title-holding corporation is "by its nature responsive to the needs and purposes of its exempt parent which established it mainly to facilitate the administration of properties."[12] Wherever the administration of one or more organizations may be so served, the title-holding corporation is available as a useful tax planning mechanism.

Should the organization to which a tax-exempt title-holding corporation makes income distributions cease to qualify for tax exemption, the holding company would, in turn, lose its entitlement to tax exemption on this basis.[13] Likewise, the sale of all of the stock of an exempt title-holding company to a private person would cause the organization to no longer qualify for tax-exempt status.[14]

(a)   Single Parent Organizations

The federal tax law references "[c]orporations organized for the exclusive purpose of holding title to property, collecting income therefrom, and turning over the entire amount thereof, less expenses, to an organization which itself is" tax-

[10] United States v. District of Columbia, 558 F. Supp. 213 (D.D.C. 1982).
[11] IRC § 501(c)(2); IRS Exempt Organizations Handbook (Internal Revenue Manual 7751) § 230.
[12] Rev. Rul. 77-429, 1977-2 C.B. 189.
[13] Rev. Rul. 68-371, 1968-2 C.B. 204.
[14] Priv. Ltr. Rul. 9414002.

exempt. This is the *single parent title-holding organization*. For this purpose, the term *expenses* includes a reasonable allowance for depreciation.[15]

In general, this type of organization cannot accumulate income.[16] That is, as a general rule, its function is to transfer the entire amount of its income, less expenses, to a tax-exempt parent.[17] If the organization is not specifically organized to do this, it cannot qualify as an exempt title-holding corporation.[18] Moreover, if the entity does not operate in this fashion, it cannot constitute this type of exempt organization.[19]

Despite the general prohibition on income accumulation, however, a tax-exempt title-holding corporation may retain part of its income each year to apply to indebtedness on property to which it holds title.[20] The transaction is treated as if the income had been transferred to the parent organization and that entity had used the income to make a capital contribution to the title-holding corporation, which, in turn, applied the contribution to the indebtedness. In rationalizing this flexibility, the IRS observed that the title-holding corporation should not be "restricted in serving the needs of the parent in connection with the administration of properties."[21]

The IRS ruled that an organization formed as a subsidiary of a tax-exempt title-holding corporation, organized for the exclusive purpose of holding title to investment property that would otherwise be held by the parent, itself qualified as an exempt title-holding corporation, inasmuch as it collected the income from the property and transferred it to its parent (which was, of course, an exempt organization).[22] In other words, an exempt title-holding organization can be the beneficiary of the functions of another exempt title-holding organization.

These organizations can be put to creative uses. In one instance, a tax-exempt title-holding corporation was utilized to hold and administer a scholarship and loan fund for a fraternity.[23] In another case, a stock corporation organized and operated to hold title to a chapter house of a college fraternity was held to qualify as an exempt title-holding organization, even though the stock was owned by members of the fraternity.[24] (Where, however, an exempt organization has no control over the title-holding organization, the latter cannot qualify for tax-exempt status.[25])

While the renting of real estate generically is a business, the IRS determined

---

[15] Rev. Rul. 66-102, 1966-1 C.B. 133.

[16] E.g., Kanawha-Roane Lands v. United States, 136 F. Supp. 631 (S.D. W. Va. 1955).

[17] Reg. § 1.501(c)(2)-1(b).

[18] E.g., Banner Bldg. Co., Inc. v. Comm'r, 46 B.T.A. 857 (1942).

[19] E.g., Eddie Cigelman Corp. v. Comm'r, 15 T.C.M. 1259 (1955); The Davenport Found v. Comm'r, 6 T.C.M. 1335 (1947).

[20] Rev. Rul. 77-429, *supra* note 12.

[21] *Id.* at 189–190.

[22] Rev. Rul. 76-335, 1976-2 C.B. 141.

[23] N.P.E.F. Corp. v. Comm'r, 5 T.C.M. 313 (1946).

[24] Rev. Rul. 68-222, 1968-1 C.B. 243. This stock was the type that did not provide any rights to receive profits (either as dividends or liquidating distributions).

[25] Rev. Rul. 71-544, 1971-2 C.B. 227; Citizens Water Works, Inc. v. Comm'r, 33 B.T.A. 201 (1935). Cf. Return Realty Corp. v. Ranieri, 359 N.Y.S.2d 611 (N.Y. Cty. 1974).

that income from the rental of realty is a permissible source of income for tax-exempt title-holding corporations.[26] That is, this rental activity is not an unrelated business. The rental of personal property (unless leased with realty), however, is treated as the conduct of an unrelated business.[27] Thus, title-holding organizations engaging in business activity—other than rental of real property—may be denied or lose their tax exemption.[28]

Consequently, the characterization of the nature of the property being rented can be determinative of an organization's status as a tax-exempt title-holding corporation. In one instance, a corporation that otherwise qualified for exemption as a title-holding entity held a leasehold interest in an office building, with all of its income derived from the subleasing of space in the building to the general public. Even though a leasehold of real property is generally classified as personal property, income derived from subleasing an office building was treated as income derived from the rental of real property.[29] The IRS reasoned that this type of income is similarly treated as rental income from real property for purposes of qualification for exemption as a title-holding corporation,[30] thereby concluding that the corporation was tax-exempt.[31]

A title-holding corporation that derives income from the rental of real property to the general public is not precluded from tax exemption. In one instance, a corporation held title to a building containing offices that were rented to the public. It collected the rents, paid the expenses incident to operation and maintenance of the building, and turned over the balance of the income to its exempt parent. The rents were not forms of unrelated business income, because there were no substantial services to the tenants.[32] The IRS wrote that the "statutory language that requires them [tax-exempt title-holding corporations] to turn over the income from the property to an exempt organization contemplates that income will be received from parties other than the exempt organization for which they hold title."[33]

A tax-exempt title-holding corporation may receive unrelated business taxable income in an amount up to 10 percent of its gross income for a tax year,

---

[26] Rev. Rul. 69-381, 1969-2 C.B. 113. Also Reg. § 1.512(b)-1(c)(2); Rev. Rul. 66-295, 1966-2 C.B. 207.

[27] Rev. Rul. 69-278, 1969-1 C.B. 148.

[28] Stanford Univ. Bookstore v. Comm'r, 29 B.T.A. 1280 (1934); Sand Springs Ry. Co. v. Comm'r, 21 B.T.A. 1291 (1931). In general, see § 28.3.

[29] IRC § 512(b)(3). See § 27.1(h).

[30] This reasoning proceeded as follows: An IRC § 501(c)(2) corporation generally cannot have unrelated business taxable income (Reg. § 1.501(c)(2)-1(a)). (This aspect of the law, however, has been altered (see *infra* note 34).) For unrelated income purposes, the term *real property* includes property described in IRC § 1250(c) (Reg. § 1.512(b)-1(c)(3)(i)). That provision encompasses certain real property that is or has been property of a character subject to the depreciation allowance rules of IRC § 167. Qualifying depreciable real property includes intangible real property, which in turn includes a leasehold of land of IRC § 1250 property. Accordingly, such a leasehold is IRC § 1250 property and thus is real property for purposes of the tax law concerning title-holding companies.

[31] Rev. Rul. 81-108, 1981-1 C.B. 327.

[32] See § 27.1(h).

[33] Rev. Rul. 69-381, *supra* note 26, at 113.

where the unrelated income is incidentally derived from the holding of real property.[34]

A tax-exempt title-holding corporation is subject to the unrelated business income tax if one of its parent organizations is subject to that tax. In one instance, a title-holding entity, with two parents, one subject to the tax, the other not, found itself in this position.[35]

Where a tax-exempt title-holding corporation holds title to property for the benefit of its parent exempt organization, the property is encumbered with a debt, and the property is not utilized for the exempt purposes of the parent organization, the title-holding corporation will be subject to the tax on unrelated debt-financed income.[36]

As noted, a title-holding corporation must, to be tax-exempt, not engage in any business other than that of holding title to property and collecting and remitting any resulting income to its parent organization.[37] For example, an organization that held title to a building housing its exempt parent, maintained the property, and operated social facilities located in the building, was held to not qualify for this tax exemption, because the social activities were "outside the scope of" those allowed to an exempt title-holding entity.[38] Likewise, a title-holding corporation had its exempt status revoked because it operated a bar and buffet in the building it maintained.[39]

A title-holding corporation may file a consolidated return with a parent entity for a tax year. When this occurs and the title-holding entity pays net income to the parent, or would pay net income but for the fact that the expenses of collecting the income exceed its income, the title-holding corporation is deemed, for purposes of the unrelated business income tax, as being organized and operated for the same purposes as the parent, as well as its title-holding purposes.[40]

Generally, contributions to a title-holding corporation are not deductible as charitable gifts. Where a tax-exempt title-holding entity engages in a charitable activity, however, contributions to it for the express purpose of funding that activity are deductible as charitable gifts for federal income tax purposes.[41] Indeed, if a title-holding corporation has a charitable organization as its parent

---

[34] See § 28.3, text accompanied by note 40.

[35] Rev. Rul. 68-490, 1968-2 C.B. 241.

[36] Priv. Ltr. Rul. 8145011. See § 29.1. An instance of the use of tax-exempt entities to hold title to property acquired with borrowed funds, prior to adoption of the unrelated debt-financed income rules, appears in Rev. Rul. 66-295, *supra* note 26; the rationale was that this type of activity was not a trade or business engaged in for profit, under the approach adopted in court opinions such as Bright Star Found., Inc. v. Campbell, 191 F. Supp. 845 (N.D. Tex. 1960).

[37] Reg. § 1.501(c)(2)-1(a).

[38] Rev. Rul. 66-150, 1966-1 C.B. 147, 148.

[39] Knights of Columbus Bldg. Ass'n of Stamford, Conn., Inc. v. United States, 88-1 U.S.T.C. ¶ 9336 (D. Conn. 1988). Occasionally, the IRS or a court will not allow an organization to qualify under this category of exempt organization because of a violation of the private inurement doctrine (see Chapter 19) (e.g., Rev. Rul. 58-566, 1958-2 C.B. 261; The Davenport Found. v. Comm'r, *supra* note 19).

[40] IRC § 511(c).

[41] Priv. Ltr. Rul. 8705041.

and the corporation engages in one or more activities that the parent itself could undertake without loss of tax exemption, the title-holding entity itself may be eligible to be recognized as a charitable organization or can convert its basis for tax exemption from that as a title-holding organization to that of a charitable entity.[42]

It was the position of the IRS that a title-holding company is ineligible for tax exemption under these rules if it has multiple unrelated parents, inasmuch as that is evidence of a pooling of assets for an active corporate venture, not a mere holding of title.[43] This matter was, however, subsequently resolved by legislation.[44]

(b) Multiparent Organizations

The *multiparent title-holding organization* was added, in 1986, to the categories of tax-exempt organizations.[45] This is an otherwise eligible corporation or trust that is organized for the exclusive purposes of acquiring and holding title to real property, collecting income from the property, and remitting the entire amount of income from the property (less expenses) to one or more qualified tax-exempt organizations that are shareholders of the title-holding corporation or beneficiaries of the title-holding trust.[46] For this purpose, the term *real property* does not include any interest as a tenant in common (or similar interest) and does not include any indirect interest; this requirement means that the title-holding entity must hold real property directly, rather than, for example, as a partner in a partnership.[47] The term *real property* also includes any personal property that is leased under, or in connection with, a lease of real property, although this rule applies only if the rent attributable to the leasing of the personal property for a year does not exceed 15 percent of the total rent for the year attributable to both the real and personal property under the lease.[48]

Tax exemption under this category of organization is available only if the

---

[42] E.g., Priv. Ltr. Rul. 9242002. For example, a supporting organization (see § 11.3(c)) often can be utilized in this regard instead of a title-holding entity, as can a single-member limited liability company (see § 4.3(d)).

[43] Gen. Couns. Mems. 39341, 37351.

[44] See *infra* § (b). In general, Blanchard, "Section 501(c)(2): Time for the Service To Clean House," 10 *Exempt Org. Tax Rev.* (No. 1) 101 (1994).

[45] IRC § 501(c)(25).

[46] IRC § 501(c)(25)(A)(iii). In 1988, the IRS modified and supplemented an earlier pronouncement (Notice 87-18, 1987-1 C.B. 455) concerning certain provisions that must be included in the articles of incorporation or trust document of an organization seeking recognition of federal tax exemption as an organization described in IRC § 501(c)(25) (Notice 88-121, 1988-C C.B. 457). If state law prevents a corporation from including the required provisions in its articles of incorporation, the provisions must be included in the bylaws of the corporation. A nonstock corporation may qualify under IRC § 501(c)(25) if its articles of incorporation or bylaws provide members with the same rights as is required for other qualifying entities. The 1988 pronouncement also stated that a multiparent title-holding organization may, under certain circumstances, acquire options to purchase real estate, hold reasonable cash reserves, and receive debt-financed income (see § 29.1) without loss of tax-exempt status.

[47] IRC § 501(c)(25)(A).

[48] IRC § 501(c)(25)(F).

corporation or trust has no more than 35 shareholders or beneficiaries, and has only one class of stock or beneficial interest.[49] Also, to be exempt as this type of title-holding organization, the corporation or trust must permit its shareholders or beneficiaries to (1) dismiss the corporation's or trust's investment adviser, following reasonable notice, upon a vote of the shareholders or beneficiaries holding a majority of interest in the corporation or trust; and (2) terminate their interest in the corporation or trust by either (or both), as determined by the corporation or the trust, selling or exchanging their stock in the corporation or interest in the trust (subject to federal or state securities law) to any qualified organization as long as the sale or exchange does not increase the number of shareholders or beneficiaries in the corporation or trust to more than 35, or having their stock or interest redeemed by the corporation or mist after the shareholder or beneficiary has provided 90 days' notice to the corporation or trust.[50]

Organizations that are eligible to acquire or hold interests in this type of title-holding organization are charitable organizations,[51] qualified pension, profit-sharing, or stock bonus plans,[52] governmental plans,[53] and governments and agencies and instrumentalities of them.[54]

For these purposes, a corporation that is a *qualified subsidiary* (wholly owned) of a tax-exempt multiparent title-holding organization is not treated as a separate organization.[55] In this instance, all assets, liabilities, and items of income, deduction, and credit of the qualified subsidiary are treated as assets, liabilities, and like items of the title-holding organization.[56] These rules allow a title-holding company to hold properties in separate corporations so as to limit liability with respect to each property.

This category of tax-exempt organization was, as noted, created in response to the position of the IRS that a title-holding company otherwise eligible for tax exemption under preexisting law[57] cannot be tax-exempt if two or more of its parent organizations are unrelated. This body of law does not modify the pre-existing law concerning the exempt status of single- or related-parent title-holding corporations.[58]

§ 18.3 LOCAL EMPLOYEES' ASSOCIATIONS

Federal income tax law provides exemption for "local associations of employees, the membership of which is limited to the employees of a designated person or

---

[49] IRC § 501(c)(25)(A)(i), (ii).
[50] IRC § 501(c)(25)(D).
[51] That is, organizations that are tax-exempt pursuant to IRC § 501(a) as entities described in IRC § 501(c)(3).
[52] That is, plans that meet the requirements of IRC § 401(a). See Chapter 16.
[53] That is, plans that are described in IRC § 414(d).
[54] See *infra* § 17.
[55] IRC § 501(c)(25)(E)(i)(I).
[56] IRC § 501(c)(25)(E)(i)(II).
[57] See *supra* § 2(a).
[58] H. Rep. 99-841, 99th Cong., 2d Sess. II-824 (1986).

persons in a particular municipality, and the net earnings of which are devoted exclusively to charitable, educational or recreational purposes."[59] The word *local* has the same meaning as is applicable with respect to certain benevolent and mutual organizations.[60]

A *local association of employees* can assume a variety of forms. For example, an association that operated a gasoline station on property owned by its members' employer qualified,[61] as did an organization that engaged only in social and recreational activities that met the approval of the members' employer.[62] By contrast, a local employees' association the membership of which was limited to the employees of a particular employer and that operated a bus for the convenience of its members was denied tax exemption,[63] as was an organization the purpose of which was to pay lump-sum retirement benefits to its members or death benefits to their survivors.[64] Employees can include retirees who were members of the association at the time of retirement.[65]

The IRS considered the tax status of an organization the membership of which was limited to the employees of an employer in a particular municipality. The organization arranged with businesses to extend discounts to its members on their purchases of specified goods and services, and sold tickets to recreational and entertainment activities to them at a discount. Basing its position on the legislative history for this category of tax-exempt organization,[66] the IRS dismissed the organization as merely a "cooperative buying service for members" and denied it tax exemption as an employees' association.[67]

The IRS took the position that a voluntary employees' beneficiary association[68] that could not meet the 85 percent source-of-income test (deleted in 1969)[69] could not qualify for tax exemption as an employees' association.[70] Thus, the IRS does not follow a case holding that a cooperative electric company is exempt as an employees' association even though it met all of the requirements for exemption under the rules for certain benevolent and mutual organizations,[71] except for the 85 percent source-of-income test.[72]

Unlike the law pertaining to voluntary employee beneficiary associations,

---

[59] IRC § 501(c)(4).

[60] Reg. §§ 1.501(c)(4)-1(b), 1.501(c)(12)-1. These benevolent and mutual organizations are the subject of *infra* § 5.

[61] Rev. Rul. 66-180, 1966-1 C.B. 144.

[62] Rev. Rul. 70-202, 1970-1 C.B. 130. Also T. J. Moss Tie Co. v. Comm'r, 18 T.C. 188 (1952), *aff'd*, 201 F.2d 512 (8th Cir. 1953); Weil Clothing Co. v. Comm'r, 13 T.C. 873 (1949).

[63] Rev. Rul. 55-311, 1955-1 C.B. 72.

[64] Rev. Rul. 66-59, 1966-1 C.B. 142.

[65] Rev. Rul. 74-281, 1974-1 C.B. 133.

[66] Hearings Before House Ways and Means Committee on Revenue Revision of 1924, 68th Cong., 1st Sess. 5–12 (1924); 65 *Cong. Rec.* 2905–2906 (1924).

[67] Rev. Rul. 79-128, 1979-1 C.B. 197.

[68] See § 16.3.

[69] *Id.*, text accompanied by note 76.

[70] Rev. Rul. 57-494, 1957-2 C.B. 315, which was declared obsolete in Rev. Rul. 82-148, 1982-2 C.B. 401.

[71] See *infra* § 5.

[72] United States v. Pickwick Elec. Membership Corp., 158 F.2d 272 (6th Cir. 1946).

there are no membership restrictions for tax-exempt employees' associations. Thus, a health club available only to salaried employees qualified as an exempt employees' association.[73] If, however, the membership criteria are too exclusive, the organization may not qualify as a local employees' association because it may "not really [be] an association of employees at all."[74]

§ 18.4 FRATERNAL ORGANIZATIONS

(a) Fraternal Beneficiary Societies

Federal income tax law provides tax exemption for fraternal beneficiary societies, orders, or associations operating under the lodge system or for the exclusive benefit of the members of a fraternity itself operating under the lodge system and providing for the payment of life, sick, accident, or other benefits to the members of the society, order, or association or their dependents.[75] These are, collectively, *fraternal beneficiary societies*.

This classic definition of a tax-exempt fraternal beneficiary society was formulated by a federal court of appeals:

> We must accordingly assume that the words "fraternal-beneficial" were used in their ordinary sense—to designate an association or society that is engaged in some work that is of a fraternal and beneficial character. According to this view, a fraternal-beneficial society . . . would be one whose members have adopted the same, or a very similar, calling, avocation, or profession, or who are working in unison to accomplish some worthy object, and who for that reason have banded themselves together as an association or society to aid and assist one another, and to promote the common cause. The term "fraternal" can properly be applied to such an association, for the reason that the pursuit of a common object, calling or profession usually has a tendency to create a brotherly feeling among those who are thus engaged. It is a well-known fact that there are at the present time many voluntary or incorporated societies which are made up exclusively of persons who are engaged in the same avocation. As a general rule such associations have been formed for the purpose of promoting the social, moral, and intellectual welfare of the members of such associations, and their families, as well as for advancing their interests in other ways and in other respects . . . Many of these associations make a practice of assisting their sick and disabled members, and of extending substantial aid to the families of deceased members. Their work is at the same time of a beneficial and fraternal character, because they aim to improve the condition of a class of persons who are engaged in a common and to unite them by a stronger bond of sympathy and interest. . . .[76]

[73] Gen. Couns. Mem. 39357.
[74] *Id.*
[75] IRC § 501(c)(8); Reg. § 1.501(c)(8)-1; Banner Bldg. Co., Inc. v. Comm'r, 46 B.T.A. 857 (1942); Royal Highlanders v. Comm'r, 1 T.C. 184 (1942).
[76] National Union v. Marlow, 74 F. 775, 778 (8th Cir. 1896). Also Employees Benefit Ass'n of Am. Steel Foundries v. Comm'r, 14 B.T.A. 1166 (1929).

On the basis of this definition, an organization of employees of a railroad company was denied tax exemption as a fraternal beneficiary society.[77] The organization was established to administer a relief fund for the payment of benefits to its members in case of sickness, accident, or death. This court characterized the organization's deficiencies in this regard as follows:

> [The organization] is entirely without any social features. Its membership is made up of individuals whose vocations are as numerous and diverse as the classifications of employment of a great railway system; the section hand, the freight hustler, the brakeman, the conductor in charge of a fast trans-continental train, the locomotive engineer, the train dispatcher, the clerk in the office, all are entitled to membership in the [a]ssociation for the mere asking, expressed in written application, provided no disability exists; and yet none of these look to the . . . [organization] for any betterment in social and laboring conditions. There is no fraternal object which moves them to seek membership in the . . . [organization] but rather the motive is mercenary. The . . . [organization] has neither lodges, rituals, ceremony; or regalia; and it owes no allegiance to any other authority or jurisdiction. It is not a "fraternal beneficiary association" operating under the lodge system . . . and, therefore, is not entitled to exemption. . . .[78]

Thus, an organization will not be classified as fraternal in nature for these purposes where the only common bond between the majority of its members is the fact of membership in the organization.[79] Moreover, mere recitation of common ties and objectives in an organization's governing instrument is insufficient; there must be specific activities in implementation of the appropriate purposes.[80]

As noted, a fraternal beneficiary organization, to qualify for tax exemption, must operate under the lodge system or for the exclusive benefit of members that operate in that manner. The phrase *operating under the lodge system* means that an organization is "carrying on its activities under a form of organization that comprises local branches, chartered by a parent organization and largely self-governing, called lodges, chapters, or the like."[81] Therefore, an organization without a parent organization or subordinate branches does not operate under the lodge system and cannot qualify for tax exemption as a fraternal beneficiary society.[82] (Moreover, this type of a mutual, self-interest type of organization that may otherwise qualify as a tax-exempt fraternal beneficiary society cannot qualify as an exempt social welfare organization."[83]) Further, the parent and local organizations must be active; mere provision for them in governing instruments is

---

[77] Philadelphia & Reading Relief Ass'n v. Comm'r, 4 B.T.A. 713 (1926).
[78] Id. at 726.
[79] Polish Army Veterans Post 147 v. Comm'r, 24 T.C. 891 (1955), *aff'd*, 236 F.2d 509 (3d Cir. 1956).
[80] Fraternal Order of Civitans of Am. v. Comm'r, 19 T.C. 240 (1952).
[81] Reg. § 1.501(c)(8)-1. Also Western Funeral Benefit Ass'n v. Hellmich, 2 F.2d 367 (E.D. Mo. 1924).
[82] Rev. Rul. 55-495, 1955-2 C.B. 259.
[83] Rev. Rul. 75-199, 1975-1 C.B. 160, *mod.* Rev. Rul. 55-495, *supra* note 82. Also Police Benevolent Ass'n of Richmond, Va. v. United States, 87-1 U.S.T.C. ¶ 9238 (E.D. Va. 1987); Rev. Rul. 81-58, 1981-1 C.B. 331.

insufficient.[84] Notwithstanding this requirement, however, an organization that did not operate under the lodge system was granted exemption as a fraternal beneficiary society because it operated exclusively for the benefit of the members of a fraternal beneficiary society that itself operated under the lodge system, by providing life, sick, and accident benefits to the members of the society or their dependents.[85]

Also, as noted, a tax-exempt fraternal beneficiary society must have an established system for the payment to its members or their dependents of life, sick, accident, or other benefits. While not every member of the society need be covered by the benefits program,[86] this type of coverage must be extended to a substantial number of members.[87] According to a federal court of appeals, the term *benefits* in this context is not confined to insurance for members against personal risks such as disability or death but may also extend to insuring them against property loss.[88] This decision overruled a lower court's determination that permissible benefits include only those insuring members against mishap to the person.[89] The IRS concluded that the term *other benefits* embraces the provision of legal expenses to defend members accused of criminal, civil, or administrative misconduct arising in the course of their employment (by a fraternal beneficiary society composed of law enforcement officers)[90] and the operation by a fraternal beneficiary society of an orphanage for surviving children of deceased members.[91] The IRS ruled that whole life insurance constitutes a life benefit that fraternal domestic societies can provide to members, even though the policies contain investment features such as cash surrender value and policy loans.[92]

Consequently, a tax-exempt fraternal beneficiary organization must both operate under the lodge system and provide for the payment of benefits to members or their dependents—although one of these features does not have to predominate over the other.[93] Both of these features, however, must be present in substantial form; neither may be a sham.[94]

As noted, the tax-exempt fraternal beneficiary society must be operated for the exclusive benefit of its members. Where benefits provided to others are incidental to the accomplishment of the society's exempt purpose, however, the organization's exemption will not be jeopardized. For example, a society that conducted an insurance operation for its members in all of the states was found to have not lost its exemption because it participated in a state-sponsored reinsur-

[84] I.T. 1516, 1-2 C.B. 180 (1922).
[85] Rev. Rul. 73-192, 1973-1 C.B. 224.
[86] Rev. Rul. 64-194, 1964-2 C.B. 149.
[87] Polish Army Veterans Post 147 v. Comm'r, *supra* note 79.
[88] Grange Ins. Ass'n of Calif. v. Comm'r, 317 F.2d 222 (9th Cir. 1963).
[89] Grange Ins. Ass'n of Calif. v. Comm'r, 37 T.C. 582 (1961).
[90] Rev. Rul. 84-48, 1984-1 C.B. 133.
[91] Rev. Rul. 84-49, 1984-1 C.B. 134; Gen. Couns. Mem. 39212.
[92] Rev. Rul. 86-75, 1986-1 C.B. 245; Gen. Couns. Mem. 39510.
[93] Rev. Rul. 73-165, 1973-1 C.B. 224.
[94] Commercial Travelers Life & Accident Ass'n v. Rodway, 235 F. 370 (N.D. Ohio 1913).

ance pool that protected participating insurers from excessive losses on major medical health and accident insurance, since any benefit derived by other insurers from participation in the pooling arrangement was "incidental to" the society's exempt purpose.[95] Similarly, the reinsurance of its policies is a fraternal beneficiary society's exempt function.[96]

A federal district court held that fraternal organizations that are otherwise tax-exempt that practice racial discrimination as to entry into membership may not be exempt.[97] This holding was based on the fact that, unlike organizations that are exempt as social clubs or voluntary employees' beneficiary associations,[98] the passive investment income of fraternal beneficiary organizations is not taxed; this the court found to be a governmental benefit warranting invocation of the Fifth Amendment. The case was initiated as a class action by a black individual allegedly denied, on the basis of race, membership in a local lodge of a fraternal beneficiary society.

Individuals' gifts to a domestic fraternal beneficiary organization are deductible where the gift is to be used exclusively for religious, charitable, scientific, literary, or educational purposes, or for the prevention of cruelty to children and animals.[99]

(b) Domestic Fraternal Societies

Federal income tax law provides tax exemption for domestic fraternal societies, orders, or associations, operating under the lodge system, the net earnings of which are devoted exclusively to religious, charitable, scientific, literary, educational, and fraternal purposes, and that do not provide for the payment of life, sick, accident, or other benefits to their members.[100] These are, collectively, *domestic fraternal societies.*

An organization not providing these benefits but otherwise qualifying as a fraternal beneficiary society[101] qualifies as a tax-exempt domestic fraternal

---

[95] Rev. Rul. 78-87, 1978-1 C.B. 160.

[96] Priv. Ltr. Rul. 7937002. Congress, by enactment of § 1012(c)(2) of the Tax Reform Act of 1986, directed the Department of the Treasury to audit and study fraternal beneficiary organizations that received gross insurance premiums in excess of $25 million in taxable years ending in 1984, and to report the results of the study and recommendations to Congress by January 1, 1988.

This report of this study was issued on January 15, 1993 ("Report to the Congress on Fraternal Beneficiary Societies"). The study found that the insurance functions of these organizations are income-producing activities that are similar in "nature and scope" to those provided by for-profit commercial insurance companies. Although the study concluded that the insurance policies of these societies "appear to serve the same markets as those served by commercial insurers" and that the large societies charge prices "that are not significantly less than those charged by comparable large mutual life insurers," it did not advocate repeal of the tax exemption for these organizations. Rather, it concluded that the "benefits of society from [their] charitable services . . . may justify continuation of tax exemption" for the insurance activities of fraternal beneficiary societies. Cf., in general, Chapter 25.

[97] McGlotten v. Connally, 338 F. Supp. 448, 459 (D.D.C. 1972).

[98] See IRC § 512(a)(3); § 28.3.

[99] IRC § 170(c)(4).

[100] IRC § 501(c)(10); Reg. § 1.501(c)(10)-1.

[101] See *supra* § (a).

society. Thus, for example, a domestic fraternal beneficiary society of farmers, which met the fraternal beneficiary society rules, except that it did not provide for the payment of the requisite benefits, although it did make its members eligible for favorable insurance rates, was denied classification as an exempt fraternal beneficiary society and was ruled to be an exempt domestic fraternal society.[102] A social welfare organization,[103] however, does not qualify for tax exemption under these rules.[104]

A domestic fraternal society meeting these basic requirements was organized to provide a fraternal framework for social contact among its members who were interested in the use of and the philosophy behind a method used in attempting to divine the future. The net income of the organization was used to provide instruction on the use of the method, supply information on the method to the public, and maintain a reference library—all charitable and educational uses. The IRS ruled that the organization qualified for tax exemption under these rules.[105]

The IRS ruled that an organization formed by a local lodge of a fraternal beneficiary society, both tax-exempt as domestic fraternal societies, to carry on the activities of the society in a particular geographical area, was itself exempt as a domestic fraternal society.[106] Because the organization was chartered and supervised by the local lodge, and was subject to the laws and edicts of the parent society, it was deemed to function as "part of the lodge system" of the fraternal society and hence qualify for exemption.

The IRS also ruled that an organization that did not conduct any fraternal activities and did not operate under the lodge system, but operated exclusively for the benefit of the members of certain related domestic fraternal societies operating under the lodge system, could not qualify as a tax-exempt domestic fraternal society.[107] The rationale for this denial of exemption was that the tax law requirements for domestic fraternal societies lack the language in the tax rules for fraternal beneficiary societies providing exemption for an organization operating for the benefit of the members of a tax-exempt fraternity (a provision enacted to cover the separately organized insurance branches of a fraternal beneficiary society).

§ 18.5 BENEVOLENT OR MUTUAL ORGANIZATIONS

Federal income tax law references tax-exempt benevolent life insurance associations of a purely local character, mutual ditch or irrigation companies, mutual or

---

[102] Rev. Rul. 76-457, 1976-2 C.B. 155.
[103] See Chapter 12.
[104] Reg. § 1.501(c)(10)-1. This distinction was upheld by the U.S. Tax Court in Zeta Beta Tau Fraternity, Inc. v. Comm'r, 87 T.C. 421 (1986).
[105] Rev. Rul. 77-258, 1977-2 C.B. 195.
[106] Rev. Rul. 73-370, 1973-2 C.B. 184. In Hip Sing Ass'n, Inc. v. Comm'r, 43 T.C.M. 1092 (1982), an organization was found to be operating under the lodge system, even though the parent organization was established subsequent to creation of the branch organizations.
[107] Rev. Rul. 81-117, 1981-1 C.B. 346.

cooperative telephone companies, or like organizations.[108] These are, collectively, *benevolent or mutual organizations*. In general, 85 percent or more of the income of these entities must consist of amounts collected from members for the sole purpose of meeting losses and expenses.[109] As discussed below, there are some exceptions to this rule in the case of mutual or cooperative telephone companies.[110]

(a) Local Life Insurance Associations

Thus, one type of organization described in these rules is the benevolent life insurance association of a purely local character. These associations basically operate to provide life insurance coverage to their members, albeit at cost because of the requirement that income be collected solely for the purpose of meeting losses and expenses.[111] Organizations *like* benevolent life insurance associations include burial and funeral benefit associations that provide benefits in cash,[112] but not in the form of services and supplies (although the latter type of organization may qualify for exemption as a mutual insurance company[113]), and an organization furnishing light and water to its members on a cooperative basis.[114] IRS rulings and court decisions provide examples of organizations considered not like benevolent life insurance associations.[115]

The phrase *of a purely local character* means "confined to a particular community, place, or district, irrespective, however, of political subdivisions,"[116] that is, a single identifiable locality.[117] This requirement does not mean that members of an otherwise qualifying benevolent life insurance association must continually reside in the local area to retain membership; it only means that persons applying for membership in the association must reside in the local geographic area at the time of application.[118] An organization is not local in character where its activities are limited only by the borders of a state,[119] although state lines are

---

[108] IRC § 501(c)(12)(A).

[109] Reg. § 1.501(c)(12)-1(a); Consumers Credit Rural Elec. Coop. Corp. v. Comm'r, 37 T.C. 136 (1961), *aff'd in pertinent part*, 319 F.2d 475 (6th Cir. 1963). This 85-percent-of-income test is applied annually, so that a cooperative can be taxable for one year and tax-exempt for another (Rev. Rul. 65-99, 1965-1 C.B. 242). In addition to meeting this test, these organizations must operate according to cooperative principles to be eligible for tax exemption (Buckeye Countrymark, Inc. v. Comm'r, 103 T.C. 547 (1994); Puget Sound Plywood, Inc. v. Comm'r, 44 T.C. 305 (1965); Rev. Rul. 72-36, 1972-1 C.B. 151).

[110] IRC § 501(c)(12)(A).

[111] IRS Exempt Organizations Handbook (IRM 7751) § (12)21.

[112] Thompson v. White River Burial Ass'n, 178 F.2d 954 (8th Cir. 1950), *aff'g* 81 F. Supp. 18 (E.D. Ark.. 1948).

[113] See *infra* § 8.

[114] Rev. Rul. 67-265, 1967-2 C.B. 205.

[115] Rev. Rul. 65-201, 1965-2 C.B. 170; Consumers Credit Rural Elec. Coop. Corp. v. Comm'r, *supra* note 109; Shelby County Mut. Relief Ass'n v. Schwaner, 21 F.2d 252 (S.D. Ill. 1927); New Jersey Automobile Club v. United States, 181 F. Supp. 259 (Ct. Cl. 1960), *cert. den.*, 366 U.S. 964 (1961); Swedish Mission Friends' Aid Ass'n v. Comm'r, 12 B.T.A. 1152 (1928).

[116] Reg. § 1.501(c)(12)-1(b).

[117] Hardware Underwriters & National Hardware Serv. Corp. v. United States, 65 Ct. Cl. 267 (1928).

[118] Rev. Rul. 83-43, 1983-1 C.B. 108.

[119] Reg. § 1.501(c)(12)-1(b).

not controlling as to what constitutes a single locality. One organization lost its tax exemption as a benevolent life insurance association by advertising in four states.[120] Another organization was denied tax exemption because it operated in 14 counties, as did another conducting its affairs in 32 counties, including three separate metropolitan trade centers.[121]

(b) Mutual Organizations

The other type of organization exempt from federal income tax by virtue of these rules encompasses mutual ditch or irrigation companies, mutual or cooperative telephone companies, and similar organizations. The IRS issued criteria in this regard in 1972.[122] These organizations are commonly mutual or cooperative electric companies and water companies.[123] Tax exemption was accorded an organization established to protect certain river banks against erosion,[124] an organization that provided and maintained a two-way radio system for its members,[125] and an electric generation and transmission cooperative that sold and serviced electric appliances.[126] The membership of cooperative companies need not be restricted to ultimate consumers,[127] nonmembers may be charged a higher rate for service than members,[128] and a government agency may be a member of a cooperative.[129] In 1983, the IRS, ruling that a cooperative organization furnishing cable television service to its members qualified for tax exemption as a like organization under these rules, observed that this category of tax exemption is applicable "only to those mutual or cooperative organizations that are engaged in activities similar in nature to the benevolent life insurance or public utility type of service or business customarily conducted by the specified organizations."[130] IRS rulings, by contrast, provide examples of organizations considered not like mutual and cooperative organizations.[131]

The IRS utilized a rather unusual rationale to enable a mutual ditch company to qualify for tax exemption under these rules, notwithstanding the fact that it did not satisfy all of the requirements enunciated by the IRS in 1972.[132] The organization, created in 1874 to maintain and operate an irrigation system for the use and benefit of its members, was unable to meet standards concerning forfeiture of a member's rights and interest upon withdrawal or termination and dis-

---

[120] Huff-Cook Mutual Burial Ass'n, Inc. v. United States, 327 F. Supp. 1209 (W.D. Va. 1971).
[121] Rev. Rul. 64-193, 1964-2 C.B. 151.
[122] Rev. Rul. 72-36, *supra* note 109, *mod.* by Rev. Rul. 81-109, 1981-1 C.B. 347; Rev. Rul. 65-174, 1965-2 C.B. 169.
[123] Rev. Rul. 67-265, *supra* note 114. Also Rev. Rul. 73-453, 1973-2 C.B. 185.
[124] Rev. Rul. 68-564, 1968-2 C.B. 221.
[125] Rev. Rul. 57-420, 1957-2 C.B. 308.
[126] Priv. Ltr. Rul. 8109002.
[127] Rev. Rul. 65-174, *supra* note 122.
[128] Rev. Rul. 70-130, 1970-1 C.B. 133.
[129] Rev. Rul. 68-75, 1968-1 C.B. 271.
[130] Rev. Rul. 83-170, 1983-2 C.B. 97, 98 *mod'g* Rev. Rul. 55-716, 1955-2 C.B. 263.
[131] Rev. Rul. 65-201, *supra* note 115; Rev. Rul. 55-311, *supra* note 63.
[132] Rev. Rul. 72-36, *supra* note 109.

tribution of gains from the sale of an appreciated asset upon dissolution, in that former shareholders were not entitled to any funds. The IRS said, however, that it was nonetheless "necessary to give some consideration to the historical context within which mutual ditch and irrigation companies were created and have operated," because prior to the enactment of these rules organizations such as the one at issue "were well established entities in a number of western states."[133] The IRS noted that, under applicable state law, these organizations (1) "issued stock representing both water rights and equitable interest in the organization's assets," which was "considered personal property and freely available," and (2) had the "power to assess the outstanding stock for the costs of operation and maintenance and to enforce any assessment lien through foreclosure and forced sale, thereby transferring a delinquent shareholder's interest to the purchaser.[134] Therefore, the IRS concluded that in view of the fact that these organizations were "operating in this manner when Congress originally enacted legislation providing for their exemption from federal income tax, and the fact that there have been no major changes in the applicable federal tax provisions in the intervening years, it is clear that Congress intended and still intends that mutual ditch and irrigation companies operated in the manner and under the circumstances described above" qualify for this category of exemption.[135] The requirements promulgated in 1972 consequently were modified accordingly.

In another case, a mutual company formed for the purpose of supplying electric power to its members was recognized by the IRS as qualifying as this type of a tax-exempt entity. Subsequently, part of the organization's distribution system located within a county was purchased by the county's public utility district. The organization's members located in that utility district were refunded their membership fee in full payment for their interest in the company, since they became served by the new utility. The company refused to meet the demand of the IRS that it distribute the gains realized from the sale on a patronage basis and thus had its exempt status revoked. Upon review, however, a federal court of appeals held that the company did not have to credit or distribute its surplus or net gains on a patronage basis to maintain its classification as an exempt mutual company.[136]

As noted,[137] the general rule is that all organizations, to be exempt from tax under these rules, must obtain at least 85 percent of their income from amounts collected from members for the sole purpose of meeting losses and expenses.[138] This requirement is applied on the basis of annual accounting periods[139] and by taking into account only income actually received each year.[140] Income from all

---

[133] Rev. Rul. 81-109, *supra* note 122, at 348.

[134] *Id.* at 348-349.

[135] *Id.* at 349.

[136] Peninsula Light Co., Inc. v. United States, 552 F.2d 878 (9th Cir. 1977). The IRS, in Rev. Rul. 78-238, 1978-1 C.B. 161, announced that it would not follow this decision.

[137] See the text accompanied by *supra* note 107.

[138] IRC § 501(c)(12)(A).

[139] Rev. Rul. 65-99, *supra* note 109.

[140] Priv. Ltr. Rul. 9809055.

sources is taken into account, including capital gains from the sale of assets[141] and investments;[142] amounts received as gifts or contributions are not regarded as income.[143] In one instance, the IRS ruled that, where an electric cooperative leased power facilities to a nonmember power company that in turn sold power to the cooperative, the entire rental income was income from a nonmember for purposes of the 85-percent-of-income requirement, rather than an offset against the cost of acquiring power.[144] In another case, an organization in good faith failed to elect the installment method of treating gain from the sale of real property, with the result that the receipt of the entire gain caused less than 85 percent of its income to be derived from its members; over the government's objection, a court allowed the organization to amend its annual information return to make the election and thus preserve its tax exemption.[145] By contrast, the IRS determined that the income derived by an exempt electric cooperative from the annual sale of its excess fuel to a commercial pipeline company that was not a member of the cooperative was not to be taken into account in determining compliance with the 85-percent-of-income requirement, in that the excess fuel was sold at cost and thus gross income was not derived from the sales.[146] A federal district court held that the 85-percent-of-income requirement was satisfied where income from tenants of members of a mutual water and electric company was considered member income; the IRS took the position that the tenants did not have any participation in the management of the company and thus could not be regarded as *members*.[147] Court decisions provide examples of organizations that failed to meet the 85-percent-of-income requirement.[148]

---

[141] Cate Ditch Co. v. United States, 194 F. Supp. 688 (S.D. Cal. 1961); Mountain Water Co. of La Crescenta v. Comm'r, 35 T.C. 418 (1960).

[142] Reg. § 1.501(c)(12)-1(a).

[143] Gen. Couns. Mem. 35921.

[144] Rev. Rul. 65-174, *supra* note 122. It was held that income from a cooperative's sale of nonfirm power to a member entity constituted member income (Buckeye Power, Inc. v. United States, 97-2 U.S.T.C. ¶ 50,580 (U.S. Ct. Fed. Cl. 1997)).

[145] Sunny Slope Water Co. v. United States, 78-2 U.S.T.C. ¶ 9685 (C.D. Cal. 1978).

[146] Rev. Rul. 80-86, 1980-1 C.B. 118.

[147] Modern Elec. Water Co. v. United States, 88-2 U.S.T.C. ¶ 9523 (E.D. Wash. 1988).

[148] Allgemeiner Arbeiter Verein v. Comm'r, 237 F.2d 604 (3d Cir. 1956), *aff'g* 25 T.C. 371 (1956); Family Aid Ass'n of the United States House of Prayer for All People v. United States, 36 F. Supp. 1017 (Ct. Cl. 1941). In Dial-Cab Taxi Owners Guild Ass'n, Inc. v. Comm'r, 42 T.C.M. 590 (1981), *aff'd in unpub. op.* (2d Cir. May 4, 1982), the organization was held to not qualify under IRC § 501(c)(12) because it was unable to carry its burden of proving that 85 percent of its income in the tax years involved was collected solely to cover losses and expenses. The court said that the organization was "acquiring a substantial net worth far in excess of its reasonably anticipated needs" and that it failed to show that the retained earnings will be used to meet losses and expenses (*id.* at 592). The court also indicated that the organization—which provided a radio dispatching service to its member taxicab owners and operated a two-way radio station to dispatch its members—may not otherwise qualify as a *like organization* because its reliance on Peninsula Light Co., Inc. v. United States, *supra* note 136, was "tenuous" (*id.* at 592, note 3).

A court held that certain bond proceeds and items of interest were not income for this purpose but were "capital investment funds" and thus that the 85-percent-of-income rule was not transgressed (Lockwood Water Users Ass'n v. United States (unreported) (D. Mont. 1990)), but the holding was reversed on appeal, with the appellate court finding that the monies were items of gross income for pur-

Some exceptions to this 85-percent-of-income requirement are applicable in the case of mutual or cooperative telephone companies. One of these exceptions is that the requirement does not apply to income received or accrued from a non-member telephone company for the performance of communication services that involve members of the mutual or cooperative telephone company.[149] These services pertain to the completion of long-distance calls to, from, or between members of the company.[150] This exception was legislated to supplant a ruling by the IRS, holding that a cooperative telephone company, providing only local telephone service to its members but obtaining connecting long-distance service by agreement with a nonmember company, could not adjust its gross income by off-setting income from long-distance tolls collected by both companies against expenses for services rendered by the nonmember company to the cooperative's members but had to include as part of its gross income all of the member and nonmember income from the long-distance service, to determine whether member income met the 85-percent-of-income requirement.[151] This statutory revision reflects the view that the performance of the "call-completion services" is a related activity and that the "payments" from another telephone company for the services should not disqualify otherwise eligible mutual or cooperative telephone cooperatives from this tax-exempt status.[152]

Another exception is that this requirement does not apply to income received or accrued from qualified pole rentals.[153] A *qualified pole rental* is any rental of a pole (or other structure used to support wires) if the pole (or other structure) is used by the telephone or electric company to support one or more wires needed to provide telephone or electric services to its members and is

---

poses of IRC § 501(c)(12)(A) (Lockwood Water Users Ass'n v. United States, 935 F.2d 274 (9th Cir. 1991)). The IRS ruled that a government grant to a tax-exempt electric power cooperative was excluded from the 85-percent member-income fraction because it was excluded from income as a non-shareholder contribution to the capital of the cooperative (under IRC § 118(a)) (Priv. Ltr. Rul. 9401035).

The IRS held that income received by a cooperative telephone company from charges to third parties (such as interexchange carriers, local exchange carriers, or other exchange carriers) for billing or collecting intrastate, interstate, or international revenues was income from the provision of a service to nonmembers (Tech. Adv. Mems. 9110041, 9111001). Thus, this income was not member source income for purposes of the requirement that 85 percent of the cooperative's income must be derived from members. The IRS also ruled that the income was not excludable from the computation of the percentage of nonmember income under the rule that includes income from nonmember sources where the provision of the services involves members of the cooperative (IRC § 501(c)(12)(B)(i)). Thus, the cooperative involved did not qualify for tax exemption for the year unless the 15 percent limit was not exceeded, in which case this income would be unrelated business income (see Part Five). Subsequently, however, the IRS announced that these positions will apply for all tax years beginning after December 31, 1990 (Notice 92-33, 1992-2 C.B. 363). Income received by a telephone cooperative allocable to billing and collection services performed in respect of long-distance calls was held to qualify as income from communication services, enabling the organization to be exempt under these rules (Golden Belt Telephone Ass'n, Inc. v. Comm'r, 108 T.C. 23 (1997)).

[149] IRC § 501(c)(12)(B)(i).
[150] H. Rep. 95-742, 95th Cong., 1st Sess. (1977); S. Rep. 95-762, 95th Cong., 2d Sess. (1978).
[151] Rev. Rul. 74-362, 1974-2 C.B. 170.
[152] Consequently, Rev. Rul. 74-362, *supra* note 151, was declared obsolete by the IRS with respect to tax years beginning after December 31, 1974 (Rev. Rul. 81-291, 1981-2 C.B. 131).
[153] IRC § 501(c)(12)(B)(ii), (C)(i).

used pursuant to the rental to support one or more additional wires for use in connection with the transmission by wire of electricity or of telephone or other communications.[154] For this purpose, the word *rental* includes any sale of the right to use the pole (or other structure).[155]

There are two other exceptions. One exception is for income received or accrued from the sale of display listings in a directory furnished to the members of the mutual or cooperative telephone company.[156] The other exception is for income received or accrued from the prepayment of certain loans.[157]

The income of a wholly owned subsidiary of a tax-exempt cooperative is not included for purposes of determining whether the exempt cooperative satisfies the 85-percent member income test.[158] (This rule assumes that the subsidiary is recognized as an entity validly separate from the cooperative.[159]) Any payments a cooperative receives from its wholly owned subsidiary must, however, be included in the calculation of the member income test.

The IRS is of the opinion that an organization that meets all of the requirements for tax exemption under these rules except for the 85-percent-of-income test cannot qualify for exemption as a social welfare organization.[160] Also, an organization carrying on two functions, one qualifying under the social club rules[161] and the other under these rules, cannot qualify for exemption under either category.[162]

§ 18.6 CEMETERY COMPANIES

The federal income tax law exemption rules reference *cemetery companies* that are owned and operated exclusively for the benefit of their members and that are not operated for profit.[163] This tax exemption also extends to a corporation chartered solely for the purpose of the disposal of bodies by burial or cremation; it may not engage in any business not necessarily incident to that purpose.

[154] IRC § 501(c)(12)(D).
[155] IRC § 501(c)(12), last sentence.
[156] IRC § 501(c)(12)(B)(iii).
[157] IRC § 501(c)(12)(B)(iv), (C)(ii).
[158] Rev. Rul. 2002-55, 2002-37 I.R.B. 529. This was a reversal of the IRS's initial position, which was that the revenue received by a for-profit subsidiary should be regarded as revenue of the parent cooperative for purposes of determining the cooperative's tax-exempt status (Tech. Adv. Mem. 9722006).
[159] See § 31.1.
[160] Cf. United States v. Pickwick Elec. Membership Corp., *supra* note 72. Tax-exempt social welfare organizations are the subject of Chapter 12.
[161] See Chapter 14.
[162] Allgemeiner Arbeiter Verein v. Comm'r, *supra* note 148.
[163] IRC § 501(c)(13).

Thus, there are three types of cemetery companies that may gain exemption under these rules.

According to the IRS, a tax-exempt cemetery company is generally one which "owns a cemetery, sells lots therein for burial purposes, and maintains these and the unsold lots in a state of repair and upkeep appropriate to a final resting place."[164] With respect to the membership category of cemetery companies, its members are those who are its "lot owners who hold such lots for bona fide burial purposes and not for purpose of resale."[165] According to a court, an exempt cemetery company need not serve exclusively public interests but may be a family cemetery organization.[166] Under certain circumstances, a cemetery company may be exempt even though it has private preferred stockholders.[167] This category of exemption applies only to organizations providing for the burial or cremation of the remains of human bodies—not pets.[168]

An organization receiving and administering funds for the perpetual care of a nonprofit cemetery itself qualifies as a tax-exempt cemetery company.[169] A nonprofit organization that provides for the perpetual care of a burial area in a community may also become so classified, even though it is not associated with a nonprofit cemetery.[170]

One of the requirements for tax exemption as a cemetery company is that the company may not be permitted by its charter to engage in any business not necessarily incident to its tax-exempt (burial) purposes.[171] The IRS construed this requirement to extend to activities, thereby ruling, for example, that operation by a cemetery company of a mortuary will deprive the company of this exemption.[172] Under this approach, the IRS also held that operation of a crematorium would likewise adversely affect the exemption,[173] although this determination was withdrawn in view of modification of the exemption statute.[174] A cemetery company may, however, sell monuments, markers, vaults, and flowers solely for use in the cemetery, where the sales proceeds are used for maintenance of the cemetery.[175]

---

[164] IRS Exempt Organizations Handbook (IRM 7751) § (13) 22.1. E.g., Resthaven Memorial Park & Cemetery Ass'n v. United States, 155 F. Supp. 539 (W.D. Ky. 1957); Forest Lawn Memorial Park Ass'n, Inc. v. Comm'r, 5 T.C.M. 738 (1946).

[165] Reg. § 1.501(c)(13)-1(a)(1). Also West Laurel Hill Cemetery Co. v. Rothensies, 139 F.2d 50 (3d Cir. 1943).

[166] The John D. Rockefeller Family Cemetery Corp. v. Comm'r, 63 T.C. 355 (1974); Du Pont de Nemours Cemetery Co. v. Comm'r, 33 T.C.M. 1438 (1974). Cf. Rev. Rul. 65-6, 1965-1 C.B. 229; Provident Nat'l Bank v. United States, 325 F. Supp. 1187 (E.D. Pa. 1971).

[167] Reg. § 1.501(c)(13)-1(b).

[168] Rev. Rul. 73-454, 1973-2 C.B. 185. A tax-exempt cemetery company can, however, establish and utilize a for-profit subsidiary (see Chapter 31) to operate a pet cemetery and mortuary (Priv. Ltr. Rul. 200152048).

[169] Rev. Rul. 58-190, 1958-1 C.B. 15.

[170] Rev. Rul. 78-143, 1978-1 C.B. 161.

[171] Reg. § 1.501(c)(13)-1(b).

[172] Rev. Rul. 64-109, 1964-1 (Part 1) C.B. 190.

[173] Rev. Rul. 69-637, 1969-2 C.B. 127.

[174] Rev. Rul. 71-300, 1971-2 C.B. 238.

[175] Rev. Rul. 72-17, 1972-1 C.B. 151.

No part of the net earnings of a tax-exempt cemetery company may inure to the benefit of any private shareholder or individual.[176] The private inurement doctrine frequently is involved in the case of a newly organized cemetery company, in relation to payments to and other relationships with the organizers. The reasoning of the IRS is that (1) where a cemetery company acquires land at an indeterminable price, to be paid on the basis of a percentage of the proceeds from the sale of individual lots from the tract, the vendor of the land has a continuing interest in the land; (2) any appreciation in value, whether it be due to the state of the market generally or the cemetery's own efforts in undertaking capital improvements and the like, will result in a benefit to the vendor of the land; and (3) continuing participation in the earnings of the cemetery company will also ordinarily result in receipt by the vendor of a total price substantially in excess of the reasonable value of the land at the time of its sale to the cemetery company.[177]

Perhaps the most important issue in relation to these rules is one that emerged as many American cemeteries became transformed from noncommercial operations (such as by religious institutions and municipal governments) to commercial businesses. As part of that process, profit-oriented enterprises sought favorable tax consequences from bootstrap sales of assets to ostensibly tax-exempt cemetery companies. When this issue was first litigated, the courts were highly tolerant of these transactions,[178] thereby generating substantial criticism.[179] Subsequently, the courts began to scrutinize the substance of these transactions more carefully, concluding that some cemetery companies were causing private inurement of net earnings by the creation of equity interests. That is, in considering transactions by which a cemetery company acquires land under the terms of an open-ended or percentage arrangement contract, in which the transferor receives a percentage of the sale price of each lot, the courts came to conclude that the substance of the transaction was to create an equity interest in the transferor because all the traditional elements of a true debt were missing: (1) There is no unqualified obligation on the part of the cemetery company to pay because the installments depend on the sale of lots; (2) there is no maturity date because the obligation is to continue until all the lots are sold; (3) there is no sum certain since the price of the lots is subject to change; (4) there is no stated interest rate; (5) there is no minimum annual payment; (6) there is no right to share with general creditors; (7) there is no paid-in capitalization of the company; and

[176] Reg. § 1.501(c)(13)-1(b). E.g., Branson v. Comm'r, 50 T.C.M. 1056 (1985). In general, see Chapter 19.
[177] Rev. Rul. 61-137, 1961-2 C.B. 118; Butler County Memorial Park, Inc. v. Comm'r, 45 T.C.M. 181 (1982).
[178] Forest Lawn Memorial Park Ass'n, Inc. v. Comm'r, 45 B.T.A. 1091 (1941); Kensico Cemetery v. Comm'r, 35 B.T.A. 498 (1937), aff'd, 96 F.2d 594 (2d Cir. 1938). Also Rose Hill Memorial Park, Inc. v. Comm'r, 23 T.C.M. 1434 (1964); Washington Park Cemetery Ass'n, Inc. v. Comm'r, 22 T.C.M. 1345 (1963).
[179] E.g., Note, "Special Treatment of Cemeteries," 40 S.C.L. Rev. 716 (1967); Lanning, "Tax Erosion and the Bootstrap Sale of a Business," 108 U. Pa. L. Rev. 623 (1960).

(8) the transferors have control of the cemetery company.[180] Thus, the IRS ruled that a nonprofit cemetery company that acquired land from a for-profit cemetery company, under an agreement providing payment to the former owners on the basis of a percentage of the sales price of each cemetery lot sold, was not a tax-exempt cemetery company, because the transferors acquired an equity interest in the cemetery company, which constituted private inurement.[181]

Another issue concerns the ability of a commercial cemetery to sequester funds in a perpetual care trust fund that would qualify as a tax-exempt cemetery company. The matter seemed to have been resolved when a court, enunciating an adjunct theory,[182] held in 1975 that this type of tax exemption was available by reason of the fact that the fund, which rendered services normally provided by the cemetery company, had the same tax status as the cemetery company itself.[183] This rationale was espoused earlier by the IRS.[184] Congress the next year, however, enacted a law providing a deduction for amounts distributed by perpetual care trust funds to taxable cemetery companies for the care and maintenance of gravesites.[185] To qualify under this provision, the fund must be a trust established pursuant to local law by a taxable cemetery for the care and maintenance of the cemetery.[186]

Contributions to tax-exempt cemetery companies are deductible for federal income tax purposes.[187] The contributions must be voluntary and made to or for the use of a nonprofit cemetery, the funds of which are irrevocably dedicated to the care of the cemetery as a whole. Contributions made to a cemetery company for the perpetual care of a particular lot or crypt are, however, not deductible.[188] While bequests or gifts to exempt cemetery companies are generally not deductible for federal estate or gift tax purposes,[189] a court allowed the estate tax deduction for a bequest to a public nonprofit cemetery because of its

---

[180] Restland Memorial Park of Dallas v. United States, 509 F.2d 187 (5th Cir. 1975); Evergreen Cemetery Ass'n v. United States, 375 F. Supp. 166 (W.D. Ky. 1974); Rose Hill Memorial Park Ass'n v. United States, 463 F.2d 425 (Ct. Cl. 1972), *cert. den.*, 414 U.S. 822 (1973); Arlington Memorial Park Ass'n v. United States, 327 F. Supp. 344 (W.D. Ark. 1971); Knollwood Memorial Gardens v. Comm'r, 46 T.C. 764 (1966).
[181] Rev. Rul. 77-70, 1977-1 C.B. 150.
[182] See § 6.8.
[183] Trustees of Graceland Cemetery Improvement Fund v. United States, 515 F.2d 763 (Ct. Cl. 1975). Also Laurel Hill Cemetery Ass'n v. United States, 427 F. Supp. 679 (E.D. Mo. 1977), *aff'd*, 566 F.2d 630 (8th Cir. 1977); Endowment Care Trust Fund of Inglewood Park Cemetery Ass'n Bd. of Trustees v. United States, 76-2 U.S.T.C. ¶ 9516 (Ct. Cl. 1976); Au v. United States, 76-1 U.S.T.C. ¶ 9370 (Ct. Cl. 1976); Albuquerque Nat'l Bank v. United States, 75-1 U.S.T.C. ¶ 9294 (D.N.M. 1975).
[184] Rev. Rul. 64-217, 1964-2 C.B. 153; Rev. Rul. 58-190, *supra* note 169. Cf. Washington Trust Bank v. United States, 444 F.2d 1235 (9th Cir. 1971), *cert. den.*, 404 U.S. 1059 (1972); Evergreen Cemetery Ass'n of Seattle v. United States, 444 F.2d 1232 (9th Cir. 1971), *cert. den.*, 404 U.S. 1050 (1971); Mercantile Bank & Trust Co. v. United States, 441 F.2d 364 (8th Cir. 1971); Arlington Memorial Park Ass'n v. United States, *supra* note 180.
[185] Pub. L. No. 528, 94th Cong., 2d Sess. (1976). Also H. Rep. No. 1344, 94th Cong., 2d Sess. (1976).
[186] IRC § 642(j); Reg. § 1.642(j). A trust established for the care of two cemetery lots for a family was held to not qualify for tax-exempt status (Cave Hill Investment Company v. United States, 2002-2 U.S.T.C ¶ 50,722 (W.D. Ky. 2002)).
[187] IRC § 170(c)(5).
[188] Rev. Rul. 58-190, *supra* note 169.
[189] Rev. Rul. 67-170, 1967-1 C.B. 272.

ostensible characteristics as a charitable entity.[190] This decision was, however, reversed on appeal.[191]

§ 18.7 CREDIT UNIONS AND MUTUAL RESERVE FUNDS

The federal income tax law exemption rules reference *credit unions* without capital stock organized and operated for mutual purposes and without profit.[192] As noted, federal credit unions organized and operated in accordance with the Federal Credit Union Act are tax-exempt as instrumentalities of the United States.[193] Credit unions otherwise exempt from federal income tax generally are those chartered under state law,[194] although in one instance the IRS recognized tax exemption under this body of law for the benefit of an organization formed by a group at a U.S. military base in a foreign country.[195] In addition to being chartered under a state credit union law, however, a credit union, to qualify under these rules, must, as noted, operate without profit and for the mutual benefit of its members.[196]

The first credit union in the United States was chartered in New Hampshire in 1909 and was recognized by the Department of the Treasury as a tax-exempt organization in 1935. The government attempted to revoke its exempt status in 1966, however, contending that the organization was operating as a commercial savings and loan association, because of the nature of its services and the alleged absence of the requisite "common bond" among its members. Courts found that the organization did not lose its exempt credit union status because it offered services such as checking accounts and real estate loans, and that the members of the credit union in fact had a common bond (it primarily served the French-speaking residents of a city) even though this commonality was not reduced to a written requirement.[197] A federal court of appeals used the occasion of its decision in this case to define the term *credit union* as follows:

---

[190] Mellon Bank v. United States, 590 F. Supp. 160 (W.D. Pa. 1984).

[191] Mellon Bank v. United States, 762 F.2d 283 (3d Cir. 1985). A court held that a cemetery association cannot qualify as a charitable organization for estate tax deduction purposes because of its function of selling burial plots and maintenance of grounds (Smith v. United States, 84-2 U.S.T.C. ¶ 13,595 (W.D. Mo. 1984)). Also Linwood Cemetery Ass'n Comm'r, 87 T.C. 1314 (1986). In general, Frederick & Porcano, "Taxation of Cemetery Organizations," 57 *Taxes* 186 (1979); Lapin, "Golden Hills and Meadows of the Tax-Exempt Cemetery," 44 *Taxes* 744 (1966).

[192] IRC § 501(c)(14); Reg. § 1.501(c)(14)-1. Also United States v. Cambridge Loan & Bldg. Co., 278 U.S. 55 (1928).

[193] Rev. Rul. 55-133, *supra* note 3.

[194] Rev. Rul. 69-282, 1969-1 C.B. 155.

[195] Rev. Rul. 69-283, *supra* note 6.

[196] Rev. Rul. 72-37, 1972-1 C.B. 152.

[197] La Caisse Populaire St. Marie v. United States, 425 F. Supp. 512 (D.N.H. 1976), *aff'd*, 563 F.2d 505 (1st Cir. 1977).

A credit union is a democratically controlled, cooperative, nonprofit society organized for the purpose of encouraging thrift and self-reliance among its members by creating a source of credit at a fair and reasonable rate of interest in order to improve the economic and social conditions of its members. A credit union is fundamentally distinguishable from other financial institutions in that the customers may exercise effective control.[198]

This category of tax exemption also extends to certain *mutual organizations* organized before September 1, 1957.[199] Prior to 1951, all savings and loan associations were exempt from taxation, as were the nonprofit corporations that insured these savings institutions. In that year, the tax exemption for savings and loan associations was repealed because Congress determined that the purpose of the exemption, which was to afford savings institutions that had no capital stock the benefit of an exemption so that a surplus could be accumulated to provide the depositors with greater security, was no longer applicable because the savings and loan industry had developed to the point where the ratio of capital account to total deposits was comparable to commercial banks.

Tax exemption for the insurers of these associations was, however, continued for those that were organized prior to September 1, 1951.[200] In 1960, Congress extended the expiration date to September 1, 1957, to accommodate a particular organization, inasmuch as that entity had been organized at a time when the savings and loan associations were essentially not taxed, due to generous bad debt reserve provisions.[201]

In 1962, a nonprofit corporation was established by a state legislature for the purpose of insuring the accounts of depositors in savings and loan associations doing business in the state, which were not insured by the Federal Savings and Loan Insurance Corporation. Legislation to extend the termination date was not enacted, in part because Congress did not want to discriminate (again) in favor of these financial institutions.[202] (This nonaction on the part of Congress was challenged, with the U.S. Supreme Court holding that Congress did not function in an arbitrary and unconstitutional manner in declining to extend the exemption beyond 1957.[203]) Similar legislation to extend the cutoff period was considered but not enacted. Thereafter, one of the organizations that would have been benefited by the legislation attempted to secure a judicial determination that it was entitled to a deduction from its income for an addition to its loss reserves but this

---

[198] *Id.*, 563 F.2d at 509.
[199] IRC § 501(c)(14)(B).
[200] At that time, Congress understood that the exemption would be limited to four private insurers (two in Massachusetts, one in Connecticut, and one in New Hampshire). S. Rep. No. 781, 82d Cong., 1st Sess. 22-29 (1951).
[201] S. Rep. No. 1881, 87th Cong., 2d Sess. 40 (1962).
[202] Savings and loan associations, like other financial institutions, were entitled to establish tax-free reserves from their earnings for losses on loans; there was opposition to exemption of these insurers from tax on the earnings of their members' capital deposits because it would, in effect, provide a method whereby the associations could accumulate reserves free of tax. Also, there was concern about the financial stability of the FSLIC.
[203] Maryland Sav.-Share Ins. Corp. v. United States, 400 U.S. 4 (1970).

was rejected on the ground that the deduction would be the equivalent of exemption of the income from tax—a result Congress had rejected.[204]

It is the position of the IRS that the only way that organizations providing insurance for shares or deposits can qualify for tax exemption is to satisfy the rules as to this category of exemption.[205] This position is predicated upon the rule of statutory construction that a specific statutory provision must prevail over more general provisions.[206] Thus, for example, the type of organization that cannot satisfy the requirements for exemption of these mutual organizations (for example, because it was organized after 1957) cannot be exempt as a business league.[207] Therefore, generally, credit unions cannot be categorized as exempt business leagues.[208]

§ 18.8 CERTAIN INSURANCE COMPANIES OR ASSOCIATIONS

(a) Existing Law

The federal tax law exemption rules reference *insurance companies or associations*, other than life insurance companies or associations (including interinsurers and reciprocal underwriters), if their net written premiums (or, if greater, their direct written premiums) for the year do not exceed $350,000.[209] Thus, this category of exemption applies not only to otherwise qualified mutual property and casualty organizations[210] but also to otherwise qualified stock property and casualty organizations. For these purposes, a company or association is treated as receiving during the tax year qualifying premiums that are received during the year by all other companies or associations that are members of the same controlled group as the insurance company or association the tax exemption of which is being determined.[211]

(b) Pre-1987 Law

For tax years beginning before January 1, 1987, this body of law described *mutual insurance companies or associations* other than life or marine (including interinsurers and reciprocal underwriters), if their gross amount received during the tax year from certain items and premiums (including deposits and assessments) did not exceed $350,000. This amount received included[212] (1) interest, dividends, rents,

---

[204] Maryland Sav.-Share Ins. Corp. v. United States, 644 F.2d 16 (Ct. Cl. 1981).

[205] Rev. Rul. 83-166, 1983-2 C.B. 96 (applicable to years beginning after November 7, 1983).

[206] E.g., HCSC-Laundry v. United States, 450 U.S. 1 (1981).

[207] See Chapter 13.

[208] Credit Union Ins. Corp. v. United States, 95-1 U.S.T.C. ¶ 50,286 (D. Md. 1995), *aff'd*, 96-2 U.S.T.C. ¶ 50,323 (4th Cir. 1996).

[209] IRC § 501(c)(15)(A).

[210] See *supra* § 7.

[211] IRC § 501(c)(15)(B). The term *controlled group* is defined in IRC § 831(b)(2)(B)(ii) (IRC § 501(c)(15)(C)).

[212] See IRC § 822(b)(1)(A)-(C), (2).

and royalties; (2) amounts received as the result of entering into leases, mortgages, or other instruments or agreements from which the organization derived interest, rents, or royalties; (3) amounts received from altering or terminating these instruments or agreements; (4) gross income from a business (other than the insurance business) carried on by the company or by a partnership of which it was a partner; and (5) premiums,[213] including deposits and assessments.[214]

An insurance company that was tax-exempt under these rules was required to be a mutual organization; all of its policyholders had to be members having common equitable ownership.[215] Also, the members had to control the company; it would lose exemption if a substantial number of policyholders were denied the right to vote for management[216] or if nonpolicyholders enjoyed voting rights equal to policyholders.[217] Further, the exempt mutual company had to provide its members with insurance at substantially actual cost, with any excess premiums eventually returned to the policyholders (as dividends or premium reductions).[218] The issuance of policies on a nonassessable basis (that is, at fixed premiums) was not a necessary prerequisite to mutuality.[219]

The requirement that insurance be provided at substantially actual cost could have operated to deny this tax exemption where the company had a guaranty fund evidenced by dividend-bearing stock entitling the holders to share in the profits of the organization or to share beyond the face amount of the certificates in the assets of the organization upon dissolution. Nonetheless, the holders of the certificate could have had voting rights without endangering the company's exemption as long as control in fact remained with its policyholder members.[220] Further, this requirement meant that exempt mutual companies could not accumulate unreasonable reserves.[221]

§ 18.9   CROP OPERATIONS FINANCE CORPORATIONS

Federal income tax law provides tax exemption for corporations organized by an exempt farmers' cooperative or association[222] or members of these organizations,

---

[213] See Reg. § 1.821-4(a).
[214] Reg. § 1.501(c)(15)-1(a). Cf. Young Men's Christian Ass'n Retirement Fund, Inc. v. Comm'r, 18 B.T.A. 139 (1929).
[215] Rev. Rul. 74-196, 1974-1 C.B. 140.
[216] Keystone Automobile Club Casualty Co. v. Comm'r, 122 F.2d 886 (3d Cir. 1941), cert. den., 315 U.S. 814 (1942).
[217] Rev. Rul. 55-240, 1955-1 C.B. 406; Rev. Rul. 58-616, 1958-2 C.B. 928.
[218] Penn Mutual Life Insurance Co. v. Lederer, 252 U.S. 523 (1920); Safeguard Mutual Fire Insurance Co. v. Comm'r, 4 T.C. 74 (1944). Also Estate of Moyer v. Comm'r, 32 T.C. 515 (1959).
[219] Ohio Farmers Indemnity Co. v. Comm'r, 108 F.2d 665 (6th Cir. 1940).
[220] Property Owners Mutual Insurance Co. v. Comm'r, 28 T.C. 1007 (1957); Holyoke Mutual Fire Insurance Co. v. Comm'r, 28 T.C. 112 (1957).
[221] Mutual Fire Ins. Co. of Germantown v. United States, 142 F.2d 344 (3d Cir. 1944); Keystone Mutual Casualty Co. v. Driscoll, 137 F.2d 907 (3d Cir. 1943); MacLaughlin v. Philadelphia Contributionship for Ins. of Houses from Loss by Fire, 73 F.2d 582 (3d Cir. 1934), cert. den., 294 U.S. 718 (1935); The Mutual Fire, Marine & Inland Insurance Co. v. Comm'r, 8 T.C. 1212 (1947); Baltimore Equitable Soc'y v. United States, 3 F. Supp. 427 (Ct. Cl. 1933), cert. den., 290 U.S. 662 (1933).
[222] See infra § 11.

for the purpose of financing the ordinary crop operations of the members or other producers, and operated in conjunction with this type of an association.[223] The *crop operations finance corporation* may retain its exemption even though it issues capital stock, where certain statutory conditions are met, or it accumulates and maintains a reasonable reserve. A tax-exempt crop financing corporation may own all the stock of a business corporation without jeopardizing its exempt status.[224]

A court denied tax exemption under these rules to a crop financing corporation, which was organized by fruit growers who were members of tax-exempt cooperatives, because the growers did not perform their activities as members of the cooperatives.[225]

§ 18.10 VETERANS' ORGANIZATIONS

(a) General Rules

Federal income tax law provides tax exemption for a post or organization of past or present members of the armed forces of the United States, or an auxiliary unit or society of these entities, or a trust or foundation operated for these entities, where (1) it is organized in the United States or any of its possessions; (2) at least 75 percent of its members are past or present members of the U.S. armed forces and substantially all of the other members are individuals who are cadets or spouses, widows, or widowers of these past or present members or of cadets; and (3) there is no private inurement.[226] These rules were revised in 1982 to enable certain *veterans' organizations* to qualify for tax exemption without having a principal amount of members who are war veterans.[227] Some veterans groups may nonetheless continue to have exemption as social welfare organizations.[228]

Although the accompanying tax regulations have not been altered to reflect revision of the statute, presumably, a veterans' organization, to qualify for tax exemption under these rules, must operate exclusively to (1) promote the social welfare of the community; (2) assist disabled and needy veterans and members of the U.S. armed forces and their dependents, and the widows and widowers and orphans of deceased veterans; (3) provide entertainment, care, and assistance to hospitalized veterans or members of the U.S. armed forces; (4) carry on programs to perpetuate the memory of deceased veterans and members of the

---

[223] IRC § 501(c)(16); Reg. § 1.501(c)(16)-1.

[224] Rev. Rul. 78-434, 1978-2 C.B. 179.

[225] Growers Credit Corp. v. Comm'r, 33 T.C. 981 (1970).

[226] IRC § 501(c)(19). The private inurement doctrine is the subject of Chapter 19.

[227] Under pre-1982 law, the membership of a tax-exempt veterans' organization had to be composed of at least 97.5 percent of war veterans or the other qualifying individuals (Reg. § 1.501(c)(19)-1(b)(2)). The term *war veteran* was defined at Reg. § 1.501(c)(19)-1(b)(1), and *war period* was defined in Rev. Rul. 78-239, 1978-1 C.B. 162.

[228] See Chapter 12.

armed forces and comfort their survivors; (5) conduct programs for religious, charitable, scientific, literary, or educational purposes; (6) sponsor or participate in activities of a patriotic nature; (7) provide insurance benefits for their members or dependents thereof, or both; and/or (8) provide social and recreational activities for their members.[229]

Income derived from members of these organizations attributable to payments for life, accident, or health insurance with respect to its members or their dependents, where the net profits are set aside for charitable purposes, is exempt from the unrelated business income tax.[230] The enactment of this general income tax exemption thus provides a category of organizations entitled to use the unrelated business income tax exemption.

A contribution to a post or organization of war veterans, or an auxiliary unit or society of, or trust or foundation for, any of these posts or organizations is deductible as a charitable gift, if the donee is organized in the United States or any of its possessions and none of its net earnings inures to the benefit of any private shareholder or individual.[231]

Prior to enactment of the tax exemption for war veterans' organizations in 1972, veterans' organizations found their exemption as social welfare organizations,[232] social clubs,[233] or charitable and educational organizations.[234] It is not clear from the legislative history underlying the exemption for veterans' organizations whether the exemption is to be the exclusive basis for exemption for these groups or whether they may continue to be eligible for exemption under one or more of the other categories. A court regarded this exemption as if it is the exclusive ground for tax exemption for veterans' organizations,[235] although the better view appears to be that this exemption was originally written for war veterans' organizations and that other veterans' organizations may, if they are otherwise qualified to do so, base their exemption on the social welfare organization, social club, or charitable and educational organization categories.

---

[229] Reg. § 1.501(c)(19)-1(c). The IRS held that a veterans' organization engaged in unrelated activities when it rented its hotel to nonmembers, sold bottled liquor, and provided banquet services to civic groups (Priv. Ltr. Rul. 8539091).

[230] IRC § 512(a)(4); Reg. § 1.512(a)-4. See § 28.3, text accompanied by note 26.

[231] IRC § 170(c)(3). Also Rev. Rul. 84-140, 1984-2 C.B. 56, *mod. and sup.*, Rev. Rul. 59-151, 1959-1 C.B. 53. A federal court of appeals concluded that a contribution to a qualified veterans' organization by an individual of long-term capital gain appreciated property was subject to the 30 percent-of-contribution base limitation (see § 2.5), because the donee satisfied the publicly supported organization test of (i.e., is "described in") IRC § 509(a)(2) (see § 11.3(b)(iv)) and thus was described in IRC § 170(b)(1)(A)(viii) (Weingarden v. Comm'r, 825 F.2d 1027 (6th Cir. 1987)). The appellate court thus rejected the conclusion of the U.S. Tax Court that the gift was limited by the 20-percent-of-contribution base limitation on the ground that Congress intended that only organizations described in IRC § 501(c)(3) are charitable donees eligible for the more liberal limitation (Weingarden v. Comm'r, 86 T.C. 669 (1986)).

[232] See Chapter 12.

[233] See Chapter 14.

[234] See Chapters 6, 7.

[235] Taxation With Representation of Wash. v. Regan, 676 F.2d 715 (D.C. Cir. 1982).

When this tax exemption category was first proposed in the House of Representatives,[236] the descriptive language was the same as that in the provision making veterans' groups eligible charitable donees.[237] In both the House Committee on Ways and Means report[238] and in statements on the House floor,[239] there were repeated references to creation of a separate category of exemption for *veterans' organizations*. The House-passed measure was amended by the Senate, which added the 75-percent membership requirement. This membership requirement was added by the Senate Committee on Finance, which regarded the amendment as an expansion of the specific exemption. (The Senate Finance Committee report characterized the House bill as providing the exemption for *war veterans' organizations*.[240]) The Finance Committee report also stated that it "intends this provision to cover any veterans organization whose membership is composed almost exclusively of military associated individuals."[241]

Nonetheless, there is nothing in the legislative history of this tax exemption for certain types of veterans' organizations that expressly precludes a veterans' organization that cannot or may not qualify under it from exemption pursuant to some other classification of exempt organization where the criteria for that classification are satisfied.

There is no federal tax law restriction on the extent of lobbying by veterans' organizations. This feature was characterized by the U.S. Supreme Court as a "subsidy" enacted by Congress as part of the nation's long-standing policy of compensating veterans for their contributions by providing them with numerous advantages.[242] Presumably, tax exemption for their organizations is likewise a subsidy, for those who have "been obliged to drop their own affairs and take up the burdens of the nation"[243] and have subjected themselves to the "mental and physical hazards as well as the economic and family detriments which are peculiar to military service and which do not exist in normal life."[244] "This policy [of subsidization]," wrote the Court, "has 'always been deemed to be legitimate.' "[245]

(b) Pre-1880 Veterans' Organizations

In 1982, Congress established another category of tax-exempt veterans' organizations, which is available for any association organized before 1880, more than 75 percent of the members of which are present or past members of the U.S. armed forces and a principal purpose of which is to provide insurance and other benefits to veterans or their dependents.[246]

[236] H.R. 11185, 92d Cong., 2d Sess. (1972).
[237] H. Rep. No. 851, 92d Cong., 2d Sess (1972).
[238] 118 *Cong. Rec.* 6033 (1972).
[239] 118 *Cong. Rec.* 29076 (1972).
[240] S. Rep. No. 1082, 92d Cong., 2d Sess. 1, 3 (1972).
[241] *Id.* at 5.
[242] Regan v. Taxation With Representation of Wash., 461 U.S. 540, 550 (1983).
[243] Boone v. Lightner, 319 U.S. 561, 575 (1943).
[244] Johnson v. Robison, 415 U.S. 361, 380 (1974).
[245] Personnel Admin. v. Feeney, 442 U.S. 256, 279, note 25 (1979).
[246] IRC § 501(c)(23).

§ 18.11 FARMERS' COOPERATIVES

An eligible *farmers' cooperative organization* is exempt from federal income taxation.[247] These farmers' cooperatives are farmers', fruit growers', or like associations organized and operated on a cooperative basis for the purpose of (1) marketing the products of members or other producers and returning to them the proceeds of sales, less the necessary marketing expenses, on the basis of either the quantity or the value of the products furnished by them; or (2) purchasing supplies and equipment for the use of members or other persons and turning over the supplies and equipment to them at actual cost plus necessary expenses.[248] A farmers' cooperative may pay dividends on its capital stock in certain circumstances,[249] permit proxy voting by its shareholders,[250] and maintain a reasonable reserve.[251] The earnings of cooperatives are generally taxed to them or their patrons; these rules give tax-exempt farmers' cooperatives certain advantages in computing the tax that are not available to other cooperatives.[252]

Farmers' cooperatives came into being because of the economic fact that a farmer "sells his products in a producers' market and makes his purchases in a retail market."[253] Thus, a farmers' marketing cooperative markets farmers' products at a price nearer retail price and makes their purchases at wholesale rather than retail. A farmers' purchasing cooperative sells supplies and equipment to its patrons at a price that leaves a balance after expenses. The cooperative's net earnings or savings are distributed to the patrons on the basis of the amount of business transacted by them, in the form of patronage dividends. *Patronage dividends* are the profits of a cooperative that are rebated to its patrons pursuant to a preexisting obligation of the cooperative to do so; the rebate must be made in an equitable fashion on the basis of the quantity or value of business done with the cooperative.

Farmers' cooperatives are associations of individuals such as farmers, fruit growers, livestock growers, and operators of dairies. Illustrations of these organizations include associations operated to facilitate the artificial breeding of members' livestock,[254] acquire and apportion the beneficial use of land for the grazing of members' livestock,[255] furnish its members a place to market their farm products,[256] process and market poultry for members and other producers,[257] market

---

[247] IRC § 521.
[248] Reg. § 1.521-1. In general, Liberty Warehouse Co. v. Burley Tobacco Growers' Coop. Mktg. Ass'n, 276 U.S. 71, 92–96 (1928).
[249] IRC § 521(b)(2); Reg. § 1.521-1(a)(2). Also Agway, Inc. v. United States, 524 F.2d 1194 (Ct. Cl. 1975); Rev. Rul. 75-388, 1975-2 C.B. 227; Rev. Rul. 73-148, 1973-1 C.B. 294.
[250] Rev. Rul. 75-97, 1975-1 C.B. 167.
[251] IRC § 521(b)(3); Reg. § 1.521-1(a)(3). Also Rev. Rul. 76-233, 1976-1 C.B. 173.
[252] According to the U.S. Tax Court, in determining the amount to be paid as patronage dividends, a cooperative may allocate all of its gain from the sale of equipment to its patrons in the year of the sale in proportion to their patronage during that year (Lamesa Coop. Gin v. Comm'r, 78 T.C. 894 (1982)).
[253] IRS Exempt Organizations Handbook (IRM 7751) § (44) 12 (1).
[254] Rev. Rul. 68-76, 1968-1 C.B. 285.
[255] Rev. Rul. 67-429, 1967-2 C.B. 218.
[256] Rev. Rul. 67-430, 1967-2 C.B. 220.
[257] Rev. Rul. 58-483, 1958-2 C.B. 277.

farm-raised fish,[258] operate a grain elevator and feed yard and process soybeans,[259] purchase raw materials for processing into completed products before their transfer to patrons,[260] and produce and market range grasses.[261] The term *like association* is limited to associations that market agricultural products or purchase supplies and equipment for those engaged in producing agricultural products.[262] Thus, the admission to membership of a substantial number of non-producers in an otherwise tax-exempt producers' cooperative would destroy the association's exemption.[263] This, in turn, raises questions as to what constitutes a *farm*[264] and a *farmer*.[265]

The specific rules in this area of the federal tax law do not define these terms. These terms are, however, referenced elsewhere in the federal tax law.[266] On the basis of these other definitions, the IRS concluded that these terms do not apply to forestry, so that a federated cooperative marketing newsprint and its member cooperatives supplying pulpwood cut from timber grown by the patron members did not qualify as tax-exempt farmers' cooperatives.[267]

Examples of organizations denied this category of tax exemption as not being like a farmers' cooperative include an association that maintained its patrons' orchards and harvested their crops,[268] an association that marketed lumber for the independent lumber-producing companies that controlled it,[269] an association that marketed building materials on a cooperative basis,[270] and an association of advertising agencies[271] and of garbage collectors.[272] An organization may be recognized as a cooperative association under state law and still be denied this form of exemption.[273]

Other requirements must be met in order to achieve this category of tax exemption, including the requirements that the association be organized and operated on a cooperative basis,[274] there be bona fide members,[275] and (where appropriate) there be producers.[276] A federal court of appeals held that a person

---

[258] Rev. Rul. 64-246, 1964-2 C.B. 154.

[259] Rev. Rul. 74-567, 1974-2 C.B. 174.

[260] Rev. Rul. 54-12, 1954-1 C.B. 93.

[261] Rev. Rul. 75-5, 1975-1 C.B. 166.

[262] Sunset Scavenger Co., Inc. v. Comm'r, 84 F.2d 453 (9th Cir. 1936).

[263] Cooperative Cent. Exch. v. Comm'r, 27 B.T.A. 17 (1932).

[264] Rev. Rul. 64-246, *supra* note 258.

[265] Rev. Rul. 55-611, 1955-2 C.B. 270.

[266] IRC §§ 61 (also Reg. § 1.61-4(d)), 175 (Reg. § 1.175-3), 180, 182 (Reg. § 1.182-2), 464(e)(1).

[267] Rev. Rul. 84-81, 1984-1 C.B. 135.

[268] Rev. Rul. 66-108, 1966-2 C.B. 154.

[269] Rev. Rul. 73-570, 1973-2 C.B. 195.

[270] Rev. Rul. 73-308, 1973-2 C.B. 193.

[271] National Outdoor Advertising Bur., Inc. v. Helvering, 89 F.2d 878 (2d Cir. 1937).

[272] Sunset Scavenger Co., Inc. v. Comm'r, *supra* note 262.

[273] Lyeth v. Hoey, 305 U.S. 188 (1938).

[274] Reg. § 1.521-1(a)(1); Eugene Fruit Growers Ass'n v. Comm'r, 37 B.T.A. 993 (1938); Rev. Rul. 71-100, 1971-1 C.B. 159; Rev. Rul. 68-496, 1968-2 C.B. 251; Rev. Rul. 55-558, 1955-2 C.B. 270.

[275] Reg. § 1.521-1(a)(3); Producers Livestock Mktg. Ass'n of Salt Lake City v. Comm'r, 45 B.T.A. 325 (1941).

[276] Farmers Coop. Creamery Ass'n of Cresco, Iowa v. United States, 81-1 U.S.T.C. ¶ 9457 (N.D. Iowa 1981); Dr. P. Phillips Coop. v. Comm'r, 17 T.C. 1002 (1951); Rev. Rul. 72-589, 1972-2 C.B. 282; Rev. Rul. 67-422, 1967-2 C.B. 217; Rev. Rul. 58-483, *supra* note 257.

who merely stores items in the cooperative's facilities but does not market any products or purchase any supplies from the cooperative is not a *producer*.[277]

To be tax-exempt as a farmers' cooperative, an organization must establish that it does not have any taxable income for its own account other than that reflected in an authorized reserve or surplus.[278] An organization engaged in both marketing farm products and purchasing supplies and equipment is exempt, as this type of cooperative, if as to each of its functions it meets the tax law requirements.[279] An organization cannot be exempt under these rules if it nets losses between the marketing function and the purchasing function.[280]

With respect to a farmers' cooperative that issues stock, for the cooperative to be tax-exempt, substantially all of the capital stock must be owned by producers who market their products or purchase their supplies and equipment through the cooperative.[281] Also, the farmers' cooperative must be able to demonstrate that the ownership of its capital stock has been restricted to participating shareholders "as far as possible."[282] While the phrase *substantially all* is not defined in the statute or regulations, it is the view of the IRS that, for this rule to be satisfied, at least 85 percent of the capital stock must be held by producers;[283] a court held that a 91 percent holding satisfied the requirement[284] and that neither a 78 percent nor a 72 percent holding met the requirement.[285]

Subsequently, a court agreed with the IRS's 85-percent-of-stock test "in concept," emphasizing that the "favorable tax treatment offered cooperatives is intended to benefit the member producers, not the cooperative as a business entity."[286] A federal court of appeals twice concluded that the test is reasonable.[287] This appellate court wrote that, inasmuch as this form of tax exemption is available "only to those cooperatives in which participation in the direction and decision making process of the cooperative is strictly limited to patrons," of "primary importance, therefore, is a shareholder's right to vote."[288] Consequently, the court of appeals enunciated this rule:

---

[277] West Cent. Coop. v. United States, 758 F.2d 1269 (8th Cir. 1985), *aff'g per curiam* (N.D. Iowa 1983).
[278] Reg. § 1.521-1(c).
[279] *Id.*
[280] Union Equity Coop. Exch. v. Comm'r, 481 F.2d 812 (10th Cir. 1973), *cert. den.*, 414 U.S. 1028 (1973).
[281] IRC § 521(b)(2).
[282] Reg. § 1.521-1(a)(2).
[283] Rev. Rul. 73-248, 1973-1 C.B. 295.
[284] Farmers Co-Op. Creamery v. Comm'r, 21 B.T.A. 265 (1930). Also Farmers' Co-Op. Milk Co. v. Comm'r, 9 B.T.A. 696 (1927).
[285] Co-Operative Grain & Supply Co. v. Comm'r, 32 T.C.M. 795 (1973), *on remand*, 407 F.2d 1158 (8th Cir. 1969), *rev'g in part and rem'g*, 26 T.C.M. 593 (1967); Petaluma Co-Op. Creamery v. Comm'r, 52 T.C. 457 (1969).
[286] Farmers Coop. Co. v. Comm'r, 85 T.C. 601, 613, 614 (1985).
[287] Farmers Coop. Co. v. Comm'r, 87-2 U.S.T.C. ¶ 9404 (8th Cir. 1987); West Cent. Coop. v. United States, *supra* note 277.
[288] Farmers Coop. Co. v. Comm'r, *supra* note 287, at 89,116.

[F]or purposes of applying the 85% test, the relevant consideration is whether the right to vote has actually accrued or been terminated by the time of the annual shareholders' meeting following the close of the tax year. In other words, if a producer who sufficiently patronizes a cooperative during the tax year to become entitled to a share of capital stock is actually entitled to vote that share at the annual shareholders' meeting following the close of that tax year, that producer should be counted as both a shareholder and as a patron for the tax year in which the right to the share accrued. Conversely, if a shareholder, by failing to patronize a cooperative, ceases to be entitled to own a share and thereby actually loses the right to vote at the annual shareholders' meeting following the close of the tax year, that shareholder should not be counted as a shareholder or patron for the tax year in which the right to the share was lost.[289]

The law provides that tax exemption "shall not be denied any such association because it has capital stock . . . if substantially all such stock . . . is owned by producers who market their products or purchase their supplies and equipment through the association."[290] It is, as noted, the position of the IRS that at least 85 percent of capital stock must be held by producers to satisfy the *substantially all* test.[291] This requirement has been upheld by the courts, with the courts agreeing that, as noted, a person that merely stores items in the cooperative's storage facilities but does not market any products or purchase any supplies from the cooperative is not a producer.[292]

The IRS issued guidelines[293] to determine whether a patron is a producer patron of a tax-exempt farmers' cooperative for purposes of applying these stock ownership requirements. These guidelines, which were subsequently abandoned, stated that the qualifying stockholders will be persons who, during the cooperative's tax year, market through the cooperative more than 50 percent of their products, who purchase from the cooperative more than 50 percent of their products, or who purchase from the cooperative more than 50 percent of their supplies and equipment of the type handled by the cooperative. A person who did not meet this 50 percent requirement could nonetheless be considered a producer for purposes of the ownership requirements if certain facts and circumstances, as stated in a 1977 IRS ruling, were present.[294] A court, however, voided the 50-percent-patronage requirement,[295] causing the IRS to revoke the test[296] and the ruling.[297] Thus, stock owned by persons who transact any amount of current and active patronage with an exempt cooperative during the cooperative's tax year will be considered stock that is counted toward the stock ownership require-

---

[289] *Id.*
[290] IRC § 521(b)(2).
[291] Rev. Rul. 73-248, *supra* note 283.
[292] West Cent. Coop. v. United States, *supra* note 277.
[293] Rev. Proc. 73-39, 1973-2 C.B. 502.
[294] Rev. Rul. 77-440, 1977-2 C.B. 199.
[295] Farmers Coop. Co. v. Comm'r, 89 T.C. 682 (1987).
[296] Rev. Proc. 90-29, 1990-1 C.B. 533.
[297] Rev. Rul. 90-42, 1990-1 C.B. 117.

ment. Moreover, a person who does not transact any patronage during the cooperative's tax year may still be considered a producer for these purposes if, on the
basis of all the facts and circumstances, it is determined that the person was unable to transact any patronage during the year because (1) the person encountered a crop failure and had nothing to market; (2) sickness, disability, death, or
other hardship prevented the person from transacting any patronage; or (3) the
cooperative deals in items (such as farm machinery) that are not normally purchased on an annual basis.[298]

Still other requirements concern the nature of permissible activities of these
tax-exempt cooperatives. With respect to marketing cooperatives, questions
have been raised as to what constitutes *marketing*.[299] The IRS has a long-standing
policy of allowing exempt farmers' cooperatives, in connection with their marketing function, to manufacture or otherwise change the basic form of their
members' products, as illustrated by the exempt farmers' cooperative that operated a cannery and facilities for drying fruit and a cooperative that operated a
textile mill, both of which marketed the processed or unprocessed products of
their member growers and distributed the proceeds to them on the basis of the
quantity of product furnished, less a charge to cover the cost of processing.[300]
Subsequently, this policy was further illustrated by an IRS ruling allowing qualification as an exempt farmers' cooperative of a cooperative association that, in
connection with its marketing function, processed its members' agricultural
products into alcohol.[301]

As to the tax-exempt purchasing cooperative, the issue may be what is encompassed by the term *supplies and equipment*.[302] Business done for or with the
federal government is disregarded in determining the right to this category of exemption.[303] Because hedging is an activity that is incidental to the marketing
function of an exempt farmers' cooperative, it may establish a commodity trading
division to serve as a commodity broker to facilitate hedging transactions for its
marketing patrons without adversely affecting its exemption.[304]

Tax exemption for a farmers' cooperative may not be denied because it has
capital stock, if the dividend rate of the stock is fixed at a rate not to exceed the
legal rate of interest in the state of incorporation or 8 percent annually,
whichever is greater, on the value of the consideration for which the stock was
issued, and if substantially all of the stock (other than nonvoting preferred stock,
the owners of which are not entitled or permitted to participate, directly or indirectly, in the profits of the organization, upon dissolution or otherwise, beyond

[298] See Rev. Proc. 90-29, *supra* note 296; Rev. Rul. 90-42, *supra* note 297.
[299] Treasure Valley Potato Bargaining Ass'n v. Ore-Ida Foods, Inc., 497 F.2d 203 (9th Cir. 1974); Rev. Rul.
67-430, *supra* note 256; Rev. Rul. 66-108, *supra* note 268; Mim. 3886, X-2 C.B. 164 (1931).
[300] Rev. Rul. 77-384, 1977-2 C.B. 198.
[301] Rev. Rul. 81-96, 1981-1 C.B. 359.
[302] Farmers Union Coop. Ass'n, Fairbury, Neb. v. Comm'r, 44 B.T.A. 34 (1941); Rev. Rul. 68-76, *supra*
note 254; Rev. Rul. 67-429, *supra* note 255; Rev. Rul. 54-12, *supra* note 260; S.M. 2288, III-2 C.B. 223
(1924).
[303] IRC § 521(b)(5); Rev. Rul. 65-5, 1965-1 C.B. 244.
[304] Rev. Rul. 76-298, 1976-2 C.B. 179.

the fixed dividends) is owned by producers who market their products or purchase their supplies and equipment through the organization.[305] It is the position of the IRS that this *substantially all* test can be satisfied only where at least 85 percent of the capital stock (other than the nonvoting preferred stock) is held by producers.[306] This test was upheld by a federal court of appeals.[307]

A tax-exempt farmers' cooperative may establish and control a subsidiary corporation as long as the activities of the subsidiary are activities that the cooperative itself might engage in as an integral part of its operations without adversely affecting its exempt status.[308] For this reason, the IRS ruled that a cooperative may establish and control a Domestic International Sales Corporation.[309]

A rule that has generated considerable attention is the limitation on the purchasing of supplies and equipment for nonmembers and nonproducers to 15 percent of the value of all of the tax-exempt cooperative's purchase of supplies and equipment.[310] By contrast, a marketing cooperative will generally not qualify for this exemption if it markets the goods of nonproducers.[311] There are exceptions to the limitation on marketing nonproducer goods, however, which may be categorized into sideline,[312] ingredient,[313] and emergency[314] purchases from nonproducers.

Still another requisite for qualification for this category of tax exemption is that any excess of gross receipts over expenses and payments to patrons (termed *earnings*) must be returned to the patrons in proportion to the amount of business done for them. The income and expenses for each function (primarily marketing and purchasing) must be accounted for separately.[315] In computing earnings, the exempt cooperative must experience only necessary expenses associated with marketing and purchasing (frequently undertaken in different departments or branches), rather than for items such as the purchase of life insurance for members.[316] Nonpatronage income may be allocated to the appropriate department of the cooperative.[317]

Also, a tax-exempt farmers' cooperative must treat its nonmember patrons the same as member patrons as respects patronage dividends. There are several cases where an association was denied tax exemption under these rules because

---

[305] IRC § 521(b)(2).

[306] Rev. Rul. 73-248, *supra* note 283.

[307] West Central Coop. v. United States, *supra* note 277. Also Co-Operative Grain & Supply Co. v. Comm'r, *supra* note 285.

[308] Rev. Rul. 69-575, 1969-2 C.B. 134.

[309] Rev. Rul. 73-247, 1973-1 C.B. 294.

[310] IRC § 521(b)(4). Also Rev. Rul. 69-417, 1969-2 C.B. 132; Rev. Rul. 67-346, 1967-2 C.B. 216; Rev. Rul. 67-223, 1967-2 C.B. 214. As for the effect of the use of subsidiaries in relation to this limitation, see Rev. Rul. 73-148, *supra* note 249; Rev. Rul. 69-575, *supra* note 308.

[311] IRC § 521(b)(1). Also Rev. Rul. 67-152, 1967-1 C.B. 147.

[312] Rev. Proc. 67-37, 1967-2 C.B. 668; Land O'Lakes, Inc. v. United States, 362 F. Supp. 1253 (S.D. Minn. 1973), *rev. and rem.*, 514 F.2d 134 (8th Cir. 1975), *cert. den.*, 423 U.S. 926 (1975); Eugene Fruit Growers Ass'n v. Comm'r, *supra* note 274.

[313] Reg. Rul. 75-4, 1975-1 C.B. 165; Rev. Rul. 67-152, *supra* note 311, Dr. P. Phillips Coop. v. Comm'r, *supra* note 276.

[314] Rev. Rul. 69-222, 1969-1 C.B. 161; Producer's Produce Co. v. Crooks, 2 F. Supp. 969 (W.D. Mo. 1932).

[315] Rev. Rul. 67-253, 1967-2 C.B. 214; Rev. Rul. 75-110, 1975-1 C.B. 167.

[316] Rev. Rul. 55-558, *supra* note 274. Also Rev. Rul. 73-93, 1973-1 C.B. 292.

[317] Rev. Rul. 67-128, 1967-1 C.B. 147; Juanita Farmers Coop. Ass'n v. Comm'r, 43 T.C. 836 (1965). Cf. Rev. Rul. 75-228, 1975-1 C.B. 278; Rev. Rul. 74-327, 1974-2 C.B. 66.

of this type of discrimination,[318] as well as a number of instances where inequality among patrons was deemed to not be present.[319]

A discussion of the circumstances under which a federated farmers' cooperative (an association the membership of which includes tax-exempt farmers' cooperative associations) may qualify for this form of exemption was the subject of an IRS ruling.[320] Two revenue procedures set forth methods acceptable for a federated cooperative and its members to establish exemption (involving the look-through principle[321]) and setting forth the general requirements in this regard.[322]

The federal tax law provisions for cooperatives generally[323] operate to treat these organizations more like a conduit than a separate taxable business enterprise. The primary reason for this treatment is to avoid penalizing (by taxing) a group of persons for collectivizing their marketing or purchasing efforts in order to take advantage of economies of scale. The conduit treatment is derived from the ability of a cooperative to deduct from its taxable income patronage dividends paid. (A farmers' cooperative generally may deduct patronage dividends to the full extent of its net income and may also deduct, to a limited extent, dividends on common stock.)

A tax-exempt cooperative may make purchases or market goods in several product lines and/or several geographic areas, or both make purchases and market goods. Many cooperatives of this type will calculate net income on an aggregate basis, netting gains from profitable products or geographic areas with losses from unprofitable ones, and thus pay patronage dividends based upon the net income so computed. The position of the IRS is that a cooperative may not net gains and losses from different operations in any manner it chooses and that netting is not permitted unless it is equitable under the circumstances.[324]

---

[318] E.g., Farmers Coop. Creamery Ass'n of Cresco, Iowa v. United States, *supra* note 276; Fertile Coop. Dairy Ass'n v. Huston, 119 F.2d 274 (8th Cir. 1951); Farmers Coop. Co. of Wahoo, Neb. v. United States, 23 F. Supp. 123 (Ct. Cl. 1938); Rev. Rul. 73-59, 1973-1 C.B. 292.

[319] E.g., Rev. Rul. 69-52, 1969-1 C.B. 161; Rev. Rul. 66-152, 1966-1 C.B. 155. Also Rev. Rul. 76-388, 1976-2 C.B. 180.

[320] Rev. Rul. 69-651, 1969-2 C.B. 135.

[321] Rev. Ruls. 72-50, 51, 52, 1972-1 C.B. 163, 164, 165.

[322] Rev. Procs. 72-16, 17, 1972-1 C.B. 738, 739.

[323] IRC § 1381 *et seq.*

[324] The caselaw is more supportive of the cooperatives', rather than the government's, position. E.g., Ford-Iroquois FS v. Comm'r, 74 T.C. 1213 (1980); Lamesa Cooperative Gin v. Comm'r, *supra* note 252; Associated Milk Producers v. Comm'r, 68 T.C. 729 (1977). In general, Butwill, "IRS Expands Availability of Patronage Dividend Deductions and Tax-Exempt Status for Cooperatives but Restricts Benefit of Package Design Expenditures," 12 *J. Agric. Tax. & Law* (No. 4) 342 (1991); Fleck, "Cooperatives—Accounting and Tax Developments: Distribution of Nonpatronage Retained Earnings," 11 *J. Agric. Tax. & Law* (No. 2) 181 (1989); Frederick, "Qualifying Farmers' Cooperatives for Section 521 Tax Status," 10 *J. Agric. Tax & Law* (No. 1) 16 (1988); Locke, "Cooperatives—Accounting and Tax Developments: 'Substantially All' Test of Section 521 Cooperatives Clarified," 10 *J. Agric. Tax. & Law* (No. 2) 181 (1988); Fleck, "Cooperatives—Accounting and Tax Developments: Losses and Netting," 9 *J. Agric. Tax & Law* (No. 4) 374 (1988); Sedo, "Cooperative Mergers and Consolidations: A Consideration of the Legal and Tax Issues," 63 *N.D.L. Rev.* (No. 3) 377 (1987); Katz, "Buying Through Cooperatives Has Tax Benefits for the Cooperative and Its Owners," 16 *Tax Accts.* 115 (1976); Comment, "Agricultural Cooperative Associations and the Equal Treatment Requirement of Section 521," 27 *Ala. L. Rev.* 611 (1976); Note, "Section 521—Exemption of Farmers Cooperatives from Tax," 25 *Drake L. Rev.* 705 (1976); Schrader & Goldberg, *Farmers' Cooperatives and Federal Income Taxes* (1975); Pearson, "Farm Cooperatives and the Federal Income Tax," 44

§ 18.12 SHIPOWNERS' PROTECTION AND INDEMNITY ASSOCIATIONS

The federal tax law provides that "[t]here shall not be included in gross income the receipts of shipowners' mutual protection and indemnity associations not organized for profit, and no part of the net earnings of which inures to the benefit of any private shareholder; but such corporations shall be subject as other persons to the tax on their taxable income from interest, dividends, and rents."[325] This law, in essence, provides federal income tax exemption for the *shipowners' protection and indemnity association.*

The return of excess dues by a fishing vessel owners' association to its members was ruled by the IRS to not be inurement of earnings to the members; therefore, the dues paid to the association were not includible in its gross income.[326] The amount paid by a member of a tax-exempt association of this type to its reserve fund to provide certain insurance protection was deemed deductible.[327]

§ 18.13 HOMEOWNERS' ASSOCIATIONS

For decades, tax-exempt *homeowners' associations* were treated as a form of exempt social welfare organization.[328] It is common for these associations to be formed as part of the development of a real estate subdivision, a condominium project, or a cooperative housing project. These associations enable their members (usually individual homeowners) to act together in managing, maintaining, and improving areas where they live. The associations' purposes include the administration and enforcement of covenants for preserving the physical appearance of the development, the ownership and management of common areas (for example, sidewalks and parks), and the exterior maintenance of property owned by the members.

Originally, as noted, the IRS regarded homeowners' associations as tax-exempt social welfare organizations.[329] The IRS, however, concerned that the requisite *community* was not being served, issued a countervailing ruling in 1974.[330] Most homeowners' associations found it difficult to meet the requirements of this

---

N.D.L. Rev. 490 (1968); Logan, "Federal Income Taxation of Farmers' and Other Cooperatives," 44 *Tex. L. Rev.* 250, 1269 (1965–1966); Wile, "Taxation of Farmers' Cooperatives and Their Patrons," 18 *S.C. Tax Inst.* 449 (1966); Blair, "Farmers' Cooperatives and Their Patrons Face New Problems in Reporting Income," 28 *J. Tax.* 180 (1968); Asbill, "Cooperatives: Tax Treatment of Patronage Refunds," 42 *Va. L. Rev.* 1087 (1956); Paul, "The Justifiability of the Policy of Exempting Farmers' Marketing and Purchasing Cooperatives from Federal Income Taxation," 29 *Minn. L. Rev.* 343 (1945).
[325] IRC § 526.
[326] Rev. Rul. 70-566, 1970-1 C.B. 128.
[327] Rev. Rul. 55-189, 1955-1 C.B. 265.
[328] See Chapter 12.
[329] Rev. Rul. 72-102, 1972-1 C.B. 149.
[330] Rev. Rul. 74-199, 1974-1 C.B. 131.

policy change.[331] The IRS also ruled that condominium management associations did not qualify for this category of exemption.[332]

Congress responded to this dilemma with an elective tax exemption provision for most of these associations.[333] This provision is in the mode of the tax treatment of exempt social clubs[334] and political organizations,[335] in that only *exempt function income* escapes unrelated business income taxation.

To qualify as a tax-exempt homeowners' association, an organization must be a condominium[336] management association or a residential real estate management association.[337] Generally, membership in these associations is confined to the developers and the owners of the units, residences, or lots.[338] Membership in either type of association is normally required as a condition of this ownership.[339]

A tax-exempt homeowners' association must meet certain requirements: (1) It must be organized and operated primarily to provide for the acquisition, construction, management, maintenance, and care of association property;[340] (2) it must pass an income test, by which at least 60 percent of the association's gross income for a tax year consists of exempt function income;[341] (3) it must pass an expenditure test, by which at least 90 percent of the annual expenditures of the association must be to acquire, construct, manage, maintain, and care for or improve its property;[342] (4) no part of the association's net earnings

---

[331] Frank, "IRS Takes Harsh Position on Exempting Condominium and Homeowners' Associations," 44 *J. Tax.* 306 (1976).

[332] Rev. Rul. 74-17, 1974-1 C.B. 130.

[333] IRC § 528; Reg. § 1.528-8. This election (IRC § 528(c)(1)(E)) is a year-to-year one; a homeowners' association may thus alternate between taxable and tax-exempt status. In a particular year, a homeowners' association may prefer taxable status to exempt status because an exempt homeowners' association is taxed at a flat 30 percent rate on income other than exempt function income (see the text accompanied by *infra* note 346), whereas a taxable homeowners' association is subject to tax on all income but at progressive and perhaps lower tax rates (see the text accompanied by *infra* note 348). Thus, the tax on nonexempt income under IRC § 528 may exceed the tax the homeowners' association would pay as a taxable entity.

In one instance, the IRS refused to excuse a homeowners' association from the requirement of filing a timely refund claim, under the mitigation rules of IRC §§ 1311-1314, in the face of the argument that the claim is dependent on a future event, namely, the grant of permission to revoke the IRC § 528 election on the ground of inadequate accounting advice (Priv. Let. Rul. 8429049). In another case, the IRS refused to grant a homeowners' association an extension of time within which to make the election, where three management companies failed to file tax returns for the association (Priv. Let. Rul. 8433077). The IRS ruled that a homeowners' association may revoke an election because of incorrect tax advice provided by a professional tax adviser (Rev. Rul. 83-74, 1983-1 C.B. 112). There is an automatic 12-month extension to make the election (Rev. Proc. 92-85, 1992-2 C.B. 490 § 4.01).

[334] IRC § 512(a)(3). See § 28.3.

[335] IRC § 527(b). See § 17.3(a).

[336] The term *condominium* is defined for these purposes in Reg. § 1.528-1(b).

[337] Reg. § 1.528-1(a). The term *residential real estate management association* is defined in Reg. § 1.528-1(c).

[338] Reg. § 1.528-1(a).

[339] *Id.* Associations of holders of timeshare interests (IRC § 528(c)(4)) are treated as homeowners' associations.

[340] Reg. § 1.528-2.

[341] Reg. § 1.528-5.

[342] Reg. § 1.528-6.

may inure to the benefit of any private shareholder or individual;[343] and (5) substantially all of the dwelling units in the condominium project or lots and buildings in a subdivision, development, or similar area must be used by individuals for residences.[344] The acts of acquiring, constructing, or providing management, maintenance, and care of association property, and of rebating excess membership dues, fees, or assessments, do not constitute private inurement. *Association property* means not only property held by it but also property commonly held by its members, property within the association privately held by the members, and property owned by a governmental unit and used for the benefit of residents of the unit.[345]

In this context, *exempt function income* means any amount received as membership dues, fees, or assessments from persons who are members of the association, namely, owners of condominium housing units (in the case of a condominium management association) or owners of real property (in the case of a residential real estate management association).[346] Taxable income includes investment income and payments by nonmembers for the use of the association's facilities, subject to a specific $100 deduction and deductions directly connected with the production of gross income (other than exempt function income).[347] The taxable income of a qualified homeowners' association is taxable at the rate of 30 percent, rather than the regular corporate rates (ranging from 15 to 35 percent, the latter for taxable income over $75,000).[348]

The House version of the Tax Reform Act of 1969 would have applied the foregoing rules to cooperative housing corporations,[349] but the 1969 Act in its final form followed the Senate bill in not allowing the exemption for these corporations.[350] Instead, the Act clarified existing law to ensure that a cooperative housing corporation is entitled to a deduction for depreciation[351] with respect to property it leases to a tenant-stockholder even though the tenant-stockholder may be entitled to depreciate his or her stock in the corporation to the extent the stock is related to a proprietary lease or right of tenancy

[343] Reg. § 1.528-7. The private inurement doctrine is the subject of Chapter 19.
[344] Reg. § 1.528-4.
[345] Reg. § 1.528-3.
[346] Reg. § 1.538-9. Annual assessments paid to a homeowners' association by its members are not deductible as real property taxes (Rev. Rul. 76-495, 1976-2 C.B. 43). An amount received by a homeowners' association in settlement of litigation on behalf of individual lot owners was deemed to constitute *membership fees* for this purpose (Rev. Rul. 88-56, 1988-1 C.B. 126). By contrast, interest earned by a homeowners' association on funds received in settlement of a pending lawsuit and held for certain repairs was ruled to be taxable (Priv. Ltr. Rul. 9042036).
[347] Reg. § 1.528-10. Qualified homeowners' associations that elect to be taxed under IRC § 528 file tax return Form 1120-H (IRC § 6012(a)(7)); Ann. 77-42, 1977-13 1 R.B. 23.
[348] IRC § 528(b). Timeshare associations (see *supra* note 339), however, are taxed at a 32 percent rate.
[349] IRC § 216(b).
[350] Thus, "[c]ooperative housing corporations and organizations based on a similar form of ownership are not eligible to be taxed as homeowners' associations" (Reg. § 1.528-1(a)).
[351] IRC § 167(a).

that is used by the tenant-stockholder in a trade or business or for the production of income.[352]

§ 18.14   HIGH-RISK INDIVIDUALS HEALTH CARE COVERAGE ORGANIZATIONS

Tax-exempt status is available for a membership organization established by a state exclusively to provide coverage for medical care[353] on a nonprofit basis to high-risk individuals through insurance issued by the organization or a health maintenance organization under an arrangement with the organization.[354]

The individuals, who must be residents of the state, must be—by reason of the existence or history of a medical condition—unable to acquire medical care coverage for the medical condition through insurance or from a health maintenance organization, or able to acquire the coverage only at a rate that is substantially in excess of the rate for the coverage through the membership organization.[355] The composition of the membership in the organization must be specified by the state.[356] For example, a state can mandate that all organizations that are subject to insurance regulation by the state must be members of the organization.[357] The private inurement doctrine[358] is applicable to this type of organization.[359]

§ 18.15   WORKERS' COMPENSATION REINSURANCE ORGANIZATIONS

(a) State-Sponsored Organizations

Tax-exempt status under federal law is available for a membership organization established before June 1, 1996, by a state exclusively to reimburse its members for losses arising under workers' compensation acts.[360]

The state must require that the membership of the organization consists of all persons who issue insurance covering workers' compensation losses in the state, and all persons and governmental entities who self-insure against these

---

[352] Park Place, Inc. v. Comm'r, 57 T.C. 767 (1972). In general, Cowan, "Working with New Rules for Condominiums, Cooperatives and Homeowners Associations," 46 *J. Tax.* 204 (1977); Reinstein, "Federal Tax Implications of Condominium Associations," 50 *Fla. Bar J.* 219 (1976); Redemske, "Income Tax Considerations for the Condominium Corporation," 7 *Tax Adv.* 608 (1976); Garrett, "The Taxability of Condominium Owners' Associations," 12 *San Diego L. Rev.* 778 (1975).
[353] This term is defined in IRC § 213(d).
[354] IRC § 501(c)(26)(A).
[355] IRC § 501(c)(26)(B).
[356] IRC § 501(c)(26)(C).
[357] H. Rep. 736, 104th Cong., 2d Sess. 36 (1996).
[358] See Chapter 19.
[359] IRC § 501(c)(26)(D).
[360] IRC § 501(c)(27)(A)(i).

losses.[361] The organization must "operate as a nonprofit organization" by returning surplus income to its members or workers' compensation policyholders on a periodic basis and by reducing initial premiums in anticipation of investment income.[362]

(b) Certain Insurance Companies

Tax exemption is also available to any organization (including a mutual insurance company) if it is created by state law and is organized and operated under state law exclusively to (1) provide workers' compensation insurance which is required by state law or with respect to which state law provides significant disincentives if the insurance is not purchased by an employer, and (2) provide related coverage which is incidental to worker's compensation insurance.[363]

The organization must provide workers' compensation insurance to any employer in the state (for employees in the state or temporarily assigned out-of-state) which seeks the insurance and meets other reasonable requirements.[364] The state must make a financial commitment with respect to the organization, either by extending the full faith and credit of the state to the initial debt of the organization or by providing the organization its initial operating capital.[365] The assets of the organization must revert to the state upon dissolution, unless state law does not permit the dissolution of the organization.[366] The majority of the board of directors or oversight body of the organization must be appointed by the chief executive officer or other executive branch official of the state, by the state legislature, or by both.[367]

§ 18.16 QUALIFIED TUITION PROGRAMS

(a) State-Sponsored Programs

Tax-exempt status is accorded *qualified tuition programs.*[368] These include programs established and maintained by a state (or an agency or instrumentality of a state) under which persons may (1) purchase tuition credits or certificates on behalf of a designated beneficiary that entitle the beneficiary to the waiver or payment of qualified higher education expenses of the beneficiary or (2) make contributions to an account that is established for the sole purpose of meeting qualified higher education expenses of the designated beneficiary of the account.[369] The phrase *qualified higher education expenses* means tuition, fees, books,

---

[361] IRC § 501(c)(27)(A)(ii).
[362] IRC § 501(c)(27)(A)(iii).
[363] IRC § 501(c)(27)(B)(i).
[364] IRC § 501(c)(27)(B)(ii).
[365] IRC § 501(c)(27)(B)(iii)(I).
[366] IRC § 501(c)(27)(B)(iii)(II).
[367] IRC § 501(c)(27)(B)(iv).
[368] IRC § 529(a).
[369] IRC § 529(b)(1).

and equipment required for the enrollment or attendance at a college, university, or certain vocational schools.[370]

This type of program must provide that purchases or contributions may be made only in cash.[371] Contributors and beneficiaries are not allowed to direct any investments made on their behalf by the program.[372] The program is required to maintain a separate accounting for each designated beneficiary.[373] A specified individual must be designated as the beneficiary at the commencement of participation in a qualified tuition program (that is, when contributions are first made to purchase an interest in the program), unless interests in the program are purchased by a state or local government or a tax-exempt charitable organization as part of a scholarship program operated by the government or charity under which beneficiaries to be named in the future will receive the interests as scholarships.[374] A transfer of credits (or other amounts) from one account benefiting one designated beneficiary to another account benefiting a different beneficiary is considered a distribution (as is a change in the designated beneficiary of an interest in a qualified tuition program) unless the beneficiaries are members of the same family.[375]

Earnings on an account may be refunded to a contributor or beneficiary, but the state or instrumentality must impose a more than de minimis monetary penalty unless the refund is used for qualified higher education expenses of the beneficiary, made on account of the death or disability of the beneficiary, or made on account of a scholarship received by the designated beneficiary to the extent the amount refunded does not exceed the amount of the scholarship used for higher education expenses.[376] These programs may not allow any interest in the program or any portion of it to be used as security for a loan.[377]

A program cannot be treated as a qualified tuition program unless it provides adequate safeguards to prevent contributions on behalf of a designated beneficiary in excess of those necessary to provide for the qualified higher education motion expenses of the beneficiary.[378]

(b) Educational Institution–Sponsored Programs

Pursuant to this body of law as originally enacted, these tuition programs could only be established and maintained by a state or agency or instrumentality of a state. Beginning in 2002, however, these plans can be established and maintained

---

[370] IRC § 529(e)(3).
[371] IRC § 529(b)(2).
[372] IRC § 529(b)(5).
[373] IRC § 529(b)(4).
[374] IRC § 529(e)(1). An interest in a qualified tuition program is not regarded as a debt for purposes of the unrelated debt-financed income rules (see § 29.1) (IRC § 529(e)(4)).
[375] The phrase *member of the family* is defined in IRC § 2032A(e)(2).
[376] IRC § 529(b)(3).
[377] IRC § 529(b)(6).
[378] IRC § 529(b)(7).

by eligible educational institutions,[379] including private institutions.[380] In order for a tuition program of a private eligible educational institution to be a qualified tuition program, assets of the program must be held in a *qualified trust*.[381] This is a trust which is organized in the United States for the exclusive benefit of designated beneficiaries, where its trustee is a bank or other person who demonstrates that it will administer the trust in accordance with certain requirements; the assets of the trust may not be commingled with other property except in a common trust fund or common investment fund.[382] The tuition program of a private eligible educational institution must receive a determination from the IRS that the program meets these requirements.[383]

(c) Other Rules

In general, no amount is includable in the gross income of a designated beneficiary under a qualified tuition program or a contributor to the program on behalf of a designated beneficiary with respect to any distribution or earnings under the program.[384] A contribution to a qualified tuition program on behalf of a designated beneficiary is not a taxable gift.[385] A distribution under a qualified tuition program is includable in the gross income of the distributee in the manner as prescribed under the annuity taxation rules[386] to the extent not excluded from gross income under other federal tax law.[387] Thus, if matching-grant amounts are distributed to or on behalf of a beneficiary as part of a qualified tuition program, the matching grant amounts still may be excluded from the gross income of the beneficiary as a scholarship.[388]

An exclusion from gross income is provided, however, for distributions made in tax years after December 31, 2001, from qualified state tuition programs to the extent that the distribution is used to pay for qualified higher education expenses. This exclusion from gross income is extended to distribution from qualified tuition programs established and maintained by an entity other than a state (or agency or instrumentality of a state) for distributions made in tax years after December 31, 2003.[389]

Amounts contributed to a qualified tuition program (and earnings on those amounts) are included in the contributor's estate for federal estate tax purposes

---

[379] This change in the law was occasioned by enactment of the Economic Growth and Tax Relief Reconciliation Act of 2001 § 402 (Pub. L. No. 107-16, 107th Cong., 1st Sess. (2001)).
[380] IRC § 529(b)(1) (as amended). The term *eligible educational institution* is defined in IRC § 529(e)(5) (see § 11.3(a), text accompanied by note 134).
[381] IRC § 529(b)(1) (as amended).
[382] See IRC § 408(a)(2), (5).
[383] IRC § 529(b)(1) (as amended).
[384] IRC § 519(c)(1).
[385] IRC § 529(c)(2).
[386] IRC § 72.
[387] IRC § 529(c)(3).
[388] H. Rep. 737, 104th Cong., 2d Sess. 122 (1996).
[389] IRC § 529(c)(3)(B) (as amended).

in the event that the contributor dies before the amounts are distributed under the program.[390]

The IRS issues private letter rulings on an ongoing basis as to plans that do or do not qualify as qualified tuition programs.[391]

§ 18.17   STATES, POLITICAL SUBDIVISIONS, INSTRUMENTALITIES, AND INTEGRAL PARTS

The states, the District of Columbia, and U.S. territories are, in a loose sense of the term, tax-exempt entities. This tax exemption does not derive from any specific provision in the federal tax statutory law, but rather is a consequence of the doctrine of *intergovernmental immunity*—the doctrine implicit in the U.S. Constitution that the federal government will not tax the states.

This tax exemption extends not only to the states as such but to component parts thereof: political subdivisions, instrumentalities, agencies, and the like. The general principle is that the "United States may not tax instrumentalities which a state may employ in the discharge of her essential governmental duties."[392]

The constitutional law basis for this tax exemption is not unlimited; however, its scope has not been delineated. The position of the U.S. Supreme Court initially was that all "governmental" functions of a state were encompassed by the exemption and that only its "proprietary" activities could be taxed by the federal government.[393] Subsequently, the Court ruled that Congress could tax any "source of revenue by whomsoever earned and not uniquely capable of being earned only by a State," even though the tax "incidence falls also on a State."[394] Apparently, the *uniquely capable* test remains the standard.[395]

Notwithstanding the existence of this constitutional law tax exemption, Congress in 1913 enacted a broader statutory immunity. In its relevant portions,[396] this statutory immunity is available only for entities that exercise an *essential governmental function*, and where the income thereby generated accrues to a state or political subdivision of the state. The IRS has long maintained that, by enacting the statutory immunity, "Congress did not desire in any way to restrict a State's participation in enterprises which might be useful in carrying out those

---

[390] IRC § 529(c)(4). Proposed regulations concerning these programs were issued on August 21, 1998 (REG-106177-97). Issuance of these regulations in final form has been delayed, due to the statutory law changes in 2001. In the interim, the IRS provided guidance on changes to record-keeping, reporting, and other requirements applicable to these programs (Notice 2001-81, 2001-52 I.R.B. 617).

[391] E.g., Priv. Ltr. Rul. 9812037. In general, Spitzer & Houston, "The New QSTPs: Not Your Grandparents' State Tuition Plan," 23 *Exempt Org. Tax Rev.* (No. 3) 457 (Mar. 1999).

[392] Helvering v. Therrell, 303 U.S. 218, 223 (1938).

[393] South Carolina v. United States, 199 U.S. 437 (1905).

[394] New York v. United States, 326 U.S. 572, 582 (1946).

[395] Massachusetts v. United States, 435 U.S. 44 (1978); Willmette Park Dist. v. Campbell, 388 U.S. 411 (1949). Cf. Davis v. Michigan Dept. of Treasury, 89-2 U.S.T.C. ¶ 9456 (Mich. Ct. App. 1989); State of S.C. v. Baker, 485 U.S. 505 (1988). Also Flint v. Stone Tracy Co., 220 U.S. 107, 172 (1911).

[396] IRC § 115(a)(1).

projects desirable from the standpoint of the State Government."[397] Thus, the IRS ruled that the income of an investment fund established by a state was excludable from gross income; even though more than one governmental entity participated in the fund, the requisite accrual was found.[398] Likewise, the IRS held that the income of an organization formed, operated, and funded by one or more political subdivisions (or by a state and one or more political subdivisions) to pool their risks in lieu of purchasing insurance to cover their public liability, workers' compensation, or employees' health obligations was excluded from gross income, as long as private interests did not, except for incidental benefits to employees of the participating state and political subdivisions, participate in or benefit from the organization.[399]

As to the type of entity that can avail itself of the broader immunity, commentators wrote that only a state or political subdivision of a state, and not a private corporation, may invoke this immunity, because only the former can perform an essential governmental function.[400] The courts appear to have reached the same conclusion, albeit for a different reason, namely, on the theory that the interposition of a corporation operates to prevent the requisite *accrual* from taking place.[401] These analyses, however, leave unanswered the question as to whether a corporation, such as a nonprofit one, can qualify for federal tax purposes as a political subdivision. The answer to this question has several ramifications, not the least of which is the ability of this type of entity to incur debt the interest on which is excludable from the recipient's gross income.[402]

In its narrowest sense, the term *political subdivision* connotes a jurisdictional or geographical component of a state, such as counties, cities, and sewer districts. Perhaps a more realistic definition of the term was provided by a federal court of appeals: The term *political subdivision* is broad and comprehensive, and denotes any division of a state made by the proper authorities thereof, acting within their constitutional powers, for the purpose of carrying out a portion of these functions of the state that by long usage and the inherent necessities of government have always been regarded as public.[403]

These considerations take on greater coloration when applied in the context of organizations that are state-owned but have charitable organization counterparts, such as state schools, colleges, universities, hospitals, and libraries.[404] Cer-

---

[397] Gen. Couns. Mem. 14407.

[398] Rev. Rul. 77-261, 1977-2 C.B. 45, *as clar. by* (on another point) Rev. Rul. 78-316, 1978-2 C.B. 304.

[399] Rev. Rul. 90-74, 1990-2 C.B. 34.

[400] Tucker & Rombro, "State Immunity from Federal Taxation: The Need for Re-examination," 43 *Geo. Wash. L. Rev.* 501, 546–547 (1975).

[401] E.g., Troy State Univ. v. Comm'r, 62 T.C. 493 (1974).

[402] IRC § 103. The U.S. Supreme Court ruled that the federal income tax exemption for mutual bond interest is not mandated by the Tenth Amendment to the U.S. Constitution or by the doctrine of intergovernmental immunity (State of S.C. v. Baker, *supra* note 395).

[403] Comm'r v. Estate of Alexander J. Shamburg, 3 T.C. 131 (1944), *aff'd*, 144 F.2d 998 (2d Cir. 1944), *cert. den.*, 323 U.S. 792 (1944). Cf. Rev. Rul. 76-550, 1976-2 C.B. 331; Rev. Rul. 76-549, 1976-2 C.B. 330. Also Crilly v. Southeastern Pa. Transp. Auth., 529 F.2d 1355 (3d Cir. 1976); Popkin v. New York State Health & Mental Hygiene Facilities Improvement Corp., 409 F. Supp. 430 (S.D.N.Y. 1976).

[404] See Chapters 6, 7.

tainly these entities are generally exempt from tax; the tax exemption derives in part from the constitutional immunity accorded the revenue of integral units of states. The exemption may likewise traced to this statutory immunity. Presumably, there is the requisite accrual; for example, the provision of education has been regarded as the exercise of an essential governmental function.[405] By contrast, courts have held that, under certain circumstances, operation of a hospital is not an essential governmental function.[406] There is no case that specifically holds that, for example, a state college or university is a political subdivision, although this conclusion may be reached by a process of negative implication.[407] The IRS, however, asserted that a state university cannot qualify as a political subdivision because it fails to possess a substantial right to exercise the power to tax, the power of eminent domain, or the police power.[408]

A third way for an organization to qualify for this type of tax-exempt status is to be an *integral part of a state*. Generally, income earned by an integral part of a state (or by a political subdivision of a state) is not subject to federal income taxation in the absence of a specific statutory authorization to tax that income.[409] The IRS developed factors to be considered in deciding whether an entity is an integral part of a state.[410]

The rules as to whether an entity is a political subdivision, instrumentality, agency, or integral part of a state continue to become more inconsistent and confusing. A court of appeals evaluated the tax status of an organization established to receive advance payments of college tuition, invest the money, and ultimately make disbursements under a program that allows its beneficiaries to attend any of the state's public colleges and universities without further tuition cost. The

---

[405] Page v. Regents of Univ. Sys. of Ga., 93 F.2d 887 (5th Cir. 1937), *rev. on other grounds sub nom.*, Allen v. Regents of the Univ. Sys. of Ga., 304 U.S. 339 (1938).

[406] Liggett & Myers Tobacco Co. v. United States, 13 F. Supp. 143 (Ct. Cl. 1936), *aff'd*, 299 U.S. 383 (1937), *reh'g. den.*, 300 U.S. 686 (1937); Cook v. United States, 26 F. Supp. 253 (D. Mass. 1939).

[407] Troy State Univ. v. Comm'r, *supra* note 401; Iowa State Univ. of Science & Technology v. United States, 500 F.2d 508 (Ct. Cl. 1974).

[408] Rev. Rul. 77-165, 1977-1 C.B. 21. In Tech. Adv. Mem. 8119061, the IRS held that a state university was not a political subdivision of the state (for purposes of eligibility for the interest exclusion for the university's obligations) because the university possessed no more than an insubstantial part of any sovereign power. The university did not have the power to tax nor the power of eminent domain, and the IRS concluded that the possession of certain powers to promulgate and enforce regulations in the areas of health and safety on the university's campus did not constitute the police power (citing Manigault v. Springs, 119 U.S. 473 (1905); Barbier v. Connelly, 113 U.S. 27 (1885)). The IRS noted that the campus police operated at the university under a scope of authority defined by state law rather than by the university, and that the campus police had the power to make arrests only for violations of the state's criminal law and not for violations of the university's rules and regulations that are not criminal in nature. The university also failed with its argument that the interest on its obligations should be tax-excludable because the obligations were issued "on behalf of" the state (principally inasmuch as the university was a state instrumentality and a land grant institution), with the IRS determining that the requisite degree of control by the state was absent, in that fewer than one-third of the university's board of trustees are government officials or appointees of the governor of the state (see § 6.9). In general, Henze, "State Universities as Political Subdivisions," 9 *J. Coll. & U.S.* 341 (1982–1983).

[409] Rev. Rul. 87-2, 1987-1 C.B. 18.

[410] Rev. Rul. 57-128, 1957-1 C.B. 311. Also Rose v. Long Island R.R. Pension Plan, 828 F.2d 910 (2d Cir. 1987).

appellate court, having found that the entity was an instrumentality of the state, concluded that it was also an integral part of the state, so that its investment income was not taxable.[411] The court ruled that a state or political subdivision of a state is not a corporation for purposes of the federal corporate income tax.[412] It wrote that the "broad constitutional immunity from federal taxation once thought to be enjoyed by states and their instrumentalities has been severely eroded by the passage of time."[413] As to the law concerning the exclusion from taxation of income accruing to the state, the court characterized the rules as "very old and somewhat cryptic."[414]

An organization created in the aftermath of a major hurricane as a vehicle for property and casualty insurers to share insurance coverage for property owners unable to obtain coverage in the "voluntary" market was held to be an integral part of a state.[415] The court considered the factors used in this context by the IRS,[416] and concluded that the organization "bears a much closer resemblance to being an integral part of the state than to being a private insurance company."[417] The court also noted the state's financial commitment to the enterprise. Overall, wrote the court, the "determinative test with respect to the financial arrangements" regarding this organization is "whether it is the [s]tate or the participating private insurance companies who ultimately may profit from its operations, and the undisputed evidence is that only the state may receive any financial benefit."[418]

The law in this regard has changed dramatically, largely due to the emergence of the check-the-box regulations, which treat, as an entity that is disregarded as a separate one for federal tax purposes, an organization that is an integral part of a state.[419] The IRS, for some time regularly issuing letter rulings concerning organizations that do or do not qualify as governmental instrumentalities by reason of the intergovernmental immunity doctrine,[420] has largely ceased doing so. Today, the

---

[411] Michigan v. United States, 40 F.3d 817 (6th Cir. 1994). The district court in this case ruled that this entity was not tax-exempt under the doctrine of intergovernmental immunity because it was not an integral part of the state and that its income could not be excluded from taxation pursuant to IRC § 115 because there was no accrual of income to the state (Michigan v. United States, 802 F. Supp. 120 (W.D. Mich. 1992)).

[412] IRC § 11. The court relied on Gen. Couns. Mem. 14407 (issued in 1935) as authority for this proposition.

[413] Michigan v. United States, *supra* note 411, 40 F.3d at 822.

[414] *Id.* at 829. Further confusing aspects of this opinion include the court's reliance on Rev. Rul. 57-128, *supra* note 410 (see § 6.9), which applies to entities that are separate from a state; the factors enumerated in the revenue ruling do not determine whether an enterprise is considered to be a separate entity or an integral part of a state. Subsequently, a statutory basis for tax-exempt status for tuition programs of this nature was enacted (see *supra* § 16).

[415] Florida Residential Property & Casualty Joint Underwriting Ass'n v. United States, 2002-1 U.S.T.C. ¶ 50,280 (N.D. Fla. 2002).

[416] Rev. Rul. 57-128, *supra* note 410.

[417] Florida Residential Property & Casualty Joint Underwriting Ass'n v. United States, *supra* note 415.

[418] *Id.* at 83,641.

[419] See § 4.1(b)(ii), text accompanied by note 42.

[420] E.g., Priv. Ltr. Rul. 8842071.

IRS issues private letter rulings on an ongoing basis as to organizations that do or do not qualify as political subdivisions[421] or that qualify as integral parts of a state.[422]

§ 18.18 NATIVE AMERICAN TRIBES

Native American tribes generally are not taxable entities for federal income tax purposes.[423] These tribes generally have governing instruments, a council, operational rules, a formal membership arrangement, and various governmental powers, such as the rights to levy taxes, enact ordinances, and maintain a police force. The assets of an Indian tribe are owned by the tribe as a community (rather than by the individual members) and the right to participate in the enjoyment of tribal property depends on continuing membership in the tribe.[424]

Any income earned by an unincorporated tribe (including that from gambling and other commercial business activities), regardless of the location of the business activities that produced the income (that is, whether on or off the tribe's reservation), is not subject to federal income tax.[425] Tribal income not otherwise exempt from federal income tax is includible in the gross income of the Indian tribal member when distributed to, or constructively received by, the member.[426]

Native American tribal corporations organized under the Indian Reorganization Act of 1934[427] share the same tax status as the native American tribe and is not taxable on income from activities carried on within the boundaries of the reservation.[428] Thus, any income earned by this type of corporation, regardless of the location of the business activities that produced the income, is not subject to federal income tax.[429] Tribal corporations organized under the Oklahoma Welfare Act[430] have the same tax status.[431]

---

[421] E.g., Priv. Ltr. Rul. 8737090.

[422] E.g., Priv. Ltr. Rul. 9507037 (updated by Priv. Ltr. Rul. 9522039). In general, Aprill, "Excluding the Income of State and Local Governments: The Need for Congressional Action," 26 *Ga. L. Rev.* 421 (Winter 1992); Rich, "State and Local Governments' and Their Instrumentalities' Escape from Federal Income Taxation: Immunity, Exemption, and Exclusion," 23 *Exempt Org. Tax Rev.* (No. 3) 463 (Mar. 1999).

[423] Rev. Rul. 67-284, 1967-2 C.B. 55, *mod. on another issue*, Rev. Rul. 74-13, 1974-1 C.B. 14. Cf. Lummi Indian Tribe v. Whatcom County, Wash., 5 F.3d 1355 (9th Cir. 1993) (real property of a tribe was held to not be exempt from state property tax).

[424] Gritts v. Fisher, 2224 U.S. 640 (1912).

[425] Rev. Rul. 94-16, 1994-1 C.B. 19.

[426] *Id.* E.g., Beck v. Comm'r, 67 T.C.M. 2469 (1994) (income received by a member of the Eastern Band of Cherokee Indians from the rental of apartment buildings located on a Cherokee reservation was held to not be exempt from federal income taxation).

[427] 25 U.S.C. § 477.

[428] Rev. Rul. 81-295, 1981-2 C.B. 15, which relied on Mescalero Apache Tribe v. Jones, 411 U.S. 145 (1973).

[429] Rev. Rul. 94-16, *supra* note 425.

[430] 25 U.S.C. § 503.

[431] Rev. Rul. 94-65, 1994-2 C.B. 14. Earlier law was clear that the fact that a native American tribe was incorporated did not alter its federal tax status (Maryland Cas. Co. v. Citizens Nat'l Bank of W. Hollywood, 361 F.2d 517 (5th Cir. 1966), *cert. den.*, Maryland Cas. Co. v. Seminole Tribe of Fla. Inc., 385 U.S. 918 (1966); Parker Drilling Co. v. Metlakatla Indian Community, 451 F. Supp. 1127 (D. Alaska 1978); Rev. Rul. 81-295, *supra* note 428).

A corporation organized by a native American tribe under state law is not the same as a native American tribal corporation organized under the Indian Reorganization Act and does not share the same tax status as the native American tribe for federal income tax purposes. This type of corporation is subject to federal income tax on any income earned, regardless of the location of the income-producing activities.[432]

§ 18.19 OTHER TAX-EXEMPT ORGANIZATIONS

There are several other types of organizations or entities that may be regarded as tax-exempt organizations in the broadest sense of the term.

Some organizations are tax-exempt as a matter of practice, not because of any specific grant of exemption but because of the ability to utilize sufficient deductions to effectively eliminate taxation. As noted, this is the principle on which the general tax exemption for cooperatives is premised.[433] Likewise, a pooled income fund[434] is generally a nontaxpaying entity because it is entitled to a deduction for distributions to beneficiaries and for long-term capital gain set aside.[435] (By contrast, a charitable remainder annuity trust or unitrust[436] is an organization expressly exempt from tax except in years in which it has unrelated business taxable income.[437]) As discussed earlier, this approach also provides "tax exemption" for perpetual care trust funds operated in conjunction with taxable cemeteries.[438]

Other entities achieve federal income tax exemption because the law regards them as organizations that, while they may have to file tax returns, do not have taxable income but instead pass that liability on to others. It is this principle that operates to exempt partnerships,[439] small business ("S") corporations,[440] and limited liability companies from federal income taxation.

[432] *Id.* IRC § 7871 provides that a qualified native American tribal government is treated as a state for certain federal income tax purposes, including the private foundation rules, unrelated business income rules, and the charitable contribution deductions. Although native American tribal governments do not have an inherent exemption from federal excise taxes, the IRS issued a ruling, founded on IRC § 7871, granting limited exemptions from some of these taxes (Rev. Rul. 94-81, 1994-2 C.B. 412).
[433] See § 3.4.
[434] IRC § 642(c)(5).
[435] Reg. § 1.642(c)-5(a)(2).
[436] IRC § 664.
[437] Reg. § 1.664-1(c).
[438] See *supra* § 6, text accompanied by note 180. Also IRC § 852(a) (concerning regulated investment companies).
[439] IRC § 701.
[440] IRC § 1372.

§ 18.20   PROPOSED EXEMPT ORGANIZATIONS

Proposals continue to abound for statutory authorization of new types of tax-exempt organizations (or, in a few instances, revision of existing exemption provisions). These proposals include the following:

1. Tax exemption for public utilities that furnish electrical power (S. 2213 (1975)).

2. Same tax exemptions and other tax treatment to recognized native American tribes as are available for governmental units (H.R. 8989 (1975); H. Rep. No. 94-1693 (1976)).

3. Tax exemption for a trust established by a taxpayer for the purpose of providing care for certain mentally incompetent relatives (H.R. 584 (1979); H.R. 10582 (1978); H.R. 3932 (1977); H.R. 9736 (1975)).

4. Tax credit for contributions to "neighborhood corporations" (S. 2192 (1975)).

5. Tax exemption for certain nonprofit corporations all of the members of which are tax-exempt credit unions (H.R. 1153 (1977); H.R. 13532 (1976)).

6. Tax exemption for certain nonprofit organizations operated for mutual purposes to provide reserve funds for and insurance of shares or deposits in certain credit unions and domestic building and loan associations (H.R. 6989 (1978); H.R. 14039 (1976)).

7. Tax exemption for certain state and local government retirement systems (S. 1587 (1977); H.R. 9109 (1977)).

8. Tax exemption for associations operated exclusively to provide worker's compensation for state and local employees (H.R. 1074 (1979); H.R. 8470 (1977)).

9. Tax exemption for a product liability self-insurance reserve trust (H.R. 394, 1677, 1678, 1947, 2341, 2693, 2926, 2935, 3252, 4729, 6489 (1979–1980); H.R. 12471 (1978); H.R. 7711 (1977)).

10. Tax exemption for certain organizations furnishing computer and fiscal management services to social service organizations (H.R. 7207 (1978)).

11. Tax exemption for an Energy Company of America (H.R. 3885, 4649, 5622 (1979)).

12. Tax exemption for organizations of professionals (H.R. 990, 4724 (1979)).

13. Tax exemption for professional liability insurance organizations (H.R. 4427 (1979)).

14. Special tax treatment of certain physicians' and surgeons' mutual protection and indemnity associations (Senate version of Tax Reform Act of 1984, H.R. 4170, 98th Cong., 2d Sess. (1984) § 866).

15. Tax exemption for local police and fire associations that provide pension and other benefits that would otherwise be provided by a state or local government, to its members (Senate version of Tax Reform Act of 1984, H.R. 4170, 98th Cong., 2d Sess. (1984)).

16. Tax exemption for certain nonprofit corporations and associations organized to provide reserve funds for domestic savings and loan associations (H.R. 6199 (1984)).

17. Separate category of tax exemption for college and university fraternities and sororities (H.R. 2189 (1985)).

18. Tax exemption for trust or corporation to facilitate collective investment in real estate by tax-exempt organizations, pension plans, and state and local governments (H.R. 3301 (1986)).

19. Tax exemption for organizations that assist in introducing into public use technology developed by operating research organizations (S. 2195 (1986)).

20. Tax exemption for self-insured workers' compensation associations (H.R. 1489 (1987); H.R. 1709 (1987)).

21. Tax exemption for certain Blue Cross and Blue Shield organizations (H.R. 2191 (1989)).

22. To deny tax-exempt status to certain politically active organizations that are linked to candidates for federal office and to require that contributions to separate political organizations that are linked to these candidates be treated as direct contributions (S. 2148 (1990)).

23. Tax exemption for industrial recapitalization funds for manufacturing industries (S. 2765 (1990)).

24. Imposition of a requirement that tax-exempt hospitals provide a certain amount of charity care and care to Medicare and Medicaid patients in order to maintain tax-exempt status (H.R. 5686 (1990), H.R. 790 (1991)).

25. Denial of tax-exempt status to educational institutions which have been found to have a policy of racial discrimination against any group in enrollment, hiring, or in other areas, until these institutions clearly and convincingly demonstrate their abandonment of the policy through the enrollment, hiring, or the taking of other vigorous, affirmative, and continued corrective action with respect to such group (H.R. 181 (1991)).

26. Denial of tax-exempt status to rural electric cooperatives that have gross receipts in excess of $25 million (H.R. 1355 (1991)).

27. Linkage of a hospital's tax-exempt status to the level of charity care that the hospital provides (H.R. 1374 (1991)).

28. Denial of tax-exempt status, and charitable donee status, to organizations which directly or indirectly perform or finance procedures which take the life of a pre-born child other than procedures required

to prevent the death of either the pregnant woman or pre-born child, so long as every reasonable effort is made to preserve the life of each (H.R. 1458 (1991)).

29. Tax exemption for common investment funds for private and community foundations (H.R. 2608 (1989), H.R. 1733, S. 588 (1991)). This proposal was the subject of § 4664 of the Revenue Act of 1992 (H.R. 11 (1992)), which passed Congress but was vetoed.

30. Tax exemption for regional health alliances, as part of overall health care reform legislation (H.R. 3600 (1993)).

31. Tax exemption for health risk pools (H.R. 3507 (1993); S. 539 (1995)).

32. Tax exemption (reinstitution of it) for the Teacher's Insurance and Annuity Association–College Retirement Equities Fund (S. 1142 (1997)).

33. To restore and make permanent the tax exemption for qualified group legal service plans (H.R. 1640 (1999), H.R. 4031 (1998)).

34. Tax exemption for organizations created by a state to provide property and casualty insurance coverage for property for which the coverage is otherwise unavailable (H.R. 4361 (1998)).

35. To deny tax exemption, on grounds of private inurement, to a charitable organization that, directly or indirectly, uses gift funds to purchase a life insurance, endowment, or annuity contract benefiting the donor or any designee of the donor, or engages in any other transaction "which provides a personal benefit directly or indirectly" to the donor or designee of the donor, where the transaction occurs after February 4, 1999 (charitable contributions would be denied for all gifts made before, on, or after date of enactment) (H.R. 572 (1999)).

36. Tax exemption for associations created by state law (before January 1, 1999) and organized and operated exclusively to provide property and casualty insurance coverage for property located within the state for which the state has determined that coverage in the authorized insurance market is limited to or unavailable at reasonable rates (S. 1136 (1999), H.R. 2488 (1999)) (see item 34).

37. To treat state developmental disabilities endowment programs as tax-exempt organizations (H.R. 4074 (2000)).

38. To suspend the tax-exempt status of designated terrorist organizations (S. 3081, S. 3082 (2002)).

PART FOUR

General Exempt
Organization Laws

CHAPTER NINETEEN

Private Inurement, Private Benefit, and Excess Benefit Transactions

The doctrine of *private inurement* is one of the most important sets of rules within the law of tax-exempt organizations—it is the fundamental defining principle distinguishing *nonprofit organizations* from *for-profit organizations*.[1] The private inurement doctrine is a statutory criterion for federal income tax exemption for nine types of exempt organizations. These categories of exempt organizations are charitable organizations,[2] social welfare organizations,[3] associations and

---

[1] See § 1.1.
[2] See Part Two.
[3] See Chapter 12.

other business leagues,[4] social clubs,[5] voluntary employees' beneficiary associations,[6] teachers' retirement fund associations,[7] cemetery companies,[8] veterans' organizations,[9] and state-sponsored organizations providing health care to high-risk individuals.[10]

Thus, aside from being organized and operated primarily for a tax-exempt purpose and otherwise meeting the appropriate statutory requirements for exemption, an organization subject to the doctrine must comport with the federal tax law prohibiting private inurement. Despite the fact that this law is applicable to several categories of tax-exempt organizations, nearly all of the law concerning private inurement has been developed involving transactions with charitable organizations.

The oddly phrased and thoroughly antiquated language of the private inurement doctrine requires that the tax-exempt organization be organized and operated so that "no part of ... [its] net earnings ... inures to the benefit of any private shareholder or individual."[11] This provision reads as though it were proscribing the payment of dividends. In fact, it is rare for a tax-exempt organization to have shareholders,[12] let alone to make payments to them. Moreover, the private inurement doctrine can be triggered by the involvement of persons other than individuals, such as corporations, partnerships, limited liability companies, estates, and trusts. The meaning of the statutory language today is barely reflected in its literal form and transcends the nearly century-old formulation: none of the income or assets of a tax-exempt organization subject to the private inurement doctrine may be permitted to directly or indirectly unduly benefit an individual or other person who has a close relationship to the organization, particularly those who are in a position to exercise a significant degree of control over it.

The *private benefit doctrine* is considerably different than, although it subsumes, the private inurement doctrine. Being an extrapolation of the operational test,[13] this doctrine is applicable only to charitable organizations. The rules pertaining to *excess benefit transactions* are applicable with respect to public charitable organizations[14] and social welfare organizations.[15]

---

[4] See Chapter 13.
[5] See Chapter 14.
[6] See § 16.3.
[7] See § 16.7, text accompanied by note 115.
[8] See § 18.6.
[9] See § 18.10(a).
[10] See § 18.14.
[11] In a fine characterization, this phraseology was termed a "nondistribution constraint" (Hansmann, "The Role of Nonprofit Enterprise," 89 *Yale L. J.* 835, 838 (1980).
[12] The law in a few states permits a nonprofit corporation to issue stock. This type of stock, however, does not carry with it rights to dividends. Thus, these rare bodies of law are not in conflict with the private inurement doctrine.
[13] See § 4.5.
[14] See §§ 11.1, 11.3.
[15] See Chapter 12.

§ 19.1 ESSENCE OF PRIVATE INUREMENT

The concept of private inurement lacks precision. One court wrote that the "boundaries of the term 'inures' have thus far defied precise definition."[16] The case law teaches that the doctrine is broad and wide-ranging. The advent of the rules concerning excess benefit transactions[17] will bring some exactitude to, albeit perhaps less application of, the doctrine. Further, the rules as to self-dealing involving private foundations[18] continue to bring many examples of private inurement transactions, as does the private benefit doctrine.[19]

The word *inure* means to gravitate toward, flow to or through, or transfer to something. In the private inurement context, the emphasis is on a flowing, of income or assets, directly or indirectly, through an organization to a person who should not be receiving the economic benefit. The term *private* is used in this setting to mean unwarranted personal benefits and other forms of non-exempt uses and purposes. Consequently, the private inurement doctrine forbids (1) the flow or transfer of income or assets of a tax-exempt organization, that is subject to the doctrine, through or away from the organization, and (2) the use of such income or assets by one or more persons closely associated with, or for the benefit of one or more other persons with some significant relationship to, the organization, for inappropriate purposes.

A pronouncement from the IRS stated that private "[i]nurement is likely to arise where the financial benefit represents a transfer of the organization's financial resources to an individual solely by virtue of the individual's relationship with the organization, and without regard to accomplishing exempt purposes."[20] Another of these observations, more bluntly expressed, was that the "inurement prohibition serves to prevent anyone in a position to do so from siphoning off any of a charity's income or assets for personal use."[21]

The purpose of the private inurement rule is to ensure that the tax-exempt organization involved is serving exempt rather than private interests. It is thus necessary for an organization subject to the doctrine to be in a position to establish that it is not organized and operated for the benefit of persons in their private capacity, such as the organization's founders, trustees, directors, officers, members of their families, entities controlled by these individuals, or any other persons having a personal and private interest in the activities of the organization.[22]

In ascertaining the presence of private inurement, the law looks to the ultimate purpose of the organization involved. If its basic purpose is to benefit

---

[16] Variety Club Tent No. 6 Charities, Inc. v. Comm'r, 74 T.C.M. 1485, 1494 (1997).
[17] See *infra* § 11.
[18] See § 11.4(a).
[19] See *infra* § 10.
[20] Gen. Couns. Mem. 38459.
[21] Gen. Couns. Mem. 39862. As noted, this summary applies, not just to charitable organizations, but to other tax-exempt organizations subject to the doctrine.
[22] Reg. §§ 1.501(a)-1(c), 1.501(c)(3)-1(c)(2). Also Ginsburg v. Comm'r, 46 T.C. 47 (1966); Rev. Rul. 76-206, 1976-1 C.B. 154.

individuals in their private capacity—without thereby serving exempt purposes—then it cannot be tax-exempt, even though exempt activities may also
be performed. Thus, a court, in concluding that an organization that purchased
and sold products manufactured by blind individuals constituted a tax-exempt
charitable organization, was not deterred in reaching this finding because of
the fact that the organization distributed a portion of its "net profits" to qualified workers at a state agency; the court in essence held that these distributions
were in furtherance of exempt purposes.[23] Conversely, incidental benefits to
private individuals will not defeat the exemption, as long as the organization
otherwise qualifies for tax-exempt status.[24]

The doctrine of private inurement does not prohibit transactions between
a tax-exempt organization subject to the doctrine and those who have a close
relationship with it. As the IRS wrote, "[t]here is no absolute prohibition
against an exempt section 501(c)(3) organization dealing with its founders,
members, or officers in conducting its economic affairs."[25] Rather, as is the case
with the excess benefit transactions rules and the doctrine of private benefit,
the private inurement doctrine requires that these transactions be tested
against a standard of *reasonableness*.[26] The standard calls for a roughly equal exchange of benefits between the parties; the law is designed to discourage what
the IRS termed a "disproportionate share of the benefits of the exchange" flowing to an insider.[27]

The reasonableness standard focuses essentially on comparability of data,
that is, on how similar organizations, acting prudently, transact their affairs in
comparable instances. Thus, the regulations pertaining to the business expense
deduction, addressing the matter of the reasonableness of compensation, provide that it is generally "just to assume that reasonable and true compensation
is only such amount as would ordinarily be paid for like services by like enterprises under like circumstances."[28] Consequently, the terms of these transactions are compared to comparable practices at comparable exempt or for-profit
organizations. Currently, the law generally holds that the relative insignifi-
cance of the private benefit provided to persons who should not have received
it cannot serve as a defense to a claim of private inurement. That precept is un-
dergoing reevaluation, in part because of the appearance of the intermediate
sanctions rules.

The core of the private inurement doctrine are the various ways to impermissibly confer private inurement.[29] Before reviewing private inurement transac-

---

[23] Industrial Aid for the Blind v. Comm'r, 73 T.C. 96 (1979).
[24] Reg. § 1.501(c)(3)-1(d)(1)(ii).
[25] Priv. Ltr. Rul. 9130002. To this group may be added trustees and directors.
[26] In contrast, the private foundation self-dealing rules generally and essentially forbid these types of
transactions.
[27] Priv. Ltr. Rul. 9130002.
[28] Reg. § 1.162(b)(3). See § 4.5(b).
[29] See *infra* § 4.

tions, however, it is necessary to summarize two other elements critical to the private inurement equation: the concepts of *net earnings*[30] and the *insider*.[31]

§ 19.2 CONCEPT OF *NET EARNINGS*

The term *net earnings* means gross earnings minus related expenses—a meaning that, as noted, seemingly applies the term, in the private inurement setting, in a technical, accounting sense.[32] For example, a state supreme court addressed this definition at length in the early decades of the federal tax law. In one opinion, this court wrote that, since the term is not defined in the statute, it "must be given its usual and ordinary meaning of what is left of earnings after deducting necessary and legitimate items of expense incident to the corporate business."[33] This approach was followed in the early years by other state courts and by federal courts.[34]

From the perspective of the law of tax-exempt organizations, however, this technical definition of the term was never quite adequate as to its sole meaning. Some courts applied the term in this restricted manner, where the facts particularly lent themselves to this approach,[35] but most court opinions on the point reflect the broader, and certainly contemporary, view that there can be inurement of net earnings in the absence of actual transfers of net income.[36]

An early proponent of this view was another state supreme court, which observed that the *net earnings* phraseology "should not be given a strictly literal construction, as in the accountant's sense" and that the "substance should control the form," so that tax exemption should not be available where private inurement is taking place, "irrespective of the means by which that result is accomplished."[37] Likewise, a federal court foresaw today's application of the term when it held that private inurement "may include more than the term net profits as shown by the books of the organization or than the difference between the gross receipts and disbursements in dollars," and that "[p]rofits may inure to the benefit of

---

[30] See *infra* § 2.

[31] See *infra* § 3.

[32] The statute, as originally written in 1913, employed the term *net income*. In 1918, the word *earnings* was substituted for *income*. There is nothing in the legislative history to suggest that this change had any substantive significance, and the commonality of the meanings of the two terms indicates that none was intended.

[33] Bank of Commerce & Trust Co. v. Senter, 260 S.W. 144, 151 (Sup. Ct. Tenn. 1924). Likewise, Southern Coal Co. v. McCanless, 192 S.W.2d 1003, 1005 (Sup. Ct. Tenn. 1946); National Life & Accident Ins. Co. v. Dempster, 79 S.W.2d 564 (Sup. Ct. Tenn. 1935).

[34] E.g., United States v. Riely, 169 F.2d 542 (4th Cir. 1948); Winkelman v. General Motors Corp., 44 F. Supp. 960 (S.D.N.Y. 1942); Inscho v. Mid-Continent Development Co., 146 P. 1014 (Kan. 1915).

[35] E.g., Birmingham Business College, Inc. v. Comm'r, 276 F.2d 476 (5th Cir. 1960); Gemological Institute of America v. Comm'r, 17 T.C. 1604 (1952), *aff'd*, 212 F.2d 205 (9th Cir. 1954); Putnam v. Comm'r, 6 T.C. 702 (1946).

[36] E.g., Edward Orton, Jr., Ceramic Foundation v. Comm'r, 9 T.C. 533 (1947), *aff'd*, 173 F.2d 483 (6th Cir. 1949); Gemological Institute of America v. Riddell, 149 F. Supp. 128 (S.D. Cal. 1957).

[37] Virginia Mason Hospital Association v. Larson, 114 P.2d 978, 983 (Wash. 1941).

shareholders in ways other than dividends."[38] This view certainly represents the current application of the private inurement doctrine—as an overall standard assessing the use of a tax-exempt organization's income and assets[39]—although the recent past brought an occasional somewhat literal interpretation.[40]

In conclusion, the contemporary concept of private inurement goes far beyond any mechanical computation and dissemination of net earnings, and embraces a much wider range of transactions and other activities.

§ 19.3 THE REQUISITE *INSIDER*

A private inurement transaction is one between a tax-exempt organization that is subject to the doctrine and a person (or persons) who has a special, close relationship with the organization. To put a name to the latter, the federal tax law appropriated the term *insider* from the federal securities laws.[41]

Generally, an *insider* is a person who has a unique relationship with the exempt organization involved, by which that person can cause application of the organization's funds or assets for the private purposes of the person by reason of the person's exercise of control or influence over, or being in a position to exercise that control or influence over, the organization.[42] An insider includes an organization's founders, trustees, directors, officers, key employees, members of the family of these individuals, and certain entities controlled by them.[43] All of these persons have been swept into the insider category, from the starting point of the

---

[38] Northwestern Municipal Ass'n v. United States, 99 F.2d 460, 463 (8th Cir. 1938).

[39] E.g., Harding Hospital, Inc. v. United States, 505 F.2d 1068 (6th Cir. 1974).

[40] A federal court found that the term *net earnings* signified funds used for expenses over and above expenses that are "ordinary and necessary" in the operation of a charitable organization (Carter v. United States, 973 F.2d 1479, 1487 (9th Cir. 1992); Hall v. Comm'r, 729 F.2d 632, 634 (9th Cir. 1984)).

A less-than-literal interpretation of these rules occurred when a court held that "paying over a portion of *gross* earnings to those vested with the control of a charitable organization constituted private inurement as well," adding that "[a]ll in all, taking a slice off the top should be no less prohibited than a slice out of net" (People of God Community v. Comm'r, 75 T.C. 127, 133 (1980) (emphasis in original).

[41] These laws prohibit, for example, insider trading.

[42] American Campaign Academy v. Comm'r, 92 T.C. 1053 (1989). It was subsequently stated that the "case law [as to private inurement] appears to have drawn a line between those who have significant control over the organization's activities and those who are unrelated third parties" (Variety Club Tent No. 6 Charities, Inc. v. Commissioner, *supra* note 16, at 1492).

[43] In the excess benefit transactions context (see *infra* § 11) and in the private foundations context (IRC § 4946), the term *disqualified person* is used to describe an insider.

The IRS expressed the view that all persons performing services for a tax-exempt organization are insiders with respect to that organization (Gen. Couns. Mem. 39670); this obviously is an expansive interpretation of the concept. It was the position of the IRS, for example, that all physicians on the medical staff of an exempt hospital are insiders in relation to the hospital (Gen. Couns. Mem. 39498); however, this stance was ameliorated in the aftermath of enactment of the intermediate sanctions law (see *infra* § 11(c), text accompanied by note 350).

statutory language with its peculiar and incomplete reference to *private shareholder or individual.*[44]

The case law is rich with court opinions concerning the involvement of insiders in private inurement transactions.

Five individuals leased property to a tax-exempt school, which constructed improvements on its property; of this group, one was the school's president, two were its vice-presidents, and one was its secretary-treasurer. These four individuals were also directors of the school and constituted its executive committee. Private inurement was found in the form of "excessive rent payments [by which] part of the net earnings of [the school] inured to the benefit of the members of the . . . group . . . and that part of the net earnings of [the school] also inured to their benefit because of the construction at its expense of buildings and improvements on real estate owned by them."[45]

A foundation failed to achieve tax-exempt status because part of its net earnings was determined to have inured to its founder. The foundation made loans for the personal benefit of this individual and his family members and friends, made research expenditures to advance his personal hobby, and purchased stock in a corporation owned by a friend of his. A court concluded that the foundation was "organized in such a fashion that [its founder] held control of its activities and expenditures; it was operated to carry out projects in which [he] was interested and some of its funds were expended for [his] benefit or [for the benefit of] members of his family."[46]

Tax exemption was denied to a college that had five family members as all of its trustees and three of them as its shareholders, because of private inurement in the form of "constant commingling of the funds of the shareholders and the [c]ollege."[47] A court concluded that this college was "operated as a business producing, or ultimately producing, substantial revenue for its operators[;] the net earnings, or substantial portions, were to be, and were in fact, distributed to these shareholders for their own personal benefit."[48]

A foundation, bearing the name of a radio personality, was established to provide musical instruction, proper living quarters, and medical assistance to young individuals interested in the field of entertainment and who were featured in the shows of this entertainer. The foundation was found to be engaging in private inurement, inasmuch as in "these circumstances [the entertainer] received a great benefit by establishing an organization whereby the recipients of the organization's charitable services were in his employ and benefiting him" and that "it was to [his] advantage as a director of a radio program and as an employer to provide these services."[49]

---

[44] It is, as noted, uncommon for a nonprofit organization to have shareholders. When they exist, presumably they must be insiders for the private inurement doctrine to apply, although the IRS suggested that the status of a person as such a shareholder automatically makes that person an insider (Priv. Ltr. Rul. 9835001).

[45] Texas Trade School v. Comm'r, 30 T.C. 642, 647 (1958), *aff'd*, 272 F.2d 168 (5th Cir. 1959).

[46] Best Lock Corp. v. Comm'r, 31 T.C. 1217, 1236 (1959).

[47] Birmingham Business College, Inc. v. Comm'r, *supra* note 35, at 479.

[48] *Id.* at 480.

[49] Horace Heidt Foundation v. United States, 170 F. Supp. 634, 638 (Ct. Cl. 1959).

A physician established an ostensible scientific research foundation; he and his father were two of the three trustees. A court found private inurement in the form of benefits to the physician in his medical practice. The foundation's laboratory, located next door to the physician's office, was, according to the government, used "on numerous occasions in his practice"; the foundation's principal activities were the treatment of patients (chiefly those of the physicians). The court accepted the government's contention that the physician's "practice and the income therefrom were materially enhanced by the establishment of the laboratory."[50]

A church disbursed substantial sums to its founder and members of his family as fees, commissions, royalties, compensation for services, rent, reimbursements for expenses, and loans; the church maintained a personal residence for these individuals. Finding impermissible private inurement, a court observed that "[w]hat emerges from these facts is the inference that the . . . [founder's] family was entitled to make ready personal use of the corporate earnings. . . . [N]othing we have found in the record dispels the substantial doubts the court entertains concerning the receipt of benefit by [this family] from [the church's] net earnings."[51] With respect to certain of the disbursements, the court stated that the "logical inference can be drawn that these payments were disguised and unjustified distributions of [the church's] earnings."[52]

A court, in part because of the advantages obtained by the physicians who organized the institution, barred the tax exemption of a hospital. The founding physicians attended to most of the patients admitted to the hospital. The court's concern was over an arrangement for management services by which these physicians were paid, and a lease of office space. The court concluded that the hospital was the "primary source of the doctors' professional income" and that this "virtual monopoly by the [physicians] of the patients permitted benefits to inure to . . . [them] within the intendment of the statute."[53]

The IRS revoked, on private inurement grounds, the tax-exempt status of a hospital organized and operated by a physician. The institution was held by a court to have distributed its earnings to the physician in the form of direct payments (compensation and loans), improvements to the property of a corporation he owned, administrative services relating to his private practice, and the free use of its facilities.[54] The same fate befell an organization established to study chiropractic methods, where the founding chiropractor sold his home, automobile, and medical equipment to the entity, and caused it to pay his personal expenses and a salary while he continued his private practice.[55] Likewise, the tax exemption of an organization was revoked because of several transactions, including the receipt of property from the founder's mother and payment

---

[50] Cranley v. Comm'r, 20 T.C.M. 20, 25 (1961).
[51] Founding Church of Scientology v. United States, 412 F.2d 1197, 1202 (Ct. Cl. 1969), *cert. den.*, 397 U.S. 1009 (1970).
[52] *Id.* at 1201.
[53] Harding Hospital, Inc. v. United States, *supra* note 39, at 1078.
[54] Kenner v. Comm'r, 33 T.C.M. 1239 (1974).
[55] The Labrenz Foundation, Inc. v. Comm'r, 33 T.C.M. 1374 (1974).

to her of an annuity, payment of a child's college education, payment of the founder's personal expenses, and purchasing and leasing real estate owned by the founder.[56]

Private inurement precluded an ostensible religious organization from achieving tax-exempt status. Its governing board consisted of its founder, his spouse, and their child. It conducted some ministry through its founder (who was also its principal donor) and made some grants to needy individuals selected by him. A court concluded that the founder's activities were "more personal than church oriented."[57] In similar circumstances, a court rejected an organization's claim of tax exemption because the organization provided its founder and his family with "housing, food, transportation, clothing and other proper needs as may from time to time arise."[58]

A court's finding that a church was ineligible for tax-exempt status was based in part on its conclusion that a portion of the net earnings of the church inured to the benefit of its founder and his family. Indicia of this private inurement included unreasonable increases in salaries and payments of directors' fees, management fees, and other payments in support of the family. The court also labeled as private inurement the founder's practice of marketing books and other items in the name of the church, and being paid royalties for the sales, as well as to personally be paid royalties attributable to the literary efforts of employees of the church. Still other forms of private inurement were analyzed by the court, including "repayment of alleged debts in unspecified amounts and unfettered control over millions of dollars in funds" belonging to entities affiliated with the church.[59]

A community organization, with homeowners as members, was held to be engaging in private inurement transactions by providing "comfort and convenience" to the residents who, by reason of being the "intended beneficiaries" of the facilities and services of the organization, were found to have a "personal interest" in the activities of the organization.[60] A modern definition of the term *insider* means a person who has a "significant formal voice in [an exempt organization's] activities generally and had substantial formal and practical control over most of [the organization's] income."[61]

The IRS has likewise adopted the view that the prohibition on private inurement relates only to circumstances where unwarranted benefits are provided to insiders. Thus, the agency ruled that private inurement was not present where a tax-exempt hospital compensated a hospital-based radiologist on the basis of a fixed percentage of the revenue of the radiology department;

---

[56] Rueckwald Foundation, Inc. v. Comm'r, 33 T.C.M. 1383 (1974).

[57] Western Catholic Church v. Comm'r, 73 T.C. 196, 211 (1979), *aff'd*, 631 F.2d 736 (7th Cir. 1980), *cert. den.*, 450 U.S. 981 (1981).

[58] Parshall Christian Order v. Comm'r, 45 T.C.M. 488, 492 (1983).

[59] Church of Scientology of California v. Comm'r, 83 T.C. 381, 492 (1984), *aff'd*, 823 F.2d 1310 (9th Cir. 1987).

[60] Columbia Park & Recreation Ass'n, Inc. v. Comm'r, 88 T.C. 1, 24, 26 (1987), *aff'd*, 838 F.2d 465 (4th Cir. 1988).

[61] Variety Club Tent No. 6 Charities, Inc. v. Comm'r, *supra* note 16, at 1493.

this conclusion was arrived at, in part, because the radiologist "did not control" the hospital.[62]

By contrast, a trust that was required to pay out its net income for tax-exempt purposes for a period of years or the lives of specified individuals was ruled by the IRS to not qualify for tax-exempt status. At the end of the income-payment period, the trust terminated and the principal reverted to the founder of the trust or his estate. The disqualifying feature in this regard was the reversionary interest, which resulted in inurement of investment gains over the life of the trust to the benefit of its creator.[63] The IRS observed that the "inurement issue . . . focuses on benefits conferred on an organization's insiders through the use or distribution of the organization's financial resources.[64]

As the foregoing indicates, the focus on the concept of the *insider* in the private inurement area over the years has been on those who are the exempt organization's founders, trustees, directors, officers, and family members. Recently, however, attention has been given to what may appear at the outset to be an independent entity, such as a vendor of services, and whether that person may be an insider with respect to a tax-exempt organization. This development has been fueled in part by IRS-conceived examples of situations where ostensibly outside fundraising and similar companies are considered disqualified persons, under the intermediate sanctions rules, in relation to charitable organizations.[65]

The state of the law, as to this matter of vendors as insiders, is uncertain, largely because of litigation as to whether a fundraising firm can be an insider with respect to a charitable organization. A trial court found a fundraising firm to be an insider under these circumstances, because of the extent to which the firm took over, controlled, and manipulated the charity to its private ends.[66] By reason of the arrangement between the parties, the charity was funded and otherwise maintained in existence by the firm. This relationship was characterized as "substantial control" by the firm, which was portrayed as "in many ways analogous to that of a founder and major contributor to a new organization."[67] On appeal, however, this decision was reversed; the appellate court could not find anything in the facts of the case to support the "theory" that the fundraising firm "seized control" of the charity "and by doing so became an insider."[68] Said the court: "There is nothing that corporate or agency law would recognize as control."[69] Writing in obvious ignorance of the intermediate sanctions rules,[70] the appellate court wrote that the lower court used the

---

[62] Rev. Rul. 69-383, 1969-2 C.B. 113, 114.

[63] Rev. Rul. 66-259, 1966-2 C.B. 214.

[64] Gen. Couns. Mem. 38459.

[65] See *infra* § 11(c), text accompanied by note 351.

[66] United Cancer Council, Inc. v. Comm'r, 109 T.C. 326 (1997).

[67] *Id.* 387. The court wrote that, for purposes of the private inurement doctrine, an insider is a person who has "significant control of the [exempt] organization's activities" (*id.*).

[68] United Cancer Council, Inc. v. Comm'r, 165 F.3d 1173, 1178 (7th Cir. 1999).

[69] *Id.*

[70] See *infra* § 11.

word *control* "in a special sense not used elsewhere, so far as we can determine, in the law, including the federal tax law."[71]

This appellate court focused on the terms of the contract between the parties, because of its view that the lower court's classification of the fundraising firm as an insider with respect to the charity was based "on the fundraising contract."[72] This position, the court of appeals wrote, "threatens to unsettle the charitable sector by empowering the IRS to yank a charity's tax exemption simply because the Service thinks the charity's contract with its major fundraiser too one-sided in favor of the fundraiser, even though the charity has not been found to have violated any duty of faithful and careful management that the law of nonprofit corporations may have laid upon it."[73]

Consequently, a tax-exempt organization subject to the private inurement doctrine should be concerned with the doctrine only where there is a transaction or transactions involving one or more *insiders* with respect to the organization. The overall rule on this point was expressed this way: the "concept of private benefit [inurement] . . . [is] limited to the situation in which an organization's *insiders* . . . [are] benefited."[74] At the same time, however, the IRS may elect to apply the intermediate sanctions penalties against the insider[75] rather than revoke tax-exempt status.[76] Moreover, even if it turns out that a transaction involving a tax-exempt organization does not involve a person who is an insider, the analysis should not necessarily end, inasmuch as the transaction could nonetheless operate for the use or benefit of an insider/disqualified person[77] or be a transgression of the private benefit doctrine.[78]

§ 19.4   TYPES OF PRIVATE INUREMENT

The concept of the private inurement transaction has many manifestations. While the most common instance of private inurement is excessive compensation, there are several other forms of private inurement, most notably sales of assets, rental

---

[71] United Cancer Council, Inc. v. Comm'r, *supra* note 68 at 1178. The intermediate sanctions rules had been in existence over three years when this was written.

[72] *Id.* at 1176.

[73] *Id.* at 1179. This court also observed: "If the charity's contract with the fundraiser makes the latter an insider, triggering the inurement clause of section 501(c)(3) and so destroying the charity's tax exemption, the charitable sector of the economy is in trouble" (at 1176). It was not the contract that made the fundraising firm an insider, however, but the actions and compensation amounts that resulted from it.

[74] Sound Health Ass'n v. Comm'r, 71 T.C. 158, 185 (1978). Occasionally, the overwhelming domination of a tax-exempt organization and wrongdoing by an insider can lead a court to a finding of private inurement, when in fact inurement is not present because the terms and conditions of the transactions involved were reasonable (e.g., Airlie Foundation, Inc. v. United States, 826 F. Supp. 537 (D.D.C. 1993), *aff'd*, 95-1 U.S.T.C. ¶ 50,279 (D.C. Cir. 1995)).

[75] As discussed, in the intermediate sanctions area, an insider is termed a disqualified person (see *infra* § 11(c)). At the present, the terms *insider* and *disqualified person* should be regarded as essentially synonymous.

[76] See *infra* § 11.

[77] A discussion of transactions of this nature is in Hopkins, *The Law of Intermediate Sanctions: A Guide for Nonprofits* (John Wiley & Sons, Inc., 2003) § 4.8.

[78] See *infra* § 10.

of property, lending of money, use of facilities or other assets, and involvement in partnerships or other joint ventures.

Although the concepts of private inurement and self-dealing in the private foundation setting are by no means precisely the same, the following summary of self-dealing transactions offers a useful sketch of the scope of transactions that can, in appropriate circumstances, amount to instances of private inurement:[79] (1) sale or exchange, or leasing, of property between a tax-exempt organization and an insider; (2) lending of money or other extension of credit between an exempt organization and an insider; (3) furnishing of goods, services, or facilities, between an exempt organization and an insider; (4) payment of compensation (or payment or reimbursement of expenses) by an exempt organization to an insider; and (5) transfer to, or use by or for the benefit of, an insider of the income or assets of an exempt organization.[80]

A set of facts that illustrates some of the distinctions between private inurement and self-dealing was provided in a case involving a tax-exempt museum that, at the outset, was structured as a private foundation. The museum made a low-interest loan to an incoming director, who became a disqualified person with respect to the museum. The IRS determined that, for every year the loan principal remained outstanding, an act of self-dealing occurs, inasmuch as the extension of credit by a private foundation is, as noted, self-dealing. The museum thereafter, however, became qualified as a public charity, thus rendering the self-dealing rules inapplicable. The IRS valued the loan as part of the director's compensation package and found the arrangement reasonable, thereby averting application of the private inurement doctrine.[81]

(a) Compensation for Services

A tax-exempt organization, subject to the private inurement doctrine, can, of course, make ordinary and necessary expenditures in furtherance of its operations without forfeiting its exempt status.[82] This includes the payment of compensation for services rendered, whether to an employee in the form of a salary, wage, bonus, commission, pension or other benefits, and/or the like, or to a ven-

---

[79] The definition of self-dealing as applied in the private foundation setting, written in 1969, is, in essence, a codification of much of the case law concerning private inurement. Yet, over 25 years later, Congress believed its specificity to be too limiting and chose, when once again legislating on the subject, to use an overarching definition when creating the excess benefit transaction (see *infra* § 11(d)).

[80] IRC § 4941(d)(1)(A)–(E). The IRS applied the self-dealing rationale on one public occasion in an instance of a transaction involving a public charity and its directors (Rev. Rul. 76-441, 1976-2 C.B. 147) and a court essentially did the same (without expressly using the term) in a case concerning a church and its ministers (Church by Mail, Inc. v. Comm'r, 48 T.C.M. 471 (1984), *aff'd*, 765 F.2d 1387 (9th Cir. 1985)).

[81] Priv. Ltr. Rul. 9530032. Today, a transaction of this nature would likely be sheltered, as to the intermediate sanctions rules, by the initial contract exception (*infra* § 11(d), text accompanied by notes 384-386).

[82] E.g., Birmingham Business College, Inc. v. Comm'r, *supra* note 35; Mabee Petroleum Corp. v. United States, 203 F.2d 872 (5th Cir. 1953); Broadway Theatre League of Lynchburg, Virginia, Inc. v. United States, 293 F. Supp. 346 (W.D. Va. 1968); Enterprise Railway Equipment Co. v. United States, 161 F. Supp. 590 (Ct. Cl. 1958).

dor, consultant, or other independent contractor in the form of fees and reimbursement of expenses. As a court observed, the law "places no duty on individuals operating charitable organizations to donate their services; they are entitled to reasonable compensation for their efforts."[83] The legislative history of the intermediate sanctions rules stated that "an individual need not necessarily accept reduced compensation merely because he or she renders services to a tax-exempt, as opposed to a taxable, organization."[84]

The private inurement doctrine mandates, however, that the compensation amount be *reasonable*. In other words, the payment of *excessive* compensation can result in a finding of private inurement.[85] Whether an amount of compensation is reasonable is a question of *fact*, to be decided in the context of each case;[86] it is not an issue of law.

The process for determining the reasonableness of compensation is much like that of valuing an item of property. It entails an appraisal—an evaluation of factors that have a bearing on the value. It is an exercise of comparing a mix of variables pertaining to the compensation of others in similar circumstances. The basic standard has been in the federal tax law for years; it is cited in the business expense regulations[87] and the intermediate sanctions regulations[88] as follows: reasonable compensation is that amount as would ordinarily be paid for like services by like enterprises under like circumstances. This alchemy—what the intermediate sanctions rules refer to as an accumulation and assessment of data as to comparability[89]—is supposed to yield the conclusion as to whether a particular item of compensation or a compensation package is *reasonable* or is *excessive*.[90]

Traditionally, the case law has dictated the criteria to be used in ascertaining the reasonableness of compensation. This approach has come to be known as utilization of the *multi-factor test*. The elements—factors—to be utilized in a particular case can vary, depending on the court. (Even though the reasonableness of compensation is a matter of fact, the selection and application of the appropriate factors can be a matter of law.) Much of the law in this field is based on case law concerning payments by for-profit corporations. This is because a payment of compensation, to be deductible as a business expense,[91] must be an

---

[83] World Family Corp. v. Comm'r, 81 T.C. 958, 969 (1983).

[84] H. Rep. 104-506, 104th Cong., 2d Sess. 56, note 3 (1996).

[85] E.g., Harding Hospital, Inc. v. United States, *supra* note 39; Birmingham Business College, Inc. v. Comm'r, *supra* note 35; Mabee Petroleum Corp. v. United States, *supra* note 82; Texas Trade School v. Comm'r, *supra* note 45; Northern Illinois College of Optometry v. Comm'r, 2 T.C.M. 664 (1943).

[86] E.g., Jones Brothers Bakery, Inc. v. United States, 411 F.2d 1282 (Ct. Cl. 1969); Home Oil Mill v. Willingham, 68 F. Supp. 525 (N.D. Ala. 1945), *aff'd*, 181 F.2d 9 (5th Cir. 1950), *cert. den.*, 340 U.S. 852 (1950).

[87] Reg. § 1.162-7(b)(3).

[88] Reg. § 53.4958-4(b)(1)(ii)(A). See *infra* § 11(d), text accompanied by note 363.

[89] Reg. § 53.4958-6(c)(2). See *infra* § 11(e), text accompanied by note 393.

[90] The process of determining reasonable compensation may include obtaining a report from an independent consultant and a ruling from the IRS. An excellent illustration of this process appeared in Priv. Ltr. Rul. 200020060, concerning the valuation of a compensation package paid to the executive of a tax-exempt charitable organization.

[91] IRC § 162(a).

ordinary and necessary outlay; the concepts of *reasonableness* and ordinary and necessary are essentially identical.[92] Also, as will be discussed, the advent of the intermediate sanctions rules has greatly informed this aspect of the law of tax-exempt organizations.

The concept of *compensation* paid to an individual or other person by an exempt organization is not confined to items such as a salary or a wage. All forms of compensation are aggregated for this purpose: bonuses, commissions, royalties, fringe benefits, retirement and pension benefits, expense allowances, insurance coverages,[93] and the like are taken into account.[94]

The factors commonly applied in the private inurement (and intermediate sanctions) setting to ascertain the reasonableness of compensation are:

- The levels of compensation paid by similar organizations (tax-exempt and taxable) for functionally comparable positions, with emphasis on comparable entities in the same community or region;

- The need of the organization for the services of the individual whose compensation is being evaluated;

- The individual's background, education, training, experience, and responsibilities;

- Whether the compensation resulted from arm's-length bargaining, such as whether it was approved by an independent board of directors;

- The size and complexity of the organization, in terms of elements such as assets, income, and number of employees;

- The individual's prior compensation arrangement;

- The individual's performance;

- The relationship of the individual's compensation to that paid to other employees of the same organization; and

- The amount of time the individual devotes to the position.[95]

If the issue is litigated, the individual whose compensation is being challenged and the IRS are likely to have expert witnesses, who produce reports and testimony incorporating some or all of these factors. The judge in the case is called upon to determine whether there has been payment of excessive compensation. Most of these cases originate in the U.S. Tax Court. Recently, however, a federal court of appeals observed (articulating a fact that, until then, no

---

[92] If the IRS or a court finds that a portion of a payment by a for-profit corporation constitutes excessive compensation, that amount is treated as a dividend and thus is not deductible by the payor corporation (e.g., Rapco, Inc. v. Comm'r, 85 F.3d 950 (2d Cir. 1996); Leonard Pipeline Contractors, Ltd. v. Comm'r, 72 T.C.M. 83 (1996), *rev'd and rem'd*, 142 F.3d 1133 (9th Cir. 1998)).

[93] E.g., Priv. Ltr. Rul. 9539016 (split-dollar life insurance plan).

[94] See *infra* § 11(d), text accompanied by notes 365–366.

[95] *Id.*, text accompanied by note 363.

court had ventured to mention) that the "judges of the Tax Court are not equipped by training or experience to determine the salaries of corporate officers; no judges are."[96]

This appellate court attacked the multi-factor test, perceiving it to be "redundant, incomplete, and unclear."[97] It was found to "not provide adequate guidance to a rational decision."[98] Rather, wrote the court, the test to be applied when determining the reasonableness of an individual's compensation package paid by a for-profit business is the *independent investor test*.[99] This test is based on the return on investment expected by the company's investors (actual or hypothetical)—a percentage determined by an expert witness. When these investors are obtaining a "far higher return than they had any reason to expect," the executive's salary is "presumptively reasonable," even if the compensation may otherwise be considered "exorbitant."[100] Under this approach, the presumption can be rebutted if the government shows that, although the executive's salary was reasonable, the company "did not in fact intend to pay him [or her] that amount as salary, that his [or her] salary really did include a concealed dividend though it need not have."[101] Also, according to this court, if the executive's salary is approved by the other owners of the corporation, who are independent of the executive—that is, who lacked an incentive to disguise a dividend as a salary—that approval "goes far" to rebut any evidence of "bad faith."[102]

It initially appeared that a court would use either the multi-factor test or the independent investor test in determining the reasonableness of executive compensation. Yet, however, another federal court of appeals, in one of these cases, applied a multi-factor test, then used the independent investor test to interpret one of the factors.[103]

Whatever the substance and progress of the independent investor test in the context of closely held for-profit corporations may turn out to be, it would seem that this test has little, if anything, to do with tax-exempt organizations, which, of course, do not have investors (in the usual sense of that term). Thus, the law in this regard as established by the courts may be evolving to the point where the tests for determining the reasonableness of compensation are different for tax-exempt organizations and for-profit organizations. If this is the outcome, it appears that the former will use a multi-factor test and the latter the independent investor test.[104]

---

[96] Exacto Spring Corp. v. Comm'r, 196 F.3d 833, 835 (7th Cir. 1999).
[97] *Id.*
[98] *Id.*
[99] This approach was first advanced in Dexsil Corp. v. Comm'r, 147 F.3d 96 (2d Cir. 1998).
[100] Exacto Spring Corp. v. Comm'r, *supra* note 96, at 835, 838.
[101] *Id.* at 839. See *supra* note 92.
[102] *Id.* at 839.
[103] Label/Graphics, Inc. v. Comm'r, 2000-2 U.S.T.C. ¶ 50,648 (9th Cir. 2000).
[104] Inexplicably, in an intermediate sanctions case, the IRS, in stating the factors it relied on in concluding that an individual's compensation, paid by a public charity, was excessive, invoked the independent investor test (writing, in the notice of deficiency, that "[i]t is not probable an outside investor would approve of such a compensation plan as reasonable") (Peters v. Comm'r, No. 8446-00 (U.S. Tax Court), docketed on August 3, 2000, and settled). In general, Note, "Determining the Deductibility of Executive Compensation: *Exacto Spring Corp. v. Commissioner*," 53 *Tax Law.* (No. 4) 919 (2000).

A large salary can be considered private inurement, particularly where the employee is concurrently receiving other forms of compensation from the organization (for example, fees, commissions, and/or royalties) and more than one member of the same family are compensated by the same organization.[105] Thus, where the control of an organization was in two ministers, whose contributions were its total receipts, all of which were paid to them as housing allowances, the tax exemption of the organization was revoked; the court said that the compensation was not "reasonable although it may not be "excessive."[106] Yet large salaries and noncash benefits received by an organization's employees can be reasonable, considering the nature of their services and skills, such as payments to physicians by a nonprofit entity that was an incorporated department of anesthesiology of a hospital.[107]

Another basis for finding private inurement is where the compensation paid annually is reasonable but the year-to-year increases of it are not justifiable. In one case, salary increases were found to be "abrupt," resulting in a "substantial" amount of compensation, leading the court to the conclusion that the salaries were "at least suggestive of a commercial rather than nonprofit operation."[108] Yet, it is also possible to cast salary increases, abrupt or otherwise, as payments for prior's years' compensation.[109]

Other forms of compensation are subject to the private inurement doctrine. For example, although a court held that an excessive parsonage allowance may constitute private inurement,[110] the same court subsequently ruled that another parsonage allowance was "not excessive as a matter of law."[111] The IRS revoked the tax-exempt status of a health care institution on the ground of several instances of private inurement, including various forms of compensation.[112]

Some compensation arrangements are not based on a salary, wage, or bonus but, in whole or in part, on a percentage of the tax-exempt organization's revenue. (In the intermediate sanctions setting, these forms of compensation are of-

[105] E.g., Founding Church of Scientology v. United States, *supra* note 51; Bubbling Well Church of Universal Love, Inc. v. Comm'r, 74 T.C. 531 (1980), *aff'd*, 670 F.2d 104 (9th Cir. 1981); Unitary Mission Church of Long Island v. Comm'r, 74 T.C. 507 (1980), *aff'd*, 647 F. 2d 163 (2d Cir. 1981).

[106] Church of the Transfiguring Spirit, Inc. v. Comm'r, 76 T.C. 1, 6 (1981). Cf. Universal Church of Scientific Truth, Inc. v. United States, 74-1 U.S.T.C. ¶ 9360 (N.D. Ala. 1973) (where the organization retained its tax exemption in part because its revenue was derived from fees for publications and its expenses included items other than the compensation of its ministers).

[107] B.H.W. Anesthesia Foundation, Inc. v. Comm'r, 72 T.C. 681 (1979). Also University of Massachusetts Medical School Group Practice v. Comm'r, 74 T.C. 1299 (1980).

[108] The Incorporated Trustees of the Gospel Worker Soc'y v. United States, 510 F. Supp. 374, 379 (D.D.C. 1981), *aff'd*, 672 F.2d 894 (D.C. Cir. 1981), *cert. den.*, 456 U.S. 944 (1982).

[109] In some circumstances, in the intermediate sanctions context (see *infra* § 11), a determination of the reasonableness of compensation for a year may take into account services performed by a disqualified person in prior years (Reg. § 53.4958-4(a)(1)).

[110] Hall v. Comm'r, *supra* note 40.

[111] Carter v. United States, *supra* note 40, at 1487.

[112] Tech. Adv. Mem. 9451001. Litigation ensued (LAC Facilities, Inc. v. United States (No. 94-604T, U.S.Ct. Fed. Cl.)); the case was settled. In general, Griffith, "Compensation and Fraud Issues Trigger First Health Care Audit Revocation of the 1990s," 6 J. Tax. Exempt Orgs. (No. 6) 259 (May/June 1995).

ten revenue-sharing arrangements.[113]) The law on this point is unclear and inconsistent. In one case, a court held that a percentage compensation arrangement amounted to private inurement, because there was no upper limit as to total compensation.[114] This court subsequently restricted the import of this decision when it held that private inurement did not occur when a tax-exempt organization paid its president a commission determined by a percentage of the contributions obtained by him. The court in the second of these cases held that the standard is whether the compensation is reasonable, rather than the manner in which it is ascertained. Fundraising commissions, that are "directly contingent on success in procuring funds," were held to be an "incentive well suited to the budget of a fledgling [charitable] organization."[115] In reaching this conclusion—and saying nothing about caps on compensation levels—the court reviewed states' charitable solicitation acts governing payments to professional solicitors, which the court characterized as "[s]anctioning such commissions and in many cases endors[ing] percentage commissions higher than" the percentage commission paid by the organization involved in the case.[116]

Another court subsequently introduced more confusion in this area when it ruled that "there is nothing insidious or evil about a commission-based compensation system" and thus that an arrangement, by which those who successfully secured contributions for a charitable organization were paid a percentage of the gift amounts, is "reasonable," despite the absence of any limit as to an absolute amount of compensation (and despite the fact that the law requires compensation to be reasonable, not the percentage by which it is determined).[117]

The IRS will likely closely scrutinize compensation programs of tax-exempt organizations that are predicated on an incentive feature by which compensation is a function of revenue received by the organization, is guaranteed, or is otherwise outside the boundaries of conventional compensation arrangements. These programs—sometimes termed *gainsharing arrangements*—have developed largely in the health care context. For example, the IRS concluded that the establishment of incentive compensation plans for the employees of a hospital, with payments determined as a percentage of the excess of revenue over a budgeted level, will not constitute private inurement, where the plans are not devices to distribute profits to principals and are the result of arm's-length bargaining, and do not result in unreasonable compensation.[118] Employing similar reasoning, the agency approved guaranteed minimum annual salary contracts pursuant to which physicians' compensation was subsidized so as to induce

---

[113] See *infra* § 11(d), text accompanied by notes 378–381.
[114] People of God Community v. Comm'r, *supra* note 40.
[115] World Family Corp. v. Comm'r, *supra* note 83, at 970.
[116] *Id.* at 969. In general, see Hopkins, *The Law of Fundraising, Third Edition* (John Wiley & Sons, Inc., 2002), § 5.13.
[117] National Foundation, Inc. v. United States, 87-2 U.S.T.C. ¶ 9602 (Ct. Cl. 1987).
[118] Gen. Couns. Mem. 39674. Also Lorain Avenue Clinic v. Comm'r, 31 T.C. 141 (1958); INFO 2002-0021.

them to commence employment at a hospital.[119] The IRS promulgated guidance concerning the tax consequences of physician recruitment incentives.[120]

The agency has explored other forms of productivity incentive programs[121] and contingent compensation plans.[122] Outside the health care field, the IRS concluded that a package of compensation arrangements for the benefit of sports coaches for schools, colleges, and universities, including deferred compensation plans, payment of life insurance premiums, bonuses, and moving expense reimbursements, did not constitute private inurement.[123] In one instance, the IRS approved of a "sharable income policy" by which a tax-exempt scientific research organization provided one-third of the revenue derived from patents, copyrights, processes, or formulae to the inventors and 15 percent of the revenue received from the licensing or other transfer of the organization's technology to valuable employees.[124]

Hospital audit guidelines issued by the IRS contain a substantive review of the law concerning unreasonable compensation.[125] Although these guidelines address private inurement transactions between hospitals and their physicians and senior executives, they apply to any category of tax-exempt organization where the private inurement rules are applicable. These guidelines reflect the fact that contemporary concerns at the IRS in this regard embrace incentive compensation plans, recruitment and retention incentives, purchases of physicians' practices, open-ended employment contracts, and compensation based on a percentage of the institutions' net revenue. IRS examiners were urged to review compensation contracts to determine whether they were negotiated at arm's length; where that is not the case (such as where a physician is also a member of the hospital's board of trustees or is a department head), the contracts were said to warrant "closer scrutiny."[126]

In some instances, an individual will receive compensation (including fringe benefits) and/or other payments from more than one organization, whether or not tax-exempt. A determination as to the reasonableness of this compensation or other payments must be made in the aggregate. Thus, for example, in the college and university examination guidelines developed by the IRS, examining agents were advised that "[i]f an employee is compensated by several entities, even if the entities have independent boards or representatives, examine the total compensation paid to such person by all entities over which

---

[119] Gen. Couns. Mem. 39498.

[120] Rev. Rul. 97-21, 1997-1 C.B. 121. In general, see Hyatt & Hopkins, *The Law of Tax-Exempt Healthcare Organizations, Second Edition* (John Wiley & Sons, Inc., 2001), Chapter 25.

[121] E.g., Gen. Couns. Mem. 36918.

[122] E.g., Gen. Couns. Mem. 32453.

[123] Gen. Couns. Mem. 39670. Cf. Copperweld Steel Co.'s Warren Employees' Trust v. Comm'r, 61 T.C.M. 1642 (1991) (where an organization was denied tax-exempt status on the basis of IRC § 501(c)(3) because its primary purpose was the provision of compensatory fringe benefits).

[124] Priv. Ltr. Rul. 9316052.

[125] IRS Audit Guidelines for Hospitals, Manual Transmittal 7(10)69-38 for Exempt Organizations Examinations Guidelines Handbook (March 27, 1992) ("Hospital Audit Guidelines") §§ 333.2, 333.3.

[126] *Id.* § 333.2(2).

the institution has significant control or influence."[127] The annual information return filed by most tax-exempt organizations[128] requires reporting of arrangements where a trustee, director, officer, or key employee of an organization received aggregate compensation of more than $100,000 from the organization and all related organizations, of which more than $10,000 was provided by the related organization.[129]

Aside from the reasonableness of compensation, it is axiomatic that a tax-exempt organization subject to the private inurement doctrine may not, without transgressing the doctrine, pay compensation where services are not actually rendered. For example, an organization was denied exempt status because it advance funds to telephone solicitors, to be offset against earned commissions, where some of the solicitors resigned, and kept the funds, before earning commissions equal to or exceeding their advances.[130]

(b) Rental Arrangements

A tax-exempt organization subject to the doctrine of private inurement generally may lease property and make rental payments for the use of property, in a transaction involving an insider.[131] The rent payments, and other terms and conditions of the arrangement, however, must be reasonable, and it should be beneficial for the exempt organization. That is, an inflated rent amount favoring the insider would be private inurement.[132]

The hospital audit guidelines pointed out that one form of private inurement is "payment of excessive rent" and stated that "[a]reas of concern" include "below market leases."[133] The guidelines observed that examining agents should be alert to the existence of "rent subsidies," noting that "[o]ffice space in the [tax-exempt] hospital/medical office building for use in the physician's private practice generally must be provided at a reasonable rental rate gauged by market data and by actual rental charges to other tenants in the same facility."[134] These guidelines stated that it is permissible for a physician to use an exempt organization's facility for both hospital duties and private practice, as long as the "time/use of [the] office [is] apportioned between hospital activities and

---

[127] Examination Guidelines for Colleges and Universities, Internal Revenue Manual, Exempt Organization Handbook 7(10)(69) § 342.

[128] See § 24.3.

[129] Form 990, Part V, line 75.

[130] Senior Citizens of Missouri, Inc. v. Comm'r, 56 T.C.M. 479 (1988). In general, Broeck, "Preventing Private Inurement by Measuring the Reasonableness of Compensation for Executives," 6 J. Tax Exempt Orgs. (No. 1) 21 (July/Aug. 1994); Steinberg, "Profits and Incentive Compensation in Nonprofit Firms," 1 Nonprofit Management & Leadership (No. 2) 137 (1990).

[131] A rental arrangement between a private foundation and a disqualified person with respect to it is likely, however, to constitute an act of self-dealing (IRC § 4941(d)(1)(A)).

[132] E.g., Founding Church of Scientology v. United States, supra note 51; Texas Trade School v. Comm'r, supra note 45.

[133] Hospital Audit Guidelines §§ 333.2(1), 333.3(1).

[134] Id. at § 333.3(7)(b).

private practice activities and a reasonable rent [is] charged for the private practice activities."[135]

The factors to be considered, in the rental arrangement context, in determining reasonableness, include the duration of the lease, and the amount and frequency of the rent payments, with all elements of the relationship evaluated in relation to comparable situations in the community.[136]

(c) Lending Arrangements

A loan involving the assets of a tax-exempt organization subject to the doctrine of private inurement, made to an insider, is likely to be closely scrutinized by the IRS.[137] As was noted, the "very existence of a private source of loan credit from an [exempt] organization's earnings may itself amount to inurement of benefit."[138]

Like rental arrangements, the terms of this type of loan should be reasonable, that is, financially advantageous to the exempt organization (or at least not be disadvantageous) and should be commensurate with the organization's purposes.[139] The factors to be considered when assessing reasonableness in this setting include the duration of the indebtedness, the rate of interest paid, the security underlying the loan, and the amount involved—all evaluated in relation to similar circumstances in the community.[140] If such a loan is not repaid on a timely basis, questions as to private inurement may well be raised.[141] Thus, for example, the tax exemption of a school was revoked, in part because two of its officers were provided by the school with interest-free, unsecured loans that subjected the school to uncompensated risks for no business purpose.[142]

A court found private inurement resulting from a loan where a nonprofit organization, formed to assume the operations of a school conducted up to that point by a for-profit corporation, required parents of its students to make interest-free loans to the corporation. Private inurement was detected in the fact that the property to be improved using the loan proceeds would revert to the for-profit corporation after a 15-year term; the interest-free feature of the loans was held to be an unwarranted benefit to individuals in their private capacity.[143]

This court earlier found private inurement in a case involving a tax-exempt hospital and its founder, who was a physician who operated a clinic lo-

---

[135] *Id.*

[136] See Hopkins, *supra* note 77, § 4.7(b).

[137] A loan by a private foundation to a disqualified person with respect to it is likely to constitute an act of self-dealing (IRC § 4941(d)(1)(B)).

[138] Founding Church of Scientology v. United States, *supra* note 51, 412 F.2d at 1202. Also Unitary Mission Church of Long Island v. Comm'r, *supra* note 105; Western Catholic Church v. Comm'r, *supra* note 57; Church in Boston v. Comm'r, 71 T.C. 102 (1978).

[139] Griswold v. Comm'r, 39 T.C. 620 (1962).

[140] See Hopkins, *supra* note 77, § 4.7(a).

[141] Best Lock Corp. v. Comm'r, *supra* note 46; Rev. Rul. 67-5, 1967-1 C.B. 123.

[142] John Marshall Law School v. United States, 81-2 U.S.T.C. ¶ 9514 (Ct. Cl. 1981).

[143] Hancock Academy of Savannah, Inc. v. Comm'r, 69 T.C. 488 (1977).

cated in the hospital building.[144] The hospital and the clinic shared supplies and services; most of the hospital's patients were also patients of the founding physician and his partner. The hospital made a substantial number of unsecured loans to a nursing home owned by the physician and a trust for his children at below-market interest rates. The court held that there was private benefit to the physician because this use of the hospital's funds reduced his personal financial risk in and lowered the interest costs for the nursing home. The court also found inurement in the fact that the hospital was the principal source of financing for the nursing home, since an equivalent risk incurred for a similar duration could be expected to produce higher earnings elsewhere. In general, the court observed, "[w]here a doctor or group of doctors dominate the affairs of a corporate hospital otherwise exempt from tax, the courts have closely scrutinized the underlying relationship to insure that the arrangements permit a conclusion that the corporate hospital is organized and operated *exclusively* for charitable purposes without any private inurement."[145]

The hospital audit guidelines state that a form of private inurement is "inadequately secured loans,"[146] and that a loan used as a recruiting subsidy is appropriate (assuming the requisite need for the physician in the first instance[147]) as long as the recruitment contract "require[s] full repayment (at prevailing interest rates)."[148] These guidelines provided the following factors, which the IRS considers in determining whether a loan made by a tax-exempt organization to an insider is reasonable: (1) generally, the loan agreement should specify a reasonable rate of interest (the prime rate plus 1 or 2 percent) and provide for adequate security, (2) the loan decision should be reviewed by the board of directors of the exempt organization and should include consideration of the history of payment of prior loans by the insider, and (3) even if determined reasonable, any variance in the terms of the loan from what the borrower could obtain from a typical lending institution must be treated, and appropriately reported, as compensation.[149]

(d) Sales of Assets

Another application of the private inurement doctrine involves the sale of assets of tax-exempt organizations to those who are insiders with respect to them. A charitable or other exempt organization may, for example, decide to sell assets relating to a program activity, because the organization no longer wishes to engage in that activity. Sometimes, for a variety of reasons, these assets are sold to one or more individuals who are insiders (usually directors or officers). As with other

---

[144] Lowry Hospital Ass'n v. Comm'r, 66 T.C. 850 (1976).
[145] *Id.* at 859 (emphasis in the original).
[146] Hospital Audit Guidelines § 333.2(1).
[147] See text accompanied by *supra* note 120.
[148] Hospital Audit Guidelines § 333.3(4).
[149] *Id.* § 333.3(10).

manifestations of these transactions, they are not prohibited; the requirement is that their terms and conditions be reasonable.

A case illustrates some of the difficulties and complexities that can arise in this context. The matter concerned the sale of the assets of an exempt hospital to an entity controlled by insiders with respect to the hospital. The court concluded that the transaction gave rise to private inurement because the sale was not at arm's length, which caused the assets to be sold for less than their fair market value.

An appraiser determined that the fair market value of the hospital in 1981 was between $3.5 and $4.3 million. The IRS issued a private letter ruling in 1982, holding that the sale would be on an arm's-length basis and would not jeopardize the organization's tax-exempt status.[150] The sale closed in 1983 with a purchase price (as ultimately determined by the court) of $6.6 million. The hospital expanded over the ensuing months and obtained a certificate of need for additional beds. The operating assets were sold in 1985 for $29.6 million, to a large health care provider. In 1990, the hospital was sold for $4.3 million.

The court found that the lawyers who negotiated the sale in 1983, "as far as the legal as distinguished from the financial aspects of the sale were concerned, acted independently and in good faith and sought to protect the interests" of their clients.[151] The court continued, however, to state that "there are serious questions as to the extent to which the negotiations adequately took into account certain financial aspects of the transaction which may cause the negotiations and the resulting sale price to be categorized as not being at arm's length and therefore giving rise to inurement."[152]

The court noted an array of elements that were either not taken into account or were inadequately taken into account in arriving at the price, including various changes in the value of assets between 1981 and 1983, valuations of adjacent properties that were transferred as part of the deal, the value of a certificate of need, the impact of changes in Medicare reimbursement policy, and the sales of the hospital in 1985 and 1990. Factoring in these elements, the court concluded that the fair market value of the assets transferred in 1983 was $7.8 million.

This court was not unmindful of the subsequent sales, particularly the one in 1985. It wrote that "evidence as to [a] latter category of events may be admitted because of its potential relevance even though it may ultimately be determined that such evidence does not have an impact on the determination of fair market value."[153] As to this case, the court cryptically wrote that "other evidence could provide a basis for concluding that the elements which impacted the 1985 sale may have been sufficiently known or anticipated at the time of the 1983 sale."[154]

---

[150] See Priv. Ltr. Rul. 8234084.
[151] Anclote Psychiatric Center, Inc. v. Comm'r, 76 T.C.M. 175, 182 (1998). Also Priv. Ltr. Rul. 9130002.
[152] Anclote Psychiatric Center, Inc. v. Comm'r, *supra* note 151, at 183.
[153] *Id.*
[154] *Id.*

The difference between $7.8 million and $6.6 million was found to be "substantial."[155] The value of $7.8 million was found to "fall outside the upper limit of any reasonable range of fair market values."[156] The negotiations between the lawyers were found to be "fatally flawed because of their apparent failure to take into account the obvious and substantial" increases in asset values over the period 1981-1983.[157] The court rejected reliance on the appraisal, in that, by the time of closing, it was more than 18 months old.

This opinion, being neither a model of clarity nor consistency,[158] nonetheless offers several lessons: (1) the fair market value of property sold by an exempt organization to one or more insiders should be established by an independent appraisal, which should not be stale, (2) an IRS favorable ruling is not necessarily protection in relation to subsequent turns of events, (3) lawyers or others negotiating this type of transaction may not blindly rely on an appraisal but must independently assure themselves that all relevant items are valued, and (4) the IRS and the courts are permitted to take into account, in assessing value, events and actions that occur *after* the sale. Apparently, it is not enough to value items that are *known* at the time; consideration must somehow be accorded those that may be *anticipated*.

This opinion is not, however, completely adverse to the interests of tax-exempt organizations. The court rejected the claim of the IRS that it is necessary to determine a "precise amount" representing the fair market value of property in a private inurement case.[159] All that is required is an amount that is "sufficiently close to the fair market value of the property at the time of the sale."[160] The court wrote that, when the amount is within a "reasonable range" of what could be considered fair market value, there cannot be private inurement.[161]

An open issue is whether, in assigning a value to an item of property for private inurement purposes, a single valuation will suffice.[162] Moreover, there is no mandated valuation method. The IRS wrote that "no single valuation method is necessarily the best indicator of value in a given case."[163] Yet, the agency has signaled its preference for various appraisal methodologies in valuing property, observing in one instance that "it would be logical to assume that an appraisal that has considered and applied a variety of approaches in reaching its 'bottom line' is

---

[155] *Id.* at 186.

[156] *Id.*

[157] *Id.* at 187.

[158] This opinion opened with the court stating that the issue of revocation "turns on the question [of] whether petitioner's sale of its hospital in May 1983 was for less than fair market value" (at 176). Yet, a few pages later, it was written that "fair market value plays an important role but is not determinative herein" (at 182).

[159] *Id.* at 182.

[160] *Id.*

[161] *Id.* A similar case unfolded in the intermediate sanctions setting (Caracci v. Comm'r, 118 T.C. 379 (2002)); see, e.g., *infra* § 11(d), text accompanied by note 374.

[162] In the charitable giving setting, where an appraisal of property is required, only a single appraisal is called for; see Hopkins, *The Tax Law of Charitable Giving, Second Edition* (John Wiley & Sons, Inc., 2000), § 22.2.

[163] Priv. Ltr. Rul. 9130002.

more likely to result in an accurate valuation than an appraisal that focused on a single valuation method."[164]

(e) Equity Distributions

With the emphasis of the federal tax law, in the private inurement area, on *net earnings* and the reference to *private shareholders*, the most literal and obvious form of private inurement is the parceling out of an exempt organization's net income to those akin to shareholders, such as members of its board of directors. It is rare, however, that private inurement is this blatant.

In one instance, nonetheless, this type of private inurement was identified. In this case, the assets of a tax-exempt hospital relating to a pharmacy were sold to an organization, which then sold pharmaceuticals to the hospital at higher prices. A court held that that practice amounted to the "siphoning off" of the hospital's income for the benefit of its stockholders.[165] Thereafter, apparently according to a preconceived plan, the corporation was dissolved and the sales proceeds distributed to its shareholders. While the court's reasoning is far from clear, it observed that "[i]t is doubtful, too, whether an organization's operation can be 'exclusively' for charitable purposes . . . when its income is being accumulated to increase directly the value of the interests of the stockholders which they expect, eventually, to receive beneficially."[166] This separation of the pharmacy from the hospital resulted in the retroactive revocation of the exempt status of the hospital.[167]

In nearly all of the states, nonprofit corporations may not be organized as entities with the ability to issue stock. Even in the few instances where tax-exempt organizations may have stockholders, the organizations may not pay dividends. In one instance, memberships in a tax-exempt hospital were found to not entitle the members to a beneficial interest in the capital or earnings of the hospital because the law of the state prohibited the corporation from paying any part of its income to members and required transfer of the assets upon dissolution for charitable purposes.[168]

(f) Assumptions of Liability

Generally, a tax-exempt organization can incur debt to purchase an asset at its fair market value, thereafter retire the debt with its receipts, and not thereby violate the private inurement proscription.[169] As is the case with the sale of an asset,

---

[164] *Id.*

[165] Maynard Hospital, Inc. v. Comm'r, 52 T.C. 1006, 1027, 1032 (1969).

[166] *Id.* at 1031.

[167] An organization once classified as a charitable one, had its tax exemption retroactively revoked because revenue was diverted to two of its officers for their personal use, including payments for school tuition, insurance, car repairs, and home landscaping (Tech. Adv. Mem. 9851001).

[168] Estate of Grace M. Scharf v. Comm'r, 316 F.2d 625 (7th Cir. 1963), *aff'g* 38 T.C. 15 (1962).

[169] E.g., Shiffman v. Comm'r, 32 T.C. 1073 (1959); Estate of Howes v. Comm'r, 30 T.C. 909 (1958), *aff'd sub nom.*, Comm'r v. Johnson, 267 F.2d 382 (1st Cir. 1959); Ohio Furnace Co., Inc. v. Comm'r, 25 T.C. 179 (1955), *app. dis.* (6th Cir. 1956). The acquisition of property by means of debt-financing may, however, generate unrelated business income (IRC § 514) (see §§ 29.1–29.4).

however, if the purchase price for an asset acquired from an insider is in excess of the property's fair market value (debt-financed or not), private inurement may result.[170]

In one instance, a nonprofit corporation was formed to take over the operation of a school conducted up to that time by a for-profit corporation. The organization assumed a liability for goodwill, which a court determined was an excessive amount. The court ruled that this assumption of liability was a violation of the prohibition on private inurement because it benefited the private interests of the owners of the for-profit corporation.[171] This court strongly suggested that any payment by a tax-exempt organization to an insider for goodwill constitutes private inurement, inasmuch as goodwill generally is a measure of the profit advantage in an established business and the profit motive is, by definition, not supposed to be a factor in the operation of an exempt organization.[172] This is a quaint and probably, in the modern era, inaccurate understanding of nonprofit organization law; no other court has expanded on the point.

(g) Employee Benefits

A tax-exempt organization can, as discussed, provide reasonable compensation, including standard benefits, to its employees. For example, a court found that payments for medical insurance is an "ordinary and necessary" expense of a tax-exempt employer.[173] An organization may not be able to qualify as an exempt charitable one, however, where the provision of employee benefits is its purpose. For example, a trust created by an employer to pay pensions to retired employees failed to qualify as a charitable entity.[174] This would be the result where the recipients are still employees providing services, in part because they do not constitute a charitable class.[175] Thus, a foundation lost its tax-exempt status because it devoted its funds to the payment of the expenses of young performers employed by the foundation's founder, who was in show business.[176] Organizations such as these may, however, qualify for tax exemption under other provisions of the federal tax law.[177]

A school's tax exemption was revoked because, for one or more of its officers, it provided interest-free, unsecured loans, paid for household items and furnishings used in their residences, made scholarship grants to their children, paid personal travel expenses, paid for their personal automobile expenses, paid the premiums on life and health insurance policies (where the premiums were not paid for other employees), and purchased season tickets for them to

---

[170] E.g., Kolkey v. Comm'r, 27 T.C. 37 (1956), aff'd, 254 F.2d 51 (7th Cir. 1958).
[171] Hancock Academy of Savannah, Inc. v. Comm'r, supra note 143.
[172] Id. at 494, note 6.
[173] Carter v. United States, supra note 40, at 1487.
[174] Rev. Rul. 56-138, 1956-1 C.B. 202.
[175] Rev. Rul. 68-422, 1968-2 C.B. 207. Also Watson v. United States, 355 F.2d 269 (3d Cir. 1965).
[176] Horace Heidt Foundation v. United States, supra note 49.
[177] E.g., IRC §§ 401, 501(c)(9), (c)(17).

sports events.[178] Yet, in another instance, a court concluded that the payment by a church of medical expenses for its minister and family did not constitute private inurement.[179]

The IRS has come around to the view that charitable and other tax-exempt organizations may establish profit-sharing and similar compensation plans without causing private inurement,[180] having earlier taken the position that the establishment of qualified profit-sharing plans resulted in *per se* private inurement.[181] This shift in position was based on the reasoning that the principles of qualification of pension and profit-sharing plans,[182] and the protections afforded by the Employee Retirement Income Security Act (enacted in 1974), are sufficient to ensure that operation of these plans would not jeopardize the tax-exempt status of the nonprofit organizations involved. Thereafter, legislation enacted in 1986 amended the employee plan rules to make it clear that tax-exempt organizations can, without jeopardy, maintain qualified profit-sharing plans[183] and extended deferred compensation rules[184] to make them applicable to tax-exempt organizations.

Tax-exempt organizations may maintain the qualified cash or deferral arrangements known as 401(k) plans.[185] A charitable organization may maintain a tax-sheltered annuity program for its employees.[186] In general, tax-exempt organizations may pay pensions, where the terms are reasonable, to their retired employees without adversely affecting their tax-exempt status.[187]

(h) Tax Avoidance Schemes

Tax-exempt organizations can be used impermissibly as vehicles to avoid income taxation. The circumstance troubling the IRS in this context is the transfer by an individual, in a business or profession, of his or her business assets to a controlled nonprofit entity solely for the purpose of avoiding taxes, who then continues to operate the business or profession as an employee of the transferee organization. Transactions of this nature are seen as lacking in substance, with the nonprofit entity manipulated for private gain.

In one instance, a physician transferred his medical practice and other assets to a controlled organization, which hired him to conduct "research," which amounted to the ongoing examination and treatment of patients; tax exemption

---

[178] John Marshall Law School v. United States, *supra* note 142. Also Chase v. Comm'r, 19 T.C.M. 234 (1960).
[179] Brian Ruud International v. United States, 733 F. Supp. 396 (D.D.C. 1989).
[180] Gen. Couns. Mem. 39674.
[181] E.g., Gen. Couns. Mem. 35869.
[182] IRC § 401.
[183] IRC § 401(a)(27).
[184] IRC § 457.
[185] IRC § 401(k)(4)(B)(i).
[186] IRC § 403(b).
[187] Rev. Rul. 73-126, 1973-1 C.B. 220. See Chapter 16.

for this organization was denied.[188] In another case, an organization, ostensibly a church, was formed by a professional nurse, who was the organization's minister, director, and principal officer. It held assets and liabilities formerly owned and assumed by the nurse, and provided the nurse with a living allowance and use of the assets, including a house and automobile. The organization was found by the IRS to not qualify as a tax-exempt organization because it "serves as a vehicle for handling the nurse's personal financial transactions."[189] In another instance, a court found that "tax avoidance" was a "substantial nonexempt purpose" of an organization, as evidenced by its promotional literature and seminars, and for that reason revoked the organization's tax-exempt status.[190]

Another court, unwilling to recognize an organization as a church because most of the organization's support was derived from, and the organization paid the living expenses of, the founder, wrote that private "inurement is strongly suggested where an individual or small group is the principal contributor to an organization and the principal recipient of the distributions of the organization, and that individual or small group has exclusive control over the management of the organization's funds."[191] Another "church" failed to gain exemption because of the transfer to it of funds used to furnish a sports car to its donor and pastor.[192]

(i) Services Rendered

An organization, the primary purpose of which is to render services to individuals in their private capacity, generally cannot qualify as a tax-exempt, charitable entity. There are exceptions to this general rule, of course, such as where the individuals benefited constitute members of a charitable class, the individual beneficiaries are considered merely instruments or means for advancement of a charitable objective, or the private benefit involved is incidental and/or unavoidable.

This type of private inurement takes many forms and involves judgments in specific cases that are difficult to quantify or generalize. For example, even though furtherance of the arts can be a charitable activity, a cooperative art gallery that exhibited and sold only its members' works was ruled to be serving their private ends—a "vehicle for advancing their careers and promoting the sale of their work"—and hence not tax-exempt, notwithstanding the fact that the exhibition and sale of works of art may sometimes be an exempt purpose.[193]

---

[188] Rev. Rul. 69-66, 1969-1 C.B. 151. Also Nittler v. Comm'r, 39 T.C.M. 422 (1979); Walker v. Comm'r, 37 T.C.M. 1851 (1978); Boyer v. Comm'r, 69 T.C. 521 (1977).

[189] Rev. Rul. 81-94, 1981-1 C.B. 330. Also Rev. Rul. 78-232, 1978-1 C.B. 69. These two rulings pertain to the *personal church* (see § 8.2(c)).

[190] Freedom Church of Revelation v. United States, 588 F. Supp. 693 (D.D.C. 1984).

[191] The Church of Eternal Life and Liberty, Inc. v. Comm'r, 86 T.C. 916 (1986).

[192] McFall v. Comm'r, 58 T.C.M. 175 (1989). Also Good Friendship Temple v. Comm'r, 55 T.C.M. 1310 (1988); Church of Modern Enlightenment v. Comm'r, 55 T.C.M. 1304 (1988); Petersen v. Comm'r, 53 T.C.M. 235 (1987).

[193] Rev. Rul. 71-395, 1971-2 C.B. 228.

Similarly, although the provision of housing assistance for low-income families may qualify as an exempt purpose, an organization that provided this form of assistance but gave preference for housing to employees of a farm proprietorship operated by the individual who controlled the organization was ruled to not qualify as a charitable organization.[194] Also, a school's tax exemption was revoked, in part because it awarded scholarships to the children of two of its officers yet did not make scholarship grants to anyone else.[195]

The provision of services to individuals, as precluded by the private inurement proscription, takes several forms. For example, an organization created to provide bus transportation for school children to a tax-exempt private school was ruled to not be eligible for exemption.[196] The IRS said that the organization served a private rather than a public interest, in that it enabled the participating parents to fulfill their individual responsibility of transporting children to school. The agency concluded: "When a group of individuals associate to provide a cooperative service for themselves, they are serving a private interest."[197] A testamentary trust established to make payments to charitable organizations and to use a fixed sum from its annual income for the perpetual care of the testator's burial lot was ruled to be serving a private interest and thus not qualify for tax exemption.[198] Further, an organization that operated a subscription "scholarship" plan, by which "scholarships" were paid to preselected, specifically named individuals designated by subscribers, was ruled to not be tax-exempt, since it was operated for the benefit of designated individuals.[199] Likewise, the furnishing of farm laborers for individual farmers, as part of the operation of a labor camp to house transient workers, was held to not be an agricultural purpose under the federal tax law but rather the provision of services to individual farmers that they would otherwise have to provide for themselves.[200] Also, a nonprofit corporation was deemed to be serving private purposes where it was formed to dredge a navigable waterway, little used by the general public, fronting the properties of its members.[201] Further, an organization that provided travel services, legal services, an insurance plan, an antitheft registration program, and discount programs to its members was held to be serving the interests of the members, thereby precluding the organization from qualifying as a tax-exempt educational organization.[202] Moreover, an organization was denied exempt status because a substantial portion of its funds was to be used to pay for the medical and rehabilitative care of an individual who was related to each of the trustees of the organization.[203]

---

[194] Rev. Rul. 72-147, 1972-1 C.B. 147.
[195] John Marshall Law School v. United States, *supra* note 142.
[196] Rev. Rul. 69-175, 1969-1 C.B. 149. Also Chattanooga Automobile Club v. Comm'r, 182 F.2d 551 (6th Cir. 1950).
[197] Rev. Rul. 69-175, *supra* note 196, at 149.
[198] Rev. Rul. 69-256, 1969-1 C.B. 150.
[199] Rev. Rul. 67-367, 1967-2 C.B. 188.
[200] Rev. Rul. 72-391, 1972-2 C.B. 249.
[201] Ginsburg v. Comm'r, *supra* note 22. Cf. Rev. Rul. 70-186, 1970-1 C.B. 128.
[202] U.S. CB Radio Association, No. 1, Inc. v. Comm'r, 42 T.C.M. 1441 (1981).
[203] Wendy L. Parker Rehabilitation Foundation, Inc. v. Comm'r, 52 T.C.M. 51 (1986). This type of organization is, in any event, precluded from tax-exempt status by reason of either IRC §§ 501(c)(3) or 501(c)(4) by reason of IRC § 501(m) (see § 22.1).

Charitable organizations frequently provide services to individuals in their private capacity when they dispense financial planning advice in the context of designing major gifts. This type of personal service made available by tax-exempt organizations has never been regarded as jeopardizing the organization's tax exemption, when undertaken by institutions such as churches, universities, colleges, and hospitals. The IRS, however, refused to accord tax exemption to an organization that engaged in financial counseling by providing tax planning services (including charitable giving considerations) to wealthy individuals referred to it by subscribing religious organizations. The court that subsequently heard the case upheld the agency's position, finding that tax planning is not an exempt activity (which, of course, it is not—outside of this context) and that the primary effect of the advice is to reduce individuals' liability for income taxes—a private benefit.[204] The court rejected the contention that the organization was merely doing what the subscribing members can do for themselves without endangering their tax exemption: fundraising.

The private inurement proscription may apply not only to individuals in their private capacity but also to corporations, industries, professions, and the like. Thus, an organization primarily engaged in the testing of drugs for commercial pharmaceutical companies was ruled to not be engaged in scientific research or testing for public safety but to be serving the private interests of the manufacturers.[205] Similarly, an organization composed of members of a particular industry to develop new and improved uses for existing products of the industry was ruled to be operating primarily to serve the private interests of its creators and thus not be tax-exempt.[206] Further, an association of professional nurses that operated a nurses' registry was held to be affording greater employment opportunities for its members and thus to be substantially operating for private ends.[207]

On occasion, application of the rule that unwarranted services to members can cause denial or loss of an organization's tax-exempt status leads to bizarre circumstances. This limitation is, from time to time, stretched—bringing about adverse tax consequences for the organization involved—far beyond what Congress surely intended in legislating the proscription on private inurement.

A classic illustration of this expansionist reading of the rule against private inurement is the holding by a court that a genealogical society, the membership of which was composed of those interested in the migrations of individuals with a common name to and within the United States, failed to qualify as a charitable organization on the ground that its genealogical activities served the private interests of its members.[208] The society's activities included research of the "family's"

[204] Christian Stewardship Assistance, Inc. v. Comm'r, 70 T.C. 1037 (1978).
[205] Rev. Rul. 68-373, 1968-2 C.B. 206. Also Rev. Rul. 65-1, 1965-1 C.B. 266.
[206] Rev. Rul. 69-632, 1969-2 C.B. 120.
[207] Rev. Rul. 61-170, 1961-2 C.B. 112.
[208] The Callaway Family Ass'n, Inc. v. Comm'r, 71 T.C. 340 (1978). This opinion presumably reinforces the IRS ruling that nonprofit genealogical societies in general qualify as tax-exempt social clubs (Rev. Rul. 67-8, 1967-1 C.B. 142) (see Chapter 14). In an opinion issued less than a month prior to the *Callaway Family Ass'n* case, the Tax Court recognized that a membership organization can qualify under IRC § 501(c)(3) where it provides information and services to both members and nonmembers (National Ass'n for the Legal Support of Alternative Schools v. Comm'r, 71 T.C. 118 (1978)).

development (primarily by collecting and abstracting historical data), preparation and dissemination of publications containing the research, promotion of scholarly writing, and instruction (by means of lectures and workshops) in the methodology of compiling and preserving historical, biographical, and genealogical research. The organization's underlying operational premise was that the growth and development of the continental United States can be understood by tracing the migratory patterns of a typical group of colonists and their descendants.

While the IRS and the court conceded that some of the society's activities were charitable and educational, they determined that the compilation and publication of the genealogical history of this "family" group was an activity that served the private interests of the organization's members. The court "note[d] specifically [the organization's] emphasis on compiling members' family lives and the [group's] family history" and held that any educational benefit "to the public created by [the organization's] activities is incidental to this private purpose."[209] This conclusion ignored the discipline known as "kinship studies," in which social history focuses extensively on families and family-related institutions, and strained to place a negative, private orientation on the term *family* when in fact the use of a family is merely a research technique by which the tracings of genealogy are undertaken pursuant to an objective standard.[210] This case presented a major threat to tax exemption for genealogical societies generally—but particularly *family associations*—because of the court's characterization of genealogical study as providing private inurement or other private benefit.[211]

Following this court's holding, the IRS acted to contain the reach of the decision. The agency ruled that a genealogical society may qualify as a tax-exempt educational organization by conducting lectures, sponsoring public displays and museum tours, providing written materials to instruct members of the general public on genealogical research, and compiling a geographical area's pioneer history.[212] This organization's membership, however, was open to all interested individuals in the area, rather than members of a "family," and the society did not conduct genealogical research for its members, although its members researched genealogies independently using the society's research materials. By contrast, the IRS also ruled that an organization cannot qualify as

---

[209] *Id.* at 344.

[210] The Tax Court distinguished the general family association from the type of family association that engages in genealogical activities for religious purposes, usually one that is operated to collect and furnish information needed by the Mormon Church to advance its religious precepts (*id.* at 345). The IRS earlier ruled that these family associations are charitable entities because they advance religion (Rev. Rul. 71-580, 1971-2 C.B. 235). Yet the definition of the term *charitable* also includes the advancement of education. The private inurement restriction applies equally to all categories of charitable organizations.

[211] Also Manning Ass'n v. Comm'r, 93 T.C. 596 (1989); Benjamin Price Genealogical Ass'n v. Internal Revenue Service, 79-1 U.S.T.C. ¶ 9361 (D.D.C. 1979). In general, Johnstone, "Section 501(c)(3) Status for Nonreligious Family Associations Barred by Recent Cases," 53 *J. Tax.* 168 (1980).

[212] Rev. Rul. 80-301, 1980-2 C.B. 180.

a charitable or educational entity where its membership is limited to descendants of a particular family, it compiled family genealogical research data for use by its members for reasons other than to conform to the religious precepts of the family's denomination, it presented the data to designated libraries, it published volumes of family history, and it promoted occasional social activities among family members.[213]

(j) Provision of Goods or Refreshments

A tax-exempt organization subject to the private inurement doctrine cannot have as its primary purpose the provision of goods or refreshments (in the nature of social or recreational activities) to individuals in their private capacity. Of course, an organization of this nature may incidentally bear the expense of meals, refreshments, and the like (such as working luncheons and annual banquets) but, in general, "[r]efreshments, goods and services furnished to the members of an exempt corporation from the net profits of the business enterprise are benefits inuring to the individual members."[214] Thus, a discussion group that held closed meetings at which personally oriented speeches were given, followed by the serving of food and other refreshments, was ruled to not be tax-exempt, inasmuch as the public benefits were remote at best and the "functions of the organization are to a significant extent fraternal and designed to stimulate fellowship among the membership."[215]

(k) Retained Interests

A charitable organization may not be organized so that one or more individuals retains a reversionary interest, by which the principal would flow to an individual upon the entity's dissolution or liquidation; instead, in this event, net assets and income must be transferred to one or more other charitable or governmental entities.[216]

By contrast, a charitable organization may, in appropriate circumstances, accept an asset subject to a life estate or other income interest for one or more individuals; the fact that only a charitable remainder interest is acquired is not private inurement. Thus, there are bodies of law concerning permissible partial interest gifts to charitable organizations, of income and remainder interests.[217] Likewise, annuity payments made in exchange for a gift of property are not a form of private inurement to the annuitants, inasmuch as the payment of the annuity merely constitutes satisfaction of the charge on the transferred asset.[218]

---

[213] Rev. Rul. 80-302, 1980-2 C.B. 182.

[214] Spokane Motorcycle Club v. United States, 222 F. Supp. 151, 153 (E.D. Wash. 1963).

[215] Rev. Rul. 73-439, 1973-2 C.B. 176.

[216] Reg. § 1.501(c)(3)-1(c)(2); Rev. Rul. 66-259, 1966-2 C.B. 214.

[217] See Hopkins, *The Tax Law of Charitable Giving, Second Edition* (John Wiley & Sons, Inc., 2000), Chapters 12 (charitable remainder trusts), 13 (pooled income funds), 15 (other gifts of remainder interests), and 16 (charitable lead trusts).

[218] Rev. Rul. 69-176, 1969-1 C.B. 150. See Hopkins, *supra* note 217, Chapter 14 (charitable gift annuities).

(l) Embezzlements

Private inurement does not occur when an insider steals money from a charitable or other tax-exempt organization. In a case where insiders stole proceeds from a charity's bingo games, private inurement was not found. The court wrote: "[W]e do not believe that the Congress intended that a charity must lose its exempt status merely because a president or a treasurer or an executive director of a charity has skimmed or embezzled or otherwise stolen from the charity, at least where the charity has a real-world existence apart from the thieving official."[219] It would be anomalous, indeed, for an exempt organization to suffer the loss and indignity of an embezzlement, only to then be required to forfeit its tax-exempt status because it was the victim of the crime.[220]

§ 19.5 PRIVATE INUREMENT AND SOCIAL WELFARE ORGANIZATIONS

The private inurement doctrine is among the statutory criteria for tax-exempt status for social welfare organizations.[221] Even before this addition to the statute (in 1996), however, the IRS and the courts were utilizing a generic version of the doctrine in connection with these organizations. For example, a social welfare organization was found to have not engaged in private benefit practices when it conferred most of its benefits on the employees of a corporation, with which the organization's founder had been affiliated, and the board of directors of which was composed solely of employees of the same corporation.[222]

A related body of law requires that a tax-exempt social welfare organization not be operated primarily for the economic benefit or convenience of its members.[223] Otherwise, social welfare organizations, to discern how the law of private inurement applies to them, must look to the law as to inurement, as it is developing with respect to charitable organizations.

§ 19.6 PRIVATE INUREMENT AND BUSINESS LEAGUES

The private inurement doctrine is applicable with respect to business leagues.[224] It is related to the proscription on unwarranted services to associations' members.[225] Thus, private inurement was deemed present with respect to an organi-

---

[219] Variety Club Tent No. 6 Charities, Inc. v. Comm'r, *supra note* 16, at 1494.

[220] In the intermediate sanctions setting, an economic benefit that a disqualified person obtains by theft or fraud cannot be treated as consideration for the performance of services (see *infra* § 11(d), text accompanied by note 371).

[221] These organizations are the subject of Chapter 12.

[222] Eden Hall Farm v. United States, 389 F. Supp. 858 (W.D. Pa. 1975).

[223] See § 12.1(b).

[224] These organizations are the subject of Chapter 13.

[225] Reg. § 1.501(c)(b)-1.

zation that used its funds to provide financial assistance and welfare benefits to its members,[226] that paid its members for expenses incurred in malpractice litigation,[227] and that distributed royalties to its members.[228]

The doctrine can apply in the context of the level of members' dues in relation to an organization's receipt of nonmember income. Today, this is an unrelated business issue,[229] although prior to the advent of those rules (in 1950) it had been held that a dues reduction subsidized by the earnings of a business constituted private inurement.[230] The IRS considered taking the position that a tiered dues structure of a tax-exempt association, with some members paying certain amounts and other members that were making payments to a related business league paying less dues, amounted to undue private benefit but elected to not get into that policy thicket.[231] Likewise, the IRS explored the matter of whether association members are being inappropriately subsidized when they pay less for publications, seminars, and the like than do nonmembers but chose to not pursue it.

A business league may receive income from nonmember sources without endangering its tax exemption where the income-producing activity is related to the exempt purposes of the association, such as a sports organization operating public championship tournaments,[232] a veterinarians' association operating a public rabies clinic,[233] an insurance agents association receiving commissions from handling insurance programs,[234] and a professional association conducting a training program for nonmembers.[235] Thus, an otherwise qualified tax-exempt business league was able to derive its support primarily from the sale of television broadcasting rights to the tournaments it sponsored, without imperiling its exemption, because this sponsorship and sale of broadcasting rights by the organization "directly promotes the interests of those engaged in the sport and by enhancing awareness of the general public of the sport as a profession."[236]

Another private inurement issue of pertinence to tax-exempt associations concerns the tax consequences of cash rebates to exhibitors who participate in their trade shows. As a general principle, a qualified business league may make cash distributions to its members without loss of tax exemption where the distributions represent no more than a reduction in dues or contributions previously paid to the organization in support of its activities.[237] The IRS extrapolated from this principle in ruling that an association may, without ad-

---

[226] Rev. Rul. 67-251, 1967-2 C.B. 196.

[227] National Chiropractor Ass'n v. Birmingham, 96 F. Supp. 874 (N.D. Iowa 1951).

[228] Wholesale Grocers Exchange v. Comm'r, 3 T.C.M. 699 (1944).

[229] See Part Five.

[230] National Automobile Dealers Ass'n v. Comm'r, 2 T.C.M. 291 (1943).

[231] Priv. Ltr. Rul. 9448036.

[232] Rev. Rul. 58-502, 1958-2 C.B. 271.

[233] Rev. Rul. 66-222, 1966-2 C.B. 223.

[234] Rev. Rul. 56-152, 1956-1 C.B. 56.

[235] Rev. Rul. 67-296, 1967-2 C.B. 22.

[236] Rev. Rul. 80-294, 1980-2 C.B. 187, 188.

[237] E.g., King County Insurance Ass'n v. Comm'r, 37 B.T.A. 288 (1938).

versely affecting its tax-exempt status, make cash rebates to member and non-member exhibitors who participate in the association's annual trade show, where the rebates represent a portion of an advance floor deposit paid by each exhibitor to insure the show against financial loss, are made to all exhibitors on the same basis, and may not exceed the amount of the deposit.[238] Because the "effect of refunding a portion of the floor deposits is to reduce the exhibitors' cost of participating in the trade show," the IRS concluded that the return of funds would not constitute private inurement.[239] If, however, a tax-exempt business league sponsoring an industry trade show, involving both member and nonmember exhibitors who are charged identical rates, makes space rental rebates only to its member-exhibitors, the rebates are considered proscribed inurement of income.[240]

§ 19.7 PRIVATE INUREMENT AND SOCIAL CLUBS

The private inurement doctrine is applicable with respect to tax-exempt social clubs.[241] For the most part, the application of the doctrine to exempt clubs focuses on the question as to whether nonmember use is generating revenue, the use of which (such as for maintenance and improvement of club facilities) redounds inappropriately to the personal advantage of the members (as reflected in reduced or not-increased dues, improved facilities, and the like).[242] Even in this context, however, use of club facilities by the general public may not constitute proscribed inurement where the club contributes net profits from a function (for example, a steeplechase[243]) to charity.[244] Infrequent public use is permissible as long as it is incidental and basically in furtherance of the club's purposes.[245] Much of this law as to private inurement has been eclipsed by guidelines as to permissible nonmember income social clubs can receive that were subsequently developed by Congress (in 1976).[246]

These clubs must be organized and operated for pleasure, recreation, and other nonprofit purposes. They must have an established membership of individuals, personal contacts and fellowship, and a commingling of members must play a material part in the life of the organization.[247] For example, this commingling requirement was satisfied in the case of a membership organiza-

---

[238] Rev. Rul. 77-206, 1977-1 C.B. 149. Also Rev. Rul. 81-60, 1981-1 C.B. 335.

[239] Rev. Rul. 77-206, *supra* note 238, at 149.

[240] Michigan Mobile Home & Recreational Vehicle Institute v. Comm'r, 66 T.C. 770 (1976).

[241] These organizations are the subject of Chapter 14.

[242] E.g., Knights of Columbus Council 3660 v. United States, 83-2 U.S.T.C. ¶ 16,410 (S.D. Ind. 1983), aff'd, 783 F.2d 69 (7th Cir. 1986); Aviation Club of Utah v. Comm'r, 162 F.2d 984 (10th Cir. 1947). See § 14.2.

[243] Rev. Rul. 68-119, 1968-1 C.B. 268.

[244] Rev. Rul. 69-636, 1969-2 C.B. 126.

[245] Rev. Rul. 60-323, 1960-2 C.B. 173.

[246] See § 14.2.

[247] Rev. Rul. 58-589, 1958-2 C.B. 266.

tion that provided bowling tournaments and recreational bowling competition for its members.[248] In this instance, the IRS ruled that the awarding of cash prizes paid from entry fees did not constitute inurement of the organization's net income because the payments were in furtherance of the members' pleasure and recreation.

The private inurement doctrine can also be applicable where an otherwise tax-exempt social club has more than one class of members. It is the position of the IRS that, where individuals are in membership classes in a club that enjoy the same rights and privileges in the club facilities but are treated differently as respects dues and initiation fees, there is private inurement because those who pay lower dues and fees are subsidized by the others.[249] Similarly, private inurement can arise where an exempt club increases the scope of its services without a corresponding increase in dues or other fees paid to the club.[250]

Another dimension to application of the private inurement doctrine in the tax-exempt social club setting involves undue dealings between a club and its members. For example, a social club was denied tax exemption because it regularly sold liquor to its members, for consumption off the club premises.[251] Likewise, a club that leased building lots to its members in addition to providing them recreation facilities was deemed not entitled to tax exemption.[252] In a somewhat comparable set of circumstances, the IRS ruled that a club, operating a cocktail lounge and café as an integral part of a motel and restaurant business, was not an exempt organization; about one-fourth of the club's "membership" consisted of individuals temporarily staying at the motel.[253] Private inurement was ruled to not be involved, however, where a tax-exempt social club paid a fixed fee to each member who brought a new member into the club, as long as the payments are "reasonable compensation for performance of a necessary administrative service."[254]

A tax-exempt social club may provide social and recreational facilities to its members who are limited to homeowners of a housing development and nonetheless qualify for tax exemption. This exemption will be precluded, however, where any of the following services are provided by the club: owning and maintaining residential streets; administering and enforcing covenants for the preservation of the architecture and appearance of the development; or providing police and fire protection, and a trash collection service to residential areas.[255]

---

[248] Rev. Rul. 74-148, 1974-1 C.B. 138.
[249] Rev. Rul. 70-48, 1970-1 C.B. 133.
[250] Rev. Rul. 58-589, *supra* note 247.
[251] Rev. Rul. 68-535, 1968-2 C.B. 219. Also Santa Barbara Club v. Comm'r, 68 T.C. 200 (1972).
[252] Rev. Rul. 68-168, 1968-1 C.B. 269. Also Lake Petersburg Ass'n v. Comm'r, 33 T.C.M. 259 (1974).
[253] Rev. Rul. 66-225, 1966-2 C.B. 227.
[254] Rev. Rul. 80-130, 1980-1 C.B. 117.
[255] Rev. Rul. 75-494, 1975-2 C.B. 214.

§ 19.8 *PER SE* PRIVATE INUREMENT

As discussed, most instances of private inurement arise in that a payment—such as compensation for services, rent, or interest—to one or more insiders is unreasonable or excessive. There are forms of private inurement, however, that have that designation because they constitute *per se private inurement*. This means that the structure of the transaction is inherently deficient; private inurement is embedded in the very nature of the transaction. It is thus irrelevant, in this context, that the economic benefit conferred on an insider in some way also furthers the organization's exempt purposes and/or that the amount paid is reasonable.

The doctrine of *per se* private inurement was most notably applied when the IRS articulated its view as to the impact on the tax-exempt status of a hospital involved in a joint venture with members of its medical staff, where the hospital sold to the venture the gross or net revenue stream derived from operation of a department of the hospital for a defined period.[256] The agency ruled that the hospital jeopardized its tax exemption, on the basis of private inurement, simply by entering into the venture.[257]

In arriving at this conclusion, the IRS revisited the position taken in three rulings issued in the 1980s. Essentially, the facts in these cases involved the purchase, by a partnership or other joint venture, of the revenue stream of a hospital program.

In the facts underlying one of these rulings, a limited partnership purchased the net revenue stream of a tax-exempt hospital's outpatient surgical program and gastroenterology laboratory.[258] The partnership consisted of a subsidiary of the hospital as the general partner; the limited partners were members of the hospital's medical staff. A limited partnership involving an exempt hospital and members of its medical staff, in the facts of another ruling, acquired the gross revenue stream derived from operation of the hospital's outpatient surgery facility.[259] This was done to provide an investment incentive to the physicians to use the hospitals' facilities. In one of these instances, a for-profit venture had established a competing ambulatory surgery center near the nonprofit hospital and was offering physicians on that hospital's staff ownership interests in the surgicenter, attempting to lure their practices.

In these situations, the hospitals continued to own and operate the facilities, and to establish the amounts charged patients for their use. At the time of the ruling request in the first of these cases, the surgical facility was utilized only 54 percent. The arrangement was undertaken to allow the hospital's medical staff physicians an opportunity to participate, on an investment basis, in the technical or facility charge component of the outpatient surgery program or gastroenterology laboratory. As part of the ruling request, the IRS was told that this

---

[256] Gen. Couns. Mem. 39862.
[257] E.g., Priv. Ltr. Ruls. 8942099 and 8820093.
[258] Priv. Ltr. Rul. 8820093 (subsequently withdrawn (Priv. Ltr. Rul. 9231047)).
[259] Priv. Ltr. Rul. 8942099 (subsequently withdrawn (Priv. Ltr. Rul. 9233037)).

arrangement would provide a financial incentive to the physicians to increase their use of the hospital's facilities, to the obvious advantage to the hospital. In these instances, the purchase price for the revenue stream was established at fair market value as the result of arm's-length negotiations, and was discounted to its present value.

The IRS recognized that "there often are multiple reasons why hospitals are willing to engage in joint ventures and other sophisticated financial arrangements with [their] physicans."[260] Two of these reasons are the "need to raise capital and to give physicians a stake in the success of a new enterprise or service." The hospital, in addition to the "hope for or expectation of additional admissions and referrals," may act "out of fear that a physician will send patients elsewhere or, worse, establish a new competing provider." The IRS nonetheless added: "Whenever a charitable organization engages in unusual financial transactions with private parties, the arrangements must be evaluated in light of applicable tax law and other legal standards."

Its analysis of these net revenue stream ventures led the IRS to conclude that there "appears to be little accomplished that directly furthers the hospitals' charitable purposes of promoting health." The reasons the hospitals entered into these arrangements were, as noted, to retain and reward the participating physicians. The IRS wrote, however, that "[g]iving (or selling) medical staff physicians a proprietary interest in the net profits of a hospital under these circumstances creates a result that is indistinguishable from paying dividends on stock."[261] Thus, the prohibition on private inurement was considered, by the agency, violated because "[p]rofit distributions are made to persons having a personal and private interest in the activities of the organization and are made out of the net earnings of the organization." The IRS added that, in these cases, the "hospital's profit interests in those [charitable] assets have been carved out largely for the benefit of the physician-investors." The IRS's lawyers opined that "[t]his is enough to constitute inurement and is per se inconsistent with exempt status."

Thus, this type of private inurement could not be successfully defended with the argument that the purchase price for the revenue streams was predicated on their fair market value and therefore was reasonable.[262] There have not been any subsequent developments in the realm of *per se* private inurement.

---

[260] Gen. Couns. Mem. 39862.

[261] See *supra*, text accompanied by note 12.

[262] In an unusual move, the IRS established a temporary amnesty program concerning these net-revenue-stream joint ventures, by which a tax-exempt hospital could rescind the arrangement and enter into a closing agreement with the IRS, preserving its exempt status (Ann. 92-70, 1992-19 I.R.B. 89).

§ 19.9   INCIDENTAL PRIVATE INUREMENT

It is the position of the IRS that there is no de minimis exception to the doctrine of private inurement.[263] That is, the agency will not accept a defense to an allegation of private inurement that it was merely *incidental*.[264]

Nonetheless, even though private inurement is present in a set of facts, a reasonable argument can be made that tax exemption should not be denied or revoked for that reason if the inurement was incidental or insignificant. As an illustration, the IRS, having reversed an initial decision, ruled that an organization of accredited educational institutions was exempt as a charitable entity because the development of standards for accreditation of colleges and universities constitutes the advancement of education.[265] The pertinence of this ruling is that, although "very few" schools that had been approved for membership in the organization were proprietary institutions, the IRS ruled that any benefit that may accrue to them because of accreditation was incidental to the purpose of improving the quality of education.

Similarly, where a business donated land and money to a charitable organization to establish a public park, its tax exemption was not jeopardized by reason of the fact that the donor retained the right to use a scenic view of the park as a brand symbol.[266] Also, in a situation involving a business that provided a substantial portion of the support of a charitable organization operating a replica of a nineteenth-century village, where the business benefited by having the village named after it, by having its name associated with the village in conjunction with its own advertising program, and by having its name mentioned in each publication of the organization, the IRS ruled that "such benefits are merely incidental to the benefits flowing to the general public."[267]

Likewise, the IRS determined that a children's day care center, operated in conjunction with an industrial company that enrolled children on the basis of financial need and the children's needs for the care and development program of the center, was tax-exempt because any benefit derived by the company or the parents of enrolled children was incidental to the public benefit resulting from operation of the center.[268] In another example, the agency concluded that an otherwise exempt educational organization may produce public interest programs for viewing via public educational channels of commercial cable television companies because any benefit to the companies was "merely

---

[263] E.g., Gen. Couns. Mem. 39862.
[264] E.g., Gen. Couns. Mem. 35855. There is no formal standard as to an incidental excess benefit transaction, either; by contrast, the law in the self-dealing context recognizes self-dealing that is "incidental and tenuous," as does the private benefit doctrine (see *infra* § 10, text accompanied by note 286).
[265] Rev. Rul. 74-146, 1974-1 C.B. 129. Also Rev. Rul. 74-575, 1974-2 C.B. 161. Cf. Rev. Rul. 81-29, 1981-1 C.B. 329.
[266] Rev. Rul. 66-358, 1966-2 C.B. 218.
[267] Rev. Rul. 77-367, 1977-2 C.B. 193.
[268] Rev. Rul. 70-533, 1970-2 C.B. 112.

incidental."[269] Further, the IRS concluded that the sale of items on consignment by a tax-exempt thrift shop did not result in loss of its exempt status, in that any benefit to the consignors was "clearly incidental" in relation to the organization's charitable purposes.[270] Also, a tax-exempt consortium of exempt universities and libraries was advised by the IRS that it may, without endangering its exemption, make its information dissemination services available to private businesses, since "[a]lthough there is some benefit to the private institutions, such benefit is incidental to this activity and, in fact, may be said to be a logical by-product of it."[271] In still another example, the IRS determined that the provision of tickets and/or admission passes to an exempt organization's shareholders,[272] to enable them to attend an agricultural fair conducted by the organization, did not rise to the level of private inurement, with the agency emphasizing the fact that only three percent of the free passes were given to shareholders.[273]

The U.S. Tax Court is in agreement with the IRS that any element of private inurement can cause an organization to lose or be deprived of tax exemption. For example, this court stated that "even if the benefit inuring to the members is small, it is still impermissible."[274] Likewise, a federal district court wrote that "any inurement, however small the benefit to the individual, is impermissible."[275]

The present state—or future—of the law on this point is probably reflected in the view of one federal court of appeals, which observed that "[w]e have grave doubts that the de minimis doctrine, which is so generally applicable, would not apply in this situation [that is, in the private inurement setting]."[276] This appellate court cited cases where a civil rights plaintiff was held to not be a prevailing party for purposes of an award of lawyers' fees where the success was considered technical or *de minimis*,[277] where it was held that only if a state's noncompliance with statutorily prescribed time periods for an administrative action was de minimis does a court have the discretion to not issue an injunction,[278] where a court concluded that if the role of illegally obtained leads in the discovery of evidence was *de minimis* the suppression of the evidence was inappropriate,[279] and where it was held that the *de minimis* rule applies in relation to the total sum involved in litigation, thereby precluding the recovery of compensation for overtime for tasks otherwise compensable under the federal labor laws where the time spent on the tasks was *de miminis*.[280]

---

[269] Rev. Rul. 76-4, 1976-1 C.B. 145.

[270] Rev. Rul. 80-106, 1980-1 C.B. 113.

[271] Priv. Ltr. Rul. 7951134.

[272] See *supra*, note 12.

[273] Tech. Adv. Mem. 9835003.

[274] McGahen v. Comm'r, 76 T.C. 468, 482 (1981), *aff'd*, 720 F.2d 664 (3d Cir. 1983). Also Unitary Mission Church of Long Island v. Comm'r, *supra* note 105.

[275] Gookin v. United States, 707 F. Supp. 1156, 1158 (N.D. Cal. 1988). Also Beth-El Ministries, Inc. v. United States, 79-2 U.S.T.C. ¶ 9412 (D.D.C. 1979).

[276] Carter v. United States, *supra* note 40, at 1486, note 5.

[277] Texas State Teachers Ass'n v. Garland Independent School District, 489 U.S. 782 (1989).

[278] Withrow v. Concannon, 942 F.2d 1385 (9th Cir. 1991).

[279] United States v. Johns, 891 F.2d 243 (9th Cir. 1989).

[280] Lindow v. United States, 738 F.2d 1057 (9th Cir. 1984). In general, Jones, "The Scintilla of Individual Profit: In Search of Private Inurement and Excess Benefit," 19 *Va. Tax Rev.* (No. 4) 575 (Spring 2000).

The state of the law in this regard is probably that articulated by a federal court of appeals, looking at a set of facts from the standpoint of the primary purpose test.[281] That court wrote that nonexempt activity of a tax-exempt charitable organization will not result in loss or denial of exemption where it is "only incidental and less than substantial" and that a "slight and comparatively unimportant deviation from the narrow furrow of tax approved activity is not fatal."[282]

§ 19.10 PRIVATE BENEFIT DOCTRINE

An organization cannot qualify as a tax-exempt charitable entity if it has transgressed the *private benefit doctrine*. The concept of private benefit is a derivative of the operational test;[283] as one court put the matter, the private benefit proscription "inheres in the requirement that [a charitable] organization operate exclusively for exempt purposes."[284] The private benefit doctrine is separate from the private inurement doctrine, yet is broader than and thus subsumes that doctrine.[285]

(a) General Rules

The private benefit doctrine differs from the private inurement doctrine in two significant respects. One is that the law recognizes the concept of *incidental* private benefit—that is, types of private benefit that will not cause loss or denial of tax-exempt status.[286] The other is that the private benefit doctrine can be applied in the absence of undue benefit to insiders.[287] As to the latter, a court noted that the private benefit doctrine embraces benefits provided to "disinterested persons."[288] Subsequently, this court wrote that impermissible private benefit can be conferred on "unrelated" persons.[289]

One of the few cases fully explicating the private benefit doctrine concerned an otherwise tax-exempt school that trained individuals for careers as political

---

[281] See § 4.4.
[282] St. Louis Union Trust Co. v. United States, 374 F.2d 427, 431-432 (8th Cir. 1967). In general, Hutton & Rowland, "The Inurement Rule and Ownership of Copyrights," 9 *Exempt Org. Tax Rev.* (No. 4) 813 (1994); Sevcik, "Inurement of Net Earnings to Shareholders or Individuals: A Challenge and a Danger to Exempt Organizations," 65 *Taxes* (No. 8) 519 (1987); Note, "'Inurement of Earnings to Private Benefit' Clause of Section 501(c)(3): A Standard Without Meaning?," 48 *Minn. L. Rev.* 1149 (1964).
[283] See § 4.5.
[284] Redlands Surgical Services v. Comm'r, 113 T.C. 47, 74 (1999), aff'd, 242 F.3d 904 (9th Cir. 2001).
[285] E.g., Church of Ethereal Joy v. Comm'r, 83 T.C. 20 (1984); Canada v. Comm'r, 82 T.C. 973 (1984); Goldsboro Art League, Inc. v. Comm'r, 75 T.C. 337 (1980); Aid to Artisans, Inc. v. Comm'r, 71 T.C. 202 (1978).
[286] E.g., Priv. Ltr. Rul. 200103083. Cf. *supra* § 9.
[287] Cf. *supra* § 3.
[288] American Campaign Academy v. Comm'r, *supra* note 42, at 1069.
[289] Redlands Surgical Services v. Comm'r, *supra* note 284, 113 T.C. at 74.

campaign professionals.[290] Nearly all of the school's graduates became employed by or consultants to Republican Party organizations or candidates. A court concluded that the school did not primarily engage in activities that accomplished educational purposes, in that it benefited private interests to more than an insubstantial extent. That is, the school was found to be substantially benefiting the private interests of Republican Party entities and candidates.[291]

The heart of this opinion is the analysis of the concept—not previously articulated—of *primary* private benefit and *secondary* private benefit. In this setting, the beneficiaries of primary private benefit were the students; the beneficiaries of secondary private benefit were the employers of the graduates. It was the existence of this secondary private benefit that caused this school to fail to acquire tax-exempt status.

The court accepted the IRS's argument that "where the training of individuals is focused on furthering a particular targeted private interest, the conferred secondary benefit ceases to be incidental to the providing organization's exempt purposes."[292] The beneficiaries, at the secondary level, were found to be a "select group."[293]

The school unsuccessfully presented as precedent several IRS rulings holding tax-exempt, as educational organizations, entities that provide training to individuals in a particular industry or profession.[294] The court accepted the IRS's characterization of these rulings, which was that the "secondary benefit provided in each ruling was broadly spread among members of an industry . . ., as opposed to being earmarked for a particular organization or person.[295] The court said that the secondary benefit in each of these rulings was, because of the spread, "incidental to the providing organization's exempt purpose."[296]

This court subsequently held that a nonprofit organization that audited structural steel fabricators in conjunction with a quality certification program conducted by a related trade association did not constitute a charitable organization, in part because it yielded inappropriate private benefit to the association and to the fabricators who were inspected.[297] The court wrote that the "development and administration of a quality certification program, at the request of and for the structural steel industry, would appear to be consistent with [the association's] mission" as a business league."[298] The court added that the "focus thus

---

[290] American Campaign Academy v. Comm'r, *supra* note 42.

[291] The court, in some portions of its opinion, seemed to be less concerned about private benefit and more troubled about assistance to a political party. For example, it wrote that the school "conducted its educational activities with [a] partisan objective" (at 1070) and operated to "advance Republican interests" (at 1072).

[292] *Id.* at 1074.

[293] *Id.* at 1076.

[294] E.g., Rev. Rul. 75-196, 1975-1 C.B. 155; Rev. Rul. 72-101, 1972-1 C.B. 144; Rev. Rul. 68-504, 1968-2 C.B. 211; Rev. Rul. 67-72, 1967-1 C.B. 125.

[295] American Campaign Academy v. Comm'r, *supra* note 42, at 1074.

[296] *Id.*

[297] Quality Auditing Co. v. Comm'r, 114 T.C. 498 (2000).

[298] *Id.* at 510.

seems to be on aiding industry participants, with any benefit to the general public being merely secondary."[299] The court thus saw more than insubstantial private benefit in two contexts: the extent to which the purported charitable organization served the association's interests in carrying out its role of industry betterment and the benefit accruing to the steel fabricators who requested audits and whose facilities were inspected by the organization.

The IRS has been advancing the private benefit doctrine as well. The most striking recent example of this was application of the doctrine, for the first time, in the private foundation setting. An individual requested access to an archive of materials, held by a foundation, concerning a distant and famous relative who had recently died, for the purpose of writing a book about the decedent. The book project was to be a commercial one; the foundation was not to be compensated for the author's use of the collection. The IRS ruled that, although provision of the materials to the author would not constitute self-dealing,[300] because the individual was not a disqualified person,[301] it would amount to substantial private benefit, which could endanger the tax-exempt status of the private foundation.[302]

Although tax-exempt charitable organizations may provide benefits to persons in their private capacity, benefits of this nature must—to avoid jeopardizing exempt status—be incidental both quantitatively and qualitatively in relation to the furthering of exempt purposes. To be quantitatively incidental, the private benefit must be insubstantial, measured in the context of the overall tax-exempt benefit conferred by the activity.[303] To be qualitatively incidental, private benefit must be a necessary concomitant of the exempt activity, in that the exempt objectives cannot be achieved without necessarily benefiting certain individuals privately.[304]

As an illustration, a nonprofit organization was formed to generate community interest in retaining classical music programming on a commercial radio station, by seeking sponsors for the programs, urging listeners to patronize the sponsors, and soliciting listener subscriptions to promote the programs; the IRS ruled that the organization could not qualify for tax exemption because these activities increased the station's revenues and thus benefited it in more than an insubstantial manner.[305] By contrast, a charitable organization that allocated Medicaid patients to physicians in private practice was held to provide qualitatively and quantitatively incidental private benefits to the physicians, including some on the organization's board of directors, inasmuch as it would be "impossible" for the or-

---

[299] *Id.*

[300] IRC § 4941. See § 11.4(a).

[301] IRC § 4941. That is, this individual was not a member of the family of the decedent (IRC § 4946(a)(1)(D)). See § 11.2(d).

[302] Priv. Ltr. Rul. 200114040.

[303] E.g., Ginsburg v. Comm'r, *supra* note 22; Rev. Rul. 75-286, 1975-2 C.B. 210; Rev. Rul. 68-14, 1968-1 C.B. 243.

[304] E.g., Rev. Rul. 70-186, 1970-1 C.B. 128.

[305] Rev. Rul. 76-206, *supra* note 238.

ganization to accomplish its exempt purposes without providing some measure of benefit to the physicians.[306]

(b) Import of Joint Venture Cases

The private benefit doctrine has been repeatedly invoked in a line of cases concerning the involvement of tax-exempt charitable organizations in partnerships and other joint ventures. The IRS has an ongoing concern that some of these ventures may constitute a means for conferring unwarranted private benefit on nonexempt participants. The agency lost these cases in the early going but recently its victories have propelled the private benefit doctrine into one of the major elements of the law of tax-exempt organizations.[307]

Originally, the IRS was of the view that involvement by a tax-exempt charitable organization as a general partner in a limited partnership would automatically lead to revocation of its exempt status, irrespective of the organization's purpose for joining the venture. This *per se* rule[308] surfaced when the IRS ruled that participation by a charitable organization in a partnership, where the organization would be the general partner and private investors would be limited partners, would be inconsistent with eligibility for exempt status in that private economic benefit would flow to the limited partners. The agency wrote that, if the charity "entered [into] the proposed partnership, [it] would be a direct participant in an arrangement for sharing the net profits of an income producing venture with private individuals and organizations of a noncharitable nature." By serving as the general partner in the project, the IRS said, the charity would be furthering the "private financial interests" of the limited partners, which would "create a conflict of interest that is legally incompatible with [the charity] being operated exclusively for charitable purposes."[309] This was the position of the IRS, even though the purpose of the partnership was to advance a charitable objective—the development and operation of a low-income housing project.

The *per se* rule was followed again the next year, when the IRS issued an adverse ruling to a charitable organization that was the general partner in a limited partnership, also created for the purpose of maintaining a low-income housing development. As before, the agency declared that the organization was a "direct participant in an arrangement for sharing the net profits of an income producing venture" with private individuals, so that the organization was "further[ing] the private financial interest of the [limited] partners."[310] The organization took the matter to court but the case was settled.[311]

---

[306] Priv. Ltr. Rul. 9615030.
[307] A larger analysis of the law concerning charitable organizations in partnerships and other ventures is Chapter 32.
[308] See *supra* § 8.
[309] Priv. Ltr. Rul. 7820058.
[310] Unnumbered private letter ruling dated Feb. 6, 1979.
[311] Strawbridge Square, Inc. v. United States (Ct. Cl. No. 471-79T).

Another IRS ruling, concerning whether certain fees derived by a tax-exempt lawyer referral service were items of unrelated business income,[312] reflected this IRS position. The agency ruled that, while flat counseling fees paid by clients and registration fees paid by lawyers were not taxable, the fees paid by lawyers to the organization based on a percentage of the fees received by the lawyers for providing legal services to clients referred to them constituted unrelated business income. The reason: the subsequently established lawyer-client relationship was a commercial undertaking and the ongoing fee arrangement with the percentage feature placed the exempt organization in the position of being in a joint venture in furtherance of these commercial objectives.[313]

The first of the court decisions, concerning a charitable organization in a joint venture, sanctioned the involvement of a charitable organization as a general partner in a limited partnership. The case concerned an arts organization that, to generate funds to pay its share of the capital required to produce a play with a tax-exempt theater, sold a portion of its rights in the play to outside investors, utilizing the limited partnership. The arts organization was the general partner, with two individuals and a for-profit corporation as limited partners. Only the limited partners were required to contribute capital; they collectively received a share of the profits or losses resulting from the production. In disagreeing with the IRS's position that the organization, solely by involvement in the limited partnership, was being operated for private interests, the court noted that the sale of the interest in the play was for a reasonable price, the transaction was at arm's length, the organization was not obligated for the return of any capital contributions made by the limited partners, the limited partners lacked control over the organization's operations, and none of the limited partners nor any officer or director of the for-profit corporation was an officer or director of the arts organization.[314]

Around that same time, the IRS approved an undertaking between a tax-exempt blood plasma fractionation facility and a commercial laboratory, by which the parties acquired a building and constructed a blood fractionation facility. This arrangement enabled the facility to become self-sufficient in its production of blood fractions, to reduce the cost of fractionating blood, and thus to be able to more effectively carry out its charitable blood program. Each party had an equal ownership of, and shared equally in the production capacity of, the facility. The IRS concluded that the exempt organization's participation in this venture was substantially related to its exempt purposes and that there was no private benefit.[315]

One of the most significant of the private benefit court cases[316] concerned the matter of whole entity joint ventures, where a health care facility places its entire operations in a venture with a for-profit entity, perhaps ceding authority over

---

[312] See Part Five.
[313] Priv. Ltr. Rul. 7952002.
[314] Plumstead Theatre Society, Inc. v. Comm'r, 74 T.C. 1324 (1980). Cf. Broadway Theatre League of Lynchburg, Va., Inc. v. United States, *supra* note 82.
[315] Priv. Ltr. Rul. 7921018.
[316] Redlands Surgical Services v. Comm'r, *supra* note 284.

all of its resources to the co-venturer.[317] A fundamental concept in this context is control, with the IRS and the courts examining relationships between public charities and for-profit organizations to ascertain whether the former have lost control of their facilities and programs to the latter. Examples include relationships reflected in management agreements, leases, fundraising contracts, and, of course, partnership, limited liability company, or other joint venture agreements.[318] In this setting, it can be irrelevant if the public charity is in fact engaging substantially in exempt activities[319] and if fees (if any) paid by the exempt organization to a for-profit entity are reasonable.[320]

The sweeping rule of law in this regard was articulated, in one of the two most radical of these cases, by a federal court of appeals, which wrote that the "critical inquiry is not whether particular contractual payments to a related for-profit organization are reasonable or excessive, but instead whether the entire enterprise is carried on in such a manner that the for-profit organization benefits substantially from the operation of" the tax-exempt organization.[321] This, to date, represents the outer reaches of the ambit of the private benefit doctrine: the thought that there can be unwarranted private benefit, conferred on a noninsider, even if the terms and conditions of the arrangement are reasonable and substantial exempt functions are occurring.

In the other of these cases, two for-profit organizations that did not have any formal structural control over the nonprofit entity, the tax exemption of which was at issue, nevertheless were found to have exerted "considerable control" over its activities.[322] The for-profit entities set fees that the nonprofit organization charged for training sessions, required the nonprofit organization to carry on certain types of educational activities, and provided management personnel paid for and responsible to one of the for-profit organizations. Pursuant to a licensing agreement with the for-profit organizations, the nonprofit entity was allowed to use certain intellectual property for 10 years; at the end of the license period, all copyrighted material, including new material developed by the nonprofit organization, was required to be turned over to the for-profit organizations.[323] The nonprofit organization was required to use its excess funds for the development of its program activities or related research. The for-profit organizations also required that trainers and local organizations sign an agreement to not compete with these activities for two years after terminating their relationship with the organizations involved.

The trial court, in this case, concluded that the nonprofit organization

---

[317] See Hyatt & Hopkins, *The Law of Tax-Exempt Healthcare Organizations, Second Edition* (John Wiley & Sons, Inc., 2001) § 22.9.

[318] In St. David's Health Care System, Inc. v. United States, 2002-1 U.S.T.C. ¶ 50,452 (W.D. Tex. 2002), the court purportedly followed the rationale of Redlands Surgical Services v. Comm'r, *supra* note 284, although it concluded that private benefit was not present in the case.

[319] See § 4.4.

[320] See *supra* § 4(a).

[321] Church by Mail, Inc. v. Comm'r, *supra* note 80, 765 F.2d at 1392.

[322] est of Hawaii v. Comm'r, 71 T.C. 1067, 1080 (1979), *aff'd*, 647 F.2d 170 (9th Cir. 1981).

[323] See *supra* § 8.

was "part of a franchise system which is operated for private benefit and . . . its affiliation with this system taints it with a substantial commercial purpose."[324] The "ultimate beneficiaries" of the nonprofit organization's activities were found to be the for-profit corporations; the nonprofit organization was "simply the instrument to subsidize the for-profit corporations and not vice versa."[325] The nonprofit organization was held to not be operating exclusively for charitable purposes.

These two cases have framed this analysis. Even without formal control over the ostensible tax-exempt organization by one or more for-profit entities, the ostensible exempt organization can be viewed as merely the instrument by which a for-profit organization is subsidized (benefited). The nonprofit organization's "affiliation" with a for-profit entity or a "system" involving one or more for-profit entities can taint the nonprofit organization, actually or seemingly imbuing it with a substantial commercial purpose. The result is likely to be a finding of private benefit (or, if an insider is involved,[326] private inurement[327]), causing the nonprofit organization to lose or be denied tax-exempt status.

Matters worsen in this context when there is actual control. This is the principal message of the decision concerning whole entity joint ventures. In that case, a tax-exempt subsidiary of a public charity (hospital) became a co-general partner with a for-profit organization in a partnership that owned and operated a surgery center. A for-profit management company affiliated with the for-profit co-general partner managed the arrangement. The subsidiary's sole activity was participation in the partnership. The court termed this relationship "passive participation [by the charitable subsidiary] in a for-profit health-service enterprise."[328] The court concluded that it was "patently clear" that the partnership was not being operated in an exclusively charitable manner. The income-producing activity of the partnership was characterized as "indivisible" as between the nonprofit and for-profit organizations. No "discrete part" of these activities was "severable from those activities that produce income to be applied to the other partner's profit."[329]

The heart of the whole entity joint venture decision is this: to the extent a public charity "cedes control over its sole activity to for-profit parties [by, in this case, entering into the joint venture] having an independent economic interest in the same activity and having no obligation to put charitable purposes ahead of profit-making objectives," the charity cannot be assured that the partnership will in fact be operated in furtherance of charitable purposes.[330] The

---

[324] est of Hawaii v. Comm'r, *supra* note 322, 71 T.C. at 1080.

[325] *Id.*

[326] See *supra* § 3.

[327] The private inurement doctrine was invoked in a case concerning a charitable organization in a partnership in Housing Pioneers, Inc. v. Comm'r, 65 T.C.M. 2191 (1993).

[328] Redlands Surgical Services v. Comm'r, *supra* note 284, 113 T.C. at 77.

[329] *Id.*

[330] *Id.* at 78.

consequence is the conferring on the for-profit party in the venture "significant private benefits."[331]

Overall, today, a tax-exempt charitable organization can participate as a general partner in a limited partnership, without endangering its exempt status, if the organization is serving a charitable purpose by means of the partnership, the organization is insulated from the day-to-day responsibilities as general partner, and the limited partners are not receiving an undue economic benefit from the partnership.[332]

(c) Perspective

The IRS is making much of the private benefit doctrine these days. Two examples illustrate this. The agency is of the view that private benefit is present when the founders of an otherwise tax-exempt school also are directors of a for-profit company that manages the school; the nature of the benefit is largely financial, and the IRS asserted that the educational activities of the school could be undertaken without conferring the benefit (such as by use of employees or volunteers).[333] It also believes that certain scholarship-granting foundations are ineligible for tax exemption, by reason of the private benefit doctrine, because the recipients are individuals who are participants in beauty pageants operated by tax-exempt social welfare organizations; private benefit is thought to be bestowed on the social welfare organizations because the grant programs serve to attract contestants to enter the pageants and on the for-profit entities that a corporate sponsors of the pageants.[334]

Traditionally, then, the private benefit doctrine has been largely applied in cases concerning relationships between public charities and individuals. The application of this doctrine, however, is being expanded to encompass arrangements between charitable organizations and for-profit entities and charitable organizations and other categories of tax-exempt organizations.[335]

---

[331] *Id.* This opinion was a major victory for the IRS, which earlier staked out, in Rev. Rul. 98-15, 1998-1 C.B. 718, the position adopted by the court. In general, Jones, "Private Benefit and the Unanswered Questions from Redlands," 89 *Tax Notes* 121 (2000). But see St. David's Health Care System, Inc. v. United States, *supra* note 318.

[332] E.g., Gen. Couns. Mem. 39862, 39732, 39546, 39444, 39005, 37789. See Chapter 32.

[333] "Private Benefit Under IRC 501(c)(3)," Topic H in the IRS Exempt Organizations Continuing Professional Education Technical Instruction Program textbook for fiscal year 2001.

[334] "Beauty Pageants: Private Benefit Worth Watching," Topic B in the IRS Exempt Organizations Continuing Professional Education Technical Instruction Program textbook for fiscal year 2002.

[335] The court of appeals that reversed the Tax Court in United Cancer Council, Inc. v. Comm'r, *supra* note 68, also remanded the case for consideration in light of the private benefit doctrine. Inasmuch as the Tax Court previously held that an act of private inurement is also an act of private benefit (American Campaign Academy v. Comm'r, *supra* note 288), the *United Cancer Council* case was shaping up to be a significant private benefit case. The case, however, was settled before the Tax Court could rule on the private benefit aspects. In general, Raby and Raby, "Private Inurement, Private Benefit, *UCC*, and Intermediate Sanctions," 24 *Exempt Org. Tax Rev.* (No. 2) 315 (May 1999).

§ 19.11   EXCESS BENEFIT TRANSACTIONS

One of the newest, yet one of the most important, augmentations to the law of tax-exempt organizations is the set of rules pertaining to *excess benefit transactions*. These rules, which in many ways parallel and overlap the private inurement doctrine, were enacted in 1996 and took effect in 1995;[336] the final regulations to accompany the rules were issued in early 2002. The tax penalties that underlay these rules are termed *intermediate sanctions*.

(a) Introduction to Intermediate Sanctions

The intermediate sanctions rules emphasize the taxation of persons who engaged in impermissible private transactions with certain types of tax-exempt organizations, rather than revocation of the tax-exempt status of these entities. With this approach, tax law sanctions—structured as penalty excise taxes—may be imposed on those persons who improperly benefited from the transaction and on certain managers of the organization who participated in the transaction knowing that it was improper.

This body of law[337] represents the most dramatic and important package of federal statutory tax law rules concerning tax-exempt organizations created since enactment of the basic statutory structure of the exempt organizations field in 1969.[338] The law as to excess benefit transactions is refocusing and reshaping application of the private inurement and private benefit doctrines, and is impacting the composition and functioning of many boards of directors of exempt organizations.

---

[336] The effective date of these rules is September 14, 1995 (Reg. § 53.4958-1(f)(1)). In the first of the reported intermediate sanctions cases, the effective date of the transactions was October 1, 1995 (Caracci v. Comm'r, *supra* note 161). The intermediate sanctions do not apply to any benefit that arose out of a transaction pursuant to a written contract that was binding on that date and continued in force through the time of the transaction, and the terms of which have not materially changed (Reg. § 53.4958-1(f)(2)).

[337] The excess benefit transactions rules are the subject of IRC § 4958. The report of the House Committee on Ways and Means, dated March 28, 1996 (H. Rep. 104-506, 104th Cong., 2d Sess. (1996)) (for purposes of this § 11, "House Report"), constitutes the totality of the legislative history of these rules. The IRS provided a brief summary of the intermediate sanctions rules in Notice 96-46, 1996-2 C.B. 212. In general, see Hopkins, *The Law of Intermediate Sanctions: A Guide for Nonprofits* (John Wiley & Sons, Inc., 2003); Hopkins & Tesdahl, *Intermediate Sanctions: Curbing Nonprofit Abuse* (John Wiley & Sons, Inc., 1997).

[338] A substantial portion of the Tax Reform Act of 1969 concerned enactment of law defining *public charities* and imposing stringent rules of operations of *private foundations* (see §§ 11.3, 11.4). Much of the motivation for creation of the foundation rules, particularly those pertaining to self-dealing (IRC § 4941)—fear of considerable abuses—is mirrored in the reason for adoption of the excess benefit transactions rules.

(b) Tax-Exempt Organizations Involved

The law as to excess benefit transactions applies with respect to tax-exempt public charities[339] and tax-exempt social welfare organizations.[340] These entities are collectively termed, for this purpose, *applicable tax-exempt organizations.*[341] Organizations of this nature include any organization described in either of these two categories of exempt organizations at any time during the five-year period ending on the date of the transaction.[342]

There are no exemptions from these rules.[343] That is, all tax-exempt public charities and all tax-exempt social welfare organizations are applicable tax-exempt organizations. A foreign organization that receives substantially all of its support from sources outside the United States, however, is not an applicable tax-exempt organization.[344]

A social welfare organization is covered by these rules if it has received recognition of tax exemption from the IRS, has filed an application for recognition of exemption, has filed an information return with the IRS as a social welfare organization, or has otherwise held itself out as a tax-exempt social welfare organization.[345]

(c) Disqualified Persons

For these purposes,[346] the term *disqualified person* means (1) any person who was, at any time during the five-year period ending on the date of the transaction involved, in a position to exercise substantial influence over the affairs of the organization (whether by virtue of being an organization manager or otherwise),[347] (2) a member of the family of an individual described in the preceding category,[348]

---

[339] A *public charity* is an organization that is tax-exempt for federal income tax purposes (IRC § 501(a)) because it is a charitable, educational, scientific, and/or like organization (that is, it is described in IRC § 501(c)(3) (see Part Two)); this type of charitable organization is not (by reason of IRC § 509(a)) a private foundation (see § 11.3). The excess benefit transactions rules do not apply to private foundations because of application to them of the self-dealing rules (IRC § 4941).

[340] A *social welfare organization* is an organization that is tax-exempt for federal income tax purposes (IRC § 501(a)) because it is described in IRC § 501(c)(4). The law of social welfare organizations is the subject of Chapter 12.

[341] IRC § 4958(e)(1); Reg. § 53.4958-2(a)(1).

[342] IRC § 4958(e)(2); Reg. § 53.4958-2(b)(1). In the case of a transaction occurring before September 14, 2000, this lookback period begins on September 14, 1995 (see *supra* note 336), and ends on the date of the transaction (Reg. § 53.4958-2(b)(1)).

[343] In other areas of the law of tax-exempt organizations, by contrast, there are exemptions from the rules for entities such as, for example, small organizations and religious organizations (e.g., §§ 23.3(b), 24.3(b)).

[344] Reg. § 53.4958-2(b)(2).

[345] Reg. § 53.4958-2(a)(3). These distinctions are required because, unlike nearly all public charities, an entity can be a tax-exempt social welfare organization without applying for recognition of exemption (see § 23.3).

[346] Cf. IRC § 4946. See § 11.2.

[347] IRC § 4958(f)(1)(A); Reg. § 53.4958-3(a)(1).

[348] IRC § 4958(f)(1)(B); Reg. § 53.4958-3(b)(1).

and (3) an entity in which individuals described in the preceding two categories own more than a 35 percent interest.[349]

A person is in a position to exercise substantial influence over the affairs of an applicable tax-exempt organization if that person is a voting member of the organization's governing body or is (or has the powers or responsibilities of) the organization's president, chief executive officer, chief operating officer, or chief financial officer.[350] Certain facts and circumstances tend to show this substantial influence, such as being the organization's founder, a substantial contributor to it, having managerial control over a discrete segment of the organization, or serving as a key adviser to a person who has managerial authority.[351] Certain facts and circumstances tend to show a lack of substantial influence, such as service as an independent contractor (such as a lawyer, accountant, or investment adviser).[352] Certain persons are deemed not to have the requisite substantial influence, such as an employee who receives economic benefits that are less than the compensation referenced for a highly compensated employee[353] and public charities.[354]

An *organization manager* is a trustee, director, or officer of the applicable tax-exempt organization, as well as an individual having powers or responsibilities similar to those of trustees, directors, or officers of the organization.[355]

The term *member of the family* is defined as being (1) spouses, ancestors, children, grandchildren, great grandchildren, and the spouses of children, grandchildren, and great grandchildren—namely, those individuals so classified under the private foundation rules,[356] and (2) the brothers and sisters (whether by whole- or half-blood) of the individual and their spouses.[357]

The entities that are disqualified persons because one or more disqualified persons own more than a 35 percent interest in them are termed *35 percent controlled entities*. These are (1) corporations in which one or more disqualified persons own more than 35 percent of the total combined voting power, (2) partnerships in which one or more disqualified persons own more than 35 percent of the profits interest, and (3) trusts or estates in which one or more dis-

---

[349] IRC § 4958(f)(1)(C); Reg. § 53.4958-3(b)(2).

[350] Reg. § 53.4958-3(c). The legislative history, however, states that an individual having the title of "trustee," "director," or "officer" is not automatically considered a disqualified person (House Report at 58). Although it has been the view of the IRS that all physicians who are on the medical staff of a hospital or similar organization are insiders for purposes of the private inurement doctrine (see *supra* § 3) (Gen. Coun. Mem. 39862), a physician is a disqualified person under the intermediate sanctions rules only where he or she is in a position to exercise substantial influence over the affairs of the organization (House Report at 58, note 12).

[351] Reg. § 53.4958-3(e)(2).

[352] Reg. § 53.4958-3(e)(3).

[353] IRC § 414(q)(1)(B)(i). An individual is a highly compensated employee in 2003 if he or she earned more than $90,000 in 2002.

[354] Reg. § 53.4958-3(d). As to this last point, other types of tax-exempt organizations can be disqualified persons in this context, such as a membership association (see Chapter 13) in relation to a related foundation (see § 30.2(a)).

[355] IRC § 4958(f)(2); Reg. § 53.4958-1(d)(2)(i).

[356] IRC § 4946(d). See § 11.2(d).

[357] IRC § 4958(f)(4); Reg. § 53.4958-3(b)(1).

qualified persons own more than 35 percent of the beneficial interest.[358] The term *voting power* includes voting power represented by holdings of voting stock, actual or constructive, but does not include voting rights held only as a director or trustee.[359] In general, constructive ownership rules apply for purposes of determining whether an entity is a 35 percent controlled entity.[360]

(d) Excess Benefit Transactions

This tax law regime has as its heart the excess benefit transaction. In the instance of one of these transactions, tax sanctions are imposed on the disqualified person or persons who improperly benefited from the transaction and perhaps on any organization manager or managers who participated in the transaction knowing that it was improper.

An *excess benefit transaction* is any transaction in which an economic benefit is provided by an applicable tax-exempt organization directly or indirectly to or for the use of any disqualified person, if the value of the economic benefit provided by the exempt organization exceeds the value of the consideration (including the performance of services) received for providing the benefit.[361] This type of benefit is known as an *excess benefit*.[362]

Payment of compensation, which is not reasonable, to a disqualified person is a type of excess benefit transaction. Compensation for the performance of services is reasonable if it is only such "amount that would ordinarily be paid for like services by like enterprises under like circumstances."[363] Generally, the circumstances to be taken into consideration are those existing at the date when the contract for services was made. When reasonableness cannot be determined on that basis, the determination is made based on all facts and circumstances, up to and including circumstances as of the date of payment. The IRS may not consider "circumstances existing at the date when the payment is questioned" in making a determination of the reasonableness of compensation.[364]

Compensation for these purposes means all items of compensation provided by an applicable tax-exempt organization in exchange for the performance of services. This includes (1) forms of cash and noncash compensation, such as salary, fees, bonuses, and severance payments; (2) forms of deferred compensation that are earned and vested, whether or not funded and whether or not the plan is a qualified one; (3) the amount of premiums paid for insurance coverage (including

---

[358] IRC § 4958(f)(3)(A); Reg. § 53.4958-3(b)(2)(i).

[359] Reg. § 53.4958-3(b)(2)(ii).

[360] IRC § 4958(f)(3)(B); Reg. § 53.4958-3(b)(2)(iii).

[361] IRC § 4958(c)(1)(A); Reg. § 53.4958-4(a)(1). The IRS ruled that an annual monetary award presented by a public charity was an exempt activity and did not involve an excess benefit transaction (Priv. Ltr. Rul. 9802045).

[362] IRC § 4958(c)(1)(B).

[363] Reg. § 53.4958-4(b)(1)(ii)(A).

[364] Reg. § 53.4958-4(b)(2)(i). By contrast, the U.S. Tax Court is of the view that, in the private inurement setting, circumstances occurring after the transaction in question can be considered in determining reasonableness (e.g., Anclote Psychiatric Center, Inc. v. Comm'r, *supra* note 151).

liability), as well as payment or reimbursement by the organization of charges, expenses, fees, or taxes not ultimately covered by the insurance coverage; and (4) other benefits, whether or not included in income for tax purposes, including payments to welfare benefit plans on behalf of the individuals being compensated, such as plans providing medical, dental, life insurance, severance pay, and disability benefits, and taxable and nontaxable fringe benefits,[365] including expense allowances or reimbursements or foregone interest on loans that the recipient must report as income for tax purposes.[366]

The criteria for determining the reasonableness of compensation and fair market value of property are not stated in the intermediate sanctions regulations. Preexisting law standards apply in determining reasonableness of this nature.[367] An individual need not necessarily accept reduced compensation merely because he or she renders services to a tax-exempt, as opposed to a taxable, organization.[368]

An economic benefit may not be treated as consideration for the performance of services unless the organization providing the benefit clearly indicates its intent to treat the benefit as compensation when the benefit is paid.[369] In determining whether payments or transactions of this nature are in fact forms of compensation, the relevant factors include whether (1) the appropriate decision-making body approved the transfer as compensation in accordance with established procedures and (2) the organization provided written substantiation that is contemporaneous with the transfer of the economic benefit at issue.[370] If an organization fails to provide this contemporaneous substantiation, any services provided by the disqualified person will not be treated as provided in consideration for the economic benefit for purposes of determining the reasonableness of the transaction.[371] These rules do not apply to nontaxable fringe benefits[372] and certain other types of nontaxable transfers (such as employer-provided health benefits and contributions to qualified pension plans).[373]

Excess benefit transactions can also include a rental arrangement, borrowing arrangement, and sales of assets between an applicable tax-exempt organization and a disqualified person. Thus, a court held that the transfers of assets by public charities to disqualified persons, where the value of the assets "far exceeded" the consideration paid for them, were excess benefit transactions.[374]

---

[365]This item, however, does not include working condition fringe benefits (IRC § 132(d)) or *de minimis* fringe benefits (IRC § 132(e)) (Reg. § 53.4958-4(a)(4)(i)).

[366] Reg. § 53.4958-4(b)(1)(ii)(B).

[367] House Report at 56. See *supra* § 4. Where two or more disqualified persons perform services as a team, in determining whether they received any excess benefit in a year, each person is treated separately, so that the total value of each person's services provided to an exempt organization in a year must be compared with the value of the benefits received by the person for that year (Priv. Ltr. Rul. 200244028).

[368] House Report at 56, note 5.

[369] IRC § 4958(c)(1)(A); Reg. § 53.4958-4(c)(1).

[370] Reg. § 53.4958-4(c)(1). These returns or forms include the organization's annual information return filed with the IRS (usually Form 990), the information return provided by the organization to the recipient (Form W-2 or Form 1099), and the individual's income tax return (Form 1040) (House Report at 57; Reg. § 53.4958-4(c)(3)(i)(A)(1)).

[371] Reg. § 53.4958-4(c)(1). An economic benefit that a disqualified person obtains by theft or fraud cannot be treated as consideration for the performance of services (*id.*).

[372] IRC § 132.

[373] The first intermediate sanctions case concerning the issue of excessive compensation was filed in the U.S. Tax Court on August 3, 2000 (Peters v. Comm'r, *supra* note 104; the case was settled).

[374] Caracci v. Comm'r, *supra* note 161, at 415.

The phraseology *directly or indirectly* means the provision of an economic benefit directly by the organization or indirectly by means of a controlled entity. Thus, an applicable tax-exempt organization cannot avoid involvement in an excess benefit transaction by causing a controlled entity to engage in the transaction.[375] An economic benefit may also be provided by an applicable tax-exempt organization indirectly to a disqualified person through an intermediary entity.[376] All consideration and benefits exchanged between a disqualified person and an applicable tax-exempt organization, and all entities the organization controls, are taken into account to determine whether an excess benefit transaction has occurred.

The following economic benefits are disregarded for these purposes: (1) the payment of reasonable expenses for members of the governing body of an organization to attend board meetings; (2) an economic benefit received by a disqualified person solely as a member of (if the membership fee does not exceed $75) or volunteer for the organization; and (3) an economic benefit provided to a disqualified person solely as a member of a charitable class.[377]

Also, to the extent to be provided in tax regulations, the term *excess benefit transaction* includes any transaction in which the amount of any economic benefit provided to or for the use of a disqualified person is determined in whole or in part by the revenues of one or more activities of the organization, but only if the transaction results in private inurement.[378] In this context, the excess benefit is the amount of the private inurement.[379] This type of arrangement is known as a *revenue-sharing arrangement*. The Department of the Treasury was instructed to promptly issue guidance providing examples of revenue-sharing arrangements that violate the private inurement prohibition.[380] The tax regulations that were issued in 2002 are silent on the subject.[381]

Under the law in existence before enactment of the intermediate sanctions rules, certain revenue-sharing arrangements have been determined by the IRS to not constitute private inurement.[382] It is to continue to be the case that not all revenue-sharing arrangements are private inurement transactions. The legislative history of the intermediate sanctions rules, however, stated that the IRS is not bound by any of its prior rulings in this area.[383]

The intermediate sanctions rules do not apply to any fixed payment made to a person pursuant to an initial contract.[384] A *fixed payment* is an amount of money or other property specified in the contract, or determined by a fixed formula specified in the contract, which is to be paid or transferred in

[375] *Id.* at 56, note 3.
[376] Reg. § 53.4958-4(a)(2).
[377] Reg. § 53.4958-4(a)(4).
[378] IRC § 4958(c)(2).
[379] *Id.*
[380] House Report at 56.
[381] A section in the regulations has been reserved for these rules (Reg. § 53.4958-5).
[382] E.g., Gen. Couns. Mem. 39674, 38905, and 38283. See House Report at 56, note 4.
[383] House Report at 56, note 4.
[384] Reg. § 53.4958-4(a)(3)(i).

exchange for the provision of specified services or property.[385] An *initial contract* is a binding written contract between an applicable tax-exempt organization and a person who was not a disqualified person immediately prior to entering into the contract.[386] A compensation package can be partially sheltered by this initial contract exception; for example, an individual can have a base salary that is a fixed payment pursuant to an initial contract and also have an annual performance-based bonus which is subject to excess benefit transaction analysis.[387]

(e) Rebuttable Presumption of Reasonableness

This body of law includes a *rebuttable presumption of reasonableness*, with respect to compensation arrangements and other transactions between an applicable tax-exempt organization and a disqualified person.[388] This presumption arises where the transaction was approved by a board of directors or trustees (or a committee of the board) of an applicable tax-exempt organization that was composed entirely of individuals who were unrelated to and not subject to the control of the disqualified person or persons involved in the transaction, obtained and relied on appropriate data as to comparability, and adequately documented the basis for its determination.[389]

The first of these criteria essentially requires an independent board. The standard as to independence, for governing bodies and committees, is based on the concept of an absence of a *conflict of interest*.[390] An individual is not regarded as a member of a governing body or committee when it is reviewing a transaction if that individual meets with the members only to answer questions, otherwise recuses himself or herself from the meeting, and is not present during debate and voting on the transaction.[391] A committee of a governing body may be composed of any individuals permitted under state law to serve on the committee and may act on behalf of the governing body to the extent permitted by state law.[392]

As to the second of these criteria, appropriate data includes compensation levels paid by similarly situated organizations, both tax-exempt and tax-

---

[385] Reg. § 53.4958-4(a)(3)(ii).

[386] Reg. § 53.4958-4(a)(3)(iii).

[387] In general, Jones, " 'First Bite' and the Private Benefit Doctrine: A Comment on Temporary and Proposed Regulation 53-4958-4T(a)(3)," 62 *U. Pitt. L. Rev.* 715 (Summer 2001). This *initial contract exception* is informally known as the *first bite rule.*

[388] This rebuttable presumption is not provided for in the Internal Revenue Code; it was created by the legislative history (House Report at 56–57), and is reflected in and amplified by the regulations (Reg. § 58.4958-6).

[389] Reg. § 53.4958-6(a).

[390] Reg. § 53.4958-6(c)(1)(iii).

[391] Reg. § 53.4958-6(c)(1)(ii).

[392] Reg. § 53.4958-6(c)(1)(i)(B).

able, for functionally comparable positions; the location of the organization, including the availability of similar specialties in the geographic area; independent compensation surveys by nationally recognized independent firms; and written offers from similar institutions competing for the services of the disqualified person.[393]

In the case of an organization with annual gross receipts of less than $1 million, when reviewing compensation arrangements, the governing body or committee is considered to have appropriate data as to comparability if it has data on compensation paid by three comparable organizations in the same or similar communities for similar services.[394]

As to the third of these criteria, adequate documentation includes an evaluation of the individual whose compensation level and terms were being established, and the basis for the determination that the individual's compensation was reasonable in light of that evaluation and data.[395] The fact that a state or local legislative or agency body may have authorized or approved a particular compensation package paid to a disqualified person is not determinative of the reasonableness of the compensation paid.[396]

For a decision to be documented adequately, the written or electronic records of the governing body or committee must note the terms of the transaction that was approved, the date it was approved, the members of the governing body or committee who were present during debate on the transaction or arrangement that was approved and those who voted on it, the comparability data obtained and relied on by the governing body or committee and how it was obtained, and the actions taken with respect to consideration of the transaction by anyone who was otherwise a member of the governing body or committee but who had a conflict of interest with respect to the transaction or arrangement.[397] If the governing body or committee determines that reasonable compensation for a specific arrangement or fair market value in a specific transaction is higher or lower than the range of comparable data received, the governing body or committee must record the basis for the determination.[398]

The documentation must be made concurrently with the determination.[399] This means that records must be prepared by the next meeting of the governing body or committee occurring after the final action or actions of the body or committee are taken. Records must be reviewed and approved by the governing

---

[393] House Report at 57; Reg. § 53.4958-6(c)(2)(i).

[394] Reg. § 53.4958-6(c)(2)(ii).

[395] House Report at 57.

[396] *Id.*, note 7. Likewise, this type of authorization or approval is not determinative of whether a revenue-sharing arrangement violates the private inurement proscription (*id.*).

[397] Reg. § 53.4958-6(c)(3)(i).

[398] Reg. § 53.4958-6(c)(3)(ii).

[399] *Id.*

body or committee as reasonable, accurate, and complete within a reasonable time thereafter.[400]

If these three criteria are satisfied, penalty excise taxes can be imposed only if the IRS develops sufficient contrary evidence to rebut the probative value of the comparability data relied on by the authorized governing body.[401] For example, the IRS could establish that the compensation data relied on by the parties was not for functionally comparable positions or that the disqualified person in fact did not substantially perform the responsibilities of the position.[402]

(f) Tax Structure

A disqualified person who benefited from an excess benefit transaction is subject to and must pay an excise tax—termed the *initial tax*—equal to 25 percent of the amount of the excess benefit.[403]

An organization manager who participated in an excess benefit transaction, knowing that it was such a transaction, is subject to and must pay an excise tax of 10 percent of the excess benefit (subject to a maximum amount of tax as to a transaction of $10,000[404]), where an initial tax is imposed on a disqualified person and if there was no correction of the excess benefit transaction within the taxable period.[405] This tax is not imposed, however, where the participation in the transaction was not willful and was due to reasonable cause.[406]

Another tax—the *additional tax*—may be imposed on a disqualified person where the initial tax was imposed and if there was no correction of the excess benefit within a specified period. This period is the *taxable period*, which means—with respect to an excess benefit transaction—the period beginning with the date on which the transaction occurred and ending on the earliest of (1) the date of mailing of a notice of deficiency[407] as to the initial tax or (2) the date on which the

---

[400] *Id.* If reasonableness of compensation cannot be determined based on circumstances existing at the date when a contract for services was made, this rebuttable presumption cannot arise until circumstances exist so that reasonableness of compensation can be determined, and the three requirements for the presumption are satisfied (Reg. § 53.4958-6(d)(1)).

The fact that a transaction between an applicable tax-exempt organization and a disqualified person does not qualify for this presumption does not create an inference that the transaction is an excess benefit transaction (Reg. § 53.4958-6(e)). (An instance of nonqualification for this presumption is in Priv. Ltr. Rul. 200244028.) The fact that a transaction qualifies for the presumption does not exempt or relieve any person from compliance with any federal or state law imposing any obligation, duty, responsibility, or other standard of conduct with respect to the operation or administration of any applicable tax-exempt organization (*id.*).

[401] Reg. § 53.4958-6(b).
[402] House Report at 57.
[403] IRC § 4958(a)(1); Reg. § 53.4958-1(a), (c)(1).
[404] IRC § 4958(d)(2); Reg. § 53.4958-1(d)(7).
[405] IRC § 4958(a)(2); Reg. § 53.4958-1(d)(1). The concepts of *participation* and *knowing* are the subject of Reg. § 53.4958-1(d)(3), (4).
[406] IRC § 4958(a)(2); Reg. § 53.4958-1(d)(1). The concepts of *willful* and *reasonable cause* are the subject of Reg. § 53.4958-1(d)(5), (6).
[407] IRC § 6212.

initial tax is assessed.[408] In this situation, the disqualified person is subject to and must pay a tax equal to 200 percent of the excess benefit involved.[409]

The term *correction* means undoing the excess benefit transaction to the extent possible and taking any additional measures necessary to place the applicable tax-exempt organization in a financial position that is not worse than that in which it would be if the disqualified person were dealing under the highest fiduciary standards.[410] The correction amount with respect to an excess benefit transaction is the sum of the excess benefit and interest (at a rate that at least equals the applicable federal rate, compounded annually) on that benefit; generally, the correction must be made using cash or cash equivalents.[411] The IRS is of the view that a proper correction also requires a change in the policies or practices of the organization involved, to accord the IRS some assurance that the infraction or infractions will not be repeated. If more than one organization manager or other disqualified person is liable for an excise tax, then all such persons are jointly and severally liable for the tax.[412]

A three-year statute of limitations applies, except in the case of fraud.[413] The IRS has the authority to abate an intermediate sanctions excise tax penalty if it is established that the violation was due to reasonable cause and not due to willful neglect, and the transaction was corrected within the appropriate taxable period.[414]

(g) Reimbursements and Insurance

Any reimbursement by an applicable tax-exempt organization of excise tax liability is treated as an excess benefit transaction itself, unless it is included in the disqualified person's compensation for the year in which the reimbursement is made.[415] The total compensation package, including the amount of any reimbursement, is subject to the requirement of reasonableness. Similarly, the payment by an applicable tax-exempt organization of premiums for an insurance policy providing liability insurance to a disqualified person for excess benefit taxes is an excess benefit transaction itself, unless the amounts of the premiums are treated as part of the compensation paid to the disqualified person and the total compensation, including the premiums, is reasonable.[416]

---

[408] IRC § 4958(f)(5); Reg. § 53.4958-1(c)(2)(ii).
[409] IRC § 4958(b); Reg. § 53.4958-1(c)(2)(i).
[410] IRC § 4958(f)(6); Reg. § 53.4958-7.
[411] Reg. § 53.4958-7(c).
[412] IRC § 4958(d)(1); Reg. § 4958-1(c)(1), (d)(8).
[413] IRC § 6501; Reg. § 53.4958-1(e)(3).
[414] IRC § 4962; Reg. § 53.4958-1(c)(2)(iii).
[415] House Report at 58.
[416] *Id.*

(h) Returns for Payment of Excise Taxes

Under the law in existence prior to enactment of the excess benefit transactions rules, charitable organizations and other persons liable for certain excise taxes are required to file returns—Form 4720—by which the taxes due are calculated and reported. These taxes are those imposed on public charities for excessive lobbying expenditures[417] and for political campaign expenditures,[418] and on private foundations and/or other persons for a range of impermissible activities.[419]

Disqualified persons and organization managers liable for payment of an intermediate sanctions excise tax are required to file Form 4720 as the return by which these taxes are paid.[420] In general, returns on Form 4720 for a disqualified person or organization manager liable for an excess benefit transaction tax are required to be filed on or before the 15th day of the fifth month following the close of the tax year of that person.[421]

(i) Scope of the Sanctions

The intermediate sanctions penalties may be imposed by the IRS in lieu of or in addition to revocation of the tax-exempt status of an applicable tax-exempt organization.[422] In general, these sanctions are to be the sole penalty imposed in cases in which the excess benefit does not rise to such a level as to call into question whether, on the whole, the organization functions as an exempt charitable or social welfare organization.[423]

Revocation of tax-exempt status, with or without the imposition of intermediate sanctions taxes, is to occur only when the applicable tax-exempt organization no longer operates as an exempt charitable or social welfare organization.[424] Existing law principles apply in determining whether an applicable tax-exempt organization no longer operates as an exempt organization. For example, the loss of tax-exempt status would occur in a year, or as of a year, the entity was involved in a transaction constituting a substantial amount of private inurement.

§ 19.12 INTERRELATIONSHIP OF DOCTRINES

The coming months and years will bring interpretations and amplification of the intermediate sanctions rules, with emphasis on what does and does not

---

[417] IRC § 4911 or 4912. See § 20.6.
[418] IRC § 4955. See § 21.2.
[419] IRC §§ 4940-4948. See Chapter 11.
[420] Reg. § 53.6011-1(b).
[421] Reg. § 53.6071-1(f)(1).
[422] *Id.* at 59.
[423] The tax regulations state the matter this way: The intermediate sanctions law does not affect the substantive standards for tax exemption for applicable tax-exempt organizations; these entities qualify for exemption only if no part of their net earnings inures to the benefit of insiders (Reg. § 53.4958-8(a)).
[424] *Id.* at 59, note 15.

constitute an excess benefit transaction, and whether a compensation package or a value assigned to property or its use is reasonable. At least in the short term, this process will draw heavily on existing law as shaped by the private inurement doctrine. Likewise, the application of the intermediate sanctions area will also meaningfully inform the substance and boundaries of the doctrines of private inurement and private benefit. Thus, a development in one of these three bodies of law is likely to directly affect the development of the other two. The intermediate sanctions rules probably will be invoked more frequently than revocation of tax-exempt status by application of the private inurement doctrine to public charities and social welfare organizations.[425]

The law concerning self-dealing in the private foundation context[426] also will be heavily interrelated with the intermediate sanctions rules. The very structure of these rules is, in many ways, patterned after the foundation rules. Of greater substance, however, is that a significant amount of the private foundation self-dealing law is directly usable in discerning the contours of the intermediate sanctions law. Likewise, a development in the intermediate sanctions area is likely to be applicable in the private foundation context.

Thus, as the years unfold, the law of tax-exempt organizations is going to be enriched by the process and outcomes resulting from the interrelationships and fertilization of the intermediate sanctions, private inurement, private benefit, and self-dealing rules.

---

[425] It is telling, nonetheless, that in the intermediate sanctions cases filed through mid-2002 (see *supra* notes 373 and 374), the IRS has proposed revocation of exemption, along with application of the sanctions, in all of them.
[426] See § 11.4(a).

CHAPTER TWENTY

Legislative Activities by Tax-Exempt Organizations

Tax policy and attempts to influence legislation have, at best, an uneasy relationship. Many criticize use of the tax system to "subsidize" lobbying; legislators often do not want to encourage the practice. This antipathy is reflected in the law of tax-exempt organizations, which, among other constraints, places limitations on the extent to which charitable organizations[1] can engage in lobbying and impedes

---

[1] That is, organizations described in IRC § 501(c)(3) and exempt from federal income taxation by reason of IRC § 501(a).

lobbying by membership associations[2] by curbing the deductibility of dues paid to them, yet encourages lobbying by veterans' organizations.[3]

At the federal level, there are seven discrete bodies of law that can pertain to attempts to influence legislation by tax-exempt organizations: two sets of rules applicable to public charities,[4] rules applicable to private foundations,[5] rules pertaining to membership associations,[6] law regulating attempts to influence legislation in the U.S. Congress,[7] law concerning lobbying by recipients of federal grants and similar payments,[8] and rules established by the Office of Management and Budget concerning the use of federal funds for lobbying by nonprofit organizations.[9] These various sets of rules contain law by which terms such as *legislation* and *influencing legislation* are defined, and costs associated with lobbying are ascertained. While there is considerable overlap as to the content of the rules, in several instances there are varied definitions of the concepts.[10]

Public charities may engage in legislative activities to the extent that lobbying is not a *substantial* part of their overall functions. The rules applicable to public charities are termed the *substantial part test* and the *expenditure test*. The essence of these tests is the basis by which substantiality in this context is measured. A charitable organization is subject to the substantial part test, unless the expenditure test is elected.

§ 20.1 MEANING OF *LEGISLATION*

A threshold concept in this setting is the meaning of the term *legislation*. In the law of tax-exempt organizations, there are three sources of law on the point.

(a) Substantial Part Test

The term *legislation*, as defined for purposes of the substantial part test, includes action by Congress, a state legislature, a local council or similar governing body,

---

[2] E.g., organization described in IRC § 501(c)(6) and exempt from federal income taxation by reason of IRC § 501(a). See Chapter 13.
[3] E.g., organizations described in IRC § 501(c)(19) and exempt from federal income taxation by reason of IRC § 501(a). See § 18.10(a).
[4] See *infra* §§ 2–4.
[5] See § 11.4(e).
[6] See *infra* § 6.
[7] 2 U.S.C. § 1601 et seq. (Lobbying Disclosure Act of 1995).
[8] 31 U.S.C. § 1352 (Byrd Amendment).
[9] Circular A-122, "Cost Principles for Nonprofit Organizations," 45 Fed. Reg. 46,022 (July 8, 1980), particularly Revised Transmittal Memorandum No. 2 (May 19, 1987).
[10] The General Accounting Office (GAO) studied the issue as to whether these various definitions of lobbying activities should be harmonized, in the interest of simplicity, uniformity, and consistency. In a report issued in 1999, the GAO, having observed that these different definitions reflect separate policy decisions made by Congress, recommended that these policies be revisited and carefully reconsidered before these laws are revised. This development substantially reduced the likelihood of any harmonization of these laws.

and the general public in a referendum, initiative, constitutional amendment, or similar procedure.[11]

Legislation generally does not include action by an executive branch of a government, such as the promulgation of rules and regulations, nor does it include action by independent regulatory agencies. Appropriations bills are items of legislation for federal tax purposes. Also, the term *legislation* includes proposals for the making of laws in countries other than the United States.[12]

It is the view of the IRS that an attempt to influence the confirmation, by the U.S. Senate, of a federal judicial nominee constitutes, for these purposes, an attempt to influence legislation.[13] This position is based upon the definition of the term *legislation* found in the expenditure test, where the term is defined to include resolutions and similar items.[14]

(b) Expenditure Test

The statute in connection with the expenditure test states that the term *legislation* includes "action with respect to Acts, bills, resolutions, or similar items by the Congress, any State legislature, any local council, or similar governing body, or by the public in a referendum, initiative, constitutional amendment, or similar procedure."[15]

The position of the IRS that an attempt to influence the confirmation, by the U.S. Senate, of a federal judicial nominee constitutes an attempt to influence legislation is reflected in the expenditure test, in examples in the regulations.[16]

(c) Associations' Dues Deductibility Test

The term *legislation*, as defined for purposes of the rules concerning the deductibility of associations' members' dues, means the same as is the case with respect to the expenditure test.[17] Thus, the term includes any action with respect to acts, bills, resolutions, or other similar items by a legislative body.[18] Also, legislation includes a "proposed treaty required to be submitted by the President to the Senate for its advice and consent from the time the President's representative begins to negotiate its position with the prospective parties to the proposed treaty."[19]

Because of the breadth of these rules,[20] however, legislative bodies are

---

[11] Reg. § 1.501(c)(3)-1(c)(3)(ii). Cf. Smith v. Commissioner, 3 T.C. 696 (1944).
[12] Rev. Rul. 73-440, 1973-2 C.B. 177.
[13] Notice 88-76, 1988-2 C.B. 392.
[14] IRC § 4911(e)(2).
[15] *Id*. Also Reg. § 56.4911-2(d)(1).
[16] Reg. § 56.4911-2(b)(4)(ii)(B), Example (6). Also Reg. § 53.4945-2(d)(2)(iii), Examples (5)–(7).
[17] IRC § 162(e)(4)(B).
[18] Reg. § 1.162-29(b)(4).
[19] *Id*.
[20] As discussed *infra* § 8(a), these rules encompass certain lobbying efforts with respect to the federal executive branch but do not apply with respect to direct lobbying in connection with local legislation.

"Congress, state legislatures, and other similar governing bodies, excluding local councils (and similar governing bodies), and executive, judicial, or administrative bodies."[21] The term *administrative bodies* includes "school boards, housing authorities, sewer and water districts, zoning boards, and other similar Federal, State, or local special purpose bodies, whether elective or appointive."[22]

§ 20.2 LOBBYING BY CHARITABLE ORGANIZATIONS

As noted, one of the criteria for qualification as a tax-exempt charitable organization is that "no substantial part of the activities" of the organization may constitute "carrying on propaganda, or otherwise attempting, to influence legislation."[23] It is irrelevant, for purposes of classification of an organization as a charitable entity under the federal tax law, that the legislation that is advocated or opposed would advance the charitable purposes for which the organization was created to promote."[24] This position should be contrasted with the state of the law prior to enactment of stautory law on the point in 1934.[25]

(a) Legislative History

The provision limiting the extent of lobbying by charitable organizations was added to the federal tax law in 1934, without benefit of congressional hearings, as the result of a floor amendment adopted by the Senate. During debate on the legislation that became the Revenue Act of 1934, Senator David A. Reed of Pennsylvania, on April 2, 1934, spoke to an amendment to restrict "partisan politics" and lobbying by charitable organizations. On that occasion, he stated that the purpose of the amendment was to prohibit tax exemption for "any organization that is receiving contributions, the proceeds of which are to be used for propaganda purposes or to try to influence legislation."[26] He said that the intent of the Committee on Finance, where the amendment originated, was to deny deductibility of a contribution as a charitable gift "if it is a selfish one made to advance the personal interests of the giver of the money."[27] Observing that he did "not reproach the draftsmen" inasmuch as "I think we gave them an impossible task," Senator Reed said that "this amendment goes much further than the committee intended

---

[21] Reg. § 1.162-29(b)(6).

[22] *Id.*

[23] IRC § 501(c)(3).

[24] Rev. Rul. 67-293, 1967-2 C.B. 185. Also Cammarano v. United States, 358 U.S. 498 (1959).

[25] There is nothing in the English common law of charity that prohibits a charitable organization from engaging in legislative activities. A federal court opinion, which sparked development of contemporary tax policy, held that charitable organizations may not engage in "[p]olitical agitation" (Slee v. Comm'r, 42 F.2d 184, 185 (2d Cir. 1930)).

[26] 78 *Cong. Rec.* 5861 (1934).

[27] *Id.*

to go."[28] He noted: "Mr. President, as that amendment is worded it would apply to the Society for the Prevention of Cruelty to Children, to the Society for the Prevention of Cruelty to Animals, or any of the worthy institutions that we do not in the slightest mean to affect."[29]

The Senate abandoned its consideration of the amendment that day and deferred it to later in the debate; on April 4, 1934, it was again taken up. At that time, Senator Byron P. Harrison of Mississippi observed that the intent of the Finance Committee was to stop deductible contributions for legislative ends.[30] Senator Reed stated that he did "not think that the committee is proud of the language in which this amendment is couched" and that the "legislative drafting counsel who drew it expressed no pride whatsoever in their product."[31] The amendment was nonetheless adopted; thereafter, Senator Reed said that "we will have from now until the conference to study the project and prepare better phraseology."[32] The language was indeed changed in conference, with deletion of the reference to "partisan politics," and the language enacted in that regard remains in the federal law today.

(b) Substantial Part Test

Although legislative activities take many forms, the federal tax law distinguishes between *direct* lobbying and indirect, or *grassroots*, lobbying. Direct lobbying includes the presentation of testimony at public hearings held by legislative committees, correspondence and conferences with legislators and their staffs, communications by electronic means, and publication of documents advocating specific legislative action. Grassroots lobbying consists of appeals to the general public or segments of the general public to contact legislators or take other specific action as regards legislative matters.[33]

An organization is regarded as attempting to influence legislation if it (1) contacts, or urges the public to contact, members of a legislative body for the purpose of proposing, supporting, or opposing legislation; or (2) advocates the adoption or rejection of legislation.[34] If a substantial part of an organization's activities is attempting to influence legislation, the organization is denominated an *action organization* and hence cannot qualify as a charitable entity.[35] For example, a fund was held to be an action organization on the ground that it

---

[28] *Id.*

[29] *Id.*

[30] 78 *Cong. Rec.* 5959 (1934).

[31] *Id.*

[32] *Id.*

[33] Roberts Dairy Co. v. Comm'r, 195 F.2d 948 (8th Cir. 1952), *cert. den.*, 344 U.S. 865 (1952); American Hardware & Equip. Co. v. Comm'r, 202 F.2d 126 (4th Cir. 1953), *cert. den.*, 346 U.S. 814 (1953). In certain circumstances, grassroots lobbying is also political campaign activity (e.g., Priv. Ltr. Rul. 9652026); see § 17.1(a), text accompanied by note 27.

[34] Reg. § 1.501(c)(3)-1(c)(3)(ii).

[35] See § 4.5(b). Also Reg. § 1.501(h)-1(a)(4).

functioned in a partisan manner as part of its efforts to further the cause of tax reform.[36]

For an organization to be denied or lose tax-exempt status because of lobbying activity, the legislative activity must be undertaken as an act of the organization itself. Thus, for example, the IRS recognized that the legislative activities of a student newspaper were not attributable to the sponsoring university.[37] Similarly, during the course of the anti-Vietnam war efforts on many college and university campuses, which included legislative activities, the principle was established that the activities by students and faculty were not official acts of the particular institutions.[38]

(c) Expenditure Test

Under the expenditure test, the definition of *legislation* includes the term *action*. The term *action* is "limited to the introduction, amendment, enactment, defeat, or repeal of Acts, bills, resolutions, or similar items."[39]

(i) Influencing Legislation. These rules define the term *influencing legislation* in two ways. One is any attempt to influence any legislation through communication with any member or employee of a legislative body[40] or with any other governmental official or employee who may participate in the formulation of the legislation (a *direct lobbying communication*).[41] The other is any attempt to influence any legislation through an attempt to affect the opinions of the general public or any segment of the public (a *grassroots lobbying communication*).[42]

A communication with a legislator or government official is a direct lobby-

---

[36] Fund for the Study of Economic Growth & Tax Reform v. Internal Revenue Service, 997 F. Supp. 15 (D.D.C. 1998), *aff'd*, 161 F.3d 755 (D.C. Cir. 1999). This appellate court opinion included a curious and oblique footnote (note 9, at 760). There the court observed that its holding in the case is "quite narrow." The court wrote that it was "not holding that any organization which studies an issue touching on legislation, reaches a conclusion with respect to that issue, and then argues the merits of that conclusion must necessarily be characterized" as an action organization. It continued: "We are simply holding that an organization which assumes a conclusion with respect to a highly public and controversial legislative issue and then goes into the business of selling that conclusion may properly be designated" an action organization.

[37] Rev. Rul. 72-513, 1972-2 C.B. 246.

[38] American Council on Education Guidelines, CCH Stand. Fed. Tax Rep. ¶ 3033.197. In general, Hopkins & Myers, "Governmental Response to Campus Unrest," 22 *Case W. Res. L. Rev.* 408 (1971); Broughton, "New Politics on the Campus, Reconstitution, The Princeton Plan," VI *The College Counsel* 119 (1971); Field, "Tax Exempt Status of Universities: Impact of Political Activities by Students," 24 *Tax Law.* 157 (1970); Goldberg, "Guarding Against Loss of Tax Exempt Status Due to Campus Politics," 33 *J. Tax.* 232 (1970); Note, "Taxation—University Political Activities and Federal Tax Exemption: American Council on Education Guidelines," 84 *Harv. L. Rev.* 463 (1970).

[39] IRC § 4911(e)(3); Reg. § 56.4911-2(d)(2).

[40] This term is defined in Reg. § 56.4911-2(d)(3).

[41] IRC § 4911(d)(1)(B); Reg. § 56.4911-2(b)(1)(i).

[42] IRC § 4911(d)(1)(A); Reg. § 56.4911-2(b)(2)(i).

ing communication only where the communication refers to *specific legislation* and reflects a view on the legislation.[43] Where a communication refers to and reflects a view on a measure that is the subject of a referendum, ballot initiative, or similar procedure, and is made to the members of the general public in the jurisdiction where the vote will occur, the communication is a direct lobbying communication (unless certain exceptions apply).[44]

A communication is regarded as a grassroots lobbying communication only where the communication refers to specific legislation, reflects a view on the legislation, and encourages the recipient of the communication to take action with respect to the legislation.[45] The phrase *encouraging the recipient to take action* with respect to legislation (also known as a *call to action*) means that the communication (1) states that the recipient should contact a legislator or an employee of a legislative body, or should contact any other government official or employee who may participate in the formulation of legislation (but only if the principal purpose of urging contact with the government official or employee is to influence legislation); (2) states the address, telephone number, or similar information of a legislator or an employee of a legislative body; (3) provides a petition, tear-off postcard, or similar material for the recipient to communicate with a legislator or an employee of a legislative body, or with any other government official or employee who may participate in the formulation of legislation (but only if the principal purpose of so facilitating contact with the government official or employee is to influence legislation); or (4) specifically identifies one or more legislators who will vote on the legislation as opposing the communication's view with respect to the legislation, being undecided with respect to the legislation, being the recipient's representative in the legislature, or being a member of the legislative committee or subcommittee that will consider the legislation.[46] The IRS considers this definition of a grassroots lobbying communication to be "very lenient," because it "will permit many clear advocacy communications to be treated as NONlobbying."[47]

The term *specific legislation* is defined as (1) legislation that has already been introduced in a legislative body and (2) a specific legislative proposal that the organization supports or opposes.[48] In the case of a referendum, ballot initiative, constitutional amendment, or other measure that is placed on the ballot

---

[43] Reg. § 56.4911-2(b)(1)(ii).

[44] Reg. § 56.4911-2(b)(1)(iii). This type of communication may be treated as nonpartisan analysis, study, or research (see text accompanied by *infra* note 114).

[45] Reg. § 56.4911-2(b)(2)(ii).

[46] Reg. § 56.4911-2(b)(2)(iii). A naming of the main sponsor(s) of the legislation for purposes of identifying it is not considered an encouragement of the recipient to take action (*id.*).

[47] 55 *Fed. Reg.* 35580 (Aug. 31, 1990) (emphasis in original). The IRS commentary on this definition adds: "This is part of the Service's attempt to maintain a careful balance between the statutory limits on electing public charities' lobbying expenditures and the desire of those organizations to involve themselves in the public policy making process to the greatest extent consistent with those statutory limits" (*id.*).

[48] Reg. § 56.4911-2(d)(1)(ii).

by petitions, an item becomes specific legislation when the petition is first circulated among the voters for signature.[49]

The regulations contain a rebuttable presumption that a *paid mass media advertisement*[50] is grassroots lobbying if it (1) is made within two weeks before a vote by a legislative body, or committee of a legislative body, on highly publicized legislation, (2) reflects a view on the general subject of the legislation, and (3) either refers to the legislation or encourages the public to communicate with legislators on the general subject of the legislation. The presumption is rebutted either by showing that the charitable organization regularly makes similar mass media communications without regard to the timing of legislation or that the timing of the communication was unrelated to the upcoming vote.[51]

Expenses incurred for nonlobbying communications can subsequently be characterized as grassroots lobbying expenditures where the materials or other communications are later used in a lobbying effort. For this result to occur, the materials must be *advocacy communications or research materials*, where the primary purpose of the organization in undertaking or preparing the communications or materials was for use in lobbying; in the case of subsequent distribution of the materials by another organization, there must be "clear and convincing" evidence of collusion between the two organizations to establish that the primary purpose for preparing the communication was for use in lobbying. In any event, this subsequent-use rule applies only to expenditures paid less than six months before the first use of the nonlobbying material in the lobbying campaign.[52]

A communication between an organization and any bona fide member of the organization made to directly encourage the member to engage in direct lobbying is itself considered direct lobbying.[53] A communication between an organization and any bona fide member of the organization made to directly encourage the member to urge persons other than members to engage in direct or grassroots lobbying is considered grassroots lobbying.[54]

A transfer is a grassroots expenditure to the extent it is earmarked[55] for grassroots lobbying purposes.[56] A transfer that is earmarked for direct lobbying purposes, or for direct lobbying and grassroots lobbying purposes, is regarded as a grassroots expenditure in full, unless the transferor can demonstrate that all or part of the amounts transferred were expended for direct lobbying purposes, in which case that part of the amounts transferred is a direct lobbying expenditure by the transferor.[57] There are rules for treating as a lobbying (direct or

[49] *Id.*
[50] Certain large-scale in-house publications and broadcasts are considered *paid mass media advertisements.*
[51] Reg. § 56.4911-2(b)(5).
[52] Reg. § 56.4911-2(b)(2)(v).
[53] IRC § 4911(d)(3)(A).
[54] IRC § 4911(d)(3)(B).
[55] Reg. § 56.4911-4(f)(4).
[56] Reg. § 56.4911-3(c)(1).
[57] Reg. § 56.4911-3(c)(2).

grassroots) expenditure transfers for less than fair market value from a public charity that has elected the expenditure test, to any noncharity that makes lobbying expenditures.[58]

(ii) Allocation Rules.   There are two allocation rules for communications that have a lobbying and a bona fide nonlobbying purpose.

One rule requires that the allocation be *reasonable*. This rule applies to an electing public charity's communications primarily with its bona fide members. More than one-half of the recipients of the communication must be members of the electing public charity for this rule to apply.[59]

The other allocation rule is for nonmembership communications. Where a nonmembership lobbying communication also has a bona fide nonlobbying purpose, an organization must include as lobbying expenditures all costs attributable to those parts of the communication that are on the same specific subject as the lobbying message. The rules define the phrase *same specific subject*.[60]

If a communication (other than to an organization's members) is both a direct lobbying communication and a grassroots lobbying communication, the communication is treated as a grassroots lobbying expenditure, unless the electing public charity demonstrates that the communication was made primarily for direct lobbying purposes, in which case a reasonable allocation is permitted.[61]

§ 20.3   MEASURING ALLOWABLE LOBBYING BY CHARITABLE ORGANIZATIONS

The rules concerning legislative activities by charitable organizations, other than private foundations, contain three essential elements: the meaning of the term *legislation*, the meaning of the term *influencing legislation*, and the concept of a *substantial* part of a charitable organization's activities.

(a) Substantial Part Test

A determination as to whether a specific activity or category of activities of a charitable organization is substantial basically is a factual one. Until enactment of the expenditure test,[62] the law did not offer any formula for computing substantial or insubstantial legislative undertakings. (It was once suggested that 5 percent of an organization's time and effort that involves legislative activities is not substantial.[63]) In reflection of this state of affairs, the Senate

---

[58] Reg. § 56.4911-3(c)(3).
[59] Reg. § 56.4911-3(a)(2)(ii).
[60] Reg. § 56.4911-3(a)(2)(i).
[61] Reg. § 56.4911-3(a)(3).
[62] See *infra* § (b).
[63] Seasongood v. Comm'r, 227 F.2d 907, 912 (6th Cir. 1955).

Finance Committee, in its report accompanying the Tax Reform Act of 1969, said that the "standards as to the permissible level of [legislative] activities under the present law are so vague as to encourage subjective application of the sanction."[64] In its report accompanying the Tax Reform Act of 1976, the Senate Finance Committee portrayed the dilemma this way: "Many believe that the standards as to the permissible level of [legislative] activities under present law are too vague and thereby tend to encourage subjective and selective enforcement."[65]

One approach to attempting to measure substantiality in this context is to determine what percentage of an organization's expenditures is devoted on an annual basis to efforts to influence legislation. Yet the limitation on influencing legislation involves more than simply a curb on spending or diversions of funds; it includes restrictions on levels of activity as well (expenditures of time). A portion of an organization's activities devoted to legislative pursuits may be regarded as more important than the organization's expenditures of funds for the purpose.[66] Indeed, particularly with the advent of lobbying by means of the Internet, in some circumstances, neither of these elements are particuarly relevant; the even more subjective factor of *influence* may have to be taken into consideration.[67]

Thus, a tax-exempt organization enjoying considerable prestige and influence might be considered as having a substantial impact on a legislative process solely on the basis of a single official position statement, an activity considered negligible when measured according to a percentage standard of time or money expended.[68] A standard such as this, however, tends to place undue emphasis on whether or not a particular legislative effort was successful, inasmuch as this evaluation is usually made on the basis of hindsight.[69]

In 1972, a federal court of appeals provided a new dimension to the concept of attempting to influence legislation, when it upheld the revocation of tax exemption of a ministry organization.[70] The court, after holding that the tax regulations properly interpreted the intent of Congress (before enactment of the expenditure test), found the following substantial legislative activities: articles constituting appeals to the public to react to certain issues, support or opposition to specific terms of legislation and enactments, and efforts to cause members of the public to contact members of Congress on various matters. Of particular consequence was the court's explicit rejection of a percentage test in determining substantiality, which was dismissed as obscuring the "complexity of balancing the organization's activ-

[64] S. Rep. No. 552, 91st Cong., 1st Sess. 47 (1969).
[65] S. Rep. No. 938 (Part 2), 94th Cong., 2d Sess. 80 (1976).
[66] League of Women Voters v. United States, 180 F. Supp. 379 (Ct. Cl. 1960), *cert. den.*, 364 U.S. 822 (1960).
[67] See *infra* § 10.
[68] Kuper v. Comm'r, 332 F.2d 562 (3d Cir. 1964), *cert. den.*, 379 U.S. 920 (1964).
[69] Haswell v. United States, 500 F.2d 1133, 1142 (Ct. Cl. 1974), *cert. den.*, 419 U.S. 1107 (1974); Dulles v. Johnson, 273 F.2d 362, 367 (2d Cir. 1959), *cert. den.*, 364 U.S. 834 (1960).
[70] Christian Echoes Nat'l Ministry, Inc. v. United States, 470 F.2d 849 (10th Cir. 1972), *cert. den.*, 414 U.S. 864 (1973).

ities in relation to its objectives and circumstances."[71] Said the court: "The political [i.e., legislative] activities of an organization must be balanced in the context of the objectives and circumstances of the organization to determine whether a substantial part of its activities was to influence or attempt to influence legislation."[72]

A subsequent court decision offered authority for the proposition that *substantiality* is not always measured by the factor of funds or time expended. The court observed, albeit reviewing the term in a different context,[73] that "[w]hether an activity is substantial is a facts-and-circumstances inquiry not always dependent upon time or expenditure percentages."[74]

(b) Expenditure Test

The expenditure test embodies a mechanical standard for measuring permissible and impermissible ranges of lobbying expenditures[75] by eligible charitable organizations, and does so in terms of the expenditure of funds and sliding scales of percentages. (The basic concept that legislative activities cannot be a substantial portion of the undertakings of a charitable organization was not altered by enactment of the expenditure test.)

These standards are formulated in terms of declining percentages of total *exempt purpose expenditures*.[76] In general, an expenditure is an exempt purpose expenditure for a tax year if it is paid or incurred by an electing public charity to accomplish the organization's exempt purposes.[77] These expenditures include (1) those expended for one or more charitable purposes, including most grants made for charitable ends; (2) amounts paid as compensation (current or deferred) of one or more employees in furtherance of a charitable purpose; (3) the portion of administrative expenses allocable to a charitable purpose; (4) lobbying expenditures; (5) amounts expended for nonpartisan analysis, study, or research;[78] (6) amounts expended for examinations of broad social, economic, and similar problems;[79] (7) amounts expended in response to requests for technical advice;[80] (8) amounts expended pursuant to the *self-defense exception*;[81] (9) amounts expended for communications to members that are not lobbying expenditures; (10) a reasonable allowance for straight-line depreciation or amortization of charitable assets;[82] and (11) certain fundraising expenditures.[83]

The term *exempt purpose* expenditure does not include (1) amounts ex-

---

[71] *Id.*, 470 F.2d at 855.

[72] *Id.*

[73] See § 7.2, particularly text accompanied by notes 22–47.

[74] The Nationalist Movement v. Comm'r, 102 T.C. 558, 589 (1994), *aff'd*, 37 F.3d 216 (5th Cir. 1994).

[75] IRC § 4911(c)(1); Reg. § 1.501(h)-3(c)(1).

[76] IRC § 4911(e)(1); Reg. § 56.4911-4(a).

[77] IRC § 4911(e)(1)(A).

[78] See *infra* § 4(b), text accompanied by note 114.

[79] See *infra* § 4(b), text accompanied by note 125.

[80] See *infra* § 4(b), text accompanied by note 115.

[81] See *infra* § 4(b), text accompanied by note 116.

[82] IRC § 4911(e)(4).

[83] IRC § 4911(e)(1)(B); Reg. § 56.4911-4(b). Cf. Reg. § 56.4911-3(a)(1).

pended that are not for purposes described in the preceding items (1) through (9), or (11); (2) the amount of transfers to members of an affiliated group,[84] made to artificially inflate the amount of exempt purpose expenditures, or to certain non-charitable organizations; (3) amounts paid to or incurred for a separate fundraising unit of the organization or an affiliated organization; (4) amounts paid to or incurred for any person that is not an employee or any organization that is not an affiliated organization, if paid primarily for fundraising, but only if the person or organization engages in fundraising, fundraising counseling, or the provision of similar advice or services; (5) amounts paid or incurred that are properly chargeable to a capital account with respect to an unrelated trade or business;[85] (6) amounts paid or incurred for a tax that is not imposed in connection with the organization's efforts to accomplish charitable purposes (such as the unrelated business income tax); and (7) amounts paid or incurred for the production of income, where the income-producing activity is not substantially related to exempt purposes (such as the costs of maintaining an endowment).[86]

For this purpose, the term *fundraising* embraces three practices: (1) the solicitation of dues or contributions from members of the organization, from persons whose dues are in arrears, or from the general public; (2) the solicitation of gifts from businesses or gifts or grants from other organizations, including charitable entities; or (3) the solicitation of grants from governmental units or any agency or instrumentality of the units.[87]

A *separate fundraising unit* of an organization "must consist of either two or more individuals a majority of whose time is spent on fundraising for the organization, or any separate accounting unit of the organization that is devoted to fundraising." In addition, "amounts paid to or incurred for a separate fundraising unit include all amounts incurred for the creation, production, copying, and distribution of the fundraising portion of a separate fundraising unit's communication."[88]

The basic permitted annual level of expenditures for legislative efforts (the *lobbying nontaxable amount*[89]) is determined by using a sliding scale percentage of the organization's exempt purpose expenditures, as follows: 20 percent of the first $500,000 of an organization's expenditures for an exempt purpose, plus 15 percent of the next $500,000, 10 percent of the next $500,000, and 5 percent of any remaining expenditures. These calculations generally are made on the basis of a four-year average.[90] The total amount spent for legislative activities in any one year by an eligible charitable organization may not exceed $1 million.[91] A sepa-

---

[84] See *infra* § 5(c).
[85] See Part Five.
[86] IRC § 4911(e)(1)(C); Reg. § 56.4911-4(c).
[87] Reg. § 56.4911-4(f)(1).
[88] Reg. § 56.4911-4(f)(2).
[89] Reg. §§ 1.501(h)-3(c)(2), 56.4911-1(c)(1).
[90] IRC § 501(h)(1). This averaging is used as the consequence of the word *normally*; the general measuring period is termed the *base years* (Reg. § 1.501(h)-3(c)(7)).
[91] IRC § 4911(c)(2); Reg. § 56.4911-1(c)(1).

rate limitation—amounting to 25 percent of the foregoing amounts—is imposed upon attempts to influence the general public on legislative matters[92] (the *grassroots nontaxable amount*).[93]

A charitable organization that has elected the expenditure test[94] and that exceeds either or both of these limitations becomes subject to an excise tax in the amount of 25 percent of the excess lobbying expenditures,[95] which tax falls on the greater of the two excesses.[96] If an electing organization's lobbying expenditures normally (that is, on an average over a four-year period[97]) exceed 150 percent of either limitation (the *lobbying ceiling amount*[98] and the *grassroots ceiling amount*[99]), it will lose its tax-exempt status as a charitable entity.[100] A charitable organization in this circumstance is not able to convert to a tax-exempt social welfare organization.[101]

§ 20.4 EXCEPTIONS TO FEDERAL TAX DEFINITION OF LOBBYING BY CHARITABLE ORGANIZATIONS

(a) Substantial Part Test

A charitable organization found to have engaged in legislative activities to a prohibited extent is deemed an action organization and thus is not entitled to continuing tax exemption.[102] Likewise, legislative activities may preclude tax exemption. One form of action organization is one as to which a "substantial part of its activities is attempting to influence legislation by propaganda or otherwise."[103] Another type of action organization is one as to which its "main or primary objective or objectives (as distinguished from its incidental or secondary objectives) may be attained only by legislation or a defeat of proposed legislation," and "it advocates, or campaigns for, the attainment of such main or primary objective or objectives as distinguished from engaging in nonpartisan analysis, study or research and making the results thereof available to the public."[104]

The IRS stated in 1970 that a charitable organization that does not initiate

---

[92] IRC § 4911(c)(3); Reg. §§ 56.4911-1(c)(2), 1.501(h)-3(c)(4).
[93] IRC § 4911(c)(4); Reg. §§ 1.501(h)-3(c)(5), 56.4911-1(c)(2).
[94] See *infra* § 5(a).
[95] IRC § 4911(a); Reg. §§ 56.4911-1(a), 1.501(h)-1(a)(3).
[96] IRC § 4911(b); Reg. § 56.4911-1(b).
[97] Reg. § 1.501(h)-3(c)(7).
[98] Reg. § 1.501(h)-3(c)(3).
[99] Reg. § 1.501(h)-3(c)(6).
[100] IRC §§ 501(h)(1), 501(h)(2); Reg. § 1.501(h)-3(b).
[101] IRC § 504; Reg. §§ 1.504-1, 1.504-2. See Chapter 12. Cf. Reg. § 1.501(c)(3)-1(c)(3)(v).
[102] See § 4.5(b).
[103] Reg. § 1.501(c)(3)-1(c)(3)(ii).
[104] Reg. § 1.501(c)(3)-1(c)(3)(iv). In general, McClintock-Trunkey Co. v. Comm'r, 19 T.C. 297 (1952), *rev'd on other issue*, 217 F.2d 329 (9th Cir. 1955).

any action with respect to pending legislation but merely responds to a request from a legislative committee to testify is not, solely because of this activity, an action organization.[105] The IRS observed that (1) proscribed attempts to influence legislation "imply an affirmative act and require something more than a mere passive response to a Committee invitation," and (2) "it is unlikely that Congress, in framing the language of this position [IRC § 501(c)(3)], intended to deny itself access to the best technical expertise available on any matter with which it concerns itself."[106]

An organization may engage in nonpartisan analysis, study, and research, and publish its results (that is, undertake activities that are educational in nature[107]), without being an action organization, as long as it does not advocate the adoption of legislation or legislative action to implement its findings.[108] That is, an organization may evaluate a subject of proposed legislation or a pending item of legislation and present to the public an objective analysis of it, as long as it does not participate in the presentation of one or more bills to a legislature and does not engage in any campaign to secure enactment of any proposals.[109] If, however, the organization's primary objective can be attained only by legislative action, it is an action organization.[110] In general, promoting activism instead of promoting educational activities can deny an organization classification as a charitable entity.[111]

As for the specific connotation of the term *propaganda*, the term is not as expansive as merely spreading particular beliefs, opinions, or doctrines. Rather, the word "connotes public address with selfish or ulterior purpose and characterized by the coloring or distortion of facts."[112] To avoid stigmatization as propaganda, therefore, a presentation must be fairly well balanced as to stating alternative viewpoints and solutions, and be motivated more by a purpose to educate than by a "selfish" purpose.[113]

(b) Expenditure Test

Five categories of activities are excluded by statute from the term *influencing legislation* for purposes of the expenditure test: (1) making available the results of nonpartisan analysis, study, or research;[114] (2) providing technical advice or

---

[105] Rev. Rul. 70-449, 1970-2 C.B. 111.

[106] Curtis, "The House Committee on Ways and Means: Congress Seen Through a Key Committee," 1966 *Wis. L. Rev.* 121, 132 (1966).

[107] See Chapter 7.

[108] Reg. § 1.501(c)(3)-1(c)(3)(iv); Weyl v. Comm'r, 48 F.2d 811 (2d Cir. 1931); Rev. Rul. 70-79, 1970-1 C.B. 127.

[109] Rev. Rul. 64-195, 1964-2 C.B. 138; I. T. 2654, Xi-2 C.B. 39 (1932).

[110] Fund for the Study of Economic Growth & Tax Reform v. Internal Revenue Service, *supra* note 36; Haswell v. United States, *supra* note 69, at 1143-1145; Rev. Rul. 62-71, 1962-1 C.B. 85.

[111] Rev. Rul. 60-193, 1960-1 C.B. 195, as modified by Rev. Rul. 66-258, 1966-2 C.B. 213.

[112] Seasongood v. Comm'r, *supra* note 63, at 910-912. Also Cochran v. Comm'r, 78 F.2d 176, 179 (4th Cir. 1935).

[113] Rev. Rul. 68-263, 1968-1 C.B. 256. In general, see § 7.2.

[114] IRC § 4911(d)(2)(A); Reg. § 56.4911-2(c)(1). See text accompanied by *supra* notes 107-111.

assistance to a governmental body or legislative committee in response to a written request by that body or committee;[115] (3) appearances before or communications to any legislative body with respect to a possible decision of that body that might affect the existence of the organization, its powers and duties, its tax-exempt status, or the deduction of contributions to it (the *self-defense exception*);[116] (4) communications between the organization and its bona fide members[117] with respect to legislation or proposed legislation of direct interest to it and them, unless the communications directly encourage the members to influence legislation or directly encourage the members to urge nonmembers to influence legislation;[118] and (5) routine communications with government officials or employees.[119]

In amplification of the fourth exception, expenditures for a communication that refers to, and reflects a view on, specific legislation are not lobbying expenditures if the communication satisfies the following requirements: (1) the communication is directed only to members of the organization; (2) the specific legislation the communication refers to, and reflects a view on, is of direct interest to the organization and its members; (3) the communication does not directly encourage the member to engage in direct lobbying;[120] and (4) the communication does not directly encourage the member to engage in grassroots lobbying.[121] An expenditure that meets all of these requirements, other than the third one, is treated as an expenditure for direct lobbying.[122] An expenditure that satisfies all of these requirements, other than the fourth one, is treated as an expenditure for grassroots lobbying.[123] The regulations provide rules for treatment, as expenditures for direct or grassroots lobbying, expenditures for any written communication that is designed primarily for members of an organization, and that refers to, and reflects a view on, specific legislation of direct interest to the organization and its members.[124]

The regulations create a sixth exception, excusing examinations and discussions of broad social, economic, and similar problems from the ambit of direct lobbying communications and grassroots lobbying communications, even if the problems are of the type with which government would be expected to deal ultimately.[125]

---

[115] IRC § 4911(d)(2)(B); Reg. § 56.4911-2(c)(3).
[116] IRC § 4911(d)(2)(C); Reg. § 56.4911-2(c)(4).
[117] Reg. §§ 56.4911-5(f)(1)-(4).
[118] IRC § 4911(d)(2)(D).
[119] IRC § 4911(d)(2)(E).
[120] Reg. § 56.4911-5(f)(6).
[121] Reg. § 56.4911-5(b).
[122] Reg. § 56.4911-5(c).
[123] Reg. § 56.4911-5(d).
[124] Reg. § 56.4911-5(e).
[125] Reg. § 56.4911-2(c)(2).

§ 20.5 OTHER ASPECTS OF THE EXPENDITURE TEST

Previous sections of this analysis contain summaries of various aspects of the expenditure test. There are, however, additional elements of this test.

(a) Election of Test

An eligible charitable organization[126] that desires to avail itself of the expenditure test must elect to come within these standards; it can do so on a year-to-year basis.[127] Charitable organizations that may not or that choose to not make the election are governed by the substantial part test.[128] Churches, conventions or associations of churches, integrated auxiliaries of churches, certain supporting organizations of noncharitable entities,[129] and private foundations may not elect to come under these rules[130]—foundations being subject to more stringent regulation in this regard.[131]

If a charitable organization has its tax exemption revoked by reason of the expenditure test and thereafter is again recognized as an exempt charitable organization, it may again elect the expenditure test.[132]

(b) Record Keeping

A public charity that is under the expenditure test must keep a record of its lobbying expenditures. These records must include (1) expenditures for grassroots lobbying, (2) amounts paid for direct lobbying, (3) the portion of amounts paid or incurred as compensation for an employee's services for direct lobbying, (4) amounts paid for out-of-pocket expenditures incurred on behalf of the organization and for direct lobbying, (5) the allocable portion of administration, overhead, and other general expenditures attributable to direct lobbying, (6) expenditures for publications or for communications with members to the extent the expenditures are treated as expenditures for direct lobbying, and (7) expenditures for direct lobbying of a controlled organization[133] to the extent included by a controlling organization[134] in its lobbying expenditures.[135] Identical record keeping requirements apply with respect to grassroots expenditures.[136]

---

[126] Reg. §§ 1.501(h)-2(b), 1.501(h)-2(e).
[127] IRC §§ 501(h)(3), 501(h)(4), 1.501(h)(6). This election, and any revocation or reelection of it, is made by filing Form 5768 with the IRS. Reg. §§ 1.501(h)-2(a), 1.501(h)-2(c), 1.501(h)-2(d).
[128] Reg. § 1.501(h)-1(a)(4).
[129] See § 11.3(c).
[130] IRC § 501(h)(5).
[131] IRC § 4945(d)(1), (e). See Chapter 11.
[132] Reg. § 1.501(h)-3(d)(4).
[133] Reg. § 56.4911-10(c).
[134] Id.
[135] Reg. § 56.4911-6(a).
[136] Reg. § 56.4911-6(b).

(c) Affiliated Organizations

The expenditure test contains methods of aggregating the expenditures of related organizations, so as to forestall the creation of numerous organizations for the purpose of avoiding the limitations of the expenditure test. Where two or more charitable organizations are members of an affiliated group[137] and at least one of the members has elected coverage under the expenditure test, the calculations of lobbying and exempt purpose expenditures must be made by taking into account the expenditures of the group.[138] If these expenditures exceed the permitted limits, each of the electing member organizations must pay a proportionate share of the penalty excise tax, with the nonelecting members treated under the substantial part test.[139]

Generally, under these rules, two organizations are deemed *affiliated* where (1) one organization is bound by decisions of the other on legislative issues pursuant to its governing instrument,[140] or (2) the governing board of one organization includes enough representatives of the other (an *interlocking governing board*[141]) to cause or prevent action on legislative issues[142] by the first organization.[143] Where a number of organizations are affiliated, even in chain fashion, all of them are treated as one group of affiliated organizations.[144] If a group of autonomous organizations controls an organization but no one organization in the controlling group alone can control that organization, however, the organizations are not an affiliated group by reason of the interlocking directorates rule.[145]

(d) Reporting

The required contents of annual information returns filed by tax-exempt organizations[146] include portions designed to make information about the legislative activities of electing charitable organizations accessible to the public. Thus, an organization subject to the expenditure test must disclose in its information return the amount of its lobbying expenditures (total and grassroots), together with the amount that it could have spent for legislative purposes without becoming subject to the 25 percent excise tax. An electing organization that is a member of an affiliated group must provide this information with respect to both itself and the entire group.[147]

---

[137] Reg. § 56.4911-7(e).
[138] IRC § 4911(f)(1); Reg. §§ 56.4911-8, 56.4911-10.
[139] IRC § 4911(f)(1)(B).
[140] Reg. § 56.4911-7(c).
[141] Reg. § 56.4911-7(b).
[142] Reg. § 56.4911-7(a)(3).
[143] IRC § 4911(f)(2); Reg. § 56.4911-7(a)(1).
[144] Reg. § 56.4911-7(d).
[145] IRC § 4911-(f)(3).
[146] See § 24.3(a).
[147] IRC § 6033(b)(8).

(e) Timing of the Election

Consequently, a charitable organization (that is not a private foundation) may attempt to influence a legislative process as long as the organization stays within the bounds of insubstantiality. Thus, a charitable organization desiring to engage in attempts to influence legislation must, in assessing the basis for insubstantiality, decide whether to utilize the substantial part test or elect the expenditure test, and must determine whether one or more exceptions provided by either test are available. In an optimum situation, a charitable organization can expend 20 percent or more of its total expenditures on attempts to influence legislation.[148]

There are many variables a charitable organization should consider when deciding whether to elect the expenditure test. For example, a charitable organization that seeks to engage entirely in grassroots lobbying is undoubtedly best advised to not make the election, because the limitation on that type of lobbying is probably more stringent under the expenditure test than under the substantial part test. Other factors to consider are these: (1) the relative certainty as to allowable lobbying afforded by the expenditure test, (2) the possibility that the IRS may enforce the substantial part test using one or more standards other than the volume of legislative activity, (3) the fact that the time expended by volunteers for lobbying is taken into account for purposes of the substantial part test and is disregarded for purposes of the expenditure test, (4) the fact that lobbying is assessed annually pursuant to the substantial part test and over a four-year average under the expenditure test, (5) the potential impact of the affiliation rules in the expenditure test, (6) the additional reporting responsibilities imposed by the expenditure test, (7) the potential of applicability of the taxes that may be imposed in instances of substantial lobbying,[149] (8) the fact that a public charity that has elected the expenditure test may satisfy its requirement to report lobbying activities to Congress using the definition of lobbying under the test,[150] and (9) the fact that a public charity that has elected the expenditure test may satisfy its requirement to report lobbying expenses to Congress by filing a copy of the schedule[151] to the entity's annual information return.[152]

---

[148] Presumably, a 20 percent lobbying expenditure, allowed by the expenditure test, is greater than what would be allowed under the substantial part test. Whether lobbying can exceed 20 percent in any one year (disregarding the expenditure test's averaging rule), without adversely affecting a charitable organization's tax-exempt status, will essentially depend upon the availability and use of one or more of the exceptions from the limitation.

[149] See *infra* § 6.

[150] Lobbying Disclosure Act of 1995, *supra* note 7 ("Act") § 1610(a)(2).

[151] See § 24.3(a).

[152] Act § 1610(c)(1). In making its good faith estimate of lobbying expenditures as required by the Act, this type of public charity may use the amounts reported under the expenditure test reporting requirements (*id.* § 1610(a)(1)). An organization that has elected to use tax law information for Act reporting purposes must inform the Secretary of the Senate and the Clerk of the House of that fact; all estimates for a year must be made under the elected procedures (*id.* § 1610(c)(2)).

Moreover, a charitable organization, remaining under the substantial part test, desiring to engage in a substantial amount of lobbying can convert to a social welfare organization[153] to pursue those activities.[154]

§ 20.6   LOBBYING EXPENDITURES BY CHARITABLE ORGANIZATIONS AND TAX SANCTIONS

If a charitable organization, otherwise tax-exempt, that has not elected to come under the expenditure test or that is ineligible to make the election, fails to meet the federal tax law requirements for exemption because of attempts to influence legislation, a tax in the amount of 5 percent of the lobbying expenditures may be imposed, for each year involved, on the organization.[155] A *lobbying expenditure* is an amount paid or incurred by a charitable organization in carrying on propaganda or otherwise attempting to influence legislation.[156]

A separate tax is applicable to each of the organization's managers (basically, its officers and directors) who agreed to the making of the lobbying expenditures (knowing that they were likely to result in revocation of the organization's tax exemption), unless the agreement was not willful and was due to reasonable cause.[157] This tax is also an amount equal to 5 percent of the lobbying expenditures and can be imposed only where the tax on the organization is imposed.

§ 20.7   LOBBYING BY SOCIAL WELFARE ORGANIZATIONS

There are no federal tax law limitations on attempts to influence legislation by tax-exempt social welfare organizations, other than the general requirement that

---

[153] See Chapter 12.

[154] In general, Kusma & Jackson, "Lobbying By Exempt Organizations: A Realistic Alternative to the 'Substantial Part' Test," 69 *Taxes* (No. 7) 422 (July 1991); Bouchillon, "Guiding Lobbying Charities into a Safe Harbor: Final Section 501(h) and 4911 Regulations Set Limits for Tax-Exempt Organizations," 61 *Miss. L. J.* 157 (Spring 1991); Troyer, Slocombe & Mallon, "Final Lobbying Regulations Provide Workable Guidance," 74 *J. Tax.* (No. 2) 124 (1991); McGovern, Accettura & Walsh Skelly, "The Final Lobbying Regulations: A Challenge for Both the IRS and Charities," 48 *Tax Notes* (No. 10) 1305 (1990); Asher & Fountain, "Lobbying by Public Charities—Living With (or Without) the New IRS Regulations," 3 *Exempt Org. Tax Rev.* (No. 11) 1261 (1991); Asher & Fountain, "Lobbying by Public Charities—Living With (or Without) the New IRS Regulations," 3 *Exempt Org. Tax Rev.* (No. 9) 1011 (1991); Murdich, "The Final Lobbying Regulations—Finally," 2 *J. Tax. Exempt Orgs.* 23 (Fall 1990); Hallenberg & Murdich, "A Second Look at the Second Set of Lobbying Regulations," 1 *J. Tax Exempt Orgs.* 29 (Winter 1990).

[155] IRC § 4912(a).

[156] IRC § 4912(d)(1).

[157] IRC § 4912(b). The burden of proof as to whether a manager knowingly participated in the lobbying expenditure is on the IRS and the fact that the excise tax is imposed on an organization does not itself establish that any manager of the organization is subject to the excise tax (H. Rep. 495, 100th Cong., 1st Sess. 1024 (1987)).

the organization must primarily engage in efforts to promote social welfare.[158] In other words, a social welfare organization can be what a charitable organization cannot be—an action organization.[159]

Thus, a tax-exempt social welfare organization may draft legislation, present petitions for the purpose of having legislation introduced, and circulate speeches, reprints, and other material concerning legislation.[160] This type of organization may appear before a federal or state legislative body, or a local council, administrative board or commission, and may encourage members of the community to contact legislative representatives in support of its programs.[161]

The IRS ruled that a tax-exempt social welfare organization can operate to inform the public on controversial subjects, "even though the organization advocates a particular viewpoint."[162] The agency noted that "seeking of legislation germane to the organization's program is recognized by the regulations . . . as permissible means of attaining social welfare purposes."[163] Offering a rationale for allowing a tax-exempt social welfare organization to engage in legislative activities, the IRS stated: "The education of the public on [controversial subjects] is deemed beneficial to the community because society benefits from an informed citizenry."[164] Likewise, the IRS extended exempt status as a charitable entity to an organization formed to educate the public on the subject of abortions, promote the rights of the unborn, and support legislative and constitutional changes to restrict women's access to abortions, recognizing that the organization "advocates objectives that are controversial."[165]

Similarly, an organization that engaged in attempts to influence legislation intended to benefit animals, animal owners, persons interested in the welfare of animals, and the community at large was considered a tax-exempt social welfare organization, although it was denied tax-exempt status as a charitable entity (as an organization operated for the prevention of cruelty to animals) because it was deemed to be an action organization.[166]

§ 20.8   LOBBYING BY ASSOCIATIONS

There is no restriction, from the standpoint of the tax exemption for membership associations and other business leagues, on the amount of legislative activity these organizations may conduct. Indeed, the IRS recognized attempts to influence legislation as a valid function for a tax-exempt business league.[167]

---

[158] See § 4.4.
[159] See §§ 4.5(b), 12.3.
[160] Rev. Rul. 68-656, 1968-2 C.B. 216.
[161] Rev. Rul. 67-6, 1967-1 C.B. 135.
[162] Rev. Rul. 68-656, *supra* note 160, at 216.
[163] *Id.* at 216-217.
[164] *Id.* at 216.
[165] Rev. Rul. 76-81, 1976-1 C.B. 156.
[166] Rev. Rul. 67-293, 1967-2 C.B. 185.
[167] Rev. Rul. 61-177, 1961-2 C.B. 117.

The federal tax law rules stringently restricting the deductibility of business expenses for legislative activities[168] have, however, meaningful consequences in this context, in that they can operate as an indirect limitation on lobbying activities by business leagues. The inability to fully deduct membership dues may have an impact on the extent of an association's membership.

(a) General Business Expense Deduction Disallowance Rules

Under these rules, generally there is no business expense deduction for any amount paid or incurred in connection with influencing legislation (whether by direct or grass roots lobbying); any attempt to influence the general public, or segments of it, with respect to legislative matters or referendums; or any direct communication with a covered executive branch official in an attempt to influence the official actions or positions of the official.[169] This deduction disallowance rule, however, basically does not apply to local legislation[170] or with respect to Indian tribal governments.[171]

In this setting, *influencing legislation* means (1) any attempt to influence legislation through a lobbying communication and (2) all activities, such as research, preparation, planning, and coordination, including deciding whether to make a lobbying communication, engaged in for a purpose of making or supporting a lobbying communication, even if not yet made.[172] A *lobbying communication* is any communication (other than one compelled by subpoena or otherwise compelled by federal or state law) with any member or employee of a legislative body or any other government official or employee who may participate in the formulation of the legislation[173] that (1) refers to specific legislation and reflects a view on that legislation or (2) clarifies, amplifies, modifies, or provides support for views reflected in a prior lobbying communication.[174] The term *specific legislation* includes a specific legislative proposal that has not been introduced in a legislative body.[175]

Covered executive branch official describes the President, the Vice President, any officer or employee of the White House Office of the Executive Office of the President, the two most senior-level officers of each of the other agencies within the Executive Office of the President, any individual serving in a position in level I of the Executive Schedule (for example, a member of the Cabinet),[176] any

---

[168] IRC § 162(e).

[169] IRC § 162(e)(1)(A), (C), (D). These rules apply with respect to expenses paid or incurred beginning in 1994. Thus, the tax regulations reflecting prior law (Reg. § 1.162-20(c)(1)–(3)) are, with two exceptions (see *infra* notes 170 and 171), no longer operational.

[170] IRC § 162(e)(2). The regulations developed under prior law (Reg. § 1.162-20) generally are pertinent to the costs of lobbying in connection with local legislation.

[171] IRC § 162(e)(7).

[172] Reg. § 1.162-29(b)(1).

[173] The term *legislation* is the subject of *supra* § 1(c).

[174] IRC § 162(e)(4)(A); Reg. § 1.162-29(b)(3).

[175] Reg. § 1.162-29(b)(5).

[176] 5 U.S.C. § 5312.

other individual designated by the President as having Cabinet-level status, and an immediate deputy of an individual in the preceding two categories.[177]

The purposes for engaging in an activity are determined on the basis of all the facts and circumstances, including whether the activity and the lobbying communication are proximate in time; the activity and the lobbying communication relate to similar subject matter; the activity is performed at the request of, under the direction of, or on behalf of a person making the lobbying communication; the results of the activity are also used for a nonlobbying purpose; and, at the time the person engages in the activity, there is specific legislation to which the activity relates.[178] In instances of activities involving lobbying and nonlobbying purposes, costs must be allocated.[179] Certain activities, such as determining the status of legislation or summarizing legislation, do not constitute lobbying.[180]

Any amount paid or incurred for research for, or preparation, planning, or coordination of, any lobbying activity subject to the general disallowance rule is treated as paid or incurred in connection with the lobbying activity.[181] The intent of this rule is to convert what might otherwise be a function constituting nonpartisan analysis, study, or research[182] into a lobbying undertaking where the research is subsequently used in an attempt to influence legislation. It is not clear how this rule is to be applied where the research is performed by one organization and the lobbying using that research is done by another, particularly where the two organizations are related.[183]

There is a *de minimis* exception for certain in-house expenditures where the organization's total amount of these expenditures for a tax year does not exceed $2,000 (computed without taking into account general overhead costs otherwise allocable to most forms of lobbying).[184] The term *in-house expenditures* means expenditures for lobbying (such as labor and materials costs) other than payments to a professional lobbyist to conduct lobbying for the organization and dues or other similar payments that are allocable to lobbying (such as association dues).[185]

An organization, although able to use any reasonable method of allocation of labor costs and general and administrative costs to lobbying activities, is authorized to use a *ratio method*, a *gross-up method*, or tax rules concerning allocation of service costs.[186] An organization may disregard time spent by an individual on lobbying activities if less than 5 percent of his or her time was so spent, although

---

[177] IRC § 162(e)(6).
[178] Reg. § 1.162-29(c)(1).
[179] Reg. § 1.162-29(c)(2). See text accompanied by *infra* note 186.
[180] Reg. § 1.162-29(c)(3).
[181] IRC § 162(e)(5)(C).
[182] See *supra* § 4(a), text accompanied by notes 107–111; § 4(b), text accompanied by note 114.
[183] See, by contrast, *supra* § 2(c)(i), text accompanied by note 52.
[184] IRC § 162(e)(5)(B)(i).
[185] IRC § 162(e)(5)(B)(ii).
[186] Reg. § 1.162-28(a)–(f). The third of these methods is the subject of IRC § 263A.

this de minimis test is not applicable with respect to *direct contact lobbying*, which is a meeting, telephone conversation, letter, or other similar means of communication with a federal or state legislator or a covered executive branch official and which otherwise qualifies as a lobbying activity.[187]

Other than a general exclusion for charitable organizations, there are no specific statutory exceptions to these rules. As noted, however, any communication compelled by subpoena, or otherwise compelled by federal or state law, does not constitute an attempt to influence legislation or an official's actions.[188]

A provision prevents a cascading of the lobbying expense disallowance rule to ensure that, when multiple parties are involved, the rule results in the denial of a deduction at only one level. Thus, in the case of an individual engaged in the trade or business of providing lobbying services or an individual who is an employee and receives employer reimbursements for lobbying expenses, the disallowance rule does not apply to expenditures of the individual in conducting the activities directly on behalf of a client or employer. Instead, the lobbying payments made by the client or employer to the lobbyist or employee are nondeductible under the general disallowance rule.[189]

This anticascading rule applies where there is a direct, one-on-one relationship between the taxpayer and the entity conducting the lobbying activity, such as a client or employment relationship. It does not apply to dues or other payments to membership organizations that act to further the interests of all of their members rather than the interests of any one particular member. These organizations are themselves subject to the general disallowance rule, based on the amount of their lobbying expenditures.[190]

There is an antiavoidance rule designed to prevent donors from using charitable organizations[191] as conduits to conduct lobbying activities, the costs of which would be nondeductible if conducted directly by the donor. That is, no deduction is allowed as a charitable contribution deduction (nor as a business expense deduction) for amounts contributed to a charitable organization if (1) the charitable organization's lobbying activities regard matters of direct financial interest to the donor's trade or business, and (2) a principal purpose of the contribution is to avoid the general disallowance rule that would apply if the contributor directly had conducted the lobbying activities.[192] The application of this anti-avoidance rule to a contributor would not adversely affect the tax-exempt status of the charitable organization as long as the activity qualified as nonpartisan analysis, study, or research[193] or was not substantial under either the sub-

---

[187] Reg. § 1.162-28(g). In general, Pecarich & Primosch, "Final Lobbying Regs. Ease the Tracking of Expenses, but Some Definitions Remain Vague," 83 *J. Tax.* (No. 5) 261 (Nov. 1995).

[188] See *supra* note 174. Also H. Rep. 213, 103d Cong., 1st Sess. 607 (1993).

[189] IRC § 162(e)(5)(A).

[190] H. Rep. 213, *supra* note 188, at 610.

[191] See Part Two.

[192] IRC § 170(f)(9).

[193] See *supra* § 4(a), text accompanied by notes 107–109; § 4(b), text accompanied by note 114.

stantial part test or the expenditure test[194] of the rules limiting the legislative activities of charitable organizations.[195]

The determination regarding a *principal* purpose of the contribution is to be based on the facts and circumstances surrounding the contribution, including the existence of any formal or informal instructions relating to the charitable organization's use of the contribution for lobbying efforts (including nonpartisan analysis), the "temporal nexus" between the making of the contribution and the conduct of the lobbying activities, and any historical pattern of contributions by the donor to the charity.[196]

(b) Association Flow-Through and Proxy Tax Rules

A flow-through rule applicable with respect to membership associations disallows a business expense deduction for the portion of the membership dues (or voluntary payments or special assessments) paid to a tax-exempt organization that engages in lobbying activities.[197] Trade, business, and professional associations, and similar organizations, generally are required to provide annual information disclosure to their members, estimating the portion of their dues that is allocable to lobbying and thus nondeductible.

The organization must disclose in its annual information return both the total amount of its lobbying expenditures and the total amount of dues (or similar payments) allocable to these expenditures.[198] For this purpose, an organization's lobbying expenditures for a taxable year are allocated to the dues received during the taxable year.[199] Any excess amount of lobbying expenditures is carried forward and allocated to dues received in the following taxable year.[200]

---

[194] See *supra* §§ 1–6. There are exemptions for these four categories of organizations based on refinements of the 90-percent-of-dues test; organizations can avail themselves of this exemption by satisfying record-keeping and annual return filing requirements or by obtaining a private letter ruling from the IRS on the point. For example, social welfare organizations, and agricultural and horticultural organizations, are treated as satisfying the exemption requirements if either (1) more than 90 percent of all annual dues are received from persons who each pay less than $50 or (2) more than 90 percent of all annual dues are received from certain tax-exempt entities. (This $50 amount is indexed for inflation; for tax years beginning in 1998, the amount is $71 (Rev. Proc. 97-57, 1997-2 C.B. 584); for tax years beginning in 1999, the amount is $72 (Rev. Proc. 98-61, 1998-2 C.B. 811); for tax years beginning in 2000, the amount is $74 (Rev. Proc. 99-42, 1999-2 C.B. 568); for tax years beginning in 2001, the amount is $76 (Rev. Proc. 2001-13, 2001-1 C.B. 337); for tax years beginning in 2002, the amount is $79 (Rev. Proc. 2001-59, 2001-52 I.R.B. 623); and for tax years beginning in 2003, the amount is $80 (Rev. Proc. 2002-70, 2002-46 I.R.B. 845).) The IRS occasionally issues rulings as to the availability of the exemption (e.g., Priv. Ltr. Rul. 9429016).
[195] H. Rep. 213, *supra* note 188, at 610, note 70.
[196] *Id.* at 610.
[197] IRC § 162(e)(3).
[198] IRC § 6033(e)(1)(A)(i). An organization that is subject to these rules may satisfy its requirement to report lobbying activities to Congress using the definition of lobbying under these rules and may satisfy its requirement to report lobbying expenses to Congress by using the amounts that are nondeductible under these rules (Lobbying Disclosure Act of 1995, *supra* note 7 § 1610(b)).
[199] IRC § 6033(e)(1)(C)(i).
[200] IRC § 6033(e)(1)(c)(ii).

The organization also is generally required to provide notice to each person paying dues (or similar payments), at the time of assessment or payment of the dues, of the portion of dues that the organization reasonably estimates will be allocable to the organization's lobbying expenditures during the year and that is, therefore, not deductible by the member.[201] This estimate must be reasonably calculated to provide organization members with adequate notice of the nondeductible amount. The notice must be provided in conspicuous and easily recognizable format.[202] These requirements of annual disclosure and notice to members are applicable to all tax-exempt organizations other than those that are charitable entities.[203]

If an organization's actual lobbying expenditures for a tax year exceed the estimated allocable amount of the expenditures (either because of higher-than-anticipated lobbying expenses or lower-than-projected dues receipts), the organization must pay a *proxy tax* on the excess amount[204] or seek permission from the IRS to adjust the following year's notice of estimated expenditures.[205] The proxy tax rate is equal to the highest corporate tax rate in effect for the taxable year;[206] the highest corporate tax rate is 35 percent.[207] If an organization does not provide its members with reasonable notice of anticipated lobbying expenditures allocable to dues, the organization is subject to the proxy tax on its aggregate lobbying expenditures for the year.

If an organization elects to pay the proxy tax rather than provide the requisite information disclosure to its members, no portion of any dues or other payments made by members of the organization is rendered nondeductible because of the organization's lobbying activities. That is, if the organization pays the tax, the dues payments are fully deductible by the members as business expenses (assuming they otherwise qualify).

This disclosure and notice element is not required, however, in the case of an organization that (1) incurs only *de minimis* amounts of in-house lobbying expenditures, (2) elects to pay the proxy tax on its lobbying expenditures incurred during the tax year,[208] or (3) establishes, pursuant to an IRS regulation or procedure, that substantially all of its dues monies are paid by members who are not entitled to deduct the dues in computing their taxable income. The concept of *de minimis* in-house expenditures in this setting is the same as that in the disallowance rules (including the $2,000 maximum).[209] Amounts paid to outside

---

[201] IRC § 6033(e)(1)(A)(ii).
[202] H. Rep. 213, *supra* note 188, at 608, note 65. As to the standard of "conspicuous and easily recognizable," the IRC § 6113 rules are used (see § 22.2).
[203] IRC § 6033(e)(1)(B). The term *charitable* in this context means all organizations that are tax-exempt by reason of IRC § 501(c)(3).
[204] IRC § 6033(e)(2)(A)(ii).
[205] IRC § 6033(e)(2)(B).
[206] IRC § 6033(e)(2)(A).
[207] IRC § 11.
[208] IRC § 6033(e)(2)(A)(i).
[209] IRC § 6033(e)(1)(B)(ii). See the text accompanied by *supra* note 184.

lobbyists, or as dues to another organization that lobbies, do not qualify for this exception.

Regarding this third component, if an organization establishes, to the satisfaction of the IRS, that substantially all of the dues monies it receives are paid by members who are not entitled to deduct their dues in any event (and obtains a waiver from the IRS), the organization is not subject to the disclosure and notice requirements (or the proxy tax).[210] In this context, the term *substantially all* means at least 90 percent.[211] Examples of organizations of this nature are (1) an organization that receives at least 90 percent of its dues monies from members that are tax-exempt charitable organizations; and (2) an organization that receives at least 90 percent of its dues monies from members who are individuals not entitled to deduct the dues payments because the payments are not ordinary and necessary business expenses.[212] Indeed, by IRS pronouncement,[213] there is a complete exemption from the reporting and notice requirements (and proxy tax) for all tax-exempt organizations, other than social welfare organizations that are not veterans' organizations;[214] agricultural organizations;[215] horticultural organizations;[216] and trade, business, and professional associations, other business leagues, chambers of commerce, and boards of trade.[217]

If the amount of lobbying expenditures exceeds the amount of dues or other similar payments for the taxable year, the proxy tax is imposed on an amount equal to the dues and similar payments; any excess lobbying expenditures are carried forward to the next taxable year.[218]

§ 20.9 CONSTITUTIONAL LAW CONSIDERATIONS

It has been repeatedly asserted that the proscription on substantial legislative activities applicable to public charities is violative of constitutional law principles.[219] Although the issues were often presented to the courts, it was not until 1982 that a litigant was successful in securing a decision finding that this provision is constitutionally deficient. Nonetheless, even that remarkable occurrence

---

[210] IRC § 6033(e)(3).

[211] H. Rep. 213, *supra* note 188, at 609.

[212] E.g., Priv. Ltr. Rul. 9534021.

[213] Rev. Proc. 95-35, 1995-2 C.B. 391.

[214] See Chapter 12.

[215] See § 15.2.

[216] See § 15.3.

[217] See Chapter 13.

[218] H. Rep. No. 213, *supra*, note 188, at 608–609. In general, Dillon, "Lobbying Provisions of H.R. 2264 for Tax-Exempt Membership Organizations," 8 *Exempt Org. Tax Rev.* (No. 5) 895 (1993); Cummings, Jr., "Tax Policy, Social Policy, and Politics: Amending Section 162(e)," 9 *Exempt Org. Tax Rev.* (No. 1) 137 (1994).

[219] E.g., Troyer, "Charities, Law-Making, and the Constitution: The Validity of the Restrictions on Influencing Legislation," 31 *N.Y.U. Inst. on Fed. Tax.* 1415 (1973); Note, "Regulating the Political Activities of Foundations," 83 *Harv. L. Rev.* 1843 (1970).

ultimately failed—almost with unintended consequences for other categories of tax-exempt organizations.

Representative of these decisions was one handed down in 1979.[220] The issues involved were the following: does this tax law limitation on legislative activities (1) impose an unconstitutional condition on the exercise of First Amendment rights (that is, the right to engage in legislative activity), (2) restrict the exercise of First Amendment rights as being a discriminatory denial of tax exemption for engaging in speech, (3) deny organizations so restricted the equal protection of the laws in violation of the Fifth Amendment, and/or (4) lack a compelling governmental interest that would justify the restrictions on First Amendment rights?

The approach of the courts on the First Amendment question has been to recognize that the lobbying of legislators constitutes an exercise of the First Amendment right of petition[221] and thus that the Amendment protects legislative activities. Oft-cited in this context is the Supreme Court declaration that the general advocacy of ideas is constitutionally protected as part of this nation's "profound national commitment to the principle that debate on public issues should be uninhibited, robust, and wide-open."[222] The courts inevitably press on to observe, however, that the federal tax law limitation does not violate First Amendment rights because it does not on its face prohibit organizations from engaging in substantial efforts to influence legislation.[223]

This position is fundamentally based on a Supreme Court pronouncement upholding the constitutionality of a tax regulation that excluded from deduction as business expenses amounts expended for the promotion or defeat of legislation.[224] There, the Court stated that the taxpayers were "not being denied a tax deduction because they engage in constitutionally protected activities, but are simply being required to pay for these activities entirely out of their own pocketbook, as everyone else engaging in similar activities is required to do under the provisions of the Internal Revenue Code."[225] Thus, if they wish to engage in substantial legislative activities, charitable organizations are required to fund these efforts from their own (after-tax) resources, and the resulting loss of tax-exempt status is not regarded as an impermissible result for engaging in constitutionally protected activities.

With respect to the second aspect of the First Amendment question, this argument is premised in part on the fact that several categories of tax-exempt

---

[220] Taxation With Representation of Washington v. Blumenthal, 79-1 U.S.T.C. ¶ 9185 (D.D.C. 1979), aff'd, 81-1 U.S.T.C. ¶ 9329 (D.C. Cir. 1981), rev. en banc sub nom., Taxation With Representation of Washington v. Regan, 676 F.2d 715 (D.C. Cir. 1982).

[221] E.g., Eastern R.R. Presidents Conference v. Noerr Motor Freight, Inc., 365 U.S. 127 (1961); Liberty Lobby, Inc. v. Pearson, 390 F.2d 489 (D.C. Cir. 1968).

[222] New York Times Co. v. Sullivan, 376 U.S. 254, 270 (1964).

[223] Taxation With Representation v. United States, 585 F.2d 1219 (4th Cir. 1978), cert. den., 441 U.S. 905 (1979).

[224] Cammarano v. United States, supra note 24.

[225] Id. at 513.

organizations are free to lobby without jeopardizing their exempt status.[226] Thus, the proposition has been that the restraint on lobbying by charitable organizations is a discriminatory revocation or denial of a tax exemption for engaging in protected speech. The courts hold that this principle relates to legislative efforts "aimed at the suppression of dangerous ideas"[227] and not to denials or revocation of tax exemptions for charitable organizations.

Similar short shrift has been given to the equal protection challenge, which is premised on the fact that similarly situated (that is, tax-exempt) organizations are accorded different treatment with respect to lobbying activities. The courts usually concede that this involves a classification that accords differing treatment to classes but that it is permissible inasmuch as the classification does not affect a "fundamental" right nor involve a "suspect" class.[228] The applicable standard of scrutiny—which this statutory limitation has been repeatedly ruled to satisfy—is whether the challenged classification is reasonably related to a legitimate governmental purpose.[229]

This standard is also deemed met where the courts evaluate the constitutionality of the proscription on substantial legislative activities in relation to the requirement that the restraint be rationally related to a legitimate government purpose.[230] Several of these purposes are usually found served: "assurance of governmental neutrality with respect to the lobbying activities of charitable organizations; prevention of abuse of charitable lobbying by private interests; and preservation of a balance between the lobbying activities of charitable organizations and those of non-charitable organizations and individuals."[231]

Thus, until 1982, all courts that considered the matter had made it clear that there is no constitutional imperfection in the federal tax antilobbying clause applicable to tax-exempt charitable organizations.[232] In that year, however, a federal court of appeals temporarily changed the complexion of the constitutional law concerning the antilobbying rule applicable to charitable entities. This appellate court agreed that this restriction on legislative activities is not violative of free speech (First Amendment) rights but—after concluding that an organization that acquires tax exemption and charitable donee status is thereby receiving a government subsidy—held that this subsidy cannot constitutionally be accorded on a discriminatory basis and that to do so is violative of equal protection (Fifth

[226] E.g., the organizations described in IRC §§ 501(c)(4), 501(c)(5), 501(c)(6), 501(c)(8), 501(c)(9), and 501(c)(19).
[227] Speiser v. Randall, 357 U.S. 513, 519 (1958), where the U.S. Supreme Court struck down a state statute that required veterans to take a loyalty oath as a condition to the receipt of a veterans' property tax exemption.
[228] E.g., San Antonio Independent School District v. Rodriguez, 411 U.S. 1 (1973); Dunn v. Blumstein, 405 U.S. 330 (1972); Shapiro v. Thompson, 394 U.S. 618 (1969).
[229] E.g., United States Department of Agriculture v. Moreno, 413 U.S. 528 (1973); Frontiero v. Richardson, 411 U.S. 677 (1973).
[230] E.g., United States v. O'Brien, 391 U.S. 367 (1968); Schenk v. United States, 249 U.S. 47 (1919).
[231] Taxation With Representation of Washington v. Blumenthal, *supra* note 220.
[232] Haswell v. United States, *supra* note 69, at 500 F.2d 1147-1150; Tax Analysts & Advocates v. Shultz, 74-2 U.S.T.C. ¶ 9601 (D.D.C. 1974), *aff'd*, 512 F.2d 992 (D.C. Cir. 1975) (where a lawsuit to declare the legislative activities provision of IRC § 501(c)(3) unconstitutional was dismissed).

Amendment) rights.[233] Therefore, the court held, the fact that tax-exempt charitable organizations are required to limit their lobbying to an insubstantial extent, while certain other exempt organizations—such as veterans' organizations—can lobby without these limits, is an unconstitutionally discriminatory allocation of this "government subsidy."[234]

The appellate court held that "[b]y subsidizing the lobbying activities of veterans' organizations while failing to subsidize the lobbying of . . . charitable groups, Congress has violated the equal protection guarantees of the Constitution."[235] While the court decided that the challenge to the lobbying restriction is "weak" if based solely on free speech claims and is "weak" if based solely on equal protection claims,[236] it concluded that the "whole of . . . [the] argument well exceeds the sum of its parts" and that a "First Amendment concern must inform the equal protection analysis in this case."[237]

As a prelude to its findings, the court concluded that a "high level of scrutiny is required" because the lobbying restriction on charitable organizations "constitutes a limitation on protected First Amendment activity" and because the equal protection argument involves "what is clearly a fundamental right."[238] Under law, this "scrutiny" requires a determination as to whether a "substantial governmental interest supports the classification."[239] The court based its conclusion on the premise that nonprofit organizations that embody the features of both tax exemption and eligibility to attract tax-deductible contributions are essentially alike. Inasmuch as the court was unpersuaded that there is a valid governmental interest to be served by treating charitable groups and veterans' groups differently on the matter of lobbying, the court ruled that the distinctions between the two classes of entities are "post hoc rationales" that are "constitutionally illegitimate."[240] Hence, the court found an unconstitutional denial of equal protection rights.

The remedy desired by the organization that initiated this case was invalidation of the lobbying restrictions on charitable organizations. This the court was disinclined to do. First, it wrote that unfettered lobbying by charitable organizations would increase the likelihood of "selfish" contributions made solely to advance the donors' personal legislative interests.[241] Second, the court concluded that Congress believes that the public interest requires limitations on lobbying by charitable organizations and that "[e]ven when they attempt to remedy constitutional violations,

[233] Taxation With Representation of Washington v. Regan, *supra* note 220.
[234] Charitable organization are those that are tax-exempt by reason of IRC § 501(c)(3) and that are charitable donees by reason of IRC § 170(c)(2); veterans' organizations are tax-exempt by reason of IRC § 501(c)(3), (4), or (19), and are charitable donees by reason of IRC § 170(c)(3).
[235] Taxation With Representation of Washington v. Regan, *supra* note 220, at 717.
[236] *Id.* As to the equal protection aspect, the court conceded that "Congress has vast leeway under the Constitution to classify the recipients of its benefits and to favor some groups over others" (*id.* at 740).
[237] *Id.* at 715.
[238] *Id.* at 730.
[239] *Id.* at 731.
[240] *Id.* at 739.
[241] *Id.* at 742.

courts must resist ordering relief that clearly exceeds the legitimate expectations of Congress."[242] The reverse approach—to place the same restrictions on veterans' groups as are imposed upon charitable groups—was far more appealing to the court and received serious consideration, but the court hesitated to strike down what it termed the "preferential treatment now accorded the lobbying of veterans' organizations," since veterans' groups were not parties to the litigation.[243] Instead, the case was ordered remanded to the district court "with the instruction that it cure the constitutionally invalid operation of Section 501(c) after inviting veterans' organizations to participate in framing the relief."[244] Before that remand could occur, however, the decision was appealed to the U.S. Supreme Court.

The Supreme Court reacted swiftly, in 1983 unanimously reversing the court of appeals.[245] In so holding, the Court reiterated its position that the lobbying restriction on charitable organizations does not infringe First Amendment rights nor regulate any First Amendment activity, that Congress did not violate the equal protection doctrine in the Fifth Amendment, and that Congress acted rationally in subsidizing (by means of tax exemption and charitable deductions) lobbying by veterans' organizations while not subsidizing lobbying by charitable organizations generally.

As to the free speech issue, the Court held that the federal tax law "does not deny . . . [a charitable organization] the right to receive deductible contributions to support its non-lobbying activity, nor does it deny . . . [a charitable organization] any independent benefit on account of its intention to lobby" but that "Congress has merely refused to pay for the lobbying out of public moneys."[246]

Noting that "[l]egislatures have especially broad latitude in creating classifications and distinctions in tax statutes,"[247] the Court concluded that the distinctions in the lobbying context made by Congress between charitable and veterans' organizations do not employ any "suspect classification," are not violative of equal protection principles, and are "within Congress' broad power in this area."[248] Moreover, the Court accepted the views that "Congress was concerned that exempt [charitable] organizations might use tax-deductible contributions to lobby to promote the private interests of their members"[249] and that "[o]ur country has a long standing policy of compensating veterans for their past contributions by providing them with numerous advantages."[250] Consequently, it appears that the proscription

---

[242] *Id.*

[243] *Id.* at 743.

[244] *Id.* at 744. In general, Brower, "Whose Voice Shall Be Heard? Lobbying Limitations on Section 501(c)(3) Charitable Organizations Held Unconstitutional in Regan v. Taxation With Representation," 28 *St. Louis U. L. J.* (No. 4) 1017 (1984); Cerasani, "Lobbying of Charitable Organizations: *Regan v. Taxation With Representation*," 37 *Tax Law.* (No. 2) 399 (1984); Crockett, "Lobbying Restrictions on Section 501(c)(3) Organizations Held Unconstitutional: First Amendment Implications of *Taxation With Representation of Washington v. Regan*," 1983 *B.Y.U.L. Rev.* 442 (1983); Hopkins, "Nonprofit Lobbying: Are the Rules Changing?," 23 *Foundation News* (No. 3) 46 (May/June 1982).

[245] Regan v. Taxation With Representation of Washington, 461 U.S. 540 (1983).

[246] *Id.* at 545, thus restating its position in Cammarano v. United States, *supra* note 24.

[247] *Id.* at 547.

[248] *Id.* at 548–550.

[249] *Id.* at 550.

[250] *Id.* at 551.

on substantial legislative activities by charitable organizations, contained in the federal tax rules, is beyond further constitutional law challenge in the courts."[251]

The enactment of the expenditure test, liberalizing the ability of public charities to engage in legislative activities, has not stemmed the flow of comment on this subject. This segment of the law of tax-exempt organizations has always been a fertile field for commentators[252] and is likely to remain so.

---

[251] A concurring opinion took the position that the lobbying restriction in IRC § 501(c)(3) is—viewed in isolation—unconstitutional but that the defect is cured by the presence of IRC § 501(c)(4). This stance rests on the premises that an IRC § 501(c)(3) organization may utilize an IRC § 501(c)(4) affiliate for lobbying purposes and that contemporary administrative policy is to allow this in-tandem relationship to function relatively unfettered (see § 30.2(b)). This concurring opinion further stated that "[a]ny significant restriction on this channel of communication, however, would negate the saving effect of [IRC] § 501(c)(4)" (*id.* at 553).

[252] In general, Fuller & Abbott, "Political Activity and Lobbying Rules for Section 501(c) Organizations," 15 *Exempt Org. Tax. Rev.* (No. 3) 383 (1996); Cobb & King, "Working Through the Maze of Lobbying Requirements for Nonprofit Organizations," 7 *J. Tax. Exempt Orgs.* 243 (May/June 1996); Knight, Knight & Marshall, "Lobbying, Campaigning, and Section 501(c)(3)—What Is Allowed?," 2 *J. Tax. Exempt Orgs.* 17 (Fall 1990); Haight, "Lobbying for the Public Good: Limitations on Legislative Activities by Section 501(c)(3) Organizations," 23 *Gonzaga L. Rev.* (No. 1) 77 (1987); Robinson, "Charitable Lobbying Restraints and Tax-Exempt Organizations: Old Problems, New Directions," 1984 *Utah L. Rev.* 337 (1984); Clark, "Church Lobbying: The Legitimacy of the Controls," 16 *Houston L. Rev.* 480 (1979); Webster & Krebs, *Associations and Lobbying Regulation* (1979); Nix, "Limitations on the Lobbying of Section 501(c)(3) Organizations—A Choice for Public Charities," 81 *W. Va. L. Rev.* 407 (1978–1979); Montgomery, "Lobbying by Public Charities Under the Tax Reform Act of 1976," 50 *Taxes* 449 (1978); Washburn, "New Tax Act Defines 'Substantial' Lobbying—But Charities Must Elect to Be Covered," 55 *Taxes* 291 (1977); Bostick, "Lobbying By Non-Profit Groups," 1 *District Lawyer* (No. 3) 21 (1977); Whaley, "Political Activities of Section 501(c)(3) Organizations," *Proceedings of Univ. S. Cal. Law Center 29th Tax Institute* 195 (1977); Weithorn, "Practitioners' Planning Guide to the New Lobbying Rules for Public Charities," 46 *J. Tax.* 294 (1977); Hyslop & Ebell, "Public Interest Lobbying and the Tax Reform Act of 1976," 7 *Envtl. Law* 283 (1977); Note, "Lobbying by Section 501(c)(3) Organizations Under the Tax Reform Act of 1976: A Proposal for Change," 30 *Tax Law.* 214 (1976); Moore, Washburn & Goldman, "Restrictions on Lobbying Activities by Charitable Organizations: Proposed Legislative Remedies," 3 *Notre Dame J. Legis.* 17 (1976); Fogel, "To the I.R.S., 'Tis Better to Give than to Lobby," 61 *A.B.A.J.* 960 (9175); Caplin & Timbie, "Legislative Activities of Public Charities," 39 *Law and Contemp. Probs.* 183 (1975); Note, "Political Speech of Charitable Organizations under the Internal Revenue Code," 41 *U. Chi. L. Rev.* 352 (1974); Geske, "Direct Lobbying Activities of Public Charities," 26 *Tax Law.* 305 (1973); Green, "Activism and the Tax Status of Exempt Organizations," 44 *P.B.A.Q.* 500 (1973); Wachtel, "David Meets Goliath in the Legislative Arena: A Losing Battle for an Equal Charitable Voice?," 9 *San Diego L. Rev.* 933 (1972); Garrett, "Federal Tax Limitations on Political Activities of Public Interest and Educational Organizations," 59 *Geo. L. J.* 561 (1971); Goldberg, "Guarding Against Loss of Tax Exempt Status Due to Campus Politics," 33 *J. Tax.* 232 (1970); Hauptman, "Tax-Exempt Private Educational Institutions: A Survey of the Prohibition Against Influencing Legislation and Intervening in Political Matters," 37 *Brooklyn L. Rev.* 107 (1970); Lehrfeld, "The Taxation of Ideology," 19 *Cath. U. L. Rev.* 50 (1969); Note, "Sierra Club, Political Activity, and Tax-Exempt Charitable Status," 55 *Geo. L. J.* 1128 (1967); Note, "Income Taxes-Deductions: In General—IRS Proposes to Revoke Sierra Club's Eligibility to Receive Deductible Contributions Because of the Club's Political Activities," 80 *Harv. L. Rev.* 1793 (1967); Borod, "Lobbying for the Public Interest—Federal Tax Policy and Administration," 42 *N.Y.U.L. Rev.* 1087 (1967); Boehm, "Taxes and Politics," 22 *Tax L. Rev.* 369 (1967); Clark, "The Limitation on Political Activities: A Discordant Note in the Law of Charities," 46 *Va. L. Rev.* 439 (1960); Note, "The Effect of Legislative Activity on the Tax Status of Religious, Charitable and Scientific Organizations," 10 *Ohio State L. J.* 414 (1957); Note, "Tax Treatment of Lobbying Expenses and Contributions," 67 *Harv. L. Rev.* 1408 (1954).

Constitutional law challenges in the lobbying context have not been confined to the realm of charitable organizations, although the success rate of these other challenges is no better than those initiated by charities. The business league/association community challenged the constitutionality of the rules by which the deductibility, as a business expense, of the dues paid by members of an association is limited as a consequence of lobbying (or political campaign activity) by the association. This challenge—on free speech and equal protection grounds—failed, and did so for the same basic reasons that the challenges in the charitable setting failed: Congress has broad latitude in creating classifications and distinctions in tax statutes[253] and Congress did not preclude associations from lobbying, but instead lawfully eliminated a tax subsidy underlying the lobbying activity.[254] As the court stated its conclusion, the "challenged provisions do not impose 'penalties' on tax-exempt associations that engage in lobbying, but merely enforce the decision of Congress to eliminate the lobbying subsidy."[255] The speech about legislation was found to encompass the "entire spectrum of possible viewpoints and is, therefore, viewpoint neutral"[256]—a finding that blunted the claim that the challenged provisions discriminate on the basis of the content of the speech. These tax provisions were held to be rationally related to a legitimate government interest and thus constitutional, in relation to both free speech and equal protection principles.[257]

§ 20.10 INTERNET ACTIVITIES

Charitable organizations may engage in legislative activities by means of the Internet. This practice is raising questions as to the application of the federal tax law to this form of advocacy. Moreover, some charitable entities are affiliated with organizations that conduct lobbying using the Internet. A message, concerning this type of activity, may be on an organization's Web site which is linked to a charity's Web site.

(a) Internet Lobbying in General

Lobbying is a form of communication and the Internet is a medium of communication. Thus, lobbying by tax-exempt organizations (and other persons) can be undertaken by means of the Internet. As is the case in other contexts, however, the federal tax law does not provide any unique treatment for transactions or activities of exempt organizations, involving attempts to influence legislation, simply because the Internet is the medium of communication.

As the IRS saliently observed, the "use of the Internet to accomplish a

---

[253] See the text accompanied by *supra* note 236.

[254] See the text accompanied by *supra* note 225.

[255] American Soc'y of Ass'n Executives v. United States, 23 F. Supp. 2d 64 (D.D.C. 1998).

[256] *Id.* at 70. This opinion was affirmed (195 F.3d 47 (D.C. Cir. 1999), *cert. den.*, 120 S.Ct. 1961 (2000)).

[257] Also American Soc'y of Ass'n Executives v. Bentsen, 848 F. Supp. 245 (D.D.C. 1994).

particular task does not change the way the tax laws apply to that task."[258] The IRS continued: "Advertising is still advertising and fundraising is still fundraising."[259] The agency also could have said: "Lobbying is still lobbying." Thus, the rules of the substantial part test and the expenditure test embrace lobbying by means of the Internet.

There are four forms of Internet communications in this setting: (1) a communication published on a publicly accessible Web page; (2) a communication posted on a password-protected portion of a Web site; (3) a communication on a listserv (or by means of other methods such as a news group, chat room, and/or forum); and (4) a communication by means of e-mail. The IRS recognized that, by "publishing a webpage on the Internet, an exempt organization can provide the general public with information about the organization, its activities, and issues of concern to the organization."[260] The agency added: "An exempt organization can provide information to subscribers about issues of concern to the organization as well as enable people with common interests to share information via the Internet through a variety of methods," referencing mailing lists and the methods referred to previously in the third category of Internet communication.[261]

An e-mail communication from a tax-exempt organization clearly can constitute an attempt to influence legislation. If the lobbying message is sent to a legislator, a member of the staff of a legislator, a member of the staff of a legislative committee, or the like, it constitutes direct lobbying. Likewise, a lobbying message can amount to indirect (or grass roots) lobbying when the elements of that definition are met.

A tax-exempt organization may post a lobbying message on the portion of its Web site that is publicly accessible. For public charities, it is not always clear whether such a posting is an attempt to influence legislation in the tax-law sense of the phrase. The answer turns in part on whether the posting of the message is considered a communication for purposes of direct lobbying or indirect lobbying. For charities under the substantial part test, the law simply is vague on the point.

For charities that have elected the expenditure test, the law in this regard is much clearer. When a charitable organization posts a lobbying message on a publicly accessible portion of its Web site and takes a position with respect to specific legislation, the message is not a direct lobbying communication. This conclusion can be extrapolated from existing law. For example, the monthly newsletter of a public charity contains an editorial column that refers to and reflects a view on specific pending legislation. The organization sends the newsletter to 10,000 nonmember subscribers, including a senator. The newsletter containing the lobbying message is not a direct lobbying communication because the newsletter was sent to the senator in her capacity as a subscriber, rather than as a legislator.[262] Consequently, the possibility that a legislator may visit the Web site of a public charity

---

[258] *IRS Exempt Organization Continuing Professional Education Text for Fiscal Year 2000*, Technical Topic I.
[259] *Id.*
[260] Ann. 2000-84, 2000-42 I.R.B. 385.
[261] *Id.*
[262] Reg. § 56.4911-2(b)(4)(i), Example (7).

and read a lobbying message that is intended for all site visitors should not convert the message into a form of direct lobbying.

There is another example that illustrates some of the subtleties in this area.[263] In expansion of the prior example, one of the senator's staff members sees the senator's copy of the newsletter, reads the editorial, and writes to the public charity requesting additional information. The charity responds with a letter that refers to and reflects a view on specific legislation. This letter likely is a direct lobbying communication.[264]

Returning to the example immediately prior to the previous one, the editorial column may be an indirect (grass roots) lobbying communication if it encourages recipients to take action with respect to the pending legislation it refers to and on which it reflects a view.[265]

Substantiality in the expenditure test context is, as noted, measured solely in terms of expenditures of funds. The Internet is far more cost-effective than other forms of communication. Consequently, it is obvious that a charitable organization that has elected the expenditure test is in a position to engage in considerably more lobbying activity when the attempts to influence legislation are made by means of the Internet.

(b) Questions Posed by IRS

The IRS issued an announcement in 2000, seeking public comment on a number of questions pertaining to use of the Internet, in the context of lobbying activity, by charitable organizations. On that occasion, the IRS wrote that "[w]hen a charitable organization engages in advocacy on the Internet, questions arise as to whether it is conducting . . . lobbying activity, and if so, to what extent." The agency added: "This situation is further complicated by the affiliation of charitable organizations with other organizations engaging in . . . lobbying activities on the Internet. The ease with which different websites may be linked electronically (through a 'hyperlink') raises a concern about whether the message of a linked website is attributable to the charitable organization."[266]

(i) General Issues. The IRS posed six general questions that are relevant to the field of lobbying, with the IRS reiterating that tax-exempt organizations "use the Internet to carry on activities that otherwise can be conducted through other media, such as radio or television broadcasts, print publications, or direct mailings."

The first of these general questions was whether a Web site maintained by a tax-exempt organization "constitute[s] a single publication or communica-

---

[263] *Id.*, Example (8).
[264] It is possible that this letter is within an exception to these rules, such as the exception for nonpartisan analysis, study, or research (see *supra* § 4(b), text accompanied by note 114). The letter is not within the scope of the exception for responses to written requests from a legislative body or committee for technical advice (see *supra* § 4(b), text accompanied by note 115) inasmuch as the letter is not in response to a written request from such a body or committee.
[265] See Reg. § 56.4911-2(b)(2).
[266] Ann. 2000-84, *supra* note 260.

tion." It is conceivable that a Web site could constitute a single *publication*, in that a single publication can encompass many subjects and messages. (Many publications, however, such as a book or journal, are devoted to a single subject.) It is highly unlikely, however, that a Web site would constitute a single *communication*. In the lobbying setting, for example, even if a charity posted a message in an attempt to influence legislation, presumably it would also have messages about its purposes and exempt programs, and perhaps also fundraising and unrelated business activity. Thus, the answer to this question should be that an exempt organization's Web site may constitute a single publication but that it is rare, if ever, that a Web site would constitute a single communication.

The IRS then asked, if a Web site is not a single publication or single communication, "how should it be separated into distinct publications or communications?" The simplest of answers would be to separate a Web site into discrete communications on the basis of the amount of space each communication occupies on the site. This is often the approach taken in the case of print publications. In some instances, however, a *primary purpose test* is applied (or at least advocated), so that if the primary purpose of a publication is to communicate a particular message, the entire publication is deemed to have communication of that message as its purpose.

This segues into the third of the general questions, which inquired into the proper methodology when allocating expenses for a Web site. Again, this allocation could be based on the amount of space devoted to each type of communication. The IRS posed the question as to whether expense allocation should be based on Web pages, noting that, unlike print publications, they may not be of equal size. At this point, the answer to this question is unclear. Once again, the cost-effectiveness of Web site publishing is relevant, in that the costs involved may be relatively small to begin with.

The expenditure test rules include guidance on the allocation of *mixed purpose expenditures*.[267] This relates to "lobbying expenditures for a communication that also has a bona fide nonlobbying purpose." The guidance here is not particularly helpful and is a bit old-fashioned. For example, some of the illustrations pertain to print publications; allocation is made in terms of "pages."[268] The regulation writers presumably did not have Web pages in mind when crafting these rules.

The IRS observed that, "[u]nlike other publications of an exempt organization, a website may be modified on a daily basis." The IRS then asked: "To what extent and by what means should an exempt organization maintain the information from prior versions of the organization's website?" Although the question is a legitimate one, it seems impractical to require a charitable or other tax-exempt organization to maintain the information posted on every prior version of its Web site. Again, the answer to this question at this point is unclear.

The matter of expense allocations can be considered in light of these last two questions combined. Isolating the costs of a Web site lobbying communication is difficult enough, without taking into account many changes in Web

---

[267] Reg. § 56.4911-3(a)(2)(i).
[268] E.g., Reg. § 56.4911-3(b), Example (2).

site content in the course of a year. When the changes are factored in, expense isolation and allocation may become nearly impossible—or more expensive than the Web site expenses themselves.

An additional complicating factor is that the time and expense involved in preparing a Web site communication may be elements that the tax-exempt organization would incur in any event. The same message may be used in other forms of communication, such as print media. That aspect of lobbying, then, may well already be accounted for, leaving the cost in connection with the Web site only that of posting the material, which is negligible.

The last of these general questions was: "To what extent are statements made by subscribers to a forum, such as a listserv or newsgroup, attributable to an exempt organization that maintains the forum?" Existing law[269] indicates that the general answer to this question is that attribution is not appropriate. At least, attribution should not be the case in the lobbying context, because the charitable organization should not be held responsible for the speech of others.[270] As noted previously, for an organization to be denied or lose tax-exempt status because of lobbying activity, the legislative activities must be undertaken as an act of the organization itself.

This question had a follow-up component: "Does attribution vary depending on the level of participation of the exempt organization in maintaining the forum (e.g., if the organization moderates discussion, acts as editor, etc.)?" Generally, the answer to this question should continue to be no. For example, if a public charity maintains a chat room and initiates a discussion of a pending item of legislation, and an individual sends a message in support of or in opposition to that legislation, that message should not be attributed to the organization. At some point, of course, the answer to the question would be yes. As an illustration, if a charitable organization announced that it was opposed to an item of legislation and requested those who participate in a forum to send messages in opposition to the legislation so that the organization could compile them and send them to legislators, that aspect of maintenance of the forum would constitute an attempt to influence legislation.

(ii) Specific Questions. The IRS posed several questions specifically pertaining to lobbying by tax-exempt organizations by means of the Internet.

The first of these questions highlighted the fact that the substantial part test essentially is a facts and circumstances test.[271] The IRS inquired as to the facts and circumstances that are relevant, in the case of charitable organizations that are subject to the substantial part test, in "determining whether lobbying communications made on the Internet are a substantial part of the organization's activities." As discussed, this element of *substantiality* is vague; it may partake of expenditures, time, influence, and/or some other factor(s). There is, therefore, an

---

[269] See *supra* § 2(b), text accompanied by notes 37–38.
[270] This aspect of Internet use has been at least partially answered in the context of the corporate sponsorship rules (see § 27.2(n)).
[271] See *supra* § 3(a).

odd situation here: The IRS may be seeking to articulate facts and circumstances that may cause Internet lobbying to be substantial when there is a basic lack of understanding as to these facts and circumstances when any other form of communication is used to influence legislation.

As discussed in the context of the general questions, in separating a Web site into distinct communications, the simplest approach would be to make the separation on the basis of the amount of space a communication occupies on the site. Although that approach might work as to the separation of communications, it alone cannot work when assessing the *effectiveness* of each of the communications. The IRS suggested two other factors, both of which are clearly relevant to the inquiry. One is location of the communication on the Web site (main page or a subsidiary page). The other is the number of hits on the site.

Another question of considerable import was alluded to earlier: "Does providing a hyperlink [by a charitable organization] to the website of another organization that engages in lobbying activity constitute lobbying by [the] charitable organization?" Surely, as long as the link itself is all that is involved, the answer to this question must be no. This is because a link from one organization to another does not generally, by itself, cause any activity of the linked organization to be attributed to the linking organization.

In the lobbying context, the *no* answer is reflected in existing law. Generally, for an organization to be denied or lose tax-exempt status because of lobbying activity, the legislative activities must be undertaken as an act of the organization itself; there generally is no attribution rule.[272] Moreover, in connection with the expenditure test, there are specific rules that dictate when the lobbying expenditures of an organization are to be attributed to another organization.[273] A mere link between organizations is insufficient to trigger these rules.

In furtherance of this question, the IRS also asked: What "facts and circumstances are relevant in determining whether the charitable organization has engaged in lobbying activity" by providing such a link? This aspect of the question not-so-subtly answers the first part of the question: The existence of a link does not automatically cause attribution of lobbying, yet attribution can arise under certain sets of circumstances. Certainly, for example, if a charitable organization was opposed to an item of legislation and were to expressly request visitors to its Web site to link with another organization's Web site for the purpose of reading an explanation as to why the legislation should be defeated, the provision of the link would constitute lobbying. Also, if the charitable organization controlled the organization to which it provided the link, that would be a major factor indicating lobbying by the charitable organization. The IRS asked whether it would make any difference if lobbying activity is on the specific Web page to which the charitable organization provides the link rather than elsewhere on the other organization's Web site. The answer to that question is yes, in that such a linkage would be a factor leading to the conclusion that provision of the link constitutes lobbying by the charitable organization.

Another question concerned charitable organizations that have elected the

---

[272] See *supra* § 2(b), text accompanied by notes 37–38.
[273] See *supra* § 5(c).

expenditure test. The IRS asked, when determining whether such a charitable organization has engaged in grass roots lobbying on the Internet, what facts and circumstances are relevant to whether the organization made a *call to action*. A communication is regarded as a grass roots communication only when three requirements are satisfied; one of them is that the communication encourages the recipients to take action with respect to the legislation.[274] This question is peculiar because the phrase *encouraging the recipient to take action* with respect to legislation is given a detailed definition.[275] Thus, for example, if the communication on an electing charity's Web site states that the reader should contact a legislator or an employee of a legislative body; provides the address, telephone number, or similar information about a legislator or an employee of a legislative body; or identifies one or more legislators who will vote on the legislation as opposing the communication's view with respect to the legislation, the communication is a call to action. If a Web site communication is not within one of the four types of ways to encourage recipients to take action, the communication cannot be a grass roots lobbying communication.

Still another question posed by the IRS was whether publication of a Web page on the Internet by a charitable organization that has elected the expenditure test constitutes an appearance in the mass media. The answer is: generically, yes, but technically, no. (As to the former, the Internet (or the Web) obviously is a form of mass media—indeed, it is the largest form of mass media.) This is because the term *mass media* is defined for these purposes to mean "television, radio, billboards and general circulation newspapers and magazines."[276] The term should include the Internet but it does not.

This type of mass media publication may be a grass roots lobbying communication if it meets the three-part grass roots lobbying definition.[277] By posing this question, however, the IRS seemed to be exploring the possibility of invocation of the special rule for certain *paid mass media advertisements*.[278] There is a rebuttable presumption—utilizing a three-part test[279]—that such an advertisement is a form of grass roots lobbying. This presumption can be overcome by a charitable organization.[280] Thus, those rules would have to be applied in a particular case to see whether the mass media publication amounts to a grass roots lobbying communication. But this analysis would be required only if the Internet were to be found to be a form of *mass media* for this purpose—which it is not.[281] As the regulations state, this special rule "generally applies only to a limited type of paid advertisements that appear in the mass media."[282]

---

[274] See *supra* § 2(c)(i), text accompanied by note 45.

[275] *Id.*, text accompanied by note 46.

[276] Reg. § 56.4911-2(b)(5)(iii)(A).

[277] See *supra* § 2(c)(i), text accompanied by note 45.

[278] Reg. § 56.4911-2(b)(5)(i).

[279] Reg. § 56.4911-2(b)(5)(ii).

[280] See *supra* § 2(c)(i).

[281] The regulation states that the term *mass media* "means" . . . ; it does not use the usual word "includes." The IRS could easily have added the Internet to this definition, but that medium was not thought of in this context when this regulation was finalized in 1990.

[282] Reg. § 56.4911-2(b)(5)(i).

Pursuing this theme, the IRS asked: "Does an email or listserv communication by the [charitable] organization constitute an appearance in mass media if it is sent to more than 100,000 people and fewer than half of those people are members of the organization?" This reference is to an aspect of the definition of the term *mass media*.[283] Thus, if the email communication or listserv communication were to be deemed the equivalent of a general circulation newspaper or magazine, the answer to this question would be yes. These communications, however, are more analogous to regular mail, which is not considered a mass media communication. As discussed, moreover, Internet communications are not mass media communications for expenditure-test purposes to begin with, so the answer to this question must be no, for two reasons.

The IRS asked: "What facts and circumstances are relevant in determining whether an Internet communication (either a limited access website or a listserv or email communication) is a communication directly to or primarily with members of the organization" for a charitable organization that is under the expenditure test? This question relates to the exception in this body of law for communications between the organization and its bona fide members.[284] The facts and circumstances are the following:

- The communication must be directed only to members of the organization. Thus, the communication cannot be posted on the organization's general Web site, but must be published in a manner that makes it accessible only by members. This would be done, as the IRS suggested, by placing the communication on the Web site where only the members have access to it (by password) or make it available only to the members by means of a listserv or email.

- The specific legislation the communication refers to, and reflects a view on, must be of *direct interest* to the organization and its members. The presence of the requisite direct interest is determined on a facts and circumstances basis. An organization in this circumstance would be well advised to explain, as part of the communication, why the legislation is of direct interest to the organization and its members (although, in many instances, that nexus will be obvious).

- The communication may not directly encourage the organization's members to engage in direct lobbying with respect to the legislation.

- The communication may not directly encourage the organization's members to engage in grass roots lobbying.[285]

[283] Reg. § 56.4911-2(b)(5)(iii)(A).
[284] See *supra* § 4(b), text accompanied by notes 117, 120–124.
[285] In general, Hopkins, *The Nonprofits' Guide to Internet Communications Law* (John Wiley & Sons, Inc., 2002), Chapter 5.

CHAPTER TWENTY-ONE

Political Campaign Activities by Tax-Exempt Organizations

With one exception—the political organization[1]—the federal tax laws concerning tax-exempt organizations do not encourage their involvement in political campaign activities. The limitations with respect to charitable organizations[2] are particularly stringent. The law in this regard concerning other types of exempt organizations is vague. Moreover, the law of tax-exempt organizations in this regard interrelates to, and sometimes is inconsistent with, the federal law regulating the financing and conduct of political campaigns.

§ 21.1 POLITICAL CAMPAIGN ACTIVITIES OF PUBLIC CHARITIES

One of the criteria for qualification as a tax-exempt charitable organization is that it must "not participate in, or intervene in (including the publishing or distributing of statements), any political campaign on behalf of (or in opposition to) any candidate for public office."[3] If a charitable organization engages in a political

---

[1] See Chapter 17.
[2] That is, organizations described in IRC § 501(c)(3) and exempt from federal income taxation by reason of IRC § 501(a)
[3] IRC § 501(c)(3).

campaign activity, it becomes classified as an *action organization*[4] and thus may be disqualified for exempt status.

(a) Legislative History

This provision forbidding political campaign activity by charitable organizations was added to the federal tax law in 1954, without benefit of congressional hearings, in the form of a floor amendment adopted in the Senate.[5] During consideration of the legislation that became the Revenue Act of 1954, Senator Lyndon B. Johnson of Texas, on July 2, 1954, offered the amendment out of concern that funds provided by a charitable foundation were being used to help finance the campaign of an opponent in a primary election. Senator Johnson said only that the purpose of the amendment is to "deny[] tax-exempt status to not only those people who influence legislation but also to those who intervene in any political campaign on behalf of any candidate for any public office."[6] The phrase "(in opposition to)" was added to the provision in 1987.

(b) Scope of the Proscription

The prohibition on involvement by a tax-exempt charitable organization in a political campaign is generally considered by the IRS to be absolute, although neither the legislative history of the provision nor the regulations provide any clarification.[7] The IRS stated that "this is an absolute prohibition," adding that "[t]here is no requirement that political campaigning be substantial."[8] Thus, the Chief Counsel of the IRS opined that "an organization described in section 501(c)(3) is precluded from engaging in *any* political campaign activities."[9]

Nonetheless, analogy may be made to a comparable statute that was also absolute on its face: section 610 of the Federal Corrupt Practices Act. That act made "[i]t . . . unlawful for . . . any corporation whatever . . . to make a contribution or expenditure in connection with" various federal elections. Nonetheless, the courts read an insubstantiality threshold into the absolute proscription of this law.[10] Further, it has been stated that a "slight and comparatively unimportant deviation from the narrow furrow of tax approved activity is not fatal."[11] It was also observed that "courts recognize that a nonexempt purpose, even

---

[4] Reg. § 1.501(c)(3)-1(c)(3)(iii).
[5] 100 *Cong. Rec.* 9604 (1954).
[6] *Id.* There is no analysis of this provision in the conference report (H. Rep. 2543, 83d Cong., 2d Sess. 46 (1954)).
[7] Reg. §§ 1.501(c)(3)-1(b)(3)(ii), (c)(iii).
[8] IRS Exempt Organizations Handbook (IRM 7751) § 370(2).
[9] Gen. Couns. Mem. 39694 (emphasis supplied).
[10] United States v. Painters Local 481, 172 F.2d 854 (2d Cir. 1949); United States v. Construction Local 264, 101 F. Supp. 873 (W.D. Mo. 1951). The repeal of the Federal Corrupt Practices Act does not alter the analysis on this point.
[11] St. Louis Union Trust Co. v. United States, 374 F.2d 427, 431-432 (8th Cir. 1967).

'somewhat beyond a de minimis level,' may be permitted without loss of exemption."[12] Thus, the Commissioner of Internal Revenue stated, in congressional testimony describing the political campaign limitation: "If political intervention is involved, the prohibition is absolute; however, some consideration may be given to whether, qualitatively or quantitatively, the organization is in the circumstance where the activity is so trivial it is without legal significance and, therefore, de minimis."[13]

There is an anomaly in this aspect of the federal tax law. This prohibition on political campaign activities is considered, at least by the IRS, to be absolute, yet there is relatively little law and guidance as to the scope of the prohibition."[14] As discussed next, this scope is believed to be broad—even though there is considerable difference between political campaign activities and political activities.

(c) Political Campaign Activities

The political campaign activities prohibition applicable to charitable organizations embodies four elements, all of which must be present for the limitation to become operative. These elements are that a charitable organization may not *participate* or *intervene* in a political campaign, the political activity that must be involved is a political *campaign*, the campaign must be with respect to an individual who is a *candidate*, and the individual must be a candidate for a *public office*.[15]

(d) Participation or Intervention

The requirement that a tax-exempt charitable organization not engage in political campaign activities is relatively clear as to its meaning. Because of this relative clarity, the matter has infrequently been the subject of discussion in court opinions or in IRS rulings. The most obvious way for a charitable organization to participate or intervene in a political campaign is to make a contribution to the political campaign of a candidate. Contributions of this nature are, however, clearly forbidden as a condition of tax exemption (and by federal campaign financing laws). The same is true for endorsements, provision of facilities, lending of employees, and the like.

The scope of this prohibition is broader, however, than that of the laws regulating political campaign financing. For example, the IRS ruled that a charitable organization may not—without loss of tax-exempt status—evaluate the qualifica-

---

[12] Living Faith, Inc. v. Comm'r, 950 F.2d 365, 370 (7th Cir. 1991).

[13] Statement of Lawrence B. Gibbs before the House Subcommittee on Oversight, March 12, 1987, in "Lobbying and Political Activities of Tax-Exempt Organizations," Hearings before the Subcommittee on Oversight, Committee on Ways and Means, House of Representatives, Serial 100-5, 96-97, 100th Cong., 1st Sess. (1987).

[14] Reg. § 1.501(c)(3)-1(c)(3)(iii)

[15] A court observed: "It should be noted that exemption is lost . . . by participation in any political campaign on behalf of *any* candidate for public office" (United States v. Dykema, 666 F.2d 1096, 1101 (7th Cir. 1981), *cert. den.*, 456 U.S. 983 (1982) (emphasis in original)).

tions of potential candidates in a school board election and then support particular slates in the campaign.[16] The agency also ruled that a charitable organization violated the prohibition on political campaign activities when it made an interest-bearing loan to an organization that used the funds for political purposes.[17] Also, a court held that an organization established with the dominant aim of bringing about world government as rapidly as possible did not qualify as a charitable organization because the activity was political in nature.[18]

Conversely, the IRS ruled that a university did not intervene in a political campaign by conducting a political science course that required the students' participation in political campaigns of their choice[19] nor by the provision of faculty advisors and facilities for a campus newspaper that published the students' editorial opinions on political matters.[20] Also, a tax-exempt broadcasting station that provided equal air time to all electoral candidates in compliance with the Federal Communications Act was ruled to not be in violation of the proscription against partisan political activities.[21] Moreover, the IRS ruled that the administration, by a charitable organization, of a payroll deduction plan to collect contributions from its employees and remit the contributions to unions representing its employees for transfer to union-sponsored political action committees would not violate the prohibition on participating in political campaigns, in part because the charity's expenses are reimbursed.[22]

Despite the requirement of a political campaign and a candidate for public office, the IRS denominated as an action organization (and thus denied recognition of tax exemption to) an organization formed for the purpose of implementing an orderly change of administration of the office of governor of a state in the most efficient and economical fashion possible by assisting the governor-elect during the period between his election and inauguration.[23] The IRS ruled that the organization's "predominant purpose is to effectuate changes in the government's policies and personnel which will make them correspond with the partisan political interests of both the Governor-elect and the political party he represents."[24] Without any statement of its reasoning, the IRS ruled that a presidential inaugural committee that sponsored inaugural activities, some of which were open to the public and some by invitation only, where donations to it were commingled with the proceeds from various fundraising affairs and activities, was not an organization organized and operated exclusively for charitable purposes.[25]

---

[16] Rev. Rul. 67-71, 1967-1 C.B. 125.
[17] Tech. Adv. Mem. 9812001.
[18] Estate of Blaine v. Comm'r, 22 T.C. 1195 (1954).
[19] Rev. Rul. 72-512, 1972-2 C.B. 246.
[20] Rev. Rul. 72-513, 1972-2 C.B. 246.
[21] Rev. Rul. 74-574, 1974-2 C.B. 160.
[22] Priv. Ltr. Rul. 200151060.
[23] Rev. Rul. 74-117, 1974-1 C.B. 128.
[24] Id.
[25] Rev. Rul. 77-283, 1977-2 C.B. 72.

An expansive reading of this prohibition on political activities was provided by a federal court of appeals, in denying tax-exempt status to a religious ministry organization for engaging in legislative activities and intervening in political campaigns.[26] The organization, by means of publications and broadcasts, attacked candidates and incumbents (presidents and members of Congress) considered too liberal and endorsed conservative officeholders. The court summarized the offenses: "These attempts to elect or defeat certain political leaders reflected . . . [the organization's] objective to change the composition of the federal government."[27] The IRS Chief Counsel's office "reluctantly" concluded in 1989 that an organization "probably" did not intervene in a political campaign on behalf of or in opposition to a candidate for public office, even though the organization ran a political advertising program that (1) was, in the words of the IRS, "mostly broadcast during a two week period around the Reagan/Mondale foreign and defense policy debate on October 21, 1984," (2) contained statements that "could be viewed as demonstrating a preference for one of the debating candidates" [Mondale], (3) "could be viewed" as having content such that "individuals listening to the ads would generally understand them to support or oppose a candidate in an election campaign," (4) involved statements that were released so close to the November vote as to be "troublesome," and (5) was clearly in violation of the IRS's voter education rules.[28]

A charitable organization was found to have engaged in prohibited political campaign activity because of language in and the timing of mailing of fundraising letters.[29] This organization had a variety of programs, all focused on a certain position along the political spectrum; its direct-mail fundraising letters were mailed mostly to individuals of this political persuasion. These letters, sent contemporaneously with election periods, implied—in the view of the IRS—that a contribution to the organization would be used in part to finance candidates for public office who share this political view. The IRS wrote that the letters were biased against candidates of opposing political aims or in favor of the candidates supporting its view of political issues; one letter was found to not entail voter education but rather "voter direction." Likewise, a charitable organization was held to have improperly intervened in a political campaign because its fundraising letters were signed by an individual who was a candidate for political office at the time; language in the letters was found to be "very much like [the candidate's] campaign statements, positions, and rhetoric."[30]

It is common for a tax-exempt charitable organization to be related to another exempt organization that is permitted to engage in some political campaign

---

[26] Christian Echoes National Ministry, Inc. v. United States, 470 F.2d 849 (10th Cir. 1972), *cert. den.*, 414 U.S. 864 (1973).

[27] *Id.* at 856. Also Monsky v. Comm'r, 36 T.C.M. 1046 (1977); Giordano v. Comm'r, 36 T.C.M. 430 (1977).

[28] Tech. Adv. Mem. 8936002. See *infra* § 1(e).

[29] Tech. Adv. Mem. 9609007.

[30] Tech. Adv. Mem. 200044038.

activity or that is permitted to establish and maintain a political action committee. If the arrangement is properly structured, the campaign activities of the other
organization or organizations will not be attributed to the charitable entity for
purposes of the political campaign prohibition. For example, a business league
established a political action committee; that fact was ruled by the IRS to not jeopardize the exempt status of a charitable organization related to the business
league.[31]

Inasmuch as organizations function only by means of the acts of individuals, who retain their civil rights to engage in political campaign activities (within
limitations), the law distinguishes between activities that are undertaken in conjunction with "official" responsibilities and those that are "personal"; only the
former activities are relevant in assessing an organization's qualification for tax
exemption in the face of political campaign efforts.[32] Political campaign activities
of individuals (such as directors or officers) will be attributed to an organization
if it has, directly or indirectly, authorized or ratified the acts or reimbursed for
contributions or other similar expenditures.[33]

It is the view of the IRS that an attempt to influence the confirmation, by the
U.S. Senate, of a federal judicial nominee does not constitute participation or intervention in a political campaign, inasmuch as the individual involved is not a
contestant for elective public office.[34]

The proscription on political campaign activity by public charities is particularly controversial as applied to religious organizations. Thus, one observer
wrote that "[r]eligion and politics have been intertwined since the birth of our nation," and that "[i]n a democracy created to reflect the social fabric of its citizens,
religious groups have always advocated moral positions to further or impede political causes and political campaigns."[35] Another commentator wrote that
"[u]nder some circumstances, nearly every religious group will be motivated by
sincere belief to engage in substantial political activity" and that "[m]oreover, political activity of some sort implicitly is required by many religions; indeed, a religion which did not have moral standards which it believed should be followed
by the society would be an anomaly."[36] A similar viewpoint is reflected in the observation that churches and other religious organizations "consider their efforts
to influence the making of public policy to be an integral part of their religious
enterprise" and "[f]or some religious persons, political activity may even be a
form of worship."[37] Still another observer said that the "involvement of religious

---

[31] Priv. Ltr. Rul. 200103084. Business leagues are the subject of Chapter 13; political organizations are
the subject of Chapter 17.
[32] Gen. Couns. Mem. 34631.
[33] Gen. Couns. Mem. 33912.
[34] Notice 88-76, 1988-2 C.B. 392.
[35] Note, "Religion and Political Campaigns: A Proposal to Revise Section 501(c)(3) of the Internal Revenue Code," 49 *Fordham L. Rev.* 536 (1981) (footnotes omitted).
[36] Note, "Religion in Politics and the Income Tax Exemption," 42 *Fordham L. Rev.* 397 (1973) (footnotes
omitted).
[37] West, "The Free Exercise Clause and the Internal Revenue Code's Restrictions on the Political Activity of Tax-Exempt Organizations," 21 *Wake Forest L. Rev.* 395, 396 (1986).

organizations in the political process . . . has long been a reality in American society."[38] The situation has been aptly summed up as follows: "[T]he IRS interpretations [of the political campaign prohibition] make compliance extremely difficult and are highly intrusive on 'free exercise' and other constitutional rights. In particular, churches must act at their peril as they attempt to walk the obscure line between loss of exemption and faithfulness to the obligation to speak out on the moral dimension of important social issues."[39]

These observations notwithstanding, the IRS was quick to revoke the tax-exempt status of a church as a result of its involvement in a political campaign. This church intervened in the 1992 presidential election by means of newspaper advertisements questioning the position of one of the candidates on certain social issues. This revocation of exemption was upheld in the courts.[40]

---

[38] Note, "Conflicts Between the First Amendment Religion Clauses and the Internal Revenue Code: Politically Active Religious Organizations and Racially Discriminatory Private Schools," 61 *Wash. U. L. Q.* 503, 508-509 (1983) (footnote omitted).

[39] Caron & Dessingue, "I.R.C. § 501(c)(3): Practical and Constitutional Implications of 'Political' Activity Restrictions," 11 *J. Law & Politics* (No. 1) 169, 178 (1985).

It is the position of the IRS that a distinction is to be made between political campaign involvement by religious institutions and the free expression on political matters by leaders of religious organizations speaking for themselves as individuals; the latter certainly is permitted. Thus, the IRS stated that "[m]inisters and others who commonly speak or write on behalf of religious organizations should clearly indicate, at the time they do so, that public comments made by them in connection with political campaigns are strictly personal and are not intended to represent their organization" ("Tax Guide for Churches and Other Religious Organizations" (Pub. 1828) (Ann. 94-112, 1994-42 I.R.B. 20, modifying Ann. 94-111, 1994-37 I.R.B. 36)). The IRS added: "Partisan comments by the employees or other representatives of an organization regarding political candidates must be avoided in official organization publications and at official church functions" (*id.*).

[40] Branch Ministries, Inc. v. Rossotti, 40 F. Supp. 2d 15 (D.D.C. 1999), *aff'd*, 211 F.3d 137 (D.C. Cir. 2000). One of the arguments asserted by this church was that it was the victim of selective prosecution by the IRS. This contention was that the agency penalizes churches on the right of the political spectrum when they engage in political campaign activity but ignores comparable activity when engaged in by churches on the left. The trial court previously held that the church made a "colorable showing" that the entity's "political and/or religious beliefs may have played an impermissible role in the revocation of their [sic] tax-exempt status" and thus that it was entitled to additional discovery on the issue of the motivation of the IRS (Branch Ministries, Inc. v. Richardson, 970 F. Supp. 11, 17 (D.D.C. 1997)). (The church had tendered to the court 65 examples of political campaign activity in or by churches.) The court, however, ultimately rejected this argument, writing that the church's evidence related "only to churches that have allowed political leaders to appear at religious services or churches that have used the pulpit to advocate a certain message" (Branch Ministries, Inc. v. Rossotti, *supra*, 40 F. Supp. 2d at 21). The court observed that the church was unable to point to "no other instance in which a church so brazenly claimed responsibility for a political advertisement in a national newspaper and solicited tax-deductible contributions for that political advertisement" (*id.*).

The staff of the Joint Committee on Taxation conducted a study as to whether the IRS is biased in its treatment of religious organizations engaged in political campaign activity. The results of this study, issued in March 2000, were that there is no credible evidence that the IRS engaged in any activity (such as issuance of determination letters or selection of organizations for examination) that was politically motivated ("Report of Investigation of Allegations Relating to Internal Revenue Service Handling of Tax-Exempt Organizations Matters" (JCS-3-00)).

In general, Morris, "Political Activity and Charitable Status at Common Law: In Search of Certainty," 23 *Exempt Org. Tax Rev.* (No. 2) 247 (Feb. 1999); Roady, "Political Activities of Tax-Exempt Organizations: Federal Income Tax Rules and Restrictions," 22 *Exempt Org. Tax Rev.* (No. 3) 401 (Dec.

(e) Voter Education Activities

A charitable organization may instruct the public on matters useful to the individual and beneficial to the community.[41] In carrying out this form of an educational purpose, an organization may operate in a political milieu, albeit cautiously. Thus, organizations have been permitted to assemble and donate to libraries the campaign speeches, interviews, and other materials of an individual who was a candidate for a "historically important elective office,"[42] conduct public forums involving debates and lectures on social, political, and international questions,[43] and conduct public forums involving congressional candidates, where there is a fair and impartial treatment of the candidates."[44] By contrast, the organization will imperil its tax exemption if it solicits the signing or endorsing of a fair campaign practices code by political candidates.[45]

In performing activities such as these, however, the organization must present a sufficiently full and fair exposition of pertinent facts to permit the public to form its own opinion or conclusion independent of that presented by the organization, although the organization may also advocate a particular position or viewpoint.[46] Thus, while a charitable organization may seek to educate the public on patriotic, political, and civic matters and even alert the citizenry to the dangers of an extreme political doctrine, it may not do so by the use of disparaging terms, insinuations, innuendoes, and suggested implications drawn from incomplete facts.[47]

There is, not surprisingly, tension between the concepts of political campaign activities and voter education activities. This is illustrated by a case involving the practice of a tax-exempt bar association (otherwise qualified as a charitable organization) of rating candidates for public office in a state's judiciary. The candidates were rated as "approved," "not approved," or "approved as highly qualified"; more than one candidate for the same office may receive

---

1998); Hill, "Can Arguments About Subjective Intent Eliminate the Political Prohibition Under Section 501(c)(3)?," 10 *J. Tax. Exempt Orgs.* (No. 4) 147 (Jan./Feb. 1998); Rich, "The Utilization of Section 501(c)(3) Organizations for Politically Motivated Activity," 22 *Exempt Org. L. Rev.* (No. 1) 45 (1998); Colvin, "An Election-Year Guide to Exempt Organization Political Activities," 7 *J. Tax. Exempt Orgs.* (No. 2) 74 (Sept./Oct. 1995); Rosenthal, "Prelates and Politics: Current Views on the Prohibition Against Campaign Activity," 52 *Tax Notes* 1122 (1991); Chisholm, "Politics and Charity: A Proposal for Peaceful Coexistence," 58 *Geo. Wash. L. Rev.* (No. 2) 308 (1990); Tesdahl, "Intervention in Political Campaigns by Religious Organizations After the Pickle Hearings—A Proposal for the 1990s," 4 *Exempt Org. Tax Rev.* (No. 9) 1165 (1991).

[41] Reg. § 1.501(c)(3)-1(d)(3). See §§ 7.4, 7.5.

[42] Rev. Rul. 70-321, 1970-1 C.B. 129.

[43] Rev. Rul. 66-256, 1966-2 C.B. 210.

[44] Rev. Rul. 86-95, 1986-1 C.B. 332. In one instance, the IRS approved of a forum where less than all of the candidates were invited because the decision "accentuate[d] the educational nature of the forums and still ensure[d] a meaningful field of candidates for worthwhile forums, while allocating for the organization's limited space and time" (Tech. Adv. Mem. 9635003).

[45] Rev. Rul. 76-456, 1976-2 C.B. 151; Rev. Rul. 66-258, 1966-2 C.B. 213. Also Rev. Rul. 60-193, 1960-1 C.B. 195.

[46] Reg. § 1.501(c)(3)-1(d)(3). Also Haswell v. United States, 500 F.2d 1133, 1143-1145 (Ct. Cl. 1974), *cert. den.*, 419 U.S. 1107 (1974).

[47] Rev. Rul. 68-263, 1968-1 C.B. 256.

the same rating. The ratings were disseminated to the public in press releases and by means of the publications of the association. A court held that this rating process did not constitute prohibited participation or intervention in political campaigns on behalf of or in opposition to candidates; the court found that the "ratings do not support or oppose the candidacy of any particular individual or recommend that the public vote for or against a specific candidate."[48] The court added that "we do not believe that the mere practice of rating candidates for elective office without more is, per se, a prohibited political activity."[49] On appeal, however, this opinion was reversed, with the appellate court concluding that the rating activity constituted participation or intervention in the political campaigns for the judgeships.[50] The court of appeals characterized the ratings as "[p]ublished expressions of . . . opinion, made with an eye toward imminent elections."[51]

A traditional distinction between political campaign activity and voter education activity has been that the latter is *nonpartisan*. This bar association case focused on this aspect of the law as well, with the appellate court finding that the prohibition on political campaign activity for charitable organizations embraces nonpartisan activity; it wrote that the "statute and pertinent regulations thereunder are not limited in their application to the partisan campaigns of candidates representing recognized political parties."[52] Writing of the rating process, the court of appeals noted that a "candidate who receives a 'not qualified' rating will derive little comfort from the fact that the rating may have been made in a nonpartisan manner."[53] By contrast, the lower court took the position that the rating activity was not campaign activity because the association engaged in the "totally passive, not active" function of merely reporting its ratings (which were not, according to that court, based on partisan or political preferences) and did "not actively seek to influence the outcome of elections."[54]

The IRS published a ruling allowing organizations that operate broadcast stations to provide equal air time to political candidates.[55] The import of this ruling as a matter of tax policy is uncertain, however, in that these organizations were required by federal communications law to provide free air time to political candidates.[56]

An IRS ruling contains two examples of voter education activities that a charitable organization may carry on without loss of tax exemption. These examples indicate that a charitable organization can (1) prepare and disseminate a compilation of the voting records of all members of Congress on a wide variety of

---

[48] Ass'n of the Bar of the City of New York v. Comm'r, 89 T.C. 599, 609-610 (1987).
[49] *Id.* at 610.
[50] Ass'n of the Bar of the City of New York v. Comm'r, 858 F.2d 876 (2d Cir. 1988), *cert. den.*, 490 U.S. 1030 (1989).
[51] *Id.*, 858 F.2d at 880.
[52] *Id.*
[53] *Id.*
[54] Ass'n of the Bar of the City of New York v. Comm'r, *supra* note 48, at 611.
[55] Rev. Rul. 74-574, *supra* note 21.
[56] See Rev. Rul. 78-160, 1978-1 C.B. 153, *rev.* by Rev. Rul. 78-248, 1978-1 C.B. 154.

major subjects, as long as there is no editorial comment and no approval or disapproval of the voting records is implied, and (2) publish the responses to its questionnaire on a wide variety of subjects from all candidates for an office, as long as no preference for a candidate is expressed. This ruling also contains two illustrations of prohibited activities: an organization may not (1) publish candidates' answers to questions that indicate a bias on the issues or (2) publish a voter guide reflecting the voting records of members of Congress on selected issues of interest to the organization.

Notwithstanding these latter two illustrations, the IRS subsequently ruled that a charitable organization may publish a newsletter containing the voting records of congressional incumbents on selected issues without prohibited involvement in political campaigns.[57] The IRS indicated that the format and content of the publication need not be neutral, in that each incumbent's votes and the organization's views on selected legislative issues can be reported, and the publication may indicate whether the incumbent supported or opposed the organization's view. Nonetheless, the IRS considered the following factors as demonstrating the absence of political campaign activity: (1) the voting records of all incumbents will be presented, (2) candidates for reelection will not be identified, (3) no comment will be made on an individual's overall qualifications for public office, (4) no statements expressly or impliedly endorsing or rejecting any incumbent as a candidate for public office will be offered, (5) no comparison of incumbents with other candidates will be made, (6) the organization will point out the inherent limitations of judging the qualifications of an incumbent on the basis of certain selected votes, by stating the need to consider such matters as performance on subcommittees and constituent service, (7) the organization will not widely distribute its compilation of incumbents' voting records, (8) the publication will be distributed to the organization's usual readership (a few thousand nationwide), and (9) no attempt will be made to target the publication toward particular areas in which elections are occurring nor to time the date of publication to coincide with an election campaign.

The position of the IRS on this issue in general is that "in the absence of any expressions of endorsement for or opposition to candidates for public office, an organization may publish a newsletter containing voting records and its opinions on issues of interest to it provided that the voting records are not widely distributed to the general public during an election campaign or aimed, in view of all the facts and circumstances, towards affecting any particular elections."[58]

The IRS concluded that the use by a charitable organization of panels of citizens to review and rate political candidates is a form of intervention or participation in the candidates' campaigns.[59] These groups of individuals questioned expert witnesses and candidates, analyzed the information and views presented, and prepared reports for public dissemination. Most of these reports included a

[57] Rev. Rul. 80-282, 1980-2 C.B. 178.
[58] Gen. Couns. Mem. 38444.
[59] Tech. Adv. Mem. 9635003.

rating of the candidates by members of the panels, including an analysis of their stands on several major issues in a box score style. The organization viewed these processes as forms of issue education and means to stimulate public dialogue, but the IRS determined that the candidates' ratings provided "political editorial opinions to the general public and went beyond the neutral forums" that are permissible.[60]

(f) Requirement of a Candidate

The Internal Revenue Code does not define the term *candidate* for purposes of the prohibition on political campaign activities by charitable organizations. The income tax regulations provide a definition of the term in the context of defining the phrase *candidate for public office*, as an "individual who offers himself, or is proposed by others, as a contestant for an elective public office, whether such office be national, State, or local."[61]

An analysis of the political campaign intervention rules by the staff of the Joint Committee on Taxation stated that "[c]lear standards do not exist for determining precisely at what point an individual becomes a candidate for purposes of the rule."[62] This analysis continued: "On the one hand, once an individual declares his candidacy for a particular office, his status as a candidate is clear."[63] The analysis added: "On the other hand, the fact that an individual is a prominent political figure does not automatically make him a candidate, even if there is speculation regarding his possible future candidacy for particular offices."[64]

(g) Requirement of a Campaign

A federal court of appeals observed that a "campaign for a public office in a public election merely and simply means running for office, or candidacy for office, as the word is used in common parlance and as it is understood by the man in the street."[65]

The term *campaign* is not otherwise defined in the federal tax law.

(h) Requirement of a Public Office

Neither the Internal Revenue Code nor the income tax regulations define the term *public office* for purposes of the political campaign activity prohibition applicable to charitable organizations.

---

[60] In general, Yablon & Coleman, "Intent Is Not Relevant in Distinguishing Between Education and Politics," 9 *J. Tax. Exempt Orgs.* (No. 4) 156 (Jan./Feb. 1998); Hill, "The Role of Intent in Distinguishing Between Education and Politics," 9 *J. Tax. Exempt Orgs.* (No. 1) 9 (July/Aug. 1997); Cerny & Lauber, Jr., "Voter Guides Must Meet IRS Guides as Permissible Voter Education," 8 *J. Tax. Exempt Orgs.* (No. 4) 147 (Jan./Feb. 1997).

[61] Reg. § 1.501(c)(3)-1(c)(3)(iii).

[62] "Lobbying and Political Activities of Tax-Exempt Organizations" 14 (JCS-5-87, Mar. 11, 1987).

[63] *Id.*

[64] *Id.*

[65] Norris v. United States, 86 F.2d 379, 382 (8th Cir. 1936), *rev'd on other grounds*, 300 U.S. 564 (1937).

The private foundation rules defining disqualified persons, however, make reference to an *elective public office*.[66] While the statute does not define the term public office in this setting, the tax regulations state:

> In defining the term "public office" . . ., such term must be distinguished from mere public employment. Although holding a public office is one form of public employment, not every position in the employ of a State or other governmental subdivision . . . constitutes a "public office." Although a determination whether a public employee holds a public office depends on the facts and circumstances of the case, the essential element is whether a significant part of the activities of a public employee is the independent performance of policy-making functions. In applying this subparagraph, several factors may be considered as indications that a position in the executive, legislative, or judicial branch of the government of a State, possession of the United States, or political subdivision or other area of any of the foregoing, or of the District of Columbia, constitutes a "public office." Among such factors to be considered in addition to that set forth above, are that the office is created by the Congress, a State constitution, or the State legislature, or by a municipality or other governmental body pursuant to authority conferred by the Congress, State constitution, or State legislature, and the powers conferred on the office and the duties to be discharged by such office are defined either directly or indirectly by the Congress, State constitution, or State legislature, or through legislative authority.[67]

The only other instance, in the law of tax-exempt organizations, where the tax regulations make reference to the term *public office* is in the context of the rules concerning political organizations, where the term public office is used in the definition of a political organization exempt function.[68] The accompanying regulations use the same definition of the term public office as is used in the setting of the private foundations' rules defining disqualified persons.[69]

The IRS Chief Counsel's office took the position that precinct committee members in a state were holders of a public office.[70] This position was based on the content of the state's law, which accorded these individuals the following characteristics: (1) the position was created by statute, (2) holders of the position swear an oath to uphold the state and U.S. constitutions in the performance of their duties, (3) they assist in the selection of election officers (characterized as an "essential function in the State's regulation of elections"), (4) they participate in the party's county central committee and state committee (characterized as "essential to the electoral process"), (5) there is a fixed term of office, and (6) the positions are "not occasional or contractual." The IRS conceded that, if the above-quoted regulation was applied to these facts, the precinct committeemen "would not be considered as holding public office because their duties entail no

[66] IRC §§ 4946(c)(1), (5).
[67] Reg. § 53.4946-1(g)(2)(i).
[68] IRC § 527(e)(2). See § 17.2.
[69] Reg. § 1.527-2(d).
[70] Gen. Couns. Mem. 39811.

independent policymaking functions." Nonetheless, the IRS pronouncement continued: "However, the additional factors to be considered as indicative of a public office and which are listed in the latter part of that regulation would support the Service's position." Thus, the IRS chief counsel's office advised that the tax exemption of the organization involved should be revoked because it encouraged its members to seek election to precinct committees and to support these candidacies.

A state court of appeals held that an individual who is a candidate for delegate to a county political convention is a candidate for state law purposes but is not a candidate for a public office.[71] The court pointed out that the state's election law does not define the word *candidate*. Thus, the court concluded, applying a "general rule of statutory construction . . . that words and phrases should be construed according to their common meaning," and that "[l]ogically, most people would believe that if an individual's name is listed on an election ballot, that individual is a candidate for something."[72] In the court's opinion, the "common meaning" of the word *candidate* includes state precinct delegates,[73] although, as noted, they are not seekers of a *public office*.

Another federal appellate court has held that the phrase *candidate for office* is "used in common parlance and as it is understood by the man in the street."[74] Relying on this observation, the above IRS pronouncement stated that, to the "average person, the appearance of precinct candidates on the general election ballot indicates that the position is a public office."[75]

(i) Treatment of Activist Organizations

Aside from the types of activity traditionally considered by the federal tax law to be action efforts—legislative and political campaign activities—there is a broad range of action or political undertakings that may be described as the type of speech or activities sheltered by free speech principles. These undertakings may be manifested in a variety of ways, such as writings, demonstrations, boycotts, strikes, picketing, and litigation, all protected by the rights of free speech and association and the right to petition (assuming the absence of any illegal activities). These activities frequently give the IRS pause in evaluating the status of an organization as a charitable entity but, unless the activities may be fairly characterized as being impermissible lobbying or electioneering, there is no basis in the law concerning action organizations (as that term is used in its technical sense) for denying an organization engaging in these activities tax-exempt status or for revoking this type of organization's tax-exempt status.

The position of the IRS on this point apparently is that this type of activity

---

[71] Templin v. Oakland City Clerk, 387 N.W. 2d 156 (Mich. Ct. App. 1986).
[72] *Id.* at 159.
[73] *Id.*
[74] Ass'n of the Bar of the City of New York v. Comm'r, *supra* note 50, 858 F.2d at 880.
[75] Gen. Couns. Mem. 39811.

can be a permissible method by which to further tax-exempt purposes.[76] These activities will jeopardize exemption, however, where they are illegal or otherwise contrary to public policy.[77] Nonetheless, where an activity is legal, the IRS generally will not deem it contrary to public policy.[78]

The tolerance of the courts in this area in general was classically illustrated by a federal district court finding that the anticonvention boycott orchestrated by the National Organization for Women (NOW), in states the legislatures of which had not ratified the proposed Equal Rights Amendment, was not in violation of antitrust laws, even though the boycott or concerted refusal to deal has been held to be an unlawful combination in restraint of trade.[79] Because the objective of NOW's convention boycott campaign was the ratification of the proposed amendment, by means of demonstrating support and generating widespread publicity for the proposed amendment, the court found that the boycott activities "were not intended as punitive . . . and were not motivated by any type of anti-competitive purpose."[80] NOW was successful in asserting that the antitrust laws do not apply to boycotts that take place in a political rather than a commercial context.[81] The essence of the NOW case is summed up in one sentence from an article quoted by the court: "There are areas of our economic and political life in which the precepts of antitrust must yield to other social values."[82]

At the same time the NOW litigation was unfolding, the IRS had before it the tax status of an organization that conducted a consumer boycott. Prior to the decision in the NOW case, the IRS concluded that the organization, which conducted a national campaign against the purchase of products from companies that manufacture infant formula and market it in developing countries by means of allegedly unethical business practices, could not qualify as a charitable entity because it was an action organization. Consequently, the organization took the matter into court,[83] but just before the case reached the briefing stage, the IRS suddenly reversed its position and issued a favorable ruling, thereby mooting the case.

Presumably, therefore, the case stands as a basis for the proposition that an organization may conduct a boycott in furtherance of charitable ends.[84] The operative legal principle appears to be that, while the conduct of a boycott may not in-

---

[76] Gen. Couns. Mem. 37858.

[77] See §§ 5.3, 5.5(f).

[78] *Id.*

[79] State of Missouri v. National Organization for Women, Inc., 467 F. Supp. 289 (W.D. Mo. 1978).

[80] *Id.* at 296.

[81] Also Eastern R.R. Presidents Conf. v. Noerr Motor Freight, Inc., 365 U.S. 127 (1961); Register of Wills for Baltimore City v. Cook, 216 A.2d 542 (Md. 1966).

[82] Handler, "Annual Review of Antitrust Developments," 71 *Yale L. J.* 75, 88 (1961).

[83] The Infant Formula Action Coalition v. United States (D.D.C. No. 79-0129).

[84] Some organizations, already possessing IRC § 501(c)(3) classification, engage in consumer boycotts (relating to, for example, the purchase of tuna, products that exploit animals, and products produced in whaling nations) but *The Infant Formula Action Coalition* case, *supra* note 83, involved an organization that conducted a boycott as its primary activity and that had its tax status reviewed by the IRS at the outset of its existence.

herently be an exempt function, a boycott can further an exempt purpose and thereby lead to charitable status. As the IRS recognized, the "performance of a particular activity that is not inherently charitable may nonetheless further a charitable purpose [and the] . . . overall result in any given case is dependent on why and how that activity is actually being conducted."[85]

Moreover, the IRS recognized that an otherwise tax-exempt charitable organization can further its exempt purposes by instituting litigation, even where the organization employs private lawyers to represent it in bringing and maintaining the litigation.[86] The IRS insists, however, that an organization's litigation activities be a "reasonable means" of accomplishing its tax-exempt purposes, and that the program of litigation not be illegal, contrary to a clearly defined and established public policy, or violative of express statutory provisions.[87]

This means-to-an-end principle thus initially characterizes activities such as demonstrations, boycotts, and litigation as "neutral" activities—from a federal tax standpoint—and allows the tax status of the organization conducting them to depend on its ability to show how tax-exempt purposes are thereby furthered. (In some instances, the IRS has publicly recognized the exempt status of organizations engaging in this type of activity, such as litigation conducted by public interest law firms.[88])

This principle has also been recognized by the courts. One court discussed the point that the purpose towards which an organization's activities are directed, and not the nature of the activities themselves, is ultimately dispositive of the organization's right to be classified as a charitable organization.[89] In a similar case, this court found that an activity (sale of handicrafts) was "neither an exempt purpose nor a nonexempt purpose but an activity carried on by . . . [the organization] in furtherance of its exempt purposes."[90]

The U.S. Supreme Court applied this principle in analogous contexts. Perhaps the most applicable of the Court's opinions is the holding that litigation activities as conducted in the public interest context of that case are modes of expression and association protected by constitutional law, and may not be barred by state authority to regulate the legal profession.[91] The Court distinguished this type of litigation from that normally instituted to resolve private differences, stating that the former is a "means for achieving lawful objectives."[92] In that case, litigation activities were perceived as neutral activities, engaged in as a means for accomplishment of the organization's ends. Likewise, boycotts, demonstrations, and the like can serve as the basis for advancing charitable purposes. As the Court has repeatedly observed, the First

---

[85] Rev. Rul. 69-572, 1969-2 C.B. 119.
[86] In general, Bachmann, *Nonprofit Litigation* (John Wiley & Sons, Inc., 1991), Chapter 4.
[87] Rev. Rul. 80-278, 1980-2 C.B. 175. The IRS, in Rev. Rul. 80-279, 1980-2 C.B. 176, took a like stance with respect to an organization that conducted mediation of internal environmental disputes.
[88] See § 6.10(d).
[89] Pulpit Resource v. Comm'r, 70 T.C. 594 (1978). See § 4.5(a).
[90] Aid to Artisans, Inc. v. Comm'r, 71 T.C. 202, 214 (1978).
[91] N.A.A.C.P. v. Button, 371 U.S. 415 (1963).
[92] *Id.* at 429.

Amendment protects advocacy, certainly of lawful ends, against governmental intrusion.[93]

A court held that litigation is an "appropriate vehicle for an organization to accomplish" its tax-exempt purpose, in a case involving the exempt status of an organization that provided legal assistance to employees whose rights were violated under compulsory unionism arrangements.[94]

In one case, the IRS had taken the position that engaging in proxy contests was not a charitable activity. There was no dispute over the obvious fact that proxy contests are not inherently charitable or educational endeavors. Upon review, however, the court involved placed the organization's activities in context, that is, in light of its overall purposes.[95] The court recognized that the mission of the organization "is to make corporate management, and thus corporations, responsible."[96] The court continued:

> It is only reasonable that corporations begin to realize that they have duties beyond simply making money for their stockholders. A corporation does not exist in a vacuum, but is part of the community for better or for worse. In the past, it has been for worse. Large corporations have contributed to many of the social problems affecting the community both directly, in hiring practices, effects on the environment, non-compliance with regulations, indifference to the consumer safety, etc. and indirectly through use of their economic power in socially irresponsible ways. As a member of the community, it is incumbent upon corporations to use their substantial economic power for the community good, rather than solely for self-enrichment, at the community's expense. The need for a swift re-orientation of the corporate perspective to its community responsibilities is imperative. The general public is in no financial, organizational or power position to undertake the task with any effectiveness.[97]

With that as background, the court discussed the proxy voting process and its impact on corporate management. After commenting that proposals to promote socially responsible programs and policies may not be voted in by stockholders, the court concluded:

---

[93] E.g., Thomas v. Collins, 323 U.S. 516 (1945); Herndon v. Lowry, 301 U.S. 242 (1937). Also Pratt v. Robert S. Odell & Co., 122 P.2d 684, 692 (Cal. Dist. Ct. App. 1942), where it was held that a corporation may expend funds in the prosecution of litigation to which it is not a party where the expenditure is a means for furthering its objects; and Register of Wills for Baltimore City v. Cook, supra note 81, at 546, where it was held that advocacy of passage of the Equal Rights Amendment is one method of accomplishing the charitable objectives of a tax-exempt trust. In this context, it should be noted that, in Village of Schaumburg v. Citizens for a Better Environment, 444 U.S. 620 (1980), the Supreme Court held that acts of fundraising are among the most protected forms of free speech. Also, as to the latter point, Riley v. National Federation of the Blind of N.C., 487 U.S. 781 (1988); Secretary of State of Maryland v. Joseph H. Munson Co., Inc., 467 U.S. 947 (1984). In general, Hopkins, *The Law of Fundraising, Third Edition* (John Wiley & Sons, Inc., 2002), § 4.3

[94] National Right to Work Legal Defense & Education Foundation, Inc. v. United States, 487 F. Supp. 801 (E.D.N.C. 1979). Cf. Retired Teachers Legal Defense Fund, Inc. v. Comm'r, 78 T.C. 280 (1982).

[95] Center on Corporate Responsibility, Inc. v. Shultz, 368 F. Supp. 863 (D.D.C. 1973).

[96] *Id.* at 874, note 21.

[97] *Id.* at 874–875, note 21.

But the questions will have been raised, the shareholders will have been educated to the wider horizon, and the seed may have been planted for future change that will require the corporation to assume some of its duties as a member of the community. The beneficiary of this activity and educational process to promote socially responsible corporations will be the public. . . .

As the Court views them, proxy contests appear to be the more direct and effective instrument of achieving the . . . [organization's] purposes, and when conducted in the public interest, as the . . . [organization] has done, they are charitable activities, in that they are the instruments (both legal and not against public policy) by which the charitable purposes are accomplished for the public good.[98]

Thus, certain activities—activist in nature—can avoid classification as political campaign activities, thereby enabling the organizations involved to qualify for tax-exempt status as public charities.[99]

---

[98] *Id.* at 875, note 21.

[99] E.g., Priv. Ltr. Rul. 8936002. In general, Morris, "Political Activity and Charitable Status at Common Law: In Search of Certainty," 23 *Exempt Org. Tax Rev.* (No. 2) 247 (Feb. 1999); Roady, "Political Activities of Tax-Exempt Organizations: Federal Income Tax Rules and Restrictions," 22 *Exempt Org. Tax Rev.* (No. 3) 401 (Dec. 1998); Hill, "Can Arguments About Subjective Intent Eliminate the Political Prohibition Under Section 501(c)(3)?," 10 *J. Tax. Exempt Orgs.* (No. 4) 147 (Jan./Feb. 1998); Rich, "The Utilization of Section 501(c)(3) Organizations for Politically Motivated Activity," 22 *Exempt Org. L. Rev.* (No. 1) 45 (1998); Fuller & Abbott, "Political Activity and Lobbying Rules for Section 501(c) Organizations," 15 *Exempt Org. Tax Rev.* (No. 3) 383 (1996); Bird, "The Exempt Organization Rules on Political Activities," 7 *J. Tax. Exempt Orgs.* 195 (Mar./Apr. 1996); Colvin, "An Election-Year Guide to Exempt Organization Political Activities," 7 *J. Tax. Exempt Orgs.* (No. 2) 74 (Sept./Oct. 1995); Rosenthal, "Prelates and Politics: Current Views on the Prohibition Against Campaign Activity," 52 *Tax Notes* 1122 (1991); Tesdahl, "Intervention in Political Campaigns by Religious Organizations After the Pickle Hearings—A Proposal for the 1990s," 4 *Exempt Org. Tax Rev.* (No. 9) 1165 (1991); Washlick, "Political Activities of Tax-Exempt Organizations," 3 *J. Tax. Exempt Orgs.* 4 (Spring 1991); Knight, Knight & Marshall, "Lobbying, Campaigning, and Section 501(c)(3)—What is Allowed?," 2 *J. Tax. Exempt Orgs.* 17 (Fall 1990); Chisholm, "Politics and Charity: A Proposal for Peaceful Coexistence," 58 *Geo. Wash. L. Rev.* (No. 2) 308 (1990); Chisholm, "Sinking the Think Tanks Upstream: The Use and Misuse of Tax Exemption Law to Address the Use and Misuse of Tax-Exempt Organizations by Politicians," 51 *U. Pitt. L. Rev.* (No. 3) 577 (1990); Sabbath, "Tax Exempt Political Education Organizations: Is the Exemption Being Abused?," 41 *Tax Law.* (No. 4) 847 (1988); Christopher, "Political Activities Become More Risky for Tax-Exempts Due to RA '87," 68 *J. Tax.* (No. 3) 136 (1988); Rosenblum, "Religion and Political Campaigns: A Proposal to Revise Section 501(c)(3) of the Internal Revenue Code," 49 *Fordham L. Rev.* 536 (1981); Crumplar, "Tax Consequences of Political Activity by Religious Organizations," V *Christian Law.* (No. 2) 29 (1975); Bailey, "Religion in Politics and the Income Tax Exemption," 42 *Fordham L. Rev.* 397 (1974); Garrett, "Federal Tax Limitations on Political Activities of Public Interest and Educational Organizations," 59 *Geo. L. J.* 561 (1971); Note, "Political Activity and Tax-Exempt Organizations Before and After The Tax Reform Act of 1969," 38 *Geo. Wash. U. L. Rev.* 1114 (1970); Amer. Ent. Inst., *Political Activities of Colleges and Universities* (1970); Lehrfeld, "How Much 'Politicking' Can a Charitable Organization Engage In?," 20 *J. Tax.* 236 (1968); Boehm, "Political Expenditures by Tax-Exempt Organizations," 14 *Prac. Law.* 13 (1968); Note, "Income Tax Disadvantages of Political Activities," 57 *Col. L. Rev.* (1957).

§ 21.2 POLITICAL EXPENDITURES BY CHARITABLE ORGANIZATIONS AND TAX SANCTIONS

The federal tax law authorizes the levy of taxes in situations where a charitable organization makes a political expenditure.[100] Generally, a *political expenditure* is any amount paid or incurred by a charitable organization in any participation in, or intervention in (including the publication or distribution of statements), any political campaign on behalf of or in opposition to any candidate for public office.[101] The IRS has the discretion, in a situation where a charitable organization engages in political campaign activity, to revoke the organization's tax-exempt status,[102] impose this tax,[103] or do both.

In an effort to discourage the use of ostensibly educational organizations operating in tandem with political campaigns, the concept of a political expenditure was expanded, so as to apply with respect to an organization "which is formed primarily for purposes of promoting the candidacy (or prospective candidacy) of an individual for public office (or which is effectively controlled by a candidate or prospective candidate and which is availed of primarily for such purposes)."[104] In these circumstances, the term *political expenditure* includes any of the following amounts paid or incurred by the organization: (1) amounts paid to or incurred by the individual for speeches or other services; (2) the travel expenses of the individual; (3) the expenses of conducting polls, surveys, or other studies, or the preparation of papers or other materials, for

---

[100] IRC § 4955.

[101] Reg. § 53.4955-1(c)(1).

[102] E.g., Branch Ministries, Inc. v. Rossoti, *supra* note 40.

[103] E.g., Tech. Adv. Mem. 9635003.

[104] Reg. § 53.4955-1(c)(2)(i), (ii). The conference report accompanying these rules stated that, for this purpose, an organization is to be "considered as effectively controlled by a candidate or prospective candidate only if the individual has a continuing, substantial involvement in the day-to-day operations or management of the organization" (H. Rep. 495, 100th Cong., 1st Sess. 1021 (1987)). The report added that an organization is not to be "considered as effectively controlled by a candidate or a prospective candidate merely because it is affiliated with such candidate, or merely because the candidate knows the directors, officers, or employees of the organization" (*id.*). The report additionally stated that, "[l]ikewise, the effectively controlled test is not met merely because the organization carries on its research, study, or other educational activities with respect to subject matter or issues in which the individual is interested or with which the individual is associated" (*id.*).

This conference report also stated that the "determination of whether the primary purposes of an organization described in . . . [these rules] are promoting the candidacy or prospective candidacy of an individual for public office is to be made on the basis of all relevant facts and circumstances" (*id.*). The report added that the "factors to be considered include whether the surveys, studies, materials, etc. prepared by the organization are made available only to one individual (the candidate) or are made available to the general public; and whether the organization pays for speeches and travel expenses for only one individual, or for speeches or travel expenses of several persons" (*id.*). The report concluded: "The fact that a candidate or prospective candidate utilizes studies, papers, materials, etc. prepared by the organization (for example, in speeches by the individual) is not to be considered as a factor indicating that the organization has a purpose of promoting the candidacy or prospective candidacy of such individual where such studies, papers, materials, etc. are not made available only to that individual" (*id.* at 1021–1022).

use by the individual; (4) the expenses of advertising, publicity, and fundraising for the individual; and (5) any other expense "which has the primary effect of promoting public recognition, or otherwise primarily accruing to the benefit, of" the individual.[105]

A political expenditure can trigger an *initial tax*, payable by the organization, of 10 percent of the amount of the expenditure. An initial tax of $2\frac{1}{2}$ percent of the expenditure can also imposed on each of the organization's managers (such as directors and officers), where he or she knew it was a political expenditure, unless the agreement to make the expenditure was not willful and was due to reasonable cause.[106] The IRS has the discretionary authority to abate these initial taxes where the organization can establish that the violation was due to reasonable cause and not to willful neglect, and timely corrects the violation.[107]

An *additional tax* can be imposed on a charitable organization, at a rate of 100 percent of the political expenditure. This tax is levied where the initial tax was imposed and the expenditure was not timely corrected. An additional tax can be imposed on the organization's manager, at a rate of 50 percent of the expenditure. This tax is levied where the additional tax was imposed on the organization and where the manager refused to agree to part or all of the correction.

As to management and as to any one political expenditure, the maximum initial tax is $5,000 and the maximum additional tax is $10,000.[108]

In this context, the concept of *correction* means "recovering part or all of the expenditure to the extent recovery is possible, establishment of safeguards to prevent future political expenditures, and where full recovery is not possible, such additional corrective action" as may be prescribed by federal tax regulations.[109]

If a tax is imposed with respect to a political expenditure under these rules, the expenditure will not be treated as a taxable expenditure under the private foundation rules.[110]

An organization that loses its federal tax-exempt status as a charitable organization because of political campaign activities is precluded from becoming tax-exempt as a social welfare organization.[111]

Under certain circumstances, the IRS is empowered to commence an action

---

[105] The conference report accompanying this legislation made it clear that these rules do not alter the existing rules as to the qualification of voter registration and voter education activities as exempt functions of charitable organizations (H. Rep. 495, *supra* note 104, at 1021). Also Reg. § 53.4955-1(c)(2)(iii).

[106] Reg. § 53.4955-1(b).

[107] IRC § 4962; Reg. § 53.4955-1(d).

[108] A tax paid under this section is reported on Form 4720 (Reg. §§ 53.6011-1(b), 53.6071-1(e)).

[109] Reg. § 53.4955-1(e). The conference report noted that the "adoption of the excise tax sanction does modify the present-law rule that an organization is not tax-exempt under [IRC] section 501(c)(3), eligible to receive tax-deductible charitable contributions, if the organization engages in any political campaign activity" (H. Rep. 495, *supra* note 104, at 1020). Also Reg. § 53.4955-1(a).

[110] See § 11.4(e).

[111] IRC § 504.

in federal district court to enjoin a charitable organization from the further making of political expenditures and for other relief to ensure that the assets of the organization are preserved for tax-exempt purposes.[112] These circumstances are the following: (1) the IRS has notified the organization of its intention to seek this injunction if the making of the political expenditures does not immediately cease; and (2) the Commissioner of Internal Revenue has personally determined that the organization has "flagrantly" participated or intervened in a political campaign on behalf of or in opposition to any candidate for public office and that injunctive relief is appropriate to prevent future political expenditures. If the federal district court finds, on the basis of "clear and convincing" evidence, the same facts as the Commissioner found, the court is authorized to enjoin the expenditures and grant other appropriate relief.

If the IRS finds that a charitable organization has flagrantly violated the prohibition against the making of political expenditures, the IRS is required to determine and assess any income and/or excise tax(es) due immediately, by terminating the organization's tax year.[113]

§ 21.3 TAXATION OF POLITICAL ACTIVITIES

A tax-exempt organization[114] that makes an expenditure for a political activity is subject to a tax.[115] This tax is determined by computing an amount equal to the lesser of the organization's net investment income[116] for the year involved or the amount expended for the political activity. This amount constitutes *political organization taxable income*[117] and is taxed[118] at the highest corporate rates.[119]

The concept of *political activity* for purposes of this tax is the same as that used for defining the exempt functions of political organizations.[120] Thus, political activity includes the function of influencing or attempting to influence the selection, nomination, election, or appointment of any individual to any federal, state, or local public office.[121] Consequently, this concept of *political activity* is broader than the concept of *political campaign activity* made applicable, as a prohibition, to charitable organizations.[122]

The prohibition applicable to charitable organizations concerns interventions or participations in political campaigns on behalf of or in opposition to can-

---

[112] IRC § 7409; Reg. § 301.7409-1.
[113] IRC § 6852; Reg. § 301.6852-1.
[114] That is, an organization described in IRC § 501(c) and exempt from federal income taxation by reason of IRC § 501(a).
[115] IRC § 527(f)(1).
[116] This term is defined in IRC § 527(f)(2).
[117] IRC § 527(c)(1), (2).
[118] IRC § 527(b).
[119] IRC § 11(b).
[120] IRC § 527(e)(2). In general, see Chapter 17.
[121] *Id.*
[122] This chapter, *passim.* (The term *charitable* organization means an organization described in IRC § 501(c)(3).)

didates for public office. This prohibition is not necessarily a bar on political activity. For example, a charitable organization can attempt to influence the nomination of an individual to a public office; this would be *political activity* (and thus could attract this special tax) but not *political campaign activity*. Indeed, it is the position of the IRS that the function of influencing or attempting to influence the appointment of any individual to a public office, where confirmation by the legislative branch is involved, constitutes influencing or attempting to influence legislation, rather than political activity.[123]

The IRS has recognized the distinction between the concept of *political campaign activity* and the broader concept of *political activity*, in the context of noting that a charitable organization can establish a separate segregated fund for the purpose of conducting political activities that are not political campaign activities. On this occasion, the IRS Chief Counsel's office wrote that an "organization described in section 501(c)(3) is precluded from engaging in any political campaign activities."[124]

Political activity that is not political campaign activity can constitute a charitable, educational, religious, or like activity, undertaken in furtherance of the tax-exempt functions of a charitable organization. Thus, the income tax regulations state that, where the prohibited activities are not engaged in as a "primary objective," the organization is not an action organization but can be regarded as "engaging in nonpartisan analysis, study, or research and making the results thereof available to the public."[125]

§ 21.4   POLITICAL ACTIVITIES OF SOCIAL WELFARE ORGANIZATIONS

Tax-exempt social welfare organizations generally are forbidden from participating or intervening in any political campaign on behalf of or in opposition to any candidate for public office.[126] The IRS has traditionally been strict in applying this restriction, as illustrated by the denial of classification as an exempt social welfare organization to a group that rated candidates for public office on a nonpartisan basis and disseminated its ratings to the general public, on the theory that its rating process was intervention or participation on behalf of those candidates favorably rated and in opposition to those less favorably rated.[127]

Nor will objectivity necessarily ward off an unfavorable determination, as evidenced by the nonprofit group that selected slates of candidates for school board elections and engaged in campaigns on their behalf, and that was accordingly denied tax exemption as a charitable organization (and thus presumably as a social welfare organization) because of these political activities, "even though its process of selection may have been completely objective and

---

[123] Notice 88-76, 1988-2 C.B. 392.
[124] Gen. Couns. Mem. 39694.
[125] Reg. § 1.501(c)(3)-1(c)(3)(iv).
[126] Reg. § 1.501(c)(4)-1(a)(2)(ii). See Chapter 12.
[127] Rev. Rul. 67-368, 1967-2 C.B. 194.

unbiased and was intended primarily to educate and inform the public about the candidates."[128]

The foregoing does not mean, however, that a tax-exempt social welfare organization is completely foreclosed from participation in governmental and political affairs. An organization the activities of which were primarily directed, on a nonprofit and nonpartisan basis, toward encouraging individuals in business to become more active in politics and government and toward promoting business, social, or civic action was held to qualify for tax exemption as a social welfare organization.[129] Likewise, a group that engaged in nonpartisan analysis, study, and research, made the results available to the public, and publicized the need for a code of fair campaign practices, was ruled to be an exempt educational organization.[130] Also, an organization that recruited college students for an internship program providing employment with local municipal agencies qualified as an exempt educational and charitable organization.[131] Thus, an exempt social welfare organization could similarly undertake these activities.

The IRS, therefore, in determining an organization's tax-exempt status in light of the requirements for a social welfare entity, carefully adheres to the distinction between those groups that actively participate or intervene in a political campaign for or against candidates for public office and those that more passively seek to stimulate public interest in improved government, better campaign practices, and the like.

This prohibition on political campaign activities by tax-exempt social welfare organizations is not absolute, however, in that the requirement is that these organizations must be *primarily* engaged in activities that promote social welfare.[132] Thus, an exempt organization primarily engaged in social welfare functions may carry on activities (such as financial assistance and in-kind services) involving participation and intervention in political campaigns on behalf of or in opposition to candidates for nomination or election to public office.[133]

§ 21.5 INTERNET ACTIVITIES

Charitable organizations may engage in political campaign activities by means of the Internet. This practice is raising questions as to the application of the federal tax law to this form of advocacy. Moreover, some charitable entities are affiliated with organizations that conduct political campaign activity using the Internet. A

---

[128] Rev. Rul. 67-71, 1967-1 C.B. 125.

[129] Rev. Rul. 60-193, 1960-1 C.B. 145.

[130] Rev. Rul. 66-258, 1966-2 C.B. 213.

[131] Rev. Rul. 70-584, 1970-2 C.B. 114.

[132] See § 4.4.

[133] Rev. Rul. 81-95, 1981-1 C.B. 332. These political campaign activities will, however, cause the organization to be subject to the tax imposed by IRC § 527(f) on the expenditures for political activities that are within the meaning of IRC § 527(e)(2) (see *supra* § 3).

message, concerning this type of activity, may be on an organization's Web site, which is linked to a charity's Web site.

(a)   Internet Political Campaign Activity in General

Political campaign activity can constitute a form of communication and the Internet is a medium of communication. Thus, political campaign activities by tax-exempt organizations (and other persons) can be undertaken by means of the Internet. As is the case in other contexts, however, the federal tax law does not provide any unique treatment to transactions or activities of exempt organizations involving political campaign activities, simply because the Internet is the medium of communication.

As the IRS saliently observed, the "use of the Internet to accomplish a particular task does not change the way the tax laws apply to that task."[134] The IRS continued: "Advertising is still advertising and fundraising is still fundraising."[135] The agency also could have said: "Political campaign activity is still political campaign activity."

There are four forms of Internet communications in this setting: (1) a communication published on a publicly accessible Web page; (2) a communication posted on a password-protected portion of a Web site; (3) a communication on a listserv (or by means of other methods such as a news group, chat room, and/or forum); and (4) a communication by means of email. The IRS recognized that, by "publishing a webpage on the Internet, an exempt organization can provide the general public with information about the organization, its activities, and issues of concern to the organization."[136] The agency added: "An exempt organization can provide information to subscribers about issues of concern to the organization as well as enable people with common interests to share information via the Internet through a variety of methods," referencing mailing lists and the methods referred to previously in the third category of Internet communication.[137]

An email communication from a tax-exempt organization clearly can constitute a political campaign activity (such as an endorsement). If an exempt organization were to send an email message or messages, urging the election of an individual to a public office, that would constitute a political campaign activity. An exempt organization may post a political campaign message on the portion of its Web site that is publicly accessible. That also would be a political campaign activity.[138]

---

[134] *IRS Exempt Organization Continuing Professional Education Text for Fiscal Year 2000*, Technical Topic I.
[135] *Id.*
[136] Ann. 2000-84, 2000-42 I.R.B. 385.
[137] *Id.*
[138] In general, Hopkins, *The Nonprofits' Guide to Internet Communications Law* (John Wiley & Sons, Inc., 2002), Chapter 6.

Insurance and Fundraising Activities

§ 22.1 **Insurance Activities**
  (a) General Rules
  (b) Commercial-Type Insurance Rules

  (c) Health Maintenance Organizations

§ 22.2 **Fundraising Disclosure**

The federal tax law contains bodies of law applicable to tax-exempt organizations that engage in certain insurance activities and certain fundraising activities. The former is a set of rules that can affect qualification for tax-exempt status, while the latter is a disclosure requirement. Also, the law concerning the taxation of unrelated business income can apply with respect to both insurance and fundraising activities.[1]

§ 22.1 INSURANCE ACTIVITIES

(a) General Rules

In general, and including the time prior to the effective date of the rules concerning commercial-type insurance,[2] nonprofit organizations that provide various types of insurance cannot qualify as charitable entities. Indeed, in some instances, organizations of this nature were unable to qualify as exempt social welfare organizations.

In the principal case in this regard, a church organized an entity to provide insurance protection against fire, storms, vandalism, and similar casualty losses on churches and other buildings. The coverage was available only to church members and their dependents. The organization's income was derived from insurance premiums, investment of surplus funds, and a nominal lifetime membership fee.

The organization contended that it was tax-exempt as a charitable entity on the ground that it advanced religion.[3] A federal court of appeals rejected that ar-

---

[1] See Part Five.
[2] See *infra* § 1(b).
[3] See § 6.4.

gument, observing that the entity "does not give succor to souls; it sells insurance coverage" and that it is "not supported by voluntary donations in whatever amounts the membership wishes to give; it extends benefits in return for a premium based generally upon the risk assumed."[4]

The court also wrote that the organization "primarily provides property insurance, an admitted economic activity" and that it "treats its surplus and profit as would any mutual insurance company."[5]

The court concluded that the "presence of a substantial non-exempt purpose—providing property insurance for its members on the basis of assessed premiums—precludes ... [the entity's] exempt status as an organization for the advancement of religion."[6] The court also found that that purpose precluded the organization's status as an exempt social welfare organization.

A similar entity met the same fate. This was a trust, affiliated with some religious schools, that operated as an insurance company, extending insurance benefits in return for premiums received based on risk assumed by the entity. These functions (including the maintenance of files, acceptance of claims, and issuance of insurance benefits) were found to constitute a "substantial private purpose" that vitiated the trust's claim that it operated exclusively for religious purposes or as a social welfare organization.[7]

A program activity of a church, such as a medical aid plan, involving a single congregation and funded with voluntary contributions taken at church services, can be a charitable undertaking.[8] In such a case, the church's doctrine considers all of its members to be needy and thus "deserving of one another's assistance, regardless of their own financial means."[9]

(b) Commercial-Type Insurance Rules

An otherwise tax-exempt charitable organization[10] or social welfare organization[11] will lose or be denied tax exemption if a substantial part of its activities consists of the provision of *commercial-type insurance.*[12] Otherwise, the activity of providing commercial-type insurance is treated as the conduct of an unrelated trade or business[13] and the income from it is taxed under the rules pertaining to taxable insurance companies.[14]

The term *commercial-type insurance* generally is any insurance of a type provided by commercial insurance companies.[15] For example, an organization

[4] Mutual Aid Ass'n of Church of the Brethren v. United States, 759 F.2d 792, 795 (10th Cir. 1985), *aff'g* 578 F. Supp. 451 (D. Kan. 1983).
[5] *Id.,* 759 F.2d at 796.
[6] *Id.*
[7] American Ass'n of Christian Schs. Voluntary Employees Beneficiary Ass'n Welfare Plan Trust v. United States, 850 F.2d 1510, 1513 (11th Cir. 1988), *aff'g* 663 F. Supp. 275 (M.D. Ala. 1987).
[8] E.g., Bethel Conservative Mennonite Church v. Comm'r, 746 F.2d 388 (7th Cir. 1984).
[9] *Id.* at 391.
[10] See Part Two.
[11] See Chapter 12.
[12] IRC § 501(m).
[13] See § 27.1(o).
[14] IRC Subchapter L. The application of these rules may require organizations affected by them to change their accounting methods; the process for doing so is the subject of Rev. Proc. 87-51, 1987-2 C.B. 650.
[15] H. Rep. 99-841, 99th Cong., 2d Sess. II-345 (1986).

was held to not qualify as a tax-exempt social welfare organization because its sole activity was the provision of certain benefits to students in a school who were injured in the course of school-related activities, in that the coverage was similar to contingent or excess insurance coverage.[16] However, this term does not include insurance provided at substantially below cost to a class of charitable recipients, incidental health insurance provided by an HMO of a kind customarily provided by these organizations,[17] property or casualty insurance provided (directly or through a qualified employer)[18] by a church or convention or association of churches for the church or convention or association of churches, and the provision of retirement or welfare benefits (or both) by a church or a convention or association of churches (directly or through a qualified organization[19]) for the employees of the church or convention or association of churches or the beneficiaries of these employees.[20] This rule is also inapplicable to income from an insurance activity conducted by a political subdivision of a government.[21]

The IRS endeavored to define the term *commercial-type insurance*, since the phrase is undefined in the statute. Following a review of tax cases defining the term *insurance*, the Chief Counsel's office concluded that the definition of commercial-type insurance "should include some form of risk-sharing and risk-distribution."[22] The IRS's lawyers also said that, despite the statutory exception for HMO insurance, "it is our opinion that in certain circumstances a health maintenance organization may be found to provide" commercial-type insurance.

Of course, for these rules to apply, the underlying activity must be the provision of *insurance* in the first instance. (The essence of the concept of insurance is that the risk of liability is shifted to at least one third party (the insurer), and that the risk is shared and distributed across a group of persons.[23]) For these purposes, the issuance of annuity contracts is considered the provision of insurance.[24] These rules do not, however, apply to a charitable gift annuity, which is defined for this purpose as an annuity where a portion of the amount paid in connection with the issuance of the annuity is allowable as a charitable

---

[16] Gen. Couns. Mem. 39703.

[17] E.g., Priv. Ltr. Rul. 9246004.

[18] That is, an organization described in IRC § 414(e)(3)(B)(ii).

[19] That is, an organization described in IRC § 414(e)(3)(A) or § 414(e)(3)(B)(ii).

[20] IRC § 501(m)(3). The management, by supporting organizations (see § 11.3(c)), for a church of regulated investment companies to provide benefits for church employees was ruled by the IRS to not cause loss of tax-exempt status of the organizations by reason of IRC § 501(m) (Priv. Ltr. Rul. 9645007).

[21] Priv. Ltr. Rul. 8836038.

[22] Gen. Couns. Mem. 39828.

[23] E.g., Sears, Roebuck & Co. v. Comm'r, 96 T.C. 61 (1991); The Harper Group v. Comm'r, 96 T.C. 45 (1991); Americo & Subsidiaries v. Comm'r, 96 T.C. 18 (1991); Humana, Inc. v. Comm'r, 88 T.C. 197 (1987), *aff'd in part, rev'd in part*, 881 F.2d 276 (6th Cir. 1989); Beech Aircraft Corp. v. United States, 797 F.2d 920 (10th Cir. 1986); Clougherty Packing Co. v. Comm'r, 84 T.C. 948 (1985), *aff'd*, 811 F.2d 1297 (9th Cir. 1987); Stearns-Roger Corp. v. United States, 774 F.2d 414 (10th Cir. 1985); Carnation Co. v. Comm'r, 71 T.C. 400 (1978), *aff'd*, 640 F.2d 1010 (9th Cir. 1981), *cert. den.*, 454 U.S. 965 (1981); Helvering v. LeGierse, 312 U.S. 531 (1941).

[24] IRC § 501(m)(4).

deduction for federal income or estate tax purposes, and the annuity is described in the special rule for annuities in the unrelated debt-financed income provisions[25] (determined as if any amount paid in cash in connection with the issuance were property).[26]

A court ruled that a nonprofit organization established to create and administer a group self-insurance pool for the benefit of tax-exempt social service paratransit providers, to provide the necessary financing for comprehensive automobile liability, risk management, and related services for pool members, did not qualify for exemption as a charitable organization because it provided commercial-type insurance.[27] The court observed that the purpose of the insurance pool "is to shift the risk of potential tort liability from each of the individual insured paratransit organizations" to the entity, which "diversifies the risk of liability for each individual member."[28] It added that the type of insurance offered "is basic automobile liability insurance, a type of insurance provided by a number of commercial insurance carriers."[29] The court, writing that the phrase commercial-type insurance encompasses "every type of insurance that can be purchased in the commercial market," rejected the contention that the rules as to commercial-type insurance apply only where the insurance is offered to the general public. As to substantiality, the court, having found claims expenses to be as high as 75 percent, held that these insurance activities "are unquestionably a substantial part of its operations."[30]

This court subsequently held that three types of hospital membership funds cannot qualify as tax-exempt because they provided forms of commercial-type insurance. One fund enabled hospitals to self-insure on a group basis against hospital professional liability; this fund and another provided centralized cooperative insurance services to its member hospitals through the employment of actuaries, risk managers, underwriters, accountants, and other insurance consultants. The third fund was created as a vehicle for member hospital employers to self-insure on a group basis against workers' compensation claims. Finding the commercial-type insurance rules applicable, the court observed that the funds "provide actuarial, accounting, underwriting, claims payment, and similar services" that are "essential to the administration of the insurance programs."[31] The court said that there "is no dispute that hospital professional liability and workers' compensation insurance are normally offered by commercial insurers."[32]

---

[25] IRC § 514(c)(5) (see § 29.3).

[26] IRC §§ 501(m)(3)(E), (5). The IRS held that a supporting organization's global capitation agreements with unrelated insurance companies and individuals do not entail the provision of commercial-type insurance (and thus not cause unrelated business income) (Priv. Ltr. Rul. 200044039).

[27] Paratransit Ins. Corp. v. Comm'r, 102 T.C. 745 (1994).

[28] Id. at 754.

[29] Id.

[30] Id.

[31] Florida Hosp. Trust Fund v. Comm'r, 103 T.C. 140 (1994).

[32] Id. at 158. This opinion was affirmed on appeal (71 F.3d 808 (11th Cir. 1996)).

Another case concerned an organization that administered a group self-insurance risk pool for a membership of nearly 500 charitable organizations that operate to fund or provide health or human services. It was formed to provide its membership with affordable insurance, which had endured periods of large premium increases, coverage reductions, and cancellations. The organization also develops educational materials and makes educational presentations, provides loss control and risk management services without charge, and serves as a resource for insurance-related questions. As to the insurance coverage, the organization provided commercial general liability, automobile liability, employer's non-owned and hired automobile liability, and miscellaneous professional liability. Observing that the organization "exists solely for the purpose of selling insurance to nonprofit exempt organizations at the lowest possible cost on a continued, stable basis," the court wrote that "[s]elling insurance undeniably is an inherently commercial activity ordinarily carried on by a commercial for-profit company."[33] The court said that, despite the fact that the insurance is provided on a low-cost basis and that loss control and risk management services are provided without charge, the "nature and operation" of the organization are commercial in nature.[34] It was noted that the organization engages in the actual underwriting of insurance policies, contracts with other firms to secure reinsurance for high claims, and ceases membership benefits when a member fails to timely pay the required premium payments.

The foregoing body of caselaw,[35] however, has been somewhat supplanted by statutory law providing tax-exempt status for charitable risk pools.[36]

As noted,[37] these rules are inapplicable to the provision of insurance by a nonprofit organization at substantially below cost to a class of charitable recipients.[38] The courts are placing great emphasis on a ruling by the IRS, issued in a different context, that the phrase *substantially below cost* entails a subsidy of at least 85 percent.[39] Thus, in one case, while the court declined to "draw a bright line" defining that phrase, it rejected the proposition that a subsidy of about 35 percent qualified.[40] In another instance, this exception was ruled not applicable where member contributions for one year were in excess of 80 percent.[41]

---

[33] Nonprofits' Ins. Alliance of Calif. v. United States, 94-2 USTC ¶ 50,593 (Ct. Fed. Cl. 1994).
[34] *Id.*
[35] See the text accompanied by *supra* notes 27–34,
[36] See § 10.6.
[37] See *supra* note 20.
[38] IRC § 501(m)(3)(A).
[39] Rev. Rul. 71-529, 1971-2 C.B. 234.
[40] Nonprofits' Ins. Alliance of Calif. v. United States, *supra* note 33.
[41] Paratransit Ins. Corp. v. Comm'r, *supra* note 27. In general, Shill, "Revocation of Blue Cross & Blue Shield's Tax-Exempt Status an Unhealthy Change? An Analysis of the Effect of the Tax Reform Act of 1986 on the Taxation of Blue Cross & Blue Shield and Health Insurance Activities," 6 *B. U. J. Tax Law* 147 (1988); McGovern, "Federal Tax Exemption of Prepaid Health Care Plans," 7 *Tax Adviser* 76 (Feb. 1976).

(c) Health Maintenance Organizations

A matter of some controversy is application of these rules concerning commercial-type insurance to health maintenance organizations (HMOs).[42] It appears relatively clear that these rules were not intended to apply to the types of services provided by these organizations.[43] Yet, the IRS applies these rules with respect to HMOs. Also, as noted, commercial-type insurance does not include arrangements that are not regarded as insurance (such as situations involving the absence of sufficient risk-shifting and risk distribution).

An organization that issued medical service contracts to groups or individuals and furnished direct medical services to the subscribers by means of a salaried staff of medical personnel was ruled by the IRS not to be an insurance company.[44] In that case, a medical clinic employed a staff of salaried physicians, nurses, and technicians to provide a major portion of the contracted medical services. If the clinic had to treat a patient with an illness or injury, the patient was treated by the clinic's salaried staff, thereby avoiding any significant additional costs. The IRS concluded that any risk the clinic incurred was predominantly normal business risk. Thus, the clinic's economic risk was fixed irrespective of the presence or extent of any illness or injury. A federal court of appeals, in finding an HMO not to be an insurance company, observed that, although the HMO did not employ physicians to provide medical services, it paid contracted physicians a "fixed annual compensation in monthly installments, not specific fees for each treatment or case."[45]

Neither the Internal Revenue Code nor the tax regulations define the term *insurance contract*. The IRS defines the term as a contract that must involve the element of shifting or assuming the risk of loss of the insured and must, therefore, be a contract under which the insurer is liable for a loss suffered by its insured.[46] Case law defines an *insurance contract* as a "contract whereby, for an adequate consideration, one party undertakes to indemnify another against loss from certain specified contingencies or peril. . . . [I]t is contractual security against possible anticipated loss."[47] Case law also has established that risk-shifting and risk distribu-

---

[42] These organizations are the subject of § 6.2(e).

[43] For example, in the conference report accompanying the Technical and Miscellaneous Revenue Act of 1988, it was stated: "[T]he provision relating to organizations engaged in commercial-type insurance activities did not alter the tax-exempt status of health maintenance organizations (HMOs). . . . the conference committee clarifies that, in addition to the general exemption for health maintenace organizations, organizations that provide supplemental health maintenance organization-type activities (such as dental or vision services) are not treated as providing commercial-type insurance if they operate in the same manner as a health maintenance organization" (H. Rep. 100-1104, 100th Cong., 2d Sess. II-9 (1988)).

[44] Rev. Rul. 68-27, 1968-1 C.B. 315.

[45] Jordan, Superintendent of Ins. v. Group Health Ass'n, 107 F.2d 239, 242, note 7 (D.C. Cir. 1939).

[46] Rev. Rul. 68-27, *supra* note 44.

[47] Empeler v. United States, 199 F.2d 508, 509–10 (7th Cir. 1962). Also Union Labor Life Ins. Co. v. Pireno, 458 U.S. 119, 127 (1982); Group Life & Health Ins. Co. v. Royal Drug Co., 440 U.S. 205, 211 (1979); Securities & Exch. Comm'n v. Variable Life Annuity Life Ins. Co., 359 U.S. 65, 71 (1959); 1 *Couch on Insurance* 2d (rev. ed.) §§ 1:2, 1:3 (1984).

tion are the fundamental characteristics of a contract of insurance.[48] Further, the risk that is transferred must be a risk of economic loss. The risk for which insurance coverage is provided is an insurance risk, that is, it must occur fortuitously and must result in an economic loss to the insurer. As one court stated, the "common definition for insurance is an agreement to protect the insured against a direct or indirect economic loss arising from a defined contingency whereby the insurer undertakes no present duty of performance but stands ready to assume the financial burden of any covered."[49]

The IRS ruled that risk-shifting occurs when a person facing the possibility of an economic loss transfers some or all of the financial consequences of the loss to the insurer.[50] The IRS also held that risk distribution refers to the operation of the statistical phenomenon known as the "law of large numbers." When additional statistically independent risk exposure units are insured, an insurance company's potential total loss increases, as does the uncertainty regarding the amount of that loss. As the uncertainty regarding the company's total loss increases, however, there is an increase in the predictability of the insurance company's average loss. Because of this increase in the predictability of average loss, there is a downward trend in the amount of capital that the company needs per risk unit to remain at a given level of solvency.[51]

These rules were applied by the IRS in the case of a tax-exempt HMO[52] with a point-of-service (POS) program.[53] The issue was whether this program was the provision of commercial-type insurance.[54]

This HMO arranges, on a prepaid basis, for the provision of comprehensive preventive and therapeutic health care services to its enrollees, who are individuals and employer groups. The HMO offers its enrollees a choice of two plans when they select their benefits. One plan is, on the basis of enrollees, the "predominant" one, while the other was cast by the IRS as "insignificant." As to the latter plan, the POS program, the issue was whether the plan is an unrelated business.

Pursuant to the POS program, an enrollee can utilize a network or a non-network of physicians as selected by the enrollee. This program is administered by a nonexempt affiliate of the HMO. In the event of an emergency, an enrollee can obtain health care services from a network or non-network specialist without prior authorization from a primary care physician. A network primary care physician who provided medical services to an enrollee under the predominant plan is paid a different fee for providing the identical services to an enrollee in the POS plan.

---

[48] See the text accompanied by *infra* note 49.

[49] E.g., Allied Fidelity Corp. v. Comm'r, 68 T.C. 1068 (1976), *aff'd*, 572 F.2d 1190 (7th Cir. 1978), *cert. den.*, 439 U.S. 835 (1978).

[50] Rev. Rul. 88-72, 1998-2 C.B. 31, *clarified by* Rev. Rul. 89-61, 1989-1 C.B. 75.

[51] Rev. Rul. 89-61, *supra* note 50.

[52] An IRC § 501(c)(4) organization. See Chapter 12.

[53] Tech. Adv. Mem. 200033046.

[54] The analysis to follow is based on the IRS's *Exempt Organizations Continuing Professional Education Technical Instruction Text for Fiscal Year 2001.*

This HMO's cost of arranging primary medical care services for each enrollee under this plan does not vary based on the extent of primary care services a network physician provided to the enrollee. Therefore, the HMO shifts to its primary care physicians a substantial portion of its risk of loss associated with arranging primary health care services for its enrollees. The HMO retains only a normal business risk. Consequently, the HMO's activities with respect to its enrollees in the predominant plan do not consist of the provision of commercial-type insurance.

Conversely, the HMO's cost of arranging primary health care services for each enrollee in the POS plan are not fixed but vary based on the extent of primary care services the primary care physician provided to the plan enrollee. Since the HMO pays primary care physicians who treated POS plan enrollees on a fee-for-service basis, the HMO bears the risk of loss associated with the cost of providing additional primary care services an enrollee in this plan may require. Therefore, the IRS concluded that the HMO retains, rather than shifts to these primary care physicians, its risk of loss associated with arranging primary health care services for its POS plan enrollees. As a result, the HMO's activities with respect to its POS plan enrollees consist of the provision of commercial-type insurance.

Inasmuch as the HMO's activities of providing commercial-type insurance for its POS plan enrollees is not substantial in relation to its total activities, these activities will not adversely affect the HMO's tax exemption. Nonetheless, the net income the HMO earns from the provision of commercial-type insurance for its POS plan enrollees is subject to the unrelated business income tax.

Comparable tax issues are raised by the operation of Medicaid-only HMOs. These are HMOs that arrange for the provision of health care services exclusively to Medicaid beneficiaries. These entities may qualify for tax exemption as charitable or social welfare organizations. Here, too, the issue arises as to whether the HMO has shifted a substantial portion of its risk of loss to its primary care providers.

The IRS stated that an example of such risk-shifting is an HMO compensating its contracted primary care providers on a capitated fee basis. Another illustration is an HMO compensating its contracted primary care providers on a fee-for-service basis, using the Medicaid-approved fee schedule, and withholding a substantial portion of the fees paid.

A Medicaid-only HMO that otherwise qualifies for tax exemption and that compensates its contracted primary care providers using the Medicaid-approved fee schedule, but does not withhold a substantial portion of the fees paid, does not—the IRS has said—adequately shift its risk of loss to the providers and thus is providing insurance.

There are, nonetheless, three arguments an HMO can muster in this context. One contention is that it has shifted a substantial portion of its risk of loss by means of a stop-loss insurance arrangement.

Generally, under these arrangements, if the total annual medical expenses incurred by the HMO on behalf of an enrollee exceed a certain amount, the insurer will absorb all or a portion of these expenses. The insurer may impose a maximum on the amount it will pay; it may cover only certain types of medical expenses, such as in-patient hospital care.

When a Medicaid-only HMO contracts with a state to arrange for the provision of health care services to its Medicaid beneficiary enrollees, the HMO is primarily liable to arrange and pay for the provision of these services to its enrollees, notwithstanding the fact that the HMO has purchased stop-loss insurance. In this situation, says the IRS, the predominant activity of the HMO is the issuance of an insurance contract to the state.

Thus, the position of the IRS is that the obtaining of an insurance contract by a Medicaid-only HMO that would indemnify the HMO for a portion of the losses it might sustain in performing its Medicaid contract with the state does not alter the fact that the HMO is primarily engaged in the business of insurance.

The IRS has left open, however, the possibility that a Medicaid-only HMO may be able to show, in an instance involving a stop-loss arrangement, that it has shifted a substantial portion of its risk of loss to an insurance company or that the portion of the risk of loss it retained was insubstantial.

The second argument a Medicaid-only HMO can muster is that it has shifted a substantial portion of its risk of loss by means of a deficit-sharing arrangement with its providers. Whether this argument prevails, says the IRS, will depend on the facts and circumstances.

One set of these circumstances that is likely to prove adverse to an HMO is a doctrine in insurance law known as the *economic family concept*. There is not a sufficient shifting of risk of loss when the shifting is only within the organization's family.

When an integrated health care delivery system forms an HMO, or when a group of hospitals which are structurally unrelated to each other forms an HMO, the member hospitals usually are the HMO's principal, if not exclusive, providers of inpatient and outpatient hospital services to the HMO's enrollees. Under a deficit-sharing arrangement between the member hospitals and the HMO, the member hospitals agree to bear a portion of the HMO's operating losses.

The IRS has written that if an HMO enters into a deficit-sharing arrangement with member hospitals that are structurally related to each other, the HMO does not shift a substantial portion of its risk of loss because it has not shifted its risk of loss outside its economic family. But, if an HMO enters into a deficit-sharing arrangement with member hospitals that are not structurally related to each other, and the hospitals are jointly and severally liable for *all* of the HMO's operating losses (that is, not just the losses attributable to services the HMO performed for the patients of the particular hospital), the IRS said that "an argument can be made" that the HMO has shifted a substantial portion of its risk of loss to these hospitals.

The final argument that may be made is that, while the HMO concededly provides insurance, it does not provide *commercial-type insurance*. Thus, a Medicaid-only HMO may contend that, even if it is providing insurance, the insurance is not of a commercial type on the ground that health insurance for Medicaid beneficiaries is not generally available commercially. This argument may go as follows: virtually no insurance companies in the community offer health insurance solely to a Medicaid population and, if they do, it is generally not affordable. This argument will fail.

The reason the argument is not meritorious, observed the IRS, is that it assumes that the Medicaid beneficiaries are the purchasers of the health care insurance. This, however, is not the case. Although a Medicaid beneficiary may select a particular provider from among a panel of them to be his or her primary care provider, he or she does not purchase or pay for the insurance. Rather, this is done by the state involved.

It is the state that solicits bids from health care organizations to arrange for the provision of health care services to Medicaid beneficiaries in selected areas of the state. It is the state that contracts with and compensates the organization, usually on a capitated fee basis. Usually, there are a number of health care insurance companies, integrated health care systems, or other health care consortiums that may offer to sell these health care insurance services to the state, even though this health care insurance is not available for purchase by the individual Medicaid beneficiaries.

Thus, the IRS has said, if the health care services these organizations provide is considered to be insurance, it is generally available commercially to the purchaser of the insurance. The case law teaches that, to be commercial-type insurance, it must be insurance that is generally available commercially; it does not have to be generally available to the public. Therefore, if the health care services offered by a Medicaid-only HMO are treated as insurance, this insurance will be regarded by the IRS as commercial-type insurance.

§ 22.2 FUNDRAISING DISCLOSURE

Federal tax law includes a provision concerning fundraising by most tax-exempt organizations.[55] These rules, however, are not applicable with respect to charitable organizations.[56]

This body of law is designed to prevent noncharitable (principally, social welfare) organizations from engaging in public fundraising activities under circumstances where donors are likely to assume that the contributions are tax deductible as charitable gifts, when in fact they are not.

---

[55] IRC § 6113.

[56] That is, this element of the legislation does not apply to organizations described in IRC § 501(c)(3). Nonetheless, the report of the House Committee on Ways and Means accompanying the legislation (H. Rep. 391, 100th Cong., 1st Sess. (1987)) observed that the Committee "is concerned that some charitable organizations may not make sufficient disclosure, in soliciting donations, membership dues, payments for admissions or merchandise, or other support, of the extent (if any) to which the payors may be entitled to charitable deductions for such payments" (at 1607). The report discussed these matters in some detail, concluding with an exhortation to the organizations representing the charitable community to "further educate their members as to the applicable tax rules and provide guidance as to how charities can provide appropriate information to their supporters in this regard" (at 1608).

Less than five years later, however, fundraising regulation law was enacted for charitable organizations. These rules include a gift substantiation requirement (IRC § 170(f)(8)) and rules pertaining to *quid pro quo* contributions (IRC §§ 6115, 6714). These bodies of law are the subject of Hopkins, *The Tax Law of Charitable Giving, Second Edition* (John Wiley & Sons, Inc., 2000), §§ 22.1(b), 23.2.

Thus, under these rules, each *fundraising solicitation* by (or on behalf of) a noncharitable tax-exempt organization is required to "contain an express statement (in a conspicuous and easily recognizable format)" that gifts to it are not deductible as charitable contributions for federal income tax purposes.[57] A fundraising solicitation that is in conformity with rules promulgated by the IRS (concerning the format of the disclosure statement in instances of use of print media, telephone, television, and radio), which include guidance in the form of "safe harbor" provisions, is deemed to satisfy the statutory requirements.[58]

Generally, this rule applies to any organization to which contributions are not deductible as charitable gifts and that (1) is tax-exempt,[59] (2) is a political organization,[60] (3) was either type of organization at any time during the five-year period ending on the date of the fundraising solicitation, or (4) is a successor to this type of an organization at any time during the five-year period.[61] This rule is inapplicable, however, to any organization that has annual gross receipts that are normally no more than $100,000. Also, where all of the parties being solicited are tax-exempt organizations, a solicitation need not include the disclosure statement (inasmuch as these grantors do not utilize a charitable contribution deduction).[62]

Further exempt from this disclosure rule is the billing of those who advertise in an organization's publications, billings by social clubs for food and beverages, billing of attendees at a conference, billing for insurance premiums of an insurance program operated or sponsored by an organization, billing of members of a community association for mandatory payments for police and fire (and similar) protection, or billing for payments to a voluntary employees' beneficiary association, as well as similar payments to a trust for pension and/or health benefits.[63]

The IRS is accorded the authority to treat any group of two or more organizations as one organization for these purposes where "necessary or appropriate" to prevent the avoidance of these rules through the use of multiple organizations. The term *fundraising solicitation* means any solicitation of gifts made in written or printed form, or by television, radio, or telephone. An exclusion is provided for letters or calls not part of a "coordinated fundraising campaign soliciting more than 10 persons during the calendar year."[64]

---

[57] IRC § 6113(a).

[58] Notice 88-120, 1988-2 C.B. 454. In one instance, a political organization (see Chapter 17) that conducted fundraising by means of telemarketing and direct mail was found to be in violation of these rules; a notice of nondeductibility of contributions was not included in its telephone solicitations or pledge statements, and the print used in some of its written notices was too small (Priv. Ltr. Rul. 9315001).

[59] That is, is described in IRC § 501(c) (other than, as noted, *supra* note 56, IRC § 501(c)(3)).

[60] That is, an organization described in IRC § 527. See Chapter 17.

[61] IRC § 6113(b). For this purpose, a fraternal organization (one described in IRC § 170(c)(4); see § 18.4) is treated as a charitable organization only with respect to solicitations for contributions which are to be used exclusively for purposes referred to in IRC § 170(c)(4).

[62] Notice 88-120, *supra* note 58.

[63] *Id.*

[64] IRC § 6113(c).

Failure to satisfy this disclosure requirement can result in imposition of penalties.[65] The penalty is $1,000 per day (maximum of $10,000 per year), albeit with a reasonable cause exception. In the case of an "intentional disregard" of these rules, however, the penalty for the day on which the offense occurred is the greater of $1,000 or 50 percent of the aggregate cost of the solicitation that took place on that day and the $10,000 limitation would be inapplicable. For these purposes, the days involved are those on which the solicitation was telecast, broadcast, mailed, otherwise distributed, or telephoned.

---

[65] IRC § 6710.

CHAPTER TWENTY-THREE

Exemption Recognition Process

Every element of gross income received by a person, including a corporation or trust, is subject to the federal income tax.[1] The presumption is that all income is taxable; income, to not be taxable, must be exempt by virtue of a specific tax law provision. Examples of this are the provisions for tax-exempt organizations.

An organization is not exempt from the federal income tax merely because it is organized and operated as a *nonprofit* entity.[2] Tax exemption is achieved only where the organization satisfies the requirements of a particular provision in the Internal Revenue Code.[3] Thus, in general, an organization that meets the appropriate statutory criteria qualifies—for that reason alone—as a tax-exempt organization. That is, whether an organization is entitled to tax exemption, on an initial or ongoing basis, is a matter of statutory law. It is Congress that, by statute, defines the categories of organizations that are eligible

---

[1] IRC § 61(a).
[2] See discussion at § 1.1.
[3] IRC §§ 501(c), 521, or 526–529; Reg. § 1.501(a)-1(a)(1).

for federal income tax exemption[4] and it is Congress that determines whether a type of tax exemption should be continued.[5]

§ 23.1 CONCEPT OF RECOGNITION OF TAX EXEMPTION

An organization's tax-exempt status may be *recognized*. This is a function of the IRS, which it exercises, where appropriate, by making a written determination that an entity constitutes a tax-exempt organization. (The role of the IRS in recognizing the tax-exempt status of organizations is part of its overall practice of evaluating the tax status of organizations.[6]) Eligibility for tax-exempt status, however, is different than recognition of that status. Thus, Congress, as noted, and not the IRS, is responsible for *granting* tax-exempt status.

As a general rule, an organization desiring tax-exempt status pursuant to the federal tax law is not required to secure recognition of tax exemption from the IRS.[7] Nonetheless, organizations of this nature may seek recognition of exempt status, and are often well-advised to do so (following standards used in ascertaining whether to seek any type of ruling from the IRS[8]). By contrast, in order for an organization to be granted tax exemption as a charitable entity or as an employee benefit organization, it must file an application for recognition of the exemption with the IRS and receive a favorable determination. Likewise, for an organization to be treated as a tax-exempt political organization, it must give notice to the IRS of its existence. Consequently, when an organization makes application to the IRS

---

[4] E.g., HCSC-Laundry v. United States, 450 U.S. 1 (1981) (where the Supreme Court held that Congress had the authority to exclude nonprofit laundry organizations from the scope of the tax exemption accorded to cooperative hospital service organizations (see § 10.4)).

[5] E.g., Maryland Sav.-Share Ins. Corp. v. United States, 400 U.S. 4 (1970) (where the Supreme Court held that Congress did not exceed its power to tax nor violate the Fifth Amendment to the Constitution in denying tax-exempt status to nonprofit insurers of deposits in savings banks and similar entities where the insurers were organized after September 1, 1957 (see § 18.5)). Likewise, for example, IRC § 501(c)(18) (see § 16.6) is applicable only to trusts created before June 25, 1959; IRC § 501(c)(20) (see § 16.6) is available to provide tax exemption for trusts under a qualified group legal services plan for tax years beginning before July 1, 1992; IRC § 501(c)(27)(A) (see § 18.15) is applicable only to entities established before June 1, 1996, and IRC § 501(c)(23) (see § 18.10(b)) is available only to an organization organized before 1880.

[6] Reg. §§ 601.201(a)(1), 601.201(d)(1).

[7] E.g., Savings Feature of Relief Dep't of B&O R.R. Co. v. Comm'r, 32 B.T.A. 295 (1935); Rev. Rul. 80-108, 1980-1 C.B. 119 (reflecting the fact that an organization qualifying for tax exemption as a social welfare organization (see Chapter 12) is not required to seek recognition of tax exemption). The tax regulations currently are incorrect on this point (Reg. § 1.501(a)-1(a)(3)). The IRS has taken the position that, if an organization has not filed an application for recognition of exemption, even if it is not required to do so, the agency will refuse acceptance of annual information returns (see § 24.3(a), note 190).

[8] In this context, the advantages to be gained by obtaining recognition of tax-exempt status include acknowledgment by the IRS that the entity qualifies for tax exemption, exemption from certain state taxes, and eligibility for preferential mailing rates. As to the latter, see Hopkins, *The Second Legal Answer Book for Fund-Raisers* (John Wiley & Sons, Inc., 2000), Chapter 8.

for a determination as to tax-exempt status, it is requesting the IRS to recognize its tax exemption, not to grant tax exemption.

Subject only to the authority of the IRS to revoke a ruling for good cause (usually a change in the facts or law), an organization whose tax-exempt status has been recognized by the IRS can rely on that determination as long as there are no substantial changes in its character, purposes, or methods of operation.[9] (Upon the occurrence of any one of these changes, the organization is required to notify the IRS and obtain a reevaluation of its tax-exempt status.[10])

§ 23.2   RECOGNITION APPLICATION PROCEDURE

The IRS promulgated rules by which a determination letter or ruling may be issued to an organization in response to the filing of an application for recognition of tax-exempt status.[11] Nearly all determinations by the IRS recognizing the tax-exempt status of organizations are in the form of *determination letters*. This is a document issued by the IRS in response to an application for recognition of exemption.[12] Where a determination as to an organization's tax exemption is made by the National Office of the IRS, the document is a *ruling*.[13]

In most instances, an organization seeking recognition of tax exemption by the IRS must file a particular form of application. An organization seeking recognition of exemption as a charitable organization is required to file Form 1023.[14] Nearly all other applicant organizations[15] file Form 1024,[16] although homeowners' associations file Form 1120-H and farmers', fruit growers', and like associations file Form 1028.[17] For a few categories of tax-exempt organization, there is no application form by which to seek recognition of tax exemption; instead, the request is made by letter.[18] Applications for recognition of tax exemption generally are filed with the IRS in Cincinnati, Ohio; occasionally, an application for recognition of exemption is filed with or referred to the IRS National Office.

---

[9] Reg. § 1.501(a)-1(a)(2).

[10] See § 4.5(a).

[11] Rev. Proc. 90-27, 1990-1 C.B. 514. These rules apply with regard to organizations seeking recognition of tax exemption under IRC §§ 501 and 521, and with respect to revocation and modification of exemption determination letters and rulings. Rev. Proc. 72-5, 1972-1 C.B. 709 states the information that must be included on applications for recognition of tax exemption filed by certain religious and apostolic organizations (see § 8.7). Rev. Proc. 80-30, 1980-1 C.B. 685 applies in instances involving the tax exemption of funds underlying pension, annuity, profit-sharing, and stock bonus plans.

Occasionally, the IRS will announce a process for the expediting of applications for recognition of tax exemption for charitable organizations, in aid of entities that are quickly formed to solicit contributions and provide programs in response to an emergency.

[12] Reg. § 601.201(a)(3).

[13] Reg. § 601.201(a)(2).

[14] The present Form 1023 is dated September 1998.

[15] Generally, those listed in IRC § 501(c), other than in IRC § 501(c)(3).

[16] The present Form 1024 is dated September 1998.

[17] The present Form 1028 is dated January 1997.

[18] E.g., that is the procedure in the case of multiemployer pension plan trusts (Ann. 80-163, 1980-52 I.R.B. 50).

These rules as to application for recognition of tax-exempt status are sepa-rate from those concerning requests for determination letters or rulings in the tax-exempt organizations context generally.[19] They are also separate from the procedures followed by the IRS for the issuance of determination letters and the like generally.[20]

(a) General Procedures

A determination letter or ruling recognizing tax-exempt status will be issued by the IRS to an organization, where its application for recognition of exemption and supporting documents establish that it meets the requirements of the category of exemption that it claimed as provided in the Internal Revenue Code and other re-lated law.[21] Any oral representations of additional facts or modification of facts as represented or alleged in the application must be reduced to writing over the sig-nature of an authorized individual.[22]

Tax-exempt status for an organization will be recognized by the IRS in ad-vance of operations where the entity's proposed activities are described in suffi-cient detail to permit a conclusion that the organization will clearly meet the pertinent statutory requirements. A mere restatement of purposes or a statement that proposed activities will be in furtherance of the organization's purposes does not satisfy this requirement. An applicant organization must fully describe the ac-tivities in which it expects to engage, including the standards, criteria, proce-dures, or other means adopted or planned for carrying out the activities, the anticipated sources of receipts, and the nature of contemplated expenditures.[23] The tax regulations in essence require that an applicant organization describe its character, purposes, and methods of operation.[24] They require that the applica-tion be "properly completed."[25]

An organization seeking a determination letter or ruling as to recognition of its tax-exempt status has the burden of proving that it satisfies all of the require-ments of the particular tax exemption category.[26]

---

[19] The IRS generally will issue determination letters, rulings, and information letters on any aspect of the law of tax-exempt organizations, transactions that may have an impact on an organization's tax-exempt or public charity status, or that may involve unrelated trade or business matters. The adminis-trative rules in this regard are issued at the beginning of each year (currently Rev. Proc. 98-4, 1998-1 I.R.B. 113), as are the related rules concerning the seeking of technical advice from the IRS (currently 2002-2, 2000-1 I.R.B. 82).

[20] These procedures are also issued at the outset of each year (currently Rev. Proc. 2002-1, 2002-1 I.R.B. 1), along with the general rules for seeking technical advice (currently Rev. Proc. 2002-2, 2000-1 I.R.B. 82).

[21] Reg. § 601.201(n)(1)(ii).

[22] Rev. Proc. 90-27, *supra* note 11 § 5.01.

[23] Reg. § 601.201(n)(1)(ii); Rev. Proc. 90-27, *supra* note 11 § 5.02. See § 24.8.

[24] Reg. § 1.501(a)-1(a)(2). See supra note 9. In its determination letters, the IRS adds a requirement of disclosure of an organization's sources of support.

[25] Reg. § 1.508-1(a)(2)(i) (at least in the case of organizations seeking to qualify for exemption by rea-son of IRC § 501(c)(3)).

[26] E.g., Harding Hosp., Inc. v. United States, 505 F.2d 1068 (6th Cir. 1974); Church of Spiritual Technol-ogy v. United States, 92-1 U.S.T.C. ¶ 50,305 (Fed. Cl. 1992).

The IRS, generally supported by the courts, usually will refuse to recognize an organization's tax-exempt status unless the entity tenders sufficient information regarding its operations and finances. For example, an organization submitted an application for recognition of tax exemption, stating its "long-range plan" to form a school; it was unable to substantively respond to any of the requests from the IRS for additional information. The IRS refused to recognize the organization as a tax-exempt entity; a court agreed, holding that the organization "failed to supply such information as would enable a conclusion that when operational, if ever, . . . [the organization] will conduct all of its activities in a manner which will accomplish its exempt purposes."[27] The court chided the entity for having only "vague generalizations" of its ostensibly planned activities and strongly suggested that the organization had "no plan to operate a school in the foreseeable future."[28] Likewise, a court concluded that an organization failed to meet its burden of proof as to its eligibility for tax exemption because it did not provide a "meaningful explanation" of its activities to the IRS.[29] In another such instance, a court concluded that an organization's failure to respond "completely or candidly" to many of the inquiries of the IRS precluded it from receiving a determination as to its tax-exempt status.[30]

An organization is considered to have made the required "threshold showing," however, where it describes its activities in "sufficient detail" to permit a conclusion that the entity will meet the pertinent requirements,[31] particularly where it answered all of the questions propounded by the IRS.[32] In another instance, a court observed that, although the law "requires that the organization establish reasonable standards and criteria for its operation as an exempt organization," the standard does not necessitate "some sort of metaphysical proof of future events."[33]

When the representatives of a would-be tax-exempt organization fail to submit its books and records to the IRS, an inference arises that the facts involved would denigrate the organization's cause.[34] (At the same time, it has been held

---

[27] Pius XII Academy, Inc. v. Comm'r, 43 T.C.M. 634, 636 (1982).

[28] *Id.*

[29] Public Indust., Inc. v. Comm'r, 61 T.C.M. 1626, 1629 (1991).

[30] National Ass'n of Am. Churches v. Comm'r, 82 T.C. 18, 32 (1984). Also United Libertarian Fellowship, Inc. v. Comm'r, 65 T.C.M. 2178 (1993); Church of Nature in Man v. Comm'r, 49 T.C.M. 1393 (1985); LaVerdad v. Comm'r, 82 T.C. 215 (1984); The Basic Unit Ministry of Alma Karl Schurig v. United States, 511 F. Supp. 166 (D.D.C. 1981).

[31] Rev. Proc. 90-27, *supra* note 11 § 5.02.

[32] E.g., The Church of the Visible Intelligence That Governs the Universe v. United States, 83-2 U.S.T.C. ¶ 9726 (Ct. Cl. 1983).

[33] American Science Found. v. Comm'r, 52 T.C.M. 1049, 1051 (1986).

[34] E.g., New Concordia Bible Church v. Comm'r, 49 T.C.M. 176 (1984) (*app. dis.*, 9th Cir. (1985)). Also Chief Steward of the Ecumenical Temples & the Worldwide Peace Movement & His Successors v. Comm'r, 49 T.C.M. 640 (1985); Basic Bible Church of Am., Auxiliary Chapter 11004 v. Comm'r, 46 T.C.M. 223 (1983); McElhannon v. Comm'r, 44 T.C.M. 1392 (1982); Bubbling Well Church of Universal Love, Inc. v. Comm'r, 74 T.C. 531 (1980), *aff'd*, 670 F.2d 104 (9th Cir. 1981); Founding Church of Scientology v. United States, 412 F.2d 1197 (Ct. Cl. 1969), *cert. den.*, 397 U.S. 1009 (1970); Parker v. Comm'r, 365 F.2d 792 (8th Cir. 1966), *cert. den.*, 385 U.S. 1026 (1967).

that the refusal by an organization to turn records over to the IRS, in response to a summons, does not give the IRS the authority to summarily revoke the organization's tax-exempt status.[35]) As one court stated the matter, in "order to gain [charitable] status, a taxpayer must openly and candidly disclose all facts bearing upon the organization, its operations, and its finances so that the [c]ourt may be assured that it is not sanctioning an abuse of the revenue laws by granting a claimed exemption."[36]

Where an organization cannot demonstrate, to the satisfaction of the IRS, that its proposed activities will qualify it for tax exemption, a record of actual operations may be required before a determination letter or ruling is issued.[37] In cases where an organization is unable to fully describe its purposes and activities, a refusal by the IRS to issue a determination letter or ruling is considered an initial adverse determination from which administrative appeal or protest rights will be afforded.[38]

If an application for recognition of tax exemption does not contain the requisite information, the application usually will be returned to the applicant organization (rather than to anyone on a power of attorney) without being considered on its merits, with a letter of explanation.[39] In the case of a would-be charitable organization, where an application is returned, the IRS will inform the organization of the time within which the completed application must be resubmitted in order for the application to be considered a timely notice to the IRS.[40]

A determination letter or ruling recognizing tax exemption ordinarily will not be issued if an issue involving the organization's tax-exempt status is pending in litigation or is under consideration within the IRS.[41]

An application for recognition of tax exemption may be withdrawn, upon the written request of an authorized representative of the organization, at any time prior to the issuance of an initial adverse determination letter or ruling. Where an application is withdrawn, it and all supporting documents are retained by the IRS.[42]

An organization may reapply for recognition of tax exemption if it was previously denied the recognition, where the facts involved are materially changed so that the organization is in compliance with the requirements. For example, an organization that was refused recognition of exemption because of excessive lobbying activities, by reason of the expenditure test,[43] may subsequently reapply for recognition of exemption as a charitable organization for any tax year following the first tax year as to which the recognition was denied.[44] The reapplication form

---

[35] Church of World Peace, Inc. v. Internal Revenue Serv., 715 F.2d 492 (10th Cir. 1983).
[36] The Nationalist Found. v. Comm'r, 80 T.C.M. 507 (2000).
[37] Reg. § 601.201(n)(1)(ii).
[38] Rev. Proc. 90-27, *supra* note 11 § 5.02.
[39] *Id.* at § 5.03.
[40] Reg. § 601.201(n)(1)(iii). See *infra* § 3.
[41] Reg. § 601.201(n)(1)(iv); Rev. Proc. 90-27, *supra* note 11 § 5.04.
[42] *Id.* at § 7.01.
[43] See § 20.2(c).
[44] Reg. § 1.501(h)-3(d)(1).

must include information demonstrating that the organization was in compliance with the expenditure test during the full tax year immediately preceding the date of reapplication,[45] and that the organization will not knowingly operate in a manner that would disqualify it from exemption by reason of attempts to influence legislation.[46]

The IRS has an expedited determination process, whereby an experienced employee reviews applications for determination letters recognizing tax-exempt status and decides which applications can be processed quickly without further review by an exempt organization specialist or contact with the applicant organization.[47] A properly prepared application for recognition of tax-exempt status can thus be processed by the IRS in a shorter period than might otherwise be the case.

The proper preparation of an application for recognition of tax exemption involves far more than merely responding to the questions on a government form. It is a process not unlike the preparation of a prospectus for a business in conformity with securities law requirements. Every statement made in the application should be carefully considered. Some of the questions may force the applicant organization to focus on matters that good management practices should cause it to consider, even in the absence of the application requirements.

The prime objective must be accuracy; it is essential that all material facts be correctly and fully disclosed. Of course, the determination as to which facts are material and the marshaling of these facts requires judgment. Also, the manner in which the answers are phrased can be extremely significant; in this regard, the exercise can be more one of art than science. The preparer or reviewer of the application should be able to anticipate the concerns the contents of the application may cause the IRS and to see that the application is properly prepared, while simultaneously minimizing the likelihood of conflict with the IRS. Organizations that are entitled to tax-exempt status have been denied recognition of exemption by the IRS, or at least have caused the process of gaining the recognition to be more protracted, because of unartful phraseologies in the application that motivated the IRS to muster a case that the organization does not qualify for exemption. Therefore, the application for recognition of tax exemption should be regarded as an important legal document and prepared accordingly. The fact that the application is available for public inspection only underscores the need for the thoughtful preparation of it.[48]

(b) The *Substantially Completed* Application

The application for recognition of tax exemption as submitted by an organization will not be processed by the IRS until the application is at least *substantially com-*

[45] Reg. § 1.501(h)-3(d)(2).
[46] Reg. § 1.501(h)-3(d)(3).
[47] This process is discussed in "Tax Administration: IRS Can Improve Its Process for Recognizing Exempt Organizations," 4 General Accounting Office (GAO/GCD-90-55 (June 1990)).
[48] See § 15.3.

pleted.[49] Likewise, for purposes of the declaratory judgment rules,[50] it is the position of the IRS that the 270-day period[51] does not begin until the date a substantially completed application is filed with the IRS.[52]

A substantially completed application for recognition of tax exemption is one that:

- Is signed by an authorized individual;

- Includes an employer identification number or a completed application for the number (Form SS-4);

- Includes information regarding any previously filed federal income and/or exempt organization information returns;

- Includes a statement of receipts and expenditures and a balance sheet for the current year and the three preceding years (or the years the organization was in existence, where that period is less than four years), although if the organization has not yet commenced operations, or has not completed one full accounting period, a proposed budget for two full accounting periods and a current statement of assets and liabilities is acceptable;

- Includes a narrative statement of proposed activities[53] and a narrative description of anticipated receipts and contemplated expenditures[54];

- Includes a copy of the document by which the organization was established that is signed by a principal officer or is accompanied by a written declaration signed by an authorized individual certifying that the document is a complete and accurate copy of the original or otherwise meets the requirement that it be a *conformed* copy[55];

- If the organizing document is a set of articles of incorporation, includes evidence that it was filed with and approved by an appropriate state official (such as a copy of the certificate of incorporation) or includes a copy of the articles of incorporation accompanied by a written declaration signed by an authorized individual that the copy is a complete and accurate copy of the original document that was filed with and approved by the state, and stating the date of filing with the state;

- If the organization has adopted bylaws,[56] includes a current copy of that document, verified as being current by an authorized individual; and

- Is accompanied by the correct user fee.[57]

---

[49] Rev. Proc. 90-27, *supra* note 11 § 5.06.
[50] See § 24.6(b).
[51] IRC § 7428(b)(2).
[52] Rev. Proc. 90-27, *supra* note 11 § 5.05.
[53] Also Reg. §§ 1.501(a)-1(b)(1), 1.501(c)(3)-1(b)(1)(v).
[54] Also Reg. § 1.501(a)-1(a)(3).
[55] Rev. Proc. 68-14, 1968-1 C.B. 768.
[56] Reg. § 1.501(a)-1(a)(3).
[57] Rev. Proc. 90-27, *supra* note 11 § 5.05. As to user fees, see *infra* § (d).

Of particular significance to charitable organizations, the application for recognition of tax exemption requests information concerning the composition of the entity's governing body, any relationship with other organizations, the nature of its program activities, its fundraising program, and a variety of other matters.

Where an application for recognition of tax exemption involves an issue where significant contrary authorities (such as court opinions) exist, the applicant organization is encouraged by the IRS to disclose and discuss them. Failure to do so can result in requests for additional information and may delay action on the application.[58]

If an application for recognition of tax exemption is revised at the request of the IRS, the 270-day period that applies in the declaratory judgment context[59] will not be considered by the IRS as starting until the date the application is refiled with the IRS with the requested information. If the upgraded application is mailed and a postmark is not evident, the period starts on the date the IRS received the substantially completed application.

Even though an application for recognition of tax exemption is substantially complete, the IRS has reserved the authority to obtain additional information before a determination letter or ruling is issued.[60]

The standards for a substantially completed application also apply with respect to the notice requirements for charitable organizations.[61]

(c) Issuance of Determination Letters and Rulings

Generally, an organization acquiring recognition of tax-exempt status does so by means of issuance of a determination letter by the IRS.[62] That is, the National Office of the IRS relatively infrequently issues a ruling recognizing the tax-exempt status of an organization.[63]

An IRS representative must refer to the National Office of the IRS an application for recognition of tax exemption that (1) presents questions the answers to which are not specifically covered by the Internal Revenue Code, Department of the Treasury regulations, an IRS revenue ruling, or court decision published in the *Internal Revenue Bulletin*, or (2) has been specifically reserved by an IRS revenue procedure and/or *Internal Revenue Manual* instructions for handling by the National Office for purposes of establishing uniformity or centralized control of designated categories of cases. In this instance, the National Office is to consider the application, issue a ruling di-

---

[58] Rev. Proc. 90-27, *supra* note 11 § 5.08.
[59] See § 24.6(b).
[60] Rev. Proc. 90-27, *supra* note 11 § 5.07. Also Reg. §§ 1.501(a)-1(b)(2), 601.201(h)(1)(ii), 601.201(h)(1)(iii). Cf. text accompanied by *supra* notes 27–35.
[61] Rev. Proc. 90-27, *supra* note 11 § 5.07. See § 24.3.
[62] Reg. § 601.201(n)(2)(i); Rev. Proc. 90-27, *supra* note 11 § 6.01.
[63] See text accompanied by *infra* note 69.

rectly to the organization, and send a copy of the ruling to the appropriate IRS office.[64]

If, during the course of consideration of an application for recognition of tax exemption, the applicant organization believes that its case involves an issue on which there is no published precedent, the organization may ask the IRS to request technical advice[65] from the IRS National Office.[66] If the IRS proposes to recognize the tax exemption of an organization to which the National Office had previously issued a contrary ruling or technical advice memorandum (a highly unlikely event), the IRS representative must seek technical advice from the National Office before issuing a determination letter.[67]

Some determination letters issued by the IRS are reviewed in the IRS National Office for the purpose of assuring uniform application of the statutes, regulations, rulings, and court opinions published in the *Internal Revenue Bulletin*.[68] Where the IRS National Office takes exception to a determination letter, the IRS representative involved must be advised. If the organization disagrees with the exception taken, the file is returned to the National Office. The referral is treated as a request for technical advice.[69]

Occasionally, the IRS issues exemption letters (rulings) out of its National Office. These documents are available for public inspection, along with the underlying application for recognition of exemption.[70]

A determination letter or ruling recognizing tax exemption usually is effective as of the date of formation of the organization where its purposes and activities during the period prior to the date of the determination letter or ruling were consistent with the requirements for tax exemption.[71] If the organization is required to alter its activities or to make substantive amendments to its enabling instrument, the determination letter or ruling recognizing its tax-exempt status is effective as of the date specified in the determination letter or ruling. If a nonsubstantive amendment is made, tax exemption is ordinarily recognized as of the date the entity was formed.[72]

In general, an organization can rely on a determination letter or ruling from the IRS recognizing its tax exemption. This is not the case, however, if there is a material change, inconsistent with exemption, in the character, purpose, or method of operation of the organization.[73]

---

[64] Reg. § 601.201(n)(2)(ii); Rev. Proc. 90-27, *supra* note 11 § 6.02.

[65] Reg. § 601.201(n)(2)(iv); Rev. Proc. 2003-5, *supra* note 19.

[66] Rev. Proc. 90-27, *supra* note 11 § 6.03.

[67] *Id.* at § 6.04.

[68] *Id.* at § 8.01.

[69] *Id.* at § 8.02.

[70] Notice 92-28, 1992-1 C.B. 515.

[71] Reg. § 601.201(n)(3)(i); Rev. Proc. 90-27, *supra* note 11 § 13.01. There are special requirements in this regard for charitable organizations (see §§ 24.3, 24.4).

[72] Rev. Proc. 90-27, *supra* note 11 § 13.01. *Nonsubstantive* amendments include correction of a clerical error in the enabling instrument or the addition of a dissolution clause (see § 4.3(b)), where the activities of the organization prior to the determination letter or ruling are consistent with the requirements for tax exemption (*id.*).

[73] Reg. § 601.201(n)(3)(ii); Rev. Proc. 90-27, *supra* note 11 § 13.02.

(d) User Fees

Congress enacted a program of user fees, payable to the IRS for requests for rulings, information letters, determination letters, and similar requests.[74] These fees must be accompanied by the filing of an IRS form (Form 8718).

Under the current schedule, the fee for the processing of an application for recognition of tax exemption is $500, where the applicant has gross receipts that annually exceed $10,000. For smaller organizations, the fee is $150. A group exemption[75] letter fee is $500. A user fee of $100 is charged for a request for a ruling to modify the terms or stipulations stated in an initial ruling, issued by the National Office of the IRS, recognizing the tax-exempt status of an organization.[76]

(e) The Application Form

The application forms are available from the IRS, as part of a packet that includes general instructions as to the preparation of them.

The pertinent parts of the application form for charitable organizations (Form 1023) are the following:

- Part I, which requests basic information about the applicant organization, such as its name, address, Web site, employer identification number, form of entity, and date of formation;

- Part II, which requests a description of activities, composition of and other information about the governing body, assets, and other operational information about the applicant organization;

- Part III, which requests information concerning the period of time the determination letter or ruling will cover[77] and the public charity/private foundation status of the applicant organization[78]; and

- Part IV, which requests certain financial data, including revenue, expenses, assets, and liabilities, which new applicant organizations may instead submit by means of a budget.

The application packet also contains the following:

- The form that is used to extend the statute of limitations for the assessment of the private foundation investment income tax[79] during the pendency of the advance ruling period (Form 872-C);[80]

---

[74] The program was first described in Rev. Proc. 88-8, 1988-1 C.B. 628.

[75] See *infra* § 6.

[76] Rev. Proc. 2002-8, 2002-1 I.R.B. 252. Other ruling requests in the tax-exempt organizations area generally generate a user fee of $1,775. Where the requesting organization has annual gross receipts that are less than $150,000, however, the fee is $500.

[77] See *infra* § 3, 4.

[78] See Chapter 11.

[79] See § 11.4(f).

[80] See *infra* § 4(b).

- Schedule A, to be prepared by applicant organizations that are churches;[81]

- Schedule B, to be prepared by applicant organizations that are schools, colleges, and universities;[82]

- Schedule C, to be prepared by applicant organizations that are hospitals and medical research organizations;[83]

- Schedule D, to be prepared by applicant organizations that are supporting organizations;[84]

- Schedule E, to be prepared by applicant organizations that are private operating foundations;[85]

- Schedule F, to be prepared by applicant organizations that are homes for the aged or disabled;[86]

- Schedule G, to be prepared by applicant organizations that are child care organizations;[87]

- Schedule H, to be prepared by applicant organizations that provide scholarships and comparable benefits;[88] and

- Schedule I, to be prepared by applicant organizations that are successors to for-profit organizations.[89]

- Also in the application packet is the form used to submit the user fee.[90]

Once the IRS has recognized the tax exemption of an organization, the entity cannot voluntarily relinquish it.[91] That is, there is no provision in the law for voluntary termination of tax-exempt status. The only ways an organization can shed its tax exemption is to violate the applicable organizational test[92] or the applicable operational test,[93] or to dissolve.[94]

---

[81] See § 8.3.
[82] See § 7.3.
[83] See § 6.2(a), (c).
[84] See § 11.3(c).
[85] See § 11.1(b).
[86] See § 6.2(d).
[87] See § 7.7.
[88] See § 6.5.
[89] See § 33.4.
[90] See *supra* § (d), particularly text accompanied by note 74. In prior versions of the application, the applicant organization was requested to select up to three activity codes that best correlate to the organization's actual and planned activities but that element of the application has been eliminated.
[91] Priv. Ltr. Rul. 9141050.
[92] See § 4.3.
[93] See § 4.5.
[94] See § 4.3(b).

Applications for recognition of tax exemption submitted by most tax-exempt organizations must be made available for public inspection.[95]

(f) Penalties for Perjury

The individual who signs an application for recognition of tax-exempt status does so under penalty of perjury, stating that to the best of the individual's knowledge it is true, correct, and complete. The IRS can revoke or amend an organization's exempt status if the agency determines that the organization omitted or misstated a material fact in its application or operates in a manner materially different from that originally represented in the application. If the changed or expanded activities, which were not reported, further the organization's exempt purposes or are unrelated but insubstantial, the IRS likely will not take any action against the entity.[96]

Because of the "penalty of perjury" statement, the IRS could impose a penalty, for the commission of a felony, if a representation was made willfully under the belief that it was untrue and incorrect as to every material manner.[97] The organization and its officers may be fined up to $100,000 ($500,000 in the case of a corporation) or imprisoned for up to three years, or both. A lesser violation (a misdemeanor), that does not require penalties of perjury, may involve a penalty if the organization or one or more of its officers willfully delivered the organization's application knowing it contained information that was false as to any material matter.[98] The organization and its officers may be fined up to $10,000 ($50,000 in the case of a corporation) or imprisoned not more than one year, or both.

In general, federal law imposes penalties for making false statements, making false claims, and otherwise committing perjury.

§ 23.3   SPECIAL REQUIREMENTS FOR CHARITABLE ORGANIZATIONS

There are special requirements in this regard for charitable organizations[99] that desire to be tax-exempt under federal law.

(a) General Rules

An organization that desires to be tax-exempt as a charitable organization generally must obtain a determination letter or a ruling from the IRS to that effect.[100] An

---

[95] See § 24.4(b). In general, Hopkins, "A Practical Guide on How to Apply for Section 501(c)(3) Status," 4 *J. Tax. Exempt Orgs.* (No. 4) 8 (Jan./Feb. 1993); Gessay, "Tracking a Pending Application for Federal Income Tax Exemption," 2 *J. Tax. Exempt Orgs.* 4 (Winter 1991); Gardner, "The Determination Process—Current Changes and Some in the Wind," 2 *J. Tax. Exempt Orgs.* 7 (Fall 1990).

[96] E.g., Tech. Adv. Mem. 9835003.

[97] IRC § 7206.

[98] IRC § 7207.

[99] That is, entities described in IRC § 501(c)(3) and tax-exempt by reason of IRC § 501(a).

[100] IRC § 508(a).

organization that desires recognition as a tax-exempt charitable organization as of the date of its formation generally must notify the IRS that it is applying for recognition of exemption on that basis, in conformity with a threshold notice rule. Thus, where the IRS recognizes the tax exemption of an organization that made a timely filing of the notice, the exemption is effective as of the date the organization was created. (The requisite notice is given by the timely filing with the IRS of a properly completed and executed application for recognition of tax exemption.[101]) Otherwise, the recognition of tax exemption as a charitable organization by the IRS generally is effective only on a prospective basis.[102]

This *threshold notice rule* is of two parts. One rule is that the notice to the IRS must be given within 15 months from the end of the month in which the organization was organized.[103] The IRS, however, provided an automatic 12-month extension of time for this filing,[104] thereby converting it to a 27-month period. The application is formatted to reflect which period is being used.

An organization is considered *organized* on the date it became a charitable entity.[105] In determining the date on which a corporation is organized for purposes of this exemption recognition process, the IRS looks to the date the entity came into existence under the law of the state in which it was incorporated, which usually is the date its articles of incorporation were filed in the appropriate state office.[106] This date is not the date the organizational meeting was held, by-laws adopted, or actual operations began.

In general, if any return, claim, statement, or other document is required by law to be filed before a specified date, and the document is delivered by mail after that date to the agency, officer, or office with which the document is required to be filed, it is deemed to have been filed on or before that date if the postmark stamped on the envelope or other cover in which the document was mailed was dated on or before the date prescribed for filing.[107] In application of this standard, the date of notice for purposes of the threshold notice rule is the date of the postmark stamped on the cover in which the application for recognition of tax exemption was mailed; in the absence of a postmark, the date of notice is the date the application was stamped as received by the IRS.[108]

If an organization made a nonsubstantive amendment to a governing instrument,[109] that action is not taken into account for purposes of the threshold notice rule.[110] For example, an organization may have submitted an application for

---

[101] See *supra* § 2(b).
[102] IRC §§ 508(a)(2), 508(d)(2)(B); Reg. § 1.508-2. E.g., Priv. Ltr. Rul. 8518067. As discussed *infra*, however, there are two exceptions to this rule: the automatic 12-month extension procedure (see the text accompanied by *infra* notes 103–104) and the grant of an extension of this filing time by the IRS (see the text accompanied by *infra* notes 108–110).
[103] Reg. § 1.508-1(a)(2)(i). E.g., Peek v. Comm'r, 73 T.C. 912 (1980); Rev. Rul. 90-100, 1990-2 C.B. 156.
[104] Rev. Proc. 92-85, 1992-2 C.B. 490 § 4.01.
[105] Reg. § 1.508-1(a)(2)(iii). See Form 1023, Part I, question 5.
[106] Rev. Rul. 75-290, 1975-2 C.B. 215.
[107] IRC § 7502(a)(1).
[108] Rev. Rul. 77-114, 1977-1 C.B. 152.
[109] Rev. Proc. 90-27, *supra* note 11 § 13.01.
[110] Rev. Proc. 84-47, 1984-1 C.B. 545.

recognition of tax exemption within the 15-month period and subsequently made a nonsubstantive amendment to its governing instrument; its tax exemption is still effective as of the date of its formation. Likewise, an organization may have submitted an application for recognition of tax exemption after expiration of the 27-month period and thereafter made a nonsubstantive amendment to its governing instrument; its tax exemption is effective as of the date the application was mailed to or received by the IRS, as the case may be. If an organization made a nonsubstantive amendment to its governing instrument after expiration of the threshold notice rule period, then applied for recognition of exemption within 27 months after the date of the amendment, the organization will be recognized as tax-exempt as of the date the application was mailed to or received by the IRS, not the date the amendment was made. Where a substantive amendment is made to the governing instrument, recognition of exemption is effective as of the date of the change.

The IRS has general discretionary authority, upon a showing of good cause, to grant a reasonable extension of a time fixed by the tax regulations for making an election or application for relief in respect of the federal income tax law.[111] This discretionary authority may be exercised where the time for making the election or application is not expressly prescribed by statute, the request for the extension is filed with the IRS within a period the IRS considers reasonable under the circumstances, and it is shown to the satisfaction of the IRS that granting the extension will not jeopardize the interests of the federal government. The IRS acknowledged that it can exercise this discretionary authority to extend the time for satisfaction of the threshold notice period requirement (which, as noted, is not fixed by statute).[112] The IRS outlined the information and representations that must be furnished and some factors that will be taken into consideration in determining whether an extension of this nature will be granted.[113]

An organization's eligibility to receive deductible charitable contributions also is governed by the threshold notice rule. Thus, where a charitable organization timely files the application for recognition of tax exemption, and the determination letter or ruling ultimately is favorable, the ability to receive deductible charitable gifts is effective as of the date the organization was formed.

An organization that qualifies for tax exemption as a charitable organization but files for recognition of exemption after the threshold notice period can be tax-exempt as a social welfare organization[114] for the period commencing on the date of its inception to the date tax exemption as a charitable organization

---

[111] Reg. § 1.9100-1.

[112] Rev. Proc. 84-47, *supra* note 110 § 4; Rev. Rul. 80-259, 1980-2 C.B. 192.

[113] Rev. Proc. 92-85, *supra* note 104, *mod. by* Rev. Proc. 93-28, 1993-2 C.B. 344. A request for this extension is built into the application for recognition of tax exemption (Form 1023, Part III, questions 13 (c), 13(d)).

[114] See Chapter 12.

becomes effective.[115] Contributions to social welfare organizations, however, are generally not deductible as charitable gifts,[116] so this approach is of little utility to charitable organizations that rely significantly on contributions.

(b) Exceptions

The threshold notice requirement is not applicable to

- Churches, interchurch organizations of local units of a church, conventions or associations of churches, and integrated auxiliaries of churches;[117]

- Organizations whose gross receipts in each tax year are normally not more than $5,000 (as long as they are not private foundations[118]);[119] and

- Subordinate organizations covered by a group exemption letter where the central organization has submitted to the IRS the requisite notice covering the subordinates.[120]

The IRS is authorized to exempt from the notice requirement operating educational institutions[121] and any other class of organizations as to which compliance with the requirement is not necessary to the efficient administration of the tax law rules pertaining to private foundations.[122]

The exception in these rules for organizations with gross receipts that are normally no more than $5,000 can operate to relieve a small organization from the requirement of filing an application for recognition of tax exemption during the initial years of its operation (yet still be tax-exempt) but expire as the organization receives greater amounts of financial support. Once an organization fails to meet this exception, it is required to file the notice (application for recognition of exemption) within 90 days after the close of the year in which its gross receipts exceeded the amounts permitted under the exception.[123] Thus, this notice period is used in this circumstance instead of the general threshold notice rule. An organization in this situation can, therefore, be tax-exempt as a charitable entity from its inception—no matter how many years have passed—as long as it files the application on a timely basis (under the 90-day rule).

---

[115] Rev. Rul. 80-108, *supra* note 7. This is because, as noted (see the text accompanied by *supra* notes 7–8), social welfare organizations are not required to apply for recognition of tax-exempt status. The IRS requests an organization in this circumstance to file Form 1024, page 1, with its application for recognition of exemption (Form 1023, Part III, instructions accompanying line 6).

[116] E.g., Smith v. Comm, 51 T.C.M. 1114 (1986).

[117] IRC § 508(c)(1), (2); Reg. § 1.508-1(a)(3)(i)(A). Also Gen. Couns. Mems. 36078, 37458. See §§ 8.3–8.5.

[118] See Chapter 11.

[119] IRC § 508(c)(1).

[120] See *infra* § 7.

[121] IRC § 508(c)(3)(A). These are entities described in IRC § 170(b)(1)(A)(ii). See § 7.3.

[122] IRC § 508(c)(2)(B).

[123] Reg. § 1.508-1(a)(3)(ii).

The term *normally* embodies an averaging mechanism. That is, the gross receipts of an organization are normally not more than $5,000 if, during its first tax year, it received gross receipts of no more than $7,500; during its first two tax years, it received gross receipts of no more than $12,000; and, in the case of an organization that has been in existence for three tax years, the gross receipts received by it during its immediately preceding two tax years plus the current year are not more than $15,000.[124] The IRS provided three examples of the applicability of this 90-day rule, one involving an organization that did not receive any financial support until its third year[125] and two illustrating the consequences of failing to timely satisfy the rule.[126]

(c) Limited Liability Companies

A charitable organization can be the sole member of a limited liability company (LLC) or two or more charitable organizations can be members of an LLC.[127] In the case of the single-member LLC, the LLC is a disregarded entity for federal tax purposes and thus its activities are treated as the activities of the member.[128] In this instance, then, the single-member LLC is not required to file an application for recognition of tax exemption.[129] When, however, there is a multimember LLC, the members of which are charitable organizations, the LLC can qualify as a charitable organization[130] and thus is subject to the exemption recognition process.

§ 23.4 NONPRIVATE FOUNDATION STATUS

(a) Notification to IRS

In general, every charitable organization is presumed to be a private foundation unless it is able to rebut the presumption.[131] The rebuttal process entails the filing of the requisite notice with the IRS;[132] this is done as part of the application for recognition of tax exemption.[133] Thus, generally, a charitable organization endeavoring to be a public charity[134] must successfully rebut this presumption. The time for the giving of this notice is, by IRS rule, the same as for the notice requirement with respect to tax exemption—the threshold notice rule or the 90-day rule.

---

[124] *Id.*
[125] Rev. Rul. 85-173, 1985-2 C.B. 164.
[126] Rev. Rul. 81-177, 1981-2 C.B. 132; Rev. Rul. 80-259, *supra* note 112.
[127] In general, see § 4.1(b).
[128] In general, see § 30.7.
[129] E.g., Priv. Ltr. Rul. 200134025.
[130] See § 4.3(e).
[131] IRC § 508(b). See § 11.1.
[132] IRC § 508(a).
[133] Form 1023, Part III, questions 7–14.
[134] See § 11.2.

The requirement of notification to the IRS as to nonprivate foundation status does not apply to churches, conventions or associations of churches, and integrated auxiliaries of churches.[135]

The law is vague as to the time when a notice of nonprivate foundation status must be filed to be effective. As noted, a charitable organization that is not a private foundation is able to rebut the presumption that it is a foundation by showing that it is a public charity. An organization that failed to timely file a notice may nonetheless establish its public charity status by submitting a request for a determination as to that status to the IRS.[136]

In one instance, a charitable organization (not exempt from the notice requirement) did not apply for recognition of tax exemption until after expiration of the threshold notice rule. Tax exemption of this organization was ultimately approved; it was a private foundation. Inasmuch as the organization could be treated as a charitable organization only as of the date the application was filed, however, it could not be classified as a private foundation until that date.[137] The same result obtains with respect to an organization's public charity status.[138] When an applicant organization withdraws its application for recognition of exemption in the face of issuance of an adverse determination, it also cancels its notification to the IRS that it is seeking public charity status, so that the threshold notice rule period continues to run.[139]

The IRS promulgated rules with respect to the issuance of determination letters and rulings as to public charity/private foundation status, as well as to reconsiderations, modifications, and revocations of these determinations.[140]

(b) Advance and Definitive Rulings

A tax-exempt charitable organization (not exempt from the notice requirements) that is not a private foundation will (if the notice has been given) have its public charity status evidenced in a definitive ruling and perhaps, previously, in an advance ruling. Whether the organization receives only a definitive ruling, or is issued both an advance ruling and then a definitive ruling, one is dependent on the basis on which the organization is classified as a public charity. This ruling usually is in the same document by which the organization's tax exemption was recognized by the IRS.

A *definitive ruling* is a permanent (or final) determination as to public charity status, which remains in effect absent a material change in the facts or change in the law. An *advance ruling* is a preliminary (or probationary) determination as to an organization's status as a publicly supported charity[141] that is in effect for a

---

[135] IRC § 508(c)(1)(A).
[136] Rev. Rul. 73-504, 1973-2 C.B. 190.
[137] Rev. Rul. 77-207, 1977-1 C.B. 152.
[138] Rev. Rul. 80-113, 1980-1 C.B. 58; Rev. Rul. 77-208, 1977-1 C.B. 153.
[139] Rev. Rul. 90-100, *supra* note 103.
[140] Rev. Proc. 90-27, *supra* note 11.
[141] There are three categories of publicly supported charitable organizations: the donative charity, the service provider charity, and the foundation supportive of state colleges and universities (see § 11.3(b)).

sufficient period—the *advance ruling period*—to enable the organization to attempt to qualify for a definitive ruling as to public charity status. An organization with an advance ruling that meets the applicable public support requirements during the advance ruling period becomes entitled to receive a definitive ruling on the point.[142]

A charitable organization will receive a definitive ruling at the outset if it is one of the institutions,[143] has been publicly supported during the requisite period,[144] or constitutes a supporting organization.[145] Otherwise, the charitable organization must start the process with an advance ruling.

A newly created organization seeking recognition as a tax-exempt charitable entity and also seeking nonprivate foundation status as a publicly supported organization is entitled to receive (if it so elects) a definitive ruling as to public charity status if it has completed a tax year consisting of at least eight full months (as of the time of filing the application) and if the applicable public support test is met.

This type of organization that does not satisfy a public support test over the eight-month period must request an advance ruling covering its first five tax years. (Unlike the eight-month rule, the first tax year of this five-year period can consist of any number of days.)

A charitable organization that has been in existence for at least eight full months has two options in this regard. One, as noted, is to request a definitive ruling at the outset, in which instance the organization's qualification as a publicly supported charity is initially based on the support the organization has received as of the application date. The other is to request an advance ruling; the organization's public support computation, for purposes of obtaining a definitive ruling, is based on the financial support it receives during its first five tax years. As to this choice, the IRS offers this advice: "An organization should consider this [second] option if it has not received significant public support during its first tax year or during its first and second tax years, but it reasonably expects to receive such support by the end of its fifth tax year."[146] (In both instances, the organization must, to avoid subsequent classification as a private foundation, constitute a public charity on an ongoing basis.)

A charitable "foundation" that is related to a state college or university[147]

---

[142] As part of the process of filing the application for recognition of exemption, a charitable organization will submit a budget projecting its financial support. If the projection indicates that the applicable public support test will be met, the IRS will rule that it is reasonable to conclude that the organization will qualify as a publicly supported charity, and will issue an advance ruling. Within 90 days following expiration of the advance ruling period, the organization is expected to submit to the IRS a summary of its financial support during the period (preferably on Form 8734). If that data shows that the organization has been publicly supported, the IRS will issue a definitive ruling to the organization.

[143] See § 11.3(a).

[144] See § 11.3(b).

[145] See § 11.3(c).

[146] Instructions accompanying Form 1023, Part III, line 10. The description of eligibility for definitive and advance rulings accompanied by *supra* notes 141–145 is based on the rules as stated in these instructions. The rules in this regard contained in the tax regulations are, however, quite different.

[147] See § 11.3(b)(v).

is not subject to the foregoing eight-month requirement.[148] Thus, a newly created organization, prior to the close of its first tax year consisting of at least eight months, may be issued a definitive ruling that it qualifies as this type of publicly supported charity, assuming the requisite support requirements are met.

Where an incorporated charitable organization is claiming qualification as a publicly supported entity, it is the successor to an unincorporated charitable organization, and incorporation is the only significant change in the facts, the period of time that the predecessor organization was in operation may be taken into consideration in determining qualification of the successor organization under the time requirements[149] of the rules concerning publicly supported charity classification.[150] In other words, the IRS permits the public support data for the unincorporated entity to be tacked to the public support data for the incorporated entity for purposes of ascertaining whether the corporation qualifies as a publicly supported charity.

After a decade or so after the creation by statute of the concepts of public charities and private foundations, Congress began receiving complaints from donors and grantors about the stringency of the rules concerning newly created publicly supported charities, in that the advance ruling period that was in the law at that time[151] was thought to be too short, thereby not according these new entities adequate time to qualify as publicly supported entities. Congress was reluctant to legislate on this subject, however, because the underlying rules as to advance and definitive rulings are not statutory ones. That is, Congress did not want to codify the entire procedure solely for the purpose of lengthening the advance ruling period.

This matter of expanding the opportunities for reliance by donors and grantors on the nonprivate foundation status of new charitable organizations was rectified in 1984. The conference committee finalizing the Tax Reform Act of that year directed the Department of the Treasury to extend this advance ruling period to five years.[152] The IRS, in 1986, adopted the single five-year advance ruling period discussed above. The tax regulations on this topic have yet to be amended to reflect this change in policy.

§ 23.5 SPECIAL REQUIREMENTS FOR EMPLOYEE BENEFIT ORGANIZATIONS

An organization that desires status as an *employee benefit organization*[153] as of the date of its establishment must timely notify the IRS that it is applying for recogni-

---

[148] Rev. Rul. 77-407, 1977-2 C.B. 77.
[149] Reg. §§ 1.170A-9(e)(4)(vi), 1.509(a)-3(c)(1)(iv).
[150] Rev. Rul. 73-422, 1973-2 C.B. 70. Cf. Rev. Rul. 77-116, 1977-1 C.B. 155.
[151] See *supra* note 146.
[152] H. Rep. 861, 98th Cong., 2d Sess. 109 (1984).
[153] That is, one described in IRC § 501(c)(9) (a voluntary employees' beneficiary association—see § 16.3) or IRC § 501(c)(17) (a supplemental unemployment compensation benefit trust—see § 16.4.

tion of tax exemption on that basis.[154] The 15-month rule[155] is applicable in this context, including its exceptions.[156]

These rules as to notification are generally the same as those in place for charitable organizations.[157] That is, the 15-month rule also applies in this context and the organization's tax exemption will be recognized retroactively to the date the organization was organized, where the notice is timely filed.[158]

§ 23.6   NOTICE REQUIREMENTS FOR POLITICAL ORGANIZATIONS

Basically, for an organization to be treated as a tax-exempt political organization,[159] it must *give notice* to the IRS of its existence.[160] This notice must be transmitted no later than 24 hours after the date on which the organization is established.[161] The notice must be submitted both in writing and electronically. If this notice is given after the 24-hour period, the exemption treatment is only prospective.

This notice must contain the following: the name and address of the organization and its electronic mailing address; the purpose of the organization; the names and addresses of its officers, highly compensated employees, contact person, custodian of records, and members of its board of directors; the name and address of, and relationship to, any related entities; and such other information as the IRS may require. Any material change in the information provided in the initial notice must be reported to the IRS within 30 days of the change.

The phrase *highly compensated employees*, for this purpose, means the five employees (other than officers or directors) who are expected to have the highest annual compensation over $50,000. The term *compensation* includes cash and non-cash amounts, whether paid currently or deferred, for the 12-month period that began with the date the organization was formed (if it was formed after June 30, 2000). If the organization was already in existence on June 30, 2000, it must use the accounting period that includes July 1, 2000.

An entity is a *related entity* under two circumstances: (1) the organization and that entity have significant common purposes and substantial common membership or substantial common direction or control, whether directly or indirectly; or (2) either the organization or that entity owns, directly or through one or more entities, at least a 50 percent capital or profits interest in the other.[162]

---

[154] IRC § 505(c)(1).

[155] See *supra* § 2.

[156] *Id.* (particularly text accompanied by *supra* notes 100–101, 108–110).

[157] See *supra* §§ 2, 3.

[158] Reg. § 1.505(c)-1T. The notice that is required by IRC § 505(c)(1) is given by submitting a properly completed and executed Application for Recognition of Exemption (Form 1024) to the IRS.

[159] These organizations are the subject of Chapter 17.

[160] IRC § 527(i). This notice is given by means of Form 8871.

[161] This body of law took effect on July 1, 2000.

[162] IRC § 168(h)(4).

Where an organization fails to submit the requisite notice on a timely basis, it is taxable (unless otherwise exempt, such as by reason of qualifying as a social welfare organization).[163] The taxable income of the organization is computed by taking into account any exempt function income and any directly related deductions.

This notice requirement does not apply in the case of a political organization which reasonably anticipates that it will not have gross receipts of $25,000 or more for any year.[164] The requirement also does not apply to an entity required to report under the Federal Election Campaign Act[165] as a political committee. Further, the requirement is not applicable to any other type of tax-exempt organization that is nonetheless subject to the political campaign activities tax.[166] (This latter exception is basically for social welfare and labor organizations, and associations.[167]) This rule applies, however, to most state and local political action committees and candidate committees.[168]

---

[163] These organizations are the subject of Chapter 12.

[164] This $25,000 filing threshold is not the same as for other tax-exempt organizations, which is based on the concept of receipts *normally* received (see *supra* § (b)(ii)). The form must be filed unless the political organization reasonably expects annual gross receipts to always be less than $25,000 in each tax year.

[165] 2 U.S.C. § 431 *et seq.*

[166] IRC § 527(f)(1). See § 17.3(b).

[167] See Chapters 12 and 13, and § 15.1.

[168] The history of this legislation is brief but filled with contention and acrimony. The primary elections held in 2000, as part of the presidential campaign, attracted considerable soft money from political organizations that are not required to report to the Federal Election Commission (so-called "unregulated political action committees"). Early in the year, the staff of the Joint Committee on Taxation issued a report, recommending a number of disclosure requirements for tax-exempt organizations, including greater disclosure by political organizations. Thereafter, legislation was introduced in the House of Representatives to force disclosure of the financing of political action committees (PACs) to the IRS. The first bill was H.R. 3688, 106th Cong., 2d Sess. (2000). An attempt to engraft legislation of this nature on taxpayer rights legislation (H.R. 4163, 106th Cong., 2d Sess. (2000)) failed in the Ways and Means Committee on April 5, 2000. Another bill on the subject was introduced in the House (H.R. 4168, 106th Cong., 2d Sess. (2000)), followed by comparable legislation in the Senate (S. 2582, S. 2583, 106th Cong., 2d Sess. (2000)). An attempt in the House to add this legislation to a bill to repeal a telephone excise tax (H.R. 3916, 106th Cong., 2d Sess. (2000)) failed on May 25, 2000. A disclosure proposal was added to the Senate version of the defense authorization bill (S. 2549, 106th Cong., 2d Sess. (2000)) on June 8, 2000. Efforts began to craft legislation to force disclosure of political activities by most tax-exempt organizations. A discharge petition to force consideration of H.R. 3688, *supra*, was filed on June 14, 2000. A hearing on the disclosure issue in general, by the House Subcommittee on Oversight, was held on June 20, 2000; that hearing led to the writing of the Full and Fair Political Activity Disclosure Act of 2000 (H.R. 4717, 106th Cong., 2d Sess. (2000)), which was approved by the Ways and Means Committee on June 22, 2000. The Senate Finance Committee announced hearings on disclosure legislation on June 26, 2000. The Ways and Means proposal never made it to the House floor; the House suddenly passed a bill requiring disclosure by political organizations only (H.R. 4762, 106th Cong., 2d Sess. (2000)) on June 28, 2000. The Senate passed the bill the next day, thereby negating the Senate Finance Committee hearings. The legislation was signed into law on July 1, 2000 (Pub. L. No. 106-230). This legislation was amended in 2002, with most of the changes concerning the reporting and disclosure requirements (see § 24.3(d)).

§ 23.7   GROUP EXEMPTION

An organization (such as a chapter, local, post, or unit) that is affiliated with and is subject to the general supervision or control of a central organization (usually, a state, regional, or national organization) may be recognized as a tax-exempt organization solely by reason of its relationship with the parent organization. Tax-exempt status acquired in this manner is referred to as tax exemption on a *group basis*. The advantage of the group exemption is that each of the organizations covered by a group exemption letter—termed *subordinate* organizations[169]—is relieved from filing its own application for recognition of tax exemption.

The procedures by which a group exemption may be recognized by the IRS[170] contemplate a functioning of the parent organization as an agent of the IRS, requiring that the parent organization responsibly and independently evaluate the tax-exempt status of its subordinate organizations from the standpoint of the organizational and operational tests applicable to them.[171] A parent organization is required to annually file with the IRS a list of its qualifying tax-exempt subordinate organizations; this listing amounts to an attestation by the central organization that the subordinate organizations qualify as tax-exempt organizations so that the IRS need not carry out an independent evaluation as to the tax-exempt status of the organizations. Therefore, it is essential that the central organization, in performing this agency function, exercise responsibility in evaluating the tax status of its subordinates.

Assuming that the general requirements for recognition of tax-exempt status[172] are satisfied, a group exemption letter will be issued to a central organization where the above requirements as to subordinate organizations are met, the exemption to be recognized is under the general exemption rules,[173] and each of the subordinate organizations has an organizing document (although they do not have to be incorporated). Private foundations may not be included in a group exemption letter, nor may an organization that is organized and operated in a foreign country.

Thus, a central organization applying for a group exemption letter must first obtain recognition of its own tax-exempt status and establish that all of the subordinate organizations to be included in the group exemption letter are affiliated with it, subject to its general supervision or control, exempt under the same paragraph of the general exemption rules (although not necessarily the section under which the central organization is tax-exempt), not private foundations or foreign organizations, on the same accounting period as the central organization if they are not to be included in group returns, and formed within

---

[169] This is an unfortunate choice of terminology, in that many organizations and those who manage them do not care to be regarded as *subordinates*; a preferable term would have been *affiliates*.

[170] Rev. Proc. 80-27, 1980-1 C.B. 677. Also Reg. § 601.201(n)(7).

[171] See §§ 4.3, 4.5.

[172] Rev. Proc. 90-27, *supra* note 11.

[173] IRC § 501(c). Thus, the group exemption procedures are unavailable to organizations described in IRC §§ 521 (see § 18.11), 526 (see § 18.12), 527 (see Chapter 17), 528 (see § 18.13), 529 (see § 18.16).

the 15-month period prior to the date of submission of the group exemption application (assuming this is the case and these entities are claiming charitable status and are subject to the requirements for application for recognition of tax exemption).[174] For example, with respect to this third requirement, a central organization may be tax-exempt as a charitable entity with all of the subordinates thereof exempt as social welfare organizations. Concerning the sixth requirement, the procedures state that if one or more of the subordinates have not been organized within the 15-month period, the group exemption letter will be issued only if all of the subordinates agree to be recognized as tax-exempt from the date of the application rather than the date of their creation. Subordinate charitable organizations are exempt from the notice requirements generally applicable to charitable organizations.[175]

Each subordinate organization must authorize, in writing, the central organization to include it in the application for the group exemption letter.

A central organization may be involved in more than one group exemption arrangement, such as a charitable parent organization having both charitable and social welfare/civic organization subordinates. Also, a central organization may be a subordinate organization with respect to another central organization, such as a state organization that has subordinate units and is itself affiliated with a national organization.

An instrumentality or agency of a political subdivision that exercises control or supervision over a number of organizations similar in purposes and operations, each of which may qualify for tax exemption under the same category of exempt organizations, may obtain a group exemption letter covering the organizations in the same manner as a central organization. With this approach the group exemption for organizations such as federal credit unions, state chartered credit unions, and federal land bank associations may be established.[176]

A central organization must submit to the IRS, in addition to certain information about itself, the following information on behalf of its group exemption subordinates: (1) a letter signed by a principal officer of the central organization setting forth or including as attachments (a) information verifying the existence of the foregoing six relationships and requirements, (b) a detailed description of the principal purposes and activities of the subordinates, including financial information, (c) a sample copy of a uniform or representative governing instrument adopted by the subordinates, (d) an affirmation that, to the best of the officer's knowledge, the subordinates are operating in accordance with the stated purposes, (e) a statement that each subordinate to be included within the group exemption letter has furnished the requisite written authorization, (f) a list of subordinates to be included in the group exemption letter to which the IRS has issued an outstanding ruling or determination letter relating to tax exemption, and (g), if relevant, an affirmation that no subordinate organization is a private foundation; and (2) a list of the names, addresses, and employer identification numbers

---

[174] See *supra* § 2.
[175] Reg. § 1.508-1(a)(3)(i)(c); Rev. Rul. 90-100, *supra* note 103.
[176] See § 18.7.

of subordinates to be included in the group exemption letter (or, in lieu thereof, a satisfactory directory of subordinates). Certain additional information is required if a subordinate is claiming tax-exempt status as a school. In the only court decision involving the group exemption rules, the U.S. Tax Court upheld the requirement that detailed information concerning the activities and finances of subordinates be submitted to the IRS, in holding that an organization is not eligible for classification as a central organization because the requisite information was not provided.[177]

Once a group exemption letter is issued, certain information must be submitted annually by the central organization (at least 90 days before the close of its annual accounting period) to the IRS so as to maintain the letter. This information consists of (1) information regarding any changes in the purposes, character, or method of operation of the subordinates; (2) lists of (a) subordinates that have changed their names or addresses during the year, (b) subordinates no longer to be included in the group exemption letter (for whatever reason), and (c) subordinates to be added to the group exemption letter (for whatever reason); and (3) the information summarized in the foregoing paragraph (items (1)(a) through (g)) with respect to subordinates to be added to the group exemption letter.[178]

A subordinate organization may, in lieu of filing a separate annual information return (Form 990), file in combination with the central organization. (This is an optional practice; combined filing is not required under the group exemption rules.) For this option to be available, however, each of the subordinates must be tax-exempt under the same federal tax law provision and the consolidated return must relate solely to unrelated income tax matters.[179]

There are two ways in which a group exemption letter may be terminated. When a termination occurs, the tax-exempt status of the subordinate organizations is no longer recognized by the IRS, thereby requiring (where continuing recognition of tax-exempt status is required or desired) each subordinate to file an application for recognition of tax exemption, the central organization to file for a new group exemption letter, or the subordinates (or a portion of them) to become tax-exempt by reason of their status with respect to another qualifying central organization. Termination of a group exemption letter will be occasioned where (1) the central organization dissolves or otherwise ceases to exist, (2) one or more of the subordinates fail to fulfill the qualification requirements, or (3) the central organization fails to qualify for tax exemption, to submit the information required to obtain the letter, to file the annual information return, or to otherwise comply with the reporting requirements.[180]

---

[177] National Ass'n of Am. Churches v. Comm'r, *supra* note 30.

[178] Group exemption reports are filed with the IRS Service Center in Ogden, Utah (Rev. Proc. 96-40, 1996-2 C.B. 301).

[179] Tech. Adv. Mem. 8514001. See text accompanied by *infra* notes 184–186.

[180] IRC §§ 6001, 6033. Loss of tax exemption by some members of the group does not adversely affect the group exemption ruling as it pertains to the other members in the group (Tech. Adv. Mem. 9711004).

If the IRS revokes the tax-exempt status of a central organization, the group exemption letter involved is also revoked, thereby simultaneously revoking the tax-exempt status of all of the subordinates. To regain recognition of tax exemption in this instance, or in the case of its withdrawal from the group exemption, a subordinate organization must file an application for recognition of exemption or become a member of another tax-exempt group. As of the date an organization is no longer in a group, the 27-month notice period begins to run, so that an organization desiring to maintain tax exemption on an ongoing basis must file the application within that period or timely join another group.[181]

Where a subordinate organization has an outstanding ruling of tax exemption and becomes included in a group exemption letter, the prior exemption letter is superseded.[182] The central organization, in this circumstance, is obligated to notify the affected subordinate organization(s) of this supersession.

Where the subordinates are charitable organizations, their publicly supported charity status must be considered, inasmuch as, as noted, they may not be private foundations and qualify under the group exemption rules. On the basis of standardized paragraphs promulgated by the IRS National Office, the IRS will assume—and so rule—that the subordinates have the same nonprivate foundation status as the parent charitable organization. Moreover, the IRS will, in the case of classification of subordinates as publicly supported entities, do so on the basis of definitive rulings.[183]

The group exemption arrangement is distinguishable from the consolidated return rules pertaining to the filing requirements of an affiliated group of organizations.[184] Generally, the consolidated return rules are applicable only with respect to taxable entities.[185] Tax-exempt organizations can, however, use the consolidated return option as respects unrelated business income tax returns.[186]

A central organization must, as a general rule, file an annual information return.[187] Also as a general rule, this reporting obligation is imposed upon a subordinate organization. One or more of the subordinates may, however, file with the central organization as part of a group annual information return.[188] Organizations with gross receipts not normally in excess of $25,000 each year are not required to file an annual information return.[189] Thus, a central organization may exclude from its group return those subordinates the annual gross receipts of which are normally not in excess of $25,000 per year.[190]

---

[181] Rev. Rul. 90–100, *supra* note 103.
[182] Internal Revenue Manual, Part 7600 § 7667, 23 (3).
[183] See *supra* § 4(b).
[184] IRC § 1501.
[185] IRC § 1504(b)(1); cf. IRC § 1504(e).
[186] Tech. Adv. Mem. 8514001. See § 24.3(a)(v).
[187] See § 24.3.
[188] Reg. § 1.6033-2(d).
[189] See § 24.3(b)(ii).
[190] Priv. Ltr. Rul. 8337094.

The group exemption generally is very favorable for clusters of nonprofit organizations that are affiliated. This approach to tax exemption obviates the need for each member entity in the group to file a separate application for recognition of tax exemption, and this can result in savings of time, effort, and expenses—for the organizations and for the IRS. It is, then, a streamlined approach to the establishment of tax-exempt status for related organizations.

There are, however, some disadvantages to a tax-exempt status based on the group exemption. One concerns the fact that the members of the group do not individually possess determination letters as to their tax exemption. This can pose difficulties for donors and grantors,[191] as well as problems for the organization in securing state tax exemptions. Second, there is no separate assessment of these organizations' publicly supported status.[192] Third, if a member of the group is found liable for damages, the existence of the group exemption may be used in an effort to assert "ascending" liability on the part of the central organization.

§ 23.8 INTEGRAL PART DOCTRINE

The *integral part doctrine* is a basis in law for the acquisition of tax-exempt status, by means of recognition of that status by the IRS or otherwise. There are two variants of this doctrine. One concerns an organization that obtained tax exemption because of its relationship with one or more tax-exempt entities. This type of organization is, in law, a separate entity, with tax exemption a function of the affiliation. The other application of the doctrine pertains to tax-exempt organizations that have component entities that, while appearing to be separate organizations, are not, in law, separate but are instead *integral parts* of the larger organization. These component entities are in the nature of divisions of a tax-exempt organization.

(a) Affiliated Organizations

As noted, in general, the entitlement of a nonprofit organization to tax-exempt status is derived solely from the entity's own characteristics.[193] There is, however, an exception to this general rule, which is one of two aspects of the integral part doctrine. This facet of the doctrine, applied largely with respect to tax exemption as a charitable organization, enables an organization which functions as

---

[191] A donor of a major gift may want the security of a determination letter so as to have the requisite basis for relying on the organization's representation that it is a charitable entity. A private foundation grantor may desire similar assurance to be certain that the grant constitutes a qualifying distribution (see § 11.4(b)), is not an expenditure responsibility grant (see § 11.4(e)), or is not otherwise a taxable expenditure (*id.*).

[192] This point relates to the ones in *supra* note 191. For example, private foundations rarely make grants to other private foundations and a private foundation grantor usually wants meaningful assurance that the grantee is a public or publicly supported charity.

[193] See *supra* § 1.

an integral part of the exempt activities of a related entity or entities to derive tax exemption by reason of the relationship with its affiliate or affiliates. Tax exemption of this nature is also known as a *derivative* or *vicarious* exemption.

The genesis of this element of the doctrine is language in the federal tax regulations on the subject of feeder organizations.[194] There it is stated that, as an exception to these rules, a "subsidiary" of a tax-exempt organization can be exempt "on the ground that its activities are an integral part of the activities of the parent organization."[195] As an illustration, the regulations describe a "subsidiary organization that is operated for the sole purpose of furnishing electric power used by its parent, a tax-exempt organization, in carrying out its educational activities."[196] These regulations also state that an entity seeking tax exemption as an integral part of another entity cannot primarily be engaged in an activity that would generate more than insubstantial unrelated business income for the other entity.[197]

The criteria for achieving tax exemption by reason of an affiliation with a charitable entity are in flux. The traditional view is that this aspect of the integral part doctrine applies where the activities of the organization whose tax status is being evaluated are carried on under the supervision or control of an exempt organization and could be carried on by the exempt parent organization without materially constituting an unrelated trade or business.[198] Interpretations along this line from the IRS include tax exemption for a trust existing solely as a repository of funds set aside by a nonprofit hospital for the payment of malpractice claims against the hospital and as the payor of those claims,[199] a corporation that published and sold law journals as an adjunct to a tax-exempt law school,[200] and a bookstore used almost exclusively by the faculty and students of a university with which it was associated.[201] This traditional explication of the doctrine is also found in court opinions. For example, one court ruled that a corporation operating a bookstore and restaurant that sold college texts, was wholly owned by a tax-exempt college, used college facilities without charge, served mostly faculty and students, and devoted its earnings to educational purposes was tax-exempt because it "obviously bears a close and intimate relationship to the functioning of the [c]ollege itself."[202]

---

[194] See § 28.6.

[195] Reg. § 502-1(b). Also Gen. Couns. Mem. 39830.

[196] Reg. § 1.502-1(b).

[197] *Id.*

[198] E.g., Geisinger Health Plan v. Comm'r, 100 T.C. 394, 402 (1993), *aff'd*, 30 F.3d 494 (3d Cir. 1994).

[199] Rev. Rul. 78-41, 1978-1 C.B. 148. See, however, § 22.1.

[200] Rev. Rul. 63-235, 1963-2 C.B. 210.

[201] Rev. Rul. 58-194, 1958-1 C.B. 240.

[202] Squire v. Students Book Corp., 191 F.2d 1018, 1020 (9th Cir. 1951). Also University of Md. Physicians, P.A., v. Comm'r, 41 T.C.M. 732 (1981); University of Mass. Med. School Group Practice v. Comm'r, 74 T.C. 1299 (1980); B.H.W. Anesthesia Found. Inc. v. Comm'r, 72 T.C. 681 (1979); B.S.R Group, Inc. v. Comm'r, 70 T.C. 352 (1978); Brundage v. Comm'r, 54 T.C. 1468 (1970).

The reason that the criteria associated with this doctrine in transition is that, despite this tax regulation, and wealth of caselaw and IRS rulings, a court decided that the law is not clear as to "whether there are any other necessary qualifications" surrounding the doctrine.[203] Indeed, the court also concluded that there is one additional criterion—and, "[d]istilling . . . [this body of law] into a general rule," wrote that a "subsidiary that is not entitled to exempt status on its own may only receive such status as an integral part of its . . . [charitable] parent if (i) it is not carrying on a trade or business that would be an unrelated trade or business (that is, unrelated to exempt activities) if regularly carried on by the parent, and (ii) its relationship to its parent somehow enhances the subsidiary's own exempt character to the point that, when the boost provided by the parent is added to the contribution made by the subsidiary itself, the subsidiary would be entitled to . . . [tax-exempt, charitable] status"[204] Applying this new *boost principle*, the court held that a health maintenance organization could not qualify for tax exemption on the ground that it is an integral part of a hospital system, because the plan did not receive any boost from its association with the system.[205] Noting that an entity's "mere financing of the exempt purposes of a related organization does not constitute furtherance of that organization's purpose so as to justify exemption," the court observed that "it is apparent that . . . [the plan] merely seeks to 'piggyback' off of the other entities in the [s]ystem, taking on their charitable characteristics in an effort to gain exemption without demonstrating that it is rendered 'more charitable' by virtue of its association with them.[206] Reviewing the prior caselaw, this court wrote that the electric company referenced in the tax regulations received a boost from its association with the educational institution, as did the bookstore and law journal organizations. This new articulation of the integral part doctrine prevents an organization "that is not entitled to an exemption on its own" from becoming

---

[203] Geisinger Health Plan v. Comm'r, 30 F.3d 494 (3d Cir. 1994).

[204] *Id.* at 501.

[205] The court concluded that the association of the health maintenance organization with the other entities in the hospital system "does nothing to increase the portion of the community for which . . . [the plan] promotes health—it serves no more people as a part of the [s]ystem than it would serve otherwise. It may contribute to the [s]ystem by providing more patients than the [s]ystem might otherwise have served, thus arguably allowing the [s]ystem to promote health among a broader segment of the community than could be served without it, but its provision of patients to the [s]ystem does not enhance its own promotion of health; the patients it provides—its subscribers—are the same patients it serves without its association with the [s]ystem. To the extent it promotes health among non- . . . [plan]-subscriber patients of the [s]ystem, it does so only because . . . [plan] subscribers' payments to the [s]ystem help finance the provision of health care to others" (*id.* at 502).

This appellate court earlier held that this health maintenance organization could not qualify as a charitable entity on its own merits (Geisinger Health Plan v. Comm'r, 985 F.2d 1210 (3d Cir. 1993) (see § 6.2(e)).

[206] *Id.* at 503.

"tax-exempt *merely* because it happens to be controlled by an organization that is itself exempt."[207]

There are other instances where this variant of the integral part doctrine has been applied that escaped the analysis of the boost principle court. One is the determination by the IRS that a vending machine management organization was an integral part of a tax-exempt university.[208] Another is an IRS ruling that an organization formed and controlled by a tax-exempt conference of churches, that borrowed funds from individuals and made mortgage loans at less than the commercial rate of interest to affiliated churches to finance the construction of church buildings, qualified as an integral part of the parent organization.[209] A court subsequently held, without reference to the boost principle, that two organizations did not qualify for tax exemption on the basis of the integral part doctrine; indeed, the entities were dismissed as "appendages rather than integral parts" and "superfluous corporate shells that make no cognizable contribution" to the exempt organizations's purposes.[210] This court thereafter concluded that a health maintenance organization could not be considered an integral part of a health system because its enrollees received nearly 80 percent of their physician services from physicians with no direct link to any of the organization's tax-exempt affiliates; the boost principle was not considered.[211]

---

[207] *Id.* at 502 (emphasis by the court). When this court of appeals remanded the case to the U.S. Tax Court for decision as to application of the integral part doctrine, it said the doctrine "provides a means by which organizations may qualify for exemption vicariously through related organizations, as long as they are engaged in activities which would be exempt if the related organizations engaged in them, and as long as those activities are furthering the exempt purposes of the related organizations" (Geisinger Health Plan v. Comm'r, *supra* note 205, at 1220). No mention was there made of any boost principle. (Likewise, Texas Learning Technology Group v. Comm'r, 958 F.2d 122, 126 (5th Cir. 1992).) In its subsequent opinion, the appellate court dismissed its previous summary of the doctrine as simply "dicta" and pronounced that it was "not bound by" it (Geisinger Health Plan v. Comm'r, *supra* note 203, at 499).

As to the prior law, one IRS ruling (Rev. Rul. 78-41, *supra* note 199) did not comport with the boost theory, so the court elected to "not rely on . . . [it] in our analysis" (Geisinger Health Plan v. Comm'r, *supra* note 203, at 502, note 8).

When the U.S. Tax Court considered this issue, it sought to determine whether the organization's overall functions were substantially related to the exempt function of its tax-exempt affiliates in the system; it stated that, if the organization's activities are conducted on a scale larger than is reasonably necessary to accomplish the purposes of the affiliates (see § 26.4(b)), the requisite substantial relationship would not be present (Geisinger Health Plan v. Comm'r, *supra* note 198, at 394, 406 (1993)). The court concluded that, because the health maintenance organization made sales to and provided services for individuals who are not patients of the exempt entities within the health care system, the organization's operations were not substantially related to the other components of the system and thus it could not be considered an integral part of the system (*id.* at 406–407). On appeal, this unrelated business argument was not reviewed, because the appellate court held that, inasmuch as the boost principle of the doctrine was not satisfied, there was no need to assess the other prong of this integral part test. In general, Levine, "*Geisinger Health Plan* Likely to Adversely Affect HMOs and Other Health Organizations," 79 J. Tax. (No. 2) 90 (Aug. 1993).

[208] Rev. Rul. 81-19, 1981-1 C.B. 353.

[209] Rev. Rul. 75-282, 1975-2 C.B. 201. In general, Rasman, "Third Circuit's 'Boost' Test Denies Section 501(c)(3) Status to HMO," 6 J. Tax Exempt Orgs. (No. 4) 147 (Jan./Feb. 1995).

[210] University Medical Resident Serv., P.C. v. Comm'r, 71 T.C.M. 3130, 3131–3135 (1996).

[211] IHC Health Plans, Inc. v. Comm'r, 82 T.C.M. 593 (2001).

(b) Divisions

An organization may be viewed as a composite of integrated components—being "composed of constituent parts making a whole."[212] In comparable instances, the law regards an item of property as an integral part of a larger property or process, such as bottles and cartons being an integral part of manufactured beer for purpose of state use tax exemptions[213] and executed contracts being an integral part of a baseball team for purposes of defining the team's "raw materials."[214] The fragmentation rule utilized in the unrelated business setting is predicated on this view of an organization.[215]

A tax-exempt organization may have component entities that are not separate organizations (although they may appear to be) and thus are "exempt" from tax because of the tax exemption of the host organization. For example, a tax-exempt university may have scholarship funds, a tax-exempt hospital may have research funds, and a tax-exempt charitable organization may have one or more endowment funds; these funds may have separate names and be recipients of contributions made in those names. These component entities may be little more than one of several accounts carried on a tax-exempt organization's financial records. By analogy to the terminology in the for-profit setting, these component entities are akin to divisions (as is the case with the schools of a university or the departments of a hospital).[216] The principal distinction from a tax standpoint is that the entity that is an integral part of a tax-exempt organization as a division is itself tax-exempt solely by virtue of the exemption of the host organization, while the tax exemption of a subsidiary must be obtained (if it can) by reason of the other definition of the integral part doctrine or on the merits of its own characteristics.[217]

It has been held that a principal element leading to a finding that one organization functions as an integral part of another organization is the fact that the function of the integrated organization is "essential" to the operation of the larger organization, and is an "ordinary and proper" function of the larger organization.[218] While this may be the case in general, in the tax-exempt organizations context it is largely an irrelevant criterion, inasmuch as the decision as to whether to establish the would-be integrated organization will nearly always be that of the larger organization.

---

[212] Application of Larson, 340 F.2d 965, 967 (U.S. Ct. Cust. Pat. Appl. 1965).

[213] Zoller Brewing Co. v. State Tax Comm'r, 5 N.W.2d 643 (Iowa 1942).

[214] Hollywood Baseball Ass'n v. Comm'r, 423 F.2d 494 (9th Cir. 1970), *cert. den.*, 400 U.S. 848 (1970).

[215] See § 26.2(d).

[216] By contrast, the organizations that are tax-exempt by reason of the other application of the integral part doctrine (see *supra* § (a)) or the group exemption procedures (see *supra* § 6) are comparable to a for-profit organization's subsidiaries. A somewhat similar body of federal tax law is that concerning the supporting organization (see § 11.3(c)).

[217] The *division* aspect of the doctrine assumes that the attributes of this type of component entity do not cause it to be considered a separate organization; for example, one nonprofit corporation cannot be a division of another nonprofit corporation (although it can be an integral part of one).

[218] E.g., Schwarz v. United States, 284 F. Supp. 792, 797 (U.S. Customs Ct. 1968); also Matczak v. Secretary of Health, Educ. & Welfare, 299 F. Supp. 409 (E.D.N.Y. 1969).

Thus, the use of the integral part doctrine can be an efficient manner in which to acquire tax exemption for an organization, being a considerably speedier approach than the conventional exemption application process and even more rapid than the group exemption approach.[219]

§ 23.9 ADMINISTRATIVE PROCEDURES WHERE DETERMINATION IS ADVERSE

The filing of an application for recognition of tax exemption with the IRS can, of course, lead to the issuance of an initial adverse determination. In this instance, or in the case of the issuance of a letter proposing revocation or modification of tax-exempt status,[220] the IRS will advise the organization of its right to appeal the determination by requesting appeals office consideration.[221] To initiate an appeal, the organization must submit to the IRS, within 30 days from the date of the letter, a statement of the facts, law, and arguments in support of its position. At this time, the organization must also state whether it wishes an appeals office conference.

Upon receipt of an organization's request for appeals office consideration, the person with responsibility for the case will forward the request and case file to the chief of the appropriate appeals office.[222] Any determination letter that is issued on the basis of IRS National Office technical advice may not be appealed to an appeals office as regards issues that were the subject of the technical advice.[223]

The appeals office, after considering the organization's appeal and any additional information developed in conference, will advise the organization of its decision and issue the appropriate determination letter to the organization.[224]

An organization is expected to make full presentation of the facts, circumstances, and arguments at the initial level of consideration by the appeals office, since submission of additional facts, circumstances, and arguments may result in suspension of appeal procedures and referral of the case back to the key district for additional consideration. Any oral representation of additional facts or modification of facts originally represented or alleged must be reduced to writing.[225]

---

[219] One of the current issues involving the integral part doctrine is whether the many unincorporated congregations established by the Universal Life Church are tax-exempt by reason of the church's tax-exempt status (see § 8.3). To date, the U.S. Tax Court (the only court to consider the issue) has held that the congregations cannot partake of the church's tax exemption (Stephenson v. Comm'r, 79 T.C. 995 (1982), aff'd, 748 F.2d 331 (6th Cir. 1984); Murphy v. Comm'r, 45 T.C.M. 621 (1983); Riemers v. Comm'r, 42 T.C.M. 838 (1981)).

[220] Reg. § 601.201(n)(6).

[221] Rev. Proc. 90-27, *supra* note 11 § 10.01.

[222] *Id.* at § 10.03.

[223] *Id.* at § 10.02.

[224] *Id.* at § 11.01.

[225] *Id.* at § 11.02.

If an appeals office believes that a tax exemption or private foundation status issue is not covered by published precedent, the appeals office must request technical advice from the IRS National Office. Unless the appeals office believes that the conclusions reached by the National Office should be reconsidered and promptly requests the reconsideration, the case will be disposed of by the appeals office on the basis of the decision in the technical advice memorandum.[226]

If at any time during the course of appeals office consideration, the organization believes that its case involves an issue as to which there is no published precedent, the organization may ask the appeals office to request technical advice from the National Office.[227]

If the proposed disposition by the appeals office is contrary to a prior National Office technical advice memorandum or ruling concerning tax exemption, the proposed disposition will be submitted to the Exempt Oranizations Division.[228] Unless the appeals office believes that the conclusions reached by the National Office should be reconsidered and promptly requests that consideration, the decision of the National Office must be followed by the appeals office.[229] In any event, it is clear that the Director of the Division (and perhaps, ultimately, the Commissioner of Internal Revenue) will make the final decision.

A ruling or determination letter recognizing tax exemption may be revoked or modified by (1) a notice to the organization involved, (2) enactment of legislation, (3) ratification of a tax treaty, (4) a decision of the U.S. Supreme Court, (5) issuance of temporary or final regulations, or (6) the issuance of a revenue ruling, a revenue procedure, or other statement published in the Internal Revenue Bulletin. The revocation or modification may be retroactive[230] if the organization omitted or misstated a material fact, operated in a manner materially different from that originally represented, or, in certain instances,[231] engaged in a prohibited transaction with the purpose of diverting corpus or income of the organization from its tax-exempt purpose and the transaction involved a substantial part of the corpus or income of the organization. Where there is a material change, inconsistent with tax exemption, in the character, purpose, or method of operation of an organization, revocation or modification will ordinarily take effect as of the date of the material change.[232]

Once the IRS has acted to revoke recognition of the tax exemption of an or-

---

[226] *Id.* at § 11.03.
[227] *Id.* at § 11.04; Reg. §§ 601.201(n)(2)(iv), (9).
[228] Reg. § 601.201(n)(5)(iii).
[229] Rev. Proc. 90-27, *supra* note 11 § 11.05.
[230] See § 24.1.
[231] Namely, where IRC § 503 applies; that provision denies tax exemption to supplemental unemployment benefit trusts (see § 16.4) and to certain funded pension trusts (see § 16.6) where the organization engaged in one or more *prohibited transactions* (as defined in IRC § 503(b)).
[232] Rev. Proc. 90-27, *supra* note 11 § 14.01.

ganization, it will expect the entity to begin paying income taxes.[233] Should the organization not do so, however, the IRS may be expected to commence proceedings to assess and collect the tax due. This activity is begun by the mailing to the organization of a statutory notice of deficiency. This the IRS is authorized to do following a determination that there is a tax deficiency.[234] However, because there cannot be general income tax liability for a tax-exempt organization, it is essential to the government's efforts to collect the tax that the statutory notice of deficiency be preceded by a valid letter of revocation. To have this letter, the IRS is required to act in conformity with certain procedures[235] and at least generally apprise the organization of the basis for the revocation. However, the revocation itself must be in conformity with all requirements of law, so that if, for example, the grounds upon which the revocation is based were erroneous, the revocation is not proper.[236] Likewise, if the letter of revocation was prompted by political or similar considerations that demonstrate lack of objectivity by the IRS, the revocation becomes null and void.[237] Thus, a letter of revocation can be shown to be void *ab initio* because of the considerations governing its issuance. Also, subsequent actions by the IRS indicating a continuing recognition of tax-exempt status can operate to make a prior revocation of recognition nugatory. In either event, the letter of revocation is not valid, so that the tax exemption has not been properly revoked, meaning that any notice of deficiency based upon the letter of revocation is of no force and effect.[238]

Still other procedures have been promulgated for appeals from the attempted imposition of certain taxes on most tax-exempt organizations and on certain individuals under the private foundation rules. These taxes are the excise taxes imposed by the federal tax law pertaining to private foundations,[239] the unrelated income tax,[240] the private foundation termination tax,[241] the political activities tax,[242] and the tax[243] on charitable and split-interest trusts.[244]

---

[233] See, e.g., § 24.2(a) (concerning the tax consequences of retroactive revocation of tax-exempt status of public charities). Usually, when an organization's exemption is revoked, it becomes a taxable nonprofit organization, liable for the regular federal income tax imposed on corporations. However, when the tax exemption of a social club (see Chapter 14) was revoked, the issue arose as to whether the club should be treated as a personal holding company. One of the tests for a personal holding company is that, at any time during the last half of the tax year, more than 50 percent in value of its stock is owned by or for no more than five individuals (IRC § 542(a)). The IRS treated the club's members as shareholders for this purpose, found that the stock ownership test was met, and held that the club, as a nonexempt entity, was a personal holding company (Tech. Adv. Mem. 9728004). The result was that the club became liable, not only for the regular corporate income tax, but also for a tax of 39.6 percent of the club's undistributed personal holding company income.

[234] IRC § 6212.

[235] Internal Revenue Manual § 7(10)(12).

[236] A. Duda & Sons Coop. Ass'n v. United States, 504 F.2d 970, 975 (5th Cir. 1974).

[237] Center on Corporate Responsibility, Inc. v. Schultz, 368 F. Supp. 863, 871–873 (D.D.C. 1973).

[238] Cf. Church of Scientology of Calif. v. Comm'r, 83 T.C. 381 (1984), *aff'd*, 823 F.2d 1310 (9th Cir. 1987).

[239] See § 11.4.

[240] See § 28.1.

[241] See § 11.4(f).

[242] See § 17.3.

[243] IRC § 641.

[244] IRC § 4947.

CHAPTER TWENTY-FOUR

Operational Considerations

The federal tax law imposes a battery of operational requirements on tax-exempt organizations, irrespective of whether they have received recognition of tax-exempt status from the IRS.[1] For most exempt organizations, the principal responsibility is the filing of an annual information return with the IRS. Other reporting obligations are imposed on exempt organizations, such as in instances of material changes and mandated disclosures. Most ominous is the possibility of an IRS audit and the potential revocation of exemption.

§ 24.1 CHANGES IN OPERATIONS OR FORM

Once an organization achieves tax-exempt status, that qualification can be maintained as long as the entity does not materially change its character, purposes, or methods of operation. A change in an organization's form is likely to have tax consequences. An organization's exempt status may be affected by a change in the law.

(a) Changes in Operations

An organization's tax-exempt status remains in effect as long as there are no substantial—*material*—changes in the organization's character, purposes, or methods of operation.[2] An organization and its advisors have the burden of determining whether or not a change of this nature is material or immaterial.

A material change should be communicated to the IRS as soon as possible after the change is made or becomes effective. Other changes should be reflected in due course in the organization's annual information return.[3]

A substantial change in an organization's character, purposes, or methods of operation may result in modification or revocation of the organization's tax-exempt status.[4] As noted, a change in the law may afford the IRS a basis for modifying or revoking an organization's exempt status.

There is no sanction that is automatically levied by the IRS for failure to notify the agency of a change of facts, in relation to those stated on the application for recognition of tax exemption, concerning the operations of a tax-exempt organization. This is the case even when the fact change is material. It may be that the change of facts involves a substantial expansion of exempt function activities, so that the exempt status of the entity is not imperiled. Even if new facts reveal nonexempt activities, exemption will not be disturbed if the fact change is

[1] Reg. § 1.501(a)-1(a)(2). Also Rev. Proc. 90-27, 1990-1 C.B. 514 § 13.02; Rev. Rul. 68-217, 1968-2 C.B. 260. The IRS may revoke a ruling letter that recognized an organization's tax exemption, without retroactive effect, pursuant to IRC § 7805(b), but in this case the organization would be subject to taxation on any unrelated business taxable income (see Part Five) during the IRC § 7805(b) relief period (Rev. Rul. 78-289, 1978-2 C.B. 180). It is the view of the IRS that the principle of this 1978 ruling is applicable with respect to the political activities tax (see § 17.3) (Gen. Couns. Mem. 39811).
[2] Reg. §§ 1.501(a)-1(a)(2), 601.201(n)(3)(ii).
[3] See *infra* § 3. E.g., Form 990 Part VI, question 77.
[4] Rev. Proc. 90-27, *supra* note 1 § 14.

insubstantial (although there may be unrelated business tax implications[5]). A misrepresentation of fact on the application for recognition of exemption will not necessarily have adverse consequences to the organization if the circumstances do not involve a violation of the law of tax-exempt organizations. As to the latter, for example, the IRS was told on an application that insiders with respect to a charitable organization[6] were providing the organization facilities without charge, when in fact there was a rental arrangement; when the IRS learned the truth, revocation of exemption did not occur because the IRS accepted the rent as being of fair value.[7]

Occasionally, the IRS attempts to cause a retroactive revocation of tax exemption. The government's procedural regulations state that a revocation of exemption may be retroactive in three instances: where (1) the organization omitted or misstated a material fact in the process of acquiring recognition of exemption, (2) the organization operated in a manner materially different from that originally represented, or (3) the organization engaged in a prohibited transaction.[8] A *prohibited transaction* is one in which the organization entered into the process of pursuing tax exemption for the purpose of diverting substantial corpus or income from its exempt purpose.[9]

One of the infrequent cases on the point was decided in 1979. A nonprofit organization was recognized as a tax-exempt educational entity in 1959; its function was to operate a school. In 1970, when the rules prohibiting schools from maintaining racially discriminatory policies were introduced,[10] the IRS advised the school of its concerns that the school may be engaging in discriminatory practices. In 1976, the IRS commenced a revocation procedure, which culminated in loss by the organization of its exemption by court order. The IRS attempted to revoke the school's exempt status retroactively to 1959, the date the IRS initially recognized the entity's exempt status. The court upheld revocation retroactively to 1970, however, inasmuch as the IRS had expressly provided the organization with notice of the law change in that year, rather than to 1959.[11]

Thereafter, the same court upheld a retroactive revocation of tax exemption, effective as of the date the IRS determined that the exempt functions had ceased. The case involved an organization that was granted exemption in 1936 as a religious organization engaging in missionary activities, with the exemption upheld in 1953. In 1976, the IRS proposed to revoke the exemption on the grounds that the missionary activities had ceased and were replaced by commercial publishing

---

[5] See Part Five.

[6] See § 19.3.

[7] Tech. Adv. Mem. 9835003.

[8] Reg. § 601.201(n)(6)(i). E.g., West Central Coop v. United States, 758 F.2d 1269 (8th Cir. 1985); Stevens Bros. Found. Inc. v. Comm'r, 324 F.2d 633, 641 (8th Cir. 1963), *cert. den.*, 376 U.S. 969 (1964).

[9] Reg. § 601.201(n)(6)(vii); Rev. Proc. 90-27, *supra* note 1 § 14.01.

[10] See § 5.4(a).

[11] Prince Edward School Found. v. United States, 80-1 U.S.T.C. ¶ 9295 (D.D.C. 1979), *aff'd in unpub. op.* (D.C. Cir. 1980), *cert. den.* 450 U.S. 944 (1981). Also Virginia Educ. Fund v. Comm'r, 85 T.C. 743 (1985), *aff'd*, 799 F.2d 903 (4th Cir. 1986); Estate of Clopton v. Comm'r, 93 T.C. 275 (1989).

operations, with the revocation retroactive to 1963, the year in which the exempt functions were determined to have stopped. This court agreed with the IRS and held that the organization failed to meet its burden of showing that the IRS's action of retroactive revocation of exemption was erroneous. The IRS had also determined that the organization's records showed drastic increases in salaries and accumulated surplus by 1970 and ordered the filing of tax returns by the organization as of that year; this determination was also upheld by the court.[12]

Subsequently, another court adopted a like stance with respect to a religious publishing company. The organization was formed in 1931 and was recognized as tax-exempt in 1939; in 1980, the IRS proposed to revoke the exemption, on the grounds that the organization had become operated in a commercial manner, retroactive to 1969. The court agreed with the IRS as to revocation of exemption, but held that the IRS abused its discretion in making the revocation effective as of 1969; instead, the court concluded that the retroactivity should extend back only to 1975.[13] The court was reversed, however, with the appellate court concluding that the organization was engaged in exempt functions, thereby voiding this retroactive revocation of exempt status.[14]

A comparable line of law holds that the IRS has the power to retroactively revoke a determination as to tax-exempt status if it becomes contrary to law.[15] The cases involve situations, however, where the change in the law was made by Congress.[16] Also, retroactivity of exemption may occur where the law was clear at the time the ruling was issued and the issuance was an error.[17]

An aspect of this subject that is by no means clear is the authority of the IRS to retroactively revoke the tax exemption of an organization solely for the reason that the IRS has prevailed in a case of first impression. While this type of victory for the government may be a basis for revocation, it does not appear to be a "change" in the law that would trigger retroactive revocation of exemption. Even a decision by the U.S. Supreme Court should not lead to automatic revocation of exemption of all similarly situated organizations, retroactive to the date they were established. In part, the rationale for a more reasoned approach is that an organization receiving a favorable ruling is permitted, in most circumstances,

---

[12] Incorporated Trustees of Gospel Worker Soc'y v. United States, 510 F. Supp. 374 (D.D.C. 1981), aff'd, 672 F.2d 894 (D.C. Cir. 1981), cert. den., 456 U.S. 944 (1982). Also Freedom Church of Revelation v. United States, 588 F. Supp. 693 (D.D.C. 1984).

[13] Presbyterian & Reformed Publishing Co. v. Comm'r, 79 T.C. 1070 (1982).

[14] 743 F.2d 148 (3d Cir. 1984). In another case, the IRS recognized the tax-exempt status of an organization in 1969, revoked the determination letter in 1990, and caused the revocation to be retroactive to 1984 (United Cancer Council, Inc. v. Comm'r, 109 T.C. 326 (1997), rev'd and rem'd, 165 F.3d 1173 (7th Cir. 1999)).

[15] This aspect of the law is predicated upon the authority of the IRS to apply withdrawal of an acquiescence retroactively (e.g., Dixon v. United States, 381 U.S. 68 (1965)).

[16] E.g., Bornstein v. United States, 345 F.2d 558 (Ct. Cl. 1965) (where a ruling was issued one month after a statute was enacted, the matter was reconsidered months later, and the ruling was retroactively revoked).

[17] E.g., Automobile Club of Mich. v. Comm'r, 353 U.S. 180 (1957), aff'g 230 F.2d 585 (6th Cir. 1956), aff'g 20 T.C. 1033 (1955).

to rely upon the position stated in the ruling in planning and/or consummating a transaction.[18]

Retroactive revocation of tax exemption can produce harsh results, particularly where the period embraced by the revocation covers several years. Moreover, comparable adverse tax consequences may result under state law. Also, for nearly all charitable organizations, retroactive revocation of exemption could operate to likewise retroactively revoke the organization's eligibility to receive deductible contributions, which could lead to disallowance of the tax deductions taken by the organization's donors.[19]

The facts and circumstances of a given case determine whether, in retroactively revoking an organization's tax exemption, the IRS has abused its discretion[20] and thus has caused the government to be estopped from causing a revocation to be retroactive.[21]

(b) Changes in Form

A change in organizational form generally is regarded by the IRS as the creation of a new legal entity requiring the filing of an application for recognition of exemption for the successor entity, even though the organization's purposes, methods of operation, sources of support, and accounting method remain the same as they were in its predecessor form.[22] In this determination, the IRS stated that in each of the following changes in the structure of organizations, a new application for recognition of tax exemption is warranted: (1) conversion of a trust to a corporation; (2) conversion of an unincorporated association to a corporation; (3) reincorporation of an organization, incorporated under state law, by an act of Congress; and (4) reincorporation of an organization, incorporated under the laws of one state, under the laws of another state. This determination has been endorsed by a court.[23]

Absent a change in the law or in the rulings policy of the IRS, the tax-exempt status of the predecessor entity will, in effect, be transmitted to the successor entity. This assumes, however, that the predecessor entity itself was an exempt organization and, in the case of a charitable entity, held a ruling from the IRS to that effect. Where the predecessor lacks the ruling, the organization is treated as a charitable entity only as of the date of formation of the successor entity (assuming a ruling to that effect is timely secured).[24]

When the IRS issues a ruling or determination letter recognizing the tax-exempt status of a corporation, generally the effective date is the date of incorporation or the date the entity became organized and operated for exempt

---

[18] Rev. Proc. 62-28, 1962-2 C.B. 496.

[19] See *infra* note 39.

[20] IRC § 7805.

[21] E.g., Lesavoy Found v. Comm'r, 238 F.2d 589 (3d Cir. 1957), *rev'g* 25 T.C. 924 (1956).

[22] Rev. Rul. 67-390, 1967-2 C.B. 179.

[23] American New Covenant Church v. Comm'r, 74 T.C. 293 (1980). Also Smith v. Comm'r, 51 T.C.M. 1114 (1986).

[24] Rev. Rul. 77-469, 1977-2 C.B. 196; Rev. Rul. 77-208, 1977-1 C.B. 153.

purposes.[25] When prior to incorporation an organization was formed and operated in an exempt manner and its incorporation merely had the effect of changing the form of organization from that of an unincorporated organization to a corporation, however, the ruling or determination letter embraces the period during which the organization operated in an unincorporated status.[26]

It should not be assumed that the tax status of a predecessor entity will automatically be transmitted to a successor entity. For example, as noted, the policies and views of the IRS may change, and the IRS may deny recognition of tax exemption to an organization even though it granted recognition of exemption to a predecessor organization and the material facts did not differ.[27]

The law also imposes comparable requirements in other areas. Thus, an organization that remains in existence after terminating its private foundation status[28] must file a new application for recognition of exemption if it wishes to be treated as a charitable organization, since the IRS regards it as a newly created entity.[29] Similarly, a tax-exempt corporation formed to take over the operations of an exempt unincorporated association is regarded as a new organization for purposes of filing the Social Security (FICA) tax waiver certificate.[30]

The continuity of existence of a charitable organization is of importance, notwithstanding a change in form. This is particularly the case where the organization has its nonprivate foundation status predicated on classification as a publicly supported organization, which classification contemplates a history of required financial support.[31] Where certain requirements are met, the IRS allows the financial history of the predecessor entity to be used in establishing a public support record for the successor entity.[32]

If a tax-exempt organization converts to a taxable entity[33] the termination of exempt status is ordinarily operative prospectively; retroactive loss of exemption would occur only if there had been a material misrepresentation of fact or material difference in actual operation.[34]

[25] Rev. Rul. 54-134, 1954-1 C.B. 88.
[26] *Id.*
[27] E.g., MIB, Inc. v. Comm'r, 734 F.2d 71 (1st Cir. 1984); National Right to Work Legal Defense Educ. Found., Inc. v. United States, 487 F. Supp. 801 (E.D.N.C. 1979).
[28] See Chapter 11.
[29] Rev. Rul. 74-490, 1974-2 C.B. 171.
[30] Rev. Rul. 77-159, 1977-1 C.B. 302. Also Rev. Rul. 71-276, 1971-1 C.B. 289.
[31] See § 11.3(b).
[32] Rev. Rul. 73-422, 1973-2 C.B. 70.
[33] See § 33.3.
[34] E.g. Priv. Ltr. Rul. 8446047.

§ 24.2   TAX CONSEQUENCES OF RETROACTIVE REVOCATION OF TAX-EXEMPT STATUS OF PUBLIC CHARITIES

There are numerous federal tax consequences that can flow from the revocation of the tax-exempt status of an organization that is not a private foundation,[35] where the revocation is retroactive.[36] In general, revocation of the exemption of an organization is made retroactive if the organization omitted or misstated a material fact in seeking recognition of exemption or operated in a manner materially different from that originally represented.[37] (The IRS, however, has the authority to grant relief in this regard.[38])[39]

Generally, a public charity that has its tax-exempt status retroactively revoked will be treated as a corporation for tax purposes.[40] Some organizations, however, are established as charitable trusts.[41] In addition, the corporate form may be disregarded and the tax liabilities passed through to another entity where the revoked corporation is in substance a sham that should be disregarded as the "alter ego" of a controlling individual or group[42] or where the corporation is functioning as an agent with respect to contributed funds.[43]

(a) Tax Treatments: Corporations

Where a charitable organization loses its tax-exempt status because it is operating on a commercial basis, it becomes taxed under the rules normally applicable to taxable corporations.

When a revoked charitable organization is engaged in tax-exempt activities, nonprofit, nonexempt (for example, political) activities, and/or for-profit activities, the tax outcome is dependent on whether the income is business income, investment income, or contribution income.

As to income from a related or unrelated business, a revoked organization would have gross income to the extent of receipts from trade or business activity,

---

[35] An organization is not a private foundation where it is an organization that is tax-exempt by reason of IRC § 501(c)(3), where it is also classified under IRC § 509(a)(1)-(4) as being a public charity. See Chapter 11.

[36] Many of these considerations are also applicable with respect to private foundations. In those situations, however, rules pertaining to the termination of private foundation status may be applicable.

[37] Rev. Proc. 84-86, 1984-1 C.B. 541 § 14.01.

[38] IRC § 7805(b).

[39] In these circumstances (retroactive revocation), charitable contribution deductions generally are protected until public announcement of the revocation of charitable donee status; however, the IRS may disallow a contribution deduction where the donor knew of actual or imminent revocation or was responsible for or aware of the activities that gave rise to the revocation (Rev. Proc. 82-39, 1982-2 C.B. 759, note 5 § 3.01). In the context of declaratory judgment litigation (see *infra* § 6(b)), contributions not in excess of $1,000 are deductible after notice of revocation and during the pendency of the litigation (see text accompanied by *infra* notes 348–351).

[40] IRC § 7701.

[41] IRC § 4947.

[42] Generally, however, the corporate form is respected. See § 4.1.

[43] E.g., Comm'r v. Bollinger, 485 U.S. 340 (1988); National Carbide Corp. v. Comm'r, 336 U.S. 422 (1949).

offset by deductions for related expenses.[44] Investment income, net of related expenses, would be taxable, including passive income that generally is excluded from taxation when received by a tax-exempt organization.[45]

The law on this point is more complicated where the receipts are voluntary contributions intended, by the donor or donors, to further the organization's stated tax-exempt purposes.

Generally, donated funds and the value of donated property are not considered items of income to the recipient organization.[46] For this purpose, a *gift* is a payment where the donor does not receive something of equivalent value in return. Thus, the U.S. Supreme Court wrote that a "payment of money [or transfer of property] generally cannot constitute a charitable contribution if the contributor expects a substantial benefit in return."[47] Essentially, the same rule was subsequently articulated by the Court, when it ruled that an exchange having an "inherently reciprocal nature" is not a gift and thus cannot be a charitable gift, where the recipient is a charity.[48] An earlier Supreme Court opinion stated that a gift proceeds from a "detached and disinterested generosity" and is "out of affection, respect, admiration, charity or like impulses."[49]

Therefore, while a true gift to an organization is not income,[50] the IRS may contend that the payments are in fact gross income, such as where contributions are considered income to individuals associated with an organization rather than gifts to the organization[51] or where the "contributions" are considered payments in exchange for a quid pro quo.[52] Another contention may be that the "contributions" are items of unrelated business income.[53]

It is the position of the IRS that contributions given in good faith are generally excludable by a revoked tax-exempt organization, as long as the organization also acted in good faith in soliciting the contributions.[54] It is also the view of the IRS that the intent of the donor is not determinative of the gift issue in instances of misrepresentation or fraud where "it is clear that from the outset an organization intentionally misrepresented in its solicitations that it was validly tax-exempt and would use all the donations for exempt purposes."[55] By contrast, it has been held that excludable gift treatment is not appropriate where the recipient organization, "misrepresenting itself to be a tax-exempt charity, seeks and obtains donations which it plans to, and does, use in carrying on business activities for profit and

---

[44] See § 28.2.

[45] See § 27.1.

[46] IRC § 102.

[47] United States v. American Bar Endowment, 477 U.S. 105, 116–117 (1986).

[48] Hernandez v. Comm'r, 490 U.S. 680, 692 (1989).

[49] Comm'r v. Duberstein, 363 U.S. 278, 285–286 (1960).

[50] E.g., Bail Fund of the Civil Rights Congress of N.Y. v. Comm'r, 26 T.C. 482 (1956).

[51] E.g., Webber v. Comm'r, 21 T.C. 742 (1954), *aff'd*, 219 F2d 834 (10th Cir. 1955).

[52] E.g., Foundation for Divine Mediation, Inc. v. Comm'r, 24 T.C.M. 411 (1965); Publishers New Press, Inc. v. Comm'r, 42 T.C. 396 (1964); Teleservice Co. of Wyoming Valley v. Comm'r, 27 TC. 722 (1957), *aff'd*, 254 F.2d 105 (3d Cir. 1958).

[53] E.g., Veterans of Foreign Wars, Dep't of Mich. v. Comm'r, 89 T.C. 7 (1987), *app. dis.* (6th Cir. 1988).

[54] Gen. Couns. Mem. 39813.

[55] *Id.*

thereby enriches itself.[56] Thus, where the "misrepresentation exception" is applicable, contributions to the revoked exempt organization are not excludable gifts but are items of gross income. This exception will apply where the fraudulent acts and intentions are attributable to the organization,[57] as opposed to actions by individuals in their separate capacities.[58]

The determination as to this type of corporate level responsibility is a matter of fact. Nonetheless, it is the view of the IRS's lawyers that "misrepresentation by an organization should be presumed to exist when the facts show that an organization soliciting contributions was engaged in a pattern of activities inconsistent with the basis for its exemption."[59] It is also their view that contributions are taxable pursuant to the misrepresentation exception when the organization's exemption is revoked for engaging in nonprofit, nonexempt (for example, political) activities, inasmuch as this type of activity does not "benefit" the organization.[60] Under these views, however, the misrepresentation rationale does not extend to situations where contributions initially obtained through "sincere representations" are diverted to noncharitable uses.[61]

Some "contributions" will not be regarded as gifts but as contributions to the capital of the corporation involved.[62] Contributions to capital, whether by a shareholder or a nonshareholder, are not includible in the recipient's gross income.[63] It is unlikely, however, that contributions to a revoked exempt organization would qualify as contributions to capital. Should a contribution potentially so qualify, the contribution would usually be by a "nonshareholder"; even then, the contribution probably would not be a contribution to capital, if only because the contribution would not have become a permanent part of the recipient's working capital structure.[64]

If contributions are included in the gross income of a revoked organization, the organization's tax would depend on its ability to offset expenditures against that income. Where the expenditures (including an allocable portion of fundraising costs) were for exempt purposes, a deduction will be allowed to the extent of

---

[56] Synanon Church v. Comm'r, 57 T.C.M. 602, 628 (1989). Also Altman v. Comm'r, 475 F.2d 876 (2d Cir. 1973); Peters v. Comm'r, 51 T.C. 226 (1968); Zips v. Comm'r, 38 T.C. 620 (1962), *app. dis.* (5th Cir. 1963).

[57] E.g., Asphalt Indus., Inc. v. Comm'r, 384 F.2d 229 (3d Cir. 1967).

[58] E.g., Sherin v. Comm'r, 13 T.C. 221 (1949).

[59] Gen. Couns. Mem. 39813 (see text accompanied by *supra* note 54).

[60] *Id.*

[61] *Id.* An alternative approach that would bypass the IRC § 102 issue rests on the principle that funds or assets received by persons acting under the control and for the benefit of others are not includable in the gross income of the initial recipients under the "conduit" doctrine. See § 3.4.

[62] E.g., Veterans Found. v. Comm'r, 38 T.C. 66 (1962), *aff'd*, 317 F.2d 456 (10th Cir. 1963).

[63] IRC § 118.

[64] The characteristics of nonshareholder contributions to capital are analyzed in United States v. Chicago, Burlington & Quincy R.R., 412 U.S. 401 (1973). Another consequence of this classification is that a gift accords the donee the donor's basis in the property (carryover basis) (IRC § 1015), while a contribution to capital results in zero basis to the recipient (IRC § 362(c)). Also, generally, the basis of an asset acquired or held in periods during which the organization was exempt from income tax would be the original cost or other basis of the asset, reduced by depreciation (IRC § 1016(a)(3)(B); Reg. § 1.1016-4; Polish Am. Club, Inc. v. Comm'r, 33 T.C.M. 925, 931–932 (1974)). As to capital contributions in the context of the social club rules, see § 14.2, note 65.

income from the related activity.[65] Charitable expenditures that are attributable to income from other sources (such as business or investment income) would be subject to other income tax restrictions.[66] If the expenditures represent reasonable compensation for services, the expenditures would be deductible; however, amounts in excess of reasonable compensation for services, or otherwise found not to have been intended as compensation for services, would not be deductible.[67] Amounts for expenditures by public charities that are specifically disallowed by federal tax law (such as political campaign expenses[68] or substantial lobbying expenses[69]) would not be deductible. Most expenditures for illegal activities could not be offset against contribution income.

In addition to income tax consequences, there may be excise tax consequences when the tax-exempt status of a public charity is retroactively revoked. For example, where the exempt status is revoked due to excessive lobbying, an excise tax is applicable to the organization,[70] as is the case when the revocation occurs because the organization participated in political campaign activities.[71]

(b) Tax Treatments: Individuals

If a purported organization is no more than a sham or "alter ego" of an individual, on the retroactive revocation of the tax exemption of the "organization," there would not be any tax at the organizational level.[72] Should this occur, all income (including charitable contributions) and expenditures would be attributed to the individual.[73] This result would also occur should the "organization" be considered merely a conduit in relation to an individual.[74]

Where an organization is a separate entity, and a principal of the organization obtains dominion and control over its funds (other than as a borrower or agent), the individual is taxable on the payment (unless it is a return of capital). Likewise, payments made by the organization to others, where made for the benefit of an individual, would constitute constructive payments includible in the individual's income. For these rules to apply, however, the payment must confer benefit (usually financial in nature) to the individual rather than to the corporation[75]; these rules do not apply simply because an individual has control over an

---

[65] Gen. Couns. Mem. 39813.
[66] IRC § 162 (business expense deduction) and/or § 170 (charitable contribution deduction).
[67] E.g., Kenner v. Comm'r, 33 T.C.M. 1239 (1974); Synanon Church v. Comm'r, *supra* note 56, at 633–635.
[68] See Chapter 21.
[69] See Chapter 20.
[70] IRC § 4912. See § 20.6.
[71] IRC § 4955. See § 21.2. In general, Summers, "Retroactive Loss of Exemption—The Effect on Organizations," 2 J. Tax. Exempt Org. 18 (Summer 1990).
[72] As discussed, however, this type of characterization of an organization is unlikely (see text accompanied by *supra* note 42).
[73] E.g., Universal Church of Jesus Christ, Inc. v. Comm'r, 55 T.C.M. 144 (1988); Sly v. Comm'r 56 T.C.M. 209 (1988).
[74] See text accompanied by *supra* note 61.
[75] E.g., Knott v. Comm'r, 67 T.C. 681 (1977); Rev. Rul. 79-9, 1979-1 C.B. 125.

organization's income and expenditures in his or her capacity as a director, officer, or employee. Thus, a "principal of a revoked exempt organization would not realize income merely by virtue of having authorized, or acquiesced in, a diversion of funds to nonexempt purposes, in the absence of a financial or economic benefit."[76]

Usually, this type of a payment (direct or constructive) to an individual is regarded as ordinary income in the nature of compensation for services provided. It is possible, however, for the payment to be taxed as capital gain (where made in return for property furnished to the organization) or as a dividend.[77] Nonetheless, there is authority for the conclusion that, when controlling persons divert corporate funds to their personal use, the persons are taxable in full on the amount involved without regard to the technicalities of dividend treatment.[78]

Principals of an organization that had its tax exemption revoked may be liable for the organization's taxes and/or penalties, to the extent that they obtained assets of the organization and are liable as transferees.[79] Also, courts have occasionally disregarded the corporate form to collect a corporate liability from a controlling individual, under an "alter ego" theory, even though the corporate entity was considered viable for purposes of imposing a corporate level tax.[80]

Aside from income tax consequences, an individual who is a manager of a public charity that has its tax-exempt status retroactively revoked can be liable for an excise tax where the organization lost its exemption because of substantial lobbying[81] or political campaign activities.[82]

24.3   ANNUAL REPORTING REQUIREMENTS

Nearly every organization that is exempt from federal income taxation must file an annual information return.[83] This return generally is:

---

[76] Gen. Couns. Mem. 39813.

[77] As to dividend treatment, see, e.g., Sly v. Comm'r, *supra* note 73; Kenner v. Comm'r, *supra* note 67; Grant v. Comm'r, 18 T.C.M. 601 (1959). Also Stevens Bros. Found v. Comm'r, *supra* note 8.

[78] Truesdell v. Comm'r, 89 T.C. 1280 (1987). Cf. Benes v. Comm'r, 42 T.C. 358 (1964), *aff'd*, 355 F.2d 929 (6th Cir. 1966), *cert. den.*, 384 U.S. 961 (1966); Weir v. Comm'r, 283 F.2d 675 (6th Cir. 1960); Davis v. United States, 226 F.2d 331 (6th Cir. 1955). Also DiZenzo v. Comm'r, 348 F.2d 122 (2d Cir. 1965); Leaf v. Comm'r, 33 T.C. 1093 (1960), *aff'd*, 295 F.2d 503 (6th Cir. 1961); Simon v. Comm'r, 248 F.2d 869 (8th Cir. 1957).

[79] IRC § 6901. E.g., Wade v. Comm'r, 16 T.C.M. 308 (1957).

[80] E.g., Wolfe v. United States, 798 F.2d 1241, *amended*, 806 F.2d 1410 (9th Cir. 1986), *cert. den.*, 482 U.S. 927 (1987); Harris v. United States, 764 F.2d 1126 (5th Cir. 1985).

[81] IRC § 4912. See § 20.6.

[82] IRC § 4955. See § 21.2. An IRS analysis of this aspect of the law stated that the Internal Revenue Code "does not provide clear-cut answers to many of these questions," in that the "statutory scheme is oriented toward normal, profit-making corporations" (Gen. Couns. Mem. 39813). This analysis concluded: "If the treatment of revoked [exempt] organizations continues to pose a problem, a legislative solution may be appropriate" (*id.*).

[83] IRC § 6033(a)(1); Reg. § 1.603-2(a)(1). This filing requirement applies to organizations that are tax-exempt by reason of IRC §§ 501(a) and 527. Thus, it is not applicable to those entities that are exempt pursuant to IRC §§ 521 (see § 18.11), 526 (§ 18.9), 528 (§ 18.3), or 529 (§ 18.16).

- Most tax-exempt organizations—Form 990[84]

- Small tax-exempt organizations[85]—Form 990-EZ

- Private foundations[86]—Form 990-PF

- Black lung benefit trusts[87]—Form 990-BL

Political organizations[88] also file tax returns on Form 1120-POL and homeowners' associations[89] file tax returns on Form 1120-H.

The annual information return must state the organization's items of gross income, disbursements, and other information, and it must keep appropriate records, render statements under oath, make other returns, and comply with other requirements, as the tax regulations, return instructions, and the return itself prescribes.[90] Generally, an organization must file an annual information return irrespective of whether it is chartered by, or affiliated or associated with, any central, parent, or other organization.[91]

(a) Contents of Annual Information Return

The annual information return filed with the IRS by most tax-exempt organizations—Form 990—is not merely akin to a tax return that principally requires the submission of financial information. There is also a substantial amount of other factual information that is required to be provided. This annual return is often the document that is principally used by government officials, prospective contributors, representatives of the media, and others to evaluate an exempt organization.[92]

(i) Form 990. The annual information return filed by most tax-exempt organizations must include the following items: a summary of the types of gross revenue received for the year involved;[93] its expenses for the year;[94] its net assets as of the close of the year;[95] a statement of program service accomplishments;[96] a

---

[84] Form 990 is also generally filed by nonexempt charitable trusts (IRC § 4947(a)(1)). The filing requirements for charitable trusts (IRC § 4947) are the subject of Rev. Proc. 73-29, 1973-2 C.B. 474.

[85] See *infra* § (iii).

[86] See Chapter 11.

[87] See § 16.5.

[88] See Chapter 17.

[89] See § 18.3.

[90] IRC § 6033(a)(1); Reg. § 1.6033-2. The contents of the return for charitable organizations (entities described in IRC § 501(c)(3) and tax-exempt by reason of IRC § 501(a)) are stated in IRC § 6033(b); Reg. § 1.6033-2(a)(2).

[91] Reg. § 1.6033-2(a)(1).

[92] In general, Dylewsky, "Form 990 Offers Opportunity for Exempts to Position Themselves Favorably," 6 *J. Tax. Exempt Orgs.* 120 (Nov./Dec. 1994).

[93] Form 990, Part I, lines 1–12.

[94] *Id.*, Part I, lines 13–17.

[95] *Id.*, Part I, lines 18–21; Part IV.

[96] *Id.*, Part III.

list of trustees, directors, officers, and key employees;[97] an analysis of income-producing activities;[98] and information concerning taxable subsidiaries.[99] Expenses must be reported on a functional basis.[100] Information is required with respect to cost allocations where there are joint costs for educational and fundraising purposes.[101] An organization must report aggregate compensation of directors and the like from the reporting organization and related organizations, where the aggregate compensation was more than $100,000, of which more than $10,000 was provided by a related organization.[102]

A tax-exempt organization is required to inventory its sources of revenue (such as program service revenues identified by discrete activities, membership dues, investment income, special fundraising events, and sales of inventory).[103] These items of revenue must be characterized as either unrelated business income or related (exempt function) income.[104] Each type of related income must be accompanied by an explanation as to how the income-producing activities relate to the accomplishment of exempt purposes.[105] Some revenue received by exempt organizations is excluded from unrelated business income taxation.[106] If an exempt organization has income of this nature, it must report the amount and identify an *exclusion code* corresponding with the section of the Internal Revenue Code that provides the exclusion.[107]

In determining whether an activity of a tax-exempt organization is a *business*, the IRS and the courts look to the presence or absence of a *profit motive* prompting the conduct of the activity.[108] An activity that is not conducted with this motive is not regarded as a *business*. (This means that any net loss from an activity of this nature cannot be offset against net gain from a business undertaking.[109]) To induce exempt organizations to disclose any activities that do not qualify as businesses for this purpose, the IRS utilizes a special business code.[110]

A tax-exempt organization is required to report certain other facts, including its Web site address, a statement as to any new activities, any changes made in governing documents, a liquidation or substantial contraction, relationship with another organization, political expenditures, receipt of nondeductible gifts, compliance with the requirement to disclose its application for recognition of ex-

---

[97] *Id.*, Part V.
[98] *Id.*, Part VII.
[99] *Id.*, Part IX.
[100] *Id.*, Part II.
[101] *Id.*, Part II, last question.
[102] *Id.*, Part V, question 75.
[103] *Id.*, Part VII.
[104] *Id.*, Part VII, columns (B), (E).
[105] *Id.*, Part VIII.
[106] See Chapter 27.
[107] Form 990, Part VII, columns (C), (D).
[108] See § 26.2(a).
[109] As reflected on Form 990-T, net income and net losses from unrelated businesses conducted in a year can be netted in determining any unrelated business taxable income. See § 28.1.
[110] Form 990 instructions, exclusion code 41.

emption and recent annual information returns, deductibility of membership dues (in the case of social welfare, labor, agricultural, and horticultural organizations, and business leagues), revenue items unique to social clubs, payment of taxes for excessive lobbying or political campaign activities (in the case of public charities), involvement in any excess benefit transactions (in the case of a public charity or social welfare organization). Ownership of an interest in a taxable corporation or partnership, and information about any excess benefit transaction (in the case of public charities and social welfare organizations).[111]

The accounting system used by a tax-exempt organization to maintain its books and records may be different from that reflected on the annual information return, particularly because of changes in generally accepted accounting principles.[112] A portion of the annual information return is used to reconcile these two approaches.[113]

(ii) Form 990, Schedule A. In addition to filing the annual information return, a charitable organization[114] must file an accompanying schedule requiring other information.[115]

This schedule is the means by which charitable organizations report on the compensation of the five highest paid employees,[116] the compensation of the five highest paid independent contractors for professional services,[117] certain activities,[118] eligibility for nonprivate foundation status,[119] compliance by private schools with the antidiscrimination rules,[120] and information regarding transfers, transactions, and relationships with other organizations.[121]

Charitable organizations that elected the expenditure test with respect to their lobbying activities[122] must report their lobbying expenses, including those over the four-year averaging period.[123] Organizations that have not made this election, and thus remain subject to the substantial part test,[124] are subject to other reporting requirements.[125]

---

[111] Form 990, Part VI, questions 76-77 (see *supra* § 1), 79 (§ 4.3(b)), 80 (Chapters 30–33), 81 (Chapter 17), 82, 83, (*infra* § 4), 84 (§ 22.2), 85 (§ 20.8), 86 (Chapter 14), 87 (§ 18.5), 88 (Chapters 31, 32), and 89 (§§ 20.6, 21.2, 19.11(d)).
[112] Financial Accounting Standards Boards Statements Nos. 116, 117.
[113] Form 990, Parts IV-A, IV-B.
[114] That is, an organization that is tax-exempt under IRC § 501(a) by reason of IRC § 501(c)(3).
[115] Form 990, Schedule A.
[116] Schedule A, Part I.
[117] Schedule A, Part II.
[118] Schedule A, Part III.
[119] Schedule A, Part IV. See Chapter 11.
[120] Schedule A, Part V. See § 5.4(a).
[121] Schedule A, Part VII.
[122] See § 20.5(a).
[123] Form 990, Schedule A, Part VI-A.
[124] See § 20.2(b).
[125] Form 990, Schedule A, Part VI-B.

(iii) Form 990-EZ.   To alleviate the annual reporting burden for smaller tax-exempt organizations, the IRS promulgated a less extensive annual information return. This is the two-page Form 990-EZ.

This return may be used by tax-exempt organizations that have gross receipts that are less than $100,000 and total assets that are less than $250,000 in value at the end of the reporting year.[126]

An organization can use this annual information return in any year in which it meets the two criteria, even though it was, and/or is, required to file a Form 990 in other years. The Form 990-EZ cannot be filed by private foundations. A charitable organization filing a Form 990-EZ must also file a Schedule A (Form 990) (see above).

(iv) Form 990-PF.   Private foundations[127] must file an annual information return.[128] This return is on Form 990-PF.

Private foundations must report their revenue and expenses,[129] assets and liabilities,[130] fund balances,[131] and information about trustees, directors, officers, foundation managers, other highly paid employees, and contractors.[132] Private foundations must report as to qualifying distributions,[133] calculation of the minimum investment return,[134] computation of the distributable amount,[135] undistributed income,[136] and grants programs and other activities.[137]

A private foundation must calculate the tax on its investment income[138] (unless it is an exempt operating foundation) and its qualification for the reduced tax on net investment income (assuming it is reporting that lower tax).[139] A private foundation must provide certain information regarding foundation managers,[140] loan and scholarship programs,[141] grants and contributions paid during the year or approved for future payment,[142] transfers, transactions, and relationships with other organizations,[143] and compliance with the public inspection requirements.[144]

---

[126] This is not a statutory rule; it is a threshold established by the IRS.
[127] See Chapter 11.
[128] IRC § 6033(a)-(c).
[129] Form 990-PF, Part I.
[130] Form 990-PF, Part II.
[131] Form 990-PF, Part III.
[132] Form 990-PF, Part VIII.
[133] Form 990-PF, Part XIII.
[134] Form 990-PF, Part IX.
[135] Form 990-PF, Part X.
[136] Form 990-PF, Part XIV.
[137] Form 990-PF, Part XVII.
[138] From 990-PF, Part IV, VI.
[139] Form 990-PF, Part V.
[140] Form 990-PF, Part XVI.
[141] *Id.*
[142] *Id.*
[143] Form 990-PF, Part XVIII.
[144] Form 990-PF, Part XIX.

A private foundation must report as to certain activities. These requirements are largely the same as for all reporting tax-exempt organizations.[145] The annual information return for private foundations, however, also requests information about self-dealing transactions,[146] failure to distribute income as required,[147] excess business holdings,[148] investments that jeopardize charitable purposes,[149] taxable expenditures,[150] political expenditures,[151] and substantial contributions.[152]

Additional reporting requirements are applicable to private operating foundations.[153]

The Form 990-PF must also include the following items: (1) an itemized statement of the private foundation's assets; (2) an itemized list of all grants and contributions made or approved, showing the amount of each grant or contribution, the name and address of each recipient, any relationship between any recipient and the foundation's managers or substantial contributors, and a concise statement of the purpose of each grant or contribution; (3) the address of the principal office of the foundation and (if different) of the place where its books and records are maintained; and (4) the names and addresses of the foundation's managers that are substantial contributors with respect to the foundation or that own 10 percent or more of the stock of any corporation of which the foundation owns 10 percent or more of the stock, or corresponding interests in partnerships or other entities, in which the foundation has a 10 percent or greater interest.[154]

(v) Form 990-T. Revenue and expenses associated with unrelated business activity by a tax-exempt organization are reported to the IRS on Form 990-T.[155] This is a *tax return*, rather than an *information return*.

A tax-exempt organization with unrelated business taxable income[156] must file, in addition to the Form 990 or Form 990-EZ (or, in the case of a private foundation, the Form 990-PF), a Form 990-T. It is on this form that the source (or sources) of unrelated income is reported and any tax computed.[157]

Tax-exempt organizations must report their unrelated trade or business income.[158] These reporting obligations are less where the unrelated trade or business gross income is no more than $10,000.

---

[145] See *supra* § (i).
[146] Form 990-PF, Part VII, question 10.
[147] From 990-PF, Part VII, question 11.
[148] Form 990-PF, Part VII, question 12.
[149] Form 990-PF, Part VII, question 13.
[150] Form 990-PF, Part VII, question 14.
[151] Form 990-PF, Part VII, question 14.
[152] Form 990-PF, Part VII, question 15.
[153] Form 990-PF, Part XV.
[154] IRC § 6033(c); Reg. § 1.6033-3(a).
[155] IRC § 6012(a)(2)(4); Reg. §§ 1.6012-2(e), 1.6012-3(a)(5), 1.6033-2(i).
[156] See Chapters 26, 27.
[157] Reg. § 1.6012(e).
[158] See § 28.2.

All forms of unrelated trade or business gross income must be reported, along with associated deductions.[159] Separate schedules pertain to rental income,[160] unrelated debt-financed income,[161] investment income of those organizations that must treat that type of income as unrelated business income,[162] income (other than dividends) from controlled organizations,[163] exploited exempt activity income (other than advertising income),[164] and advertising income.[165]

Under certain guidelines,[166] tax-exempt labor organizations may file copies of U.S. Department of Labor forms in lieu of Form 990, Part II, and exempt employee benefit plans may file for that purpose copies of forms otherwise filed with the IRS pursuant to the requirements of the Employee Retirement Income Security Act.

(vi) Due Dates. The annual information return (Form 990, Form 990-EZ, or Form 990-PF) and any unrelated business income tax return (Form 990-T) are due on or before the fifteenth day of the fifth month following the close of the tax year.[167] Thus, the return for a calendar year organization should be filed by May 15 of each year. One or more extensions may be obtained. These returns are filed with the IRS service center in Ogden, Utah.[168]

At the time a private foundation files its annual return, a copy of the return must be sent to the attorney general of one or more states, including the state in which the foundation was created and in which the foundation's principal office is located.[169]

The filing date for an annual information return (Form 990, Form 990-EZ, or Form 990-PF) may fall due while the organization's application for recognition of tax-exempt status is pending with the IRS. In that instance, the organization should nonetheless file the information return (rather than a tax return) and indicate on it that the application is pending.[170]

(vii) Penalties. Failure to timely file the appropriate information return, or failure to include any information required to be shown on the return

---

[159] Form 990-T, Parts I, II.

[160] Form 990-T, Schedule C. See § 27.1(h).

[161] Form 990-T, Schedule E. See §§ 29.1-29.4.

[162] Form 990-T, Schedule F. See § 28.3. These organizations are social clubs (see Chapter 14), voluntary employees beneficiary associations (see § 16.3), and supplemental unemployment benefit trusts (see § 16.4).

[163] Form 990-T, Schedule G. See §§ 27.1(n), 33.1.

[164] Form 990-T, Schedule H. See § 26.4(e).

[165] Form 990-T, Schedule I. See § 26.5(f).

[166] Rev. Proc. 79-6, 1979-1 C.B. 485.

[167] IRC § 6072(e); Reg. § 1.6033-2(e). This due date is also applicable with respect to Form 4720 (the tax return by which certain excise taxes imposed on private foundations, public charities, and others are paid).

[168] Ann. 96-63, 1996-29 I.R.B. 18.

[169] Reg. § 1.6033-3(c).

[170] Reg. § 1.6033–2(c).

(or failure to show the correct information) absent reasonable cause, can give rise to a $20 per day penalty, payable by the organization, for each day the failure continues, with a maximum penalty for any one return not to exceed the lesser of $10,000 or five percent of the gross receipts of the organization for one year.[171] An additional penalty may be imposed at the same rate and maximum of $10,000 on the individual(s) responsible for the failure to file, absent reasonable cause, where the return remains unfiled following demand for the return by the IRS.[172] There is a much larger penalty on organizations having gross receipts in excess of $1 million for a year; in this circumstance, the per-day penalty is $100 and the maximum penalty is $50,000.[173] An addition to tax for failure to timely file a federal tax return, including a Form 990-T, may also be imposed.[174]

In one instance, an organization required to file a Form 990 submitted an incomplete return by omitting material information from the form, and failed to supply the missing information after being requested to do so by the IRS and did not establish a reasonable cause for its failure to file a complete return. Under these circumstances, the filing of the incomplete return is a failure to file the return for purposes of the penalty.[175] The IRS observed that the legislative history underlying the pertinent law "shows that Congressional concern was to ensure that information requested on exempt organization returns was provided timely and completely so that the Service would be provided with the information needed to enforce the tax laws."[176] The IRS added:

> Form 990 and accompanying instructions issued by the Service request information that is necessary in order for the Service to perform the duties and responsibilities placed upon it by Congress for proper administration of the revenue laws. These duties and responsibilities include making exempt organization returns available for public inspection as well as conducting audits of exempt organizations to determine their compliance with statutory provisions. When a return is submitted that has not been satisfactorily completed, the Service's ability to perform its duties is seriously hindered, and the public's right to obtain meaningful information is impaired. Thus, when material information is omitted, a return is not completed in

---

[171] IRC § 6652(c)(1)(A), (c)(3). A private foundation is deemed to have reasonable cause for failure to comply with the requirements of IRC § 6033, as well as §§ 6011, 6056, 6104, and 6151, for filing of returns and payment of taxes until 90 days after it is issued a letter containing a determination of private foundation status from the IRS, thereby immunizing it from application of penalty provisions IRC §§ 6651 and 6652 with respect to a tax year for which, prior to the due date for filing Form 990-PF the organization has filed notice (on Form 1023) claiming not to be a private foundation (Rev. Proc. 79-8, 1979-1 C.B. 487).

[172] IRC § 6652(c)(1)(B); Reg. § 301.6652-2. Two or more organizations exempt from taxation under IRC § 501, one or more of which is described in IRC § 501(c)(2) (see § 18.2(a)) and the other(s) of which derive income from IRC § 501(c)(2) organization(s), are eligible to file a consolidated return Form 990 (and/or Form 990-T) in lieu of separate return, (IRC § 1504(e)).

[173] IRC § 6652(c)(1)(A), last sentence.

[174] IRC § 6651(a)(1).

[175] Rev. Rul. 77-162, 1977-1 C. B. 4011.

[176] Id., citing S. Rep. 552, 91st Cong., 1st Sess. 52 (1969).

the manner prescribed by the form and instructions and the organization has not met the filing requirements of section 6033(x)(1) of the Code.[177]

A related point is that, in the case of failure to file a return, the tax may be assessed, or a proceeding in court for the collection of the tax may be begun without assessment, at any time.[178] In the above-discussed situation, the organization was considered[179] to have failed to file any return at all and, therefore, the period of limitations on assessment and collection of the tax[180] was ruled to have not started.[181]

(viii) Assessments. The IRS generally must assess any tax within three years of the due date of the return or the date on which the return involved is actually filed, whichever is later.[182] A six-year statute of limitations applies, however, if an excise tax return "omits an amount of such tax properly includible thereon which exceeds 25 percent of the amount of such tax reported thereon"; this extended period does not apply, in the case of the private foundation and certain other taxes, where there is adequate disclosure in the return to the IRS.[183] In one case, a private foundation timely filed its annual information return, reflecting certain salary payments to an officer; believing the payments to be reasonable, the foundation did not file a return showing any excise taxes due. A court held that, under these facts, only the annual information return was due, that adequate disclosure was made on that return, and that the six-year statute of limitations was inapplicable (thereby precluding the IRS from assessing the tax because the deficiency notice was mailed more than three years after the organization's returns were filed).[184]

It is the practice of the IRS to omit from its listing of organizations to which deductible gifts may be made[185] those organizations that fail to establish their nonfiling status with the IRS. This practice was upheld by the Chief Counsel of the IRS.[186] The continuing validity of this procedure was temporarily cast in doubt because of a court opinion,[187] although the lawyers at the IRS

---

[177] Rev. Rul. 77-162, *supra* note 175 at 401.

[178] IRC § 6501(c)(3).

[179] IRC § 6652(c)(1)(A).

[180] IRC § 6501(c)(3).

[181] In general, reliance on the advice of a competent tax advisor can constitute reasonable cause for a failure to file a return, for purposes of the IRC § 6651(a)(1) addition to tax, and the IRC § 6652(c)(1)(A) or § 6652(c)(1)(B) penalty (e.g., Waco Lodge No. 166, Benevolent & Protective Order of Elks v. Comm'r, 42 T.C.M. 1202 (1981), *aff'd in part and rev'd in part*, 696 F.2d 372 (5th Cir. 1983); Coldwater Seafood Corp. v. Comm'r, 69 T.C. 966 (1978); West Coast Ice Co. v. Comm'r, 49 T.C. 345 (1968)).

[182] IRC § 6501(a).

[183] IRC § 6501(e)(3).

[184] Cline v. Comm'r, 55 T.C.M. 540 (1988).

[185] Publication No. 78, "Cumulative List of Organizations Described in Section 170(c) of the Internal Revenue Code."

[186] Gen. Couns. Mem. 39389.

[187] Estate of Clopton v. Comm'r, *supra* note 11.

ultimately concluded that the opinion did not raise any concerns with respect to the practice.[188]

(ix) Miscellaneous. The filing of an annual information return is also the opportunity for the changing of annual accounting periods by most tax-exempt organizations. An exempt organization desiring to change its annual accounting period may effect the change by timely filing its annual information return with the IRS for the short period for which the return is required, indicating in the return that a change of accounting period is being made. If an organization is not required to file an annual information return or a tax return reflecting unrelated income, it is not necessary to otherwise notify the IRS that a change of accounting period is being made. If, however, an organization has previously changed its annual accounting period at any time within the 10 calendar years ending with the calendar year that includes the beginning of the short period resulting from the change of an annual accounting period, and if the organization had a filing requirement at any time during the 10-year period, it must file an application for a change in accounting period (Form 3115) with the IRS.[189]

Special rules apply with respect to the filing of annual information returns by organizations under a group exemption.[190]

(b) Exceptions to Reporting Requirements

This requirement of filing an annual information return does not apply to several categories of tax-exempt organizations.

Some of these exceptions are mandatory,[191] while others are at the discretion of the IRS.[192]

(i) Churches and Certain Other Religious Organizations. Churches (including an interchurch organization of local units of a church), their integrated

---

[188] Gen. Couns. Mem. 39809.

[189] Rev. Proc. 85-58, 1985-2 C.B. 740, *supp. by* Rev. Proc. 76-9, 1985-1 C.B. 547, as *mod. by* Rev. Proc. 79-2, 1979-1 C.B. 482. This simplified procedure is inapplicable to farmers' cooperatives (see § 18.11), shipowners' protective associations (see § 18.12), political organizations (see Chapter 17), or homeowners' associations (see § 18.13). These entities change their annual accounting period by filing the form with the IRS National Office.

The IRS provided relief from the filing of an application for change in accounting method for tax-exempt organizations changing their method so as to comply with the Statement of Financial Accounting Standards No. 116 issued by the Financial Accounting Standards Board (Notice 96-30, 1996-1 C.B. 378).

[190] Reg. 1.6033-2(d). The group exemption rules are the subject of § 23.6.

The IRS has taken the position that it will not accept annual information returns filed by tax-exempt organizations that have not filed an application for recognition of tax exemption, including in situations where the filing of the application is not required (see § 23.1) (INFO-2000-0260). The IRS is instructing organizations either to file the application or to begin filing income tax returns.

[191] IRC § 6033(a)(2)(A).

[192] IRC § 6033(a)(2)(B).

auxiliaries, and conventions or associations of churches do not have to file annual information returns.[193]

The definitions given the terms *church, integrated auxiliary of a church,* and *convention or association of churches* are discussed elsewhere.[194]

Also, the reporting requirements do not apply to the exclusively religious activities of any *religious order.*[195]

(ii) Small Organizations. The requirement of filing an annual information return is inapplicable to certain organizations (other than private foundations) the gross receipts[196] of which in each year are normally not more than $5,000.[197]

Other organizations may be relieved from filing annual information returns where a filing of these returns by them is not necessary to the efficient administration of the internal revenue laws, as determined by the IRS.[198] This category of organizations[199] embraces:

1. Religious organizations;[200]

2. Educational organizations;[201]

3. Charitable organizations or organizations for the prevention of cruelty to children or animals,[202] if the organizations are supported by funds contributed by the federal or a state government or are primarily supported by contributions from the general public;

4. Organizations operated, supervised, or controlled by or in connection with a religious organization;

5. Certain fraternal beneficiary organizations;[203] and

---

[193] IRC § 6033(a)(2)(A)(i); Reg. § 1.6033-2(g)(1)(i). Religious orders (see § 8.6) do not file Form 990; instead, because they are treated as partnerships for tax purposes, they file the partnership return (Form 1065).

[194] See §§ 8.3-8.5.

[195] IRC § 6033(a)(2)(A)(iii); Reg. § 1.6033-2(g)(1)(iii). See § 8.6.

[196] The term *gross receipts* means total receipts without any reduction for costs or expenses, including costs of goods sold (Form 990, part 1, line 8). For this purpose, insurance premiums collected by the local lodge of a tax-exempt fraternal beneficiary society from its members, maintained separately without use or benefit, and remitted to its parent organization that issued the insurance contracts, were ruled by the IRS to not be gross receipts of the local lodge (Rev. Rul. 73-364, 1973-2 C.B. 393).

[197] IRC § 6033(a)(2)(A)(ii). The rules for calculating this $5,000 limitation appear in Reg. § 1.6033-2(g)(3). This threshold amount is, in actuality, $25,000 (see *infra* note 205).

[198] IRC § 6033(a)(2)(B); Reg. § 1.6033-2(g)(6).

[199] IRC § 6033(a)(2)(C).

[200] See Chapter 8.

[201] IRC § 170(b)(1)(A)(ii). See Chapter 7, § 11.3(a).

[202] IRC § 501(c)(3). See § 10.1.

[203] IRC § 501(c)(8). See § 18.4(a).

6. A corporation organized under an act of Congress if it is wholly owned by the United States or any agency or instrumentality of the United States or a wholly owned subsidiary of the United States.[204]

In the exercise of this discretionary authority, the IRS announced that organizations, other than private foundations, with gross receipts not normally in excess of $25,000, do not have to file annual information returns.[205]

(iii) Other Exempted Organizations. As noted, other organizations may be relieved from filing annual information returns where a filing of these returns by them is not necessary to the efficient administration of the internal revenue laws, as determined by the IRS.[206] This discretion in the IRS also has been exercised to except from the filing requirement:

1. An educational organization (below college level) that is qualified as a school, has a program of a general academic nature, and is affiliated with a church or operated by a religious order;[207]

2. Mission societies sponsored by or affiliated with one or more churches or church denominations, more than one-half of the activities of which are conducted in, or directed at persons in, foreign countries;[208]

3. State institutions, the income of which is excluded from gross income on the ground that the income is accruing to the state;[209]

4. A foreign organization (other than a private foundation) which normally does not receive more than $25,000 in gross receipts annually from sources within the United States[210] and which does not have any significant activity (including lobbying or political activity) in the United States;[211]

5. A governmental unit;[212] and

6. An affiliate of a governmental unit.[213]

---

[204] IRC § 501(c)(1). Also Reg. § 1.6033-2(g)(1)(vi). See § 18.1. The IRS ruled that the National Credit Union Administration and the tax-exempt federal credit unions under its supervision are organizations described in IRC § 501(c)(1) and thus are not required to file annual information returns (Rev. Rul. 89-94, 1989-2 C.B. 233).

[205] Ann. 82-88, 1982-25 I.R.B. 23. For purposes of the $25,000 rule, a tax-exempt organization is exempt from filing an annual information return where (1) during its first year, it received (including pledges) gross receipts of $37,500 or less; (2) during a period of more than one year of its existence and less than three years, it received, as an average of gross receipts experienced in the first two tax years, gross receipts of $30,000 or less; and (3) during its existence of more than three years, it received, as an average of gross receipts, $25,000 or less (*id.*).

[206] IRC § 6033(a)(2)(B).

[207] Reg. 1.6033-2(g)(1)(vii). See § 7.3. Also Rev. Rul. 78-316, 1978-2 C.B. 304. For this purpose, the rules as to *affiliation* are the same as those discussed in § 8.5.

[208] IRC § 115; Reg. § 1.6033-2(g)(1)(iv).

[209] Reg. § 1.6033-2(g)(l)(v).

[210] IRC § 861-865; Reg. § 53.4948-1(b).

[211] Rev. Proc. 94-17, 1994-1 C.B. 579.

[212] Rev. Proc. 95-48, 1995-2 C.B. 418, *supp'g* Rev. Proc. 83-23, 1983-1 C.B. 687.

[213] *Id.*

For purposes of the fifth of these items, an entity is a *governmental unit* if it is (1) a state or local governmental unit as defined in the rules providing an exclusion from gross income for interest earned on bonds issued by these units,[214] (2) it is entitled to receive deductible charitable contributions as a unit of government,[215] or (3) it is an Indian tribal government or a political subdivision of this type of government.[216]

For purposes of the sixth of these items, an entity is an *affiliate of a governmental unit* if it is a tax-exempt organization[217] and meets one of two sets of requirements. One is that it has a ruling or determination letter from the IRS that (1) its income, derived from activities constituting the basis for its exemption, is excluded from gross income under the rules for political subdivisions and the like,[218] (2) it is entitled to receive deductible charitable contributions[219] on the basis that contributions to it are for the use of governmental units, or (3) it is a wholly owned instrumentality of a state or political subdivision of a state for employment tax purposes.[220] The other is available for an entity that does not have a ruling or determination letter from the IRS but (1) it is either operated, supervised, or controlled by governmental units, or by organizations that are affiliates of governmental units, or the members of the organization's governing body are elected by the public at large, pursuant to local statute or ordinance, (2) it possesses two or more of certain affiliation factors,[221] and (3) its filing of an annual information return is not otherwise necessary to the efficient administration of the internal revenue laws.[222] An organization can (but is not required to) request a ruling or determination letter from the IRS that it is an affiliate of a governmental unit.[223]

(c) Limited Liability Companies

A tax-exempt organization can be the sole member of a limited liability company (LLC) or two or more exempt organizations can be members of an LLC.[224] In the case of the single-member LLC, the LLC is a disregarded entity for federal tax purposes and thus its activities are treated as the activities of the member.[225] In

---

[214] IRC § 103; Reg. 1.103-1(b). See § 6.9.

[215] IRC § 170(c)(1). See § 18.18.

[216] IRC §§ 7701(a)(40), 7871. This tripartite definition of *governmental unit* is in Rev. Proc. 95-48, *supra* note 212, § 4.01.

[217] That is, as described in IRC § 501(c).

[218] IRC § 115. See § 18.17.

[219] IRC § 170(c)(1).

[220] IRC §§ 3121(b)(7), 3306(c)(7). This definition is provided by Rev. Proc. 95-48, *supra* note 212, § 4.02(a).

[221] Rev. Proc. 95-48, *supra* note 212 § 4.03.

[222] *Id.* § 4.02(b). Relevant facts and circumstances as to whether an annual return is necessary include those provided at *id.* § 4.04.

[223] *Id.* § 5. The IRS is considering making changes to the Form 990 (Ann. 2002-87, 2002-39 I.R.B. 624).

[224] In general, see § 4.1(b).

[225] In general, see § 30.7.

this instance, then, the single-member LLC is not required to file annual information returns; rather, the activities of the LLC are reported as activities of the exempt member.[226] Where, however, there is a multi-member LLC, the members of which are exempt organizations, the LLC may be able to qualify as an exempt organization[227] and if so would be subject to the annual reporting requirements.

(d) Political Organizations Reporting Requirements

(i) General Rules. A political organization,[228] other than those involved only in state or local electoral activities and subject to comparable state disclosure laws, which accepts a contribution or makes an expenditure for an exempt (political) function during a year must file quarterly reports with the IRS in the case of a year in which a federal election is held. Also, preelection and postelection reports may be required. Otherwise, generally, the reports are due semiannually. A political organization has the option of filing these reports monthly. Whatever the choice, the organization must file on the same schedule basis for the entire calendar year.[229]

This report must contain the following: the amount and date of each expenditure made to a person if the aggregate amount of expenditures to the person during the year is at least $200; the purpose of the contribution if it is at least $500; the name and address of the person (in the case of an individual, including the individual's occupation and employer); the name and address (including occupation and employer in the case of an individual) of all contributions which contributed an aggregate amount of at least $200 to the organization during the year; and the amount of such contribution.[230]

This set of rules does not apply to a person required to report under the Federal Election Campaign Act as a political committee; a state or local committee of a political party or political committee of a state or local candidate; an organization which reasonably anticipates that it will not have gross receipts of $25,000 or more for any year; another type of tax-exempt organization that is subject to the political campaign activities tax; or independent expenditures (as that term is defined in the Federal Election Campaign Act).[231]

There are penalties for failure to comply with this requirement (by filing late, insufficiently, or incorrectly). The penalty is 35 percent of the total amount of

---

[226] E.g., Priv. Ltr. Rul. 200134025.

[227] See § 4.3(e).

[228] See Chapter 17.

[229] IRC § 527(j)(2). This return is Form 8872. These rules are summarized in Rev. Rul. 2000-44, 2000-43 I.R.B. 409. These rules were first enacted in 2000 (P.L. 106-230, 106th Cong., 2d Sess. (2000); see § 23.6, note 168). The exception for state and local political organizations and certain other changes in this aspect of the law were enacted in 2002 (P.L. 107-276, 107th Cong., 2d Sess. (2002)) and made retroactive to 2000. This law change followed a decision by a federal district court, striking down as unconstitutional the requirements of the law that political organizations disclose their expenditures and that they disclose contributions associated with state and local elections (National Fed'n of Republican Assemblies v. United States, 2002-2 U.S.T.C. ¶ 50,620 (S.D. Ala. 2002)). In general, Tobin, "Campaign Finance Disclosure and Section 527 of the Code: A Look at the District Court's Opinion in *National Federation of Republican Assemblies*," 38 *Exempt Org. Tax Rev.* (No. 1) 43 (Oct. 2002).

[230] IRC § 527(j)(3).

[231] IRC § 527(j)(5).

contributions and expenditures not properly reported.[232] Political organizations are also required to file income tax returns.[233]

(ii) Filing Dates.   Political organizations that choose to file monthly generally must file their reports by the 20th day after the end of the month; the reports must be complete as of the last day of the month. The year-end report, however, is due by January 31 of the following year.

If, however, the year is one in which a regularly scheduled election is to be held, the organization filing monthly does not file the reports regularly due on November and December (that is, the monthly reports for October and November). Instead, the organization must file a report 12 days before the general election (or 15 days before the general election if posted by registered or certified mail) that contains information through the 20th day before the general election. The organization must also file a report no more than 30 days after the general election which contains information through the 20th day after the election. Rather than a December monthly report, the year-end report is due by January 31 of the following year.

As noted above, political organizations that choose to not file on a monthly basis must file semiannual reports in nonelection years. These reports are due on July 31 for the first half of the year and, for the second half of the year, on January 31 of the following year.

In an election year, these political organizations must file quarterly reports which are due on the 15th day after the last day of the quarter, except that the return for the final quarter is due on January 31 of the following year. These organizations must also file preelection reports with respect to any election for which they receive a contribution or make an expenditure. These reports are due 12 days before the election (15 days if posted by registered or certified mail) and must contain information through the 20th day before the election. These organizations must also file a post-general election report, due 30 days after the general election and containing information through the 20th day after the election.

§ 24.4   DOCUMENT AVAILABILITY REQUIREMENTS

As this chapter and the previous one indicate, the following general categories of documents containing information about tax-exempt organizations must be filed with the IRS: the application for recognition of tax exemption and supporting documents (such as governing instruments, exhibits, and legal memoranda), any statements as to changes in material facts, and annual information returns. Another document on file at the IRS is, of course, a copy of the ruling as to exempt (and, where applicable, private foundation) status.

(a) Availability Through IRS

The application for recognition of tax exemption and any supporting documents filed by most exempt organizations[234] must be made accessible to the

---

[232] IRC § 527(j)(1).
[233] IRC § 6012(a)(6). These returns are Form 1120-POL.
[234] Those described in IRC § 501(c) or § 501(d).

public by the IRS where a favorable determination letter is issued to the organization.[235] Where there is no prescribed application form, the documents filed with the IRS that led to the issuance of an exemption ruling become publicly available under these rules. These rules are triggered by a finding that an organization is exempt for any year, even though the organization may subsequently lose its exemption.

Information contained in the application or supporting documents may relate to a trade secret, patent, process, style of work, or apparatus. An organization, the application for recognition of exemption of which is open to public inspection, may request in writing that the information be withheld. The information will be withheld from public inspection if the IRS determines that disclosure of it would adversely affect the organization.[236]

Once an organization's application for recognition of exemption, and related and supporting documents, become open to public inspection, the determination letter (ruling) issued by the IRS also becomes publicly available. Also open to inspection under these rules are any technical advice memoranda issued with respect to any favorable ruling. A favorable ruling recognizing an organization's tax-exempt status may be issued by the National Office; these rulings and the underlying applications for recognition of tax exemption are available for inspection in the IRS Freedom of Information Reading Room in Washington, D.C.[237]

Certain determinations issued by the IRS in the tax-exempt organizations context, however, are not open to public inspection. These include (1) unfavorable rulings issued in response to applications for recognition of exemption, (2) rulings revoking or modifying a favorable ruling, (3) technical advice memoranda relating to a disapproved application for recognition of exemption, and (4) any letter filed with or issued by the IRS relating to an organization's status as a nonprivate foundation or as a private operating foundation.[238]

An application and related materials may be inspected at the appropriate IRS service center. Inspection may also occur at the National Office of the IRS; a request for inspection should be directed to the Assistant to the Commissioner (Public Affairs), 1111 Constitution Avenue, N.W., Washington, D.C. 20224.[239]

The excise tax return filed by private foundations (Form 4720) is disclosable to the public.[240] This return as filed by a person other than a foundation (as well as one filed in the intermediate sanctions context) is not disclosable. Therefore, if disclosure of the return filed by a person other than a private foundation is not

---

[235] IRC § 6104(a)(1)(A). This disclosure requirement is confined to papers submitted in support of the application by the organization (Reg. § 301.6104(a)-1(e)). It does not apply to papers submitted by any other person, such as a member of Congress (Lehrfeld v. Richardson, 132 F.3d 1463 (D.C. Cir. 1998)).
[236] Reg. § 301.6104(a)-5.
[237] Notice 92-28, 1992-1 C. B. 515.
[238] Reg. § 301.6104(a)-1(i). Also Tax Analysts v. Internal Revenue Service, 2002-2 U.S.T.C. ¶ 50,665 (D.D.C. 2002)); Christian Coalition International v. United States, 90 A.F.T.R. 2d 6010 (E.D. Va. 2002).
[239] Reg. § 301.6104(a)-6.
[240] Reg. § 1.6033-2(a)(2)(ii)(j).

desired, the person should file separately rather than jointly with the foundation, inasmuch as the joint filing is disclosable.[241]

These document availability rules are applicable to the notice that must be filed by political organizations to establish their tax-exempt status[242] and to the reports that they must file.[243]

The IRS is required to make publicly available, at its offices and on the Internet, a list of all political organizations that file this notice, and the name, address, electronic mailing address, custodian of records and contact person for these organizations.[244] This information must be made available not later than five business days after the notice is received.

(b) Disclosure by Exempt Organizations

A tax-exempt organization is required to disclose, and generally is required to disseminate, its most recent three annual information returns and application for recognition of exemption, although there are exceptions from the document dissemination rules.[245] The effective date of these dissemination requirements is June 8, 1999.[246]

(i) General Rules. Under the law in effect before 1999, the general rules were that a tax-exempt organization[247] must make its application for recognition of exemption[248] available for public inspection without charge at its principal, regional, and district offices during regular business hours.[249] In addition, it must make its annual information returns available for public inspection without charge in the same offices during regular business hours.[250] Each return must be made available for a period of three years, beginning on the date the return is required to be filed or is actually filed, whichever is later.[251]

---

[241] T.D. 7785, 1981-2 C.B. 233.

[242] See § 23.6.

[243] See § 4(c).

[244] IRC § 6104(a)(3).

[245] IRC § 6104(d).

[246] Reg. § 301.6104(d)-3(h). Generally, the names and addresses of donors need not be disclosed (IRC § 6104(d)(3)(A)) (but see infra note 254) and certain information can be withheld from public inspection, such as trade secrets and patents (IRC § 6104(d)(3)(B), (a)(1)(D)).

[247] That is, an organization described in IRC § 501(c) or (d).

[248] See § 23.2. This requirement embraces papers submitted in support of the application and any documents issued by the IRS with respect to the application (IRC § 6104(d)(5)).

[249] IRC § 6104(d)(1)(A). This requirement is inapplicable with respect to an application filed before July 15, 1987, unless the organization that filed it had a copy of it on that date (Reg. § 301.6104(d)-3(b)(3)(iii)(B)).

[250] IRC § 6104(d)(1)(A).

[251] IRC § 6104(d)(2). IRS rules (Notice 88-120, 1988-2 C.B. 454) reinforce the point that exact copies of these documents are required. This means that, for charitable (IRC § 501(c)(3)) organizations, the compensation of key employees must be disclosed.

Organizations that are covered by a group exemption (see § 23.6) and do not file their own annual information returns, and that receive a request for inspection, must acquire a copy of the group return from the central organization and make the material available to the requestor within a reasonable amount of time (Notice 88-120, *supra*). Alternatively, the requestor can request, from the central organization, inspection of the group return at the principal office of the parent organization (*id.*). Similar rules apply with respect to the document dissemination requirements (Reg. § 6104(d)-3(f)).

In addition, as of the 1999 effective date, the general rule is that a tax-exempt organization must provide a copy without charge, other than a reasonable fee for reproduction and actual postage costs, of all or any part of any application for recognition of exemption or return required to be made available for public inspection to any individual who makes a request for the copy in person or in writing.[252]

Subsequently, these rules were made applicable to private foundations. Separate regulations to this end became final in early 2000,[253] making foundations subject to these disclosure requirements as of March 13, 2000.[254]

(ii) Rules as to Inspection. A tax-exempt organization must make its application for recognition of exemption available for public inspection without charge at its principal, regional, and district offices during regular business hours.[255] Likewise, an exempt organization must make its annual information returns available for public inspection without charge in the same offices during regular business hours.[256] Each annual information return must be made available for a period of three years.

(iii) Rules as to Copies. Generally, a tax-exempt organization must provide copies of the documents, in response to an in-person request, at its principal, regional, and district offices during regular business hours. Also generally, the organization must provide the copies to a requestor on the day the request is made.[257]

In the case of an in-person request, when unusual circumstances exist so that fulfillment of the request on the same business day places an unreasonable burden on the exempt organization, the copies must be provided on the next business day following the day on which the unusual circumstances cease to exist or the fifth business day after the date of the request, whichever occurs first. *Unusual circumstances* include receipt of a volume of requests that exceeds the organization's daily capacity to make copies, requests received shortly before the end of regular business hours that require an extensive amount of copying, and requests received on a day when the organization's managerial staff capable of fulfilling the request is conducting special duties. *Special duties* are activities such as student registration or attendance at an off-site meeting or convention, rather than regular administrative duties.[258]

If a request for a document is made in writing, the tax-exempt organization must honor it if the request:

---

[252] IRC § 6104(d)(1)(B); Reg. § 301.6104(d)-3(d).
[253] T. D. 8861.
[254] In contrast to the general rule (*supra* note 246), private foundations are required to disclose information as to their donors.
[255] Reg. § 301.6104(d)-3(a).
[256] *Id.*
[257] Reg. § 301.6104(d)-3(d)(1)(i).
[258] Reg. § 301.6104(d)-3(d)(1)(ii).

- Is addressed to, and delivered by mail, electronic mail, facsimile, or a private delivery service to a principal, regional, or district office of the organization.

- Sets forth the address to which the copy of the document should be sent.[259]

A tax-exempt organization receiving a written request for a copy must mail the copy within 30 days from the date it receives the request. If, however, an exempt organization requires payment in advance, it is only required to provide the copy within 30 days from the date it receives payment. An exempt organization must fulfill a request for a copy of the organization's entire application or annual information return or any specific part or schedule of its application or return.[260]

A tax-exempt organization may charge a reasonable fee for providing copies. A fee is *reasonable* if it is no more than the per-page copying fee charged by the IRS for providing copies. It can also include actual postage costs. The requestor may be required to pay the fee in advance.[261]

(iv) Failure to Comply.   If a tax-exempt organization denies an individual's request for inspection or a copy of an application or return, and the individual wishes to alert the IRS to the possible need for enforcement action, he or she may send a statement to the appropriate IRS district office, describing the reason why the individual believes the denial was in violation of these requirements.[262]

(v) Widely Available Exception.   A tax-exempt organization is not required to comply with requests for copies of its application for recognition of exemption or an annual information return if the organization has made the document widely available.[263] The rules as to public inspection of the documents nonetheless continue to apply.

A tax-exempt organization can make its application or a return *widely available* by posting the document on a Web page that the organization establishes and maintains. It can also satisfy the exception if the document is posted as part of a database of similar documents of other exempt organizations on a Web page established and maintained by another entity.[264]

The document is considered widely available only if:

- The Web page through which it is available clearly informs readers that the document is available and provides instructions for downloading it.

---

[259] Reg. § 301.6104(d)-3(d)(2)(i).
[260] Reg. § 301.6104(d)-3(d)(2)(ii).
[261] Reg. § 301.6104(d)-3(d)(3).
[262] Reg. § 301.6104(d)-3(g).
[263] IRC § 6104(d)(4); Reg. § 301.6104(d)-4(a).
[264] Reg. § 301.6104(d)-4(b)(2)(i).

- The document is posted in a format that, when accessed, downloaded, viewed, and printed in hard copy, exactly reproduces the image of the application or return as it was originally filed with the IRS, except for any information permitted by statute to be withheld from public disclosure.

- Any individual with access to the Internet can access, download, view, and print the document without special computer hardware or software required for that format, and can do so without payment of a fee to the exempt organization or to another entity maintaining the Web page.[265]

The organization maintaining the Web page must have procedures for ensuring the reliability and accuracy of the documents that it posts on the page. It must take reasonable precautions to prevent alteration, destruction, or accidental loss of the document when printed on its page. In the event a posted document is altered, destroyed, or lost, the organization must correct or replace the document.[266]

(vi) Harassment Campaign Exception. If the IRS determines that a tax-exempt organization is the subject of a harassment campaign and that compliance with the requests that are part of the campaign would not be in the public interest, the organization is not required to fulfill a request for a copy that it reasonably believes is part of the campaign.[267]

A group of requests for a tax-exempt organization's application or returns is indicative of a harassment campaign if the requests are part of a single coordinated effort to disrupt the operations of the organization, rather than to collect information about it. This is a facts-and-circumstances test; factors include a sudden increase in the number of requests, an extraordinary number of requests made by means of form letters or similarly worded correspondence, evidence of a purpose to deter significantly the exempt organization's employees or volunteers from pursuing the organization's exempt purpose, requests that contain language hostile to the organization, direct evidence of bad faith by organizers of the purported harassment campaign, evidence that the organization has already provided the requested documents to a member of the purported harassment group, and a demonstration by the exempt organization that it routinely provides copies of its documents on request.[268]

A tax-exempt organization may disregard any request for copies of all or part of any document beyond the first two received within any 30-day period or the first four received within any one-year period from the same individual or the same address, irrespective of whether the IRS has determined that the organization is subject to a harassment campaign.[269]

---

[265] *Id.*
[266] Reg. § 301.6104(d)-4(b)(2)(iii).
[267] IRC § 6104(d)(4); Reg. § 301.6104(d)-5(a).
[268] Reg. § 301.6104(d)-5(b).
[269] Reg. § 301.6104(d)-5(c).

There is a procedure to follow for applying to the IRS for a determination that the organization is the subject of a harassment campaign. (There is no form.) The organization may suspend compliance with respect to the request, as long as the application is filed within 10 days after harassment is suspected, until the organization receives a response from the IRS.[270]

(vii) Penalties. A person failing to allow inspection of an organization's annual information returns is subject to a penalty of $20 per day for each day the failure continues, absent reasonable cause, with a maximum penalty per return of $10,000.[271] A person failing to allow inspection of an organization's application for recognition of tax exemption must, absent reasonable cause, pay $20 per day for each day the failure continues.[272] A person who willfully fails to comply with these inspection requirements is subject to a penalty of $5,000 with respect to each return or application.[273]

(viii) Political Organizations. These document availability rules are applicable to the notice that must be filed by political organizations to establish their tax-exempt status[274] and to the reports that they must file.[275]

With the annual information return a public document, it is important that it be accurately and completely prepared. This is easier to state than to do, for the preparers of today's annual information return often are expected to make determinations as to which there is little guidance, in law and in accounting, as to how to do them. These judgments include functional accounting of expenses,[276] allocations as between types of legislative activities,[277] separation of related and unrelated activities,[278] and the availability of a host of exceptions to unrelated income taxation.[279] Nonetheless, the annual information return is now an excellent means by which to present an organization's programs and other activities in the best possible light to the public, the media, and the IRS (perhaps thereby avoiding an audit). The return also is an effective tool for the management of a tax-exempt organization to use to assess the programmatic and financial progress of the organization.[280]

---

[270] Reg. § 301.6104(d)-5(d), (e).

[271] IRC § 6652(c)(1)(C), (3).

[272] IRC § 6652(c)(1)(D), (3).

[273] IRC § 6685. In general, Sullivan, "New IRS Regulations Will Make Information About Nonprofit Health Care Providers Widely Available," 24 *Exempt Org. Tax Rev.* (No. 2) 307 (May 1999); Ellingsworth & Horning, "New Public Disclosures Rules Present Opportunities and Challenges to Exempt Organizations," 23 *Exempt Org. Tax Rev.* (No. 1) 55 (Jan. 1999).

[274] See § 23.6.

[275] See § 4(c).

[276] See *supra* § 3(a)(i).

[277] See § 20.2.

[278] See Chapter 26.

[279] See Chapter 27.

[280] In early 2000, the staff of the Joint Committee on Taxation issued a report containing a massive set of proposals to substantially expand the disclosure requirements imposed on tax-exempt organizations. In general, Faber, "The Joint Committee Staff Disclosure Recommendations: What They Mean for Exempt Organizations," 28 *Exempt Org. Tax Rev.* (No. 1) 31 (April 2000).

24.5   DISCLOSURE REGARDING CERTAIN INFORMATION OR SERVICES

A tax-exempt organization[281] must pay a penalty if it fails to disclose that information or services it is offering is available without charge from the federal government.

Specifically, if (1) a tax-exempt organization offers to sell (or solicits money for) specific information or a routine service for any individual that could be readily obtained by the individual without charge (or for a nominal charge) from an agency of the federal government, (2) the exempt organization, when making the offer or solicitation, fails to make an "express statement (in a conspicuous and easily recognizable format)" that the information or service can be so obtained, and (3) the failure is due to "intentional disregard" of these requirements, the organization must pay a penalty.[282]

This requirement applies only if the information to be provided involves the specific individual solicited. Thus, for example, the requirement applies with respect to obtaining the social security earnings record or the social security identification number of an individual solicited, while the requirement is inapplicable with respect to the furnishing of copies of newsletters issued by federal agencies or providing copies of or descriptive material on pending legislation. Also, this requirement is inapplicable to the provision of professional services (such as tax return preparation, grant application preparation, or medical services), as opposed to routine information retrieval services, to an individual even if they may be available from the federal government without charge or at a nominal charge.[283]

The penalty, which is applicable for each day on which the failure occurred, is the greater of $1,000 or 50 percent of the aggregate cost of the offers and solicitations that occurred on any day on which the failure occurred and with respect to which there was this type of failure.[284]

§ 24.6   REVOCATION OF EXEMPTION: ADMINISTRATIVE AND LITIGATION PROCEDURES

The IRS is authorized to revoke an organization's tax exemption, notwithstanding an earlier recognition of its exemption by IRS ruling or court order, where the organization violates one or more of the requirements for the applicable exempt status. If the recognition of exemption was by court order, the IRS

---

[281] That is, an entity described in IRC §§ 501 (c) or (d) and exempt from federal income tax under IRC § 501(a) (see Part Two), or a political organization as defined in IRC § 527(e) (see Chapter 17).

[282] IRC § 6711(a). IRS guidelines (Notice 88-120, *supra* note 251) state that if materials and/or services are available from the federal government for less than $2.50 (including postage and handling costs), the materials are considered by the IRS as being available from the federal government at a nominal charge.

[283] Notice 88-120, *supra* note 251.

[284] IRC § 6711(b).

is not collaterally estopped from subsequently revoking the exemption where the ground for disqualification is different from that asserted in the prior court proceeding.[285]

If an organization's tax-exempt (or, where applicable, nonprivate foundation) status is revoked (or adversely modified) by the IRS, its administrative remedies are much the same as if the original application for that status had been denied.[286]

The principle of procedural due process, embodied in the Fifth Amendment to the U.S. Constitution, does not require the IRS to initiate a judicial hearing on the qualification of an organization for tax-exempt status before revoking the organization's favorable determination letter. This point was addressed by the Supreme Court in 1974.[287] It was reaffirmed nearly 20 years later, when another court found that the Supreme Court's analysis is still the law, that the revocation did not infringe on the organization's exercise of First Amendment rights,[288] and that, even if the organization had a property interest in the IRS's prior recognition of its exempt status, the revocation was not a deprivation of property without procedural due process.[289]

(a) General Rules

Facing revocation of tax-exempt status and having exhausted its administrative remedies, an organization's initial impulse may be to seek injunctive relief in the courts, to restrain the IRS from taking such action. The Anti-Injunction Act,[290] however, provides that, aside from minor exceptions, "no suit for the purpose of restraining the assessment or collection of any tax shall be maintained in any court by any person."[291] Despite the explicitly inflexible language

---

[285] Universal Life Church, Inc. v. United States, 86-1 U.S.T.C ¶ 9271 (Cl. Ct. 1986).

[286] Rev. Proc. 90-27, *supra* note 1 § 14.02; § 23.8. The protest and conference rights before a final revocation notice is issued are not applicable to matters where delay would be prejudicial to the interests of the IRS (such as in cases involving fraud, jeopardy, or the imminence of the expiration of the statute of limitations, or where immediate action is necessary to protect the interests of the federal government) (Rev. Proc. 90-27, *supra* § 14.03).

[287] Bob Jones Univ. v. Simon, 416 U.S. 725 (1974), *aff'g* 472 F.2d 903 (4th Cir. 1973), *reh. den.*, 476, F.2d 259 (4th Cir. 1973).

[288] This argument was based on the fact that the organization involved, a charitable (IRC § 501c(3)) entity, has a First Amendment (free speech) right to solicit charitable contributions. See Hopkins, *The Law of Fundraising, Third Edition* (John Wiley & Sons, Inc., 2002), § 4.3.

[289] United Cancer Council, Inc. v. Comm'r, 100 T.C. 162 (1993).

The church audit rules (see *infra* § 8(b)) require that a church tax examination take no more than two years to complete (*id.*, text accompanying note 518). A federal court of appeals held that the revocation of the exempt status of a church cannot be defended against on the ground that the IRS failed to complete its audit of the church within the requisite period (Music Square Church v. United States, 218 F.3d 1367 (Fed. Cir. 2000)).

[290] IRC § 7421(a).

[291] Also the Tax Exception to the Declaratory Judgment Act, 28 U.S.C. § 2201. E.g., American Soc'y of Ass'n Executives v. Bentsen, 848 F Supp. 245 (D.D.C. 1994) (holding that both statutes deprived the court of jurisdiction over challenge of the constitutionality of the law denying the business expense deduction for dues paid to exempt associations that engaged in lobbying (see § 20.8)); Alpine Fellowship Church of Love & Enlightenment v. United States, 87-1 U.S.T.C. ¶ 9203 (N.D. Cal. 1987).

of the statute, the U.S. Supreme Court carved out a narrow exception, in that a preenforcement injunction against tax assessment or collection may be granted only if it is clear that under no circumstances could the government ultimately prevail and if equity jurisdiction otherwise exists (that is, a showing of irreparable injury, no adequate remedy at law, and advancement of the public interest).[292] Generally, loss of exempt status will not bring an organization within the ambit of this exception, under Supreme Court rulings[293] and other cases.[294] An exception may be available in this context but success will require rather unusual factual circumstances.[295]

An organization facing loss of tax-exempt status or similar adverse treatment from the IRS may petition the U.S. Tax Court for relief following the issuance of notice of tax deficiency (if one can be found)[296] or may pay the tax and sue for a refund in federal district court or the U.S. Court of Federal Claims following expiration of the statutory six-month waiting period.[297] The organization, however, may well become defunct before any relief can be obtained in this fashion, particularly where the ability to attract charitable contributions is a factor, since denial of exempt status also means (where applicable) loss of advance assurance by the IRS of deductibility of contributions. The U.S. Supreme Court recognized the seriousness of this dilemma but concluded that "although the congressional restriction to postenforcement review may place an organization claiming tax-exempt status in a precarious financial position, the problems presented do not rise to the level of constitutional infirmities, in light of the powerful governmental interests in protecting the administration of the tax system from premature judicial interference . . . and of the opportunities for review that are available.[298]

---

[292] Enochs v. Williams Packing & Navigation Co., 370 U.S. 1 (1962). E.g., Investment Annuity v. Blumenthal, 437 F. Supp. 1095 (D.D.C. 1977), 442 F. Supp. 681 (D.D.C. 1977), rev'd, 609 F.2d 1 (D.C. Cir. 1979); State of Minn., Spannaus v United States, 525 F.2d 231 (8th Cir. 1975).

[293] Bob Jones Univ. v. Simon, supra note 287; "Americans United" Inc. v. Walters, 416 U.S. 752 (1974), rev'g 477 F.2d 1169 (D.C. Cir. 1973). Also United States v. American Friends Serv. Comm., 419 U.S. 7 (1974); Cattle Feeders Tax Comm. v. Shultz, 504 F.2d 462 (10th Cir. 1974); Vietnam Veterans Against the War, Inc. v. Voskuil, 389 F. Supp. 412 (E.D. Mo. 1974).

[294] E.g., Crenshaw County Private School Found. v. Connally, 474 F.2d 1185 (5th Cir. 1973); Judicial Watch, Inc. v. Rossotti, 223 F. Supp. 2d 698 (D. Md. 2002); National Council on the Facts of Overpopulation v. Caplin, 224 F. Supp. 313 (D.D.C. 1963); Israelite House of David v. Holden, 14 F.2d 701 (W.D. Mich. 1926).

[295] Center on Corporate Responsibility, Inc. v. Shultz, 368 F. Supp. 863 (D.D.C. 1973). In The Founding Church of Scientology of Washington, D.C., Inc. v. Director, Federal Bureau of Investigation et al., 84-1 U.S.T.C. ¶ 9468 (D.D.C. 1984), the organization was permitted to seek an injunction against the IRS for allegedly engaging in illegal law enforcement and information-gathering activities in violation of the organization's constitutional rights, inasmuch as the lawsuit was not related to tax assessment or collection.

[296] IRC §§ 6212, 6213. E.g., Golden Rule Church Ass'n v. Comm'r, 41 T.C. 719 (1964). The role and responsibilities of the Chief Counsel of the IRS in tax-exempt organization cases docketed in the U.S. Tax Court is the subject of Rev. Proc. 78-9, 1978-1 C.B. 563.

[297] IRC § 7422; 28 U.S.C. §§ 1346(x)(1), 1491. In the absence of the timely filing of a claim for refund (a jurisdictional prerequisite to this type of court action), this type of suit may not be maintained. Also The American Ass'n of Commodity Traders v. Department of the Treasury, 79-1 U.S.T.C. ¶ 9183 (D.N.H. 1978), aff'd, 598 F.2d 1233 (1st Cir. 1979).

[298] Bob Jones Univ. v. Simon, supra note 287, 416 U.S., at 747–748.

(b) Declaratory Judgment Rules

Federal tax law provides for declaratory judgments as to the tax status of charitable organizations.[299] This law authorizes federal court jurisdiction in cases of actual controversy involving determinations (or failures to make a determination) by the IRS with respect to the tax status of charitable organizations. This jurisdiction is vested in the U.S. District Court for the District of Columbia, the U.S. Court of Federal Claims, and the U.S. Tax Court.[300]

This declaratory judgment procedure is designed to facilitate relatively prompt judicial review of four categories of tax-exempt organizations issues.[301] This procedure is not, however, intended to supplant the preexisting avenues available for exempt organizations for judicial review. Jury trials are not available in these types of cases.[302]

(i) General Requirements. These rules create a remedy in a case of actual controversy involving a determination by the IRS with respect to the initial qualification or classification or continuing qualification or classification of an entity as a charitable organization for tax exemption purposes[303] and/or charitable contribution deduction purposes,[304] a private foundation,[305] or a private operating foundation.[306] The remedy is also available in the case of a failure by the IRS to make a determination as respects one or more of these issues.[307] The remedy is

---

[299] IRC § 7428. E.g., The Church of the New Testament v. United States, 783 F.2d 771 (9th Cir. 1986).

[300] The U.S. Tax Court is the only one of these courts where this type of a declaratory judgment case can be pursued without the services of a lawyer; these *pro se* cases will be dismissed for that reason in the other two courts (e.g., Point of Wisdom No. 1 v. United States, 77 A.F.T.R. 2d 986 (D.D.C. 1996)).

[301] Congress enacted a similar declaratory judgment procedure for ascertaining the tax qualifications of employee retirement plans, as part of the Employee Retirement Income Security Act (IRC § 7476). E.g., Federal Land Bank Ass'n of Asheville, N.C. v. Comm'r, 67 T.C. 29 (1976), *rev. and rem.*, 573 F.2d 179 (4th Cir. 1978), 74 T.C. 1106 (1980) (*on remand*).

[302] The Synanon Church v. United States, 83-1 U.S.T.C. ¶ 9230 (D.D.C. 1983).

[303] That is, an organization described in IRC § 501(c)(3) and exempt from federal income taxation by reason of IRC § 501(a). Reasoning that the question as to whether a trust is a charitable trust within the meaning of IRC § 4947(a)(1) (see § 11.4(f)) is "inextricably related" to the issue of whether it is qualified under IRC § 501(c)(3), the Tax Court held that it has declaratory judgment jurisdiction to decide the IRC § 4947(a)(1) issue (Allen Eiry Trust v. Comm'r, 77 T.C. 1263 (1981)). In this case, however, the court declined to take jurisdiction over the question as to whether the trust is qualified to have its income exempt from tax under IRC § 115 (see § 18.17). The court also declined jurisdiction in an instance where the organization was dissolved prior to the filing of the petition for declaratory relief, on the ground that there was not an actual controversy (Nat'l Republican Found. v. Comm'r, 55 T.C.M. 1395 (1988)). Likewise, where an audit by the IRS is undertaken and the organization's tax-exempt status is not altered, there is no actual controversy (Founding Church of Scientology of Washington, D.C., Inc. v. United States, 92-1 U.S.T.C. ¶ 50,302 (Cl. Ct. 1992)).

[304] IRC § 170(c)(2).

[305] IRC § 509(a).

[306] IRC § 4942(j)(3).

[307] IRC § 7428(x)(2). Thus, the rulings and determination letters in cases subject to the declaratory judgment procedure of IRC § 7428 are those issued pursuant to the procedures stated in Rev. Proc. 90-27, *supra* note 1. The withdrawal of an application for recognition of tax exemption is not a failure to make a determination under IRC § 7428(a)(2) (*id.* § 7.02).

pursued in one of the three above-noted courts, which is authorized to "make a declaration" with respect to the issues.

A *determination* within the meaning of these rules[308] is a final decision by the IRS affecting the tax qualification of a charitable organization.[309] The term does not encompass an IRS ruling passing on an organization's proposed transactions, in that this type of ruling does not constitute a denial or revocation of an organization's tax-exempt status nor does it jeopardize the deductibility of contributions to it; thus, absent a final determination, a declaratory judgment is premature.[310] The same principle applies to an IRS ruling concerning an organization's public charity entity classification.[311] In the case of a church, a final report of an IRS agent (the 30-day letter) constitutes the requisite final determination.[312]

A topic of some controversy is whether a tax-exempt organization can litigate, under these declaratory judgment rules, its public charity classification where the IRS accords public charity status to it but in a category different from that requested by the organization. In the first case on the point, the U.S. Tax Court held that it is a justiciable issue[313] for an organization to assert that it is not a private foundation because it is a church rather than a publicly supported organization.[314] The court said that, in this type of an instance, the organization has received the requisite adverse ruling, if only because the organization had requested a definitive ruling yet received only an advance ruling;[315] the IRS unsuccessfully asserted that the declaratory judgment jurisdiction becomes available only where the ruling is "fully adverse."[316]

The U.S. Court of Appeals for the Fifth Circuit, however, endeavored to narrow the reach of this Tax Court decision.[317] While the appellate court agreed that the "receipt of a favorable ruling on a non-private [foundation] status that is a different and less advantageous status that [sic] the one which is the subject of the ruling request will not defeat" declaratory judgment jurisdication,[318] the court said it would "not . . . [interpret] the statute to allow court review of an adverse holding by the Service which has no present effect on a taxpayer's

---

[308] IRC § 7428(a)(1).

[309] Rev. Proc. 90-27, *supra* 1 note, § 12.04.

[310] New Community Senior Citizen Hous. Corp. v. Comm'r, 72 T.C. 372 (1979). In one case, the U.S. Tax Court held that the requirement that there be a final adverse determination means that the court lacks jurisdiction to review a determination issued by the IRS only after the organization agreed to not conduct a certain activity in consideration of receipt of the otherwise favorable determination, because the ruling is not "adverse" in relation to the proposed activity (AHW Corp. v. Comm'r, 79 T.C. 390 (1982)).

[311] Urantia Found. v. Comm'r, 77 T.C. 507 (1981), *aff'd*, 684 F.2d 521 (7th Cir. 1982).

[312] IRC § 7611(g).

[313] Under IRC § 7428(a)(1)(B).

[314] See § 11.3.

[315] See § 23.4(b).

[316] Friends of the Soc'y of Servants of God v. Comm'r, 75 T.C. 209 (1980). Also Foundation of Human Understanding v. Comm'r, 88 T.C. 1341 (1987).

[317] CREATE, Inc. v. Comm'r, 634 F.2d 803 (5th Cir. 1981).

[318] *Id.* at 813.

classification" as a private foundation or nonfoundation.[319] The principal issue before this court of appeals concerned an organization that was ruled to be a donative publicly supported organization; however, the IRS had also ruled, contrary to the position of the organization, that contributions from another organization were subject to the 2 percent limitation on allowable "public" contributions.[320] The court rejected the contention that the Tax Court had jurisdiction to entertain the action, concerning proper application of the 2 percent limitation, since the organization was accorded initial classification as a publicly supported charity and since the IRS had not failed to make the requisite determination. Thus, the court concluded that the necessary *actual controversy* was not present and that the organization can litigate the applicability of the 2 percent rule when and if that rule causes the IRS to attempt to adversely classify the organization under the public charity classification rules.[321] Likewise, the U.S. Court of Appeals for the Sixth Circuit held that the courts lack declaratory judgment jurisdiction where an organization is seeking reclassification under the public charity rules.[322]

A pleading may be filed under these rules "only by the organization the qualification or classification of which is at issue."[323] Prior to utilizing the declaratory judgment procedure, an organization must have exhausted all administrative remedies available to it within the IRS.[324] The refusal by an organization to turn records over to the IRS, during the pendency of a contest of the IRS summons, cannot be considered a failure to exhaust administrative remedies that could result in a loss of declaratory judgment rights.[325] For the first 270 days after a request for a determination is made, an organization is

---

[319] *Id.* at 812.

[320] See Chapter 11.

[321] Inherent in the opinion is the court's concern about overburdening the judicial system with too many IRC § 7428 declaratory judgment cases, for it spoke of a contrary holding giving rise to a "significant volume of § 7428 litigation, some of which would be needless" (CREATE, Inc. v. Comm'r, *supra* note 317, at 812).

[322] Ohio County & Ind. Agric. Soc'ys v. Comm'r, 610 F.2d 448 (6th Cir. 1979), *cert. den.*, 446 U.S. 965 (1980).

[323] IRC § 7428(b)(1). Thus, for example, as regards an unincorporated organization that applied for recognition of tax exemption and subsequently, during the administrative process, incorporated, when the IRS denied exemption for the unincorporated entity, the corporation (being a separate legal entity) was held to lack standing to seek a declaratory judgment on the qualification as an exempt organization of the unincorporated organization (American New Covenant Church v. Comm'r, *supra* note 23). By contrast, a surviving exempt corporation in a merger was held to be able to litigate, under these rules, the issue of exemption of the merged entity; the appellate court looked to state law to determine that the suit could be said to be maintained by "the organization" (Baptist Hosp., Inc. v. United States, 851 F.2d 1397 (Fed. Cir. 1988), *rev'g* 87-1 U.S.T.C. ¶ 9290 (Ct. Cl. 1987)). A director of an exempt organization lacks standing to bring an action pursuant to these rules (Fondel v. United States, 99-1 U.S.T.C. ¶ 50,188 (Fed. Cir. 1999)).

[324] In The Sense of Self Soc'y v. United States, 79-2 U.S.T.C. ¶ 9673 (D.D.C. 1979), the court ruled that the organization failed to exhaust its administrative remedies because it did not respond to the IRS' "repeated" requests for information. Cf. Change-All Souls Hous. Corp. v. United States, 671 F.2d 463 (Ct. Cl. 1982).

[325] Church of World Peace, Inc. v. Internal Revenue Service, 715 F.2d 492 (10th Cir. 1983).

deemed to not have exhausted its administrative remedies, assuming a determination has not been made during that period.[326] After this 270-day period has elapsed, the organization may initiate an action for a declaratory judgment. Thus, however, if the IRS makes an adverse determination during this jurisdictional period, an action can be initiated. Nonetheless, all actions under these rules must be initiated within 90 days after the date on which the final determination by the IRS is made.[327] In the case of a church, the receipt of a final report of an IRS agent is deemed to constitute the exhaustion of administrative remedies.[328]

A *determination* can, in this context, include a proposed revocation of an organization's tax-exempt status or public charity classification. In one case, an exempt charitable organization received a letter in which the IRS proposed to revoke its public charity status; in response, it filed a written protest and thereafter filed a petition for a declaratory judgment (under the 270-day rule). After the court petition was filed, the IRS issued a final determination letter revoking the public charity classification of the organization. At issue was whether the court had jurisdiction as the result of the filing of the petition. The IRS contended the court did not, inasmuch as the petition was filed before the final adverse letter was issued. The court disagreed, finding that the proposed revocation was sufficient to create the requisite actual controversy and that the written protest constituted the requisite request for a determination.[329]

In the case, the court concluded that the administrative appeals process had been completed and that the 270-day period had run its course. By contrast, where the administrative process is ongoing and where the IRS has merely threatened to issue a notice of proposed revocation, the courts will decline to assume declaratory judgment jurisdiction.[330] Emphasizing the requirement of an *actual controversy*, a court observed that "[w]e find no grounds for believing that Congress intended this [declaratory judgment] section to grant us plenary authority to supervise examinations of exempt organizations."[331] This determination was upheld, with the appellate court rejecting the claim of jurisdiction in that the IRS was "still only in the investigative stage and has not issued any ruling affecting . . . [the organization's] tax exempt status, directly or indirectly."[332]

In one instance, a court concluded that it had declaratory judgment jurisdiction over a case, where the IRS notified a tax-exempt organization that the

---

[326] IRC § 7428(b)(2). Withdrawal of an application for recognition of tax exemption (Form 1023) is not an exhaustion of administrative remedies (Rev. Proc. 90-27, supra note 1 § 7.02). The filing of an application for recognition of exemption is not a required administrative step for organizations claiming status as a church (see § 23.3(b)) (Universal Life Church, Inc. (Full Circle) v. Comm'r, 83 T.C. 292 (1984)).

[327] IRC § 7428(b)(3). E.g., Metropolitan Community Serv., Inc. v. Comm'r, 53 T.C.M. 810 (1987).

[328] IRC § 7611(g).

[329] J. David Gladstone Found. v. Comm'r, 77 T.C. 221 (1981).

[330] High Adventure Ministries, Inc. v. Comm'r, 80 T.C. 292 (1983).

[331] *Id.* at 302.

[332] 726 F.2d 555, 557 (9th Cir. 1984).

agency was considering revocation of its exempt status, even though the complaint in the case was filed before the IRS issued its final adverse determination letter to the organization.[333] Prior to the filing of the court petition, the IRS issued a technical advice memorandum stating that the organization's exemption should be revoked. The government argued that, at the time the petition was filed, there was no actual controversy because the IRS had not yet revoked or officially "proposed revocation" of the organization's exempt status. The court, however, held that the organization's "continuing classification was unquestionably at issue between the parties throughout the entire administrative proceeding."[334] This court wrote that, after the "issuance of the technical advice memorandum, final revocation was inevitable" and thus "[t]here can be no other conclusion but that an actual controversy existed on the date . . . [the organization] filed its petition herein.[335]

In this case, there was no "failure to make a determination" and there was no "request for a termination." The government did not issue a "proposed revocation" and the organization never filed a "written protest." The court examined the administrative status of the case, however, and compared it to the administrative status of an organization that receives a proposed revocation, and concluded that the correspondence from the IRS was "in substance, procedurally the same" as a written protest.[336] The court concluded that, by the time the matter was substantively considered by the IRS, a full and complete administrative record had been developed.

In the course of issuance of a favorable determination letter recognizing an organization's tax-exempt status, the IRS not infrequently conditions its ruling on the organization's agreement to not engage in a particular activity. A court held that this type of favorable final ruling does not constitute the requisite adverse determination.[337] Indeed, the court starkly wrote that organizations which have exempt status "have been left with only one means of obtaining judicial review: to engage in the proposed activities despite . . . [the IRS's] adverse ruling, thereby to risk revocation, and to test . . . [the IRS's] position in court in the event of actual revocation."[338] If an organization concludes that it cannot risk loss of exemption, the court suggested that a new entity be formed to undertake the activities at issue and, if necessary, litigate the matter.[339]

According to the IRS, this 270-day period does not begin until the date a *substantially completed* application for recognition of tax exemption is sent to the agency.[340]

(ii) Exhaustion of Administrative Remedies. As respects the exhaustion of administrative remedies requirement, the IRS is of the view that the following

---

[333] Anclote Psychiatric Center, Inc. v. Comm'r, 95 T.C. 371 (1992).
[334] *Id.* at 377.
[335] *Id.*
[336] *Id.* at 378.
[337] AHW Corp. v. Comm'r, 79 T.C. 390 (1982).
[338] *Id.* at 394-395.
[339] *Id.* at 398, note 5.
[340] Rev. Proc. 90-27, *supra* note 1 at § 5.05.

steps and remedies must be exhausted prior to proper initiation of a declaratory judgment action:

1. The filing of a substantially completed application for recognition of tax exemption,[341] or the filing of a request for a determination of public charity/private foundation status;

2. The timely submission of all additional information requested to perfect an application for recognition of exemption or request for determination of public charity/private foundation status;

3. In appropriate cases, requesting appropriate relief under the rules[342] regarding applications for extensions of the time for making an election or application for relief from tax;[343] and

4. Exhaustion of all administrative appeals available within the IRS,[344] as well as appeal of a proposed adverse ruling in National Office original jurisdiction exemption application cases.[345]

According to the IRS, an organization cannot be deemed to have exhausted its administrative remedies prior to the earlier of (1) the completion of the foregoing steps and the sending of a notice of final determination by certified or registered mail, or (2) the expiration of the 270-day period in a case where the IRS has not issued a notice of final determination and the organization has taken, in a timely manner, all reasonable steps to secure a ruling or determination.[346]

Further, the IRS stated that the foregoing steps "will not be considered completed until the Service has had a reasonable time to act upon the appeal or protest, as the case may be."[347] (As noted, nonetheless, once the statutory 270 days have elapsed, the action can be initiated, without regard to the pace of the IRS in relation to these steps.)

(iii) Deductibility of Contributions. To protect the financial status of an allegedly charitable organization during the litigation period, the law provides for circumstances under which contributions made to the organization during that period are deductible[348] even though the court ultimately decides against the organization.[349] Basically, this relief can only be accorded where the IRS is propos-

---

[341] See § 23.2(b).

[342] Reg. § 1.9100.

[343] Rev. Proc. 79-63, 1979-2 C.B. 578.

[344] Rev. Proc. 90-27, *supra* note 1 §§ 10, 11.

[345] *Id.* at § 12.01.

[346] *Id.* at § 12.02.

[347] *Id.* at § 12.03. The U.S. District Court for the District of Columbia held that it lacks subject matter jurisdiction in these cases until the IRS makes an adverse determination or the 270-day period (commenced by the filing of a substantially completed application for recognition of exemption) has elapsed (New York County Health Servs. Review Org., Inc. v. Comm'r, 80-1 U.S.T.C. ¶ 9398 (D.D.C. 1980)).

[348] IRC § 170(c)(2).

[349] IRC § 7428(c)(1).

ing to revoke, rather than initially deny, an organization's charitable status. The total deductions to any one organization from a single donor, to be so protected during this period, however, may not exceed $1,000.[350] (Where an organization ultimately prevails in a declaratory judgment case, this $1,000 limitation on deductibility becomes inapplicable, so that all gifts are fully deductible within the general limitations of the charitable deduction rules.[351]) This benefit is not available to any individual who was responsible, in whole or in part, for the actions (or failures to act) on the part of the organization that were the basis for the revocation of tax-exempt status.[352]

When the IRS revokes an organization's tax exemption, that action is usually the result of an audit of the organization's activities for one or more years. When a revocation of exemption occurs, the IRS inevitably makes a public announcement that the organization is no longer exempt and that contributions to it are no longer deductible. Thus, for example, once such a revocation occurs, and the organization does not take any affirmative steps to restore its exemption, a gift to the organization would not be tax-deductible, even when made in a year subsequent to one of the audit years. A court in a declaratory judgment case only has jurisdiction in relation to the audit years, inasmuch as the requisite determination with respect to those years has been made. As to the subsequent years, court jurisdiction does not exist because there is no determination with respect to those years. The remedy available to an organization in these circumstances is to file an application for recognition of exemption for the subsequent period. The manner in which the IRS responds to the filing will determine whether the organization needs to proceed in court for those years—in any event, that response will be the determination needed to vest a court with declaratory judgment jurisdiction.[353]

(iv) Administrative Record. The U.S. Tax Court is the only one of the three jurisdictions to adopt procedural rules for actions filed under these rules.[354] The single most significant feature of these rules is the decision of the court to generally confine its role to review of the denial by the IRS of a request for a determination of tax exemption based solely on the facts contained in the administrative record, that is, not to conduct a trial *de novo* at which new evidence maybe

---

[350] IRC § 7428(c)(2)(A).

[351] See § 2.5.

[352] IRC 7428(c)(3). The IRS publishes, in the Internal Revenue Bulletin, the names of organizations that are challenging, under IRC § 7428, the revocation of their status as organizations entitled to receive deductible charitable contributions, so as to inform potential donors to these organizations of the protection, to the extent provided under IRC § 7428(c), for their contributions made during the litigation period (Ann. 85-169, 1985-48 I.R.B. 40). In general, Kittrell, "Administrative Prerequisites for Declaratory Judgments about Tax Issues," 66 *A.B.A.J.* 1570 (1980); Roady, "Declaratory Judgments for 501(c)(3) Status Determinations: End of a 'Harsh Regime'," 30 *Tax Law.* 765 (1977).

[353] The Synanon Church v. United States, *supra* note 302.

[354] Rules of Practice and Procedure, U.S. Tax Court, Title XXI.

adduced.[355] (This approach does not apply where the exemption has been revoked.) Thus, in one case, the court refused to permit information orally furnished to IRS representatives during a conference at the administrative level to be introduced in evidence during the pendency of the case before it.[356] Likewise, it was held that the administrative record may consist only of material submitted by either the applicant organization or the IRS, so that materials submitted by third parties are inadmissible.[357] Similarly, the court is to base its decision upon only theories advanced in the IRS notice or at trial, and not on arguments advanced anew by the IRS during the litigation.[358]

The U.S. Tax Court suggested that, if an organization that has been denied tax exemption and did not prevail before it has material information previously excluded from the administrative record, the organization may file a new application for recognition of exemption and that the principles of *res judicata* would not preclude the court from reviewing a denial of the subsequent application.[359]

The general Tax Court scheme for the processing of these declaratory judgment cases is being adopted, on a case-by-case basis, by both the U.S. District Court for the District of Columbia and the U.S. Court of Federal Claims. This approach includes basic reliance on the administrative record, with court review *de novo* only in unusual cases.[360]

---

[355] *Id.*, Rule 217(a). E.g., The Nationalist Movement v. Comm'r, 64 T.C.M. 1479 (1992); Dr. Erol Bastug, Inc. v. Comm'r, 57 T.C.M. 562 (1989); Colorado State Chiropractic Soc'y, Inc. v. Comm'r, 56 T.C.M. 1018 (1989); Liberty Ministries Int'l v. Comm'r, 48 T.C.M. 105 (1984); Unitary Mission Church of Long Island v. Comm'r, 74 T.C. 507 (1980). The U.S. Tax Court is concerned about "fishing expeditions" in these situations (e.g., Wisconsin Psychiatric Servs. v. Comm'r, 76 T.C. 839, 846 (1981)). This court has allowed supplementation of the administrative record in a denial-of-exemption case (First Libertarian Church v. Comm'r, 74 T.C. 396 (1980)). The U.S. District Court for the District of Columbia, however, appears more willing to review facts beyond the administrative record (e.g., Freedom Church of Revelation v. United States, 588 F. Supp. 693 (D..D.C. 1984); Incorporated Trustees of the Gospel Worker Soc'y v. United States, *supra* note 12; cf. Airlie Found., Inc. v. United States, 92-2 U.S.T.C. ¶ 50,462 (D.D.C. 1992)). Because the Tax Court will render a declaratory judgment in a nonrevocation case on the petition, the answer, and the administrative record, it has held that a motion for summary judgment in that court is "superfluous" and "pointless" (Pulpit Resource v. Comm'r, 70 T.C. 594, 602 (1978)).

[356] Houston Lawyer Referral Serv., Inc. v. Comm'r, 69 T.C. 570 (1978). Also Church in Boston v. Comm'r, 71 T.C. 102 (1979).

[357] Church of Spiritual Technology v. United States, 90-1 U.S.T.C. ¶ 50,097 (Ct. Cl. 1989). A court ruled that transcripts from the criminal trials and the grand jury materials from the criminal case, involving the founder and executive director of an organization, were part of the administrative record in a subsequent case where the organization's ongoing tax-exempt status was at issue (Airlie Found., Inc. v. United States, *supra* note 355).

[358] Peoples Translation Service/Newsfront Int'l v. Comm'r, 72 T.C. 42 (1979); Goodspeed Scholarship Fund v. Comm'r, 70 T.C. 515 (1978); Schuster's Express, Inc. v. Comm'r, 66 T.C. 585 (1976), *aff'd*, 562 F.2d 39 (2d Cir. 1977).

[359] Houston Lawyer Referral Serv., Inc. v. Comm'r, *supra* note 356, at 577–578.

[360] E.g. Southwest Va. Professional Standards Review Org., Inc. v. United States, 78-2 U.S.T.C. ¶ 9747 (D.D.C. 1978); Animal Protection Inst., Inc. v. United States, 78-2 U.S.T.C. ¶ 9709 (Ct. Cl. 1978).

In Synanon Church v. United States, 579 F. Supp. 967 (D.D.C. 1984), *aff'd*, 87-1 U.S.T.C. ¶ 9347 (D.C. Cir. 1987), the court dismissed the case on the ground of fraud upon the court, based upon the court's finding that the organization destroyed material records.

The U.S. Tax Court will not consolidate a declaratory judgment case with a regular tax deficiency case, even where the issues are the same and a trial may be available in both instances (Centre for Int'l Understanding v. Comm'r, 84 T.C. 279 (1985)).

An organization's fate before a court may well depend on the quality of the contents of the administrative record. The applicant organization, significantly, generally controls what comprises the administrative record. Even when the record includes responses to IRS inquiries, it is the organization that decides the phraseology of the answers and what, if anything, to attach as exhibits. It is, therefore, important that the administrative record be carefully constructed, particularly in instances where there is a reasonable likelihood that an initial determination case will be unsuccessful at the IRS level and thus ripen into a declaratory judgment case.

As an illustration, a court had before it the issue as to whether an organization that operated a mountain lodge as a retreat facility could qualify as a tax-exempt religious organization. The opinion in the case reflected the court's view that this type of organization can so qualify under appropriate circumstances, yet the organization involved lost the case primarily because the administrative record did not show that the recreational facilities were used for exempt purposes or otherwise used only in an insubstantial manner.[361] By contrast, where the administrative record is able to show that an organization is advancing exempt purposes by means of a religious retreat, the courts will not deprive the organization of exemption, even where the retreats are held in an environment somewhat more attractive than the wilderness.[362]

The impact of this declaratory judgment procedure on the administrative practice before the IRS cannot be underestimated. In the past, the IRS could be confident that, with rare exception, its determination as to a charitable organization's tax status was the final one. That is, because of the large amount of legal fees, other expenses, and time required to litigate, the agency knew that judicial review of one of its decisions in this area would be highly unlikely.

With the advent of the declaratory judgment rules, all this has dramatically changed. No longer can the IRS make its decisions with the luxury of assuming their finality. Now, the agency, in approaching this decision-making process, must do so with awareness of the greatly increased possibility of a challenge in court. This means that the IRS, obviously reluctant to have a rebuff in the casebooks as precedent, may well be forced to issue favorable rulings in instances where the contrary would otherwise be the case. Also, these procedures can force the IRS to act more quickly than it may otherwise be disposed to do.

In one episode, the IRS refused to rule on a request for recognition of exemption, saying that the issue raised was under study. Once the 270-day administrative remedies period expired, the organization launched a lawsuit. Within 60 days after the complaint was filed, the Department of justice made it known that

---

The Tax Court ruled that an IRC § 7428 declaratory judgment petition may be dismissed for failure of the organization to prosecute the case (Basic Bible Church of America v. Comm'r, 86 T.C. 110 (1986)).

[361] The Schoger Foundation v. Comm'r, 76 T.C. 380 (1981). The organization argued that the administrative record did not show that the recreational facilities were used in an insubstantial manner but this failed because, under the U.S. Tax Court Rules of Practice and Procedure (Rule 217(c)(2)(i)), the organization had the burden of showing that the determination of the IRS is incorrect. Cf. Alive Fellowship of Harmonious Living v. Comm'r, 47 T.C.M. 1134 (1984).

[362] Junaluska Assembly Hous., Inc. v. Comm'r, 86 T.C. 1114 (1986).

the IRS was willing to issue a favorable ruling (thereby mooting the case). Thus, soon after instituting a declaratory judgment request, the organization came into possession of a favorable ruling, under circumstances where, if this form of relief were not available, the IRS probably would not have acted for some time or would have issued an unfavorable determination.[363]

(v) Development of Law. These procedures are not solely of consequence to the new organization that is struggling to obtain its tax exemption and/or its private foundation/public charity status. They are also of immense significance to the established charitable (including educational, religious, and scientific) organization or institution, the tax status of which is, or appears to be, immune from revocation or other disturbance. This declaratory judgment provision is having a considerable impact on development of the law applicable to charitable organizations.

The courts are holding a variety of organizations to be tax-exempt entities, in rejection of IRS positions. As illustrations, the courts have concluded, notwithstanding the opposition of the IRS, that health maintenance organizations,[364] professional standards review organization foundations,[365] consumer credit counseling agencies,[366] and private schools providing custodial services for young pupils[367] can qualify for exemption. The courts, however, are also upholding the IRS position, such as in the case of genealogical societies,[368] communal groups,[369] and certain scholarship funds.[370] Interpretations of the private foundation definition rules have gone for and against the government.[371]

Consequently, the growing use of these procedures creates a significant impact on the law encompassing the reach of the tax exemption for charitable organizations. This can be of considerable importance in the continuing preservation of organizations' tax-exempt and/or private foundation classifications.

Moreover, the breadth of the issues being raised by these cases is fostering the rapid development of law in areas related to tax exemption other than as respects the exemption categories themselves. Chief among these areas being ex-

---

[363] Infant Formula Action Coalition v. United States (C.A. No. 79-0129, D.D.C.); also Fair Campaign Practices Comm., Inc. v. United States (C.A. No. 77-0830, D.D.C.).

[364] Sound Health Assn v. Comm'r, 71 T.C. 158 (1978).

[365] Virginia Professional Standards Review Found. v. Blumenthal, 466 F. Supp. 1164 (D.D.C. 1979).

[366] Consumer Credit Counseling Serv. of Ala., Inc. v. United States, 78-2 U.S.T.C. ¶ 9660 (D.D.C. 1978).

[367] San Francisco Infant School, Inc. v. Comm'r, 69 T.C. 957 (1978); Michigan Early Childhood Center, Inc. v. Comm'r, 37 T.C.M. 808 (1978). Also § 7.7.

[368] The Callaway Family Ass'n, Inc. v. Comm'r, 71 T.C. 340 (1978); Benjamin Price Genealogical Ass'n v Internal Revenue Service, 79-1 U.S.T.C. ¶ 9361 (D.D.C. 1979). Also Manning Ass'n v Comm'r, 93 T.C. 596 (1989) (holding that an association of descendants of a settler from England in the U.S. in the 1600s did not qualify for tax exemption as an educational organization, in part because of the compilation of genealogical information).

[369] Beth-El Ministries, Inc. v. United States, 79-2 U.S.T.C. ¶ 9412 (D.D.C. 1979).

[370] Miss Georgia Scholarship Fund, Inc. v. Comm'r, 72 T.C. 267 (1979). Cf. Wilson v. United States, 322 F.Supp. 830 (D. Kan. 1971).

[371] E.g., William F., Mabel E., & Margaret K. Quarrie Charitable Fund v. Comm'r, 70 T.C. 182 (1978), aff'd, 603 F.2d 1274 (7th Cir. 1979).

plored and expounded on is the doctrine of private inurement.[372] Many of these cases under review and being decided are turning on the question of whether private interests are being unduly served. Thus, two courts have found that genealogical societies improperly (for tax exemption purposes) provide personal services to members when the societies help their members research their ancestry.[373] One set of cases has resulted in opinions that there is unwarranted private inurement with respect to a religious organization because of its communal structure, where meals, lodging, and other life necessities are provided to the ministers.[374] Other decisions contain analyses as to why particular facts may concern educational efforts,[375] or may involve private inurement, or why the inurement that is present is either insubstantial or unavoidable and incidental.[376]

These cases are also triggering examinations of the requirement that tax-exempt organizations be organized and operated exclusively for exempt purposes. The parameters of this requirement are being tested by cases that involve questions such as whether, or the extent to which, a charitable organization can operate at a profit or can provide services to members.[377]

The courts in these declaratory judgment cases are also paying close attention to the technical essentials of the organizational test.[378] In one case, a court ruled that an organization could not qualify for tax exemption because of a defect in its articles of organization, in that the articles did not expressly preclude the possibility of a violation of the test by operation of state law.[379]

Current and future developments in this area will continue to have an enormous impact on the revision and expansion of the federal tax law applicable to charitable organizations. These procedures are contributing to the federal tax law affecting charitable organizations on many fronts.

(c) Other Approaches

Other options may be open, as to court jurisdiction, for the organization confronted with revocation (or denial) of tax-exempt status. Where charitable

---

[372] See Chapter 19.

[373] See *supra* note 368.

[374] See *supra* note 369.

[375] Big Mama Rag, Inc. v. United States, 631 F.2d 1030 (D.C. Cir. 1980), *rev'g and rem'g*, 494 F. Supp. 473 (D.D.C. 1979); Afro-American Purchasing Center, Inc. v. Comm'r, 37 T.C.M. 184 (1978).

[376] Christian Stewardship Assistance, Inc. v. Comm'r, 70 T.C. 1037 (1978), *aff'd*, 647 F.2d 170 (9th Cir. 1981); est of Hawaii v. Comm'r, 71 T.C. 1067 (1979); Federation Pharmacy Servs., Inc. v. Comm'r, 72 T.C. 687 (1979), *aff'd*, 625 F.2d 804 (8th Cir. 1980).

[377] Pulpit Resource v. Comm'r, *supra* note 355; National Ass'n for the Legal Support of Alternative Schools v. Comm'r, 71 T.C. 118 (1978); Aid to Artisans, Inc. v. Comm'r, 71 T.C. 202 (1978); Christian Manner Int'l, Inc. v. Comm'r, 71 T.C. 661 (1979); Peoples Translation Service/ Newsfront Int'l v. Comm'r, *supra* note 358; Industrial Aid for the Blind v. Comm'r, 73 T.C. 96 (1979); The Schoger Found. v. Comm'r, *supra* note 361.

[378] See § 4.3.

[379] General Conference of the Free Church of America v. Comm'r, 71 T.C. 920 (1979). In general, Lehrfeld, "Section 501(c)(3) Appeals—Declaratory Judgments for Establishing Exemption," 43 N.Y.U. *Inst. on Fed. Tax.* 18 (1985); Winslow & Ash, "Forum Shopping Has Distinct Advantages in Seeking Declaratory Judgments on Exemption," 51 *J. Tax.* 112 (1979); McGovern, "The New Declaratory Judgment Provision for 501(c)(3) Organizations: How It Works," 47 *J. Tax.* 222 (1977).

contributions are involved, a "friendly donor" may bring an action contesting the legality of the IRS disallowance of the charitable deduction (which generally will involve the same issues) as those relating to exemption.[380] A lawsuit of this nature, however, requires a plaintiff who is willing to be subjected to a tax audit and the organization may lose control over the management of the litigation. An organization may also sue for refund of Federal Unemployment Tax Act (FUTA) taxes,[381] excise taxes,[382] or wagering taxes.[383] While these avenues of review can take much more time than a declaratory judgment action, they offer the distinct advantage of enabling the organization to initiate the litigation in a federal court geographically proximate to it.

Conventional declaratory judgment suits[384] are of no avail in this setting, as the Declaratory Judgment Act expressly excludes controversies over federal taxes from its purview.[385]

One of the considerations in determining the nature of litigation in the tax-exempt organizations context is the likelihood of the award of reasonable litigation costs. This type of award can be made in the case of a civil proceeding brought by or against the federal government in connection with the determination, collection, or refund of any federal tax.[386] This award is accorded to the prevailing party that establishes that the position of the government in the proceeding "was not substantially justified" and has substantially prevailed with respect to the amount in controversy or the "most significant issue or set of issues presented.[387] However, an award is not available with respect to any declaratory judgment proceeding, other than a proceeding that involves the revocation of a determination that the organization is a charitable entity.[388]

Once an organization has secured a final determination from a court that it is tax-exempt, and if the material facts and law have not changed since court consideration, the IRS will, on request, issue a ruling or determination letter recognizing the exemption. If, however, the organization did not previously file an application for recognition of exempt status, the IRS will not issue the ruling or determination letter until the application is submitted.[389]

---

[380] E.g., Teich v. Comm'r, 48 T.C. 963 (1967), aff'd, 407 F.2d 815 (7th Cir. 1969); Krohn v. United States, 246 F. Supp. 341 (D. Col. 1965); Kuper v. Comm'r, 332 F2d 562 (3d Cir. 1964), cert. den., 379 U.S. 902 (1964); Bolton v. Comm'r, 1 T.C. 717 (1943).

[381] IRC § 3306(c)(8).

[382] IRC § 4253(h).

[383] IRC § 4421. Also Rochester Liederkranz, Inc. v. United States, 456 F.2d 152 (2d Cir. 1972); Hessman v. Campbell, 134 F. Supp. 415 (S.D. Ind. 1955).

[384] 28 U.S.C. §§ 2201-2202.

[385] E.g., Ecclesiastical Order of the ISM of AM, Inc. v. Internal Revenue Service, 725 F.2d 398 (6th Cir. 1984); Mitchell v. Riddell, 401 F.2d 842 (9th Cir. 1968), cert. den., 394 U.S. 456 (1969); In re Wingreen Co., 412 F.2d 1048 (5th Cir. 1969); Jolles Found., Inc. v. Moysey, 250 F.2d 1966 (2d Cir. 1957); The Church of the New Testament, Its Members & Friends v. United States, 85-1 U.S.T.C. ¶ 9227 (E.D. Col. 1984); Int'l Tel. & Tel. Corp. v. Alexander, 396 F. Supp. 1150 (D. Del. 1975); Kyron Found. v. Dunlop, 110 F. Supp. 428 (D.D.C. 1952).

[386] IRC § 7430(a).

[387] IRC § 7430(c)(2).

[388] IRC § 7430(b)(3).

[389] Rev. Proc. 80-28, 1980-1 C.B. 680.

Absent relief administratively or in the courts, an organization facing loss of tax-exempt status has no choice but to accept the revocation, discontinue the disqualifying activity (if its activities are sufficiently separable), and reestablish its exemption,[390] or spin the disqualifying activity off into a taxable subsidiary[391] or an auxiliary exempt organization[392] and reestablish its exemption. Or, the organization may attempt an alternative to formal exempt status, such as by operating as a nonexempt cooperative.[393]

§ 24.7 THIRD-PARTY LITIGATION

As noted at the outset, an organization's tax-exempt status may be maintained absent a material change in the pertinent facts or a change in the law.[394] The organization generally will have control over the former circumstances but relatively little opportunity to affect the latter. One way, however, to have an impact on the development of the law of tax-exempt organizations is to bring a third-party lawsuit.

(a) Third-Party Lawsuits in General

A third-party suit in this context is an action brought by one or more persons as a challenge to an IRS policy in administering the law of tax-exempt organizations or other tax law. The person bringing the suit is rarely doing so as a "taxpayer," and this type of a suit is not framed as a conventional U.S. Tax Court or refund suit. The defendants usually are the Secretary of the Treasury and/or the Commissioner of Internal Revenue. Depending on the outcome of the suit, the resulting change in law can have considerable implications for one or more categories of exempt organizations.

The third-party policy suit challenging a principle of the law of tax-exempt organizations is an amalgam of a series of "public interest" suits in the tax field[395]

---

[390] Compare Danz v. Comm'r, 18 T.C. 454 (1952), aff'd, 231 F.2d 673 (9th Cir. 1955), cert. den., 352 U.S. 828 (1956), reh. den., 353 U.S. 951 (1957), with John Danz Charitable Trust v. Comm'r, 32 T.C. 469 (1959), aff'd, 284 F.2d 726 (9th Cir. 1960).

[391] American Inst. for Economic Research, Inc. v. United States, 302 F.2d 934 (Ct. Cl. 1962), cert. den., 372 U.S. 976 (1963); Rev. Rul. 54-243, 1954-1 C.B. 92.

[392] Center on Corporate Responsibility, Inc. v. Shultz, supra note 295.

[393] See § 3.4. In general, Friedland, "Constitutional Issues in Revoking Religious Tax Exemptions: Church of Scientology of California v. Commissioner," 39 U. Fla. L. Rev. 565 (1985); Yaffa, "The Revocation of Tax Exemptions and Tax Deductions for Donations to 501(c)(3) Organizations on Statutory and Constitutional Grounds," 30 U.C.L.A. L. Rev. 156 (1982).

The proposed revocation of the tax-exempt status of the public charity known as the Bishop Estate, in Hawaii, and the IRS's insistence on resignation or removal of its trustees as a condition of settlement (which occurred) stimulated discussion as to the propriety of the IRS's stance in the case. E.g., Brody, "A Taxing Time for the Bishop Estate: What Is the IRS's Role in Charity Governance?," 21 Univ. Hawaii L. Rev. (No. 2) 537 (Winter 1999).

[394] See text accompanied by supra notes 2–4.

[395] E.g., Tax Analysts & Advocates v. Shultz, 376 F. Supp. 889 (D.D.C. 1974); Tax Analysts & Advocates v. Internal Revenue Service, 362 F. Supp. 1298 (D.D.C. 1973); Common Cause v. Shultz, 73-2 U.S.T.C. ¶ 9592 (D.D.C. 1973).

and a variety of tax suits raising constitutional questions. As respects the latter, in the principal case, the courts involved concluded that racially discriminatory private schools were not entitled to federal tax exemption.[396] Comparable cases, with fainter relationships to constitutional principles, led to decisions that racially discriminatory fraternal organizations were not entitled to exemption,[397] although racially discriminatory social clubs[398] were not barred from exempt status,[399] that charitable organizations will not lose their exemption because they discriminate in their membership policies on the basis of sex,[400] and that unions that expend membership dues for partisan political campaigns do not for that reason forfeit their exempt status.[401]

These cases have given rise, however, to cases that strictly involve "policy" questions—questions previously answered only by the Department of the Treasury in its regulations, the IRS in its rulings, or the courts in passing on the tax status of particular organizations who were parties to the suit. One of the most prominent cases in this category caused a federal appellate court to consider IRS policy as to the criteria for a tax-exempt hospital and pronounce a revision of that policy valid.[402] A lawsuit unsuccessfully sought to enjoin Treasury and IRS officials from granting charitable status to otherwise charitable organizations that substantially provide commercial travel services and from refusing to enforce the unrelated business income tax provisions.[403] Similarly, a for-profit consulting company failed in its attempt to cause the revocation of the exempt status of a nonprofit research organization for the latter's refusal to include the company's product in its research and testing program.[404] Likewise, individuals who claimed they were forced out of the restaurant business because of the competitive activities of exempt social clubs were unsuccessful in their effort to have the clubs' exemptions revoked.[405]

The continuing viability of these types of cases is questionable, inasmuch as the U.S. Supreme Court discourages this type of litigation.[406] It accomplishes this objective by issuing opinions articulating its concept of the law of standing.[407] In

---

[396] Green v. Kennedy, 309 F. Supp. 1127 (D.D.C. 1970); *app. dis. sub nom.* Cannon v Green, 398 U.S. 956 (1970), *cont. sub nom.* Green v. Connally, 330 F. Supp. 1150 (D.D.C. 1971), *aff'd on intervenors' appeal sub nom.*, Coit v. Green, 404 U.S. 997 (1971). See § 5.4(a).

[397] See § 18.4(a).

[398] See Chapter 14.

[399] McGlotten v. Connally, 338 F. Supp. 448 (1972).

[400] McCoy v. Shultz, 73-1 U.S.T.C. ¶ 9233 (D.D.C. 1973).

[401] IRC § 501(c)(5). Marker v. Connally, 485 F.2d 1003 (D.C. Cir. 1973), *aff'g* 837 F. Supp. 1301 (D.D.C. 1972).

[402] Eastern Ky. Welfare Rights Org. v. Simon, 560 F.2d 1278 (D.C. Cir. 1974), *rev'g* 370 F. Supp. 325 (D.D.C. 1973). Also Penn v. San Juan Hosp., Inc., 528 F.2d 1181 (10th Cir. 1975).

[403] American Soc'y of Travel Agents v. Simon, 75-1 U.S.T.C. ¶ 9454 (D.D.C. 1975), *aff'd*, 556 F.2d 145 (D.C. Cir. 1977), *cert. den.*, 435 U.S. 947 (1978). Also Pharmaceutical & Diagnostic Serv's, Inc. v. Univ. of Utah, 1989 U.S. Dist. LEXIS 11857 (D. Utah 1989); Council of British Soc. in S. Calif. v. United States, 78-2 U.S.T.C. ¶ 9744 (C.D. Cal. 1978).

[404] Research Consulting Assocs., Inc. v. Electric Power Research Inst., 626 F. Supp. 1330 (D. Mass. 1986).

[405] Drake v. North Dakota, 1995 U.S. Dist. LEXIS 8967 (D.N.D. 1995).

[406] Simon v. Eastern Ky. Welfare Rights Org., 426 U.S. 26 (1976).

[407] See *infra* § (b).

one instance the Court, in a case initiated by indigents and organizations of indigents seeking judicial review of IRS criteria for exempting nonprofit hospitals from income tax, held that the plaintiffs lacked standing to bring the suit within the framework of Article III of the U.S. Constitution, which requires the existence of an authentic "case or controversy." Nonetheless, the Court stated that "[we] do not reach . . . the question of whether a third party *ever* may challenge the IRS treatment of another."[408]

Still, the standing test as formulated in this decision was designed to curb the type of litigation represented by that case. The Court summarized the standing requirement as follows: "when a plaintiff's standing is brought into issue the relevant inquiry is whether, assuming justiciability of the claim, the plaintiff has shown an injury to himself that is likely to be redressed by a favorable decision."[409] The Court's interpretation of that requirement in this context means that an organization's "abstract concern with a subject that could be affected by an adjudication does not substitute for the concrete injury required by Article III."[410] Thus, the plaintiffs in the case lost because they could not demonstrate the needed "concrete injury" (stated in a previous decision as the requisite "personal stake in the outcome of the controversy"[411]) and because, even if the hospitals had caused injury, the plaintiffs proceeded not against those institutions but against federal officials. (The second, "non-constitutional" standing requirement that the interest of a plaintiff be "arguably within the zone of interests to be protected or regulated" by the statutory framework within which his or her claim arises[412] went unconsidered in the opinion.[413])

The author of a concurring opinion in this case observed that "I cannot now imagine a case, at least outside the First Amendment area, where a person whose own tax liability was not affected ever could have standing to litigate the federal tax liability of someone else."[414] This gratuitous comment is, however, unduly sweeping. For example, an organization ruled by the IRS to be a supported organization[415] would have standing to bring suit against the Secretary of the Treasury and Commissioner of Internal Revenue contesting the legality of the determination on the ground that the alleged supporting organization was not in compliance with the statute's essentials (thereby depriving the alleged supported

---

[408] Simon v. Eastern Ky. Welfare Rights Org., *supra* note 406, at 37 (emphasis added).

[409] *Id.* at 38.

[410] *Id.* at 40, citing Sierra Club v. Morton, 405 U.S. 727 (1972).

[411] Worth v. Seldin, 422 U.S. 490, 498 (1975).

[412] Ass'n of Data Processing Serv. Org. v. Camp, 397 U.S. 150, 153 (1969). In Wright v. Regan, 81-2 U.S.T.C. ¶ 9504 (D.C. Cir. 1981), the court held that the parents of black children in public schools had standing to bring a class action suit claiming that IRC § 501(a) promoted discrimination by permitting recognition of tax exemption of racially discriminatory private schools. Also Tax Analysts v. Blumenthal, 566 F.2d 130 (D.C. Cir. 1977), *cert. den.*, 434 U.S. 1086 (1977).

[413] Commentary on the *Eastern Kentucky* case appears in Note, 30 *Tax Law.* 490 (1977); Note, 1977 *Wis. L. Rev.* 247 (1977); Note, 29 *Tax Law.* 361 (1976); Note, 7 *U. Toledo L. Rev.* 278 (1975); Note, 73 *Col. L. Rev.* 1502 (1973).

[414] Simon v. Eastern Ky. Welfare Rights Org., *supra* note 406, at 46.

[415] See Chapter 11.

organization of funds) and thus should be classified as a private foundation (and be liable for taxes imposed on these entities).

A justice criticized his brethren for not deciding the case against the plaintiffs on the ground that the case involved largely hypothetical situations and hence was not a ripe controversy. He also complained that the majority unnecessarily and erroneously treated the "injury-in-fact" standing requirement in direct conflict with prior decisions of the Court, in part by laying down a standard of pleading of facts not "in keeping with modern notions of civil procedure."[416]

On this latter point, this justice stated that, in Administrative Procedure Act cases, "standing is not to be denied merely because the ultimate harm alleged is a threatened future one rather than an accomplished fact."[417] (The "ultimate harm" alleged in the case was that tax-exempt hospitals, as encouraged by the IRS, would cease providing medical services to indigents.) The justice did some hypothesizing of his own,[418] wondering if, as the result of the opinion, "minority school children [will] now have to plead and show that in the absence of illegal governmental 'encouragement' of private segregated schools, such schools would not 'elect to forego' their favorable tax treatment, and that this will 'result in the availability' to complainants of an integrated educational system"[419] or if "black Americans [will] be required to plead and show that in the absence of illegal government encouragement, private institutions would not 'elect to forego' favorable tax treatment, and that this will 'result in the availability' to complain[an]ts of services previously denied."[420]

This justice found the "most disturbing aspect" of the opinion to be the Court's "insistence on resting its decision regarding standing squarely on the irreducible Art. III minimum of injury in fact, thereby effectively placing its holding beyond congressional power to rectify."[421] He added: "Thus, any time Congress chooses to legislate in favor of certain interests by setting up a scheme of incentives for third parties, judicial review of administrative action that allegedly frustrates the congressionally intended objective will be denied, because any complainant will be required to make an almost impossible showing."[422] He stated the ultimate objective well: "In our modern-day society, dominated by complex legislative programs and large-scale governmental involvement in the everyday lives of all of us, judicial review of administrative action is essential both for protection of individuals illegally harmed by that action . . . and to ensure that the attainment of congressionally mandated goals is not frustrated by illegal action."[423]

---

[416] Simon v. Eastern Ky. Welfare Rights Org., *supra* note 406, at 62.

[417] *Id.* at 61.

[418] *Id.* at 63.

[419] Citing Green v. Kennedy, *supra* note 396.

[420] Citing McGlotten v. Connally, *supra* note 399; Pitts v. Wisconsin Dep't of Revenue, 333 F. Supp. 662 (E.D. Wis. 1971).

[421] Simon v Eastern Ky. Welfare Rights Org., *supra* note 406, at 64.

[422] *Id.*

[423] *Id.* at 65. In general, Sheldon & Bostock, "Supreme Court Severely Limits Third Party's Right to Contest Exempt Status," 45 J. Tax. 140 (1976).

(b) Standing

The impact of the U.S. Supreme Court's pronouncement on this subject has been somewhat ameliorated as the result of enactment of the declaratory judgment procedures for contesting loss or denial of tax-exempt and similar status for charitable organizations.[424] Although third-party suits are not involved as such, these procedures are greatly enhancing the likelihood and frequency of court review of IRS determinations in the tax-exempt organizations field.

Despite the government's attempts to invoke the doctrine of sovereign immunity, the courts have generally held that the doctrine does not bar actions against government officials who allegedly are acting in excess of their statutory authority or discretion or in an unconstitutional manner.[425] The general prohibition on injunctive relief[426] was held to not be a bar to these suits because they bear no relation to the assessment or collection of taxes.[427] The Declaratory Judgment Act likewise was found to not be a bar to jurisdiction, on the ground that its scope is coterminous with the injunctive relief rule.[428]

Aside from these and other alleged bars to jurisdiction, the courts have held that various statutes provide jurisdiction. Thus, jurisdiction in these cases has been fully asserted on the basis of the Administrative Procedure Act[429] and the Declaratory Judgment Act, the pendent jurisdiction rules,[430] and the more conventional jurisdictional basis.[431] Still another hurdle these suits, in many instances, have cleared is *standing*, which is a prerequisite of any court action. Basically, a plaintiff must be able to demonstrate a direct injury and the requisite personal stake in the controversy.[432] The focus of these principles is far from clear,[433] as the above-discussed U.S. Supreme Court decision indicates.

The future of third-party suits in the tax-exempt organizations field is uncertain, in view of the above-discussed Supreme Court opinion and the decision of Congress to confine the exempt organizations declaratory judgment procedure to use "by the organization the qualification or classification of which is at issue."[434] In the first case to be considered by a court of appeals following the

---

[424] See *supra* § 6(b).

[425] E.g., Dugan v. Rank, 372 U.S. 609 (1963); State Highway Comm'n of Mo. v. Volpe, 479 F.2d 1099 (8th Cir. 1973). So held in Eastern Ky. Welfare Rights Org. v. Simon, *supra* note 402; McGlotten v. Connally, *supra* note 399.

[426] IRC § 7421(a).

[427] Eastern Ky. Welfare Rights Org. v. Simon, *supra* note 402; McGlotten v. Connally, *supra* note 399.

[428] E.g., Jules Hairstylists of Md. v. United States, 268 F. Supp. 511 (D. Md. 1967), aff'd, 389 F.2d 389 (4th Cir. 1968), *cert. den.*, 391 U.S. 934 (1968). So held in, e.g., Eastern Ky. Welfare Rights Org. v. Simon, *supra* note 402; "Americans United" Inc. v. Walters, *supra* note 293, at 447 F.2d 1176.

[429] 5 U.S.C. §§ 702, 703.

[430] 28 U.S.C. §§ 2282, 2284. E.g., Zemel v. Rusk, 381 U.S. 1 (1965).

[431] 28 U.S.C. §§ 1331, 1340, 1361.

[432] Frothingham v. Mellon, 262 U.S. 447 (1923); Flast v. Colien, 392 U.S. 83 (1968); Ass'n of Data Processing Serv. Org. v. Camp, *supra* note 412; Tax Analysts & Advocates v. Simon, 390 F. Supp. 927 (D.D.C. 1975).

[433] United States v. Richardson, 418 U.5. 166 (1974); Schlesinger v. Reservists Comm. to Stop the War, 418 U.S. 208 (1974); United States v. Students Challenging Regulatory Agency Procedures, 412 U.S. 669 (1973).

[434] IRC § 7428(b)(1).

■   **703**   ■

Court's ruling, the appellate court had deferred its consideration of the case pending the Court's determination and, once the Court ruled, affirmed the lower court's dismissal of the case but on the ground of lack of standing.[435] The court concluded that the plaintiff organization failed to demonstrate any actual injury resulting from the administration of the tax laws, with respect to third parties, governing exempt organizations.

Certainly this line of litigation produced much uncertainty about the appropriate tax treatment of particular activities and programs of tax-exempt organizations.[436] Moreover, these cases generated considerable controversy as to the proper roles of the courts, the IRS, and the Department of the Treasury in formulating the law of tax-exempt organizations.[437]

Nonetheless, third-party litigation over tax exemption issues continues. As illustrations, the debate over the tax status of private schools with racially discriminatory policies was resumed, in part, because the original litigation was reopened,[438] and the challenge on equal protection grounds to the disparate treatment of charitable and veterans' groups that lobby was, for a while, successful.[439]

One of the most striking examples of third-party litigation in the tax-exempt organizations setting arose in mid-1982, when a federal district court ruled that a variety of organizations and individuals had standing to challenge the constitutionality of the government's alleged refusal to enforce the restrictions in the general rules for charitable organizations on legislative and political campaign involvements[440] against a church.[441] The plaintiffs in the case sued the Secretary of the Treasury and the Commissioner of Internal Revenue on the ground that they failed in their responsibility to revoke the exempt status of the church because of its alleged legislative and electioneering activities. These activities were seen by the plaintiffs, which included a charitable organization, as being in direct conflict with the limitations on lobbying and electioneering in the tax law under which the church and its affiliates continue to be exempt. By contrast, the plaintiffs asserted that the IRS refused to grant to organizations with opposing views (such as the plaintiff exempt organization) exemption as charitable entities where they engage in comparable legislative and electioneering activities. The plaintiffs contended that this was discriminatory tax policy that was unconstitutional, illegal, and unfair.

Before considering the claims of these plaintiffs on their merits, the court had to dispose of a variety of motions, including the government's motion to dis-

---

[435] American Soc'y of Travel Agents, Inc. v. Simon, *supra* note 403.

[436] E.g., Jackson v. Statler Found., 496 F.2d 623 (2d Cir. 1974).

[437] Tannenbaum, "Public Interest Tax Litigation Challenging Substantive I.R.S. Decisions," 27 *Nat'l Tax J.* 373 (1974); Worthy, "Judicial Determinations of Exempt Status: Has the Time Come for a Change of Systems?," 40 *J. Tax.* 324 (1974).

[438] Wright v. Regan, 656 F.2d 820 (D.C. Cir. 1981).

[439] Taxation With Representation of Wash. v. Regan, 676 F.2d 715 (D.C. Cir. 1982).

[440] See Chapters 20, 21.

[441] Abortion Rights Mobilization, Inc. v. Regan, 544 F. Supp. 471 (S.D.N.Y. 1982). Also 552 F. Supp. 364 (S.D.N.Y. 1982).

miss for lack of standing. The court considered three bases for standing: establishment clause standing, voter standing, and equal protection standing. The essential elements for standing, said the court, are a "distinct and palpable injury" to the plaintiff, a "fairly traceable causal connection between the claimed injury and the challenged conduct," and a showing that the "exercise of the Court's remedial powers would redress the claimed injuries."[442]

As to establishment clause standing, most of the plaintiffs were found to have failed the injury-in-fact test. Said the court: "Plaintiffs' devotion to . . . [its] position does not identify an interest that the allegedly illegal activities have damaged; it only explains why plaintiffs have chosen to complain about a particular government impropriety—renewal of the church defendants' [IRC] § 501(c)(3) status."[443] The plaintiffs who were members of the clergy, however, were found to have shown "compelling and personalized injuries flowing from the tacit government endorsement of the . . . [church's] position on . . . [issues] that are sufficient to confer standing on them to complain of the alleged establishment clause violations."[444] In language that suggested the government was going to lose the case on the merits, the court ruled that the "causation" and "redressability" tests were also satisfied. As to the former, the court said: "The granting of a uniquely favored tax status to one religious entity is an unequivocal statement of preference that gilds the image of that religion and tarnishes all others."[445] As to the latter, the court observed: "A decree ordering the termination of this illegal practice and restoring all sects to equal footing will redress this injury."[446]

Concerning voter standing, the underlying issue was whether some arbitrary government action diluted the strength of voters in one group at the expense of those in another group. Finding this type of standing in the plaintiffs, the court concluded: "Plaintiffs claim that allegedly unconstitutional government conduct and illegal private conduct has distorted the electoral and legislative process by creating a system in which members of the public have greater incentive to donate funds to the . . . [church] than to politically active . . . groups and in which each dollar contributed to the church is worth more than one given to non-exempt [that is, noncharitable donee] organizations."[447] Once again, in language highly suggestive of victory to the plaintiffs (at least at the district court level), the court stated: "An injunction against that discriminatory policy will restore the proper balance between adversaries in the abortion debate."[448]

As to the equal protection basis for standing, the court rejected the contention

---

[442] *Id.* at 476-477.
[443] *Id.* at 478.
[444] *Id.* at 479.
[445] *Id.* at 480.
[446] *Id.*
[447] *Id.* at 482.
[448] *Id.* Cf. Keane v. Baker, 1987 W.L. 8052 (W.D.N.Y. 1987) (where, in holding that a defeated candidate for public office lacked standing to sue the IRS in an attempt to cause revocation of the tax-exempt status of an organization allegedly involved in political campaign activities on behalf of his opponent, a court rejected broad applicability of the concept of voter standing).

that the plaintiffs could prevail on Fifth Amendment grounds. The court also found that the litigation was outside the reach of the Anti-Injunction Act[449] and that conventional declaratory relief[450] was not available to the plaintiffs.[451]

In 1984, however, the U.S. Supreme Court issued an opinion that made successful third-party lawsuits more difficult to structure.[452] The Court held that parents of black children in public schools lacked standing to bring an action to force the IRS to adopt more stringent rules to deny tax-exempt status and deductible contributions to racially discriminatory private schools.[453] While the proponents of this litigation did not claim that their children were denied access to private schools, they claimed direct injury in the form of denigration suffered by reason of the grant of exempt status to educational institutions that discriminate against members of their race.

The Court analyzed the case or controversy requirement of Article III of the U.S. Constitution, from which, as noted, the concept of standing is derived. To successfully achieve standing, wrote the Court, a plaintiff must allege personal injury "fairly traceable" to a defendant's allegedly unlawful conduct and likely to be redressed by the requested relief.[454] In the case, the Court ruled that this denigration injury does not constitute judicially cognizable injury, nor does any adverse impact on the plaintiffs' "equal educational opportunities" that may be occasioned as the result of the tax exemption and charitable deduction. As to the latter claim, the Court ruled that the injury alleged is not fairly traceable to any conduct of the IRS.

---

[449] IRC § 7421. E.g., In re Heritage Village Church & Missionary Fellowship, Inc., 851 F.2d 104 (4th Cir. 1988).

[450] IRC § 2201.

[451] A similar suit, challenging the tax-exempt status of the World Zionist Organization American Section, Inc., Jewish Agency American Section, Inc., United Israel Appeal, Inc., United Jewish Appeal, Inc, Jewish National Fund, Inc., and Americans for a Safe Israel, Inc., was filed in 1983. The case was dismissed in 1985, however, shortly after the Supreme Court decisions finding any correlation between tax exemption for allegedly racially discriminatory public schools and denigration of black individuals to be "speculative" (see *infra* notes 452–455) with the court observing that it would be "more fanciful still to assume here that the government of Israel is so responsive to changes in U.S. tax laws that the withdrawal of benefits from U.S. contributors will work any alteration whatsoever in the character of its occupation of territory it now holds by force in the Middle East" (Khalaf et al. v. Regan et al., 85-1 U.S.T.C. ¶ 9269 (D.D.C. 1985)). Likewise, an exempt organization formed to advance civil and religious liberties, other religious organizations and then-officials, and individual members of the clergy of various denominations were found to lack standing as taxpayers, citizens, and voters, and as victims of stigmatization, to sue the President, the Secretary of the Treasury, and the United States Ambassador to the Vatican to enjoin the funding of a diplomatic mission to the Vatican and to enjoin the ambassador from engaging in ambassadorial activity (Americans United for Separation of Church & State v. Reagan, 786 F.2d 194 (3d Cir. 1986)).

Litigation against employees of the Department of the Treasury and IRS is likely to be unsuccessful, in that these employees are insulated from lawsuits where reasonable grounds existed for the belief that the challenged actions were appropriate and they acted in good faith (e.g., The Ecclesiastical Order of the ISM of AM, Inc. v. Chasin, 653 F. Supp. 1200 (E.D. Mich. 1986), *aff'd*, 845 F.2d 113 (6th Cir. 1988); Judicial Watch, Inc. v. Rossotti, 223 F. Supp. 2d 698 (D. Md. 2002)).

[452] Allen v. Wright, 468 U.S. 737 (1984).

[453] See § 5.4(a).

[454] Allen v. Wright, *supra* note 452, at 751.

It thus appeared that lawsuits brought solely to challenge governmental policies, absent the requisite direct injury, would fail on the standing issue. The Court counseled "against recognizing standing in a case brought, not to enforce specific legal obligations whose violation works in direct harm, but to seek a restructuring of the apparatus established by its legal duties."[455]

Notwithstanding this Supreme Court decision, however, the court in the church case maintained its position on the standing issue.[456] Unlike the Court, the district court found the requisite direct link between the injury that was the subject of the complaint and governmental action. Finding a "quasi-official imprimatur accorded the anti-abortion activities of the [c]hurch through tax exemptions and the restrictions placed on the establishment clause plaintiffs' political activities by [IRC] § 501(c)(3)," the court held that "[r]edress will come directly from the government's consistent enforcement of the tax laws, not from any change in the political activities of the [c]hurch."[457] Added the court: "The injury alleged . . . [in the case] is unequal footing in the political arena, a condition completely traceable [to] and within the control of the IRS."[458] The court in the case wrote that, the Supreme Court "did not close the door on private suits challenging government grants of tax exemption."[459]

Subsequently, however, a federal court of appeals decided that the district court in this case lacked jurisdiction over the matter because the plaintiffs failed to satisfy the standing requirements.[460] The appellate court explored the principles of clergy standing, taxpayer standing, and voter standing as they applied in the context of this case, as well as jurisdiction predicated upon the doctrine of "competitive advocate standing." The court wrote that the clergy plaintiffs "have not been injured in a sufficiently personal way to distinguish themselves from other citizens who are generally aggrieved by a claimed constitutional violation."[461] Taxpayer standing was rejected because of violation of the "basic rule . . . that taxpayers do not have standing to challenge how the federal government spends tax revenue."[462] Voter standing was not found since the plaintiffs' "asserted basis for standing has nothing to do with voting."[463] Competitive advocate standing was held absent "since by their [plaintiffs'] own admission they choose not to match the [c]hurch's alleged electioneering with their own," so that the plaintiffs are not competitors.[464] Addressing the point that, if no one among this diverse group of plaintiffs has standing in this case, then no one could have standing to raise these issues, the appellate court summarily observed that the

---

[455] *Id.* at 761.
[456] Abortion Rights Mobilization, Inc. et al. v. Regan, 603 F. Supp. 970 (S.D.N.Y. 1985).
[457] *Id.* at 973.
[458] *Id.* at 974, 971.
[459] *Id.* at 971.
[460] In re: United States Catholic Conference & Nat'l Conference of Catholic Bishops, 885 F.2d 1020 (2d Cir. 1989).
[461] *Id.* at 1024–1025.
[462] *Id.* at 1027.
[463] *Id.* at 1028.
[464] *Id.* at 1029.

"lack of a plaintiff to litigate an issue may suggest that the matter is more appropriately dealt with by Congress and the political process."[465] By reason of this holding that none of the plaintiffs in this case had standing, the appellate court concluded that the district court lacked subject matter jurisdiction. Subsequently, the U.S. Supreme Court declined to review this case, thereby ending a decade of litigation over the issue.[466]

Consequently, it appears that nearly all forms of third-party litigation will not satisfy the requirements of standing as interpreted by the Supreme Court.[467] In any event, a somewhat functional equivalent of the third-party suit is available. The congressional committee reports constituting part of the legislative history of the Tax Reform Act of 1976 stated that Congress's silence on third-party litigation "constitutes neither an implied endorsement nor an implied criticism of such 'third-party' suits."[468] Nonetheless, Congress indicated its intent that the courts should be reasonably "generous" in accepting amicus curiae briefs and permitting appearances by third parties in these suits.[469]

24.8 THE IRS AUDIT

(a) General Rules

The IRS is empowered to audit the activities and records of tax-exempt organizations. This examination activity is designed to assure that exempt organizations are in compliance with all pertinent requirements of the federal tax law.[470] Consequently, the likelihood of an IRS audit continues to be a concern to organizations as a factor affecting continuation of their exemption (and, where applicable, their private foundation status), susceptibility to the tax on unrelated income, deferred

---

[465] *Id.* at 1031.
[466] Abortion Rights Mobilization, Inc. v. United States Catholic Conference, *cert. den.*, 495 U.S. 918 (1990). In general, Dunec, "Voter Standing: A New Means for Third Parties to Challenge the Tax-Exempt Status of Nonprofit Organizations?," 16 *Hastings Const. L. Quar.* (No. 3) 453 (1989); Shimazaki, "Abortion Politics: The Roman Catholic Church's Tax-Exempt Status in Jeopardy Under Section 501(c)(3) of the Internal Revenue Code," 1988 *B.Y.U.L. Rev.* (No. 4) 799 (1988); Goldberg, "Standing for Public and Quasi-Public Interest Tax Litigants," 1978 *Wash. U. L. Q.* 571 (1978).
[467] A candidate for the U.S. presidency was found to lack standing to sue the Secretary of the Treasury to revoke the tax-exempt status of a debate-sponsoring organization on the ground that she was excluded from the debates (Fulani v. Brady, 729 F. Supp. 158 (D.D.C. 1990), *aff'd*, 935 F.2d 1324 (D.C. Cir. 1991)). Also Fulani v. Bentsen, 809 F. Supp. 1112 (S.D.N.Y. 1994), *aff'd*, 35 F.3d 49 (2d Cir. 1994); Fulani v. League of Women Voters Educational Fund, 882 F.2d 621 (2d Cir. 1989); Fulani v. Brady, 809 F. Supp. 1112 (S.D.N.Y. 1993); Fulani v. Brady, 149 F.R.D. 501 (S.D.N.Y. 1993). In general, Note, "Fighting Exclusion from Televised Presidential Debates: Minor Party Candidates' Standing to Challenge Sponsoring Organizations' Tax-Exempt Status," 90 *Mich. L. Rev.* 838 (Feb. 1992).
[468] E.g., S. Rep. 938, 94th Cong., 2d Sess. 212, note 6 (1976).
[469] *Id.*
[470] In general, McGovern, "IRS Audits of Exempt Organizations: News and Tips for the General Practitioner," 17 *Exempt Org. Tax Rev.* (No. 1) 125 (1997); Faber, "How to Handle an IRS Audit of a Tax-Exempt Organization," 16 *Exempt Org. Tax Rev.* (No. 5) 753 (1997); Arnold, Jr., "How the IRS Approves, Processes and Audits Tax-Exempt Organizations," 20 *Prac. Acct.* (No. 10) 62 (1987).

compensation and retirement programs, tax-exempt bond financing, and employment tax issues.

An IRS audit usually is initiated in the field, that is, by a local IRS office. The examiners involved are specialists in tax-exempt organizations matters. The Tax-Exempt Entities and Governmental Entities Division in the IRS National Office establishes the procedures and policies for the conduct of exempt organizations audit programs. Tax-exempt organizations audits are coordinated in the IRS office in Dallas, Texas.

The IRS, from time to time, initiates audit programs targeted at particular categories of tax-exempt organizations, such as health care organizations, institutions of higher education, associations, private foundations, and social clubs. Nonetheless, audits are typically commenced on the basis of the size of the organization and the length of time that has elapsed since any prior audit. Often, an audit is undertaken as the result of an information return or a tax return,[471] inasmuch as one of the functions of the IRS is to ascertain the correctness of returns.[472] Other reasons for the development of an audit include media or third-party reports of alleged wrongdoing by a taxpayer, including investigations by a state's attorney general.

Some examinations are *office examinations* where contact by the IRS with a taxpayer is by IRS office interview.[473] A *correspondence audit* involves an IRS request for additional information from a taxpayer by letter, fax, or e-mail correspondence.[474] Other examinations are, as noted, *field examinations*, in which one or more IRS agents review the books and records of the person under examination on the person's premises.[475]

One of the problems with IRS audit practices in the past has been that a typical audit focused on an organization, ignoring subsidiaries, joint ventures, and other affiliates, and/or did not include matters outside the technical exempt organizations field, such as employment taxes. This deficiency (from the government's standpoint) was remedied with development of the *coordinated examination program*.[476] With this program, complex issues are addressed and managed using a team audit approach. The objectives of the coordinated examination program are to perform effectively planned and managed coordinated examinations, secure support for district assistance where appropriate, and accumulate and disseminate novel examination techniques, issues unique to specific organizations, tax avoidance and examination schemes, and other useful examination information.

A coordinated examination case focuses on a domestic or foreign organization, along with controlled entities, the organizational structure of which, or geo-

---

[471] Reg. § 601.103(b).
[472] IRC § 7602(a).
[473] Reg. § 601.105(b)(2).
[474] *Id.*
[475] Reg. § 601.105(b)(3).
[476] The coordinated examination program is the subject of IRS Exempt Organizations Guidelines Handbook (IRM 7(10)(18) 69), which provides the procedures and guidelines that have been developed to promote uniformity and consistency in the management of coordinated examination cases.

graphic dispersion or other examination problems, warrant application of the coordinated case procedures. These examinations are susceptible to interdistrict coordination, team audit techniques, and case manager participation. Corporations, trusts, and other forms of entities effectively controlled by the primary organization or otherwise related to the primary organization are components of the case.

The factors used in determining whether a case qualifies for the coordinated examination procedure include the amount of assets of the organization (usually more than $50 million), the gross receipts of the organization (again, usually more than $50 million), the number of controlled or otherwise related entities, the national import of the case, the team members, specialists, support agents, and the total direct examination staff-days involved.

In recent years, the coordinated examination program has concentrated on colleges, universities, and health care organizations. In this connection, the IRS has promulgated various audit guidelines.[477] The IRS is nearing completion of its audits of these entities. The future or direction of the coordinated examination procedure is unclear.[478]

Another relatively contemporary IRS examination technique is the *package audit*. This type of audit arises out of the review of one or more annual information returns and/or unrelated business income tax returns. It entails ascertainment as to whether the tax-exempt organization is filing or has filed all other required federal tax returns, such as employment tax returns, other information returns, employee benefit plan returns, and the returns of related entities.

The records that must be produced on audit are likely to include all organizational documents (such as articles of organization, bylaws, resolutions, and minutes of meetings), documents relating to tax status (such as the application for recognition of exemption and IRS rulings as to exempt and private foundation status), financial statements (including underlying entry books and records), and newsletters and other publications. The items that must be produced will depend on the type of audit being conducted; the audit may or may not encompass payroll records, pension plan matters, returns of associated individuals or subsidiary organizations, and the like. A related element is the attitude and competence of the revenue agent(s), and the degree to which the organization is prepared to cooperate in the audit. In some circumstances, the organization may find it appropriate to produce information only on the presentation of a subpoena.[479]

The techniques for coping with IRS personnel on the occasion of an audit are easily summarized but their deployment and success will depend heavily on the personalities involved. Certainly, the key staff and legal counsel of the au-

---

[477] See, e.g., *infra*, §§ (c), (d).

[478] Zeigler, "Preparation is the Best Response to the CEP Possibility," 10 *J. Tax. Exempt Orgs.* (No. 2) 79 (Sep./Oct. 1998).

[479] A discussion of enforcement proceedings in connection with IRS administrative summonses appears in *United States v. Church of Scientology of Calif.*, 520 F.2d 818 (9th Cir. 1975). In general, the U.S. Supreme Court broadly construes the IRS summons power (e.g., *United States v. Lasalle Nat'l Bank*, 437 U.S. 298 (1978), *rev'g and rem'g* 554 F.2d 302 (7th Cir. 1977)).

dited organization should be in the process from the beginning, and it is advisable to select one person who will serve as liaison with the IRS during the audit. The duration of and the procedures to be followed during the audit should be ascertained at the outset, and records should be maintained as to information and documents examined or copies by the revenue agents. Interviews should be monitored by the liaison person, with appropriate records made; at least some of the questioning should occur only in the presence of legal counsel.

Where issues arise, one or both sides may decide to pursue the technical advice procedure[480] or the matter may be taken up with the IRS by means of the conference(s) procedure.[481]

(b) Church Audits

Special statutory rules govern federal tax inquiries and churches.[482] For these purposes, a *church* includes any organization claiming to be a church or a convention or association of churches,[483] but the term does not include church-supported schools or other organizations that are incorporated separately from the church.[484]

An inquiry of a church's tax liabilities—a *church tax inquiry*—may be commenced by the IRS only where the appropriate IRS regional commissioner (or higher official) reasonably believes, on the basis of facts and circumstances recorded in writing, that the organization may not qualify for tax exemption as a church, may be carrying on an unrelated trade or business,[485] or otherwise be engaged in nonexempt activities.[486] A church tax inquiry commences when the IRS requests information or materials from a church of a type contained in church records, other than routine requests for information or inquiries regarding matters that do not primarily concern the tax status or liability of the church.[487]

---

[480] See § 23.2(a).

[481] Details of the IRS Audit Procedures for Exempt Organizations appear in the Internal Revenue Manual. IR Manual MT 4(11) 00-6.

Also, the staff of the Joint Committee on Taxation, in March 2000, published a summary of the IRS tax-exempt organizations examination process ("Report of Investigation of Allegations Relating to Internal Revenue Service Handling of Tax-Exempt Organization Matters" § V (JCS-3-00)).

[482] IRC § 7611. A court characterized these rules as follows: "The IRS has broad authority with respect to tax inquiries," although Congress "has scaled back these powers with respect to church tax inquiries"; also this provision "provides certain procedural protections to insure that the IRS does not embark on an impermissibly intrusive inquiry into church affairs" (United States v. Church of Scientology of Boston, Inc., 739 F. Supp. 46, 47 (D. Mass. 1990), *aff'd*, 933 F.2d 1074 (1st Cir. 1991)).

These rules superseded restrictions on the audits of churches for unrelated income tax purposes (IRC § 7605(c)) (e.g., United States v. Church of World Peace, 775 F.2d 265 (10th Cir. 1985)). These rules are inapplicable, however, where the inquiry is directed at one or more church leaders personally, rather than the church (e.g., St. German of Alaska E. Orthodox Catholic Church et al. v. United States, 653 F. Supp. 1342 (S.D.N.Y. 1987), *aff'd*, 840 F.2d 1087 (2d Cir. 1988)). Cf. Assembly of Yahveh Beth Israel et al. v. United States, 87-1 U.S.T.C. ¶ 9353 (D. Col. 1984).

[483] IRC § 7611(h)(1). See §§ 8.3, 8.4.

[484] H. Rep. No. 861, 98th Cong., 2d Sess. 1102 (1954).

[485] See Part Five.

[486] IRC §§ 7611(a)(1)(A), (2).

[487] IRC § 7611(h)(2).

Prior to commencement of an investigation, the IRS must provide written notice to the church, containing a general explanation of the federal statutory tax law provisions authorizing the investigation or that may otherwise be involved in the inquiry, a general explanation of the church's administrative and constitutional rights in connection with the audit (including the right to a conference with the IRS before any examination of church records), and an explanation of the concerns that gave rise to the investigation and the general subject matter of the inquiry.[488]

The explanation of the concerns and general subject matter of the inquiry must be "sufficiently specific to allow the church to understand the particular area of church activities or behavior which is at issue in the inquiry."[489] For example, as to an inquiry regarding unrelated business income, the notice should indicate the general activities of the church that may result in unrelated income, and, as to an inquiry regarding tax-exempt status, the notice should indicate the general aspects of the church's operations or activities that have given rise to questions regarding its tax-exempt status. The IRS "is not to be precluded from expanding its inquiry beyond the concerns expressed in the notice as a result of facts and circumstances which subsequently come to its attention (including, where appropriate, an expansion of an unrelated income inquiry to include questions of tax-exempt status, or vice-versa)."[490]

The notice requirement does not require the IRS to share particular items of evidence with a church or to identify its sources of information regarding church activities, where provision of the information would be damaging to the inquiry or to the sources of IRS information.[491] The facts and circumstances that form the basis for a reasonable belief under these rules must be derived from information lawfully obtained by the IRS and the information obtained from informants used by the IRS for this purpose must not be known to be unreliable.[492]

The general explanation of applicable administrative and constitutional provisions "should make reference to the various stages of the church audit procedures . . . (including the right to a preexamination conference) and the principle of separation of church and state under the First Amendment," although the explanation is "not required to explain the possible legal or constitutional ramifications of any particular church audit."[493]

The IRS may examine church records or religious activities—a *church tax examination*—only if, at least 15 days prior to the examination, the IRS provides written notice to the church and to the appropriate IRS regional counsel of the proposed examination.[494] This notice is in addition to the notice of commencement of a tax inquiry previously provided to the church. A church tax examination is any examination, for purposes of making a determination as described in

---

[488] IRC §§ 7611(a)(1)(B), (3).
[489] H. Rep. No. 861, *supra* note 484, at 1102.
[490] *Id.*
[491] *Id.*
[492] H. Rep. No. 861, *supra* note 445, at 1101.
[493] *Id.*
[494] IRC §§ 7611(b)(1),(2)(A).

the *church tax inquiry* definition, of church records at the request of the IRS or of the religious activities of any church.[495]

The notice of examination must include a copy of the church tax inquiry notice previously provided to the church, a description of the church records and activities that the IRS seeks to examine, and a copy of all documents that were collected or prepared by the agency for use in the examination, and that are required to be disclosed under the Freedom of Information Act[496] and supplemented by the federal tax law concerning disclosure and confidentiality of tax return information.[497] The documents that must be supplied under this requirement are "limited to documents specifically concerning the church whose records are to be examined and will not include documents relating to other inquiries or examinations or to IRS practices and procedures in general."[498] Disclosure to the church is "subject to the restrictions of present law regarding the disclosure of the existence or identity of informers."[499] The description of materials to be examined in the notice of examination and the documents disclosed by the IRS to the church do not restrict the ability of the IRS to examine the church records or religious activities that are properly within the scope of the examination.

The appropriate IRS regional commissioner is required, as part of the notice of examination, to offer the church an opportunity to meet with an IRS official to discuss, and attempt to resolve, the concerns that gave rise to the examination and the general subject matter of the inquiry. The organization may request this meeting at any time prior to the examination. If the church requests a meeting, the IRS is required to schedule the meeting within a reasonable time and may proceed to examine church records only following that meeting.[500] The holding of one meeting with the church is "sufficient to satisfy the requirement" and churches cannot utilize this requirement "in order to unreasonably delay an examination."[501]

The purpose of a meeting between the church and the IRS is to discuss the relevant issues that may arise as part of the inquiry, in an effort to resolve the issues of tax exemption or liability without the necessity of an examination of church records. The church and the IRS are expected to "make a reasonable effort to resolve outstanding issues at the meeting" and the IRS is expected to "remind the church at the meeting, in general terms, of the stages of the church audit procedures and the church's rights under such procedures," although the IRS is not required to "reveal information at the meeting of a type properly excludable from a written notice (including information regarding the identity of third-party witnesses or evidence provided by such witnesses)."[502]

---

[495] IRC § 7611(h)(3).
[496] 5 U.S.C. § 552.
[497] IRC § 6103.
[498] H. Rep. No. 861, *supra* note 484, at 1103-1104.
[499] *Id.* at 1104.
[500] IRC §§ 7611(b)(2), (3)(A)(iii).
[501] H. Rep. No. 861, *supra* note 484, at 1104.
[502] *Id.*

The notice of examination may be sent to a church not less than 15 days after the notice of commencement of a church tax inquiry was provided.[503] Thus, at least 30 days must pass between the first notice and the actual examination of church records. If the IRS does not send a notice of examination within 90 days after sending the notice of inquiry, the inquiry must be terminated.[504] This 90-day period is suspended during any period for which the two-year period for duration of a church audit (discussed below) would be suspended;[505] however, the 90-day period "is not to be suspended because of the church's failure to comply with requests for information made prior to the notice of examination."[506] If an inquiry or examination is terminated under this rule, any further inquiry or examination regarding the same or similar issues within a five-year period must have the approval of the IRS.[507]

At the same time as the notice of an examination is provided to a church, the IRS is required to provide a copy of the same notice to the appropriate IRS regional counsel. The regional counsel is then allowed 15 days from issuance of the notice in which to file an advisory objection to the examination.[508] This regional commissioner is expected to "take any objection by the regional counsel into account when determining whether to proceed with the examination."[509]

The IRS may examine church records only to the extent necessary to determine the liability for, and the amount of, any federal tax.[510] This may include examinations to determine the initial or continuing qualification of the organization as a tax-exempt entity,[511] to determine whether the organization qualifies to receive tax-deductible contributions, or to determine the amount of tax, if any, to be imposed on the organization.[512]

All regularly kept church corporate and financial records, including (but not limited to) corporate minute books, contributor lists, and membership lists, constitute church records.[513] The term *church records* includes "private correspondence between a church and its members that is in the possession of the church" but does "not include records previously filed with a public official or . . . newspapers or newsletters distributed generally to the church members."[514] Records held by third parties (such as cancelled checks or other records in the possession

---

[503] IRC § 7611(b)(3)(B).
[504] IRC § 7611(c)(1)(B).
[505] IRC § 7611(c)(2).
[506] H. Rep. No. 861, *supra* note 484, at 1104.
[507] IRC § 7611(f).
[508] IRC § 7611(b)(3)(C).
[509] H. Rep. No. 861, *supra* note 484, at 1105.
[510] IRC § 7611(b)(1)(A).
[511] That is, exempt from federal income tax pursuant to IRC § 501(a) by reason of description in IRC § 501(c)(3).
[512] The scope of the records of a church that the IRS may examine is discussed in United States v. C. E. Hobbs Found. for Religious Training & Educ., Inc., 93-2 U.S.T.C. ¶ 50,588 (9th Cir. 1993); United States v. Church of Scientology v. United States, 973 F.2d 715 (9th Cir. 1992), petition to the U.S. Supreme Court (No. 92-2002) dismissed on Oct. 6, 1993.
[513] IRC § 7611(h)(4).
[514] H. Rep. No. 861, *supra* note 484, at 1106.

of a bank) are not church records, so that the IRS is permitted access to these records without regard to the church audit procedures. As under general law, either the IRS or a third-party record keeper generally is required to inform a church of any IRS requests for materials.[515]

The IRS may not determine that a church is not entitled to tax exemption or assess tax for unrelated business income against a church solely on the basis of third-party records, without complying with the church audit procedures. (This rule does not apply to assessments of tax other than for unrelated business income, such as for social security or other employment taxes.) The IRS may not use information obtained from third-party bank records to avoid the purposes of the church audit procedures.[516]

The IRS may examine the religious activities of an organization claiming to be a church (or a convention or association of churches) only to the extent necessary to determine if the organization actually is a church for any period.[517]

The IRS is required to complete any church tax inquiry or examination, and make a final determination with respect to the examination or inquiry, not later than two years after the date on which the notice of examination is supplied to the church.[518] The running of this two-year period is suspended for any period during which (1) a judicial proceeding brought by the church against the IRS with respect to the church tax inquiry or examination is pending or being appealed, (2) a judicial proceeding brought by the IRS against the church or any official of the church to compel compliance with any reasonable IRS request for examination of church records or religious activities is pending or being appealed, or (3) the IRS is unable to take actions with respect to the church tax inquiry or examination by reason of an order issued in a suit involving access to third-party records.[519] The two-year period is also suspended for any period in excess of 20 days, but not in excess of six months, in which the church fails to comply with any reasonable IRS request for church records or other information. This two-year period can be extended by mutual agreement of the church and the IRS.[520]

For examinations regarding revocation of tax-exempt status, where no return is filed, the IRS is limited initially to an examination of church records that are relevant to a determination of tax status or liability for the three most recent taxable years preceding the date on which the notice of examination (the second notice) is sent to the church.[521] If the church is proven to not be exempt for any of these years, the IRS may examine relevant records and assess tax (or proceed without assessment), as part of the same audit, for a total of six years preceding the notice of examination date.[522]

[515] *Id.*
[516] *Id.*
[517] IRC § 7611(b)(1)(B).
[518] IRC § 7611(c)(1)(A).
[519] IRC § 7609.
[520] IRC § 7611(c)(2).
[521] IRC § 7611(d)(2)(A)(i).
[522] IRC § 7611(d)(2)(A)(ii).

For examinations relating to unrelated business income, where a return was not filed, the IRS may assess or collect tax for the six most recent years preceding the date on which the notice of examination is sent, with no additional limit on the period of church records that may be examined.[523] For examinations involving issues other than revocation of tax-exempt status or unrelated business income (such as examinations relating to Social Security or other employment taxes) there is no limitation period where a return has not been filed.

The special limitation periods for church tax liabilities are not to be construed to increase an otherwise applicable limitation period.[524] Thus, as under general law, a three-year limitation period applies where a church filed a tax return before an examination was held and did not substantially understate income. There is no limitation period in a case of fraud, willful tax evasion, or knowing failure to file a return that should have been filed. The applicable limitation period may be extended by mutual agreement of the church and the IRS.

The appropriate IRS regional counsel must approve, in advance and in writing, (1) any determination as to whether an organization has tax-exempt status as a church, (2) the determination of whether the organization is a church that is eligible to attract tax-deductible contributions, or (3) the issuance of a notice of tax deficiency to a church following a church tax examination (or in cases where the deficiency procedures are inapplicable, the assessment of any underpayment of tax by the church following a church tax examination). The regional counsel must state in writing that the IRS has substantially complied with the church audit procedures.[525]

The IRS must approve, in writing, any second investigation or examination of a church, unless the first investigation or examination resulted in (1) revocation of tax exemption or an assessment of tax or (2) a request by the IRS for any significant changes in church operational practices (including the adequacy or sufficiency of records maintained to reflect income). This rule applies only to second audits involving the same or similar issues as the prior audit. This approval requirement is inapplicable where the second audit does not involve the same or similar issues as the preceding inquiry or examination and the requirement applies only to second audits beginning within five years of the date on which the notice of examination was sent to the church during the prior audit (or, if no notice of examination was sent, the date of the notice of commencement of inquiry). This five-year period is suspended for periods during which the two-year period for completion of an audit is suspended (unless the prior audit was actually concluded within two years of the notice of examination). In determining whether a second audit involves issues similar to those of a prior audit, the "substantive factual issues involved in the two audits, rather than legal classifications, will govern" and, specifically, "unrelated business income from different sources will be considered different issues" for these purposes.[526]

---

[523] IRC § 7611(d)(2)(B).
[524] IRC § 7611(d)(2)(C).
[525] IRC § 7611(d)(1).
[526] H. Rep. No. 861, *supra* note 484, at 1110.

The church audit procedures are inapplicable to any inquiry or examination of any person other than a church, any termination assessment[527] or jeopardy assessment,[528] any case involving a knowing failure to file a return or a willful attempt to defeat or evade tax, or a criminal investigation.[529]

Inquiries or examinations "which relate primarily to the tax status or liability of persons other than the church (including the tax status or liability of a contributor or contributors to the church), rather than the tax status or liability of the church itself, will not be subject to the church audit procedures"; these inquiries or examinations may include those regarding the "inurement of church funds to a particular individual or to another organization, which may result in the denial of all or part of such individual's or organization's deduction for charitable contributions to the church," the "assignment of income or services or excessive contributions to a church," or a "vow of poverty by an individual or individuals followed by a transfer of property or an assignment of income or services to the church."[530] The IRS "may inquire of a church regarding these matters without being considered to have commenced a church tax inquiry and may proceed to examine church records relating to these issues (including enforcement of a summons for access to such records) without following the requirements applicable to church tax examinations, subject to the general rules regarding examinations of taxpayer books and records."[531]

Inquiries or examinations "conducted outside the church audit procedures will be limited to the determination of facts and circumstances specifically relating to the tax liabilities of the individuals or other organizations in question" and the IRS may not "make use of inquiries or examinations regarding individuals' or other organizations' tax liabilities to avoid the intended purpose of the church audit procedures."[532] However, the "failure of a church to respond to repeated inquiries regarding individuals' or other organizations' tax liabilities will be considered a reasonable basis for commencement of a church tax inquiry."[533]

"[R]outine IRS inquiries to a church will not be considered to commence a church tax inquiry and therefore will not trigger application of the church audit procedures."[534] Nonetheless, "[re]peated failure by a church or its agents to reply

---

[527] IRC § 6851.

[528] IRC § 6861.

[529] IRC § 7611(i).

[530] H. Rep. No. 861, *supra* note 484, at 1111.

[531] *Id.* at 1111–1112.

[532] *Id.* at 1112.

[533] *Id.*

[534] *Id.* "Routine questions for [this] include (but are not limited to) questions regarding (1) the filing or failure to file any tax return or information return by the church, (2) compliance with income tax or FICA tax withholding responsibilities by the church, (3) any supplemental information needed to complete the mechanical processing of any incomplete or incorrect return filed by the church, (4) information necessary to process applications for exempt status, letter ruling requests, or employment tax exemption requests by the church, and information identifying a church that is used by the IRS to update its Cumulative List of Tax Exempt Organizations and other computer files, and (5) confirmation that a specific business is or is not owned or operated by a church" (*id.*).

to such routine inquiries will be considered a reasonable basis for commencement of a church tax inquiry under the applicable church audit procedures."[535] Also, the IRS may "request a church to provide information necessary to locate third-party records (for example, bank records), including information regarding the church's chartered name, state and year of incorporation, and location of checking and savings accounts, without following the church audit procedures; failure to provide this type of information is to be a factor, but not a conclusive factor, in determining if there is reasonable cause for commencing a church tax inquiry."[536]

As stated, the church audit procedures do not apply to any case involving a knowing failure to file a return or a willful attempt to defeat or evade tax. "[N]othing in the church audit procedures will inhibit IRS inquiries, examinations, or criminal investigations of tax protestor or other tax avoidance schemes posing as religious organizations, including (but not limited to) tax avoidance schemes posing as mail-order ministries or storefront churches, whether such schemes are limited to one particular taxpayer or encompass a group of taxpayers."[537]

The exclusive remedy for any IRS violation of the church audit procedures is as follows: failure of the agency to substantially comply with (1) the requirement that two notices be sent to the church, (2) the requirement that the appropriate IRS representative approve the commencement of a church tax inquiry, or (3) that an offer of an IRS conference with the church be made (and a conference held if requested), will result in a stay of proceedings in a summons proceeding to gain access to church records (but not in dismissal of the proceeding) until a court determines that these requirements have been satisfied.[538] The two-year limitation on the duration of a church audit is not suspended during these stays of summons proceedings; however, the IRS may correct the violations without regard to the otherwise applicable time limits prescribed under the church examination procedures.[539] In determining whether a stay is necessary, a court "will consider the good faith of the IRS and the effect of any violation of the proper examination procedures."[540]

Otherwise, there is no judicial remedy for IRS violation of the church examination procedures. The failure of the IRS to comply with these rules may not be raised as a defense or as an affirmative ground for relief in a judicial proceeding, including a summons proceeding to gain access to church records, a declaratory judgment proceeding involving a determination of tax-exempt status,[541] or a proceeding to collect unpaid tax. Additionally, failure to substantially comply with the requirement that two notices be sent, that the appropriate IRS representative approve an inquiry, and that a conference be offered (and the conference held if

[535] *Id.*
[536] *Id.*
[537] *Id.* at 1113.
[538] IRC § 7611(e)(1).
[539] *Id.*
[540] H. Rep. No. 861, *supra* note 484, at 1114.
[541] That is, a proceeding under IRC § 7428. See *supra* § 6(b).

requested) may not be raised as a defense or as an affirmative ground for relief in a summons proceeding or any other judicial proceeding other than as specifically previously stated.[542] A church or its representatives cannot "litigate the issue of the reasonableness of the [IRS representative's] belief in approving the commencement of a church tax inquiry . . . in a summons proceeding or any other judicial proceeding," although this does not derogate from a church's "right to raise any substantive or procedural argument which would be available to taxpayers generally in the appropriate proceeding."[543]

(c) Hospital Audits

The IRS, in recent years, has been making the audit of tax-exempt hospitals and other health care entities a matter of special priority. In reflection of this, the IRS developed audit guidelines specific to these types of exempt organizations (although many of the guidelines are equally applicable to other types of exempt entities).[544]

The guidelines encompass nearly all aspects of qualification for tax-exempt status by hospitals, with emphasis on private inurement and private benefit situations;[545] they also focus on joint venture arrangements[546] and unrelated business income circumstances.[547]

The tax exemption of nonprofit hospitals today rests on the *community benefit standard*.[548] In determining whether a hospital meets this standard, IRS agents are expected to consider (1) whether the hospital has a governing board composed of "prominent civic leaders" rather than hospital administrators, physicians, and the like, (2) if the organization is part of a multi-entity hospital system, whether the minutes reflect "corporate separateness," (3) whether admission to the medical staff is open to all qualified physicians in the area, consistent with the size and nature of the facilities, (4) whether the hospital operates a full-time emergency room open to everyone, regardless of ability to pay, and (5) whether the hospital provides nonemergency care to everyone in the commu-

---

[542] IRC § 7611(e)(2).

[543] H. Rep. No. 861, *supra* note 484, at 1114. An illustration of the applicability of these rules so as to preclude an audit of a church appears in United States v. Church of Scientology of Boston, Inc., *supra* note 482, interpreting, in this context, United States v. Powell, 679 U.S. 48 (1964). Also United States v. Church of World Peace, *supra* note 482; United States v. Church of Scientology Flag Serv. Org. Inc., 90-1 U.S.T.C. ¶ 50,019 (M.D. Fla. 1989); United States v. Church of Scientology Western United States, 92-2 U.S.T.C. ¶ 50,441 (9th Cir. 1992).

In general, Walker & Holub, "Audit of Church-Related Schools and Churches," 24 *Cath. Law.* 184 (1979); Worthing, "The Internal Revenue Service as a Monitor of Church Institutions: The Excessive Entanglement Problem," 45 *Fordham L. Rev.* 929 (1977); Shaw, "Tax Audits of Churches," 22 *Cath. Law.* 247 (1976).

[544] IRS Audit Guidelines for Hospitals ("Hospital Audit Guidelines"), Manual Transmittal 7(10)69-38 for Exempt Organizations Examinations Guidelines Handbook (Mar. 27, 1992).

[545] See Chapter 19.

[546] See § 32.3.

[547] See Part Five.

[548] See § 7.6.

nity who is able to pay either privately or through third parties (such as Medicare and Medicaid).[549]

These guidelines contain criteria for assessing whether an "open staff policy" exists at a hospital, for determining whether use of an emergency room is restricted, and for examining whether nonemergency services are available to everyone in the community who has the ability to pay. Examining agents are admonished to determine whether a hospital engages in the practice known as patient dumping.[550]

The guidelines contain a discussion of private inurement and private benefit, and differentiate between the two doctrines. The IRS recognized two key distinctions between these two concepts. First, the agency reiterated its position that even a "minimal amount" of private inurement may result in loss of tax-exempt status, while private benefit is tested against a threshold of insubstantiality. Second, private inurement applies only with respect to "insiders," while private benefit can accrue to anyone. An *insider* is defined in these guidelines as individuals "whose relationship with an organization offers them an opportunity to make use of the organization's income or assets for personal gain." (The IRS considers a physician an insider in relation to a hospital in which he or she practices and/or is a member of the hospital's governing body.[551])

The following guidelines for determining private inurement or private benefit are applicable with respect to any tax-exempt organization where either set of rules applies:

1. Identify the members of the board of directors or trustees and key staff members. Examine any business relationships or dealings with the hospital. Note transactions where supplies or services are provided at prices exceeding competitive market prices or on preferred terms. Be alert for any loan agreement at less than prevailing interest rates. Scrutinize any business arrangements under which hospitals finance the construction of medical buildings owned by staff doctors on favorable financial terms.

2. Review contracts and leases. Scrutinize any contracts under which the hospital requires doctors to conduct private practices on hospital premises.

3. Review the minutes of the board of directors' executive committee and finance committee for indications of transactions with physicians, administrators, and board members.

4. Review the articles of incorporation, bylaws, minutes, filings with regulatory authorities, correspondence, brochures, newspaper articles, and the like, to determine the existence of related parties.

---

[549] Hospital Audit Guidelines, § 333.1(1).
[550] *Id.* §§ 333.1(2), (3).
[551] *Id.* § 333.2(1)-333.2(3). See, however, § 19.11(c), text accompanied by note 350.

5. Determine whether the hospital is engaged in commercial or industrial research or testing benefiting private individuals or firms rather than scientific or medical research benefiting the general public.

6. Review third-party reports (such as CPA audit reports, management letters, and annual reports) to determine whether the hospital's activities further an exempt purpose or serve private interests.

7. To determine whether medical staff or board members have an economic interest in, or significant dealings with, the hospital, review any conflict-of-interest statements.[552]

These guidelines focus on the matter of unreasonable compensation and require examining agents to inquire as to recruiting incentives, incentive compensation arrangements, below-market loans, below-market leases, and hospital purchases of a physician's practice. An extensive list of "common compensation arrangements" between physicians and hospitals is provided.[553]

The guidelines also focus on joint ventures, pointing out that a variety of forms may be involved, such as a cooperative agreement or the creation of a separate legal entity. Examples of the items or services involved in these joint ventures include clinical diagnostic laboratory services, medical equipment leasing, durable medical equipment, and other outpatient medical or diagnostic services.[554]

Agents are advised to carefully examine joint ventures between taxable and tax-exempt parties in search of private inurement or private benefit. The facts must be reviewed to determine whether the partnership involved serves a charitable purpose, whether and how participation by the exempt entity furthers an exempt purpose, and whether the arrangement permits the exempt entity to act exclusively in furtherance of its exempt purposes. A variety of private inurement issues in this context are explored, as are possible violations of the federal anti-kickback law.[555]

Sixteen types of "financial analyses" by examining agents are requested.[556] These include:

1. Review income and expenditures of affiliated entities, to determine whether nonexempt purposes, inurement, serving of private interests, or unrelated business income may be present.

2. Look for lobbying or political activities or expenditures; determine whether the hospital has elected the expenditure test as to lobbying expenditures.

---

[552] *Id.* § 333.2(4)-333.2(10).
[553] *Id.* § 333.3.
[554] *Id.* § 333.4.
[555] *Id.*
[556] *Id.* § 333.5.

3. Reconcile the hospital's books with the figures on its information return (Form 990).

4. Review Medicare cost reports for indications of insider transactions or unrelated activities.

5. Review the correspondence files on large gifts and grants; look for unusual transactions that may prohibit the "donor" from receiving a charitable deduction.

6. Check the value shown on the books for donated property against any appraisals in the file; if any property was sold, note the difference between the book value and the selling price.

7. Review the travel ledger accounts of the administrative department and the board of directors; be alert for personal items such as spouse's travel and ensure that there has been "proper accounting."

8. Where private individuals or outside entities operate the hospital cafeteria, gift shop, pharmacy, parking lot, etc., determine whether the agreements with these individuals or firms provide for reasonable payments to the hospital.

The guidelines contain rules for analyzing a hospital's balance sheet.[557] These are:

1. Review the general ledger control account for receivables from officers, trustees, and members of the medical staff, and analyze for private benefit and additional compensation; review loan or other agreements underlying these transactions.

2. Check notes receivable for interest-free loans to insiders (for example, a mortgage loan to an administrator given as an inducement to accept or continue employment at the hospital); these arrangements must be scrutinized for inurement, proper reporting, and so on.

3. Review property records to determine whether any assets are being used for personal purposes that should be taxable income to the user (for example, vehicles, residential property held for future expansion, etc.).

4. Review trust funds to see whether the trusts should be filing separate returns.

5. Review investment portfolios and check for controlled entities.

6. Review the ledger accounts and check for notes and mortgages payable that could lead to unrelated debt-financed income issues.[558]

[557] Id. § 333.6.
[558] See §§ 29.1–29.4.

7. Analyze any self-insurance trust or fund set up by the hospital to provide liability insurance.[559]

Concerning the unrelated income aspects of audits, IRS agents are advised to be particularly inquisitive as respects these "[s]pecific examples common in [the] health care field"[560]: laboratory testing, pharmacy sales, cafeterias, coffee shops, gift shops, parking facilities, medical research, laundry services, leasing of medical buildings, supply departments, and services to other hospitals.

(d) College and University Audits

The IRS issued examination guidelines for its agents to use during the audits of colleges and universities.[561] These guidelines provide factors to be considered in determining how a college or university is structured. Emphasis was placed on accounting methods, financial information, compensation arrangements, fringe benefit issues, joint ventures,[562] scholarships and fellowships, and unrelated business income issues.[563] Attention was also placed on the fundraising efforts of, and contributions to, these entities. Like the guidelines for hospital audits,[564] the college and university examination guidelines contain material that is equally applicable to other types of tax-exempt organizations.

These guidelines[565] apply with respect to three categories of exempt colleges and universities: (1) private institutions that are tax-exempt[566] and are not private foundations,[567] (2) public institutions the income (other than unrelated business income) of which is excluded from federal taxation,[568] and (3) public institutions that have received recognition of tax exemption from the IRS.[569]

Agents are instructed to obtain and review the following items in analyzing the institution's size, structure, and activities: the school bulletin and course catalogue, the school telephone directory, minutes of meetings of the governing board, as well as committees and other groups, student newspapers, alumni

---

[559] See, however, § 10.6.

[560] *Id.* § 333.8(1). In general, Bedard & Gribens, "CEP Audits Often Are Revenue Raisers for IRS and Bad News for Health Organizations," 8 *J. Tax. Exempt Orgs.* 3 (July/Aug. 1996); Theisen & Pelfrey, "Preparing an Exempt Health Care Organization for an IRS Audit," 6 *J. Tax. Exempt Orgs.* 208 (Mar./Apr. 1995); Bedard & Gribens, "Coordinated Examinations Highlight Current Scrutiny of Health Care Organizations," 6 *J. Tax. Exempt Orgs.* 28 (July/Aug. 1994); Broccolo & Peregrine, " New Hospital Audit Guidelines: The IRS Gets Down to Business," 5 *Exempt Org. Tax Rev.* 653 (1992).

[561] Examination Guidelines for Colleges and Universities (College and University Audit Guidelines), Internal Revenue Manual, Exempt Organizations Handbook 7(10)(69), reproduced in Ann. 94-112, 1994-37 I.R.B. 36.

[562] See § 32.3.

[563] See Part Five.

[564] See *supra* § 8(c).

[565] College and University Audit Guidelines § 342.

[566] That is, are tax-exempt under IRC § 501(a) by reason of being described in IRC § 501(c)(3). See § 7.3.

[567] That is, are classified under IRC § 509(a)(1) by reason of description in IRC § 170(b)(1)(A)(ii). See § 11.3(a).

[568] This exclusion of income is by reason of IRC § 115. See §§ 6.9, 18.17.

[569] This refers to tax exemption pursuant to IRC § 501(c)(3).

bulletins and magazines, any catalogue or descriptive list of the publications of the institution, a description of the institution's accounting system, the requisition and purchase order files, information that must be disclosed by coaches concerning athletically related income from sources outside the institution, possible conflicts of interest involving federally sponsored research, a description of the computer hardware and software, and formats of files and records maintained, and the institution's materials as to its racially nondiscriminatory policies.[570] Other documentation to be reviewed includes the appropriate audited financial statements, reports prepared for accreditation audits, information concerning state and local real property tax exemptions and information required by the U.S. Office of Management and Budget.[571] The guidelines contain detailed instruction on examination of financial statements,[572] employment taxes and fringe benefits,[573] cafeteria plans, retirement and pension plans, and other deferred compensation arrangements[574] contributions to the institution and other aspects of fundraising,[575] research and contracts,[576] scholarships and fellowships,[577] legislative and political expenses,[578] bookstores,[579] other unrelated business income tax considerations,[580] and related entities.[581]

As to the matter of related entities, the examining agents are advised to interpret the term *related* broadly and to include any organization the primary activity of which is to support a college or university or its programs.[582] These related entities will include separately incorporated schools or departments, athletic booster clubs, foundations, endowment funds, scholarship funds, joint ventures (including those with unitrusts), and partnerships.[583] Auditors are encouraged to identify related entities.[584]

---

[570] College and University Audit Guidelines, §§ 342.2, 342.31.

[571] *Id.* at §§ 342.32, 342.33.

[572] *Id.* at § 342.4.

[573] *Id.* at §§ 342.5, 342.7.

[574] *Id.*, § 342.6. See Chapter 16.

[575] *Id.* at § 342.9.

[576] *Id.* at § 342.10.

[577] *Id.* at § 342.11.

[578] *Id.* at § 342.12. See Chapters 20, 21.

[579] *Id.* at § 342.13. See § 26.5(a)(i).

[580] *Id.* at § 342.14.

[581] *Id.* at § 342.15.

[582] *Id.* at § 342.15(1).

[583] *Id.* at § 342.15(4)-(9).

[584] *Id.* at § 342.45. In general, Cerny & Mallon, "Extensive New IRS Audit Guidelines Intensify Scrutiny of Colleges and Universities," 78 *J. Tax.* (No. 5) 298 (May 1993); Harding, Jr. & McClellan, "Commentary on the IRS Proposed Examination Guidelines for College and University Audits," 9 *Exempt Org. Tax. Rev.* (No. 3) 589 (1994); Whaley, "IRS Proposes Strict College and University Examination Guidelines," 4 *J. Tax Exempt Orgs.* (No. 6) 3 (May/June 1993).

The Commerciality Doctrine and Unrelated Business Income Taxation

CHAPTER TWENTY-FIVE

The Commerciality Doctrine

Occasionally, as part of the law of tax-exempt organizations, the courts will create law or develop law that is engrafted onto statutory criteria. This phenomenon is most obvious and extensive in connection with the evolution and application of the *commerciality doctrine*. These principles are impacting the law concerning qualification for exemption, principally for charitable organizations, and in the process helping shape the law of unrelated business activities.

Despite its enormous effect to date, the commerciality doctrine is somewhat of an enigma. In writing the law of tax-exempt organizations over the decades, Congress did not create the doctrine. With one exception,[1] the word *commercial* does not appear in the federal statutory law concerning exempt organizations. Nor, with one exception (discussed below), is the term to be found in the applicable income tax regulations. It is, then, a doctrine created by the courts.

§ 25.1 ORIGIN OF DOCTRINE

The commerciality doctrine, as it relates to the activities of tax-exempt organizations, is an overlay body of law that the courts have engrafted onto the statutory and regulatory rules.

(a) Nature of Doctrine

The commerciality doctrine is essentially this: A tax-exempt organization is engaged in a nonexempt activity when that activity is engaged in in a manner that is considered *commercial*. An act is a commercial one if it has a direct counterpart

---

[1] IRC § 501(m), denying tax exemption to certain organizations that provide *commercial-type* insurance. See § 22.1.

in, or is conducted in the same manner as is the case in the realm of for-profit organizations. (Having stated the essence of the doctrine, it must also be said that the doctrine is unevenly applied.)

The doctrine appears to be born of the basic fact that United States society is composed of three sectors: the business (for-profit) sector, the governmental sector, and the nonprofit sector. Generally, the governmental sector is not viewed as an operator of businesses (there are, of course, exceptions to this), so that sector is not a factor in this analysis (other than as the source of regulation).

The United States is essentially a capitalist society, so the business sector is, in several ways, the preferred sector. While entities in the business sector are seen as being operated for private ends (for example, profits to shareholders), with the overall result a capitalist (albeit rather regulated) economy for the society, the nonprofit sector is seen as being operated for public ends (the general good of society).[2] Many today still perceive of nonprofit organizations as entities that do not and should not earn a profit, are operated largely by volunteers, and are not "run like a business."[3]

Out of these precepts (some of which are false) is emanating the view that organizations in the nonprofit sector should not *compete* with organizations in the business sector. Thus, over recent years, the nonprofit community has heard much about competition between for-profit organizations (usually, *small* business) and nonprofit organizations—with the word *competition* almost always preceded by the word *unfair*.[4]

This doctrine thus involves a *counterpart* test. When a court sees an activity being conducted by a member of the business sector and the same activity being conducted by a member of the nonprofit sector, it often, motivated by some form of intuitive offense at the thought that a nonprofit organization is doing something that "ought to" be done or is being done by a for-profit organization, concludes that the nonprofit organization is conducting that activity in a commercial manner. This conclusion then leads to a finding that the commercial activity is a nonexempt function with adverse consequences in law for the nonprofit organization with respect to either unrelated income taxation or tax exemption.

Consequently, the federal tax law pertaining to nonprofit organizations is being shaped by a doctrine that rests in part upon untrue premises and that has crept into the law by actions of courts which, consciously or unconsciously, ignored the Internal Revenue Code and the underlying regulations, and developed law with these premises in mind.

For example, the debate over whether credit unions should continue to be tax-exempt is a classic illustration of the counterpart test. A report from the Congressional Research Service, a division of the Library of Congress, made reference to the fact that "many believe that an economically neutral tax system requires that financial institutions engaged in similar activities should have the same tax treatment."[5] Citing differences between credit unions and other financial institutions, organizations like the National Credit Union Administration ar-

[2] See § 1.1(b).
[3] See § 4.9.
[4] See § 26.2(b).
[5] "Should Credit Unions Be Taxed?," CRS Analysis No. I B 89066 (Sept. 18, 1990).

gue for the ongoing exemption, while organizations like the American Bankers Association disagree.

Another example is the debate over the criteria for tax exemption for hospitals. This issue concerns the question as to whether the basis for tax exemption for hospitals should continue to be the community benefit standard[6] or whether it should be revised to reflect a charity care standard.[7]

(b) Internal Revenue Code

Usually, when endeavoring to understand a point of federal tax law, one first turns to the Internal Revenue Code. In searching for the law embodied by the commerciality doctrine as it applies to tax-exempt organizations, however, a perusal of the pages of the Code is basically futile. That is, the commerciality doctrine, as a general standard of law, is not in the Code.

Nonetheless, a significant element of the doctrine was added to the Internal Revenue Code in 1986. This occurred as the result of the decision by Congress to deny tax-exempt status to organizations such as Blue Cross and Blue Shield organizations that are providers of health care insurance. The thought was that this type of insurance is being provided by the business sector, that these types of nonprofit organizations "look like" and compete with for-profit organizations, and that tax exemption for insurance providers is no longer appropriate.[8] This legislation is a classic illustration of the points made above, concerning the business sector preference and the counterpart test.

Thus, Congress wrote a rule that provides that an organization cannot be tax-exempt as a charitable organization[9] or a social welfare organization[10] if a substantial part of its activities consists of the provision of *commercial-type* insurance.[11] Although this term is not defined in the Internal Revenue Code, the legislative history stated that "commercial-type insurance generally is any insurance of a type provided by commercial insurance companies."[12] This is an appli-

---

[6] See § 6.2(a).

[7] See Hyatt & Hopkins, *The Law of Tax-Exempt Healthcare Organizations, Second Edition* (John Wiley & Sons, Inc., 2001), Chapter 26. Still another illustration of the point is the question of the ongoing tax exemption for fraternal beneficiary societies. A study conducted by the Department of the Treasury, which led to a report in early 1993 (see § 18.4(a), note 96), concluded that the insurance products offered by these organizations are essentially the same as those provided by commercial insurers; it observed that the large fraternal beneficiary societies "conduct their insurance operations in a manner similar to commercial insurers." The report dismissed this commerciality, however, stating that these societies "do not use their exemption to compete unfairly with commercial insurers in terms of price or to operate inefficiently." Nonetheless, this conclusion is wholly inconsistent with contemporary court opinions and IRS policy. As will be discussed, in those quarters, commercial practices are automatically considered unrelated activities, leading to denial or revocation of exemption or to unrelated income taxation. This report concluded that there must be more than commerciality—there must also be unfair competition.

[8] See § 22.1.

[9] That is, an organization described in IRC § 501(c)(3) (see Part Two).

[10] That is, an organization described in IRC § 501(c)(4) (see Chapter 12).

[11] IRC § 501(m).

[12] H. Rep. 841, 99th Cong., 2d Sess. II-345 (1986).

cation of the counterpart test: If the activity is found in the business sector, it is an inappropriate activity for conduct in the nonprofit organization sector.

Organizations that seek to be tax-exempt must meet an *operational test*—a test that facilitates an evaluation of activities in relation to the achievement of tax-exempt functions.[13] The operational test is most refined in the body of law concerning charitable organizations.[14] The regulations also amplify the Internal Revenue Code usage of words such as *charitable* and *educational*.[15]

A provision of the Internal Revenue Code taxes the net income derived from tax-exempt organizations from *unrelated business activities*.[16] These activities are those that are not substantially related to the exercise or performance by the exempt organization of its exempt purpose or function.[17] The need of the organization for the revenue derived from a business or the use it makes of the profits derived from it cannot be used as a basis for demonstrating relatedness.[18]

Absent an applicable statutory exception, an activity is taxable as an unrelated one where the activity is a trade or business, the business is regularly carried on, and the conduct of the business is not substantially related (other than through the production of funds) to the organization's performance of its exempt function.[19]

Pursuant to the statutory law, an "activity does not lose identity as trade or business merely because it is carried on within a larger aggregate of similar activities or within a larger complex of other endeavors that may, or may not, be related to the exempt purposes of the organization."[20] This is the *fragmentation rule*.

(c) Tax Regulations

The tax regulations exist to explain and, in some instances, amplify the law as stated in the statutory law. Yet, when it comes to the commerciality doctrine as it is being conceived and interpreted by the courts today, it is nowhere to be found in the regulations.

The income tax regulations are silent on the matter of commercial operations as the concept relates to a determination as to whether an activity is substantially related to the accomplishment of exempt purposes.[21] With one minor exception (concerning commercial advertising), the same is true with respect to the definition of the term *trade or business*.[22]

The term *commercial* is used in the regulations as part of the elements for determining whether or not a business is regularly carried on. Thus, the regulations state that specific business activities of an exempt organization are ordinarily

---

[13] See § 4.5.
[14] Reg. § 1.501(c)(3)-1(c).
[15] Reg. § 1.501(c)(3)-1(d)(2), (3).
[16] IRC § 511(a).
[17] IRC § 513(a); Reg. § 1.513-1(a).
[18] *Id.*
[19] Reg. § 1.513-1(a).
[20] IRC § 513(c).
[21] Reg. § 1.513-1(d).
[22] Reg. § 1.513-1(b).

deemed to be regularly carried on if they "manifest a frequency and continuity, and are pursued in a manner, generally similar to comparable commercial activities of nonexempt organizations."[23]

To determine whether an activity is substantially related to an organization's exempt purposes, it is necessary to examine the "relationship between the business activities which generate the particular income in question—the activities, that is, of producing or distributing the goods or performing the services involved—and the accomplishment of the organization's exempt purposes."[24]

A business is related to exempt purposes where the conduct of the business activity has a *causal relationship* to the achievement of exempt purposes and it is substantially related where the causal relationship is a substantial one.[25] For a business to be substantially related to exempt purposes, the production or distribution of the goods or the performance of the services from which the gross income is derived must "contribute importantly to the accomplishment of those purposes."[26] Whether activities productive of gross income contribute importantly to the accomplishment of one or more exempt purposes "depends in each case upon the facts and circumstances involved."[27]

As noted, this regulatory definition of relatedness does not make any reference to the commerciality doctrine. Rather, this definition of relatedness is a causal relationship test. Thus, under the regulations, a business may be regularly carried on (that is, be commercially conducted) and not be taxed, where there is a substantial causal relationship between the activity and the accomplishment of exempt purposes. In other words, the IRS regulations contemplate a nontaxable, related business that is commercially carried on.

(d) Beginnings of the Doctrine

The commerciality doctrine is not the consequence of some grand pronouncement by the Supreme Court or, for that matter, any court. The doctrine just evolved, growing from loose language in court opinions, which in turn seems to have reflected judges' personal views as to what the law ought to be (rather than what it is). The commerciality doctrine appears to be the product of what is known in the law as *dictum*: a gratuitous remark by a judge that need not have been uttered to resolve the case. The term stems from the Latin "simplex dictum," meaning an "assertion without proof," and later "obiter dictum," which means a statement "lacking the force of an adjudication." The commerciality doctrine has, over the years, however, very much taken on the force of an adjudication.

The doctrine was initiated far before Congress enacted the unrelated income rules in 1950. It was first mentioned, at the federal level, in 1924, by the U.S. Supreme Court.[28] The case concerned a tax-exempt religious order that was

---

[23] Reg. § 1.513-1(c)(1), (2)(ii).
[24] Reg. § 1.513-1(d)(1).
[25] Reg. § 1.513-1(d)(2).
[26] *Id.*
[27] *Id.*
[28] Trinidad v. Sagrada Orden de Predicadores de la Provincia del Santisimo Rosario de Filipinas, 263 U.S. 578 (1924).

operated for religious purposes, but that engaged in other activities which the government alleged destroyed the basis for its exemption; the order had extensive investments in real estate and stockholdings that returned a profit, as well as some incidental sales of wine, chocolate, and other articles. The Supreme Court found that the order was exempt as a religious entity, justifying its investment and business efforts by writing that "[s]uch [religious] activities cannot be carried on without money."[29]

In this case, the Court did not articulate a commerciality doctrine. The Court characterized the government's argument as being that the order "is operated also for business and *commercial* purposes."[30] The Court rejected this characterization, writing that there is no "competition" and that while the "transactions yield some profit [it] is in the circumstances a negligible factor."[31] Thus, in this case, the Supreme Court did not enunciate the commerciality doctrine; however, by using the word in describing the government's position, the commerciality doctrine was born.

The rules that flowed out of this Supreme Court opinion are known today as the *operational test*, which is stated in the tax regulations.[32] The opinion laid down the rule that a charitable organization can engage in business activities for profit, without loss of exemption, if its net income is destined for charitable uses. This rule, known as the *destination-of-income test*, was ended by Congress in 1950, when it enacted the law of *feeder organizations*.[33] An analysis of the cases applying the destination-of-income test and of its transition out of existence was provided in a 1957 appellate court opinion.[34]

Repeal of the destination-of-income test, however, did not extinguish what has been termed the *activities standard*.[35] This standard is used where a nonprofit organization engages in activities that, while commercial, further exempt purposes.[36] Today, the activities standard survives as the operational test.

The 1924 Supreme Court opinion established another point: Where an organization's activities are a *negligible factor* (as was the sale by the order of wine and chocolate), they are considered *incidental* in relation to exempt purposes and thus have no adverse effect on the exemption.[37] This aspect of the law is today reflected in the rule that a charitable organization must be operated exclusively for exempt purposes, with today's understanding that the word *exclusively* actually means *primarily*. The word *exclusively* is in the Internal Revenue Code and in the tax regulations the word is *primarily*.[38]

The Supreme Court formally articulated the commerciality doctrine in 1945,

---

[29] *Id.* at 581.
[30] *Id.* (emphasis added).
[31] *Id.* at 582.
[32] Reg. § 1.501(c)(3)-1(c)(1). See § 4.5.
[33] IRC § 502. See § 28.6.
[34] Lichter Found. v. Welch, 247 F.2d 431 (6th Cir. 1957).
[35] Fides Publishers Ass'n v. United States, 263 F. Supp. 924 (N.D. Ind. 1967).
[36] *Id.* at 933–934.
[37] Trinidad v. Sagrada Orden de Predicadores de la Provincia del Santisimo Rosario de Filipinas, *supra* note 28, at 582.
[38] Reg. § 1.501(c)(3)-1(c)(1). See § 4.6.

when reviewing a case concerning the tax exemption of a chapter of the Better Business Bureau, which was seeking exempt status as an educational organization.[39] On this occasion, the Court said that the *exclusivity* requirement "plainly means that the presence of a single non-educational purpose, if substantial in nature, will destroy the exemption regardless of the number or importance of truly educational purposes."[40] The Court found a noneducational purpose in the promotion of a profitable business community. The Court, in the closest that it has come to expressly articulating the commerciality doctrine, said that the organization had a "commercial hue" and that its "activities are largely animated by this commercial purpose."[41]

(e)   Focus on Publishing

The commerciality doctrine flourished during a period in the early 1960s, in the context of the courts' scrutiny of nonprofit publishing organizations, which is understandable given the fact that publishing occurs in both the business and nonprofit sectors, and thus facilitates easy application of the counterpart doctrine.

An early case to invoke the commerciality doctrine, replete with the counterpart test, was decided in 1961.[42] The organization published and sold religious literature in furtherance of the purpose of upgrading the quality of teaching materials for Bible instruction in Sunday schools. It generated what the court termed "very substantial" profits.[43] The court rejected the argument that profits alone preclude tax exemption. The court wrote: "If the defendant [IRS] seeks by this distinction ["slight" versus "very substantial" profits] to suggest that where an organization's profits are very large a conclusion that the organization is noncharitable must follow, we reject such a suggestion."[44] But then the court added these fateful words: "If, however, defendant means only to suggest that it is at least some evidence indicative of a *commercial* character we are inclined to agree."[45]

This court found the organization to be directly involved in the conduct of a trade or business for profit, with religious objectives "incidental."[46] Application of the counterpart test was articulated in a footnote, with the court observing "that there are many commercial concerns which sell Bibles, scrolls, and other religious and semi-religious literature which have not been granted exemption as to that part of their businesses."[47] Consequently, the court found that the organization's activities were of a "nonexempt character."[48] The court declined to apply the unrelated income tax rules to these facts. Thus, this 1961 opinion is devoid of

---

[39] Better Business Bureau of Wash., D.C. v. United States, 326 U.S. 279 (1945).
[40] *Id.* at 283.
[41] *Id.* at 283–284.
[42] Scripture Press Found. v. United States, 285 F.2d 800 (Ct. Cl. 1961).
[43] *Id.* at 803.
[44] *Id.*
[45] *Id.* (emphasis added).
[46] *Id.* at 805.
[47] *Id.* at 806, note 11.
[48] *Id.* at 807.

any discussion of related and unrelated activities. The court obviously thought that the organization's primary activities were unrelated ones, since the exemption was revoked, but the word *commercial* was used rather than the word *unrelated*. The opinion offers no definition of the word commercial and contains no indication as to why the court used it.

In one of these cases, decided in 1956, a court held that an organization that sold religious publications and charged admission fees to conclaves was tax-exempt because the "activities bear an intimate relationship to the proper functioning of" the organization.[49] The court made no mention of a commerciality doctrine. Earlier, in 1954, this court held that an organization organized to prepare and publish a widely accepted system for indexing library collections (the Dewey Decimal Classification System) was exempt.[50] Again, there was no mention of any commerciality doctrine. The commerciality doctrine appears, on the basis of this 1961 opinion, to take into account at least three elements: the scope of an organization's net profits, the extent of accumulated surplus revenue (capital), and amounts expended for what the court deems to be tax-exempt functions.

As it turned out, another court had another nonprofit publishing organization before it the next year. This organization disseminated publications (principally newsletters and books) containing investment advice to subscribers and other purchasers. Rejecting the argument that the organization was engaged in educational activities, the court held that the organization was not entitled to tax exemption because "its purpose is primarily a business one."[51] Once again, there was no discussion by the court as to whether the business was related or unrelated.

This court did not need to use the word *commercial*; the proper terminology would have been *unrelated business*. Instead, in this 1962 opinion, the court wrote passages such as the organization is "in competition with other commercial organizations providing similar services,"[52] the organization's "investment service in all its ramifications may be educational, but its purpose is primarily a business one,"[53] and the "totality of these activities is indicative of a business, and . . . [the organization's] purpose is thus a commercial purpose and nonexempt."[54] With that, the commerciality doctrine, and its counterpart test and the concern about competition between the sectors, was irrevocably launched. The doctrine was becoming a part of the law of tax-exempt organizations.

In 1963, a court rejected the government's contention that the publication and sale of religious magazines, books, pamphlets, Bibles, records, tape recordings, and pictures amounted to commercial activity.[55] In 1964, this court was faced with another case involving the operation of alleged commercial enter-

---

[49] Saint Germain Found. v. Comm'r, 26 T.C. 648, 658 (1956).
[50] Forest Press, Inc. v. Comm'r, 22 T.C. 265 (1954).
[51] American Inst. for Economic Research v. United States, 302 F.2d 934, 938 (Ct. Cl. 1962).
[52] *Id.* at 938.
[53] *Id.*
[54] *Id.* at 937.
[55] A.A. Allen Revivals, Inc. v. Comm'r, 22 T.C. 1435 (1963).

prises, this time concerning a religious organization that conducted training projects. The court rejected the commerciality doctrine, with the observation that "we regard consistent nonprofitability as evidence of the absence of commercial purposes."[56]

Still another case involving a religious publishing organization was considered by a federal district court in 1967. This court refined the commerciality doctrine by distinguishing between organizations that have commercial activities as a part of their overall activities and those that have commercial activities as their sole activity.[57] Organizations that retained their tax exemption in the prior cases were grouped in the first category;[58] the other organizations were placed in the second category. The court thus relied on the other cases[59] in concluding that the publishing company was not exempt. The nonexempt purpose[60] was portrayed as the "publication and sale of religious literature at a profit."[61] The court said its conclusion could not be otherwise—"If it were, every publishing house would be entitled to an exemption on the ground that it furthers the education of the public."[62]

In 1968, another federal district court came to the identical result. A publisher of religious materials was denied tax exemption because it was "clearly engaged primarily in a business activity, and it conducted its operations, although on a small scale, in the same way as any commercial publisher of religious books for profit would have done."[63] The fact that the organization's ultimate purpose was a religious one did not, for that court, confer exemption.

The next year, this opinion was reversed on appeal. The case was won before the appellate court on the ground that the organization did not have "operational profits."[64] The court concluded that the "deficit operation reflects not poor business planning nor ill fortune but rather the fact that profits were not the goal of the operation."[65] Although the nonprofit organization involved in the case prevailed, this opinion went a long way toward establishment of the point that the existence of profit is evidence of commerciality.

Thus, the 1960s witnessed court cases that invoked and solidified the commerciality doctrine. After this flurry of activity involving publishing organizations, not much happened with the doctrine for over a decade. Then, in 1978, came the first of the contemporary commerciality doctrine cases.

In 1978, a court had occasion to review the previous cases discussing the commerciality doctrine. Once again, it had before it an organization the sole ac-

---

[56] The Golden Rule Church Ass'n v. Comm'r, 41 T.C. 719, 731 (1964).

[57] Fides Publishers Ass'n v. United States, *supra* note 35.

[58] This includes cases like Saint Germain Found. v. Comm'r, *supra* note 49; The Golden Rule Church Ass'n v. Comm'r, *supra* note 56; A.A. Allen Revivals, Inc. v. Comm'r, *supra* note 55.

[59] Scripture Press Found. v. United States, *supra* note 42; American Inst. for Economic Research v. United States, *supra* note 51.

[60] Following the rationale in Better Business Bureau of Wash., D.C. v. United States, *supra* note 39.

[61] Fides Publishers Ass'n v. United States, *supra* note 35, at 935.

[62] *Id.*

[63] Elisian Guild, Inc. v. United States, 292 F. Supp. 219, 221 (D. Mass. 1968).

[64] Elisian Guild, Inc. v. United States, 412 F.2d 121, 125 (1st Cir. 1969).

[65] *Id.* at 125.

tivity of which was religious publishing. Essentially, the purpose of the organization under review was to disseminate sermons to ministers to improve their religious teachings. The court allowed the organization to be tax-exempt on the ground that the sale of religious literature was an "integral part of and incidental to" the entity's religious purpose.[66]

That same year, the court was called upon to determine whether an organization that purchased, imported, and sold artists' crafts could be tax-exempt. The IRS contended that the organization was a "commercial import firm."[67] The organization argued that its purpose was to help disadvantaged artisans in poverty-stricken countries to subsist and preserve their craft and to furnish services to tax-exempt museums by providing museum stores with representative handicrafts from disadvantaged countries. Once again, the court came down on the side of exemption, concluding that the organization engaged in the purchase, import, and sale activities, not as an end unto themselves, but as a means of accomplishing exempt purposes. This organization thus escaped characterization as a commercial organization.

In early 1979, this court went the other way. The court concluded that the primary purpose of the organization involved was the publication and sale of books written by its founder. In concluding that the principal purpose served by this organization was commercial in nature, the court focused on the fact of annual profits and its distribution and marketing practices. Although the conclusion reached was that the organization was principally commercial, the case had considerable overtones of private inurement.[68]

Later that same year, the court analyzed the facts involving an organization operated to purchase and sell products manufactured by blind individuals. The court found that the principal purpose of the organization was to provide employment for the blind, thereby alleviating the hardship these disabled individuals experience in securing and holding regular employment. The fact that the organization generated a profit was disregarded.[69]

Early in 1980, the same court considered the case of an organization that benefited the poor of the Navajo Nation by assisting in the organization and operation of businesses that employ or are owned by residents of the Navajo Reservation. Its most substantial source of revenue was the leasing of oil well drilling equipment. The court denied the organization tax exemption on the ground that it was operated primarily for commercial purposes. The court articulated the commerciality doctrine as follows: "Profits may be realized or other nonexempt purposes may be necessarily advanced incidental to the conduct of the commercial activity, but the existence of such nonexempt purposes does not require denial of exempt status so long as the organization's dominant purpose for conducting the activity is an exempt purpose, and so long as the nonexempt activity is merely incidental to the exempt purpose."[70] The organization's activities were found to be in violation of the operational test.

[66] Pulpit Resource v. Comm'r, 70 T.C. 594, 611 (1978).
[67] Aid to Artisans, Inc. v. Comm'r, 71 T.C. 202, 208 (1978).
[68] Christian Manner Int'l v. Comm'r, 71 T.C. 661 (1979).
[69] Industrial Aid for the Blind v. Comm'r, 73 T.C. 96 (1979).
[70] Greater United Navajo Dev. Enters., Inc. v. Comm'r, 74 T.C. 69, 79 (1980).

The next year, a federal district court concluded that an organization that published religious literature should lose its tax exemption because it evolved into a commercial entity. Originally formed as a missionary organization, it, the court ruled, became an organization with a "commercial hue" and a "highly efficient business venture."[71] In reaching this conclusion, the court noted that the organization adhered to publishing and sales practices followed by comparable commercial publishers, had shown increasing profits in recent years, experienced a growth in accumulated surplus, and had been paying substantially increased salaries to its top employees.

Late in 1982, this court issued an opinion concerning still another religious publishing house, again concluding that its exemption should be revoked. The court decided that the organization had become too profitable and thus commercial.[72] Once again, the court found a "commercial hue," derived from profits, wide profit margins, development of a professional staff, and competition with commercial publishers.[73] The opinion was, however, reversed, with the appellate court "troubled by the inflexibility of the Tax Court's approach."[74] The court of appeals proffered no clarity; while it was bothered by the facts, it could not bring itself to revoke the exemption of the organization. Thus, the court of appeals said that "success in terms of audience reached and influence exerted, in and of itself, should not jeopardize the tax-exempt status of organizations which remain true to their stated goals."[75] Yet the court also wrote that if an exempt "organization's management decisions replicate those of commercial enterprises, it is a fair inference that at least one purpose is commercial."[76]

In 1983, a court concluded that an ostensibly religious organization could not qualify for tax exemption because its principal purpose is "tax avoidance" counseling.[77] The court was clearly displeased at that element of the facts and, in a sense, the case is more one of private benefit rather than commerciality. The court noted that the information provided by the organization "is no different from that furnished by a commercial tax service."[78]

About three years went by before a court considered another commerciality case. Before a court was an organization that was formed to assist in the process of technology transfer, which is the transfer of technology from universities and research institutions to industry.[79] The court concluded that its major activity was the provision of patenting and licensing services, and that the activity was primarily commercial in nature.[80]

In 1986, a court held that a religious retreat center was not an organization

---

[71] Incorporated Trustees of Gospel Worker Soc'y v. United States, 510 F. Supp. 374, 381 (D.D.C. 1981), aff'd, 672 F.2d 894 (D.C. Cir. 1981), cert. den., 456 U.S. 944 (1981).
[72] Presbyterian & Reformed Publishing Co. v. Comm'r, 79 T.C. 1070 (1982).
[73] Id. at 1083.
[74] Presbyterian & Reformed Publishing Co. v. Comm'r, 743 F.2d 148, 152 (3d Cir. 1984).
[75] Id. at 158.
[76] Id. at 155.
[77] The Ecclesiastical Order of the Ism of Am, Inc. v. Comm'r, 80 T.C. 833, 843 (1983).
[78] Id. at 839.
[79] See § 9.5.
[80] Washington Research Found. v. Comm'r, 50 T.C.M. 1457 (1985). (This opinion was "overturned" by Congress when it enacted § 1605 of the Tax Reform Act of 1986 (see H. Rep. 841, 99th Cong., 2d Sess. II-827 (1986)).)

that is commercial in nature, because it did not compete with commercial entities.[81] The entity was held to be an integral part of a conference of the United Methodist Church. The organization was portrayed as a general contractor for the construction of housing on its own property to promote increased religious activity. The fact that the organization charged fair market prices was held to be required to avoid charges of private inurement.

(f) Contemporary Application of the Doctrine

The latter half of the 1980s brought little attention to the commerciality doctrine. The focus instead, particularly with respect to religious organizations, was on unrelated business activities, rather than loss of exemption. In none of these opinions did the court involved endeavor to discuss the origins and scope of the commerciality doctrine.

The 1990s continued to bring cases involving the commerciality doctrine. In the first of these cases, the court concluded that the commerciality doctrine was the basis for denial of tax-exempt status, as a charitable and religious entity, to an organization associated with the Seventh-day Adventist Church that operated, in advancement of church doctrine, vegetarian restaurants and health food stores.[82] The court wrote that the organization's "activity was conducted as a business and was in direct competition with other restaurants and health food stores."[83] The court added: "Competition with commercial firms is strong evidence of a substantial nonexempt purpose."[84]

When this case was considered on appeal, the appellate court affirmed the lower court decision.[85] The appellate court opinion specifically stated the factors that the court relied upon to find commerciality and thus offered the best contemporary explication of the commerciality doctrine. These factors were that (1) the organization sold goods and services to the public (this factor alone was said to make the operations "presumptively commercial"), (2) the organization was in "direct competition" with for-profit restaurants and food stores, (3) the prices set by the organization were based on pricing formulas common in the retail food business (with the "profit-making price structure loom[ing] large" in the court's analysis and the court criticizing the organization for not having "below-cost pricing"), (4) the organization utilized promotional materials and "commercial catch phrases" to enhance sales, (5) the organization advertised its services and food ($15,500 expended for advertising over two years), (6) the organization's hours of operation were basically the same as for-profit enterprises, (7) the guidelines by which the organization operated required that its management have "business ability" and six

---

[81] Junaluska Assembly Hous., Inc. v. Comm'r, 86 T.C. 1114 (1986).

[82] Living Faith, Inc. v. Comm'r, 60 T.C.M. 710 (1990).

[83] Id. at 713.

[84] Id.

[85] Living Faith, Inc. v. Comm'r, 950 F. 2d 365 (7th Cir. 1991). In another case, a court concluded that an organization's principal activity was the "operation of a number of canteen-style lunch trucks," which is a commercial activity, and upheld revocation of the organization's tax exemption (New Faith, Inc. v. Comm'r, 64 T.C.M. 1050 (1992)). Likewise, a nonprofit organization, the activities of which were the same as a temporary service agency, was denied tax-exempt status because it was "essentially a commercial venture" (At Cost Services, Inc. v. Comm'r, 80 T.C.M. 573 (2000)).

months training, (8) the organization did not utilize volunteers but paid salaries (totalling $63,000 in one year and more than $25,000 in another year), and (9) the organization did not receive charitable contributions.

The IRS has applied the commerciality doctrine in the context of ascertaining whether a tax-exempt charitable organization should lose its exempt status because its fundraising costs are too "high."[86] Further, it has been held that an organization selling religious tapes was a nonexempt commercial organization,[87] and that an organization operating prisoner rehabilitation programs is not eligible for tax exemption because of commercial activities.[88]

The commerciality doctrine is being applied in some of the cases involving the provision of *commercial-type insurance*.[89] For example, in one of these cases, the court wrote that the "various factors to consider in determining whether an organization promotes a forbidden nonexempt purpose" under the rules concerning charitable organizations include the "manner in which an organization conducts its activities; the commercial hue or nature of those activities; the competitive nature of the activities; the existence of accumulated profits; and the provision of free or below cost services."[90] The organization, the tax status of which was at issue in the case, was characterized by the court as existing "solely for the purpose of selling insurance to nonprofit exempt organizations at the lowest possible cost on a continued, stable basis"; the court continued with the observation that "[s]elling insurance undeniably is an inherently commercial activity ordinarily carried on by a commercial for-profit company."[91] The court added that, although the organization "may not possess every attribute characteristic of a mutual insurance company, it possesses a majority of the qualifying characteristics, which only further enhances the determination that . . . [it] is presumptively commercial in nature."[92] In another of these cases, a court concluded that a group of self-insurance pools had a "commercial hue."[93]

The commerciality doctrine, as a court-founded rule of law, has come to be widely accepted in the courts. This phenomenon has occurred, and is occurring, as other judicial and administrative doctrines are coming to the fore. These other doctrines include competition between nonprofit and for-profit organizations,[94] the private benefit doctrine,[95] the commensurate test,[96] and the unrelated business rules.[97]

---

[86] E.g., United Cancer Council, Inc. v. Comm'r, 109 T.C. 326 (1997), *rev'd and rem'd*, 165 F.3d 1173 (7th Cir. 1999); this opinion is discussed at § 19.4(a).
[87] United Missionary Aviation, Inc. v. Comm'r, 60 T.C.M. 1152 (1990), *rev'd and rem'd*, 985 F.2d 564 (8th Cir. 1989), *cert. den.*, 506 U.S. 816 (1992).
[88] Public Indust., Inc. v. Comm'r, 61 T.C.M. 1626 (1991).
[89] See § 22.1.
[90] Nonprofits' Ins. Alliance of Calif. v. United States, 94-2 U.S.T.C. ¶ 50,593 (Fed. Cl. 1994).
[91] *Id.*
[92] *Id.*
[93] Paratransit Ins. Corp. v. Comm'r, 102 T.C. 745, 754 (1994). Subsequently, Congress enacted a limited tax exemption for certain charitable risk pools (see § 10.6).
[94] See *supra* note 4.
[95] See § 19.10.
[96] See § 4.7.
[97] See Chapters 26 and 27. E.g., the IRS applied the commerciality doctrine in concluding that an activity was an unrelated business (Tech. Adv. Mem. 200021056).

§ 25.2 CONTEMPORARY PERSPECTIVE ON DOCTRINE

One of the requirements for qualification as a tax-exempt charitable organization is that the entity be operated exclusively for one or more tax-exempt purposes.[98] This is, in essence, a *primary purpose* rule.[99]

Pursuant to the exclusively doctrine, the IRS or a court may conclude that an organization is not operated exclusively for a tax-exempt purpose because its operation is similar to a commercial enterprise operated on a for-profit basis.[100] In many of the court opinions focusing on this point, the courts have expressed concern about the *commercial hue* of the organization.[101]

There is more to the commerciality doctrine than the generation of profits. It partakes, as well, of other doctrines discussed throughout, such as, as noted, the matter of competition with for-profit organizations, the private inurement and private benefit rules, and the commensurate test. The IRS may, however, use the existence of a profit to characterize the activity as being commercial in nature, thus placing at issue the question as to whether the organization's activities are devoted exclusively to tax-exempt purposes.

The competition issue is the most troublesome, particularly when the lines of demarcation between nonprofit and for-profit organizations are, in some instances, blurring. Nonprofit organizations are becoming increasingly reliant on revenue in the form of fees for services. For-profit organizations are more concerned than ever about their public image and the extent to which they can provide assistance to their communities. For-profit organizations are entering domains of producing and providing services that were once the sole province of nonprofit organizations. Laws are changed to promote greater parity between the sectors, such as the Office of Management and Budget regulations, which require tax-exempt organizations pursuing government contracts to calculate tax revenues foregone. Management of nonprofit organizations is becoming more sophisticated.

Two categories of charitable organizations continue to evolve: Those that are supported largely by gifts (*donative* organizations)[102] and those that are supported principally by exempt function revenue (*service provider* organizations).[103] As this trend continues, it will force new pressures on the concept of tax exemption. New rationales for exemption may emerge. The battles that are building over the ground rules for exemptions for hospitals[104] and credit unions[105] must be appreciated from this perspective. A sort of "domino theory" may be in the works in this setting. One commentator is of the view that "if nonprofit hospitals lose their exemption, federal corporate tax exemption for most or all of the second [commercial] nonprofit sector may then be in doubt."[106]

[98] See § 4.6.
[99] See § 4.4.
[100] See Chapter 25.
[101] See § 26.2(b).
[102] See § 11.3(b)(i).
[103] See § 11.3(b)(iv).
[104] See text accompanying *supra* notes 6–7.
[105] See text accompanying *supra* note 5.
[106] Hansmann, "The Two Nonprofit Sectors: Fee for Service Versus Donative Organizations," in *The Future of the Nonprofit Sector* 95 (Jossey-Bass, Inc., 1989).

The undermining effect of the commerciality doctrine on the future of the nonprofit sector cannot be underestimated. Recall the underlying premise of the commerciality doctrine, which is that there are two sectors that can engage in commercial activities but the bias is that those activities should be conducted only by the for-profit sector—the United States being a capitalist society. The business sector is, in several ways, the preferred sector. This view is that of the Treasury Department, such as was expressed in 1987, where an assistant secretary testified before the House Subcommittee on Oversight that the "role of the quasi-governmental, not-for-profit sector should . . . be restricted to that of supplementing, and not supplanting, the activities of for-profit businesses."[107]

The emerging commerciality doctrine is the backdrop against which the unrelated business laws can be viewed. This is in part because, in the view of some, the concept of relatedness and unrelatedness is outmoded, and should be replaced by a commerciality test.[108] Even if the commerciality doctrine does not operate to cause denial or loss of tax-exempt status, the doctrine remains a significant force in determining what is an unrelated trade or business.[109]

---

[107] "Unrelated Business Income Tax," Statement of O. Donaldson Chapeton, Deputy Assistant Secretary (Tax Policy), Department of the Treasury, Hearings before the Subcommittee on Oversight, House Committee on Ways and Means, House of Representatives, 100th Cong., 1st Sess. 35 (1987).

[108] Bennett & Rudney, "A Commerciality Test to Resolve the Commercial Nonprofit Issue," 36 *Tax Notes* (No. 14) 1065 (1987).

[109] In general, Washlick, "The Commerciality Standard Changes the Rules of UBIT Planning," 4 *J. Tax. Exempt Orgs.* 15 (Nov./Dec. 1992); Hopkins, "Is the Rationale for Tax-Exempt Organizations Changing?," 4 *J. Tax. Exempt Orgs.* 13 (Spring 1992); Hopkins, "The Most Important Concept in the Law of Tax-Exempt Organizations Today: The Commerciality Doctrine," 5 *Exempt Org. Tax Rev.* (No. 3) 459 (1992); Brown, "Religious Nonprofits and the Commercial Manner Test," 99 *Yale L. J.* (No. 7) 1631 (1990).

CHAPTER TWENTY-SIX

Unrelated
Business Activities

One of the most significant components of the law of tax-exempt organizations is the body of law that defines, and taxes the net income from, exempt organizations' unrelated trade or business activities. Exempt organizations are permitted to engage in some activities that are not related to their exempt purposes. This type of undertaking is termed an *unrelated business*. Nearly all of what exempt organizations otherwise do is considered related business activity.

§ 26.1 INTRODUCTION

Taxation of the unrelated business income of tax-exempt organizations, a feature of the federal tax law introduced in 1950, is predicated on the concept that this approach is a more effective and workable sanction for enforcement of this aspect of the law of exempt organizations than denial or revocation of exempt status because of unrelated business activity.[1] This aspect of the law is rested on two concepts: activities that are unrelated to an exempt organization's purposes are to be segregated from related business activities and the net income from unrelated business activities is taxed essentially in the same manner as the net income earned by for-profit organizations.[2] That is, the unrelated business income tax applies only to income generated by active business activities that are unrelated to an exempt organization's tax-exempt purposes.

The primary objective of the unrelated business rules is to eliminate a source of unfair competition with for-profit businesses, by placing the unrelated business activities of tax-exempt organizations on the same tax basis as the nonexempt business endeavors with which they compete.[3] The House Ways and Means Committee report that accompanied the Revenue Act of 1950 contained the observation that the "problem at which the tax on unrelated business income is directed here is primarily that of unfair competition," in that exempt organizations can "use their profits tax-free to expand operations, while their competitors can expand only with the profits remaining after taxes."[4] The Senate Committee on Finance reaffirmed this position nearly three decades later when it noted that one "major purpose" of the unrelated business rules "is to make certain that an exempt organization does not commercially exploit its exempt status for the purpose of unfairly competing with taxpaying organizations."[5]

This rationale for the unrelated business rules has begun to be subjected to revisionist theories, namely, the view that other objectives are equally important. Thus, a federal appellate court observed that, "although Congress enacted the [unrelated business income rules] to eliminate a perceived form of unfair competition, that aim existed as a corollary to the larger goals of producing revenue and achieving equity in the tax system."[6] Another appellate court, electing more reticence, stated that "while the equalization of competition between taxable and tax-exempt entities was a major goal of the unrelated business income tax, it was by no means that statute's sole objective."[7] At a minimum, however, elimination

---

[1] An analysis of developments leading to enactment of the unrelated business rules is in Myers, "Taxing the Colleges," 38 *Cornell L. Q.* 388 (1953).

[2] See § 28.1.

[3] Reg. § 1.513-1(b).

[4] H. Rep. No. 2319, 81st Cong., 2d Sess. 36-37 (1950). Also S. Rep. No. 2375, 81st Cong., 2d Sess. 28-29 (1950).

[5] S. Rep. No. 94-938, 94th Cong., 2d Sess. 601 (1976).

[6] Louisiana Credit Union League v. United States, 693 F.2d 525, 540 (5th Cir. 1982).

[7] American Medical Ass'n v. United States, 887 F.2d 760, 772 (7th Cir. 1989).

of this type of competition clearly was Congress's principal aim; the tax regulations proclaim that it was the federal legislature's "primary objective."[8]

Generally, unrelated business activities must be confined to something less than a substantial portion of a tax-exempt organization's overall activities.[9] This is a manifestation of the *primary purpose test*.[10] According to traditional analysis, if a substantial portion of an exempt organization's income is from unrelated sources, the organization cannot qualify for tax exemption.[11] The IRS may deny or revoke the exempt status of an organization where it regularly derives over one-half of its annual revenue from unrelated activities.[12]

Although there generally are no specific percentage limitations in this area,[13] it is common to measure substantiality and insubstantiality in terms of percentages of expenditures or time.[14] Thus, generally, if a substantial portion of a tax-exempt organization's income is from unrelated sources, the organization cannot qualify for exemption. For example, a court barred an organization from achieving exempt status where the organization received about one-third of its revenue from an unrelated business.[15]

Still, this is not the approach always taken by the IRS or the courts. As the IRS framed the matter, there is no "quantitative limitation" on the amount of unrelated business in which a tax-exempt organization may engage.[16] Likewise, a court wrote that "[w]hether an activity [of an exempt organization] is substantial is a facts-and-circumstances inquiry not always dependent upon time or expenditure percentages."[17]

Yet there are countervailing principles. The IRS, from time to time, applies the *commensurate test*, which compares the extent of a tax-exempt organization's resources to its program efforts.[18] Pursuant to this test, an organization may derive a substantial portion of its revenue in the form of unrelated business income, yet nonetheless be exempt because it also expends a significant amount of time on exempt functions. Thus, in one instance, although a charitable organization derived 98 percent of its income from an unrelated business, it remained exempt because 41 percent of the organization's activities, as mea-

---

[8] Reg. § 1.513-1(b).

[9] Rev. Rul. 66-221, 1966-2 C.B. 220 (holding that a volunteer fire department was tax-exempt, notwithstanding an incidental amount of unrelated business activities).

[10] See § 4.4.

[11] E.g., People's Educ. Camp Soc'y, Inc. v. Comm'r, 331 F.2d 923 (2d Cir. 1964), *cert. den.*, 379 U.S. 839 (1964); Indiana Retail Hardware Ass'n v. United States, 366 F.2d 998 (Ct. Cl. 1966); Rev. Rul. 69-220, 1969-1 C.B. 154.

[12] E.g., Gen. Couns. Mem. 39108.

[13] See, however, § 28.3, text accompanied by notes 38-39.

[14] Similar definitional issues pertain with respect to the limits on allowable lobbying by public charities (see § 20.3).

[15] Orange County Agricultural Soc'y, Inc. v. Comm'r, 893 F.2d 647 (2d Cir. 1990), *aff'g* 55 T.C.M. 1602 (1988).

[16] Tech. Adv. Mem. 200021056.

[17] The Nationalist Movement v. Comm'r, 102 T.C. 558, 589 (1994), *aff'd*, 37 F.3d 216 (5th Cir. 1994). Also Manning Ass'n v. Comm'r, 93 T.C. 596 (1989); Church in Boston v. Comm'r, 71 T.C. 102 (1978).

[18] See § 4.7.

sured in terms of expenditure of time, constituted exempt programs.[19] Utilizing another approach, the IRS permitted an organization to remain exempt, even though two-thirds of its operations were unrelated businesses, inasmuch as the purpose for the conduct of these businesses was achievement of charitable purposes.[20] On that occasion, the IRS said that one way in which a business may be in furtherance of exempt purposes "is to raise money for the exempt purpose of the organization, notwithstanding that the actual trade or business activity may be taxable." The agency reiterated that the "proper focus is upon the purpose of [the organization's] activities and not upon the taxability of its activities."[21]

An organization may qualify as a tax-exempt entity, although it operates a trade or business as a substantial part of its activities, where the operation of the business is in furtherance of the organization's exempt purposes. In determining the nature of a primary purpose, all of the circumstances must be considered, including the size and extent of the trade or business and of the activities that are in furtherance of one or more exempt purposes.[22] For example, an organization that purchased and sold at retail products manufactured by blind individuals was held by a court to qualify as an exempt charitable organization because its activities resulted in employment for the blind, notwithstanding its receipt of net profits and its distribution of some of these profits to qualified workers.[23]

Funds received by a tax-exempt organization as an agent for another organization are not taxable income to the exempt organization and thus are not unrelated business income.[24]

The unrelated business rules are applicable to nearly all categories of tax-exempt organizations.[25] These rules are inapplicable to governmental entities, however, other than colleges and universities that are agencies or instrumentalities of a government or political subdivision of a government, or that are owned or operated by a government or such political subdivision or by any agency or instrumentality of one or more governments or political subdivisions of them; the rules also apply to any corporation wholly owned by one or more of these colleges or universities.[26] These rules also do not apply to instrumentalities of the federal government,[27] certain religious and apostolic organizations,[28] farmers' cooperatives,[29] and shipowners' protection and indemnity associations.[30]

---

[19] Tech. Adv. Mem. 9711003.
[20] Tech. Adv. Mem. 200021056.
[21] The fact that a business generates net income for exempt activities is alone insufficient to cause the business to be regarded as a related one (see *infra* text accompanied by note 159).
[22] Reg. § 1.501(c)(3)-1(e)(1).
[23] Industrial Aid for the Blind v. Comm'r, 73 T.C. 96 (1979).
[24] E.g., Priv. Ltr. Rul. 7823048.
[25] IRC § 511(a)(2)(A).
[26] IRC § 511(a)(2)(B).
[27] See § 18.1.
[28] See § 8.7.
[29] See § 18.11.
[30] See § 18.12.

The portion of a tax-exempt organization's gross income that is subject to the tax on unrelated business income is generally includible in the computation of unrelated business taxable income when three factors are present: the income is from a *trade or business*,[31] the business is *regularly carried on* by the exempt organization,[32] and the conduct of the business is not substantially related to the performance by the organization of its exempt functions.[33] In addition, there are certain types of income and certain types of activities that are exempt from unrelated business income taxation.[34]

In recent years, considerable attention has been accorded the phenomenon of tax-exempt organizations that are considered to be operating in a commercial manner[35] or unfairly competing with for-profit organizations.[36] Some of the activities that are under review as being ostensibly commercial or competitive are those that are *related*, rather than *unrelated*, businesses.[37]

§ 26.2 DEFINITION OF *TRADE OR BUSINESS*

As noted, some or all of the gross income of a tax-exempt organization may be includible in the computation of unrelated business income where it is income from a *trade or business*.

(a) General Principles

The statutory definition of the term *trade or business*, used for unrelated business law purposes, states that it includes "any activity which is carried on for the production of income from the sale of goods or the performance of services."[38] This definition is sweeping and encompasses nearly every activity that a tax-exempt organization may undertake. Indeed, the federal tax law views an exempt organization as a cluster of businesses, with each discrete activity susceptible to evaluation independently from the others.[39]

The definition of the term *trade or business*, however, also embraces an activity that otherwise possesses the characteristics of a business as that term is defined by the federal income tax law in the business expense deduction setting.[40] This definition, then, is even more expansive than the statutory one, being in-

---

[31] See infra § 2.
[32] See infra § 3.
[33] See *infra* § 4. In general, Reg. § 1.513-1(a).
[34] See Chapter 27.
[35] See Chapter 25.
[36] E.g., At Cost Services, Inc. v. Comm'r, 80 T.C.M. 573 (2000). See *infra* § (c).
[37] E.g., Priv. Ltr. Rul. 200051049 (concerning the operation of fitness centers, that compete with for-profit health clubs, by exempt hospitals and universities). In general, Horvitz, "Financing Related Commercial Activities of Exempt Universities," 55 *Taxes* 457 (1977); Note, "Profitable Related Business Activities and Charitable Exemption Under Section 501(c)(3)," 44 *Geo. Wash. L. Rev.* 270 (1976).
[38] IRC § 513(c).
[39] See the discussion of the *fragmentation rule* (*infra* § (f)).
[40] Reg. § 1.513-1(b). The business expense deduction is the subject of IRC § 162.

formed by the considerable body of law as to the meaning of the word *business* that has accreted in the federal tax law generally.

There is a third element to consider in this regard, stemming from the view that, to constitute a business, an income-producing activity of a tax-exempt organization must have the general characteristics of a trade or business. Some courts of appeals have recognized that an exempt organization must carry out extensive business activities over a substantial period of time to be considered engaged in a trade or business.[41] In one case, a court held that the proceeds derived by an exempt organization from gambling operations were not taxable as unrelated business income, inasmuch as the organization's functions in this regard were considered insufficiently "extensive" to warrant treatment as a business.[42] In another instance, the receipt of payments by an exempt association pursuant to involvement in insurance plans was ruled to not constitute a business because the association's role was not extensive and did not possess the general characteristics of a trade or business.[43] This aspect of the analysis, however, is close to a separate test altogether, which is whether the business activities are regularly carried on.[44]

Where an activity carried on for profit constitutes an unrelated business, no part of the business may be excluded from classification as a business merely because it does not result in profit.[45]

Traditionally, the government has almost always prevailed on the argument that an activity of a tax-exempt organization constitutes a trade or business. In recent years, however, courts have been more willing to conclude that an exempt organization's financial undertaking does not rise to the level of a business.[46]

(b) Requirement of Profit Motive

The most important element in the federal tax law as to whether an activity is a trade or business, for purposes of the business expense deduction (aside from the underlying statutory definition), is the presence of a *profit motive*. The courts have exported the profit objective standard into this aspect of the law of tax-exempt organizations.

The Supreme Court held that the principal test in this regard is that the "taxpayer's primary purpose for engaging in the activity must be for income or profit."[47] In the tax-exempt organization's context, the Court said that the inquiry should be whether the activity "was entered into with the dominant

---

[41] E.g., in the tax-exempt organizations context, Professional Insurance Agents v. Comm'r, 726 F.2d 1097 (6th Cir. 1984). E.g., in the business expense deduction context, Zell v. Comm'r, 763 F.2d 1139 (10th Cir. 1985); McDowell v. Ribicoff, 292 F.2d 174 (3d Cir. 1961), *cert. den.*, 368 U.S. 919 (1961).
[42] Vigilant Hose Company of Emmitsburg v. United States, 2001-2 U.S.T.C. ¶ 50,458 (D. Md. 2001).
[43] American Academy of Family Physicians v. United States, 91 F.3d 1155 (8th Cir. 1996).
[44] See *infra* § 3.
[45] IRC § 513(c).
[46] E.g., Laborer's Int'l Union of North America v. Comm'r, 82 T.C.M. 158 (2001).
[47] Comm'r v. Groetzinger, 480 U.S. 23, 35 (1987).

hope and intent of realizing a profit."[48] An appellate court stated that the "existence of a genuine profit motive is the most important criterion for . . . a trade or business."[49]

Various federal courts of appeal have applied the profit motive element to ascertain whether an activity of a tax-exempt organization is a business for purposes of the unrelated business rules. For example, an appellate court employed an *objective profit motivation test* to ascertain whether an exempt organization's activity is a business. This court wrote that "there is no better objective measure of an organization's motive for conducting an activity than the ends it achieves."[50] Subsequently, this court held that an activity of an exempt organization was a business because it "received considerable financial benefits" from performance of the activity, which was found to be "persuasive evidence" of a business endeavor.[51] On this latter occasion, the court defined as a business the situation where a "non-profit entity performs comprehensive and essential business services in return for a fixed fee."[52] Thereafter, this appellate court wrote simply that for an activity of a tax-exempt organization to be a business, it must be conducted with a "profit objective."[53] Another appellate court observed that an insurance company's payments to an exempt association were not taxable, in that "it does not matter whether the payments were brokerage fees, gratuities, to promote goodwill, or interest," since the association was not engaging in business activity for a profit.[54] Other courts of appeals have adopted this profit motive test.[55]

A court concluded, in the case of a tax-exempt labor union[56] that collected per capita taxes from unions affiliated with it, that, other than the services the union provides its members and affiliated unions in furtherance of its exempt purposes, the union "provide[d] no goods or services for a profit and therefore cannot be a trade or business."[57]

The IRS applies the profit motive test. In one example, a tax-exempt health care provider sold a building to another provider organization; it was used to operate a skilled nursing and personal care home. The selling entity

---

[48] United States v. American Bar Endowment, 477 U.S. 105, 110, note 1 (1986). The Court cited for this proposition the appellate court opinion styled Brannen v. Comm'r, 722 F.2d 695 (11th Cir. 1984).

[49] Professional Insurance Agents v. Comm'r, *supra* note 41, at 1102.

[50] Carolinas Farm & Power Equipment Dealers Ass'n, Inc. v. United States, 699 F.2d 167, 170 (4th Cir. 1983).

[51] Steamship Trade Ass'n of Baltimore, Inc. v. Comm'r, 757 F.2d 1494, 1497 (4th Cir. 1985).

[52] *Id.* This latter statement, however, is a mischaracterization of the law. There is no requirement, for an activity to be a business, that the endeavor be *comprehensive* nor is there a requirement that the activity be *essential*. Also, the mode of payment is irrelevant; whether the payment is by fixed fee, commission, or some other standard has no bearing on whether the income-producing activity is a business.

[53] West Va. State Medical Ass'n v. Comm'r, 882 F.2d 123, 125 (4th Cir. 1989), *cert. den.*, 493 U.S. 1044 (1990).

[54] American Academy of Family Physicians v. United States, *supra* note 43, at 1159-1160.

[55] E.g., Louisiana Credit Union League v. United States, *supra* note 6; Professional Ins. Agents v. Comm'r, *supra* note 41.

[56] See § 15.1.

[57] Laborer's Int'l Union of North America v. Comm'r, *supra* note 46, at 160.

provided food service to the patients for about seven months, at a net loss; the IRS characterized the food service operation as merely an "accommodation" to the purchasing entity.[58] Finding the activity to not be conducted in a manner characteristic of a commercial enterprise—that is, an operation motivated by profit—the IRS looked to these factors: there was no evidence, such as a business plan, that a food service business was being started; the organization did not take any steps to expand the food service to other unrelated organizations; the organization did not actively solicit additional clientele for a meal (or food catering) business; the organization did not take any steps to increase the per-meal charge, which was substantially below cost; and the service relationship between the organizations was not evidenced by a contract. On another occasion, the IRS concluded that, although the development of a housing project and sales of parcels of land was an unrelated business of an exempt planned community, the provision of water, sewer, and garbage services in conjunction with the project lacked a profit motive, so that the income received for the services was not taxable as unrelated business income.[59]

A tax-exempt organization may have more than one activity that it considers a business. An activity of this nature may generate net income or it may generate a net loss. When calculating net taxable unrelated business income, an exempt organization may offset the loss from one business against the gain from another business in determining taxable income. If the loss activity, however, consistently (year-in and year-out) produces losses, the IRS may take the position that the activity is not a business, because of absence of a profit motive, and disallow the loss deduction. Occasional losses, however, should not lead to this result.

(c) Factor of Competition

The presence or absence of competition—fair or unfair—is not among the criteria, in a statute or regulation, applied in assessing whether an activity of a tax-exempt organization is an unrelated business. This is the case notwithstanding the fact that concern about competition between exempt and for-profit organizations is the principal reason for and underpinning of the unrelated business rules.[60]

Thus, an activity of a tax-exempt organization may be wholly noncompetitive with an activity of a for-profit organization and nonetheless be an unrelated business. For example, in an opinion finding that the operation of a bingo game by an exempt organization was an unrelated business, a court wrote that the "tax on unrelated business income is not limited to income earned by a trade or business that operates in competition with taxpaying entities."[61] Yet, in a case concerning an exempt labor union which collected per capita taxes from unions affiliated with it, a court concluded that the imposition of these taxes, which en-

---

[58] Tech. Adv. Mem. 9719002.
[59] Tech. Adv. Mem. 200047049.
[60] See *supra* § 1, text accompanied by notes 2–7.
[61] Clarence LaBelle Post No. 217 v. United States, 580 F.2d 270, 272 (8th Cir. 1978).

abled the union to perform its exempt functions, "simply is not conducting a trade or business," in part because the union was not providing any services in competition with taxable entities.[62]

(d) Commerciality

Where there is competition, a court may conclude that the activity of a tax-exempt organization is being conducted in a commercial manner[63] and thus is an unrelated business. For example, the operation of a television station by an exempt university was held to be an unrelated business because it was operated in a commercial manner; the station was an affiliate of a national television broadcasting company.[64]

Historically, the IRS has used the commerciality doctrine in assessing an organization's qualification for tax-exempt status; the doctrine was not used to ascertain the presence of an unrelated business. This appears to be changing, however, with the IRS employing the doctrine in rationalizing that a business is an unrelated one.[65]

(e) Charging of Fees

Many tax-exempt organizations charge fees for the services they provide; where the business generating this revenue is a related one, the receipts are characterized as *exempt function revenue*.[66] Universities, colleges, hospitals, museums, planetariums, orchestras, and like institutions generate exempt function revenue, without adverse impact as to their exempt status.[67] Organizations such as medical clinics, homes for the aged, and blood banks impose charges for their services and are not subject to unrelated income taxation (or deprived of exemption) as a result.[68] Indeed, the IRS, in a ruling discussing the tax status of homes for the aged as charitable organizations, observed that the "operating funds [of these homes] are derived principally from fees charged for residence in the home."[69] Similarly, the IRS ruled that a nonprofit theater may charge admission for its performances and nonetheless qualify as an exempt charitable organization.[70] Other fee-based exempt charitable entities include hospices,[71] organizations providing specially designed housing for the elderly,[72] and organizations

---

[62] Laborers' Int'l Union of North America v. Comm'r, *supra* note 46, at 160.
[63] See Chapter 25.
[64] Iowa State Univ. of Science & Technology v. United States, 500 F.2d 508 (Ct. Cl. 1974).
[65] E.g., Tech. Adv. Mem. 200021056.
[66] See, e.g., § 11.3(b)(iv).
[67] IRC § 170(b)(1)(A)(ii), (iii); Reg. § 1.170A-9(e)(1)(ii); Reg. § 1.501(c)(3)-1(d)(3)(ii), Ex. (4).
[68] E.g., Rev. Rul. 72-124, 1972-1 C.B. 145; Rev. Rul. 70-590, 1970-2 C.B. 116; Rev. Rul. 66-323, 1966-2 C.B. 216, *mod. by* Rev. Rul. 78-145, 1978-1 C.B. 169.
[69] Rev. Rul. 72-124, *supra* note 68, at 145.
[70] Rev. Rul. 73-45, 1973-1 C.B. 220.
[71] Rev. Rul. 79-17, 1979-1 C.B. 193.
[72] Rev. Rul. 79-18, 1979-1 C.B. 194.

providing housing for the disabled.[73] Moreover, for some types of publicly supported charities, exempt function revenue is regarded as support enhancing public charity status.[74] Several categories of exempt organizations, such as business associations, unions, social clubs, fraternal groups, and veterans' organizations are dues-based entities.

Yet the receipt of fee-for-service revenue occasionally is regarded in some quarters as evidence of the conduct of an unrelated business. For example, the contention is made from time to time that an organization, to be charitable in nature, must provide its services and/or sell its goods without charge. In fact, the test is, for charitable and other exempt organizations, how the fees received are expended; the rendering of services without charge is not a prerequisite to tax-exempt status.

In one instance, the IRS opposed tax exemption for nonprofit consumer credit counseling agencies. The agencies asserted that their services, provided to individuals and families, as well as facilitating speakers and disseminating publications, were educational in nature as being forms of instruction of the public on subjects (such as budgeting) useful to the individual and beneficial to the community.[75] They also contended that their activities were charitable because they advance education and promote social welfare.[76] The IRS sought to deny these agencies exempt status on the ground that they charge a fee for certain services, even though the fee was nominal and waived in instances of economic hardship. This effort was rebuffed in court.[77] Thereafter, the IRS's office of chief counsel advised that if the "activity [of consumer credit counseling] may be deemed to benefit the community as a whole, the fact that fees are charged for the organization's services will not detract from the exempt nature of the activity" and that the "presence of a fee is relevant only if it inhibits accomplishment of the desired result."[78] (Earlier, the chief counsel's office wrote that the fact that a charitable organization charges a fee for a good or service "will be relevant in very few cases," that the "only inquiry" should be whether the charges "significantly detract from the organization's charitable purposes," and that the cost issue is pertinent only where the activities involved are commercial in nature.[79]) At about the same time, the IRS ruled that an organization that is operated to provide legal services to indigents may charge, for each hour of legal assistance provided, a "nominal hourly fee determined by reference to the client's own hourly income."[80]

There have been instances where the IRS determined that an organization is charitable in nature, and thus tax-exempt, because it provides services that

[73] Rev. Rul. 79-19, 1979-1 C.B. 195.
[74] IRC § 509(a)(2). See § 11.3(b)(iv).
[75] Reg. § 1.501(c)(3)-1(d)(3) (i) (b). See § 7.4.
[76] Reg. § 1.501(c)(3)-1(d)(2). See § 6.6.
[77] Consumer Credit Counseling Service of Ala., Inc. v. United States, 78-2 U.S.T.C. ¶ 9660 (D.D.C. 1978).
[78] Gen. Couns. Mem. 38459.
[79] Gen. Couns. Mem. 37257.
[80] Rev. Rul. 78-428, 1978-2 C.B. 177.

are free to the recipients. This is, however, an independent basis for finding a charitable activity, usually invoked where the services, assistance, or benefits provided are not inherently charitable in nature. This distinction may be seen in the treatment by the IRS of cooperative service organizations established by colleges and universities. In one instance, a computer services sharing organization was ruled to be an exempt charitable organization because the IRS concluded that the services provided to the participating institutions of higher education were charitable as advancing education; no requirement was imposed that the services be provided without charge.[81] In another instance, a similar organization was found to be charitable even though the services it rendered to the participating educational institutions were regarded as non-exempt functions (being "administrative"); the distinguishing feature was that the organization received less than 15 percent of its financial support from the colleges and universities that received the services.[82] Thus, the recipient entities were receiving the services for, at most, a nominal charge. Had this latter organization been providing only an insubstantial extent of administrative services and a substantial amount of exempt services, its exemption would have been predicated on the basis that it was engaging in inherently exempt activities; the 15-percent rule was employed only as an alternative rationale for exemption as a charitable entity.[83]

Thus, the law does not require, as a condition of tax exemption or avoidance of unrelated income, that the organization provide services without charge.[84] Likewise, the fact that an exempt organization charges a fee for the provision of goods or services, while perhaps an indicator that the underlying activity is a *business*, should not lead to an automatic conclusion that the business is an unrelated one.

(f) Fragmentation Rule

The IRS has the authority to tax net income from an activity as unrelated business taxable income, where the activity is an integral part of a cluster of activities that is in furtherance of a tax-exempt purpose. To ferret out unrelated business, the IRS regards an exempt organization as a bundle of activities and evaluates each of the activities in isolation to determine if one or more of them constitutes a trade or business. This assessment process is known as *fragmentation*.

The *fragmentation rule* states that an "activity does not lose identity as trade or business merely because it is carried on within a larger aggregate of similar activities or within a larger complex of other endeavors which may, or may not, be related to the exempt purpose of the organization."[85] Thus, as noted, the IRS is

---

[81] Rev. Rul. 74-614, 1974-2 C.B. 164, *amp. by* Rev. Rul. 81-29, 1981-1 C.B. 329.
[82] Rev. Rul. 71-529, 1971-2 C.B. 234.
[83] In general, see § 10.5.
[84] The "position that the test of a charitable institution is the extent of free services rendered, is difficult of application and unsound in theory" (Southern Methodist Hosp. & Sanatorium of Tucson v. Wilson, 77 P.2d 458, 462 (Ariz. 1943)).
[85] IRC § 513(c); Reg. § 1.513-1(b).

empowered to fragment the operations of a tax-exempt organization, operated as an integrated whole, into its component parts in search of one or more unrelated businesses.

The fragmentation rule was fashioned to tax the net income derived by a tax-exempt organization from the soliciting, selling, and publishing of commercial advertising, even where the advertising is published in a publication of an exempt organization that contains editorial matter related to the exempt purposes of the organization.[86] That is, the advertising functions constitute an unrelated business even though the overall set of publishing activities amounts to one or more related businesses; the advertising is an integral part of the larger publication activity.[87]

There are no stated limits as to the level of detail the IRS may pursue in application of the fragmentation rule. A tax-exempt university may find the agency's examiners probing its campus bookstore operations, evaluating goods for sale on nearly an item-by-item basis. An exempt association may watch as the IRS slices up its various services to members into numerous businesses. An exempt charitable organization may be surprised to see the IRS carve its fundraising program into a range of business activities.

A tax-exempt blood bank that sold blood plasma to commercial laboratories, was found by the IRS to not be engaging in unrelated business when it sold by-product plasma and salvage plasma, because these plasmas were produced in the conduct of related businesses, but was ruled to be engaged in unrelated business when it sold plasmapheresed plasma and plasma it purchased from other blood banks.[88] An exempt organization, the primary purpose of which was to retain and stimulate commerce in the downtown area of a city where parking facilities were inadequate, was ruled to be engaged in related businesses when it operated a fringe parking lot and shuttle service to the downtown shops, and an unrelated business by conducting a park-and-shop plan.[89]

The use of a tax-exempt university's golf course by its students and employees was ruled to not be unrelated businesses, while use of the course by alumni of the university and major donors to it were found to be unrelated businesses.[90] The fragmentation rule was applied to differentiate between related and unrelated travel tours conducted by an educational and religious organization.[91] An exempt charitable organization was held to be a dealer in certain parcels of real property and thus engaged in unrelated business with respect to those properties, even though the principal impetus for the acquisition and sale of real property by the organization was achievement of exempt

---

[86] The caption of IRC § 513(c), which also contains the basic definition of the term *business* (see *supra* § (a)), is "Advertising, etc." The rules by which advertising revenue is cast as unrelated business income are the subject of *infra* § 5(f).

[87] Reg. § 1.512(a)-1(f).

[88] Rev. Rul. 78-145, 1978-1 C.B. 169.

[89] Rev. Rul. 79-31, 1979-1 C.B. 206.

[90] Tech. Adv. Mem. 9645004.

[91] Tech. Adv. Mem. 9702004. See *infra* § 5(h).

purposes.[92] An exempt monastery, the members of which made and sold caskets, was ruled to be engaged in a related business as long as the caskets were used in funeral services conducted by churches that are part of the religious denomination supporting the monastery but was held to be conducting an unrelated business where the caskets were used in services conducted by other churches.[93] An exempt organization established to benefit deserving women, in part by enabling them to sell foodstuffs and handicrafts, was held to operate a consignment shop as a related business but a retail gift shop and a small restaurant were found to be unrelated businesses.[94]

(g) Nonbusiness Activities

Not every activity of a tax-exempt organization that generates a financial return is a trade or business for purposes of the unrelated business rules. As the Supreme Court observed, the "narrow category of trade or business" is a "concept which falls far short of reaching every income or profit making activity."[95] Specifically in the exempt organization's context, an appellate court wrote that "there are instances where some activities by some exempt organizations to earn income in a noncommercial manner will not amount to the conduct of a trade or business."[96]

The most obvious of the types of non-business activities is the management by a tax-exempt organization of its own investment properties. Under the general rules, concerning the business expense deduction, defining *business activity*, the management of an investment portfolio composed wholly of the manager's own securities does not constitute the carrying on of a trade or business. The Supreme Court held that the mere derivation of income from securities and keeping of records is not the operation of a business.[97] On that occasion, the Court sustained the government's position that "mere personal investment activities never constitute carrying on a trade or business."[98] Subsequently, the Court stated that "investing is not a trade or business."[99] Likewise, a court of appeals observed that the "mere management of investments . . . is insufficient to constitute the carrying on of a trade or business."[100]

---

[92] Priv. Ltr. Rul. 200119061.

[93] Priv. Ltr. Rul. 200033049.

[94] Tech. Adv. Mem. 200021056.

[95] Whipple v. Comm'r, 373 U.S. 193, 197, 201 (1963).

[96] Steamship Trade Ass'n of Baltimore, Inc. v. Comm'r, *supra* note 51, at 1497. Also Adirondack League Club v. Comm'r, 458 F.2d 506 (2d Cir. 1972); Blake Constr. Co., Inc. v. United States, 572 F.2d 820 (Ct. Cl. 1978); Monfore v. United States, 77-2 U.S.T.C. ¶ 9528 (Ct. Cl. 1977); Oklahoma Cattlemen's Ass'n, Inc. v. United States, 310 F. Supp. 320 (W.D. Okla. 1969); McDowell v. Ribicoff, *supra* note 41.

[97] Higgins v. Comm'r, 312 U.S. 212 (1941).

[98] *Id.* at 215.

[99] Whipple v. Comm'r, *supra* note 95, at 202.

[100] Continental Trading, Inc. v. Comm'r, 265 F.2d 40, 43 (9th Cir. 1959), *cert. den.*, 361 U.S. 827 (1959). Also VanWart v. Comm'r, 295 U.S. 112 (1935); Deputy v. duPont, 308 U.S. 488 (1940) (concurring opinion); Moller v. United States, 721 F.2d 810 (Fed. Cir. 1983); Comm'r v. Burnett, 118 F.2d 659 (5th Cir. 1941); Rev. Rul. 56-511, 1956-2 C.B. 170.

This principle of law is applicable in the tax-exempt organizations context. For example, the IRS ruled that the receipt of income by an exempt employees' trust from installment notes purchased from the employer-settlor was not income from the operation of a business, noting that the trust "merely keeps the records and receives the periodic payments of principal and interest collected for it by the employer."[101] Likewise, the agency held that a reversion of funds from a qualified plan to a charitable organization did not "possess the characteristics" required for an activity to qualify as a business.[102] For a time, there was controversy over whether the practice, engaged in by some tax-exempt organizations, of lending securities to brokerage houses for compensation was an unrelated business;[103] the IRS ultimately arrived at the view that securities lending is a form of "ordinary or routine investment activities" and thus is not a business.[104] A court held that certain investment activities conducted by a charitable organization were not businesses.[105]

Other similar activities do not rise to the level of a business. In one instance, a tax-exempt association of physicians was held to not be taxable on certain payments it annually received by reason of its sponsorship of group insurance plans that were available to its members and their employees, with the court writing that the payments "were neither brokerage fees nor other compensation for commercial services, but were the way the parties decided to acknowledge the . . . [association's] eventual claim to the excess reserves while . . . [the insurance company involved] was still holding and using the reserves."[106] In another case, an exempt dental society that sponsored a payment plan to finance dental care was held to not be taxable on refunds for income taxes and interest on amounts paid as excess reserve funds from a bank and as collections on defaulted notes.[107] A comparable position was taken by a court in concluding that an exempt organization did not engage in an unrelated business by making health insurance available to its members, in that the organization did not control the financial result of the insurance activities.[108]

In still another case, a court held that the proceeds derived by a tax-exempt organization from gambling operations were not taxable as unrelated

---

[101] Rev. Rul. 69-574, 1969-2 C.B. 130, 131.

[102] Priv. Ltr. Rul. 200131034.

[103] E.g., Stern & Sullivan, "Exempt Organizations Which Lend Securities Risk Imposition of Unrelated Business Income Tax," 45 *J. Tax.* 240 (1976).

[104] Rev. Rul. 78-88, 1978-1 C.B. 163. This issue was subsequently further resolved by statute (see § 27.1(d)).

[105] The Marion Found. v. Comm'r, 19 T.C.M. 99 (1960).

[106] American Academy of Family Physicians v. United States, *supra* note 43, at 1159. Nonetheless, the IRS remains of the view that these types of oversight and like activities with respect to insurance programs constitute unrelated business (e.g., Tech Adv. Mem. 9612003 (concerning a charitable organization, fostering competition in a sport (see § 10.2), that provided certain administrative services in connection with an insurance program covering its members for practices and other sports activities)).

[107] San Antonio Dist. Dental Soc'y v. United States, 340 F. Supp. 11 (W.D. Tex. 1972).

[108] Carolinas Farm & Power Equip. Dealers Ass'n, Inc. v. United States, 541 F. Supp. 86 (E.D. N. Car. 1982), *aff'd, supra* note 50. Cf. § 27.1(o).

business income, in that the economic activity did not constitute a business.[109] The operations involved the use of "tip jars," with the exempt organization's role confined to applying for gambling permits and purchasing the tip-jar tickets; the significant and substantial portion of the gambling activities was the sale of the tickets at participating taverns. The exempt organization's functions in this regard were considered insufficiently "extensive" to warrant treatment as a business.[110]

(h) Real Estate Activities

A tax-exempt organization may acquire real property under a variety of circumstances and for a variety of reasons. The acquisition may be by purchase or by contribution. Often, this is undertaken to advance exempt purposes or to make an investment. The activity may be, or may be seen as being, part of dealings in the ordinary course of a business. When exempt functions are not involved, the dichotomy becomes whether the exempt organization is a passive investor or is a dealer in property. Often, the issue arises when the property, or portions of it, is being sold; the exempt organization may be liquidating an investment or selling property to customers in the ordinary course of business.

The elements to take into account in this evaluation are many. One is the purpose for which the property was acquired. Others are the length of time the property was held; the purpose for which the property was held; the proximity of the sale to the purchase of the property; the activities of the exempt organization in improving and disposing of the property; and the frequency, continuity, and size of the sales of the property.

In the absence of use of the property for exempt functions, the factor of frequency of sales tends to be the most important of the criteria.[111] Even in this context, the activity may not be characterized as a business if the sales activity results from unanticipated, externally introduced factors that make impossible the continued preexisting use of the property. The IRS places emphasis on the presence of and the reasons for improvements on the land.

The exception in the law for capital gain,[112] which interrelates with these rules, is not available when the property is sold in circumstances in which the exempt organization is a dealer in the property. When dealer status exists or is imposed, the property is considered to be property sold in the ordinary course of business, giving rise to ordinary income.

The standard followed in making these determinations, as to whether property is held primarily for sale in the ordinary course of business or is held for investment, is a primary purpose test. In this setting, the word *primary* has been interpreted to mean "of first importance" or "principally."[113] By this standard, the

---

[109] Vigilant Hose Co. of Emmitsburg v. United States, *supra* note 42.
[110] On occasion, as an alternative argument, the IRS will assert that the tax-exempt organization is involved in a joint venture with one or more for-profit entities and attempt to tax net revenues received by the exempt organization on that basis (see § 32.3).
[111] In part, this is due to the *regularly carried on test* (see *infra* § 3).
[112] See § 27.1(j).
[113] Malat v. Riddell, 383 U.S. 569 (1966).

IRS ruled, ordinary income would not result unless a "sales purpose" is "dominant."[114]

In a typical instance, the IRS reviewed a proposed sale of certain real estate interests held by a public charity. In the case, substantially all of the property was received by bequest and had been held for a significant period of time. The decision was made to sell the property (liquidate the investment) due to the enactment of legislation adverse to the investment, so as to receive fair market value. Availability of the property for sale was not advertised to the public. Applying the primary purpose test, the IRS concluded that the proposed sales did not involve property held primarily for sale to customers in the ordinary course of business.[115]

By contrast, a charitable organization purchased real estate, divided it into lots, and improved the lots. The project evolved into the equivalent of a municipality. Lots were sold to the general public pursuant to a marketing plan involving real estate companies. The IRS concluded that the subdivision, development, and sale of the lots was a business that was regularly carried on, "in a manner that is similar to a for-profit residential land development company." The organization advanced the argument that the land development and sales were done in furtherance of exempt purposes, by attracting members who participate in its educational programs.[116] But the IRS concluded that the relationship between the sales of lots for single family homes and the organization's goal of increasing program attendance was "somewhat tenuous." Therefore, the IRS held that the resulting sales income was unrelated business income.[117]

Even if the primary purpose underlying the acquisition and holding of real property is advancement of exempt purposes, the IRS may apply the fragmentation rule[118] in search of unrelated business. As the IRS stated the matter in one instance, a charitable organization "engaged in substantial regularly carried on unrelated trade [or] business as a component of its substantially related land purchase activity."[119] In the matter, the IRS looked to substantial and frequent sales of surplus land that was not intended for exempt use, and found that those sales were unrelated businesses. The same factors were used to reach that conclusion as are used in the general context, such as the sale of land shortly after its purchase and the extent of improvements.

(i) Efficiencies of Operation

On occasion, a court will focus on the fact that a tax-exempt organization is operating in a fashion that is considered "efficient," "effectively managed," "run like a

---

[114] Priv. Ltr. Rul. 9316032.
[115] *Id.*
[116] An argument of this nature was accepted in Junaluska Assembly Housing, Inc. v. Comm'r, 86 T.C. 1114 (1986).
[117] Tech. Adv. Mem. 200047049.
[118] See *supra* § (f).
[119] Priv. Ltr. Rul. 200119061.

business," and the like.[120] This can lead to a finding that the organization, or an activity of it, is—for that reason alone—a business undertaking.[121]

(j) Occasional Sales

Another illustration of a transaction involving a tax-exempt organization that is not a business undertaking is the occasional sale of an item of property. For example, the IRS held that a sale of property by an exempt entity was not under circumstances where the property was held primarily for sale to customers in the ordinary course of business.[122] By contrast, as noted, the subdivision, development, and sale of real estate parcels by an exempt organization was held by the IRS to be a business carried on in a manner similar to the activities of for-profit residential land development companies.[123]

This aspect of the law, however, is closely analogous to the *regularly carried on* test.[124]

§ 26.3   DEFINITION OF *REGULARLY CARRIED ON*

As noted, gross income of a tax-exempt organization may be includable in the computation of unrelated business income where the trade or business that produced the income is *regularly carried on* by the organization.

(a) General Principles

In determining whether a trade or business from which a particular amount of gross income is derived by a tax-exempt organization is *regularly carried on*,[125] regard must be had to the frequency and continuity with which the activities productive of the income are conducted and the manner in which they are pursued. This requirement is applied in light of the purpose of the unrelated business income rules, which is to place tax-exempt organization business activities on the same tax basis as the nonexempt business endeavors with which they compete.[126] Thus, for example, specific business activities of a tax-exempt organization will ordinarily be deemed to be *regularly carried on* if they manifest a frequency and

---

[120] See § 4.9.

[121] E.g., The Incorporated Trustees of the Gospel Worker Soc'y v. United States, 510 F. Supp. 374 (D.D.C. 1981), aff'd, 672 F.2d 894 (D.C. Cir. 1981), cert. den., 456 U.S. 944 (1981); Presbyterian & Reformed Publishing Co. v. Comm'r, 79 T.C. 1070 (1983).

[122] Priv. Ltr. Rul. 9316032.

[123] Tech. Adv. Mem. 200047049. See *supra* § (h).

[124] See *infra* § 3.

[125] IRC § 512.

[126] See *supra* § 1. This is one of only two aspects of the unrelated business rules where the commerciality doctrine (see Chapter 25) is expressly taken into account in the statute or tax regulations. The other aspect is the subject of § 22.1.

continuity, and are pursued in a manner generally similar to comparable commercial activities of nonexempt organizations.[127]

An illustration of this body of law is the case of a tax-exempt organization that published a yearbook for its membership. The publication contained advertising; the organization contracted on an annual basis with a commercial firm for solicitation of advertising sales, printing, and collection of advertising charges. Although the editorial materials were prepared by the staff of the organization, the organization, by means of its contract with the commercial firm, was ruled by the IRS to be "engaging in an extensive campaign of advertising solicitation" and thus to be "conducting competitive and promotional efforts typical of commercial endeavors."[128] Therefore, the income derived by this organization from the sale of advertising in its yearbook was deemed to be unrelated business income.

By contrast, a one-time sale of property (as opposed to an ongoing income-producing program) by a tax-exempt organization is not an activity that is regularly carried on and thus does not give rise to unrelated business income.[129] For example, an exempt organization that was formed to deliver diagnostic and medical health care and that developed a series of computer programs concerning management and administrative matters, such as patient admissions and billings, payroll, purchases, inventory, and medical records, sold some or all of the programs to another exempt organization comprising three teaching hospitals affiliated with a university; the income derived from the sale was held to be from a "one-time only operation" and thus not taxable as unrelated business income.[130] Likewise, the transfer of investment assets from a public charity to its supporting organization[131] is exempt from unrelated business taxation under this rule,[132] as is the infrequent sale of parcels of real estate.[133]

(b) Determining Regularity

Where income-producing activities are of a kind normally conducted by nonexempt commercial organizations on a year-round basis, the conduct of the activities by a tax-exempt organization over a period of only a few weeks does not constitute the regular carrying on of a business.[134] For example, the operation of a sandwich stand by a hospital auxiliary organization for two weeks at a state fair is not the regular conduct of a business.[135] The conduct of year-

---

[127] Reg. § 1.513-1(c)(1).
[128] Rev. Rul. 73-424, 1973-2 C.B. 190, 191.
[129] See *supra* § 2(i).
[130] Priv. Ltr. Rul. 7905129.
[131] See § 11.3(c).
[132] E.g., Priv. Ltr. Rul. 9425030.
[133] The gain from transactions of this nature may be protected from taxation by the exclusion for capital gain (see § 27.1(j)).
[134] Reg. § 1.513-1(c)(2)(i).
[135] *Id.*

round business activities for one day each week, such as the operation of a commercial parking lot once a week, however, constitutes the regular carrying on of a business.[136]

If income-producing activities are of a kind normally undertaken by nonexempt commercial organizations only on a seasonal basis, the conduct of the activities by a tax-exempt organization during a significant portion of the season ordinarily constitutes the regular conduct of a business.[137] For example, the operation of a track for horse racing for several weeks in a year is the regular conduct of a business where it is usual to carry on the business only during a particular season.[138] Likewise, where a distribution of greeting cards celebrating a holiday was deemed to be an unrelated business, the IRS measured regularity in terms of that holiday's season.[139]

In determining whether intermittently conducted activities are regularly carried on, the manner of conduct of the activities must, as noted, be compared with the manner in which commercial activities are normally pursued by nonexempt organizations.[140] In general, tax-exempt organization business activities that are engaged in only discontinuously or periodically will not be considered regularly carried on if they are conducted without the competitive and promotional efforts typical of commercial endeavors.[141] As an illustration, the publication of advertising in programs for sports events or music or drama performances will not ordinarily be deemed to be the regular carrying on of a business.[142] Conversely, where the nonqualifying sales are not merely casual but are systematically and consistently promoted and carried on by the organization, they meet the requirement of regularity.[143]

In determining whether a business is regularly carried on, the functions of a service provider with which a tax-exempt organization has contracted may be attributed to the exempt organization for these purposes. This is likely to be the case where the contract denominates the service provider as an agent of the exempt organization, in that the activities of an agent are attributed to the principal for law analysis purposes. In such a circumstance, the time expended by the service provider is attributed to the exempt organization for purposes of determining regularity.[144]

Noncompetition under a covenant not to compete, characterized as a "one-

---

[136] S. Rep. No. 2375, *supra* note 4, at 106–107.
[137] *Id.*
[138] *Id.* Also Rev. Rul. 68-505, 1968-2 C.B. 248.
[139] Priv. Ltr. Rul. 8203134.
[140] Reg. § 1.513-1(c)(1), (2)(ii).
[141] Reg. § 1.513-1(c)(2)(ii). Also Adam v. Comm'r, 60 T.C. 996 (1973).
[142] *Id.*
[143] *Id.* A leasing arrangement that was "one-time, completely fortuitous" was held to involve a business not regularly carried on (Museum of Flight Found. v. United States, 63 F. Supp. 2d 1257 (W.D. Wash. 1999)), whereas a lease of extended duration can constitute a business that is regularly carried on (Cooper Tire & Rubber Co. Employees' Retirement Fund v. Comm'r, 306 F.2d 20 (6th Cir. 1962)).
[144] National Collegiate Athletic Ass'n v. Commr, 92 T.C. 456 (1989), *aff'd, infra* note 153.

time agreement not to engage in certain activities," is not a taxable business inasmuch as the "activity" is not "continuous and regular."[145]

(c) Fundraising and Similar Activities

Fundraising activities, by charitable and other tax-exempt organizations, can constitute unrelated business activities.[146] Inasmuch as these activities rarely are inherently exempt functions, the rules as to *regularity* are often the only basis on which the income from these activities is not taxed as unrelated business income.

Certain intermittent income-producing activities occur so infrequently that neither their recurrence nor the manner of their conduct will cause them to be regarded as trades or businesses that are regularly carried on.[147] For example, fundraising activities lasting only a short time are not ordinarily treated as being regularly carried on if they recur only occasionally or sporadically.[148] Furthermore, activities will not be regarded as regularly carried on merely because they are conducted on an annual basis.[149] It is for this reason that many special event fundraising activities, such as dances, auctions, tournaments, car washes, and bake sales, do not give rise to unrelated business income.[150] In one instance, a court concluded that a vaudeville show conducted one weekend per year was an intermittent fundraising activity and thus not regularly carried on.[151]

(d) Preparatory Time

An issue of some controversy is whether the time expended by a tax-exempt organization in preparing for a business undertaking should be taken into account in assessing whether the activity is regularly carried on. The IRS asserts that this preparatory time should be considered, even where the event itself occupies only one or two days each year.[152] This preparatory time argument, however, has been rejected on the occasions it was considered by a court.[153] In the principal case, a federal court of appeals held that the preparatory time argument is inconsistent with the tax regulations, which do not mention the concept. The court referenced the example concerning operation of the sandwich

---

[145] Ohio Farm Bureau Fed., Inc. v. Comm'r, 106 T.C. 222, 234 (1996). This opinion caused the IRS to issue Gen. Couns. Mem. 39891, revoking Gen. Couns. Mem. 39865 (which held that refraining from competition in this context was a business activity).

[146] See *infra* § 5(g). In general, Hopkins, *The Law of Fundraising, Third Edition* (John Wiley & Sons, Inc., 2002), § 5.7.

[147] Reg. § 1.513-1(c)(2)(iii).

[148] *Id.*

[149] *Id.*

[150] E.g., Orange County Builders Ass'n, Inc. v. United States, 65-2 U.S.T.C. ¶ 9679 (S.D. Cal. 1965).

[151] Suffolk County Patrolmen's Benevolent Ass'n, Inc. v. Comm'r, 77 T.C. 1314 (1981).

[152] E.g., Tech. Adv. Mem. 9147007.

[153] National Collegiate Athletic Ass'n v. Comm'r, 914 F.2d 1417 (10th Cir. 1990); Suffolk County Patrolmen's Benevolent Assn, Inc. v. Comm'r, *supra* note 151.

stand at a state fair,[154] denigrating the thought that preparatory time should be taken into account as follows: "The regulations do not mention time spent in planning the activity, building the stand, or purchasing the alfalfa sprouts for the sandwiches."[155]

Nonetheless, the IRS is in disagreement with these holdings,[156] and writes private letter rulings and technical advice memoranda that are openly contrary to these cases. One of these instances concerned a tax-exempt organization which sponsored a concert series open to the public occupying two weekends each year, one in the spring and one in the fall. The preparation and ticket solicitation for each of the concerts usually occupied up to six months. Taking into account the preparatory time involved, the IRS concluded that the concerts were unrelated business activities that were regularly carried on.[157]

§ 26.4   DEFINITION OF *SUBSTANTIALLY RELATED*

As noted, gross income of a tax-exempt organization may be includible in the computation of unrelated business income where it is income from a trade or business that is regularly carried on and that is not *substantially related* to the exempt purposes of the organization.[158] (The fact that the organization needs or uses the funds for an exempt purpose does not make the underlying activity a related business.[159]) Thus, it is necessary to examine the relationship between the business activity that generates the income in question—the activity, that is, of producing or distributing the goods or performing the services involved—and the accomplishment of the organization's exempt purposes.[160]

To determine whether the conduct of an activity by a tax-exempt organization is substantially related to its exempt purpose, it is necessary to ascertain the organization's *primary* purpose or purposes, and then ascertain the organization's primary purpose in conducting the activity. Where the primary purpose behind the conduct of the activity is to further an exempt purpose, the activity meets the substantially related test. According to the IRS, this exercise entails examination of the "nature, scope and motivation" for conducting the activity.[161] As an example, the IRS concluded that the construction and operation of a regulation-size 18-hole golf course, replete with warm-up area, snack bar, and pro shop, was substantially related to the purposes of an exempt school operated to rehabilitate court-referred juveniles, inasmuch as the course was utilized primarily as part of the school's vocational education and career development department.[162]

---

[154] See text accompanied by *supra* note 135.
[155] National Collegiate Athletic Assn v. Comm'r, *supra* note 153, at 1423.
[156] AOD No. 1991-015.
[157] Tech. Adv. Mem. 9712001. The IRS acquiesced in the *Suffolk County Patrolmen's Ass'n* case (*supra* note 151) (AOD 1249 (1984). That acquiescence had no bearing in this instance, the IRS said, inasmuch as the preparatory time in that case was "much shorter."
[158] IRC § 513(a); Reg. § 1.513-1(a).
[159] Cf. text accompanied by *supra* note 21.
[160] Reg. § 1.513-1(d)(1).
[161] Priv. Ltr. Rul. 200151061.
[162] *Id.*

(a) General Principles

A trade or business is *related* to tax-exempt purposes of an organization only where the conduct of the business activity has a causal relationship to the achievement of an exempt purpose (again, other than through the production of income); it is *substantially related* only if the causal relationship is a substantial one.[163] Thus, for the conduct of a business from which a particular amount of gross income is derived to be substantially related to exempt purposes, the production or distribution of the goods or the performance of the services from which the gross income is derived must contribute importantly to the accomplishment of these purposes.[164] Where the production or distribution of the goods or the performance of services does not contribute importantly to the accomplishment of the exempt purposes of an organization, the income from the sale of the goods or the performance of the services does not derive from the conduct of related business.[165] A court wrote that resolution of the substantial relationship test requires an examination of the "relationship between the business activities which generate the particular income in question ... and the accomplishment of the organization's exempt purposes."[166]

Certainly, gross income derived from charges for the performance of a tax-exempt function does not constitute gross income from the conduct of an unrelated business.[167] Thus, income is not taxed when it is generated by functions such as performances by students enrolled in an exempt school for training children in the performing arts, the conduct of refresher courses to improve the trade skills of members of a union, and the presentation of a trade show for exhibiting industry products by a trade association to stimulate demand for the products.[168] Also, dues paid by bona fide members of an exempt organization are forms of related income.[169]

Whether activities productive of gross income contribute importantly to the accomplishment of an organization's exempt purpose depends in each case on the facts and circumstances involved.[170] A court observed that each of these instances requires a case-by-case identification of the exempt purpose involved and an analysis of how the activity contributed to the advancement of that purpose.[171] By reason of court opinions and IRS rulings, there have been many determina-

---

[163] Reg. § 1.513-1(d)(2).
[164] *Id.*
[165] *Id.*
[166] Louisiana Credit Union League v. United States, 693 F.2d 525, 534 (5th Cir. 1982).
[167] Reg. § 1.513-1(d)(4)(i).
[168] *Id.*
[169] E.g., Rev. Rul. 67-109, 1967-1 C.B. 136. However, certain forms of associate members dues are taxable as unrelated business income (see *infra* § 5(d)(iii), § 27.2(l)).
[170] Reg. § 1.513-1(d)(2).
[171] Hi-Plains Hosp. v. United States, 670 F.2d 528 (5th Cir. 1982). Also Huron Clinic Foundation v. United States, 212 F. Supp. 847 (D.S.D. 1962).

tions over the years as to whether particular activities are related businesses[172] or unrelated businesses.[173]

One of these determinations is particularly illustrative of these points of law. In the case, a tax-exempt charitable organization, the purpose of which was enabling needy women to support themselves, operated three businesses, each of equal size: a consignment shop, a gift shop, and a tearoom. The IRS concluded that the consignment shop was a related business, and that the gift shop and tearoom were unrelated businesses. As to the gift shop, the organization argued that it was a related business because the items in the gift shop enhanced the items in the consignment shop and attract customers. The IRS agreed that there was a causal relationship between the organization's exempt purposes and the operation of the gift shop (recognizing that the gift shop items were purchased "with the intent of imbuing the consignment items with an aura of sophistication and tastefulness"); the relationship, however, was found to not be substantial. The tearoom as well failed to be classified as a related business.[174]

(b) Size and Extent Test

In determining whether an activity contributes importantly to the accomplishment of a tax-exempt purpose, the *size and extent* of the activity must be considered in relation to the nature and extent of the exempt function that it purportedly serves.[175] Thus, where income is realized by an exempt organization from an activity that is generally related to the performance of its exempt functions, but the activity is conducted on a scale that is larger than reasonably necessary for performance of the functions, the gross income attributable to the portion of the activity that is in excess of the needs associated with exempt functions constitutes gross income from the conduct of an unrelated business.[176] This type of income is not derived from the production or distribution of goods or the performance of services that contribute importantly to the accomplishment of any exempt purpose of the organization.[177]

For example, one of the activities of a tax-exempt trade association, which had a membership of businesses in a particular state, was to supply companies (members and nonmembers) with job injury histories on prospective employees. Despite the association's contention that this service contributed to the accomplishment of its exempt purposes, the IRS ruled that the operation was an unrelated business, in that the activity went "well beyond" any mere development and promotion of efficient business practices.[178] The IRS adopted a similar pos-

---

[172] See *infra* § 4(f).
[173] See *infra* § 4(g).
[174] Tech. Adv. Mem. 200021056.
[175] Reg. § 1.513-1(d)(3). One court discussed the point that, in a search for unrelated activity, there should be an examination of the scale on which the activity is conducted (Hi-Plains Hosp. v. United States, *supra* note 171).
[176] Reg. § 1.513-1(d)(3).
[177] *Id.* In essence, the size and extent test is an application of the fragmentation rule (see *supra* § 2(d)).
[178] Rev. Rul. 73-386, 1973-2 C.B. 191, 192.

ture in ruling that a retail grocery store operation, formed to sell food in a poverty area at below-market prices and to provide job training for unemployed residents in the area, could not qualify for tax exemption because the operation was conducted on a "much larger scale than reasonably necessary" for the training program.[179] Similarly, the IRS ruled that the provision of private duty nurses to unrelated exempt organizations, by an exempt health care organization that provided temporary nurses and private duty nurses to patients of related organizations as related businesses, was an activity performed on a scale "much larger" than necessary for the achievement of exempt functions.[180]

By contrast, a tax-exempt organization formed to provide a therapeutic program for emotionally disturbed adolescents was the subject of a ruling from the IRS that a retail grocery store operation, almost fully staffed by adolescents to secure their emotional rehabilitation, was not an unrelated business because it was operated on a scale no larger than reasonably necessary for its training and rehabilitation program.[181] A like finding was made in relation to the manufacture and marketing of toys, which was the means by which an exempt organization accomplished its charitable purpose of training unemployed and underemployed individuals.[182]

(c) Same State Rule

Ordinarily, gross income from the sale of items that result from the performance of tax-exempt functions does not constitute gross income from the conduct of an unrelated business if the item is sold in substantially the *same state* it is in upon completion of the exempt functions.[183] Thus, in the case of a charitable organization engaged in a program of rehabilitation of disabled individuals, income from the sale of items made by them as part of their rehabilitation training was not gross income from the conduct of an unrelated business. The income in this instance was from the sale of products, the production of which contributed importantly to the accomplishment of the organization's exempt purposes, namely, rehabilitation of the disabled.[184] Conversely, if an item resulting from an exempt function is utilized or exploited in further business endeavors beyond that reasonably appropriate or necessary for disposition in the state it is in on completion of exempt functions, the gross income derived from these endeavors is from the conduct of unrelated business.[185]

As an illustration, in the case of an experimental dairy herd maintained for

---

[179] Rev. Rul. 73-127, 1973-1 C.B. 221, 222. Under similar facts, a nonprofit organization that operated restaurants and health food stores in accordance with the tenets of a church was denied tax-exempt status as a charitable entity on the ground that it was operated for substantially commercial purposes (*Living Faith, Inc. v. Comm'r*, 60 T.C.M. 710 (1990), *aff'd*, 950 F.2d 365 (7th Cir. 1991)).

[180] Priv. Ltr. Rul. 9535023.

[181] Rev. Rul. 76-94, 1976-1 C.B. 171.

[182] Rev. Rul. 73-128, 1973-1 C.B. 222.

[183] Reg. § 1.513-1(d)(4)(ii).

[184] *Id.*

[185] *Id.*

scientific purposes by a tax-exempt organization, income from the sale of milk and cream produced in the ordinary course of operation of the project is not gross income from the conduct of unrelated business. If, however, the organization utilized the milk and cream in the further manufacture of food items, such as ice cream and pastries, the gross income from the sale of these products would be from the conduct of unrelated business—unless the manufacturing activities themselves contributed importantly to the accomplishment of an exempt purpose of the organization.[186] Similarly, a charitable organization that operated a salmon hatchery as an exempt function was able to sell a portion of its harvested salmon stock in an unprocessed condition to fish processors in an untaxed business. By contrast, when it converted the fish into salmon nuggets (fish that was seasoned, formed into nugget shape, and breaded), the sale of the fish in that state was an unrelated business.[187]

(d) Dual Use Rule

An asset or facility of a tax-exempt organization that is necessary to the conduct of exempt functions may also be utilized for nonexempt purposes. In these *dual use* instances, the mere fact of the use of the asset or facility in an exempt function does not, by itself, make the income from the nonexempt endeavor gross income from a related business. The test is whether the activities productive of the income in question contribute importantly to the accomplishment of exempt purposes.[188] For example, an exempt museum may have an auditorium that is designed and equipped for showing educational films in connection with its program of public education in the arts and sciences. The theater is a principal feature of the museum and is in continuous operation during the hours the museum is open to the public. If the museum were to operate the theater as a motion picture theater for public entertainment during the evening hours when the museum is otherwise closed, gross income from that operation would be gross income from the conduct of an unrelated business.[189] Similarly, a mailing service operated by an exempt organization was ruled to be an unrelated trade or business even though the mailing equipment was also used for exempt purposes.[190]

Another illustration is the athletic facilities of a college or university, which, while used primarily for educational purposes, may also be made available for members of the faculty, other employees of the institution, and members of the general public. Income derived from the use of the facilities by those who are not students or employees of the institution is likely to be unrelated business

---

[186] *Id.*
[187] Priv. Ltr. Rul. 9320042.
[188] Reg. § 1.513-1(d)(4)(iii).
[189] *Id.*
[190] Rev. Rul. 68-550, 1968-2 C.B. 249.

income.[191] For example, the IRS ruled that the operation by a tax-exempt school of a ski facility for the general public was the conduct of an unrelated business, while use of the facility by the students of the school for recreational purposes and in its physical education program were related activities.[192] Likewise, a college that made available its facilities and personnel to an individual not associated with the institution for the conduct of a summer tennis camp was ruled to be engaged in the conduct of an unrelated business.[193]

The provision of athletic or other activities by an educational institution to outsiders may be a tax-exempt function, inasmuch as the instruction of individuals on the subject of a sport can be an educational activity.[194] As illustrations, the IRS held that the following were exempt educational activities: the conduct of a summer hockey camp for youths by a college,[195] the conduct of four summer sports camps by a university,[196] and the operation of a summer sports camp by a university-affiliated athletic association.[197] Similarly, the IRS determined that a college may operate a professional repertory theater on its campus that is open to the general public[198] and that a college may make its facilities available to outside organizations for the conduct of conferences[199]—both activities being in furtherance of exempt purposes.

This area of the law intertwines with the exclusion from unrelated income taxation for rent received by tax-exempt organizations.[200] For example, a college may lease its facilities to a professional sports team for the conduct of a summer camp and receive nontaxable lease income, as long as the college does not provide food or cleaning services to the team.[201] By contrast, where the institution provides services, such as cleaning, food, laundry, security, and grounds maintenance, the exclusion for rent is defeated.[202]

This dichotomy is reflected in the treatment the IRS accorded a tax-exempt school that used its tennis facilities, which were utilized during the academic year in the institution's educational program, in the summer as a public tennis club operated by employees of the school's athletic department. Because the school not only furnished its facilities, but operated the tennis club through its own employees who rendered substantial services for the participants in the club, the IRS held that the operation of the club was an unrelated business and that the income derived from the club's operation was not sheltered by the exclusion for rental income.[203] The IRS also observed that, however, if the school

---

[191] E.g., Tech. Adv. Mem. 9645004 (concerning dual use of a university's golf course).
[192] Rev. Rul. 78-98, 1978-1 C.B. 167.
[193] Rev. Rul. 76-402, 1976-2 C.B. 177.
[194] E.g., Rev. Rul. 77-365, 1977-2 C.B. 192. In general, see § 7.4.
[195] Priv. Ltr. Rul. 8024001.
[196] Priv. Ltr. Rul. 7908009.
[197] Priv. Ltr. Rul. 7826003.
[198] Priv. Ltr. Rul. 7840072.
[199] Priv. Ltr. Rul. 8020010.
[200] See § 27.1(h).
[201] Priv. Ltr. Rul. 8024001.
[202] Priv. Ltr. Rul. 7840072.
[203] Rev. Rul. 80-297, 1980-2 C.B. 196.

had furnished its tennis facilities to an unrelated individual without the provision of services (leaving it to the lessee to hire the club's administrators) and for a fixed fee not dependent on the income or profits derived from the leased property, the rental income exclusion would have been available.[204] In a comparable ruling, the IRS determined that, when a university that leased its stadium to a professional sports team for several months of the year and provided the utilities, grounds maintenance, and dressing room, linen, and stadium security services, it was engaged in an unrelated business and was not entitled to the rental income exclusion.[205]

(e) Exploitation Rule

Activities carried on by a tax-exempt organization in the performance of exempt functions may generate good will or other intangibles that are capable of being exploited in commercial endeavors. Where an exempt organization exploits this type of intangible in commercial activities, the fact that the resultant income depended in part on the conduct of an exempt function of the organization does not make it gross income from a related business. In these cases, unless the activities contribute importantly to the accomplishment of an exempt purpose, the income that they produce is gross income from the conduct of an unrelated business.[206]

Thus, the rules with respect to taxation of advertising revenue received by tax-exempt organizations treat advertising as an exploitation of exempt publication activity.[207] As another illustration of this *exploitation rule*, where access to athletic facilities of an educational institution by students is covered by a general student fee, outside use may trigger the exploitation rule; if separate charges for use of the facilities are imposed on students, faculty, and outsiders, any unrelated income is a product of the dual-use rule.[208]

(f) Related Business Activities

There are many determinations by the courts and the IRS that activities by tax-exempt organizations are related businesses. For example, a furniture shop operated by an exempt halfway house and staffed by its residents was found to be a related business.[209] An organization that promoted professional automobile racing was held to not receive unrelated business income from the conduct of a product certification program, because the program was part of the organization's regulatory activities designed to prevent trade abuses in the automobile

---

[204] *Id.*
[205] Rev. Rul. 80-298, 1980-2 C.B. 197. The dual use rule is, in some ways, an application of the fragmentation rule (see *supra* § 2(f)).
[206] Reg. § 1.513-1(d)(4)(iv).
[207] See *infra* § 5(f).
[208] E.g., Priv. Ltr. Rul. 7823062.
[209] Rev. Rul. 75-472, 1975-2 C.B. 208.

racing business.[210] The certification of the accuracy and authenticity of export documents by an exempt chamber of commerce, for the purpose of providing an independent verification of the origin of exported goods, was ruled to be a related business because the activity "stimulates international commerce by facilitating the export of goods and, thus, promotes and stimulates business conditions in the community generally."[211]

A tax-exempt national conservation education organization was ruled to be engaging in related activities, by the sale of stationery items, serving items, desk accessories, nature gift items, emblem items, toys, and wearing apparel, because each of the product lines served to stimulate the public about wildlife preservation.[212] The operation of a restaurant and cocktail lounge by certain exempt organizations, such as social clubs and veterans' organizations, for their members is an activity that is in furtherance of their exempt purposes.[213]

Other court opinions and IRS rulings providing illustrations of *related* business activities conducted by tax-exempt organizations include these: the sponsorship of championship tournaments by an association organized to promote a sport;[214] the charging of activity fees to libraries of for-profit organizations for computer-stored library cataloging services;[215] the operation of a beauty shop and barber shop by a senior citizens' center;[216] the sale of members' horses by a horsebreeders' association;[217] the sale of greeting cards and art reproductions by a museum;[218] the conduct of weekly dances by a volunteer fire company;[219] the tax collection activities by a social welfare organization on behalf of its member municipalities;[220] sponsorship of a bank payment plan for the membership of a professional society;[221] gambling receipts from members of social and fraternal organizations;[222] the conduct of an employment program providing training and work experience for the disabled;[223] loan organization and servicing activities;[224] a project to facilitate court proceedings by telephone;[225] the operation of a lawyer referral service by a bar association;[226] the performance of management services for a charitable orga-

---

[210] Priv. Ltr. Rul. 7922001.

[211] Rev. Rul. 81-127, 1981-1 C.B. 357, 358.

[212] Priv. Ltr. Rul. 8107006.

[213] Priv. Ltr. Rul. 8120006.

[214] Rev. Rul. 58-502, 1958-2 C.B. 271, as clarified by Rev. Rul. 80-294, 1980-2 C.B. 187. Cf. Mobile Arts & Sports Ass'n v. United States, 148 F. Supp. 315 (S.D. Ala. 1957).

[215] Priv. Ltr. Rul. 7816061.

[216] Rev. Rul. 81-61, 1981-1 C.B. 355.

[217] Priv. Ltr. Rul. 8112013.

[218] Rev. Rul. 73-104, 1973-1 C.B. 263.

[219] Rev. Rul. 74-361, 1974-2 C.B. 159. Also Rev. Rul. 68-225, 1968-1 C.B. 283; Rev. Rul. 67-296, 1967-2 C.B. 212; Rev. Rul. 67-219, 1967-2 C.B. 210; Rev. Rul. 64-182, 1964-1 (Part 1) C.B. 186. Maryland State Fair & Agric. Soc'y, Inc. v. Chamberlin, 55-1 U.S.T.C. ¶ 9399 (D. Md. 1955).

[220] Kentucky Mun. League v. Comm'r, 81 T.C. 156 (1983).

[221] San Antonio Dist. Dental Soc'y v. United States, *supra* note 107.

[222] Gen. Couns. Mem. 39061.

[223] Priv. Ltr. Rul. 8349072.

[224] Priv. Ltr. Rul. 8349051.

[225] Priv. Ltr. Rul. 8351160.

[226] Priv. Ltr. Rul. 8417003.

nization;[227] the provision of group insurance and workers' compensation self-insurance for member counties by a social welfare organization;[228] the provision of worker's compensation insurance coverage to county government employees by a social welfare organization;[229] the provision of veterinary services by a tax-exempt humane society;[230] a low-cost animal neutering service;[231] the operation of a health club for individuals reflective of the community;[232] the conduct of research and counseling activities for the purpose of promoting business in foreign countries;[233] the sales of products in connection with the conduct of educational programs;[234] the sale of computer software by an organization formed to make new scientific technology widely available for the benefit of the public;[235] the sale of life memberships in a rural lodge used only for religious and educational purposes;[236] the operation of an arena (including concessions and leases);[237] the management of a project to restore historic property;[238] the operation of golf courses to promote rehabilitation of disadvantaged youth;[239] the construction and operation of a recreational complex and ancillary activities;[240] the performance of art conservation services for private collectors;[241] the sale of posters and other promotional items carrying the organization's program message;[242] the publication and sale by a shipowners' and operators' organization of common tariffs:[243] the operation of a medical malpractice peer review program by a medical society;[244] the operation of a mobile cancer screening program;[245] the activities of a trade association as a "certified frequency coordinator" (as designated by the Federal Communications Commission) for its industry;[246] the leasing of a theater by a performing arts organization for musical productions;[247] the sale of insurance by a charitable organization on the lives of donors;[248] the licensing of an educational institution's curriculum to other colleges and universities;[249] the conduct of

---

[227] Priv. Ltr. Rul. 8422168.
[228] Priv. Ltr. Rul. 8442092.
[229] Tech. Adv. Mem. 8443009.
[230] Tech. Adv. Mem. 8450006.
[231] Tech. Adv. Mem. 8501002.
[232] Tech. Adv. Mem. 8505002.
[233] Priv. Ltr. Rul. 8505047.
[234] Priv. Ltr. Rul. 8512084.
[235] Priv. Ltr. Rul. 8518090.
[236] Priv. Ltr. Rul. 8523072.
[237] Priv. Ltr. Rul. 8623081.
[238] Priv. Ltr. Rul. 8628049.
[239] Priv. Ltr. Rul. 8626080.
[240] Priv. Ltr. Rul. 8624127.
[241] Priv. Ltr. Rul. 8606074.
[242] Priv. Ltr. Rul. 8633034.
[243] Priv. Ltr. Rul. 8709072.
[244] Priv. Ltr. Rul. 8730060.
[245] Priv. Ltr. Rul. 8749085.
[246] Priv. Ltr. Rul. 8802079.
[247] Gen. Couns. Mem. 39715.
[248] Priv. Ltr. Rul. 8820061.
[249] Priv. Ltr. Rul. 8824018.

teleconferencing activities;[250] the operation of a second-hand store;[251] the teaching of computer programming courses for employees of a corporation;[252] the operation of nursing homes by a health care organization;[253] the operation of physical, occupational, and speech therapy, injury prevention, pediatric services, and adult day-care programs;[254] the cleaning up of spills of oil and oil products;[255] the conduct of services relating to the use of an organization's mailing list;[256] the operation of a birthing center by a church;[257] the sponsor- ship of gospel concerts by a broadcast ministry;[258] the receipt of income from Medicare, Medicaid, or private insurance programs for the operation of inter- mediate care facilities;[259] the operation by a charitable organization of a park- ing garage for the benefit of its member charities;[260] the performance of pre-acquisition student loan services by a public charity;[261] the provision by a health care entity of temporary nurses to a related exempt organization;[262] the sale of books by a religious organization that were written by its founder;[263] the provision of services by a community development organization to a com- munity development bank;[264] the conduct by an agricultural organization of activities promoting cooperative programs among farmers in a state;[265] the de- velopment and operation by a business league of a tracking system for al- imony and support payments;[266] the conduct by a public charity of market development and investment programs intended to promote investment in foreign countries;[267] the operation of a center for regional economic develop- ment, and for educational and cultural activities;[268] the sale of caskets by an exempt cemetery company;[269] the conduct of national amateur athletic con- tests;[270] the sale of medical diagnostic literature and equipment;[271] the rental of office space and rooms, and the provision of food service, with respect to an educational facility operated by a charity;[272] lease of the assets of a hospital

[250] Priv. Ltr. Rul. 8643091.
[251] Priv. Ltr. Rul. 8643049.
[252] Priv. Ltr. Rul. 9137002.
[253] Priv. Ltr. Rul. 9237090.
[254] Priv. Ltr. Rul. 9241055.
[255] Priv. Ltr. Rul. 9242035.
[256] Priv. Ltr. Rul. 9249001.
[257] Priv. Ltr. Rul. 9252037.
[258] Priv. Ltr. Rul. 9325062.
[259] Priv. Ltr. Rul. 9335061.
[260] Priv. Ltr. Rul. 9401031.
[261] Priv. Ltr. Rul. 9403022.
[262] Priv. Ltr. Rul. 9535023.
[263] Priv. Ltr. Rul. 9535050.
[264] Priv. Ltr. Rul. 9539015.
[265] Ohio Farm Bureau Fed. Inc. v. Comm'r, *supra* note 145.
[266] Priv. Ltr. Rul. 9633044.
[267] Priv. Ltr. Rul. 9651046.
[268] Priv. Ltr. Rul. 9810038.
[269] Priv. Ltr. Rul. 9814051.
[270] Priv. Ltr. Rul. 9821049.
[271] Priv. Ltr. Rul. 9821063.
[272] Priv. Ltr. Rul. 9824048.

district to a charitable organization that was to operate the hospital;[273] the sale of a corporate charter, licenses to conduct an insurance business, and deposits with state regulatory departments by an exempt property and casualty insurance company;[274] the administration of state education assistance programs by a state-controlled charity;[275] the provision of lobbying services by a business league for the benefit of its member health care providers;[276] the provision of services by a community development organization as the managing member of a limited liability company used as a financing vehicle;[277] the provision of office automation training services by a charitable organization for job seekers with vocational advantages;[278] the participation by a charitable organization in home buyer assistance programs for low- and moderate-income families;[279] the operation by a charitable organization of a mushroom growing and processing facility predominantly to employ poor and drug-addicted individuals;[280] the sale of a commodity code by an organization of federal and state purchasing agencies;[281] the provision of credit enhancement services to developers of, and predevelopment and construction lending to projects that result in, affordable housing;[282] the conduct by a library of a remote access project, fee-based services, research assistance for library users, business information collection, and library management training;[283] the operation by a charitable organization of a rural health infrastructure loan program;[284] the operation by a private operating foundation of a guest house;[285] the reorganization of an educational institution;[286] the operation of a fee-for-services plan by an exempt retirement home;[287] the operation by a public charity of noncommercial television and radio stations;[288] the use by a charitable organization of a vessel to provide ferry service for a limited time in the context of an emergency;[289] the leasing of industrial buildings by a charitable organization to promote development of an economically distressed county;[290] payments to a pension plan trust to induce it to lend its securities;[291] the addition of a warehouse facility to a charitable organization's manufacturing program for the development of disabled individuals;[292]

---

[273] Priv. Ltr. Rul. 9825030.
[274] Priv. Ltr. Rul. 9853026.
[275] Priv. Ltr. Rul. 199905027.
[276] Priv. Ltr. Rul. 199905031.
[277] Priv. Ltr. Rul. 199909056.
[278] Priv. Ltr. Rul. 199910053.
[279] Priv. Ltr. Rul. 199910061.
[280] Priv. Ltr. Rul. 199920041.
[281] Tech. Adv. Mem. 199922055.
[282] Priv. Ltr. Rul. 199929049.
[283] Priv. Ltr. Rul. 199945062.
[284] Priv. Ltr. Rul. 199949045.
[285] Priv. Ltr. Rul. 200030027.
[286] E.g., Priv. Ltr. Rul. 200150032.
[287] Priv. Ltr. Rul. 200150038.
[288] Priv. Ltr. Rul. 200151047.
[289] Priv. Ltr. Rul. 200204051.
[290] Priv. Ltr. Rul. 200213027.
[291] Priv. Ltr. Rul. 200220028.
[292] Priv. Ltr. Rul. 200241050.

and the renovation of a conference center and redevelopment of commercial rental property.[293]

Private letter rulings from the IRS provide additional illustrations of related business activity.[294]

(g) Unrelated Business Activities

There are many determinations by the courts and the IRS that activities by tax-exempt organizations are *unrelated* businesses. For example, the presentation of commercial programs and the sale of air time were ruled to be activities not substantially related to the exempt purposes of a tax-exempt broadcasting station.[295] The operation of a miniature golf course in a commercial manner, by a charitable organization operating to provide for the welfare of young individuals, was determined to constitute an unrelated business.[296] The operation of dining facilities for the general public by an exempt social club or exempt veterans' organization is an unrelated business.[297]

Other court opinions and IRS rulings providing illustrations of unrelated business activities include these: the provision of pet boarding and grooming services, for pets owned by the general public, by an organization operated to prevent cruelty to animals;[298] carrying on of commercially sponsored research, where the publication of the research is withheld or delayed significantly by the organization beyond the time reasonably necessary to establish ownership rights;[299] weekly operation of a bingo game by a social welfare organization;[300] sale of membership lists to commercial companies by educational organizations;[301] publication of academic works;[302] receipt of commissions from sales of cattle by an agricultural organization for its members;[303] sale of certain blood and blood components by a blood bank to commercial laboratories;[304] management of health and welfare plans by a business league for a fee;[305] furnishing of

---

[293] Priv. Ltr. Rul. 200225044.

[294] E.g., Priv. Ltr. Rul. 8640007.

[295] Rev. Rul. 78-385, 1978-2 C.B. 174.

[296] Rev. Rul. 79-361, 1979-2 C.B. 237.

[297] Rev. Rul. 68-46, 1968-1 C.B. 260.

[298] Rev. Rul. 73-587, 1973-2 C.B. 192.

[299] Rev. Rul. 76-296, 1976-2 C.B. 141.

[300] Clarence LaBelle Post No. 217 v. United States, *supra* note 61, Smith-Dodd Businessman's Ass'n, Inc. v. Comm'r, 65 T.C. 620 (1975). Also Rev. Rul. 59-330, 1959-2 C.B. 153.

[301] Rev. Rul. 72-431, 1972-2 C.B. 281.

[302] Priv. Ltr. Rul. 7839042. Also Oklahoma Dental Ass'n v. United States, 75-2 U.S.T.C. ¶ 9682 (W.D. Okla. 1975); Western Catholic Church v. Comm'r, 73 T.C. 196 (1979), *aff'd*, 631 F.2d 736 (7th Cir. 1980), *cert. den.*, 450 U.S. 981 (1981).

[303] Rev. Rul. 69-51, 1969-1 C.B. 159.

[304] Rev. Rul. 66-323, 1966-2 C.B. 216, as *mod. by* Rev. Rul. 78-145, *supra* note 88.

[305] Rev. Rul. 66-151, 1966-1 C.B. 152. Also Cooper Tire & Rubber Co., Employees' Retirement Fund v. United States, *supra* note 143; Rev. Rul. 69-633, 1969-2 C.B. 121; Rev. Rul. 69-69, 1969-1 C.B. 159; Rev. Rul. 68-505, 1968-2 C.B. 248; Rev. Rul. 68-267, 1968-1 C.B. 284; Duluth Clinic Foundation v. United States, 67-1 U.S.T.C. ¶ 9226 (D. Minn. 1967); Rev. Rul. 66-47, 1966-1 C.B. 149; Rev. Rul. 62-191, 1962-2 C.B. 146; Rev. Rul. 60-228, 1960-1 C.B. 200; Rev. Rul. 60-86, 1960-1 C.B. 198; Rev. Rul. 58-482, 1958-2 C.B. 273; Rev. Rul. 57-466, 1957-2 C.B. 311; Rev. Rul. 57-313, 1957-2 C.B. 316; Rev. Rul. 55-449, 1955-2 C.B. 599.

laborers by a religious organization (usually its members) to forest owners to plant seedlings on cleared forest land;[306] the sale of heavy-duty appliances to senior citizens by a senior citizens' center;[307] the performance of administrative services performed by a business league in connection with vacation pay and guaranteed annual income accounts established by a collective bargaining agreement;[308] the provision of veterinary services for a fee by an animal cruelty prevention society;[309] the operation of a commuting program by a labor union for its members;[310] the distribution of business directories to new residents in a community;[311] the sale of work uniforms by a union;[312] the operation of a central payroll and records system;[313] the sale of printing services to other persons (including exempt organizations);[314] the provision of commercial hospitalization review services by a professional standards review organization;[315] the sales of liquor by a veterans' organization;[316] the sale of a computer-based information retrieval and message service provided by a for-profit business;[317] the sale of information about real estate used to prepare market evaluations and house appraisals;[318] the provision of arbitration and mediation, and other alternative dispute resolution services for the benefit of consumers;[319] the conduct of utilization review services and drug-free workplace programs for private businesses by a professional standards review organization;[320] the sale of herbs and herb products by an exempt scientific research organization to private practitioners and the general public;[321] the operation by a low-income housing corporation of a temporary storage business open to the general public;[322] the storage by an agricultural organization of trailers, campers, motor homes, boats, and automobiles;[323] the operation by a business league of a recycling facility;[324] and the use by the public of a golf course maintained by an exempt planned community.[325]

---

[306] Rev. Rul. 76-341, 1976-2 C.B. 307. Also Shiloh Youth Revival Centers v. Comm'r, 88 T.C. 565 (1987).
[307] Rev. Rul. 81-62, 1981-1 C.B. 355.
[308] Steamship Trade Ass'n of Baltimore, Inc. v. Comm'r, *supra* note 51.
[309] Priv. Ltr. Rul. 8303001.
[310] Tech. Adv. Mem. 8226019.
[311] Priv. Ltr. Rul. 8433010.
[312] Tech. Adv. Mem. 8437014.
[313] Tech. Adv. Mem. 8446004.
[314] Priv. Ltr. Rul. 8452074.
[315] Priv. Ltr. Rul. 8511082.
[316] Priv. Ltr. Rul. 8530043.
[317] Priv. Ltr. Rul. 8814004.
[318] Priv. Ltr. Rul. 9043001.
[319] Priv. Ltr. Rul. 9145002.
[320] Priv. Ltr. Rul. 9436002.
[321] Tech. Adv. Mem. 9550001.
[322] Tech. Adv. Mem. 9821067.
[323] Tech. Adv. Mem. 9822006.
[324] Tech. Adv. Mem. 9848002.
[325] Tech. Adv. Mem. 200047049.

Private letter rulings from the IRS provide additional illustrations of unrelated business activity.[326]

Occasionally, a situation will arise where monies are paid to an agent of a tax-exempt organization, who in turn pays the monies over to the organization, with the monies taxable as unrelated business income. This situation occurs, for example, in connection with an exempt religious order, which requires its members to provide services for a component of the supervising church and to turn over their remuneration to the order under a vow of poverty. Under these circumstances, the payments for services are income to the order and not to the member.[327] Where the individual is not acting as agent for the order and is performing services (as an employee) of the type ordinarily required by members of the religious order, however, the income is to the individual, and the unrelated income tax is avoided, because the monies are received by the orders as charitable contributions.

(h) Interrelationship with Commerciality Doctrine

Traditionally, the unrelated business rules and the commerciality doctrine[328] have developed along parallel, rather than intersecting, lines. Recently, however, the IRS has begun integrating the commerciality doctrine into its analyses as to whether an activity is a related or unrelated business.

A striking example of this approach was provided in an instance of an organization that operated a tearoom in conjunction with a consignment shop and a gift shop. The organization contended that the tearoom was a related business because it served to attract the type of individuals to the organization's facilities who will be willing to purchase items from the consignment shop, which itself was a related business. There was considerable merit to this argument; entities such as museums have relied on it for years. For example, the operation of an eating facility that helped to attract visitors to a museum and enhanced the efficient operation of the museum by enabling its staff to remain on the premises throughout the workday was held by the IRS to contribute importantly to the accomplishment of the museum's exempt purposes and thus constitute a related business.[329] In the instance of the tearoom, however, the IRS relied on the principal case articulating the com-merciality doctrine,[330] concluding that "where the operation of an eating facility is presumptively commercial, competes directly with other restaurants, uses profit-making pricing formulas, engages in advertising, has hours of operation competitive with commercial enterprises,

---

[326] E.g., Priv. Ltr. Rul. 9128003.
[327] Rev. Rul. 76-323, 1976-2 C.B. 18, *clar. by* Rev. Rul. 77-290, 1977-2 C.B. 26. Also Rev. Rul. 77-436, 1977-2 C.B. 25; Rev. Rul. 68-123, 1968-1 C.B. 35.
[328] See Chapter 25.
[329] Rev. Rul. 74-399, 1974-2 C.B. 172.
[330] Living Faith, Inc. v. Comm'r, 950 F.2d 365 (7th Cir. 1991).

and the underlying organization does not have plans to solicit donations," the facility is a nonexempt function.[331]

§ 26.5   CONTEMPORARY APPLICATIONS OF THE UNRELATED BUSINESS RULES

Myriad activities undertaken by various types of tax-exempt organizations provide contemporary applications of the unrelated business income rules. Traditionally, colleges and universities raised the most issues as to related and unrelated business endeavors, although in recent years health care institutions have achieved the dubious distinction of being first in this regard. Other exempt organizations that are currently generating significant unrelated business issues are museums, associations, and labor, agricultural, and horticultural organizations.

(a) Educational Institutions

The principal business of tax-exempt colleges, universities, and schools[332] is the education of students; income generated by this related activity in the form of tuition, fees, assessments, dormitory rent, and food service revenue is not taxable. Another major exempt function at these institutions is research; this activity is not normally taxed, either because it is inherently an exempt function or is sheltered from tax by statute.[333]

The legislative history of the unrelated business income rules states that a wheat farm operated by a tax-exempt agricultural college as part of its educational program is a related business and income from a university press is exempt "in the ordinary case" since it is derived from an activity that is substantially related to the purposes of the university.[334]

By contrast, an activity such as the manufacture and sale of automobile tires by a tax-exempt college ordinarily is an unrelated business; this type of activity does not become substantially related simply because some students performed minor clerical or bookkeeping functions as part of their educational program.[335] By contrast, the IRS determined that the sale of handicraft articles by an exempt vocational school, made by its students as part of their regular courses of instruction, was a related trade or business.[336] Likewise, the IRS held that a exempt university may publish, as a related business, scholarly works written by its faculty and students.[337]

(i) Bookstore Operations.   For colleges, universities, and some schools, operation of their bookstores yields opportunities for unrelated business income

---

[331] Tech. Adv. Mem. 200021056.
[332] Essentially, these are institutions referenced in IRC § 170(b)(1)(A)(ii) (see § 11.3(a)).
[333] See §§ 9.2, 27.1(l).
[334] S. Rep. No. 2375, *supra* note 4, at 107.
[335] *Id.* A college or university may operate a health and physical fitness center, with many of its programs qualifying as related business activities (Priv. Ltr. Rul. 9732032).
[336] Rev. Rul. 68-581. 1968-2 C.B. 250.
[337] Priv. Ltr. Rul. 9036025.

issues.[338] While the operation of these stores generally is a tax-exempt function,[339] there are some sales that can attract the tax on unrelated business income. There are three categories of business activities in this context: related business, business activities that are protected from taxation by a statutory exception, and unrelated business.

Related business activities include the sale of items such as course books, supplies, tapes, compact discs, athletic wear necessary for participation in the institution's athletic, and physical education programs, computer hardware and software,[340] and items that induce school spirit, including t-shirts, tote bags, pennants, and mugs.

Another category of sales that are not taxable are those that are within the ambit of the *convenience doctrine*, in that the business activity is for the benefit of the students.[341] Items protected from taxation by this doctrine include sundry articles, film, cards, health and beauty aids, and novelty items.

For the most part, all other sales are unrelated business transactions. It is the view of the IRS that items that have a useful life of more than one year cannot be the subject of the convenience doctrine.[342] Taxable sales can thus be those of articles such as wearing apparel, appliances, stuffed animals, wall posters, wristwatches, and plants.[343] Sales of items to the general public, as opposed to students and faculty, can be unrelated business activity.

(ii) Athletic Events. It is an understatement to say that the preparation for and participation in athletic events is a major function of today's tax-exempt educational institution. The revenue that a college, university, or school derives as charges for admission to athletic events is income from a related business inasmuch as the activities are substantially related to the institution's educational program.[344]

Revenue generated by the telecasting and radio broadcasting of these events also is not taxable, in that this activity is related to the institutions' educational mission.[345] As the IRS observed, an "audience for a game may con-

---

[338] Some institutions lease the bookstore operation to unrelated parties, with the resulting rent nontaxable (see § 27.1(h)).

[339] Squire v. Students Book Corp., 191 F.2d 1018 (9th Cir. 1951); Rev. Rul. 58-194, 1958-1 C.B. 240.

[340] The IRS, in its college and university examination guidelines (see § 24.8(d)), stated that "[a]lthough the sale of one computer to a student or faculty member may be substantially related to exempt purposes, the sale of multiple computers, in a single year, to a single student or the sale of a computer to someone who is not a student, officer or employee of the institution may result in unrelated business income" (*id.* § 342.(13)(5)).

[341] See § 27.2(b).

[342] Gen. Couns. Mem. 35811.

[343] E.g., Priv. Ltr. Rul. 8025222.

[344] H. Rep. No. 2319, *supra* note 4, at 37, 109; S. Rep. No. 2375, *supra* note 4, at 107. "[A] university would not be taxable on income derived from a basketball tournament sponsored by it, even where the teams were composed of students from other schools" (H. Rep. No. 2319, *supra*, at 37; S. Rep. No. 2375, *supra* note 4, at 29).

[345] Tech. Adv. Mem. 7851004. However, the original position of the IRS on this point was that the income from telecasting and radio broadcasting of athletic events, including bowl games, was unrelated business income. This view was altered in the face of enactment of legislation to the contrary (§ 27.2(n)).

tribute importantly to the education of the student-athlete in the development of his/her physical and inner strength." Further, "[a]ttending the game enhances student interest in education generally and in the institution because such interest is whetted by exposure to the school's athletic activities." Finally, the "games (and the opportunity to observe them) foster those feelings of identification, loyalty, and participation typical of a well-rounded educational experience."[346]

The IRS ruled that a tax-exempt organization that sponsored a post-season all-star college football game for the benefit of a state university did not jeopardize its exempt status because of, nor realize unrelated income from the sale of, television broadcast rights of the games since broadcasting of the games "contributes importantly" to the accomplishment of its exempt purposes;[347] that payments received by a state university for the sale of radio and television broadcasting rights to its basketball and football games were not unrelated business income because the carrying on the sporting events was substantially related to the university's exempt purposes;[348] that income received by an exempt organization that promoted professional automobile racing from the sale of television broadcast rights to the races it sanctions did not constitute unrelated income because the television coverage effectively popularized automobile racing;[349] that income derived from the sale by an exempt organization that sponsored and sanctioned amateur athletics of television rights to broadcast its athletic events was not unrelated income because the television medium was used to disseminate its goals and purposes to the public;[350] that an exempt organization promoting interest in a particular sport that sold television rights to championship golf tournaments that it sponsored did not incur unrelated income because the grant of the rights was directly related to its exempt purposes;[351] that the income received by an exempt amateur sports organization for the licensing of television broadcasting rights was not unrelated income because the broadcasting of the sports events was substantially related to the organization's exempt purpose of promoting international goodwill;[352] and that payments to be received from the sale of radio and television broadcasting rights to an athletic event were not items of unrelated income because the promotion of the event (the organization's exempt purpose) was furthered by the broadcasting of it.[353]

The IRS issued a ruling, holding that the sale of exclusive television and radio broadcasting rights to athletic events to an independent producer by a

---

[346] Priv. Ltr. Rul. 7930043.
[347] Priv. Ltr. Rul. 7948113 (which also held that the proceeds from admissions to the game, sales of the program of the game, and sales of advertising in the program were not taxable as unrelated income).
[348] Priv. Ltr. Rul. 7930043.
[349] Priv. Ltr. Rul. 7922001.
[350] Priv. Ltr. Rul. 7851003.
[351] Priv. Ltr. Rul. 7845029.
[352] Priv. Ltr. Rul. 8303078.
[353] Priv. Ltr. Rul. 7919053.

tax-exempt national governing body for amateur athletics was not unrelated business because the "broadcasting of the organization's sponsored, supervised, and regulated athletic events promotes the various amateur sports, fosters widespread public interest in the benefits of its nationwide amateur athletic program, and encourages public participation" and, therefore, the sale of the broadcasting rights and the broadcasting of the events was an exempt function.[354] The IRS issued a similar ruling with respect to the sale of broadcasting rights to a national radio and television network by an organization created by a regional collegiate athletic conference composed of exempt universities to hold an annual athletic event.[355]

The IRS asserted that the payment by a business, of a sponsorship fee to a college, university, or bowl association in connection with the telecasting or radio broadcasting of an athletic event, was unrelated business income because the package of "valuable services" received by the business was not substantially related to exempt purposes and amounted to advertising services.[356] This matter was generally resolved by the enactment of legislation concerning the *qualified sponsorship payment*.[357]

(iii) Travel Tours. The IRS is concerned that a college, university, or school, or alumni or alumnae association, will offer a travel tour as an educational experience, yet in fact it is a social, recreational, or other form of vacation opportunity and thus an unrelated business.

In a 1977 unpublished technical advice memorandum, the IRS ruled that a travel tour program conducted by an alumni association of a university was an unrelated trade or business. The program was available to all members of the association and their families; in the year at issue, the association made four mailings announcing nine tours to between 27,500 and 34,900 individuals. The memorandum stated that "[al]though the tours include sightseeing, there is no formal educational program conducted in connection with them; nor is there any program for contacting and meeting with alumni in the countries visited." The IRS determined that (1) the activities of the alumni association in working with commercial travel agencies in the planning and preparation of the tours, mailing out the tour announcements, and receiving reservations constituted a trade or business; the travel tours were inherently recreational, not educational,[358] and thus did not contribute importantly to a tax-exempt (edu-

---

[354] Rev. Rul. 80-295, 1980-2 C.B. 194.

[355] Rev. Rul. 80-296, 1980-2 C.B. 195. These two public rulings, along with Rev. Rul. 80-294, 1980-2 C.B. 187, capture the essence of the foregoing (notes 348–353) and like private letter rulings. In general, Jensen, "Taxation, the Student Athlete, and the Professionalization of College Athletics," 1987 *Utah L. Rev.* (No. 1) 35 (1987); Thompson & Young, "Taxing the Sale of Broadcast Rights to College Athletics—An Unrelated Trade or Business?," 8 *J. Coll. & Univ. L.* 331 (1981–2); Kaplan, "Intercollegiate Athletics and the Unrelated Business Income Tax," 80 *Col. L. Rev.* 1430 (1980); Note. "University TV Receipts Not Unrelated Business Income," 50 *J. Tax.* 184 (1979).

[356] Tech. Adv. Mem. 9147007.

[357] See § 27.2(n). The taxation of advertising revenue is the subject of *infra* § (f).

[358] Rev. Rul. 67-327, 1967-2 C.B. 187. Also Rev. Rul. 84-55, 1984-1 C.B. 29, holding that the travel expenses incurred by an alumnus in participation in a university's continuing education program in foreign countries are not deductible because they are personal outlays. Cf. IRC § 170(k).

cational) purpose; the unrelated business was regularly carried on; and this commercial endeavor exploited an intangible asset, namely, the association's membership.[359]

An alumni association travel tour program that is structured as an authentic educational activity is not an unrelated trade or business.[360] The policy of the IRS with respect to travel tours generally is that some are related and some unrelated, depending on how they are structured, what they consist of, and what they accomplish. Tours that feature "bona fide educational methodologies"—such as organized study, reports, lectures, library access, and reading lists—are likely to be considered educational in nature. Pursuant to a primary purpose test, tours that devote a significant amount of time to endeavors such as sightseeing are not usually exempt functions. Tours that are "not significantly different from commercially sponsored" tours are probably unrelated businesses, as are extension (or add-on) tours.[361]

The law in this regard has evolved in the form of regulations on the unrelated business tax aspects of travel and tour activities of tax-exempt organizations.[362]

(iv) Rental of Facilities.   A tax-exempt educational institution may provide athletic facilities, dormitories, and other components of the campus to persons other than its students, such as for seminars or the training of professional athletes. The income derived from the provision of the facilities in these circumstances is likely to be regarded by the IRS as unrelated business income where the institution is providing collateral services such as meals or maintenance; a mere leasing of facilities would likely generate passive rental income excluded from taxation.[363] The provision of dormitory space may be an activity that is substantially related to an exempt purpose, however, as the IRS ruled in an instance of rental of dormitory rooms primarily to individuals under age 25 by an exempt organization the purpose of which was to provide for the welfare of young people.[364]

(b) Health Care Providers

Hospitals and other health care providers[365] have as their principal business the promotion of health; income generated by this related activity in the form of

---

[359] This technical advice memorandum is the basis of Rev. Rul. 78-43, 1978-1 C.B. 164. The IRS revoked the tax-exempt status of a charitable organization in 1995, because of the extent of its conduct of golf and tennis tours, ostensibly undertaken in furtherance of exempt purposes (Tech. Adv. Mem. 9540002).

[360] Rev. Rul. 70-534, 1970-2 C.B. 113.

[361] Tech. Adv. Mem. 9702004.

[362] See *infra* § 26.5(k).

[363] See § 27.1(h).

[364] Rev. Rul. 76-33, 1976-1 C.B. 169. In general, Keeling, "Property Taxation of Colleges and Universities: The Dilemma Posed by the Use of Facilities for Purposes Unrelated to Education," 16 *J. Coll. & Univ. L.* 623 (1990). Behrsin; "College and University Leasing Activities Evoke IRS Scrutiny," 57 *Taxes* 431 (1979).

[365] Essentially, these are institutions referenced in IRC § 170(b)(1)(A)(iii) (see § 11.3(a)).

revenue from patients (whether by means of Medicare, Medicaid, insurance, or private pay) is not taxable.[366]

(i) *Various Related Businesses.*   Tax-exempt hospitals operate many businesses that are necessary to their exempt function. Thus, an exempt hospital may operate a gift shop, which is patronized by patients, visitors making purchases for patients, and its employees, without incurring the unrelated business income tax.[367] The IRS observed: "By providing a facility for the purchase of merchandise and services to improve the physical comfort and mental well-being of its patients, the hospital is carrying on an activity that encourages their recovery and therefore contributes importantly to its exempt purposes."[368] The same rationale is extended to the hospital operation of a cafeteria and coffee shop primarily for its employees and medical staff,[369] the hospital operation of a parking lot for its patients and visitors,[370] and the hospital operation of a guest accommodation facility.[371]

In one instance, a tax-exempt hospital had as its primary activity the operation of a clinic that provided various rehabilitation services to handicapped persons, including those with hearing deficiencies. The hospital tested and evaluated the hearing of its patients with the deficiencies and recommended types of hearing aids as may be necessary in each case. The hospital also sold hearing aids and fitted them to ensure maximum assistance to the patients in the correction or alleviation of their hearing deficiencies. The IRS ruled that the sale of hearing aids as an integral part of the hospital's program was not an unrelated business because it "contributes importantly to the organization's purpose of promoting the health of such persons."[372] Likewise, the IRS determined that a hospital was not conducting an unrelated business when it allowed its physicians and facilities to be used in reading and diagnosing electrocardiogram tests for an exempt hospital that lacked the physicians and facilities to provide the service.[373] Similarly, an exempt health care provider was held to not be engaging in an unrelated trade or business when it provided supplemental staffing services to hospitals and nursing homes.[374] Further, an exempt hospital was ruled to be operating, as a related business, outpatient clinics (faculty physician practices).[375]

---

[366] S. Rep. No. 2375, *supra* note 4, at 107.

[367] Rev. Rul. 69-267, 1969-1 C.B. 160.

[368] *Id.*

[369] Rev. Rul. 69-268, 1969-1 C.B. 160.

[370] Rev. Rul. 69-269, 1969-1 C.B. 160. Also Ellis Hosp. v. Fredette, 279 N.Y.S. 925 (N.Y. 1967); Rev. Rul. 81-29, 1981-1 C.B. 329.

[371] Priv. Ltr. Rul. 9404029. In holding that the operation of a motel by a supporting organization of a university's medical center (including a hospital), for the benefit of patients and their relatives and friends, was a related business, the IRS observed that "[p]roviding a temporary living facility for patients and their friends or family members . . . advances one of the purposes of the hospital which is to provide health care for members of the community" (Tech. Adv. Mem. 9847002).

[372] Rev. Rul. 78-435, 1978-2 C.B. 181.

[373] Priv. Ltr. Rul. 8004011.

[374] Tech. Adv. Mem. 9405004.

[375] Priv. Ltr. Rul. 200211051.

The *convenience doctrine*—applicable with respect to businesses that are conducted for the benefit of patients—is of considerable import in the health care setting.[376] The IRS defined the term *patient* of a health care provider.[377]

A hospital may be able to develop real estate by constructing condominium residences to be used as short-term living quarters by its patients, as a related business.[378] The provision of ancillary health care services by charitable health care providers by means of a health maintenance organization (an exempt social welfare entity[379]), with income in the form of capitated payments for the services of employee-physicians and physicians who are independent contractors, was ruled to be a related business.[380]

(ii) Sales of Pharmaceuticals. The sale of pharmaceutical supplies by a tax-exempt hospital to private patients of physicians who have offices in a medical building owned by the hospital is considered by the IRS to constitute the conduct of an unrelated business.[381] The IRS also outlined the circumstances in which an exempt hospital derives unrelated business income from the sale of pharmaceutical supplies to the general public.[382] By contrast, the sale of pharmaceutical supplies by a hospital pharmacy to its patients is not the conduct of an unrelated trade or business.

A federal court of appeals considered this issue and concluded that sales of pharmaceuticals by a tax-exempt hospital to members of the general public gave rise to unrelated business taxable income.[383] The concept of the *general public* encompassed the private patients of the hospital-based physicians, on the rationale that sales by the pharmacy to the patients were related to the purchaser's visit to his or her private physician at offices rented from the hospital and were not related to the use of services provided by the hospital. Another consideration was that exempt hospital-operated pharmacies unfairly compete with commercial pharmacies.

By contrast, another appellate court concluded that sales of pharmaceuticals by a tax-exempt hospital to nonhospital private patients of physicians located in the hospital did not produce unrelated business income because the sales were important in attracting and holding physicians in a community that lacked any medical services for eight years prior to the establishment of the hospital.[384] This appellate court ruled that the trial court was in error in defining the organization's function solely as that of providing a hospital, and held that another purpose was to attract physicians to the community and provide facilities

[376] Rev. § 27.2(b).
[377] Rev. Rul. 68-376, 1968-2 C.B. 246.
[378] Priv. Ltr. Rul. 8427105.
[379] See Chapter 12.
[380] Priv. Ltr. Rul. 9837031.
[381] Rev. Rul. 68-375, 1968-2 C.B. 245. Cf. Rev. Rul. 69-463, 1969-2 C.B. 131.
[382] Rev. Rul. 68-374, 1968-2 C.B. 242.
[383] Carle Found. v. United States, 611 F.2d 1192 (7th Cir. 1979), *cert. den.*, 449 U.S. 824 (1980).
[384] Hi-Plains Hosp. v. United States, 670 F.2d 528 (5th Cir. 1982), *rev'g and rem'g* 81-1 U.S.T.C. ¶ 9214 (N.D. Tex. 1981).

to retain them. Thus, this appellate court concluded that the "availability of the hospital's pharmacy for use by the doctor's private patients is causally related to inducing doctors to practice" at the hospital.[385] The court distinguished this case from the holding of the other court of appeals, stating that the facts in the previous case "give no indication that the hospital had any difficulty in attracting doctors to its staff."[386]

(iii) Testing Services. It is the view of the IRS that the performance of diagnostic laboratory testing, otherwise available in the community, by a tax-exempt hospital, upon specimens from private office patients of the hospital's staff physicians, generally constitutes an unrelated business.[387] The IRS concluded that there was no substantial causal relationship between the achievement of a hospital's exempt purposes and the provision of the testing to nonpatients, and that there are commercial laboratories that can perform the testing services on a timely basis. Nonetheless, the IRS noted that there may exist "unique circumstances" that cause the testing to be related activities, such as emergency laboratory diagnosis of blood samples from nonpatient drug overdose or poisoning victims in order to identify specific toxic agents, where referral of these specimens to other locations would be detrimental to the health of hospital nonpatients, or in situations where other laboratories are not available within a reasonable distance from the area served by the hospital or are clearly unable or inadequate to conduct tests needed by hospital nonpatients.[388]

A court held that income received by a tax-exempt teaching and research hospital for the performance of pathological diagnostic tests on samples submitted by physicians associated with the hospital was not unrelated business taxable income.[389] The court found that the performance and interpretation of these outside pathology tests by the hospital's pathology department were substantially related to the performance by the hospital of its exempt functions because the tests contributed importantly to the teaching functions of the hospital. Further, the court concluded that the testing was a related activity because it increased the doctors' confidence in the quality of the work performed by the pathology department and it was convenient in the event of surgery, in that the pathologist who interpreted the test could interpret the biopsy.[390]

---

[385] *Id.* at 531.

[386] *Id.* at 533.

[387] Rev. Rul. 85-110, 1985-2 CB. 166.

[388] *Id.* at 168. Laboratory testing services provided by a university's dental school were ruled to be related activities because a unique type of diagnostic dental service and testing was provided, and there were no commercial laboratories that provided a comparable service (Priv. Ltr. Rul. 9739043).

[389] St. Luke's Hosp. of Kansas City v. United States, 494 F. Supp. 85 (W.D. Mo. 1980). The IRS agreed to follow this aspect of the decision (Rev. Rul. 85-109, 1985-2 C.B. 165).

[390] Also Anateus Lineal 1948, Inc. v. United States, 366 F. Supp. 118 (W.D. Ark. 1973). In general, Mancino, "The Unrelated Business Income Taxation of Nonprofit Hospitals," 4 *Exempt Org. Tax Rev.* (No. 1) 35 (1991); Kannry, "How Hospitals Can Minimize Their Potential Exposure to the Unrelated Business Income Tax," 43 *J. Tax.* 166 (1975).

From time to time, the IRS rules that analysis and testing activities conducted by hospitals and other health care entities in laboratories are the conduct of exempt functions.[391]

(iv) Fitness Centers and Health Clubs.   Another area of controversy is whether fitness centers and health clubs, operated as a program of a tax-exempt hospital, are unrelated businesses. In this setting, the IRS looks to the breadth of the group of individuals being served. If the fees for use of a health club are sufficiently high to restrict use of the club's facilities to a limited segment of a community, the club operation will be a non-exempt one—an unrelated business activity.[392] By contrast, where the health club provides a community-wide benefit for the community the organization serves, operation of the club is an exempt function (related business).[393] This latter position is predicated on the rule in the general law of charity that the promotion of the happiness and enjoyment of the members of the community is considered to be a charitable purpose.[394] Thus, in one instance, the IRS blended these two definitions of *charity* in finding that a health club was exempt because its "operations promote health in a manner which is collateral to the providing of recreational facilities which advances the well-being and happiness of the community in general."[395] Similarly, a fitness center was held to be exempt inasmuch as it furthered the accomplishment of certain of the other programs of the health organization that operated it (including an occupational and physical therapy program), its facilities and programs were specially designed for the needs of the handicapped and the treatment plans of patients in other programs, its fee structure was designed to make it available to the general public, and it offered a range of programs and activities that focused on wellness.[396]

(v) Physical Rehabilitation Programs.   Organizations that maintain physical rehabilitation programs often provide housing and other services which are available commercially. Yet, the IRS ruled that an organization which provided specially designed housing to physically handicapped individuals at the lowest feasible cost and maintained in residence those tenants who subsequently became unable to pay the monthly fees was a tax-exempt charitable entity.[397] The IRS similarly ruled that the rental to individuals under age 25 and low-income individuals of all ages of dormitory rooms and similar residential accommodations was a related business.[398] The IRS likewise ruled that a halfway house, organized to provide room, board, therapy, and counsel-

---

[391] E.g., Priv. Ltr. Rul. 9851054.
[392] Rev. Rul. 79-360, 1979-2 C.B. 236.
[393] Tech. Adv. Mem. 8505002.
[394] *Restatement (Second) of Trusts* § 374 (1959); IV Scott, *The Law of Trusts* § 374.10 (3d ed. 1967).
[395] Tech. Adv. Mem. 8505002. A similar facility operated by a university was ruled to entail related business activities (Priv. Ltr. Rul. 9732032).
[396] Priv. Ltr. Rul. 9329041.
[397] Rev. Rul. 79-19, 1979-1 C.B. 195.
[398] Rev. Rul. 76-33, *supra* note 364.

ing for individuals discharged from alcoholic treatment centers was an exempt charitable organization; its operation of a furniture shop to provide full-time employment centers for its residents was considered a related business.[399] Also, the IRS ruled that an organization which provided a residence facility and therapeutic group living program for individuals recently released from a mental institution was an exempt charitable organization.[400] An organization with the purpose of providing rehabilitative and pre-vocational counseling to the handicapped and developmentally disabled received a ruling that its residential and day care facilities were related activities.[401] Another entity, a charitable organization which maintained nursing homes and ancillary health facilities, was ruled to be engaged in the following related businesses: programs offering physical therapy, occupational therapy, speech therapy, injury prevention, pediatric services, and adult care, as well as the provision of day care for its employees.[402]

Lifestyle rehabilitation programs can also present this dichotomy. For example, the IRS ruled that the operation of a miniature golf course in a commercial manner by a tax-exempt organization, the purpose of which was to provide for the welfare of young people, constituted an unrelated trade of business.[403] The IRS also ruled, however, that an exempt organization, formed to improve the life of abused and otherwise disadvantaged children by means of the sport and business of golf, did not conduct an unrelated activity in operation of a golf course because the opportunity to socialize and master skills through the playing of the game were "essential to the building of self-esteem and the ultimate rehabilitation of the young people" in the organization's programs.[404]

(vi) Other Health Care Activities. In other instances, the IRS ruled that the rental of pagers to staff physicians by a hospital is not an unrelated business;[405] the sale by a hospital of silver recovered from x-ray film is not an unrelated activity;[406] and the leasing of space and the furnishing of services to practitioners is not an unrelated activity by the lessors.[407] Still other related business in the health care setting are operation of mobile cancer screening units;[408] sales and rentals of durable medical equipment to patients of a health care organization;[409] the provision by an exempt hospital of services such as ultrasound and general radiology, outpatient dialysis, acute dialysis, critical life support, home health, occupational health, electrocardiogram computer, well-

---

[399] Rev. Rul. 75-472, 1975-2 C.B. 208.
[400] Rev. Rul. 72-16, 1972-1 C.B. 143.
[401] Priv. Ltr. Rul. 9335061.
[402] Priv. Ltr. Rul. 9241055.
[403] Rev. Rul. 79-361, *supra* note 296.
[404] Priv. Ltr. Rul. 8626080.
[405] Tech. Adv. Mem. 8452011.
[406] Tech. Adv. Mem. 8452012.
[407] Priv. Ltr. Rul. 8452099.
[408] Priv. Ltr. Rul. 8749085.
[409] Priv. Ltr. Rul. 8736046.

ness and prevention, employee physicals, and storage of medical and administrative records;[410] the operation of home care services;[411] the operation of an adult foster care home;[412] the transfer to and operation of blood-related clinical service programs by a charitable organization;[413] and the operation of an assisted living facility.[414]

The provision of services by and among organizations within a hospital system, such as the leasing of property and the sale of services, generally will not give rise to unrelated business taxable income.[415] Designation of a health care provider as the preferred provider of services for patients of another charitable organization and its statewide affiliates is not the creation of an unrelated business.[416] The operation of a call center by an exempt ambulance service provider was ruled to be a related business.[417]

(c) Museums

Tax-exempt museums operate related businesses when they maintain collections and make them accessible to the general public; admissions fees and the like are income from related business. Some museum business operations are nontaxable by reason of the lines of law referenced above, pertaining to parking lots, snack bars, and the like. The operation of a dining room, cafeteria, and snack bar by an exempt museum for use by its staff, employees, and members of the public usually are related activities.[418] Food service operations of this nature are considered related businesses when they are merely "convenient eating places" for visitors and employees, as opposed to endeavors "designed to serve as a public restaurant."[419]

The most difficult issues in the unrelated trade or business context presented by museum operations relate to sales to the general public. Where, for example, a tax-exempt museum sells to the public greeting cards that display printed reproductions of selected works from the museum's collection and from other art collections, the sales activity is substantially related to the museum's exempt purpose.[420] The rationale for this conclusion is that (1) the sale of

---

[410] E.g., Priv. Ltr. Rul. 8736046.
[411] In general, see Hyatt & Hopkins, *The Law of Tax-Exempt Healthcare Organizations, Second Edition* (New York: John Wiley & Sons, Inc., 2001), Chapter 10.
[411] Priv. Ltr. Rul. 9822039.
[412] Priv. Ltr. Rul. 199943053.
[413] Priv. Ltr. Rul. 199946036.
[414] Priv. Ltr. Rul. 199946037.
[415] E.g., Priv. Ltr. Rul. 8822065.
[416] Priv. Ltr. Rul. 9839040.
[417] Priv. Ltr. Rul. 200222031. In general, Hyatt & Hopkins, *supra* note 411, particularly Chapter 24.
[418] Rev. Rul. 74-399, *supra* note 329. Cf. Rev. Rul. 69-268, 1969-1 C.B. 160.
[419] E.g., Priv. Ltr. Rul. 200222030. The IRS, however, is not this tolerant outside the museum setting (e.g., Tech. Adv. Mem. 200021056, holding that a gift shop and tea room operated in conjunction with an exempt craft and foodstuff business were unrelated activities).
[420] Rev. Rul. 73-104, *supra* note 218.

the cards "contributes importantly to the achievement of the museum's exempt educational purposes by stimulating and enhancing public awareness, interest, and appreciation of art"; and (2) a "broader segment of the public may be encouraged to visit the museum itself to share in its educational functions and programs as a result of seeing the cards."[421]

The IRS applies the fragmentation rule, to segment the retailing activities of tax-exempt museums.[422] For example, museums traditionally have sold greeting cards, slides, instructional literature, and metal, wood, and ceramic copies of art works. In recent years, some museums have begun selling novelty items, clothing, and the like. To the extent that the items being sold are "expensive," "lavish," or otherwise "luxury" items, there is a greater likelihood that the IRS will presume the sales activity to be an unrelated business.

Where an item sold by a tax-exempt museum is priced at a "low cost,"[423] and bears the museum's logo, the IRS generally finds the sales activity to be related, because it enhances public awareness of and encourages greater visitation to the museum. Again, however, as the price of items bearing a museum's logo increases, so too will the likelihood that the IRS will find the sales activity to be substantially unrelated to the museum's exempt purposes. Nonetheless, the sale of, for example, clothing bearing a reference to a museum is arguably *per se* substantially related to the museum's exempt purposes—since it publicizes the museum and attracts visitors—irrespective of the price paid for the clothing.

One of the most difficult issues in this context lies in the distinction drawn by the IRS between museum *reproductions* and *adaptations*. For the most part, the IRS considers the sales of reproductions to be sales that are related to the museum's tax-exempt purposes, although the IRS may resist that conclusion where the items, while copies of items originally created by master period craftsmen, are not contemporaneously made in a manner commensurate with the period. The IRS is much more likely to question the relatedness of sales of adaptations, which are items that may incorporate or reflect original art but differ significantly in form from the original work. Nonetheless, an adaptation may have intrinsic artistic merit or historical significance in its adaptive form (so that a sale of it by a museum is a related activity) or it may bear a museum's logo or otherwise reference the museum (so that it enhances public awareness of the museum and encourages the public to visit the museum, thereby making the sale of it a related activity).

In application of the fragmentation rule, the IRS will attempt to determine the motivation behind the museum's sale of an item. For example, the IRS's general counsel has advised the IRS that it should apply a test to determine whether or not the primary purpose of the article sold is *utilitarian*.[424] According to this test, if the "primary purpose of the article is utilitarian and the utilitarian aspects are the predominant reasons for the production and sale of

---

[421] *Id.*
[422] Rev. Rul. 73-105, 1973-1 C.B. 264.
[423] Reg. § 1.513-1(b). See text accompanying *infra* note 545. Also § 27.2(j).
[424] Gen. Couns. Mem. 38949.

the article, it should not be considered related." Conversely, if the "utilitarian or ornamental aspects are merely incidental to the article's relation to an exempt purpose, then the article should be considered related." In most instances, the IRS finds that a museum regularly sells both related and unrelated items. The IRS counsel readily admitted that application of the utilitarian standard is easiest when "reproductions or adaptations of items contained in the [m]useum's collection" are considered (sales of them are clearly related) or when "items of a souvenir, trivial, or convenience nature" are considered (sales of these are clearly unrelated). "The difficult task," conceded the IRS counsel, "lies in identifying those items that raise classification problems, such as those that are arguably reproductions with utilitarian, ornamental, or decorative aspects and those that present an interpretation of some theme related to an exempt purpose."

The museum evaluated by the IRS counsel and the IRS agreed that the items sold in the museum can be classified as follows: (1) replicas or reproductions of items or artifacts in the collections or exhibitions; (2) reproductions, adaptations, or examples of items that are not on exhibit, but that are representative of, and designed to encourage interest in, historical periods or artistic, scientific, or technological developments that are featured in the museum collections, or that are related to areas of museum involvements; (3) arts and crafts works by artists, or by native and/or foreign groups, whose works are in the collections or have been included in museum exhibitions; (4) arts and crafts items representing similar forms that can be found in the various museum collections designed to illustrate the techniques and historical development of these forms; (5) arts and crafts kits, tools, and instruments designed to encourage a personal experience of various arts and crafts forms; (6) books and records relating to art, science, history, and other areas of museum involvement; (7) educational toys and games for children, based on museum exhibits or relating to areas of museum involvement; (8) scientific and aviation models, tools and specimens, and other educational items that encourage interest and personal participation in the sciences; (9) posters, postcards, note cards, and calendars, with photographs, drawings, or depictions relating to areas of museum involvement; (10) souvenirs of the museum; and (11) convenience items. The IRS counsel did not attempt to classify the sale of each of these categories of sale items as related or unrelated business but, instead, noted that "[t]hese judgments are not, of course, easy to make."

Thus the IRS, in application of the fragmentation rule, also applies a primary purpose test. If the article sold by a tax-exempt museum is predominantly utilitarian, sales of it produce unrelated income, as is the case with items sold primarily to generate income. If an article is primarily related to the museum's exempt function and any utilitarian aspects are incidental, sales income is related income. One specific guideline is provided: "If the primary purpose of an article that interprets some facet of the [m]useum's collection is to encourage personal learning experiences about the [m]useum's collection even though not an accurate depiction of an item in the collection, the article should be considered related."

The current emphasis of the IRS in this regard is on the primary purpose for the production and sale of each item in the museum. As noted, the sale of reproductions of items found in the collection is not unrelated business, as is the case with the sales of adaptations of artistic utilitarian items in the collection, particularly where the items are sold with descriptive literature showing their artistic, cultural, or historic connections with the museum's collections or exhibits. Museum sales of original art or craft may, however, be unrelated business, since these activities are inconsistent with the purpose of exhibiting art for the public benefit.[425]

The IRS in 1986 again addressed the subject of the tax treatment of retail sales of items by a tax-exempt museum.[426] In that instance, the IRS inventoried the various items sold by the museum, fragmenting them into categories such as furniture, china, fabrics, wallpaper, lamps, note cards, cooking accessories, handicrafts, and gift items. The IRS observed that, to be exempt from the tax on unrelated income, items sold in museum gift shops must be substantially related to the accomplishment of the museum's tax-exempt purpose. This relationship, said the IRS, "must extend specifically to the particular subject matter of the museum in which the items are sold as contrasted to being educational generally." The IRS added: "The characterization of a sales activity as an unrelated trade or business does not hinge on whether the activities may have a commercial hue or are in competition with for-profit entities such as furniture stores, or roadside gift stands offering souvenir items with a regional flavor."

In this case, the IRS said that the museum's retail sales inventory is to be evaluated in the context of its tax-exempt purpose (to preserve and protect the cultural and historical heritage unique to a particular city in the seventeenth through nineteenth centuries). The IRS proceeded through the various categories of items, finding the sale of nearly all of them related. Thus, all of the furniture sales were held to be related activities because of the educational value, despite the fact that the "items are sturdy enough for practical use in the home." The china sales were found related because of the design of the items and accompanying descriptive literature. The sales of fabric and wallpaper were found related because of the original designs and derivations from documented research. Lamp sales were related despite the "utilitarian adaptation of the modern electric lamps from various artifacts" because the original design was not distorted. Most of the sales of the other items were held related because of authenticated design motifs, decorations portraying historical scenes, and/or accompanying literature. This rationale embraced chandeliers, artwork, kitchen accessories, cookbooks, lawn furniture, toys, and games. The only sales that were found unrelated were those of a cast iron trivet (merely bearing the museum's logo), soaps, colognes, and bath oils.

This museum did more than sell at retail from its store; it also engaged in catalog sales. Applying the fragmentation rule, the IRS found that the catalog operation itself was a tax-exempt function, in that it was of educational value because it carried articles and illustrations generally supportive of the museum's tax-exempt purpose. Rejected was the view that the income from catalog sales

---

[425] Priv. Ltr. Rul. 8326008. Cf. (on this last point) Goldsboro Art League v. Comm'r, 75 T.C. 337 (1980).
[426] Tech. Adv. Mem. 8605002.

should be divided into related and unrelated income on an allocable basis in relation to the listing of related and unrelated items.

In technical advice made public late in 1995, the IRS once again had occasion to review the tax treatment of sales of items by a tax-exempt museum.[427] As before, the IRS stated that the museum's primary purpose for selling a particular item is determinative of whether the sale is a related or unrelated activity. Thus, where the primary purpose behind the production and sale of an item is to further the organization's exempt purpose, the sale is a related one. In a departure from previous pronouncements, however, the IRS added that this is the case even though the item has a utilitarian function or value.[428] By contrast, where the primary purpose underlying production and sale of an item is to generate income, the activity is an unrelated business. On this occasion, the IRS stated that there are a number of differing factors to be considered in ascertaining this primary purpose, including (1) the degree of connection between the item and the museum's collection, (2) the extent to which the item relates to the form and design of the original item, and (3) the overall impression conveyed by the article. If the "dominant impression" individuals gain from viewing or using the article relates to the subject matter of the original article, picture, or likeness, substantial relatedness would be established. If the noncharitable use or function predominated, however, the sale is an unrelated business activity.

In this case, the IRS addressed the fact that much of the museum's sales are off-site. The IRS wrote that the museum has "many outlets and utilizes many vehicles to advertise and sell its wares," namely, retail stores, gift shops, an outlet located in another city, mail order catalogues, advertisements in various publications, a corporate/conference program, and more. The IRS held, however, that the sole fact that sales are off-site does not make them unrelated; this is true even when the sales are in a commercial manner and in competition with for-profit companies. The reason: the off-site sales enhance a broader segment of the public's understanding of the collection and may encourage more individuals to visit the museum.

In another of these instances, a tax-exempt museum, which sponsored programs for children, maintained a shop; the IRS found that the sale of certain tots' and childrens' items constituted unrelated businesses. Nonetheless, items that were reproductions or adaptations of articles displayed in the collections and exhibits were held saleable in related business. The IRS reiterated its general view that, where the primary purpose behind the production and sale of an item is utilitarian, ornamental souvenir in nature, or only generally educational, the matter entails unrelated business activity.[429]

The IRS ruled that a tax-exempt museum may operate an art conservation laboratory and perform conservation work for other institutions and collectors for a fee, without incurring unrelated business income.[430] Likewise, the IRS ruled

---

[427] Tech. Adv. Mem. 9550003.
[428] See text accompanied by *supra* note 424.
[429] Tech. Adv. Mem. 9720002.
[430] Priv. Ltr. Rul. 8432004.

that a museum store may sell items in furtherance of the exempt museum's exempt purpose, other than those that have utilitarian purposes.[431]

(d) Associations

A tax-exempt association (or, technically, business league[432]) is subject to the unrelated income rules. The basic related business function of an exempt association is the provision of services to its members in exchange for dues; thus, this type of dues income is related revenue.

(i) Service to Members. The IRS ruled that a variety of services performed by tax-exempt associations for their members are unrelated businesses.[433] Illustrations of this approach include the sale of equipment by a tax-exempt association to its members,[434] the management of health and welfare plans for a fee by an exempt business league,[435] the provision of insurance for the members of an exempt association,[436] the operation of an executive referral service,[437] the publication of ordinary commercial advertising for products and services used by the legal profession in an exempt bar association's journal,[438] the conduct of a language translation service by an exempt trade association that promoted international trade relations,[439] the publication and sale, by an association of credit unions to its members, of a consumer-oriented magazine designed as a promotional device for distribution to the members' depositors,[440] the provision of mediation and arbitration services by an exempt business league,[441] the advertising and administrative services provided by an exempt business league with respect to a for-profit discount purchasing service,[442] and the operation by an exempt association of members in the trucking industry of an alcohol and drug testing program for members and nonmembers.[443]

Nonetheless, the IRS is not always successful in this context, as illustrated by the finding of a court that the sales of preprinted lease forms and landlord's manuals by a tax-exempt association of apartment owners and managers is a related activity.[444] By contrast, the IRS concluded that the sale of television time to

---

[431] Tech. Adv. Mem. 8605002.
[432] See Chapter 13.
[433] See § 13.4.
[434] Rev. Rul. 66-338, 1966-2 C.B. 226.
[435] Rev. Rul. 66-151, *supra* note 305.
[436] Rev. Rul. 74-81, 1974-1 C.B. 135.
[437] Tech. Adv. Mem. 8524006.
[438] Rev. Rul. 82-139, 1982-2 C.B. 108. In this ruling, the IRS also held that the publication of legal notices by a bar association was not an unrelated trade or business.
[439] Rev. Rul. 81-75, 1981-1 C.B. 356.
[440] Rev. Rul. 78-52, 1978-1 C.B. 166.
[441] Priv. Ltr. Rul. 9408002.
[442] Tech. Adv. Mem. 9440001.
[443] Tech. Adv. Mem. 9550001.
[444] Texas Apartment Ass'n v. United States, 869 F.2d 884 (5th Cir. 1989).

governmental and nonprofit organizations at a discount by an exempt association of television stations was a related business.[445]

Sometimes, there can be a conflict between the IRS and the courts in this setting. For example, the sale of standard legal forms by a local bar association to its member lawyers, which purchased the forms from the state bar association, was ruled by the IRS to be an unrelated business because the activity did not contribute importantly to the accomplishment of the association's exempt functions.[446] A court held, however, that the sale of standard real estate legal forms to lawyers and law students by an exempt bar association was an exempt function because it promoted the common business interests of the legal profession and improved the relationship among the bench, bar, and public.[447]

In one instance, the IRS examined seven activities of a tax-exempt trade association and found all of them to be productive of unrelated income. These activities were the sale of vehicle signs to members, the sale to members of embossed tags for inventory control purposes, the sale to members of supplies and forms, the sale to members of kits to enable them to retain sales tax information, the sale of price guides, the administration of a group insurance program, and the sale of commercial advertising in the association's publications. Moreover, since the majority of the income of the organization was derived from these activities and the majority of the time of the organization's employees was devoted to them, the IRS revoked the association's tax exemption.[448]

(ii) Insurance Programs.   It is common for a tax-exempt association to be involved in the provision of various forms of insurance for its members. The state of the law on this point is that nearly any form of insurance program of an association—endorsement or otherwise—is an unrelated activity.

An association can become involved in a variety of insurance programs in several ways. An association may have little relationship to an insurance offering except to make its name and membership records available to the insurer. It may endorse a particular insurance policy or have a role in the processing of claims. By contrast, the association may be directly involved in the management of an insurance program or may operate a self-insurance fund. The insurance coverage (on a group basis or otherwise) may range over life, health, disability, legal liability, worker's compensation, product liability, and similar subjects. The insureds may be the association's employees, members, and/or employees of members.

At the outset of the evolution of the development of law on this issue, where an insurance company provided insurance coverage for a tax-exempt association's members (and/or its employees) and the association was the mere sponsor, it appeared that this minimal involvement in the insurance process was not an unrelated trade or business. In one instance, an exempt association pro-

---

[445] Priv. Ltr. Rul. 9023081.
[446] Rev. Rul. 78-51, 1978-1 C.B. 165.
[447] San Antonio Bar Ass'n v. United States, 80-2 U.S.T.C. ¶ 9594 (W.D. Tex. 1980).
[448] Priv. Ltr. Rul. 7902006.

vided an insurance company with information about its membership, mailed a letter about the insurance coverage, and allowed the insurer to use the association's name and insignia on brochures. For this, the association received a percentage of the premiums paid by its members to the insurance company. The matter was litigated, with the court concluding that the association was merely passively involved and thus that the activity did not become a trade or business.[449] Another court concluded that this type of remuneration, sometimes termed an *administrative allowance*, paid to an exempt association for its efforts in administering an accident and health insurance program for its members, did not constitute unrelated income, because the association's activities in this regard did not rise to the level of a business,[450] but this holding was reversed on appeal.[451] Similar logic was applied in a decision regarding fees received by an exempt business league in return for its sponsorship of a bank payment plan made available to its members.[452]

Today, however, it is clear that, where a tax-exempt association actively and regularly manages an insurance program for its members, for a fee, and a substantial portion of its income and expenses is traceable to the activity, the management undertaking will be regarded by the IRS as an unrelated business.[453] The IRS initially permitted exempt associations to escape taxation of insurance income by structuring the payments as royalties,[454] but subsequently reversed its position and ruled that the payments are taxable income for services rendered.[455] If the provision of insurance is an association's sole or principal activity, the IRS will deny recognition of, or deprive it of, exemption, as illustrated by the denial of tax exemption to an organization that provided group worker's compensation insurance to its members[456] and to an organization that provided insurance and similar plans for its members.[457]

The approach of the courts in this area is essentially the same as that of the IRS. The Court of Claims, for example, found that a significant portion of an association's income was from the performance of services to members, including billing and collecting insurance premiums and distributing claim forms (with the association's income set as a percentage of premiums collected) and therefore held that the association did not qualify for tax exemption.[458] The U.S. Tax Court

---

[449] Oklahoma Cattlemen's Ass'n v. United States, *supra* note 96.

[450] Carolinas Farm & Power Equip. Dealers Ass'n., Inc. v. United States, *supra* note 108.

[451] *Supra* § 2(g).

[452] San Antonio Dist. Dental Soc'y v. United States, *supra* note 107.

[453] Rev. Rul. 66-151, *supra* note 305. Also Rev. Rul. 60-228, *supra* note 305.

[454] See § 27.1(g). This position of the IRS was stated in Priv. Ltr. Rul. 8828011.

[455] Priv. Ltr. Rul. 9029047. In reaching this conclusion, the IRS took into consideration not only the insurance-related activities of the association but also the activities of its agent, which the IRS attributed to the association under authority of National Water Well Ass'n, Inc. v. Comm'r, 92 T.C. 75 (1989). Further, the IRS held that the membership list exception (see § 27.2(k)) governed the tax consequences of the transaction, in that the payments for services were inseparable from payments for use of the association's membership list; the IRS held that the exception was inapplicable.

[456] Rev. Rul. 76-81, 1976-1 C.B. 156.

[457] Rev. Rul. 67-176, 1967-1 C.B. 140.

[458] Indiana Retail Hardware Ass'n v. United States, 366 F.3d 998 (Ct. Cl. 1966).

adopted a like rationale, combining insurance activities with the sale of educational materials, jewelry, emblems, and supplies to conclude that an association failed to qualify for exemption because of substantial unrelated business activity.[459] This decision was followed by a holding that the promotional and administrative fees received by an exempt professional association of independent insurance agents for the promotion of group insurance programs for its members constituted unrelated business income.[460]

One of the first courts to rule directly on the point upheld the IRS position. The court determined that a commission paid a tax-exempt organization on the writing of new and renewal insurance policies by an insurance company, the coverage plans of which the organization endorsed, was unrelated business income.[461] Subsequently, the U.S. Tax Court echoed that decision, holding that the promotional and administrative fees received by an exempt business league from insurance companies for the sponsorship of insurance programs for the benefit of its membership were taxable as unrelated income.[462] In so holding, the Tax Court rejected the reasoning of the two decisions finding that this type of income is merely passively derived and thus not taxable.[463] The court held that, since the activity was engaged in with the intent to earn a profit, the activity must be considered a trade or business.[464] Also, the court was of the view that the enactment in 1969 of a statutory definition of the term *trade or business* overruled the passive income concept utilized in the other cases.[465] An appellate court agreed, holding that the organization was engaged in a taxable business activity because it "engaged in extensive activity over a substantial period of time with intent to earn a profit."[466]

Thus, the remaining major substantive issue in this area is no longer whether a tax-exempt association can have its tax status adversely affected by, or must treat as an unrelated trade or business, the active conduct of an insurance program, but whether there is a way for an association to be only passively involved in an insurance activity. The IRS does not believe the court decision finding this passive involvement[467] to be correct; rather, the IRS holds that initiation of an insurance program by an association, negotiation with the broker, and general

---

[459] Associated Master Barbers & Beauticians of America, Inc. v. Comm'r, 69 T.C. 53 (1977).
[460] Professional Ins. Agents of Mich. v. Comm'r, 78 T.C. 246 (1982), *aff'd*, 726 F.2d 1097 (6th Cir. 1984). Also Professional Ins. Agents of Wash. v. Comm'r, 53 T.C.M. 9 (1987); Long Island Gasoline Retailers Ass'n, Inc. v. Comm'r, 43 T.C.M. 815 (1982).
[461] Louisiana Credit Union League v. United States, 501 F. Supp. 934 (E.D.La. 1980), *aff'd*, 693 F.2d 525 (5th Cir. 1982).
[462] Professional Ins. Agents of Mich. v. Comm'r, *supra* note 460.
[463] See *supra* notes 449, 450.
[464] See *supra* § 2(b).
[465] See *supra* § 2(a).
[466] Professional Ins. Agents of Mich. v. Comm'r, 726 F.2d 1097, 1102 (6th Cir. 1984). Also Professional Ins. Agents of Wash. v. Comm'r, *supra* note 460; Texas Farm Bur. v. United States, 822 F. Supp. 371 (W.D. Tex. 1993), *aff'd and rev'd*, 95-1 U.S.T.C. ¶ 50,297 (5th Cir. 1995); Independent Ins. Agents of Huntsville, Inc. v. Comm'r, 63 T.C.M. 2468 (1992), *aff'd*, 998 F.2d 898 (11th Cir. 1993) Illinois Ass'n of Professional Ins. Agents, Inc. v. Comm'r, 49 T.C.M. 925 (1985).
[467] See *supra* note 499.

support of and promotion of the program are services to the association's members, in the private capacity, and thus an unrelated business.[468] Consequently, in the view of the IRS, once the insurance activity rises to the level of a business,[469] it is an unrelated activity, and all association insurance activities constitute more than mere passive involvements.[470]

One solution may be to have the insurance program conducted by a separate entity, such as a trust or corporation, albeit controlled by the parent tax-exempt association. This approach requires care that the separate entity is in fact a true legal entity, with its own governing instruments, governing board, and separate tax return filing obligation.[471] If it is a mere trusteed bank account or the like of the association, the IRS will regard the program as an integral part of the association itself.[472] If it is an authentic separate legal entity, any tax liability would be confined to that imposed on the net income of the entity, which presumably would have no basis for securing tax exemption.[473] If the entity transfers funds to the parent association, however, the funds may be taxable to the association as unrelated business income.[474] Likewise, the funds may be taxable to the association if the separate entity is regarded as an agent of the association.[475]

A court case recognized that the acquisition and provision of insurance can be an exempt function of a tax-exempt business league.[476] In this instance, the organization's purposes included counseling governmental agencies with regard to insurance programs, accepting and servicing insurance written by the agencies, and otherwise acting as an insurance broker for the governmental agencies. Finding this function to be an "important public service" (because the activity resulted in the best comprehensive insurance program for each agency and eliminated political corruption in the procurement of insurance), the court held that the net brokerage commissions received by the business league were not taxable as being from an unrelated trade or business. In so holding, the court placed some reliance on an IRS ruling that the provision for equitable distribution of high-risk insurance policies among member insurance companies is an exempt undertaking.[477]

[468] E.g., Priv. Ltr. Rul. 7840014.
[469] See *supra* § 2.
[470] In the first appellate court decision following the pronouncement of the Supreme Court in the *American Bar Endowment* case (*infra* note 562), a court concluded that the performance of promotional and administrative services by an association in connection with the sale of insurance to its members is an unrelated activity (Illinois Ass'n of Professional Ins. Agents, Inc. v. Comm'r, 86-2 U.S.T.C. ¶ 9702 (7th Cir. 1986), *aff'g* 49 T.C.M. 925 (1985)). Also National Water Well Ass'n, Inc. v. Comm'r, *supra* note 455.
[471] See § 24.3.
[472] Priv. Ltr. Rul. 7847001.
[473] North Carolina Oil Jobbers Ass'n, Inc. v. United States, 78-2 U.S.T.C. ¶ 9658 (E.D.N.C. 1978); New York State Ass'n of Real Estate Bds. Group Ins. Fund v. Comm'r, 54 T.C. 1325 (1970).
[474] See § 27.1(n).
[475] See *supra* § 3(b), text accompanied by note 144.
[476] Independent Ins. Agents of N. Nev., Inc. v. United States, 79-2 U.S.T.C. ¶ 9601 (D. Nev. 1979). This position of the IRS extends to insurance programs maintained by tax-exempt social welfare membership organizations (see Chapter 12) (e.g., Priv. Ltr. Rul. 9441001).
[477] Rev. Rul. 71-155, 1971-1 C.B. 152.

If a tax-exempt association provides insurance for its own employees, it can do so without adverse tax consequences by contracting with an insurance provider or by establishing a voluntary employees beneficiary association, which is itself exempt.[478] This type of organization is one that provides "for the payment of life, sick, accident, or other benefits to the members of such association or their dependents or designated beneficiaries."[479]

Separate consideration must be given the insurance programs of tax-exempt fraternal beneficiary societies,[480] as their exempt purpose is to provide for the payment of qualifying benefits to their members and their dependents.[481] The IRS recognized that these benefits are in the nature of insurance, in holding that a society may not, as an exercise of an exempt function, provide additional insurance for terminated members.[482]

(iii) Associate Member Dues.   Another issue for tax-exempt associations is the tax treatment of dues derived from associate members (or affiliate or patron members). In some instances, the IRS will tax these dues as forms of unrelated business income, on the ground that the member is paying for a specific service or to gain access to the regular membership for purposes of selling products or services.[483] Thus, in one instance, the IRS recommended taxation of associate member dues, where the associates allegedly joined only to obtain coverage under the association's automobile, health, dental, and farm owners' insurance programs.[484] In another instance, the IRS recommended taxation as advertising income the dues paid by associate members for listings in a variety of publications, allegedly to make them accessible to the regular members; the IRS recast the dues as *access fees*.[485] Taxation of dues is more likely where the associate members do not receive exempt function benefits, serve as directors or officers, vote on association matters, or otherwise lack any meaningful right or opportunity to participate in the affairs of the organization.

The first court opinion on the point held that dues collected by a tax-exempt labor organization[486] from persons who were not regular active members of the organization, who became members so as to be able to participate in a health insurance plan sponsored by the organization, constituted unrelated business income.[487] The court concluded that this special class of members was created to generate revenue and not to contribute importantly to an exempt

---

[478] See § 16.3.
[479] In general, Greif & Goldstein, "Rulings Holding Insurance Plans of Exempt Orgs. Taxable May Threaten Exemptions," 50 *J. Tax.* 294 (1979); Claytor, "When Will Business Activities Cause Trade Associations to Forfeit Their Exempt Status?," 49 *J. Tax.* 104 (1978).
[480] See § 18.4(a).
[481] *Id.*
[482] Priv. Ltr. Rul. 7937002.
[483] This issue is identical to that raised in the context of tax-exempt labor unions (see text accompanied by *infra* notes 498–501).
[484] Tech. Adv. Mem. 9416002.
[485] Tech. Adv. Mem. 9345004.
[486] See § 15.1.
[487] National League of Postmasters v. Comm'r, 69 T.C.M. 2569 (1995), *aff'd*, 86 F.3d 59 (4th Cir. 1996).

purpose. The fact that the organization generated substantial net revenues through the sale of these memberships was considered evidence that revenue-raising was the principal intent underlying the establishment of the membership category.

The IRS stated that, in the case of tax-exempt labor, agricultural, and horticultural organizations,[488] dues payments from associate members will not be regarded as unrelated business income unless, for the relevant period, the membership category was formed or availed of for the principal purpose of producing unrelated income.[489] This aspect of the law was subsequently altered by statute, however, in that certain dues payments to exempt agricultural or horticultural organizations are exempt from unrelated business income taxation.[490] Nonetheless, this IRS position continues to be its view with respect to labor organizations (and to agricultural and horticultural entities that do not qualify for the exception); indeed, the IRS indicated that it will follow this approach with respect to associations generally.[491]

(iv) Other Association Business Activity. It is the position of the IRS that a tax-exempt business league can engage in charitable activities, without incurring an unrelated income tax, even though the activities are technically unrelated to the business league's purposes.[492]

The position of the IRS is that the operation of an employment service by a tax-exempt association is an unrelated activity.[493] This approach embraces registry programs[494] but not job training programs.[495]

Tax-exempt associations are experiencing a conflict in the federal tax law as respects the classification of an activity as being a related service for members or an unrelated business. In the absence of statutory or administrative regulatory authority on the point, the courts are formulating standards. For example, a federal court of appeals applied three factors in resolving the issue as to whether an activity is substantially related to an association's exempt purposes: (1) whether the fees charged are directly proportionate to the benefits received; (2) whether participation is limited to members and thus is of no benefit to those in the industry who are nonmembers; and (3) whether the service provided is one commonly furnished by for-profit entities.[496] In subsequent application of these criteria, the

---

[488] See Chapter 15.

[489] Rev. Proc. 95-21, 1995-1 C.B. 686.

[490] See § 27.2(l).

[491] Rev. Proc. 97-12, 1997-1 C.B. 631, *mod.* Rev. Proc. 95-21, *supra* note 489. Associate member dues received by a professional association were found to not be taxable because the associate member category was not formed or availed of for the principal purpose of producing unrelated business income; voting rights were held to not be the sole criterion in this evaluation (Tech. Adv. Mem. 9742001). Associate member dues received by a union were, however, held taxable as unrelated income because the membership category was availed of for the principal purpose of producing this type of income (Tech. Adv. Mem. 9751001).

[492] Tech. Adv. Mem. 8418003.

[493] Rev. Rul. 61-170, 1961-2 C.B. 112.

[494] Priv. Ltr. Rul. 8503103.

[495] Rev. Rul. 67-296, 1967-2 C.B. 22.

[496] Carolinas Farm & Power Equip. Dealers Ass'n, Inc. v. United States, *supra* note 50, at 171.

court found that an association's administration of vacation pay and guaranteed annual income accounts for its members under a collective bargaining agreement was unrelated to its exempt negotiation and arbitration activities, because each member benefited in proportion to its participation in the activity, only the association's members were eligible to participate in the service, and the functions could be performed by for-profit entities.[497]

(e) Labor and Agricultural Organizations

One of the principal issues in the unrelated income context for tax-exempt labor unions[498] is the taxation of revenue (dues) derived from associate members (sometimes termed limited benefit members) who joined the organization solely to be able to participate in the organization's health insurance plans. The evolving view is that this dues revenue is taxable.[499] When this issue was initially litigated, the government lost, basically on the ground that the courts lacked the authority to define the bona fide membership of exempt labor unions.[500] The prevailing view, however, is that the same rules that apply with respect to associations[501] apply in the case of labor organizations.

In other applications of the unrelated income rules to tax-exempt labor organizations, the IRS found to be taxable income derived by an exempt labor organization from the operation of semiweekly bingo games[502] and from the performance of accounting and tax services for some of its members.[503]

Tax-exempt agricultural organizations are likewise subject to the tax on unrelated business income. As an illustration, the IRS ruled that the following is taxable: income received by an exempt agricultural organization from the sale of supplies and equipment to members,[504] commissions from the sale of members' cattle,[505] income from the sale of supplies to seedsmen,[506] and income from the operation of club facilities for its members and their guests.[507]

Federal tax law provides an exclusion from the unrelated income taxation rules for income received by a tax-exempt organization used to establish, maintain, or operate a retirement home, hospital, or similar facility for the exclusive

---

[497] Steamship Trade Ass'n of Baltimore, Inc. v. Comm'r, *supra* note 51, where the appellate court endorsed Rev. Rul. 66-151, *supra* note 305. Cf. Rev. Rul. 82-138, 1982-2 C.B. 106; Rev. Rul. 65-164, 1965-1 C.B. 238.

[498] See § 15.1.

[499] American Postal Workers Union, AFL-CIO v. United States, 925 F.2d 480 (D.C. Cir. 1991); National Ass'n of Postal Supervisors v. United States, 90-2 U.S.T.C. ¶ 50,445 (Ct. Cl. 1990), *aff'd*, 944 F. 2d 859 (Fed. Cir. 1991).

[500] American Postal Workers Union, AFL-CIO, v. United States, 90-1 U.S.T.C. ¶ 50,013 (D.D.C. 1989), *rev'd, supra* note 499.

[501] See *supra* § (d).

[502] Rev. Rul. 59-330, 1959-2 C.B. 153. Cf. § 27.2(h).

[503] Rev. Rul. 62-191, 1962-2 C.B. 146.

[504] Rev. Rul. 57-466, 1957-2 C.B. 311.

[505] Rev. Rul. 69-51, 1969-1 C.B. 159.

[506] Priv. Ltr. Rul. 8429010.

[507] Rev. Rul. 60-86, 1960-1 C.B. 198.

use and benefit of the aged and infirm members of the organization, where the income is derived from agricultural pursuits and conducted on grounds contiguous to the facility and where the income does not provide more than 75 percent of the cost of maintaining and operating the facility.[508]

(f) Advertising Activities

Generally, the net income derived by a tax-exempt organization from the sale of advertising is taxable as unrelated business income.[509] Despite the extensive body of regulatory and case law in this area concerning when and how advertising revenue may be taxed, however, there is little law on the question as to what constitutes *advertising*. In one instance, a court considered the publication of "business listings," consisting of "slogans, logos, trademarks, and other information which is similar, if not identical in content, composition and message to the listings found in other professional journals, newspapers, and the 'yellow pages' of telephone directories," and found them to qualify as advertising.[510]

Under the rules defining what is a *trade or business*,[511] income from the sale of advertising in publications of tax-exempt organizations (even where the publications are related to the exempt purpose of the organization) generally constitutes unrelated business income, taxable to the extent it exceeds the expenses directly related to the advertising. If, however, the editorial aspect of the publication is carried on at a loss, the editorial loss may be offset against the advertising income from the publication. Thus, there will be no taxable unrelated trade or business income because of advertising where the publication as a whole is published at a loss. This rule embodies a preexisting regulation[512] that was promulgated in an effort to carve out (and tax) income from advertising and other activities in competition with taxpaying business, even though the advertising may appear in a periodical related to the educational or other tax-exempt purpose of the organization.

These rules are not intended to encompass the publication of a magazine with little or no advertising, which is distributed free or at a nominal charge not intended to cover costs. This type of publication would likely be published basically as a source of public information and not for the production of income. For a publication to be considered an activity carried on for the production of income, it must be contemplated that the revenues from advertising in the publication or

---

[508] Pre-1976 IRC § 512(b)(4). Although this provision was removed from the Internal Revenue Code as one of the "deadwood" provisions of the Tax Reform Act of 1976, it remains preserved in the law.

[509] IRC § 513(c).

[510] Fraternal Order of Police, Illinois State Troopers Lodge No. 41 v. Comm'r, 87 T.C. 747, 754 (1986), *aff'd*, 833 F.2d 717 (7th Cir. 1987).

[511] IRC § 513(c). See *supra* § 2.

[512] Reg. § 1.513-1(b). This regulation became effective on December 13, 1967. IRC § 513(c) became effective on December 31, 1969. As respects tax years beginning between these dates, the regulation is of no effect, as an impermissible administrative enlargement of the scope of the statutory unrelated business income law (Massachusetts Medical Soc'y v. United States, 514 F.2d 153 (1st Cir. 1975); American College of Physicians v. United States, 530 F.2d 930 (Ct. Cl. 1976)).

the revenues from sales of the publication, or both, will result in net income (although not necessarily in a particular year). Nonetheless, for the tax on unrelated business income to apply, the advertising activity must also constitute a trade or business that is regularly carried on. Further, the tax is inapplicable where the advertising activity is a tax-exempt function.[513]

As an example, a tax-exempt association of law enforcement officials published a monthly journal containing conventional advertising featuring the products or services of a commercial enterprise. The IRS ruled that the regular sale of space in the journal for the advertising was carried on for the production of income and constituted the conduct of trade or business, which was not substantially related to the organization's exempt functions.[514] The "controlling factor in this case," said the IRS, was that the "activities giving rise to the income in question constitute the sale and performance of a valuable service on the part of the publisher, and the purchase of that service on the part of the other party to the transaction."[515]

In a similar situation, the IRS ruled that income derived by a tax-exempt membership organization from the sale of advertising in its annual yearbook was unrelated business income.[516] Preparation of the editorial materials in the yearbook was largely done by the organization's staff, which also distributed it. An independent commercial firm was used, under a full year contract, to conduct an intensive advertising solicitation campaign in the organization's name and the firm was paid a percentage of the gross advertising receipts for selling the advertising, collecting from advertisers, and printing the yearbook. The IRS stated that by "engaging in an extensive campaign of advertising solicitation, the organization is conducting competitive and promotional efforts typical of commercial endeavors."[517]

Initially, it appeared that the courts were willing to accede to this approach by the IRS. In the principal case, a tax-exempt medical organization was found to be engaging in an unrelated business by selling advertising in its scholarly journal. The court rejected the contention that the purpose of the advertising was to educate physicians, holding instead that its primary purpose was to raise revenue. In reaching this conclusion, the court reviewed the content, format, and positioning of the advertisements, and concluded they were principally commercial in nature. The court, however, set forth some standards as to when journal advertising might be an exempt function, such as advertising that comprehensively surveys a particular field or otherwise makes a systematic presentation on an appropriate subject.[518]

These findings of the court were reversed on appeal, with the appellate court holding that the content of the advertisements was substantially related to

---

[513] E.g., Priv. Ltr. Rul. 7948113 (holding that proceeds from the sale of advertising in the program published in promotion of a postseason all-star college football game are not unrelated income).

[514] Rev. Rul. 74-38, 1974-1 C.B. 144, *clar. by* Rev. Rul. 76-93, 1976-1 C.B. 170.

[515] Rev. Rul. 74-38, *id.*, at 145.

[516] Rev. Rul. 73-424, *supra* note 128.

[517] *Id.* at 191.

[518] The American College of Physicians v. United States, 83-2 U.S.T.C. ¶ 9652 (Ct. Cl. 1983).

the organization's educational purpose.[519] The court noted that the advertisements only appeared in bunches, at the beginning and end of the publications; were screened with respect to subject matter, with the contents controlled; and were indexed by advertiser. Also, only advertisements directly relevant to the practice of internal medicine were published. This decision, then, established the principle that advertising is like any other trade or business, in that it is not automatically an unrelated activity, in that it can be an information dissemination (educational) function.

This dispute as to the tax treatment of advertising revenue in the unrelated income context, specifically whether the IRS is correct in asserting that all net income from advertising in tax-exempt publications is always taxable, was resolved by the U.S. Supreme Court, in 1986, when it held, after reviewing the history of the regulations promulgated in 1967[520] and of the statutory revisions authored in 1969,[521] that it is possible to have related advertising.[522] The Court said that the standard is whether the conduct of the exempt organization in selling and publishing the advertising is demonstrative of a related function, rather than a determination as to whether the advertising is inherently educational.

The Supreme Court observed that in ascertaining relatedness, it is not sufficient to merely cluster the advertising in the front and back of the tax-exempt publication. Other facts that tended to mitigate against relatedness were that all advertising was paid, the advertising was for established products or services, advertising was repeated from one month to another, or the advertising concerned matters having "no conceivable relationship" to the exempt purpose of the sponsoring exempt organization.[523] The test, said the Court, quoting from the trial court's opinion, is whether the organization uses the advertising to "provide its readers a comprehensive or systematic presentation of any aspect of the goods or services publicized;" as the Court wrote, an exempt organization can "control its publication of advertisements in such a way as to reflect an intention to contribute importantly to its . . . [exempt] functions."[524] This can be done, said the Court, by "coordinating the content of the advertisements with

[519] The American College of Physicians v. United States, 743 F.2d 1570 (Fed. Cir. 1984).
[520] See *supra* note 512.
[521] IRC § 513(c).
[522] United States v. American College of Physicians, 475 U.S. 834 (1986). A court found the advertising of a tax-exempt trade association to be taxable because it was not substantially related to the organization's exempt purposes and there was "[n]o systematic effort" made "to advertise products that relate to the editorial content of the magazine, and no effort . . . made . . . to limit the advertisements to new products" (Florida Trucking Ass'n, Inc. v. Comm'r, 87 T.C. 1039 (1986)). Displays and listings in a yearbook published by a tax-exempt labor organization (see § 15.1) were found to be the result of unrelated business (State Police Ass'n of Massachusetts v. Comm'r, 97-2 U.S.T.C. ¶ 50,627 (1st Cir. 1997)).
[523] United States v. American College of Physicians, *supra* note 522, at 849.
[524] *Id.*

the editorial content of the issue, or by publishing only advertisements reflecting new developments."[525]

The foregoing may be contrasted with the situation involving a charitable organization that raised funds for a tax-exempt symphony orchestra. As part of this effort, the organization published an annual concert book that was distributed at the orchestra's annual charity ball. The IRS ruled that the solicitation and sale of advertising by volunteers of the organization was not an unrelated taxable activity because the activity was not regularly carried on and because it was conducted as an integral part of the process of fundraising for charity.[526] Thus, part of a successful contention that the unrelated income tax should not apply in the advertising context would seem to be a showing that the advertising activity ties in with other organization activity. Yet the same type of organization that engaged in the sale of advertising over a four-month period by its paid employees, for publication in concert programs distributed free at symphony performances over an eight-month period, was found by the IRS to be carrying on an unrelated business.[527] In that ruling, the IRS observed:

> It is a matter of common knowledge that many non-exempt organizations make a regular practice of publishing and distributing a seasonal series of special interest publications covering only a portion of each year with a format that includes substantial amounts of advertising matter. It would not be unusual for such an organization to concentrate its efforts to sell the advertising space thus made available during similar periods of intensive activity that would frequently last for no more than three or four months of each year. Since it is likewise further apparent that the activities giving rise to the advertising income here in question do not otherwise substantially differ from the comparable commercial activities of nonexempt organizations, those activities of the subject organization are regularly carried on within the meaning of section 512 of the Code.[528]

Similarly, a tax-exempt business league that sold a membership directory, but only to its members, was held to not be engaged in an unrelated trade or business.[529] The directory was considered to contribute importantly to the achievement of the organization's exempt purposes by facilitating communication among its members and encouraging the exchange of ideas and expertise, resulting in greater awareness of collective and individual activities of the

---

[525] *Id.*, at 849–850. Subsequently, a court found that a tax-exempt organization's advertising did not contribute importantly to the carrying out of any of its tax-exempt purposes, although it was willing to explore the argument to the contrary and found that the subject matter of some of the advertising was related to the organization's exempt purpose (Minnesota Holstein-Friesian Breeders Ass'n v. Comm'r, 64 T.C.M. 1319 (1992)). The court concluded that the primary purposes underlying the advertising were commercial: stimulating demand for the advertised products and raising revenue for the tax-exempt organization.
[526] Rev. Rul. 75-201, 1975-1 C.B. 164.
[527] Rev. Rul. 75-200, 1975-1 C.B. 163.
[528] *Id.* at 164.
[529] Rev. Rul. 79-370, 1979-2 C.B. 238.

membership. The principal aspect governing the outcome of this matter, however, was the fact that the sale of the directory, done in a noncommercial manner, did not confer any private benefit on the organization's members.

Income attributable to a publication of a tax-exempt organization basically is regarded as either *circulation income* or (if any) *gross advertising income*.[530] Circulation income is the income attributable to the production, distribution, or circulation of a publication (other than gross advertising income), including amounts realized from the sale of the readership content of the publication. Gross advertising income is the amount derived from the unrelated advertising activities of an exempt organization publication.

Likewise, the costs attributable to a tax-exempt organization publication are characterized as *readership costs* and *direct advertising costs*.[531] A reasonable allocation may be made as between cost items attributable both to an exempt organization publication and to its other activities (such as salaries, occupancy costs, and depreciation).[532] Readership costs are, therefore, the cost items directly connected with the production and distribution of the readership content of the publication, other than the items properly allocable to direct advertising costs. Direct advertising costs include items that are directly connected with the sale and publication of advertising (such as agency commissions and other selling costs, artwork, and copy preparation), the portion of mechanical and distribution costs attributable to advertising lineage, and any other element of readership costs properly allocable to the advertising activity.

As noted, a tax-exempt organization (assuming it is subject to the unrelated business income rules in the first instance) is not taxable on its advertising income where its direct advertising costs equal such (gross) income. Even if gross advertising income exceeds direct advertising costs, costs attributable to the readership content of the publication qualify as costs deductible in computing (unrelated) income from the advertising activity, to the extent that the costs exceed the income attributable to the readership content.[533] There are limitations on this rule, however, including the conditions that its application may not be used to realize a loss from the advertising activity nor to give rise to a cost deductible in computing taxable income attributable to any other unrelated activity. If the circulation income of the publication exceeds its readership costs, any unrelated business taxable income attributable to the publication is the excess of gross advertising income over direct advertising costs.

Another set of rules requires an allocation of membership dues to circulation income where the right to receive the publication is associated with membership status in the tax-exempt organization for which dues, fees, or other

---

[530] Reg. § 1.512(a)-1(f)(3).

[531] Reg. § 1.512(a)-1(f)(6).

[532] Once a reasonable method of allocation is adopted, it must be used consistently (Reg. § 1.512(a)-1(f)(6)(i)). One court held that the application of a ratio used in previous years for this purpose is not a "method"; it is the output of a method which cannot be automatically applied each year (National Ass'n of Life Underwriters, Inc. v. Comm'r, 94-2 U.S.T.C. ¶ 50,412 (D.C. Cir. 1994), *rev'g* 64 T.C.M. 379 (1992)).

[533] Reg. § 1.512(a)-1(f)(2)(ii), (d)(2).

charges are received.[534] There are three ways of determining the portion of membership dues that constitute a part of circulation income (*allocable membership receipts*):

1. If 20 percent or more of the total circulation of the publication consists of sales to nonmembers, the subscription price charged to the nonmembers is the amount allocated from each member's dues to circulation income. It was held that the term *total circulation* means paid circulation, that is, it does not include distribution of a publication without charge to a tax-exempt organization's nonmembers.[535] It has also been held that this term means the actual number of copies of the publication distributed for compensation without regard to how the copies were purchased; in the case, members of an exempt association paid for subscriptions, by means of dues, and they designated nonmember recipients of the publication, who were considered part of the total circulation base.[536]

2. If rule (1) is inapplicable and if the membership dues from 20 percent or more of the members of the organization are less than the dues received from the remaining members because the former category of members does not receive the publication, the amount of the dues reduction is the amount used in allocating membership dues to circulation income.

3. Otherwise, the portion of membership receipts allocated to the publication is an amount equal to the total amount of the receipts multiplied by a fraction, the numerator of which is the total costs of the publication and the denominator of which is these costs plus the costs of the other exempt activities of the organization.[537]

---

[534] Reg. § 1.512(a)-1(f)(4). The IRS initially took the position that the requirement that membership receipts must be allocated on a pro rata basis to circulation income of a tax-exempt organization's periodical (Reg. § 1.512(a)-1(f)(4)(iii)) requires that the "cost of other exempt activities of the organization" must be offset by the income produced by the activities (the "net cost" rule) (Gen. Couns. Mem. 38104), but subsequently concluded that the gross cost of the other tax-exempt activities must be used in computing the denominator of the formula (Gen. Couns. Mems. 38205, 38168).

[535] American Hosp. Ass'n v. United States, 654 F. Supp. 1152 (N.D. Ill. 1987).

[536] North Carolina Citizens for Business & Indus. v. United States, 89-2 U.S.T.C. ¶ 9507 (Cl. Ct. 1989).

[537] The reference to the "costs of the other exempt activities" means the total costs or expenses incurred by an organization in connection with its other tax-exempt activities, not offset by any income earned by the organization from the activities (Rev. Rul. 81-101, 1981-1 C.B. 352).

An organization, such as a business league (Chapter 13), may have within it an integral fund that is a charitable organization, and the costs of the fund can be included in the formula used to calculate the business league's net unrelated business taxable income derived from advertising, thereby reducing the tax liability of the business league (American Bar Ass'n v. United States, 84-1 U.S.T.C. ¶ 9179 (N.D. Ill. 1984)).

These regulations, particularly the third pro rata allocation method rule, were challenged in court on substantive and procedural grounds; while the challenge was initially successful, it essentially failed on appeal (American Medical Ass'n v. United States, 887 F.2d 760 (7th Cir. 1989), *aff'g and rev'g* 608 F. Supp. 1085 (N.D. Ill. 1987), 668 F. Supp. 1101 (N. D. Ill. 1987), 668 F. Supp. 358 (N.D. Ill. 1988), 691 F. Supp. 1170 (N.D. Ill. 1988)). The basic assertion, which was ultimately rejected, was that a tax-exempt organization can deduct, as direct advertising costs, the readership content costs of periodicals distributed for the purpose of generating advertising revenue.

These rules become more intricate where a tax-exempt organization publishes more than one publication for the production of income. (A publication is published for the production of income if the organization generally receives gross advertising income from the publication equal to at least 25 percent of its readership costs and the publication activity is engaged in for profit.) In this case, the organization may treat the gross income from all (but not just some) of the publications and the deductible items directly connected with the publications on a consolidated basis in determining the amount of unrelated business taxable income derived from the sale of advertising. (Thus, an organization cannot consolidate the losses of a publication not published for the production of income with the profit of other publications that are so published.) This treatment must be followed consistently and, once adopted, is binding, unless the organization obtains the requisite permission from the IRS to change the method.[538]

It is the position of the IRS, as supported by the U.S. Tax Court, that the specific rules concerning the computation of net unrelated income derived from advertising are inapplicable in a case where the "issue of whether the . . . [organization's] publication of the readership content of the magazines is an exempt activity has not been decided, stipulated to, or presented for decision" and where the IRS "has not sought to apply such regulations, maintaining that they cannot be applied due to the . . . [organization's] failure to produce credible evidence of its advertising and publishing expenses."[539]

---

[538] IRC § 446(e); Reg. § 1.446-1(e).

[539] CORE Special Purpose Fund v. Comm'r, 49 T.C.M. 626, 630 (1985). Notwithstanding the differences in the manner in which tax-exempt social clubs are treated for purposes of unrelated taxation (see § 28.3), the rules concerning the taxation of advertising revenue are applicable to them (Chicago Metropolitan Ski Council v. Comm'r, 104 T.C. 341 (1995)). In general, Reap, "Getting the Most from Periodical Advertising Income," 4 *Exempt Org. Tax Rev.* (No. 8) 1065 (1991); Geske, "Unrelated Business Taxable Income and Advertising Revenue of Exempt Organization Periodicals," 4 *Exempt Org. Tax Rev.* (No. 3) 311 (1991); Schnee & Brock, "Opportunities Exist to Reduce Unrelated Business Income from Advertising Revenue," 74 *J. Tax.* (No. 4) 240 (1991); Littman, "Advertising and the Unrelated Business Income Tax after *United States v. American College of Physicians*," 49 *Ohio St. L. Jour.* (No. 2) 625 (1988); Gallagher, " 'Substantially Related': The Magic Words for Nonprofit Organizations: *United States v. American College of Physicians*," 21 *U.S.F.L. Rev.* (No. 4) 795 (1987); Huffaker & Gut, "Supreme Court Holds Advertising Revenue Was Not Substantially Related Income," 65 *J. Tax.* (No. 1) 2 (July 1986); Gross, "New Developments Regarding Advertising Income of Tax-Exempt Organizations," 24 *Am. Bus. L. J.* (No. 1) 116 (1986); Shillingburg, "*American College of Physicians v. United States*: An Ending—A Beginning—Or?," 64 *Taxes* (No. 9) 539 (1986); Simpson, "Taxation of Income from Advertising in Exempt Organizations' Publications," 10 *Estates, Gifts, & Trusts J.* (No. 6) 184 (1985); Weinberg & Nixon, "What Are the Implications of the Federal Circuit's Holding in *American College*?," 62 *J. Tax.* (No. 4) 242 (1985); Gregory, Jr., "Fed. Circuit Holds ABE Insurance Program Does Not Constitute Unrelated Business Income," 63 *J. Tax.* (No. 4) 244 (1985); Kannry, "Taxing Advertising," IX *The Philanthropy Monthly* (No. V) 26 (1976); Kannry, "How to Mitigate the Impact of New Regs. on Exempt Organization's Advertising Income," 45 *J. Tax.* 304 (1976); Sugarman & Vogt, "The New Advertising Regulations and Their Application to Exempt Organizations," 54 *Taxes* 196 (1976); Spevack, "Taxation of Advertising Income of Exempt Organizations' Publications," 21 *Cath. Law.* 268 (1975); Endicott, "Proposed Changes in the Taxation of Advertising Income of Exempt Organization Publications," 2 *Tax Adv.* 710 (1971); Lehrfeld, "The Unfairness Doctrine: Commercial Advertising Profits as Unrelated Business Income," 23 *Tax Law.* 349 (1970); Weithorn & Liles, "Unrelated Business Income Tax: Changes Affecting Journal Advertising Revenues," 45 *Taxes* 791 (1967).

(g) Fundraising Activities

Fundraising practices of charitable organizations and the unrelated business rules have long had a precarious relationship. For this purpose, the term *fundraising* means the solicitation of contributions, grants, and other forms of financial support, usually by charitable organizations.[540] Fundraising activities are almost always distinct from program activities. These activities are often *businesses*.[541]

(i) Fundraising as Unrelated Business. The type of fundraising undertaking that is most likely to be considered a business is the *special event*. These events include functions such as auctions, dinners, sports tournaments, dances, theater events, fairs, car washes, and bake sales.[542] Sometimes a court applies the statutory definition of the term *business*[543] in concluding that the event is an unrelated business; on other occasions, a court will utilize other criteria—such as competition or commerciality—to find that the event is or is not an unrelated business.[544]

Conventional fundraising, namely the solicitation and collection of contributions and grants, technically is a business (or, perhaps, two or more businesses). Yet neither the IRS nor a court has characterized the practices as business—let alone unrelated business.

A case concerned a tax-exempt school that solicited charitable contributions by means of mailing of packages of greeting cards as inducements to prospective donors. The IRS asserted that the school was actually involved in the unrelated business of selling greeting cards. The tax regulations, however, provide that an "activity does not possess the characteristics of a trade or business . . . when an organization sends out low cost articles incidental to the solicitation of charitable contributions."[545] The government asserted that this rule was inapplicable in this case because the funds involved were not "gifts," but the court disagreed, writing that to read the law in that narrow manner would "completely emasculate the exception."[546] The court held that the case turned on the fact that the unrelated business rules were designed to prevent exempt organizations from unfairly competing with for-profit entities,[547] and that the school's fundraising program

---

[540] The federal tax law does not generally define the term *fundraising*. The tax regulations promulgated in connection with the *expenditure test* (see § 20.2(c)), however, provide that the term embraces three practices: the solicitation of dues or contributions from members of the organization, from persons whose dues are in arrears, or from the general public; the solicitation of gifts from businesses or gifts or grants from other organizations, including charitable entities; or the solicitation of grants from a governmental unit or any agency or instrumentality of the unit (Reg. § 56.4911-4(f)(1)).

[541] See *supra* § 2.

[542] The IRS, in the instructions that accompany the annual information return filed by most tax-exempt organizations (see § 24.3), states: "These activities [fundraising special events] only incidentally accomplish an exempt purpose. Their sole or primary purpose is to raise funds that are other than contributions to finance the organization's exempt activities."

[543] See *supra* § 2(a).

[544] See *supra* § 2(b)–(e).

[545] Reg. § 1.513-1(b). See § 27.2(j).

[546] Hope School v. United States, 612 F.2d 298, 302 (7th Cir. 1980).

[547] See *supra* § 2(a).

did not give it an "unfair competitive advantage over taxpaying greeting card businesses."[548]

Greeting cards and similar items, when used in conjunction with the solicitation of charitable contributions, are termed *premiums*. This fundraising practice has spawned considerable litigation and IRS ruling activity. An unrelated business may be present where the value of the premium approximates the amount of the "gift." Also, if the premiums are mailed with the gift solicitation, the result probably is charitable giving; if the premiums are made available following the "gifts," there may be commercial activity. Thus, a court wrote, in a case involving a greeting card program of a national veterans' organization, that "when premiums are advertised and offered only in exchange for prior contributions in stated amounts," the activity is commercial, but if the organization "had mailed the premiums with its solicitations and had informed the recipients that the premiums could be retained without any obligation arising to make a contribution," the activity is not a business because it is not a competitive practice.[549] Another court ruled that the revenue derived by a veterans' organization from the distribution of cards to its members constituted unrelated business income, concluding that the organization was acting with a profit motive and that the card program was the "sale of goods."[550] IRS rulings reflect this approach as well.[551] Yet, another court held, without referencing the other two cases, that the revenue generated by a veterans' organization from the dissemination of greeting cards was not income from an unrelated business but rather contributions resulting from a fundraising program.[552]

One of the earliest examples of a fundraising event cast as a business was an IRS ruling, issued in 1979, holding that a religious organization that conducted, as its principal fundraising activity, bingo games and related concessions, three nights each week, was engaged in an unrelated business.[553] The IRS concluded that the games "constitute a trade or business with the general public, the conduct of which is not substantially related to the exercise or the performance by the organization of the purpose for which it was organized other than the use it makes of the profits derived from the games."[554]

A court ruled that the conduct by a charitable organizaiton of weekly and monthly lotteries was activity regularly carried on and thus was a taxable busi-

---

[548] Hope School v. United States, *supra* note 546, at 304.
[549] Disabled American Veterans v. United States, 650 F.2d 1179, 1187, 1186 (Ct. Cl. 1981).
[550] Veterans of Foreign Wars, Dep't of Mich. v. Comm'r, 89 T.C. 7, 38 (1987). Cf. Veterans of Foreign Wars of the United States, Dep't of Mo., Inc. v. United States, 85-2 U.S.T.C. ¶ 9605 (W.D. Mo. 1984).
[551] E.g., Priv. Ltr. Ruls. 8203134, 8232011.
[552] The American Legion Dep't of N.Y. v. United States, 93-2 U.S.T.C. ¶ 50,417 (N.D.N.Y. 1993).
[553] Priv. Ltr. Rul. 7946001. Also P.L.L. Scholarship Fund v. Comm'r, 82 T.C. 196 (1984); Piety, Inc. v. Comm'r, 82 T.C. 193 (1984).
[554] This organization was unable to utilize the exemption from unrelated income taxation accorded to bingo games (see § 27.2(h)) because, under the law of the state in which it was organized, the games constituted, at that time, an illegal lottery.

ness because the gambling activities were not substantially related to the organization's charitable purposes.[555]

Another court case concerned the tax status of a membership organization for citizens' band radio operators, which used insurance, travel, and discount plans to attract new members.[556] The organization contended that it was only doing what many tax-exempt organizations do to raise contributions, analogizing these activities to fundraising events. The court rejected this argument, defining a *fundraising event* as a "single occurrence that may occur on limited occasions during a given year and its purpose is to further the exempt activities of the organization."[557] These events were contrasted with activities that are "continuous or continual activities which are certainly more pervasive a part of the organization than a sporadic event and [that are] . . . an end in themselves."[558]

A nonprofit school consulted with a tax-shelter investments firm in search of fundraising methods, with the result being a program in which individuals would purchase various real properties from the school, which the school would simultaneously purchase from third parties; both the sellers and the buyers were clients of the investments firm. There were about 22 of these transactions during the years at issue, from which the school received income reflecting the difference between the sales prices and the purchase prices. Finding the "simultaneous purchase and sale of real estate . . . not substantially related to the exercise or performance of [the school's] . . . exempt function," a court held that the net income from the transactions was unrelated income.[559]

At issue before a court was whether income, received by a charitable organization as the result of assignments to it of dividends paid in connection with insurance coverage purchased by members of a related professional association at group rates, was taxable as unrelated business income. The trial court wrote that, where the tax-exempt organization involved in an unrelated business case is a charitable one, the court "must distinguish between those activities that constitute a trade or business and those that are merely fundraising."[560] The court said that this distinction is not always readily apparent, in that charitable activities are "sometimes so similar to commercial transactions that it becomes very difficult to determine whether the organization is raising money 'from the sale of goods or the performance of services' [the statutory definition of a *business*[561]] or whether the goods or services are provided merely as an incident to a fundraising activity." Nonetheless, the court held that the test is whether the activity in question is "operated in a competitive, commercial manner," which is a "question of fact and turns upon the circumstances of each case." "At bottom," the court wrote, the "inquiry is whether the actions of the participants conform

---

[555] United States v. Auxiliary to the Knights of St. Peter Claver, Charities of the Ladies Court No. 97, 92-1 U.S.T.C. ¶ 50,176 (S.D. Ind. 1992).
[556] U.S. CB Radio Association, No. 1, Inc. v. Comm'r, 42 T.C.M. 1441 (1981).
[557] *Id.* at 1444.
[558] *Id.*
[559] Parklane Residential School, Inc. v. Comm'r, 45 T.C.M. 988, 992 (1983).
[560] American Bar Endowment v. United States, 84-1 U.S.T.C. ¶ 9204 (Ct. Cl. 1984).
[561] See *supra* § 2(a).

with normal assumptions about how people behave in a commercial context" and "[i]f they do not, it may be because the participants are engaged in a charitable fundraising activity."

In this case, the court stressed the following elements: the activity involved was a pioneering idea at its inception, it was originally devised as a fundraising effort and was subsequently so presented, the "staggering amount of money" and the "astounding profitability" that was generated by the activity, the degree of the organization's candor toward its members and the public concerning the operation and revenue of the program, and the fact that the activity was operated with the consent and approval of the organization's membership. Concerning the third element, substantial profits and consistently high profit margins are usually cited as reasons for determining that the activity involved is a business. In this case, however, the amounts of money involved were so great that they could not be rationalized in conventional business analysis terms; the only explanation that was suitable to the court was that the "staggering amount" of money was the result of successful charitable fundraising.

Notwithstanding this rational analysis, the Supreme Court overturned the opinion.[562] The Court found of consequence the facts that the organization negotiated premium rates with insurers, selected the insurers that provided the coverage, solicited the membership of the association, collected the premiums, transmitted the premiums to the insurer, maintained files on each policyholder, answered members' questions concerning insurance policies, and screened claims for benefits. In deciding that this bundle of activities amounted to an unrelated business, the Court observed that the charitable organization "prices its insurance to remain competitive with the rest of the market," that the Court "can easily view this case as a standard example of monopoly pricing," and that the case "presents an example of precisely the sort of unfair competition that Congress intended to prevent."[563]

The Court in this case concluded that the "only valid argument in the charitable organization's favor, therefore, is that the insurance program is billed as a fundraising effort."[564] But the Court summarily rejected this contention—in language that highlights why most fundraising efforts are unrelated businesses—writing that that "fact, standing alone, cannot be determinative, or any exempt organization could engage in a tax-free business by 'giving away' its product in return for a 'contribution' equal to the market value of the product."[565]

Currently popular fundraising techniques that raise questions as to application of the unrelated income rules are forms of *commercial co-venturing* and *cause-related marketing*. The former involves situations where a charitable organization consents to be a recipient of funds under circumstances where a commercial business agrees to make payments to it, with that agreement advertised,

---

[562] United States v. American Bar Endowment, 447 U.S. 105 (1986).

[563] *Id.* at 112–114.

[564] *Id.* at 115.

[565] *Id.* Revisions in this program led the IRS to conclude that it was no longer an unrelated business (Priv. Ltr. Rul. 8725056).

where the amount of the payment is predicated on the extent of products sold or services provided by the business to the public during a particular time period. The latter involves the public marketing of products or services by or on behalf of a tax-exempt organization, or some similar other use of an exempt organization's resources. A manifestation of the latter can be seen in the participation by exempt organizations in affinity card programs, in which an exempt membership organization is paid a portion of the revenues derived from the marketing of credit cards to its members, where the initial position of the IRS was that, while the participation (licensing of mailing lists) is an exploitation of the organization's exempt function,[566] the resultant revenues are not taxable because they constitute passive royalty income.[567] The IRS subsequently determined that an affinity card program is an unrelated business, that the payments are not exempt royalty income, and that the resulting revenue is taxable as income from a third party's use of the organization's membership mailing lists.[568]

Nonetheless, the U.S. Tax Court, following its stance with respect to the exclusion for royalty income in general,[569] ruled that affinity card revenue is excludable from unrelated income taxation when it is structured, as reflected in the pertinent agreement with one or more for-profit participants, as royalty income.[570] The court rejected the government's arguments that the exempt organization involved participated in a joint venture with regard to the affinity card program or that it was engaged in the business of selling financial services to its members. Finding that the organization made available its name, marks, and mailing list for use by the for-profit participant, and that those items were intangible property, the court ruled that the "financial consideration received by . . . [the organization] under the agreement was in consideration of such use" and thus that the resulting revenue was excludable royalty income.[571]

On appeal, however, the appellate court crafted a different definition of the term *royalty*,[572] and reversed the Tax Court as to the affinity card revenue, remanding the case for reconsideration.[573] Nonetheless, even with this revised definition of the term *royalty*, the Tax Court again concluded that the organization's affinity card revenue was excludable as royalty income.[574]

---

[566] See *supra* § 4(e).

[567] Priv. Ltr. Rul. 8747066.

[568] Gen. Couns. Mem. 39727. Priv. Ltr. Rul. 8747066 (see *supra* note 567) was revoked by Priv. Ltr. Rul. 8823109. As to the mailing list approach, the IRS determined that the statutory exception (see § 27.2(k)) was not available because the lists were provided to noncharitable organizations. In general, Cerny & Lauber, "Logos, UBIT, and a Strict IRS Approach to Affinity Card Programs," 2 *J. Tax Exempt Orgs.* 9 (Winter 1991).

[569] See § 27.1(a), text accompanied by notes 17–21.

[570] Sierra Club, Inc. v. Comm'r, 103 T.C. 307 (1994). Also Mississippi State University Alumni, Inc. v. Comm'r, 74 T.C.M. 458 (1997); Oregon State University Alumni Assn, Inc. v. Comm'r, 71 T.C.M. 1935 (1996) *aff'd*, 99-2 U.S.T.C. ¶ 50,879 (9th Cir. 1999); Alumni Ass'n of the Univ. of Oregon, Inc. v. Comm'r, 71 T.C.M. 2093 (1996), *aff'd*, 99-2 U.S.T.C. ¶ 50,879 (9th Cir. 1999).

[571] Sierra Club, Inc. v. Comm'r, *supra* note 570 at 344.

[572] See § 27.1(g), text accompanied by notes 42–44.

[573] Sierra Club, Inc. v. Comm'r, 86 F.3d 1526 (9th Cir. 1996).

[574] Sierra Club, Inc. v. Comm'r, 77 T.C.M. 1569 (1999).

The IRS held that the regular sales of membership mailing lists by a tax-exempt educational organization to colleges and business firms for the production of income was an unrelated business.[575] By contrast, the IRS ruled that the exchange of mailing lists by an exempt organization with similar exempt organizations does not give rise to unrelated business income (namely, barter income of an amount equal to the value of the lists received).[576] In this ruling, the IRS ruled that the activity was not a business because it was not carried on for profit but rather to obtain the names of potential donors. Likewise, this exchange funciton was held to be substantially related to the organization's exempt function as being a "generally accepted method used by publicly supported organizations to assist them in maintaining and enhancing their active donor files."[577] Nonetheless, where an exempt organization exchanges mailing lists so as to produce income, it is the position of the IRS that the transaction is economically the same as a rental and thus is an unrelated business.[578]

(ii) Application of Exceptions. Thus, many fundraising endeavors of charitable and other tax-exempt organizations are businesses and are not related practices. Yet, they often escape taxation because of one or more exceptions.

The exception that is most frequently utilized to shelter fundraising activities from taxation is the one for business activities that are not regularly carried on.[579] The typical special event, for example, is usually not regularly carried on,[580] although on occasion the inclusion of preparatory time will convert the activity into a taxable unrelated business.[581] The IRS ruled, for example, that the net proceeds resulting from the annual conduct by a charitable organization of a ball and golf tournament were not taxable because the events were not regularly carried on.[582]

In one case, a court concluded that the annual fundraising activity of a tax-exempt charitable organization, consisting of the presentation and sponsoring of a professional vaudeville show, conducted one weekend per year, was a business that was not regularly carried on.[583] The court concluded: "The fact that an organization seeks to insure the success of its fundraising venture by beginning to

---

[575] Rev. Rul. 72-431, *supra* note 301.

[576] Priv. Ltr. Rul. 8127019.

[577] *Id.*

[578] Priv. Ltr. Rul. 8216009.

[579] See *supra* § 3. A charitable organization, however, may be found to be engaged in an unrelated business for conducting this type of a fundraising event where it is done for the benefit of another charity (Rev. Rul. 75-201, 1975-1 C.B. 164).

[580] E.g., Priv. Ltr. Rul. 200128059 (concerning an annual charity ball and annual golf tournament).

[581] See *supra* § 3(d).

[582] Priv. Ltr. Rul. 200128059.

[583] Suffolk County Patrolmen's Benevolent Ass'n, Inc. v. Comm'r, *supra* note 151. The court took this opportunity to observe that the IRS "apparently believes that all fundraisers of exempt organizations are conducted by amateurs in an amateurish manner," that "[w]e do not believe that this is, nor should be, the case," and that it is "entirely reasonable for an exempt organization to hire professionals in an effort to insure the success of a fundraiser [i.e., fundraising event]" (at 1323).

■ 812 ■

plan and prepare for it earlier should not adversely affect the tax treatment of the income derived by the venture."[584]

Conventional fundraising—the solicitation and collection of gifts and grants—however, is usually regularly carried on, yet there have not been any assertions that these activities are taxable, even though they may be businesses and are not related to exempt purposes.

Other exceptions may be available in the fundraising setting. For example, a business, albeit regularly carried on, in which substantially all of the work is performed for the organization by volunteers is not taxable.[585] The same is the case for the sale of merchandise substantially all of which has been received by the organization as gifts.[586] Activities carried on primarily for the convenience of the organization's members, students, patients, officers, or employees are not taxable.[587] The receipts from certain gambling activities (bingo games) are exempted from related business income taxation.[588]

(iii) Tax Planning Consulting. It is common for charitable organizations that engage in fundraising efforts to provide financial and tax planning information to prospective donors. This may entail modest amounts of information, such as direction as to valuation of property or the extent of the charitable deduction. In other settings, by contrast, the financial and tax information can be substantial and complex. This is particularly the case with respect to planned giving, where charities are directly involved in charitable gift planning and preparation of documents, such as charitable remainder trusts, other trust arrangements, and wills.

A fundamental precept of the federal tax law concerning charitable organizations is that they may not, without jeopardizing their tax-exempt status, be operated in a manner that causes persons to derive a private benefit from their operations.[589] Occasionally, these elements conflict, in that the provision of tax planning information and services by charitable organizations to prospective contributors is considered the provision of impermissible private benefit. While it would seem nearly inconceivable to seriously contend that, when a charitable organization works with a prospective donor to effect a sizable gift that will generate significant tax and other advantages for the donor, by reason of a charitable contribution deduction and other benefits, the organization is imperiling its tax exemption because it is conferring a private benefit, this is the import of three court opinions.

One case concerned the tax-exempt status of an organization that engaged in financial counseling by providing tax planning services, including charitable giving considerations, to wealthy individuals referred to it by subscribing religious organizations. The counseling given by the organization consisted of ad-

---

[584] *Id.* at 1324.
[585] See § 27.2(a).
[586] See § 27.2(c).
[587] See § 27.(b).
[588] See § 27.2(h).
[589] See Chapter 19.

vice on how a contributor may increase current or planned gifts to these religious organizations, including the development of a financial plan that, among other objectives, resulted in a reduction in federal income and estate taxes. The position of the IRS was that this organization could not qualify for federal income tax exemption because it served the private interests of individuals by enabling them to reduce their tax burden. The organization's position was that it was engaging in activities that exempt charitable organizations may generally undertake without loss of their tax exemption. A court agreed with the government, holding that the organization's "sole financial planning activity, albeit an exempt purpose furthering . . . [exempt] fundraising efforts, has a nonexempt purpose of offering advice to individuals on tax matters that reduces an individual's personal and estate tax liabilities."[590] The court dryly stated that "[w]e do not find within the scope of the word charity that the financial planning for wealthy individuals described in this case is a charitable purpose."[591]

In this opinion, the court singled out the planned giving techniques for portrayal as methods that gave rise to unwarranted private benefit by this organization. The example was given of the creation of a charitable remainder trust, where the donor receives "considerable lifetime advantages," such as the flow of income for life, reduced capital gain taxes in instances involving appreciated property, and lower probate costs.[592] (The court could have recited other benefits, such as the charitable contribution deduction, the calculation of the deduction based on the full fair market value of property, and the benefits of (free to the donor) professional money and property management.) These were cast as "real and substantial benefits" that inure to the contributors as the consequence of the organization's activities, with these benefits "substantial enough to deny exemption."[593]

In another case, this court held that a religious organization could not be tax-exempt because it engaged in a substantial nonexempt purpose, which was the counseling of individuals on the purported tax benefits accruing to those who become ministers of the organization.[594] The court decided that the organization was akin to a "commercial tax service, albeit within a narrower field (i.e., tax benefits to ministers and churches) and a narrower class of customers (i.e., . . . [the organization's] ministers)," and thus that it served private purposes.[595] The many

---

[590] Christian Stewardship Assistance, Inc. v. Comm'r, 70 T.C. 1037, 1041 (1978).

[591] *Id.* at 1043.

[592] *Id.* at 1044.

[593] *Id.* This was, indeed, a sweeping conclusion for the court to reach, at least without noting that charitable organizations engage in these practices all the time. (The problem in this case, apparently, was that the financial and tax planning functions were in a separate organization.) Congress provided the benefits to donors who make contributions by means of charitable remainder trusts (IRC § 664). It was unusual for the court to suggest that, when charities make their supporters aware of, and donors elect to avail themselves of, these benefits, the donee charitable organization should in turn lose its tax exemption. Indeed, the court subsequently somewhat circumscribed the reach of this conclusion (see the text accompanying *infra* note 598).

[594] The Ecclesiastical Order of The Ism of Am, Inc. v. Comm'r, 80 T.C. 833 (1983), *aff'd*, 740 F.2d 967 (6th Cir. 1984), *cert. den.*, 471 U.S. 1015 (1985).

[595] *Id.*, 80 T.C. at 839. Also Universal Life Church v. United States, 87-2 U.S.T.C. ¶ 9617 (Ct. Cl. 1987).

detailed discussions by the organization in its literature of ways to maximize tax benefits led the court to observe that although the organization "may well advocate belief in the God of Am [the diety worshipped by the members of the organization], it also advocates belief in the God of Tax Avoidance."[596] In words that have considerable implications for fundraising for charitable purposes generally, the court wrote that a "substantial nonexempt purpose does not become an exempt purpose simply because it promotes the organization in some way."[597] The court apparently grasped the larger portent of its opinion and attempted to narrow its scope by noting that "[w]e are not holding today that any group which discusses the tax consequences of donations to and/or expenditures of its organization is in danger of losing or not acquiring tax-exempt status."[598] That, of course, was the essence of its holding in the prior case.

The court thereafter held that an organization, the membership of which was "religious missions," was not entitled to tax-exempt status as a religious organization because it engaged in the substantial nonexempt purpose of providing financial and tax advice.[599] The court was heavily influenced by a rush of cases before it concerning, in the words of the court, "efforts of taxpayers to hide behind the cover of purported tax-exempt religious organizations for significant tax avoidance purposes."[600] As the court saw the facts of this case, each member mission was the result of individuals attempting to create churches involving only their families so as to convert after-tax personal and family expenses into deductible charitable contributions. The central organization provided sample incorporation papers, tax seminars, and other forms of tax advice and assistance to those creating the missions. Consequently, the court was persuaded that the "pattern of tax avoidance activities which appears to be present at the membership level, combined with . . . [the organization's] admitted role as a tax advisor to its members" justified the conclusion that the organization was ineligible for tax exemption.[601]

These three court opinions can be read as meaning that, where an organization's only function is the provision of financial and tax planning services, it cannot constitute a tax-exempt charitable organization, even where its only "customers" are other charitable, educational, and religious entities. At the same time, particularly when read out of context, some of the court's pronouncements on this point make little sense and are hardly synchronous with real world fundraising practices. In light of this expansive interrelationship of the unrelated business rules and the private benefit doctrine, the court's disclaimer in the second of these cases[602] looms large.[603]

---

[596] *Id.* at 840.
[597] *Id.* at 841.
[598] *Id.* at 842. This decision was affirmed (740 F.2d 967 (6th Cir. 1984), *cert. den.,* 471 U.S. 1015 (1985)).
[599] National Association of American Churches v. Comm'r, 82 T.C. 18 (1984).
[600] *Id.* at 29–30.
[601] *Id.* at 32.
[602] See the text accompanied by *supra* note 598.
[603] In general, Hopkins, *The Law of Fundraising, Third Edition* (John Wiley & Sons, Inc., 2002) § 5.7.

(h) Travel and Tour Activities

Travel tour activities that constitute a business that is not substantially related to a tax-exempt organization's purposes are an unrelated business. Whether travel tour activities conducted by an exempt organization are substantially to an exempt purpose is determined by an analysis of all of the relevant facts and circumstances, including how a travel tour is developed, promoted, and operated.[604]

The balance of the law, as stated in the regulations, on this point must be extracted from examples. An absence of "scheduled instruction or curriculum related to the destination being visited"[605] can lead to a finding of an unrelated business. Thus, for example, it is not a related business for a tax-exempt university alumni association to operate a tour program for its members and guests, where a faculty member is a guest on the tour and participants are encouraged to continue their "lifelong learning" by joining a tour.[606] Conversely, a tour conducted by teachers and directed to students enrolled in degree programs at educational institutions can be a related business, particularly where five or six hours per day are devoted to organized study, preparation of reports, lectures, instruction, and recitation by the students; a library of material is available; examinations are given at the end of the tour; and academic credit is offered for participation in the tour.[607]

A tax-exempt membership organization can exist to foster cultural unity and educate Americans about their country of origin. Tours of this organization that are designed to "immerse participants in [the country's] history, culture and language" may be related businesses, particularly where "[s]ubstantially all of the daily itinerary" is devoted to instruction and visits to places of historical significance. If the trips, however, consist of optional tours and destinations of principally recreational interest, and lack instruction or curriculum, they will likely be unrelated businesses.[608]

A tour where the participants assist in data collection to facilitate scientific research can qualify as a related business.[609] An archaeological expedition with a significant educational component can constitute a related business.[610] A tour enabling participants to attend plays and concerts will be an unrelated business, where the emphasis is on social and recreational activities, rather than a "coordinated educational program."[611]

Advocacy travel can qualify as related business. For example, travel tours for a tax-exempt organization's members to Washington, D.C., where the participants spend substantially all of their time over several days attending meetings with legislators and government officials, and receiving briefings on policy de-

---

[604] Reg. § 1.513-7(a).
[605] Reg. § 1.513-7(b), Example (1).
[606] *Id.*
[607] Reg. § 1.513-7(b), Example (2).
[608] Reg. § 1.513-7(b), Example (4).
[609] Reg. § 1.513-7(b), Example (5).
[610] Reg. § 1.513-7(b), Example (6).
[611] Reg. § 1.513-7(b), Example (7).

velopments related to the issue that is the organization's focus, are related businesses.[612] This is the case even though the participants have some time in the evenings to engage in social and recreational activities.

(i) Provision of Services

In general, net income from the provision of services by a tax-exempt organization to another organization, including another exempt organization, is unrelated business income. This is because it is not automatically an exempt function for one exempt organization to provide services to another, even where both organizations have the same category of exempt status. For example, the IRS ruled that the provision of administrative services by an exempt association to a tax-exempt voluntary employees' beneficiary association, where the latter entity provided a health and welfare benefit plan for the former entity's members' employees, was an unrelated business.[613] Likewise, the provision of management services by an exempt association to a charitable organization it founded was ruled by the IRS to be an unrelated business.[614] Indeed, the provision of management services by a nonprofit organization to unaffiliated charitable organizations led to the revocation of the organization's exemption as a charitable entity.[615]

There are two exceptions to this general rule. One is that, under certain circumstances, it can be a related business for a tax-exempt organization to provide services of this nature to another exempt entity. As an illustration, an exempt business association with an aggressive litigation strategy placed the litigation function in a separate exempt organization because of a substantial risk of counterclaims and other retaliatory actions against the association and its members; the IRS concluded that the provision by the association of management and administrative services to the other exempt organization was in furtherance of the association's exempt purposes.[616] Likewise, the IRS ruled that a national charitable organization engaged in related business activities when it provided certain coordination services for its chapters in connection with a new program it was implementing.[617] Additionally, an exempt organization that was an arm of an association of public school boards which administered the association's cash/risk management funds was found to be engaged in the charitable activity of lessening the burdens of government.[618]

Also, the provision of professional, managerial, and administrative services among a group of interrelated health care organizations, directly or by means of a partnership, was ruled to be a bundle of related businesses.[619] Similarly, the lease and management of a computer system to a partnership, by a supporting organiza-

---

[612] Reg. § 1.513-7(b), Example (3).
[613] Tech. Adv. Mem. 9550001.
[614] Tech. Adv. Mem. 9811001.
[615] Tech. Adv. Mem. 9822004.
[616] Tech. Adv. Mem 9608003.
[617] Priv. Ltr. Rul. 9641011.
[618] Tech. Adv. Mem. 9711002.
[619] Priv. Ltr. Rul. 9839039.

tion of a university's medical center, which system was used for billing, collection, and recordkeeping of the partners, was found to be a related business because the partners were physicians comprising the faculty of the university's medical school and teaching hospital.[620] Further, the IRS ruled that a graduate educational institution was engaged in a related business when it provided "central services" to a group of affiliated colleges (such as campus security, a central steam plant, accounting services, and a risk and property insurance program).[621] Other IRS rulings are issued from time to time on this point.[622]

The other exception is where the tax-exempt organizations are related entities, usually as parent or subsidiary. In the health care context, for example, the IRS now has a ruling policy that the provision of services by and to related entities is not an unrelated business. This policy was articulated in a ruling concerning the tax consequences of creation of a health care delivery system by means of a joint operating agreement. The arrangement entails what the IRS terms the provision of *corporate services* by and among exempt organizations (in the case of this type of system, several hospitals and a parent supporting organization). The IRS stated that, if the participating exempt organizations are in a parent and subsidiary relationship, corporate services provided between them necessary to their accomplishment of their exempt purposes are treated as other than an unrelated business and the financial arrangements between them are viewed as *merely a matter of accounting*.[623] Indeed, in this ruling, the IRS extended the matter-of-accounting rationale to relationships that are analogous to parent-subsidiary arrangements, which was the case under the facts involved under this particular joint operating agreement.

This outcome obviously was welcome news for tax-exempt organizations desiring to utilize joint operating agreements. But, from the larger perspective, the development was a transformative one for many other exempt organizations. Inasmuch as the tax law rationale underlying these agreements could not be confined to that context, it meant that, in any situation in which an exempt organization had a parent-subsidiary relationship with another exempt organization, the provision of corporate services could be protected from unrelated business taxation by this rationale. It also meant that the matter-of-accounting rationale could be extended to any arrangement where the relationship between two exempt organizations was analogous to that of parent and subsidiary.

The first time this parent-subsidiary rationale was used outside the health care setting was in connection with a typical situation: where a tax-exempt social welfare organization provided corporate services to its related foundation.[624] This

---

[620] Tech. Adv. Mem. 9847002.
[621] Priv. Ltr. Rul. 9849027.
[622] E.g., Priv. Ltr. Rul. 199910060.
[623] Priv. Ltr. Rul. 9651047. In constructing this rationale, the IRS utilized the accounting concept heretofore reserved for the feeder organization rules (see § 28.6, note 73) and the unrelated debt-financed income rules (see § 29.3, text accompanied by note 83).
[624] Priv. Ltr. Rul. 200022056.

arrangement was held not to generate unrelated business income, because of the "close structural relationship" between the two organizations.

As to arrangements where the relationship is analogous to that of parent and subsidiary, the first illustration was provided in the case of two charitable organizations that managed health care facilities; they entered into a management agreement with a third such organization. Each of these entities was independent of the others. By reason of the agreement, these two charitable organizations were found by the IRS to have ceded to the third organization "significant financial, managerial and operational authority over their affairs, including exclusive authority over capital and operating budgets, strategic plans, managed care contracting, the ability to allocate or reallocate services among the health care facilities [they] manage, and the ability to monitor and audit compliance with directives." The IRS ruled that these two organizations were "effectively under the common control" of the third organization. Therefore, the IRS held that these organizations were "within a relationship analogous to that of a parent and subsidiary," so that the provision of these corporate services would not result in unrelated business income.[625]

(j) Share-Crop Leasing

An unrelated business tax issue that is of concern to the IRS and that is being addressed in the courts is the proper tax treatment to be accorded share-crop revenue received by tax-exempt organizations.

This subject is informed by two bodies of law: the existence or nonexistence of a general partnership or joint venture for tax purposes[626] and the interpretation of the *passive rent rules*.[627]

A share-crop lease arrangement may involve land that is owned by a tax-exempt organization and leased by the organization to a farmer. Under the terms of the lease, the tenant is exclusively responsible for managing and operating the farm property. The tenant is also required to prepare a farm operating plan, including a schedule of crops to be grown on the land and seeding or planting rates, chemicals and fertilizers to be used, conservation practices and tillage plans, livestock breeding and market schedules, nutrition and feeding schedules, and harvesting and storage plans. After the operating plan is complete, the tenant is usually required to submit the plan to the exempt organization for review.[628]

Operation of all aspects of the farm is the sole responsibility of the tenant. The tenant is responsible for general farming operations, including cultivation

---

[625] E.g., Priv. Ltr. Rul. 200108045.
[626] See Chapter 32.
[627] See § 27.1(h).
[628] The final college and university examination guidelines omitted a discussion of crop leasing, due to the litigation throughout 1993 (see text accompanied by *infra* notes 638–652. The proposed guidelines (Ann. 93-2, 1993-2 I.R.B. 39), however, contained this analysis (in § 342.12(2)): the text is based on that summary.

of the land, planting, fertilizing, harvesting and marketing crops, and all aspects of livestock husbandry. The tax-exempt organization is generally responsible for all of the costs associated with the land and fixed improvements, including the costs of wells and pumps, irrigation equipment, and initially required limestone and rock phosphates. The tenant or the landlord may provide equipment and tools required to farm the land. The allocation of the proceeds of the sale of any crops and/or livestock raised on the property between the exempt organization and the tenant is negotiated between them and is generally comparable to percentage crop rents negotiated between other landlords and farm operators in the community.[629]

Under the terms of the typical share-crop lease, although the tenant farmer is required to submit a detailed farm operating plan to the tax-exempt organization for review, which provides an opportunity for control to some extent by the exempt organization over the farming operations, the IRS is of the view that "it does not follow that under the terms of such a farm lease that the exempt organization manages and directs the operation of the property to a significant extent."[630] The IRS also stated that, even if the requirement of a farm operating plan provides control over how a tenant conducts the farming activity, "it does not rise to a level of control that would require treating crop shares as other than rental from real property."[631] The IRS observed that it is "significant that under such a farm lease there is no sharing of expense and the exempt organization does not provide financing for its tenants."[632]

The determination of whether an amount received pursuant to a share-crop lease constitutes excludable rent is a two-step process. First, there must be a determination as to whether a particular share-crop arrangement constitutes a lease or some other arrangement. It is necessary to compare the particular share-crop arrangement with standard share-crop arrangements in a particular locality to determine whether the agreement constitutes a lease under local law and whether an amount received according to the agreement constitutes rent. Most share-crop arrangements, however, are in the nature of leases that produce rental income. There are cases where the IRS will find that a particular sharecrop agreement creates a joint venture rather than a lease; in these circumstances, it will be asserted that the income under the agreement does not constitute rent,[633] so that the income is taxable.[634] Second, if it is found that a share-crop agreement constitutes a lease producing rental income, the determination must be made as to whether the exclusion for rental income applies. In cases where the IRS asserts that the underlying agreement is not a lease, it generally will be asserted as a

[629] Id.
[630] Id.
[631] Id.
[632] Id.
[633] Id. § 342.12(3)(a).
[634] See § 27.1(h).

back-up argument that the exclusion for rent does not apply because the rent is in any event based on the profit from the farm.[635]

When a tax-exempt organization shares the crop produced by a tenant farmer, the rent is in fact based on a percentage of receipts or sales and is not barred from treatment as rent from real property for these purposes. When the sharing is combined with a substantial sharing of farm costs with the tenant, however, the rent is in effect based on the profit from the farm and the income is not protected by the exclusion.[636]

A federal district court was the first to issue an opinion grappling with the question as to whether income received by a tax-exempt organization, as rent from a share-crop lease, was a form of passive income (and thus not subject to un-related income taxation) or revenue from participation in a joint venture that is not in furtherance of an exempt purpose (and thus subject to the tax). The court concluded that the income was "true rent" that is based on a fixed percentage of receipts from the farm production within the scope of the statutory exclusion[637] and thus was not taxable.[638]

The tax-exempt organization in this case owned a farm that was managed by a bank; the organization entered into a share-crop agreement with two indi-viduals. Their rent was 50 percent of farm production after the crop was divided at the grain elevator. They made the farming decisions; they and the bank were billed separately for the shared expenses and never assumed one another's debts. The parties to the lease did not share in each other's profits or losses. The court reviewed the applicable state law and concluded that there was no evidence that this relationship was a joint venture or a partnership.

The government's alternative argument was that the rent from the share-crop agreement was based on a percentage of income or profits and thus was not exempt from tax under a special exception.[639] This assertion led the court to review the legislative history of this provision and to conclude that, in enact-ing it, Congress sought to tax property rentals that are measured by reference to the net income from the property. The court again reviewed the terms of the lease and state law which recognized that rent may be paid as a portion of crops. It said that if the farm were leased on a cash-rent basis, the rent would be excludable from tax.[640] The court wrote that it "seems anomalous that iden-tical activities undertaken on a share-crop lease should be taxable."[641] The court noted the "long history" of share-crop leases in the particular state; the absence of a "clear directive from Congress to the contrary" led it to hold that

---

[635] Ann. 93-2, *supra* note 628 § 342.12(3)(b).

[636] *Id.* § 342.12(4).

[637] IRC § 512(b)(3)(A)(i), (B)(ii).

[638] Harlan E. Moore Charitable Trust v. United States, 812 F. Supp. 130, 135 (C.D. Ill. 1993), *aff'd*, 9 F.3d 623 (7th Cir. 1993).

[639] IRC § 512(b)(3)(B)(ii).

[640] IRC § 512(b)(3)(A)(i).

[641] Harlan E. Moore Charitable Trust v. United States, *supra* note 638, 812 F. Supp., at 135.

division of the crops under this share-crop lease was a receipt of rent and not a division of profits.[642]

In a subsequent case, another court held that rents received under share-crop leases by a charitable trust were excluded from unrelated business income taxation.[643] The trust, by means of a bank that managed the property, operated farmland, paid necessary expenses, made necessary improvements, and rented the farmland; the land was rented under share-crop leases. Thus, the trust supplied the farm and buildings on it, materials necessary for repairs and improvements on the farm, and skilled labor for making permanent improvements. The trust was responsible for 50 percent of the cost of seed, fertilizer, limestone, herbicides, and insecticides. These leases obligated the tenant to be responsible for all machinery, equipment, power, and labor necessary to farm the land. The parties were to confer for the purpose of planning land use and sharing certain costs. Liability for all accidents relative to farming was conferred on the tenant. The amount of rent payable to the trust under these leases was fixed at 50 percent of the harvested corn, oats, soybean, and wheat.

Generally, to be excluded from unrelated income taxation, rent must be passive income. Thus, rent is taxable as unrelated income if the "determination of the amount of such rent depends in whole or in part on the income or profits derived by any person from the property leased."[644] Nonetheless, rent may be excluded from unrelated income taxation when the amount of rent is based on a "fixed percentage or percentages of receipts or sales."[645] These two provisions were termed by the court the "passive rent test."[646] The court wrote that, in order to "exclude rents from . . . [unrelated business income taxation], rents must in substance qualify as rent, as opposed to actually representing a return of profits by the tenant or a share of profits retained by the landlord as either a partner or joint venturer . . . and not violate the . . . passive income test."[647]

The IRS contended that these arrangements were either general partnerships or joint ventures and that the payments under the leases represented a return of profits that were taxable. This contention was rested largely on the provisions in the leases concerning land use planning and cost sharing.

The court disagreed with the IRS's characterization of the facts. It found that the trust "did not itself or through its managing agent participate in the day-to-day operations of the farm to a degree which would support the existence of a joint venture or partnership with the tenant."[648] The court singled out the provision concerning liability for farming accidents as evidence that the arrangement was not a joint venture or a partnership. Also, the court noted that the trust was not required to contribute to losses, there were no provisions to

[642] Id.
[643] Trust U/W Emily Oblinger v. Comm'r, 100 T.C. 114 (1993).
[644] IRC § 512(b)(3)(B)(ii).
[645] Id.
[646] Trust U/W Emily Oblinger v. Comm'r, *supra* note 643, at 121.
[647] Id. at 117.
[648] Id. at 120.

carry over losses from one year to reduce payments to the trust in later years, and the leases were typical of share-crop leases used in the region. The court then found that the rent involved did not violate the passive rent test. The tax regulations state that an amount is excluded from "rents from real property" if, considering the lease and the surrounding circumstances, the arrangement does not conform with normal business practice and is in reality used as a means of basing the rent on income or profits.[649] The court wrote that this test is "intended to prevent avoidance of unrelated business income tax where a profit-sharing arrangement will, in effect, make the lessor an active participant in the operation of the property."[650]

As noted, an exception is provided for amounts based on a fixed percentage or percentages of receipts or sales. In asserting that the arrangements violated the passive rent test, the IRS emphasized the trust's splitting of the expenses, its involvement in the farming operations, and its receipt of a percentage of production as rent, rather than a percentage of receipts. The court disagreed, finding the leases to amount to the "equivalent of the tenant's reducing the crops to cash and then giving . . . [the trust] its share of the total receipts collected."[651] In conclusion, wrote the court, the "passive rent test was not violated since . . . [the trust's] rent was not determined, in whole or in part, on the net profits or income derived from the property."[652]

(k) Retirement Plan Reversions

A tax-exempt organization may maintain a qualified pension or other retirement plan to provide retirement benefits to its employees.[653] Generally, the assets of the plan must be used exclusively for the employees and their beneficiaries,[654] and the contributions of an employer to a qualified plan are deductible in the year in which the contributions are paid.[655] This type of plan may be terminated; in that instance, all benefits accrued to the date of termination must become completely vested and nonforfeitable, and plan benefits must be distributed to the participants in the plan or annuities providing for the payment of comparable benefits must be purchased and distributed to the participants. Where the plan is terminated and assets remain after the satisfaction of all liabilities to plan participants and other beneficiaries, and if the excess of assets is attributable to actuarial error, the employer is permitted to recover the excess assets.[656] Generally, this excess must be included in the gross income of the employer.

---

[649] Reg. § 1.512(b)-1(c)(2)(iii)(b).
[650] Trust U/W Emily Oblinger v. Comm'r, *supra* note 643, at 122.
[651] *Id.* at 123.
[652] *Id.* In so holding, the court favorably cited the opinion in Harlan E. Moore Charitable Trust v. Comm'r, *supra* note 638. Also Independent Order of Odd Fellows Grand Lodge of Iowa v. United States, 93-2 U.S.T.C. ¶ 50,448 (S.D. Iowa 1993); White's Iowa Manual Labor Inst. v. Comm'r, 66 T.C.M. 389 (1993).
[653] See § 16.1.
[654] IRC § 401(a)(2).
[655] IRC § 401(a)(1)(A).
[656] Reg. § 1.401-2(b)(1).

Where the employer organization is a tax-exempt organization that is subject to the rule that all income other than exempt function income is taxable as related business income,[657] such as a social club,[658] generally the amount of the reversion is includable in the organization's unrelated business income because it is not exempt function income.[659] This body of law does not contain the general requirement that there must be a *trade or business* before the income can be taxable.[660]

This type of income of a tax-exempt organization with these characteristics may, however, be excluded from taxation by reason of the *tax benefit rule*. Under the exclusionary portion of this rule, gross income does not include income attributable to the recovery during a tax year of any amount deducted in any prior tax year to the extent that amount did not reduce the amount of income tax involved.[661] By contrast, under the inclusionary aspect of this rule, where the amount previously deducted from gross income generates a tax benefit and is then recaptured in a subsequent year, the recaptured amount is includible in gross income in the year of the recapture.[662] Consequently, to the extent that this type of tax-exempt organization deducted contributions to a defined benefit plan in determining its taxable nonexempt function income, the inclusionary aspect of the tax benefit rule would be applicable.[663]

Where the employer organization is a tax-exempt organization that is not subject to this rule concerning taxation of nonexempt function income, the tax consequences of a reversion of plan assets are different. Because (1) the operation of the plan is not a business[664] but rather an administrative function that is part of the overall operations of the exempt organization and (2) the funds that revert upon termination of the plan are a one-time source of income rather than income from an activity that is regularly carried on,[665] the reverted funds are generally not taxable as unrelated business income.[666]

The tax benefit rule can apply in this setting as well. In general, an organization that is not subject to this special rule of unrelated income taxation is usually exempt from taxation and thus would not derive any tax benefit from contributions to a qualified pension plan. This is another application of the exclusionary aspect of the tax benefit rule. This type of organization, however, could receive a tax benefit from a contribution to a qualified plan if it deducted the amount of the contribution from any unrelated business taxable income.[667] In that case, by operation of the inclusionary aspects of the tax benefit rule, the re-

[657] See § 28.3.
[658] See Chapter 14.
[659] Gen. Couns. Mem. 39717.
[660] See § 14.3.
[661] IRC § 111(a).
[662] IRC § 61; Rev. Rul. 68-104, 1968-1 C.B. 361; Gen. Couns. Mem. 39744.
[663] Gen. Couns. Mem. 39717.
[664] See § 14.3.
[665] See *supra* § 3.
[666] Gen. Couns. Mem. 39806.
[667] See § 28.2.

covery of the previously deducted amounts would be unrelated business taxable income to the tax-exempt organization.[668]

(l) Internet Activities

Recent years have brought extensive use of the Internet by tax-exempt organizations, with several implications for development of the federal tax law pertaining to related and unrelated business activities. There has been little guidance, however, from the IRS in this area. Law will evolve in this field, nonetheless, from the agency and the courts.

One aspect of this subject is clear: The federal tax law does not provide any unique treatment to transactions or activities of tax-exempt organizations simply because the Internet is the medium. The IRS saliently observed: "[T]he use of the Internet to accomplish a particular task does not change the way the tax laws apply to that task. Advertising is still advertising and fundraising is still fundraising."[669] Overall, the unrelated business rules are still the unrelated business rules.

The Internet use that implicates the unrelated business rules concerns marketing, merchandising, advertising, and the like. In general, as noted, it should be assumed that as the law develops the IRS will generally remain consistent with its positions with respect to advertising, merchandising, and publishing in the offline world.

A significant issue in this context is the matter of tax-exempt organizations' Web site hypertext links to related or recommended sites. These exchanges may be treated by the IRS the same as mailing list exchanges.[670] Compensation for a linkage may be unrelated business income. (An absence of compensation may entail private benefit or the like.[671]) The purpose of the link may be determinative: Is its purpose furtherance of exempt purposes—such as a reference of the site visitor to additional (educational) information—or is it part of an unrelated activity (including advertising)?

Also involved are corporate sponsorships, inasmuch as some tax-exempt organizations seek corporate support to underwrite the production of all or a portion of the organization's Web site. These relationships may be short-term or continue on a long-term basis. The financial support may be acknowledged by means of display of a corporate logo, notation of the sponsor's Web address and/or 800 number, a "moving banner" (a graphic advertisement, usually a moving image, measured in pixels), or a link. The issue is whether the support is a qualified sponsorship payment (in which case the revenue is not taxable)[672] or is advertising income (which generally is taxable as unrelated business

---

[668] Gen. Couns. Mem. 39806.
[669] IRS Exempt Organizations Continuing Professional Education Text for Fiscal Year 2000, Topic I, Part 1.
[670] See *supra* § 5(g)(i), text accompanied by notes 575–578.
[671] See Chapter 19.
[672] See § 27.2(n).

income).[673] Use of a link in an acknowledgment may change the character of a corporation's payment, converting it from nontaxable sponsorship to taxable advertising income. This is one area where the IRS has provided formal guidance.[674]

Another problem relates to the rule that qualified sponsorship payments do not include payments that entitle the sponsors to acknowledgments in regularly scheduled printed material published by or on behalf of the tax-exempt organization.[675] Here the issue is the characterization of Web site materials. Most of the material made available on exempt organizations' Web sites is prepared in a manner that is distinguishable from the methodology used in the preparation of periodicals.

Other aspects of this area include the virtual trade show and the extent to which the traditional rules excluding trade show income from unrelated business taxation[676] may apply. Online storefronts, replete with virtual shopping carts, on tax-exempt organizations' Web sites may be subject to the same analysis the IRS applies in the context of museum gift shop sales.[677] Still other aspects of this subject include the tax treatment of online auctions, and affiliate and other co-venture programs with merchants (including booksellers). (A principal issue is whether any resulting income is a tax-excludable royalty.[678]) The IRS wrote that it is "hoped that all members of the exempt organizations [community] will be involved in the development of new policies which will build upon principles developed over time and adapt to allow exempt organizations to take advantage of the technological innovations of the new millennium."[679]

The IRS, late in 2000, sought comment on a range of questions pertaining to Internet activities by tax-exempt organizations in the unrelated business income context.[680] The agency explored whether a Web site maintained by a tax-exempt organization constitutes a "single publication or communication." (Presumably, a site can be considered a single *publication* but rarely should it be regarded as a single *communication*.) The IRS also asked about the methodology for separating a Web site into "distinct" publications and communications. These exercises will generate new and interesting applications of the fragmentation rule.[681] Related to this, as evidenced by an IRS question, is the process to use in allocating expenses for the components of a site.

Other questions asked pertained to the prospects of attribution to a tax-exempt organization of statements made by subscribers to a forum maintained by the exempt organization, the circumstances under which the payment of a percentage of sales from customers referred by the exempt organization to an-

---

[673] See *supra* § 5(f).
[674] See § 27.2(n), text accompanied by note 305.
[675] *Id.*, text accompanied by note 307–308.
[676] See § 27.2(f).
[677] See *supra* § 5(c).
[678] See § 27.1(g).
[679] IRS Continuing Professional Education Text, *supra* note 669.
[680] Ann. 2000-84, 2000-42 I.R.B. 385.
[681] See *supra* § 2(f).

other site would be related business income, and the extent to which an exempt organization should keep records as to prior versions of its Web site.

One of these questions was: "To what extent are business activities conducted on the Internet regularly carried on?" This was followed by the question: "What facts and circumstances are relevant in making this determination?" Regularity of business operations on an exempt organization's Web site, and the relevant facts and circumstances, are determined using the same criteria as are applied in any other context.[682]

[682] See *supra* § 3. This subject is treated in greater detail in Chapter 2 of Hopkins, *The Nonprofits' Guide to Internet Communications Law* (John Wiley & Sons, Inc., 2002). In general, Cain, "Marketing Activities in the Non-Profit Sector—Recent Lessons Regarding Tax Implications," 36 *Amer. Bus. Law J.* (Vol. 2) 349 (Winter 1999); Hansmann, Kaplan & Jett, "Handling the UBIT Problems of Churches and Religious Organizations," 6 *J. Tax. Exempt Orgs.* (No. 2) 74 (Sep./Oct. 1994); Tesdahl, "Three Easy Ways to Avoid UBIT," 8 *Exempt Org. Tax Rev.* (No. 5) 937 (Nov. 1993); "Unfair Competition and the Unrelated Business Income Tax," 75 *Va. L. Rev.* (No. 3) 605 (1989); Gallagher III, "The Taxation of Investments by Pension Funds and Other Tax-Exempt Entities," 67 *Taxes* (No. 12) 981 (1989); Jones, Shortway, & Borhorst, "When Pension Trusts Participate: The Impact of the Unrelated Business Income Rules," 5 *Real Estate Finance* (No. 2) 91 (1988); Bennett, "Unfair Competition and the UBIT," 41 *Tax Notes* (No. 7A) 759 (1988); Rosen, "When Will Business Income of an Organization Be Sheltered by Its Tax-exempt Status?," 40 *Tax. for Accts.* (No. 4) 222 (1988); Wittenbach & Gallagher, "The Tax Implications to Exempt Organizations of Six Income-producing Activities," 16 *Tax Adv.* (No. 3) 170 (1985); Fant III, "Doing Well While Doing Good, and the Pitfalls of the Unrelated Business Income Tax," 63 *Taxes* (No. 12) 862 (1985); Walter, "Unrelated Business Income—Division, Characterization and Allocation," 19 *Univ. of Miami Philip E. Heckerling Inst. on Est. Plan.* 7 (1985); Kennedy, "Considerations in the Determination of Tax on Unrelated Business Income," 15 *Tax Adv.* (No. 6) 342 (1984).

In recent years, there have been efforts to revise the statutory law concerning the taxation of unrelated business income. In general, Comment, "Making Tax-Exempts Pay: The Unrelated Business Income Tax and the Need for Reform," 4 *Admin. L. J. Am. U.* 527 (Winter 1991); Owens, "Current Developments in the Unrelated Business Area—IRS Perspective," 4 *Exempt Org. Tax Rev.* (No. 7) 923 (1991); Sanders & Cobb, "Impact of Proposals To Revise the Unrelated Business Income Rules," 2 *Exempt Org. Tax Rev.* (No. 6) 694 (1990); Haley, "The Taxation of the Unrelated Business Activities of Exempt Organizations: Where Do We Stand? Where Do We Seem to Be Headed?," 7 *Akron Tax J.* (No. 2) 61 (1990); Spitzer, "Reform of the UBIT: An Open Letter to Congress," 43 *Tax Notes* (No. 2) 195 (1989); Aprill, "Lessons from the UBIT Debate," 45 *Tax Notes* (No. 9) 1105 (1989); Turner & Lambert, "Why the Furor Over UBIT," 165 *J. Act.* (No. 5) 78 (1988); Troyer, "Changing UBIT: Congress in the Workshop," 41 *Tax Notes* (No. 11) 1221 (1988); Kalick, "Reorganizing for the UBIT," 41 *Tax Notes* (No. 7A) 771 (1988); Hasson, Jr., "An Early Warning: UBIT Changes Ahead," 127 *Trusts & Ests.* (No. 7) 43 (1988).

CHAPTER TWENTY-SEVEN

Exceptions to
Unrelated Income Taxation

Notwithstanding the fact that, pursuant to the general rules, an activity may constitute an unrelated trade or business that is regularly carried on, the activity may escape federal income taxation under one or more statutory exceptions.

There are two basic categories of these exceptions. Some of them appear in the law concerning a variety of modifications. Others are expressly denominated as exceptions.

§ 27.1 MODIFICATIONS

In determining unrelated business taxable income, both gross income derived from an unrelated trade or business and business deductions are computed with certain *modifications*.[1]

---

[1] IRC § 512(b).

(a) Concept of Passive Income

The unrelated business rules were enacted to ameliorate the effects of competition between tax-exempt organizations and for-profit (taxable) organizations by taxing the net income of exempt organizations from unrelated business activities.[2] The principle underlying this statutory scheme is that the business endeavors must be *active* ones for competitive activity to result. Correspondingly, income derived by a tax-exempt organization in a passive manner generally is income that is not acquired as the result of competitive activity; consequently, most forms of passive income are not taxed as unrelated business income.[3]

Therefore, passive income—such as dividends, interest, payments with respect to securities loans, annuities, royalties, certain rents (generally of real estate), income from certain option-writing activities, income from interest rate and currency swaps, income from equity and commodity swaps, income from notional principal contracts and the like, and gain from the disposition of property—is generally excluded from unrelated business taxable income, along with directly connected deductions.[4]

The legislative history of these provisions indicates that Congress believed that passive income should not be taxed under these rules "where it is used for exempt purposes because investments producing incomes of these types have long been recognized as proper for educational and charitable organizations."[5]

Thus, for example, a tax-exempt organization can capitalize a for-profit corporation without endangering the tax exemption of the exempt organization, a tax-exempt organization can own all of the stock of a for-profit corporation without endangering its tax exemption,[6] the for-profit corporation can pay dividends to the exempt organization without jeopardizing the tax exemption of the nonprofit entity, and the dividend income received by the exempt entity will not be taxable as unrelated income.[7]

There may be forms of passive income incurred by tax-exempt organizations that may not be strictly within the technical meaning of one of the specific

---

[2] See § 26.1.

[3] Two significant exceptions to this rule concern income from unrelated debt-financed property (see *infra* notes 56, 81, and 87, §§ 29.1-29.4) and income from cont.olled subsidiaries (see *infra* §§ 27.1(b), 31.3).

[4] IRC §§ 512(b)(1)-(3), (5). Also Reg. § 1.512(b)-1(a)-(d); State National Bank of El Paso v. United States, 509 F.2d 832 (5th Cir. 1975); Louis W. Hill Family Found. v. United States, 347 F. Supp. 1225 (D. Minn. 1972); Rev. Rul. 69-430, 1969-2 C.B. 129; Rev. Rul. 69-178, 1969-1 C.B. 158; Rev. Rul. 69-69, 1969-1 C.B. 159; Rev. Rul. 67-218, 1967-2 C.B. 213; Rev. Rul. 60-206, 1960-1 C.B. 201.

A U.S. Tax Court decision expanded the possibility that what once may have been considered a passive activity is now to be treated as an active business enterprise, by holding that nearly any activity engaged in for the production of income (the expenses of which are deductible under IRC § 212) can be converted into a business activity by the intensification of participation by the taxpayer in the activity (Hoopengarner v. Comm'r, 80 T.C. 538 (1983)). In general, Hopkins & Kaplan, "Could *Ditunno* and *Hoopengarner* result in expanding the scope of unrelated business?," 60 J. Tax. (No. 1 40 (1984).

[5] H. Rep. No. 2319, 81st Cong., 2d Sess. 38 (1950). Also S. Rep. No. 2375, 81st Cong., 2d Sess. 30-31 (1950).

[6] There are, however, special rules for private foundations in this regard (see § 11.4(c)).

[7] E.g., Priv. Ltr. Rul. 8244114. See Chapter 31.

terms referenced in the passive income rules, yet which are nonetheless outside the framework of unrelated income taxation.

Occasionally, the IRS takes the position that the only items of income that can be regarded as passive income are those that are specifically referenced in the statutory modification rules. This has led to conflict, with the matter usually resolved in favor of tax-exempt organizations by Congress, such as in the instances of the writing of options[8] and the lending of securities.[9]

The legislative history of the unrelated business income tax provisions is clear on the point that Congress, in enacting these rules, did not intend and has not authorized taxation of the passive income of tax-exempt organizations, and that a technical satisfaction of the definitional requirements of the terms used in the passive income rules is not required. Thus, the Senate Finance Committee observed in 1950 that the unrelated income tax was to apply to "so much of . . . [exempt organizations'] income as rises from active business enterprises which are unrelated to the tax exempt purposes of the organizations."[10] This committee added: "The problem at which the tax on unrelated business income is directed is primarily that of unfair competition."[11] Speaking of the exclusion for passive sources of income, the committee stated:

> Dividends, interest, royalties, most rents, capital gains and losses and *similar items* are excluded from the base of the tax on unrelated income because your committee believes that they are "passive" in character and are not likely to result in serious competition for taxable businesses having similar income. Moreover, investment-producing incomes of these types have long been recognized as a proper source of revenue for educational and charitable organizations and trusts.[12]

Therefore, it seems unmistakable that passive income, regardless of type, is generally excluded from unrelated business income taxation.[13]

Recent illustrations of the IRS acceptance of this viewpoint is the development of regulations[14] concerning the exclusion of income derived from certain notional principal contracts[15] and other forms of a tax-exempt organization's ordinary and routine investments.[16]

The foregoing analysis notwithstanding, there is a component of this law that rejects the premise that, for an item of income to be excluded from unrelated business income taxation (absent a specific statutory exclusion), it must be passive in nature. That is, there is a view that an item of income—once classified as a

---

[8] See text accompanied by *supra* note 4 and *infra* notes 109–110.
[9] See *infra* § 1(d).
[10] S. Rep. No. 2375, *supra* note 5, at 27 (emphasis supplied).
[11] *Id.* at 28.
[12] *Id.* at 30-31 (emphasis supplied).
[13] Also H. Rep. No. 2319, *supra* note 5, at 36–38.
[14] Reg. § 1.512(b)-1(a)(2).
[15] Reg. § 1.512(b)-1(a).
[16] See text accompanied by *infra* notes 93–100.

royalty or other similar item—is excludable from unrelated income taxation irrespective of whether it is passively derived.

At the present, only the U.S. Tax Court has expressed this view, which arose in the course of consideration of whether payments for the use of mailing lists and payments from the operation of an affinity card program constitute excludable *royalties*. This court held that, if the arrangement is properly structured, mailing lists payments are royalties and thus that they are excludable from unrelated business income taxation even if they are not forms of passive income.[17] The court also so held in the case of affinity card program payments.[18] The essence of this view is that, although Congress *believed* these types of income to be passive,[19] that does not necessarily mean that they always must be passive.[20] Stated in the reverse, this view holds that a statutorily classified item of excludable income remains excludable irrespective of whether the income is passive or is derived from the active conduct of a trade or business. The validity of this view was, however, substantially eroded by a subsequent appellate court opinion.[21]

(b) Dividends

Dividends paid to a tax-exempt organization generally are not taxable as unrelated business income.[22] Basically, a *dividend* is a share allotted to each of one or more persons who are entitled to share in the net profits generated by a business undertaking, usually a corporation; it is a payment out of the payor's net profits.

There are some exceptions to this exclusion, principally dividends that are unrelated debt-financed income[23] and those that are from controlled foreign offshore insurance captives.[24] Generally, however, dividends paid to tax-exempt organizations from controlled corporations are not taxable.[25]

(c) Interest

Interest paid to a tax-exempt organization generally is not taxable as unrelated business income.[26] Basically, *interest* is compensation that one person pays to another for the use of money.

---

[17] Sierra Club, Inc. v. Comm'r, 65 T.C.M. 2582 (1993); Disabled American Veterans v. Comm'r, 94 T.C. 60 (1990), *rev'd on other grounds*, 942 F.2d 309 (6th Cir. 1991).
[18] Sierra Club, Inc. v. Comm'r, 103 T.C. 307 (1994). See *infra* § 1(g).
[19] See text accompanied by *supra* note 5.
[20] This view is based on additional language in the committee reports indicating that the exception for dividends, interest, annuities, royalties, and the like "applies not only to investment income [a concept broader than passive income], but also to such items as business interest on overdue open accounts receivable" (S. Rep. No. 2375, *supra* note 5, at 108; H. Rep. No. 2319, *supra* note 5, at 110).
[21] See text accompanied by *infra* notes 42–44.
[22] IRC § 512(b)(1).
[23] See § 29.1-29.4.
[24] See *infra* § 1(p).
[25] See *infra* § 1(n), § 31.3.
[26] IRC § 512(b)(1).

There are some exceptions to this exclusion, principally interest that is unrelated debt-financed income[27] and that is paid by a controlled corporation.[28]

The IRS from time to time issues private letter rulings as to what constitutes excludable interest in this context.[29]

(d) Securities Loan Payments

Qualified payments with respect to loans of securities are generally excluded from unrelated business income taxation.[30] These amounts are not excluded from this tax, however, if they constitute unrelated debt-financed income.[31]

This exclusion is available for the lending of securities to a broker and the return of identical securities.[32] For this nontaxation treatment to apply, the security loans must be fully collateralized and must be terminable on five business days' notice by the lending organization. Further, an agreement between the parties must provide for reasonable procedures to implement the obligation of the borrower to furnish collateral to the lender with a fair market value on each business day the loan is outstanding in an amount at least equal to the fair market value of the security at the close of business on the preceding day.

(e) Certain Consideration

Amounts received or accrued as consideration for entering into agreements to make loans are excluded from unrelated business income taxation.[33] This exclusion is not available where the income is unrelated debt-financed income.[34]

(f) Annuities

Income received by a tax-exempt organization as an annuity generally is not taxable as unrelated business income.[35] Basically, an *annuity* is an amount of money, fixed by contract between the annuitor and the annuitant, that is paid annually, either in one sum or in installments (such as semiannually or quarterly).

This exclusion is not available where the income is unrelated debt-financed income[36] or is from a controlled corporation.[37]

---

[27] See §§ 29.1-29.4.
[28] See *infra* § 1(n), § 31.3.
[29] E.g., Priv. Ltr. Rul. 9108021.
[30] IRC § 512(b)(1).
[31] See §§ 29.1-29.4.
[32] IRC § 512(a)(5).
[33] IRC § 512(b)(1).
[34] See §§ 29.1-29.4.
[35] IRC § 512(b)(1).
[36] See §§ 29.1-29.4.
[37] See *infra* § 1(n), § 31.3.

(g) Royalties

Generally, a royalty paid to a tax-exempt organization is excludible from unrelated income taxation.[38]

Basically, a *royalty* is a payment for the use of a valuable intangible right, such as a trademark, trade name, service mark, logo, or copyright, regardless of whether the property represented by the right is used; royalties also include the right to a share of production reserved to the owner of property for permitting another to work mines and quarries or to drill for oil or gas.[39] Royalties have also been characterized as payments that constitute passive income, such as the compensation paid by a licensee to the licensor for the use of the licensor's patented invention.[40]

It was the stance of the U.S. Tax Court that a royalty is a payment for the use of valuable intangible property rights (irrespective of whether the income was passive).[41] A federal appellate court, however, is of the view that the Tax Court's definition of the term *royalty* is overly broad, in that a royalty "cannot include compensation for services rendered by the owner of the property."[42] This position, then, is a compromise between the approach of the Tax Court and that of the IRS on the point. Thus, the appellate court wrote that, to the extent the IRS "claims that a tax-exempt organization can do nothing to acquire such fees," the agency is "incorrect."[43] Yet, the court continued, "to the extent that . . . [the exempt organization involved] appears to argue that a 'royalty' is any payment for the use of a property right—such as a copyright—regardless of any additional services that are performed in addition to the owner simply permitting another to use the right at issue, we disagree."[44]

Thus, despite the exclusion for royalty income, it is the position of the IRS that monies will be taxed, even if they are characterized as royalties, when the tax-exempt organization is actively involved in the enterprise that generates the revenue, such as through the provision of services.[45] Frequently, the IRS will view the relationship between the parties as that of partners or joint venturers.[46] A common instance of this treatment is the insistence by the IRS that the funds an exempt organization receives for an endorsement are taxable, while the organization asserts that the monies are royalties for the use of its name and logo.[47] An approach to resolution of this issue is to make partial use of the royalty exclusion by

[38] IRC § 512(b)(2).

[39] E.g., Fraternal Order of Police III. State Troopers Lodge No. 41 v. Comm'r, 833 F.2d 717, 723 (7th Cir. 1987).

[40] Disabled Am. Veterans v. United States, 650 F.2d 1178, 1189 (Ct. Cl. 1981).

[41] Sierra Club, Inc. v. Comm'r, *supra* note 18, at 337; Sierra Club, Inc. v. Comm'r, *supra* note 17, at 2586-2588; Disabled Am. Veterans v. Comm'r, *supra* note 17, 94 T.C., at 70.

[42] Sierra Club, Inc. v Comm'r, 86 F.3d 1526, 1532 (9th Cir. 1996).

[43] *Id.* at 1535.

[44] *Id.*

[45] E.g., National Water Well Ass'n, Inc. v. Comm'r, 92 T.C. 75 (1989).

[46] E.g., Tech. Adv. Mem. 9509002.

[47] E.g., Priv. Ltr. Rul. 9450028.

means of two contracts: one for the taxable services and one for the royalty arrangement.[48]

Additional litigation has somewhat transfored the IRS's stance in this regard. This process began when an appellate court ruled that a tax-exempt organization could treat income as a royalty even when the organization provided some services.[49] It was furthered when the Tax Court held that revenue was royalty income under this new definition.[50] The IRS's position further eroded when the Tax Court again held, in two opinions, that mailing list rental payments qualified as royalties.[51] The denouement of the government's stance probably came when two other appellate court opinions on the subject of royalty income went against it.[52]

By the close of 1999, the IRS realized that this series of defeats was insurmountable—that the courts were not going to accept its interpretation of the scope of the tax-excludable royalty. The IRS National Office, late in that year, communicated with its exempt organizations specialists in the field, essentially capitulating on the point; a memorandum distributed to them stated bluntly that cases should be resolved "in a manner consistent with the existing court cases."[53] This memorandum added that "it is now clear that courts will continue to find the income [generated by activities such as mailing list rentals and affinity card programs] to be excluded royalty income unless the factual record clearly reflects more than unsubstantial services being provided." Two factors were highlighted by the IRS as establishing nontaxable royalty income: where the involvement of the exempt organization is "relatively minimal" and where the exempt organization "hired outside contractors to perform most services associated with the exploitation of the use of intangible property."[54]

Earlier, the U.S. Tax Court held that a tax-exempt organization that received

---

[48] There is support for this approach in Texas Farm Bureau, Inc. v. United States, 53 F.3d 120 (5th Cir. 1995), in which the contracts involved did not expressly cast the revenues at issue as royalties.

[49] See text accompanied by *supra* notes 42-44.

[50] Sierra Club, Inc. v. Comm'r, 77 T.C.M. 1569 (1999). This case was heard on remand; the first decision is the subject of *supra* note 18. In general, Tsilas, "Sierra Club, Inc. v. Commissioner: Why is the IRS Continuing to Fight a Losing Battle?," 24 *Exempt Org. Tax Rev.* (No. 3) 487 (June 1999); Lauber & Mayer, "Tax Court Rules (Again) on Sierra Club Affinity Card Income," 24 *Exempt Org. Tax Rev.* (No. 2) 311 (May 1999).

[51] Common Cause v. Comm'r, 112 T.C. 332 (1999); Planned Parenthood Fed'n of Am., Inc. v. Comm'r, 77 T.C.M. 2227 (1999). Also Mississippi State University Alumni, Inc. v. Comm'r, 74 T.C.M. 458 (1999).

[52] Oregon State Univ. Alumni Ass'n., Inc. v. Comm'r, Alumni Ass'n. of Univ. of Ore., Inc. v. Comm'r., 193 F.3d 1098 (9th Cir. 1999), *aff'g* 71 T.C.M. 1935 (1996), 71 T.C.M. 2093 (1996).

[53] Memorandum from Jay H. Rotz, IRS Exempt Organizations Division, National Office, dated December 16, 1999. This is not to say that the government loses every case on this point. When the tax-exempt organization participates in and maintains control over significant aspects of the activities that generate the income, the courts will reject the contention that the revenue is an excludible royalty (e.g., Arkansas State Police Ass'n, Inc. v. Comm'r, 81 T.C.M. 1172 (2001), *aff'd*, 282 F.3d 556 (8th Cir. 2002)). In general, Light, "Denial of the Royalty Exclusion Because of Excessive Participation in *Arkansas State Police Association v. Commissioner*," 55 *Tax Law.* (No. 1) 351 (Fall 2001).

[54] An issue under consideration at the IRS is whether there should be an allocation of a single payment between compensation for the use of intangible property and compensation for more than insubstantial services.

income from the rental of mailing lists was not taxable on that income because it was properly characterized as royalties, notwithstanding the extent of activities the organization engaged in to preserve and enhance the list.[55] The court seemed to state that it was irrelevant in this setting as to whether or not the royalty income was passive. It appears, nonetheless, that the active endeavors of the organization that the court acknowledged were activities to preserve and enhance the asset (maintain the list) rather than the provision of services to others in connection with rental activities. On appeal, however, it was held that the organization was collaterally estopped from bringing the case in the first instance, in that the same issue was litigated previously.[56]

Mineral royalties, whether measured by production or by gross or taxable income from the mineral property, are excludable in computing unrelated business taxable income. Where, however, a tax-exempt organization owns a working interest in a mineral property, and is not relieved of its share of the development costs by the terms of any agreement with an operator, income received is not excludable from unrelated income taxation.[57] The holder of a mineral interest is not liable for the expenses of development (or operations) for these purposes where the holder's interest is a net profit interest not subject to expenses that exceed gross profits. Thus, a tax-exempt university was ruled to have excludable royalty interests, where the interests it held in various oil and gas producing properties were based on the gross profits from the properties reduced by all expenses of development and operations.[58]

The IRS ruled that patent development and management service fees deducted from royalties collected from licensees by a tax-exempt charitable organization for distribution to the beneficial owners of the patents were not within this exception for royalties; the IRS said that "although the amounts paid to the [exempt] organization are derived from royalties, they do not retain the character of royalties in the organization's hands" for these purposes.[59] Similarly, the IRS decided that income derived by an exempt organization from the sale of advertising in publications produced by an independent firm was properly characterized as royalty income.[60] By contrast, the IRS determined that amounts received from licensees by an exempt organization, which was the legal and

---

[55] Disabled Am. Veterans v. Comm'r, 94 T.C. 60 (1990). In general, Sperzman & Washlick, "Mailing Lists Revisited: The Disabled American Veterans in Tax Court," 47 *Tax Notes* (No. 11) 1377 (1990).

[56] Disabled Am. Veterans v. Comm'r, 942 F.2d 309 (6th Cir. 1991). The previous litigation is reflected in Disabled Am. Veterans v. United States, 650 F.2d 1178 (Ct. Cl. 1981), *aff'd and rem'd*, 704 F.2d 1570 (Fed. Cir. 1983). In general, Schadler, "The Courts Point the Way to Royalty Treatment for UBIT Purposes," 9 *J. Tax Exempt Orgs.* (No. 6) 244 (May/June 1998); Elfenbein & Crigler, "*Sierra Club* Provides Trailmarks for Royalties," 8 *J. Tax Exempt Orgs.* 99 (Nov./Dec. 1996); Cerny & Lauber, "Ninth Circuit Rules on Sierra Club Mailing List and Affinity Card Income," 14 *Exempt Org. Tax Rev.* (No. 2) 255 (Aug. 1996); Desilets, Jr., "Payments Received for Use of an Exempt Organization's Name and Logo: Royalties or UBIT?," 13 *Exempt Org. Tax. Rev.* 147 (Jan./Feb. 1996); Kirschten & Brown, "The IRS Narrows the UBIT Royalty Exclusion," 1 *J. Tax Exempt Orgs.* 20 (Spring 1989).

[57] Reg. § 1.512(b)-1(b).

[58] Priv. Ltr. Rul. 7741004.

[59] Rev. Rul. 73-193, 1973-1 C.B. 262, 263. Also Rev. Rul. 69-179, 1969-1 C.B. 158.

[60] Priv. Ltr. Rul. 7926003.

beneficial owner of patents assigned to it by inventors for specified percentages of future royalties, constituted excludable royalty income.[61] A federal court of appeals held that income consisting of 100 percent of the net profits in certain oil properties, received by an exempt organization from two corporations controlled by it, constituted income from overriding royalties and thus was excluded from taxation.[62]

A matter of some concern to the IRS has been the proper tax treatment of payments to a tax-exempt organization, the principal purpose of which is the development of a U.S. team for international amateur sports competition, in return for the right to commercially use the organization's name and logo. The organization entered into licensing agreements that, in consideration of the annual payment of a stated sum, authorized use of the organization's name and logo in connection with the sale of products. The initial position of the IRS was that payments must be measured according to the use made of a valuable right to be characterized as a royalty and thus be excludable from unrelated income taxation. The IRS became sufficiently persuaded, on the basis of caselaw precedent,[63] however, that fixed-sum payments for the right to use an asset qualify as excludable royalties, although it continues to adhere to the position that absent the statutory exclusion, the income would be taxable as being from an unrelated trade or business.[64]

Subsequently, the IRS ruled that certain payments a labor organization received from various business enterprises for the use of its trademark and similar properties were royalties.[65] This conclusion was reached even though the organization retained the right to approve the quality or style of the licensed products and services, and the payments were sometimes set as flat annual payments.[66]

The IRS from time to time issues private letter rulings as to what constitutes excludable royalties in this context.[67]

Unrelated debt-financed income is not subject to this exclusion,[68] nor is royalty income from a controlled corporation.[69]

---

[61] Rev. Rul. 76-297, 1976-2 C.B. 178. Also J. E. and L. E. Mabee Found., Inc. v. United States, 533 F.2d 521 (10th Cir. 1976), *aff'g* 389 F. Supp. 673 (N.D. Okla. 1975).

[62] United States v. The Robert A. Welch Found., 334 F.2d 774 (5th Cir. 1964), *aff'g* 228 F. Supp. 881 (S.D. Tex. 1963). The IRS refused to follow this decision, as stated in Rev. Rul. 69-162, 1969-1 C.B. 158. In general, Holloman, "Are Overriding Royalties Unrelated Business Income?," 24 *Oil & Gas Tax Q.* 1 (1975).

[63] Comm'r v. Affiliated Enters., Inc., 123 F.2d 665 (10th Cir. 1941), *cert. den.*, 315 U.S. 812 (1942). Also Comm'r v. Wodehouse, 337 U.S. 369 (1949); Rohmer v. Comm'r, 153 F.2d 61 (2d Cir. 1946), *cert. den.*, 328 U.S. 862 (1946); Sabatini v. Comm'r, 98 F.2d 753 (2d Cir. 1938).

[64] Priv. Ltr. Rul. 8006005.

[65] Rev. Rul. 81-178, 1981-2 C.B. 135. By contrast, other payments were held to not be royalties because the personal services of the organization's members were required.

[66] The IRS cited the following authority for its conclusion: Uhlaender v. Henrickson, 316 F. Supp. 1277 (D. Minn. 1970); Cepeda v. Swift & Co., 415 F.2d 1205 (8th Cir. 1969); Comm'r v. Wodehouse, *supra* note 63; Rohmer v. Comm'r, *supra* note 63, Sabatini v. Comm'r, *supra* note 63; Comm'r v. Affiliated Enters., Inc., *supra* note 63.

[67] E.g., Priv. Ltr. Rul. 8708031.

[68] See §§ 29.1-29.4.

[69] See *infra* § 1(n), § 31.3.

(h) Rent

Another exclusion from unrelated business income taxation is available with respect to certain rents.[70] The principal exclusion is for rents from real property.[71]

    (i) General Rules.   Rent is a form of income that is paid for the occupa-
tion or other use of property. In general, this exclusion is available for rental income where the tax-exempt organization is not actively involved in the
enterprise that generates the revenue, such as through the provision of services
to tenants.

    The exclusion from unrelated business taxable income for rents is some-
times misunderstood, inasmuch as not all income labeled *rent* qualifies for the
exclusion. Where a tax-exempt organization carries on activities that constitute
an activity carried on for trade or business, even though the activities involve
the leasing of real estate, the exclusion will not be available.[72] For example, an
exempt organization may own a building and lease space in it, and the income
from this activity will constitute excludable rent even where the organization
performs normal maintenance services, such as the furnishing of heat, air conditioning, and light, the cleaning of public entrances, exits, stairways, and lobbies, and the collection of trash. Where, however, the organization undertakes
functions beyond these maintenance services, such as services rendered primarily for the convenience of the occupants (for example, the supplying of
cleaning services), the payments will not be considered as being from a passive
source but instead from an unrelated trade or business (assuming that the activity is regularly carried on and is not substantially related to the organization's
tax-exempt purposes).[73]

    The contractual relationship between the parties, from which the ostensi-
ble rental income is derived, must be that as reflected in a *lease*, rather than a *license*, for the exclusion for rental income to be available. A lease "confers upon a
tenant exclusive possession of the subject premises as against all the world, including the owner."[74] The difference is the conferring of a privilege to occupy
the owner's property for a particular use, rather than general possession of the
premises. Thus, a tax-exempt organization that conferred to an advertising
agency the permission to maintain signs and other advertisements on the wall
space in the organization's premises was held to receive income from a license
arrangement, rather than a rental one, so that the exclusion for rental income
was not available.[75]

---

[70] IRC § 512(b)(3).
[71] IRC § 512(b)(3)(a)(i).
[72] In general the rental of real estate constitutes the carrying on of a trade or business (e.g., Hazard v. Comm'r, 7 T.C. 372 (1946)).
[73] Reg. § 1.512(b)-1(c)(5). Rev. Rul. 69-69, *supra* note 4; Rev. Rul. 58-482, 1958-2 C.B. 273. The distinction between these permitted and impermissible services is discussed in Rev. Rul 69-178, *supra* note 4.
[74] Union Travel Associates, Inc. v. International Associates, Inc., 401 A.2d 105 (D.C. Ct. App. 1979).
[75] Priv. Ltr. Rul. 9740032.

As a general rule, the exclusion for rent is not applicable where the relationship between the parties is a partnership[76] or a joint venture.[77]

Consequently, where the requisite profit motive is absent, even if the arrangement is a partnership or joint venture in the broad sense of ownership of property and sharing of net rents, there presumably is no partnership or joint venture for federal tax purposes because of the lack of an intent of a return of profits and because the relationship does not involve a working interest or operational control of the "business." Thus, where the income is truly rent and where the relationship is a passive one (of investor only), the exclusion for rental income is available.[78]

The exclusion from unrelated business taxable income for rents of personal property leased with real property is limited to instances where the rent attributable to the personalty is incidental (no more than 10 percent).[79] Moreover, the exclusion is not available where the rent attributable to personalty is tied to the user's income or profits or if more than 50 percent of the total rent is attributable to the personalty leased. Thus, where the rent attributable to personalty is between 10 percent and 50 percent of the total, only the exclusion with respect to personalty is lost.[80]

Unrelated debt-financed income is not subject to this exclusion,[81] however, nor is royalty income from a controlled corporation.[82]

(ii) Passive Rent Test. Notwithstanding these general rules, the exclusion for rent does not apply if the determination of the amount of the rent depends in whole or in part on the income or profits derived by any person from the property leased (other than an amount based on a fixed percentage or percentages of receipts or sales).[83] This is the *passive rent test.*

An amount is excluded from consideration as rents from real property if, considering the lease and all of the surrounding circumstances, the arrangement does not conform with normal business practice and is in reality a means of basing the rent on income or profits.[84] This rule is intended to prevent

---

[76] See §§ 32.1, 32.2.

[77] See § 32.3.

[78] United States v. Myra Found., 382 F.2d 107 (8th Cir. 1967), where it was held that a foundation that was a lessor of farmland and received a portion of the crops produced by the tenant as rent was not subject to the unrelated business tax on the rent. Also Rev. Rul. 67-218, *supra* note 4. Cf. Reg. § 1.512(c)-1.

[79] IRC § 512(b)(3).

[80] Reg. § 1.512(b)-1(c)(2). Also Rev. Rul. 67-218, *supra* note 4; Rev. Rul. 60-206, *supra* note 4. In general, Greif, "Tax Implications of an Exempt Organization Constructing and Operating a Building," 6 *Tax Adv.* 354 (1975); Reed, "Exemptions from Unrelated Business Tax—Rental Income," 21 *Cath. Law.* 282 (1975); Johnson, "Rental and Investment Income of Many Exempt Organizations May Be Taxable," 41 *J. Tax.* 170 (1974).

[81] IRC § 512(b)(4). See §§ 29.1-29.4.

[82] See *infra* § 1(n), § 31.3. A leasing arrangement can be a related activity, in which case the revenue is not taxable (e.g., Museum of Flight Found. v. United States, 63 F. Supp. 2d 1257 (W.D. Wash. 1999)).

[83] IRC § 512(b)(3)(B)(ii).

[84] Reg. §§ 1.512(b)-1(c)(2)(iii)(b), 1.856-4(b)(3), 1.856-4(b)(6) (other than (b)(6)(ii)). The latter set of regulations is part of the rules pertaining to real estate investment trusts.

avoidance of the unrelated business income tax where a profit-sharing arrangement would, in effect, make the lessor an active participant in the operation of the property.

As noted, an exception is provided for amounts based on a fixed percentage or percentages of sales. These amounts are customary in rental contracts and are generally considered to be different from the profit or loss of the lessee. Generally, rents received from real property are not disqualified solely by reason of the fact that the rent is based on a fixed percentage of total receipts or sales of the lessee. The fact that a lease is based on a percentage of total receipts, however, would not necessarily qualify the amount received or accrued as rent from real property. For example, an amount would not qualify as rent from real property if the lease provided for an amount measured by varying percentages of receipts and the arrangement did not conform with normal business practices but was used as a means of basing the rent on income or profits.[85]

This passive rent test can be applied, for example, in determining whether income from share-crop leasing is excludable rent or taxable rental income.[86] In one of these instances, the IRS argued that, even if there was a landlord-tenant relationship, the rents were nonetheless taxable as unrelated business income because they were not in conformance with the passive rent test.[87] The government contended that, because of the splitting of the expenditures by the tax-exempt organization/landlord, its involvement in the farming operation, and its receipt of a percentage of production as rents, rather than a percentage of receipts, the exempt organization violated the passive rent test. The court disagreed. The exempt organization's rental fee was based solely on a fixed percentage of the crops. The organization shared the costs of some of the expenses related to farming; the tenant, however, bore the entire cost of damages, claims, interest, and other liabilities. The share-crop lease explicitly exonerated the exempt organization from any liability, claim, and/or damages. Thus, the court held that the crop shares to the exempt organization were rental income based on a percentage of the receipts of the harvest. This, wrote the court, is the "equivalent of the tenant's reducing the crops to cash and then giving . . . [the exempt organization] its share of the total receipts collected."[88] "It is not," the court continued, a "percentage of profits or net income."[89]

Income passively received from the rental of real property, such as that from a valid landlord-tenant relationship where the landlord receives nothing more than net rental payments, is not taxable.[90]

---

[85] Reg. § 1.856-4(b)(3).

[86] The law concerning share-crop leases in the unrelated business income tax context is the subject of § 26.5(h).

[87] Trust U/W Emily Oblinger v. Comm'r, 100 T.C. 114 (1993).

[88] *Id.* at 123.

[89] *Id.* Also Harlan E. Moore Charitable Trust v. United States, 812 F. Supp. 130 (C.D. Ill. 1993), *aff'd*, 9 F.3d 623 (7th Cir. 1993).

[90] The State National Bank of El Paso v. United States, 75-2 U.S.T.C. ¶ 9868 (W.D. Tex. 1975). Cf. Rev. Rul. 54-420, 1954-2 C.B. 128, *rendered obsolete* by Rev. Rul. 77-278, 1977-2 C.B. 485.

The IRS from time to time issues private letter rulings as to what constitutes excludable rent in this context.[91]

On occasion, rental income is derived from the operation of a related business, so that the revenue is nontaxable for that reason. In one instance, a public charity with a training program shared office space with a business league that owned the building, in part because the tenants of the league provided volunteer teaching faculty to the charitable organization; the charity accorded the business league the right to allow the tenants use of its research equipment in exchange for maintenance of the equipment; the IRS held that the value of the maintenance services was phantom rent that was not taxable.[92]

(i) Other Investment Income

The IRS ruled that the interest earned by a tax-exempt organization pursuant to *interest rate swap agreements* is not taxable as unrelated business income.[93]

A typical transaction of this type proceeds as follows: The tax-exempt organization purchases a debt security; the instrument evidencing the indebtedness provides that the organization will receive interest payments from the issuer that are keyed to the six-month Eurodollar rate; the organization contracts with an unrelated third party to provide it with payments equal to a fixed rate of return on all or a specified part of the principal amount of the debt security; the fixed rate of return is set so as to provide the organization with a return that is a specified spread of basis points over the seven-year U.S. Treasury bill rate; the organization provides the third party with payments equal to a floating rate of return on all or part of the principal amount of the debt security; the floating rate of return is calculated in the same manner as the floating rate interest payments described in the second stage of the transaction; the funds used to acquire the debt security and the funds used to make the swap payments are not borrowed;[94] and all payments made and received by the organization are in U.S. dollars.

The anticipated result of the interest rate swap is to provide the tax-exempt organization with interest payments that are preferable, from its investment standpoint, to those provided for in the floating rate note.

The IRS concluded that these swap transactions are "ordinary or routine investment activities undertaken in connection with the management of . . . [the organization's] securities portfolio." The IRS analogized to the securities lending practice,[95] finding the swap transaction "similar," in that the "securities will be acquired and the swap agreements will be entered into as part of an investment strategy designed to stabilize the return on the floating rate debt securities."

---

[91] E.g., Priv. Ltr. Rul. 9246032.

[92] Priv. Ltr. Rul. 9615045. In general, Nugent, "Possible Approaches for Avoiding UBIT on Real Estate Investments," 37 *Exempt Org. Tax Rev.* (No. 2) 285 (Aug. 2002).

[93] Priv. Ltr. Rul. 9042038.

[94] This is done to prevent debt-financed income taxation. See §§ 29.1-29.4.

[95] See *supra* § 1(d).

In addition to the foregoing forms of investment income, income from notional principal contracts,[96] and other substantially similar income from ordinary and routine investments to the extent determined by the IRS, are excluded in computing unrelated business taxable income.[97] This exclusion embraces interest rate and currency swaps, as well as equity and commodity swaps.

These exclusions do not apply to income derived from (and deductions in connection with) debt-financed property,[98] gains or losses from the sale, exchange, or other disposition of any property,[99] gains or losses from the lapse or termination of options to buy or sell securities,[100] interest and annuities derived from (and deductions in connection with) controlled organizations,[101] and income earned by brokers or dealers (including organizations that make a market in derivative financial products[102]).[103]

(j) Capital Gains

Excluded from unrelated business income taxation generally are gains from the sale, exchange, or other disposition of capital gain property.[104] This exclusion for capital gains does not extend to dispositions of inventory or property held primarily for sale to customers in the ordinary course of a business.[105] The IRS applies eight factors in determining whether property is being sold in the ordinary course of business: the purpose for which the property was acquired, the cost of it, the activities of the owner in the improvement and disposition of the property, the extent of improvements made to the property, the proximity of the sale to the purchase, the purpose for which the property was held, prevailing market conditions, and the frequency, continuity, and size of the sales.[106] For example, the IRS ruled that the gain from the sale by tax-exempt organizations of leased fee interests in condominium apartments to lessees was not taxable because of the exclusion for capital gain.[107]

Nonetheless, there is an exception from this second limitation[108] that excludes

---

[96] Reg. § 1.863-7.
[97] Reg. § 1.512-(b)-1(a)(2).
[98] See §§ 29.1-29.4.
[99] See *infra* § 1(j).
[100] *Id.*
[101] See *infra* § 1(n), § 31.3.
[102] Reg. § 1.954-2T(a)(4)(iii)(B).
[103] In general, Note, "Tax-Exempt Entities, Notional Principal Contracts, and the Unrelated Business Income Tax," 105 *Harv. L. Rev.* 1265 (April 1992); Ben-Ami, "UBIT and Portfolio Investments for Exempt Organizations," 2 *J. Tax Exempt Orgs.* 12 (Spring 1990).
[104] IRC § 512(b)(5).
[105] IRC § 512(b)(5)(A), (B); Reg. § 1.512(b)-1(d). In general, Kaltreider v. Comm'r, 255 F.2d 833 (3d Cir. 1958), *aff'g* 28 T.C. 121 (1957); Buono v. Comm'r, 74 T.C. 187 (1980).
[106] E.g., Priv. Ltr. Rul. 9619069.
[107] E.g., Priv. Ltr. Rul. 9629030.
[108] IRC § 512(b)(5)(B).

gains and losses from the sale, exchange, or other disposition of certain real property and mortgages acquired from financial institutions that are in conservatorship or receivership.[109] Only real property and mortgages owned by a financial institution (or held by the financial institution as security for a loan) at the time when the institution entered conservatorship or receivership are eligible for the exception.

This exclusion is limited to properties designated as *foreclosure property* within nine months of acquisition and disposed of within $2\frac{1}{2}$ years of acquisition.[110] The $2\frac{1}{2}$-year disposition period may be extended by the IRS if the extension is necessary for the orderly liquidation of the property. No more than one half by value of properties acquired in a single transaction may be designated as disposal property. This exception is not available for properties that are improved or developed to the extent that the aggregate expenditures on development do not exceed 20 percent of the net selling price of the property.[111] This rule concerning an exclusion of gains from certain dispositions of property also excludes all gains, in connection with the organization's investment activities, from the lapse or termination of options to buy or sell securities or real property, as well as all gains from the forfeiture of good-faith deposits (that are consistent with established business practice) for the purchase, sale, or lease of real property in connection with the organization's investment activities.[112] Under prior law, the income from the writing of options (premiums) was generally treated as ordinary income—and thus was subject to the unrelated business income tax.[113] (Premiums received for options that are exercised are treated as part of the gain or loss on the sale of the property involved, that is, usually as capital gain or loss.) In the opinion of the Senate Committee on Finance, a law change was necessary because taxation of this type of income is "inconsistent with the generally tax-free treatment accorded to exempt organizations' income from investment activities."[114]

The IRS from time to time issues private letter rulings as to what constitutes excludable capital gains in this context.[115]

Unrelated debt-financed income, however, is not subject to this exclusion.[116]

(k) Loan Commitment Fees

The law was unclear as to whether loan commitment fees constitute unrelated business taxable income. A *loan commitment fee* is a nonrefundable charge made

---

[109] IRC § 512(b)(16).

[110] IRC §§ 512(b)(16)(B), 514(c)(9)(H)(v). As to the latter reference, see § 29.3.

[111] IRC § 512(b)(15)(A).

[112] IRC § 512(b)(5). This rule applies to the disposition of timber, to the extent it qualifies as sale of the timber (IRC § 631(b)); income from the cutting of timber held short-term may qualify as an excludible royalty (see *supra* § (g)).

[113] Rev. Rul. 66-47, 1966-1 C.B. 137.

[114] S. Rep. No. 1172, 94th Cong., 2d Sess. 3 (1976), accompanying Pub. L. No. 94-396.

[115] E.g., Priv. Ltr. Rul. 9247038.

[116] IRC § 512(b)(4). See §§ 29.1-29.4.

by a lender to reserve a sum of money with fixed terms for a specified period of time. This type of charge compensates the lender for the risk inherent in committing to make the loan (such as for the lender's exposure to interest rate changes and for potential lost opportunities). Today, however, an exclusion from such tax treatment applies; the reference is to "amounts received or accrued as consideration for entering into agreements to make loans."[117]

(l) Research Income

Income derived from research[118] for government is excluded from unrelated business income taxation, as is income derived from research for anyone in the case of a tax-exempt college, university, or hospital, and of "fundamental research" units.[119] According to the legislative history, the term *research* includes "not only fundamental research but also applied research such as testing and experimental construction and production."[120] With respect to the separate exemption for college, university, or hospital research, "funds received for research by other institutions [do not] necessarily represent unrelated business income," such as a grant by a corporation to a foundation to finance scientific research if the results of the research are to be made freely available to the public.[121] Without defining the term *research*, the IRS was content to find applicability of this rule because the studies were not "merely quality control programs or ordinary testing for certification purposes, as a final procedural step before marketing."[122]

In employing the term *research* in this context, the IRS generally looks to the body of law defining the term in relation to what is considered tax-exempt scientific research.[123] Thus, the issue is usually whether the activity is being carried on as an incident to commercial or industrial operations; if it is, it will almost assuredly be regarded by the IRS as an unrelated trade or business.[124] In one instance, the IRS found applicability of the exclusion because the studies undertaken by a tax-exempt medical college in the testing of pharmaceutical products under contracts with the manufacturers were held to be more than "mere quality control programs or ordinary testing for certification purposes, as a final procedural step before marketing."[125] In another instance, the exclusion was

---

[117] IRC § 512(b)(1).
[118] The concept of scientific research is discussed in § 9.2.
[119] IRC § 512(b)(7)–(9). See Reg. § 1.512(b)-1(f). Also Rev. Rul. 54-73, 1954-1 C.B. 160; IIT Research Inst. v. United States, 9 Cl. Ct. 13 (1985).
[120] H. Rep. No. 2319, *supra* note 5, at 37.
[121] S. Rep. No. 2375, *supra* note 5, at 30.
[122] Priv. Ltr. Rul. 7936006.
[123] Rev. Rul. 76-296, 1976-2 C.B. 141. Cf. IRC § 41 (which provides a tax credit for certain research). In general, Kertz, "University Research and Development Activities: The Federal Income Tax Consequences of Research Contracts, Research Subsidiaries and Joint Venturers," 13 J. Coll. & Univ. L. 109 (1986); Kertz, "Tax Exempt Organizations and Commercially Sponsored Scientific Research," 9 J. Coll. & Univ. L. 69 (1982-1983).
[124] Rev. Rul. 68-373, 1968-2 C.B. 206.
[125] Priv. Ltr. Rul. 7936006.

held to be applicable to contract work done by an exempt educational institution for the federal government in the field of rocketry.[126]

College and university audit guidelines issued by the IRS[127] include a section on research activities by these institutions. The auditing agent is directed to determine whether "purported research is actually the conduct of an activity incident to a commercial enterprise (e.g., testing, sampling or certifying of items to a known standard)";[128] determine whether the research is conducted by the institution or by a separate entity;[129] review the institution's safeguards for managing and reporting conflicts of interest and any requirements imposed by any federal agency sponsoring research;[130] review the institution's policy regarding ownership of intellectual property;[131] review research arrangements with government sponsors and joint venture or royalty-sharing arrangements with industry sponsors;[132] determine who holds the patent or right to license technology derived from the research;[133] determine whether the institution is investing in licensee firms, either directly or through venture capital funds;[134] obtain a list of all publications that discuss the institution's search activities;[135] if the institution conducts government-funded research, review copies of audit reports from the funding agency;[136] and review sample closed research projects.[137]

(m) Certain Deductions

Also excluded are all deductions directly connected with income in the form of dividends, interest, payments with respect to securities loans, amounts received or accrued as consideration for entering into agreements to make loans, annuities, royalties, and rents.[138] Similarly excluded are capital losses.[139]

There are limitations on the availability of the charitable contribution deduction, as allowed in the unrelated income tax context.[140] This deduction may not exceed 10 percent of unrelated business taxable income, otherwise computed.

In computing unrelated business taxable income, there is a specific deduction of $1,000.[141] This deduction is allowed, in the case of a diocese, province of a religious order, or a convention or association of churches, with respect to each

---

[126] Priv. Ltr. Rul. 7924009.
[127] See § 24.8(d) (College and University Audit Guidelines).
[128] *Id.* § 342.(10)(3).
[129] *Id.* § 342.(10)(2).
[130] *Id.* § 342.(10)(4).
[131] *Id.* § 342.(10)(5).
[132] *Id.* § 342.(10)(6)(a).
[133] *Id.* § 342.(10)(6)(b).
[134] *Id.* § 342.(10)(7).
[135] *Id.* § 342.(10)(8).
[136] *Id.* § 342.(10)(9).
[137] IRC § 512(b)(1)-(3).
[138] IRC § 512(b)(5).
[139] College and University Audit Guidelines § 342.(10)(10).
[140] IRC § 512(b)(10); Reg. § 1.512(b)-1(g).
[141] IRC § 512(b)(12); Reg. § 1.512(b)-1(h)(1).

parish, individual church, district, or other local unit.[142] This deduction is intended to eliminate imposition of the unrelated income tax in cases where the exaction of it would involve excessive costs of collection in relation any payments received by the government.[143]

(n) Revenue from Controlled Organizations

Payments of interest, annuities, royalties, and/or rents (but not dividends) by a controlled organization to a tax-exempt, controlling organization can be taxable as unrelated income, notwithstanding the fact that these forms of income are generally otherwise nontaxable as passive income.[144] The purpose of this provision is to prevent an exempt organization from housing an unrelated activity in a separate but controlled organization and receiving nontaxable income by reason of the passive income rules (for example, by renting unrelated income property to a subsidiary.)[145]

The rules in this regard changed dramatically in 1997.[146]

(i) Pre-1998 Law. Pursuant to the law before its revision in 1997, a tax-exempt organization controlled another organization where it had at least an 80 percent interest in it.[147] This control element can be manifested by stock or by an interlocking of directors, trustees, or other representatives of the two organizations.[148]

When stock was the control mechanism, it had to constitute at least 80 percent of the total combined voting power of all classes of stock entitled to vote and at least 80 percent of the total number of shares of all other classes of stock of the corporation.[149] Thus, this type of control was not present when the classes of stock issued by the subsidiary were split between related tax-exempt organizations. For example, an exempt trade association with a related supporting foundation was not considered to control a for-profit subsidiary when the association held all of the subsidiary's voting stock and the foundation held all of its nonvoting stock (such as preferred shares). Likewise, there was

---

[142] Reg. § 1.512(b)-1(h)(2). Also Rev. Rul. 68-536, 1968-2 C.B. 244.
[143] H. Rep. No. 2319, *supra* note 5, at 37; S. Rep. No. 2375, *supra* note 5, at 30.
[144] IRC § 512(b)(13); Reg. § 1.512(b)-1(l). Also, J.E. & L.E. Mabee Found., Inc. v. United States, *supra* note 61; United States v. The Robert A. Welch Found., *supra* note 62; Campbell v. Carter Found. Prod. Co., 322 F.2d 827 (5th Cir. 1963), *aff'g in part* 61-2 U.S.T.C. ¶ 9630 (N.D. Tex. 1961).
[145] S. Rep. No. 91-552, 91st Cong., 1st Sess. 73 (1969); In general, Crosby Valve & Gage Co. v. Comm'r, 380 F.2d 146 (1st Cir. 1967); Bird, "Exempt Organizations and Taxable Subsidiaries," 4 *Prac. Tax Law.* (No. 2) 53 (1990); Heinlen, "Commercial Activities of Exempt Organizations—Joint Ventures and Taxable Subsidiaries," *N. Ky. L. Rev.* (No. 2) 285 (1989); Nagel, "The Use of For-Profit Subsidiaries by Non-Profit Corporations," 17 *Col. Law.* (No. 7) 1293 (1998).
[146] The Taxpayer Relief Act of 1997 altered the rules in this context, effective for tax years beginning after August 5, 1997. This law does not apply to payments made during the first two tax years beginning on or after that date if the payments were made pursuant to a binding written contract in effect as of June 8, 1997, and at all times thereafter before the payment.
[147] IRC § 368(c).
[148] Reg. § 1.512(b)-1(l)(4).
[149] Reg. § 1.512(b)-1(l)(4)(i)(a).

no control element applied where a second-tier subsidiary paid income to an exempt organization.[150]

When the subsidiary was a nonexempt organization, income paid to the tax-exempt parent organization was regarded as unrelated business taxable income to the extent it would have been unrelated business taxable income if earned directly by the exempt parent. In the case of an exempt subsidiary, the rules applied in the proportion that the subsidiary's income was unrelated business taxable income.[151]

(ii) Post-1997 Law. The law in this regard was changed significantly in 1997.[152] The control test was revised, constructive ownership rules were added, and the rules for determining how income is taxed under this regime were altered. This law change occurred because its purpose had been frustrated, in that it was too narrowly written and easily circumvented.[153]

Under the new rules, the percentage threshold for determining control was considerably reduced, from 80 percent to a more-than-50-percent standard. Thus, in the case of a corporation, *control* means ownership by vote or value of more than 50 percent of the stock in the corporation.[154] In the case of a partnership, control is ownership of more than 50 percent of the profits interest or capital interests in the partnership.[155] In an instance of a trust or any other case, control is measured in terms of more than 50 percent of the beneficial interests in the entity.[156]

Preexisting constructive ownership rules are engrafted onto this area for purposes of determining ownership of stock in a corporation.[157] Similar principles apply for purposes of determining ownership of interests in any other entity.[158] For example, if 50 percent or more in value of the stock in a corporation is owned, directly or indirectly, by or for any person, that person is considered as owning any stock owned, directly or indirectly, by or for the corporation, in the proportion which the value of the stock the person so owns bears to the value of all of the stock in the corporation.[159] Likewise, if 50 percent or more in value of the stock in a corporation is owned, directly or indirectly, by or for any person, the corporation is considered as owning the stock owned, directly or indirectly, by or for that person.[160] There are attribution rules that apply with respect to stock owned by members of a family, partnerships, estates, and trusts.[161]

---

[150] See § 31.3.
[151] Reg. § 1.512(b)-1(l)(2), (3).
[152] Taxpayer Relief Act of 1997 § 1041(a).
[153] H. Rep. 105-148, 105th Cong., 1st Sess. 491 (1997).
[154] IRC § 512(b)(13)(D)(i)(I).
[155] IRC § 512(b)(13)(D)(i)(II).
[156] IRC § 512(b)(13)(D)(i)(III).
[157] IRC §§ 512(b)(13)(D)(ii), 318.
[158] IRC § 512(b)(13)(D)(ii).
[159] IRC § 318(a)(2)(C).
[160] IRC § 318(a)(3)(C).
[161] IRC § 318(a)(1), (2)(A), (B), and (3)(A), (B).

Thus, when a controlling organization receives, directly or indirectly, a specified payment from a controlled entity (whether or not tax-exempt), the controlling entity may have to treat that payment as income from an unrelated business.[162] The term *specified payment* means interest, annuity, royalties, or rent.[163] A specified payment must be treated as unrelated business income to the extent the payment reduced the net unrelated income of the controlled entity or increased any net unrelated loss of the controlled entity.[164] The controlling organization may deduct expenses that are directly connected with amounts that are treated as unrelated business income under this rule.[165]

In the case of a controlled entity that is not tax-exempt, the term *net unrelated income* means the portion of the entity's taxable income that would be unrelated business taxable income if the entity were exempt and had the same exempt purposes as the controlling organization.[166] When the controlled entity is exempt, *net unrelated income* means the amount of the unrelated business taxable income of the controlled entity.[167] The term *net unrelated loss* means the net operating loss adjusted under rules similar to those pertaining to net unrelated income.[168] Consequently, the allocation-of-income rule embodied in prior law has been replaced by this look-through approach.

(o) Commercial-Type Insurance Activities

In the case of tax-exempt charitable and social welfare organizations, commercial-type insurance activities are treated as unrelated trades or businesses.[169] These exempt organizations are subject to tax on the income from these insurance activities (including investment income that might otherwise be excluded from taxation) under the rules by which for-profit insurance companies are taxed.[170]

(p) Foreign Source Income

A look-through rule characterizes certain foreign source income, namely, income from insurance activities conducted by offshore captives of tax-exempt organizations, as unrelated business income.[171] Generally, U.S. shareholders of controlled

---

[162] IRC § 512(b)(13)(A). Examples of indirect payments appear in J. E. & L. E. Mabee Found., Inc. v. United States, *supra* note 61, and Gen. Couns. Mem. 38878.

[163] IRC § 512(b)(13)(C). The term thus does not include capital gain, enabling a controlling organization to sell appreciated property to a controlled entity without generating unrelated business income. Cf. IRC § 4040(c).

[164] IRC § 512(b)(13)(A).

[165] *Id.*

[166] IRC § 512(b)(13)(B)(i)(I).

[167] IRC § 512(b)(13)(B)(i)(II).

[168] IRC § 512(b)(13)(B)(ii).

[169] If these commercial-type insurance activities constitute a substantial part of the organization's activities, the organization cannot be tax-exempt (see § 22.1).

[170] IRC § 501(m)(2).

[171] IRC § 512(b)(17)(A).

foreign corporations must include in income their shares of the foreign entities' income, including certain insurance income.[172] The IRS treated these income inclusions as dividends, so that the income to exempt organizations was excludible from tax.[173] Today, however, this look-through rule overrides the former treatment of this type of income as dividends.[174]

This rule is not applicable to amounts that are attributable to the insurance of risks of the tax-exempt organization itself, certain of its exempt affiliates,[175] or an officer or director of, or an individual who (directly or indirectly) performs services for, the exempt organization (or certain exempt affiliates), provided that the insurance primarily covers risks associated with the individual's performance of services in connection with the exempt organization (or exempt affiliates).[176]

(q) Religious Order Rule

The unrelated business income tax does not apply to a tax-exempt religious order or educational institution maintained by the order, with respect to a trade or business, even though the business is unrelated, if the business provides services under license issued by a federal regulatory agency, if less than 10 percent of its net income is used for unrelated activities, and if the business was carried on before May 27, 1969.[177]

§ 27.2 EXCEPTIONS

In addition to the exceptions provided in the rules concerning modifications, there are various other exceptions from unrelated business income taxation.

(a) Businesses Conducted by Volunteers

Exempt from the scope of taxable unrelated trade or business is a business in which substantially all of the work in carrying on the business is performed for the tax-exempt organization without compensation.[178] An example of applicability of

---

[172] IRC §§ 951(a)(1)(A), 953.

[173] E.g., Priv. Ltr. Rul. 8819034. See text accompanied by *supra* note 4.

[174] This look-through rule was enacted as part of the Small Business Job Protection Act of 1996 (Pub. L. No. 188, 104th Cong., 2d Sess. (1996)).

[175] The determination as to whether an entity is an *affiliate* of an organization is made under rules similar to those applied in the tax-exempt entity leasing context (see § 29.5(c)). Also, two or more organizations generally are regarded as affiliates if the organizations are colleges, universities, hospitals, or other medical entities and they participate in an insurance arrangement that provides for any profits from the arrangement to be returned to the policyholders in their capacity as such (see § 29.5(c)).

[176] IRC § 512(b)(17)(B). In general, Stretch, Cooper & Snowling, "UBIT Rules Are Expanded to Include Income from Foreign Captives: Congressional Revenue Raisers Pick Another Pocket," 16 *Exempt Org. Tax Rev.* (No. 16) 29 (Jan. 1997).

[177] IRC § 512(b)(15).

[178] IRC § 513(a)(1). Also Rev. Rul. 56-152, 1956-1 C.B. 56.

this exception is an exempt orphanage operating a secondhand clothing store and selling to the general public, where substantially all of the work in operating the store is performed by volunteers.[179] Another illustration of this rule is the production and sale of phonograph records by a medical society, where the services of the performers were provided without compensation.[180] Still another illustration of this exception concerned a trade association that sold advertising in a commercial, unrelated manner, but avoided unrelated income taxation of the activity because the work involved was provided solely by volunteers.[181]

As to the scope of this exception, Congress apparently intended to provide an exclusion from the definition of unrelated trade or business only for those unrelated business activities in which the performance of services is a material income-producing factor in carrying on the business and substantially all of the services are performed without compensation.[182] In reliance upon the legislative history underlying this rule, the IRS ruled that the rental of heavy machinery under long-term lease agreements requiring the lessees to provide insurance, pay the applicable taxes, and make and pay for most repairs, with the functions of securing leases and processing rental payments performed without compensation, was not an unrelated trade or business excluded under this exception since there is "no significant amount of labor regularly required or involved in the kind of business carried on by the organization" and thus the performance of services in connection with the leasing activity is not a material income-producing factor in the business.[183]

A membership entity of an art museum published and sold a book containing recipes, all of which were contributed. Inasmuch as substantially all of the work in preparing and selling the cookbook was performed by volunteers, the IRS ruled that the activity was not an unrelated business, by reason of this exception.[184]

A court ruled that this exemption was defeated in part because free drinks provided to the collectors and cashiers in connection with the conduct of a bingo game by a tax-exempt organization were considered "liquid compensation."[185] This position was, however, rejected on appeal.[186] This court subsequently held that this exception was not available, in the case of an exempt organization that regularly carried on gambling activities, because the dealers and other individuals received tips from patrons of the games.[187] In another case, this court found that an exempt religious order that operated a farm was not taxable on the in-

[179] S. Rep. No. 2375, *supra* note 5, at 108.
[180] Greene County Med. Soc'y Found. v. United States, 345 F. Supp. 900 (W.D. Mo. 1972).
[181] Priv. Ltr. Rul. 9302023.
[182] H. Rep. No. 2319, *supra* note 5, at 37; S. Rep. No. 2375, *supra* note 5, at 107-108.
[183] Rev. Rul. 78-144, 1978-1 C.B. 168.
[184] Tech. Adv. Mem. 8211002. Having reached this conclusion, the IRS declined to apply the exception for contributed merchandise (see *infra* § 2(c)).
[185] Waco Lodge No. 166, Benevolent & Protective Order of Elks v. Comm'r, 42 T.C.M. 1202 (1981).
[186] 696 F.2d 372 (5th Cir. 1983).
[187] Executive Network Club, Inc. v. Comm'r, 69 T.C.M. 1680 (1995).

come derived from the farming operations because the farm was maintained by the uncompensated labor of the members of the order.[188]

(b) Convenience Businesses

Also excluded from unrelated income taxation is a business, in the case of a tax-exempt charitable organization or a state college or university, that is carried on by the organization primarily for the convenience of its members, students, patients, officers, or employees.[189] An example of applicability of this exception is a laundry operated by an exempt college for the purpose of laundering dormitory linens and the clothing of students.[190] (A laundry operated by a college apart from its campus primarily for the purpose of making a profit from laundering the clothing of the general public would, however, be an unrelated business and outside the scope of this exception.) As another illustration, the provision by an exempt hospital of mobile services to its patients by means of specially designed vans was ruled to be a convenience business.[191]

A court expanded this concept by holding that physicians on the staff of a teaching hospital were "members" of the hospital, in that the term "refers to any group of persons who are closely associated with the entity involved and who are necessary to the achievement of the organization's purposes."[192] The IRS disagrees with this opinion, however, taking the position that the "hospital's staff physicians are neither 'members' nor 'employees' of the hospital in their capacities as private practitioners of medicine."[193]

The exemption for revenue derived from an activity carried on primarily for the convenience of an organization's members was unsuccessfully invoked in a situation involving advertising in the organization's monthly journal. The lower court rejected the argument, deciding that the primary purpose of the advertising was to raise revenue.[194] On appeal, the higher court wrote that it could not conclude that the finding was clearly erroneous.[195]

Read literally, this exception pertains only to the classes of individuals who have the requisite relationship directly with the exempt organization; for example, it applies with respect to services carried on by an exempt hospital for the convenience of *its* patients. The IRS ruled, however, that the doctrine was

---

[188] St. Joseph Farms of Ind. Bros. of the Congregation of Holy Cross, Southwest Province, Inc. v. Comm'r, 85 T.C. 9 (1985), *app. dis.* (7th Cir. 1986). Cf. Shiloh Youth Revival Centers v. Comm'r, 88 T.C. 565 (1987).

[189] IRC § 513(a)(2). Also Rev. Rul. 81-19, 1981-1 C.B. 354; Rev. Rul. 69-268, 1969-1 C.B. 160; Rev. Rul. 55-676, 1955-2 C.B. 266; College and University Audit Guidelines, *supra* note 127 § 342.(13). Cf. Carle Found. v. United States, 611 F.2d 1192 (7th Cir. 1979), *cert. den.,* 449 U.S. 824 (1980).

[190] Reg. § 1.513-2(b); S. Rep. No. 2375, *supra* note 5, at 108.

[191] Priv. Ltr. Rul. 9841049.

[192] St. Luke's Hosp. of Kansas City v. United States, 494 F. Supp. 85, 92 (W.D. Mo. 1980).

[193] Rev. Rul. 85-109, 1985-2 C.B. 165, 166.

[194] The American College of Physicians v. United States, 83-2 U.S.T.C. ¶ 9652 (Cl. Ct. (1983)).

[195] The American College of Physicians v. United States, 743 F.2d 1570 (Fed. Cir. 1984), *rev'd*, 475 U.S. 834 (1986).

available when an exempt organization's activities were for the convenience of patients of another, albeit related, exempt entity.[196] At the same time, the IRS refused to extend the doctrine to embrace spouses and children of a university's students.[197]

(c) Sales of Gift Items

Unrelated trade or business does not include a business, conducted by a tax-exempt organization, that constitutes the selling of merchandise, substantially all of which has been received by the organization by means of contributions.[198] This exception is available for thrift shops that sell donated clothes, books, furniture, and similar items (merchandise) to the general public.[199]

Despite its origin, however, this exception is not confined to businesses that are thrift shops, either independent stores or thrift shops operated by tax-exempt organizations, such as schools. For example, the IRS ruled that an exempt organization could solicit contributions of home heating oil from individuals who had converted to gas heat, extract the oil from fuel tanks, and sell it to the general public, and not be involved in an unrelated business by reason of this exception.[200] Likewise, the IRS held that a charitable organization may maintain a property donation program, where contributed vehicles and other properties are sold to generate funds, with the program not considered an unrelated business by virtue of this exception.[201]

As noted, substantially all of the merchandise involved must have been contributed. In one instance, the IRS held that the exception was available where less than 5 percent of total sales was of purchased items.[202] For this exception to be utilized, however, the tax-exempt organization itself must be in the requisite business; it is not enough to have the business owned and operated by an independent contractor who merely uses an exempt organization's name and pays over certain receipts to the exempt organization.[203]

(d) Businesses of Employees' Associations

Excluded from unrelated business income taxation is a business, in the case of a tax-exempt local association of employees[204] organized before May 27, 1969, that

---

[196] Priv. Ltr. Rul. 9535023.
[197] Tech. Adv. Mem. 9645004.
[198] IRC § 513(a)(3).
[199] Reg. § 1.513-1(e), last sentence; Rev. Rul. 71-581, 1971-2 C.B. 236.
[200] Priv. Ltr. Rul. 8116095.
[201] Priv. Ltr. Rul. 200230005.
[202] Priv. Ltr. Rul. 8122007.
[203] Tech. Adv. Mem. 8041007. Likewise, when the thrift stores were in a separate corporation, the operation of them was not imputed to a related tax-exempt organization for purposes of this exception (Disabled American Veterans Service Found., Inc. v. Comm'r, 29 T.C.M. 202 (1970)).
[204] IRC § 501(c)(4). See § 18.3.

is the selling by the organization of items of work-related clothing and equipment and items normally sold through vending machines, through food-dispensing facilities, or by snack bars, for the convenience of its members at their usual places of employment.[205] The IRS ruled that this type of association may change its form, from unincorporated entity to a corporation, without losing its grandfathered status.[206]

(e) Entertainment Activities

Another exception from unrelated business income taxation is applicable with respect to the conduct of entertainment at fairs and expositions.[207] This rule applies to charitable, social welfare, labor, agricultural, and horticultural organizations[208] that regularly conduct, as a substantial tax-exempt purpose, an agricultural and educational fair or exposition.[209] This exemption from the unrelated income tax overrides an IRS pronouncement.[210]

The term unrelated trade or business does not include qualified *public entertainment activities* of an eligible organization.[211] This term is defined to mean any "entertainment or recreational activity of a kind traditionally conducted at fairs or expositions promoting agricultural and educational purposes, including, but not limited to, any activity one of the purposes of which is to attract the public to fairs or expositions or to promote the breeding of animals or the development of products or equipment."[212]

Unrelated income taxation is not to occur with respect to the operation of a *qualified public entertainment activity* that meets one of the following conditions: the public entertainment activity is conducted (1) in conjunction with an international, national, state, regional, or local fair or exposition, (2) in accordance with state law that permits that activity to be conducted solely by an eligible type of tax-exempt organization or by a governmental entity, or (3) in accordance with state law that permits that activity to be conducted under license for not more than 20 days in any year and that permits the organization to pay a lower percentage of the revenue from this activity than the state requires from other organizations.[213]

To qualify under this rule, the tax-exempt organization must regularly conduct, as a substantial exempt purpose, a fair or exposition that is both agricultural

---

[205] IRC § 513(a)(2).
[206] Priv. Ltr. Rul. 9442013. In so ruling, the IRS relied on Rev. Rul. 54-134, 1954-1 C.B. 88 (holding that an IRS ruling recognizing the tax-exempt status of a corporation, where there was a mere change in form from unincorporated status, embraces the period of unincorporation as well).
[207] IRC § 513(d)(1), (2).
[208] IRC § 501(c)(3), (4), or (5). See Chapters 5–10, 12, 15, respectively.
[209] IRC § 513(d)(2)(C).
[210] Rev. Rul. 68-505, 1968-2 C.B. 248.
[211] IRC § 513(d)(1).
[212] IRC § 513(d)(2)(A).
[213] IRC § 513(d)(2)(B).

and educational. The Senate Finance Committee report that accompanied these rules stated that a book fair held by an exempt university is not sheltered by this provision since this type of a fair is not agricultural in nature.[214]

A charitable, social welfare, labor, agricultural, or horticultural organization is not to be considered as not entitled to tax exemption solely because of its qualified public entertainment activities.

(f) Trade Show Activities

Another exception from unrelated business income taxation is applicable with respect to the conduct of trade shows by certain tax-exempt organizations. The rule with respect to trade show activities[215] is available for exempt labor, agricultural, and horticultural organizations, business leagues,[216] and charitable and social welfare organizations[217] that regularly conduct, as a substantial exempt purpose, shows that stimulate interest in and demand for the products of a particular industry or segment of industry or that educate persons in attendance regarding new developments or products or services related to the exempt activities of the organization. This provision overrules contrary IRS determinations.[218]

Under these rules, the term unrelated trade or business does not include qualified convention and trade show activities of an eligible organization.[219] This term is defined to mean any "activity of a kind traditionally conducted at conventions, annual meetings, or trade shows, including but not limited to, any activity one of the purposes of which is to attract persons in an industry generally (without regard to membership in the sponsoring organization) as well as members of the public to the show for the purpose of displaying industry products or services, or to educate persons engaged in the industry in the development of new products and services or new rules and regulations affecting the industry."[220]

A *qualified convention and trade show activity* is a convention and trade show activity that is (1) carried on by a qualifying organization; (2) conducted in conjunction with an international, national, state, regional, or local convention, annual meeting, or show; (3) sponsored by a qualifying organization that has as one of its purposes in sponsoring the activity the promotion and stimulation of interest in and demand for the products and services of the industry involved in general or the education of persons in attendance regarding new developments or products and services related to the exempt activities of the organization; and (4)

---

[214] S. Rep. No. 94-938, 94th Cong., 2d Sess. 602 (1976).
[215] IRC § 513(d)(1), (3).
[216] IRC § 501(c)(5), (6). See Chapters 15, 13, respectively.
[217] IRC § 501(c)(3), (4). See Chapters 5–10, 12, respectively.
[218] Rev. Ruls. 75-516 through 75-520, 1975-2 C.B. 220-226. Also Rev. Rul. 67-219, 1967-1 C.B. 210; Rev. Rul. 58-224, 1958-1 C.B. 242. Subsequently, these rulings were revoked or rendered obsolete by the IRS (Rev. Rul. 85-123, 1985-2 C.B. 168).
[219] IRC § 513(d)(1).
[220] IRC § 513(d)(3)(A); Reg. § 1.513-3(c)(4).

designed to achieve this purpose through the character of the exhibits and the extent of the industry products displayed.[221]

The income that is excluded from taxation by these rules is derived from the rental of display space to exhibitors. This is the case even though the exhibitors who rent the space are permitted to sell or solicit orders, as long as the show is a qualified trade show or a qualified convention and trade show.[222] This exclusion is also available with respect to a "supplier's exhibit" that is conducted by a qualifying organization in conjunction with a qualified convention or trade show.[223] This exclusion is not available, however, to a stand-alone suppliers' exhibit that is not a qualified convention show.[224] Nonetheless, income from a suppliers' show is not taxable where the displays are educational in nature and are displays at which soliciting and selling are prohibited.[225]

There is, moreover, an aspect of this issue that may resolve the tax issue for many tax-exempt organizations not expressly covered by these rules. This relates to the fact that an unrelated business must be *regularly carried on* before the revenue from the business can be taxed as unrelated income.[226] Thus, the net income derived by an exempt organization (irrespective of the statutory basis for its tax exemption) from the conduct of a trade show would not be taxable as unrelated income if the trade show is not regularly carried on. A court case gives support to the premise that the conduct of a typical trade show is not an activity that is regularly carried on.[227] This court held that an organization that annually sponsored a vaudeville show did not generate any unrelated income from the activity because the show was not regularly carried on—rather, it was an "intermittent activity."[228] Consequently, to the extent that an annual trade show of an exempt organization can be regarded as an intermittent activity, it would not give rise to unrelated income, irrespective of the exempt status of the organization and without regard to invocation of these special rules. It must be noted, however, that in measuring regularity, the IRS looks not only to the time expended in conducting the activity itself but also to the time expended in preparing for the activity and any time expended after, yet related to, the activity.[229]

---

[221] IRC § 513(d)(3)(B). E.g., Orange County Agric. Soc'y, Inc. v. Comm'r, 893 F.2d 647 (2d Cir. 1990), aff'g 55 T.C.M. 1602 (1988); Ohio County & Independent Agricultural Soc'y Delaware County Fair v. Comm'r, 43 T.C.M. 1126 (1982).

[222] Reg. § 1.513-3(d)(1).

[223] Reg. § 1.513-3(c), Ex. (2). A *supplier's exhibit* is one in which the exhibitor displays goods or services that are supplied to, rather than by, the members of the qualifying organization in the conduct of the members' own trade or business (Reg. § 1.513-3(d)(2)).

[224] Reg. § 1.513-3(e), Ex. (4). The legislative history of these statutory rules suggests, however, that the exclusion is applicable with respect to wholly suppliers' shows (S. Rep. No. 94-938, *supra* note 214, at 601-603).

[225] Rev. Rul. 75-516, *supra* note 218. In general, Fones, "Taxation of Trade Shows and Public Entertainment Activities," 64 *A.B.A.J.* 913 (1978).

[226] See § 26.3.

[227] Suffolk County Patrolmen's Benevolent Ass'n, Inc. v. Comm'r, 77 T.C. 1314 (1982).

[228] *Id.* at 1321, 1322.

[229] See § 26.3(d).

A tax-exempt organization may sponsor and perform educational and supporting services for a trade show (such as use of its name, promotion of attendance, planning of exhibits and demonstrations, and provision of lectures for the exhibits and demonstrations) without having the compensation for its efforts taxed as unrelated income, as long as the trade show is not a sales facility.[230] The IRS ruled that this type of activity both stimulates interest in and demand for services of the profession involved (the organization being an exempt business league) and educates the members on matters of professional interest.

(g) Hospital Services

An exception from unrelated business income taxation is applicable with respect to the performance of certain services for small hospitals. It generally is the position of the IRS that income that a tax-exempt hospital derives from providing services to other exempt hospitals constitutes unrelated business income to the hospital that is the provider of the services, on the theory that the providing of services to other hospitals is not an activity that is substantially related to the exempt purpose of the provider hospital.[231] Congress acted to reverse this rule in the case of small hospitals.

This special rule[232] applies where a tax-exempt hospital[233] provides services only to other exempt hospitals, as long as each of the recipient hospitals has facilities to serve no more than 100 inpatients and the services would be consistent with the recipient hospitals' exempt purposes if performed by them on their own behalf. The services provided must be confined to certain ones.[234]

This law change was implemented to enable a number of small hospitals to receive services from a single institution instead of providing them directly or creating a separate organization to provide the services. Language in the legislative history, however, is somewhat broader than the specifics of the statutory rule, inasmuch as the Senate Finance Committee explanation stated that a "hospital is not engaged in an unrelated trade or business simply because it provides services to other hospitals if those services could have been provided on a tax-free basis, by a cooperative organization consisting of several tax-exempt hospitals."[235]

Another requirement for this exception is that the service must be provided at a fee not in excess of actual cost, including straight-line depreciation and a reasonable rate of return on the capital goods used to provide the service.[236] The Medicare program formulations are a "safe harbor" for use in complying with the limitations on fees. Thus, a rate of return on capital goods will be considered reasonable as long as it does not exceed, on an annual basis, a percentage that is

---

[230] Rev. Rul. 78-240, 1978-1 C.B. 170.
[231] Rev. Rul. 69-633, 1969-2 C.B. 121. See § 26(j).
[232] IRC § 513(e).
[233] IRC § 170(b)(1)(A)(iii). See §§ 6.2(a), 11.3(a).
[234] IRC § 501(e)(1)(A). See § 10.4.
[235] S. Rep. No. 94-938 (Part 2), 94th Cong., 2d Sess. 76 (1976).
[236] IRC § 513(e)(3).

based on the average of the rates of interest on special issues of public debt obligations issued to the Federal Hospital Insurance Trust Fund for each of the months included in the tax year of the hospital during which the capital goods are used in providing the service. Determinations as to the cost of services and the applicable rate of return are to be made as prescribed in the Medicare rules,[237] which permit a health care facility to be reimbursed under the Medicare program for the reasonable cost of its services, including, in the case of certain proprietary facilities, a reasonable return on equity capital.[238]

(h) Bingo and Other Games of Chance

Bingo game income realized by most tax-exempt organizations is not subject to unrelated business income taxation.[239] This exclusion applies where the bingo game[240] is not conducted on a commercial basis and where the games do not violate state or local laws.[241] It is the view of the IRS that this exception applies only to gambling activities in which all wagers are placed, all winners are determined, and all prizes are distributed in the presence of the players of the game, so that the conduct of a "pull-tab operation" is not embraced by the exception.[242] This view was reflected in a court opinion holding that proceeds attributable to an organization's "instant bingo" activities were not protected by the exception because individuals could play and win in isolation.[243] By virtue of the way the organizations are taxed, the bingo game exception is not applicable to social clubs, voluntary employees' beneficiary associations, political organizations, and homeowners' associations.[244]

The term *unrelated trade or business* does not include any trade or business which consists of the conduct of games of chance, conducted after June 30, 1981, which, under state law (in effect as of October 5, 1983), can be conducted only by nonprofit organizations.[245] This exception, however, is applicable only with respect to North Dakota law.[246]

---

[237] 42 USC § 1395x(v)(1)(A), (B).

[238] Reg. § 1.513-6(a)(3).

[239] IRC § 513(f).

[240] IRC § 513(f)(2)(A).

[241] H. Rep. No. 95-1608, 95th Cong., 2d Sess. (1978). E.g., Waco Lodge No. 166, Benevolent & Protective Order of Elks v. Comm'r, *supra* note 185 (where this exception was held unavailable because the bingo game was illegal under state law as being a "lottery").

[242] Tech. Adv. Mem. 8602001.

[243] Julius M. Israel Lodge of B'nai B'rith No. 2113 v. Comm'r, 70 T.C.M. 673 (1995), *aff'd*, 98 F.3d 190 (5th Cir. 1996). Also Variety Club Tent No. 6 Charities, Inc. v. Comm'r, 74 T.C.M. 1485 (1997).

[244] See Chapter 14, § 16.3, Chapter 17, and § 18.13, respectively. Cf. Clarence LaBelle Post No. 217 v. United States, 580 F.2d 270 (8th Cir. 1978); Smith-Dodd Businessman's Ass'n, Inc. v. Comm'r, 65 T.C. 620 (1975).

[245] Tax Reform Act of 1984 § 311.

[246] Tax Reform Act of 1986 § 1834. This clarification in 1986 would have caused retroactive taxation of this type of revenue derived by tax-exempt organizations in states other than North Dakota. The Technical Corrections and Miscellaneous Revenue Act of 1988 (§ 6201), however, made the 1986 clarification effective for games of chance conducted after October 22, 1986 (the date of enactment of the 1986 technical correction), so that revenue derived by exempt organizations from games of chance conducted prior to the 1986 effective date in any state is governed by rules enacted in 1984. The IRS issued an explanation of the law on this point (Ann. 89-138, 1989-45 I.R.B. 41).

(i) Pole Rental Activities

In the case of a mutual or cooperative telephone or electric company,[247] the term *unrelated trade or business* does not include engaging in qualified pole rentals.[248]

(j) Low-Cost Articles

Another exception from unrelated business income taxation is available only to tax-exempt organizations eligible to receive tax-deductible charitable contributions,[249] for activities relating to certain distributions of *low-cost articles* incidental to the solicitation of charitable contributions.[250] While this statutory provision is generally reflective of a similar rule stated in the income tax regulations,[251] there is one important refinement, which is that the term *low-cost article* is defined as any article (or aggregate of articles distributed to a single distributee in a year) that has a cost not in excess of $5 (adjusted for inflation[252]) to the organization that distributes the item or on behalf of which the item is distributed.[253] These rules also require that the distribution of the items be unsolicited and be accompanied by a statement that the distributee may retain the low-cost article irrespective of whether a charitable contribution is made.[254]

(k) Mailing Lists

Another exception from unrelated business income taxation available to the category of tax-exempt organizations eligible for the low-cost articles exception[255] is applicable to the exchanging or renting of membership or donor mailing lists with or to other of these exempt organizations.[256]

---

[247] See § 18.5.

[248] IRC § 513(g). For the definition of *qualified pole rentals*, see § 18.5.

[249] That is, an organization described in IRC § 501, where it qualifies as a charitable donee under IRC § 170(c)(2) or § 170(c)(3) (namely, as a charitable or veterans' organization).

[250] IRC § 513(h)(1)(A).

[251] Reg. § 1.513-1(b).

[252] IRC § 513(h)(2)(C). The IRS calculated that the low-cost-article cost threshold was $5.71 for years beginning in 1991 and $6.01 for years beginning in 1992 (Rev. Proc. 92-58, 1992-2 C.B. 410), was $6.20 for years beginning in 1993 (Rev. Proc. 92-102, 1992-2 C.B. 579), was $6.40 for years beginning in 1994 (Rev. Proc. 93-49, 1993-2 C.B. 581), was 6.60 for years beginning in 1995 (Rev. Proc. 94-72, 1994-2 C.B. 811), was $6.70 for years beginning in 1996 (Rev. Proc. 95-53, 1995-2 C.B. 445), was $6.90 for years beginning in 1997 (Rev. Proc. 96-59, 1996-2 C.B. 390); was $7.10 for years beginning in 1998 (Rev. Proc. 97-57, 1997-2 C.B. 584); was $7.20 for years beginning in 1999 (Rev. Proc. 98-61, 1998-2 C.B. 811); was $7.40 for years beginning in 2000 (Rev. Proc. 99-42, 1999-2 C.B. 568); was $7.60 for years beginning in 2001 (Rev. Proc. 2001-13, 2001-1 C.B. 337), was $7.90 for years beginning in 2002 (Rev. Proc. 2001-59, 2001-52 I.R.B. 623), and is $8.00 for years beginning in 2003 (Rev. Proc. 2002-70, 2002-46 I.R.B. 845).

[253] IRC § 513(h)(2).

[254] IRC § 513(h)(3).

[255] See *supra* § 2(j).

[256] IRC § 513(h)(1)(B). The purpose of this provision is to "overrule" the decision in Disabled Am. Veterans v. United States, *supra* note 40. Also Disabled Am. Veterans v. Comm'r, 68 T.C. 95 (1994).

Absent this exception, however, the rental or exchange of a mailing list by a tax-exempt organization, when regularly carried on, is considered by the IRS to be a taxable unrelated business. This is not a problem from an economic standpoint when the activity involves a list rental,[257] in that taxes can be paid from the resulting net income. When the activity is a list exchange, however, there is no income from the transaction available to pay the tax; it is nonetheless the view of the IRS that these exchanges are unrelated businesses.[258] In calculating the amount of "income" of this nature, the IRS advised that the method to use should be in accordance with the rules concerning facilities used for related and unrelated purposes; thus, expenses and deductions are to be allocated between the two uses on a reasonable basis.[259] According to the IRS, the "actual calculating of the costs and expenses associated with or allocable to the rental or exchange activities and the income they generate is a factual determination."[260]

If properly structured, however, a mailing list rental or exchange program involving a noncharitable tax-exempt organization can avoid unrelated business income taxation by reason of treatment of the income as an excludable royalty.[261]

(l) Certain Associate Member Dues

If a tax-exempt agricultural or horticultural organization[262] requires annual dues not exceeding $100 (indexed for inflation[263]) to be paid in order to be a member of the organization, no portion of the dues may be considered unrelated business income because of any benefits or privileges to which these members are entitled.[264]

---

[257] Rev. Rul. 72-431, 1972-2 C.B. 281.

[258] Tech. Adv. Mem. 9502009.

[259] See § 28.2.

[260] In the technical advice memorandum (*supra* note 258), the IRS ruled that these exchanges are not a disposition of property causing the realization of gain or loss for tax purposes (IRC § 1001), in that capital assets (IRC § 1222) are not involved; this holding precluded application of the exception from income taxation for capital gains (see *supra* § 1(j)). It also held that the nontaxation rules concerning like-kind exchanges (IRC § 1031) are inapplicable, because the title to the lists does not pass and the rights to the properties acquired by the parties are not perpetual (Koch v. Comm'r, 37 T.C.M. 1167 (1978); Rev. Rul. 55-749, 1955-2 C.B. 295). An earlier technical advice memorandum, concluding that exchanges of mailing lists between tax-exempt organizations did not give rise to unrelated business income (8128004), was thereafter prospectively revoked by the IRS (Tech. Adv. Mem. 9635001).

[261] So held in Sierra Club, Inc. v. Comm'r, *supra* note 42. Also American Academy of Ophthalmology, Inc. v. Comm'r (Tax Ct. No. 21657-94) (where the IRS abandoned its mailing list revenue taxation stance in the aftermath of the *Sierra Club* holding). See the discussion in *supra* § 1(g).

[262] See §§ 15.2, 15.3.

[263] IRC § 512(d)(2). For years beginning in 1998, this threshold was $109 (Rev. Proc. 97-57, *supra* note 252); for years beginning in 1999, this threshold was $110 (Rev. Proc. 98-61, *supra* note 252); for years beginning in 2000, this threshold was $112 (Rev. Proc. 99-42, *supra* note 252); for years beginning in 2001, this threshold was $116 (Rev. Proc. 2001-13, *supra* note 252); for years beginning in 2002, this threshold was $120 (Rev. Proc. 2001-59, *supra* note 252); and for years beginning in 2003, this threshold is $122 (Rev. Proc. 2002-70, *supra* note 252).

[264] IRC § 512(d)(1).

The term *dues* is defined as any "payment required to be made in order to be recognized by the organization as a member of the organization."[265] If a person makes a single payment that entitles the person to be recognized as a member of the organization for more than 12 months, the payment can be prorated for purposes of applying the $100 cap.[266]

(m) S Corporations

A tax-exempt organization may be a shareholder in an *S corporation*, which is a corporation that is treated for federal income tax purposes as a partnership.[267] The authorization to own this type of a security is a revision of prior law.[268]

This type of interest is considered as an interest in an unrelated business.[269] Items of income, loss, or deduction of an S corporation flow through to tax-exempt organization shareholders as unrelated business income.[270] Gain or loss on the disposition of stock in an S corporation results in unrelated business income.[271]

(n) Corporate Sponsorship Payments

A payment made by a corporation to sponsor an event or activity of a tax-exempt organization may be a contribution or may be taxable as unrelated business income. This type of payment usually is a transfer of a relatively large amount of money by a for-profit business to a charitable organization. Sponsorship payments received by exempt organizations that are *qualified* are not subject to unrelated business income taxation. That is, the activity of soliciting and receiving these payments is not an unrelated business.[272]

This is a safe-harbor rule. Therefore, a corporate sponsorship payment that is not a qualified one is not necessarily taxable. Rather, the tax treatment of it is evaluated under the unrelated business rules generally. Thus, the transaction would be evaluated as to whether it is a business,[273] whether it is regularly carried on,[274] whether it is subject to an exception for income or activities,[275] and the like.

A *qualified sponsorship payment* is a payment made by a person, engaged in a trade or business, to a tax-exempt organization, with respect to which there is no arrangement or expectation that the person will receive, from the exempt organization, a substantial return benefit.[276] It is irrelevant whether the sponsored activ-

---

[265] IRC § 512(d)(3).
[266] H. Rep. No. 104-737, 104th Cong., 2d Sess. 14 (1996).
[267] IRC §§ 1361-1363.
[268] IRC § 1361(c)(6).
[269] IRC § 512(e)(1)(A).
[270] IRC § 512(e)(1)(B)(i).
[271] IRC § 512(e)(1)(B)(ii). In general, Hoyt, "Subchapter S Stock Owned by Tax-Exempt Organizations: Solutions to Legal Issues," 22 *Exempt Org. L. Rev.* (No. 1) 25 (1998).
[272] IRC § 513(i)(1); Reg. § 1.513-4(a).
[273] See § 26.2.
[274] See § 26.3.
[275] See this chapter, above items.
[276] IRC § 513(i)(2)(A); Reg. § 1.513-4(c)(1).

ity is related or unrelated to the recipient tax-exempt organization's exempt purpose. It is also irrelevant whether the sponsored activity is temporary or permanent. The word *payment* means the payment of money, transfer of property, or performance of services.[277]

A *substantial return benefit* is a benefit, other than certain uses or acknowledgments and other than certain disregarded benefits.[278] Benefits are disregarded if the aggregate fair market value of all the benefits provided to the payor or persons designated by the payor in connection with the payment during the organization's tax year is not more than 2 percent of the amount of the payment.[279] If the aggregate fair market value of the benefits exceeds 2 percent of the amount of the payment, then (unless it is a shielded use or acknowledgment) the entire fair market value of the benefits is a substantial return benefit.[280]

Benefits provided to the payor or a designated person may include advertising; an exclusive provider arrangement; goods, facilities, services, or other privileges; and/or exclusive or nonexclusive rights to use an intangible asset (such as a trademark, patent, logo, or designation) of the exempt organization.[281]

A substantial return benefit does not include the use or acknowledgment of the name, logo, or product lines of the payor's trade or business in connection with the activities of the exempt organization. While a use or acknowledgment does not include advertising, it may include an exclusive sponsorship arrangement; logos and slogans that do not contain qualitative or comparative descriptions of the payor's products, services, facilities, or company; a list of the payor's locations, telephone numbers, or Internet address; value-neutral descriptions, including displays or visual depictions, of the payor's product-line or services; and/or reference to the payor's brand or trade names and product or service listings.[282]

Logos or slogans that are an established part of a payor's identity are not considered to contain qualitative or comparative descriptions. Mere display or distribution, whether for free or remuneration, of a payor's product by the payor or the exempt organization to the general public at the sponsored activity is not considered an inducement to purchase, sell, or use the payor's product and thus will not affect the determination of whether a payment is a qualified sponsorship payment.[283]

The term *advertising* means any message or other programming material which is broadcast or otherwise transmitted, published, displayed, or distributed, and which promotes or markets any trade or business, or any service, facility or product.[284] The term includes messages containing qualitative or comparative language, price information or other indications of savings or value,

---

[277] Reg. § 1.513-4(c)(1).
[278] Reg. § 1.513-4(c)(2)(i).
[279] Reg. § 1.513-4(c)(2)(ii).
[280] *Id.*
[281] Reg. § 1.513-4(c)(2)(iii).
[282] Reg. § 1.513-4(c)(2)(iv).
[283] *Id.*
[284] Reg. § 1.513-4(c)(2)(v).

an endorsement, or an inducement to purchase, sell, or use any company, service, facility, or product.[285] A single message that contains both advertising and an acknowledgment is advertising.[286]

These rules are inapplicable to activities conducted by a payor on its own. For example, if a payor purchases broadcast time from a television station to advertise its product during commercial breaks in a sponsored program, the activities of the tax-exempt organization are not thereby converted to advertising.[287]

An arrangement that acknowledges the payor as the exclusive sponsor of a tax-exempt organization's activity, or the exclusive sponsor representing a particular trade, business, or industry, generally does not, by itself, result in a substantial return benefit.[288] For example, if in exchange for a payment, an exempt organization announces that its event is sponsored exclusively by the payor (and does not provide any advertising or other substantial return benefit to the payor), the payor has not received a substantial return benefit. An arrangement that limits the sale, distribution, availability, or use of competing products, services, or facilities in connection with an exempt organization's activity generally results in a substantial return benefit.[289] For example, if, in exchange for a payment, an exempt organization agrees to allow only the payor's products to be sold in connection with an activity, the payor has received a substantial return benefit.[290]

To the extent that a portion of a payment would (if made as a separate payment) be a qualified sponsorship payment, that portion of the payment and the other portion of the payment are treated as separate payments.[291] Thus, if there is an arrangement or expectation that the payor will receive a substantial return benefit with respect to any payment, then only the portion, if any, of the payment that exceeds the fair market value of the substantial return benefit is a qualified sponsorship payment.[292] If the exempt organization, however, does not establish that the payment exceeds the fair market value of a substantial return benefit, then no portion of the payment constitutes a qualified sponsorship payment.[293]

Again, the unrelated business treatment of a payment, or portion of a payment, that is not a qualified sponsorship payment is determined by application of the general rules. For example, payments related to the provision of facilities, services, or other privileges by a tax-exempt organization to a payor, or designated person; advertising; exclusive provider arrangements; a license to use intangible assets of an exempt organization; or other substantial return benefits, are evalu-

---

[285] IRC § 513(i)(2)(A).

[286] *Id.*

[287] *Id.*

[288] Reg. § 1.513-4(c)(2)(vi)(A).

[289] Reg. § 1.513-4(c)(2)(vi)(B).

[290] In general, Irvine, "Does Exclusivity Create Liability for UBIT?," 14 *J. Tax. of Exempt Orgs.* (No. 1) 19 (July/Aug. 2002).

[291] IRC § 513(i)(3).

[292] Reg. § 1.513-4(d)(1).

[293] *Id.*

ated separately in determining whether the exempt organization realizes unrelated business income.[294]

The *fair market value* of a substantial return benefit provided as part of a sponsorship arrangement is the price at which the benefit would be provided between a willing recipient and a willing provider of the benefit, neither being under any compulsion to enter into the arrangement and both having reasonable knowledge of relevant facts, and without regard to any other aspect of the sponsorship arrangement.[295]

In general, the fair market value of a substantial return benefit is determined when the benefit is provided. If the parties enter into a binding, written sponsorship contract, however, the fair market value of any substantial return benefit provided pursuant to that contract is determined on the date the parties enter into the sponsorship contract. If the parties make a material change to a sponsorship contract, it is treated as a new sponsorship contract as of the date the material change is effective. A *material change* includes an extension or renewal of the contract, or a more-than-incidental change to any amount payable (or other consideration) pursuant to the contract.[296]

To the extent necessary to prevent avoidance of the rules concerning determination of substantial return benefits and allocation of payments, where a tax-exempt organization fails to make a reasonable and good faith valuation of a substantial return benefit, the IRS may determine the portion of a payment allocable to the substantial return benefit and/or may treat two or more related payment as a single payment.[297]

The existence of a written sponsorship agreement does not, in itself, cause a payment to fail to be a qualified sponsorship payment. The terms of the agreement, not its existence or degree of detail, are relevant to the determination of whether a payment is a qualified sponsorship payment. Similarly, the terms of the agreement and not the title or responsibilities of the individuals negotiating the agreement determine whether a payment, or a portion of a payment, made pursuant to the agreement is a qualified sponsorship payment.[298]

The term *qualified sponsorship payment* does not include any payment, the amount of which is contingent, by contract or otherwise, on the level of attendance at one or more events, broadcast ratings, or other factors indicating the degree of public exposure to the sponsored activity. The fact that a payment is contingent on sponsored events or activities actually being conducted does not, by itself, cause the payment to fail to be a qualified sponsorship payment.[299]

Qualified sponsorship payments in the form of money or property—but not services—are contributions received by the tax-exempt organization involved. For organizations that are required to or need to compute public support,[300] these

[294] Reg. § 1.513-4(d)(1)(i).
[295] Reg. § 1.513-4(d)(1)(ii).
[296] Reg. § 1.513-4(d)(1)(iii).
[297] Reg. § 1.513-4(d)(2).
[298] Reg. § 1.513-4(e)(1).
[299] IRC § 513(i)(2)(B)(i); Reg. § 1.513-4(e)(2).
[300] See § 11.3(b).

payments are contributions for that purpose.[301] The fact that a payment to an exempt organization constitutes a qualified sponsorship payment, that is treated as a contribution to the payee organization, does not determine whether the payment is deductible by the payor.[302] The payment may be deductible as a charitable contribution[303] or as a business expense.[304]

The tax regulations address the matter of the import of Web site links by means of two examples. The essence of these examples is that the mere existence of a link, from the sponsored tax-exempt organization to the corporate sponsor, does not cause a payment to fail to be a qualified sponsorship payment but material on the linked site can cause the payment to entail a substantial return benefit.[305]

This safe harbor rule does not apply to payments made in connection with qualified convention and trade show activities.[306] It also does not apply to income derived from the sale of an acknowledgement or advertising in the periodical of a tax-exempt organization.[307] The term *periodical* means regularly scheduled and printed material published by or on behalf of an exempt organization that is not related to and primarily distributed in connection with a specific event conducted by the exempt organization.[308] There are separate rules governing the sale of advertising in exempt organization periodicals.[309] For purposes of the corporate sponsorship rules, at least, the phrase printed material includes material that is published electronically.[310]

[301] Reg. § 1.513-4(e)(3).
[302] *Id.*
[303] IRC § 170. See § 2.5.
[304] IRC § 162.
[305] Reg. § 1.513-4(d)(f), Examples 11 and 12.
[306] IRC § 513(i)(2)(B)(ii)(II); Reg. § 1.513-4(b). See *supra* § (f).
[307] IRC § 513(i)(2)(B)(ii)(I); Reg. § 1.513-4(b).
[308] *Id.*
[309] See § 26.5(f).
[310] Reg. § 1.513-4(b). A history of the law leading to these rules is in Hopkins, *The Law of Fundraising, Third Edition* (John Wiley & Sons, Inc. 2002) § 5.16; Woods, "Tax Treatment of Corporate Sponsorship Payments to Exempt Organizations: Final Regulations," 38 *Exempt Org. Tax Rev.* (No. 2) 205 (Nov. 2002); Henderson; "The Tax Treatment of Corporate Sponsorship Payments and the Aftermath of the Cotton Bowl Ruling," 13 *Exempt Org. Tax Rev.* (No. 5) 789 (May 1996).

CHAPTER TWENTY-EIGHT

Unrelated Income Taxation and Feeder Organizations

Even though an organization achieves exemption from the federal income tax,[1] it nonetheless remains potentially taxable on any unrelated business income.[2]

§ 28.1 TAX STRUCTURE

The unrelated income rates payable by most tax-exempt organizations are the corporate rates.[3] Some organizations, such as trusts, are subject to the individual income rates.[4]

The tax law features the following three-bracket structure for corporations:

Taxable Income	Rate (percent)
$50,000 or less	15
$50,000–$75,000	25
Over $75,000	34

An additional 5 percent surtax is imposed on taxable income between $100,000 and $335,000, causing a marginal tax rate of 39 percent on taxable income in that range.[5] This tax structure is inapplicable to the taxation of insurance companies,[6] which is the tax law paradigm that is used to tax organizations that cannot qualify as charitable organizations or social welfare organizations because a sub-

---

[1] IRC § 501(a).

[2] IRC § 501(b).

[3] IRC § 11. See IRC § 12(1).

[4] IRC § 1(E). A court discussed the applicability of the corporate and trust rates in this context, in holding that a tax-exempt voluntary employees' beneficiary association is taxable at the trust, not the corporate, rates (The Sherwin-Williams Co. Employee Health Plan Trust v. United States, 2002-2 U.S.T.C. ¶ 50,721 (N. D. Ohio)).

[5] IRC § 11(b).

[6] IRC § 11(c)(2). See IRC § 801 *et seq.* (IRC Subchapter L).

stantial part of their activities consists of the provision of commercial-type insurance.[7]

Tax-exempt organizations must make quarterly estimated payments of the tax on unrelated business income, under the same rules that require quarterly estimated payments of corporate income taxes.[8] Revenue and expenses associated with unrelated business activity are reported to the IRS on a tax return (Form 990-T).[9]

§ 28.2 DEDUCTION RULES

Generally, the term *unrelated business taxable income* means the gross income derived by a tax-exempt organization from an unrelated trade or business, regularly carried on by the organization, less business deductions that are directly connected with the carrying on of the trade or business.[10] For purposes of computing unrelated business taxable income, both gross income and business deductions are computed with certain modifications.[11]

Generally, to be *directly connected with* the conduct of an unrelated business, an item of deduction must have a proximate and primary relationship to the carrying on of that business. In the case of a tax-exempt organization that derives gross income from the regular conduct of two or more unrelated business activities, unrelated business taxable income is the aggregate of gross income from all unrelated business activities, less the aggregate of the deductions allowed with respect to all unrelated business activities.[12] Expenses, depreciation, and similar items attributable solely to the conduct of unrelated business are proximately and primarily related to that business and therefore qualify for deduction to the extent that they meet the requirements of relevant provisions of the federal income tax law.[13] A loss incurred in the conduct of an unrelated activity may be offset against the net gain occasioned by the conduct of another unrelated activity only where the loss activity is conducted with a profit objective.[14]

[7] IRC § 501(m)(2)(B). See § 22.1.
[8] IRC §§ 6655(a)–(d). A tax-exempt organization is generally subject to an addition to tax for any underpayment of estimated tax on its unrelated business income (IRC § 6655(a), (g)(3)). A tax-exempt organization does not have an underpayment of estimated tax if it makes four timely estimated tax payments that total at least 100 percent of the tax liability shown on its return for the current taxable year (IRC § 6655(d)(1)(B)). A tax-exempt organization may determine its estimated unrelated income tax payments (filed by means of Form 990-W) under one of three annualized income installment methods: a standard option, option 1, and option 2; Form 8842 must be annually filed to elect option 2.
[9] IRC § 6012(a)(2), 6012(a)(4). See § 24.3(a)(v).
[10] IRC § 512(a)(1).
[11] See § 27.1. A tax-exempt organization is not entitled to an expense deduction for funds transferred from one internal account to another (Women of the Motion Picture Industry v. Comm'r, 74 T.C.M. 1217 (1997)).
[12] Reg. § 1.512(a)-1(a).
[13] E.g., IRC §§ 162, 167. Reg. § 1.512(a)-1(b).
[14] E.g., West Va. State Med. Ass'n v. Comm'r, 91 T.C. 651 (1988), *aff'd*, 882 F.2d 123 (4th Cir. 1989), *cert. den.*, 493 U.S. 1044 (1990). See § 26.2(a).

§ 28.2 DEDUCTION RULES

Where facilities and/or personnel are used both to carry on tax-exempt activities and to conduct unrelated trade or business, the expenses, depreciation, and similar items attributable to the facilities and/or personnel, such as overhead or items of salary, must be allocated between the two uses on a reasonable basis.[15] Despite the statutory rule that an expense must be directly connected with an unrelated business, the regulations merely state that the portion of the expense allocated to the unrelated business activity is, where the allocation is on a reasonable basis, proximately and primarily related to the business activity.[16] Once an item is proximately and primarily related to a business undertaking, it is allowable as a deduction in computing unrelated business income in the manner and to the extent permitted by federal income tax law generally.[17]

Both the U.S. Tax Court and the U.S. Court of Appeals for the Second Circuit found the regulations to be in conformity with the statutory requirements, in a case concerning the proper allocation of fixed expenses of the operation of a fieldhouse by a university where the facility was used for both tax-exempt and unrelated purposes.[18] Therefore, the critical question in this context is whether a particular method of allocation is *reasonable*. The university contended that fixed expenses should be allocated on the basis of relative times of actual use, so that the portion of the deductible expenses is determined by means of a ratio, the numerator of the fraction of which is the total number of hours the facility is used for unrelated purposes and the denominator of which is the total number of hours the fieldhouse is used for both related and unrelated activities. By contrast, the IRS argued that the allocation should be on the basis of total time available for use, so that the denominator of the fraction is the total number of hours in the tax year. The two courts found for the university.

The essential argument of the IRS was that the allocation is not reasonable because the outcome is a deductible expense that is not directly connected with the unrelated activity. The appellate court reasoned, however, that it was merely following the government's own regulations. A dissent took the position that the regulation must be read in conjunction with the statute, so that the *directly connected with* language is a requirement that is in addition to those expressly contained in the regulations.[19]

Gross income may be derived from an unrelated trade or business that exploits a tax-exempt function. Generally, in these situations, expenses, depreciation, and similar items attributable to the conduct of the tax-exempt function are not deductible in computing unrelated business taxable income. Since the items are incident to a function of the type that is the chief purpose of the organization to conduct, they do not possess a proximate and primary relationship to the unre-

---

[15] Reg. § 1.512(a)-1(c). In Disabled American Veterans v. United States, 704 F.2d 1570 (Fed. Cir. 1983), *aff'g and rem'g* 82-2 U.S.T.C. ¶ 9440 (Cl. Ct. 1982), the U.S. Court of Appeals for the Federal Circuit approved an allocation of expenses proposed by the Claims Court whereby the veterans' organization is to allocate its fundraising expenses between the taxable and tax-exempt portions of its solicitation program.

[16] Reg. § 1.512(a)-1(c).

[17] *Id.*

[18] Rensselaer Polytechnic Inst. v. Comm'r, 732 F.2d 1058 (2d Cir 1984), *aff'g* 79 T.C. 967 (1982).

[19] *Id.*, 732 F.2d 1058 at 1063–1066.

lated trade or business. Therefore, they do not qualify as being directly connected with that business.[20]

A tax-exempt organization will be denied business expense deductions in computing its unrelated business taxable income if it cannot adequately substantiate that the expenses were incurred or that they were directly connected with the unrelated activity. In one instance, an organization derived unrelated business income from the sale of advertising space in two magazines, and incurred expenses in connection with solicitation of the advertising and publication of the magazines. A court basically upheld the position of the IRS, which disallowed all of the claimed deductions (other than those for certain printing expenses) because the organization failed to establish the existence or relevance of the expenses.[21] The court found that the organization did not maintain adequate books and records, failed to accurately allocate expenses among accounts, and had insufficient accounting practices. During pretrial discovery, the organization failed to provide the requisite documentation. This led to a court order to produce the material, the response to which was labeled by the court as "evasive and incomplete."[22] Consequently, the court imposed sanctions, which essentially prevented the organization from introducing at trial any documentary evidence embraced by the government's request in discovery. The court rejected the organization's effort to prove its expenses at trial by testimony and to use its accountant's audit as evidence of the facts stated in the report. Thus, most of the claimed expenses were not allowed. Those that the court allowed over the government's objection were ascertained by the court on the basis of an approximation by the court.[23]

§ 28.3 SPECIAL RULES

Federal tax law provides a definition of *unrelated business taxable income* specifically applicable to foreign organizations that are subject to the tax on unrelated income.[24] Basically, foreign organizations are taxed on their unrelated business taxable income that is *effectively connected* with the conduct of a trade or business within the United States and on unrelated income derived from sources within the United States even though not so effectively connected.

In the case of certain veterans' organizations,[25] the term *unrelated business taxable income* does not include any amount attributable to payments for life, sick, accident, or health insurance with respect to members of the organizations or

---

[20] Reg. § 1.512(a)-1(d).
[21] CORE Special Purpose Fund v. Comm'r, 49 T.C.M. 626 (1985).
[22] *Id.*, at 629.
[23] In general, Lyons & Hall, "Allocating and Substantiating Income and Expenses for Tax-Exempt Organizations," 8 *J. Tax. Exempt Orgs.* 107 (Nov./Dec. 1996), Bloom, "Offsetting Expenses Against UBI Can Be an Allocation Headache for Tax-Exempts," 8 *J. Tax. Exempt Orgs.* 33 (July/Aug. 1996); Blazek, "Accentuate the Negative: Maximizing Deductions on Form 990-T," 4 *J. Tax. Exempt Orgs.* (No. 6) 24 (May/June 1993).
[24] IRC § 512(a)(2).
[25] See § 18.10.

their dependents that is set aside for the purpose of providing for the payment of insurance benefits or for a charitable purpose.[26]

Special rules are applicable to social clubs,[27] voluntary employees' beneficiary associations,[28] supplemental unemployment benefit trusts,[29] and group legal services organizations.[30] These rules[31] apply the unrelated business income tax to all of these organizations' net income other than so-called *exempt function income*.[32] For example, a tax-exempt voluntary employees' beneficiary association was required to pay the unrelated business income tax on revenue allocable to temporary excess office space, notwithstanding the court's belief that the space was acquired, in the exercise of sound business judgment, in anticipation of growth of the organization.[33]

Exempt function income is of two types: gross income from amounts (such as dues or fees) paid by members of the organization as consideration for the provision of goods, facilities, or services in furtherance of tax-exempt purposes, and income that is set aside for a charitable[34] purpose or (other than in the case of a social club) to provide for the payment of life, sick, accident, or other benefits, subject to certain limitations.[35]

It had been the position of the IRS that a title-holding company[36] must lose its tax-exempt status if it generates any amount of certain types of unrelated business taxable income.[37] The federal tax law was amended in 1993, however, to permit an exempt title-holding company to receive unrelated business taxable income (that would otherwise disqualify the company for tax exemption) in an amount up to 10 percent of its gross income for the tax year, provided that the unrelated business taxable income is incidentally derived from the holding of real property.[38] For example, income generated from fees for parking or from the operation of vending machines located on real property owned by a title-holding

---

[26] IRC § 512(a)(4).

[27] IRC § 501(c)(7) (see Chapter 14).

[28] IRC § 501(c)(9) (see § 16.3).

[29] IRC § 501(c)(17) (see § 16.4).

[30] IRC § 501(c)(20) (see § 16.6).

[31] IRC § 512(a)(3), as amended by Tax Reform Act of 1984 § 511(b).

[32] IRC § 512(a)(3)(B). Interest on obligations of a state (see IRC § 103(a)) received by a tax-exempt social club is not included in gross income for purposes of IRC § 512(a)(3) (Rev. Rul. 76-337, 1976-2 C.B. 177).

[33] Uniformed Servs. Benefit Ass'n v. United States, 727 F. Supp. 533 (W. D. Mo. 1990).

[34] IRC § 170(c)(4).

[35] IRC § 512(a)(3)(E). In a case involving an organization described in IRC § 501(c)(9) (see § 16.3), a court held that, in determining its unrelated business taxable income, the amount of investment income that it set aside to provide for the payment of reasonable costs of administration directly connected with providing for the payment of health care benefits was subject to the limitation prescribed by IRC § 512(a)(3)(E)(i) and that, in making the calculation, the amount of assets that were set aside may not be reduced by the amount of the reserve (as described in IRC § 419A(c)(2)(A)) for postretirement medical benefits (Sherwin-Williams Co. Employee Health Plan Trust v. Comm'r, 115 T.C. 440 (2000)).

[36] See § 18.2.

[37] IRS Notice 88-121, 1988-2 C.B. 457. Also Reg. § 1.501(c)(2)-1(a).

[38] IRC § 501(c)(2), last sentence; IRC § 501(c)(25)(G)(i).

company generally qualifies for the 10 percent *de minimis* rule, but income derived from an activity that is not incidental to the holding of real property (such as manufacturing) does not qualify.[39] Permissible unrelated business income is nonetheless subject to taxation.

Also, a tax-exempt title holding company will not lose its tax exemption if unrelated business taxable income that is incidentally derived from the holding of real property exceeds the 10 percent limitation, where the organization establishes to the satisfaction of the IRS that the receipt of unrelated business taxable income in excess of the 10 percent limitation was "inadvertent and reasonable steps are being taken to correct the circumstances giving rise to such income."[40]

A tax-exempt organization and a single-parent title-holding corporation[41] may file a consolidated annual information return for a tax year. When this is done, and where the title-holding corporation pays any amount of its net income over the year to the exempt organization (or would have paid the amount but for the fact that the expenses of collecting the income exceeded its income), the corporation is treated as if it was organized and operated for the same purpose(s) as the other exempt organization (in addition to its title-holding purpose).[42] The effect of this rule is to exclude from any unrelated income taxation the income received by the exempt parent organization from the title-holding corporation.

§ 28.4 PARTNERSHIP RULES

If a trade or business regularly carried on by a partnership, of which a tax-exempt organization is a member, is an unrelated trade or business with respect to the organization, in computing its unrelated business taxable income the organization must include its share (whether or not distributed and subject to certain modifications[43]) of the gross income of the partnership from the unrelated trade or business and its share of the partnership deductions directly connected with the gross income.[44] This rule (known as a *look-through rule*) applies irrespective of whether the tax-exempt organization is a general or limited partner.[45] The courts reject the thought that income derived by an exempt organization from a limited partnership interest is, for that reason alone, not taxable because a limited partnership interest is a passive investment by which the organization lacks any ability to actively engage in the management, operation, or control of the partnership.[46]

---

[39] H. Rep. No. 103-111, 103d Cong., 1st Sess. 618 (1993).

[40] IRC § 501(c)(2), last sentence; IRC § 501(c)(25)(G)(ii).

[41] See § 18.2(a).

[42] IRC § 511(c).

[43] See § 27.1.

[44] IRC § 512(c)(1), Reg. § 1.512(c)-1. E.g., Priv. Ltr. Rul. 7934008.

[45] Rev. Rul. 79-222, 1979-2 C.B. 236; Service Bolt & Nut Co. Profit Sharing Trust et al. v. Comm'r, 78 T.C. 812 (1982).

[46] Service Bolt & Nut Co. Profit Sharing Trust v. Comm'r, 724 F.2d 519 (6th Cir. 1983), *aff'g* 78 T.C. 812 (1982).

An illustration of this rule was provided when the IRS ruled that income from utility services, to be provided in the context of the provision of telecommunications services, will be rental income to exempt organizations that is excluded from unrelated business income taxation;[47] this income will flow to the exempt organizations from partnerships and limited liability companies.[48]

The look-through rule also applies when a partnership, of which a tax-exempt organization is a member, engages in activities that are related to the exempt purposes of the exempt organization. In this situation, any income generated by the related business is not subject to taxation as unrelated business income.[49]

§ 28.5 SMALL BUSINESS CORPORATION RULES

Tax-exempt charitable organizations[50] are allowed to be shareholders in small business corporations (also known as *S corporations*[51]).[52] Items of income or loss of a small business corporation flow through to these organizations as unrelated business income, irrespective of the source or nature of the income.[53] Thus, for example, unlike the partnership rules,[54] passive income of a small business corporation flows to an exempt charitable organization as unrelated business income.

If a charitable organization has acquired by purchase stock in a small business corporation (whether the stock was acquired when the corporation was a regular corporation—also known as a *C corporation*[55]—or an S corporation) and receives a dividend distribution with respect to the stock, the shareholder generally must reduce its basis in the stock by the amount of the dividend.[56]

---

[47] See § 27.1(h).
[48] Priv. Ltr. Rul. 200147058.
[49] E.g., Priv. Ltr. Rul. 9839039. Oddly, in finding income to be from a related business, the IRS applied the look-through rule to income derived by a tax-exempt organization from a partnership—but the exempt organization was not a member of the partnership (Tech. Adv. Mem. 9847002).

In general, Kennedy, "Guidelines for Avoiding the Unrelated Business Income Tax on Exempt Organizations," 12 *Tax Law.* (No. 1) 56 (1983); Van Wert, "Retail Sales by Exempt Organizations: When Will They Be Subject to the UBT?", 56 *J. Tax.* 104 (Feb. 1982); Myers & Myers, Jr., "How Art-Oriented Exempt Organizations Can Skirt the Unrelated Business Income Tax," 49 *J. Tax.* 150 (Sept. 1978); Warren, "Taxable Income of Qualified Trusts," 61 *A.B.A.J.* 981 (1975); Webster, "Unrelated Business Income," 23 *Tax Law.* 471 (1970); Note, "Unrelated Business Income of Tax Exempt Organizations," 19 *De Paul L. Rev.* 525 (1970); Note, "The Macaroni Monopoly: The Developing Concept of Unrelated Business Income of Exempt Organizations," 81 *Harv. L. Rev.* 1280 (1968); Comment, "Preventing the Operation of Untaxed Business by Tax-Exempt Organizations," 32 *U. Chi. L. Rev.* 581 (1965).
[50] That is, organizations that are tax-exempt pursuant to IRC § 501(a) because of description in IRC § 501(c)(3).
[51] That term is derived from the fact that the tax treatment of these corporations is the subject of IRC Subtitle A, Chapter 1, subchapter S (§§ 1361–1363).
[52] See § 27.2(m).
[53] IRC § 512(C)(1)(B)(1).
[54] See *supra* § 4.
[55] That term is derived from the fact that the tax treatment of these corporations is the subject of IRC Subtitle A, Chapter 1, subchapter C (§§ 301–385).
[56] IRC § 512(e)(2).

Any gain that may be received on the disposition of stock in an S corporation also is automatically treated as unrelated business income.[57]

§ 28.6 FEEDER ORGANIZATIONS

Federal tax law provides that an "organization operated for the primary purpose of carrying on a trade or business for profit shall not be exempt from taxation under [IRC] section 501 on the ground that all of its profits are payable to one or more organizations exempt from taxation under section 501."[58] This type of nonexempt entity is a *feeder organization*, inasmuch as it is a business operation that "feeds" monies to one or more tax-exempt organizations. In determining the primary purpose of an organization, all pertinent circumstances are considered, including the size and extent of the trade or business and the size and extent of the activities of the exempt organization.[59] If an organization carries on a trade or business but not as a primary function, the organization may be exempt, although the income from the trade or business may be taxed as unrelated business taxable income.[60]

The feeder organization rules were added to the federal tax law in 1950, as a legislative overturning of the court-derived *destination-of-income test*. Pursuant to this test, as articulated by the U.S. Supreme Court in 1924,[61] the destination of an organization's income was considered to be of greater consequence than the source and use of the income (the emphasis now as the result of enactment of the feeder organization rules) for purposes of determining exemption from taxation. That is, under this test, where a for-profit organization contributed all of its net income for charitable purposes, the organization itself was considered a charity. The principal problem with this standard, however, was that tax-exempt business operations were able to competitively undercut for-profit organizations that were not related to or otherwise supporting tax-exempt organizations.

---

[57] IRC § 512(e)(1)(B)(ii).

[58] IRC § 502(a).

[59] Reg. § 1.502-1(a).

[60] Reg. § 1.502-1(c). See Chapters 26–27.

[61] Trinidad v. Sagrada Orden de Predicadores de la Provincia del Santisimo Rosario de Filipinas, 263 U.S. 578 (1924). Cases involving application of the destination-of-income test, for the benefit of the organizations involved, are Roche's Beach, Inc. v. Comm'r, 96 F.2d 776 (2d Cir. 1938); Bohemian Gymnastic Ass'n Sokol of City of New York v. Higgins, 147 F.2d 774 (2d Cir. 1945); Debs Memorial Radio Fund, Inc. v. Comm'r, 148 F.2d 948 (2d Cir. 1945); Comm'r v. Orton, 173 F.2d 483 (6th Cir. 1949); Consumer-Farmer Milk Coop. v. Comm'r, 186 F.2d 68, 70 (2d Cir. 1950), *cert. den.*, 341 U.S. 931 (1951); Willingham v. Home Oil Mill, 181 F.2d 9 (5th Cir. 1950); Scofield v. Rio Farms, Inc., 205 F.2d 68 (5th Cir. 1953); Lichter Found. v. Welch, 247 F.2d 431 (6th Cir. 1957). Cases where the government prevailed, the test notwithstanding, are Universal Oil Prods. Co. v. Campbell, 181 F.2d 451 (7th Cir. 1950), *cert den.*, 340 U.S. 850 (1950); United States v. Community Servs., 189 F.2d 421 (1951), *cert. den.*, 342 U.S. 932 (1952); Ralph H. Eaton Found. v. Comm'r, 219 F.2d 527 (9th Cir. 1955); John Danz Charitable Trust v. Comm'r, 231 F.2d 673 (9th Cir. 1955), *cert. den.*, 352 U.S. 828 (1956); Riker v. Comm'r, 244 F.2d 220 (9th Cir. 1957).

A summary of the law prior to enactment of the destination-of-income test and the transition into the feeder organization rules is provided in Lichter Found. v. Welch, *supra* at 434–437.

The House Committee on Ways and Means report accompanying the Revenue Act of 1950 stated that the feeder organization provision was intended to

> prevent the exemption of a trade or business organization under . . . [the predecessor to IRC § 501(c)(3)] on the grounds that an organization actually described in . . . [that section] receives the earnings from the operations of the trade or business organization. In any case it appears clear to your committee that such an organization is not itself carrying out an exempt purpose. Moreover, it obviously is in direct competition with other taxable business.[62]

The impact of the feeder organization rules may be vividly seen in the case of the SICO Foundation, which was a nonstock corporation that owned controlling interests in several corporations engaged in the business of selling and distributing petroleum products.[63] Its net income was distributed to teachers' colleges for scholarship purposes. The SICO Foundation was in court in 1952 seeking tax-exempt status for tax years prior to 1951. Following the destination of income test, the court found the organization to be educational in nature and hence exempt.[64] But, when its tax status for years 1951, 1952, and 1953 was litigated, the court held that enactment of the feeder organization rules in 1950[65] caused the organization to lose its exempt status. Concluded the court: "That it gave all its profits to an educational institution availeth it nothing [except perhaps a charitable contribution deduction] in the mundane field of taxation, however much the children in our schools have profited from its beneficence."[66]

One vestige of the destination of income test remains, however. Under the rules defining the meaning of the term *gross income*,[67] the value of services is not includible in gross income when the services are rendered directly and gratuitously to a charitable organization.[68] Thus, a parimutuel race track corporation was able to distribute charity day race proceeds to a charitable organization, which agreed to absorb any losses arising from the event and to assume all responsibility for the promotion, and not include any of the proceeds in its gross income for federal income tax purposes.[69] Where, by contrast, the race track corporation was the promoter of the charity day racing event, rather than the agent of the charity, the proceeds from the event were taxable to the corporation.[70]

---

[62] H. Rep. No. 2319, 81st Cong., 2d Sess. 41 (1950). Also S. Rep. No. 2375, 81st Cong., 2d Sess. 35 (1950).

[63] SICO Found. v. United States, 295 F.2d 924 (Ct. Cl. 1961), *reh'g den.*, 297 F.2d 557 (Ct. Cl. 1962).

[64] The SICO Co. v. United States, 102 F. Supp. 197 (Ct. Cl. 1952).

[65] 26 U.S.C. § 101.

[66] SICO Found. v. United States, *supra* note 63, at 925.

[67] IRC § 61(a).

[68] Reg. § 1.61-2(c).

[69] Rev. Rul. 77-121, 1977-1 C.B. 17.

[70] Rev. Rul. 72-542, 1972-2 C.B. 37. In this instance, however, the corporation receives a business expense deduction under IRC § 162 or a charitable contribution deduction under IRC § 170 for the proceeds turned over to charity (Rev. Rul. 77-124, 1977-1 C.B. 39; Rev. Rul. 72-542 *supra*).

The distinctions at play in the feeder organization context are frequently difficult to initially discern. For example, the IRS accorded tax-exempt status to a nonprofit corporation controlled by a church, where the organization's function was to print and sell educational and religious material to the church's parochial system at a profit, with the profits returned to the system.[71] But, an organization formed by a church to operate a commercial printing business (which generated a substantial profit) and to print religious materials for the church at cost (about 10 percent of its activities), where all net income was paid over to the church, was ruled a feeder organization and thus not exempt.[72] The distinguishing feature was the fact that an overwhelming percentage of the organization's activities in the latter instance were the provision of commercial services to other than the related tax-exempt organization.

The government's position is that where a subsidiary organization of a tax-exempt parent would itself be exempt, because its activities are an integral part of the activities of the parent, the tax-exempt status of the subsidiary will not be lost because the subsidiary derived a profit from its dealings with the parent.[73] For example, the income tax regulations contain an illustration of a subsidiary organization operated for the sole purpose of furnishing electric power used by the parent organization (an exempt educational institution) in carrying on its tax-exempt activities, the subsidiary is itself a charitable entity.[74] Likewise, a graduate school providing a variety of services to a group of affiliated colleges was ruled not to be a feeder organization, inasmuch as it was controlled and supervised by the colleges and the services were regarded as an integral part of the activities of the colleges.[75] Where a subsidiary of an exempt parent is operated for the primary purpose of carrying on a trade or business that would be an unrelated trade or business if regularly carried on by the parent, the subsidiary would not be exempt.[76] The regulations contain the example of a subsidiary of an exempt parent that is not exempt because it is operated primarily for the purpose of furnishing electric power to consumers other than the parent.

The income tax regulations accompanying the feeder organizations law contain an observation that has no basis in statutory law and that has nothing to do with that rule. This is the comment that "if the subsidiary organization is owned by several [that is, more than one] unrelated exempt organizations, and is operated for the purpose of furnishing electric power to each of them, it is not exempt since such business would be an unrelated trade or business if regularly carried on by any one of the tax-exempt organizations."[77] On this point, the regulations have it backwards, for the feeder organization rules do not even apply

---

[71] Rev. Rul. 68-26, 1968-1 C.B. 272. Also Pulpit Resource v. Comm'r, 70 T. C. 594 (1978).

[72] Rev. Rul. 73-164, 1973-1 C.B. 223.

[73] Reg. § 1.502-1(b). A technical parent-subsidiary relationship need not be present (Rev. Rul. 68-26, *supra* note 71); the revenue flowing to the exempt organization is disregarded for tax purposes, because the "profits" are essentially regarded as a matter of accounting among the organizations.

[74] *Id.*

[75] Priv. Ltr. Rul. 9849027.

[76] Reg. § 1.502-1(b).

[77] *Id.*

until there is an organization "operated for the primary purpose of carrying on a trade or business for profit." Thus, the Senate Finance Committee report accompanying the Senate version of the measure that became the Revenue Act of 1950 stated that the provision "applies to organizations operated for the primary purpose of carrying on a trade or business for profit, as for example, a feeder corporation whose business is the manufacture of automobiles for the ultimate profit of an educational institution."[78] These rules do not purport to define this type of organization and nothing in its history indicates that it was intended to denominate as a feeder an organization controlled by and serving only tax-exempt organizations. As discussed,[79] this statement is one of the rationales of the IRS for denying exempt status to consortia and other organizations performing joint activities for exempt organizations,[80] even though this rationale was rejected in the first cases where it was considered.[81] In one of these cases, the court first questioned the relationship of this regulation to the statute: "Charitably put (no pun intended), the Court has difficulty in finding any basis in the statute . . . [concerning feeder organizations] for . . . [this] portion of the regulations."[82] Second, the court dismissed the applicability of these rules in the context of "shared services" organizations consortia: "What does this [the feeder organization rule] have to do with two or more such [tax-exempt] organizations setting up a not-for-profit corporation, wholly controlled by them, and not serving the public, in order to effect economies in their own charitable operations? The Court in . . . [a prior case] gave no effect to the regulation, nor does this Court."[83]

As the government progressed to success in defeating tax exemption for cooperative hospital laundry organizations,[84] it abandoned its argument against consortia based on this interpretation of the feeder rules. The argument was rejected by the federal district court involved,[85] jettisoned by the government on appeal,[86] and thus not considered by the U.S. Supreme Court.[87] The U.S. Tax Court, however, accepted this argument.[88]

With the emphasis on determination of unrelated business taxable income, rather than deprivation of tax-exempt status, the IRS has retreated somewhat as concerns vigorous assertion of the feeder organization rules.[89] Also, the

---

[78] S. Rep. No. 2375, *supra* note 62, at 116.
[79] See § 6.8.
[80] Rev. Rul. 69-528, 1969-2 C.B. 127.
[81] Hospital Bur. of Standards & Supplies v. United States, 158 F. Supp. 560, 563 (Ct. Cl. 1958); United Hosp. Serv., Inc. v. United States, 384 F. Supp. 776 (S.D. Ind. 1974).
[82] United Hosp. Serv., Inc. v. United States, *supra* note 81, at 782.
[83] *Id.*
[84] See §§ 6.8. 10.4.
[85] HCSC Laundry v. United States, 473 F. Supp. 250 (E.D. Pa. 1979).
[86] HCSC Laundry v. United States, 624 F.2d 428, 432, note 6 (3d Cir. 1980).
[87] HCSC Laundry v. United States, 450 U.S. 1 (1981).
[88] Associated Hosp. Servs., Inc. v. Comm'r, 74 T.C. 213 (1980), *aff'd unrep. dec.* (5th Cir. 1981). In a case involving a cooperative organization outside the health care setting, the IRS advanced, then withdrew, the feeder organization argument (The Council for Bibliographic and Information Technologies v. Comm'r, 63 T.C.M. 3186, 3187–3188 (1992)).
[89] E.g., Rev. Rul. 66-296, 1966-2 C.B. 215; Rev. Rul. 66-295, 1966-2 C.B. 207.

courts have infrequently construed the feeder rules against the affected organizations.[90]

For purposes of these rules,[91] the term *trade or business* does not include (1) the derivation of most types of rents,[92] (2) any trade or business in which substantially all the work in carrying on the trade or business is performed for the organization without compensation,[93] or (3) any trade or business that consists of the selling of merchandise, substantially all of which has been received by the organization as gifts or contributions.[94] For example, a thrift shop may avoid feeder organization status because the work is performed by volunteers[95] or because the merchandise was received as gifts.[96]

---

[90] Cases where IRC § 502 was not applied include Industrial Aid for the Blind v. Comm'r, 73 T.C. 96 (1979); E. Orton, Jr. Ceramic Found. v. Comm'r, 56 T.C. 147 (1971); Duluth Clinic Found. v. United States, 67-1, U.S.T.C. ¶ 9926 (D. Minn. 1967); Bright Star Found. v. Campbell, 191 F. Supp. 845 (N.D. Tex 1960). The feeder organization rule was applied in, e.g., Veterans Found. v. United States, 281 F.2d 912 (10th Cir. 1960); Disabled Veterans Serv. Found., Inc. v. Comm'r, 29 T.C.M. 202 (1970).

[91] IRC § 502(b).

[92] See § 27.1(h).

[93] See § 27.2(a).

[94] See § 27.2(c).

[95] Rev. Rul. 80-106, 1980-1 C.B. 113.

[96] Rev. Rul. 71-581, 1971-2 C.B. 236.

CHAPTER TWENTY-NINE

Unrelated Debt-Financed Income and Tax-Exempt Entity Leasing Rules

The unrelated debt-financed income rules cause certain forms of income received by tax-exempt organizations, which would otherwise be exempt from taxation, to be subject to the unrelated business income tax. The tax-exempt entity leasing rules require certain persons who engage in certain leasing transactions involving exempt organizations to compute their depreciation deduction over a longer recovery period than might otherwise be the case.

§ 29.1 OVERVIEW OF DEBT-FINANCED INCOME RULES

Prior to the enactment of the Tax Reform Act of 1969, most charitable organizations and certain other tax-exempt organizations were subject to the unrelated business income tax on rental income from real property to the extent the property was acquired with borrowed funds. There was an important exception, however, that excluded rental income from a lease of five years or less and, further, the tax was not applicable to all exempt organizations. Moreover, there was a question as to whether the tax applied to income from the leasing, by an exempt organization, of assets constituting a going business.

In the years immediately preceding enactment of the 1969 Act, some tax-exempt organizations were using their tax privileges to purchase businesses and investments on credit, frequently at what was more than the market price, while contributing little or nothing themselves to the transaction other than their tax exemption. A typical factual situation in this regard was as follows:

> A sells an incorporated business to B, a charitable foundation, which makes a small (or no) down payment and agrees to pay the balance of the purchase price only out of profits to be derived from the property. B liquidates the corporation and then leases the business assets to C, a new corporation formed to operate the business. A (collectively, the stockholders of the original business) manages the business for C and frequently holds a substantial minority interest in C. C pays 80 percent of its business profits as "rent" to B, who then passes on 90 percent of those receipts to A until the original purchase price is paid in full. B has no obligation to pay A out of any funds other than the "rent" paid by C.[1]

The tax results of this type of transaction provided capital gain to the seller, a rent deduction for the operator, and no tax on the tax-exempt organization.

In this manner, a business was able to realize increased after-tax income and a tax-exempt organization was able to acquire the ownership of a business valued at $1.3 million without the investment of its own funds.[2] Immediately prior to the Tax Reform Act of 1969, a court upheld the acquisition of 24 businesses by a charitable organization in this manner in the period 1945 to 1954.[3]

The response of Congress to the problems in this area was enactment of revamped unrelated debt-financed income rules. In 1969, Congress acted to impose a tax on the investment income of tax-exempt institutions that is traceable in one way or another to borrowed funds. This was done by the addition to the Internal Revenue Code of rules that impose a tax on *unrelated debt-financed income*.[4]

In computing a tax-exempt organization's unrelated business taxable income, there must be included with respect to each debt-financed property that is unrelated to the organization's exempt function—as an item of gross income derived from an unrelated trade or business—an amount of income from the property, subject to tax in the proportion in which the property is financed by the debt.[5] Basically, deductions are allowed with respect to each debt-financed property in the same proportion.[6] The allowable deductions are those that are directly connected with the debt-financed property or its income, although any depreciation may only be computed on the straight-line method.[7] For example, if a commercial business property is acquired by an exempt organization subject to an 80 percent mortgage, 80 percent of the income and 80 percent of the deductions are taken into account for these tax purposes. As the mortgage is paid, the percentage taken into account usually diminishes. Capital gains on the sale of unrelated debt-financed property are also taxed in the same proportions.[8]

---

[1] H. Rep. 91-413 (Part 1), 91st Cong., 1st Sess. 45 (1969).

[2] Comm'r v. Brown, 380 U.S. 563 (1965).

[3] University Hill Found. v. Comm'r, 51 T.C. 548 (1969), *rev'd*, 446 F.2d 701 (10th Cir. 1971), *cert. den.*, 405 U.S. 965 (1972). Also Anderson Dairy, Inc. v. Comm'r, 39 T.C. 1027 (1963); Shiffman v. Comm'r, 32 T.C. 1073 (1959); Ohio Furnace Co., Inc. v. Comm'r, 25 T.C. 179 (1955).

[4] An example of an interpretation of pre-1969 IRC § 514 appears in Rev. Rul. 70-132, 1970-1 C.B. 138.

[5] IRC §§ 514(a)(1), 512(b)(4).

[6] IRC § 514(a)(2).

[7] IRC § 514(a)(3).

[8] Reg. § 1.514(a)-1.

§ 29.2 DEBT-FINANCED PROPERTY

The term *debt-financed property* means, with certain exceptions, all property (for example, rental real estate, tangible personalty, and corporate stock) that is held to produce income (for example, rents, royalties, interest, and dividends) and with respect to which there is an acquisition indebtedness[9] at any time during the tax year (or during the preceding 12 months, if the property is disposed of during the year).[10]

Excepted from the term debt-financed property is (1) property where substantially all (at least 85 percent) of its use is substantially related (aside from the need of the tax-exempt organization for income or funds) to the exercise or performance by the organization of its exempt purpose or, if less than substantially all of its use is related, to the extent that its use is related to the organization's exempt purpose,[11] (2) property to the extent that its income is already subject to tax as income from the conduct of an unrelated trade or business,[12] (3) property to the extent that the income is derived from research activities and therefore excluded from unrelated business taxable income,[13] and (4) property to the extent that its use is in a trade or business exempted from tax because substantially all the work is performed without compensation, the business is carried on primarily for the convenience of members, students, patients, officers, or employees, or the business is the selling of merchandise, substantially all of which was received as gifts or contributions.[14] For purposes of the first of these types of properties, substantially all of the use of property is considered substantially related to the exercise or performance of an organization's tax-exempt purpose if the property is real property subject to a lease to a medical clinic, where the lease is entered into primarily for purposes that are substantially related to the lessor's exempt purposes.[15] For purposes of the first, third, and fourth property types, the use of any property by a tax-exempt organization that is related to an organization is treated as use by the related organization.[16]

An illustration of a situation where property that is debt-financed did not yield unrelated debt-financed income, because the use of the property was substantially related to a tax-exempt use, was provided by the case of an exempt organization, created to encourage business development in a particular area, that constructed a building to lease, at below-market rates, to an industrial tenant for the purpose of attracting new industry to the area. Once the lease was

---

[9] See *infra* § 3.

[10] IRC § 514(b)(1).

[11] IRC § 514(b)(1)(A). Unrelated debt-financed income is triggered to the extent that the financing occurred in connection with the acquisition of property used for an exempt purpose but the loan proceeds were instead invested (Southwest Tex. Elec. Coop., Inc. v. Comm'r, 95-2 U.S.T.C. ¶ 50,565 (5th Cir. 1995), *aff'g* 68 T.C.M. 285 (1994)).

[12] IRC § 514(b)(1)(B). This rule does not apply in the case of income excluded under IRC § 512(b)(5) (principally, capital gain). See § 27.1(j).

[13] IRC § 514(b)(1)(C). See § 27.1(l).

[14] IRC § 514(b)(1)(D). See § 27.2(c).

[15] IRC § 514(b), last sentence.

[16] IRC § 514(b)(2).

executed, the organization completed the building (which was initially financed by the business community) to suit the needs of the tenant; the completion of the building was financed by subjecting the property to a mortgage. Because the leasing of the building under these circumstances was an activity designed to attract industry to the community, the IRS concluded that the activity contributed importantly to the organization's exempt purpose and hence did not constitute debt-financed property subject to these tax rules.[17] Another example of this rule was provided in the case of an exempt medical foundation that rented mortgaged property to a medical clinic that had a close working relationship with the foundation; the leased property was held to be related to the foundation's exempt purpose of providing medical training, so that the rental income was determined to be nontaxable.[18]

Also, for purposes of the first of these categories of property, the principles established under the general unrelated income rules[19] are applicable in determining whether there is a substantial relationship between the property and the tax-exempt purposes of the organization.[20] These principles were adversely applied to an exempt organization that was operated for educational purposes essentially in the same manner as a museum in that it promoted the appreciation of history and architecture by acquiring, restoring, and preserving buildings of historical and/or architectural significance and opened the restored buildings to the general public for a nominal admission fee. The organization acquired certain historically or architecturally significant buildings by assumption of outstanding mortgages and leased them at a fair rental value, subject to a covenant to ensure that the historical architecture of the buildings was maintained by the lessees, for uses that neither bear any relationship to the buildings' historical or architectural significance nor accommodate viewing by the general public. Because this leasing did not contribute importantly to the accomplishment of the organization's educational purpose and had no causal relationship to the achievement of that purpose, the IRS found that substantially all the use of the buildings was not substantially related to the organization's exempt purposes and thus that the leased buildings constituted debt-financed property.[21]

Property owned by a tax-exempt organization and used by a related exempt organization or by an exempt organization related to the related exempt organization is not treated as debt-financed property to the extent the property is used by either organization in furtherance of its tax-exempt purpose.[22] Two exempt organizations are related to each other if more than 50 percent of the members of one organization are members of the other organization.[23] In one instance, the IRS held that a charitable organization may acquire a building, use

---

[17] Rev. Rul. 81-138, 1981-1 C.B. 358, *amp'g* Rev. Rul. 70-81, 1970-1 C.B. 131. Cf. Rev. Rul. 58-547, 1958-2 C.B. 275.

[18] Gundersen Med. Found., Ltd. v. United States, 536 F. Supp. 556 (W.D. Wis. 1982). Also Rev. Rul. 69-464, 1969-1 C.B. 132.

[19] IRC § 513. See Chapter 26.

[20] Reg. § 1.514(b)-1(b)(1). See § 26.4.

[21] Rev. Rul. 77-47, 1977-1 C.B. 157.

[22] Reg. § 1.514(b)-1(c)(2)(i).

[23] Reg. § 1.514(b)-1(c)(2)(ii)(c).

a portion of it, and lease the other portion to a related charitable organization and a related business league for their offices and activities and that the building will not be treated as debt-financed property.[24] The organization acquiring the building had as its membership all of the active members of the business league who had contributed to it, and the membership of the other charitable organization consisted of those active members of the business league who were elected to and served on the governing body of the business league; the members of one of the charitable organizations would not necessarily be members of the other.

The *neighborhood land rule* provides an exemption from the debt-financed property rules for interim income from neighborhood real property acquired for a tax-exempt purpose. The tax on unrelated debt-financed income does not apply to income from real property, located in the neighborhood of other property owned by the tax-exempt organization, which it plans to devote to exempt uses within 10 years of the time of acquisition.[25] This rule applies after the first five years of the 10-year period only if the exempt organization satisfies the IRS that future use of the acquired land in furtherance of its exempt purposes before the expiration of the period is reasonably certain;[26] this process is to be initiated by filing a ruling request at least 90 days before the end of the fifth year.[27] A more generous 15-year rule is established for churches; it is not required that the property be in the neighborhood of the church.[28]

If debt-financed property is sold or otherwise disposed of, a percentage of the total gain or loss derived from the disposition is included in the computation of unrelated business taxable income.[29] The IRS recognizes, however, that the unrelated debt-financed income rules do not render taxable a transaction that would not be taxable by virtue of a nonrecognition provision of the federal tax law if it were carried out by an entity that is not tax-exempt.[30] The occasion was a transfer, subject to an existing mortgage, of an apartment complex, which had appreciated in value, by an exempt hospital to its wholly owned taxable subsidiary in exchange for additional stock in the subsidiary. Because of the operation of federal tax rules that provide for the nonrecognition of gain or loss in certain circumstances,[31] including those involving this hospital, the transaction did not result in a taxable gain for the hospital.

---

[24] Priv. Let. Rul. 7833055. The IRS cautioned that the charitable organization should charge the business league a fair market value rent, for if it did not it would be conferring a financial benefit upon a non–IRC § 501(c)(3) organization, which might adversely affect its tax-exempt status.

[25] IRC § 514(b)(3)(A)-(C). Where a tax-exempt organization did not own the original site property in the neighborhood, since the property was owned by a supporting organization (see § 11.3(c)) with respect to the organization, the IRS concluded that the neighborhood land rule nonetheless applied because of the supported organization's "interrelated nature" with the property by means of the supporting organization (Priv. Ltr. Rul. 9603019).

[26] IRC § 514(b)(3)(A).

[27] Reg. § 1.514(b)-1(d)(1)(iii). Where an exempt organization failed to seek this ruling, because the IRS was satisfied with the plans the organization submitted for the future use of the property, it granted administrative relief (Reg. § 301.9100-1(a)) by extending the filing period (Priv. Ltr. Rul. 9603019).

[28] IRC § 514(b)(3)(E). In general, Reg. § 1.514(b)-1.

[29] Reg. § 1.514(a)-1(a)(1)(v).

[30] Rev. Rul. 77-71, 1977-1 C.B. 156.

[31] IRC §§ 351, 357.

§ 29.3   ACQUISITION INDEBTEDNESS

Income-producing property is considered to be unrelated debt-financed property (making income from it, less deductions, taxable) only where there is an acquisition indebtedness attributable to it. *Acquisition indebtedness*, with respect to debt-financed property, means the unpaid amount of the indebtedness incurred by the tax-exempt organization in acquiring or improving the property, the indebtedness incurred before any acquisition or improvement of the property if the indebtedness would not have been incurred but for the acquisition or improvement, and the indebtedness incurred after the acquisition or improvement of the property if the indebtedness would not have been incurred but for the acquisition or improvement and the incurring of the indebtedness was reasonably foreseeable at the time of the acquisition or improvement.[32]

If property is acquired by a tax-exempt organization subject to a mortgage or other similar lien, the indebtedness thereby secured is considered an acquisition indebtedness incurred by the organization when the property is acquired, even though the organization did not assume or agree to pay the indebtedness.[33] Some relief is provided, however, with respect to mortgaged property acquired as a result of a bequest or devise. That is, the indebtedness secured by this type of mortgage is not treated as acquisition indebtedness during the 10-year period following the date of acquisition. A similar rule applies to mortgaged property received by gift, where the mortgage was placed on the property more than five years before the gift and the property was held by the donor more than five years before the gift.[34]

A tax-exempt charitable organization acquired an undivided interest in income-producing rental property subject to a mortgage; the property was leased for purposes unrelated to the organization's exempt purposes. To liquidate its share of the mortgage, the organization prepaid its proportionate share of the mortgage indebtedness, thereby receiving releases of liability from the mortgagee and the co-owners. The lien securing payment of the mortgage nonetheless extended to the entire rental property and the mortgagee was not to release the lien until the entire principal of the mortgage was paid by the co-owners. The IRS ruled that the organization, by satisfying the full amount of its indebtedness under the mortgage, did not have any acquisition indebtedness.[35]

By contrast, a charitable organization purchased mineral production payments with borrowed funds to obtain income for its grant-making program, receiving from each payment the difference between the aggregate amount payable to the lender of the borrowed funds and the total amount of the production payment, with the difference generally amounting to 1/16 of 1 percent of each payment purchased. The IRS held that the indebtedness incurred to purchase the

---

[32] IRC § 514(c)(1). An interest in a qualified tuition program (see § 18.16) is not regarded as a debt for purposes of these rules (IRC § 529(e)(4)). Trading in commodity futures contracts by a tax-exempt organization does not give rise to acquisition indebtedness (Gen. Couns. Mem. 39620).

[33] IRC § 514(c)(2)(A).

[34] IRC § 514(c)(2)(B).

[35] Rev. Rul. 76-95, 1976-1 C.B. 172.

production payment was an acquisition indebtedness and that, accordingly, the payments were debt-financed property.[36]

The regulations accompanying the statutory unrelated debt-financed income rules provide, in effect, a special rule for debts for the payment of taxes, stating that "in the case where State law provides that a tax lien attaches to property prior to the time when such lien becomes due and payable, such lien shall not be treated as similar to a mortgage until after it has become due and payable and the organization has had an opportunity to pay such lien in accordance with State law."[37] Prior to enactment of the Tax Reform Act of 1976, however, the IRS took the position that a lien arising from a special assessment imposed by a state or local government on land for the purpose of making improvements on the land, with the improvements financed by the sale of bonds secured by the lien, constituted acquisition indebtedness, even though (like the property tax lien) the installment payments were due in future periods. In 1976, Congress took action to reverse this position so that, as respects tax years that began after December 31, 1969, where state law provides that a lien for taxes or for assessments made by the state or a political subdivision of the state attaches to property prior to the time when the taxes or assessments become due and payable, the indebtedness does not become acquisition indebtedness (that is, the lien is not regarded as similar to a mortgage[38]) until and to the extent that the taxes or assessments become due and payable and the organization has had an opportunity to pay the taxes or assessments in accordance with state law.[39] The Senate Finance Committee noted that "it is not intended that this provision apply to special assessments for improvements which are not of a type normally made by a State or local governmental unit or instrumentality in circumstances in which the use of the special assessment is essentially a device for financing improvements of the sort that normally would be financed privately rather than through a government."[40]

Other exemptions from the scope of acquisition indebtedness are as follows:

1. The term does not include indebtedness that was necessarily incurred in the performance or exercise of an organization's tax-exempt purpose or function, such as the indebtedness incurred by an exempt credit union[41] in accepting deposits from its members.[42] It has been held, however, that the purchase of securities on margin and with borrowed funds is not inherent in (meaning essential to) the performance or exercise of a credit union's exempt purposes or function, so that a portion of the resulting income is taxable as debt-financed income.[43]

2. The term does not include an obligation to pay an annuity that (a) is the sole consideration issued in exchange for property if, at the time of the

---

[36] Rev. Rul. 76-354, 1976-2 C.B. 179.

[37] Reg. § 1.514(c)-1(b)(2).

[38] IRC § 514(c)(2)(A).

[39] IRC § 514(c)(2)(C).

[40] S. Rep. No. 94-938 (Part 2), 94th Cong., 2d Sess. 86 (1976).

[41] See § 18.7.

[42] IRC § 514(c)(4).

[43] Alabama Central Credit Union v. United States, 646 F. Supp. 1199 (N.D. Ala. 1986).

exchange, the value of the annuity is less than 90 percent of the value of the property received in the exchange; (b) is payable over the life of one individual who is living at the time the annuity is issued, or over the lives of two individuals living at that time; and (c) is payable under a contract that does not guarantee a minimum amount of payments or specify a maximum amount of payments and does not provide for any adjustment of the amount of the annuity payments by reference to the income received from the transferred property or any other property.[44]

3. The term does not include an obligation to finance the purchase, rehabilitation, or construction of housing for low and moderate income persons to the extent that it is insured by the Federal Housing Administration.[45]

4. The term does not include a tax-exempt organization's obligation to return collateral security pursuant to a securities lending arrangement, thereby making it clear that, in ordinary circumstances, payments on securities loans are not debt-financed income.[46]

The IRS ruled that a tax-exempt employees' trust (which was, in general, subject to tax on unrelated business taxable income[47]), which was a partner in a partnership that was organized to make investments in securities, could experience unrelated debt-financed income.[48] The partnership borrowed money to invest in securities and became primarily liable for repayment of the debt and for payment of interest on the debt, with the partners secondarily liable on a pro rata basis. The IRS held that the indebtedness was an acquisition indebtedness because it was incurred to acquire property for investment purposes, the incurring of the debt was not inherent in the performance of the trust's exempt function (namely, to receive employer and employee contributions and to use them and increments on them to provide retirement benefits to the plan participants[49]), and the investment property was not substantially related to the exercise of the trust's exempt purposes. Thus, whether the trust's investment activity can result in unrelated business taxable income under these rules is determined by whether its share of any partnership income was derived from or on account of debt-financed property.[50] Subsequently, a court held that the income from securities purchased on margin by a qualified profit sharing plan was unrelated debt-financed income, in that this type of indebtedness was not inherent in the exercise of the trust's exempt function.[51] Similarly, another court concluded that, when an exempt organi-

---

[44] IRC § 514(c)(5).
[45] IRC § 514(c)(6). In general, Reg. § 1.514(c)-1.
[46] IRC § 514(c)(8). See § 27.1(d).
[47] Rev. Rul. 71-311, 1971-2 C.B. 184.
[48] Rev. Rul. 74-197, 1974-1 C.B. 143.
[49] Reg. § 1.401-1(a)(2)(i).
[50] Reg. § 1.702-1(a).
[51] Elliot Knitwear Profit Sharing Plan v. Comm'r, 71 T.C. 765 (1979), aff'd, 614 F.2d 347 (3d Cir. 1980). Also Ocean Cove Corp. Retirement Plan & Trust v. United States, 657 F. Supp. 776 (S.D. Fla. 1987); Alabama Central Credit Union v. United States, *supra* note 43.

zation withdrew the accumulated cash values in life insurance policies and reinvested the proceeds in income-paying investments, it created an acquisition indebtedness and thus unrelated debt-financed income, even though the organization did not have an obligation to repay the funds.[52] Likewise, a court held that the interest earned on certificates of deposit obtained by an exempt organization was taxable as debt-financed income because the certificates were acquired using the proceeds of a loan that was collateralized with other certificates of deposit previously purchased by the organization.[53]

By contrast, the IRS examined similar practices engaged in by a trust forming part of a leveraged employee stock ownership plan (ESOP).[54] (An ESOP is a technique of corporate finance designed to build beneficial equity ownership of shares in an employer corporation into its employees substantially in proportion to their relative income without requiring any cash outlay on their part, any reduction in pay or other employee benefits, or the surrender of any rights on the part of the employees.[55]) This type of trust generally acquires stock of the employer with the proceeds of a loan made to it by a financial institution. Consequently, the IRS concluded that a leveraged ESOP's capital growth and stock ownership objectives were part of its tax-exempt function[56] and "borrowing to purchase employer securities is an integral part of accomplishing these objectives."[57] Thus, the borrowing was not acquisition indebtedness and the securities thereby purchased were not debt-financed property. But the IRS cautioned that these circumstances are "distinguishable from a situation in which a pension or profit sharing plan that satisfies the requirements of [IRC] section 401(a) borrows money to purchase securities of the employer; in the latter situation the exempt trusts borrowing to purchase employer securities could result in unrelated business income within the meaning of [IRC] section 512."[58]

For these purposes, the term *acquisition indebtedness* generally does not include indebtedness incurred by a qualified organization in acquiring or improving any real property.[59] A *qualified organization* is an operating educational institution,[60] any affiliated support organization,[61] and a tax-exempt multiparent

---

[52] Mose & Garrison Siskin Memorial Found., Inc. v. United States, 603 F. Supp. 91 (E.D. Tenn. 1985), *aff'd*, 790 F.2d 480 (6th Cir. 1986).

[53] Kern County Elec. Pension Fund v. Comm'r, 96 T.C. 845 (1991), *aff'd in unpub opinion* (9th Cir. 1993).

[54] IRC § 4975(e)(7).

[55] S. Rep. No. 94-938, 94th Cong., 2d Sess. (1976).

[56] IRC § 401(a).

[57] Rev. Rul. 79-122, 1979-1 C.B. 204, 206.

[58] *Id.* Cf. Rev. Rul. 79-349, 1979-2 C.B. 233.

[59] IRC § 514(c)(9)(A).

[60] That is, one described in IRC § 170(b)(1)(A)(ii). See § 11.3(a).

[61] That is, one described in IRC § 509(a)(3). See § 11.3(c). When a supporting organization affiliated with an operating educational institution is the sole member of a limited liability company (SMLLC) (see §§ 4.1, 30.7), and the SMLLC receives real property encumbered by debt, it and the supporting organization will be afforded these exemptions for purposes of determining debt-financed income (Priv. Ltr. Rul. 200134025).

title-holding organization,[62] as well as any trust that constitutes a pension trust.[63] Nonetheless, in computing the unrelated income of a shareholder or beneficiary of a disqualified holder (namely, a multiparent title-holding organization[64]) of an interest in a multiparent title-holding entity attributable to the interest, the holder's pro rata share of the items of income that are treated as gross income derived from an unrelated business (without regard to the exception for debt-financed property) is taken into account as gross income of the disqualified holder derived from an unrelated business; the holder's pro rata share of deductions are likewise taken into account.[65]

Thus, under this exception, income from investments in real property is not treated as income from debt-financed property and therefore as unrelated business income. Mortgages are not considered real property for purposes of this exception.[66]

This exception for real property in the debt-financed income rules is available for investments only if the following six restrictions are satisfied:

1. Where the purchase price for an acquisition or improvement of real property is a fixed amount determined as of the date of the acquisition or completion of the improvement (the *fixed price restriction*);[67]

2. Where the amount of the indebtedness, any amount payable with respect to the indebtedness, or the time for making any payment of that amount, is not dependent (in whole or in part) on revenues, income, or profits derived from the property (the *participating loan restriction*);[68]

3. Where the property is not, at any time after the acquisition, leased by the qualified organization to the seller or to a person related[69] to the seller (the *leaseback restriction*);[70]

4. In the case of a pension trust, where the seller or lessee of the property is not a disqualified person[71] (the *disqualified person restriction*);[72]

5. Where the seller or a person related to the seller (or a person related to the plan with respect to which a pension trust was formed) is not provid-

---

[62] That is, one described in IRC § 501(c)(25). See § 18.2(b).

[63] That is, one described in IRC § 401. The definition of *qualified organization* is the subject of IRC § 514(c)(9)(C).

[64] IRC § 514(c)(9)(F)(iii). An entity that is this type of shareholder or beneficiary, however, is not a disqualified holder if it otherwise constitutes a qualified organization by reason of being an educational institution, a supporting organization of an educational institution, or a pension trust (*id.*).

[65] IRC § 514(c)(9)(F)(i), (ii). The purpose of this rule is to prevent the benefits of this exception from flowing through the title-holding company to its shareholders or beneficiaries (unless those organizations themselves are qualified organizations (see *supra* note 63).

[66] IRC § 514(c)(9)(B), last sentence.

[67] IRC § 514(c)(9)(B)(i).

[68] IRC § 514(c)(9)(B)(ii).

[69] As described in IRC § 267(b) or 707(b).

[70] IRC § 514(c)(9)(B)(iii).

[71] As described in IRC § 4975(e)(2)(C), (E), (H).

[72] IRC § 514(c)(9)(B)(iv).

ing financing in connection with the acquisition of the property (the *seller-financing restriction*);[73]

6. If the investment in the property is held through a partnership, where certain additional requirements are satisfied by the partnership, namely, (a) the partnership satisfies the rules in the foregoing five circumstances, and (b)(i) all of the partners are qualified organizations,[74] (ii) each allocation to a partner of the partnership is a qualified allocation,[75] or (iii) the partnership meets the rules of a special exception (the *partnership restrictions*).[76]

Nonetheless, the leaseback restriction and the disqualified person restriction are relaxed to permit a limited leaseback of debt-financed real property to the seller (or a person related to the seller) or to a disqualified person;[77] and the fixed price restriction and the participating loan restriction are relaxed for certain sales of real property foreclosed on by financial institutions.[78]

An example of the flexibility of the potential application of the unrelated debt-financed income rules was the suggestion that this type of income is realized by tax-exempt organizations in the lending of securities transaction.[79] This

---

[73] IRC § 514(C)(9)(B)(v).

[74] For this purpose, an organization cannot be treated as a qualified organization if any income of the organization is unrelated business income (IRC § 514(c)(9)(B), penultimate sentence).

[75] A *qualified allocation* is one described in IRC § 168(h)(6) (see *infra* § 5(g), text accompanied by note 130).

[76] IRC § 514(c)(9)(B)(vi). This special exception is the subject of IRC § 514(c)(9)(E). Rules similar to those of this situation also apply in the case of any pass-thru entity other than a partnership and in the case of tiered partnerships and other entities (IRC § 514(c)(9)(D)).

[77] This exception applies only where (1) no more than 25 percent of the leasable floor space in a building (or complex of buildings) is leased back to the seller (or related party) or to the disqualified person and (2) the lease is on commercially reasonable terms, independent of the sale and other transactions (IRC § 514(c)(9)(G)). A leaseback to a disqualified person remains subject to the prohibited transaction rules (IRC § 4975).

The fixed price restriction and the participating loan restriction are not subject to this refinement. Thus, for example, income from real property acquired with seller financing, where the timing or amount of payment is based on revenue, income, or profits from the property, generally continues to be treated as income from debt-financed property, unless another exception applies.

[78] For this purpose, the term *financial institutions* includes financial institutions in conservatorship or receivership, certain affiliates of financial institutions, and government corporations that succeed to the rights and interests of a receiver or conservator (IRC § 514(c)(9)(H)(iv)).

This exception is limited to instances where (1) a qualified organization obtained real property from a financial institution that acquired the property by foreclosure (or after an actual or imminent default), or the property was held by the selling financial institution when it entered into conservatorship or receivership; (2) any gain recognized by the financial institution with respect to the property is ordinary income; (3) the stated principal amount of the seller financing does not exceed the financial institution's outstanding indebtedness (including accrued but unpaid interest) with respect to the property at the time of foreclosure or default; and (4) the present value of the maximum amount payable pursuant to any participation feature cannot exceed 30 percent of the total purchase price of the property (including contingent payments) (IRC § 514(c)(9)(H)(i)–(iii), (v)).

In general, Ferguson & Brown, "More Investment Options Are Available for Tax-Exempt Organizations," 4 *J. Tax. Exempt Orgs.* (No. 4) 22 (Jan./Feb. 1993); McDowell, "Taxing Leveraged Investments of Charitable Organizations: What Is the Rationale?," 39 *Case W. Res. L. Rev.* (No. 3) 705 (1988–1989).

[79] See § 27.1(d).

conclusion was arrived at by way of the contention that the exempt institution is not actually lending the securities but is "borrowing" the collateral, thereby making—so the argument goes—the entire interest (and perhaps the dividend or interest equivalent) taxable.

This matter was clarified, however, by enactment of a special rule[80] and earlier by an IRS ruling that the income from the investment of the collateral posted by the broker is not unrelated debt-financed income, since the organization did not incur the indebtedness "for the purpose of making additional investments."[81]

The intent of these rules is to treat an otherwise tax-exempt organization in the same manner as an ordinary business enterprise to the extent that the exempt organization purchases property through the use of borrowed funds.[82] The IRS recalled this intent in passing on the tax status of indebtedness owed to an exempt labor union by its wholly owned subsidiary title-holding company resulting from a loan to pay debts incurred to acquire two income-producing office buildings. The IRS ruled that this *interorganizational indebtedness* was not an acquisition indebtedness because the "very nature of the title-holding company as well as the parent-subsidiary relationship show this indebtedness to be merely a matter of accounting between the organizations rather than an indebtedness as contemplated by" these rules.[83]

The income of a tax-exempt organization that is attributable to a short sale of publicly traded stock through a broker is not unrelated debt-financed income and thus is not taxable as unrelated business income.[84] This is because, although a short sale creates an obligation, it does not create an indebtedness for tax purposes[85] and thus there is no acquisition indebtedness. This position of the IRS is not intended to cause any inference with respect to a borrowing of property other than publicly traded stock sold short through a broker. Securities purchased on margin by a tax-exempt organization constitute debt-financed property, which generates unrelated business income.[86]

§ 29.4 COMPUTATION OF UNRELATED DEBT-FINANCED INCOME

The computation of unrelated debt-financed income (the amount subject to tax) is made by applying to the total gross income (and deductions attributable) to debt-financed property the following fraction: the average acquisition indebtedness for the tax year over the average adjusted basis of the property during the tax year.

For purposes of the numerator of this fraction, acquisition indebtedness is to be averaged over the tax year.[87] This averaging mechanism precludes a tax-

---

[80] IRC § 514(c)(8) (see text accompanied by *supra* note 45).
[81] Rev. Rul. 78-88, 1978-1 C.B. 163, 164.
[82] H. Rep. No. 91-413, 91st Cong., 1st Sess. 46 (1969).
[83] Rev. Rul. 77-72, 1977-1 C.B. 157, 158. This rationale was also applied to avoid the prospect of unrelated business income taxation resulting from use of joint operating agreements in the health care context (see § 26.5(j)).
[84] Rev. Rul. 95-8, 1995-1 C.B. 107.
[85] Deputy v. du Pont, 308 U.S. 488 (1940).
[86] E.g., Henry E. & Nancy Horton Bartels Trust for the Benefit of the University of New Haven v. United States, 209 F.3d 147 (2d Cir. 2000).
[87] IRC § 514(c)(7).

exempt organization from avoiding a tax by using other available funds to pay off the indebtedness immediately before any fixed determination date. If debt-financed property is disposed of during the year, *average acquisition indebtedness* means the highest acquisition indebtedness during the preceding 12 months. Absent this rule, a tax-exempt organization could avoid tax by using other resources to discharge indebtedness before the end of one tax year and dispose of property after the beginning of the next tax year.

For purposes of the denominator of this fraction, adjusted basis is the average adjusted basis for the portion of the year during which the property is held by the tax-exempt organization. The use of average adjusted basis is only for purposes of determining the fraction. Where property is disposed of, gain or loss will, as usual, be computed with reference to adjusted basis at the time of disposition.

The essence of the foregoing rules[88] may be illustrated by the following example:

> A tax-exempt organization acquires property for the production of income on July 1, 2003, for $100,000, of which $80,000 is financed (that is, there is an $80,000 acquisition indebtedness). As of December 31, 2003, the organization has satisfied $10,000 of the debt, by one payment (on September 1, 2003) and has claimed $2,500 in straight-line depreciation. For 2003, 75.9 percent of the income (less appropriate deductions) from the property is taxable.
>
> To determine this percentage, the average acquisition indebtedness for 2003 must be computed. This amount is $75,000, ascertained as follows:

(1) Debt	(2) Months Outstanding	(3) (1) × (2)
$80,000	3	$240,000
70,000	3	210,000
	6	$450,000

> (3) divided by (2) equals $75,000, which is the weighted average for the six-month period involved.
>
> To determine the average adjusted basis, it is necessary to compute the basis at the beginning (here, $100,000) and at the end of the tax year ($97,500, that is, original basis less depreciation). The average adjusted basis ($100,000 divided by $97,500 divided by 2) is $98,750.
>
> The applicable percentage thus becomes 75.9 percent ($75,000/$98,750).

If property is distributed by a corporation in liquidation to a tax-exempt organization, the exempt organization uses the basis of the distributing corporation, with adjustment for any gain recognized on the distribution either to the exempt organization or to the taxable corporation. An example of the former would be where an exempt organization had an acquisition indebtedness applicable to its stock in the distributing corporation and an illustration of the latter would be an instance of recapture of depreciation.[89] This rule is designed to pre-

[88] IRC § 514(a)–(c).
[89] IRC §§ 1245, 1250.

vent an exempt organization from acquiring the property in a taxable subsidiary to secure accelerated depreciation during the first several years of the life of the property, enabling the subsidiary to pay off a large part of the indebtedness during those years, after which the exempt organization would obtain a stepped-up basis on liquidation of the subsidiary.[90] If property is used partly for exempt and partly for nonexempt purposes, the income and deductions attributable to the exempt uses are excluded from the computation of unrelated debt-financed income and allocations are made, where appropriate, for acquisition indebtedness, adjusted basis, and deductions assignable to the property.[91]

§ 29.5 TAX-EXEMPT ENTITY LEASING RULES

The federal income tax law contains a body of law concerning certain situations where tax-exempt organizations lease real and/or personal property in practices known as *tax-exempt entity leasing*. These rules have two purposes. One is to impose restrictions on the federal tax benefits of leasing property (including relationships evidenced by service contracts) to exempt organizations. The other is to place restrictions on the federal tax benefits available to investors in partnerships composed of taxable and exempt entities.

These rules are intended to remedy three perceived abuses. One concern was that lessors indirectly made investment tax incentives available to tax-exempt organizations through reduced rents. Another concern was that exempt organizations were being encouraged to enter into sale-leaseback transactions with taxpayers that resulted in substantial revenue losses to the federal government. The third perceived abuse was that partnerships that included exempt and taxable entities could allocate all tax losses to taxable entities, while exempt entities shared in profits and cash distributions.

(a) Introduction

During the early 1980s, Congress became concerned that, in some cases, the tax-exempt status of nonprofit organizations was being abused by techniques designed to shift to taxpaying persons the tax benefits of ownership of property (chiefly, the depreciation deduction[92]) that in actuality was owned by the tax-

---

[90] IRC § 514(d); Reg. § 1.514(d)-1.

[91] IRC § 514(e); Reg. §1.514(e)-1. Also Florida Farm Bur. Fed'n v. Comm'r, 65 T.C. 1118 (1975). In general, Krasity & Indenbaum, "Tax-Exempt Organizations and Section 514: The Taxation of Income Generated by Bond Reserve Funds and Similar Accounts," 19 *J. Real Estate Tax.* (No. 2) 137 (1992); Indenbaum & Krasity, "Tax-Exempt Entities and Limited Partnerships; Section 514(c)(9)(E)'s Inadequate Response to the Problem of Unrelated Debt-Financed Income," 18 *J. Real Estate Tax.* (No. 1) 37 (1990); Weitz, "Unresolved Issues Remain for Qualified Organizations in Real Estate Partnerships," 73 *J. Tax.* 332 (1990); Williamson, Duren & Grigorian, "How Exempt Organizations Can Avoid Unrelated Debt-Financed Income on Realty," 6 *J. Tax. Inv.* (No. 4) 236 (1989); Larson, "Tax Exempt Organizations and Unrelated Debt Financed Income: Does the Problem Persist?," 61 *N. D. L. Rev.* (No. 1) 31 (1985); Beller, "Exempt Organizations: Taxation of Debt-Financed Income," 24 *Tax Law.* 489 (1971).

[92] IRC § 168.

exempt organizations. Generally, of course, the depreciation deduction and other tax benefits of property ownership (such as the former investment tax credit[93]) are not available for property owned by exempt organizations inasmuch as they are not usually taxable, and thus usually do not have a need for deductions and credits. A specific provision disallowed the investment tax credit for property leased to or otherwise used by an exempt organization.[94] Until the federal tax law was revised in 1984, however, a comparable provision was not in the depreciation deduction rules.

A number of transactions involving sales and leasebacks by tax-exempt organizations or governmental units achieved considerable publicity in the months preceding the 1984 tax law revisions.[95] One result of this attention was a congressional report on the subject.[96]

Consequently, even though a tax-exempt organization is not generally permitted to have the benefits of the depreciation deduction that normally accompany the ownership of property, Congress believed that some exempt organizations were indirectly enjoying these tax benefits by leasing property, with the value of the tax deductions available to the lessor reflected in the lease payments. The result was enactment of the tax-exempt entity leasing rules.[97]

In general, the depreciation deduction is determined by utilizing, as phrased in the statute, the applicable depreciation method, the applicable recovery period, and the applicable convention.[98] The applicable recovery periods run from 3 years to 31.5 years, with the 31.5-year period for nonresidential real property.[99]

The law embodies the concept of *alternative depreciation systems*.[100] The alternative depreciation systems utilize the straight line method (without regard to salvage value), the applicable convention, and recovery periods that run from the appropriate class life[101] to 40 years, with the 40-year period for nonresidential real property.[102] The alternative depreciation system is to be used, *inter alia*, with respect to tax-exempt use property.[103]

---

[93] Pre-1986 IRC § 38.

[94] Pre-1986 IRC § 48(a)(4).

[95] For example, Doyle & Hartle, "Tax Avoidance 101," *Wash. Post*, June 2, 1983; "Selling a Bridge," *N. Y. Times*, April 10, 1983; "Financing of Art Center Is Somewhat Convoluted," *Wash. Post*, April 3, 1983; Curran, "Intriguing Twists in Real Estate," *Fortune*, March 21, 1983; Webb, Jr., "Associations Can Use the Tax Benefits of Leasing—At Least for Now," 34 *Ass'n Mgmt.* 141 (Aug. 1982). In general, Henze II & Simpkins, "Should Tax-Exempt Lessees Profit from Tax Benefits?," 8 *Review of Tax. of Indiv.* (No. 3) 240 (Summer 1984); McIlwain, "The Sale and Leasing Back of Real Estate by Tax-Exempt Organizations," 14 *Coll. Law Digest* (No. 6) 154 (1984).

[96] "Tax and Budget Issues Related to Leasing by Non-taxable Entities," Report of Subcommittee on Oversight, House Committee on Ways and Means, U.S. House of Representatives, May 25, 1983.

[97] IRC § 168(h).

[98] IRC § 168(a).

[99] IRC § 168(c).

[100] IRC § 168(g).

[101] IRC § 168(g)(3).

[102] IRC § 168(g)(2).

[103] IRC § 168(g)(1)(B).

(b) Summary of Rules

The essence of the tax-exempt entity leasing rules is to cause investors to compute their depreciation deduction over a longer recovery period where the property is *tax-exempt use property.*

(c) Definition of *Tax-Exempt Entity*

For purposes of these rules, the term *tax-exempt entity* includes any organization that is tax-exempt under the federal income tax law (other than a farmers' cooperative[104]).[105]

(d) Definition of *Related Entity*

For purposes of these rules, one entity is *related* to another entity if the two entities have "significant common purposes and substantial common membership" or "directly or indirectly substantial common direction or control."[106]

An entity is related to another entity if either entity owns (directly or through one or more entities) a 50 percent or greater interest in the capital or profits of the other entity.[107]

An entity is related to another entity with respect to a transaction if the transaction is part of an attempt by the entities to avoid the application of these rules.[108]

(e) Recovery Periods

The tax-exempt entity rules apply with respect to both tangible personal property and real property. Where these rules apply, the depreciation deduction must be determined by using the straight-line method (without regard to salvage

---

[104] See § 18.11.

[105] IRC § 168(h)(2)(A)(ii). Governmental bodies and their instrumentalities are also considered tax-exempt entities (IRC § 168(h)(2)(A)(i), (D)), as are certain foreign organizations (IRC §§ 168(h)(2)(A)(iii), 168(h)(2)(B), 168(h)(2)(C)). Special rules deem certain previously tax-exempt organizations to be tax-exempt entities where they were tax-exempt during the five-year period ending on the date the property involved was first leased to the organization (IRC § 168(h)(2)(E)(i)), with a special election for IRC § 501(c)(12) organizations (IRC § 168(h)(2)(E)(ii)). This rule applies to successor corporations (IRC § 168(h) (2) (E) (iii)). Property is *first used* by an organization when the property is first placed in service under a lease to the organization (IRC § 168(h)(2)(E) (iv) (I)). Also, property is first used by an organization, in the case of property leased to (or held by) a partnership (or other pass-through entity) in which the organization is a member, on the later of when the property is first used by the partnership (or other pass-through entity) or when the organization is first a member of the partnership (or other pass-through entity) (IRC § 168(h) (2) (E) (iv) (II)).

[106] IRC § 168(h)(4)(B).

[107] IRC § 168(h)(4)(C).

[108] IRC § 168(h)(4)(D).

value).[109] The recovery period, however, must always be at least 125 percent of the lease term.[110]

Real property must be depreciated over a 40-year recovery period if it is subject to these rules.[111] Again, the recovery period must always be at least 125 percent of the lease term.[112]

(f) Definition of *Tax-Exempt Use Property*

Tax-exempt use property means that portion of any tangible property (other than nonresidential real property) that is leased[113] to a tax-exempt entity.[114]

In the case of nonresidential real property, the term *tax-exempt use property* means any portion of the property that is leased to a tax-exempt organization by means of a disqualified lease.[115] These rules, however, apply to property only if the portion of the property leased to an exempt entity by means of a disqualified lease is more than 35 percent of the property.[116]

A *disqualified lease* is any lease of a property to a tax-exempt organization, where one or more of the following four features or events are or were present:

1. Part or all of the property was financed (directly or indirectly) by a tax-exempt obligation[117] and the exempt organization (or a related entity) participated in the financing.

2. Under the lease, there is a fixed or determinable price purchase or sale option that involves the entity (or a related entity) or there is the equivalent of a sale option.

3. The lease has a lease term in excess of 20 years.[118]

---

[109] IRC § 168(g)(2)(C)(iii). The recovery period for qualified technological equipment (see *infra* note 113) is generally five years (IRC § 168(h)(3)).

[110] IRC § 168(g)(3)(A). Options to renew are taken into account in determining a lease term and two or more successive leases that are part of the same transaction (or a series of related transactions) with respect to the same or substantially similar property are treated as one lease (IRC § 168(i)(3)(A)).

[111] IRC § 168(g)(2). Earlier, this property would otherwise be depreciable over a 15-year recovery period under pre-1984 rules. The Tax Reform Act of 1984 (§ 111), however, generally converted the recovery period to 18 years, with the recovery period extended to 19 years in 1985 (Pub. L. No. 99-121 § 103) (pre-1986 IRC § 168(j)(2)(F)).

[112] IRC § 168(g)(3)(A). For purposes of the definition of a *lease term* (see *supra* note 110) in the case of real property, an option to renew at fair market value, determined at the time of renewal, is not taken into account (IRC § 168(i)(3)(B)).

[113] The term *lease* includes any grant of a right to use property (IRC § 168(h)(7)) and may include *service contracts* (IRC § 7701(e)).

[114] IRC § 168(h)(1)(A). Property is not considered tax-exempt use property merely by reason of a *short-term lease* (IRC § 168(h)(1)(C)), nor if it is a certain type of *qualified technological equipment* (IRC § 168(h)(3)).

[115] IRC § 168(h)(1)(B)(i).

[116] IRC § 168(h)(1)(B)(iii). For purposes of these rules, improvements to a property (other than land) are not treated as a separate property (IRC § 168(h)(1)(B)(iv)).

[117] That is, an obligation the interest on which is exempt from tax under IRC § 103.

[118] See *supra* notes 110, 112.

4. The lease occurs after a sale (or other transfer) of the property by, or lease of the property from, the tax-exempt entity (or a related entity) and the property has been used by the entity (or a related entity) before the sale (or other transfer) or lease.[119]

The fourth of these items embraces the sale-leaseback feature that triggered the invocation of these rules. It requires that the property be *used* by the tax-exempt organization (or a related entity) prior to the sale or other transfer and any subsequent leasing arrangement. Also, this type of leasing arrangement does not become a disqualified lease where the property is leased within three months after the date the property is first used by the exempt organization (or a related entity).[120]

In the case of any property that is leased to a partnership, the determination as to whether any portion of the property is tax-exempt use property is made by treating each exempt organization partner's share[121] of the property as if it is being leased to the partner.[122] This rule also applies in the case of any pass-through entity other than a partnership and in the case of tiered partnerships and other entities.[123]

The term *tax-exempt use property* does not include any portion of a property if the portion is predominantly used by the tax-exempt entity (directly or through a partnership of which the entity is a partner) in an unrelated business.[124] As respects nonresidential real property, the rule that tax-exempt use property means that portion of the property leased to an exempt entity in a disqualified lease[125] applies only if the portion of the property leased to a tax-exempt entity in a disqualified lease is more than 35 percent of the property.[126] Any portion of a property used in unrelated business is not to be treated as leased to an exempt entity in a disqualified lease.[127]

This is best illustrated by an example. Assume that a tax-exempt entity leases 100 percent of a building for a term of 21 years (a disqualified lease). Eighty percent of the building is used in the tax-exempt organization's unrelated trade or business and 20 percent is used in its tax-exempt function. No portion of the building constitutes tax-exempt use property because the portion used in a disqualified lease (20 percent) is less than 35 percent of the property.[128]

(g) Partnership Arrangements

It is becoming more common for a tax-exempt organization to utilize property owned by a partnership in which the organization is a partner.[129] The tax-exempt

---

[119] IRC § 168(h)(1)(B)(ii).
[120] IRC § 168(h)(1)(B)(v).
[121] IRC § 168(h)(6)(C).
[122] IRC § 168(h)(5)(A).
[123] IRC § 168(h)(5)(B).
[124] IRC § 168(h)(1)(D).
[125] IRC § 168(h)(1)(B)(i).
[126] IRC § 168(h)(1)(B)(iii).
[127] IRC § 168(h)(1)(D), last sentence.
[128] H. Rep. 99-426, 99th Cong., 1st Sess. 878 (1986); S. Rep. 99-313, 99th Cong., 2d Sess. 895 (1986).
[129] See Chapter 32.

entity leasing rules may, however, cause the property in a partnership to be treated as tax-exempt use property.

The rules provide that if any property, which would not otherwise be tax-exempt use property, is owned by a "partnership which has both a tax-exempt entity and a person who is not an exempt entity as partners," and any allocation to the exempt entity of partnership items is not a qualified allocation, an amount equal to the exempt organization's proportionate share of the property is treated as tax-exempt use property.[130]

A *qualified allocation* is any allocation to a tax-exempt organization that (1) is consistent with allocation to the organization of the same distributive share of each item of income, gain, loss, deduction, credit, and basis, and the share remains the same during the entire period the organization is a partner in the partnership, and (2) has substantial economic effect.[131]

A tax-exempt organization's *proportionate share* of property owned by a partnership is determined on the basis of the organization's share of partnership items of income or gain, whichever results in the largest proportionate share.[132] If an exempt organization's share of partnership items of income or gain varies during the period the organization is a partner in a partnership, the proportionate share is the highest share the organization may receive.[133]

These rules also apply in the case of any *pass-through* entity other than a partnership and in the case of tiered partnerships and other entities.[134]

Following the creation of these rules, there were efforts to avoid them by causing a taxable entity controlled by a tax-exempt organization to be a partner in a partnership (where the allocation of partnership items was not a qualified one[135] in lieu of the exempt organization. Congress acted to thwart this technique by causing the taxable subsidiary to be considered an exempt organization for purposes of the tax-exempt entity leasing rules.

This result was occasioned by introduction of the term tax-exempt controlled entity.[136] A *tax-exempt controlled entity* means any corporation (not otherwise an exempt entity) if 50 percent or more (in value) of the stock in the corporation is held by one or more tax-exempt entities.[137] In the case of a corporation the stock of which is publicly traded on an established securities market, stock held by an exempt entity is not taken into account for this purpose unless the entity holds at least 5 percent (in value) of the stock in the corporation.[138] Also,

---

[130] IRC § 168(h)(6)(A).
[131] IRC § 168(h)(6)(B). The concept of *substantial economic effect* is the subject of IRC § 704(b)(2).
[132] IRC § 168(h)(6)(C)(i).
[133] IRC § 168(h)(6)(C)(ii).
[134] IRC § (168)(h)(6)(E).
[135] See *supra* note 131.
[136] IRC § 168(h)(6)(F)(i).
[137] IRC § 168(h)(6)(F)(iii)(I).
[138] IRC § 168(h)(6)(F)(iii)(II).

related entities[139] are treated as one entity[140] and an exempt entity is treated as holding stock that it holds constructively.[141]

A tax-exempt controlled entity can irrevocably elect to not be treated as an exempt entity for these purposes.[142] The consequence of this election is that any gain recognized by an exempt entity on any disposition of an interest in a tax-exempt controlled entity (and any dividend or interest received or accrued by an exempt entity from the tax-exempt controlled entity) is treated as unrelated business taxable income.[143]

[139] See *supra* § (d).
[140] IRC § 168(h)(6)(F)(iii)(II).
[141] IRC § 168(h)(6)(F)(iii)(III). The constructive ownership rules are those of IRC § 318, determined without regard to the 50-percent limitation in IRC § 318(a)(2)(C).
[142] IRC § 168(h)(6)(F)(ii)(I).
[143] IRC § 168(h)(6)(F)(ii)(II). For this purpose, only dividends that are properly allocable to income of the tax-exempt controlled entity that was not taxed are taken into account (IRC § 168(h)(6)(F)(ii)). (The unrelated business income rules are the subject of Part Five; see, particularly, IRC § 512(b)(13), discussed in §§ 27.1(n), 31.3.)

Inter-Organizational Structures and Operational Forms

Combinations of Tax-Exempt Organizations

One of the most striking and significant contemporary practices of tax-exempt organizations is the structuring of activities, which in an earlier era were or would have been in a single exempt entity, so that they are undertaken by two or more related organizations, either exempt or taxable.

    This chapter contains an analysis of combinations of tax-exempt organizations, while the following two chapters discuss the utilization by exempt organizations of other types of entities.

§ 30.1 BIFURCATION BASICS

The reasons for the advent of combinations of tax-exempt organizations are varying and manifold. In the early years, the law mandated most of the structuring, such as the placement of lobbying activities by a charitable organization[1] into a separate organization[2] or the placement of property with a potential for incurring liability into a title-holding corporation.[3] Likewise, as discussed in the next chapter,

---

[1] That is, an organization described in IRC § 501(c)(3) and exempt from federal income taxation under IRC § 501(a).
[2] See § 20.7.
[3] See § 18.2.

the law frequently dictated the placement by an exempt organization of a substantial unrelated business in a for-profit subsidiary.

Cutbacks in government funding and reductions in traditional forms of revenue (such as dues) have caused many tax-exempt organizations to become more innovative and entrepreneurial in the search for operating monies, spawning both exempt and for-profit subsidiaries. More sophisticated management of and advisors to exempt organizations have also led to extensive utilization of one or more separate organizations.

Underlying the concept of interorganizational forms is the precept that a tax-exempt organization may be perceived as a bundle of activities.[4] In this setting, then, the management, legal, and/or other considerations should be regarded as determining whether the activities of an exempt organization are properly housed in one legal entity or whether one or more of the activities of the organization are to be spun off and placed in one or more other legal entities. For example, a charitable organization may consist of a bundle of publication, seminar, research, scholarship, administrative, and lobbying activities; to retain its exempt status, it may, as noted, have to place the legislative activities in a separate organization. As another example, a business association[5] may consist of a bundle of membership service, industry promotion, certification, lobbying, administrative, and research activities; to attract deductible charitable gifts and foundation grants to support its research activities, it generally will have to place the research activities in a separate organization.[6]

The early manifestation of this phenomenon as reflected in federal tax law was simple *bifurcation*: the assignment of activities to two related organizations. Frequently, both of the organizations were tax-exempt, such as, as noted, the use of an exempt title-holding corporation by another exempt organization or the use of an exempt fundraising organization by a government college or university.[7] In some instances, as noted in the next chapter, one of the two related organizations is taxable, such as a for-profit business with a related foundation or an exempt organization with a for-profit subsidiary.

The concept of bifurcation in the tax-exempt organizations context was given a meaningful boost and degree of acceptance by Congress when the supporting organization rules[8] were enacted in 1969. On that occasion, Congress gave recognition to the widespread application of the bifurcation principle in the exempt organizations setting. These rules gave another official sanction to the idea of housing related activities in two (or more) exempt organizations.[9]

As managers of and planners for tax-exempt organizations became more sophisticated, they utilized the bifurcation concept more readily. Thus, it became more common, for example, for the leadership of a trade or business association to establish a related foundation, political action committee, and/or for-profit

[4] This is the principle underlying the *fragmentation rule* (see § 26.2(d)).
[5] See Chapter 13.
[6] See *infra* § 2.
[7] See §§ 17.2, 11.3(b)(v).
[8] See § 11.3(c).
[9] As noted in Chapter 31, Congress earlier recognized the use by a tax-exempt organization of a related for-profit subsidiary but, until recently, that technique was not frequently utilized.

subsidiary. Soon, however, the pattern of using two organizations, where before there might be or was only one, began to be augmented by the use of many organizations. Thus, for example, today the leadership of that association would be likely to more readily implement the utilization of all three related entities, so that the association's activities become allocated among four organizations.

Today, the health care community is leading the way in organizational restructuring. Yesterday's tax-exempt hospital often is today's multiorganizational system, replete with several health care entities, a fundraising foundation, a management company, and an array of other exempt and taxable organizations. These systems may well entail 20, 30, or more organizations, coordinated by an exempt managing entity.[10] Frequently, in a structure that is also being utilized outside the health care setting, there is a *holding company*, or management company, that coordinates the system.

While it is by no means necessary for a tax-exempt organization to spread its activities over tens of exempt and taxable organizations, the basic concepts of restructuring and the potential for use of various operational forms offer great opportunities and flexibility for today's exempt organization in the performance of its exempt functions and in the financing of its operations in the most legally efficacious and efficient manner. As an illustration of these points, an exempt fraternal beneficiary society[11] that conducted a variety of charitable activities deemed it appropriate to reorganize and establish five additional exempt organizations, including four public charities: a school,[12] a home for the aged,[13] a title-holding company,[14] a publicly supported charity,[15] and a supporting organization[16] for the three other charitable entities.[17]

§ 30.2   CHARITABLE ORGANIZATIONS AS SUBSIDIARIES

One of the more common developments in recent years in the law of tax-exempt organizations is the establishment by an exempt organization, which is not itself

---

[10] Health care provider reorganizations and combinations are discussed in Hyatt & Hopkins, *The Law of Tax-Exempt Healthcare Organizations, Second Edition* (John Wiley & Sons, Inc., 2001), Part Five. In general, Hill, "Separation Is the Key to Using Complex Structures in Exempt Organizations," 6 *J. Tax. Exempt Orgs.* (No. 5) 195 (Mar./Apr. 1995).
[11] See § 18.4(a).
[12] See § 11.3(a).
[13] See § 11.3(b)(iv).
[14] See § 18.2(a).
[15] See § 11.3(b)(i).
[16] See § 11.3(c).
[17] Priv. Ltr. Rul. 9527043. For bifurcation to be successful, the same considerations that are discussed at § 31.1 apply: The entities must be separate, bona fide legal organizations and not operated so closely that the activities of one are considered the activities of the other (sham arrangements).
A court case that the IRS lost could have had enormous adverse implications for these forms of restructuring had the IRS prevailed, in that the government asserted six forms of private benefit in the arrangement, including the payment of rent, use of common employees, overlapping boards of directors, and similarity of organizations' names (Bob Jones Univ. Museum & Gallery, Inc. v. Comm'r, 71 T.C.M. 3120 (1996)). In the case, a taxable nonprofit university spun off a tax-exempt educational museum to be operated on the university's campus.

a charitable organization, of an auxiliary charitable organization for program operation and/or fundraising purposes. The auxiliary charitable organization functions in tandem with the sponsoring (or parent) organization to achieve common objectives.[18] Frequently termed a *related foundation*, the related charitable organization is rarely a private foundation, due to its ability to qualify as a publicly supported organization or a supporting organization.[19]

(a) Charitable Subsidiaries of Associations

Typical of this pattern is the charitable organization related to a trade, business, or professional association that qualifies as a tax-exempt business league.[20] The association-related foundation can engage in many activities, principally publishing, seminars, research, scholarships, fellowships, awards, and a variety of services. These activities—which can qualify as charitable, educational, and/or scientific programs—are either activities previously undertaken by the association or activities initiated by the foundation, or a combination of both. The foundation's activities can be funded by gifts and grants, leaving the association's revenues (such as membership dues) to support the remaining association activities.

When properly organized and operated, the auxiliary charitable organization is eligible to receive deductible charitable contributions and grants from private foundations and others. The foundation can administer its own programs, can make grants to other entities (including its parent organization) in furtherance of charitable purposes, or can utilize a combination of both approaches. Of course, where the auxiliary charitable organization is not properly organized or operated, it will lose or not obtain recognition of tax-exempt status.[21]

Many business leagues engage in charitable activities. While doing so will not adversely affect their tax-exempt status as long as the charitable activities are in furtherance of their exempt purposes, deductible charitable gifts cannot and private foundation grants most likely will not be made available to a business league.[22] By transferring the charitable activities to a separate foundation, however, the programs become eligible for a variety of tax-enhanced fundraising undertakings. For example, a medical society may wish to have a scholarship fund for medical students, which, by being placed in a separate organization, can qualify as a charitable organization for both tax exemption and tax-deductible charitable giving purposes. In addition to the tax advantages, this technique has the virtue of concentrating the fundraising function in a separate organization, where its governing board realizes (or should realize) that fundraising is a principal reason for the existence of the subsidiary.

As noted, the auxiliary charitable organization may properly make grants to its parent association, as long as it can be clearly demonstrated that the grants are for one or more qualifying charitable purposes. This type of grant must be tar-

[18] Historically, the IRS has been tolerant of the use by a tax-exempt organization of a related subsidiary organization (e.g., Rev. Rul. 58-143, 1958-1 C.B. 239 (revoked on another issue)).
[19] See § 11.3(b), (c).
[20] See Chapter 13. In general, Tenenbaum, "Subsidiaries and Related Foundations: Maximizing the Returns and Minimizing the Risks to Your Association," 14 *Exempt Org. Tax. Rev.* (No. 1) 105 (July 1996).
[21] E.g., Priv. Ltr. Rul. 9017003.
[22] See Chapter 13.

geted for specific charitable programs and not used by the association to defray the cost of general operations.

In most instances, the auxiliary charitable organization is a true subsidiary of the related association, meaning that it is controlled by the association.[23] Of course, control of this nature is not mandatory, in that the foundation can be a freestanding organization, but most associations, taking into account the investment in the related foundation, are unwilling to forgo the opportunity to at least loosely control the foundation.

Also, as noted, the association-related foundation will almost certainly not be a private foundation. These foundations are frequently publicly supported, in that they receive the requisite amount of gifts, grants, and/or exempt function revenue. For example, an association-related foundation may have a program of conferences and publications, and generate sufficient qualifying support in the form of admissions fees and publications sales.[24] If an association-related foundation relies on gifts and grants for nonprivate foundation status, the related association and/or its members can be contributors, although this form of support will generally be confined as to its qualification as public support.[25] If these two approaches are unavailable, the association-related foundation can usually qualify as a supporting organization in relation to the association, where the association itself satisfies the first of these support tests.[26]

Despite the need to adhere to certain legal requirements as to organization and operation of an association-related foundation,[27] the advantages to a business league associated with an auxiliary charitable organization usually outweigh the few complexities. The ability of the association-related foundation to attract grants and deductible charitable contributions, and perhaps forms of exempt function revenue, means that, for the furtherance of the objectives concurrently served by the two organizations, there is access to financial support that otherwise would not be forthcoming. The use of a charitable organization by a business league makes support of eligible programs by private foundations much more likely, since (assuming the charitable organization is not a private foundation) the administrative rigors of the expenditure responsibility rules[28] are thereby avoided.

The growing complexity of the law of tax-exempt organizations is offering the managers of these organizations more opportunities to properly structure the organizations' functions. Developing law is producing greater flexibility in these regards, making use of the auxiliary charitable organization for trade and professional associations a useful management and fundraising technique.

(b) Charitable Subsidiaries of Other Noncharitable Exempt Organizations

Despite the growing frequency of the practice, business leagues are by no means the only type of noncharitable tax-exempt organization that can make effective

---

[23] See Chapter 31.
[24] See § 11.3(b)(iv).
[25] See § 11.3(b)(i).
[26] See § 11.3(c).
[27] See Chapter 33.
[28] See § 11.4(e).

use of an auxiliary charitable organization. Indeed, any exempt organization that operates or otherwise funds charitable programs is in this category.

Auxiliary charitable organizations are usually most useful to membership organizations, because they provide the means by which the members can assist in the funding of programs of direct consequence to themselves and simultaneously deduct the payments as charitable gifts. This is one of the principal reasons that an auxiliary charitable organization can be so useful in relation to the objectives of a business league.

Business leagues are not, however, the only form of tax-exempt membership organization. Membership organizations also include social welfare organizations,[29] labor organizations,[30] social clubs,[31] and veterans' organizations.[32] For example, an organization may be classified as a social welfare organization solely because of the extent of its legislative activities; its charitable functions may be housed in a related foundation. Similarly, a college or university fraternity or sorority can make effective use of an auxiliary charitable organization as a source of funding of charitable and educational programs of, or sponsored by, the fraternity or sorority,[33] and/or by means of the set-aside deduction for the funding of charitable programs.[34]

Nonetheless, there is no requirement that a tax-exempt organization must be a membership organization to utilize an auxiliary charitable organization. Indeed, any type of exempt organization (or, for that matter, a taxable organization) can potentially make effective use of a related foundation. The same federal tax considerations that are discussed in the context of foundations related to business leagues[35] apply with respect to any auxiliary charitable organization, including the rules pertaining to nonprivate foundation status (although the special rule for supporting organizations of noncharitable entities also applies only with respect to social welfare organizations and labor organizations).[36]

(c) Charitable Subsidiaries of U.S. Charitable Organizations

The general reason for the establishment by a noncharitable organization (whether tax-exempt or taxable) of a charitable organization is to attract deductible charitable contributions and perhaps private foundation and other grants. Thus, it may appear that the establishment of a charitable organization by a charitable organization solely for fundraising purposes would be of little utility inasmuch as the qualifying gifts and grants could be made directly to the parent entity.

In some instances, however, the establishment of a separate fundraising entity by a charitable organization is warranted. Usually the objective in these circumstances is to concentrate the fundraising function in a single organization, essentially by creating a governing board and other support systems and re-

---

[29] See Chapter 12.
[30] See § 15.1.
[31] See Chapter 14.
[32] See § 18.10.
[33] E.g., Priv. Ltr. Rul. 8739055.
[34] See §§ 11.4(b), 28.3.
[35] See *supra* § 2(a).
[36] See Chapter 12 and § 15.1.

sources that are present principally or solely to enhance fundraising. This enhancement can also occur by creating a governing body of which substantial contributors (and/or those that can lead to them) can be members and by giving the fundraising entity a name that is more conducive to fundraising than that of the parent. Further, the subsidiary may have a characteristic that the parent entity lacks, such as the ability to maintain a pooled income fund.[37]

Many of the federal tax considerations reflected above likewise pertain to the auxiliary charitable organization of a charitable parent. Thus, for example, the auxiliary charitable organization can avoid private foundation classification by using one of the three approaches generally available.[38] In some situations, the charitable parent will be one of the tax-recognized institutions, such as a church, university, college, or hospital. Indeed, the auxiliary charitable organization serving a governmental college or university is expressly referenced in the federal tax law.[39] Likewise, the supporting organization rules generally contemplate a charitable parent and a charitable subsidiary.[40]

For the most part, however, the use of an auxiliary charitable organization by a charitable organization is done to enhance the nontax aspects of fundraising, by concentrating the fundraising function with a group that has fundraising as its principal, if not sole, responsibility.[41] Other uses include a function that the charitable organization parent could itself perform without jeopardizing its tax-exempt status, such as the maintenance by a hospital of a separate charitable fund from which to pay malpractice claims[42] or the maintenance by a college of an endowment fund in a separate charitable organization.[43]

Another application of the charitable subsidiary approach in this context can be seen in the reorganization phenomenon, where management considerations dictate the use of several charitable organizations.[44] While this relationship can result in instances of derivative tax exemptions, the exemption as a charitable organization may not be available on this basis where the entity is providing services to both exempt and nonexempt organizations, without suitable limitations on the scope of the latter.[45]

(d) Charitable Subsidiaries of Foreign Charitable Organizations

A U.S. organization that otherwise qualifies as a charitable entity and that carries on part or all of its charitable activities in foreign countries is not precluded because of these activities from qualifying as a charitable organization.[46] For example, the charitable activity of "relief of the poor and distressed or of the underprivileged" is nonetheless charitable where the beneficiaries of the assis-

---

[37] See § 18.19.
[38] See Chapter 11.
[39] See § 11.3(b)(v).
[40] See § 11.3(c).
[41] E.g., Priv. Ltr. Rul. 9019004.
[42] Rev. Rul. 78-41, 1978-1 C.B. 148.
[43] E.g., Priv. Ltr. Rul. 9242002.
[44] See *supra* § 1.
[45] E.g., Gen. Couns. Mem. 39684. In general, see § 23.7(a).
[46] Rev. Rul. 71-460, 1971-2 C.B. 231.

tance are outside the United States. Thus, the IRS ruled tax-exempt as a charitable group an organization formed to help poor rural inhabitants of developing countries[47] and an organization created for the purpose of assisting underprivileged people in Latin America to improve their living conditions through educational and self-help programs.[48]

The foregoing distinctions are well illustrated by the tax treatment accorded the *friends organization*. This is an organization formed to solicit and receive contributions in the United States and to expend the funds on behalf of a charitable organization in another country. Its support may be provided in a variety of ways, including program or project grants, provision of equipment or materials, or scholarship or fellowship grants.

Charitable contributions made directly to an organization not created or organized in the United States, a state or territory, the District of Columbia, or a possession of the United States are not deductible.[49] Also, contributions to a U.S. charity that transmits the funds to a foreign charity are deductible only in certain limited circumstances.

An IRS ruling provided five illustrations of supporting domestic charities and the tax treatment to be given contributions to them.[50] One example involved a mere conduit entity formed by a foreign organization. The second example involved a mere conduit entity formed by individuals in the United States. The third example involved a tax-exempt U.S. charitable organization that agrees to solicit and funnel contributions to a foreign organization. The fourth example involved a U.S. charitable organization that frequently makes grants to charities in a foreign country in furtherance of its exempt purposes, following review and approval of the uses to which the funds are to be put. The fifth example involved a U.S. charitable organization that formed a subsidiary organization in a foreign country to facilitate its tax-exempt operations there, with certain of its funds transmitted directly to the subsidiary.

This ruling stated a rationale of earmarking and of nominal as opposed to real donees, and thus concluded that contributions to the U.S. entities in the first, second, and third examples were not deductible. Contributions to the U.S. organization described in the fourth example were deductible because there was no earmarking of contributions and "use of such contributions will be subject to control by the domestic organization."[51] Contributions to the U.S. organization described in the fifth example were deductible because the "foreign organization [was] merely an administrative arm of the domestic organization,"[52] with the domestic organization considered the "real recipient"[53] of the contributions.

These rules were amplified, with the IRS describing the necessary attributes of the friends organization (in essence, the entity in the fourth example of the earlier

---

[47] Rev. Rul. 68-117, 1968-1 C.B. 251.
[48] Rev. Rul. 68-165, 1968-1 C.B. 253. Also Rev. Rul. 80-286, 1980-2 C.B. 179.
[49] IRC § 170(c)(2)(A); Rev. Rul. 63-252, 1963-2 C.B. 101. Also Tobjy v. Comm'r, 51 T.C.M. 449 (1986); Erselcuk v. Comm'r, 30 T.C. 962 (1958); Welti v. Comm'r, 1 T.C. 905 (1943).
[50] Rev. Rul. 63-252, *supra* note 49.
[51] *Id.*, at 104.
[52] *Id.*, at 105.
[53] *Id.*

ruling).[54] Again, the IRS emphasized the earmarking problem,[55] stating that the "test in each case is whether the organization has full control of the donated funds, and discretion as to their use, so as to insure that they will be used to carry out its functions and purposes."[56] The point of this fourth example was subsequently illustrated.[57]

These rules concerning prohibited *earmarking* and *conduits* contemplate two separate organizations: the domestic (U.S.) entity and the foreign entity. Where, therefore, the domestic and foreign activities are housed in one entity (such as a corporation), and that entity qualifies as a domestic charitable organization, the rules do not apply and the contributions to the organization are deductible as charitable gifts. Thus, a court held that a charitable entity organized under the law of a state and operating a private school in France was fully qualified as a recipient of deductible contributions from U.S. sources.[58] The organization did not have any employees, activities, or assets in the U.S. and all expenditures were in France. These facts led the IRS to contend that the U.S. corporation was a mere "shell" and functioned solely to funnel contributions to a foreign organization (namely, the school). But the court refused to go much beyond the fact that the corporation was a valid legal entity[59] and that the charitable giving rules do not require a substantial operational nexus in the United States in order to qualify as an eligible recipient of deductible gifts.[60]

---

[54] Rev. Rul. 66-79, 1966-1 C.B. 48.

[55] Citing Rev. Rul. 62-113, 1962-2 C.B. 10.

[56] Rev. Rul. 66-79, *supra* note 54, at 51.

[57] Rev. Rul. 75-65, 1975-1 C.B. 79. A lawsuit challenging the deductibility of contributions made by U.S. donors to U.S.-based Jewish organizations, claiming that these organizations were mere conduits of the contributions to Israel, was initiated in 1983. The case was dismissed in early 1985, however, shortly after the Supreme Court decisions finding any correlation between tax exemption for allegedly racially discriminatory public schools and denigration of black individuals to be "speculative" (see § 5.4(a)), with the court observing that it would be "more fanciful still to assume here that the government of Israel is so responsive to changes in U.S. tax laws that the withdrawal of benefits from U.S. contributors will work any alteration whatsoever in the character of its occupation of territory it now holds by force in the Middle East" (Khalaf et al. v. Regan et al., 85-1 U.S.T.C. ¶ 9269, at 87,592 (D.D.C. 1985)).

[58] Bilingual Montessori School of Paris, Inc. v. Comm'r, 75 T.C. 480 (1980).

[59] IRC § 170(c)(2)(A).

[60] This holding created a substantial exception to the IRS's conduit rationale and exalts much form over substance (e.g., Maryland Savings-Share Insurance Corp. v. United States, 644 F.2d 16, 31 (Ct. Cl. 1981), where the court wrote of mere "different mechanics for achieving the same result"). The charitable giving rules do not differentiate between corporations but rather between organizations, and in any event a corporation for tax purposes can be different from a corporation for state law purposes. Thus, irrespective of the status of the U.S. corporation, it would not have been difficult for the court to find the school to be a "corporation" for federal tax law purposes. The fact that the domestic entity was recognized as an IRC § 501(c)(3) organization eligible for gifts deductible for estate and gift tax purposes would not have precluded this finding. Also, the court explored the legislative history and found that the rationale expressed in it—that the charitable deduction for gifts to foreign charities is not available because there are no economic and social benefits for the U.S. government—supports its conclusions. There can be no such U.S. benefits resulting from the conduct of a school in France, however, whether operated by a U.S. entity or not. The legislative history states that if the gift recipient "is a domestic organization the fact that some portion of its funds is used in other countries for charitable and other purposes . . . will not affect the deductibility of the gift" (H. Rep. No. 1860, 75th Cong., 3d Sess. (1938)) but this statement does not necessarily mean that the same result occurs where all of the funds, and assets, are so used in other countries.

Assuming, however, that the friends organization has been properly created and operated so as to qualify as a charitable entity for purposes of charitable giving and tax exemption, a determination must also be sought as to whether it is a private foundation.[61] This type of entity can qualify as a publicly supported organization if it can demonstrate sufficient support from the general public.[62] Inasmuch as grants from substantial contributors often cannot be fully utilized in computing the public support fraction, however, a form of publicly supported charity status may not be available. This leaves the supporting organization rules.

These rules require the supporting organization to stand in one of three required relationships to the supported organization (the foreign organization). Because the charitable giving rules stress the independence of the qualified friends organization from the foreign charity, the weakest of the supporting relationships should be relied upon in establishing its nonprivate foundation status. This is the relationship defined in the regulations accompanying the supporting organization rules as *operated in connection with*. In connection with this relationship, the *responsiveness test* can be met by causing one or more of the officers of the foreign organization to be a director or officer of the U.S. organization.[63] The *integral part test* can be met by demonstrating that the U.S. entity makes payments of substantially all of its income to the foreign entity.[64] In essence, the balance is to show some independence between the U.S. and foreign entities to qualify for deductible contributions but to establish a sufficient relationship between them to satisfy the requirements of the supporting organization rules.

As to the charitable contribution deduction, however, the IRS ruled that contributions to a U.S. charity that solicits contributions for a specific project of a foreign charity are deductible only under certain circumstances. Contributions made directly to a foreign organization are not deductible.[65] Organizations formed in the United States for the purpose of raising funds and merely transmitting them as a conduit to a foreign charity are not eligible to attract deductible charitable contributions.[66] Conversely, where a domestic organization makes grants to a foreign charity out of its general fund following review and approval of the specific grant or where the foreign organization is merely an administrative arm of the domestic organization, contributions to the domestic charity are deductible.[67] The test is whether the domestic organization is the real recipient of the contributions, as it must be for the charitable contribution deduction to be allowed. The domestic organization must have full control over the donated funds and discretion as to their use.[68]

[61] See Chapter 11.
[62] IRC §§ 509(a)(1) (§ 170(b)(1)(A)(vi)), and 509(a)(2).
[63] Reg. § 1.509(a)-4(i)(2)(ii)(b). See § 11.3(c). The IRS, not overly enamored with the operated in connection with relationship, tends to strictly construe the responsiveness test and the integral part test (e.g., Tech. Adv. Mem. 9730002).
[64] Reg. § 1.509(a)-4(i)(3)(iii)(a). See § 11.3(c).
[65] IRC § 170(c)(2)(A).
[66] Rev. Rul. 63-252, *supra* note 49.
[67] *Id.*
[68] Rev. Rul. 75-434, 1975-2 C.B. 205; Rev. Rul. 66-79, *supra* note 54. Also see Rev. Rul. 75-65, *supra* note 57. A related issue is the availability of the estate tax deduction for charitable transfers to foreign governments or political subdivisions thereof, as discussed in Rev. Rul. 74-523, 1974-2 C.B. 304, and the cases cited therein. In general, Sanders, "Support and Conduct of Charitable Operations Abroad," *1st Annual Notre Dame Inst. on Charitable Giving, Foundations, & Trusts* 33 (1976).

As a general rule, a contribution by a corporation to a charitable organization is deductible only if the gift is to be used within the United States or its
possessions exclusively for permissible charitable purposes.[69] Where the recipient charitable organization is itself a corporation, however, this restriction is inapplicable.[70]

Because of the U.S.–Canada tax treaty, the general rule that contributions to
a foreign charity are not deductible does not apply in the case of certain contributions to Canadian charities.[71] In order for the contribution to be deductible, the
Canadian organization must be one that, if it were a U.S. organization, would be
eligible for deductible charitable contributions. In addition, the deduction may
not exceed the charitable deduction allowable under Canadian law, computed as
though the corporation's taxable income from Canadian sources was its aggregate income.

§ 30.3   TAX-EXEMPT SUBSIDIARIES
OF CHARITABLE ORGANIZATIONS

The previous section of this chapter summarized circumstances where, in an in-
tandem relationship between two tax-exempt organizations, the parent exempt
organization is a noncharitable organization and the subsidiary is a charitable organization. This arrangement can, however, be reversed.

Thus, another application of these precepts occurs where a charitable organization has a noncharitable, albeit tax-exempt, subsidiary. This will occur where
a charitable organization, which is engaging in or planning to engage in an activity that may or would jeopardize its exempt status, spins off to or initiates that
potentially disqualifying activity in a separate organization that qualifies under
another category of exemption. For example, a charitable organization may be
concerned about the extent of its legislative activities[72] and thus elect to operate
them out of an exempt social welfare organization.[73] Other functions that a charitable organization cannot properly pursue itself can be housed in a noncharitable
exempt organization, such as a title-holding corporation or a business league.[74]
For example, as to the use of a business league (although not as a subsidiary) by
a charitable organization, the IRS ruled that a charitable entity could advance
its charitable purpose of lessening the burdens of government[75] by purchasing an

---

[69] IRC § 170(c)(2), last sentence. This limitation does not apply with respect to contributions by
individuals nor to contributions from a small business corporation (an *S corporation*) (Priv. Ltr. Rul.
9703028).

[70] This results from the fact that IRC § 170(c)(2) opens with the phrase that a "corporation, trust, or
community chest, fund, or foundation" may qualify as a charitable donee, while the restriction in the
last sentence of IRC § 170(c)(2) applies to a gift to a "trust, chest, fund, or foundation." E.g., Rev. Rul.
69-80, 1969-1 C.B. 65.

[71] Rev. Proc. 59-31, 1959-2 C.B. 949.

[72] See Chapter 20.

[73] See Chapter 12.

[74] See § 18.2, Chapter 13, respectively.

[75] See § 6.3.

office building and leasing it to a business league for job creation and world trade purposes, where the business league would sublease the property to appropriate businesses.[76] This technique generally cannot work, however, in the context of political activities,[77] in that a charitable organization usually cannot properly establish a related political action committee.[78]

The use by a charitable organization of entities such as charitable remainder trusts and pooled income funds[79] can also be viewed as illustrative of this technique.

Thus, the use by a charitable organization of noncharitable tax-exempt subsidiaries is still another application of the concept of bifurcation in the exempt organizations setting. When coupled with other combinations of exempt organizations, as well as with the use of taxable subsidiaries by exempt organizations,[80] it is clear that there are many occasions and opportunities warranting the splitting of functions of exempt organizations and the housing of them in separate entities.

§ 30.4 OTHER COMBINATIONS OF TAX-EXEMPT ORGANIZATIONS

There are combinations of tax-exempt organizations where none of the entities involved are charitable ones. The most common of these arrangements entails the use of political action committees, title-holding corporations, and employee benefit funds.

As discussed, several types of tax-exempt organizations utilize political action committees.[81] The usual users of these entities are business leagues[82] and labor organizations;[83] occasionally, social welfare organizations[84] and other exempt organizations will have occasion to create and operate a related political organization.

Any type of tax-exempt organization can have a related title-holding corporation. The usual model is a parent exempt organization and a title-holding entity.[85] Unrelated exempt organizations can, however, share a title-holding corporation.[86]

Various employee benefit funds are themselves tax-exempt organizations[87]

---

[76] Priv. Ltr. Rul. 9246032.

[77] See Chapter 21.

[78] See Chapter 17. An illustration as to how close to the edge a charitable organization can go in this regard was provided in the case of a public charity that was permitted by the IRS to administer a payroll deduction plan to collect political contributions from its employees and remit the contributions to unions representing its employees for transfer to union-sponsored political action committees (Priv. Ltr. Rul. 200151060).

[79] See § 18.19.

[80] See Chapter 31.

[81] See § 17.1(a).

[82] See Chapter 13.

[83] See § 15.1.

[84] See Chapter 12.

[85] See § 18.2(a).

[86] See § 18.2(b).

[87] See Chapter 16.

and can be related to other exempt organizations. This includes pension and retirement funds in general, and voluntary employees' beneficiary associations.[88]

Still other combinations of tax-exempt organizations entail groupings that go far beyond bifurcation, involving perhaps tens of these entities. This is most common in the health care field, where contemporary systems of health care providers and related entities can involve a multitude of exempt organizations.[89] These systems may involve partnerships and/or other forms of joint ventures,[90] or they may be created by means of joint operating agreements;[91] or they may entail less formal relationships, cast perhaps as affiliations;[92] often, these clusters of entities are orchestrated by one or more supporting organizations.[93] Collectives of this nature are also arising outside the health care field, principally in the realm of education.[94]

§ 30.5   TREATMENT OF CONTRIBUTIONS AND OTHER PAYMENTS

As a consequence of these in-tandem arrangements, it is not uncommon for a payment by a third party to be made to one organization, with some or all of the payment directed to another organization. The tax treatment accorded some or all of the payment (such as deductibility as a charitable contribution) can depend on whether the payment is deemed made to the initial payee or whether it or a portion of it is deemed made to another, sometimes related, organization that is the transferee of the initial payee. In many of these instances, the initial payee organization is regarded as the agent of the organization that is the ultimate recipient of the payment, so that the payor is considered, for tax purposes, to have made the payment directly to the ultimate transferee, notwithstanding the flow of the payment through one or more intermediate organizations (conduit entities).[95]

For example, a contribution to a tax-exempt organization is deductible as a charitable gift only where the recipient is a qualified donee.[96] Nonetheless, contributions to an exempt social club[97] were held to be deductible, where the club functioned as an authorized agent for one or more charitable organizations, enabling the members of the club to, when purchasing tickets for a social event, direct that the amount of their total payment in excess of the price of the tickets be

---

[88] *Id.* at § 3. There can be combinations of entities where some are tax-exempt and some are taxable. This includes the use of for-profit subsidiaries (see Chapter 31) and partnerships (see Chapter 32). Related to a for-profit organization can be a political action committee, a private foundation, and/or one or more employee benefit funds.

[89] E.g., Priv. Ltr. Rul. 9840049. In general, see Hyatt & Hopkins, *supra* note 10, Chapter 20.

[90] See Chapter 32.

[91] See § 26.5(j).

[92] E.g., Priv. Ltr. Rul. 9809054.

[93] See § 11.3(c). Also, Hopkins & Blazek, *Private Foundations: Tax Law and Compliance* (John Wiley & Sons, Inc., 1997) § 15.7(i).

[94] E.g., Priv. Ltr. Rul. 9840051.

[95] Cf. *supra* § 2(d).

[96] IRC § 170(c). See § 2.5.

[97] See Chapter 14.

transferred to charitable organizations and deduct, as charitable gifts, that portion of the payment to the club that was paid over to the charitable organizations.[98] In this type of instance, the initial payee organization is considered the mere conduit of some or all of the payments and thus the federal tax consequences of the payment are determined as if the payment (or a portion of it) was made directly to the ultimate recipient.

Likewise, charitable gift deductibility treatment was accorded additional amounts paid by customers of a utility company, when paying their bills to the company, where the additional amounts were earmarked for a tax-exempt charitable organization that assisted individuals with emergency energy-related needs.[99] Again, the utility company was considered the agent of the charitable organization; the company did not exercise any control over the funds and segregated them from its own funds. In a similar instance, contributions paid to an exempt title-holding company[100] for purposes of maintaining and operating a historic property were once ruled by the IRS to be deductible as charitable gifts, where the gifts were segregated from the company's funds and otherwise clearly devoted to charitable ends.[101] In this instance, however, the ruling was withdrawn,[102] although the effect of the withdrawal was not made retroactive.[103] Similarly, the IRS ruled that an exempt charitable organization may maintain a property donation program, with the contriutions of property qualifying for a contribution deduction, where the transfers are to a for-profit fundraising entity, in that the entity was functioning as an agent of the charity.[104]

Similarly, a contribution to a charitable entity is not deductible as a charitable gift where the ultimate recipient is not a qualified donee. For example, a contribution to a tax-exempt university for the general use of an exempt fraternity or sorority on its campus is not deductible, in that the recipient of the funds is a social club. By contrast, a contribution of this nature would be deductible if the use of the funds is confined to charitable or educational purposes.[105] Thus, where an exempt university owns the property and leases it to fraternities and sororities as part of its overall program of provision of student housing, contributions to the university for fraternity or sorority housing are deductible.[106]

Another variant of these principles is the rule that amounts paid to a tax-exempt organization for transfer to a political action committee do not, when promptly and directly transferred, constitute political campaign expenditures by

---

[98] Rev. Rul. 55-192, 1955-1 C.B. 294.
[99] Rev. Rul. 85-184, 1985-2 C.B. 84.
[100] See § 18.2(a).
[101] Priv. Ltr. Rul. 8705041.
[102] Priv. Ltr. Rul. 8826012.
[103] Priv. Ltr. Rul. 8836040. The IRS did not provide any explanation for the withdrawal of this ruling, although it may be surmised that the IRS was concerned that this form of deductible charitable giving could become prevalent, with difficulties inherent in enforcing the rules.
[104] Priv. Ltr. Rul. 200230005. Cf. Kaplan v. Comm'r, 43 T.C. 663 (1965) (concerning a property donation program operated by a for-profit corporation on behalf of a tax-exempt hospital, although the issue of agency was not raised).
[105] Rev. Rul. 60-367, 1960-2 C.B. 73.
[106] E.g., Priv. Ltr. Rul. 9733015.

the exempt organization.[107] A transfer is considered *promptly* and *directly* made if (1) the procedures followed by the organization satisfy the requirements of applicable federal and state campaign laws; (2) the organization maintains adequate records to demonstrate that the amounts transferred do in fact consist of political contributions or dues, rather than investment income; and (3) the political contributions or dues transferred were not used to earn investment income for the payor organization.[108]

Consequently, a payment to an organization (whether or not tax-exempt) can be treated, for federal tax purposes, as a payment to another organization (whether or not tax-exempt) where the initial payee is the agent of the ultimate transferee, the funds are clearly earmarked by the payor for the ultimate payee, and the funds are not subject to the control of (for example, invested for the benefit of) the initial payee.[109]

§ 30.6   MERGERS

Notwithstanding the variety of these in-tandem arrangements, occasionally two of these organizations are merged. Likewise, on occasion, two unrelated tax-exempt organizations merge. With one exception, there is not any statutory law on the point.[110]

When a merger of this nature occurs, both of the organizations involved often have the same tax-exempt status. Usually, the two organizations in this type of a merger are public charitable organizations.[111] The rationale for these mergers varies. In one instance, the merger served to change the state of incorporation.[112] In another, the merger was intended to reduce the administrative burdens of operating two or more organizations.[113] In still another, the merger was undertaken to eliminate what had become a superfluous organization.[114] In one instance, a supporting organization for a boys' school and a supporting organization for a girls' school merged to form one supporting organization, following a merger of the two schools.[115] As another illustration, an organization operating independent living housing for the elderly merged into a publicly supported organization, followed by a consolidation with a home for the elderly, all for the purpose of promot-

---

[107] See § 17.4. E.g., Priv. Ltr. Rul. 7903079.

[108] Reg. § 1.527-6(e).

[109] Thus, an association of banks that made contributions to charitable organizations on behalf of its members was found to be merely a "disbursing agent" for the banks, so that the member banks received charitable contribution deductions for the gifts (First National Bank of Omaha v. Comm'r, 17 B.T.A. 1358 (1929), *aff'd* 49 F.2d 70 (8th Cir. 1931)).

[110] This exception pertains to the special termination tax rules that apply with respect to the mergers of private foundations (see § 11.4(f)).

[111] That is, public institutions, publicly supported charitable organizations, or supporting organizations (see Chapter 11).

[112] Priv. Ltr. Rul. 9309037.

[113] E.g., Priv. Ltr. Rul. 9314059.

[114] Priv. Ltr. Rul. 9303030 (a supporting organization (see § 11.3(c)) merged into a supported organization).

[115] Priv. Ltr. Rul. 9317054.

ing efficient management, facilitating long-term planning, and enhancing philanthropy for the neediest elderly.[116] Likewise, efficiencies were achieved when five business leagues[117] were consolidated into one.[118]

Occasionally, both of the merging organizations will be tax-exempt organizations, but under differing categories. For example, a lobbying organization[119] related to a public charitable organization may merge into the public charity, or a foundation related to a trade or professional organization[120] may merge into the association. In examples of this type of merger, a single-parent title-holding corporation[121] merged into a publicly supported charity;[122] and two multiparent title-holding companies[123] merged.[124]

These mergers usually do not adversely affect the tax-exempt status or the public charity status of the surviving organization, or cause any unrelated business income.[125]

An infrequent occurrence will be a merger of a for-profit organization into a tax-exempt organization. This can be done without endangering the exempt status of the surviving organization, and generally without causing unrelated business income for the exempt organization.[126] In one instance, a taxable corporation was merged into an exempt social welfare organization.[127] The activities of the corporation were consistent with the exempt organization's purposes.[128] The exempt organization issued "special notes" to the shareholders of the for-profit corporation in exchange for their stock. Again, the rationale for the merger was that the combination would reduce duplicative operations and expenses.[129]

---

[116] Priv. Ltr. Rul. 199914051.

[117] That is, organizations described in IRC § 501(c)(6) (see Chapter 13).

[118] Priv. Ltr. Rul. 199916053.

[119] That is, an organization described in IRC § 501(c)(4) (see Chapter 12).

[120] That is, an organization described in IRC § 501(c)(6) (see Chapter 13).

[121] That is, an organization described in IRC § 501(c)(2) (see § 18.2(a)).

[122] Priv. Ltr. Rul. 9840053.

[123] That is, organizations described in IRC § 501(c)(25) (see § 18.2(b)).

[124] Priv. Ltr. Rul. 9840054.

[125] E.g., Priv. Ltr. Ruls. 9738055, 9738056 (hospitals (see § 6.2(a)) merging into unrelated supporting organizations (see § 11.3(c)); Priv. Ltr. Rul. 9522022 (merger of two supplemental unemployment benefit trusts (see § 16.4)); Priv. Ltr. Rul. 9530008 (merger of a supporting organization into a private foundation (see § 11.3(c))); Priv. Ltr. Rul. 9530036 (merger of two trade associations (see Chapter 13)); Priv. Ltr. Rul. 9533015 (merger of a social club into a public charity (see Chapter 14)); Priv. Ltr. Rul. 9548019, as modified by Priv. Ltr. Rul. 9551009 (merger of two supporting organizations, followed by transfer to the survivor entity of the assets of a private foundation and 14 charitable trusts).

[126] See, however, § 31.2(d) (discussion of liquidations of for-profit subsidiaries into tax-exempt parents).

[127] That is, an organization described in IRC § 501(c)(4)(see Chapter 12).

[128] Priv. Ltr. Rul. 9346015.

[129] In general, Harris, "Structuring Affiliations Between Exempt and Nonexempt Organizations," 6 J. Tax. Exempt Orgs. (No. 4) 155 (Jan./Feb. 1995).

§ 30.7   USE OF SINGLE-MEMBER LIMITED LIABILITY COMPANIES

The advent of the limited liability company (LLC)[130] has brought use of the single-member LLC and the multimember LLC into the tax-exempt organizations context. Initially, the focus was on the LLC in which an exempt organization was not the only member. In these instances, there may be a mix of exempt and nonexempt members,[131] or all of the members may be exempt organizations.[132]

More recently, use of the single-member LLC (SMLLC), where the member is a tax-exempt organization,[133] is emerging. The SMLLC can be a form of exempt subsidiary organization, in that the LLC is a separate legal entity, it is exempt from federal income taxes,[134] it is wholly owned by the exempt member, and it can perform exempt functions.

Generally, SMLLCs are disregarded for federal income tax purposes. A disregarded LLC is regarded as a branch or a division of its member owner. (Thus, although an SMLLC is a separate legal entity for most purposes, it is treated as a component of its owner for federal income tax purposes, and in that sense is not literally a subsidiary of the member.) In one instance, the IRS wrote that, when the sole member of an LLC is a tax-exempt organization, the function of the LLC is treated as an "activity" of the exempt organization.[135]

A disregarded (single-member) LLC is not required to file an application for recognition of tax exemption.[136] The exempt owner of an SMLLC treats the operations and finances of the LLC as its own for purposes of the annual information return filing requirements.[137] The interplay of the law of exempt organizations and the rules as to SMLLCs also are being manifested in other contexts.[138]

Creative uses of the SMLLC by tax-exempt organizations will be abounding. One of them pertains to the acceptance by charitable organizations of gifts of property that may carry with them exposure of the donee to legal liability (such as environmental or premises tort liability). Previously, a charitable organization could attempt to shield its other assets from liability by placing the gift property in a separate exempt entity, such as a supporting organization[139]

---

[130] In general, see § 4.1(b).

[131] See §§ 32.3, 32.4.

[132] See § 32.6.

[133] To date, the tax-exempt organizations utilizing an SMLLC have been confined to charitable (IRC § 501(c)(3)) entities, but that may soon change.

[134] An LLC with two or more tax-exempt charitable members can itself qualify as a charitable organization (see § 4.3(e)).

[135] Priv. Ltr. Rul. 200134025.

[136] In general, see § 23.3(c).

[137] In general, see § 24.3(c).

[138] E.g., § 29.3, note 61.

[139] See § 11.3(c).

or a title-holding company.[140] Among the difficulties with this approach is the need to file an application for recognition of tax exemption for the new entity and/or file annual information returns on its behalf. As an alternative, however, a charitable organization can utilize an SMLLC as a vehicle to receive and hold each contribution of property separately, thus presumably obtaining the desired liability protection.[141]

[140] See § 18.2
[141] E.g., Priv. Ltr. Rul. 200134025.

CHAPTER THIRTY-ONE

Tax-Exempt Organizations and For-Profit Subsidiaries

It is common, if not frequently essential, for a tax-exempt organization to utilize one or more for-profit, taxable subsidiaries.

The reasons for this phenomenon are manifold, including situations where the activity to be housed in the subsidiary is an unrelated one and the activity is too extensive to be conducted within the tax-exempt organization, the management of an exempt organization does not want to report the receipt of any unrelated income and so shifts it to a separate subsidiary, insulation of the assets of the parent exempt organization from potential liability, expansion of the sources of capital, use of it in a partnership, and/or the management of an exempt organization simply is enamored with the idea of use of a for-profit subsidiary.[1]

In most instances, the first of these three reasons is the prevalent if not the sole one. For example, a tax-exempt educational organization licensed to and otherwise utilized a for-profit subsidiary to maximize, for membership and business purposes, the operation of its Web site.[2] An unrelated business may be operated as an activity within an exempt organization, as long as the primary purpose of the organization is the carrying out of one or more exempt functions or the commensurate test is satisfied.[3] With one exception, there is no fixed percentage of unrelated activity that may be engaged in by an exempt organization.[4]

---

[1] In general, Sanders, *Joint Ventures Involving Tax-Exempt Organizations, Second Edition* (John Wiley & Sons, Inc., 2000) § 4.6(a).

[2] Priv. Ltr. Rul. 200225046.

[3] Reg. § 1.501(c)(3)-1(e)(1). Also Reg. § 1.501(c)(3)-1(c)(1).

[4] The one exception is a 10-percent limit on the unrelated business activities of title-holding companies (see § 28.3).

Therefore, if a tax-exempt organization engages in one or more unrelated activities where the activities are substantial in relation to exempt activities, the use of a for-profit subsidiary is necessary, assuming exemption is to be retained.[5] Indeed, tax exemption cannot be maintained as a matter of law if there is a substantial non-exempt activity or set of activities.[6]

§ 31.1 STRUCTURAL CONSIDERATIONS

There are several matters of structure to be taken into account when contemplating the use of a for-profit subsidiary by a tax-exempt organization. These include choice of form and the control mechanism.

(a) Establishing a For-Profit Subsidiary

Essentially, the factors to be considered in determining whether a particular activity should be housed in a tax-exempt organization or a for-profit organization are the same as those that should be weighed when there is contemplation of the commencement of a business that potentially may be conducted in either an exempt or for-profit form. These factors are the value of or need for tax exemption, the motives of those involved in the enterprise (for example, a profit motive), the desirability of creating an asset (such as stock that is appreciating in value and/or the means for transfer of ownership) for equity owners of the enterprise (usually shareholders), and the compensatory arrangements contemplated for the employees.

The law is clear that a tax-exempt organization can have one or more exempt (or at least nonprofit) subsidiaries and/or one or more for-profit subsidiaries.[7] Thus, the IRS observed that a tax-exempt organization can "organize, capitalize and own, provide services and assets (real and personal, tangible and intangible) to a taxable entity without violating the requirements for [tax] exemption, regardless of whether the taxable entity is wholly or partially owned."[8] Indeed, the IRS acknowledged that the "number of subsidiaries or related entities an exempt organization can create for the purpose of conducting business activities is not set."[9] With respect to for-profit subsidiaries, the exempt parent organization can own some or all of the equity (usually stock) of the for-profit subsidiary (unless the parent is a private foundation, in which case special rules

---

[5] In Orange County Agric. Soc'y, Inc. v. Comm'r, 893 F.2d 529 (2d Cir. 1990), the court discussed the fact that the operation of a substantial unrelated business by a tax-exempt organization is likely to result in loss of the organization's exemption.

[6] Better Business Bur. of Washington, D.C. v. United States, 326 U.S. 279 (1945).

[7] E.g., Priv. Ltr. Rul. 9016072 (where a tax-exempt organization owned a for-profit subsidiary and that subsidiary in turn owned a network of for-profit subsidiaries).

[8] Priv. Ltr. Rul. 199938041.

[9] Priv. Ltr. Rul 8706012.

apply[10]).[11] For example, a public charity created a for-profit management corporation, to provide services to it and two other exempt organizations, and provided it operating funds in exchange for 100 percent of the subsidiary's stock.[12]

The IRS from time to time issues private determinations concerning the use of for-profit subsidiaries by tax-exempt organizations.[13]

(b) Choice of Form

Just as in forming a tax-exempt organization,[14] consideration should be given to choice of organizational form when establishing a for-profit subsidiary. Most will be corporations, inasmuch as a corporation is the most common of the business forms, provides a shield against liability for management and the exempt parent, and enables the exempt parent to own the subsidiary by holding all or at least a majority of its stock.[15]

Some taxable businesses are organized as sole proprietorships; however, this approach is of no avail in the tax-exempt organization context since the business activity conducted as a sole proprietorship is an undertaking conducted directly by the exempt organization and thus does not lead to the desired goal of having the related activity in a separate entity.

Some taxable businesses are structured as partnerships; however, the participation by a tax-exempt organization in a partnership can involve unique legal complications.[16]

Some states allow businesses to be conducted by means of "business trusts," so this approach may be available to a tax-exempt organization. Before this approach (or any other approach involving a vehicle other than a corporation) is used, however, it is imperative that those involved are certain that the corporate form is not the most beneficial. One important consideration must be that of stock ownership, as stock is an asset that can appreciate in value and can be sold in whole or in part.

Another alternative is use of a limited liability company for this purpose.[17] This aspect of the law is evolving and offers interesting opportunities for tax-exempt organizations.[18]

In some instances, an activity can be placed in a taxable nonprofit organi-

---

[10] See § 11.4(c).
[11] The extent of stock ownership may determine whether income from a subsidiary to a tax-exempt parent is taxable (see *infra* § 3). A transfer without consideration from a taxable corporation to a charitable organization, which is its sole stockholder, is a dividend rather than a charitable contribution (Rev. Rul. 68-296, 1968-1 C.B. 105).
[12] Priv. Ltr. Rul. 9308047.
[13] E.g., Priv. Ltr. Rul. 8706012.
[14] See § 4.1.
[15] Charitable organizations may be shareholders in small business corporations (*S corporations*) (IRC § 1361(b)(1)(B), (c)(7)(B)). The applicability of the unrelated business income rules in this context is the subject of § 27.2(m).
[16] See Chapter 32.
[17] E.g., Priv. Ltr. Rul. 9637050.
[18] See § 30.7.

zation.[19] This approach is a product of the distinction between a nonprofit organization and a tax-exempt organization.[20] The former is a state law concept; the latter essentially is a federal tax concept. Assuming state law permits (in that an activity may be *unrelated* to the parent's exempt functions, yet still be a *nonprofit* one), a business activity may be placed in a nonprofit, albeit taxable, corporation.[21] There may be some advantage (such as public relations) to this approach.

(c) Control

Presumably, a tax-exempt organization will, when forming a taxable subsidiary, intend to maintain control over the subsidiary. Certainly, after capitalizing the enterprise,[22] nurturing its growth and success, and desiring to enjoy some profits from the business, the prudent exempt organization parent usually would not want to place the activity in a vehicle over which it cannot exercise ongoing control.

Where the taxable subsidiary is structured as a business corporation, the tax-exempt organization parent can own the entity and ultimately control it simply by owning the stock (received in exchange for the capital contributed).[23] The exempt organization parent as the stockholder can thereafter select the board of directors of the corporation and, if desired, its officers.

If the taxable subsidiary is structured as a nonprofit corporation, three choices are available. The tax-exempt organization parent can control the subsidiary by means of interlocking directorates. Alternatively, the subsidiary can be a membership corporation, with the parent entity the sole member. In the third— and least utilized—approach, the entity can be structured as a nonprofit organization that can issue stock, in which case the exempt organization parent would control the subsidiary by holding its stock. If the latter course is chosen and if the nonprofit subsidiary is to be headquartered in a (foreign) state where stock-based nonprofit organizations are not authorized, the subsidiary can be incorporated in a state that allows nonprofit organizations to issue stock and thereafter be qualified to do business in the home (domestic) state.

(d) Attribution Considerations

For federal income tax purposes, a parent corporation and its subsidiary are respected as separate entities as long as the purposes for which the subsidiary is

---

[19] Still another approach is use of a tax-exempt subsidiary. This technique is discussed throughout (e.g., § 11.3(c) (supporting organizations), § 18.2 (title-holding companies), § 20.7 (lobbying arms of charitable organizations), and § 30.2(d) (fundraising vehicles for foreign charitable organizations)).

[20] See §§ 1.1(a), 1.2.

[21] Of course, in this situation, the subsidiary, then, is not a for-profit one.

[22] See *infra* § 2(a).

[23] E.g., text accompanied by *supra* note 4.

formed are reflected in authentic business activities.[24] That is, where an organization is established with the bona fide intention that it will have some real and substantial business function, its existence will generally not be disregarded for tax purposes.[25]

By contrast, where the parent organization so controls the affairs of the subsidiary that it is merely an extension of the parent, the subsidiary may not be regarded as a separate entity.[26] In an extreme situation (such as where the parent is directly involved in the day-to-day management of the subsidiary), the establishment and operation of an ostensibly separate subsidiary may be regarded as a sham perpetrated by the parent and thus ignored for tax purposes; with this outcome, the tax consequences are the same as if the two "entities" were one.[27]

The position of the IRS on this subject can be traced through three pronouncements from its Office of Chief Counsel. In 1968, the IRS was advised by its lawyers that an attempt to attribute the activities of a subsidiary to its parent "should be made only where the evidence clearly shows that the subsidiary is merely a guise enabling the parent to carry out its . . . [disqualifying] activity or where it can be proven that the subsidiary is an arm, agent, or integral part of the parent."[28] In 1974, the IRS Chief Counsel advised that to "disregard the corporate entity requires a finding that the corporation or transaction involved was a sham or fraud without any valid business purpose, or the finding of a true agency or trust relationship between the entities."[29] In 1984, the IRS's lawyers reviewed a situation where a separate for-profit corporation provided management and operations services to several tax-exempt hospitals. Although the IRS rulings division was inclined otherwise, its lawyers advised that, where a subsidiary is organized for a bona fide business purpose and the exempt parent is not involved in the day-to-day management of the subsidiary, the activities of the subsidiary cannot be attributed to the parent for purposes of determining the

---

[24] E.g., Comm'r v. Bollinger, 485 U.S. 340 (1988); Moline Properties, Inc. v. Comm'r, 319 U.S. 436 (1943); National Carbide Corp. v. Comm'r, 336 U.S. 422 (1949); Britt v. United States, 431 F.2d 227 (5th Cir. 1970). Also Sly v. Comm'r, 56 T.C.M. 209 (1988), Universal Church of Jesus Christ, Inc. v. Comm'r, 55 T.C.M. 143 (1988) (where a debt collection business was said to be "operating under the thinnest of veils in an attempt to give itself the appearance of a religious enterprise" (at 153)).

[25] Britt v. United States, *supra* note 24.

[26] E.g., Krivo Industrial Supply Co. v. National Distillers & Chemical Corp., 483 F.2d 1098 (5th Cir. 1973); Orange County Agric. Soc'y, Inc. v. Comm'r, 55 T.C.M. 1602 (1988), *aff'd, supra* note 5.

[27] Gen. Couns. Mem. 39598. In a similar set of circumstances, courts are finding nonprofit organizations to be the alter ego of the debtor, with the result that the assets of the organization are made available to IRS levies (see the cases collected in § 4.1, note 22).

In the reverse situation, where a for-profit entity controls a tax-exempt organization (such as by day-to-day management of it), the exemption of the controlled entity may be jeopardized (see, e.g., United Cancer Council, Inc. v. Comm'r, 109 T.C. 326 (1997), *rev'd and rem'd,* 165 F.3d 1173 (7th Cir. 1999); §§ 19.4, 33.3). Nonetheless, management of an exempt organization by a for-profit company generally does not raise these concerns (e.g., Priv. Ltr. Rul. 9715031).

[28] Gen. Couns. Mem. 33912.

[29] Gen. Couns. Mem. 35719.

parent's exempt status.[30] In the third instance, this was the outcome irrespective of the fact that the parent exempt organization owned all of the stock of the subsidiary corporation.

Thus, the contemporary posture of the IRS in this regard can be distilled to two tests, which are that, for the legitimacy of a for-profit subsidiary to be respected, it must engage in an independent, bona fide function and not be a mere instrumentality of the tax-exempt parent. As to the former, the IRS's lawyers wrote that

> the first aspect [in determining the authenticity of a for-profit subsidiary] is the requirement that the subsidiary be organized for some bona fide purpose of its own and not be a mere sham or instrumentality of the [exempt] parent. We do not believe that this requirement that the subsidiary have a bona fide business purpose should be considered to require that the subsidiary have an inherently commercial or for-profit activity. The term "business" . . . is not synonymous with "trade or business" in the sense of requiring a profit motive.[31]

As to the latter, the IRS's lawyers observed that

> the second aspect of the test is the requirement that the parent not be so involved in, or in control of, the day-to-day operations of the subsidiary that the relationship between parent and subsidiary assumes the characteristics of the relationship of principal and agent, i.e., that the parent not be so in control of the affairs of the subsidiary that it is merely an instrumentality of the parent.[32]

At one point, the IRS demonstrated some proclivity to treat two organizations in this situation as one where the entities' directors and officers are the same. For example, the IRS ruled that the activities of a for-profit subsidiary are to be attributed to its exempt parent, for purposes of determining the ongoing tax exemption of the parent, where the officers and directors of the two organizations are identical.[33]

The rationale underlying this ruling rests on the premise that, when the tax-exempt parent is involved in the day-to-day management of the subsidiary, the activities of the subsidiary are imputed to the parent. In this ruling, the IRS stated that an exempt parent is "necessarily" involved in the day-to-day management of the subsidiary simply because the officers and directors of the parent serve as the officers and directors of the subsidiary. Thus, because of this structural overlap, the IRS attributed the activities of the subsidiary to the parent. Once this attribution occurs, the impact of the attribution must be ascertained to determine whether the parent will remain exempt.

---

[30] Gen. Couns. Mem. 39326.
[31] Gen. Couns. Mem. 39598.
[32] *Id.*
[33] Priv. Ltr. Rul. 8606056.

In the case, the attribution to the tax-exempt parent of the activities of the for-profit subsidiary was not fatal to the parent because the involvement was deemed to be insubstantial. (The exempt parent was a scientific research organization; the subsidiary developed and manufactured products that were derived from patentable technology generated out of the parent's research activities. The parent's average annual income was $50 million; the subsidiary's was $10,000 to $70,000.) The for-profit subsidiary was capitalized by the parent (for between $10,000 and $100,000). The parent maintained a controlling interest in the subsidiary. There was an overlapping of employees as between the parent and subsidiary. Likewise, there was a sharing of facilities and equipment. These relationships were evidenced by employment contracts and lease agreements. Separate books and records of the two entities were maintained.

The principles of law do not, however, support the conclusion of the IRS in this ruling, which is that overlapping directors and officers of two organizations automatically results in an attribution of the subsidiary's activities to the parent. The case law is instructive in that this can be the consequence where the facts show that the arrangement is a sham; however, this cannot be a mechanical and inexorable outcome. Indeed, in subsequent rulings, the IRS's rulings division has been guided by this advice from its lawyers:

> Control through ownership of stock, or power to appoint the board of directors, of the subsidiary will not cause the attribution of the subsidiary's activities to the parent. We do not believe that [a prior general counsel memorandum] should be read to suggest, by negative inference, that when the board of directors of a wholly owned subsidiary is made up entirely of board members, officers, or employees of the parent there must be attribution of the activities of the subsidiary to the parent.[34]

Contemporary rulings from the IRS evidence an abandonment of this earlier approach.[35]

Indeed, the IRS subsequently distilled the law on the point as follows: "The activities of a separately incorporated subsidiary cannot ordinarily be attributed to its parent organization unless the facts provide clear and convincing evidence that the subsidiary is in reality an arm, agent or integral part of the parent."[36] In that instance, the IRS offered a most munificent application of this aspect of the law, concluding that the activities of a for-profit subsidiary were not to be attributed to the tax-exempt organization that was its parent, notwithstanding extensive and ongoing in-tandem administrative and programmatic functions. That is, the IRS observed that the two entities will "maintain a close working relationship," they will be "sharing investment leads," they will coinvest in companies, the subsidiary will rent office space from the exempt parent, the subsidiary will purchase administrative and professional services from the

---

[34] Gen. Couns. Mem. 39598.
[35] E.g., Priv. Ltr. Rul. 9245031 (the "activities of [the] subsidiary cannot be attributed to [the] [p]arent").
[36] Priv. Ltr. Rul. 200132040.

parent, and the subsidiary will reimburse its parent for the services of some of the parent's employees.

There was somewhat of an aberration in these regards, in a situation involving a law issue concerning tax-exempt cooperatives. These entities must, to be exempt, receive at least 85 percent of their income from amounts collected from members for the sole purpose of meeting losses and expenses.[37] The IRS initially ruled that the gross receipts of a wholly owned subsidiary of such a cooperative must be aggregated with the receipts of the subsidiary for purposes of calculating the 85-percent-member-income test.[38] The rationale for this approach was based on cooperative principles, where a subsidiary must be created to perform a function that the parent cooperative might engage in as an integral part of its operations without adversely affecting its exempt status.[39] This ruling was met with stiff opposition from the industry and members of Congress; the IRS subsequently ruled, using conventional analysis, that the income of a subsidiary is not included for purposes of determining whether the parent cooperative satisfied the member-income test.[40] In this latter ruling, the IRS reiterated the point that a corporation is a separate taxable entity for federal income tax purposes if the corporation is formed for valid business purposes, and is not a sham, agency, or instrumentality.[41]

Thus, the IRS is highly unlikely to attribute the activities of a for-profit subsidiary of a tax-exempt organization to the parent entity, by reason of the foregoing elements of law. The use of for-profit subsidiaries in the contemporary exempt organizations setting has become too customary for this form of attribution to occur, absent the most egregious of facts.[42]

§ 31.2   FINANCIAL CONSIDERATIONS

(a) Capitalization

Assets of a tax-exempt organization that are currently being used in an unrelated business activity may, with little (if any) legal constraint, be spun off into an affiliated for-profit organization. The extent to which a for-profit corporation can be capitalized using exempt organization assets (particularly charitable ones), however, is a matter involving far more strict confines.

A tax-exempt organization can, as noted, invest a portion of its assets and engage in a certain amount of unrelated activities. At the same time, the governing board of an exempt organization must act in conformity with basic

---

[37] See § 18.5, text accompanied by note 109.
[38] Priv. Ltr. Rul. 9722006.
[39] E.g., Rev. Rul. 69-575, 1969-2 C.B. 134.
[40] Rev. Rul. 2002-55, 2002-37 I.R.B. 529.
[41] For this proposition, the IRS cited Comm'r v. Bollinger, *supra* note 24; Moline Properties, Inc. v. Comm'r, *supra* note 24.
[42] This does not mean that revenue from a for-profit subsidiary to an exempt parent is not taxable; in fact, just the opposite is often the case (see *infra* § 3).

fiduciary responsibilities, and the organization cannot (without jeopardizing its exemption) contravene the prohibitions on private inurement and private benefit.[43]

IRS private letter rulings suggest that only a small percentage of a tax-exempt organization's resources ought to be transferred to controlled for-profit subsidiaries.[44] These percentages approved by the IRS are usually low and, in any event, probably pertain only to cash. (Many IRS rulings in this area do not state the amount of capital involved.[45]) In some cases, a specific asset may—indeed, perhaps must—be best utilized in an unrelated activity, even though its value represents a meaningful portion of the organization's total resources.[46] Also, the exempt parent may want to make subsequent advances or loans to the subsidiary.

The best guiding standard in this regard is that of the prudent investor. In capitalizing a subsidiary, a tax-exempt organization should only part with an amount of resources that is reasonable under the circumstances and that can be rationalized in relation to amounts devoted to programs and invested in other fashions. Relevant to all of this is the projected return on the investment, in terms of income and capital appreciation. If a contribution to a subsidiary's capital seems unwise, the putative parent should consider a loan (albeit one bearing a fair rate of interest and accompanied by adequate security).[47]

In all instances, it is preferable that the operation of the subsidiary furthers (if only by providing funds for) the exempt purposes of the parent.[48] Certainly, circumstances where exempt purposes are thwarted by reason of operation of a for-profit subsidiary are to be avoided.

(b) Compensation

The structure of a tax-exempt parent and a taxable subsidiary may generate questions and issues as to compensation of employees.

The compensation of the employees of the taxable subsidiary is subject to an overarching requirement that the amount paid may not exceed a reasonable salary or wage.[49] The compensation of the employees of the parent tax-exempt organization is subject to a like limitation, by reason of the private inurement, private benefit, and/or excess benefit transaction doctrines.[50] An individual may be

---

[43] See Chapter 19.
[44] E.g., Priv. Ltr. Rul. 8505044.
[45] E.g., Priv. Ltr. Rul. 9305026.
[46] In one instance, the amount of capital transferred was characterized by the IRS as "substantial," although the exempt parent was not a charitable entity; it was a tax-exempt social welfare organization (see Chapter 12) (Priv. Ltr. Rul. 9245031).
[47] Payments by a tax-exempt organization to its subsidiary for services provided, with the payments from revenues generated by the services, are likely to be considered by the IRS to be compensation for services rather than contributions to capital (Priv. Ltr. Rul. 200227007).
[48] E.g., Priv. Ltr. Rul. 8709051.
[49] IRC § 162.
[50] See Chapter 19.

an employee of both the parent and subsidiary organizations; in that circumstance, a reasonable allocation of compensation as between the entities is required.[51] Also, if an officer, director, trustee, or key employee received aggregate compensation of more than $100,000 from an exempt organization and one or more of its related organizations, of which more than $10,000 was provided by a related organization, that fact must be reported to the IRS, with an explanation.[52] The employees of a for-profit subsidiary of a parent exempt organization may be included in one or more employee benefit plans of the parent, without endangering the exempt status of the parent, as long as the costs of the plan are allocated among the two employers on a per-capita basis.[53]

The employees of the tax-exempt parent could participate in deferred compensation plans[54] or perhaps tax-sheltered annuity programs.[55] Deferred salary plans may also be used by the subsidiary, as may qualified pension plans. Both the parent and the subsidiary may utilize 401 (k) plans.[56]

Use of a taxable subsidiary may facilitate the offering of stock options to employees, to enable them to share in the growth of the corporation. The subsidiary similarly may offer an employee stock ownership plan, which is a plan that invests in the stock of the sponsoring company.[57] The subsidiary may issue unqualified options to buy stock or qualified incentive stock options.[58]

(c) Sharing of Resources

Generally, a tax-exempt organization and its for-profit subsidiary may share resources without adverse consequences, as a matter of the law of tax-exempt organizations, to the exempt entity. That is, the two organizations may share office facilities, equipment, supplies, and the like. Particularly where the exempt entity is a charitable one, however, all relevant costs must be allocated on the basis of actual use and each organization must pay fair market value for the resources used.[59]

It is generally preferable for the tax-exempt organization to reimburse the for-profit entity for the exempt organization's use of resources, to avoid even a perception that the funds of an exempt organization are being used to subsidize a for-profit organization. Nonetheless, this approach often is impractical where the exempt organization is the parent entity.

---

[51] One of the burgeoning issues in this regard is potential misuses of for-profit subsidiaries, such as by unduly shifting expenses to them, excess and/or additional compensation paid by them, and lack of disclosure of the relationship; sometimes, there are also conflict-of-interest issues.

[52] Form 990, Part V. In general, see § 24.3.

[53] E.g., Priv. Ltr. Rul. 9242039.

[54] IRC § 457.

[55] IRC § 403(b).

[56] See § 16.1(d)(ii), text accompanied by note 13.

[57] IRC § 4975(e)(7).

[58] E.g., Priv. Ltr. Rul. 9242038.

[59] E.g., Priv. Ltr. Rul. 9308047. Where, however, the charitable organization is a private foundation, caution is required in this regard, in that this type of resource sharing is likely to be self-dealing (see § 11.4(a)).

(d) Liquidations

The federal tax law causes recognition of gain or loss by a for-profit corporation in an instance of a liquidating distribution of its assets (as if the corporation had sold the assets to the distributee at fair market value) and in the event of liquidating sales. There is an exception for liquidating transfers within an affiliated group (which is regarded as a single economic unit), so that the basis in the property is carried over from the distributor to the distributee in lieu of recognition of gain or loss.

This nonrecognition exception is modified for eligible liquidations in which an 80 percent corporate shareholder receives property with a carryover basis, to provide for nonrecognition of gain or loss with respect to any property actually distributed to that shareholder. Nonetheless, this nonrecognition rule under the exception for 80 percent corporate shareholders is generally not available where the shareholder is a tax-exempt organization. That is, any gain or loss generally must be recognized by the subsidiary on the distribution of its assets in liquidation as if the assets were sold to the exempt parent at their fair market value.[60] (Gain or loss is not recognized by the parent entity on its receipt of the subsidiary's assets pursuant to the liquidation.[61]) This nonrecognition treatment is available in the tax-exempt organizations context, however, where the property distributed is used by the exempt organization in an unrelated business immediately after the distribution. If the property subsequently ceases to be used in an unrelated business, the exempt organization will be taxed on the gain at that time.[62]

In one instance, a tax-exempt home health and hospice agency formed a wholly owned for-profit subsidiary to provide home companion services and operate an assisted living facility. Years later, the parent organization expanded its programs and facilities, and determined that the activities conducted by the subsidiary could be undertaken by the parent without adversely affecting the parent's exempt status. The parent organization proceeded to liquidate the subsidiary and transfer to it all of the assets, which had appreciated in value, in the subsidiary. The IRS ruled that the gain attributable to the distribution of the subsidiary's assets to the parent organization on liquidation would be excludable from taxation as unrelated business income by reason of the exclusion from taxation of capital gains.[63] This ruling was silent on the tax consequences of transfer of the appreciated assets by the subsidiary.[64]

---

[60] IRC § 337(b)(2)(A).

[61] IRC § 332(a).

[62] IRC § 337(b)(2)(B)(ii). Cf. Centre for Int'l Understanding v. Comm'r, 62 T.C.M. 629 (1991) (applying the liquidation rules of IRC § 337(c)(2)(A)). Regulations were issued in final form, under authority of IRC § 337(d), concerning the liquidation of for-profit entities into tax-exempt organizations, when the relationship is not that of parent and subsidiary. The rules in this regard are essentially the same as those that apply to liquidations of subsidiaries, although they also apply when a for-profit corporation converts to an exempt entity (see §§ 33.4(b), (c), 33.5).

[63] Priv. Ltr. Rul. 9438029.

[64] In general, this ruling did not utilize the liquidation rules of IRC §§ 332 and 337. It is not clear from this ruling whether the assets in the subsidiary were to be used in related or unrelated activities by the exempt parent after the liquidation. If the assets were to be used in related activities, the gain should have been recognized and taxable to the subsidiary (IRC § 337(b)(2)(A)).

In another instance, one of the functions of a charitable entity was the publication and circulation of religious materials. This organization had a for-profit subsidiary that engaged in both exempt and commercial printing activities. Once it decided to discontinue the commercial printing operations, the exempt parent proposed to liquidate the subsidiary and distribute its assets to the parent organization. The IRS ruled that any gain or loss must be recognized by the subsidiary on the distribution of its assets in liquidation (as if they were sold to the exempt parent at fair market value) to the extent the assets are to be used in related business activities.[65]

§ 31.3   TREATMENT OF REVENUE FROM SUBSIDIARY

While not always the case, most tax-exempt organizations develop an unrelated business with the anticipation that it will serve as a source of revenue. Thus, the development within, or shifting of the unrelated business to, a taxable subsidiary should be done in such a way as to not preclude or inhibit the flow of income from the subsidiary to the parent.

The staff and other resources of an affiliated business are usually those of the tax-exempt organization parent. Thus, the headquarters of the taxable subsidiary are likely to be the same as its parent. This means that the taxable subsidiary may have to reimburse the exempt organization parent for the subsidiary's occupancy costs, share of employees' time, and use of the parent's equipment and supplies. Therefore, one way for dollars to flow from the subsidiary to the parent is as this form of reimbursement, which would include an element of rent.

Another type of relationship between a tax-exempt organization parent and a taxable subsidiary is that of lender and borrower. That is, in addition to funding its subsidiary by means of a capital contribution (resulting in a holding of equity by the parent), the parent may find it appropriate to lend money to its subsidiary. Inasmuch as a no-interest loan to a for-profit subsidiary by a tax-exempt organization parent may endanger the exempt status of the parent, and trigger problems under the below-market interest rules,[66] it would be appropriate for a loan to bear a fair market rate of interest. Therefore, another way for dollars to flow from the subsidiary to the parent is in the form of interest.

The business activities of a for-profit subsidiary may be to market and sell a product or service. When done in conformity with its tax-exempt status, the parent can license the use of its name, logo, acronym, and/or some other feature that would enhance the sale of the product or service provided by the subsidiary. For

---

[65] Priv. Ltr. Rul. 9645017. This ruling expressly addressed the point that, to the extent the assets were to be used by the parent in unrelated activities, any gain would not be recognized during the pendency of that type of use (IRC § 337(b)(2)(B)(ii)).
[66] IRC § 7872.

this license, the subsidiary would pay to the parent a royalty—another way of transferring dollars from a for-profit subsidiary to a tax-exempt parent.

A conventional way of transferring money from a corporation to its stock-holders is for the corporation to distribute its earnings and profits to them. These distributions are dividends and represent yet another way in which a taxable subsidiary can transfer dollars to its tax-exempt parent.

Certain types of income are exempted from taxation as unrelated income—principally the various forms of passive income.[67] Were it not for a special rule of federal tax law, a tax-exempt organization could have it both ways: avoid taxation of the exempt organization on unrelated income by housing the activity in a subsidiary and thereafter receive passive, nontaxable income from the subsidiary.

Congress, however, was mindful of this potential double benefit and thus legislated a rule that is an exception to the general body of law that exempts passive income from taxation: Otherwise passive nontaxable income that is derived from a controlled taxable subsidiary is generally taxed as unrelated income. Thus, when a tax-exempt organization parent receives rents, interest, or most other forms of passive income from a controlled taxable subsidiary, those revenues will generally be taxable.[68]

There is no tax deduction, however, for the payment of dividends. Consequently, when a for-profit subsidiary pays a dividend to its tax-exempt organization parent, the dividend payments are not deductible by the subsidiary. Therefore, Congress determined that it would not be appropriate to tax revenue to an exempt organization parent where it is not deductible by the taxable subsidiary.[69]

§ 31.4   SUBSIDIARIES IN PARTNERSHIPS

There is a dimension to the use of a taxable subsidiary by a tax-exempt organization parent that is alluded to in the discussion of exempt organizations in partnerships.[70] This is the attempt by a charitable organization to avoid endangering its exempt status because of involvement in a partnership as a general partner by causing a taxable subsidiary to be the general partner in its stead.[71]

This can be an effective stratagem as long as all of the requirements of the law as to the bona fides of the subsidiary are satisfied, including the requirement

---

[67] See § 27.1.

[68] IRC § 512(b)(13).

[69] See § 27.1(n).

[70] See § 29.5(g), Chapter 32.

[71] E.g., Gen. Couns. Mem. 39598. One area of the federal tax law concerning tax-exempt organizations where the use of a for-profit subsidiary in a partnership, instead of an exempt organization, generally will not alter the tax outcome is the set of rules pertaining to tax-exempt entity leasing (see § 29.5(g)). On occasion, some or all of these results can be accomplished by the use of a tax-exempt subsidiary (e.g., Priv. Ltr. Rul. 8638131).

that the subsidiary be an authentic business entity. As discussed,[72] however, if the tax-exempt organization parent is intimately involved in the day-to-day management of the subsidiary, the IRS may impute the activities of the subsidiary to the parent, thereby endangering the exempt status of the parent by treating it as if it were directly involved as a general partner of the limited partnership.[73]

An illustration of this use of a partnership was presented in an IRS ruling.[74] A tax-exempt hospital wanted to expand its provision of medical rehabilitation services; a for-profit corporation that managed the rehabilitation program at the hospital was a subsidiary of the nation's largest independent provider of comprehensive rehabilitation services. The hospital, through this subsidiary, sought a joint venture with its for-profit parent to utilize its expertise and methodologies, and to operate the rehabilitation facility as a venture so that the expansion would not jeopardize the institution's role as a community hospital. The joint venture was structured so that it was between the hospital and a system of which it was a component, and a wholly owned for-profit subsidiary of the for-profit parent entity and its subsidiary. The IRS ruled favorably in the case, concluding that the hospital's participation in the venture was consistent with its purposes of promoting health.[75]

§ 31.5 EFFECT OF FOR-PROFIT SUBSIDIARIES ON PUBLIC CHARITY STATUS

Just as it is possible for the existence of a for-profit subsidiary to have an adverse impact on the tax-exempt status of an organization (by an attribution of the activities for tax purposes[76]), so too is there potential that the presence of a for-profit subsidiary will have a pernicious effect on the public charity status of the exempt charitable parent organization.

(a) Publicly Supported Organizations

Any impact of a for-profit subsidiary organization on the status of a tax-exempt charitable organization that is its parent, where the parent is classified as a publicly supported organization, is derived from funding of the parent by the subsidiary. If the funding is in the form of a charitable contribution, it may be regarded for tax purposes as a dividend.[77]

---

[72] See *supra* § 1(d).

[73] In one instance, the IRS, without explanation, expressly ignored a tax-exempt organization's use of a for-profit subsidiary as the general partner in a partnership, reviewing the facts as though the exempt organization was directly involved in the partnership (Tech. Adv. Mem. 8939002).

[74] Priv. Ltr. Rul 9352030.

[75] In general, see § 6.2.

[76] See *supra* § 1(d).

[77] See *supra* § 1, note 9.

Where a parent charitable organization has its non–private foundation status based on classification as a donative type of publicly supported charity,[78] a transfer of money or property to it by a subsidiary will, if treated as a dividend, not qualify as public support.[79] Moreover, where the item or items transferred to the publicly supported donative parent are considered gifts, they wold not constitute public support to the extent the amount exceeded the 2 percent limitation threshold.[80]

If the parent organization is not a private foundation by reason of categorization as a service provider type of publicly supported charity,[81] any amount paid to it by a subsidiary would not be public support if the amount was regarded as a dividend.[82] Moreover, a payment of this nature accorded dividend treatment would be investment income, as to which there is a one-third limitation with respect to receipt of this type of revenue.[83] If the item or items transferred to the publicly supported service provider parent are considered gifts, they would not constitute public support where the subsidiary is a disqualified person[84] with respect to the parent organization.[85]

(b) Supporting Organizations

Some tax-exempt charitable organizations are able to become classified as public charities by virtue of the rules concerning supporting organizations.[86]

Because the public charity status of a supporting organization is not derived from the nature of its funding, the considerations pertaining to publicly supported organizations discussed previously are inapplicable (although a transfer from a for-profit subsidiary to a supporting organization may nonetheless be considered a dividend).

The public charity classification of a charitable organization that is a supporting organization is rested on the rule that it must be operated exclusively to support or benefit one or more eligible public charitable organizations.[87] There was a school of thought that held that a supporting organization cannot have a for-profit subsidiary because, to do so would be a violation of the exclusively requirement. There was some merit to this position, since the term *exclusively* means, in this setting, *solely*,[88] as opposed to its definition in the context of charitable organizations generally, where the term means *primarily*.[89]

---

[78] See § 11.3(b)(i).
[79] Reg. § 1.170A-9(e)(2).
[80] Reg. § 1.170A-9(e)(6)(i).
[81] See § 11.3(b)(iv).
[82] IRC § 509(a)(2)(A); Reg. § 1.509(a)-3(a)(2).
[83] IRC § 509(a)(2)(B); Reg. § 1.509(a)-3(a)(3)(i).
[84] See § 11.2.
[85] IRC § 509(a)(2)(A); Reg. § 1.509(a)-3(b)(2).
[86] See § 11.3(c).
[87] IRC § 509(a)(3)(A). See § 11.3(c).
[88] Reg. § 1.509(a)-4(e)(1).
[89] See § 4.6.

Contentions to the contrary included the view that, where the reason for organizing and utilizing the subsidiary is to assist in the supporting or benefiting of one or more eligible public charities, there should not be a prohibition on the use of for-profit subsidiaries in this manner. This issue arose when the IRS ruled that, as long as a supporting organization does not actively participate in the day-to-day management of a for-profit subsidiary and both entities have a legitimate economic and business purpose and operations, the supporting organization can utilize a for-profit subsidiary without jeopardizing its tax-exempt status.[90] This ruling was silent on the matter of the impact of the use of the subsidiary on the organization's supporting organization classification. The IRS subsequently held, however, that a supporting organization can have a for-profit subsidiary and not disturb its status as a supporting entity.[91]

---

[90] Priv. Ltr. Rul. 9305026.

[91] Priv. Ltr. Rul. 9637051. The IRS ruled as to the tax consequences of a liquidation of a for-profit subsidiary into a supporting organization (Priv. Ltr. Rul. 9645017) (in general, see *supra* § 2(d)).

Tax-Exempt Organizations, Partnerships, and Joint Ventures

One of the most important developments involving tax-exempt organizations in the modern era is the use of related organizations. This phenomenon is reflected, for example, in the use of subsidiaries by exempt organizations.[1] What is striking, nonetheless, is the contemporary willingness—and, in some instances, necessity—of many exempt organizations to simultaneously use different forms of related entities, be they for-profit or nonprofit, trust or corporation, taxable or nontaxable. This includes participation by exempt organizations in partnerships or other forms of joint venture.

§ 32.1 PARTNERSHIPS BASICS

A partnership is a form of business entity, recognized in the law as a separate legal entity, as is a corporation or trust. It is usually evidenced by a document, which is a partnership agreement, executed between persons who are the partners; the persons may be individuals, corporations, and/or other partnerships. Each partner owns one or more interests, called units, in the partnership.

    The term *partnership* is defined in the federal tax law to include a "syndicate, group, pool, joint venture, or other unincorporated organization, through or by means of which any business, financial operation, or venture is carried on, and

---

[1] See Chapters 30 and 31.

which is not . . . a trust or estate or a corporation."[2] This term is broadly applied. For example, co-owners of income-producing real estate who operate the property (either directly or through an agent of one or more of them) for their joint profit are operating a partnership.[3]

A partnership usually entails a profit motive. Thus, a court defined a partnership as a "contract of two or more persons to place their money, efforts, labor, and skill, or some or all of them, in lawful commerce or business, and to divide the profit and bear the loss in definite proportions."[4]

Partners are of two types: general and limited. The types are delineated principally by their role in the venture (active or passive) and the extent of the partners' liability for the acts of the partnership. Generally, liability for the consequences of a partnership's operations rests with the general partner or partners, while the exposure to liability for the functions of the partnership for the limited partners is confined to the amount of the limited partner's contribution to the partnership. A general partner is liable for satisfaction of the ongoing obligations of the partnership and can be called on to make additional contributions of capital to it. Every partnership must have at least one general partner. Sometimes where there is more than one general partner, one of them is designated the managing general partner.

Many partnerships have only general partners, who contribute cash, property, and/or services. This type of partnership is termed a *general partnership*. The interests of the general partners may or may not be equal. In this type of partnership, which is essentially akin to a joint venture,[5] generally all of the partners are equally liable for satisfaction of the obligations of the partnership and can be called upon to make additional capital contributions to the entity.

Some partnerships, however, need or want to attract capital from sources other than the general partners. This capital can come from investors, who are termed limited partners. Their interest in the partnership is, as noted, limited in the sense that their liability is limited. The liability of a limited partner is confined to the amount of the capital contribution—the investment. The limited partners are in the venture to obtain a return on their investment and perhaps to procure some tax advantages. A partnership with both general and limited partners is termed a *limited partnership*.

The partnership is the entity that acquires the property, develops it (if necessary), and sometimes continues to operate and maintain the property. Where a tax-exempt organization is the general partner, it is not the owner of the property (the partnership is) but nonetheless it can have many of the incidents of ownership, such as participation in the cash flow generated by the property, a preferential leasing arrangement, and/or the general perception by the outside world that the property is owned by the exempt organization. The exempt organization may lease space in property owned by the partnership. The exempt entity may have

---

[2] IRC § 7701(a)(2).
[3] Rev. Rul. 54-369, 1954-2 C.B. 364; Rev. Rul. 54-170, 1954-1 C.B. 213.
[4] Whiteford v. United States, 61-1 U.S.T.C. ¶ 9301, at 79,762 (D. Kan. 1960).
[5] See *infra* § 3.

an option to purchase the property from the partnership after the passage of a stated period of time.

Partnerships do not pay taxes—and, in this sense, are themselves tax-exempt organizations.[6] They are conduits—technically, flow-through entities—of net revenue to the partners, who bear the responsibility for paying tax on their net income. Partnerships are also conduits of the tax advantages of the ownership of property, and thus can pass through preference items such as depreciation and interest deductions.

If an entity fails to qualify under the federal tax laws as a partnership, it will be treated as an *association*, which means taxed as a corporation. When that happens, as a general rule the entity will have to pay taxes and the ability to pass through tax advantages to the equity owners is lost.[7]

In many instances, it is clear that the parties in an arrangement intend to create and operate a partnership. In some cases, however, the law will treat an arrangement as a general partnership (or other joint venture) for tax purposes, even though the parties involved intended (or insist they intended) that their relationship is something else (such as landlord and tenant or payor and payee of royalties). The issue often arises in the unrelated business context, where a tax-exempt organization is asserting that certain income is passive in nature (most frequently, rent or royalty income) and the IRS is contending that the income was derived from active participation in a partnership (or joint venture).[8]

Federal tax law is inconsistent in stating the criteria for ascertaining whether a partnership is to be found as a matter of law. The U.S. Supreme Court stated that "[w]hen the existence of an alleged partnership arrangement is challenged by outsiders, the question arises whether the partners really and truly intended to join together for the purpose of carrying on business and sharing in the profits or losses or both."[9] The Court added that the parties' "intention is a question of fact, to be determined from testimony disclosed by their 'agreement considered as a whole, and by their conduct in execution of its provisions.' "[10] In one instance, a court examined state law and concluded that the most important element in determining whether a landlord-tenant relationship or joint venture agreement exists is the intention of the parties. This court also held that the burden of proving the existence of a partnership is on the party who claims that that type of relationship exists (usually, the IRS).[11]

---

[6] See § 1.2.

[7] Moreover, the partnership must have effective ownership of the property for these deductions to be available, rather than have the ownership be by the exempt organization/general partner (e.g., Smith v. Comm'r, 50 T.C.M. 1444 (1985)).

[8] See, e.g., § 26.5(h).

[9] Comm'r v. Tower, 327 U.S. 280, 286-287 (1946).

[10] *Id.* at 287 (citations omitted). These principles are equally applicable in determining the existence of a joint venture (e.g., Estate of Smith v. Comm'r, 313 F.2d 724 (8th Cir. 1963), *aff'g in part, rev'g in part, and remanding* 33 T.C. 465 (1959); Luna v. Comm'r, 42 T.C. 1067 (1964); Beck Chemical Equip. Corp. v. Comm'r, 27 T.C. 840 (1957)).

[11] Harlan E. Moore Charitable Trust v. United States, 812 F. Supp. 130, 132 (C.D. Ill. 1993), *aff'd*, 9 F.3d 623 (7th Cir. 1993).

Conversely, another court declared that it is "well settled that neither local law nor the expressed intent of the parties is conclusive as to the existence or nonexistence of a partnership or joint venture for federal tax purposes."[12] The court stated that the standard to follow is "whether, considering all the facts—the agreement, the conduct of the parties in execution of its provisions, their statements, the testimony of disinterested persons, the relationship of the parties, their respective abilities and capital contributions, the actual control of income and the purposes for which it is used, and any other facts throwing light on their true intent—the parties in good faith and acting with a business purposes intended to join together in the present conduct of the enterprise."[13]

This court wrote that the "realities of the taxpayer's economic interest rather than the niceties of the conveyancer's art should determine the power to tax."[14] The court added: "Among the critical elements involved in this determination are the existence of controls over the venture and a risk of loss in the taxpayer."[15] Finally, the court said that it is not bound by the "nomenclature used by the parties," so that a document titled, for example, a lease, may as a matter of law be a partnership agreement.[16]

This dichotomy was illustrated by a case involving a tax-exempt charitable organization and its tenant-farmer; the issue was whether the relationship was landlord-tenant, partnership, or other joint venture.[17] The question before the court was whether the rent, equaling 50 percent of the crops and produce grown on the farm, constituted rent that was excludable from taxation as unrelated business income.[18] The court looked to state law to ascertain the meaning to be given the term *rent*. It observed that the written contracts at issue contained provisions usually found in leases, the tenant furnished all of the machinery and labor in the production of crops, and the tenant generally made decisions with a farm manager as to the day-to-day operation of the farm. The court concluded that the contracts as a whole clearly reflected the intention of the parties to create a landlord-tenant relationship, rather than a partnership.

The IRS unsuccessfully contended that this charitable organization, by furnishing the seed and one-half of the cost of fertilizer, weed spray, and combining, engaged in farming as a partner or joint venturer. The court observed that these types of arrangements were not uncommon in share-crop leases, and noted that the furnishing of these items ordinarily increased the crop yield and the net return of both the landlord and tenant substantially more than the amount invested by each for the items. The court also analyzed the effect on the

---

[12] Trust U/W Emily Oblinger v. Comm'r, 100 T.C. 114 (1993). The court cited a number of court opinions as authority for this proposition, relying principally on Haley v. Comm'r, 203 F.2d 815 (5th Cir. 1953), *rev'g and rem'g* 16 T.C. 1509 (1951).

[13] Trust U/W Emily Oblinger v. Comm'r, *supra* note 12, at 118, citing Comm'r v. Culbertson, 337 U.S. 733, 742 (1949). Also Luna v. Comm'r, *supra* note 10, at 1077–1078.

[14] Trust U/W Emily Oblinger v. Comm'r, *supra* note 12, at 118.

[15] *Id.* at 118–119.

[16] *Id.* at 119.

[17] United States v. Myra Found., 382 F.2d 107 (8th Cir. 1967).

[18] See § 27.1(h)(i). This case was decided before enactment of the *passive rent rules*.

landlord-tenant relationship of the hiring by the charitable organization of the farm manager for the supervision of the tenant-farmer. The manager advised the tenant on topics such as crops, seed, weed spray, and fertilizer; decisions were made by the mutual agreement of the tenant and the manager. The court concluded that the utilization of the farm manager did not adversely affect the landlord-tenant relationship, and found that the arrangement was not that of a partnership (or other joint venture).

As a general rule, a partnership is a useful and beneficial way for one or more individuals or organizations to acquire, finance, own, and/or operate property. There can be problems with this approach, however, in the tax-exempt organizations context.[19]

§ 32.2   THE TAX EXEMPTION ISSUE

The IRS is not enamored with the thought of tax-exempt organizations (particularly charitable ones) in partnerships, other than as limited partners in a prudent investment vehicle.[20] To date, the controversy has centered on exempt charitable organizations in partnerships, although some or all of the principles of law being developed could apply to other types of exempt organizations, particularly social welfare organizations and business leagues.[21]

The concern of the IRS is that substantial benefits may be provided to the for-profit participants in a partnership (usually the limited partners) with a tax-exempt organization where the exempt organization is a general partner. This uneasiness in the agency has its origins in arrangements involving exempt hospitals and physicians, such as a limited partnership formed to build and manage a medical office building, with a hospital as the general partner and investing physicians as limited partners.[22] Where these substantial benefits are present, the IRS usually will not be hesitant to deploy the doctrines of private inurement, excess benefit transaction, and/or private benefit.[23] Yet the

---

[19] The foregoing is, by necessity, an overview of the law of partnerships. For a comprehensive analysis of these entities (from a tax-exempt organizations perspective), see Sanders, *Joint Ventures Involving Tax-Exempt Organizations, Second Edition* (John Wiley & Sons, Inc., 2000) (*Joint Ventures*), particularly Chapters 1, 3, and 4.

[20] E.g., Gordanier, Jr., "Structuring Securities Partnerships for Tax-Exempt and Foreign Investors," 7 *J. Partnership Tax.* (No. 2) 24 (1990); Menna, "Leveraged Real Estate Investments by Tax-Exempt and Taxable Investors: Comparing the Forms of Investment," 17 *J. Real Estate Tax.* (No. 3) 231 (1990); Williamson & Blum, "Tax Planning for Real Estate Ownership and Investment by Tax-Exempt Entities," 16 *J. Real Estate Tax.* (No. 2) 139 (1989).

[21] See Chapters 12, 13.

[22] The history of the position of the IRS in these regards is detailed in *Joint Ventures*, at § 4.2.

[23] The IRS is not averse to using its authority in this context. For example, the agency created the private inurement *per se* doctrine in the health care context as a basis for revocation of hospitals' tax-exempt status using a joint venture theory (see § 19.8). The IRS revoked the exemption of hospitals for engaging in private inurement transactions (e.g., Priv. Ltr. Rul. 9130002). In general, Hyatt & Hopkins, *The Law of Tax-Exempt Healthcare Organizations, Second Edition* (John Wiley & Sons, Inc., 2001), particularly Chapters 4, 22. The IRS concludes from time to time that the exempt status of other types of charitable organizations should be terminated because of private inurement (e.g., Tech. Adv. Mem. 9335001 (concerning a private foundation)). In general, Chapter 19.

law, in general, is now clear that an exempt charitable organization may participate as a general partner in a partnership, without adversely affecting its exempt status.[24]

It is the position of the IRS that a tax-exempt charitable organization will lose or be denied exemption if it participates as the, or a, general partner in a limited partnership, unless the principal purpose of the partnership is to further charitable purposes.[25] Even where the partnership can so qualify, the exemption is not available if the charitable organization/general partner is not adequately insulated from the day-to-day management responsibilities of the partnership and/or if the limited partners are to receive an undue economic return. The IRS recognizes that a charitable organization can be operated exclusively for exempt purposes, and simultaneously be a general partner and satisfy its fiduciary responsibilities with respect to the other partners.[26]

Confusion as to the ability of tax-exempt charitable organizations to participate as general partners in limited partnerships was added when a court held, without recognition let alone discussion of the considerable body of law developed on the point, that an organization did not qualify as an exempt entity where it was a co-general partner in limited partnerships, where the other general partner was a for-profit corporation and the limited partners were individuals, and where the purpose of the partnerships was to operate low-income housing projects. The court said that the organization's participation violated the operational test[27] in that the operation of the partnerships would cause federal and state tax benefits to flow to the nonexempt partners.[28] By reason of the organization's involvement in the partnerships, the underlying properties would receive property tax reductions. The partnership would be eligible, under federal tax law, for general business credits and low-income housing credits; pursuant to management agreements, the organization had the responsibility for ensuring that the partnership complied with the business tax credit requirements. The organization received, as compensation, percentages of state tax savings. The court concluded that the "keystone of . . . [this] entire plan is of course to lend [the organization's] exempt status to achieving the objective of property tax reduction."[29] The organization also was deprived of exempt status by reason of the private inurement doctrine[30] because its "activities here serve the commercial purposes of the for-

---

[24] On one occasion, the IRS ruled that the tax-exempt status of a charitable organization should not be revoked; the issue was its participation as a general partner in seven limited partnerships (Priv. Ltr. Rul. 8938001). On another occasion, the IRS held that a hospital organization continued to qualify as an exempt charitable entity, notwithstanding its function as the sole partner of a limited partnership, where some of the limited partnership interests were held by related individuals (Tech. Adv. Mem. 200151045).

[25] Gen. Couns. Mem. 39005.

[26] Gen. Couns. Mem. 39546.

[27] See § 4.5.

[28] Housing Pioneers, Inc. v. Comm'r, 65 T.C.M. 2191 (1993).

[29] *Id.* at 2195.

[30] See Chapter 19.

profit partners in the limited partnerships of which . . . [the organization] is a general partner."[31]

Prior to a review of the law concerning charitable organizations in partnerships, it is appropriate to trace the evolution of this body of law.

(a) Evolution of the Law

Originally, the IRS was of the view that involvement by a charitable organization in a limited partnership as general partner was the basis for automatic revocation of tax exemption, irrespective of the purpose of the partnership. This view, predicated on the private inurement doctrine, is known as the *per se rule*.

The *per se rule* surfaced in 1978, when the IRS ruled that participation by a charitable organization in a partnership, where the organization was the general partner and private investors were limited partners, was contrary to the organization's tax-exempt status in that private economic benefit was conveyed to the limited partners.[32] In this ruling, the IRS staked out this position:

> [I]f you [the charitable organization] entered [into] the proposed partnership, you would be a direct participant in an arrangement for sharing the net profits of an income producing venture with private individuals and organizations of a non-charitable nature. By agreeing to serve as the general partner of the proposed . . . project, you would take on an obligation to further the private financial interests of the other partners. This would create a conflict of interest that is legally incompatible with you being operated exclusively for charitable purposes.

Thus, the IRS posture on the matter was clear: A tax-exempt charitable organization would lose its exemption if it functioned as the general partner of a limited partnership on the ground that it was furthering the private interests of the limited partners. This was the IRS position, even though the purpose of the partnership was to advance a charitable objective (in the case, the development and operation of a low-income housing project).

The *per se rule* was advanced again in 1979, with the IRS issuing an adverse ruling to a charitable organization that was the general partner in a limited partnership (also again, having the purpose of maintaining a low-income housing project). As before, the IRS pronounced the organization a "direct participant in an arrangement for sharing the net profits of an income producing venture" with private individuals, so that the organization is "further[ing] the private financial interest of the [limited] partners."[33]

Several months later, the issue became the subject of litigation.[34] Before the

---

[31] Housing Pioneers, Inc. v. Comm'r, *supra* note 28, at 2196. This opinion was affirmed but on the ground that the organization failed to show that it was a qualified nonprofit organization for purposes of the low-income housing tax credit (IRC § 42(h)(5)(B)) (95-1 U.S.T.C. ¶ 50,126 (9th Cir. 1995)).
[32] Priv. Ltr. Rul. 7820058.
[33] Priv. Ltr. dated Feb. 6, 1979.
[34] Strawbridge Square, Inc. v. United States (Ct. Cl. No. 471-79T).

court was the case of the charitable organization that was the subject of the 1979 ruling and that held a one percent interest in a partnership as a general partner, a for-profit corporation that held a 4.5 percent interest as the other general partner, and an unspecified number of individuals that held the balance of the partnership interests as limited partners. At issue was the tax-exempt status of the charitable organization. There is no opinion in the case, however, because it was settled and the matter was dismissed in 1980.

The *per se rule* was temporarily abandoned by the IRS, and as the result of the settlement the charitable organization was allowed to serve as a general partner in the limited partnership without endangering its tax exemption. The organization ultimately prevailed because it was able to demonstrate a relatively limited involvement in both the finances as well as overall control and management of the project. The organization also was successful in showing that the other general partner was, by reason of provisions in the partnership agreement, primarily responsible for managing the financial and business aspects of the project, thereby permitting it to function primarily in furtherance of its exempt purposes without having to become unduly involved in the nonexempt aspects of the venture.

The terms of the settlement proved to be a harbinger of the IRS position to come. Nonetheless, the IRS continued to pursue application of the *per se rule* in other cases.

For example, an IRS private letter ruling issued in 1979, concerning the issue as to whether certain fees derived by tax-exempt lawyer referral services were items of unrelated income, reflected this IRS position.[35] The IRS ruled that, while flat counseling fees paid by clients and registration fees paid by lawyers were not taxable, the fees paid by lawyers to the organization based on a percentage of the fees received by them for providing legal services to clients referred to them constituted unrelated income. The reason: The subsequently established lawyer-client relationship was a commercial undertaking and the ongoing fee arrangement with the percentage feature placed the organization in the position of being in a joint venture in furtherance of those commercial objectives.

This perseverance on the part of the IRS also is mirrored in another case, this one concerning syndication of a play. In this instance, a tax-exempt theater was struggling in its efforts to stage a production (about the U.S. Supreme Court). Needing financial assistance, it underwrote its production costs with funds provided by private investors. The IRS sought to revoke the organization's exempt status for attempting to sustain the arts in this fashion but lost, both at trial and on appeal.[36] Again, the matter involved a partnership that was being used to further the exempt ends of the general partner. The courts in the case placed emphasis on the facts that the partnership had no interest in the exempt organization or its other activities, the limited partners had no control over the way in which the exempt organization operated or managed its affairs, and none of the limited

---

[35] Priv. Ltr. Rul. 7952002.
[36] Plumstead Theatre Soc'y, Inc. v. Comm'r, 74 T.C. 1324 (1980), *aff'd*, 675 F.2d 244 (9th Cir. 1982).

partners nor any officer or director of a corporate limited partner was an officer or director of the charitable organization.

The first manifestation of a relaxation of the stance of the IRS in these regards appeared in 1983 in the form of an IRS general counsel memorandum.[37] On that occasion, the IRS chief counsel's office opined that it was possible for a charitable organization to participate as a general partner in a limited partnership without jeopardizing its tax exemption. The IRS's lawyers advised that two aspects of the matter should be reviewed: (1) whether the participation may be in conflict with the goals and purposes of the charitable organization, and (2) whether the terms of the partnership agreement contain provisions that "insulate" the charitable organization from certain of the obligations imposed on a general partner. In this instance, the limited partnership (another low-income housing venture) was found to further the organization's charitable purposes and several specific provisions of the partnership agreement were deemed to provide the requisite insulation for the charitable organization/general partner. Thus, the organization was permitted to serve as the partnership's general partner and simultaneously retain its exemption.

This position of the IRS Chief Counsel opened the way for many favorable private letter rulings concerning charitable organizations in partnerships. Each of these partnerships was held to be in furtherance of charitable objectives, such as the construction and operation of a medical office building on the grounds of a hospital, the purchase and operation of a CAT scan at a hospital, and low-income housing projects. To date, the IRS has yet to issue a private letter ruling denying a charitable organization tax-exempt status because of its involvement as a general partner in a limited partnership.[38] Indeed, the IRS frequently concludes that an exempt charitable organization can participate as a general partner in a limited partnership without endangering its exempt status.[39] Also, on occasion, a charitable organization can achieve exempt purposes by involvement in a partnership as a limited partner.[40]

(b) Current State of the Law

(i) General Rules.   The current position of the IRS as to whether a charitable organization will have its tax-exempt status revoked (or recognition denied) if it functions as a general partner in a limited partnership is the subject of a three-part test,[41] which is the successor to the *per se rule.*[42]

---

[37] Gen. Couns. Mem. 39005.

[38] This observation is made with the understanding that the facts in some of these rulings are altered at the request of the IRS and that some ruling requests in this area are withdrawn in anticipation of the issuance of an adverse ruling.

[39] E.g., Priv. Ltr. Rul. 8338127.

[40] E.g., Priv. Ltr. Rul. 9608039.

[41] This was articulated in Gen. Couns. Mem. 39005 (see text accompanying *supra* note 37).

[42] In general, Hopkins, "Tax Consequences of a Charity's Participation as a General Partner in a Limited Partnership Venture: A Commentary on the McGovern Analysis," 30 *Tax Notes* (No. 4) 361 (1986), written in response to McGovern, "The Tax Consequences of a Charity's Participation as a General Partner in a Limited Partnership Venture," 29 *Tax Notes* 1261 (1985).

Under this three-part test, the IRS first looks to determine whether the charitable organization/general partner is serving a charitable purpose by means of the partnership. If the partnership is advancing a charitable purpose, the IRS applies the remainder of the test. Should the partnership fail to adhere to the charitability standard, however, the charitable organization/general partner will be deprived of its tax-exempt status.

The balance of the test is designed to ascertain whether the charity's role as general partner inhibits its charitable purposes. Here, the IRS looks to means by which the organization may, under the particular facts and circumstances, be insulated from the day-to-day responsibilities as general partner and whether or not the limited partners are receiving an undue economic benefit from the partnership. It remains the view of the IRS that there is an inherent tension between the ability of a charitable organization to function exclusively in furtherance of its exempt functions and the obligation of a general partner to operate the partnership for the benefit of the limited partners. This tension is the same perceived phenomenon that the IRS, when applying its *per se rule*, chose to characterize as a "conflict of interest."

An instance of application of this test appeared in an IRS private letter ruling made public in 1985.[43] In that case, a charitable organization became a general partner in a real estate limited partnership that leased all of the space in the property to the organization and a related charitable organization. The IRS applied the first part of the test and found that the partnership was serving exempt ends because both of the tenants were charitable organizations. (The IRS general counsel memorandum underlying this ruling[44] noted that, if the lessee organization that was not the general partner had not been a charitable entity, the general partner would have forfeited its tax exemption.) On application of the rest of the test, the IRS found that the general partner was adequately insulated from the day-to-day management responsibilities of the partnership and that the limited partners' economic return was reasonable.

In this ruling, the IRS offered the following guidance in explication of the second and third elements of the test:

> If a private interest is served [by a limited partnership in which a charitable organization is the general partner], it must be incidental in both a qualitative and quantitative sense. In order to be incidental in a qualitative sense, it must be a necessary concomitant of the activity which benefits the public at large. In other words, the activity can be accomplished only by benefiting certain private individuals. To be incidental in a quantitative sense, the private benefit must not be substantial after considering the overall public benefit conferred by the activity.

The IRS added that if the charitable organization in the partnership is "serving a private interest, other than incidentally, then its participation in a limited

[43] Priv. Ltr. Rul. 8541108.
[44] Gen. Couns. Mem. 39444.

partnership [as general partner] will [adversely] affect its exempt status." As discussed next, however, considerable clarity has been subsequently provided in this area of the federal tax law as the IRS formulated its policies concerning the involvement of hospitals and other health care institutions in partnerships where physicians practicing at the hospitals are limited partners in these partnerships.

A commentator identified the following favorable factors or categories that the IRS looks to in evaluating a tax-exempt charitable organization's involvement as a general partner in a limited partnership: (1) limited contractual liability of the tax-exempt partner; (2) limited rate of return on the capital invested by the limited partners (a stated ceiling that is, under the circumstances, reasonable); (3) an exempt organization's right of first refusal on the sale of partnership assets; (4) the presence of additional general partners obligated to protect the interest of the limited partners; (5) lack of control over the venture or the exempt organization by the for-profit limited partners (that is, there is no limited partner serving as a director or officer of the exempt organization) except during the initial start-up period; (6) absence of any obligation to return the limited partners' capital from the exempt organization's funds; (7) absence of profit as a primary motivation; (8) all transactions with partners are at arm's length; (9) management contract terminable for cause by the venture, with a limited term, renewal subject to approval of the venture, and preferably with an independent entity; (10) effective control in the exempt organization over major decisions as to the venture; and (11) written commitment in the joint venture governing document to the fulfillment of charitable purposes in the event of a conflict with a duty to maximize profit.[45]

Conversely, unfavorable factors include (1) disproportionate allocation of profits and/or losses in favor of the limited partners; (2) commercially unreasonable loans by the exempt organization to the partnership; (3) inadequate compensation received by the exempt organization for services it provides or excessive compensation paid by the exempt organization in exchange for services it receives; (4) control of the exempt organization by the limited partners or lack of sufficient control by the exempt organization to ensure that it is able to carry out its charitable activities; (5) abnormal or insufficient capital contributions by the limited partners; (6) profit motivation by the exempt partner; and (7) guarantee of the limited partner's projected tax credits or return on investment to the detriment of the general partner.[46]

Until mid-1994, the IRS position with respect to charitable organizations in partnerships was represented solely by the three-part test. At this time, however, a private letter ruling appeared which added requirements to the basic test.[47] The

---

[45] *Joint Ventures* § 4.2(h)(i). If the tax-exempt organization/general partner is shielded too much, however, the partnership may lose its tax status as a partnership (that is, a nontaxable flow-through entity). Should that occur, the entity may become an association taxable as a corporation (IRC § 7701(a)(3)) (see text accompanied by *supra* note 2). The IRS's office of Chief Counsel raised this issue for the benefit of the agency's reviewers (Gen. Couns. Mem. 39546).

[46] *Joint Ventures* § 4.2(h)(ii).

[47] Priv. Ltr. Rul. 9438030.

IRS observed that the organization was "governed by an independent board of directors" composed of church and community leaders, and that it had no other relationship with any of the commercial companies involved in the project. The IRS added that no information indicated that the organization was controlled by or "otherwise unduly influenced" by the limited partners or any company involved in the development or management of the project.

(ii) Health Care Institutions. Recently, nearly all of the federal tax law in this setting has developed as the result of the innovative financing techniques, including partnerships, by or for the benefit of hospitals and other health care organizations, institutions, and systems.

One of the manifestations of this phenomenon was the IRS's position with respect to the sale of a hospital department's net revenue stream to a limited partnership (or joint venture) involving the hospital and physicians practicing in the department. The IRS held that this use of hospital assets was private inurement *per se* (that is, the amount of the funds flowing to the physicians was not evaluated against a standard of reasonableness), causing the hospital to lose its tax exemption.[48] In formulating its position in this regard, the chief counsel's office of the IRS used the occasion (in late 1991) to restate and update the analysis the agency uses in evaluating the participation of hospitals in a partnership arrangement.

The IRS's lawyers emphasized that the participation by a tax-exempt hospital as a general partner in a limited partnership is not inconsistent with exemption on a *per se* basis.[49] In each partnership situation, the IRS determines the presence or absence of private inurement or more than incidental private benefit[50] by evaluating all of the facts and circumstances, applying a standard of review termed "careful scrutiny." This three-step analysis is as follows:

1. Does the partnership further a charitable purpose?

2. If so, does the partnership agreement reflect an arrangement that permits the exempt organization to act primarily in furtherance of its exempt (charitable) purposes?

3. If so, does the arrangement cause the exempt organization to convey an impermissible private benefit to the limited partners?[51]

The third criterion requires a finding, if the hospital is to continue to be tax-exempt, that the benefits received by the limited partners are incidental to the exempt purposes advanced by the partnership. Thus, according to this analytical approach, a

---

[48] See § 19.8.

[49] Gen. Couns. Mem. 39862. The IRS bluntly stated that it "no longer contends that participation [by a charitable organization] as a general partner in a partnership is *per se* inconsistent with [tax] exemption."

[50] E.g., Gen. Couns. Mem 37789.

[51] In stating these factors, the IRS reaffirmed the ongoing validity of Gen. Couns. Mem. 39005 (see *supra* note 37), 39444 (see *supra* note 44), and 39546 (see *supra* note 45).

hospital's participation in a partnership or joint venture is inconsistent with its exemption if it does not further a charitable purpose, or if there is either inadequate protection against financial loss by the hospital or inappropriate or excessive financial gain flowing to the limited partners (investors/physicians).

The IRS, in evaluating these situations, looks to see "what the hospital gets in return for the benefit conferred on the physician-investors." The agency is least likely to find a basis for revocation of tax exemption because of hospital partnerships where a "new health care provider or resource was made available to the community."[52] Of importance also is whether the partnership itself became a "property owner or service provider, subject to all the attendant risks, responsibilities, and potential rewards." By contrast, in the net revenue stream partnerships, the IRS saw insufficient community benefit; the partnership was viewed as a "shell type of arrangement where the hospital continues to own and operate the facilities in question and the joint venture invests only in a profits interest." The arrangement was perceived as only incidentally promoting health; the IRS believed that the hospitals "engaged in these ventures largely as a means to retain and reward members of their medical staffs; to attract their admissions and referrals; and to preempt the physicians from investing in or creating a competing provider."

Another feature the IRS deplores is the situation where the general partner (such as a hospital or a taxable subsidiary of the hospital) is liable for partnership losses and is required to maintain a loss reserve, while the limited partners are not burdened with much risk. The net revenue stream arrangement did not, the IRS wrote, result in "improved patient convenience, greater accessibility of physicians, or any other direct benefit to the community."

The IRS has identified the following legitimate purposes (absent private inurement per se) for involvement of a hospital in a partnership (or joint venture): the raising of needed capital, the bringing of new services or a new provider to a community, the sharing of a risk inherent in a new activity, and/or the pooling of diverse areas of expertise. Prior pronouncements from the IRS reflect the following factors favored by the agency: a limited contractual liability of the tax-exempt partner, a limited (reasonable) rate of return on the investment by the limited partners, a right in the exempt organization of first refusal on the disposition of an asset of the partnership, the involvement of other general partners obligated to protect the interests of the limited partners, and the absence of any obligation to return the limited partners' capital from the resources of the exempt general partner. For example, the IRS held that a charitable organization, created by 10 unrelated exempt hospitals, could remain exempt, even though it, as its only function, became a sole general partner in a limited partnership, including individuals as limited partners, because the purpose of the partnership was furtherance of exempt purposes (operation of a lithotripsy center) and because the benefit to nonexempt limited partners (including physicians) was incidental.[53]

---

[52] E.g., Gen. Couns. Mem. 39732.
[53] Tech. Adv. Mem. 200151045.

The IRS's audit guidelines for the examination of tax-exempt hospitals[54] summarize the fact situations that may cause private inurement to arise: where participation in the venture imposes on the exempt organization obligations that conflict with its exempt purposes; where there is a disproportionate allocation of profits and losses to the nonexempt (usually, limited) partners; where the exempt partner makes loans to the partnership that are commercially unreasonable (that is, they have a low interest rate or inadequate security); where the exempt partner provides property or services to the partnership at less than fair market value; and/or where a nonexempt partner receives more than reasonable compensation for the sale of property or services to the joint venture.[55]

The IRS is likely to pursue a private inurement rationale where there is a "complete lack of symmetry in upside opportunities and downside risks for the physician-investors." At the same time, the position struck by the IRS in the context of hospitals and physicians in partnerships should not "be read to imply that a typical joint venture that involves true shared ownership, risks, responsibilities, and rewards and that demonstrably furthers a charitable purpose should be met automatically with suspicion or disapproved merely because physician-investors have an ownership interest."

On occasion, a tax-exempt hospital or hospital system will create a taxable subsidiary and cause that entity to be a (or the) general partner in a limited partnership.[56]

These pronouncements by the IRS in the health care context have added considerable clarity to the dimensions of the federal tax law concerning the permissible and impermissible participation, in general, of tax-exempt charitable organizations in partnerships.

§ 32.3 JOINT VENTURES

A tax-exempt organization may enter into a joint venture with a for-profit organization, without adversely affecting its exempt status, as long as doing so furthers exempt purposes and the joint venture agreement does not prevent it from acting exclusively to further those purposes. A joint venture does not present the private inurement problems that the IRS associates with participation by charitable organizations as general partners in limited partnerships. By contrast, an involvement in a joint venture by an exempt organization would lead to loss (or denial) of exemption if the primary purpose of the exempt organization is to participate in the venture and if the function of the venture is unrelated to the exempt purposes of the exempt organization.

A court defined a *joint venture* as an association of two or more persons with intent to carry out a single business venture for joint profit, for which purpose

---

[54] IRS Audit Guidelines for Hospitals, Manual Transmittal 7(10)69-38 for Exempt Organizations Examinations Guidelines Handbook (March 27, 1992). See § 24.8(c).
[55] *Id.* § 342
[56] In general, see § 31.4.

they combine their efforts, property, money, skill, and knowledge, but they do so without creating a formal partnership, trust, or corporation.[57] Thus, two or more entities (including tax-exempt organizations) may operate a business enterprise as a joint venture.[58]

Generally, when a tax-exempt organization acquires an interest in a joint venture (such as by transfer of funds), the event is not a taxable one, because the action is a one-time activity and thus is not a business that is regularly carried on.[59] That is, the exempt organization is not likely to be characterized as being in the business of establishing or investing in partnerships.[60]

Where the purpose of the joint venture is investment, the joint venture will be looked through to determine the nature of the revenue being received by the tax-exempt organization. It is rare that the investment income will be exempt function revenue. Usually, the income is passive investment income and thus is not taxed.[61] But if the participation in the joint venture is the principal activity of the exempt organization and the purpose of the venture is not an exempt one for the organization, it will, as observed, lose (or be denied) exempt status by reason of participation in the venture.

A tax-exempt organization may become involved in a joint venture with a for-profit organization in advancement of an exempt purpose. Again, the look-through principle applies, with the revenue derived by the exempt organization from the venture characterized as related revenue. For example, an exempt charitable organization participating as a general partner in a venture, with a for-profit entity, to own and operate an ambulatory surgical center was determined by the IRS to be engaging in a related activity.[62] Likewise, the IRS ruled that a joint venture between a charitable organization and a for-profit one, for the purpose of organizing and operating a free-standing alcoholism/substance abuse treatment center, would not jeopardize the exempt status of the charitable organization.[63] Still another illustration is an IRS ruling that an exempt hospital may, without endangering its exempt status, participate with a for-profit organization for the purpose of providing magnetic resonance imaging services in an under-served community.[64] Other IRS private letter rulings provide examples of joint ventures that did not adversely affect the exempt status of the exempt organization involved.[65]

A joint venture of this nature may be structured as a limited liability company.[66]

[57] Whiteford v. United States, *supra* note 4, at 79,762.
[58] Stevens Bros. Found., Inc. v. Comm'r, 324 F.2d 633 (8th Cir. 1963).
[59] See § 26.3.
[60] E.g., Priv. Ltr. Rul. 8818008.
[61] See § 27.1.
[62] Priv. Ltr. Rul. 8817039.
[63] Priv. Ltr. Rul. 8521055.
[64] Priv. Ltr. Rul. 8833038.
[65] E.g., Priv. Ltr. Rul. 8621059.
[66] E.g., Priv. Ltr. Rul. 9637050. See § 32.4. A limited liability company is an entity formed under state law; it has the attributes of a corporation for purposes of limiting liability, yet it can, under the *check-the-box* regulations (see § 4.1(b)), be treated as a partnership for federal income tax purposes (e.g., Priv. Ltr. Rul. 9839039).

The IRS is concerned, nonetheless, about situations where the involvement of a tax-exempt organization in a joint venture gives rise, or may give rise, to private inurement.[67] For example, it is the view of the IRS, as noted, that an exempt hospital endangers its exemption because of its involvement in a joint venture with members of its medical staff, where the hospital sold to the joint venture the net revenue stream of a hospital department for a stated period of time.[68] In this situation and others that are similar, the application of the private inurement doctrine is triggered by the inherent structure of the joint venture and not by whether the compensation is reasonable.[69]

In some instances, the IRS will characterize an arrangement between parties as a joint venture, for tax purposes.[70] That is, the agency may attempt to overlay the joint venture structure on a set of facts, irrespective of the intent of the participants. This can occur, for example, as an alternative to an assertion that a tax-exempt organization is directly engaged in an unrelated business.[71] As an illustration, in a case in which a court held that an exempt labor union[72] was not engaged in an unrelated business when it collected per capita taxes from its affiliated unions, the IRS retorted with the (unsuccessful) contention that the revenue should nonetheless be taxed because the unions were involved in a "joint enterprise."[73] Another example of this point was provided when, having lost the argument that a form of gambling—"tip jars" placed by an exempt organization in taverns so that the patrons could purchase tip-jar tickets to provide revenue to the organization—was not an unrelated business, the IRS's (unsuccessful) riposte was that the exempt organization and the taverns were engaged in a joint venture, with the activities of the employees of the taverns imputed to the exempt organization.[74]

A tax-exempt organization may also enter into a joint venture with another exempt organization, in furtherance of the exempt purposes of both of them.[75] For example, two public charities organized to develop, construct, own, and operate a medical center formed a limited liability company to develop, construct, own, and operate an outpatient ambulatory surgery center; the IRS ruled that the charities will continue to engage in the promotion of health[76] directly and through the operation of the joint venture.[77]

---

[67] See Chapter 19.
[68] Gen. Couns. Mem. 39862.
[69] See § 19.8.
[70] See text accompanied by *supra* notes 6-16.
[71] See Part Five.
[72] See § 15.1.
[73] Laborer's International Union of North America v. Comm'r, 82 T.C.M. 158, 160 (2001).
[74] Vigilant Hose Co. of Emmitsburg v. United States, 2001-2 U.S.T.C. ¶ 50,458 (D. Md. 2001).
[75] E.g. Priv. Ltr. Rul. 9249026.
[76] See § 6.3.
[77] Priv. Ltr. Rul. 200117043.

§ 32.4 WHOLE HOSPITAL JOINT VENTURES

There are developments brewing in the health care field that are generating significant implications for all public charities and perhaps other types of tax-exempt organizations that are in, or are contemplating participation in, a joint venture. This matter concerns the *whole hospital joint venture*.

(a) Overview of the Law

As discussed, a tax-exempt health care organization, as well as nearly any other type of exempt organization, can participate in a joint venture with a for-profit entity and not adversely affect the organization's exempt status, as long as the purpose of involvement of the exempt organization in the joint venture is furtherance of exempt purposes.[78] In this type of joint venture, the exempt entity utilizes its assets (usually only some of them) in furtherance of a charitable purpose.

The whole hospital joint venture is much different from a conventional joint venture. With this approach, the hospital or other tax-exempt entity transfers the entirety of its assets to the joint venture, with the for-profit organization perhaps assuming control over the assets and managing the day-to-day operations of the venture. For example, ownership of one or more hospitals might be transferred. The exempt health care organization does not directly engage in health care activities; it receives income and other distributions attributable to its ownership interest in the venture. There usually is a board of directors of this joint venture. Technically, the venture is a partnership[79] or a limited liability company.[80]

A whole hospital joint venture can lead to access to managed care contracts, greater efficiency of operations, and additional funding of charitable programs. From the standpoint of the for-profit entity, the venture provides a means to "acquire" a hospital without having to engage in an outright purchase of the institution.

Thus, the fundamental distinction between joint ventures in general and whole hospital joint ventures—one that may determine whether the tax-exempt organization is able to obtain or maintain exemption—is that, in instances of the former, the exempt entity continues to engage in health care functions while, in the latter case, the entity is an owner of the venture which itself controls the assets and operates the programs underlying the health care activity. This raises the question, unresolved at this time, as to whether participation in a whole hospital joint venture would cause the hospital or other health care organization to lose or be denied exempt status. Other issues are the possibility of private inurement or private benefit to the for-profit entity in the venture,[81] imposition of the

---

[78] See *supra* § 3.
[79] See *supra* § 1.
[80] See *supra* § 3, text accompanied by note 65.
[81] See Chapter 19.

intermediate sanctions penalties,[82] and/or the likelihood that income from the venture is unrelated business income to the exempt hospital.[83] Further complicating this area of the law is the impact of any new rules on entities outside the health care field, such as on tax-exempt organizations that are managed by for-profit companies,[84] as well as on nuances concerning the future viability of these ventures.[85]

(b) IRS Guidance

The IRS stated its position with respect to whole hospital joint ventures in 1998.[86] Two situations were sketched in which involvement by a tax-exempt hospital in one of these ventures does or does not jeopardize the hospital's exempt status.

(i) Fact Situation 1. The first of these situations concerned a non-profit corporation that owned and operated an acute care charitable hospital (H1), which concluded that it could better serve its community if it obtained additional funding. A for-profit corporation (FP1) that owned and operated a number of hospitals was interested in providing financing for the hospital if it could earn a reasonable rate of return. These two entities formed a limited liability company (LLC1).

H1 contributed all of its operating assets, including the hospital, to LLC1. FP1 also contributed assets to LLC1. In return, H1 and FP1 received ownership interests in LLC1 proportional and equal in value to their respective contributions.

LLC1's governing instruments provided that it is to be managed by a governing board consisting of three individuals selected by H1 and two individuals selected by FP1. H1 intended to appoint community leaders who have experience with hospital matters but who were not on the hospital staff and did not otherwise engage in business transactions with the hospital. These documents also provided that the governing instruments may be amended only by the approval of both owners and that a majority of three board members must approve certain major decisions relating to the operation of LLC1 (such as the budget, distributions of earnings, and selection of key executives).

These governing documents further required that any LLC1-owned hos-

---

[82] See § 19.11.

[83] See Part Five.

[84] Under current law, this utilization of management companies is quite common and appropriate (see, e.g., Priv. Ltr. Rul. 9715031). Cf. Priv. Ltr. Rul. 9709014.

[85] In general, Boisture & Varley, "Emphasis on Control by Exempt General Partners May Indicate Restrictive Rules on Joint Ventures," 9 *J. Tax. Exempt Orgs.* (No. 3) 109 (Nov./Dec. 1997); Sullivan, "Whole-Hospital Joint Ventures," 19 *Exempt Org. Tax. Rev.* (No. 1) 45 (Jan. 1998); Tsilas, "Whole Hospital Joint Ventures—Do Exempt Organizations Really Know What They're Getting Themselves Into?," 17 *Exempt Org. Tax. Rev.* (No. 2) 273 (Aug. 1997); Fondo & Jedrey, "States Move to Limit Joint Ventures with For-Profit Health Care Providers," 9 *J. Tax Exempt Orgs.* (No. 1) 3 (July/Aug. 1997); Greenwalt & Legget, "Whole-Hospital Joint Ventures With Taxable Entities Raise Tax Questions for Exempts," 6 *J. Tax Exempt Orgs.* (No. 4) 163 (Jan./Feb. 1995).

[86] Rev. Rul. 98-15, 1998-1 C.B. 718. In general, *Joint Ventures* § 4.2(e).

pital be operated in a manner that advances charitable purposes by promoting health for a broad cross-section of its community. They stated that the board members' duty to adhere to this requirement overrides any obligation they may have to operate LLC1 for the financial benefit of its owners. Thus, the community benefit standard took precedence over the considerations of maximizing profitability.

The governing documents provided that all returns of capital and distributions of earnings made to the owners of LLC1 must be proportional to their ownership interests in the venture. The terms of these instruments were legal, binding, and enforceable under state law.

LLC1 entered into an agreement with a management company (MC1) for the purpose of providing day-to-day management services to LLC1. MC1 was not related to H1 or FP1. This contract was for a five-year term and was renewable for additional five-year periods by mutual consent. MC1 was paid a management fee based on the gross revenues of LLC1. The terms and conditions of the contract were reasonable and comparable to what other management firms receive for comparable services for similarly situated hospitals. LLC1 may terminate this agreement for cause.

None of the directors, officers, or key employees of H1 who were involved in the decision to form LLC1 were promised employment or any other inducement by FP1 or LLC1 and their related entities if the transaction were approved. None of these individuals had any interest, directly or indirectly, in FP1 or any of its related entities.

H1 intended to use any distributions it received from LLC1 to fund grants to support activities that promote the health of H1's community and to help the indigent obtain health care. Substantially all of H1's grant-making will be funded by distributions from LLC1. H1's projected grant-making program and its participation as an owner of LLC1 constituted H1's only activities.

(ii) Fact Situation 2.   The second of these situations concerned a nonprofit corporation that owned and operated an acute care charitable hospital (H2), which concluded that it could better serve its community if it obtained additional funding. A for-profit corporation (FP2) that owned and operated a number of hospitals and provided management services to several other hospitals, was interested in providing financing for the hospital if it could earn a reasonable rate of return. These two entities formed a limited liability company (LLC2).

H2 contributed all of its operating assets, including the hospital, to LLC2. FP2 also contributed assets to LLC2. In return, H2 and FP2 received ownership interests in LLC2 proportional and equal in value to their respective contributions.

LLC2's governing instruments provided that it is to be managed by a governing board consisting of three individuals selected by H2 and three individuals selected by FP2. H2 intended to appoint community leaders who have experience with hospital matters but who were not on the hospital staff and do not otherwise engage in business transactions with the hospital. These documents also provided that the governing instruments may be amended only by the approval of both owners and that a majority of board members must approve certain major decisions relating to the operation of LLC2 (such as the budget, distributions of earnings, and selection of key executives).

These governing documents further provided that LLC2's purpose was to construct, develop, own, manage, operate, and take other action in connection with operating the health care facilities it owned and to engage in other health-care-related activities. The documents also provided that all returns of capital and distributions of earnings made to LLC2's owners must be proportional to their ownership interests in LLC2.

LLC2 entered into an agreement with a management company (MC2) for the purpose of providing day-to-day management services to LLC2. MC2 was a wholly owned subsidiary of FP2. This contract was for a five-year term and was renewable for additional five-year periods at the discretion of MC2. MC2 was be paid a management fee based on the gross revenues of LLC2. The terms and conditions of the contract, other than its renewal terms, were reasonable and comparable to what other management firms receive for comparable services for similarly situated hospitals. LLC2 may terminate this agreement only for cause.

As part of the agreement to form LLC2, H2 agreed to approve the selection of two individuals to serve as MC2's chief executive officer and chief financial officer. These individuals previously worked for FP2 in hospital management and had business expertise. They worked with MC2 to oversee the day-to-day management of LLC2. Their compensation was comparable to what like executives are paid at similarly situated hospitals.

H2 intended to use any distributions it received from LLC2 to fund grants to support activities that promote the health of H2's community and to help the indigent obtain health care. Substantially all of H2's grant-making was funded by distributions from LLC2. H2's projected grant-making program and its participation as an owner of LLC2 constituted H2's only activities.

(iii) Summary of Guidance. In this guidance, the IRS articulated some precepts of law never before publicly stated by the agency:

1. The rule that activities of a partnership are often considered to be the activities of a tax-exempt partner is termed the *aggregate principle*. This principle applies for purposes of the operational test.[87]

2. The activities of a limited liability company are considered the activities of a nonprofit organization that is an owner of the company when evaluating whether the nonprofit entity is operated primarily for charitable purposes.[88]

3. A charitable organization may form and participate in a partnership, including a limited liability company, and meet the operational test if participation in the partnership furthers a charitable purpose, the part-

---

[87] See § 4.5(c).
[88] See § 4.4.

nership arrangement permits the exempt organization to act primarily in furtherance of tax-exempt purposes, and there is only incidental benefit to the for-profit partners.[89]

Two more of these rules are central to the findings by the IRS in this guidance:

4. A tax-exempt charitable organization may enter into a management contract with a private party, according that party authority to conduct activities on behalf of the organization and direct use of the organization's assets, as long as the charity retains ultimate authority over the assets and activities being managed, and the terms and conditions of the contract (including compensation and the term) are reasonable.

5. If a private party is allowed to control or use the nonprofit organization's activities or assets for the benefit of the private party, and the benefit is not merely incidental, the organization will not qualify for tax exemption.

In application of these principles, H1's tax exemption was preserved. H1's exempt functions consisted of the health care services it will provide through LLC1, and its grant-making activities are to be funded with income distributed by LLC1. H1's capital interest in LLC1 is equal in value to the assets it contributed to the venture. The returns from LLC1 to its owners will be proportional to their investments. The governing instruments of LLC1 clearly reflect exempt functions and purposes. The appointees of H1 will control the board of LLC1. The renewal feature of the contract is favorable to H1.

Under these facts, H1 can ensure that the assets it owns and the activities it conducts through LLC1 are used primarily to further tax-exempt purposes. Thus, H1 can ensure that the benefit to FP1 and other private parties, such as MC1, will be incidental to the accomplishment of charitable ends.

It was stipulated that the terms and conditions of the management contract were reasonable, and that the grants by H1 were intended to support education and research, and assist the indigent.

The IRS acknowledged that when H2 and FP2 formed LLC2, and H2 contributed its assets to LLC2, H2 will—like H1—be engaged in activities that consist of the health care services to be provided through LLC2 and the grant-making activities it conducted using income distributed by LLC2. The IRS said, however, that H2 will fail the primary purpose test, because there was no binding obligation in LLC2's governing instruments for it to serve charitable purposes or otherwise benefit the community. Thus, LLC2 had the ability to deny care to segments of the community, such as the indigent.

The control element was significant in the second set of facts. H2 shared control of LLC2 with FP2. This means that H2 cannot initiate programs within

---

[89] These principles are the essence of the law as summarized *supra* (§ 2(b)(i)) but this was the first time that the IRS stated them in a precedential document.

LLC2 to serve new health needs in the community without consent of at least one board member appointed by FP2. Inasmuch as FP2 is a for-profit entity, the IRS stated that it "will not necessarily give priority to the health needs of the community over the consequences for [FP's] profits."

MC2 had "broad discretion" over LLC2's activities and assets that may not always be under the supervision of LLC2's board. For example, MC2 could enter into all but "unusually large" contracts without board approval. Also, MC2 could unilaterally renew the management agreement.

The consequence of all of this for H2 is that FP2 was receiving benefits resulting from the conduct of LLC2 that were private in nature and not incidental. The operational test was failed by H2 when it participated in the formation of LLC2, contributed its operating assets to H2, and then served as an owner of LLC2.[90]

(iv) Subsequent Caselaw. The IRS's position with respect to whole hospital joint ventures was basically adopted wholesale when the issue was first litigated.[91] The court concluded that the tax-exempt health care entity involved in the venture (a surgical center) "ceded effective control" over its sole activity to for-profit parties that had an independent economic interest in the same property.[92] The documents made it clear that the partnership lacked any obligation to place charitable purposes ahead of profit-making objectives. Significant private benefits were found to be conferred by the charitable entity on private parties, to the extent that the organization was no longer exempt because it failed the primary purpose test and the operational test.

In this case, the structure of the management of the venture was fatal to the charitable participant. The trial court observed that it could exert influence by blocking actions proposed to be taken by the managing directors but it could not initiate action without the consent of at least one of the appointees of the for-profit co-venturer. The nonprofit organization was perceived as lacking sufficient control unilaterally to cause the venture to respond to community needs for new health services, modify the delivery or cost structure of its present health services to better serve the community, or terminate the management company involved if it were determined to be managing the venture in a manner inconsistent with charitable objectives. Indeed, the management contract, an arrangement like the one posited in the IRS's guidance, was portrayed by the court as a "salient indicator" of the charity's surrender of effective control over the operations of the venture.

---

[90] In general, Louthian, III, "Revenue Ruling Brings New Life to Joint Ventures but Kills Off a GCM," 10 *J. Tax Exempt Orgs.* (No. 1) 3 (July/Aug. 1998); Mancino, "New Ruling Provides Guidance, Raises Questions for Joint Ventures Involving Exempt Organizations," 88 *J. Tax* (No. 5) 294 (May 1998); Griffith, "Revenue Ruling 98-15: Dimming the Future of All Nonprofit Joint Ventures?," 20 *Exempt Org. Tax. Rev.* (No. 3) 405 (1998); Peregrine & Sullivan, "Rev. Rul. 98-15 Confirms Traditional Tax Planning Approach for 'Typical' Joint Venture," 20 *Exempt Org. Tax. Rev.* (No. 2) 220 (1998).
[91] Redlands Surgical Servs. v. Comm'r, 113 T.C. 47 (1999), *aff'd*, 242 F.3d 904 (9th Cir. 2001). In general, *Joint Ventures* § 4.2(f).
[92] Redlands Surgical Servs v. Comm'r *supra* note 91, 113 T.C. at 78.

In the other case on the point, the government lost.[93] This court concluded that there were "exceptional protections" in place to preclude the venture from being operated to serve private interests. For example, the venture agreement required that hospitals owned by the venture operate in accord with the community benefit standard, with the tax-exempt entity unilaterally able to dissolve the venture if that is not done. Other facts, such as enabling the charitable entity to appoint the chair of the venture's governing board and unilaterally remove its chief executive officer, led the court to conclude that "these provisions clearly protect the non-profit, charitable pursuits [of the exempt organization] as well as any community board could."[94]

This court wrote that "not all joint ventures between non-profit and for-profit organizations are either *per se* exempt or *per se* non-exempt."[95] It said that it was following the statement of the law laid down in the previous case, "without deciding whether it is in fact the governing standard."[96] The court said that it is "difficult to imagine a corporate structure more protective of an organization's charitable purpose than the one at issue in this case."[97] Language in the venture agreement led the court to the conclusion that the exempt partner had "substantially more control" than the for-profit partner (even though each entity appointed 50 percent of the governing board).[98] Although this court did not expressly articulate the points, it held that the exempt organization did not cede control of its resources to the for-profit partner, that charitable objectives were ahead of profit-making ones in the case, and that there was no unwarranted private benefit.[99]

§ 32.5   ANCILLARY JOINT VENTURES

The law as to tax-exempt organizations and joint ventures has evolved to the point where there are essentially three types of these ventures. In one, the entirety of the exempt organization is in the venture.[100] In another, the primary operations of the exempt organization are in the venture. In the third approach, concerning the *ancillary joint venture*, something less than primary operations of the exempt organization is in the venture.

The aggregate principle and the control test presumably are applicable in connection with the first two types of these ventures. Certainly, the operational test[101] is. In the ancillary joint venture setting, however, the context is different.

---

[93] St. David's Health Care System, Inc. v. United States, 2002-1 U.S.T.C. ¶ 50,452 (W.D. Tex. 2002).

[94] *Id.* at 84,253.

[95] *Id.*

[96] *Id.* at 84,254.

[97] *Id.*

[98] *Id.*

[99] In general, Griffith, "St. David's TAM: Goliath's Hidden Slingshot," 38 *Exempt Org. Tax Rev.* (No. 2) 195 (Nov. 2002); Griffith, "Redefining Joint Venture Control Requirements: St. David's vs. Goliath?," 37 *Exempt Org. Tax Rev.* (No. 2) 255 (Aug. 2002).

[100] See *supra* § 4.

[101] See § 4.5.

The IRS is of the view, which seems to be correct, that the aggregate principle applies when determining if there is unrelated business.[102] When the involvement in a venture is a small portion of the exempt organization's overall activities, however, the operational test is not implicated (assuming the organization continues to be operated primarily for exempt purposes[103]).

Assuming that the tax-exempt organization (to date, only a public charity) must retain control of its assets in connection with entire and primary involvement in a joint venture, the question remains as to whether control is needed in the ancillary joint venture setting. In its first ruling on the point, the IRS took the position that control was necessary in that context for a charitable organization to retain its exempt status.[104] If a charitable organization is involved in an ancillary joint venture and does not retain control of the assets it transferred, it nonetheless is not clear that that fact automatically means that the charity's participation in the venture is an unrelated business. Likewise, involvement of a charitable organization in a venture under these circumstances should not mechanically mean that undue private benefit is conferred.[105] Further developments in this area must be awaited as the policy regarding these types of ventures is being shaped.

§ 32.6 INFORMATION REPORTING

If a partnership in which a tax-exempt organization is a partner regularly carries on a trade or business that would constitute an unrelated trade or business if directly carried on by the exempt organization, the organization generally must include its share of the partnership's income and deductions from the business in determining its unrelated income tax liability.[106]

A partnership generally must furnish to each partner a statement reflecting the information about the partnership required to be shown on the partner's tax return or information return.[107] The statement must set forth the partner's distributive share of the partnership income, gain, loss, deduction, or credit required to be shown on the partner's return, along with any additional information as provided by IRS forms or instructions that may be required to apply particular provisions of the federal tax law to the partner with respect to items related to the partnership.[108]

---

[102] Priv. Ltr. Rul. 200118054.

[103] See § 4.4.

[104] Priv. Ltr. Rul. 200118054 (concerning a venture to operate an ambulatory surgery center, involving a public charity and a group of physicians). This ruling is confusing, in part because the facts indicate that the "primary business" of the charity is a set of unidentified activities, so the involvement of the charity in the venture (which utilized a limited liability company) must be less than primary, yet the law analysis speaks of a "nonprofit organization whose principal activity is the ownership of a membership interest in a limited liability company."

[105] See § 19.10(b), text accompanied by notes 328–332.

[106] See § 28.4.

[107] IRC § 6031(b).

[108] Temp. Reg. § 1.6031(b)-1T.

The instructions accompanying the statement for partners (Schedule K-1, Form 1065) require the partnership to identify whether the partner is a tax-exempt organization. Also, the partnership must attach a statement furnishing any other information needed by the partner to file its return that is not shown elsewhere on the schedule.

The federal tax statutory law provides that, in the case of any partnership regularly carrying on a trade or business, it must furnish to the partners the information necessary to enable each tax-exempt partner to compute its distributive share of partnership income or loss from the business.[109] The conference report underlying this rule stated that it "emphasize[d] that the IRS should monitor and enforce the present-law reporting requirements and, where appropriate, should provide further guidance to partnerships through regulations or instructions as to how such information must be furnished" and that "information that must be furnished to tax-exempt partners under this provision is to be reflected by such organization on Form 990 or Form 990-T in the manner prescribed by Treasury regulations or by the IRS instructions for such Forms."[110]

Partnerships of tax-exempt organizations, including those comprised wholly of exempt organizations, must annually file federal information returns.[111]

§ 32.7 ALTERNATIVES TO PARTNERSHIPS

As the foregoing indicates, tax-exempt charitable organizations should avoid substantive participation in partnerships as general partner where the purpose of the partnership is not itself advancement of charitable objectives.

One way for a charitable organization to avoid the dilemma is to establish a wholly owned organization, usually a for-profit corporation, that would serve as the general partner in the partnership. This approach has been upheld by the IRS in private letter rulings.[112] As discussed, however, the tax-exempt entity leasing rules make this approach somewhat less attractive.[113]

Another approach is for tax-exempt organizations to avoid partnerships altogether and utilize a leasing arrangement. This works best in situations such as where an exempt organization acquires unimproved land and subsequently desires to have it improved, perhaps for its offices. The organization can acquire the land and enter into a long-term ground lease with a developer or develop-

---

[109] IRC § 6031(d). This reporting requirement applies without regard to the modifications of IRC §§ 512(b)(8)-(15) (see § 27.1(l)-(n), (q)).
[110] H. Rep. 100-1104, 100th Cong., 2d Sess. 13 (1988). As to these reporting requirements, see § 24.3.
[111] IRC § 6031. This return is Form 1065. E.g., Priv. Ltr. Rul. 8925092. In determining the tax year (the current year) of a partnership (IRC § 706(b)), a partner that is tax-exempt (IRC § 501(a)) is disregarded if the partner was not subject to tax on any income attributable to its investment in the partnership during the partnership's tax year immediately preceding the current year (Reg. § 1.706-1(b)(5)).
[112] E.g., Priv. Ltr. Rul. 7820057. In general, Rev. Rul. 68-296, 1968-1 C.B. 105.
[113] See § 29.5(g).

ment group. The developer would construct the building, perhaps giving it the organization's name and otherwise providing all external appearances of the structure being the organization's own building. This leaves the developer or development group in the position of fully utilizing all of the tax advantages. The exempt organization can lease space in the building, perhaps pursuant to a "sweetheart" lease, and may be accorded an option to purchase the building after the passage of years.[114] In this way, the organization fixes its headquarters expenses and seemingly owns the building from the outset, while avoiding jeopardizing its tax exemption and allocating the tax benefits to those who can utilize them.[115]

Another alternative to a partnership is the limited liability company.[116] A limited liability company often is the vehicle utilized to structure and operate a joint venture.[117] The principal attribute of a limited liability company, from the standpoint of tax-exempt organizations, is that it is treated as a partnership for federal tax purposes, which means that the entity itself does not pay taxes.[118] One or more exempt organizations can own interests in a limited liability company and a limited liability company can engage wholly in exempt activities. Thus, an exempt organization can utilize a limited liability company for the performance of exempt functions; these functions are in a separate entity, that entity does not pay federal income taxes, and any income that flows from the limited liability company to the exempt organization shareholder is not taxable, by reason of the partnership look-through rule.[119]

In some instances, a pooled income fund can be employed as an alternative to a limited partnership.[120] Where the facts cause the relationship between the

---

[114] E.g., Priv. Ltr. Rul. 8715055.

[115] In general, Bean, "Tax Exempt Organizations' Investment in Leveraged Real Estate," 5 *Prac. Tax Law.* (No. 2) 67 (1991); Brenman, "A Lesson in Fractions: How to Attract Capital from Tax-Exempt Investors," 8 *J. Part. Tax* (No. 1) 70 (1991); Kirchick & Cavell, "Tax-Exempt Organizations in Real Estate Transactions: A General Survey," 41 *U.S.C. Inst. on Fed. Tax* 24 (1989).

[116] See *supra* note 65.

[117] See § 32.4.

[118] See § 32.1.

[119] This look-through rule is the subject of § 28.4. An illustration of these points was the use by a group of health care organizations in the United States of a limited liability company to partner with public hospitals in a foreign country to establish and operate a charitable hospital in that country; the hospital itself was operated by the limited liability company (Priv. Ltr. Rul. 9839039).

[120] Pooled income funds are the subject of IRC § 642(c)(5). In general, see Hopkins, *The Tax Law of Charitable Giving, Second Edition* (John Wiley & Sons, Inc., 2000), Chapter 12.

pooled income fund and the tax-exempt charitable organization that is the remainder interest beneficiary of the pooled income fund to be manifested in a lease, however, the tax-exempt entity leasing rules make the fund, as an investment vehicle, somewhat unattractive.[121]

---

[121] The depreciation deduction (and perhaps other tax benefits) can flow through a pooled income fund to the income beneficiaries of the fund in determining their federal income tax liability (e.g., Priv. Ltr. Rul. 8347010). This feature can provide useful tax incentives to donors to charity by means of a pooled income fund, when coupled with the income tax charitable deduction that is occasioned by reason of the transfer of cash or property to the fund. As a general rule, the depreciation deduction available to the income beneficiaries is not computed by applying the tax-exempt entity leasing rules. Where, however, the property that is the (or a) medium of investment of the pooled income fund is located on the premises of the tax-exempt charitable organization that maintains the fund or is otherwise available to those who are served by that charity, the tax-exempt entity leasing rules are likely to be applicable. This is because of the provision of these rules that includes within the definition of a *lease* the grant of the *right to use* property, thereby causing the grant of a right to use property to be a *disqualified lease* (Reg. § 1.168(j)-IT,Q-5, A-5).

In general, Mancino, "Joint Ventures With Non-Exempts Require Special Tax Planning," 10 *J. Tax. Exempt Orgs.* (No. 2) 51 (Sept./Oct. 1998); Sanders and Cobb, "Recent IRS Rulings Provide New Standards for Joint Ventures Involving Charities," 18 *Exempt Org. Tax Rev.* (No. 2) 213 (Nov. 1997); Korman & Gaske, "Joint Ventures Between Tax-Exempt and Commercial Health Care Providers," 16 *Exempt Org. Tax. Rev.* (No. 5) 773 (May 1997); Weitz, "Unresolved Issues Remain for Qualified Organizations in Real Estate Partnerships," 73 *J. Tax.* (No. 5) 332 (1990); Gartrell, "Unrelated Business Taxable Income in Limited Partnerships After the Revenue Act of 1987," 16 *J. Real Estate Tax* (No. 1) 29 (1988); Odell, "Special Partners—Exempt and Foreign Entities," 46 *N.Y.U. Inst. on Fed. Tax* 29 (1988); Hardee, Jacobson & Talisman, "Tax-Exempt Organizations: Use of Pass-Through Entities," 2 *Prac. Tax Law* (No. 4) 23 (1988); Feder & Scharfstein, "Leveraged Investment in Real Property Through Partnerships by Tax-Exempt Organizations after the Revenue Act of 1987—A Lesson in How the Legislative Process Should Not Work," 42 *Tax Law* (No. 1) 55 (1988); Kertz & Hasson, Jr., "University Research and Development Activities: The Federal Income Tax Consequences of Research Contracts, Research Subsidiaries and Joint Ventures," 13 *J. Coll. & Univ. Law* (No. 2) 109 (1986); Lehrfeld, "Charities and Partnerships: A Many-Faceted Issue," 44 *NYU Ann. Inst. on Fed. Tax* 39-1 (1986); Sanders, "Syndication with Tax-Exempt Organizations as Partners," 2 *J. Tax. Inv.* (No. 4) 341 (1985); Charyk, "The Partnership Corner: New Problems Involving Real Estate Partnerships with Tax-Exempt Partners," 12 *J. Real Estate Tax* (No. 4) 380 (1985); Flaherty, "Exempt Organizations and Real Estate Syndications After the Tax Reform Act of 1984," 12 *J. Coll. & Univ. Law* (No. 1) 61 (1985); Schill, "The Participation of Charities in Limited Partnerships," 93 *Yale L. J.* 1355 (1984); Yanowitz & Purcell, "Using the Investment Partnership as a Charitable Activity: A Means/End Analysis," 60 *J. Tax.* (No. 5) 214 (1984); Kaplan, "Real Estate Opportunities for Tax-Exempt Organizations: Potential and Pitfalls After *Plumstead Theatre*," 61 *Taxes* 291 (1983); Braitman, "Creative Uses of Real Estate for Financing Tax-Exempt Organizations," 13 *NYU Conf. on Char. Orgs.*, Chapter 8 (1983); Bromberg, "Federal Income Tax Consequences of Medical Office Buildings," *Official J. Healthcare Financial Mgmt. Ass'n* (No. 11) 11 (1982); Becker, "Partnerships with Historic Preservation Organizations in Real Estate Development," 1 *Preservation Law Rep.* 2052 (1982); Stoner & Pineo, "Tax-Exempt Organizations and Limited Partnerships," 54 *Taxes* 339 (1976).

CHAPTER THIRTY-THREE

Organizational and Operational Considerations

The establishment of tax-exempt organizations and interrelationships between exempt and other organizations entail a variety of organizational and operational considerations.

§ 33.1 ORGANIZATIONAL CONSIDERATIONS

The organizational considerations involve the form of the organizations, the composition of the governing boards, and the matter of control (if any) as between the various organizations.

(a) Form

To be a separate legal entity, an organization must fit within a legally recognized form. (In some instances, the law will treat an activity or bundle of activities as a separate organization, despite the intent and/or the preferences of those who administer the activity or activities.[1]) Therefore, the essence of interorganizational

---

[1] For example, the IRS has the authority to classify an activity as a corporation for federal income tax purposes under IRC § 7701(a)(3).

structures dictates the existence of two or more separate legal entities, as contrasted with the structure where an activity (although accorded some form of formal recognition) is an integral component of an organization.[2]

As noted, generally a tax-exempt organization must be structured in one of three forms: a corporation, a trust, or an unincorporated association.[3] If it is a corporation, the organization almost always must be a nonprofit, nonstock corporation; some states provide for a stock-based nonprofit corporation. Occasionally, a for-profit organization will convert to a tax-exempt organization.[4]

A for-profit entity can be structured as a corporation, partnership, or other type of joint venture. While a business can be operated as a sole proprietorship, this approach is of no utility in the tax-exempt organizations context because, by definition, it means that the for-profit activity will be housed in the exempt organization.[5]

Therefore, assuming the presence of a tax-exempt organization, in this context it will be presumed to be either the parent or subsidiary of or under common control with, another legal entity, be it tax-exempt or taxable.

(b) Governing Boards

Both tax-exempt organizations and for-profit organizations must have one or more managers.[6] Depending upon the form of the legal entity, the requirements of state law, the nomenclature preferred by the individuals involved, and similar considerations, there will be one or more directors or trustees.

A trust may well have only one trustee. In some states, a corporation need only have one director. In most instances, however, both a tax-exempt organization and a for-profit organization will have a governing board of three or more individuals, and that body is termed the *board of directors* or *board of trustees*.

Of course, an individual may be a member of the governing board of more than one organization. Therefore, an individual may be a member of the boards of two or more related tax-exempt organizations and for-profit organizations. Indeed, the governing boards of organizations may be identical. (The

---

[2] See § 23.7.

[3] See § 4.1. There are some exceptions to this statement. One is that, under certain circumstances, a limited liability company can qualify as a tax-exempt organization (see § 4.3). Another is that the IRS is indicating, in the health care context, that it will recognize professional corporations of physicians as exempt charitable organizations; this has typically occurred in connection with states where the corporate practice of medicine doctrine requires physicians to use the professional corporation vehicle.

The IRS recognized that a tax-exempt business league (see Chapter 13) may have within it a fund that can be recognized as a charitable entity for federal income tax purposes (Rev. Rul. 54-243, 1954-1 C.B. 92). This type of fund, however, may not be a legal entity for other law purposes, such as state law (e.g., eligibility to take title to property).

[4] E.g., Priv. Ltr. Rul. 8851039. See see *infra* § 4.

[5] Depending essentially upon the nature and size of the for-profit activity, it may or may not adversely affect the tax-exempt organization's exempt status or cause unrelated business income.

[6] The term *manager* is used in this context because of the use of that term in federal tax law in referencing both directors and officers of organizations (IRC §§ 4946(a)(1)(B), 4946(b)(1), 4958(f)(1))) (see §§ 11.2(b), 19.11(c)).

law may, however, regard two or more organizations as one under certain circumstances and identical boards would likely be one criterion used to reach that conclusion.[7])

As a generalization, the objective should be to minimize the extent to which the governing boards of two or more organizations (where at least one is a tax-exempt organization) are overlapping. It is clear that there can be interlocking of these directorates without jeopardizing an organization's exempt status, but the prudent practice is to have interlocking boards only to the extent necessary to achieve control (assuming that is desired). In some instances, interlocking directorates are required to achieve a particular result in the law, such as supporting organization classification.[8] Yet, in other circumstances, there may be reasons to keep the overlap to a minimum, such as with a charitable fundraising organization associated with a charitable parent, where the intent is to broaden the fundraising base of the charitable subsidiary.

The law, in some contexts, regards the existence of overlapping directorates as significant, such as in determining the tax treatment of income received by one organization from another[9] or the extent of the depreciation deduction allowed to partners in a partnership involving a controlled subsidiary of a tax-exempt organization.[10]

Particularly with respect to public charities, there is almost no federal tax law regulating the composition of the organizations' board of directors. Two exceptions prove this general rule: the body of law pertaining to the required and/or permissible configuration of the governing board of a supporting organization[11] and that relating to the board of an organization seeking to qualify as a donative publicly supported organization by means of the facts-and-circumstances test.[12] Nonetheless, despite the absence of any statutory authority[13] the IRS is more frequently utilizing the concept of the *independent board* or the *community-representative board* in the development of tax policy in the tax-exempt organizations field. One of the most dramatic examples of this is the IRS's insistence that health care organizations, to be tax-exempt, must adhere to the *community benefit doctrine*, which includes the element of a community board.[14]

---

[7] In Greater United Navajo Development Enterprises, Inc. v. Comm'r, 74 T.C. 69 (1980), *aff'd in unpub. op.* (9th Cir., Dec. 23, 1981), two corporations with the same directors, officers, and staff were regarded by both the IRS and the court as one organization. The IRS ruled, however, that the directors and/or officers of a tax-exempt organization and a controlled for-profit company may be the same individuals (Priv. Ltr. Rul. 8244114). See § 31.1(d).

[8] See § 11.3(c).

[9] See §§ 27.1(n), 31.3.

[10] See § 29.5(g).

[11] See § 11.3(c).

[12] See § 11.3(b)(ii).

[13] See § 19.11.

[14] See Hyatt & Hopkins, *The Law of Tax-Exempt Healthcare Organizations, Second Edition* (John Wiley & Sons, Inc., 2001), Chapter 6. As a court observed, the "purpose of the community board is to ensure that the community's interests are given precedence over any private interests" (St. David's Health Care System, Inc. v. United States, 2002-1 U.S.T.C. ¶ 50,452 (W. D. Tex. 2002) at 84,253). The court also wrote that the purpose of this type of board is "more complex than giving wealthy self-styled philanthropists something to do on the rare occasion that they are not playiing golf" (*id.*).

This is frequently the case in instances of private inurement and private benefit.[15] For example, the make-up of the board of directors is being invoked by the IRS in instances of examinations for private inurement and benefit activities and transactions by tax-exempt hospitals and other health care providers. As an illustration, as part of the development of its policy with respect to physician recruitment and retention arrangements, the IRS forced a hospital to concede that its board of trustees lacked awareness of and control over these transactions by the institution, agree to have the board's executive committee review and approve the major physician service agreements, adopt a conflict of interest policy applicable to the hospital's trustees and officers, and agree to a set of recruitment guidelines requiring board approval of every financial package provided to recruited physicians.[16] In another instance, the IRS found private inurement at a hospital, including unreasonable compensation; the IRS observed that the salary of the chief executive officer and president of the institution was "not determined by an independent compensation committee."[17] Further, a reorganization of a hospital system was approved by the IRS,[18] with any private benefit found to be incidental; the IRS emphasized the fact that "there is broad community representation on the boards of directors of the . . . [exempt, charitable] members of the system."[19]

The IRS is increasingly invoking a requirement of an independent or community-based board in other settings. For example, the involvement of a public charity as a general partner in a limited partnership was sanctioned by the IRS, using pre-existing criteria[20] but inexplicably adding the observation that the organization was governed by an "independent board of directors made up of church and community leaders," in finding the absence of any unwarranted service of private interests.[21] In another instance, concerning a close operating relationship between a charitable organization and a for-profit fundraising company where the IRS had raised questions as to private inurement and private benefit, the IRS became satisfied that the organization could retain tax exemption once its board of directors was enlarged to provide for control by individuals other than its founder (who was also the sole shareholder of the fundraising company) and her family; the IRS noted that this alteration of board composition "should do much to provide assurance" that the charity will operate "independently" of the company.[22]

The existence and functioning of independent boards has taken on greater significance in the aftermath of enactment of the intermediate sanctions rules. In

---

[15] In general, see Chapter 19.

[16] Closing agreement with Hermann Hospital, dated Sept. 16, 1994, in *Daily Tax Report* (BNA) (No. 200), Oct. 19, 1994, at L-1.

[17] Tech. Adv. Mem. 9451001, recommending revocation of the tax-exempt status of the organization involved.

[18] See Hyatt & Hopkins, *supra* note 14, particularly Chapter 20.

[19] Priv. Ltr. Rul. 9426040.

[20] See § 32.2.

[21] Priv. Ltr. Rul. 9438030.

[22] Tech. Adv. Mem. 9417003.

that context, for example, a rebuttable presumption that the terms and conditions of a transaction are reasonable arises where certain criteria are met, including approval of the transaction by an *independent board* or an independent committee of the board.[23]

(c) Control

One organization may control another organization, or two or more organizations may be under common control. This is the case irrespective of whether the organizations are tax-exempt or taxable. Thus, an exempt organization may control one or more other exempt organizations and/or for-profit organizations, just as a for-profit organization may control one or more exempt organizations.[24]

Essentially, there are three ways by which one organization controls another: interlocking directorates, a membership, or stock.

Inasmuch as few nonprofit organizations are stock-based, a tax-exempt organization is usually controlled by another exempt organization by means of an interlocking directorate. This control mechanism can take many forms, such as by enabling the board of directors of the parent exempt organization to name at least a majority of the board of directors of the subsidiary exempt organization or by causing at least a majority of the board of directors of the subsidiary exempt organization to consist of individuals holding named offices (for example, president, past-president, or treasurer) of the parent exempt organization. Any combinations of these or other forms is permissible; it is the mere fact of the majority overlap of directors that vests control in the parent organization.

On occasion, one tax-exempt organization will control another exempt organization by means of a membership feature. With this approach, the controlled entity is structured as a membership organization; the controlling entity usually is the sole member of the membership entity. The control element in this instance is manifested in the power and authority accorded the member.

Where a tax-exempt organization is formed pursuant to a nonprofit corporation act that allows the issuance of stock, the exempt organization can be controlled by another exempt organization by reason of ownership of at least a majority of the stock. In this situation, the control is achieved by the stock ownership, so that the composition of the board of directors of the exempt subsidiary is, in a sense, irrelevant, although in many instances the parent exempt organization will want more immediate control over the operations of the exempt subsidiary than mere stock ownership can give and thus will also have a substantial representation on the board of directors of the subsidiary.[25]

The control mechanism represented by the interlocking directorate and/or a membership feature will be provided for in the governing instruments of the tax-exempt subsidiary.

A for-profit organization can control a exempt organization by means of the same two devices: interlocking directorates and/or stock ownership.

---

[23] See § 19.11(e).
[24] See *supra* notes 8, 9.
[25] This aspect of the structure may cause attribution problems. See *infra* § (d), § 31.1(d).

Most for-profit organizations are corporations, so that the ownership of a for-profit organization by a tax-exempt organization will likely be the subject of stock ownership. Just as above, an exempt organization may control a for-profit organization by means of an interlocking directorate (although ultimate control is always vested in the stockholders(s)).[26]

(d) Attribution Considerations

Close operation of one or more tax-exempt organizations can cause the activities of one to be attributed to another. The legal considerations in this regard are much the same as those in the context of exempt organizations and for-profit subsidiaries.[27] That is, the organizations will be respected as separate legal entities as long as each of them has real and substantial program functions. By contrast, when one organization so controls the affairs of another entity that the latter is merely an extension, arm, or agent of the former, one or more of the organizations may not be regarded, for tax purposes, as a separate legal entity. That is, an entity may be disregarded for tax purposes; the IRS may regard the arrangement as a sham.

In the context of exempt organizations and for-profit subsidiaries, the IRS wrote that the law is as follows: "The activities of a separately incorporated subsidiary cannot ordinarily be attributed to its parent organization unless the facts provide clear and convincing evidence that the subsidiary is in reality an arm, agent or integral part of the parent."[28] The *clear and convincing evidence* standard is undoubtedly the standard to be used in this context.

It is common, for example, for a business league to operate in tandem with a related charitable organization (a "foundation"). A social welfare organization may utilize a related charitable organization as well. There are many of these combinations.[29] The attribution of the activities of one tax-exempt organization to another could adversely affect the exempt status of one of them.

Again, just as is the case with tax-exempt organizations and for-profit subsidiaries, if the proper structure and operations are in place, the separateness of the exempt organizations involved will be respected. This was illustrated in an instance in which a charitable organization and a business league operated in tandem; the charity had control over the business league by means of an identical board of directors. The business league proposed to establish a political action committee (PAC). Under the facts of the case, the IRS was persuaded that the political activities of the PAC were "sufficiently segregated and insulated by safeguards" implemented by the charitable organization and the business league, so that the activities of the PAC were not attributable to ei-

---

[26] Special rules apply in this regard to private foundations. See § 11.4(c).
[27] See § 33.1(d).
[28] Priv. Ltr. Rul. 200132040.
[29] They are collected at §§ 30.2–30.4.

ther of the other organizations in any manner that would jeopardize their tax-exempt status.[30]

§ 33.2   OPERATIONAL CONSIDERATIONS

There are certain criteria that must be met to ensure that the appropriate relationship between a noncharitable organization and an auxiliary charitable organization is maintained. Some of these criteria are dependent on whether the charitable organization is to be operated as a subsidiary of the noncharitable organization or whether the two organizations are to operate as independent entities.

In most instances, where a tax-exempt organization controls and operates another organization (whether exempt or taxable), the headquarters of both organizations will be at the same location. Thus, for example, the foundation that is related to a trade association will usually be located in the same offices as is the association. This fact gives rise to several operational considerations, mostly involving funding.

(a) Expenses

Again, the organizations involved are separate legal entities, with their own governing boards, officers, bank accounts, and the like. Unless the organizations involved have the same federal tax status (and even then it is not a desirable practice), their monies should not be commingled (as contrasted with exchanged). This prohibition against commingling dictates the use of separate bank accounts.[31]

These considerations, however, do not preclude the organizations from functioning in close operational conjunction. Therefore, whether it is a professional society in relation to its foundation or a charitable organization in relation to its lobbying arm, the two organizations may share office space, personnel, furniture, equipment, and the like.[32] Indeed, this is the case irrespective of the number of organizations involved. Moreover, it is the practice of the IRS to rule that the sharing of assets, personnel, facilities, and services, and the allocation of costs, among the organizations will not produce unrelated business income—even when there might be this type of income were the organizations unrelated.[33]

Where the parent is a tax-exempt organization other than a charitable organization[34] and the subsidiary is a charitable organization, the subsidiary may reimburse the parent for its allocable use of the resources of the parent, as long as

---

[30] Priv. Ltr. Rul. 200103084. Organizations in these arrangements, however, need to be concerned with potential application of the private benefit doctrine (e.g., Quality Auditing Company v. Comm'r, 114 T.C. 498 (2000)). In general, see § 19.10.

[31] E.g., Regan v. Taxation With Representation of Wash., 461 U.S. 540, 544, note 6 (1983).

[32] Center on Corp. Responsibility, Inc. v. Shultz, 368 F. Supp. 863, 866, note 2 (D.D.C. 1973).

[33] E.g., Priv. Ltr. Rul. 9527043. See § 26.5(j).

[34] That is, an organization described in IRC § 501(c)(3) (see Part Two).

the reimbursement amounts are reasonable. (When this is done, a desirable practice is to have a written agreement between the parties stating the terms of the relationship.[35]) This is not a form of commingling of funds but rather a reasonable expenditure of funds for administrative and program purposes. Alternatively, the parent may forgo reimbursement, with the amounts involved regarded as a grant of the funds by the parent to the subsidiary.[36]

It is preferable to avoid having a noncharitable organization reimburse a charitable organization for expenses incurred on its behalf to eliminate the potential contention that charitable funds are being expended for noncharitable purposes. Where this practice cannot be avoided, however, the relationship should be memorialized in writing, and the terms and conditions of the relationship must be fair and reasonable.

There is not a prescribed accounting practice for allocating expenses in this context.[37] Therefore, a system should be used that is reasonable.[38] For example, the costs associated with occupancy can be reimbursed on the basis of floor space utilized by the parties, the costs associated with the utilization of personnel can be reimbursed on the basis of time records, and the costs associated with the use of equipment can be reimbursed on the basis of actual use.[39]

Of course, an organization can avoid allocations and reimbursements to the extent that services and supplies can be acquired and paid for directly. But avoidance of interorganizational sharing may be undesirable or impractical, if not impossible, particularly in the early years of the relationship.

The foregoing considerations also apply to a relationship between a tax-exempt organization and a for-profit organization. Where the services and supplies are provided by the for-profit organization to the exempt organization, there may be reimbursement; where the circumstances are reversed, there must be reimbursement, and it must be fair and reasonable.

When a tax-exempt organization performs administrative, management, or similar *corporate services* for another organization, the general position of the IRS is that any net revenue resulting from the provision of the services is unrelated

---

[35] E.g., Priv. Ltr. Rul. 9012045.

[36] If the parent organization is forgoing revenue that might be taxable (such as rent that would be unrelated business taxable income), the IRS may apply the rules concerning allocation of income and deductions among taxpayers (IRC § 482) to cause the parent to have taxable income. These allocation rules are applicable to tax-exempt organizations (Reg. § 1.482-1(a)(1)).

[37] See Gross, Jr., Larkin, & McCarthy, *Financial and Accounting Guide for Not-For-Profit Organizations, Sixth Edition* (John Wiley & Sons, Inc., 2000), at § 15.8.

[38] It would not be inappropriate to analogize to the concept of the *mixed purpose expenditure* contained in the regulations that accompany the expenditure test lobbying rules (see Chapter 20), which require, in the case of this type of an expenditure, "a reasonable allocation, based on all the facts and circumstances" (Reg. § 56.4911-2(d)). Also, there are cost allocation rules available to membership associations and certain other organizations that can be alluded to in this setting (see § 20.8).

[39] These principles are not unlike the rules pertaining to the allocation of expenses between tax-exempt and unrelated activities (see § 28.2), although those rules may be somewhat more strict due to the requirement that the expenses allocable to an unrelated activity are only those that are incurred directly in connection with the unrelated activity.

business taxable income. This is the case irrespective of whether the organization receiving the services is exempt. In other words, it is not automatically an exempt function for one exempt organization to provide services to another, even where both organizations have the same category of exempt status. Yet, under certain circumstances, it can be a related business for a tax-exempt organization to provide services to another exempt entity or it can be other than an unrelated business where services are provided by and among related entities.[40]

(b) Gifts and Grants

A charitable organization may be the recipient of one or more gifts or grants from its parent, whether or not the parent is tax-exempt.[41] Where the parent is a taxable organization, the payment may be regarded by the parties as a gift (although it may be characterized for tax purposes as a (nondeductible) dividend).

Where the charitable organization is endeavoring to be a publicly supported organization,[42] the parent will be considered a donor or grantor for purposes of measuring public support. This is presumably the case irrespective of whether the grant is made directly or by means of reimbursements forgone. Consequently, where the parent is a tax-exempt organization, the related charitable organization may have to be structured as a supporting organization[43] where the organization is to receive a large portion of its funding from the parent.[44] There are exceptions to this precept, such as grants from an exempt hospital[45] or university[46] to a publicly supported organization.[47] Where the parent is a for-profit organization, the related charitable organization will probably be a private foundation.[48]

A charitable organization can make a grant to a noncharitable organization (although this is generally inadvisable where the grantor is a private foundation[49]), as long as the grant is properly restricted for charitable purposes. For example, a "foundation" related to a trade association can make a grant to the association as long as the grant is restricted for charitable purposes (such as a seminar or a research project). Generally, however, the preferable practice is for the charitable program to be maintained and funded directly by the charitable organization.

---

[40] See § 26.5(i).
[41] E.g., Priv. Ltr. Rul. 8640052.
[42] See § 11.3(b).
[43] See § 11.3(c).
[44] For example, a parent organization that is a large donor or grantor will likely be considered a *substantial contributor* and thus a *disqualified person* for purposes of qualification under IRC § 509(a)(2) (see § 11.2(a)).
[45] IRC § 170(b)(1)(A)(iii).
[46] IRC § 170(b)(1)(A)(ii).
[47] IRC § 509(a)(2)(A).
[48] See Chapter 11.
[49] See § 11.4(b).

§ 33.3 CONVERSION FROM EXEMPT TO NONEXEMPT STATUS

As has been discussed throughout, organizations can be nonprofit, tax-exempt entities or for-profit entities. On occasion, an entity of one type is desirous of converting to an entity of the other type. While both can be accomplished, the federal and state law on the point is scant.[50]

The state law on the subject concerns form and procedure. Most states have separate nonprofit corporation acts and business (for-profit) corporation acts; mergers from one to the other are not always permissible. Thus, a change in form is often required, entailing liquidations and reformations. The federal tax law on the subject focuses primarily on the need for new determinations as to tax status and disclosure of certain facts as part of any new application for recognition of exempt status.[51]

A tax-exempt organization may decide to shed that status and convert to a for-profit entity. (There is no prohibition in law as to doing that.) For example, a public charity may determine that the rules for maintaining exempt status as a charitable entity are too onerous or those involved in its operations may wish to partake of its profits; operation as a for-profit entity may thus be more attractive.

(a) State Law

Nearly every tax-exempt organization is a creature of the law of a state or the District of Columbia. (In a rare instance, an exempt organization is established by a specific state statute or, even less frequently, is created by federal law.) These organizations almost always are shaped as one of three types of entity: nonprofit corporation, unincorporated association, or trust.[52]

The unincorporated association is the least, of these three categories, likely option for a nonprofit entity. The articles of organization of this type of organization is termed a *constitution*. It will undoubtedly have bylaws and otherwise function much in the nature of a corporation.

Some organizations are formed as trusts. The articles of organization of this type of entity is a *declaration of trust* or a *trust agreement*. Trusts, particularly charitable ones, are uniquely treated under state law and this treatment may vary from state to state.

The third form that a tax-exempt entity can assume is that of the nonprofit corporation—the form that is most commonly used today. (The balance of this chapter is predicated on the assumption that the nonprofit and for-profit entities

---

[50] The law on this subject is most pronounced when it involves the termination of a charitable organization's status as a private foundation (IRC § 507; see § 11.4(f)). This is a separate body of law that is uniquely applicable to private foundations; the observations in this chapter are based on the assumption that the charitable organizations discussed in it are not private foundations.

[51] The process for obtaining a determination or ruling as to recognition by the IRS of tax-exempt status is the subject of § 23.2.

[52] See *supra* § 1(a).

involved are corporations.) The corporate form is advantageous because the law as to its formation and operation is usually quite clear, and because it can provide a shield against personal liability for those individuals who are its directors and officers.[53]

As noted, nearly every state has a nonprofit corporation act and a for-profit corporation act. These are separate statutes; the extent of any interplay between them is a matter of state law, which can vary from state to state. For example, it may not be possible for a nonprofit corporation in a particular state to amend its *articles of incorporation* so as to become a for-profit corporation under the law of that state. This is because of the fundamental difference between the two types of corporations.[54]

Likewise, the issue of whether a nonprofit corporation can merge into a for-profit corporation, particularly where the survivor of the merger is the for-profit entity, can be problematic. In any event, the transformation of a tax-exempt charitable organization can easily attract the attention of a state's attorney general.

Suppose a tax-exempt charitable entity, organized as a nonprofit corporation, is desirous of becoming a for-profit organization, organized as a for-profit corporation. Theoretically, the easiest way to accomplish this is to amend the corporate documents and convert to the for-profit form. As noted, however, state law may not allow for this transformation, and it raises great problems under the federal tax law.[55]

Another approach would be to create a for-profit corporation and then merge the nonprofit corporation into it. Again, state law may preclude the merger of a nonprofit and a for-profit organization.

A third approach would be to create the for-profit corporation, liquidate the nonprofit corporation, and transfer the remaining assets and income of the nonprofit corporation to the for-profit corporation. As discussed next, however, this type of transfer must, for federal tax reasons, entail a sale or exchange of the assets for fair market value.

(b) Federal Tax Law

There is no federal law procedure by which a tax-exempt organization can initiate withdrawal of its exempt status; while the IRS recognizes the exempt status of nonprofit organizations, it does not "de-recognize" them.[56] Thus, the only way for an exempt organization to lose its exemption is to violate one or more

---

[53] The subject of personal liability in the nonprofit organization context is outside the scope of this book. See, however, Hopkins, *Starting and Managing a Nonprofit Organization: A Legal Guide, Third Edition,* (John Wiley & Sons, Inc., 2001), Chapter 19.

[54] However, an IRS private letter ruling reflects a factual situation in which a state's law apparently permits a nonexempt nonprofit corporation to convert to a stock-based for-profit corporation (Priv. Ltr. Rul. 9545014).

[55] See text accompanied by *infra* § 3(b).

[56] Once the IRS has recognized the tax-exempt status of an organization, the organization cannot voluntarily relinquish it (Priv. Ltr. Rul. 9141050). That is, there is no provision in the law for voluntary termination of exempt status.

aspects of the organizational test and/or the operational test. These tests find their origin in the language of the statute giving rise to the exemption, which speaks of an organization being both *organized* and *operated* for one or more exempt purposes.[57]

The organizational test focuses on the organizing instrument of the entity, to determine the presence of all required provisions in the document (such as a clause preserving the assets for charitable purposes upon dissolution) and to assure that prohibited language is not present.[58] If, for example, the articles of organization[59] of a tax-exempt charitable organization are amended to allow its net earnings to inure to one or more persons in their private capacity,[60] the organization is no longer qualified for tax exemption.[61] In general, an organization's articles of organization must limit its purposes to one or more exempt ones and may not empower the organization to engage in nonexempt activities other than insubstantially.[62]

The concern of the operational test is with an organization's programs. In the case of a charitable organization, the requirement is that the entity be operated at least primarily for tax-exempt purposes.[63] For example, the rationale for exemption for a charitable organization might be that it is engaged in activities that primarily promote health.[64] Where, however, the operational test is violated so that the organization is no longer functioning primarily for exempt purposes (such as by engaging in one or more forms of private inurement), the organization is no longer qualified for tax exemption.[65]

In addition, an organization is not organized or operated exclusively for one or more tax-exempt charitable purposes unless it serves a public, rather than a private, interest.[66] This rule, like the private inurement prohibition, requires the absence of transactions that benefit insiders with respect to the organization, such as directors, officers, substantial contributors, and persons

---

[57] IRC § 501(c)(3); Reg. § 1.501(c)(3)-1(a)(1). If an organization fails to meet either of these tests, it is not tax-exempt (*id.*). These tests thus are applicable with respect to tax-exempt charitable organizations. In a sense, most other categories of exempt organizations have organizational and operational tests as well, although none of them are as well-developed as those for charitable entities.

[58] Reg. § 1.501(c)(3)-1(b)(1). See § 4.3.

[59] An organization's *articles of organization* is the document (articles of incorporation, constitution, trust agreement, and the like) by which an organization is created (Reg. § 1.501(c)(3)-1(b)(2)).

[60] The private inurement doctrine is the subject of Chapter 19.

[61] Reg. § 1.501(c)(3)-1(b)(4).

[62] Reg. § 1.501(c)(3)-1(b)(1). Although the statute (IRC § 501(c)(3)) states that a charitable organization must be organized and operated *exclusively* for charitable purposes, the true state of the law is that the word *substantially* or *primarily* is substituted for the word *exclusively* (Better Business Bur. v. United States, 326 U.S. 279 (1945)) (see § 4.4). This construction of the terminology not only tolerates an *incidental* amount of nonexempt activity, it allows for a meshing of the unrelated business rules (see Part Five). (This is the case even though the U.S. Supreme Court articulated the principle five years before the unrelated business law was enacted.)

[63] Reg. § 1.501(c)(3)-1(c)(1). The term *exempt purposes* means those charitable purposes for which the organization was organized and is operated (Reg. § 1.501(c)(3)-1(a)(2)). See § 4.5.

[64] Rev. Rul. 69-545, 1969-2 C.B. 117.

[65] Reg. § 1.501(c)(3)-1(c)(2).

[66] Reg. § 1.501(c)(3)-1(d)(1)(ii).

controlled by insiders.[67] (Particularly where the membership is small, insiders can include members.)

In the case of transgression of either the organizational test or the operational test, the organization becomes a non-tax-exempt (that is, taxable) entity. It nonetheless remains a nonprofit organization under state law. Therefore, without additional action, the entity is a taxable, nonprofit organization. Further steps under state law are usually required to convert the entity to a for-profit corporation or to merge it into a new or existing for-profit corporation.[68]

Where the tax-exempt organization is a charitable one, the most difficult problem to overcome is the proscription of the dissolution clause. The organization, to be initially recognized as a charitable entity, was required to have this clause in its articles of organization. This clause mandates that, upon dissolution or liquidation, the net assets and remaining income of the organization be preserved for charitable purposes.[69] A blatant violation of this rule would be transfer, upon dissolution, of assets to an organization's members or shareholders.[70] This aspect of the organizational test prevents a charitable organization from accumulating assets and income in the tax-exempt charitable mode and then simply converting to a taxable entity.[71]

There may be conflict between federal and state law on this point. That is, state law may allow certain liquidating distributions that are impermissible under federal tax precepts. For example, where the articles of organization of a church failed to contain the requisite dissolution clause, tax-exempt status was denied, particularly in light of the fact that the law in the state of organization permitted certain distributions of assets to members of nonprofit corporations.[72] In another case, a charitable contribution deduction was denied where the donee organization could, under state law, distribute its assets upon dissolution to its founders (in this instance, the donors).[73] As an appellate court stated, "if there is substantial possibility that upon dissolution, accumulated assets will find their

---

[67] *Id.* The federal tax regulations do not specifically use the term *insider*; the term used is "private shareholder or individual" (Reg. § 1.501(a)-1(c)) or "private interests" (Reg. § 1.501(c)(3)-1(d)(1)(ii)).

[68] Where this type of conversion is allowable under state law, the IRS regards it as a non-taxable reorganization within the meaning of IRC § 368(a)(1)(E) (Priv. Ltr. Rul. 9545014).

[69] Reg. § 1.501(c)(3)-1(b)(4).

[70] *Id.*, last sentence.

[71] In a sense, this statement is overly broad. A statement of law or a provision in articles of organization does not, in a literal sense, "prevent" an individual from doing anything. This form of violation of the organizational test would, from a federal tax standpoint, merely cause loss of the organization's tax-exempt status—a result that is to occur in any event because of the organization's conversion to a taxable entity. Nonetheless, this development would still leave the organization as a nonprofit one, with potential problems under state law (see *supra* § 3(a)). Further, the attorney general of the particular state may intervene to preserve the assets for charitable purposes.

For certain other categories of tax-exempt organizations, the federal tax law is not so stringent. For example, a social club (see Chapter 14) may make liquidating distributions to its members (e.g., Mill Lane Club, Inc. v. Comm'r, 23 T.C. 433 (1954); Rev. Rul. 58-501, 1958-2 C.B. 262). Also, a fraternal beneficiary association (see § 18.4(a)) may convert to a for-profit entity (Priv. Ltr. Rul. 8938072).

[72] General Conference of Free Church of Am. v. Comm'r, 71 T.C. 920 (1979).

[73] Calvin K. of Oakknoll v. Comm'r, 69 T.C. 770 (1978).

way into private hands, exemption is barred."[74] That statement is equally applicable in the revocation context.

Suppose, for example, that a tax-exempt charitable hospital decides to convert to a taxable for-profit hospital. It cannot merely create a for-profit corporation and transfer all of the income and assets of the charitable entity to it.[75] While the assets of the charitable organization may be transferred to the for-profit corporation, the recipient corporation must pay fair market value for them. This outcome leaves the charitable entity with no assets other than an amount of funds equal to the fair value of the assets (property) it once had.

To continue with this example, the charitable organization will no longer function as a hospital (although it may continue to operate in a manner that promotes health). Thus, there will almost certainly be a material change in circumstances, requiring the charitable entity to report the development to the IRS[76] and summarize its new programs for the promotion of health. The surviving charitable organization may, as illustrations, become a freestanding medical research organization, a foundation operating in tandem with the newly formed for-profit organization, or an entity operating a gift shop in conjunction with the for-profit hospital.[77] This new mode of operation may cause the charitable entity to become another type of public charity or become a private foundation.[78]

This matter becomes more complex where the successor for-profit entity is controlled by physicians who are insiders with respect to the tax-exempt hospital. In one case, a tax-exempt, charitable hospital transferred its pharmacy operations to an organization controlled by its trustees to function on a

---

[74] Monterey Pub. Parking Corp. v. United States, 27 A.F.T.R. 2d 71-378, 380 (6th Cir. 1971).

[75] See *supra* note 71.

[76] See § 24.1(a).

[77] It is the position of the IRS that a nonprofit organization, the primary activity of which is the operation of a gift shop and a gift cart within a proprietary hospital for the purpose of selling candy, flowers, newspapers, books, magazines, sundries, and other small gift items to patients, visitors, and employees of the hospital is a charitable entity because the organization's activity primarily improves the physical comfort and mental well-being of the hospital's patients, thereby encouraging their recovery and only incidentally benefits the proprietary hospital (Gen. Couns. Mem. 39762). The IRS termed these "recuperative sales of nonmedical items" (*id.*) and found the private benefit derived by the for-profit hospital to be incidental in both a qualitative and quantitative sense, in that the overall benefit to the general public substantially overrode any benefit to private individuals and that the private benefit was a necessary concomitant of the beneficial activity, following the criteria stated in Gen. Couns. Mem. 37789. (The doctrine of private benefit is the subject of § 19.10.)

[78] E.g., Hoyt, "Creating Supporting Organizations of Community Foundations from Hospital Sales," 17 *Exempt Org. Tax Rev.* (No. 2) 265 (Aug. 1997). If the entity became a free-standing medical research organization, it presumably would gain tax-exempt status by reason of IRC § 501(c)(3) as a scientific organization (see Chapter 9) and become a publicly supported organization by reason of IRC §§ 170(b)(1)(A)(vi) and 509(a)(1) or IRC § 509(a)(2) (see § 11.3(b)). (An example where the successor public charity status in these circumstances was that of IRC § 509(a)(2) is in Priv. Let. Rul. 8234085.) It could not, however, be a medical research organization as that term is used in IRC § 170(b)(1)(A)(iii) (see § 11.3(a)) because the required related hospital must be a tax-exempt one. If the entity became a foundation in relation to the for-profit institution, it may well become a private foundation as is the case with most company-related foundations.

for-profit basis. The for-profit entity sold pharmaceuticals to the hospital at prices higher than those previously paid by it. Subsequently, the assets of the pharmacy were sold to another charitable organization. The exemption of the hospital was retroactively revoked, on the basis of private inurement, on the ground that the transaction was merely a device to funnel profits from the exempt hospital to its trustees.[79]

Although it is infrequent, a tax-exempt organization may decide to sell one or more of its assets; generally, it can do so as long as fair value is received on the sale. For the most part, the status of the purchaser is irrelevant.[80] For example, the IRS approved the sale of assets from an exempt hospital to another exempt organization,[81] to a partnership formed by the board of directors of a hospital,[82] and to unrelated purchasers.[83]

Nonetheless, where the purchaser of assets from a tax-exempt, charitable entity is an organization that was created by individuals related to it to the extent that they are treated as insiders,[84] such as physicians practicing at a hospital or members of the hospital's governing board, the transaction will be accorded strict scrutiny. This type of transaction has several ramifications, other than the matter of tax exemption; they include the impact on the qualification for any exempt bond financing[85] and conflicts of interest.

As to the bounds of this scrutiny, it is frequently advised in these circumstances that the services of one or more competent appraisers be obtained. The purpose of this is to be able to demonstrate that the fair market value of the transferred assets was obtained on an independent basis.[86] In one instance, however, that act of prudence proved inadequate to preclude loss of the selling hospital's tax-exempt status.

In that case, a tax-exempt organization that operated a hospital, and had research and educational functions, determined to sell the hospital to gain income for the other exempt functions. Because of the highly specialized nature of the hospital facility, there was a limited market for its sale. Thus, the hospital

---

[79] Maynard Hosp., Inc. v. Comm'r, 52 T.C. 1006 (1969).

[80] Again, the assumption of this chapter is that the selling organization is not a private foundation (see *supra* note 50). In instances where the selling organization is a private foundation and one or more of the purchasers are disqualified persons with respect to it, the sale would almost certainly be an act of self-dealing, with resulting adverse federal tax consequences (see § 11.4(a)).

[81] Priv. Ltr. Rul. 9010073.

[82] Priv. Ltr. Rul. 8234084.

[83] Priv. Ltr. Rul. 8519069.

[84] See text accompanied by *supra* note 67.

[85] IR-90-60. In Rev. Rul. 77-416, 1977-2 C.B. 34, the IRS ruled that interest on municipal bonds continued to be excludable from gross income under IRC § 103 following the sale by a city of an electric system to a private utility company, where the sale proceeds were placed in an escrow account as substituted security for the system revenues originally pledged as security for the bonds. The full reasoning underlying this ruling is contained in Gen. Couns. Mem. 37158 (with heavy emphasis on the facts that considerable time passed before the facility was sold and other evidence that the transaction was "legitimate," that is, "nonprearranged"), with a somewhat similar situation analyzed in Gen. Couns. Mem. 37783.

[86] This approach to sales to insiders is critical because of the intermediate sanctions rules (see § 19.11).

was sold to a for-profit entity controlled by its board of directors. Basically, the organization went about this process in the appropriate manner. It secured a valuation from a qualified independent appraiser; the property was sold at that value, which was $8.3 million (principally in cash and notes). No loan abatements or other special concessions were offered to the directors as purchasers of the hospital facility. The exempt organization took steps to ensure that it would use arm's-length standards in future dealings with the hospital. A ruling was obtained from the IRS to the effect that the transaction would not adversely affect the tax exemption of the organization.[87]

Soon after the sale, the purchasing organization began receiving inquiries as to resale of the facility. The new organization added beds to the hospital and obtained a certificate of need for additional beds. Less than two years after the initial sale of the hospital facility by the tax-exempt organization, it was resold; the resale price was $29.6 million. Each member of the board of the for-profit selling organization received in excess of $2.3 million as his or her share of the sales proceeds. The attorney general of the state involved filed a lawsuit, alleging that the initial sales price was not fair and reasonable. The court agreed, also concluding that the directors of the exempt organization acted with a lack of due diligence. At trial, the facilities were appraised using five appraisal methodologies; the conclusion was that the value of the assets at the time of sale by the exempt organization was approximately $18 million to $21 million. A subsequent analysis by the IRS set the value of the facility at $24 million.

The factual issue before the IRS was whether the tax-exempt organization received fair market value when it sold its hospital facility. A detailed analysis of the appraisals led the IRS to the conclusion that fair market value had not been received. The appraisals done for the court and the IRS were based on various appraisal methodologies; the appraisal relied upon by the selling exempt organization used one of these methods. The IRS conceded that "no single valuation method is necessarily the best indicator of value in a given case."[88] But, added the IRS, "it would be logical to assume that an appraisal that has considered and applied a variety of approaches in reaching its 'bottom line' is more likely to result in an accurate valuation than an appraisal that focused on a single valuation method." Having resolved that factual issue, the IRS concluded as a matter of law that the exempt organization, in selling the hospital facility for substantially less than its fair market value, contravened the private inurement doctrine. Accordingly, the organization's exempt status was revoked, effective as of the date of the sale of the facility.[89] In so doing, the IRS observed: "There is no absolute prohibition against an exempt section 501(c)(3) organization dealing with its founders, members, or officers in conducting its economic affairs." There is no

---

[87] Priv. Ltr. Rul. 8234085 (in which the IRS stated that the "proposed sale as described will not benefit those in a controlling position with respect to you by virtue of the ability of such persons to unfairly manipulate the transaction"). In this ruling, the IRS observed that the transaction presented the converse of the situations in Rev. Rul. 76-441, 1976-2 C.B. 147 (see text accompanied by *infra* notes 93–94).
[88] Priv. Ltr. Rul. 9130002.
[89] *Id.*

doubt, however, that transactions of this nature will be subject to special scrutiny, with the IRS concerned about a (in the language of the ruling) "disproportionate share of the benefits of the exchange" flowing to the insiders. Thus, in this case, there was nothing inherently improper about the organization's decision to cease being a hospital and to sell the appropriate assets to an organization controlled by its directors.

The organization in this case followed the correct approach in acquiring an independent appraisal. In most circumstances, this should have been enough.[90] When, however, the directors resold the hospital facility after approximately only a two-year period and experienced a $21.3 million profit and a lawsuit by the state's attorney general (with the court having found a breach of fiduciary responsibility), the IRS found private inurement.[91]

This type of sale of assets, in whole or in part, does not give rise to taxable gain or loss under the unrelated trade or business tax rules. The one-time sale of an asset, principal or otherwise, used directly in furtherance of the selling organization's exempt function lacks the frequency, continuity, and commercial manner to be considered as an unrelated trade or business.[92]

As an alternative to sale of assets and/or total conversion, a tax-exempt organization may lease assets to a non-exempt organization, particularly where doing so advances the lessor's exempt purposes.[93] In one instance, an exempt hospital leased its clinic facilities to a for-profit corporation controlled by physicians formally employed by the clinics without endangering its exempt status.[94]

---

[90] For example, in the charitable contribution deduction context, gifts of property in excess of $5,000 in value are generally required to be the subject of a *qualified appraisal* by a *qualified appraiser* (Reg. § 1.170A-13(c)). There is no requirement for more than one appraisal nor is there a requirement that an appraisal be based on a "variety of approaches." Indeed, these rules require a qualified appraisal to state "the" method of valuation (Reg. § 1.170A-13(c)(3)(ii)). Moreover, these rules allow a donor to obtain more than one appraisal and use the most desirous one in substantiating the charitable deduction (Reg. § 1.170A-13(c)(5)(iii)). In general, Hopkins, *The Tax Law of Charitable Giving, Second Edition* (John Wiley & Sons, Inc., 2000) § 22.2. In subsequent private letter rulings, moreover, the IRS approved the use of a single valuation method (e.g., Priv. Ltr. Ruls. 9538026, 9538031). In general, see Hopkins, *The Law of Intermediate Sanctions: A Guide for Nonprofits* (John Wiley & Sons, Inc., 2003) § 4.5.

[91] E.g., Caracci v. Comm'r, 118 T.C. 379 (2002); Anclote Psychiatric Center, Inc. v. Comm'r, 76 T.C.M. 175 (1998).

[92] Reg. § 1.513-1(c)(1). E.g., Priv. Ltr. Rul. 8234084. In general, Fox IV & Kelly, "Sales of Not-For-Profit Hospitals to For-Profit Corporations," 137 *Trusts & Estates* (No. 11) 38 (Oct. 1998); Mancino, "Converting the Status of Exempt Hospitals and Health Care Organizations," 9 *J. Tax Exempt Orgs.* (No. 1) 16 (July/Aug. 1997).

[93] E.g., Gundersen Med. Found. Ltd. v. United States, 536 F. Supp. 556 (W.D. Wis. 1982).

[94] Priv. Ltr. Rul. 8204057. In general, Sawyer, "When The Party's Over: Hospital Conversion Issues and Strategies," 25 *Exempt Org. Tax Rev.* (No. 2) 203 (Aug. 1999); Fremont-Smith, "The Role of Government Regulation in the Creation and Operation of Conversion Foundations," 23 *Exempt Org. Tax Rev.* (No. 1) 37 (Mar. 1999); Mancino, "Intermediate Sanctions and Changes in Use Are Factors in Conversion of Tax Status," 9 *J. Tax Exempt Orgs.* (No. 2) 58 (Sept./Oct. 1997).

§ 33.4 CONVERSION FROM NONEXEMPT TO EXEMPT STATUS

A for-profit organization may decide to convert to a tax-exempt organization. (Like the reverse, there is no prohibition in law as to doing so.)

(a) State Law

Nearly every for-profit organization is subject to the law of a state or the District of Columbia. These organizations are usually organized as corporations. (Again, the balance of this chapter is predicated on the assumption that the nonprofit and for-profit entities involved are corporations.)

Nearly every state has a nonprofit corporation act and a for-profit corporation act. These are separate statutes; the extent of any interplay between them is a matter of state law, which can vary from state to state. For example, it may not be possible for a for-profit corporation in a particular state to amend its articles of incorporation so as to become a nonprofit corporation under the law of that state. Likewise, it can be problematic as to whether a for-profit corporation can merge into a nonprofit corporation.[95]

Suppose a hospital, organized as a for-profit corporation, is desirous of becoming a tax-exempt organization, organized as a charitable entity. As is the case when the conversion is to be the reverse, theoretically, the easiest way to accomplish this is to amend the corporate documents and convert to the nonprofit form. As noted, however, state law may not allow for this transformation.

Another approach would be to create a nonprofit corporation and then merge the for-profit corporation into it. Again, state law may preclude the merger of a nonprofit and a for-profit organization.

A third approach would be to create the nonprofit corporation, transfer the assets and income of the for-profit corporation to the nonprofit corporation, and dissolve the for-profit corporation. Presumably, there would not be a state law prohibition as to this type of transaction.

(b) Federal Tax Law

Unlike the state of the law concerning the process by which a tax-exempt organization converts to a for-profit one, there are considerable guidelines at the federal tax level for converting a for-profit entity to an exempt one.

The essential principles in this area in the healthcare context are reflected in a revenue ruling published by the IRS in 1976.[96] The transaction in that ruling involved the purchase by a nonprofit hospital corporation of all of the assets of a for-profit hospital; the purchase was not at arm's length, in that the owners of the for-profit entity created the nonprofit organization and over one-half of the board of directors of the nonprofit entity were stockholders of the for-profit institution.

---

[95] See text accompanied by *supra* § 4(a).
[96] Rev. Rul. 76-91, 1976-1 C.B. 149.

The nonprofit entity was held to qualify as an exempt charitable organization; the IRS ruled that there was no private inurement.

The chief tax issue in a transaction of this nature is the appropriate selling price. In this case, the owners obtained an independent appraisal of the tangible assets and then computed the value of the intangible assets (which was substantial) by the capitalization of excess earnings formula.[97] The purchase was made using the price arrived at by this method. The nonprofit organization satisfied the IRS that the intangible assets had a direct and substantial relationship to the performance of the exempt functions of the hospital. These assets, in the case of a hospital, were said to include accreditation for an internship or residency program, good labor relations, an active medical staff, and a favorable location.

Another example of these principles is contained in a subsequent revenue ruling also published by the IRS in 1976.[98] One aspect of the ruling concerned an otherwise qualifying nonprofit organization that purchased or leased the assets of a former for-profit school and employed the former owners, who were not related to the directors of the nonprofit entity, at salaries commensurate with their responsibilities. The IRS determined that the nonprofit school operated to serve a public interest where it purchased the for-profit school's personal property at fair market value in an arm's-length transaction and paid a fair rental value for use of the land and buildings. In the ruling, the IRS concluded that the organization was operating exclusively for educational and charitable purposes.

The ruling also discussed another situation concerning a nonprofit organization which, after receiving as a gift all of the stock of a for-profit school, dissolved the school and assumed all of its liabilities, which included notes owed to the former owners, all of whom comprised the board of directors of the recipient organization. Financial information showed that the liabilities of the school exceeded the fair market value of its assets; consequently, the IRS ruled that the nonprofit donee organization was substantially serving the directors' private interests in honoring the notes and thus that the organization failed to qualify for tax exemption. Said the IRS, the "directors were, in fact, dealing with themselves and will benefit financially from the transaction."[99]

In general, it is the view of the IRS that where an organization purchases assets from an independent party, a presumption exists that the purchase price (arrived at through negotiations) represents fair market value. Where the purchaser is controlled by the seller (or there is a close relationship between the two) at the time of the sale, however, this presumption will not be available because the elements of an arm's length transaction are not present.[100]

Although there are no regulations or rulings on the subject, the IRS, in the application for recognition of tax-exempt status as a charitable organization,[101]

[97] This formula is the subject of Rev. Rul. 68-609, 1968-2 C.B. 327.
[98] Rev. Rul. 76-441, *supra* note 87.
[99] *Id.* at 148.
[100] Rev. Rul. 76-91, *supra* note 96.
[101] Form 1023, Schedule I.

established an inventory of the items of information it must have concerning the predecessor and successor organizations in order to issue a favorable ruling or determination letter to the nonprofit organization. (This body of information is in addition to the information requested of all nonprofit organization applicants.) The form presupposes that the applicant nonprofit organization is an entity separate from the predecessor for-profit organization,[102] thus reflecting the presumption that a for-profit organization cannot be transformed into a nonprofit organization.[103]

The specific items of information a successor nonprofit organization must provide the IRS as part of the exemption recognition process are (1) the name of the predecessor organization; (2) the nature of the activities of the predecessor organization; (3) the names and addresses of the owners or principal stockholders of the predecessor organization; (4) their share or interest in the predecessor organization; (5) the business or family relationship between the owners or principal stockholders and principal employees of the predecessor organization and the officers, directors, and principal employees of the applicant nonprofit organization; (6) whether any property or equipment formerly used by the predecessor organization has been or will be rented to the successor organization (if so, copies of leases and like contracts must be attached); (7) whether the successor organization is or will be leasing or otherwise making available any space or equipment to the owners, principal stockholders, or principal employees of the predecessor organization (if so, a list of the tenants must be included, along with a copy of each lease); and (8) whether any new operating policies were initiated as a result of the transfer of assets from the for-profit organization to the nonprofit organization. Additionally, the applicant nonprofit organization must attach (1) a copy of the agreement of sale or other contract that sets forth the terms and conditions of the sale of the predecessor organization or of its assets to the nonprofit organization and (2) an appraisal[104] by an independent qualified expert showing the fair market value at the time of sale of the facilities or property interest sold.

Likewise, if a for-profit organization is endeavoring to convert to a nonprofit organization and be a tax-exempt social welfare organization[105] or a business league,[106] and is requesting a determination from the IRS as to recognition of tax-exempt status, it must reveal as part of the exemption application the name of the predecessor organization, the period during which it was in existence, and the reasons for its termination, as well as submit copies of all documents by which any transfer of assets was effected.[107]

---

[102] For this purpose, a *for-profit* organization includes any organization in which a person may have a proprietary or partnership interest, hold corporate stock, or otherwise exercise an ownership interest (Form 1023, Schedule I, last sentence). The organization need not have operated for the purpose of making a profit (*id.*).

[103] See *supra* §§ 3(a), 4(a).

[104] See *supra* note 90.

[105] See Chapter 12.

[106] See Chapter 13.

[107] Form 1024, Part II, question 4.

If a for-profit organization sells assets to a nonprofit organization, the seller would be liable for taxes on any gain, just as would be the case were any other purchaser involved. There are special rules in this regard in the case of liquidations.[108]

If assets and/or income are contributed to a tax-exempt charitable organization by a for-profit organization, a charitable contribution deduction would likely result. This deduction may be limited by one or more factors, such as the percentage limitation on annual corporate charitable deductions[109] and the restrictions on the deductibility of gifts of inventory by businesses.[110]

(c) Gain or Loss Recognition

A conversion of a for-profit corporation into a tax-exempt one can cause recognition of gain or loss by the converting corporation. This type of a transaction is treated essentially the same as a liquidation of the corporation, when the assets transferred are all or substantially all of the assets of the corporation. That is, the corporation must recognize gain or loss as if the assets transferred had been sold at their fair market values.[111]

§ 33.5   RECOGNITION OF GAIN OR LOSS

As a general rule, when a for-profit corporation is liquidated into one or more tax-exempt organizations, the taxable corporation must recognize gain or loss in the transaction.[112]

The basic rule is that if a taxable corporation transfers all or substantially all[113] of its assets to one or more tax-exempt organizations, the corporation must recognize gain or loss as if the assets transferred had been sold at their fair market values.[114] This gain or loss must be recognized immediately before the transfer.

This general rule does not apply, however, when the transferred assets are used by the recipient tax-exempt organization in an unrelated business.[115] If assets used to any extent in an unrelated business are disposed of by the exempt organization, any gain must be included in the exempt entity's unrelated business taxable income. To the extent that the exempt organization ceases to use the assets in an unrelated activity, the organization is treated as having disposed of the assets, on the date of the cessation, for their fair market value.[116]

---

[108] See § 31.2(d).

[109] IRC § 170(b)(2). See § 2.5, text accompanied by note 149; Priv. Let. Rul. 9703028.

[110] IRC § 170(e)(3). See § 2.5, text accompanied by note 151.

[111] See *infra* § 5.

[112] IRC § 337(d) and accompanying tax regulations. These rules are similar to those pertaining to liquidations of for-profit subsidiaries into tax-exempt parents (see § 31.2(d)).

[113] For this purpose, the term *substantially all* means the same as it does in the corporate reorganization context (IRC § 368(a)(1)(C)).

[114] Reg. § 1.337(d)-4(a)(1).

[115] See Part Five.

[116] Reg. § 1.337(d)-4(b)(1).

In general, a taxable corporation's change in status (conversion) to a tax-exempt organization is treated as if it had transferred all of its assets to the exempt organization immediately before the change in status became effective.[117] This rule does not apply, however, to (1) a corporation previously exempt[118] which regains its exempt status within three years from the later of a final adverse adjudication on the corporation's exempt status or the filing of a federal income tax return; (2) a corporation previously exempt or that applied for but did not receive recognition of exemption[119] before January 15, 1997, if the corporation is tax-exempt within three years from January 28, 1999; (3) a newly formed corporation that is exempt (other than as a social club[120]) within three tax years from the end of the year in which it was formed; (4) a newly formed corporation that is exempt as a social club within seven years from the end of the tax year in which it was formed; (5) a corporation previously exempt as a mutual or cooperative organization[121] that lost its exemption solely because it failed the 85-percent-member-income requirement and then regained exempt status, as long as in each intervening year it meets all of the requirements for this exemption except for the income requirement; and (6) a corporation previously taxable that becomes an exempt property or casualty insurance company (whose written premiums do not exceed $350,000)[122] where it is the subject of a court-supervised rehabilitation, conservatorship, liquidation, or similar state proceeding affecting premium income.[123]

If, during the first tax year following the transfer of an asset or the corporation's change to tax-exempt status, the asset is used by the exempt organization partly or wholly in an unrelated activity, the taxable corporation must recognize a pro rata amount of gain or loss. The corporation may rely on a written representation from the exempt organization estimating the percentage of the asset's anticipated use in an unrelated activity for that year, using a reasonable method of allocation, unless the corporation has reason to believe that the exempt organization's representation is not made in good faith.[124]

If, for any tax year, the percentage of an asset's use in the unrelated activity later decreases from the estimate used in computing gain or loss when the asset was transferred, the tax-exempt organization must recognize the part of the deferred gain or loss in an amount that is proportionate to the decrease in use in the unrelated activity, and the gain or loss recognized must be subject to unrelated business income taxation.[125]

---

[117] Reg. § 1.337(d)-4(a)(2).
[118] These references to tax exemption are to exemption by reason of IRC § 501(a).
[119] See § 23.1.
[120] See Chapter 14.
[121] See § 18.5.
[122] See § 18.8.
[123] Reg. § 1.337(d)-4(a)(3). In a case involving the second of these exceptions, the IRS required as a condition of the ruling that the organization file an application for recognition of exemption, even though the regulations state that the filing of the application is not required to obtain the exemption if the applicant is not otherwise required to file, as this organization was not required to do (Priv. Ltr. Rul. 200217044).
[124] Reg. § 1.337(d)-4(b)(1)(i).
[125] Reg. § 1.337(d)-4(b)(1)(ii).

The tax-exempt organization must use the same reasonable method of allocation for determining the percentage it uses the assets in an unrelated activity as it uses for other tax purposes (such as determining the amount of depreciation deductions). Also, the exempt organization must use this reasonable method of allocation for each year that it holds the assets.[126]

Notwithstanding the foregoing, there can be continuing deferral of recognition of gain or loss to the extent that the tax-exempt organization disposes of assets in a transaction that qualifies for nonrecognition of gain or loss,[127] but only to the extent that the replacement is used in an unrelated activity.[128]

For these purposes, a *tax-exempt organization* is (1) an entity that is exempt from tax other than as a homeowners' association or a political organization;[129] (2) a charitable remainder trust;[130] (3) a governmental entity;[131] (4) an Indian tribal government or corporation;[132] (5) an international organization; (6) an entity whose income is excluded from taxation by reason of being a political subdivision and the like;[133] and (7) an entity that is not taxable "for reasons substantially similar" to those applicable to an entity in these previous categories, unless it is otherwise excluded from this law by statute or IRS action.[134]

§ 33.6   STATE ACTION DOCTRINE

(a)   State Action Doctrine in General

Tax-exempt organizations are, nearly always, *private*—that is, nongovernmental—entities.[135] Thus, the operations of exempt organizations are usually not subject to constitutional law principles.[136] These principles, embedded in the U.S. Constitution and made applicable to the states by the Fourteenth Amendment to the Constitution, include free speech rights, due process, and equal protection. Consequently, whereas *state action* is subject to Fourteenth Amendment scrutiny, private conduct normally is not. The purpose of the state action doctrine is to treat otherwise private organizations as components of a state for the purpose of applying federal constitutional law standards in situations in which the state is responsible for the conduct at issue in the particular case.

The distinction between state action and private operations sometimes is not clear; as the Supreme Court observed, it is called upon from time to time to

---

[126] Reg. § 1.337(d)-4(b)(1)(iv).
[127] IRC § 1031 or 1033 (concerning certain property exchanges or conversions).
[128] Reg. § 1.337(d)-4(b)(1)(iii).
[129] IRC § 501(a) (listed in IRC § 501(c)) or 529.
[130] See § 18.19.
[131] See § 18.17.
[132] See § 18.18.
[133] See § 18.17.
[134] Reg. § 1.337(d)-4(c)(2). In general, Prather, "Treasury Issues Final Section 337(d) Regulations on Transfers to Exempt Organizations," 10 *J. Tax Exempt Orgs.* (No. 5) 208 (Mar./April 1998).
[135] Cf. §§ 6.9, 18.17.
[136] Cf. § 1.7.

"plot a line" between the two.[137] The placement of this line can cause the operations of an ostensibly private tax-exempt organization to be tested against constitutional law principles, as if the organization were a state entity or one that is an integral part of the state. The courts' obligation in this setting is threefold: to "'preserv[e] an area of individual freedom by limiting the reach of federal law' and avoi[d] the imposition of responsibility on a State for conduct it could not control,"[138] as well as assure that constitutional law standards are invoked "when it can be said that the State is *responsible* for the specific conduct of which the plaintiff complains."[139] The Supreme Court explained why this dichotomy is not always apparent: "If the Fourteenth Amendment is not to be displaced, therefore, its ambit cannot be a simple line between States and people operating outside formally governmental organizations, and the deed of an ostensibly private organization or individual is to be treated sometimes as if a State had caused it to be performed."[140] The Court wrote that state action may be found if there is such a "close nexus between the State and the challenged action" that seemingly private behavior "may be fairly treated as that of the State itself."[141]

The determination as to whether the state action doctrine is applicable to a tax-exempt organization, by attributing its activity to a government, is made pursuant to a facts and circumstances test; the "criteria lack rigid simplicity."[142] The Court held, for example, that a challenged activity may be state action when it results from a state's exercise of "coercive power";[143] when a state provides "significant encouragement, either overt or covert";[144] when a private organization operates as a "willful participant in joint activity with the State or its agents";[145] when the "private actor" is controlled by an "agency of the State";[146] when it has been delegated a public function by a state;[147] or when it is "entwined with governmental policies" or when government is "entwined in [its] management or control."[148]

This background led the Court to the conclusion that the "character of a legal entity is determined neither by its expressly private characterization in statutory law, nor by the failure of the law to acknowledge the entity's inseparability

---

[137] Brentwood Academy v. Tennessee Secondary School Athletic Ass'n, 531 U.S. 288, 295 (2001). Also National Collegiate Athletic Ass'n v. Tarkanian, 488 U.S. 179, 191 (1988); Jackson v. Metropolitan Edison Co., 419 U.S. 345, 349 (1974).

[138] National Collegiate Athletic Ass'n v. Tarkanian, *supra* note 137, at 191, quoting Lugar v. Edmondson Oil Co., 457 U.S. 922, 936–937 (1982).

[139] Blum v. Yaretsky, 457 U.S. 991, 1004 (1982) (emphasis in the original).

[140] Brentwood Academy v. Tennessee Secondary School Athletic Ass'n, *supra* note 137, at 295.

[141] Jackson v. Metropolitan Edison Co., *supra* note 137, at 351.

[142] Brentwood Academy v. Tennessee Secondary School Athletic Ass'n, *supra* note 137, at 295.

[143] Blum v. Yaretsky, *supra* note 139, at 1004.

[144] *Id.*

[145] Lugar v. Edmonson Oil Co., *supra* note 138, at 941 (internal quotation marks omitted).

[146] Pennsylvania v. Board of Directors of City Trusts of Philadelphia, 353 U.S. 230, 2317 (1957).

[147] West v. Atkins, 487 U.S. 42 (1988).

[148] Evans v. Newton, 382 U.S. 296, 299, 301 (1966).

from recognized government officials or agencies."[149] In one instance, a privately endowed college was held to be a state actor and enforcement of its private founder's limitation of admission to whites attributable to a state, because, consistent with the terms of the settlor's gift, the college's board of directors was a state agency established by state law.[150] In another case, private trustees to whom a city had transferred a park were nonetheless state actors barred from enforcing racial segregation, because the park served the public purpose of providing community recreation and the "municipality remain[ed] entwined in [its] management [and] control."[151]

A state action doctrine case arose when a state university suspended its basketball coach in order to comply with rules and recommendations of a national association of colleges and universities that regulates the sport. The coach charged the association with state action, arguing that the university had delegated its functions to the association, clothing the latter with authority to make and apply the university's rules. The Court, however, concluded that the association's policies were shaped not by this state university alone, but by several hundred member institutions, most of them having no connection with the state involved; the association's connection with the state was seen as too insubstantial to ground a state action claim.[152]

Yet, the Court in this case, in dictum, mused that the "situation would, of course, be different if the [association's] membership consisted entirely of institutions located within the same State, many of them public institutions created by the same sovereign."[153] In support of this surmise, the Court approvingly cited two lower court cases in which an athletic association was treated as a state actor. One entailed a challenge to a state high school athletic association that kept boys from playing on girls' interscholastic volleyball teams in a state.[154] The other involved a parochial school's attack on the racially segregated system of interscholastic high school athletics maintained by the athletic association.[155]

The law in this area significantly changed in 2001, when the Court, in another athletic association case, held that the nonprofit corporation association was to be treated as part of a state's government and thus was bound by constitutional law principles.[156] The association in this case was organized to regulate interscholastic sport among the public and private high schools in the state that were its members. The membership included nearly all of the state's public high schools; these schools constituted 84 percent of the association's membership. The association's governing body was its "board of control" and its legislative council was its rulemaking entity. The membership of these bodies, by direction of the association's bylaws, was confined to high school principals, assistant

[149] Brentwood Academy v. Tennessee Secondary School Athletic Ass'n, *supra* note 137, at 296.
[150] Pennsylvania v. Board of Directors of City Trusts of Philadelphia, *supra* note 146.
[151] Evans v. Newton, *supra* note 148, at 301.
[152] National Collegiate Athletic Ass'n v. Tarkanian, *supra* note 137.
[153] *Id.* at 193, note 13.
[154] Clark v. Arizona Interscholastic Ass'n, 695 F.2d 1126 (9th Cir. 1982), *cert. den.*, 464 U.S. 818 (1983).
[155] Louisiana High School Athletic Ass'n v. St. Augustine High School, 396 F.2d 224 (5th Cir. 1968).
[156] Brentwood Academy v. Tennessee Secondary School Athletic Ass'n, *supra* note 137.

principals, and superintendents elected by the member schools. Although the association's staff members were not paid by the state, they were eligible to participate in the state's public retirement system for its employees. Member schools paid dues to the association; the bulk of its revenue was gate receipts at member teams' football and basketball tournaments.

The constitution, bylaws, and rules of this association set standards of school membership and the eligibility of students to play in interscholastic games. The state board of education had, on several occasions, reviewed, approved, and reaffirmed its approval of these rules, including the recruiting rule at issue in this case. The association's board of control concluded that a school (the plaintiff in the case) violated the recruiting rule, and placed the school's athletic program on a four-year probation, declared its teams ineligible to compete in playoffs for two years, and imposed a fine. At the time these penalties were imposed, all of the voting members of the board of control and the legislative council were public school administrators.

As noted, the Supreme Court held that this association was subject to constitutional law principles by application of the state action doctrine. The majority wrote: "The nominally private character of the [a]ssociation is overborne by the pervasive entwinement of public institutions and public officials in its composition and workings, and there is no substantial reason to claim unfairness in applying constitutional standards to it."[157] The Court stressed the following facts. The membership of the association consisted largely of public schools. All of the members were schools within the state. Representatives of member schools selected the members of the association's governing board and council; membership on the board was restricted to principals, assistant principals, and superintendents. The schools obtained membership in this "service organization" and "[gave] up sources of their own income to the collective association."[158] Interscholastic athletics played an integral part in the public education in the state. The association would not be "recognizable," the Court wrote, were it not for the "public school officials, who do not merely control but overwhelmingly perform all but the purely ministerial acts by which the [a]ssociation exists and functions in practical terms."[159]

These facts were said to reflect the "entwinement of public school officials with the [a]ssociation from the bottom up."[160] Also, the state was said to have "provided for entwinement from the top down."[161] This was reflected in the fact that state board of education members served ex officio on the association's board and council, and the association's employees were treated as state employees to the extent of being eligible for membership in the state retirement system. The state board was said to acknowledge the association's official character by "winks and nods."[162] The dissent, summarized later in this section, was said

[157] *Id.* at 298.
[158] *Id.* at 299.
[159] *Id.* at 300.
[160] *Id.*
[161] *Id.*
[162] *Id.* at 301.

to insist on formality as to state involvement, but the majority wrote that "if formalism were the sine qua non of state action, the doctrine would vanish owing to the ease and inevitability of its evasion, and for just that reason formalism has never been controlling."[163]

The essence of the dissent in this case is that the Court extended the state action doctrine beyond the bounds of precedent and dictates of the law. As to precedent, the dissent stated that, until this case, "we have found a private organization's acts to constitute state action only when the organization performed a public function; was created, coerced, or encouraged by the government; or acted in a symbiotic relationship with the government."[164] Prior to this case, according to the dissent, the Court had "never found state action based upon mere 'entwinement.'"[165] As to the dictates of the law, the dissenters wrote that the majority's holding "not only extends state-action doctrine beyond its permissible limits but also encroaches upon the realm of individual freedom that the doctrine was meant to protect."[166]

Aside from the case law, the dissent asserted that "common sense" dictated that the association's action could not "fairly" be attributed to the state and thus could not constitute state action.[167] The Court's minority stressed the following facts. It led with the fact that the association is a "private corporation."[168] There was no requirement that a school join the association. There was no set percentage of public school members. The association's rules were not enforced by a state agency but by its governing board. The state did not create the association, did not fund it, and did not exempt it from tax. Only 4 percent of the association's revenue was derived from member schools. The state never had any involvement in the action taken by the association in this case.

The association, wrote the minority, had not performed a function that had been traditionally reserved to the state. The organization of scholastic sports was neither a traditional nor an exclusive public function of the states, said these justices. The fact that the association served public schools did not render the provision of the service a traditional and exclusive public function, according to the dissent. The dissent further noted that the state had never promulgated regulations concerning interscholastic sports and had not encouraged the association in the enforcement of its recruiting rule.

Consequently, where there is "public entwinement in the management and control of ostensibly separate trusts or corporations," the state action doctrine is likely to apply to these tax-exempt organizations.

(b) State Action Doctrine as Applied to Social Clubs

The U.S. Constitution, in the Fifth and Fourteenth Amendments, prohibits racial discrimination by government and government-supported private institutions.

---

[163] *Id.* note 4.
[164] *Id.* at 305.
[165] *Id.*
[166] *Id.*
[167] *Id.* at 306.
[168] *Id.*

In general, private organizations may lawfully discriminate, absent applicability of the *state action* doctrine by which government is deemed to have sufficiently supported or encouraged the private discrimination as to amount to a constitutional law violation.[169]

The relationship between the state action doctrine and tax exemptions for social clubs and other nonprofit organizations has been the focus of several cases. This relationship as regards social clubs was the subject of a case in which a black individual, allegedly denied membership in a lodge of a fraternal organization solely because of his race, brought a class action to enjoin the granting of tax benefits to nonprofit fraternal organizations that exclude nonwhite individuals from membership.[170] The issue thus became whether tax exemptions and deductions cause the benefited private organizations to have the requisite imprimatur of government, that is, whether exemptions and deductions amount to a grant of federal funds to them. When such a "grant" is involved, the state action doctrine will bring the protections of the Constitution to the otherwise "private" acts.

In this case, the court concluded that a tax-exempt social club's policy of racial discrimination would not preclude tax exemption, although the exemption given to fraternal organizations[171] requires the absence of discriminatory practices. The rationale underlying this distinction in treatment turned on the peculiar manner in which social clubs are taxed; because they are taxed on all receipts other than exempt-function income, there is no state action-type "benefit" but only a matter of defining appropriate subjects of taxation, whereas fraternal organizations, being taxed only on unrelated business taxable income, do receive a government benefit in that investment income goes untaxed.[172]

Congress concluded that it is "inappropriate" for a tax-exempt social club to have a "written policy" of discrimination on account of race, color, or religion. Accordingly, Congress, in 1976, enacted a rule that bars tax exemption for

---

[169] Cases discussing the state action doctrine (in areas other than but including the private club context) have flourished over the years (e.g., Burton v. Wilmington Parking Auth., 356 U.S. 715 (1961); United States v. Texas Educ. Agency, 532 F.2d 380 (5th Cir. (1976); Golden v. Biscayne Bay Yacht Club, 530 F.2d 16 (5th Cir. 1976); Doe v. Charleston Area Med. Center, Inc., 529 F.2d 638 (4th Cir. 1975); New York City Jaycees, Inc. v. United States Jaycees, Inc., 512 F.2d 856 (2d Cir. 1975); Greenya v. George Washington Univ., 512 F.2d 556 (D.C. Cir. 1975); Barrett v. United Hosp., 375 F. Supp. 791 (S.D.N.Y. 1974), *aff'd*, 506 F.2d 1395 (2d Cir. 1974); Coleman v. Wagner College, 429 F.2d 1120 (2d Cir. 1970); Taylor v. Maryland School for the Blind, 409 F. Supp. 148 (D. Md. 1976); Hollenbaugh v. Board of Trustees of Carnegie Free Library of Connellsville, Pa., 405 F. Supp. 629 (W.D. Pa. 1975); McMenamin v. Philadelphia County Democratic Executive Committee of Philadelphia, 405 F. Supp. 998 (E.D. Pa. 1975); Berrios v. Inter American Univ., 409 F. Supp. 769 (D. P. R. 1975); Falkenstein v. Department of Revenue, 350 F. Supp. 887 (D. Or. 1972), *app. dis.*, 409 U.S. 1099 (1973)). Also Note, "State Action and the United States Junior Chamber of Commerce," 43 *Geo. Wash. L. Rev.* 1407 (1975). Further, Reitman v. Mulkey, 387 U.S. 369 (1967); Evans v. Newton, *supra* note 148; Pennsylvania v. Board of Directors of City Trusts of Philadelphia, *supra* note 146; Shelley v. Kraemer, 334 U.S. 1 (1948); Steele v. Louisville & Nashville Railroad, 323 U.S. 192 (1944); Civil Rights Cases, 109 U.S. 3 (1883).

[170] McGlotten v. Connally, 338 F. Supp. 448 (D.D.C. 1972).

[171] IRC § 501(c)(8). See § 18.4(a).

[172] Golden v. Biscayne Bay Yacht Club, *supra* note 169; Olzman v. Lake Hills Swim Club, Inc., 495 F.2d 1331 (2d Cir. 1974); Cornelius v. Benevolent Protective Order of Elks, 382 F. Supp. 1182 (D. Conn. 1974); Moose Lodge v. Irvis, 407 U.S. 163 (1972). Cf. Pitts v. Department of Revenue, 333 F. Supp. 662 (E.D. Wis. 1971).

social clubs maintaining any of these types of discriminatory policies.[173] It is the position of the IRS that this proscription on discriminatory practices does not extend to exempt social clubs that limit membership on the basis of ethnic or national origin.[174]

In 1980, Congress refined this requirement to allow tax-exempt social clubs that are affiliated with fraternal beneficiary societies[175] to retain tax exemption even though membership in the clubs is limited to members of a particular religion. Also, this law change allows certain alumni clubs, which are limited to members of a particular religion in order to further the religion's teachings or principles, to retain their exemption as social clubs.[176]

§ 33.7   CORPORATE RESPONSIBILITY LEGISLATION

Historic federal accounting reform and corporate responsibility legislation was signed into law on July 30, 2002.[177] This measure is focused on publicly traded companies and large accounting firms, not tax-exempt organizations. The emergence of this law, however, raises a number of questions for exempt organizations.

(a) Definitions

There are certain terms that are essential to understand for appreciation of the scope of this body of law as it relates to tax-exempt organizations.

An *audit committee* is a committee established "by and amongst" the board of directors of an issuer for the purpose of overseeing the accounting and financial reporting processes of the issuer and audits of the financial statements of the issuer.[178]

---

[173] IRC § 501(i).

[174] Priv. Ltr. Rul. 8317004.

[175] See § 18.4(a).

[176] IRC § 501(i), last sentence. In general, Patasnick, "Applying for Tax-Exempt Status May Be Costly for Social Clubs," 9 *J. Tax. Exempt Orgs.* (No. 2) 55 (Sept./Oct. 1997); Chiechi & Munk, "When Can Social Clubs Offset Investment Income With Losses from Nonmember Activities?," 73 *J. Tax.* (No. 3) 184 (1990); Banspach, "Social Clubs and the Profit Motive Test: Allowability of Excess Deductions Against Investment Income," 27 *San Diego L. Rev.* (No. 1) 81 (1990); Graham, "Social Clubs: Establishing the Right to Exemption Under Section 501(c)(7) and a Proposal for Expanding the Scope of Exemption," 33 *Tax Law.* 881 (1980); Crawford, "New Laws Indicate Scope of Exempt Clubs' Revenues from Investments, Nonmembers," 47 *J. Tax.* 48 (1977); Crawford, "Country Clubs: The Money Side," XXIX *Golf J.* (No. 2) 28 (1976); Moffet, "The Problems of Section 501(c)(7) Organizations," 54 *Taxes* 4 (1976); Denny, "Professional and Social Organizations," 25 *Tul. Tax Inst.* 2200 (1975); Horn, "Unrelated Business Income of Social Clubs," 49 *Taxes* 738 (1971); Ginstling, "Social Clubs Coming Under Closer IRS Scrutiny; Nonmember Use Can Kill Exemption," 23 *J. Tax.* 162 (1966); Gasperow, "Tax Problems of Country Clubs," *J. Acct.* 60 (Oct. 1964).

[177] Sarbanes-Oxley Act of 2002, Pub. L. 107–204, 116 Stat. 745 (for purposes of this section, "Act").

[178] Act § 2(a)(3).

An *audit report* is a document prepared following an audit performed for purposes of compliance by an issuer with the securities laws, and in which a public accounting firm either states the opinion of the firm regarding a financial statement, report, or other document, or asserts that such an opinion cannot be expressed.[179]

A *code of ethics* means standards that are reasonably necessary to promote (1) honest and ethical conduct, including the handling of conflicts of interest, (2) full, fair, accurate, timely, and understandable disclosure in reports of an issuer, and (3) compliance with applicable governmental rules and regulations.[180]

A *financial expert* is an individual who has (1) an understanding of generally accepted accounting principles and financial statements, and (2) experience in the preparation or auditing of financial statements, the application of these principles, experience with internal accounting controls, and an understanding of audit committee functions.[181]

An *issuer* is a for-profit corporation, the stock of which is registered pursuant to the federal securities laws, and that is otherwise required to comply with those laws, including the filing of reports (also known as a *public company*).[182]

The term *non-audit services* means any professional services provided to an issuer by a registered public accounting firm, other than those provided to an issuer in connection with an audit or review of the financial statements of an issuer.[183]

A *public accounting firm* is a legal entity (such as a corporation or partnership) that is engaged in the practice of public accounting or preparing or issuing audit reports.[184] A *registered public accounting firm* is a public accounting firm that is registered with the new Oversight Board.[185]

(b) Principal Features of the Law

(i) Public Company and Accounting Oversight Board. The Public Company and Accounting Oversight Board (Board), the members of which will be appointed by the Securities and Exchange Commission (SEC), was established.[186] The Board has five full-time members, with five-year terms, two of which may be certified public accountants. These members must be "prominent," of "integrity and reputation," have a "demonstrated commitment to the interests of investors and the public," and have an "understanding of the responsibilities for and nature of the financial disclosures required of issuers under the securities laws and the obligations of accountants with respect to the preparation and issuance of audit reports with respect to such disclosures."

---

[179] Act § 2(a)(4).
[180] Act § 406(c).
[181] Act § 407(b).
[182] Act § 2(a)(7).
[183] Act § 2(a)(8).
[184] Act § 2(a)(11).
[185] Act § 2(a)(12).
[186] Act § 101.

The purpose of the Board is to "oversee the audit of public companies that are subject to the securities laws, and related matters, in order to protect the interests of investors and further the public interest in the preparation of informative, accurate, and independent audit reports for companies the securities of which are sold to, and held by and for, public investors." The Board is required to submit an annual report to the SEC.

The Board is not part of the federal government but rather is a District of Columbia nonprofit corporation. It can be dissolved, however, only by Congress. It is empowered to accept contributions. The statute is silent as to the tax-exempt status of the Board (the Act is not tax legislation).

The Board's duties include the following: (1) registration of public accounting firms that prepare audit reports for issuers; (2) adoption of auditing, quality control, ethics, independence, and other standards relating to the preparation of audit reports for issuers; (3) conduct inspections of registered public accounting firms; (4) conduct investigations and disciplinary proceedings concerning, and impose sanctions on registered public accounting firms and persons associated with these firms, (5) otherwise promote "high professional standards among, and improve the quality of audit services offered by, registered public accounting firms and associated persons thereof"; and (6) enforce compliance with this law, rules of the Board, and related securities laws.

(ii) Board Funding. The Board is required to establish an "annual accounting support fee" for purposes of establishing and maintaining the Board.[187] These fees (and fees to fund an accounting standards setting body) are paid by and allocated among issuers.

Funds collected by the Board from the assessment of penalties are used to fund a "merit scholarship program" for undergraduate and graduate students enrolled in accredited accounting degree programs. This program is administered by the Board or an entity selected by it.

(iii) Registration with Board. It is unlawful for a person that is not a registered public accounting firm to prepare or issue, or to participate in the preparation or issuance of, an audit report with respect to an issuer.[188] The legislation detailed the contents of the application for registration, which includes a listing of clients (issuers) and the fees paid by them for audit and other services. These applications generally are publicly available.

Each registered public accounting firm pays a registration fee and an annual fee.

(iv) Standards. The Board is establishing "auditing and related attestation standards, such quality control standards, and such ethical standards" to be used by registered public accounting firms in the preparation and issuance of audit reports.[189]

---

[187] Act § 109.
[188] Act § 102.
[189] Act § 103.

These rules must include a seven-year records retention requirement, a rule as to second partner review of audit reports, and rules describing in each audit report the scope of the auditor's "internal control structure and procedures of the issuer."

In this connection, the Board may establish advisory groups. It is to "cooperate on an ongoing basis" with these groups and with professional groups of accountants.

(v) Inspections. The Board will be conducting a "continuing program of inspections" to assess compliance by registered public accounting firms (and associated persons) with this law, rules of the SEC and the Board, or professional standards, in connection with its performance of audits, issuance of audit reports, and related matters.[190]

If a firm regularly provides audit reports for more than 100 issuers, the inspection must be annually. Otherwise, the review must be at least once every three years. The Board can adjust this inspection schedule and conduct special inspections.

(vi) Investigations. The Board is to establish "fair procedures" for the investigation and disciplining of registered public accounting firms (and associated persons).[191] These investigations pertain to alleged violations of this law, Board rules, and securities laws pertaining to the preparation and issuance of audit reports.

The statute detailed the procedures these investigations are to follow, including disciplinary procedures, sanctions, and suspensions.

(vii) Nonaudit Services. The law amended the securities laws to generally make it unlawful for a registered public accounting firm, that performs for an issuer an audit, to provide to that issuer, contemporaneously with the audit, any nonaudit service.[192] The Board has the authority to grant exemptions.

These services include bookkeeping services, financial information systems design and implementation, appraisal services, fairness opinions, actuarial services, internal audit outsourcing services, investment adviser services, and legal services.

(viii) Audit Partner Rotation. The statute amended the securities laws to make it unlawful for a registered public accounting firm to provide audit services to an issuer if the lead (or coordinating) audit partner, or the audit partner responsible for reviewing the audit, has performed audit services for that issuer in each of the five previous fiscal years of the issuer.[193]

The statute provides for a study of mandatory rotation of registered public accounting firms.[194]

---

[190] Act § 104.
[191] Act § 105.
[192] Act § 201.
[193] Act § 203.
[194] Act § 207.

(ix) Audit Committees.   The law in essence mandated the creation and functioning of audit committees of issuers.[195] This is done, in part, by requiring the SEC to in turn direct the national securities exchanges and associations to prohibit the listing of the securities of issuers who fail to establish and use these committees.

The audit committee of an issuer must be directly responsible for the appointment, compensation, and oversight of the work of a registered public accounting firm employed by the issuer for the purpose of preparing or issuing an audit report or related work. Each such registered public accounting firm must report directly to the audit committee.

Each member of an audit committee must be a member of the board of directors of the issuer involved. He or she may not accept any consulting, advisory, or other compensation from the issuer.

The SEC is to issue rules to require each issuer to disclose whether or not, and if not why not, the audit committee of the issuer is comprised of at least one member who is a financial expert.

(x) Corporate Responsibility.   The law requires that the principal executive officer and principal financial officer of an issuer certify each annual or quarterly report filed by the issuer in compliance with the securities laws.[196] This includes certification that the report does not contain any untrue statement of a material fact or failure to state a material fact "necessary in order to make the statements made . . . not misleading."

If an issuer is required to prepare an accounting restatement due to the "material noncompliance" of the issuer, as a result of misconduct, with a financial reporting requirement under the securities laws, the chief executive officer and chief financial officer of the issuer must reimburse the issuer for any bonus or other incentive-based or equity-based compensation received by that individual from the issuer during a prior 12-month period.[197] This disgorgement rule can also encompass profits realized from the sale of stock of the issuer.

It is generally unlawful for an issuer to extend or maintain credit in the form of a personal loan to or for any director or executive officer of that issuer.[198] This includes the use of a subsidiary for this purpose.

A person who is the beneficial owner of more than 10 percent of any class of registered equity security must file a statement with the SEC. This includes nonprofit organizations.

The SEC is to issue rules requiring each issuer to disclose whether or not, and if not why not, the issuer has adopted a code of ethics for senior financial officers.[199]

[195] Act § 301.
[196] Act § 302.
[197] Act § 304.
[198] Act § 402.
[199] Act § 406.

(xi) Lawyers. This law requires the SEC to issue rules setting forth minimum standards of professional conduct for lawyers practicing before the SEC.[200] These rules require a lawyer to report evidence of a "major violation of securities law or breach of fiduciary duty or similar violation by the company" to the chief legal counsel or the chief executive officer of the company.

If there is not an appropriate response to the evidence presented, including remedial measures, the lawyer is to report the evidence to the audit committee of the issuer or another committee of the board.

(xii) Disgorgement Funds. If the SEC obtains a disgorgement order against a person for violation of the securities laws, and that includes a civil penalty, the penalty is to be added to and become part of a disgorgement fund for the benefit of the victims of the violation.[201]

The SEC is authorized to accept and utilize gifts, bequests, and devises for one or more of these funds. (The law does not address the point but these contributions are deductible as charitable gifts.)

(xiii) Real Time Disclosures. This law amended the securities laws to require reporting issuers to disclose to the public, on a "rapid and current basis," additional information concerning material changes in the financial condition or operations of the issuer, in "plain English."[202] This type of disclosure may include "trend and qualitative information and graphic presentations."

(xiv) Other Provisions. The SEC is to issue rules for the disclosure of material off-balance sheet transactions.[203] An accountant who conducts an audit of an issuer is required to maintain all audit or review workpapers for five years.[204] There is a new criminal law provision concerning the knowing destruction or falsification of corporate records with intent to impede or influence a federal investigation.[205]

(c) Application of Law to Tax-Exempt Organizations

This body of law does not, as noted, apply to tax-exempt organizations (other than the criminal law rule concerning destruction of evidence). Again, it applies to, and with respect to, *issuers* and *public accounting firms.*

Nonetheless, those who manage tax-exempt organizations, and perhaps those who make contributions to them, may want to give consideration to some or all of the following: whether (1) the accounting firm retained by an exempt organization should be a registered public accounting firm; (2) an exempt organization should have an audit committee or similar body; (3) an exempt organization

---

[200] Act § 307.
[201] Act § 308.
[202] Act § 409.
[203] Act § 401.
[204] Act § 802.
[205] Act § 1102.

should develop a code of ethics for its senior officers (this would go beyond a conflict-of-interest policy); (4) an exempt organization should require certification of its financial statements and/or annual information returns by its executive; (5) an exempt organization should have a policy of prohibiting loans to its senior executives; (6) in an instance of a need for an accounting restatement by an exempt organization, due to some form of misconduct, any bonuses and/or the like to executive personnel should be reimbursed; (7) an exempt organization should follow the rules as to audit partner rotation; (8) an exempt organization should separate audit and nonaudit service providers; (9) an exempt organization's lawyers should be required to report breaches of fiduciary responsibility to its executive and (10) there should be a rule requiring real-time disclosures by tax-exempt organizations.[206]

Although there is no immediate impetus for enactment of corporate responsibility legislation applicable to tax-exempt organizations, corporate responsibility principles may become directly or indirectly applicable to exempt entities as the result of revision of the annual information return.[207] The IRS is in the process of revising that document;[208] indications are that one or more of the questions on the forthcoming return will reflect corporate responsibility concepts (for example, adoption of conflict of interest policies and/or use of independent audit committees).

---

[206] A proposal, which was in the House version of this legislation, requiring issuers to increase disclosure to the SEC of their charitable contributions and of company executives' (and their family members') positions on the boards of tax-exempt organizations was abandoned.
[207] See § 24.3.
[208] See § 24.3(b), note 223.

APPENDIX A

Sources of the Law

The law as described in this book is derived from many sources. For those not familiar with these matters and wishing to understand just what the "law" regarding tax-exempt organizations is, the following explanation should be of assistance.

FEDERAL LAW

At the federal (national) level in the United States, there are three branches of government as provided for in the U.S. Constitution. Article I of the Constitution established the U.S. Congress as a bicameral legislature, consisting of the House of Representatives and the Senate. Article II of the Constitution established the Presidency. Article III of the Constitution established the federal court system.

Congress

The legal structure underlying the federal law for nonprofit organizations in the United States has been created by Congress. Most of this law is manifested in the tax law and thus appears in the Internal Revenue Code (which is officially codified in Title 26 of the United States Code and referenced throughout the book as the "IRC" (see Chapter 1, note 2)). Other laws written by Congress that can affect nonprofit organizations include the postal, employee benefits, antitrust, labor, political campaign financing, corporate responsibility, and securities laws.

Tax laws for the United States must originate in the House of Representatives (U.S. Constitution, Article I § 7). Consequently, most of the nation's tax laws are formally initially written by the members and staff of the House Committee on Ways and Means, although much of this work is performed by the staff of the Joint Committee on Taxation, which consists of members of the House and Senate. Frequently, these laws are generated by work done at the subcommittee level, usually the Subcommittee on Oversight or the Subcommittee on Select Revenue Measures.

Committee work in this area within the Senate is undertaken by the Committee on Finance. The Joint Committee on Taxation again provides assistance in this regard. Nearly all of this legislation is finalized by a House-Senate conference committee, consisting of senior members of the House Ways and Means Committee and the Senate Finance Committee.

A considerable amount of the federal tax law for nonprofit organizations is found in the "legislative history" of these statutory laws. Most of this history is in congressional committee reports. Reports from committees in the House of Representatives are cited as "H. Rep." (see, e.g., Chapter 1, note 35); reports from committees in the Senate are cited as "S. Rep." (see, e.g., Chapter 1, note 103); conference committee reports are cited as "H. Rep." (see, e.g., Chapter 10, note 39). Transcripts of the debate on legislation, formal statements, and other items are printed in the Congressional Record ("*Cong. Rec.*"). The Congressional Record is published every day one of the houses of Congress is in session and is cited as "_____ *Cong. Rec.* _____ (daily ed., [date of issue])." The first number is the annual volume number; the second number is the page in the daily edition on which the item begins. Periodically, the daily editions of the Congressional Record are republished as a hard-bound book and are cited as "_____ *Cong. Rec.* _____([year])" (see, e.g., Chapter 5, note 29). As before, the first number is the annual volume number and the second is the beginning page number. The bound version of the Congressional Record then becomes the publication that contains the permanent citation for the item.

A Congress sits for two years, each of which is termed a "session." Each Congress is sequentially numbered. For example, the 107th Congress met during the calendar years 2001–2002. A legislative development that took place in 2002 is referenced as occurring during the 107th Congress, 2d Session ("107th Cong., 2d Session (2002)").

A bill introduced in the House of Representatives or Senate during a particular Congress is given a sequential number in each house. For example, the 1,000th bill introduced in the House of Representatives in 2002 is cited as "H.R. 1000, 107th Cong., 2d Sess. (2002)" (see, e.g., Chapter 5, note 108); the 500th bill introduced in the Senate in 2002 is cited as "S. 500, 107th Cong., 2d Sess. (2002)" (see, e.g., Chapter 18 § 20).

Executive Branch

A function of the Executive Branch in the United States is to administer and enforce the laws enacted by Congress. This "executive" function is performed by departments and agencies, and "independent" regulatory commissions (such as the Federal Election Commission or the Securities and Exchange Commission). One of these functions is the promulgation of regulations, which are published by the U.S. government in the "Code of Federal Regulations" ("CFR"). When adopted, regulations are printed in the *Federal Register* ("Fed. Reg.") (see, e.g., Chapter 5, note 103). The federal tax laws are administered and enforced overall by the Department of the Treasury.

One of the ways in which the Department of the Treasury executes these functions is by the promulgation of regulations ("Reg."), which are designed to interpret and amplify the related statute (see, e.g., Chapter 1, note 58). These regulations (like other rules made by other government departments, agencies, and commissions) have the force of law, unless they are overly broad in relation to the accompanying statute or are unconstitutional, in which case they can be rendered void by a court.

Within the Department of the Treasury is the Internal Revenue Service ("IRS"). The IRS is, among its many roles, a tax-collecting agency. The IRS, while headquartered in Washington, D.C. (its "National Office"), has regional and field offices throughout the country.

The IRS's jurisdiction over tax-exempt organizations is principally lodged within the office of the Director, Exempt Organizations, who is responsible for planning, managing, directing, and executing nationwide activities for exempt organizations. The Director reports to the Tax Exempt Entities/Government Entities Division Commissioner. The Director supervises the activities of the offices of Customer Education and Outreach, Rulings and Agreements, and Examinations.

The IRS (from its National Office) prepares and disseminates guidance interpreting tax statutes and tax regulations. This guidance has the force of law, unless it is overly broad in relation to the statute and/or Treasury regulation involved, or is unconstitutional. IRS determinations on a point of law are termed "revenue rulings" ("Rev. Rul."); those that are rules of procedure are termed "revenue procedures" ("Rev. Proc.").

Revenue rulings (which may be based on one or more court opinions) and revenue procedures are sequentially numbered every calendar year, with that number preceded by a two- or four-digit number reflecting the year of issue. For example, the fiftieth revenue ruling issued in 2002 is cited as "Rev. Rul. 2002-50." Likewise, the twenty-fifth revenue procedure issued in 2002 is cited as "Rev. Proc. 2002-25."

These IRS determinations are published each week in the Internal Revenue Bulletin ("I.R.B."). In the foregoing examples, when the determinations are first published, the revenue ruling is cited as "Rev. Rul. 2002-50, 2002-____ I.R.B. ____," with the number after the hyphen being the number of the particular issue of the weekly Bulletin and the last number being the page number within that issue on which the item begins. Likewise, the revenue procedure is cited as "Rev. Proc. 2002-25, 2002-____ I.R.B. ____." Every six months, the Internal Revenue Bulletins are republished as hard-bound books, with the resulting publication termed the Cumulative Bulletin ("C.B."). The Cumulative Bulletin designation then becomes the permanent citation for the determination. Thus, the permanent citations for these two IRS determinations are "Rev. Rul. 2002-50, 2002-1 C.B. ____" (see, e.g., Chapter 3, note 119) and "Rev. Proc. 2002-25, 2002-1 C.B. ____" (see, e.g., Chapter 4, note 2), with the first number being the year of issue, the second number (after the hyphen) indicating whether the determination is published in the first six months of the year ("1" as in the example) or the second six months of the year ("2"), and the last number being the page number within that semiannual bound volume at which the determination begins.

The IRS considers itself bound by its revenue rulings and revenue procedures. These determinations are the "law," particularly in the sense that the IRS regards them as precedential, although they are not binding on the courts.

The IRS also issues forms of "public" law in the name of "notices" and "announcements." A notice is initially published in the Internal Revenue Bulletin and then republished in the Cumulative Bulletin (see, e.g., Chapter 23, note 70). An announcement, however, although published in the Internal Revenue Bulletin, is not republished in the Cumulative Bulletin (see, e.g., Chapter 24, note 223).

By contrast to these forms of "public" law, the IRS (again from its National Office) also issues "private" or nonprecedential determinations. These documents principally are private letter rulings and technical advice memoranda. These determinations may not be cited as legal authority (IRC § 6110(j)(3)). Nonetheless, these pronouncements can be valuable in understanding IRS thinking on a point of law and, in practice (the statutory prohibition notwithstanding), these documents are cited as IRS positions on issues, such as in court opinions, articles, and books.

The IRS issues private letter rulings in response to written questions (termed "ruling requests") submitted to the IRS by individuals and organizations. An IRS district office may refer a case to the IRS National Office for advice (termed "technical advice"); the resulting advice is provided to the IRS district office in the form of a technical advice memorandum. In the course of preparing a revenue ruling, private letter ruling, or technical advice memorandum, the IRS National Office may seek legal advice from its Office of Chief Counsel; the resulting advice was provided, until recently, in the form of a general counsel memorandum (see, e.g., Chapter 4, note 227). These documents are eventually made public, albeit in redacted form.

Private letter rulings ("Priv. Ltr. Rul.") and technical advice memoranda ("Tech. Adv. Mem.") are identified by seven- or nine-digit numbers, as in "Priv. Ltr. Rul. 200226007" (see, e.g., Chapter 4, note 228). (A reference to a technical advice memorandum appears in Chapter 4, note 207.) The first two (or four) numbers are for the year involved (here, 2002), the next two numbers reflect the week of the calendar year involved (here, the twenty-sixth week of 2002), and the remaining three numbers identify the document as issued sequentially during the particular week (here, this private letter ruling was the seventh one issued during the week involved).

The Judiciary

The federal court system has three levels; trial courts (including those that initially hear cases where a formal trial is not involved), courts of appeal ("appellate" courts), and the U.S. Supreme Court. The trial courts include the various federal district courts (at least one in each state, the District of Columbia, and the U.S. territories), the U.S. Tax Court, and the U.S. Court of Federal Claims. There are thirteen federal appellate courts (the U.S. Court of Appeal for the First through the Eleventh Circuits, the U.S. Courts of Appeals for the District of Columbia, and the U.S. Court of Appeals for the Federal Circuit).

Cases involving tax-exempt organization issues at the federal level can originate in any federal district court, the U.S. Tax Court, and the U.S. Court of Federal Claims. Under a special declaratory judgment procedure available only to charitable organizations (IRC § 7428), cases can originate only with the U.S. District Court for the District of Columbia, the U.S. Tax Court, and the U.S. Court of Federal Claims. Cases involving tax-exempt organizations are considered by the U.S. Courts of Appeal and the U.S. Supreme Court.

Most opinions emanating from a U.S. district court are published by the West Publishing Company in the "Federal Supplement" series ("F. Supp." or "F. Supp. 2d"). Thus, a citation to one of these opinions appears as "_____ F. Supp. _____" or "____. Supp. 2d ____," followed by an identification of the court and the year of the opinion. The first number is the annual volume number, the other number is the page in the book on which the opinion begins (see, e.g., Chapter 1, note 69). Some district court opinions appear sooner in Commerce Clearinghouse or Prentice Hall publications (see, e.g., Chapter 3, note 2); occasionally, these publications will contain opinions that are never published in the Federal Supplement series.

Most opinions emanating from a U.S. court of appeals are published by the West Publishing Company in the "Federal Reporter" series (usually "F.2d" or "F.3d"). Thus, a citation to one of these opinions appears as "_____ F.2d _____" or "_____ F.3d _____," followed by an identification of the court and the year of the opinion. The first number is the annual volume number; the other number is the page in the book on which the opinion begins (see, e.g., Chapter 1, note 66). Appellate court opinions appear sooner in Commerce Clearinghouse or Prentice Hall publications (see, e.g., Chapter 3, note 132); occasionally these publications contain opinions that are never published in Federal Second or Federal Third series. Opinions from the U.S. Court of Federal Claims are also published in the Federal Second or Federal Third.

Opinions from the U.S. Tax Court are published by the U.S. government and are usually cited as "_____ T.C. _____," followed by the year of the opinion (see, e.g., Chapter 2, note 81). Some Tax Court opinions that are of lesser precedential value are published as "memorandum decisions" and are cited as "_____ T.C.M. _____" followed by the year of the opinion (see, e.g., Chapter 3, note 122). As always, the first number of these citations is the annual volume number, the second number is the page in the book on which the opinion begins.

U.S. district court and Tax Court opinions may be appealed to the appropriate U.S. court of appeals. For example, cases in the states of Maryland, North Carolina, South Carolina, Virginia, and West Virginia are appealable (from either court) to the U.S. Court of Appeals for the Fourth Circuit. Cases from any federal appellate or district court, the U.S. Tax Court, and the U.S. Court of Federal Claims may be appealed to the U.S. Supreme Court.

The U.S. Supreme Court usually has discretion as to whether to accept a case. This decision is manifested as a "writ of certiorari." When the Supreme Court agrees to hear a case, it grants the writ ("*cert. gr.*"); otherwise, it denies the writ ("*cert. den.*") (see, e.g., Chapter 3, note 6).

In this book, citations to Supreme Court opinions are to the "United States Reports" series, published by the U.S. government, when available ("_____ U.S. _____," followed by the year of the opinion) (see, e.g., Chapter 1, note 21). When the United States Reports series citation is not available, the "Supreme Court Reporter" series, published by the West Publishing Company, reference is used ("_____ S. Ct. _____," followed by the year of the opinion). As always, the first number of these citations is the annual volume number, the second number is the page in the book on which the opinion begins. There is a third way to cite Supreme Court cases, which is by means of the "United States Supreme Court Reports—Lawyers' Edition" series, published by The Lawyers Co-Operative Publishing Company and the Bancroft-Whitney Company, but that form of citation is not used in this book. Supreme Court opinions appear earlier in the Commerce Clearinghouse or Prentice Hall publications.

In most instances, court opinions are available on Westlaw and LEXIS in advance of formal publication.

STATE LAW

The Legislative Branches

Statutory laws in the various states are created by their legislatures. There are a few references to state statutory laws in this book (although most, if not all, of the states have such forms of law relating, directly or indirectly, to tax-exempt organizations).

The Executive Branches

The rules and regulations published at the state level emanate from state departments, agencies, and the like. For tax-exempt organizations, these departments are usually the office of the state's attorney general and the state's department of state. There are no references to state rules and regulations in this book (although most, if not all, of the states have such forms of law relating to tax-exempt organizations).

The Judiciary

Each of the states has a judiciary system, usually a three-tiered one modeled after the federal system. Cases involving nonprofit organizations are heard in all of these courts. There are a few references to state court opinions in this book (see, e.g., Chapter 6, note 373) (although most, if not all, of the states have court opinions relating, directly or indirectly, to tax-exempt organizations).

State court opinions are published by the governments of each state and the principal ones by the West Publishing Company. The latter sets of opinions (referenced in this book) are published in "Reporters" relating to court developments in various regions throughout the country. For example, the "Atlantic Reporter" contains court opinions issued by the principal courts in the states of Connecticut, Delaware, Maine, Maryland, New Hampshire, New Jersey, Pennsylvania, Rhode Island, and Vermont, and the District of Columbia, while the "Pacific Reporter" contains court opinions issued by the principal courts of Arizona, California, Colorado, Idaho, Kansas, Montana, Nevada, New Mexico, Oklahoma, Oregon, Utah, Washington, and Wyoming.

PUBLICATIONS

Articles, of course, are not forms of the "law." However, they can be cited, particularly by courts, in the development of the law. Also, as research tools, they contain useful summaries of the applicable law. In addition to the many law school "law review" publications, the following (not an inclusive list) periodicals contain material that is of help in following developments concerning tax-exempt organizations.

Bruce R. Hopkins' *Nonprofit Counsel* (John Wiley & Sons, Inc.)
The Chronicle of Philanthropy
Daily Tax Report (Bureau of National Affairs, Inc.)
Exempt Organization Tax Review (Tax Analysts)
Foundation News (Council on Foundations)

SOURCES OF THE LAW

The Journal of Taxation (Warren, Gorham & Lamont)
The Journal of Taxation of Exempt Organizations (Faulkner & Gray)
The Philanthropy Monthly (Non-Profit Reports, Inc.)
Tax Law Review (Rosenfeld Launer Publications)
The Tax Lawyer (American Bar Association)
Tax Notes (Tax Analysts)
Taxes (Commerce Clearinghouse, Inc.)

APPENDIX B

Internal Revenue Code Sections

Following are the provisions of the Internal Revenue Code of 1986, as amended, which comprise the statutory framework for the law of tax-exempt organizations, coupled with references (by chapter or chapter section) to the portion(s) of the book where the provision is discussed:

Section 41—tax credit for increasing scientific research activities [Chap. 9 § 2, 11.1(f)].

Section 68—floor on certain income tax deductions, including charitable deduction [2.5].

Section 74(b)—rule concerning prizes and awards transferred to charitable organizations [11.4].

Section 84—tax on appreciated property gifts to political organizations [17].

Section 103—exclusion for interest on governmental obligations [6.9, 18.7].

Section 115—exclusion from gross income for revenues of political subdivisions and the like [6.9, 18.7].

Section 117—exclusion from gross income for qualified scholarships [4.5, 6.5, 11.4 (e)].

Section 162(e)—denial of business expense deduction for expenses of most lobbying and political campaign activities; flow-through rule relating to dues; "anti-cascading rule" that operates to ensure that lobbying expense disallowance rule results in denial of deduction at only one level [20.8].

Section 168(h)—tax-exempt entity leasing rules [29.5].

Section 170—income tax deduction for charitable contributions [2.5, 3.2(b), 5].

Section 170(b)(1)(E)(ii)—pass-through foundation rules [11.1(d)].

Section 170(b)(1)(E)(iii)—conduit foundation rules [11.1(e)].

Section 192—income tax deduction for contributions to black lung benefit trusts [16.5].

Section 274(a)(3)—denial of business expense deduction for payment of club dues [14.1].

Section 277—treatment of deductions incurred by certain nonexempt membership organizations [3.4, 13.6, 14.3].

Section 318—indirect control test for purposes of taxing revenue from controlled entities [27.1(n)(ii)].

Section 337(b)(2)—recognition of gain or loss for property distributed to tax-exempt parent in liquidation of subsidiary [33.5].

Section 337(d)—recognition of gain or loss for property distributed to tax-exempt organization generally in liquidation [31.2(d)].

Section 401(a)—general rules for qualified pension, profit-sharing and like plans [4.9, 16.1, 19.4(i)].

Section 401(k)(4)(B)(i)—maintenance of 401(k) plans by tax-exempt organizations [16.1(d), 19.4(i)].

Section 403(b)—treatment of certain annuity contracts provided by charitable organizations to their employees [3.2(e), 16.1(e), 19.4(i)].

Section 419—welfare benefit fund rules [14.2, 16.2].

Section 457—deferred compensation plans of tax-exempt organizations [3.2(e), 16.1(f), 19.4(i)].

Section 501(a)—source of tax exemption for nearly all exempt organizations [3.1].

Section 501(b)—tax-exempt organizations subject to tax on unrelated business income [28.1].

Section 501(c)(1)—tax exemption for instrumentalities of the United States [18.1].

Section 501(c)(2)—tax exemption for single-parent title-holding corporations [18.2(a)].

Section 501(c)(3)—tax exemption for charitable, educational, religious, scientific, and similar entities [5–11].

Section 501(c)(4)—tax exemption for social welfare organizations [12].

Section 501(c)(5)—tax exemption for agricultural, horticultural, and labor organizations [15].

Section 501(c)(6)—tax exemption for business leagues, including trade, business, and professional associations [13].

Section 501(c)(7)—tax exemption for social clubs [14].

Section 501(c)(8)—tax exemption for certain fraternal beneficiary societies [18.4(a)].

Section 501(c)(9)—tax exemption for voluntary employees' beneficiary associations [16.3].

Section 501(c)(10)—tax exemption for certain domestic fraternal societies [18.4(b)].

Section 501(c)(11)—tax exemption for teachers' retirement fund associations [16.6].

Section 501(c)(12)—tax exemption for benevolent or mutual organizations [18.5].

Section 501(c)(13)—tax exemption for certain cemetery companies [18.6].

Section 501(c)(14)—tax exemption for certain credit unions and mutual reserve funds [1.2, 18.7].

Section 501(c)(15)—tax exemption for certain insurance companies or associations [18.8].

Section 501(c)(16)—tax exemption for crop operations finance corporations [18.9].

Section 501(c)(17)—tax exemption for supplemental unemployment benefit trusts [16.4].

Section 501(c)(18)—tax exemption for certain pension plan trusts [16.7].

Section 501(c)(19)—tax exemption for veterans' organizations [18.10(a)].

Section 501(c)(21)—tax exemption for black lung benefit trusts [16.5].

Section 501(c)(22)—tax exemption for multiemployer benefit trusts [16.7].

Section 501(c)(23)—tax exemption for certain veterans' organizations [1.2, 18.10(b)].

Section 501(c)(24)—tax exemption for certain employee benefit trusts [16.7].

Section 501(c)(25)—tax exemption for multiparent title-holding corporations or trusts [18.2(b)].

Section 501(c)(26)—tax exemption for high-risk individuals health care coverage organizations [18.14].

Section 501(c)(27)—tax exemption for workers' compensation reinsurance organizations [1.2, 18.15].

Section 501(d)—rules for religious and apostolic organizations [8.7].

Section 501(e)—cooperative hospital service organizations [6.8, 10.4].

Section 501(f)—cooperative educational service organizations [6.8, 10.5].

Section 501(g)—definition of term *agricultural* [15.2].

Section 501(h)—election of expenditure test as to lobbying [20.5(a)].

Section 501(i)—prohibition on discrimination by social clubs [14.5].

Section 501(j)—rules for certain amateur sports organizations [10.2].

Section 501(k)—rules for certain child care organizations [7.7].

Section 501(l)—list of specified exempt U.S. instrumentalities [18.1].

Section 501(m)—rules concerning issuance of commercial-type insurance [1.2, 22.1, 25, 27.1(o)].

Section 501(n)—tax exemption for qualified charitable risk pools [1.2, 10.6].

Section 501(o)—treatment of hospitals participating in provider-sponsored organizations [6.2(a)].

Section 502—feeder organizations [23.7(a), 28.6].

Section 503—denial of tax exemption to certain organizations engaged in prohibited transactions [23.8].

INTERNAL REVENUE CODE SECTIONS

Section 504—rules as to status of nonexempt charity because of lobbying or political campaign activities [12.3, 20.3(b), 21.2].

Section 505—additional requirements for certain employee benefit funds [16.2].

Section 507—rules by which the private foundation status of charitable organizations is terminated [11.4].

Section 508—special rules for charitable organizations, including notice requirements [4.3(a), 11.1(a), 11.1(g), 23.3, 23.4].

Section 509—description of charitable organizations that are not private foundations [11.3].

Section 509(a)(1)—rules as to certain charitable institutions and donative publicly supported charitable organizations [11.3(a), (b)].

Section 509(a)(2)—rules as to service provider publicly supported charitable organizations [11.3(b)(iv)].

Section 509(a)(3)—rules as to supporting organizations [4.1, 11.3(c)].

Section 509(a)(4)—rules for organizations that test for public safety [11.3(d)].

Section 511—imposition of tax on unrelated business income [28.1].

Section 512—definition of unrelated business income [14.3, 26.1, 27.1, 29.1].

Section 512(b)—various modifications in computing unrelated business income [27.1].

Section 512(c)—special unrelated business rules for partnerships [28.4].

Section 512(d)—nontaxation of certain associate member dues [27.2(l)].

Section 512(e)—taxation of interests in S corporations [27.2(m), 31.1(b)].

Section 513—general unrelated business rules [26, 27].

Section 513(c)—definition of *trade or business* [26.2].

Section 513(d)—trade show and like activities rules [27.2(f)].

Section 513(e)—rules as to certain hospital services [6.8, 27.2(g)].

Section 513(f)—rules as to bingo games [27.2(h)].

Section 513(g)—rules as to certain pole rentals [27.2(i)].

Section 513(h)—rules as to rentals of lists and distribution of low-cost articles [27.2(j)].

Section 513(i)—nontaxation of qualified sponsorship payments [27.2(n)].

Section 514—rules as to unrelated debt-financed income [29.1–29.4].

Section 521—tax-exempt farmers' cooperatives [18.11].

Section 526—tax-exempt shipowners' protection and indemnity associations [18.12].

Section 527—tax-exempt political organizations and tax on political activities [17].

Section 527(f)(1)—tax on political expenditures [17.3, 21.3].

Section 528—tax-exempt homeowners' associations [18.13].

Section 529—tax exemption for qualified state tuition programs [18.16].

Section 642(c)(5)—qualifying pooled income funds [2.5, 11.4(f), 18.19, 32.6].

Section 664—qualifying charitable remainder trusts [2.5, 11.4(f), 18.19].

Sections 1381–1383—nonexempt cooperatives [3.4].

Section 2055—estate tax charitable contribution deduction [2.5, 5].

Section 2501(a)(5)—gift tax exemption for transfers to political organizations [3.4, 17.1].

Section 2522—gift tax charitable contribution deduction [2.5, 5].

Section 3121—employment tax definitions [3.2(h)].

Section 3306(c)—employment tax definitions [3.2(e)].

Section 4421—exemption from wagering taxes [3.2(h)].

Section 4462(h)—exemptions from harbor maintenance tax [32.2(h)].

Section 4911—rules concerning lobbying by public charities under expenditure test [20].

Section 4912—excise tax on excess lobbying amounts by public charities under substantial part test [20.6].

Section 4940—excise tax on investment income of private foundations [11.4(f)].

Section 4940(d)(1)—exempt operating foundation rules [11.1(c)].

Section 4941—private foundation self-dealing rules [11.4(a)].

Section 4942—private foundation mandatory distribution rules [11.4(b)].

Section 4942(j)(3)—private operating foundation rules [11.1(6)].

Section 4943—private foundation excess business holdings rules [11.4(c)].

Section 4944—private foundation rules concerning jeopardizing investments [11.4(d)].

Section 4945—private foundation rules concerning taxable expenditures [11.4(e)].

Section 4946—definition of *disqualified person* for purposes of private foundation rules [11.2].

Section 4947—application of private foundation rules to certain non-exempt trusts [11.4(f), 24.2].

Section 4948—application of private foundation rules to foreign organizations [11.4(f)].

Section 4951—taxes on self-dealing with black lung benefit trusts [16.5].

Section 4952—taxes on taxable expenditures by black lung benefit trusts [16.5].

Section 4953—taxes on excess contributions to black lung benefit trusts [16.5].

Section 4955—taxes on certain political expenditures [21.2].

Section 4958—intermediate sanctions with respect to public charities and social welfare organizations [19.11].

Section 4961—abatement of private foundation additional taxes [11.4].

Section 4962—abatement of public charity and private foundation initial taxes [11.4].

Section 4976—taxes with respect to funded welfare benefit plans [14.1, 16.3, 16.4, 16.6].

Section 5276(c)—exemption from occupational tax for U.S. instrumentalities [3.2(h)].

Section 6011—requirement of return for payment of certain excise taxes, including those imposed for excess benefit transactions [7, 11, 19.11, 20.6, 21.2].

Section 6012—requirement of income tax returns [24.3(a)(v)].

Section 6031—requirement of partnership tax returns [32.5].

Section 6033—requirement of filing of annual information returns [24.3].

Section 6033(e)(1)(A)—dues nondeductibility disclosure rule for associations; imposition of proxy tax [20.8].

Section 6050—information return concerning certain transfers of property to charity [2.5].

Section 6071—authority in IRS to prescribe time for filing a return, where filing date not set by statute [11, 19.11, 20.6, 21.2].

Section 6072(e)—time for filing returns [24.3(a)(vi)].

Section 6104—required publicity of information from certain exempt organizations and trusts [24.4].

Section 6110—rules as to public inspection of written determinations [24.2].

Section 6113—disclosure as to nondeductibility of contributions [3.3, 22.2].

Section 6154(h)—estimated unrelated income quarterly tax payments [28.1].

Section 6501(1)—limitations on assessments or collections; special rule for Chapter 42 taxes [24.3(a)(viii)].

Section 6651(a)(1)—addition to tax for failure to timely file unrelated business income tax (and other tax) return [24.3(a)(viii)].

Section 6652(c)(1)(A), (B)—penalties for failure to file annual information return [24.3(a)(viii)].

Section 6652(c)(1)(C)—penalties for failure to provide public access to annual information return [24.4].

Section 6652(c)(1)(D)—penalties for failure to provide public access to application for recognition of exemption [24.4].

Section 6652(d)(1)—rules concerning failure to file a return [6.10(d), 24.3].

Section 6653(b)—penalty for evading taxes due [8.2].

Section 6655(g)(3)—penalties for failure by a tax-exempt organization to pay estimated unrelated business income taxes [28.1].

Section 6673—use of Tax Court as delaying tactic [8.2].

Section 6684—penalties with respect to liability for Chapter 42 taxes [11.4].

Section 6710—penalties for failure to disclose that contributions are nondeductible [22.2].

Section 6711—penalties for failure to disclose that certain information or service is available from federal government [3.3, 24.5].

Section 6852—termination assessments for flagrant political expenditures by public charitable organizations [21.2].

Section 6901—rules as to transferred assets [24.2].

Section 7409—action to enjoin flagrant political expenditures by public charitable organizations [21.2].

Section 7421(a)—prohibition of restraint on assessment or collection of taxes [24.6(a)].

Section 7428—declaratory judgment provision for charitable organizations [24.6(b)].

Section 7454(b)—burden of proof in foundation manager cases [11].

Section 7611—church audit rules [24.8(b)].

Section 7701—definition of *partnership* and *corporation* [4.1, 32.1, 32.2(I), 33.1].

Section 7805(b)—discretion in IRS to grant relief [24.1].

Section 7871—rules as to Indian tribal governments [18.18].

APPENDIX C

68 Categories of Tax-Exempt Organizations

Agricultural organizations [IRC § 501(c)(5)]

Amateur sports, promotion of, organizations [IRC § 501(c)(3)]

Apostolic organizations [IRC § 501(d)]

Associations, membership [IRC § 501(c)(3), (6)]

Associations of churches [IRC §§ 501(c)(3), 170(b)(1)(A)(i), 509(a)(1)]

Black lung benefits trusts [IRC § 501(c)(21)]

Boards of trade [IRC § 501(c)(6)]

Benevolent organizations [IRC § 501(c)(12)]

Business leagues [IRC § 501(c)(6)]

Cemetery companies [IRC § 501(c)(13)]

Chambers of commerce [IRC § 501(c)(6)]

Charitable organizations [IRC § 501(c)(3)]

Charitable remainder trusts [IRC § 664]

Charitable risk pools [IRC §§ 501(n), 501(c)(3)]

Child care organizations [IRC §§ 501(k), 501(c)(3)]

Churches [IRC §§ 501(c)(3), 170 (b)(1)(A)(i), 509(a)(1)]

Conventions of churches [IRC §§ 501(c)(3), 170 (b)(1)(A)(i), 509(a)(1)]

Cooperative hospital service organization [IRC §§ 501(e), 501(c)(3)]

Cooperative service organizations of educational institutions [IRC §§ 501(f), 501(c)(3)]

Credit unions [IRC § 501(c)(14)]

Crop operations finance corporations [IRC § 501(c)(16)]

Cruelty, prevention of on behalf of children or animals [IRC § 501(c)(3)]

Domestic fraternal societies [IRC § 501(c)(10)]

Educational institutions [IRC §§ 501(c)(3), 170(b)(1)(A)(ii), 509(a)(1)]

Educational organizations, in general [IRC § 501(c)(3)]

Employee trusts, certain [IRC § 501(c)(24)]

Farmers' cooperatives [IRC § 521]

Foundations supporting public colleges and universities [IRC §§ 170 (b)(1)(A)(iv), 509 (a)(1)]

Fraternal beneficiary societies [IRC § 501(c)(8)]

Funded pension trusts, certain [IRC § 501(c)(18)]

Governmental units [IRC §§ 170(b)(1)(A)(v), 509(a)(1)]

Health care providers [IRC §§ 501(c)(3), 170(b)(1)(A)(iii), 509(a)(1)]

High-risk individuals health care coverage organizations [IRC § 501(c)(26)]

Homeowners' associations [IRC § 528]

Horticultural organizations [IRC § 501(c)(5)]

Indian tribes [IRC § 7871]

Instrumentalities of federal government [IRC § 501(c)(1)]

Insurance companies, certain [IRC § 501(c)(15)]

Integral parts of government [no statute]

Integrated auxiliaries of churches [IRC §§ 501(c)(3), 170(b)(1)(A)(i), 509(a)(1)]

Labor organizations [IRC § 501(c)(5)]

Literary organizations [IRC § 501(c)(3)]

Local associations of employees [IRC § 501(c)(4)]

Medical research organizations [IRC §§ 501(c)(3), 170(b)(1)(A)(iii), 509(a)(1)]

Multiemployer pension plan trusts [IRC § 501(c)(22)]

Mutual organizations [IRC § 501(c)(12), (14)]

Retirement and pension funds [IRC § 401]

Political organizations [IRC § 527]

Political subdivisions [including IRC § 115]

Prepaid tuition plans [IRC § 529]

Private foundations [IRC §§ 501(c)(3), 509(a)]

Professional football leagues [IRC § 501(c)(6)]

Publicly supported charitable organizations, in general [IRC §§ 501(c)(3), 170(b)(1)(A)(vi), 509(a)(1), 509(a)(2)]

Real estate boards [IRC § 501(c)(6)]

Religious organizations, in general [IRC § 501(c)(3)]

Scientific organizations [IRC § 501(c)(3)]

Shipowners' protection and indemnity associations [IRC § 526]

Social clubs [IRC § 501(c)(7)]

Social welfare organizations [IRC § 501(c)(4)]

Supplemental unemployment benefit trusts [IRC § 501(c)(17)]

Supporting organizations [IRC §§ 501(c)(3), 509(a)(3)]

Teachers' retirement fund associations [IRC § 50l(c)(11)]

Testing for public safety organizations [IRC §§ 501(c)(3), 509(a)(4)]

Title-holding corporations, single parent [IRC § 501(c)(2)]

Title-holding corporations, multiparent [IRC § 501(c)(25)]

Veterans' organizations [IRC § 501(c)(19), (23)]

Voluntary employees' beneficiary associations [IRC § 501(c)(9)]

Workers' compensation organizations [IRC § 501(c)(27)]

Table of Cases

TABLE OF CASES

Table of IRS Revenue Rulings and Revenue Procedures

Revenue Rulings	Book Sections	Revenue Rulings	Book Sections	Revenue Rulings	Book Sections
53-44	§ 14.1	55-449	§ 26.4(g)	56-249	§ 16.4
54-12	§ 18.11	55-495	§§ 12.1(a), 18.4(a)	56-305	§ 14.1
54-73	§ 27.1(l)			56-403	§ 5.5(a)
54-134	§§ 24.1(b), 27.2(d)	55-516	§ 12.1(a)	56-475	§ 14.1
		55-558	§ 18.11	56-486	§ 6.6
54-170	§ 32.1	55-587	§§ 6.6, 7.4	56-511	§ 26.2(g)
54-243	§§ 4.1, 33.1(a)			57-128	§§ 6.10, 18.17
		55-611	§ 18.11		
54-282	§ 15.2	55-656	§§ 6.3(h), 13.4	57-187	§ 6.10
54-296	§ 6.10			57-297	§§ 12.1(b), 12.4
54-369	§ 32.1	55-676	§ 27.2(b)		
54-394	§ 12.1(a)	55-715	§§ 13.4, 13.5	57-313	§ 26.4(g)
54-420	§ 27.1(h)(iii)			57-420	§ 18.5(b)
54-442	§ 13.1	55-716	§§ 12.1(a), 14.1, 18.5(b)	57-449	§ 5.5(a)
55-133	§§ 18.1, 18.7			57-453	§ 13.4
		55-749	§ 27.2(j)	57-466	§§ 15.2, 26.4(g),
55-156	§ 12.1(b)	56-65	§§ 13.1, 13.2, 13.4		26.5(e)
55-176	§ 14.1				
55-189	§ 18.12				
55-192	§ 30.5	56-84	§§ 13.2, 13.4	57-467	§§ 5.5(c), 6.3(d)
55-230	§ 15.2				
55-240	§ 18.8(b)	56-138	§§ 5.5(a), 19.4(g)§	57-493	§ 12.4
55-261	§ 6.3(i)			57-494	§ 18.3
55-311	§§ 12.1(a), 18.3, 18.5(b)	56-152	§§ 19.6, 27.2(a)	57-574	§ 8.7
				57-588	§ 15.2
55-319	§ 6.10	56-185	§§ 6.3(a), 6.3(d)	58-117	§ 12.1(b)
55-406	§ 6.1			58-143	§§ 15.1, 30.2(a)
55-439	§ 12.4	56-225	§ 12.2	58-147	§ 6.9
55-444	§ 13.2	56-245	§ 15.2	58-190	§ 18.6

TABLE OF IRS REVENUE RULINGS AND REVENUE PROCEDURES

Revenue Rulings	Book Sections	Revenue Rulings	Book Sections	Revenue Rulings	Book Sections
58-194	§§ 6.6, 7.6, 23.7(a), 26.5(a)(i)	60-193	§§ 4.3(c), 12.3, 20.4(a), 21.1(e), 21.4	63-235	§§ 6.6, 23.7(a)
58-209	§ 3.4			63-252	§ 30.2(d)
58-224	§§ 13.2, 27.2(f)	60-206	§§ 27.1(a), 27.1(h)(i)	64-108	§§ 4.6, 13.4
58-265	§ 6.10	60-228	§§ 26.4(g), 26.5(d)(ii)	64-109	§ 18.6
58-293	§ 4.1			64-117	§ 6.6
58-294	§§ 13.1, 13.2	60-243	§ 6.10	64-118	§§ 6.6, 14.1
58-328	§ 8.7	60-323	§§ 14.2, 19.7	64-128	§ 7.3(a)
58-482	§§ 26.4(g), 27.1(h)	60-324	§ 14.2	64-174	§ 6.7
		60-351	§§ 7.5, 7.6	64-175	§ 6.7
58-483	§ 18.11	60-367	§ 30.5	64-182	§§ 4.5(a), 4.7, 6.9, 26.4(f)
58-501	§§ 14.4, 33.3(b)	60-384	§§ 4.1, 6.10	64-187	§ 12.4
		61-72	§ 6.3(d)	64-192	§ 7.5
58-502	§§ 19.6, 26.4(f)	61-87	§§ 6.6, 7.6	64-193	§ 18.5(a)
		61-137	§ 18.6	64-194	§ 18.4(a)
58-547	§ 29.2	61-153	§ 12.1(a)	64-195	§§ 7.4, 20.4(a)
58-566	§ 18.2(a)	61-158	§ 12.1(b)		
58-588	§ 14.2	61-170	§§ 13.4, 19.4(i), 26.5(d)(iv)	64-217	§ 18.6
58-589	§§ 14.1, 19.4(f), 19.7			64-231	§ 6.3(d)
				64-246	§ 18.11
		61-177	§§ 13.1, 20.8	64-274	§ 6.6
58-616	§ 18.8(b)			64-275	§ 7.4
59-6	§§ 7.4, 15.1	62-17	§ 15.1	64-286	§ 6.9
		62-23	§ 7.3(a)	64-313	§ 12.1(b)
59-41	§ 6.10	62-66	§ 6.10	64-315	§ 13.5
59-129	§ 8.3	62-71	§ 20.4(a)	65-1	§§ 5.5(e), 9.2, 19.4(i)
59-151	§ 18.10(a)	62-113	§ 30.2(d)		
59-152	§ 6.10	62-167	§§ 12.1(a), 14.1	65-2	§§ 6.7, 7.4
59-234	§ 13.4			65-5	§ 18.11
59-310	§§ 5.5(a), 6.4	62-191	§§ 15.1, 26.4(g), 26.5(e)	65-6	§ 18.6
59-330	§§ 15.1, 26.4(g), 26.5(e)			65-14	§ 13.2
		63-15	§ 6.9	65-60	§ 9.2
		63-20	§ 6.10	65-61	§ 10.3
59-391	§§ 13.1, 13.5	63-190	§§ 12.1(a), 14.1	65-63	§ 14.2
				65-64	§ 14.4
60-86	§§ 15.2, 26.4(g), 26.5(e)	63-208	§ 6.9	65-99	§§ 18.5(a), 18.5(b)
		63-209	§ 6.9		
		63-220	§§ 6.6, 7.6	65-164	§§ 13.1, 26.5(d)(iv)
60-143	§ 6.6	63-234	§ 7.6		

TABLE OF IRS REVENUE RULINGS AND REVENUE PROCEDURES

Revenue Rulings	Book Sections	Revenue Rulings	Book Sections	Revenue Rulings	Book Sections
65-174	§ 18.5(b)	66-179	§§ 6.4, 7.5, 12.1(a), 13.1, 14.1, 15.3	67-5	§19.4(c)
65-191	§§ 6.6, 7.4			67-6	§§ 6.7, 12.2, 12.3, 20.7
65-195	§ 12.1(a)				
65-201	§§ 12.2, 18.5(a), 18.5(b)			67-7	§ 15.1
		66-180	§ 18.3	67-8	§§ 14.1, 19.4(i)
65-219	§ 14.2	66-212	§ 16.3	67-71	§§ 12.3, 21.1(d), 21.4
65-244	§ 13.4	66-219	§ 4.1		
65-270	§§ 6.7, 7.4	66-220	§§ 6.5, 7.5, 7.6	67-72	§§ 6.6, 7.4, 19.10(a)
65-271	§ 6.7				
65-298	§§ 5.5(a), 7.4, 9.2, 9.4	66-221	§ 26.1	67-77	§ 13.1
		66-222	§ 19.6	67-109	§§ 12.1(a), 26.4(a)
		66-223	§ 13.1		
65-299	§ 12.1(a)	66-225	§ 19.7		
65-536	§ 27.1(m)	66-255	§ 7.5	67-128	§ 18.11
66-46	§ 6.7	66-256	§§ 7.5, 21.1(e)	67-138	§§ 6.1, 6.7, 7.5
66-47	§§ 26.4(g), 27.1(j)	66-257	§§ 5.5(a), 6.1	67-139	§§ 7.5, 14.1
66-59	§ 18.3	66-258	§§ 12.3, 20.4(a), 21.1(e), 21.4	67-148	§ 7.4
66-79	§ 30.2(d)			67-149	§§ 6.6, 6.9
66-102	§ 18.2(a)				
66-103	§§ 6.6, 6.7	66-259	§§ 19.3, 19.4(k)	67-150	§§ 6.1, 7.4
66-104	§§ 5.5(e), 7.6	66-260	§ 13.1	67-151	§ 10.1
66-105	§ 15.2	66-273	§ 12.1(a)	67-152	§ 18.11
66-108	§ 18.11	66-295	§§ 18.2(a), 28.6	67-170	§§ 5.5(d), 18.6
66-146	§§ 6.4, 6.7	66-296	§ 28.6	67-175	§ 13.1
66-147	§§ 7.5, 9.4	66-323	§§ 6.3(h), 26.2(e), 26.4(g)	67-176	§§ 13.2, 26.5(d)(ii)
66-148	§ 12.1(a)			67-182	§ 13.4
66-149	§ 14.2			67-216	§§ 7.5, 15.2
66-150	§§ 12.1(b), 14.1, 18.2(a)	66-338	§§ 13.4, 26.5(d)(i)	67-217	§§ 6.6, 7.6
		66-354	§§ 12.1(a), 13.4, 15.1, 16.3	67-218	§§ 27.1(a), 27.1(h)(i)
66-151	§§ 13.1, 13.2, 26.4(g), 26.5(d)(i), 26.5(d)(ii), 26.5(d)(iv)	66-358	§§ 6.4, 19.9	67-219	§§ 13.2, 26.4(f), 27.2(f)
		66-359	§ 10.1	67-223	§ 18.11
66-152	§ 18.11	66-360	§ 12.1(b)	67-249	§ 14.1
66-177	§ 4.1	67-4	§§ 5.5(b), 6.6, 6.9, 7.5	67-250	§§ 6.1, 6.7, 7.5
66-178	§ 6.7			67-251	§ 19.6

TABLE OF IRS REVENUE RULINGS AND REVENUE PROCEDURES

Revenue Rulings	Book Sections	Revenue Rulings	Book Sections	Revenue Rulings	Book Sections
67-252	§§ 13.4, 15.2		12.2, 19.10(a)	68-263	§§ 20.4(a), 21.1(e)
67-253	§ 18.11	68-15	§§ 6.4, 6.7, 7.5	68-264	§ 13.4
67-264	§ 13.1			68-265	§§ 13.2, 13.4
67-265	§§ 18.5(a), 18.5(b)	68-16	§§ 6.6, 7.4	68-266	§ 14.1
		68-17	§§ 6.1, 6.7, 7.5	68-267	§ 26.4(g)
67-284	§ 18.18			68-296	§§ 31.1(a), 32.7
67-290	§ 6.10	68-26	§§ 4.5(a), 6.5, 8.2(a), 8.2(b), 28.6		
67-291	§ 6.6			68-306	§ 6.5
67-292	§§ 6.4, 6.11(a), 7.3(c)			68-307	§ 7.5
		68-27	§§ 6.3(e), 22.1(c)	68-371	§ 18.2
67-293	§§ 12.3, 20.2, 20.7	68-45	§ 12.1(b)	68-372	§ 7.3(b)
		68-46	§§ 12.1(b), 26.4(g)	68-373	§§ 9.2, 10.3, 19.4(i), 27.1(l)
67-294	§ 12.1(a)				
67-295	§ 13.1	68-70	§§ 6.7, 7.5		
67-296	§§ 19.6, 26.4(f), 26.5(d)(iv)	68-71	§§ 7.4, 7.5	68-374	§ 26.5(b)(ii)
		68-72	§§ 6.5, 7.4	68-375	§ 26.5(b)(ii)
		68-73	§ 6.3(h)	68-376	§ 26.5(b)(i)
67-302	§ 14.2	68-75	§ 18.5(b)	68-422	§§ 5.5(a), 19.4(g)
67-325	§§ 5.4(a), 5.5, 5.5(a)	68-76	§ 18.11		
		68-104	§ 26.5(k)	68-438	§§ 6.7, 7.5
67-327	§§ 7.4, 26.5(a)(iii)	68-117	§§ 6.1, 30.2(d)	68-455	§ 12.1(b)
				68-489	§ 5.5(b)
67-342	§ 7.5	68-118	§ 12.1(a)	68-490	§ 18.2(a)
67-343	§ 13.1	68-119	§ 19.7	68-496	§ 18.11
67-344	§ 13.1	68-123	§§ 8.8, 26.4(g)	68-504	§§ 5.5(a), 7.4, 19.10(a)
67-346	§ 18.11				
67-367	§§ 5.5(a), 19.4(i)	68-157	§ 7.6	68-505	§§ 26.3(b), 26.4(g), 27.2(e)
		68-164	§ 7.5		
67-368	§§ 12.3, 21.4	68-165	§§ 6.1, 7.4, 30.2(d)	68-534	§ 15.1
67-390	§ 24.1(b)			68-535	§ 19.7
67-391	§§ 6.4, 7.5	68-166	§ 6.1	68-536	§ 27.1(m)
67-392	§§ 6.7, 7.4	68-167	§§4.5(a), 6.1, 7.6	68-538	§ 7.6
67-393	§ 13.1			68-550	§ 26.4(d)
67-394	§ 13.1	68-168	§ 19.7	68-563	§§ 6.5, 8.2(a)
67-422	§ 18.11	68-175	§ 7.3(a)	68-564	§ 18.5(b)
67-428	§§ 14.1, 14.2	68-182	§§ 13.1, 13.2	68-581	§ 26.5(a)
				68-609	§ 33.4(b)
67-429	§ 18.11	68-217	§ 24	68-638	§ 14.2
67-430	§ 18.11	68-222	§ 18.2(a)	68-655	§ 6.7
68-14	§§ 6.4, 7.5,	68-224	§ 12.1(a)	68-656	§§ 12.3, 20.7
		68-225	§ 26.4(f)	68-657	§ 13.1

TABLE OF IRS REVENUE RULINGS AND REVENUE PROCEDURES

Revenue Rulings	Book Sections	Revenue Rulings	Book Sections	Revenue Rulings	Book Sections
69-16	§ 6.5	69-280	§ 12.2	69-633	§§ 3.4, 6.9,
69-51	§§ 26.4(g),	69-281	§§ 12.2,		10.4,
	26.5(e)		14.1		26.4(g),
69-52	§ 18.11	69-282	§ 18.7		27.2(g)
69-66	§ 19.4(h)	69-283	§§ 18.1,	69-634	§ 13.1
69-68	§ 14.1		18.7	69-635	§ 14.1
69-69	§§ 26.4(g),	69-381	§ 18.2(a)	69-636	§ 19.7
	27.1(a),	69-383	§ 19.3	69-637	§ 18.6
	27.1(h)	69-384	§ 12.1(a)	69-651	§ 18.11
69-80	§ 30.2(d)	69-385	§§ 12.1(b),	70-4	§§ 6.7,
69-96	§ 3.4		12.4		12.1(a)
69-106	§ 13.2	69-386	§ 15.1	70-31	§§ 13.1,
69-144	§ 16.3	69-387	§ 13.1		13.4
69-160	§ 10.4	69-400	§§ 6.6,	70-32	§ 14.1
69-161	§ 6.1		7.4	70-48	§ 19.7
69-162	§ 27.1(g)	69-417	§ 18.11	70-79	§§ 6.4,
69-174	§ 6.1	69-430	§ 27.1(a)		6.7, 7.5,
69-175	§ 19.4(i)	69-441	§§ 6.1,		20.4(a)
69-176	§ 19.4(k)		7.5	70-80	§ 13.2
69-177	§ 7.6	69-459	§ 6.10	70-81	§§ 13.1,
69-178	§§ 27.1(a),	69-463	§ 25.5(b)(ii)		13.5, 29.2
	27.1(h)	69-464	§ 29.2	70-95	§ 13.2
69-179	§ 27.1(g)	69-492	§ 7.3(a)	70-129	§ 6.6
69-217	§ 14.2	69-526	§§ 6.3(i),	70-130	§ 18.5(b)
69-219	§ 14.2		9.1, 9.2	70-132	§ 29.1
69-220	§§ 14.2, 14.3,	69-527	§ 14.1	70-186	§§ 6.4,
	26.1	69-528	§§ 6.9,		6.11(a),
69-222	§ 18.11		28.6		19.4(i),
69-232	§§ 14.3,	69-538	§ 6.6		19.10(a)
	14.4	69-545	§§ 6.1,	70-187	§ 13.1
69-256	§§ 4.3(a),		6.3,	70-188	§ 16.4
	4.3(b),		6.3(a),	70-189	§ 16.4
	19.4(i)		6.3(e),	70-202	§ 18.3
69-257	§ 6.6		33.3(b)	70-244	§ 13.1
69-266	§§ 4.6,	69-572	§§ 5.5(b),	70-270	§ 11.1(g)
	6.3(i),		6.9,	70-321	§§ 6.6,
	19.4(j)		21.1(i)		7.5,
69-267	§ 26.5(b)(i)	69-573	§§ 6.6,		21.1(e)
69-268	§§ 26.5(b)(i),		14.1	70-372	§ 15.2
	26.5(c),	69-574	§ 26.2(g)	70-411	§ 16.3
	27.2(b)	69-575	§§ 18.11,	70-449	§ 20.4(a)
69-269	§ 26.5(b)(i)		31.1(d)	70-533	§§ 4.5(b),
69-278	§ 18.2(a)	69-632	§§ 5.5(e),		6.1,
69-279	§§ 4.3(a),		9.1, 13.1,		7.3(a),
	4.3(b)		19.4(i)		19.9

TABLE OF IRS REVENUE RULINGS AND REVENUE PROCEDURES

Revenue Rulings	Book Sections	Revenue Rulings	Book Sections	Revenue Rulings	Book Sections
70-534	§§ 7.4, 26.5(a)(iii)	71-529	§§ 6.6, 6.9, 7.6, 22.1(b), 26.2(e)	72-430	§ 7.3(a)
70-535	§ 12.1(b)			72-431	§§ 26.4(g), 26.5(g)(i), 27.2(k)
70-536	§ 16.4				
70-562	§ 6.10	71-544	§ 18.2(a)	72-512	§ 21.1(d)
70-566	§ 18.12	71-545	§ 7.3(c)	72-513	§§ 20.2(b), 21.1(d)
70-583	§§ 6.1, 6.4, 7.4	71-553	§ 6.9		
		71-580	§§ 6.5, 19.4(i)	72-542	§ 28.6
70-584	§§ 6.4, 6.6, 7.4, 12.3, 21.4	71-581	§§ 26.5(g), 27.2(c), 28.6	72-559	§§ 4.6, 5.5(b), 6.1
70-585	§§ 6.1, 6.7			72-560	§§ 6.4, 7.5
70-590	§§ 6.3(h), 7.5, 26.2(e)	71-614	§ 26.2(c)	72-589	§ 18.11
		72-16	§§ 6.3(h), 7.4, 26.5(b)(v)	73-45	§§ 6.7, 26.2(e)
70-591	§ 13.2				
70-604	§ 12.2			73-59	§ 18.11
70-640	§§ 4.6, 7.5	72-17	§ 18.6	73-93	§ 18.11
70-641	§§ 6.3(g), 7.5, 13.1, 13.3	72-36	§§ 18.5(a), 18.5(b)	73-104	§§ 26.4(f), 26.5(c)
		72-37	§ 18.7	73-105	§§ 4.5(a), 26.5(c)
71-29	§ 6.4	72-50	§ 18.11		
71-97	§ 6.6	72-51	§ 18.11	73-126	§ 19.4(g)
71-99	§ 6.4	72-52	§ 18.11	73-127	§§ 7.6, 26.4(b)
71-100	§ 18.11	72-101	§§ 6.6, 7.3, 19.10(a)	73-128	§§ 5.5(b), 6.1, 7.4, 7.6, 26.4(b)
71-131	§ 6.10				
71-132	§ 6.10				
71-155	§§ 13.1, 13.4, 26.5(d)(ii)	72-102	§§ 12.2, 18.13		
		72-124	§§ 5.5(a), 5.5(c), 6.3(d), 26.2(e)	73-148	§ 18.11
71-156	§ 16.4			73-164	§ 28.6
71-175	§ 13.4			73-165	§ 18.4(a)
71-276	§ 24.1(b)			73-192	§ 18.4(a)
71-300	§ 18.6	72-147	§ 19.4(i)	73-193	§ 27.1(g)
71-311	§ 29.3	72-209	§ 6.3(i)	73-247	§ 18.11
71-395	§§ 6.7, 19.4(i)	72-211	§§ 13.1, 13.4	73-248	§ 18.11
				73-285	§§ 6.5, 6.7
71-413	§ 6.6	72-228	§§ 6.7, 7.5	73-306	§ 12.1(b)
71-421	§§ 7.4, 14.1			73-307	§§ 12.2, 16.4
71-447	§ 5.4(a)	72-355	§§ 3.4, 17		
71-460	§§ 4.1, 30.2(d)	72-369	§§ 4.5(a), 4.6, 6.9	73-308	§ 18.11
71-504	§ 13.3			73-313	§§ 4.6, 5.5(e), 6.3(g), 6.3(i)
71-505	§ 13.3	72-391	§§ 15.1, 15.2, 19.4(i)		
71-506	§§ 7.5, 9.4, 13.3			73-349	§ 12.1(b)

TABLE OF IRS REVENUE RULINGS AND REVENUE PROCEDURES

Revenue Rulings	Book Sections	Revenue Rulings	Book Sections	Revenue Rulings	Book Sections
73-364	§ 24.3(b)(ii)	74-148	§§ 14.1, 19.7	74-587	§§ 6.7, 6.11(e)
73-370	§ 18.4(b)				
73-386	§ 26.4(b)	74-167	§ 15.1	74-595	§ 7.5
73-411	§§ 4.6, 13.5	74-168	§ 14.2	74-596	§ 15.1
		74-194	§ 10.1	74-600	§ 7.3(b)
73-422	§§ 23.4(b), 24.1(b)	74-195	§ 15.2	74-604	§ 12.2
		74-196	§ 18.8(b)	74-614	§§ 6.6, 6.9, 26.2(e)
73-424	§§ 26.3(a), 26.5(f)	74-197	§ 29.3		
		74-199	§§ 3.4, 17, 18.13	74-615	§ 7.5
73-434	§ 7.3(a)			75-4	§ 18.11
73-439	§ 19.4(i)			75-5	§ 18.11
73-440	§ 20.1(a)	74-224	§ 8.4	75-38	§§ 4.3(a), 11.1(g)
73-452	§ 13.1	74-228	§ 13.4		
73-453	§ 18.5(g)	74-246	§ 6.4	75-65	§ 30.2(d)
73-454	§ 18.6	74-281	§ 18.3	75-74	§§ 6.1, 6.11(d)
73-455	§ 11.2(a)	74-287	§ 11.2(b)		
73-504	§ 23.4(a)	74-308	§ 13.4	75-75	§ 6.11(d)
73-520	§ 14.1	74-318	§ 3.4	75-76	§ 6.11(d)
73-543	§ 7.3(a)	74-319	§ 3.4	75-97	§ 18.11
73-567	§§ 6.3(g), 13.1	74-327	§ 18.11	75-110	§ 18.11
		74-361	§§ 6.4, 12.1(a), 12.4, 26.4(f)	75-145	§ 26.4(g)
73-569	§ 7.5			75-196	§§ 5.5(a), 5.5(e), 7.3(c), 7.4, 19.10(a)
73-570	§ 18.11				
73-587	§ 26.4(g)				
74-13	§ 18.18	74-362	§ 18.5		
74-14	§ 6.10	74-368	§ 11.1(g)	75-197	§ 6.3(h)
74-15	§ 6.10	74-399	§§ 26.4(h), 26.5(c)	75-198	§§ 5.5(a), 6.1, 6.3(d), 6.3(i)
74-16	§ 7.4				
74-17	§§ 12.2, 18.13	74-443	§ 10.4		
		74-540	§ 11.1(b)		
74-18	§ 16.3	74-475	§ 17	75-199	§§ 12.1(a), 18.4(a)
74-21	§§ 3.4, 17	74-488	§ 15.2		
74-23	§ 17	74-489	§ 14.2	75-200	§ 26.5(f)
74-30	§ 14.1	74-490	§ 24.1(b)	75-201	§§ 26.5(f), 26.5(g)(iii)
74-38	§ 26.5(f)	74-493	§ 10.4		
74-81	§§ 13.4 26.5(d)(i)	74-518	§ 15.2	75-207	§ 6.11(a)
		74-523	§ 30.2(d)	75-215	§ 7.3(a)
74-99	§ 12.2	74-553	§§ 6.3(g), 9.2, 13.1	75-228	§ 18.11
74-116	§ 13.1			75-231	§ 5.4(a)
74-117	§ 21.1(d)	74-563	§ 12.2	75-252	§ 6.4
74-118	§ 15.2	74-567	§ 18.11	75-258	§§ 3.4, 6.6
74-146	§§ 5.5(e), 6.6, 6.9, 19.9	74-572	§ 6.3(a)		
		74-574	§§ 21.1(d), 21.1(e)	75-282	§§ 6.3(b), 6.5, 6.9, 23.8(a)
74-147	§ 13.1	74-575	§§ 6.5, 19.9		

TABLE OF IRS REVENUE RULINGS AND REVENUE PROCEDURES

Revenue Rulings	Book Sections	Revenue Rulings	Book Sections	Revenue Rulings	Book Sections
75-283	§ 6.1	76-31	§ 15.1	76-402	§ 26.4(d)
75-284	§§ 6.6, 7.4	76-33	§§ 26.5(a)(iv),	76-408	§ 6.7
75-285	§ 6.7, 7.5		26.5(b)(v)	76-409	§ 13.4
75-286	§§ 6.4,	76-37	§ 6.0	76-410	§ 13.1
	12.2,	76-38	§ 13.4	76-417	§ 7.3(a)
	19.10(a)	76-81	§§ 20.7,	76-418	§ 6.4
75-287	§§ 13.1,		26.5(d)(ii)	76-419	§ 6.7
	15.2	76-91	§ 33.4(b)	76-420	§ 15.1
75-288	§ 15.1	76-93	§ 26.5(f)	76-440	§§ 11.3(b)(i),
75-290	§ 23.3(a)	76-94	§ 26.4(b)		11.3(b)(iv)
75-359	§§ 6.9, 6.10	76-95	§ 29.3	76-441	§§ 19.4,
75-384	§§ 5.5(f),	76-147	§§ 6.7, 12.2		33.3(b),
	6.4,	76-152	§§ 6.7, 7.3(b)		33.4(b)
	12.1(a)	76-167	§ 7.3(a)	76-442	§ 5.5(e)
75-385	§§ 5.5(a),	76-204	§§ 6.6,	76-443	§ 7.5
	6.1		6.11(a),	76-452	§ 6.3(a)
75-386	§ 12.2		15.2	76-455	§ 9.2
75-387	§ 11.3(b)(iv)	76-205	§§ 6.5,	76-456	§ 21.1(e)
75-388	§ 18.11		6.7, 7.5	76-457	§ 18.4(b)
75-434	§§ 6.5,	76-206	§§ 6.7,	76-495	§ 18.13
	30.2(d)		19.1,	76-549	§ 18.17
75-436	§ 6.10		19.10(a)	76-550	§ 18.17
75-470	§§ 6.7,	76-207	§§ 13.1,	77-3	§ 6.1
	7.3(b)		13.5	77-4	§ 7.5
75-471	§§ 5.5(e),	76-233	§ 18.11	77-5	§ 15.1
	6.7	76-241	§ 15.2	77-42	§ 6.1
75-472	§§ 6.3(h),	76-244	§§ 5.5(a),	77-43	§ 16.4
	7.4,		6.1	77-46	§ 15.1
	26.4(f),	76-296	§§ 9.3,	77-47	§ 29.2
	26.5(b)(v)		26.4(g),	77-68	§§ 6.3(i),
75-473	§ 15.1		27.1(l)		6.6, 7.4
75-492	§ 7.3(a)	76-297	§ 27.1(g)	77-69	§ 6.3(g)
75-494	§§ 12.2,	76-298	§ 18.11	77-70	§ 18.6
	14.1, 19.7	76-323	§§ 8.8,	77-71	§ 29.2
75-516	§ 27.2(f)		26.4(g)	77-72	§ 29.3
75-517	§ 27.2(f)	76-335	§ 18.2(a)	77-111	§§ 4.6, 6.7,
75-518	§ 27.2(f)	76-336	§ 6.6		6.11(e)
75-519	§ 27.2(f)	76-337	§ 28.3	77-112	§ 13.1
75-520	§ 27.2(f)	76-341	§ 26.4(g)	77-114	§ 23.3(a)
76-4	§§ 7.5,	76-354	§ 29.3	77-116	§ 23.4(b)
	19.9	76-366	§ 7.6	77-121	§ 28.6
76-5	§ 6.11(d)	76-384	§ 7.3(a)	77-124	§ 28.6
76-18	§ 11.4(a)	76-388	§ 18.11	77-153	§ 15.2
76-21	§ 6.1	76-399	§ 15.2	77-154	§ 15.1
76-22	§ 6.1	76-400	§ 13.1	77-159	§ 24.1(b)

TABLE OF IRS REVENUE RULINGS AND REVENUE PROCEDURES

Revenue Rulings	Book Sections	Revenue Rulings	Book Sections	Revenue Rulings	Book Sections
77-162	§ 24.3(a)(vii)	78-52	§ 26.5(d)(i)	78-310	§§ 6.6, 6.9, 7.4
77-165	§§ 6.10, 18.17	78-68	§§ 6.4, 6.6, 12.1(a)	78-315	§ 11.1(b)
77-206	§ 19.6	78-69	§§ 6.4, 12.1(a)	78-316	§§ 18.17, 24.3(b)(iii)
77-207	§ 23.4(a)	78-70	§ 13.5	78-384	§§ 6.6, 6.11(a)
77-208	§§ 23.4(a), 24.1(b)	78-81	§ 12.3	78-385	§§ 6.5, 7.5, 8.2(a), 26.4(g)
77-214	§ 3.4	78-82	§ 7.3(a)		
77-232	§§ 6.10, 13.3	78-84	§ 6.11(b)		
77-246	§§ 5.5(a), 6.1	78-85	§§ 5.5(e), 12.2	78-426	§§ 9.2, 10.3
77-258	§ 18.4(b)	78-86	§ 4.6, 12.1(a)	78-427	§ 6.3(i)
77-261	§ 18.17	78-87	§ 18.4(a)	78-428	§§ 6.1, 26.2(e)
77-272	§§ 5.4(a), 6.6, 7.4	78-88	§§ 26.2(g), 29.3	78-429	§ 12.2
77-278	§ 27.1(h)(ii)	78-95	§ 11.3(b)(i)	78-434	§ 18.9
77-283	§ 21.1(d)	78-98	§ 26.4(d)	78-435	§ 26.5(b)(i)
77-290	§§ 8.3, 26.4(g)	78-99	§ 7.5	79-9	§ 24.2(b)
		78-100	§ 8.7	79-11	§ 17.1(a)
77-295	§ 8.7	78-131	§§ 6.7, 12.1(a)	79-12	§ 17.1(a)
77-365	§§ 5.4(c), 7.4, 26.4(d)	78-132	§ 12.1(b)	79-13	§ 17.1(a)
77-366	§§ 4.4, 6.5, 7.4	78-143	§ 18.6	79-17	§§ 6.1, 26.2(e)
77-367	§§ 7.3(b), 19.9	78-144	§ 27.2(a)	79-18	§§ 5.5(a), 6.1, 26.2(e)
		78-145	§§ 6.3(h), 26.2(e), 26.2(f), 26.4(g)		
77-381	§ 8.5			79-19	§§ 6.1, 26.2(e), 26.5(b)(v)
77-384	§ 18.11				
77-407	§ 23.4(b)	78-160	§ 21.1(e)		
77-416	§ 33.3(b)	78-188	§ 8.2(a)	79-26	§§ 6.6, 7.2
77-429	§§ 18.2, 18.2(a)	78-189	§ 8.2(a)	79-31	§ 26.2(f)
		78-190	§ 8.2(a)	79-99	§ 5.4(a)
77-430	§ 6.5	78-225	§ 13.5	79-122	§ 29.3
77-436	§ 26.4(g)	78-232	§§ 8.2(c), 19.4(h)	79-128	§ 18.3
77-440	§ 18.11			79-130	§ 7.3(a)
77-469	§ 24.1(b)	78-238	§ 18.5(g)	79-222	§ 28.4
78-41	§§ 6.3(b), 6.9, 23.8(a), 30.2(c)	78-239	§ 18.10(a)	79-316	§ 12.1(b)
		78-240	§ 27.2(g)	79-323	§ 6.10
		78-248	§ 21.1(e)	79-349	§ 29.3
		78-287	§ 15.1	79-358	§§ 6.1, 6.3(i)
78-42	§§ 6.6, 15.1	78-288	§ 15.1	79-359	§ 6.5
78-43	§ 26.5(a)(iii)	78-289	§ 24.0	79-360	§§ 6.2(h), 26.4(g), 26.5(b)(iv)
78-50	§ 12.1(a)	78-305	§ 7.2		
78-51	§ 26.5(d)(i)	78-309	§ 7.3(a)		

■ 1055 ■

Revenue Rulings	Book Sections	Revenue Rulings	Book Sections	Revenue Rulings	Book Sections
79-361	§§ 26.4(g), 26.5(b)(v)	81-19	§§ 23.8(a), 27.2(b)	82-138	§§ 13.1, 26.5(d)(iv)
79-369	§§ 6.7, 7.5	81-28	§§ 6.1, 6.3(i)	82-139	§ 26.5(d)(i)
79-370	§ 26.5(f)	81-29	§§ 5.5(b),	82-148	§ 18.3
80-21	§ 7.3(a)		5.5(e), 6.6,	82-216	§ 17.0
80-63	§ 12.2		6.9, 19.9,	83-43	§ 18.5(a)
80-86	§ 18.5(b)		26.2(e),	83-74	§ 18.13
80-103	§ 17.3(a)		26.5(b)(i)	83-104	§ 5.4(a)
80-106	§§ 19.9, 28.6	81-58	§§ 12.1(b),	83-140	§ 7.3(a)
80-107	§ 12.1(b)		18.4(a)	83-153	§§ 11.3(b)(i),
80-108	§§ 23.1,	81-59	§ 15.2		11.3(b)(iv)
	23.3(a)	81-60	§§ 15, 19.6	83-157	§ 6.3(a)
80-113	§ 23.4(a)	81-61	§ 26.4(f)	83-164	§ 13.1
80-114	§ 6.3(i)	81-62	§ 26.4(g)	83-166	§§ 10.4, 18.7
80-124	§ 16.4	81-68	§ 16.4	83-170	§§ 12.1(a),
80-130	§ 19.7	81-69	§ 14.3		14.1, 18.5(g)
80-200	§ 6.11(f)	81-75	§ 26.5(d)(i)	84-48	§ 18.4(a)
80-205	§ 12.1(a)	81-94	§§ 8.2(c),	84-49	§ 18.4(a)
80-206	§ 12.1(b)		19.4(h)	84-55	§ 26.5(a)(iii)
80-215	§ 6.7	81-95	§§ 12.3,	84-81	§ 18.11
80-259	§§ 23.3(a),		17.3(b),	84-140	§ 18.10(a)
	23.3(b)		21.4	85-1	§ 6.4
80-278	§§ 5.5(b),	81-96	§ 18.11	85-2	§ 6.4
	6.11(a),	81-101	§ 26.5(f)	85-109	§§ 26.5(g)(iii),
	21.1(i)	81-108	§ 18.2(a)		27.2(b)
80-279	§§ 5.5(b),	81-109	§ 18.5(g)	85-110	§ 26.5(b)(iii)
	6.11(a),	81-116	§§ 4.6,	85-115	§ 17.3(a)
	21.1(i)		12.1(a)	85-123	§ 27.2(f)
80-282	§ 21.1(e)	81-117	§ 18.4(b)	85-160	§ 4.3(a)
80-286	§§ 6.6,	81-127	§§ 13.1,	85-173	§ 23.3(b)
	6.11(f),		26.4(f)	85-184	§ 30.5
	7.4,	81-138	§§ 13.1,	85-199	§ 16.3
	30.2(d)		13.5, 29.2	86-49	§ 6.7
80-287	§ 13.4	81-174	§ 13.4	86-75	§ 18.4(a)
80-294	§§ 19.6,	81-175	§ 13.4	86-95	§ 21.1(e)
	26.4(f),	81-177	§ 23.3(b)	86-98	§§ 12.1(a),
	26.5(a)(ii)	81-178	§ 27.1(g)		12.1(b),
80-295	§ 26.5(a)(ii)	81-209	§ 6.10		13.4
80-296	§ 26.5(a)(ii)	81-276	§§ 5.5(e),	87-2	§§ 6.10, 18.17
80-297	§ 26.4(d)		6.3(g), 6.4,	87-119	§ 17.1(a)
80-298	§ 26.4(d)		11.3(b)(i)	87-126	§ 12.1(b)
80-301	§ 19.4(i)	81-284	§§ 6.7,	88-56	§ 18.13
80-302	§ 19.4(i)		6.11(e)	88-72	§ 22.1(c)
80-309	§ 6.3(i)	81-291	§ 18.5(b)	88-115	§ 17.3(a)
80-316	§ 10.4	81-295	§ 18.18	89-61	§ 22.1(c)

TABLE OF IRS REVENUE RULINGS AND REVENUE PROCEDURES

Revenue Rulings	Book Sections	Revenue Rulings	Book Sections	Revenue Rulings	Book Sections
89-74	§ 8.2(l)	79-2	§ 24.3(a)(ix)	95-35	§ 20.8(b)
89-94	§§ 18.1,	79-6	§ 24.3(a)(v)	95-48	§ 24.3(b)(iii)
	24.3(b)(ii)	79-8	§ 24.3(a)(vii)	95-53	§ 27.2(j)
90-36	§ 13.6	79-63	§ 24.6(b)(ii)	96-32	§ 6.1
90-42	§ 18.11	80-27	§ 23.7	96-40	§ 23.7
90-74	§ 18.17	80-28	§ 24.6(c)	96-59	§§ 20.8(a),
90-100	§§ 23.3(a),	80-30	§ 23.2		27.2(j)
	23.4(a),	81-7	§ 11.3(b)(iv)	97-12	§ 26.5(d)(iii)
	23.4(g), 23.7	82-2	§§ 4.1, 4.3(b)	97-57	§§ 20.8(a),
93-73	§ 8.2	82-39	§ 24.2		27.2(j),
94-16	§ 18.18	83-23	§ 24.3(b)(iii)		27.2(l),
94-65	§ 18.18	83-36	§ 24.4(a)	98-1	§ 23.2
94-81	§ 18.18	84-47	§ 23.3(a)	98-2	§ 23.2
95-8	§ 29.3	84-86	§ 24.2	98-4	§§ 23.2,
97-21	§ 19.4(a)	85-58	§ 24.3(a)(ix)		24.4(a)
98-15	§§ 4.5(c),	86-43	§ 7.2	98-5	§§ 23.2,
	19.10(g)	87-51	§ 22.1(g)		23.2(c)
	32.4(b)	88-8	§ 23.2(d)	98-8	§ 23.2(d)
2000-44	§ 24.3(d)	90-27	§§ 17.3(b),	98-12	§ 26.5(d)(iii)
2002-37	§ 31.1(d)		23.2,	98-61	§§ 20.8(a),
2002-43	§ 11.4(a)		23.2(a)–		27.2(j),
2002-49	§ 23.6		23.2(c),		27.2(l)
2002-55	§ 18.5(b)		23.3(a),	99-42	§§ 20.8(a),
59-31	§ 30.2(d)		23.4(g),		27.2(j),
62-28	§ 24.1(a)		23.7,		27.2(l)
67-37	§ 18.11		23.9, 24,	2000-44	§§ 23.6,
68-14	§ 23.2(b)		24.1(a),		24.3(c)(i)
71-17	§ 14.2		24.6,	2001-3	§§ 20.8(a),
71-39	§§ 5.5(b),		24.6(b)(i),		27.2(j)
	6.11(d)		24.6(g)(ii)	2001-13	§§ 27.2(j),
72-5	§ 23.2	90-29	§ 18.11		27.2(k)
72-16	§ 18.11	91-20	§ 8.6	2001-59	§§ 27.2(j)
72-17	§ 18.11	92-58	§ 27.2(j)		27.2(k)
72-54	§ 5.4(a)	92-85	§§ 18.13,	2002-1	§ 23.2
73-29	§ 24.3		23.3(a)	2002-2	§ 23.2
73-39	§ 18.11	92-102	§ 27.2(j)	2002-4	§ 23.2
75-13	§ 6.11(d)	93-28	§ 23.3(a)	2002-5	§§ 23.2,
75-50	§§ 5.4(a),	93-49	§ 27.2(j)		23.2(c),
	5.4(c)	94-17	§ 24.3(b)(iii)		23.2(d)
76-9	§ 24.3(a)(ix)	94-72	§ 27.2(j)	2002-8	§ 23.2(d)
78-9	§ 24.6(a)	95-21	§ 26.5(d)(iii)		

Table of IRS Private Determinations Cited in Text

PRIVATE LETTER RULINGS AND TECHNICAL ADVICE MEMORANDA

Private Determination	Book Sections	Private Determination	Book Sections	Private Determination	Book Sections
7740009	8.7	7924009	27.1(1)	8120006	26.4(f)
7741004	27.1(g)	7926003	27.1(g)	8122007	27.2(c)
7742008	17.1(a)	7930005	10.3(a)	8127019	26.5(g)(i)
7816061	26.4(f)	7930043	26.5(ii)	8128004	27.2(k)
7820007	10.3	7934008	28.4	8141019	14.2
7820057	32.7	7935043	6.10	8145011	18.2(a)
7820058	19.10(b),	7936006	27.1(l)	8147008	17.4
	32.2(a)	7937002	18.4(a),	8147009	17.1(a)
7823048	26.1, 26.2(e)		26.5(d)(ii)	8202019	17.4
7823062	26.4(e)	7944018	15.1	8203134	26.3(b),
7826003	26.4(d)	7946001	26.5(g)(i)		26.5(g)(i)
7833055	29.2	7946009	17.4	8204057	33.3(b)
7838028	8.8	7948113	26.5(a)(ii),	8211002	27.2(a)
7838108	14.2		26.5(f)	8216009	26.5(g)(i)
7839042	26.4(g)	7951134	6.9, 19.9	8226019	26.4(g)
7840014	26.5(d)(ii)	7952002	19.10(b),	8232011	26.5(g)(i)
7840072	26.4(d)		32.2(a)	8234084	19.4(d)
7845029	26.5(a)(ii)	8004011	26.5(b)(i)	8234085	33.3(b)
7847001	25.5(d)(ii)	8006005	27.1(g)	8242003	14.2
7851003	26.5(a)(ii)	8020010	26.4(d)	8244114	27.1(a),
7851004	26.5(a)(ii)	8024001	26.4(d)		33.1(b)
7902006	13.4,	8025222	26.5(a)(i)	8303001	26.4(g)
	26.5(d)(i)	8032039	6.9	8303078	26.5(a)(ii)
7903079	30.5	8037103	10.2	8306056	9.5
7905129	26.3(a)	8040014	7.3(b)	8317004	33.6(b)
7908009	26.4(d)	8041007	27.2(c)	8326008	26.5(c)
7919053	26.5(a)(ii)	8107006	26.4(f)	8332072	26.4(f)
7921018	19.10(b)	8109002	18.5(b)	8337092	14.4
7922001	13.1,	8112013	26.4(f)	8337094	23.7
	26.4(f),	8116095	27.2(c)	8338127	32.2(a)
	26.5(a)(ii)	8119061	18.17	8347010	32.7

TABLE OF IRS PRIVATE DETERMINATIONS CITED IN TEXT

Private Determination	Book Sections	Private Determination	Book Sections	Private Determination	Book Sections
8349051	26.4(f)	8541108	32.2(b)(i)	8833038	32.3
8351160	26.4(f)	8542003	14.2	8836038	22.1(b)
8402014	8.5	8602001	27.2(h)	8836040	30.5
8409055	10.3	8604006	31.4	8842025	31.3
8416065	8.5	8605002	26.5(c)	8842071	18.17
8417003	26.4(f)	8606056	9.5, 31.1(d)	8851039	33.1(a)
8418003	26.5(iv)	8606074	26.4(f)	8910001	5.4(b)
8422168	26.4(f)	8621059	31.4, 32.3	8925092	32.6
8422170	13.1	8623006	13.2	8936002	21.1(d),
8426001	14.2	8623081	26.4(f)		21.1(i)
8427105	26.5(b)(i)	8624127	26.4(f)	8938001	32.2
8429010	15.2, 26.5(e)	8626080	26.4(f),	8938072	33.3(b)
8429049	18.13		26.5(b)(v)	8939002	31.4
8432004	26.5(c)	8628001	17.4	8942099	19.8
8433010	26.4(g)	8628049	26.4(f)	9002036	6.6
8433077	18.13	8633034	26.4(f)	9003045	13.1
8437014	26.4(g)	8634001	7.3(b)	9010073	33.3(b)
8442064	4.9	8638131	31.4	9012045	33.2(a)
8442092	26.4(f)	8640007	26.4(f)	9014004	11.6(d)
8443009	26.4(f)	8640052	33.2(b)	9014061	6.6
8444097	7.3(b)	8643049	26.4(f)	9016072	31.1(a)
8446004	26.4(g)	8643091	26.4(f)	9017003	30.2
8446008	14.2	8650001	17(a)	9019004	30.2(c)
8446047	24.1(b)	8705041	18.2(a), 30.5	9023081	26.5(d)(i)
8450006	26.4(f)	8706012	31.1(a)	9027003	7.4
8452011	26.5(b)(vi)	8708031	27.1(g)	9029047	26.5(d)(ii)
8452012	26.5(b)(vi)	8709051	31.2(a)	9032005	13.1
8452074	26.4(g)	8709072	26.4(f)	9036025	26.5(a)
8452099	26.5(b)(vi)	8715055	32.7	9042004	17.4
8501002	26.4(f)	8725056	26.5(g)(i)	9042036	18.13
8502003	17(b)	8730060	26.4(f)	9042038	27.1(i)
8503103	26.5(d)(iv)	8736046	26.5(b)(vi)	9043001	26.4(g)
8505002	6.3(h)	8737090	18.17	9050002	13.1
8505044	31.2(a)	8739055	30.2(b)	9105001	17.4
8505047	26.4(f)	8747066	26.5(g)(i)	9105002	17.4
8511082	26.4(g)	8749085	26.4(f),	9108021	27.1(c)
8512058	16.3		26.5(b)(vi)	9110041	18.5(b)
8512084	9.5, 26.4(f)	8802079	26.4(f)	9111001	18.5(b)
8514001	23.7, 23.7(a)	8814004	26.4(g)	9128003	13.4, 26.4(g)
8516001	17.4	8817039	32.3	9130002	19.1, 19.4(d),
8518067	23.3(a)	8818008	32.3		32.2, 33.3(b)
8518090	26.4(f)	8819034	27.1(p)	9130008	17.1(a)
8519069	33.3(b)	8820061	26.4(f)	9137002	26.4(f)
8521055	32.3	8820093	19.8	9141050	23.2(d),
8523072	26.4(f)	8822065	26.5(b)(vi)		33.3(b)
8524006	13.4	8823109	26.5(g)(i)	9145002	26.4(g)
8530043	26.4(g)	8824018	26.4(f)	9147007	26.3(d),
8539091	18.10(a)	8826012	30.5		26.5(a)(ii)
8541008	14.2	8828011	26.5(d)(ii)	9216033	16.3

TABLE OF IRS PRIVATE DETERMINATIONS CITED IN TEXT

Private Determination	Book Sections	Private Determination	Book Sections	Private Determination	Book Sections
9217001	6.7	9401035	18.5(b)	9538026	33.3(b)
9220010	12.1	9403022	26.4(f)	9538031	33.3(b)
9231047	19.8	9404029	26.5(b)(i)	9539015	26.4(f)
9233037	19.8	9405004	26.5(b)(i)	9539016	19.4(a)
9237034	5.5(e)	9408002	26.5(d)(i)	9540002	4.6,
9237090	26.4(f)	9414002	18.2		26.5(a)(iii)
9241055	26.4(f),	9414044	16.3	9542002	10.4
	26.5(b)(v)	9416002	26.5(d)(iii)	9545014	33.3(b)
9242002	18.2(a),	9417003	33.1(b)	9548019	30.6
	30.2(c)	9425030	26.3(a)	9550001	13.1, 26.4(g),
9242035	26.4(f)	9425032	17.3(a)		26.5(d)(i),
9242038	31.2(b)	9426040	33.1(b)		26.5(i)
9242039	31.2(b)	9428029	16.5	9550003	26.5(c)
9243008	9.5	9428030	16.5	9551009	30.6
9244003	17.2	9429016	20.8(a)	9603019	29.2
9245031	31.1(d),	9434041	6.3(b)	9608003	26.5(i)
	31.2(a)	9436002	26.4(g)	9608039	11.3(b)(i),
9246004	22.1(b)	9438029	31.2(d)		11.3(b)(iv),
9246032	27.1(h)(ii),	9438030	32.2(b)(i)		32.2(a)
	30.3	9440001	13.2,	9609007	21.1(d)
9247038	27.1(j)(i)		26.5(d)(i)	9612003	26.2(g)
9249001	26.4(f)	9441001	26.5(d)(ii)	9615030	19.10(a)
9249026	32.3	9442013	27.2(d)	9615045	27.1(h)(ii)
9252037	26.4(f)	9442025	6.3(b)	9619069	27.1(j)(i)
9302023	27.2(a)	9448036	19.6	9629030	27.1(j)(i)
9303030	30.6, 31.4	9450028	27.1(g)	9631004	5.5(a)
9305026	31.2(a),	9451001	19.4(a),	9633044	26.4(f)
	31.5(b)		33.1(b)	9635001	27.2(k)
9308047	31.1(a),	9451067	11.4(d)	9635003	21.1(e),
	31.2(d)	9502009	27.2(k)		21.1(i)
9309037	30.6	9506046	31.3	9637050	31.1 (b),
9314058	6.2	9507037	18.17		32.3
9314059	30.6	9509002	27.1(g)	9637051	31.5(b)
9316032	26.2(h),	9516006	17.1(a)	9641011	26.5(i)
	26.2(j)	9522022	30.6	9645004	26.2(f),
9316052	9.5, 19.4(a)	9522039	18.17		26.4(d)
9317054	30.6	9527031	9.5	9645007	22.1(b)
9320042	26.4(c)	9527043	30.1, 33.2(a)	9645017	31.2(d),
9325062	26.4(f)	9530008	30.6		31.5(b)
9329041	6.3(h),	9530024	6.4	9646002	7.3(b)
	26.5(b)(iv)	9530032	19.4	9651046	26.4(f)
9335001	32.2	9530036	30.6	9651047	6.3(f),
9335061	26.4(f),	9533015	14.2, 30.6		26.5(i)
	26.5(b)(v)	9534021	20.8(b)	9652026	17.1(a),
9338003	31.3	9535023	26.4(b),		17.1(b),
9345004	26.5(d)(iii)		26.4(f),		20.2(b)
9346015	30.6		27.2(b)	9702004	7.4,
9352030	31.4	9535043	11.2(b)		26.2(f),
9401031	26.4(f)	9535050	26.4(f)		26.5(a)(iii)

TABLE OF IRS PRIVATE DETERMINATIONS CITED IN TEXT

Private Determination	Book Sections	Private Determination	Book Sections	Private Determination	Book Sections
9703028	30.2(d)	9837031	26.5(b)(i)	200021056	4.5(a), 6.1,
9709014	32.4(a)	9839039	26.5(i),		7.6, 25.1(f),
9710030	6.3(a)		28.4,		26.1, 26.2(d),
9711002	26.2(d),		32.3,		26.2(f),
	26.5(i)		32.7		26.4(a),
9711003	4.7, 26.1	9839040	26.5(b)(vi)		26.4(h),
9711004	23.7	9840049	30.4		26.5(a)
9712001	26.3(d)	9840050	16.3	200022056	26.5(j)
9715031	31.1(d),	9840051	30.4	200030027	26.4(f)
	32.4(a)	9840053	30.6	200033046	22.1(c)
9719002	26.2(b)	9840054	30.6	200033049	26.2(f),
9720002	26.5(c)	9841049	27.2(b)		26.4(f),
9722006	18.5(b)	9847002	26.5(b)(i),		26.4(g)
9730002	30.2(d)		26.5(i),	200037053	11.6(e)
9731038	6.1		28.4	200044038	21.1(d)
9732022	15.2	9847006	17.3(a)	200044039	22.1(b)
9732032	6.3(h),	9848002	26.4(g)	200047049	26.2(b),
	7.5,	9849027	26.5(i),		26.2(h),
	26.5(a),		28.6		26.2(j),
	26.5(b)(iv)	9850025	17.3(b)		26.4(g)
9733015	30.5	9851001	19.4(b)	200051046	14.4
9736047	6.3(h)	9851054	26.5(b)(iii)	200051049	6.3(h), 26.1
9738055	30.6	9853026	26.4(f)	200102056	16.5
9738056	30.6	199905027	26.4(f)	200103083	19.10(a)
9739043	26.5(b)(iii)	199905031	26.4(f)	200103084	21.1(d),
9740032	27.1(h)(i)	199909056	26.4(f)		33.1(d)
9742001	26.5(d)(iii)	199910053	26.4(f)	200108045	26.5(i)
9751001	26.5(d)(iii)	199910060	26.5(i)	200108048	26.5(j)
9802045	19.11(d)	199910061	26.4(f)	200114040	19.10(a)
9808037	17.1(a)	199912033	12.1(b),	200117043	32.3
9809054	30.4		14.2	200118054	32.5
9809055	18.5(b)	199914051	30.6	200119061	26.2(f)
9810038	26.4(f)	199916053	30.6	200128059	26.5(g)(ii)
9811001	26.5(i)	199917079	6.2	200131034	26.2(g)
9812001	21.1(d)	199920041	26.4(f)	200132040	31.1(d),
9812037	18.16(c)	199922055	26.4(f)		33.1(d)
9814051	26.4(f)	199925051	17.1(a)	200133036	14.2
9821049	26.4(f)	199929049	26.4(f)	200134025	4.1(b)(ii),
9821063	26.4(f)	199938041	31(1)(a)		23.3(c),
9821067	26.4(g)	199943053	26.5(b)(vi)		24.3(c),
9822004	26.5(i)	199945062	26.4(f)		29.3(c), 30.7
9822006	26.4(g)	199946036	26.5(b)(vi)	200147058	28.4
9822039	26.5(b)(vi)	199946037	26.5(b)(vi)	200150032	26.4(f)
9824048	26.4(f)	199949045	26.4(f)	200150038	26.4(f)
9825030	26.4(f)	200003053	16.3	200151045	10.4, 32.2,
9835001	19.3	200009051	16.3		32.2(b)(ii)
9835003	19.9,	200020056	13.1	200151047	26.4(f)
	23.2(f),	200022056	26.5(i)	200151060	21.1(d), 30.3
	24.1(a)	200020060	19.4(a)	200151061	26.4

TABLE OF IRS PRIVATE DETERMINATIONS CITED IN TEXT

Private Determination	Book Sections	Private Determination	Book Sections	Private Determination	Book Sections
20015248	18.6	200220028	26.4(f)	200225046	31.0
200204051	26.4(f)	200222030	7.3(b), 7.6,	200227007	31.2(a)
200206056	16.4		26.5(c)	200230005	27.2(c), 30.5
200211051	26.5(b)(i)	200222031	26.5(b)(vi)	200233024	6.3(i)
200211053	16.3	200223067	13.1	200241050	26.4(f)
200213027	26.4(f)	200225041	16.3	200244028	19.11(d),
200217044	33.5	200225044	26.4(f)		19.11(e)

PRIVATE LETTER RULINGS AND TECHNICAL ADVICE MEMORANDA

Private Determination	Book Sections	Private Determination	Book Sections	Private Determination	Book Sections
14407	18.17	38283	4.9,	39389	24.3(a)(viii)
31433	6.3(i)		19.11(d)	39411	13.4
32453	19.4(a)	38437	7.3(a)	39444	19.10(b),
33207	4.3(b)	38444	21.1(e)		32.2(b)(i),
33912	21.1(d),	38458	13.4		32.2(b)(ii),
	31.1(d),	38459	5.5(b),		33.3(b)
	31.4		6.6,	39459	19.3
34608	13.4		7.4, 19.1,	39498	19.3, 19.4(a)
34631	21.1(d)		26.2(e)	39508	6.3(i)
35719	31.1(d),	38497	6.11(e)	39510	18.4(a)
	31.4	38577	10.3	39524	5.4(a)
35811	26.5(a)(i)	38699	8.3	39525	5.4(a)
35855	19.9	38735	6.3(e)	39546	19.10(b),
35862	15.1	38827	8.7, 8.8		32.2,
35869	19.4(g)	38873	27.1(n)(ii)		32.2(b)(i),
35921	18.5(b)	38881	6.1		32.2(b)(ii),
36078	23.3(b)	38905	19.11(d)		33.3(b)
36918	19.4(a)	38949	26.5(c)	39574	5.4(a)
37126	4.3(b)	38982	8.3	39598	31.1(d), 31.4
37158	33.3(b)	39005	19.10(b),	39612	5.5(b)
37159	6.11(d)		32.2, 32.2(a),	39613	7.7
37257	26.2(e)		32.2(b)(i),	39620	29.3
37351	18.2(a)		32.2(b)(ii),	39622	7.7
37458	23.3(b)		33.3(b)	39633	4.3(a)
37726	15.1	39061	24.4(f)	39670	19.3, 19.4(a)
37783	33.3(b)	39063	14.1	39674	19.4(a),
37789	19.10(b),	39105	13.4		19.4(g),
	32.2(b)(ii),	39108	13.1		19.11(d)
	33.3(b)	39115	14.2	39684	30.2(c)
37858	5.3, 21.1(i)	39211	18.4(a)	39692	10.4
37942	15.1	39288	5.5(b)	39694	21.1(b), 21.3
38104	26.5(f)	39326	31.1(d), 31.4	39703	22.1(b)
38168	26.5(f)	39341	18.2(a)	39715	24.4(f)
38205	26.5(f)	39343	14.2	39717	26.5(k)
38248	8.1(b)	39357	18.3	39721	13.3

TABLE OF IRS PRIVATE DETERMINATIONS CITED IN TEXT

Private Determination	Book Sections	Private Determination	Book Sections	Private Determination	Book Sections
39727	26.5(g)(i)	39806	26.5(k)		19.9,
39732	19.10(b),	39809	24.3(a)(viii)		19.10(b),
	32.2(b)(ii),	39811	17.1(b),		19.11(c),
	33.3(b)		21.1(h),		32.2(b)(ii),
39744	26.5(k)		24.0		32.3
39748	11.6(e)	39813	24.2(a),	39865	26.3(b)
39757	5.4(a),		24.2(b)	39866	31.4
	7.7	39828	6.3(e),	39872	7.7
39762	32.2(b)(ii),		22.1(b)	39873	16.3
	33.3(b)	39830	23.8(a)	39875	11.6(e)
39775	10.2	39837	17.4	39877	17.3(a)
39776	10.5	39862	19.1, 19.8,	39891	26.3(b)

Table of Cases Discussed in
Bruce R. Hopkins' *Nonprofit Counsel*

The following cases, referenced in the text, are discussed in greater detail in one or more issues of the author's monthly newsletter, as indicated.

Case	Book Sections	Newsletter Issue
Abortion Rights Mobilization, Inc. v. Regan	24.7(b)	Aug. 1986
Abortion Rights Mobilization, Inc. v. United States Catholic Conference	24.7(b)	Aug. 1988
Alpha Medical, Inc. v. Comm'r	19.4(a)	July 1999
American Civil Liberties Union Found. v. Crawford	8.1	June 2002
Arlie Found., Inc. v. United States	19.3, 24.6(b)	July 1993
Alabama Cent. Credit Union v. United States	29.3	June 1987
Alive Fellowship of Harmonious Living v. Comm'r	8.2, 24.6(b)	May 1984
Allen v. Wright	5.4(b), 24.7(b)	Aug. 1984, July 1985
Alumni Ass'n of the University of Oregon, Inc. v. Comm'r	26.5(g), 27.1(g)	Dec. 1999
American Academy of Family Physicians v. United States	26.2(a), 26.2(e)	June 1995, Oct. 1996
American Ass'n of Christian Schs. Voluntary Employees Beneficiary Ass'n Welfare Plan Trust v. United States	12.1(b), 16.3	Sept. 1987
American Campaign Academy v. Comm'r	4.5(a), 4.5(b), 7.3, 7.4, 19.3, 19.10	July 1989, June 2001

Case	Book Sections	Newsletter Issue
American College of Physicians v. United States	4.9, 26.5(f), 27.2(b)	Oct. 1984, June 1986
American Hosp. Ass'n v. United States	26.5(f)	May 1987
American Medical Ass'n v. United States	26.1, 26.5(f)	Oct. 1987, Nov. 1987, Jan. 1990
American Postal Workers Union, AFL-CIO v. United States	15.1, 26.5(e)	Feb. 1990, Apr. 1991
American Society of Ass'n Executives v. United States	20.8	Jan. 1999, Jan. 2000, July 2000
Anclote Psychiatric Center, Inc. v. Comm'r	19.4	June 1992, Sept. 1998
Ass'n of the Bar of the City of N.Y. v. Comm'r	21.1(e), 21.1(i)	Nov. 1987, Nov. 1998
At Cost Services, Inc. v. Comm'r	6, 19, 25	Jan. 2001
Atlanta Athletic Club v. Comm'r	14.3, 14.4	Mar. 1993
Bethel Conservative Mennonite Church v. Comm'r	4.3(b), 4.4	Dec. 1984
Bob Jones Univ. Museum Gallery, Inc. v. Comm'r	30.1	Aug. 1996
Boy Scouts of America v. Dale	1.7	Nov. 1999, Aug. 2000
Branch Ministries, Inc. v. Richardson	21.1(e)	Sept. 1997
Branch Ministries v. Rossotti	21.1, 21.3, 24.6	June 1999, July 2000
Brentwood Academy v. Tennessee Secondary Schools Athletic Ass'n	33.5(a)S	Apr. 2001
Brook, Inc., v. Comm'r	14.3	Oct. 1986
Brown Shoe Co. v. Comm'r	14.2	Oct. 2001
Buder v. United States	6.10(b)	Dec. 1993
Calhoun Academy v. Comm'r	5.4(a)	Apr. 1990
Camps Newfound/Owatonna, Inc. v. Town of Harrison	1.1, 1.1(a), 11.3(b)	July 1997
Caracci v. Comm'r	19.11	July 2002
Chicago Metro. Ski Council v. Comm'r	26.5(f)	May 1995
Chief Steward of the Ecumenical Temples & Worldwide Peace Movement v. Comm'r	4.3(b), 4.5(a), 23.2(a)	May 1985
Christian Coalition International v. United States	23.1	Nov. 2002

Case	Book Sections	Newsletter Issue
Church by Mail, Inc. v. Comm'r	19.4	Oct. 1984
Church of Ethereal Joy v. Comm'r	8.2, 19.10	Sept. 1984
Church of Spiritual Tech. v. United States	4.6, 23.2(a), 24.6(b)	Dec. 1989
Cleveland Athletic Club, Inc. v. United States	14.3	Feb. 1986
Colorado State Chiropractic Soc'y v. Comm'r	4.3(a), 24.6(b)	Dec. 1989
Columbia Park & Recreation Ass'n, Inc. v. Comm'r	12.2, 19.3	Feb. 1987
Common Cause v. Comm'r	27.1(g)	Aug. 1999
CORE Special Purpose Fund v. Comm'r	26.5(f), 28.2	May 1985
Credit Union Ins. Corp. v. United States	13.1, 18.7	July 1995, Sept. 1996
Dexsil v. Comm'r	19.4(a)	Aug. 1998, Jan. 2000
Disabled Am. Veterans v. Comm'r	27.1(a), 27.1(g)	Apr. 1990
Easter House v. United States	4.9	Aug. 1987
Ecclesiastical Order of the Ism of Am. v. Comm'r	8.2, 24.6(c), 25.1(e), 25.6(g)	Dec. 1985
est of Hawaii v. Comm'r	19.10	June 2001
Exacto Spring Corp. v. Comm'r	19.4(a)	Jan. 2000
Executive Network Club, Inc. v. Comm'r	27.2(a)	Mar. 1995
Florida Hosp. Trust Fund v. Comm'r	22.1	Sept. 1994, Mar. 1996
Fondel v. United States	24.6(b)	Oct. 1996, Mar. 1999
Founding Church of Scientology v. United States	8.2	July 1992
Fraternal Order of Police, Ill. State Troopers Lodge No. 41 v. Comm'r	25.5(f), 27.1(g)	Nov. 1986
Fulani v. League of Women Voters Educ. Fund	24.7(b)	Sept. 1989
Fund for Anonymous Gifts v. Internal Revenue Serv.	4.5(a)	July 1997, June 1999
Fund for the Study of Economic Growth & Tax Reform v. Internal Revenue Serv.	20.2	Feb. 1999
Geisinger Health Plan v. Comm'r	6.2, 6.2(e), 23.7(a)	Mar. 1993, Sept. 1994
Good News Club v. Milford Central School	8.1	Aug. 2001
Harlan E. Moore Charitable Trust v. United States	26.5(h), 27.1(h), 32.1	Apr. 1993

TABLE OF CASES DISCUSSED IN BRUCE R. HOPKINS' *NONPROFIT COUNSEL*

Case	Book Sections	Newsletter Issue
Henry E. & Nancy Horton Bartels Trust for the Benefit of the University of New Haven v. United States	26, 29.2, 29.3	July 2000
High Adventure Ministries, Inc. v. Comm'r	24.6(b)	Apr. 1984
Housing Pioneers, Inc. v. Comm'r	4.1, 32.2	Apr. 1995, Sept. 1995
IHC Health Plans, Inc. v. Comm'r	6.2(e), 23.7(a)	Dec. 2001
IIT Research Inst. v. United States	9.1, 9.2	Dec. 1985
Illinois Ass'n of Professional Ins. Agents, Inc. v. Comm'r	7.6, 26.5(d)	Nov. 1986
Judicial Watch, Inc. v. Rossotti	21, 24.8	Nov. 2002
Julius M. Israel Lodge of B'nai Brith No. 2113 v. Comm'r	27.2(h)	Dec. 1995
Junaluska Assembly Hous., Inc. v. Comm'r	4.4, 4.9, 8.2, 24.6(b), 25.1(e)	Aug. 1986
Knights of Columbus Bldg. Ass'n v. United States	3.1, 6.8, 18.2(a)	Sept. 1988
Laborer's Int'l Union of North Am. v. Comm'r	15.1, 26.2(e), 32.3	Oct. 2001
Lehrfeld v. Richardson	24.4	Mar. 1998
Lima Surgical Assocs., Inc., Voluntary Employees' Beneficiary Ass'n Plan Trust v. United States	16.3	Sept. 1990, Dec. 1991
Living Faith, Inc. v. Comm'r	4.5(a), 21.1(b), 25.1(e), 26.4(b)	Nov. 1990, Feb. 1992
Lutheran Social Servs. v. United States	8.3, 8.4, 8.5	May 1984, June 1985
Manning Ass'n v. Comm'r	7.4, 19.4(g), 24.6(b), 26.1	Jan. 1990
Mellon Bank v. United States	5.3, 6.10(f), 18.6	Aug. 1984, July 1985
Michigan v. United States	18.17	Dec. 1994
Morganbesser v. United States	15.1	Mar. 1992
Music Square Church v. United States	24.8(b)	Sept. 2000
National Ass'n of Am. Churches v. Comm'r	23.2(a), 23.6, 26.5(g)	Feb. 1984
National Ass'n of Postal Supervisors v. United States	15.1, 26.5(e)	Oct. 1990, Dec. 1991
National Collegiate Athletic Ass'n v. Comm'r	26.3(b), 26.3(d)	Apr. 1989, Nov. 1990
National Federation of Republican Assemblies v. United States	17, 24.3(d)	Nov. 2002
National Found., Inc. v. United States	4.5(a), 19.4(a)	Jan. 1998

Case	Book Sections	Newsletter Issue
St. David's Health Care System, Inc. v. United States	4.4, 6.2, 19.10, 32.4	Aug. 2002
St. Louis Science Fiction, Ltd. v. Comm'r	6.7, 7.4	July 1985
Self-Realization Bhd., Inc. v. Comm'r	8.2	Sept. 1984
Senior Citizens of Mo., Inc., v. Comm'r	19.4(a)	Mar. 1989
Service Bolt & Nut Co. Profit Sharing Trust v. Comm'r	28.4	Apr. 1984
Sherwin-Williams Co. Employee Health Plan Trust v. Comm'r	16.3, 28.3	Jan. 2001
Sierra Club, Inc. v. Comm'r	27.1(a), 27.1(g)	July 1993, Oct. 1994, Aug. 1996, May 1999
Skillman Family Reunion Fund, Inc., The v. United States	14.5	June 2002
Sklar v. Comm'r	8.2(a)	April 2002
Smith v. United States	4.4, 18.6	May 1985
Southwest Tex. Elec. Coop., Inc. v. Comm'r	29.2	Dec. 1995
Spiritual Outreach Soc'y v. Comm'r	8.3	Apr. 1991
Sta-Home Health Agency of Carthage, Inc. v. Comm'r	19.11	Feb. 2000
Sta-Home Health Agency of Greenwood, Inc. v. Comm'r	19.11	Feb. 2000
Sta-Home Health Agency of Jackson, Inc. v. Comm'r	19.11	Feb. 2000
State Police Ass'n v. Comm'r	26.5(f)	Nov. 1997
Stichting Pensioenfonds Voor de Gezondheid v. United States	15.1	Jan. 1998
Sunrise Constr. Co. v. Comm'r	16.3	May 1987
Tax Analysts v. Internal Revenue Service	23.1	Nov. 2002
Tennessee Baptist Children's Homes, Inc. v. United States	8.5	July 1985
Texas Farm Bureau v. United States	26.5(d), 27.1(g)	Aug. 1995
Texas Learning Technology Group v. Comm'r	23.7(a)	May 1992
Triune of Life Church, Inc. v. Comm'r	4.9	Sept. 1985
Trust U/W Emily Oblinger v. Comm'r	26.5(h), 27.1(h), 32.1	May 1993
Twin Oaks Community, Inc. v. Comm'r	8.7	Jan. 1987
Tupper v. United States	15.1	Mar. 1998

TABLE OF CASES DISCUSSED IN BRUCE R. HOPKINS' *NONPROFIT COUNSEL*

Case	Book Sections	Newsletter Issue
United Cancer Council, Inc. v. Comm'r	4.7, 19.3, 19.4(a), 24.1(a), 24.6, 25.1(e), 33.1(c)	Jan. 1998, Apr. 1999
United States v. American Bar Endowment	7.6, 24.2(a), 26.2(a), 26.5(g)	Apr. 1984, Aug. 1986
United States v. Chicago, Burlington & Quincy Railroad Co.	14.2	Oct. 2001
United States v. Church of Scientology	24.8(b)	Sept. 1990
United States Catholic Conference & Nat'l Conference of Catholic Bishops, In Re	27.7(b)	Oct. 1989, Nov. 1989
University Med. Resident Servs., P.C. v. Comm'r	6.3, 6.5	Oct. 1996
Variety Club Tent No. 6 Charities, Inc. v. Comm'r	19.4	Mar. 1998
Veterans of Foreign Wars, Dep't of Mich. v. Comm'r	24.2(a), 26.5(g)	Aug. 1987
Veterans of Foreign Wars, Dep't of Mo., Inc. v. United States	26.5(g)	Dec. 1984
Vigilant Hose Co. of Emmitsburg v. United States	12, 26.2, 32.3, 32.4	Aug. 2001
Wayne Baseball, Inc. v. Comm'r	4.4, 6.10(c), 7.4	Dec. 1999
Wendy L. Parker Rehabilitation Found., Inc. v. Comm'r	19.4(g)	Nov. 1986
West Va. State Med. Ass'n v. Comm'r	14.3, 26.2(a), 28.2	Nov. 1988
Westward Ho v. Comm'r	4.6	June 1992
Women of the Motion Picture Indus. v. Comm'r	28.2	Mar. 1998

Table of IRS Private Determinations Discussed in Bruce R. Hopkins' *Nonprofit Counsel*

The following IRS private letter rulings, technical advice memoranda, and general counsel memoranda, referenced in the text, are discussed in greater detail in one or more issues of the author's monthly newsletter, as indicated.

Private Determination	Book Sections	Newsletter Issue	Private Determination	Book Sections	Newsletter Issue
8306056	9.5	Dec. 1993	9438030	32.2(b)	Nov. 1994
8505044	31.2(a)	May 1985	9448036	19.6	Jan. 1995
8512084	9.5	Dec. 1993	9506046	31.3	Mar. 1995
8606056	31.1(d)	Apr. 1986	9530024	6.3	Nov. 1995
8621059	31.4, 32.3	Aug. 1986	9534021	20.8(b)	July 1995
8706012	31.1(a)	Apr. 1987	9542002	10.4	Dec. 1995
9017003	30.2	July 1990	9550001	13.1,	
9029047	26.5(d)	Sept. 1990		26.4(g)	Feb. 1996
9042038	27.1(i)	Jan. 1991	9603019	29.2	Mar. 1996
9130002	19.4(1), 32.2	Nov. 1991	9608003	26.5(j)	Apr. 1996
9242002	18.2(a)	Dec. 1992	9615030	19.10	June 1996
9243008	9.5	Dec. 1992	9615045	27.1(h)(i)	July 1996
9305026	31.2(a),	Apr. 1993,	9619069	27.1(j)(i)	Aug. 1996
	31.5(b)	Apr. 1997	9635001	27.2(k)	Nov. 1996
9316052	9.5, 19.4(a)	Dec. 1993	9635003	21.1(e)	Nov. 1996
9338003	31.3	Nov. 1993	9637050	31.1(b), 32.3	Nov. 1996
9345004	26.5(d)(iii)	June 1994	9637051	31.5(b)	Apr. 1997
9416002	26.5(d)(iii)	June 1994	9641011	26.5(g)	Dec. 1996
9425032	17.3(a)	Aug. 1994	9645004	26.2(d)	Jan. 1997
9434041	6.2(b)	Oct. 1994	9645017	31.2(d),	Feb. 1997,
9438029	31.2(d)	Nov. 1994		31.5(b)	Apr. 1997

TABLE OF IRS PRIVATE DETERMINATIONS IN
BRUCE R. HOPKINS' *NONPROFIT COUNSEL*

Private Determination	Book Sections	Newsletter Issue	Private Determination	Book Sections	Newsletter Issue
9651047	6.2(f), 26.5(g)	Jan. 1997	9835001	19.3S	Nov. 1998
			9835003	24.1	Nov. 1998
9652026	17.1(a)	Jan. 1998	9839039	32.3	Dec. 1998
9702004	26.2(d), 26.5(a)(iii)	Mar. 1997	9841003	16.3	Jan. 1999
9710030	6.2(a)	July 1997, Sept. 1997	9847002	6.2(b), 11.3(c), 26.2(d), 26.5(b)(I), 26.5(j), 27.2(b), 28.4	Mar. 1999
9711002	26.5(j)	May 1997			
9711003	4.7	June 1997			
9711004	23.6	June 1997			
9712001	26.3(d)	June 1997	9847006	17.3	Jan. 1999
9720002	26.5(c)	Sept. 1997	9849027	26.5(j), 28.6	Mar. 1999
9722006	18.5, 31.5	Feb. 1999, Nov. 2002	9853001	26.4, 27.1(h)	Mar. 1999
			199901002	26.4, 27.1(h)	Mar. 1999
9731038	6.1	Oct. 1997	199932052	6.3	Oct. 1999
9732022	15.2	Oct. 1997	199938041	31.1	May 2000
9732032	26.5(a)	Oct. 1997	200020056	13.1	July 2000
9739043	26.5(b)(iii)	Dec. 1997	200020060	11.4, 19.4(a)	Aug. 2000
9740032	27.1(h)(i)	Dec. 1997	200021056	4.4, 25.1, 26, 27.2(a)	Aug. 2000
9742001	26.5(d)(iii)	Dec. 1997			
9747003	18.10	Jan. 1998	200022056	13.1, 26.5(j)	July 2000, May 2001
9750056	30.4	Feb. 1998			
9751001	26.5(d)(iii)	Feb. 1998	200026013	18.17	Aug. 2000
9751020	30.4	Feb. 1998	200027056	17, 27.1(j), 31	Sept. 2000
9803001	25, 26.5(b)(iv)	Apr. 1998	200037053	11.3(b), 11.6(e)	Dec. 2000
9805001	12	Mar. 1998			
9811001	26.5(j)	May 1998	200044038	21.1(e)	Jan. 2001
9812001	17.3, 19.10, 21.2, 21.3	May 1998	200044039	6.2, 11.3(c), 22.1	Jan. 2001
9815061	12, 18.4, 18.10, 14	July 1998	200051046		Feb. 2001
			200051049		Feb. 2001
9816027	27.1(g)	June 1998	200108045		May 2001
9821049	26.4, 27.1(g), 27.1(h)	Aug. 1998	200114040		June 2001
			200117043		July 2001
9821063	7.6, 19.10, 26.4	Aug. 1998	200118054		July 2001
			200119061		Aug. 2001
9821067	26.4, 27.1(h)	Aug. 1998	200128059		Sep. 2001
9822004	26.5(j)	Oct. 1998	200133036		Oct. 2001
9822006	27.1(h), 27.2(a)	Oct. 1998	200133037		Oct. 2001
			200132040		Nov. 2001
9822039	26.5(b)(i)	Oct. 1998	200134025		Nov. 2001
9825030	6.2, 24.3(b)(iii)	Aug. 1998	200147058		Jan. 2002
			200151060		Mar. 2002

TABLE OF IRS PRIVATE DETERMINATIONS IN
BRUCE R. HOPKINS' *NONPROFIT COUNSEL*

Private Determination	Book Sections	Newsletter Issue	Private Determination	Book Sections	Newsletter Issue
200152048		Mar. 2002	200225044	26.4	Sept. 2002
200203069	5.5(a),		200225046	31	Oct. 2002
	31	May 2002	200230005	19, 22.1(a),	
200204051	6.3	Apr. 2002		22.1(b),	
200217044	33.4,			22.2,	
	33.5	July 2002		27.2	Oct. 2002
200222030	26.5(c)	Sept. 2002	200243057	19.11	Dec. 2002

Table of IRS Private Letter Rulings, Technical Advice Memoranda, and General Counsel Memoranda

The following citations, to pronouncements from the Internal Revenue Service issued in the context of specific cases, are coordinated to the appropriate footnotes (FN) in the suitable chapters.

Citations are to IRS private letter rulings, technical advice memoranda, and general counsel memoranda, other than those specifically referenced in footnotes, directly pertinent to the material discussed in the text. Seven-number items are either private letter rulings or technical advice memoranda; five-number items are general counsel memoranda.

While these pronouncements are not to be cited as precedent (IRC § 6110(j)(3)), they are useful in illuminating the position of the IRS on the subjects involved.

FN	Private Letter Rulings, etc.	FN	Private Letter Rulings, etc.	FN	Private Letter Rulings, etc.
Chapter 3		144	9132005	101	7851096, 8327066,
85	39782	149	8142024, 8204016,		33752, 37462, 39082,
93	8337006		32689, 34682,		39117
Chapter 4			36130, 37596,	126	8910001, 39792
11	8705078, 8709069,		38686	144	37858
	8810048	150	39684	153	8024109
15	9014063, 9629020	178	39288, 39716	157	9307027
44	200150027	200	9036001	161	8736046
58	8936050, 9526033	260	9243008,	162	8405083
79	30808		9316052	163	8827074
80	200151045	**Chapter 5**		166	9631004
82	39736	70	39800	174	9351027, 38050
92	8501082	96	35986, 37462	175	9718034

FN	Private Letter Rulings, etc.	FN	Private Letter Rulings, etc.	FN	Private Letter Rulings, etc.
177	9214031	176	9047049, 39348	370	7909026, 7935043,
182	37257, 37787,	187	9249026		8347031, 8348025,
	38459	189	9530025, 9530026,		8944068
194	9408026		9537035–9537053	376	8630021
		193	9408026	382	8349017, 8438027,
Chapter 6		195	39733		8511032
5	9718034	196	7823052	391	8836056
6	9752064	197	9731038	393	8425019, 8425031,
13	8801067, 9311034,	201	199932052		8425032, 8425038,
	9411037	227	8629045, 9802045		8425064, 8426029,
17	8637141	228	8429102, 8629045,		8429012, 8429028,
21	9325061		9048046, 9237027		8430026, 8430044,
32	9411037	241	39562		8431024, 8431025,
70	9204033	243	9118012		8432038, 8432050,
77	9043059, 9535023	255	9539013		8435027, 8435028,
87	200233024	260	9247030		8435080, 8435089,
90	8633038	262	9002036, 9025073,		8435102, 8436042,
92	9241055, 9242002		9306034		8437021, 8437038,
93	8251089, 8251096,	263	9002036, 9306034		8437040, 8437041,
	8736046, 8936045,	264	39360		8437068, 8437082,
	8936046, 9527035	269	38050		8437095, 8438019,
102	9307027	270	9407005, 9526033		8441014, 8442081,
108	9412002	272	32961, 33217		8443031, 8443077,
109	9246004, 38735,	275	9014063		8444019, 8444053,
	39057, 39487, 39799,	287	8705078		8445027, 8447013,
	39828, 39829, 39830	288	37518		8447059, 8447084,
125	9714011, 9716021,	289	37518		8447102, 8448020,
	9721031, 9722042,	292	8536099, 9014063,		8448021, 8450009,
	9738038–9738054		35936, 35966, 37180,		8452018, 8501077,
141	38686, 38894, 39120		38401, 38322		8502026, 8502037,
143	8237052, 8509044,	307	9210026		8502071, 8503031,
	8509073, 8511082,	315	8334001, 8849072		8505010, 8506035,
	8625081, 9408026,	318	8734007		8506048, 8507018,
	39340	320	8906062, 35945		8507034, 8514019,
152	32896, 36827	323	7816061, 7905129,		8516027, 8516048,
153	9325061		7951134		8516093, 8517026,
160	9210032, 9735048	324	7902019, 8920084		8517027, 8518072,
164	9001011	333	7816061		8522024, 8524111,
174	9411037, 9541003,	339	8753049, 9242002,		8534020, 8534056,
	9629002		9635037, 39562		8536027, 8536037,
175	8723052, 9243008,	359	8839024		8537014, 8537040,
	9246032, 9246033,	365	8351103		8541025, 8542010,
	9629002, 38693,	369	8448020, 8717020,		8543014, 8544015,
	39347, 39348, 39682,		8721022, 8921061,		8544027, 8546060,
	39685, 39852		9347001		8603034, 8607010,

FN	Private Letter Rulings, etc.	FN	Private Letter Rulings, etc.	FN	Private Letter Rulings, etc.
393 *cont'd*	8607040, 8609020, 8609033, 8610025, 8611036, 8620036, 8621085, 8622034, 8639024, 8639039, 8650008, 34704	127 *cont'd*	8425115, 8425118, 8425123, 8425130–8425135, 8426022, 8426023, 8426045, 8426047, 8426068, 8426091, 8426107–8426109, 8427096–8427099, 8427103, 8427104, 8428108, 8428115, 8428110–8428113, 8429065–8429068, 8429106, 8429107, 8429110, 8430073, 8431067–8431069, 8431075, 8431081–8431083, 8432068–8432070, 8432076–8432078 8432110, 8433053, 8433054, 8433111 8434064–843067, 8435047, 8435086, 8435158–8435161, 8435168, 8435171–8435174, 8435090–8435098, 8436036, 8436037, 8436039, 8436040, 8436050, 8437070, 8437076, 8437090, 8437101, 8437102, 8437104, 8437112, 8437114, 8438045, 8438061, 8438062, 8438066, 8439014, 8439015, 8439081, 8439097, 8439102, 8439103, 8440092, 8440093, 8440097–8440100, 8441046, 8441065, 8442065–8442073, 8442075, 8442093, 8442097–8442101,	127 *cont'd*	8442110, 8442132, 8442134–8442141, 8443049–3443051, 8443081, 8443090–8443092, 8444085, 8444087–8444089, 8444095, 8444096, 8445074–8445078, 8445080, 8445101–8445107, 8446033, 8446037, 8447066, 8447067, 8447088–8447090, 8448041–8448043, 8448045, 8448049, 8448055–8448058, 8448070, 8449068, 8450072–8450074, 8451051, 8452070–8452073, 8452075, 8452081–8452084, 8453096–8453101, 8501061, 8501062, 8502062, 8502063, 8502076–8502078, 8502085–8502090, 8502096, 8502101, 8503040, 8503042, 8503071, 8503078–8503082, 8504052, 8504057, 8504081, 8505061–8505064, 8505077, 8506067, 8506078–8506080, 8506084, 8506101, 8506103, 8506119, 8508082–8508085, 8508100, 8508104, 8509068, 8509101, 8510041, 8510042, 8510058–8510060, 8510090, 8510091,
394	8342022, 8412064				
397	7823052, 9526033				
399	39055				
420	8429051, 9240001, 39047, 39883				
421	9048046, 9539015				
423	39633				

Chapter 7

FN	Private Letter Rulings, etc.
86	8705078
90	8823088
95	9325061
107	9211002, 9211004
110	8645017
128	8909004
130	8846002
139	9414003
146	9019046
170	8751007, 8811021, 9036025, 9851052
171	9210026
196	9048046, 9237027
220	8930052
222	9638001
238	9335061, 39622

Chapter 8

FN	Private Letter Rulings, etc.
110	37622, 37503, 37391, 37247
125	8626100, 8626101, 8627044, 8628077, 8629051, 8641069–8641072, 8643055
127	8422171, 8422174, 8423078, 8423079, 8424056, 8424098, 8425058, 8425076,

TABLE OF IRS PRIVATE LETTER RULINGS

FN	Private Letter Rulings, etc.	FN	Private Letter Rulings, etc.	FN	Private Letter Rulings, etc.
127 *cont'd*	8511051–8511053, 8511069, 8511070, 8512075, 8512076, 8512080, 8512091, 8512092, 8514056–8514059, 8514061, 8514062, 8514078, 8514083, 8514084, 8514086, 8514096, 8514097, 8515065, 8516059, 8516097, 8516102, 8516108, 8516109, 8516115, 8516136, 8516137, 8517059–8517061, 8517065, 8518055, 8510856, 8518081–8518086, 8518091, 8518092, 8519035, 8519036, 8520047, 8520052, 8520064, 8520067, 8520071, 8520118, 8520119, 8521013, 8521100, 8521104, 8521105, 8522080–8522083 8522085, 8523082, 8523087, 8523091, 8523094, 8523095, 8523101, 8523104, 8523106–8523111, 8524065–8524069, 8525076, 8525088–8525090, 8526083, 8527045, 8527049, 8527067, 8529051, 8529052, 8529098, 8529105, 8530054–8530058, 8530134, 8531051, 8531066, 8531067, 8532014, 8532015, 8532024, 8532044,	127 *cont'd*	8532047, 8532060, 8532069, 8532095–8532097, 8533020, 8533079, 8534062, 8534086, 8534087, 8535060, 8535061, 8535119, 8536089, 8536090–8536094, 8537059, 8537060, 8537102–8537107, 8538067, 8539090, 8540032, 8540083, 8540089, 8541106, 8541109, 8541110, 8542059, 8542066, 8542096, 8542097, 8543048, 8543057–8543063, 8543090, 8544087, 8546100–8546106, 8546113, 8546114, 8546116, 8546124, 8546130, 8546132, 8546136, 8546137, 8547059, 8547060, 8547068–8547073, 8548081, 8549064, 8550048, 8550049, 8550052, 8550054–8550056 8550074–8550076, 8551048–8551050, 8551052–8551059, 8551067–8551070, 8551078–8551080, 8551081, 8552108, 8601056, 8601057, 8601059–8601062, 8601064, 8601065, 8601068–8601072, 8602048, 8602065, 8603089–8603095, 8603097, 8603107–8603109,	127 *cont'd*	8603122–8603124, 8604081, 8604083, 8604084, 8604090, 8604091, 8604094, 8605048, 8605050, 8606070, 8606071, 8606073, 8606076, 8608081, 8608082, 8609070, 8609071, 8610079, 8610080, 8610084, 8611047, 8611049, 8611080–8611083, 8614045, 8615045, 8615047, 8615049, 8615058–8615062, 8615088–8615090, 8616057, 8616062–8616065, 8616096, 8618045, 8618046, 8618066, 8619048–8619050, 8619054–8619060, 8619063–8619066, 8620059–8620063, 8620081, 8620083, 8621102, 8621114, 8622046–8622048, 8622052–8622054, 8622057, 8622061, 8623045, 8623052, 8624080–8624083, 8624091, 8624093, 8624094, 8624128, 8624152, 8624166 8624168, 8625089, 8625102–8625105, 8626100, 8626101, 8627044, 8628077, 8629051, 8631061, 8631072, 8631073, 8631080, 8631083, 8631092, 8631093, 8631097–8631099, 8631107, 8631108,

FN	Private Letter Rulings, etc.
127 cont'd	8631110, 8631111, 8631113–8631117, 8633037, 8634061, 8634064, 8635056, 8635057, 8638124, 8641069–8641072, 8833001, 9624001, 36078, 36993, 37116
163	9448017, 39614
171	9518021
188	9434002
198	7838029–7838036
200	33574, 36254, 36787, 37503

Chapter 9

FN	Private Letter Rulings, etc.
14	8723061–8723064
15	9240001, 39883
18	7852997, 8028004
19	9627023
29	9346006
50	8512084
51	9017052
52	9311032, 9722032

Chapter 10

FN	Private Letter Rulings, etc.
7	9851001
16	9211004, 39459, 39560, 39775
19	9129040, 39459, 39560
32	39799, 9851054
61	36738, 39598

Chapter 11

FN	Private Letter Rulings, etc.
362	200149045
396	200150039

Chapter 12

FN	Private Letter Rulings, etc.
1	9149004, 9201039, 39574, 39866
24	8923001
34	37518
59	9044060
62	9811003, 9815061
104	39763
128	8829072
133	8828058, 8838052

Chapter 13

FN	Private Letter Rulings, etc.
2	9517036
40	200020056
56	9349022
69	9029035
107	39721
116	37853
151	8826004
180	9429002, 9429003
181	9124004

Chapter 14

FN	Private Letter Rulings, etc.
18	39773
41	9533015
62	9043019
65	200133037, 200134021
86	9212002
87	39688
94	8809087, 8812006, 9043003, 9044022, 39717
96	8729001
105	39658
106	8816004
113	8905002, 8920002, 8922067, 8943009, 9043019, 39773
114	8728002, 9246043
123	8737060, 8738075, 8919062, 8951062, 9025001, 9027044, 9040018, 9307004, 9608002, 9629032, 9630001, 9824045, 9844012
124	8724045, 8740002
125	9225001

Chapter 15

FN	Private Letter Rulings, etc.
6	39698
81	8739066, 39672

Chapter 16

FN	Private Letter Rulings, etc.
31	9802038
33	9507009

FN	Private Letter Rulings, etc.
34	9413042
37	9147059, 9325041, 9332044, 9438017, 9641034
38	9437016
40	9145031, 9145032, 39834
43	39817
50	199930040
52	9641034, 200028007, 39879
55	9139003, 39621, 39879
58	8822089, 8925091, 8936070, 9006051, 9014065, 9115035, 9252038, 9446036, 9720034, 200023052, 200024054, 39801
61	9505019, 9551007, 200038054
62	9401033, 9438017
67	20006056
68	9410048, 9413042
69	9213029
71	8936070, 200003054
75	9214032, 9233027, 9242014, 9325054, 9351042, 9401033, 9410048, 9508032, 9640024, 9640025, 9646034, 9649037
78	8717062, 8833039, 8937038
89	8937038
90	9402034, 200006056
94	8951061, 9645022
95	8721092
100	9522023
103	9402034, 9403023
104	8629086, 8929087, 9403023
105	9403023

FN	Private Letter Rulings, etc.	FN	Private Letter Rulings, etc.	FN	Private Letter Rulings, etc.
Chapter 17		248	8807025, 8811003,	398	9348021, 9515014
13	8850014		9034043, 9229011	399	9244003
17	8650001, 9249002,	274	8626002	403	8719023, 9109030,
	9652026, 9725036,	276	9310031		9149007
	39694	280	9217003, 9314001	412	9439008, 200238001
19	9320002	285	8750002	420	9130036, 9611044
50	9622002	290	39522	421	8630021, 8639024,
60	9409003	297	39819		8645036, 8705015,
66	9603017	312	9309012		8705038, 8705054,
73	9433001	314	9132038		8710016, 8713030,
86	7903079, 9042004,	318	9021013		8719023, 8721022,
	9245001	333	8627011, 8644065,		8721061, 8722030,
88	8901050		8729071, 8801003,		8725010, 8725024,
89	39694		8804009, 8815019,		8725033, 8728057,
90	8852037		8824029, 8827054,		8728058, 8729038,
			8831043, 8910024,		8733018, 8737090,
Chapter 18			8934038, 8940025,		8738036, 8740015,
3	39859		8944029, 9003091,		8743032, 8747010,
25	9213027		9007022, 9035045,		8748017, 8748031,
28	8751006, 9130008		9030014, 9042045,		8748024, 8749030,
37	9308047		9045019, 9102008,		8751017, 8752011,
55	9721034		9133024, 9201022,		8752022, 8753008,
75	9113038, 39735		9201022, 9214020		8803020, 8803022,
92	39575		9233025, 9242018,		8803033, 8803035,
108	9539003, 9542039,		9250023, 9315020,		8803057, 8804028,
	9551010, 9551036		9348018, 9406032,		8804058, 8806028,
123	8812016, 9149007,		9413046, 9735021,		8806062, 8809038,
	9715045		9816008, 9850011,		8809047, 8809051,
138	199908001		199931045, 200034006		8810060, 8810062,
139	9110041, 9111001	346	8524011, 9038018		8810084, 8814018,
144	8816004, 39724	391	9825035,		8815009, 8815010,
146	9510066		200030030,		8815027, 8816022,
148	9510066, 9722006		200024055,		8816040, 8819046,
151	9111001		200231020, 200232035		8819055, 8820030,
164	8639074, 9231045	392	9130026		8821030, 8821046,
167	39865	397	7821037, 8107117,		8823034, 8823035,
172	8902003, 9626021		8147094, 8313060,		8824015, 8825034,
180	9102015		8314050, 8342022,		8825081, 8825087,
207	39885		8425032, 8453038,		8825096, 8825100,
209	199914052		8603034, 8609020,		8826026, 8826037,
214	39864		8621085, 8633034,		8826048, 8829041,
226	9747003, 199924057–		8650008, 8721061,		8829062, 8831047,
	199924059, 200011050		8728057, 8728058,		8832020, 8832047,
227	8741004, 9315002		8728073, 200008024,		8832056, 8832066,
231	9315002		200008039		8832067, 8834031,

TABLE OF IRS PRIVATE LETTER RULINGS

FN	Private Letter Rulings, etc.	FN	Private Letter Rulings, etc.	FN	Private Letter Rulings, etc.
421	8835034, 8836056,	421	9045021, 9046039,	421	9613007, 9622019
cont'd	8836038, 8839014,	*cont'd*	9046042, 9046060,	*cont'd*	(withdrawn by
	8839024, 8839039,		9049025, 9050052,		9631011),
	8839083, 8842070,		9050055, 9103009,		9624013, 9627016,
	8842071, 8847032,		9106007, 9106023,		9630018, 9631008,
	8849023, 8850037,		9106026, 9107032,		9635017, 9637037,
	8850038, 8850063,		9109020, 9110004,		9646018, 9646026,
	8920056, 8920023,		9110022, 9110062,		9627016, 9706006,
	8920037, 8921024,		9113021, 9114055,		9706007, 9722029,
	8921055, 8923024,		9115016, 9115037,		9723042, 9725022,
	8925010, 8925014,		9129043, 9137019,		9731023, 9740005,
	8925015, 8925028,		9140046, 9140050,		9741002, 9742003,
	8926078, 8927058,		9140070, 9142019,		9746035, 9746057,
	8928061, 8929039,		9143057, 9145042,		9809013, 9819023,
	8930036, 8931008,		9149011, 9151026,		9819029, 9823012,
	8931061, 8931068,		9201027, 9205020,		9829024, 9830006,
	8931069, 8932031,		9206012, 9212010,		9831025, 9835045,
	8933011, 8934009,		9217032, 9218014,		9836014, 9844029,
	8934026, 8934052,		9238011, 9238024,		9845018, 9846029,
	8935012, 8936028,		9240024, 9243044,		9848025, 9849003,
	8938018, 8938044,		9245007, 9247014,		9852019, 9852020,
	8939047, 8940032,		9247015, 9248024,		9852043, 9853022,
	8940034, 8941052,		9249015, 9342029,		199905026, 199909048,
	8942037, 8943051,		9347001,		199911047, 199913041,
	8943053, 8944008,		9401003–9401006,		199916045, 199916050,
	8944031, 8944032,		9401010, 9402028,		199924046, 199924063,
	8944068, 8948057,		9403025, 9405024,		199928011, 199928035,
	8948060, 8950050,		9409040, 9410034,		199930028, 199931042,
	8951048, 8951057,		9411017, 9412027,		199942008, 199952049,
	8951012, 8952016,		9421008, 9421009,		199952083, 200003052,
	8952036, 9002016,		9423038, 9424007,		200019023, 200022019,
	9004034, 9012031,		9425029, 9435031,		200031045, 200040016,
	9015057, 9017052,		9436048, 9436052,		200007015, 200003052,
	9025062, 9026015,		9440012, 9443032,		200008024, 200008039,
	9026054, 9026055,		9443034, 9505015,		200023022, 200151015,
	9027025, 9027028,		9506037, 9507019,		200201001, 200210025,
	9027038, 9028033,		9522043, 9523008,		39761
	9032012, 9033062,		9524028, 9530017,	422	9627016, 9809013,
	9034041, 9035013,		9530018, 9533040,		9822011, 9823029,
	9035024, 9037019,		9540007, 9541030,		9852018, 199906036,
	9037046, 9038036,		9544024,		199928011,
	9041054, 9041070,		9545015–9545017,		199923029,
	9042059, 9042060,		9546012, 9546014,		200012084,
	9043017, 9043035,		9549030, 9552045,		200210024,
	9043047, 9043067,		9605006, 9609034,		200222007

FN	Private Letter Rulings, etc.	FN	Private Letter Rulings, etc.	FN	Private Letter Rulings, etc.
Chapter 19		**Chapter 23**		68	8722082, 9735047,
62	9525056	102	9145001		32896, 36827
80	9231045, 9621035	150	8906008	69	9217001
86	9112006, 9201035	152	8649001	73	9325061
114	8731032	170	9145039	82	9401031
118	38394	181	39833	84	9242035
121	35638	218	39830	88	36827
132	8838047	219	39830	90	9720035
175	8807081, 8808070	**Chapter 24**		95	8822057
180	9025089, 37180,	2	9141050	96	8840020, 8841041
	38283, 39670	3	8935063	97	8806056, 9318047
181	32518, 35865	4	9446033, 9446034	105	9042038
235	9428035	32	8906008	123	9438040, 9505020,
290	39876	38	9408066		9509041, 9510039,
303	9530024–9530026	181	8728057, 8728058,		200148085
Chapter 20			8728073	128	8651086, 8708052,
14	39694	193	8642083, 8709049,		8841041
39	39694		8724057, 8738039,	129	8829003, 8932004,
42	9244003		8747032, 8818046,		9309002
93	9622002		8819037, 8819057,	131	8717002, 8717063,
115	9507020		8819071, 8825044,		8733037, 8734005,
116	9507020		8834010, 9040038,		8901064, 8934050,
118	9332042		9103047, 9253044,		8936013, 9003059,
138	9332042, 9347034		9310045, 9510068,		9017058, 9018049,
210	9510047, 9534021,		9518021, 9619024		9240937, 9337027,
	9602026, 9636016	196	9803015		9340061, 9340062,
213	199919038	205	9152046		9349022
Chapter 21		209	8710016, 8715013,	132	9425031
34	39694		8725010, 8725024,	148	8922064, 9407005,
85	8906062		8738077, 8823091,		9413020
115	9433001		8926078, 8932031,	150	9417003
133	9117001		8944068, 9029043,	153	9137002, 9417003,
Chapter 22			9150055, 9348021,		9509002, 9721001
12	8725056, 9201039,		9401010, 9409040,	159	8641001
	39718, 39737, 39799,		9421009, 9436052,	164	9302023
	39828, 39829, 39866		9540007, 200049035,	170	9539005
15	39761		200049036	171	8819005, 9723046
17	9752023	212	9411011	176	9535023
19	9645007	213	9825030	181	9750056
20	39829	**Chapter 25**		182	9641011, 9728034,
24	39655, 39764	79	9243008, 9316052		9715041
26	9108021, 9110012,	**Chapter 26**		184	8732029,
	9743054	23	9338043		9041045,
57	9042043, 39826	33	9120029		9350045
				207	9014069

FN	Private Letter Rulings, etc.	FN	Private Letter Rulings, etc.	FN	Private Letter Rulings, etc.
216	9107030, 9110012, 9137002	387	8721103, 8809092, 8921091, 8941082, 9023041	516	8932004
220	9428035			521	8726069, 9302023
226	8432003	393	9736047	530	9023001, 9023002, 9204007, 9402005
227	8743081, 8743086, 8743087, 9347036	395	9750056, 9803001	533	9247001
		396	9110042, 9226055	534	8834006, 8835001, 9023001, 9023002, 9217002, 9402005, 9419003, 9734002
228	9349024	402	9750056		
232	9110042, 9329041	409	200041030		
		410	8809092, 8817017		
234	8643091	413	199917084	535	8403013
240	9149002	415	8626102, 8640052–8640054, 8640056, 8640057, 8645064, 8833002	537	9248001
242	8643049, 9141053, 9150052, 9152039			562	9623035
				565	8725058
249	9107030			566	9736046
283	200147059, 200149044, 200216036, 200222032, 200230004	418	8949093	568	9315001, 9321005
		420	8814001, 9138003	577	9250001
		422	8641060	613	9822004
287	200150033, 200150035	437	9645027	616	9608003, 9711002, 9718029
294	9321072, 9321087, 9323035, 9812031, 9814048, 200234071, 200242041, 200243056	438	8815002		
		446	9147054, 9550001, 9527001	618	9752023, 200108048
		453	8707003, 8842002, 9037063, 9548001, 39723	622	200031057, 200033050, 200108048
302	9137049			623	9814039, 9819049, 9853026, 199924065, 199943049, 199949038, 200032046, 200036049, 200108048, 20033025, 200238051
308	9128003	454	9220054		
323	9853001	455	9220054, 9306030, 9318005, 9535004 (withdrawn by 9542046), 9612003, 39827		
326	9138003, 9145002, 9147005, 9320050, 9323035, 39864				
343	8025222				
347	9137002, 39860	457	8841003	624	200108048
352	8641090	469	8734004, 39735	625	200108046, 200108047, 200108049
356	9231001	471	9550001		
359	9521004	475	9029047		
360	8846002	495	9428035		
363	8650083	496	8852002	**Chapter 27**	
364	9014069	499	9325003	1	9012058
366	39843	500	9128002	4	8708031, 9442035
367	39762	509	9137002, 9147054, 9205037, 39860	10	9042038
370	8735004, 8815031, 8817066, 9730941, 9739042			13	8836037
		510	8947002, 9044071, 9234002, 9304001, 9345004, 9724006	20	9826046
				25	199914042, 199928042
372	8736046			32	9030048
377	8736046, 8817017, 9445024	513	9023003, 199914035		
		514	9302035	39	9231045

TABLE OF IRS PRIVATE LETTER RULINGS

FN	Private Letter Rulings, etc.	FN	Private Letter Rulings, etc.	FN	Private Letter Rulings, etc.
45	9151001, 9309002, 9306030, 39827	76	9450045	162	8729005, 8832084, 8833002, 8903083,
57	8839016	80	8713072, 8822096, 8932042		8922047, 9010073
59	9346014	81	8822057, 9551019		9045003, 9108016,
61	8827017	82	200032050		9308047, 9324026,
65	9316045, 9319042, 9419033, 9503024, 9552019	91	9245036, 9246032, 9246033, 9301024, 9315021, 9703025, 9850020		9404004, 9438029, 9506046, 9535022, 9547039, 9601047, 9642054, 9705028
67	8222066, 8645050, 8717066, 8717078, 8721102, 8728060, 8808002, 8808003, 8810097, 8824054, 8828011, 8845073, 8846005, 8922084, 8941011, 8941062, 8948023, 9015038, 9023091, 9024026, 9043039, 9108021, 9316052, 9404003, 9404004, 9417036, 9417042, 9417043, 9419033, 9436001, 9440001, 9441001, 9450028, 9703025, 9705001, 9709029, 9714016, 9723001, 9724006, 9810030, 9816027, 200046039, 200149035, 200149043, 20019037, 200225046, 39615	93	9136037	171	199928042, 199952086
		104	9108034, 9108043, 9127045, 9128030, 9132040, 9132061, 9144032–9144035, 9150047, 9204048, 9247038, 9252028, 9547040, 9551021	174	8641061, 8831007, 8932004, 8942070, 9033056, 9302023, 9544029, 9605001, 9704012
		106	9619068	186	39786
		107	9616039, 9619068, 9619069, 9630031, 9631025, 9631029, 9652028, 9704010, 9745025, 200246032	188	8832043, 39752
				189	8736046, 9241055
				195	9023081
		112	200151046, 200151062	209	8915005, 9217001
				210	8728080
		115	9108034, 9108043, 9128030, 9132040, 9132061, 9144032, 9144035, 9150047, 9252028 (modified by 9428037), 9308040, 9316032, 9319044, 9401029, 9407005, 9411018, 9411019, 9412039, 9414002, 9432019, 9629032, 9651014, 9803024, 9826046, 9844004, 9853034, 199952071, 200041038, 200219037, 200237027	220	39734
				227	9302035, 9303030
				231	9232003
				232	8920084
				239	9726030
				244	9652004
				246	8721005, 9029047, 9316045, 9321005, 9724006, 39638
70	9139029, 9212030, 9231045, 9234043, 9551019, 35957, 39568			269	200029055
71	9450045, 200041031, 200147058, 200148057, 200148074			**Chapter 28**	
				15	9147008, 9149006, 39863
72	8950072, 9139029, 9141051, 9146047, 9702003			17	9324002
				26	9145003, 9328003
				28	9141003, 9141004, 9145031, 9145032, 9147059, 9216033, 9242014, 9247039
73	8445005, 8720005, 8802009, 8925029, 39825	125	8201024	31	9247039, 9517035, 9841003
		154	199941048		

FN	Private Letter Rulings, etc.	FN	Private Letter Rulings, etc.	FN	Private Letter Rulings, etc.
32	8905002, 8943009, 9721034, 9310034, 9344028, 9628022, 199932050, 39773, 200003036	44	9042043, 9108021, 9110012, 9527033, 9743054, 200150040, 200233023, 39826	10 *cont'd*	8725087, 8727074, 8727075, 8727081, 8728070, 8728075, 8728076, 8729082, 8729084, 8730055–8730057, 8730068, 8732044, 8732092, 8735043, 8735044, 8735069–8735071, 8736041, 8737086, 8737101, 8741085, 8742068, 8742074, 8742082, 8744059, 8744062, 8744064, 8744065, 8745044, 8746053, 8746071, 8747033, 8747057–8747060, 8747077, 8748050, 8748061, 8749064, 8750070, 8752051, 8752056, 8752088, 8752090, 8752095, 8753044, 8753049, 8753052, 8753053, 8753056, 8802012, 8802085, 8803009, 8803072, 8803083, 8803084, 8806009, 8806055, 8806070, 8806080, 8807007, 8807010, 8807049, 8808007, 8808073, 8808082, 8809093, 8809100, 8810033, 8810077, 8811015, 8812076, 8814008, 8814046, 8814047, 8816020, 8817051, 8818005, 8818038, 8818041, 8819057, 8819069, 8819071, 8820074, 8820091, 8821062, 8822092,
35	8728008, 8728009, 8925091, 9016039, 9310034, 9351042, 9410048, 9413042, 9818001	45	9012001		
		51	8945038		
		59	8818008, 8923077, 9031052, 9047069, 9218006, 9218007		
44	9319044, 9750056	61	9450045, 200137061		
58	39778	63	9508031		
73	39684, 39874	72	9128020		
76	9527035	75	9002030		
95	9033056	76	200224014		
		81	8721104, 8721107, 9042038		
Chapter 29		83	9619077		
8	8708031, 8717066, 200003048	84	9637053, 9642051		
		86	9717004		
10	8738006, 9144044, 199952089	113	9010011		
11	8522040, 8651091, 8906003, 8935058, 9147058, 9204048, 9726005	**Chapter 30**			
		10	8626102, 8627056–8627060, 8627104, 8628052, 8628069, 8639089, 8642062, 8645063, 8645083, 8649081, 8650061, 8709051, 8710083, 8712062, 8712068, 8714053, 8715007, 8715048, 8715058, 8717045, 8717076, 8718066, 8718074, 8718075, 8719030, 8720048, 8721072–8721075, 8721087, 8722066, 8722067, 8722072, 8722081, 8722091, 8722093–8722098, 8722109, 8723037, 8723071, 8723079, 8724070, 8725049, 8725072–8725074,		
18	8748064–8748065, 9024085, 9315021				
22	9246032, 9246033				
25	8950073, 9047040				
27	200125096				
28	9241052				
29	9651001				
32	8044023, 8104098, 8107114, 8110164, 8338138, 8738006, 8807082, 9031052, 9407023, 9703026, 200041038, 200233032				
34	9010025, 9431001, 9533014				
38	9533014				
42	8822057				

TABLE OF IRS PRIVATE LETTER RULINGS

FN	Private Letter Rulings, etc.	FN	Private Letter Rulings, etc.	FN	Private Letter Rulings, etc.
10	8823044, 8823059,	10	8951071, 9001041,	10	9538026–9538031,
cont'd	8823087, 8824004,	*cont'd*	9002037, 9003036,	*cont'd*	9541007–9541014,
	8825018, 8825077,		9003060, 9008088,		9542009, 9542039,
	8825104, 8827006,		9009009, 9011049,		9542043, 9542044,
	8827016, 8827028,		9013049, 9014016,		9544028,
	8827059, 8827060,		9014050, 9016053,		9544033–9544036,
	8828010, 8830005,		9022055, 9024034,		9551006, 9551039,
	8830005, 8830038,		9028075, 9030039,		9552021, 9608006,
	8830083, 8831010,		9034073, 9104023,		9608037, 9608038,
	8834089, 8807007,		9109057, 9110018,		9615031, 9630013,
	8837016, 8837042,		9112025, 9128037,		9635028, 9635029,
	8837053, 8837062,		9134025, 9135054,		9635037, 9636026,
	8839005, 8839019,		9136031, 9138056,		9646032, 9651015,
	8841004, 8841011,		9139025, 9142035,		9651026,
	8845020, 8845027,		9151041, 9151049,		9740001–9740002,
	8846004, 8846019,		9152040, 9203041,		9747029–9747032,
	8846057, 8847009,		9215047, 9216035,		9750054–9750056,
	8849080, 8850026,		9217042, 9226044,		9751020, 9752062,
	8850054, 8850069,		9233042, 9234042,		9804054, 9804061,
	8901051, 8901052,		9235054, 9235056,		9805038, 9809054,
	8901065, 8903017,		9238041,		9814040, 9814042,
	8904038, 8904039,		9243045–9243047,		9814043, 9817034,
	8907060, 8909056,		9231041, 9318048,		9819047, 9839038,
	8912042, 8913051,		9318049, 9326055,		9839042, 9842030,
	8914057, 8917073,		9333046, 9343024,		9842037, 9844032,
	8918079, 8920021,		9347031, 9347032,		9847033, 9848038
	8920054, 8920055,		9350037, 9401034,	17	9740001–9740004
	8920085, 8921060,		9403029, 9404027,	33	9002036, 9014061
	8922065, 8922079,		9408024, 9409038,	41	9119069, 9547013
	8925049, 8925069,		9424027,	45	9242002
	8925089, 8925090,		9425006–9425009,	46	9629020
	8926083, 8926086,		9426040, 9435030,	49	9135003
	8929009, 8929038,		9438039, 9438046,	50	8714050
	8929050, 8932010,		9442035,	54	9031051
	8932012, 8934004,		9447051–9447053,	74	9119069, 9242002
	8934030, 8934031,		9448027–9448029,	75	9246033
	8935040, 8940012,		9450034, 9501037,	91	199924065, 199949038
	8941007, 8941012,		9501040, 9503021,	92	9839038, 9839042
	8941015, 8941061,		9511035, 9511036,	98	8810048
	8941073, 8941083,		9511038, 9511046,	99	8417019, 9335022
	8942102, 8943008,		9513003, 9517052,	107	7903079, 9042004
	8943049, 8944014,		9519057, 9521014,	111	200236049
	8944059, 8945062,		9527013, 9527043,	113	9435029, 9752062,
	8947041, 8948022,		9531005, 9533007,		9752063, 9752065,
	8950052, 8950070,		9535017, 9535018,		9752067, 9839032

FN	Private Letter Rulings, etc.
114	9425009
118	9623057, 9623059, 9623060, 9738055, 9738056, 9620027, 200150026
126	200149035

Chapter 31

FN	Private Letter Rulings, etc.
4	9308047
9	8304112, 8606056, 8705087, 8706012, 8709071, 8720048, 8749058, 8749059, 8805059, 8810082, 8811003, 8819034, 8821044, 8833002, 8840056, 8846053, 8901012, 8901050, 8903083, 8909029, 8925051, 8934064, 8952076, 9005068, 9024068, 9024026, 9024086, 9030063, 9033069, 9108016, 9119060, 9131058, 9245031, 9308047, 9311031, 9316052, 9341024, 9346013, 9402031–9402933, 9408026, 9417036, 9417042, 9417043, 9421006, 9438041, 9447043, 9523027, 9528020, 9530009, 9535022, 9539014, 9542045 (amended by 9720036), 9547039, 9626021, 9630014, 9637051, 9705028, 9721038, 9726010, 9720031, 9722032, 199941048
24	8934064, 9242038, 9408026, 9421006, 199941051

FN	Private Letter Rulings, etc.
27	199929006
30	39598, 39646, 39866
31	39776
35	8625078, 8720048, 8732040, 8743070, 8840056, 8934064, 9027050, 9305026, 9734026, 9734027, 9734036, 9734037, 9734039, 9734040, 199938041, 200149043
44	8839002
45	8709051, 9305026
62	8849072, 9136032, 9148051
68	8729005, 8832084, 8833002, 8903083, 8922047, 9010073, 9027051, 9045003, 9108016, 9308047, 9404004, 9438029, 9535022, 9547039, 9705028
71	9105029, 9303030, 9305026, 39866

Chapter 32

FN	Private Letter Rulings, etc.
22	9230001, 9350044
38	8628049, 8705089, 8715039, 9715040, 8717057, 8723065, 8724060, 8727080, 8806057, 8807012, 8814047, 8817039, 8818008, 8820093, 8833009, 8901054, 8909036, 8912003, 8912041, 8915065, 8917055, 8931083, 8936047, 8936077, 8938002, 8939024, 8940039, 8941006, 8942099, 8943050, 8943064, 9021050, 9029034, 9109066, 9122061, 9122062,

FN	Private Letter Rulings, etc.
38 cont'd	9122070, 9147058, 9318033, 9319044, 9323030, 9345057, 9349032, 9352030, 9438030, 9502035 (updating 8528080), 9603839, 9642051, 9736039, 9736043, 9739001, 9709014, 9718036, 9722032, 39732
39	200211052
62	8925052, 8945063
65	8621060, 8903060, 8912003, 8925052, 8936073, 8945063, 9029034, 9035072, 9105029, 9105031, 9215046, 9308034, 9323030, 9352030, 9407022, 9518014, 9517029, 200206058
66	9637050, 9645018, 9739036–9739039
71	8925051, 9547039
75	200044040
99	8921203, 8932085, 8941006, 8949034, 9001030, 9521013

Chapter 33

FN	Private Letter Rulings, etc.
17	9451001
28	199913044–199913046
32	8944017
40	8640054, 8640056, 8640057
82	8219066, 9538026–9538031
122	200139006

Index

IMPORTANT NOTE:

Because of the rapidly changing nature of information in this field, this product may be updated with annual supplements or with future editions. Please call 1-877-762-2974 or email us at subscriber@wiley.com to receive any current update at no additional charge. We will send on approval any future supplements or new editions when they become available. If you purchased this product directly from John Wiley & Sons, Inc., we have already recorded your subscription for this update service.